PENGUIN BOOKS

THE QUICKWAY CROSSWORD DICTIONARY

THE QUICKWAY CROSSWORD DICTIONARY

Compiled by
COLONEL H. W. HILL CMG, DSO
and revised by his son
ROWLAND G. P. HILL
11th edition

'Open locks, whoever knocks'

PENGUIN BOOKS

PENGUIN BOOKS

Published by the Penguin Group
Penguin Books Ltd, 27 Wrights Lane, London W8 5TZ, England
Penguin Books USA Inc., 375 Hudson Street, New York, New York 10014, USA
Penguin Books Australia Ltd, Ringwood, Victoria, Australia
Penguin Books Canada Ltd, 10 Alcorn Avenue, Toronto, Ontario, Canada M4V 3B2
Penguin Books (NZ) Ltd, 182–190 Wairau Road, Auckland 10, New Zealand

Penguin Books Ltd, Registered Offices: Harmondsworth, Middlesex, England

First published by Frederick Warne & Co. Ltd 1953
Eleventh edition published by Viking 1988
Published in Penguin Books 1990
3 5 7 9 10 8 6 4

Copyright © Frederick Warne & Co. Ltd, 1988
All rights reserved

Printed in England by Clays Ltd, St Ives plc

CONTENTS

PREFACE   vii

A HISTORY OF THE CROSSWORD PUZZLE   ix

CROSSWORD MISCELLANY   xi

CATEGORY CLASSIFICATION   xv

THE CROSSWORD CURE   xvi

GENERAL INFORMATION

Groups of a Kind   1

The Chemical Elements   2

Gaseous Emanations   2

Weights and Measures   3

Coins and Monies: Ancient and Modern   11

Alphabets   19

French Revolutionary Calendar   19

The 12 Signs of the Zodiac   19

The 9 Planets and their Satellites   20

Constellations in the Heavens   20

Major Stars   20

Months of the Jewish Year   21

Books of the Bible   21

The Seven Major Ecumenical Councils (in Asia Minor)   21

British Prime Ministers   22

Presidents of the United States   22

Nobel Prize Winners in Literature   23

Counties of the British Isles   24

The 50 United States of America   24

The 12 Provinces of Canada   26

The 15 Union Republics of the Soviet Union   26

The 6 Socialist Republics of Yugoslavia   26

African Countries   27

Other Recent Changes of Name   29

Polynesia   30

Melanesia   31

Micronesia   32

The 12 Caesars and Later Roman Emperors   33

CLASSICAL MISCELLANY

The Sevens   39

The Threes and The Fours   40

Some Others   41

Offspring of Zeus   42

Consorts of Zeus   42

Brothers and Sisters of Zeus   43

Offspring of Poseidon   43

Trojan War   43

Argonautica, on Board and Ashore   45

TWO-LETTER WORDS   47

THREE-LETTER WORDS   50

FOUR-LETTER WORDS   62

FIVE-LETTER WORDS   99

SIX-LETTER WORDS   163

SEVEN-LETTER WORDS   271

EIGHT-LETTER WORDS   417

GENERAL INFORMATION

A Sweep Around the World in Mythology   581

PREFACE

This Dictionary has been specially compiled to meet the exacting needs of modern crossword enthusiasts. All the distinctive features of *The Quickway Key*—of which over 100,000 copies have been sold—have been retained; but notable additions have been made. These include a far greater number of CLUE words, a wide range of synonyms, and a complete vocabulary of the Eight-Letter Words.

The distinctive features are:

1. All CLUE words having the same number of letters are grouped together.
2. Every line begins with a possible CLUE word.
3. All CLUE words are printed in capital letters.
4. Classification code letters, such as **ar** = architecture, **md** = medicine, etc. are placed at the extreme right-hand edges of the lines, on the basis of the equivalents. A detailed list is given on page xi.
5. A very wide range of the latest words has been recorded, of which few may be found in any other one dictionary. Words in brackets indicate, not synonyms or equivalents, but areas in which the word in question is to be encountered.
6. Participles and past tenses of verbs have frequently been recorded, especially when in the passive they form adjectival phrases.

These distinctive features materially reduce the time that has to be spent in the search for interesting clues.

A large number of dictionaries have been consulted; these include *The Shorter Oxford Dictionary*, *The Century*, *Chambers's*, *Nuttall's*, *Webster's Collegiate Dictionary*; also etymological and classical dictionaries, Roget's *Thesaurus* and Nuttall's *Synonyms and Antonyms*. Clue words have been taken from encyclopaedias, *The Statesman's Year Book*, Dr. Brewer's *Reader's Handbook*, and authoritative books on Glass, China, Pewter, Curios, etc.

Words such as **CRITH, HELITE, CHENAR, LIBIDO, ZYGOTE**, etc., have been collected from scientific books and reports dealing with Modern Chemistry, Electricity, Physics, Zoology, Botany, Engineering, Physiology, etc., also from books on Theosophy and New Thought. Store catalogues and the special catalogues referring to wireless apparatus, tools, seeds, drapery, and other trades have been ransacked. A wide range of terms dealing with sports and pastimes has been included, as for example: **SCRUM, CAPPED, STANCE, DORMY, ROQUET, BURNED, GOLD, HYPE, OXER, CRAPS.**

Australian, South African, Canadian, Indian, American, and foreign words, such as **COOEE, TREK, MUSH, BHYLE, PRONTO, DUCE, TCHEKA**, are represented.

The mythological names include many Greek, Roman, Norse, Egyptian, Chaldean, and Hindu Gods.

Nearly all English words have in the course of centuries passed through many variations in their spellings. For example, in Murray's *New English Dictionary* the spelling of the word 'POWDER' has between the thirteenth and seventeenth centuries passed through the following variations, *poudre, pudre, puder, powdre, powdir, powdyr, pouder, powdere, poudire, pouldre, pulder, poulder, powlder*; and to these might be added the Scots variations of *pouther* and *powther*. A number of variations in spelling have been collected, but the range of variations recorded in different dictionaries is so large that those now given should not be regarded as exhaustive.

The selection of suitable definitions or synonyms for the words of three or four letters seldom presents any difficulty; in fact, these short words often have so many completely different meanings that more than one line is required to indicate possible clue solutions. For example, **BOX** may refer to a receptacle, a shrub, a driver's seat, a box at the theatre, an affair of fisticuffs, or to some occult nautical rite in which a compass is involved.

The longer words are usually more definite in their meanings; but **BESTED** and **WORSTED** may in some cases be synonymous terms, whilst **CLEAVE** may imply either 'adhere to' or 'split asunder'. Crossword setters, however, have a somewhat similar outlook to that master of the English language, Humpty Dumpty, who declared that: 'When *I* use a word, it means just what I choose it to mean—neither more nor less'. And further, being bound by no inhibition of compunction in splitting up words to suit the nefarious purpose, the setter may insist that **BOOKS-HOP** is a voluminous dance in spite of any exact or meritorious definition while evolving his uncanny mystification.

Similarly, there are those who insist upon providing a clue such as 'five o'clock disappointment' for 'no tea' (spelt 'NO-T' i.e. 'NOT'), or 'up to his neck in the sea' for the philosopher Seneca (SE-NEC(K)-A) and, recently, that two auxiliaries acting correctly thus BE/HAVE.

This particular aspect of crosswords has been delightfully epitomized in the sonnet commemorating the 5,000th Crossword in *The Times*, reproduced on the facing page by the kind permission of its author.

The various items enumerated under the heading GENERAL INFORMATION will frequently be found of special value in elucidating clues without the necessity of delving into a selection of reference books.

The compiler wishes to express his thanks to those numerous correspondents who so kindly forwarded valuable suggestions. It is his hope that this new volume will be found to fulfil the multifarious requirements of earnest crossword solvers and setters and so enhance the pleasures of the crossword hour.

H. W. HILL

POST SCRIPT

For this 11th edition, our third further revision and enlargement, once again several thousand new words and very many more amplifications of definition and meaning have been added throughout this volume.

Further, on this occasion, the GENERAL INFORMATION section, (now in two parts) has been increased multifold with a wealth of coinage and a greatly increased load of weights and expanse of measures from many realms, past and present.

Other new listings include Nobel Prize winners (Literature), the Roman Emperors, the states and capitals within the USA, CANADA, SOVIET UNION, and YUGOSLAVIA, together with the island groupings of POLYNESIA and the postwar changes of names of the states and capitals in AFRICA and elsewhere.

The classic epics are now recalled with particulars about The Trojans and their besiegers, also concerning the Argonauts, together with a mass of revelations concerning Zeus and others, their affectionados and progeny, as well as a world-wide summary of gods, goddesses and associated characters and creatures of many mythologies.

It is also a pleasure to include a History of the Crossword Puzzle and an augmented 'Miscellany' in lighter vein.

Once again, we are indebted to many crossword enthusiasts for public-spirited efforts in sending in details, corrections, suggestions that are indeed welcomed and incorporated whenever possible.

R. G. P. H. and I. E. H.

PUBLISHER'S NOTE

The preparation of this, the 11th Edition has once again been undertaken by the author's son Rowland G.P. Hill and also Ingrid Hill for this third revision. Nevertheless, this resulting, greatly enlarged, volume remains substantially in the style of the 8 editions compiled (1923-51) by the late Col. H.W. Hill.

A History of the Crossword Puzzle
What is a fifteen-letter definition of one of the two or three most popular inventions of the twentieth century?

The answer, of course, is 'crossword puzzle'. On December 21st, 1913, the first crossword puzzle ever set appeared in the *New York World* and the craze spread like wildfire. By 1925 it had crossed the Atlantic and Britain rapidly became a nation of crossword addicts. That bastion of dignity, *The Times*, however, was characteristically cautious. It was not until 1930, after a lively debate in the letters column, that it finally succumbed. The crossword was here to stay. Today 99 per cent of the world's daily newspapers and most Sunday papers carry a crossword and regular solvers are counted in multi-millions.

While the shape of the crossword puzzle derives from the word-square, with its repetition in both directions, the notion of differentiated verticals and horizontals probably derives from the acrostic: Greek 'akros', (at the end), and 'stichos', (line of verse). The sybils or prophetesses of ancient Greece used this form of riddle as fortune-telling devices and Cicero records this in De Divinatione. This led in due course to the double acrostic form favoured by our Queen Victoria.

However, it was in 1913 that Arthur Wynne of Liverpool, England, then with the *New York Sunday World*, was determined to introduce something fresh; so he began on a geometric shape – a diamond-shaped 'word-hanger' and gave it the name 'word-cross'.

Soon, the name was transposed to 'crossword', from the subtitle 'find the missing *cross words*', and the enthusiastic public began to send in their own creations; Wynne began to change a word here and there—the right of the crossword editor to suit the readers. It was the solvers, however, who insisted on rules: such as no obscure abbreviations; minimum use of (only well known) foreign words; definitions in dictionary form; that the grid pattern shall interlock all over; a set minimum of squares shall be black; a limit to the number of letters in isolation (unkeyed); and that the design be symmetrical.

This, is turn, led to a greater familiarity with all the shortest words; so much so that the **ZOO** was regarded as home for the **EMU** and animals from **AI** to **YAK**; the most important river was the **PO**, and Egypt was only famous for **IBIS** and **ISIS**, while **ERSE** was the celebrated language of all time!

Not long after this, the then editor of The Bookman found | that | the | crossword | had | actually brought back many dying but acceptable words, to the extent that those previously unfamiliar with specific terms like **APSE** and **NAVE** in a cathedral, or more general words such as **AVER**, **IRE**, **NEE**, **EMIT**, **ERR**, **ELATE** etc. had now become aware of these words. Such was the come-back of vocabulary and usage that this new vehicle for wordpower had brought about, even if cliché use was a resultant hazard.

Reaction soon set in with the urge to discard 'limited vocabulary', make use of reference books, and for an undeniable educational value to bring the standard to a great art worthy of its exalted ancestors.

By 1925 there were about 10 million fans in America. Schools began to make use of them and university psychologists compared crossword ability with IQ tests and found parallel results. Further, a new national habit was revealed in changed situations, in everyday life.

To take one instance, The Baltimore and Ohio Railroad installed dictionaries in each carriage of commuter trains for the convenience of passengers, many of whom took crossword books when on long journeys; and one witness said that 'everyone is going about with knobs of knowledge sticking out on their foreheads like the buffers on a railway engine'.

One New York magistrate was faced with the frustrating task of distracting an intent group of twenty-one solvers; when one defendant pleaded innocent of failure to appear to the charge by explaining he had a longstanding engagement with a crossword, the judge promptly sentenced him to ten days in the workhouse!

Another incident related the effect on a would-be solver who was joined by two others in a noisy restaurant. When closing time had passed none of the three would budge, so the police had to threaten arrest of the first of the three. Thereupon that guilty party expressed delight at the prospect of further, uninterrupted, solitary solving being offered to him!

In the third printing of *The Times Crossword Puzzle Book* in 1925—that vintage year for solvers—the following warning was given to solvers to alert readers to the possible two symptoms that might result once the contagion set in:

1. If you want to do any more work the rest of the day, put down this book now. If you insist on going ahead, say goodbye to everything else.
2. This is your problem: Do you want to own a book which will delight and distract you (and perhaps shatter the serenity of your home) for at least one hundred hours?

Again, a Broadway revue, 'Puzzles of 1925' included a skit on a Sanatorium for crossword fans seeking a cure, and in that year England reeled with horror as collectively 5 million working hours a day in America—most of them in office time—were spent on poring over a puzzle. 'But that couldn't happen here!'

However, Arthur Wynne had already sold six puzzles to the *Sunday Express*, and thereby earned the title of Crossword Originator and Constructor on both sides of the Atlantic. Soon, in that year, *The Times* was forced to eat its words. 'Who would have thought . . . that the crossword puzzle had come to stay? To most of us it looked like a transatlantic craze which could not be expected to take root in solid, unimaginative English minds.'

What a comeback for those, knowledgeable in the classics and such mysteries, to make use of a mine of 'irrelevance' and so-called 'useless information'.

It only remains to add that, just as everything stops for tea, so, even with newsprint rationing in wartime, the crossword remained a feature which many brains felt to be a necessity, for balance of mind and outlook.

Thus, in its inimitable, modest, way the crossword has invaded the international scene leaving a trail of possessed solvers in its wake.

Abridged and adapted from 'A History of the Crossword Puzzle' by Michelle Arnot; Papermac. This book also contains samples of not only the first, but other famous crosswords, as they originally appeared.

R. G. P. H.

CROSSWORD MISCELLANY

TO THE EDITOR OF THE TIMES

Sir,

Much have I travelled in another life,
Taken the golden road to Samarkand,
Rolled down to Rio, wandered down the Strand
(Bananaless), asked after Laban's wife.
I swore, "I will not cease from mental strife
Nor shall my pencil slumber in my hand
Till I have re-discovered Penguinland
And found a cricketer's Malayan knife."

In vain; the tangled clues still tantalize
And synonyms elude, like runic rhymes.
So would-be solvers with lack-lustre eyes,
Confronted with the anagram for limes,
Look at each other with a wild surmise
Silent, upon a crossword in The Times.

Your faithfully,
ELTON EDGE

---

50 YEARS AGO

From the Manchester Guardian Weekly, December 12, 1924

The world is a puzzling place, but man is not to be deterred from the delights of additional and self-inflicted bewilderment. At one time he found his pleasure in the manipulation of bits and pieces in a jig-saw. Then came the more intellectual diversion of acrostics. Now we are asked to revel in an import from America called 'cross words'. The acrostic in its time must have done valuable work for the Bible Society, since the more obscure names of the Old Testament have a knack of beginning and ending with the vowels that otherwise defy the puzzle-maker, while they are also fairly hard to remember. The new pastime must be a great comfort to the salesmen of dictionaries, glossaries, and the like, and the old complaint that the average man's vocabulary is limited to some five or six hundred words out of the treasury that is open to him may be dissipated by the present quest of verbal oddities. The complete 'cross word' enthusiast is led up hills of chemistry into dales of botany, he must even put his nose to the English grammar and be quite sure where the species 'adverb' begins and ends. The thing beneath the word need not excite him; it is the raiment of letters that he seeks, and he must be sure to get them in their proper order. The young lady who thought that to write was human but to spell divine might profit by the new pastime, but people who are more deeply interested in things than in words will wonder, like the charity boy confronted with the alphabet, whether it is worth going through so much to learn so little. However, the nominalists appear to be a large, happy, and busy faction, but this only increases one's fears as to the fate of a family in which there should be a lonely realist railing at all this quest of the shy noun or dim elusive epithet. May not the result of such a clash become upon occasion — cross words?

Within that decade the first edition of this book—in pocket diary format, with a pencil—was already in evidence, especially among those travelling to and from the City. Later editions were enlarged to the present size.

Cryptic

March 5, 1976.

Sir, — Returning home from my local **hammam** I was somewhat **esurient** and so visited our **spence** and set the table complete with **ortolan** but my fear was **adipose**, so I stopped eating and performed a quick **antiphon** with my wife, before retiring to bed.

All the words in bold appeared in this week's crossword puzzles, and if they are known and understood by your average reader I will eat my **zucchetta**.

W. L. Fraser,

Glasgow

Crosswords Keep Man Young at 110

Britain's oldest living person, Mr. Alfred Harrow, notches up his 110th birthday on 21st November 1976. Even in recent years he has kept a wonderfully alert mind doing crosswords . . . 'I have to keep my mind alert,' he says.

Evening Standard

A situation of Royal gravity: one up and one down

William Rufus was hunting one day in the New Forest, when William Tell (the memorable crackshot, inventor of the crossbow puzzle) took unerring aim at a reddish apple which had fallen on to the King's head, and shot him through the heart.

W. C. Sellar and R. T. Yeatman

OUR MELLIFLUOUS BARD DOES IT AGAIN

Together with his contemporaries (Chaucer, Spencer, Dryden, Obs and Trad) our own William Shakespeare once again appears in this volume, introducing a unit of honeyed sound/capacity. This arose from the Tudor delight in gardens, leafy bowers and walks, mells and malls— a setting lending a counter point of interest to enhance consorts of viols, recorders and gambas, (and nightingales too). While they were concerned to fill a mell with melody, nowadays we would employ garden orchestras and transistor radios. This unit of pleasant sound bordering on the herbaceous, appears as 'PHILOMEL' and, as such, treads dainty a measure among the bulk of more weighty items.

THE ARDEN CHRONICLER

INFRA-DIG, AND CROSS-HERBS

It. was in last August that it all began, when my three neighbours, whose territories meet by my corner (where my herb garden had recently spread itself across), assembled under my gaze—leaving me to be ravaged by an attack of anti-socialitis or join a conspiracy of literary mendelism for crossing herbs in a mould of literal garbage.

Having caught the pestilence before another dose could be expected, but I resisted the virus germanely. Then, led by the voice of an opera singer, my other neighbours soon summoned in all their relatives and friends, and I had to submit to an exchange of words in a climate where they came up like mushrooms in the night.

From being comfortably bedded borderers we felt reduced to being mere squares in perforated patchwork plot as the conspiracy grew. Cries of 'I've found it!' and 'Here's the solution we need' echoed, blinding us with acidic science as we looked on helplessly and gradually the next stage of the rot—competitionism—took over. This was soon leading each and all of us to abandon everything else in our insatiable state— swept away as we were, with only the Post Office prospering. While we drained our resources away on lower grade species from magazines and even pictorials, and weighing in cryptograms all to be planted with herbiage verbiage.

Very Infra-dig indeed—but that's how we became—then, one day, the Opera singer struck gold! We questioned our pacemaker to the depths, and gradually fathomed out where he had cast his lead so successfully. In a fit of DTs and DIYs he seemed to have turned totally analphabetic, and only partially restored by a course of numeracy therapy. As he proudly displayed his cheque, we came to learn that he now lived in an environment of littlewords, with phrases like 'help yourself' and 'have some more'; but otherwise he poopoohed us all with '1x2' and so on.

Well, we have become even more infra-dig too—in fact, more in for a dig than ever. We have evacuated and excavated our herb gardens, and, standing at the Green end, have turned the garden hoses on. We are, each of us, busy filling in our own pools, either for a lucky dip or a last SOS; remaining, like Seneca, up to the neck in the sea . . .

—from the under-Lyme Engraver

No more cross words

From Mr John Ruffle
Sir, On a recent visit to Egypt a friend purchased a copy of The Times for £E2.50 (approx. £1.25p) and was (I think) delighted to find that the crossword had been accurately completed.

I have tried asking my supplier what he will charge for this remarkable service. Mr and Mrs Beeching (February 20) might also be interested if you could provide details of how it can be arranged.

©John Ruffle

The Times, 27 Feb 1987

No more cross words

From Mr and Mrs John Beeching
Sir, We were delighted this morning to find our crossword puzzles printed on separate sheets of paper, allowing a blissful return to the period of companionable silence after breakfast when we each apply ourselves to the puzzle most suited to our talents.

Thank you for your efforts in bringing this about.

©John Beeching
Cicely Beeching

The Times, 20 Feb 1987

WORDY MIGHT-HAVE-BEENS

Many of us think that words mean what we can remember what we thought they meant, in the manner that two famous historians described history as being not what we thought but what we can remember. We have done just that, as other methods are self-defeating.

Readers Digest tells us that 'it pays to increase your word power' and this was clear to Sir Winston Churchill, who roused, cajoled, admonished and conciliated people of all nations during an era of unparalleled tribulation. He used strong words to convey his vigorous thoughts, such as imponderable, vitiate, ignoble, verbiage, juncture, brazen, subventions, and bemused.

We therefore dwell on the unknown weightlessness implicit in imponderable as a unit of slimming, as well as lack of seriousness or gravity in astronautical travel. Vitiate suggests a graduate of avoidance, according to the Boolean law of credibility, applied to hyper non-existensialism, or missing evidence.

Ignoble must rank as democratic in opposition to the Lords, and verbiage as a screen in the Dunsinane tradition of foliage rather than the modern smoke version. But then Shakespeare wrote all his plays on words, and depended on pitprops and malaprops to uphold his staging.

Likewise Brunel found himself in the position of King Lear's Gloucester in having his observant eyes outgauged at a juncture near Clapham Heath, and thereby losing his foresight together with his broad-minded, western, lines of development.

Further, while showing arrears or being topless may be the rule for nudists, these could be actionable matters for the Queen's Bench over which the royal motto proclaims "My God, and I'm right", despite the questionable exposure of a thigh and a garter long ago at Court.

After the bronze age we find few brazen images or artifacts until horse brasses became popular, and top brass denoted support for an iron lady, and her generals. We hope that the discovery through scientific subventions encompassing nuclear magnetics will lead to chips with everything. How much can a polar bear?

Thus, in conclusion, we are bemused artistically by the Three Graces comprising Faith with Hope, and, as any vintner knows, the greatest of the three is Clarity.

E. & O.E.

This book is also dedicated to William Tell master of the cross-bow puzzle. Though his son was the apple of his eye he solved the order of the day by scoring on the apple and avoiding the eye. He was, indeed, well clued up, not routinely but routely (swiss: Rutli).

—The Editor Regrets—

Due to lack of space, Mary Poppins's favourite panegyric word will not appear in this edition. It has 34 letters and is 'Supercalifragilisticexpialidocious'.
For a sample, please apply to your nearest chemist, with prescription.

(printed on film posters)

'OPEN LOCKS, WHOEVER KNOCKS'

We wish to acknowledge with thanks and express our appreciation of kind and helpful letters suggesting the adoption of various new words or listings for the General Information section or items for our miscellany.

These are all welcomed and carefully considered as contributions to the worldwide community linked by crosswords and various word games and contents.

R. G. P. HILL and I. E. HILL

CATEGORY CLASSIFICATION

ac	acoustics	lw	law
ae	aeronautics	ma	mathematics
ag	agriculture	md	medicine and medical
am	automation	me	measurements
ar	architecture	ml	metallurgy
as	astronomy	mn	mining
au	automobiles	mo	mountaineering
ba	bacteriology	mt	meteorology
bc	biochemistry	mu	music
bd	building	nc	nuclear (physics)
bl	biology	nm	numismatics, coins
br	brewing	nt	nautical
bt	botany	nv	navigation
ce	civil engineering	oc	oceanography
cf	combining form	pb	plumbing
ch	chemistry	pc	psychology, psychiatry
.ck	cookery	pg	photography
cn	cinema	pl	physiology
cp	computers	pm	pharmaceutics
cr	carpentry	pp	paper
cy	cytology	pr	printing
ec	ecology	ps	physics
eg	engineering	pt	paints, painting
el	electrical, electronics	rd	radar
fd	foundry	rl	religion
fr	forestry	ro	radio
gl	geology	rw	railways
gn	genetics	sp	space
go	geography	sv	surveying
gp	geophysics	tc	telecommunications
gs	glass	to	tools
hd	heraldry	tv	television
hr	horology	tx	textiles
hy	hydraulics	vt	veterinary
jn	joinery	wv	weaving
le	leather-working	zo	zoology
lt	light		

Note: Language and nationality abbreviations are found closer to the definition, within parenthesis, but not in bold type, which is reserved for the above classifications.

Sc. = Scottish
Fr. = French
Rus. = Russian
Scand. = Scandinavian
Jap. = Japanese

Gr. = Greek
It. = Italian
Lat. = Latin
Turk. = Turkish

Ind. = Indian
Jew. = Jewish
Sp. = Spanish
Aust. = Australian, etc.

Various literary abbreviations are also given:

obs. = obsolete
sl. = slang

Shak. = Shakespeare

Spens. = Spenser

THE CROSSWORD CURE

To The Times *Crossword Editor*

O nameless coiner of the cryptic clue,
  O master of delusive definition,
Embracing in your panoramic view
  A world of miscellaneous erudition,
Once more I pay the homage due
  To your wise conduct of your Inquisition,
Bringing a daily boon and breathing space
To the tired runners in a mad world's race.

You leave no fruitful avenues unexplored
  That minister to innocent hilarity,
But never strike a harsh or jarring chord,
  Or find a virtue in unveiled vulgarity.
Rumour and gossip are by you ignored;
  You season ridicule with kindly charity,
Yet on occasion with unerring eyes
Transfix malicious folly as it flies.

You jog my memory with your mental jerks;
  To you, in fine, I owe a double debt
For while the old machinery still works
  And shows no sign of breaking down as yet—
Thanks to the stimulus of your quips and quirks—
  You teach me to remember, and forget.
For Hell's most grisly gangsters have no power
To crash the gate that guards the Crossword hour.

C. L. GRAVES

The above poem, which appeared in *The Times* of July 23, 1941, is reproduced by the kind permission of the author's son.

GENERAL INFORMATION

GROUPS OF A KIND

Terms of the Chase

3 NYE of pheasants
RAG of colts

4 BEVY of roes or quails
CAST of hawks
CETE of badgers
DOWN of hares
DULE of turtles
FALL of woodcock
GANG of elks
HERD of cranes, curlew, deer
LEPE of leopards
NEST of rabbits
PACE of asses
PACK of hounds
ROUT of wolves
SORD of mallards
SUTE of mallards
STUD of mares
TEAM of oxen
WISP of snipe

5 BROOD of hens
CHARM of goldfinches
COVEY of partridges
DOYLT of tame swine
DROVE of kine
FLOCK of sheep
PLUMP of wild fowl
PRIDE of lions
SEDGE of herons
SHOAL of fish
SIEGE of herons
SKEIN of geese (flying)
SKULK of foxes
SLOTH of bears
SWARM of bees
TRIBE of goats
TROOP of monkeys
WATCH of nightingales

6 BARREN of mules
COLONY of gulls
COVERT of coots
DESERT of lapwings
GAGGLE of geese
HARRAS of horses
FLIGHT of doves
KENNEL of raches
KINDLE of kittens

LABOUR of moles
LITTER of whelps
MUSTER of peacocks
SCHOOL of porpoises
SPRING of teal

7 BADLING of ducks
CLOWDER of cats
COMPANY of widgeon
DOPPING of sheldrake
SOUNDER of swine

8 BUILDING of rooks
FESNYING of ferrets
RICHESSE of martens
SINGULAR of boars

9 BADELYNGE of ducks
COWARDICE of curs

10 CHATTERING of choughs
EXALTATION of larks
SHREWDNESS of apes

11 MURMURATION of starlings

12 CONGREGATION of plovers

Miscellaneous

5 BLAST of hunters
BLUSH of boys
LYING of pardoners
SKULK of friars
STALK of foresters
STATE of princes

6 MELODY of harpers
RAYFUL of knaves

7 DRAUGHT of butlers
POVERTY of pipers

8 FIGHTING of beggars
SUBTILNE of sergeants

9 MORBIDITY of majors
SAFEGUARD of porters

WANDERING of tinkers

10 DISGUISING of tailors
OBSERVANCE of hermits
SIMPLICITY of subalterns

11 DRUNKENSHIP of cobblers
SUPERFLUITY of nuns

12 MALAPERTNESS of pedlars

13 INCREDIBILITY of cuckolds

Modern

4 BAND of musicians
NEST of machine guns
PARK of artillery
GANG of thieves
ROPE of pearls
TUFT of grass

5 CASTE of flower pots
CLUMP of trees
CROWD of people
FLEET of cars
HORDE of savages
POSSE of savages
SHEAF of corn
SKEIN of silk
STAND of arms
TRUSS of hay

6 BUDGET of papers
FLIGHT of aeroplanes
GALAXY of beauty
PUNNET of strawberries
TROUPE of actors

7 CLUSTER of stars
COMPANY of actors

8 SEQUENCE of cards

9 COMMUNITY of saints
GATHERING of the clans

Name	Symbol	Name	Symbol	Name	Symbol
3 TIN	Sn	GALLIUM	Ga	SELENIUM	Se
		HAFNIUM	Hf	TANTALUM	Ta
		HOLMIUM	Ho	THALLIUM	Tl
4 GOLD	Au	IRIDIUM	Ir	TITANIUM	Ti
IRON	Fe	KRYPTON *	Kr	TUNGSTEN	W
LEAD	Pb	LITHIUM	Li	VANADIUM	V
NEON *	Ne	MERCURY	Hg		
ZINC	Zn	NEUTRON *	Nu	**9** ALUMINIUM	Al
		NIOBIUM	Nb	BERYLLIUM	Be
5 ARGON *	A	RHENIUM	Re	COLUMBIUM	Cb
BORON	B	RHODIUM	Rh	GERMANIUM	Ge
XENON *	Xe	SILICON	Si	LANTHANUM	La
		SULPHUR	S	MAGNESIUM	Mg
6 BARIUM	Ba	TERBIUM	Tb	MANGANESE	Mn
CARBON	C	THORIUM	Th	NEODYMIUM	Nd
CERIUM	Ce	THULIUM	Tm	PALLADIUM	Pd
COBALT	Co	URANIUM	U	POTASSIUM	K
COPPER	Cu	WOLFRAM	W	RUTHENIUM	Ru
ERBIUM	Er	YTTRIUM	Y	STRONTIUM	Sr
HELIUM *	He			TELLURIUM	Te
INDIUM	In	**8** ANTIMONY	Sb	YTTERBIUM	Yb
IODINE	I	CHLORINE *	Cl	ZIRCONIUM	Zr
NICKEL	Ni	CHROMIUM	Cr		
OSMIUM	Os	EUROPIUM	Eu	**10** DYSPROSIUM	Dy
OXYGEN *	O	FLUORINE *	F	GADOLINIUM	Gd
RADIUM	Ra	GLUCINUM	Gl	MOLYBDENUM	Mo
SILVER	Ag	HYDROGEN *	H	PHOSPHORUS	P
SODIUM	Na	ILLINIUM	Il		
		LUTETIUM	Lu	**12** NEOYTTERBIUM	Yb
7 ARSENIC	As	MASURIUM	Ma	PRASEODYMIUM	Pr
BISMUTH	Bi	NITROGEN *	N		
BROMINE	Br	PLATINUM	Pt		
CADMIUM	Cd	RUBIDIUM	Rb	* GASES	
CAESIUM	Cs	SAMARIUM	Sm		
CALCIUM	Ca	SCANDIUM	Sc		

GASEOUS EMANATIONS

5 NITON from Radium

6 IONIUM from Uranium

8 ACTINIUM from Thorium
POLONIUM from Radium

2

With some approximate English equivalents

A	acre, ampere, electric current	Int.
B	bel, power comparison unit	Int.
C	colomb, charge	Int.
F	farad, capacitance	Int.
G	magnetic flux density, gram = 0.035 oz	Int.
H	henry, inductance	Int.
J	joule, energy	Int.
K	kelvin, temperature	Int.
L	litre = 1 qt (liq.)	Int.
M	metre, length = 39.37 ins	Int.
N	newton, force	Int.
S	second, time, angle, lat., long.	Int.
T	tesla, magnetic flux density, tonne, metric ton	Int.
V	volt, voltage	Int.
W	watt, power	Int.

2 Letters

AP	apothecaries measure	Int.
AV	avoirdupois (avdp), weight	Int.
BU	bushel, 4 pecks (2219.3 cu ins); 0.036 cu m (Br. Imp.)	Britain
BU	TSUBO = 3.306 sq m (area)	Japan
CD	candela, luminous intensity	Int.
CI	curie, unit of activity of radioactive substance	Int.
CM	centimetre = 0.394 ins	Int.
DB	decibel (dB), unit of noise	Int.
DL	decilitre (10 dl = 1 litre)	Int.
DR	dram, 27.34 grains, 0.06 oz, 1.771 gram	U.S.
EL	1 metre (old EL = 27.08 ins)	Netherlands
FT	foot = 12 ins, 0.33 yds, 30.48 cm	Int.
GB	gilbert (Gb), magnetomotive force (magnetic potential)	Int.
GI	gill (Br. Imp.), 5 fl oz, 8.66 cu ins, 142.06 cu cm	Britain
GI	gill (liq.), 4 fl oz, 7.21 cu ins, 118.29 ml	U.S.
GO	0.18 litre	Japan
GR	grain, 0.036 dram, 0.002 oz, 0.06 gram	Int.
HZ	hertz (Hz), frequency	Int.
HU	51.77 litres	China
IN	inch, $\frac{1}{12}$ foot, $\frac{1}{36}$ yard, 2.54 cm	Int.
KG	kilogram, 2.2 lbs	Int.
KM	kilometre, 0.6 mile	Int.
KW	kilowatt, 1.3 horsepower; kilowatt-hour/KWh.	Int.

LB	pound, 16 oz, 7000 grains, 0.453 kg	Int.
LI	$\frac{3}{4}$ mile = 360 pu	China
LM	lumen, luminous flux	Int.
LX	lux, illumination	Int.
MI	mile, 5280 ft, 320 rods, 1760 yds, 1.609 km	Int.
ML	millilitre	Int.
MM	millimetre, 0.04 in	Int.
NT	nit, luminance	Int.
OE	oersted (Oe), magnetic field strength	Int.
OZ	ounce, 28 grams, 16 drams, 437.5 grains	Int.
PE	$\frac{3}{4}$ metre	Portugal
PK	peck (dry), 8 qt, 537.605 cu in, 8.809 litres	U.S.
PK	peck (Br. Imp.), 2 gals, 554.8385 cu ins, 0.009 cu m	Britain
PT	pint (liq.), 4 gi, 28.875 cu ins, 0.473 litre	U.S.
PT	pint (dry), $\frac{1}{2}$ qt, 33.600 cu ins, 0.550 litre	U.S.
PT	pint (Br. Imp.), 4 gi, 34.677 cu ins, 568.26 cu cm	Britain
PU	70.5 ins = 5 ch'ih	China
QT	quart (liq.), 2 pts, 57.75 cu ins, 0.946 litre	U.S.
QT	quart (dry), 2 pts, 67.20 cu ins, 1.101 litres	U.S.
QT	quart (Br. Imp.), 2 pts, 69.35 cu ins, 1.136 litres	Britain
RD	rod, 5.50 yds, 16.5 ft, 5.029 m	Int.
RI	2.440 miles	Japan
SB	stilb (Sb), unit of luminance	Int.
SE	118.615 sq yds (0.9918 are)	Japan
SR	steradian, solid angle	Int.
ST	stokes, kinematic viscosity	Int.
TO	18.03 litres = 4.77 U.S. gals	Japan
TU	100.142 miles = 250 li	China
WA	WAH, 2 m	Thailand
WB	weber, magnetic flux	Int.
YD	yard, 3 ft, 36 ins, 0.914 m	Int.

3 Letters

AAM	30–35 gals	E. Indies
ARE	100 sq m, 119.6 sq yds	Int.
AUM	31 Imp. gal	S. Africa
BAT	BAHT, TICAL, 15 grams (231.5 grains)	Thailand
BEL	power comparison unit	Int.
CAB	3 pts	Hebrew

3

CHO	1815 sq ft (3000 bu/area; 360 shaku/length)	Japan
COR	8½ bushels	Hebrew
CWT	hundredweight; 45.35 kg (short), 50.80 kg (long)	Britain
DWT	pennyweight	Britain
ELL	(Eng.) 45 ins, (Sc.) 37 ins, (Jersey) 4 ft	Britain
ERG	unit of energy; 1 erg = 10^{-7} joules	Int.
FEN	5.76 grains (silver weight)	China
FOD	0.3138 m, 1.029 ft	Denmark
FOT	11.689 ins; 10 fot = 1 stäng	Sweden
FOU	bushel	Scotland
FUT	FOUTE 1 Eng. ft	U.S.S.R.
GAL	gallon (liq.), 4 qt (231 cu ins), 3.785 litres	U.S.
GAL	gallon (Br. Imp.), 4 qt (277.4 cu ins), 4.545 litres	Britain
GIN	KATI, CATTY 1¾ lbs	Malaysia
GUZ	GUDGE 27–36 ins	E. Indies
GUZ	GUEZA, ZER 1 m (40.95 ins)	Iran
HIN	6 qts	Hebrew
KAN	1 litre; 1¾ lbs (Hong Kong)	Netherlands
KEN	1.82 m, 5.96 ft	Japan
KIN	0.600 kg, 1.32 lbs	Japan
KON	CATTY 1¾ lbs	Korea
KUP	10 ins	Thailand
LOG	¼ pt	Hebrew
LOT	10 grams (new), ½ oz (old)	Germany
LUX	unit of light (lx); 1 1m over an area of 1m squared	Int.
MIL	one thousandth of an inch	U.S./G.B.
MIL	MILL 1.000 archins (new mil)	Turkey
MIN	minim, $\frac{1}{60}$ fluidram, 0.0591 cu cm (Br. Imp.)	Britain
MIN	minim, $\frac{1}{60}$ fluidram, 0.0616 cu cm	U.S.
MNA	1½ kg = 1.172 oke	Greece
MOU	806.65 sq yds (or 920.41 sq yds)	China
MUD	1 hectolitre	Netherlands
NIN	$\frac{10}{12}$ in	Thailand
NIT	(nt) luminance; 1 candela per m squared	Int.
NIU	1 in	Thailand
OCK	1 kg; (1881) 1 ock = 100 drachms; new batman = 10 ocks, kantar = 10 batmans	Turkey
OHM	resistance V/A	Int.
OKA	3 lbs	Egypt
OKE	1.28 l (liq.); 1.28 kg (old); 2.8 lbs	Bulgaria
OKE	400 drams	Cyprus
ONS	100 grams	Netherlands

PIC	PIK 2 ft (Greece picki 0.64m)	Cyprus
PIE	11.73 in	Rome
PIK	DIRAA 0.58 m	U.A.R.
PIN	half a firkin	Britain
POT	0.966 litre	Denmark
RAD	radian, plane angle; radiation absorbed dose, 0.01 joule/kg (100 ergs/ gramme)	Int.
RAI	¾ acre	Thailand
REM	roentgen equivalent man; 1 rem = 1 rad × Q.F.	Int.
RIO	ounce	Japan
ROD	5.50 yds, 16.5 ft, 5.029 m	Int.
SEN	40.6 m, 44 yds	Thailand
SHO	1.804 litres	Japan
SUN	1 in	Japan
TAN	133 lbs	China
TOD	2 stone	Britain
TON	20 cwt, 0.907 m/tons (short), 1.016 m/tons (long)	Int.
TOU	10 litres	China
TUN	252 gals	Britain
VAT	1 hectolitre	Netherlands
WAH	WA 2 m	Thailand
WEY	13 stone	Britain
ZAK	1 hectolitre	Netherlands
ZAR	1 m	Iran
ZER	GUZ, GUEZA 1 m (40.95 ins)	Iran

4 Letters

ACRE	4840 sq yds, 0.405 hectare, 4046 sq m	Britain
ATTO	(a) 10^{-18}	Int.
AUNE	1 m, (France 1.18 m), (Jersey 4 ft)	Belgium
BAHT	BAT, TICAL, 15 grams (231.5 grains)	Thailand
BALE	10 reams	Britain
BATH	6 gals	Hebrew
BUTT	108 gals	Britain
CHEE	TAHIL 1¾ oz = 10 chee = 100 hoon	Malaysia
CHEK	14⅜ ins	Hong Kong
CH'IH	14.1 ins (customs), 5 ch'ih = 1 pu	China
CHIN	CATTY 1¾ lbs (customs)	China
CHUO	1.815 sq ft (customs)	China
COSS	1.82 km, 1¾ miles	India
CRAN	ca. 750 herrings	Britain
CU CM	0.06 cu in	Int.
CU FT	1728 cu ins, 0.0370 cu yd, 0.028 cu m	Int.
CU IN	0.00058 cu ft, 16.387 cu cm	Int.
DECI	(d) 10^{-1}; 1 dm = 0.1 m	Int.

WEIGHTS AND MEASURES

Term	Definition	Region
DEKA	DECA (da) 10; 1 dekametre = 10 metres	Int.
DITO	1 cm	Italy
DOLA	DOLIA, 96 doli = 1 zolotnick	U.S.S.R.
DOSE	quantity of radiation (absorbed energy), see rad, rem	
DRAH	22 ins	Morocco
DRAM	27.343 grams, 0.0625 oz, 1.7718452 grains	Int.
DUIM	1 in	U.S.S.R./ Netherlands
DYNE	unit of force; 1 dyne = 10^{-5} newton	Int.
ELLA	1 yd	Sabah/N. Borneo
ELLE	60 cm; (Latvian S.S.R.) 0.53 m	Switzerland
EPHA	bushel	Hebrew
FL DR	fluidram, 60 minims (0.22 cu in), 29.572 ml	U.S.
FL DR	fluidram, 60 minims (0.21 cu in), 3.5516 cu cm	Britain
FL OZ	fluid ounce (Br. Imp.), 8 fluidrams, 28.413 cu cm	Britain
FOOT	12 ins, 0.333 yd, 30.48 cm	Int.
FUNT	FOUNTE 0.90 lb (U.S.S.R.), 405.5 grams	Poland
FUSZ	12 zolls = 1.037 ft (Vienna), $1\frac{3}{4}$ fusz = 1 m	Switzerland
GIGA	(G) 10^9; 1 GHz = 10^9 hertz	Int.
GILL	4 fl oz (7.218 cu ins), 118.29 ml	U.S.
GILL	5 fl oz (Br. Imp.), 8.669 cu in, 142.0652 cu cm	Britain
GRAM	0.035 oz	Int.
GRAO	0.769 gr, 0.18 in	Portugal
HAND	(horses) 4 in	Britain
HAT'H	MOOLUM, CUBIT, 18 ins	India
HIDE	120 acres	Britain
HOON	TAHIL, CHEE, $1\frac{3}{4}$ oz = 10 chee = 100 hoon	Malaysia
IMMI	1.5 litres	Switzerland
INCH	0.083 ft, 0.027 yd, 2.540 cm, 25 mm	Int.
JOCH	57.55 ares = 1.422 acres	Austria
KATI	CATTY, GIN $1\frac{3}{4}$ lbs	Malaysia
KELA	$\frac{1}{2}$ bushel	Egypt
KHAT	1 cm	Turkey
KILO	(k) 10^3; 1 km = 1000 m; comput.: 2^{10} = 1 kilobyte = 1024 bytes	Int.
KILO	kilogram, 2.2 lbs	Int.
KNOT	6.080 ft; 1 nt mile/hour = 0.514 4444 m/s	Britain
KOKU	180.39 litres (see TO)	Japan
KOSS	2000 yds	India
KUNG	78.96 ins (customs)	China
KWAN	KUWAN, 3.75 kg, 8.26 lbs	Japan
KYAT	16.33 grams	Burma
LAST	30 hectolitres	Netherlands
LINE	LIGNE, 2.26 mm	Paris
LINK	7.92 in	U.S./G.B.
MACE	$93\frac{3}{4}$ gr (Sabah/N. Borneo), $58\frac{3}{4}$ gr	China
MARC	MARK 0.2448 kg (old)	France
MEGA	(M) 10^6; 2^{20}, 1 megabyte = 1048576 bytes	Int.
MIJL	1 int. nautical mile	Netherlands
MILE	5280 ft, 320 rods, 1760 yds, 1.609 km	Int.
MILE	nautical, 6080.20 ft (formerly)	U.S.
MILE	nautical/admiralty, 6080 ft	Britain
MILE	nautical/international, 1853 m	Int.
MILE	postal, 4714 ft	Austria
MOIO	$2\frac{3}{4}$ qts	Portugal
MUDD	1 bushel	Morocco
NAIL	$2\frac{1}{4}$ ins	Britain
NANO	(n) 10^{-9}; 1 nm = 10^{-9} m	Int.
NATR	2 lbs	Ethiopia
OKET	1 oz avoirdupois (av)	Ethiopia
ONCA	28.68 grams	Portugal
ONCE	30.59 grams (old)	France
PAAL	$1\frac{1}{2}$ m	Indonesia
PACK	240 lbs	Britain
PALM	1 decimetre (dm)	Netherlands
PARA	90 lbs	Sabah/N. Borneo
PECK	2 gals	Britain
PHOT	intensity of illumination (1 1m/sq cm), 1 phot = 104 lux	Int.
PICO	(p) 10^{-12}; 1 pF = 10^{12} farad	Int.
PIED	11.81 ins = 10 pouces (Belgium), 12.79 ins	Canada
PIED	de roi 0.3248 m	Paris
PINT	(liquid) 28.875 cu ins, 0.473 litre	U.S.
PINT	(dry) $\frac{1}{2}$ qt (33.67 cu ins), 568.260 cu cm	Britain
PINT	(Br. Imp.) 4 gi (34.67 cu ins), 568.260 cu cm	Britain
PIPA	500 litres, 429 litres (old)	Portugal
PIPE	126 gals	Britain
POLE	$16\frac{1}{2}$ ft	Britain
POND	$\frac{1}{2}$ kilogram	Netherlands
POOD	36.113 lbs	U.S.S.R.
PUND	500 grams, (Sweden 425.1 grams)	Scandinavia
REAM	20 quires (of 24 sheets: paper)	Britain
REED	152 ins	Hebrew
RODE	3.138 m	Denmark
ROOD	40 perches, $\frac{1}{4}$ acre	Britain

ROTL	ROTTOLA, RATEL, 0.9905 lb (customs)	U.A.R.
SACK	2 weys	Britain
SAWK	20 in	Thailand
SEAH	14 pts	Hebrew
SEAM	(glass) 24 stone	Britain
SEER	1.061 lbs (Sri Lanka), 2.057 lbs (government)	India
SIHR	16 miseals, 1136 gr weight	Iran
SHIH	157.89 lbs	China
SKOT	low-intensity lighting	Int.
SQ IN	0.007 sq ft, 6.4516 sq cm	Int.
SQ MI	640 acres, 102 400 sq rods, 2.589 sq km	Int
SQ RD	30.25 sq yds, 0.006 acre, 25.293 sq m	Int.
SQ YD	1296 sq ins, 9 sq ft, 0.836 sq m	Int.
STAB	1 m (3¾ old fuss)	Germany
TAEL	1¾ oz (Hong Kong), 936¼ grams	Thailand
TAEL	10 momme (Japan), 1¾ oz (silver weight)	China
TANK	68.1 grams (72 tanks = 1 seer)	Bombay
TENG	(basket) 2218.2 cu ins (varies)	Burma
TERA	(T) 10^{12}; 1 Tm = 10^{12} m	Int.
TOLA	180 grains; legal weight of rupee	India
TORR	unit of pressure (vacuum), 133.322 newtons/sq m	Int.
T'SUN	1.41 ins	China
VARA	83.5 cm–l m, 33–43 ins (varies)	S. America/ U.S.
VISS	3.60 lbs (3.65 old)	Burma
VOLT	(V) W/A voltage	Int.
WATT	kilowatt, 1.3 horsepower	Int.
X-RAY	unit of length, 1.002 × 10^{-13} m	Int.
YARD	3 ft, 36 ins, 0.9144 m	Int.
YLEM	hypothetical density (10^{16} kg m^{-3})	Int.
ZOLL	3 cm (ca. 1 in. old)	Switzerland

5 Letters

ANKER	7½ gals	S. Africa
ANKER	38.25 litres (or 30 stoof)	Latvian S.S.R.
ARDEB	5.61 bushels = 100 sq m = 119.6 sq yds	Egypt
ASSAY	ton, 29.16 grams	U.S.
BAHAR	BEHAR 450 lbs	Arabian Peninsula
BARYE	unit of pressure (old); 1 barye = 0.1 pascal	Int.

BERRI	1.67 km, 1.04 miles (old)	Turkey
BRACA	2.20 m	Portugal
BRAZA	1.732 m	Argentina
CABLE	100 fathoms	Britain
CABOT	10 pots (19.75 litres)	Jersey
CANCH	6 cubits	Hebrew
CANDY	500 lbs (560 lbs Bombay)	India
CANNA	2 yds	Malta
CARAT	metric, 200 milligrams	Int.
CATTY	1¾ lbs	China
CAWNY	1 acre	India
CENTI	(c) 10^{-2}	Int.
CHAIN	66 ft, 22 yds	Britain
CHANG	10 ch'ih = 11 ft 9 ins (1200 grams/3 lbs Thailand)	China
CHEKI	509 lbs	Turkey
CH'IEN	(1 lb), 58¾ grains (silver weight)	China
CHING	121 sq ft	China
CH'ING	72 600 sq ft	China
CLOVE	7 lbs	Britain
COOMB	4 bushels	Britain
COVID	CUBIT 18–21 ins (Tamil Nadu/ Madras)	India
CUBIT	18 ins	Britain
CURIE	(Ci) unit of activity of radioactive substance	Int.
DEBYE	10^{-18} e.s.u.; 1 d = 3.335 64 × 10^{-30} coulomb metre	Int.
DIRAA	PIK 0.58 m	Egypt
DOLIA	DOLA 96 doli = 1 zolotnick	U.S.S.R.
DUCAT	53.873 grains (gold weight)	Vienna
EIMER	29-30.7 litres	Germany
EPHAH	bushel	Hebrew
FADEN	4.077 steres	Latvian S.S.R.
FANAN	THANAN 1 litre	Thailand
FARAD	(F) capacitance	Int.
FEMTO	(f) 10^{-15}	Int.
FOUTE	FUT, 1 Eng. ft	U.S.S.R.
GAUSS	(G) magnetic flux density; 1 G = 10^{-4} tesla	Int.
GISLA	360 lbs of rice (Tanzania)	Zanzibar
GRAIN	0.0365 dram, 0.002 oz, 0.06 grams, $\frac{1}{24}$ pennyweight	Britain
GRANO	0.757 grain	Rome
GREIN	0.065 gram	Netherlands
GROSS	12 dozen	Britain
GUDGE	GUZ, 27–36 in	India

GUEZA	GUZ, ZER, 24–44 ins; 1 m (government)	Iran
HECTO	(h) 10^2	Int.
HENRY	(H) inductance	Int.
HERTZ	(Hz) frequency	Int.
HOMER	8 bushels	Hebrew
JOULE	heat, energy (1 joule = 1 watt second)	Int.
KANEH	6 cubits	Hebrew
KANNA	2.62 litres	Sweden
KANNE	1 litre (formerly 1.06 liq./0.91 dry qt U.S.)	Germany
KERAT	$1\frac{1}{8}$ ins (old), 3.09 grains weight (old)	Turkey
KETTE	CHAIN 10 m	Germany
KIKEH	ca. 1 bushel (varies)	Turkey
KODDI	7.58 litres	Arabian Peninsula Cyprus
KOUZA	9 Br. Imp. qts	Malaysia
KOYAN	$5333\frac{3}{4}$ lbs	Bulgaria
KRINA	20 litres	
KUWAN	KWAN, 3.75 kg = 8.267 lbs	Japan
LATRO	1.917 m	Czechoslovakia
LIANG	LEANG, $1\frac{3}{4}$ oz, 16 liang = 1 chin = $\frac{3}{4}$ lb	China
LIBRA	ca. 1 lb	S. America/ Malta
LIBRA	ARRATEL, 1.012 lbs	Portugal
LIGNE	2.26 mm	Paris
LIPPY	$\frac{1}{2}$ gal	Scotland
LITRE	1.057 liq./0.908 dry qt	U.S.
LITRE	2 pts (1 qt/liq.) Br. Imp.	Britain
LIVRE	1 kg (Greece 1 lb)	Belgium
LOKET	ca. 0.59 m	Czechoslovakia
LUMEN	(lm) luminous flux; 1 lm = ($\frac{1}{4}$pi) cd.	Int.
MAAS	1.837 litres (Switzerland 1.5 l)	Germany
MAHND	2.04 lbs	Arabian Peninsula
MARCO	8 oncas, 229.5 grams	Portugal
MARCO	3550 grains	Spain
MAUND	82.286 lbs (government)	India
METRE	3.3 ft, 1.1 yds	Int.
METZE	61.5 litres	Austria
MICRO	(μ) 10^{-6}	Int.
MILHA	1.297 miles	Portugal
MILLI	(m) 10^{-3}; 1 mm = 10^{-3} m	Int.
MINIM	(min) $\frac{1}{60}$ fl. drams (0.003 cu ins), 0.061 mm	Int.

MKONO	45.72 cm	E. Africa
MOMME	$\frac{1}{1000}$ kwan = 10 fun, 3.75 grams	Japan
OBOLE	10–12 grams	Greece
OCQUE	3 lbs	Greece
OKIEH	1 oz	Egypt
ONCIA	436.165 grains	Rome
PALMO	0.22 m (Spain 0.20 m)	Portugal
PARAH	25.4 litres, (China 15 gals)	Sri Lanka
PECUL	133 lbs	China
PERCH	POLE, 1 rod (U.S.); $30\frac{1}{4}$ sq yds ($5\frac{1}{2}$ yds)	Britain Malta
PIEDE	11 ins	
PFUND	500 grams (zollpfund)	Switzerland, Austria Germany
PFUND	419 grams	Latvian S.S.R.
PICKI	PIK, PIC, 0.64–0.67 m	Greece
PICUL	132.3-133 lbs (ca.) Malaysia, Hong Kong	Japan Sabah/N.
PICUL	180 lbs weight of water	Borneo France
PINTE	0.931 litre	
POIDE	de marc 0.2448 kg = 8 oz	France
POISE	dynamic viscosity; 1 poise = 0.1 pascal second	Int.
POUCE	27.07 mm, 1.066 ins (old)	France
POUND	0.45 kg, 16 oz, 7000 grains	Int.
QIRAT	209 sq yds	Egypt
QUART	(Br. Imp.) 2 pts (69.35 cu ins), 1.136 litres	Britain
QUART	(liq.) 2 pts, 57.75 cu in, 0.946 litre	U.S.
QUART	(dry) 2 pts, 67.20 cu in, 1.101 litres	U.S.
QUIRE	24 sheets of paper	Britain
RATEL	1.014 lbs	Iran
RATEL	ROTL, ROTTOLO, 0.9905 lb (customs)	Egypt
ROEDE	1 dekametre	Netherlands
SAJEN	7 ft	U.S.S.R.
SHAKU	$\frac{10}{33}$ m, 12 ins, 3.306 sq dm, 18.039 cu cm	Japan
SHENG	1.035 litres	China
STERE	1 cu m	Netherlands/ France
STILB	(sb) luminance; 1 candela/sq cm; 1 sb = 10^4 nits	Int.
STONE	14 lbs	Britain

STOPA	0.288 m	Poland
TAHIL	1¾ oz = 10 chee = 100 hoon	Malaysia
TESLA	(T) magnetic flux density (1 weber per m squared)	Int.
THERM	unit of heat (gas), 100.000 btu	Int.
TOISE	1.949 m	France
TONDE	131.4 litres (liq.), 139.1 litres (dry)	Denmark
TONNE	(t) metric ton = 1000 kg (Br. Imp. ton = 1016 kg)	Int.
TONOS	3307 lbs	Greece
TOVAR	128.2 kg	Bulgaria
TSUBO	4 sq yds	Japan
UNGUL	1 in	India
VEDRO	10 schtoffs, 12.3 litres (Bulgaria 10 l), 3 gals	U.S.S.R.
VERST	VERSTA 0.66288 mile, 1166 yds	U.S.S.R.
WISSE	1 stere	Netherlands
YOJAN	ca. 5 miles	E. Indies

6 Letters

ALMUDE	16.7 litres	Portugal
AMPERE	electric current, force = 2 × 10⁻⁷ newton/m of length	Int.
ANOMAN	AMMOMAM, AMOMAM, 5.77 U.S. bushels	Sri Lanka
ARCHIN	ARSHIN, ARSIN, (cloth) 27 ins; 1 m (39.37 ins)	Turkey
ARPENT	100 sq perches, 51.07 m.ares (Quebec 180 Fr. ft)	France
ARROBA	14.68–15 kg, 32 lbs	Portugal/Brazil
ARSHIN	28 ins, 0.7112 m	U.S.S.R.
ARTABA	66 litres	Iran
BANDLE	2 ft	Eire
BARILE	58.34 litres	Rome
BARREL	36 gal cask	Britain
BATMAN	6½ lbs (varies)	Iran
BRASSE	1.62 m	France
BUNDER	1 hectare	Netherlands
BUNDLE	2 reams	Britain
BUSHEL	8 gals	Britain
CANTAR	KANTAR, 124.45 lbs (old weight)	Turkey
CAWNIE	1.322 acres (Tamil Nadu)	India
CENTAL	100 lbs	U.S.
CHAPAH	1.8 lbs	Sabah/N. Borneo

CHARKA	0.123 litre	U.S.S.R.
CHOPIN	quart	Scotland
CHUPAH	3.125 lbs of water at 62°F (as a measure of capacity)	Singapore
CHUPAH	36 oz of water	Malacca
COVADO	0.66 m	Arabian Peninsula
COVIDO	19 ins	Arabian Peninsula
DECARE	1000 sq m	France
DENARO	1 gram; (old/Rome 18.17 grams)	Italy
DIRHEM	1.761 dr (customs); (Cairo 3.12 grams)	Egypt
DJERIB	1 hectare, 2½ acres	Turkey
DOENUM	DONUM, 25 acres	Turkey
DRACHM	(fluid) 0.961 U.S. fluid dram	Britain
ENDAZE	25½ ins	Turkey
FANEGA	ca. 55.5 litres (Argentina 137 litres) (Costa Rica 11 bu)	S. America/Portugal
FATHOM	6 ft	Britain
FEDDAN	1.038 acres	Egypt
FIRKIN	9 gals	Britain
FOUNTE	0.90282 lbs	U.S.S.R.
FRASCO	2⅜ litres	Argentina
GALLON	(gal) 0.004 cu m	U.S./Britain
KANTAR	CANTARO, 99.049 lbs = 100 rotls; 45 kg/cotton	Egypt
KANTAR	100 lbs	Ethiopia
KARWAR	100 batmans	Iran
KEDDAH	2.0625 litres	Egypt
KELVIN	(K) temperature, 1 K = 1° C	Int.
KOILON	33.12 litres	Greece
KORREL	0.1 gram	Netherlands
KULMET	10.93 litres	Latvian S.S.R.
KWARTA	1 litre	Poland
LIBBRA	1 kg; 339 grams (old)	Italy
LINIYA	0.1 in; 1 archine = 280 liniyas	U.S.S.R.
MAATJE	0.1 litre, 1 dl	Netherlands
MICRON	millionth part of a metre	France
MIGLIO	0.925 mile	Rome
MISCAL	10 grams; 71 grains (old)	Iran
MUSCAL	1½ drams	Turkey
NEWTON	(N) force; 1 kg with acceleration of 1 m/s per s.	Int.
NOGGIN	small cup, ¼ pt	Britain
PARMAK	1 arsin (1m) = 10 parmak = 100 khats (cm)	Turkey

PARSEC	(as tron.) 3.2616 light years	Int.
PASCAL	(Pa) 1 newton per sq m (air pressure)	Int.
POTTLE	4 pts	Britain
RADIAN	(rad) plane angle; (1 rad = 57.296° = 57°17′45″)	Int.
RATTEL	ROTTLE, 1.02 lbs	Arabian Peninsula
ROTOLO	1$\frac{3}{4}$ lbs	Malta
ROTTOL	1.6 litres (old)	Turkey
SAGENE	7 ft	U.S.S.R.
SCHENE	7$\frac{1}{2}$ miles	Egypt
SECOND	(s) second 60th of an hour ($\frac{1}{60}$ of a min.)	Int.
SEIDEL	0.354 litre	Austria
SHTOFF	1 qt	U.S.S.R.
SKEPPE	17.39 litres	Denmark
STOKES	(St) kinematic viscosity; 1 St = 10⁻⁴ m squared/s	Int.
STREEP	1 mm	Netherlands
STRICH	1 mm	Germany
STUNDE	4.8 km	Switzerland
TALBOT	luminous energy	Int.
THANAN	FANAN, 1 litre	Thailand
TIERCE	42 gals	Britain
TOMAND	187.17 lbs of rice	Arabian Peninsula
VERSTA	VERST, 0.66288 mile, 1166 yds	U.S.S.R.
VISHAN	3 lbs	India
YOJANA	ca. 5 miles	India

7 Letters

BRACCIO	d'ara, 0.7 m (a cubit)	Italy
CALORIE	unit of heat; 1 calorie = 4.1868 joules	Int.
CANDELA	(cd) luminous intensity	Int.
CANTARA	1 arroba	Spain
CANTARO	KANTAR, 99.0492 lbs = 100 rotls; 44.5 kg	Egypt
CAPICHA	263 litres	Iran
CELSIUS	thermometer, 0°C = 32F (30°C = 85F, 100°C = 212F)	Int.
CENTNER	50 kg	C. Europe/ Denmark
CENTRAD	$\frac{1}{100}$ of a radian (rad) plane angle	Int.
CHALDER	96 bushels	Britain
CHENICA	1.359 litres	Iran

COULOMB	.(C) electric unit of charge	Int.
DARIBAH	15.84 hectolitres	Egypt
DECIARE	$\frac{1}{10}$ are	France
DECIBEL	(dB) unit of noise; $\frac{1}{10}$ of a bel (B)	Int.
DIOPTER	optical measure	Greece
DRACHMA	3.906 grams approx (Netherlands); 3.21 (Turkey) 3.2 grams	Greece
ESTADIO	258 m (old)	Portugal
FALTCHE	143.22 ares	Moldavian S.S.R.
FURLONG	220 yds	U.S./Britain
HECTARE	2.5 acres	Int.
GANTANG	1 Br. Imp. gal (Malaysia); 144 oz weight of water as measure of capacity	Sabah/N. Borneo
GARNETZ	3.28 litres	U.S.S.R.
GILBERT	(Gb) magnetomotive force; 1 Gb = 10/ 4π ampere-turns	Int.
KLAFTER	2.0740 yds; (Switzerland 1.9685 yds)	Austria
KULIMET	11.48 litres	Estonian S.S.R.
LAMBERT	unit of brightness (obs.)	Int.
MEGA-ERG	a million ergs	Greece
MILLIER	1000 kg	France
OERSTED	(Oe) magnetic field strength; 1 Oe = 10³/4π Am⁻¹	Int.
PECHEUS	0.648 m	Greece
PERSAKH	6000 guz, 3.88 miles	Iran
POUNDAL	unit of force	Int.
PULGADA	0.914 in	Spain
QUANTAR	99 lbs	Egypt
QUARTER	28 lbs; 8 Br. Imp. bu (8.257 U.S. bu)	Britain
QUINTAL	100 libras, 101.4 lbs (France 1 cwt)	S. America/ Spain
QUINTAL	58.752 kg, 129.5 lbs	Portugal
QUINTAL	(metric) 100 kg = 220.46 lbs	Int.
ROTTOLO	ROTH, RATEL, 0.9905 lb (customs)	Egypt
SCHEPEL	1 decalitre	Netherlands
SCRUPLE	(s ap) 20 grains, 0.3333 dram, 1.295 grams	Int.

SIEMENS (s) electric conductance — Int.

SKJEPPE 17.37 litres — Norway

STREMMA 10 ares — Greece

THERMIE unit of heat/calory — France

VERCHOK 1.75 ins — U.S.S.R.

VIERTEL 7.73 litres (Switzerland 15 litres) — Denmark

VIRGATE a quarter of a hide — Britain

WICHTJE 1 gram — Netherlands

8 Letters

ANGSTROM unit, 1 angstrom = 10^{-10} m — Int.

APOSTILB unit of luminance, 10^{-4} lambert — Int.

ASSAY-TON 29.167 grams — U.S.

BOISSEAU 15 litres — Belgium

BOUTYLKA 1.625 U.S. liquid pints — U.S.S.R.

CENTIARE a square metre — France

CENTIBAR meteorological measure — France

CHALDRON 25 cwt of coal — France

CHITTACK 5 tolas, 900 grains — Bengal

DAKTYLOS 25.4 mm — Greece

DECAGRAM 10 grams — Int.

DECIGRAM $\frac{1}{10}$ gram — Int.

FLUIDRAM 60 minim (0.2255 cu in) 29.572 ml — U.S.

FLUIDRAM (Br. Imp.) 60 minim (0.2167 cu in) 3.55 cu cm — Britain

FOOT-RULE a 12 in measure — Britain

HIYAKA-ME 5 797 198 grains — Japan

HIYAK-KIN 132½ lbs — Japan

HOGSHEAD a large cask — France

KASSABAH 3.8824 yds — Egypt

KILODYNE 1000 dynes — France

KILOGRAM 1000 grams; 2.2 lbs — Int.

KILOWATT 1000 watts; 1.3 horsepower (1 h.p. = 0.75 kw) — Int.

KORTONDE 138.97 litres — Norway

MUTCHKIN about a pint — Scotland

NEUTRINO 7×10^{-32} grams, beam without mass — Int.

PARASANG PERSAKH, 6000 guz, 3.99 miles — Iran

PASSEREE 5 seers — Bengal

PHAROAGH 10 mills (10 000 km); 2 hours' journey (old) — Turkey

PHILOMEL unit of sound capacity (Shakespeare) — Britain

POLEGADA 27.77 mm — Portugal

PUNCHEON a large cask — France

QUADRANT an arc of 90° — France

QUARTERN a gill; 4 lbs — Britain

SCHEFFEL 50 litres (old 16 metzen/Prussia) — Germany

SCHOPPEN ½ litre (Switzerland 0.375 litre) — Germany

SERPLATH 80 stone — Scotland

SKALPUND (skaal-pund) ½ kg (Sweden 425 grams/0.937 lb) — Norway

SULTCHEK cu m (whose sides equal a parmak/dm) — Turkey

THANGSAT 21.3 litres — Thailand

THORLAND unit of illumination — Int.

TONELADA 793.15 kg — Portugal

YARDLAND usually 30 acres — Britain

ZOLOTNIK 65.8306 grains, 96 doli — U.S.S.R.

COINS AND MONIES: ANCIENT AND MODERN

2 Letters

AS   Roman bronze coin
AT   Laotian monetary unit (1 kip = 100 at)
BU   17/18 cent. Japanese ($\frac{1}{4}$ of a ryo)
LI   old Chinese monetary unit ($\frac{1}{100}$ of a tael)
PU   ancient Chinese currency
XU   Vietnamese monetary unit (1 dong = 100 xu)

3 Letters

AES   Roman money (Grave, Rude, Signatum)
AKA   Ceylonese gold piece (Sri Lanka)
ATT   Siamese (Thailand) copper coin ($\frac{1}{64}$ of the tical)
BAT   BAHT, TICAL Thai monetary unit (100 satangs = 1 baht)
BIT   West Indian money of a/c
BOB   British shilling (obs.)
BUN   penny, British late 19 cent.
COB   Spanish monetary unit
DAM   DAWM, Indian copper coin
DUA   Malayan 19 cent. hat money (2 ampat)
ECU   French five-franc piece
FEI   Oceanian monetary unit, see YAP
FEN   Chinese monetary unit (100 fen = 1 yuan)
FIL   Iraqi monetary unit (1000 fils = 1 ID); Jordanian; Yemeni (Aden); Bahraini; Kuwaiti
FUN   Korean copper coin, late 19 cent.
HAO   Vietnamese monetary unit (10 hao = 1 dong)
HAT   money, coinage of Pahang/Malay, 19 cent.
JOE   Portuguese Joao (in English)
JON   North Korean monetary unit (100 jon = 1 won)
KAS   17 cent. copper coin for Tranquebar/India (Danish col.)
KIP   Laotian monetary unit (1 kip = 100 at)
LAT   Latvian monetary unit; 17/19 cent. Siamese (Thailand) silver tongue money
LEK   Albanian monetary unit (1 lek = 100 qindars)
LIS   French 17 cent. gold and silver coin
LEU   Romanian monetary unit, pl. LEI (1 leu = 100 bani)
LEV   Bulgarian monetary unit, pl. LEVA (1 lev = 100 stotinki)
MAS   Indonesian (Sumatra) 13/18 cent. small gold coin
MIL   proposed coin, 1/1000
ORE   Scandinavian monetary unit (100 öre = 1 krona)
PIE   Indian monetary unit ($\frac{1}{12}$ of the anna)

PUL   Russian and Georgian copper coin 15/19 cent.
PYA   Burmese monetary unit (100 pyas = 1 kyat)
REE   REI, Portuguese money of a/c
RIX   19 cent. Ceylonese dollar
RYO   Japanese monetary unit (10 ryos = 1 oban)
SEN   Japanese monetary unit (100 sen/1 yen); Indonesian (100/1 rupiah); Cambodian (100/1 riel)
SHU   old Japanese coin ($\frac{1}{16}$ of a ryo)
SOL   Peruvian monetary unit (1 sol = 100 centavos); old French halfpenny
SOU   French five-centime piece
WON   N and S Korean monetary unit (1 won = 100 jon/chon)
YAP   Micronesian (Caroline I.) stone discs used as currency (Fei)
YEN   Japanese monetary unit (1 yen = 100 sen)

4 Letters

ADLI   ADLEA, old Indian silver coin, Tripoli (20 cent.)
AKÇE   AKÇA (OTMANI), first Ottoman silver coin ($\frac{2}{3}$ of a para)
ANGE   D'OR, French 14 cent. gold coin
ANNA   Indian copper coin ($\frac{1}{16}$ of a rupee) from 17 cent. onwards
ATIA   18 cent. copper coin of Portuguese India ($6\frac{1}{4}$ Port. reis)
AURA   Icelandic monetary unit (100 aurar = 1 krona)
BAHT   Thai monetary unit (1 baht = 100 satangs)
BANU   Romanian monetary unit, pl. BANI (100 bani = 1 leu)
BEKA   Hebrew monetary unit ($\frac{1}{2}$ shekel)
BELL   money: Chinese copper coinage; French Revolution
BIRR   Ethiopian monetary unit (1 birr = 100 cents)
BONK   colloq. for Javanese old copper coins ($\frac{1}{2}$ stuiver, 8 stuivers)
BUCK   the US dollar (colloq.)
CASH   2000 years old Chinese bronze currency ($\frac{1}{1000}$ of a tael)
CEDI   Ghanaian monetary unit (1 cedi = 100 pesewas)
CENT   decimal coinage of various countries
CHIP   a counter; a sovereign
CHON   South Korean monetary unit (100 chon = 1 won)
DALA   late 19 cent. Hawaiian silver coin
DAWM   DAM, Indian copper coin
DEKA   10 cent. small Ceylonese (Sri Lanka) gold coin

11

DEMY late 14 cent. half-piece of Scottish gold coin

DIME US 10-cent piece

DOIT Dutch half-farthing 16–19 cent.

DONG Vietnamese monetary unit (old 60 dong = 1 tien/tael)

DURO Spanish monetary unit (5 pesetas)

FALS copper coin of Persia and Umayad and Abbasid caliphates

FYRK Swedish monetary unit ($\frac{1}{4}$ of an öre)

GANI Italian 14 cent. token currency (dodkin)

GELD ancient tribute; Ger. for money

GROS French 13 cent. silver coinage (gros tournois)

HVID 15 cent. Danish silver coin

HWAN WON Korean monetary unit

ISAR other name for 17–19 cent. German river gold ducats (Flussgelddukaten)

JOAO 18–19 cent. Portuguese gold coin (6400 reis)

JOEY 4d. piece (Joseph Hume); later 3d. piece

KASU 18 cent. Indian (Mysore) copper coins

KINA Papuan (New Guinea) monetary unit; (Australian dollar)

KOBO Nigerian monetary unit (1 naira = 100 kobo)

KRAN 19 cent. Persian silver coin (1000 dinar)

KYAT Burmese monetary unit (100 pyas = 1 kyat)

LAKH Indian monetary unit, 100 000 rupees

LARI Indian/Maldive Islands monetary unit (100 lari = 1 rupee); old Persian silver wire money

LIRA Italian monetary unit (pl. LIRE); Turkish monetary unit (100 kurus = 1 lira)

MAHE BICHE, French for pice

MARK German monetary unit (100 Pfennige = 1 Mark)

MERK Scottish 13s. 4d. (thistle merk); money of a/c

MITE a very small coin

MOCO late 18 cent. San Domingo coin; centre piece of Sp. dollar

OBAN Japanese oval gold coin (1 oban = 10 ryos)

OBOL B.C. Greek silver coin ($\frac{1}{6}$ of a drachm); Charon's ferry fee, 1$\frac{1}{2}$d.

ONZA Sp. and Latin American 8 escudos gold piece

PALA Ceylonese (Sri Lanka) deka

PARA Yugoslavian monetary unit (1 dinar = 100 paras); money in Turkish and old coin ($\frac{1}{40}$ of the piastre)

PEÇA PEZA, 18 cent. Portuguese gold coin (4 escudos)

PESO Filipino monetary unit (1 peso = 100 centavos); monetary unit of Mexico, Cuba, and various S. American countries

PICE Indian monetary unit, Nepalese monetary unit (100 pice = 1 rupee), ($\frac{1}{4}$ of an anna)

PITI old Indonesian tin coin (1 Spanish real = 4000 piti)

POGH ancient Armenian copper coin

POND S. African pound (Eng. gold sovereign)

PULS Afghani monetary unit (1 afghani - 100 puli)

PUNT Irish monetary unit

QUID a sovereign; a pound (colloq.)

RAND monetary unit of S. Africa and various nearby countries

REAL old Spanish ($\frac{1}{4}$ of a peseta) and Portuguese monetary unit; Dominican Rep. monetary unit (8 reales = 1 peso)

REIS plural of REAL

RIAL Persian monetary unit (1 rial = 100 dinars); Moroccan (old)

RIEL Cambodian monetary unit (1 riel = 100 sen)

RING money, first coins of Australia

RUBA 10 cent. Sicilian monetary unit ($\frac{1}{4}$ dinar)

RYAL gold coin; the rose noble

SALT money, primitive African currency

SENT Estonian monetary unit (100 sent = 1 kroon)

SKAR Tibetan copper coin

SPUR RYAL, colloq. for $\frac{1}{2}$ ryal

SYLI Guinean monetary unit (1 syli = 100 cauris)

TAEL old Chinese monetary unit (1000 bronze cash = 1 tael)

TAKA Bangladeshi monetary unit (1 taka = 100 paisa)

TARO 16–18 cent. Maltese silver coin (12 tari = 1 scudo); early Sicilian gold coin

VELD POND, S. African (Boer) gold coin

WARK Ethiopian 19 cent. gold coin

WIRE money, Persian Lari (thin bars of silver)

YANG 19 cent. Korean silver coin

YUAN Chinese monetary unit (Yuan Shi Kai)

5 Letters

ABBEY CROWN, 16 cent. 20 shillings gold piece

ACKEY 18/19 cent. silver coin (Gold Coast)

ADLEA ADLI, old Indian silver coin; Tripoli (20 cent.)

AGNEL 13 cent. French gold coin (mouton d'or)

ALBUS German "Weisspfennig" (grossus albus/white groat) 14/15 cent.

ALTUN Turkish 15 cent. gold coin

ALTYN Russian (Tartar) silver coin 17 cent. (3 kopeks)

AMANI early 20 cent. Afghani gold coin (1 amani = 30 afghani)

AMPAT Malay hat money

ANGEL old English gold coin

ASPER 13/15 cent. Middle Eastern base silver coin

AUREI Roman gold coins

BAIZA Omani monetary unit (1000 baizas = 1 rial/R.O.)

BELGA Belgian coin

BETSO small Venetian coin

BICHE French for 18 cent. pice

BRASS money (colloq.)

BRICK TEA, ancient Chinese and Tibetan currency ($2\frac{1}{2}$ lbs = 1 tael)

BRIOT CROWN for Charles I

BUTUT Gambian monetary unit (100 butut = 1 dalasi)

CANOE DOLLAR, Canadian silver dollar

COLON Costa Rican monetary unit (1 colon = 100 centimos); El Salvadorian monetary unit

CROWN five-shilling piece

DALER Scandinavian Thaler (riksdaler)

DARIC gold coin of Darius (Persia) (1 daric = 20 sigloi)

DENGA 14/15 cent. Russian coin (silver penny)

DINAR Yugoslavian monetary unit (1 dinar = 100 paras); various Moslem countries; ancient Arab gold coin

DOBLA a number of old gold coins; 16 cent. double scudo

DOBRA 14 cent. Portuguese gold coin

DUCAT Italian old gold coin

EAGLE former US gold coin (10 dollars)

FANAM Indian monetary unit, gold (ancient), silver (modern) ($\frac{1}{8}$ of a rupee)

FUANG 19 cent. Siamese (Thai) monetary unit ($\frac{1}{8}$ of a Bat)

FUGIO CENT, first US coin

FRANC monetary unit of various countries

GERSH Ethiopian monetary unit, silver ($\frac{1}{10}$ of a talari)

GIGOT 16 cent. Brabantian copper coin (Flemish negenmanneke)

GRAMO late 19 cent. Spanish private gold coin

GRANO Maltese monetary unit; old copper coin of Naples and Sicily

GROAT silver 4d. piece

GROOT 13 cent. Dutch silver gros

HARDI 14 cent. gold and silver piece of England and dominion of France

HECTE Greek monetary unit ($\frac{1}{6}$ of the statar)

HENRI D'OR French gold coin, 16 cent.

HOLEY DOLLARS, ring money

HUSUM DALER, 16 cent. Danish daler

IMADI Yemeni precursor to the riyal

JUSTO 15 cent. Portuguese gold coin (= 2 cruzados)

KAIKI SHOHO, ancient Japanese gold coin

KAKIM ancient Siamese (Thai) bars currency

KARAN KRAN, Persian silver piece

KNIFE money, simple **B.C.** Chinese bronze coinage

KOBAN 16/19 cent. Japanese gold coin ($\frac{1}{10}$ of the oban)

KOPEK Russian monetary unit (100 kopeks = 1 rouble)

KRONA Scandinavian monetary unit (1 krona = 100 öre)

KRONE Austrian monetary unit, gold or silver

KROON Estonian monetary unit

LEONE 17 cent. Venetian silver coin (= 10 lire)

LEPTA Greek monetary unit

LIARD old French farthing

LIBRA 19 cent. Peruvian monetary unit; Roman pound

LITAS Lithuanian monetary unit, pl. LITU

LITRA 6 cent. **B.C.** Sicilian monetary unit

LIVRE old French franc (20 sols = 1 livre)

LOCHO Venezuelan monetary unit

LOUIS D'OR, 20-franc piece

MASSE D'OR, 14 cent. French gold coins

MEDIO Venezuelan monetary unit

MINIM tiny Roman bronze coins

MOHUR 15-rupee gold coin

MOKKO East Indian islands drum currency

MONGO Mongolian monetary unit (100 mongos = 1 tugrik)

NAIRA Nigerian monetary unit (1 naira = 100 kobo)

NGWEE Zambian monetary unit (100 ngwee = 1 kwacha)

NOBLE old English coin, 6s. 8d.

ONCIA 14 cent. Italian money of a/c; gold coin

ONLIK old Turkish silver coin (= 10 paras)

ORTUG old Swedish silver coin

PADMA TANKA, S. Indian **B.C.** gold coin

PAISA PICE, Indian monetary unit (100 paisa = 1 rupee); Bangladeshi monetary unit (100 paisa = 1 taka); Bhutani monetary unit

PAOLO Italian cities

PENCE plural of penny, British

PENGO Hungarian silver unit

PENNI Finnish monetary unit (100 penniä = 1 markka)

PENNY British copper coin

PIECE OF EIGHT = peso

PLACK Scottish 15/16 cent. billon coin

PLATE money, Swedish copper plates (platmynt)

POUND monetary unit of Britain and various countries

QUART D'ECU, French silver coin (= 15 sols)

RIYAL Sudanese monetary unit (1 Sud. pound = 10 riyals); monetary unit of Arabian Peninsula

ROYAL D'OR, French Louis IX gold coin

RUPEE Indian monetary unit (1 rupee = 100 paisa); Nepalese, Pakistani, Mauritian monetary unit

RUPIA Portuguese rupee (Goa and Diu)

SAIGA 7 cent. Merovingian coin

SALUT D'OR European medieval gold coin

SAUDI Arabian gold sovereign

SCEAT SCEATT 7 cent. English coin, base silver or copper

SCUDO old Italian "shield" currency, gold or silver; pl. SCUDI

SEMIS half a Roman as

SENGI Zairean monetary unit (10 000 sengi = 1 zaire)

SHAKI Persian silver coin (= 10 kazbegi)

SICCA RUPEE, colloq. for E. India Co. rupee

SOLDI old Italian gold coin; pl. of soldo

SOLDO Italian sol or sou (halfpenny)

SPADE money, Chinese **B.C.** coinage

SRANG early 20 cent. Tibetan silver currency

STICA STYCA, small Saxon coin

SUCRE Ecuadorian monetary unit (1 sucre = 100 centavos)

SWORD DOLLAR, 16 cent. Scottish silver ryal

SYCEE boat-shaped Far Eastern silver ingot

TAKOE ⅛ of an ackey (Gold Coast)

TALAR a special 19 cent. thaler

TANGA 17 cent. Portuguese East Indian coin

TARIN old Sicilian silver coin

THIRD GUINEA, old English gold coin

THREE PENCE, British coin from 16 cent. (obs.)

TICAL Thai monetary unit (bat or baht); old Burmese monetary unit

TICCY S. African 3d. piece

TIGER tongue money, old weight-related silver bar currency of Indochina

TILLA old Afghani and Turkestani gold coin

TOMAN Persian gold unit

TRIME US 3-cent silver piece

UNCIA ancient Roman monetary unit ($\frac{1}{12}$ of the as)

UNITE English/Scottish 17 cent. gold piece; "Faciam Eos in Gentem Unam"

VLIES old Dutch gold or silver coin

WITTE special 14 cent. albus

ZAIRE Zairean monetary unit (1 zaire = 100 makuta = 10 000 sengi)

ZLOTY Polish monetary unit (1 zloty = 100 groszy)

6 Letters

ABACIS old Portuguese Indian and E. African silver coin

ABBASI old Persian coin (base metal) and Georgian coin (silver)

ABDERA ancient Thracian coins

ADOLFS D'OR, Swedish 5-thaler coin, gold

AGOROT Israeli monetary unit (100 agorot = 1 Israeli pound)

AMANIA Afghani monetary unit

ANCHOR money, 19 cent. British silver coins

AUREUS Roman precursor of the solidus, gold

BALBAO Panamanian monetary unit (1 balboa = 100 centesimos)

BAMBOO money, inscribed Chinese "stick" currency

BAUBEE BAWBEE, Scottish billon coin

BEZANT Byzantine gold coin (Nomisma)

BONNET PIECE, Scottish 16 cent. gold coin

BULLET money, 14/19 cent. Siamese (Thail) monetary unit, gold or silver

BUKSHA old Yemeni monetary unit

CANOPY type penny, William the Conqueror era

CARLIN 13 cent. Sicilian monetary unit, gold or silver

CARLIN D'OR, old English monetary unit, pure gold (salute)

CAURIS Guinean monetary unit (100 cauris = 1 syli)

CEITIL old Portuguese copper coin

CHO-GIN 18 cent. Japanese silver bar

CONDOR old Chilean monetary unit

COPANG Japanese gold coin

COPPER one penny (colloq.)

COWRIE shell money, Far East and Africa

CUARTO old Bolivian half-peso; ¼ of a Real

DALASI Gambian monetary unit (1 dalasi = 100 butut)

DECIME S. American 10-centavos

DENARO Italian denier, 8 cent.

DENIER Carolingian silver penny (12 deniers = 1 solidus)

DINERO old Spanish silver penny; Peruvian 10-centavo coin; Spanish for money

DIOBOL ancient Greek silver coin (⅔ of a drachma)

DIRHAM	Moroccan monetary unit (1 dirham = 100 M. francs); Iraqi (20 dirhams = 1 dinar); monetary unit Arab Emirates
DIRHEM	ancient Arab and Ottoman coin
DIZAIN	old French decimal coin (10 deniers)
DOBLON	old Uruguayan coin, gold
DODKIN	old coin of poor metal
DOLLAR	monetary unit of the USA and various countries
DOPPIA	18 cent. Sardinian gold unit
DRACHM	DRACHMA, Greek monetary unit, both ancient and modern
EIRAKU	SEN, cash-type Japanese bronze coins
ESCUDO	Portuguese monetary unit (1 escudo = 100 centavos); Chilean monetary unit (100 centesimos); old Spanish monetary unit
FALUCE	Ceylonese (Sri Lanka) monetary unit, $\frac{1}{4}$ of a fanam
FILLER	Hungarian monetary unit (100 filler = 1 forint)
FLORIN	silver 2-shilling piece
FOLLIS	Byzantine bronze coin
FORINT	Hungarian monetary unit (1 forint = 100 filler)
GADHYA	PAISA, old Indian base silver coin
GEORGE	D'OR, 18 cent. five thaler coin, gold
GEORGE	NOBLE, 16 cent. English gold coin (6s. 8d.)
GIULIO	papal "grosso largo"
GOTHIC	CROWN, Victorian
GOTHIC	FLORIN, superseded godless florin, 19 cent.
GOURDE	Haitian 19 cent. silver coin
GRINNA	Russian monetary unit, silver (= 10 kopeks); money of a/c
GROSSO	Italian monetary unit, pl. GROSSI
GROSZY	Polish monetary unit (100 groszy = 1 zloty)
GUINEA	21 shillings
GULDEN	Dutch monetary unit, German (old) monetary unit
GYLLEN	16 cent. Swedish gulden
HALALA	Yemeni monetary unit, bronze and copper (obs.)
HALERU	Czechoslovakian monetary unit (100 haleru = 1 koruna), (Heller)
HALLER	HELLER
HEAUME	D'OR and d'argent, 14 cent. Flemish
HELLER	German, Austrian, Swiss monetary unit (penny)
ICHIBU	GIN, 19 cent. Japanese coin (= 1 bu)

JAITIL	Indian 14 cent. (50 jaitils = 1 tankah)
KAPANG	KEPING
KENGEN	DAIHO, ancient Japanese bronze sen
KEPING	18/19 cent. Malay & Sumatran copper coins
KHOUMS	Mauritanian monetary unit (5 khoums = 1 ouguiya)
KORONA	Hungarian monetary unit, silver (Austrian krone)
KORUNA	Czechoslovakian monetary unit (1 koruna = 100 haleru)
KURUSH	Turkish monetary unit (100 kurus = 1 lira)
KWACHA	Zambian monetary unit (1 kwacha = 100 ngwee); Malawi monetary unit (1 k. = 100 tambala)
LAUREL	17 cent. twenty-shilling piece
LEPTON	Greek coin, copper ($\frac{1}{8}$ of an obol)
MACATA	old Guatemalan monetary unit
MACUTA	Portuguese African monetary unit 18/19 cent. (= 50 reis)
MAKUTA	Zairean monetary unit (100 makuta = 1 zaire)
MANCUS	European designation of old Arab gold dinar
MARKKA	Finnish monetary unit (1 markka = 100 penniä)
MATONA	Ethiopian monetary unit, copper or nickel
MAUNDY	money, British royal "give aways"
MAZUNA	Moroccan monetary unit, 19 cent.
MISCAL	18 cent. Spanish silver piastre; monetary unit of Chinese Turkestan
NICKEL	US 5-cent piece
OCTAVO	OCHAVO, old Spanish silver coin; Mexican copper coin
OSELLA	16 cent. Venetian gift coin
OTMANI	Ottoman monetary unit, silver (see AKÇE)
OBOLUS	OBOL, ancient Greek coin
PAGODA	Indian gold coin
PAHANG	Malay hat money
PARDAO	Portuguese Indian monetary unit, xeraphim
PATACA	17 cent. Arab silver and money of a/c; old Brazilian monetary unit
PATACA	18 cen. Brabantian and Westphalian monetary unit, silver
PATACA	18 cent. Algerian money of a/c; African name for Maria Theresa thaler
PATACA	Macauan monetary unit (1 pataca = 100 avos)
PATARD	15 cent. Dutch silver piece

PERPER early 20 cent. Montenegran silver unit; old Ragusan monetary unit

PESETA Spanish monetary unit

PLAQUE old Dutch billon coin

PRAGER GROSCHEN, late 13 cent. Bohemian coin, silver

PRUTAH old Indonesian monetary unit

QINDAR Albanian monetary unit (100 qindars = 1 lek)

QUARTO old Spanish monetary unit ($\frac{1}{4}$ real)

QUIRSH Saudi Arabian monetary unit (20 quirsh = 1 Saudi riyal)

RAPPEN Swiss monetary unit (100 rappen = 1 Swiss francs)

ROUBLE Russian monetary unit (1 rouble = 100 kopek)

RUPIAH Indonesian monetary unit (1 rupiah = 100 sen)

SANESE D'ORO, 14 cent. North Italian (Sienna) coin, gold

SATANG Thai monetary unit

SEQUIN Venetian gold coin (Zecchino); Ottoman monetary unit

SESINO 18 cent. Italian copper or billon coin ($\frac{1}{2}$ soldo)

SHEKEL Jewish half crown

SIERRA LEONE, late 18 cent. silver coin

SIGLOS ancient Persian silver piece ($\frac{1}{20}$ of a gold daric)

SIXAIN old French monetary unit (= 6 deniers)

SOMALO old Somali monetary unit

SOOKOO SUKU, old Malayan coin, silver

SOVRAN poetical sovereign

STATER ancient Greek gold or silver coin

STIVER West Indian Dutch Stuiver

SUELDO 19 cent. Bolivian coin, silver (8 sueldi = 1 peso)

TALARI Abyssinian coin, silver

TALBOT 15 cent. Anglian, gold

TALENT old Hebrew monetary unit; ancient weight unit

TANGKA 18 cent. Tibetan monetary unit, base silver

TANKAH various old Indian coins

TANNER British sixpence (obs.)

TESTER Henry VIII shilling

TESTON TESTONE/TESTOON, 16 cent. shilling; Italian silver coin

THALER 15/20 cent. German monetary unit, silver (Guldengroschen)

TICKEY S. African 3d. piece

TOMAUN Persian gold coin

TORNEZ 14 cent. Portuguese coin, silver (French gros tornois)

TOSTAO 16 cent. Portuguese coin, headless

TRIENS small Byzantine gold coin ($\frac{3}{4}$ of a solidus)

TRIPLE UNIT, largest English Civil War gold coin, 17 cent.

TUGRIK Mongolian monetary unit (1 tugrik = 100 mongos)

UNGARO Italian for the Hungarian 17 cent. ducat

VIERER old Swiss coin, silver (2 vierer = 2 rappen)

VINTEM 15 cent. Portuguese silver coin (= 20 reis); old Brazilian copper coin

WOLSEY GROAT, English, 16 cent. special coin

YUZLIK large, old Turkish silver coin equal to 100 paras

ZECHIN SEQUIN, Venetian monetary unit

7 Letters

ACRAGAS ancient Greek monetary unit (Sicily)

AFGHANI Afghani monetary unit (1 afghani = 100 puli)

ALTILIK 19 cent. Ottoman 6-piastre piece, base silver

ANGELET half an angel, 17 cent.

ANGELOT a Louis XI gold coin

ANGOLAR Angolan escudo

ANGSTER 14/19 cent. Swiss coin, silver or copper

ASHRAFI 15/18 cent. Persian coin, gold (replaced by the toman)

BAIOCCO Italian papal coin ($\frac{1}{100}$ of the scudo)

BARHINA Portuguese coin, gold (1 bahrina = 400 reis)

BOLIVAR Venezuelan monetary unit (1 bolivar = 2 reales = 100 centimes)

BRILLEN DUKAT, 17 cent. Danish coin, gold

BRILLEN THALER, 16 cent. German monetary unit

BRIQUET French for Dutch vuurijzer, 15 cent. silver coin

BULLION pieces, gold or silver objects valued on carat-mass content

BUQSHAH (Sana) Yemeni monetary unit (40 buqshahs = 1 riyal)

CADIERE late 15 cent. gold piece; silver coin of Charles V and VI

CAROLIN old Swedish coin, gold or silver

CAROLUS gold coin of Charles V (Spanish) Habsburg Emperor

CAVALLO 15 cent. Sicilian copper coin ($\frac{1}{200}$ of a ducat)

CENTAVO S. American monetary unit, various countries

CENTIME	one-hundredth of a franc (various countries)	**MILREIS**	old Brazilian and Portuguese coin
CHALKOS	Greek monetary unit (Alexander the Great), copper ($\frac{1}{48}$ of the drachm)	**MOIDORE**	Portuguese 4-cruzado piece (= 4000 reis); 18 cent. Brazilian monetary unit
CORDOBA	Nicaraguan monetary unit (1 cordoba = 100 centavos)	**NOMISMA**	Byzantine gold coins; Greek for money
CORONAT	KWARTNIK, 14/15 cent. Polish monetary unit ($\frac{1}{2}$ groschen)	**NONSUNT**	16 cent. Scottish 12-penny groat; Northumberland shillings
CRUSADO	old Portuguese monetary unit	**NOVODEL**	Russian coins (or imitations)
CRUZADO	15 cent. Portuguese gold coin; new Brazilian monetary unit	**NUMMIUM**	Byzantine bronze unit, pl. nummia
DAALDER	Dutch thaler; Charles V silver coin	**ORMONDE**	money, minted in Ireland 1643
DENARII	pence	**OUGUIYA**	Mauritanian monetary unit (1 ouguiya = 5 khoums)
DENNING	17 cent. Danish equivalent of Russian denga	**PAHLEVI**	former Persian gold unit, superseded the toman
DHARANA	Indian old punch-marked coins (Ceylonese purana)	**PAOLINO**	Italian silver scudo, 15/16 cent.
DOBLONE	Italian 4 or 8 scudi gold pieces	**PARISIS**	D'OR, 11 cent. French gold coins
DOUZAIN	old French shilling (12 deniers)		
DRACHMA	Greek monetary unit (1 drachma = 100 lepta), ancient and modern	**PATAGON**	Dutch early 17 cent., silver (= 48 stuivers)
DUPLONE	18/19 cent. Swiss gold coin (16 francs)	**PEACOCK**	RUPEE, 19 cent. Burmese coin, gold or silver
ENRIQUE	15 cent. Spanish gold coin	**PESEWAS**	Ghanaian monetary unit (100 pesewas = 1 new cadi)
ESCALIN	17 cent. Dutch silver coin	**PFENNIG**	German copper coin
ESPADIN	15 cent. Portuguese $\frac{1}{2}$ justo	**PHOENIX**	18 cent. Sicilian gold coin; 19 cent. Greek silver coin (= 100 lepta)
ESPHERA	Goan (Portuguese) 16 cent. gold coin		
EKPWELE	Equatorial Guinean peseta (1 ekpwele = 100 centimos)	**PIASTRE**	PIASTER, Egyptian monetary unit (100 piasters = 1 E. pound); Sudanese monetary unit; old European name for Spanish peso and variations
FERDING	Swedish silver farthing, 16 cent.		
FILIPPO	16/18 cent. Spanish coin, silver		
FOLLARO	Italian Byzantine copper coin	**PISTOLE**	DOUBLOON, old Spanish double escudo, gold
GAZETTA	old Venetian copper coin		
GODLESS	FLORIN (Victoria/Britain) omitting "Dei Gratia", not valid in heaven	**POLTINA**	Russian $\frac{1}{2}$ rouble
		QUARTER	US quarter of a dollar
GUARANI	Paraguayan monetary unit (1 guarani = 100 centimos)	**QUETZAL**	Guatemalan monetary unit (1 quetzal = 100 centavos)
GUERCHE	19 cent. Ethiopian coin, silver ($\frac{1}{8}$ of the talari)	**QUINTAR**	QINDAR, Albanian monetary unit
GUILDER	Dutch florin	**ROYALIN**	18 cent. Danish colonial monetary unit (Tranquebar/India), silver
HIBERNO	Viking coin, Ireland		
JACOBUS	gold coin of James I		
KAZBEGI	Persian Safavid copper coin	**RUSPONE**	18 cent. Florentine monetary unit, gold (= 3 ducats)
LEMPIRA	Honduran monetary unit (100 centavos); old Brazilian monetary unit	**SANTIMS**	early 20 cent. Latvian (100 santims = 1 lats)
LEOPARD	14 cent. English 3-shilling gold coin	**SAN TOME**	THOME, Portuguese Indian 16 cent. gold piece
MANCHIR	first Ottoman copper coin, 14 cent.	**SAPEQUE**	Indochinese dong
		SESTINO	15 cent. Neapolitan billon piece
MANILLA	W. African copper coin	**SEXTANS**	ancient Roman bronze coin
MARENGO	Napoleonic 20 franc gold piece	**SILIQUA**	Byzantine silver coin ($\frac{1}{24}$ of a solidus)
MATAPAN	13 cent. Venetian grosso		

SOLIDUS — old Roman gold coin (= 72 Roman libra)

SOSLING — 15 cent. Danish six-penny coin, silver

SOVRANO — SOUVERAIN D'OR, old Dutch gold coin

STAMPEE — French W. Indies 18 cent. sous

STOOTER — 16 cent. Dutch coin, base silver ($\frac{1}{20}$ of a daalder)

STUIVER — 15 cent. Dutch coin, base silver

TALLERO — old Italian thaler; 20 cent. It. Eritrean

TAMBALA — Malawian monetary unit (100 tambala = 1 kwacha)

TAMPANG — Malay hat money

TESTOON — old Italian silver coin

TESTRIL — tester; a sixpence

THISTLE — crown, dollar, merk, British 16/17 cent.

THISTLE — NOBLE, 16 cent. British large gold piece

THRYMSA — 6 cent. Anglo-Saxon monetary unit ($\frac{1}{3}$ of a solidus)

TRIBUTE — penny, Judaean Roman denarius

TRIOBOL — day-money for a judge in ancient Greece ($\frac{1}{2}$ drachm)

UGORSKY — Russian name for Hungarian 15 cent. gold coin

UNICORN — Scottish 15 cent. gold piece

ZLATNIK — first Russian gold coins

ZOLOTYE — Russian gold coins; Crimean campaign reward, 17 cent.

8 Letters

ADELAIDE — TOKENS, Australian one pound gold tokens

AGNUS DEI — type of penny of Aethelred II

ALBERTIN — 16 cent. Dutch (Spanish) gold coin

AMBROSIN — Milanese coin

ASSIGNAT — paper currency, French Revolution

BAZARUCO — Portuguese Indian 16 cent. coin, base metal

CAROLOUS — KAROLUS, French dizain

CENTIMOS — Equatorial Guinean monetary unit (100 centimos = 1 ekpwele)

CHUCKRAM — Indian 18/20 cent. (4 chuckrams = 1 gold fanam)

CLEMENTI — papal silver coin (15 baiocchi)

CROSAZZO — Genoese 17 cent. silver coin

CRUZEIRO — Brazilian monetary unit (1 cruzeiro = 100 centavos)

DENARIUS — main silver coin of the Roman Empire

DIDRACHM — ancient Greek 2-drachma

DINHEIRO — 12/14 cent. Portuguese billon denier

DOHOZARI — 19 cent. tiny Persian gold coin

DOUBLOON — Spanish monetary unit (2 pistoles)

DREILING — 15 cent. German 3 pfennig, billon

DUCATONE — Italian 16/18 cent. silver coin

DUCATOON — Venetian silver coin

FARTHING — a quarter of a penny

FLORENCE — Edward III gold florin

FLORETTE — variations of French 15 cent. gros

FREDERIK — D'OR, Danish 19 cent. gold coin

GENOVINO — 12 cent. Genoese gold coin

GIGLIATO — 14 cent. silver coin of Charles II of Naples

GIUSTINA — 16 cent. Venetian silver coin (8 lire)

GORY-OBAN — 19 cent. Japanese $\frac{1}{2}$ oban gold coin

GROSCHEN — Austrian monetary unit (100 groschen = 1 schilling); monetary unit of Holy Roman Empire, silver

GROSSONE — papal 14/18 cent. silver coin

GULDINER — GULDENGROSCHEN, 15 cent. European silver coin (before thaler)

HALFMARK — old English coin, 6s. 8d.

HATPIECE — 16 cent. English monetary unit, gold (80s.)

HEMIOBOL — ancient Athenian and Corinthian $\frac{1}{2}$ obol

HEXAGRAM — Byzantine silver coin

IMPERIAL — Russian 10-rouble gold coin, 18 cent.

JOHANNES — old Portuguese coin

KAHAVANU — 9 cent. Ceylonese (Sri Lanka) gold coin

KREUTZER — old Austrian copper coin

KWARTNIK — Polish 14/15 cent. $\frac{1}{2}$ groschen

MAGDALON — Provençal 15 cent. gold florin

MARAVEDI — MARABOTINO, old Spanish copper coin

MILLIMES — Tunisian monetary unit (1000 millimes = 1 dinar)

MOCENIGO — a kind of 15 cent. Italian lira

MURAJOLA — Italian billon coins of low silver content

NAPOLEON — French 20-franc gold coin

NGULTRUM — Bhutani monetary unit (1 ngultrum = 2 tikchung = 100 paisa)

PAVILLON — D'OR, 14 cent. French gold coin

PHILIPPI — 4 cent. B.C. Macedonian (Black Sea) currency

PICCIOLO — old Maltese copper coin

COINS AND MONIES: ANCIENT AND MODERN

PLAPPART	14 cent. Swiss billon coin (15 Heller)	**SIXPENCE**	old English silver coin
QUADRANS	Roman copper coin (temncius), $\frac{1}{4}$ as	**SKILLING**	old Scandinavian shilling
		SPINTRIA	old porno tokens (tesserae)
QUATRUNX	Roman 4 oz coin (triens)	**SREBENIK**	10 cent. Russian silver coins
QUINCUNX	Roman 5 oz coin	**STAMENON**	Byzantine solidus
ROSE-RYAL	English gold coin of James I (30s.)	**STERLING**	gold or silver purity of British coinage
SCELLINO	Somalian monetary unit	**STOTINKA**	Bulgarian (100 stotinki = 1 lev)
SCYPHATE	Byzantine monetary unit	**TESSERAE**	old Roman tickets or tokens
SEMUNCIA	Roman $\frac{1}{2}$ uncia	**TIKCHUNG**	Bhutani monetary unit (2 tikchung = 1 ngultrum)
SEQUENCE	marks, Roman B.C. denarii		
SESTERCE	Roman silver coin	**VIRGINIA**	Virginian 18 cent. copper coin
SHILLING	old English 12 pence; monetary unit of Austria and various other countries	**XERAPHIM**	Portuguese Indian silver coin
		ZECCHINO	old Italian ducat
		ZERMABUB	early 18 cent. Ottoman gold coin

ALPHABETS

Greek

ALPHA	**NU**
BETA	**XI**
GAMMA	**OMICRON**
DELTA	**PI**
EPSILON	**RHO**
ZETA	**SIGMA**
ETA	**TAU**
THETA	**UPSILON**
IOTA	**PHI**
KAPPA	**CHI**
LAMBDA	**PSI**
MU	**OMEGA**

Hebrew

ALEPH	**LAMED**
BETH	**MEM**
GIMEL	**NUN**
DALETH	**SAMECH** or **SAMEKH**
HE	**AIN** or **AYIN**
VAU	**PE**
ZAIN or **ZAYIN**	**TZADDI** or **ZADE**
CHETH or **HETH**	**KOPH**
TETH	**RESH**
JOD or **YOD**	**SCHIN** or **SHIN**
CAPH or **KAPH**	**TAU**

FRENCH REVOLUTIONARY CALENDAR

French Republic 1794

VENDEMIAIRE	Vintage	**Sept.**	**GERMINAL**	Seed	**Mar.**
BRUMAIRE	Fog	**Oct.**	**FLOREAL**	Blossom	**Apr.**
FRIMAIRE	Sleet	**Nov.**	**PRAIRAL**	Pasture	**May**
NIVOSE	Snow	**Dec.**	**MESSIDOR**	Harvest	**June**
PLUVIOSE	Rain	**Jan.**	**THERMIDOR, FERVIDOR**	Heat	**July**
VENTOSE	Wind	**Feb.**	**FRUCTIDOR**	Fruit	**Aug.**

THE 12 SIGNS OF THE ZODIAC

Spring	Summer	Autumn	Winter
ARIES Ram	**CANCER** Crab	**LIBRA** Balance	**CAPRICORNUS** Goat
TAURUS Bull	**LEO** Lion	**SCORPIO** Scorpion	**AQUARIUS** Water Carrier
GEMINI Twins	**VIRGO** Virgin	**SAGITTARIUS** Archer	**PISCES** Fishes

THE 9 PLANETS AND THEIR SATELLITES

MARS	**NEPTUNE**	**SATURN cont.**	**PLUTO**	**JUPITER**
Deimos	Triton	Phoebe	**URANUS**	Io
Phobos	Nereid	Tethys	Ariel	Europa
EARTH	**SATURN**	Janus	Titania	Callisto
Luna	Rhea	Iapetus	Oberon	Ganymede
VENUS	Dione	Hyperion	Umbriel	**MERCURY**
	Mimas	Enceladus	Miranda	
	Titan			

CONSTELLATIONS IN THE HEAVENS

3 ARA
LEO

4 CRUS
CRUX
LYRA
URSA MAJOR
URSA MINOR

5 ARIES
CETUS
DRACO
HYDRA
INDUS
LEPUS
LIBRA
LUPOS
MUSCA
ORION
VIRGO

6 AQUILA
AURIGA
BOOTES
CANCER

CARINA
CORONA
CORVUS
CRATER
CYGNUS
DORADO
FORNAX
GEMINI
PUPPIS
TAURUS
TUCANA

7 CENTAUR
CEPHEUS
COLUMBA
PEACOCK
PEGASUS
PHOENIX
PERSEUS
SCORPIO
SERPENS

8 AQUARIUS
ERIDANUS

HERCULES
PLEIADES

9 ANDROMEDA
CENTAURUS (Alpha &
Beta Centauri)
DELPHINUS
OPHIUCHUS

10 CANIS MAJOR
CANIS MINOR
CARSIOPEIA
TRIANGULUM
URSUS MAJOR
URSUS MINOR

11 CAPRICORNUS
SAGITTARIUS

CANES VENATICI
CORONA BOREALIS
PISCIS AUSTRALIS
TRIANGULUM
AUSTRALIS

MAJOR STARS

4 BETA Centaurus
ENIF Pegasus
KAUS Sagittarius
MIRA Cetus
VEGA Lyra

5 ACRUX Crux
ALGOL Perseus
ALPHA Centaurus
ANKAA Phoenix
AVIOR Triangle
DENEB Cygnus
DUBHE Ursus Major
HADAR Centaurus
HAMAL Aries
MIZAR Ursus Major
NUNKI Sagitarrius
RIGIL (KENT) Centaurus
SABIK Ophiuchi
SPICA Virgo

6 ACAMAR Eridanus
ADHARA Canis Major
ALIOTH Ursa Major

ALKAID Ursa Minor
ALNAIR Crux
ALTAIR Aquila
CASTOR Gemini
DIPHDA Cetus
ELNATH Taurus
GACRUX Crux
GEINAH Corvus
HYADES Taurus
KOCHAB Ursa Minor
MARKAB Pegasus
MENKAR Cetus
MIMOSA Crux
MIRFAK Perseus
POLLUX Gemini
SHAUFA Scorpio
SIRIUS Canis Major
SUHAIL Velori

7 AINILAM Orion
ALPHARD Hydra
ANTARES Scorpio
CANOPUS Carina
CAPELLA Aurga

ELTANIN Draco
MENKENT Centaurus
PEACOCK Pavo
POLARIS Ursa Minor
PROCYON Ursa Minor
REGULUS Leo
SCHEDAR Cassiopeia

8 ACHERNAR Eridanus
ALPHECCA Corona
Borealis
ARCTURUS Bootes
DENEBOLA Leo
ZUBENUBI Libra

9 ALDEBARAN Taurus
ALPHERATZ
Andromedra
BELLATRIX Orion
FOMALHAUF Pisces

10 RASALHAGUE Ophiuchi
BETELGEUSE Orion

11 MIAPLACIDUS Carina

MONTHS OF THE JEWISH YEAR

TISHRI	TEBET	NISAN or ABIB	TAMMUS
HESHVAN	SHEBAT	IYAR	AB
KISLEV	ADAR or VEADAR	SIVAN	ELUL

BOOKS OF THE BIBLE

Old Testament (39)

GENESIS	1st KINGS	ECCLESIASTES	AMOS
EXODUS	2nd KINGS	SONG OF SOLOMON	OBADIAH
LEVITICUS	1st CHRONICLES	(SONG OF SONGS)	JONAH
NUMBERS	2nd CHRONICLES	ISAIAH	MICAH
DEUTERONOMY	EZRA	JEREMIAH	NAHUM
JOSHUA	NEHEMIAH	LAMENTATIONS	HABAKKUK
JUDGES	ESTHER	EZEKIEL	ZEPHANIAH
RUTH	JOB	DANIEL	HAGGAI
1st SAMUEL	PSALMS	HOSEA	ZACHARIAS
2nd SAMUEL	PROVERBS	JOEL	MALACHI

The Apocrypha (13)

ESDRAS	BARUCH
TOBIT	EPISTLE OF JEREMY
JUDITH	SONG OF THE THREE HOLY CHILDREN
ESTHER	HISTORY OF SUSANNA
THE WISDOM OF SOLOMON	BEL AND THE DRAGON
ECCLESIASTICUS	THE PRAYER OF MANASSES
	MACCABEES

New Testament (27)

GOSPEL OF ST MATTHEW	1st EPISTLE TO TIMOTHY
GOSPEL OF ST MARK	2nd EPISTLE TO TIMOTHY
GOSPEL OF ST LUKE	EPISTLE TO TITUS
GOSPEL OF ST JOHN	EPISTLE TO PHILEMON
ACTS OF THE APOSTLES	EPISTLE TO THE HEBREWS
EPISTLE TO THE ROMANS	1st PETER
1st EPISTLE TO THE CORINTHIANS	2nd PETER
2nd EPISTLE TO THE CORINTHIANS	1st JOHN
EPISTLE TO THE GALATIANS	2nd JOHN
EPISTLE TO THE EPHESIANS	3rd JOHN
EPISTLE TO THE PHILIPPIANS	JAMES
EPISTLE TO THE COLOSSIANS	JUDE
1st EPISTLE TO THE THESSALONIANS	THE REVELATION
2nd EPISTLE TO THE THESSALONIANS	

THE SEVEN MAJOR ECUMENICAL COUNCILS (IN ASIA MINOR)

NICEA (Iznik)	325 A.D.	CONSTANTINOPLE (Istanbul)	533 A.D.
CONSTANTINOPLE (Istanbul)	381 A.D.	ISTANBUL	680–681 A.D.
EPHESUS (Efes)	431 A.D.	NICEA (Iznik)	787 A.D.
CHALCEDON (Kadikoy) (Istanbul)	451 A.D.		

BRITISH PRIME MINISTERS

From 1770

Lord NORTH
Lord ROCKINGHAM
Lord SHELBURNE
Duke of PORTLAND
William PITT
Henry ADDINGTON
William PITT
Lord GRENVILLE
Spencer PERCEVAL
Lord LIVERPOOL
George CANNING
Lord GODERICH
Duke of WELLINGTON
Lord GREY
Lord MELBOURNE
Sir Robert PEEL
Lord MELBOURNE
Sir Robert PEEL
Lord John RUSSELL
Lord DERBY
Lord ABERDEEN

Lord PALMERSTON
Lord DERBY
Lord PALMERSTON
Lord John RUSSELL
Lord DERBY
Benjamin DISRAELI
W. E. GLADSTONE
Benjamin DISRAELI,
Lord BEACONSFIELD
W. E. GLADSTONE
Lord SALISBURY
W. E. GLADSTONE
Lord SALISBURY
W. E. GLADSTONE
Lord ROSEBERY
Lord SALISBURY
A. J. BALFOUR
Sir H. CAMPBELL-BANNERMAN
H. H. ASQUITH**
David LLOYD GEORGE
A. BONAR LAW

Stanley BALDWIN
J. R. MACDONALD
Stanley BALDWIN
J. R. MACDONALD**
Stanley BALDWIN
Neville CHAMBERLAIN**
W. Spencer
CHURCHILL**
Clement ATTLEE**
Sir W. CHURCHILL
Sir Anthony EDEN
Harold MACMILLAN**
Sir Alec DOUGLAS-
HOME
Harold WILSON**
Edward HEATH
Harold WILSON**
James CALLAGHAN
Margaret THATCHER***
John MAJOR

** and *** signify the number of consecutive terms of office

PRESIDENTS OF THE UNITED STATES

George WASHINGTON
John ADAMS
Thom. JEFFERSON
James MADISON
James MONROE
John Quincy ADAMS
Andrew JACKSON
Martin van BUREN
William HARRISON
John TYLER
James Knox POLK
Zachary TAYLOR
Millard FILLMORE
Franklin PIERCE

James BUCHANAN
Abraham LINCOLN
Andrew JOHNSON
Ulysses GRANT
Rutherford HAYES
James GARFIELD
Chester ARTHUR
Grover CLEVELAND
Benjamin HARRISON
Grover CLEVELAND
William McKINLEY
Theodore ROOSEVELT
William TAFT
Woodrow WILSON

Warren HARDING
Calvin COOLIDGE
Herbert HOOVER
F. D. ROOSEVELT
Harry TRUMAN
Dwight D.
EISENHOWER
John F. KENNEDY
Lyndon B. JOHNSON
Richard M. NIXON
Gerald R. FORD
James E. CARTER
Ronald REAGAN
George BUSH

since 1901

1901	Sully PRUDHOMME	Fr.
1902	Theodor MOMMSEN	Ger.
1903	B. BJORNSON	Nor.
1904	Frédéric MISTRAL & J. ECHEGARAY y EIZAGUIRRE	Fr. & Spain
1905	H. SIENKIEWICZ	Pol.
1906	Giosue CARDUCCI	Italy
1907	Rudyard KIPLING	Brit.
1908	Rudolf EUKEN	Ger.
1909	Selma LAGERLOF	Sweden
1910	Paul von HEYSE	Ger.
1911	Maurice MAETERLINCK	Belg.
1912	Gerhart HAUPTMANN	Ger.
1913	Sir R. TAGORE	India
1914	no award	-
1915	Romain ROLLAND	Fr.
1916	V. von HEIDENSTAM	Sweden
1917	Karl GJELLERUP & H. PONTOPPIDAN	Den.
1918	no award	-
1919	Carl SPITTELER	Switz.
1920	Knut HAMSUN	Nor.
1921	Anatole FRANCE	Fr.
1922	J. BENAVENTE y MARTINEZ	Spain
1923	William Butler YEATS	Ire.
1924	Wladyslaw REYMONT	Pol.
1925	George Bernard SHAW	Ire.
1926	Grazia DELEDDA	Italy
1927	Henri BERGSON	Fr.
1928	Sigrid UNDSET	Nor.
1929	Thomas MANN	Ger.
1930	Sinclair LEWIS	U.S.
1931	Erik Axel KARLFELDT	Sweden
1932	John GALSWORTHY	Brit.
1933	Ivan BUNIN	U.S.S.R.
1934	Luigi PIRANDELLO	Italy
1935	no award	-
1936	Eugene O'NEILL	U.S.
1937	Roger MARTIN du GARD	Fr.
1938	Pearl BUCK	U.S.
1939	Frans Eemil SILLANPAA	Fin.
1940– 1943	no awards	-
1944	J. V. JENSEN	Den.
1945	Gabriela MISTRAL	Chile
1946	Hermann HESSE	Switz.
1947	André GIDE	Fr.
1948	T. S. ELIOT	Brit.
1949	William FAULKNER	U.S.
1950	Bertrand RUSSELL	Brit.
1951	Pär LAGERKVIST	Sweden
1952	François MAURIAC	Fr.
1953	Sir Winston CHURCHILL	Brit.
1954	Ernest HEMINGWAY	U.S.
1955	Halldor LAXNESS	Ice.
1956	Juan Ramon JIMENEZ	Spain
1957	Albert CAMUS	Fr.
1958	Boris PASTERNAK (declined award)	U.S.S.R.
1959	Salvatore QUASIMODO	Italy
1960	Saint-John PERSE	Fr.
1961	Ivo ANDRIC	Yugos.
1962	John STEINBECK	U.S.
1963	George SEFERIS	Gr.
1964	Jean-Paul SARTRE	Fr.
1965	Mikhail SHOLOKHOV	U.S.S.R.
1966	Shmuel Yosef AGNON & Nelly SACHS	Isr. & Sweden
1967	Miguel Angel ASTURIAS	Guat.
1968	Kawabata YASUNARI	Japan
1969	Samuel BECKETT	Ire.
1970	Aleksandr SOLZHENITSYN	U.S.S.R.
1971	Pablo NERUDA	Chile
1972	Heinrich BOLL	Ger.
1973	Patrick WHITE	Austr.
1974	Eyvind JOHNSON & Harry MARTINSON	Sweden
1975	Eugenio MONTALE	Italy
1976	Saul BELLOW	U.S.
1977	Vicente ALEIXANDRE	Spain
1978	Isaac Bashevis SINGER	U.S.
1979	Odysseus ELYTIS	Gr.
1980	Czeslaw MILOSZ	U.S.
1981	Elias CANETTI	Bulg.
1982	Gabriel Garcia MARQUEZ	Colombia
1983	William GOLDING	Brit.
1984	Jaroslav SEIFERT	Czech.
1985	Claude SIMON	Fr.
1986	Elie WIESEL	U.S.
1987	Joseph BRODSKY	U.S./U.S.S.R.
1988	Negbeh MAHFOUZ	Egypt
1989	Camilo José CELA	Spain
1990	Octavio PAZ	Mexico
1991	Nadine GORDIMER	S.A.

COUNTIES OF THE BRITISH ISLES

England and Wales

3 MON*

4 AVON
BEDS
CAMS
GLAM*
GLOS
KENT
OXON
TYNE &
   WEAR

5 BERKS
BUCKS
CARDS*
CARMS*
CLWYD
DERBY
DEVON
DYFED
ESSEX
FLINT*
GWENT
HANTS
HERTS
HUNTS*
LANCS
LEICS
LINCS
NOTTS
PEMBS*
POWYS
SALOP**
WILTS
WORCS
YORKS

6 BRECON*
DORSET
DURHAM
LONDON
OXFORD
RADNOR*
STAFFS
SURREY
SUSSEX

7 BEDFORD
CUMBRIA
DENBIGH*
GWYNEDD
LINCOLN
NORFOLK
RUTLAND*
SUFFOLK
WARWICK

8 ANGLESEY*
CARDIGAN*
CHESHIRE
CORNWALL
HEREFORD
HERTFORD
MONMOUTH*
PEMBROKE*
SOMERSET
STAFFORD

Scotland

3 AYR*

4 BUTE*
FIFE
ROSS*

5 ANGUS*
BANFF*
ELGIN*
MORAY*
NAIRN*
PERTH*

6 ARGYLL*
FORFAR*
LANARK*
ORKNEY

7 BERWICK*
BORDERS
CENTRAL
KINROSS*
LOTHIAN
PEEBLES*
RENFREW*
SELKIRK*
TAYSIDE
WIGTOWN*

8 ABERDEEN*
AYRSHIRE*
CROMARTY*
DUMFRIES &
   GALLOWAY
GRAMPIAN
HIGHLAND
ROXBURGH*
STIRLING*

Ireland

4 CORK†
DOWN
LEIX†
MAYO†

5 CAVAN†
CLARE†
KERRY†
LOUTH†
MEATH†
SLIGO†

6 ANTRIM
ARMAGH
CARLOW†
DUBLIN†
GALWAY†
OFFALY†
TYRONE
ULSTER (P)

7 DONEGAL†
KILDARE†
LEITRIM†
MUNSTER (P)†
WEXFORD†
WICKLOW†

8 KILKENNY†
LAOIGHIS
LEINSTER (P)†
LIMERICK†
LONGFORD†
MONAGHAN†

* Counties which no longer exist after local government reorganization in 1974.
**Name for Shropshire from 1974 to 1980.
† Counties of the Republic of Ireland.

THE 50 UNITED STATES OF AMERICA

State/Abbrev.		Joined/no.	Approx. Pop.	Capital
4 IOWA	Ia.	1846/29th	2.9 mill.	DES MOINES
OHIO	O.	1803/17th	10.8	COLUMBUS
UTAH	Uh.	1896/45th	1.5	SALT LAKE CITY
5 IDAHO	Id., Ida.	1890/43rd	1.0	BOISE
MAINE	Me.	1820/23rd	1.2	AUGUSTA
TEXAS	Tex.	1845/28th	14.5	AUSTIN

State/Abbrev.	Joined/no.	Approx. Pop.	Capital
6 **ALASKA** Ala.	1959/49th	0.5	JUNEAU
HAWAII	1959/50th	1.0	HONOLULU
KANSAS Kan.	1861/34th	2.4	TOPEKA
NEVADA Nev.	1864/36th	0.8	CARSON CITY
OREGON Ore., Oreg.	1859/33rd	2.7	SALEM
7 **ALABAMA** Ala.	1819/17th	3.9	MONTGOMERY
ARIZONA Ariz.	1912/48th	2.8	PHOENIX
FLORIDA Fla.	1845/27th	10.0	TALLAHASSEE
GEORGIA Ga.	orig. 13	5.5	ATLANTA
INDIANA Ind.	1816/19th	5.5	INDIANAPOLIS
MONTANA Mont.	1889/41st	0.8	HELENA
NEW YORK N.Y.	orig. 13	17.6	ALBANY
VERMONT Vt.	1791/14th	0.6	MONTPELIER
WYOMING Wyo.	1890/44th	0.5	CHEYENNE
8 **ARKANSAS** Ark.	1836/25th	2.3	LITTLE ROCK
COLORADO Colo.	1876/38th	2.9	DENVER
DELAWARE Del.	orig. 13	0.6	DOVER
ILLINOIS Ill.	1818/21st	11.5	SPRINGFIELD
KENTUCKY Ky., Ken.	1792/15th	3.7	FRANKFORT
MARYLAND Md.	orig. 13	4.3	ANNAPOLIS
MICHIGAN Mich.	1837/26th	9.3	LANSING
MISSOURI Mo.	1821/24th	5.0	JEFFERSON CITY
NEBRASKA Neb.	1867/37th	1.6	LINCOLN
OKLAHOMA Okla.	1907/46th	3.1	OKLAHOMA CITY
VIRGINIA Va.	orig. 13	5.4	RICHMOND
9 **LOUISIANA** La.	1812/18th	4.3	BATON ROUGE
MINNESOTA Minn.	1858/32nd	4.1	ST. PAUL
NEW JERSEY N.J.	orig. 13	7.4	TRENTON
NEW MEXICO N.M.	1912/47th	1.3	SANTA FE
TENNESSEE Tenn.	1796/16th	4.6	NASHVILLE
WISCONSIN Wis.	1848/30th	4.8	MADISON
10 **CALIFORNIA** Cal.	1850/31st	23.7	SACRAMENTO
WASHINGTON Wash.	1889/42nd	4.2	OLYMPIA
11 **CONNECTICUT** Conn.	orig. 13	3.2	HARTFORD
MISSISSIPPI Miss.	1817/20th	2.6	JACKSON
NORTH DAKOTA N.D., N.Dak.	1889/39th	0.7	BISMARCK
SOUTH DAKOTA S.Dak., S.D.	1889/40th	0.7	PIERRE
RHODE ISLAND R.I.	orig. 13	1.0	PROVIDENCE
12 **NEW HAMPSHIRE** N.H.	orig. 13	1.0	CONCORD
PENNSYLVANIA Penn.	orig. 13	12.0	HARRISBURG
WEST VIRGINIA W.Va.	1863/35th	2.0	CHARLESTON
13 **MASSACHUSETTS** Mass.	orig. 13	5.8	BOSTON
NORTH CAROLINA N.C.	orig. 13	5.9	RALEIGH
SOUTH CAROLINA S.C.	orig. 13	3.2	COLUMBIA

COLUMBIA (District) D.C. (site of the capital of the U.S.)   WASHINGTON D.C.

THE 12 PROVINCES OF CANADA

State	Population	Capital
YUKON Territory	ca. 18,500	WHITEHORSE
QUEBEC	ca. 6.1 million	QUEBEC
ALBERTA	ca. 1.7 million	EDMONTON
ONTARIO	ca. 8.3 million	TORONTO
MANITOBA	ca. 1.0 million	WINNIPEG
NOVA SCOTIA	ca. 0.9 million	HALIFAX
NEW BRUNSWICK	ca. 0.7 million	FREDERICTON
NEWFOUNDLAND	ca. 0.6 million	ST. JOHN'S
SASKATCHEWAN	ca. 1.0 million	REGINA
BRITISH COLUMBIA	ca. 2.5 million	VICTORIA
PRINCE EDWARD ISLAND	ca. 0.2 million	CHARLOTTETOWN
NORTHWEST TERRITORIES	ca. 35,000	YELLOWKNIFE
District of Franklin		
District of Keewatin		
District of Mackenzie		

THE 15 UNION REPUBLICS OF THE FORMER SOVIET UNION

State	Population	Capital
UZBEK S.S.R.* (Uzbekistan)	ca. 12 million	TASHKENT
KAZAKH S.S.R. (Kazakhstan)	ca. 14.5 million	ALMA-ATA
KIRGIZ S.S.R. (Kirgizstan, Kirghiz/Kirgiziya)	ca. 3 million	FRUNZE
LATVIAN S.S.R.	ca. 2.4 million	RIGA
RUSSIAN SOVIET FEDERATED S.R.	ca. 134 million	MOSCOW
TADZHIK S.S.R. (Tajikistan, Tadzhikstan)	ca. 3.5 million	DUSHANBE
TURKMEN S.S.R. (Turkmenistan, Turkmeniya)	ca. 2.5 million	ASHKHABAD
ARMENIAN S.S.R.	ca. 3.1 million	YEREVAN
ESTONIAN S.S.R.	ca. 1.4 million	TALLINN
GEORGIAN S.S.R. (Sakartvelo, Gruziya)	ca. 5 million	TBILISI (Tiflis)
MOLDAVIAN S.S.R.	ca. 3.9 million	KISHINYOV
UKRAINIAN S.S.R. (Ukraine)	ca. 50 million	KIEV
AZERBAIJAN S.S.R. (Azerbaydzhan)	ca. 5.8 million	BAKU
LITHUANIAN S.S.R.	ca. 3.3 million	VILNIUS
BELORUSSIAN S.S.R. (Byelorussia, Belorussia/White Russia)	ca. 9.1 million	MINSK

*S.S.R. = Soviet Socialist Republic

THE FORMER 6 SOCIALIST REPUBLICS OF YUGOSLAVIA (JUGOSLAVIJA)

State	Population	Capital
SERBIA (Srbija) (includes the 2 Autonomous Provinces of Vojvodina and Kosovo/Kosmet)	ca. 8.5 million	BELGRADE
CROATIA (Hrvatska)	ca. 4.5 million	ZAGREB
SLOVENIA (Slovenija)	ca. 1.8 million	LLUBLJANA
MACEDONIA (Makedonija)	ca. 1.7 million	SKOPJE
MONTENEGRO (Crna Gora)	ca. 0.5 million	TITOGRAD
BOSNIA AND HERZEGOVINA (Bosna i Hercegovina)	ca. 4.1 million	SARAJEVO

with present & former names

Country	Capital
4	
CHAD/TSCHAD	N'DJAMENA (Fort-Lamy)
MALI (col. French Soudan)	BAMAKO
TOGO (col. Togoland)	LOME
5	
BENIN (col. Dahomey)	PORTO-NOVO
CONGO (Brazzaville)	BRAZZAVILLE
EGYPT (Arab Republic of Egypt)	CAIRO
GABON (col. part of French Equatorial Africa)	LIBREVILLE (Freetown)
GHANA (col. Gold Coast & part of Togoland)	ACCRA
KENYA	NAIROBI
LIBYA	TRIPOLI
NIGER	NIAMEY (Zinder/Damagaram)
SUDAN, The	KHARTOUM
ZAIRE (col. Belgian Congo)	KINSHASA (Leopoldville)
6	
ANGOLA (col. Portuguese West Africa)	LUANDA
GAMBIA, The	BANJUL (Bathurst)
GUINEA	CONAKRY
MALAWI (col. Nyasaland)	LILONGWE (Zomba)
RWANDA (Kinyarwanda) (col. Ruanda)	KIGALI
UGANDA	KAMPALA
ZAMBIA (col. Northern Rhodesia)	LUSAKA
7	
ALGERIA	ALGIERS
BURUNDI (Kirundi) (col. Ruanda & Urundi)	BUJUMBURA
COMOROS islands (Grande Comore & Moheli & Anjouan)	MOCONI (Moheli & Anjouan)
LESOTHO Kingdom (Sesotho) (col. Basutoland)	MASERU
LIBERIA	MONROVIA
MOROCCO	RABAT
NAMIBIA (col. South West Africa)	WINDHOEK (national) SWAKOPMUND (summer)
NIGERIA Federal Republic (col. British protectorates of Northern & Southern Nigeria)	LAGOS
SENEGAL (together with Gambia: Senegambia)	DAKAR
SOMALIA (col. Br. & It. Somaliland)	MOGADISCIO
TUNISIA	TUNIS
8	
BOTSWANA (col. Bechuanaland)	GABORONE
CAMEROON (Col. Kamerun)	YAOUNDE
DJIBOUTI (col. Afars & Issas, Fr. Somaliland)	DJIBOUTI
ETHIOPIA (ancient Abyssinia)	ADDIS ABABA
MALAGASY/MADAGASIKARA (col. Madagascar)	ANTANANARIVO
TANZANIA (col. Tanganyika & Zanzibar)	DAR ES SALAAM
ZIMBABWE (col. Southern Rhodesia)	HARARE (Salisbury)
9	
CAPE VERDE islands (Windward & Leeward groups)	PRAIA
MAURITIUS (in the Indian Ocean, incl. islands of Rodrigues, Cargados Carajos Shoals, Agalega)	PORT LOUIS
SWAZILAND Kingdom	MBABANE (administrative) LOBAMBA (royal & legislative)

27

Country

Capital

10 **BOKINA FASO** (col. Upper Volta)　OUAGADOUGOU
IVORY COAST　ABIDJAN
MAURITANIA　NOUAKCHOTT
MOZAMBIQUE (col. Portuguese East Africa)　MAPUTO
SEYCHELLES (archipelago of ca. 85 islands)　VICTORIA

11 **SIERRA LEONE**　FREETOWN
SOUTH AFRICA　CAPETOWN (legislative)
　PRETORIA (administrative)
　BLOEMFONTEIN (judicial)

GUINEA-BISSAU (col. Portuguese Guinea)　BISSAU
WESTERN SAHARA (col. Spanish Sahara,　EL AAIUN (chief town, formerly capital)
divided 1976 between Morocco and
Mauritania; Southern region: Rio de Oro;
Northern region: Saguia el Hamra)
EQUATORIAL GUINEA (col. Spanish Guinea)　MALABO (Santa Isabel)
incl. Macias Nguema Biyogo (Fernando Po/
Poo) and Pagolu islands
SAO TOME E PRINCIPE (islands)　SAO TOME
CENTRAL AFRICAN REPUBLIC (col.　BANGUI
Oubangui-Chari)

Note:　French-speaking Central Africa today comprises the territories of Central African
Republic, Congo/Brazzaville, Gabon, and Zaire.

Country	Status	Capital
5 YEMEN (formerly South Yemen)	People's Democratic Republic	ADEN
YEMEN (SAN'A) (Yemen P.D.R. & Yemen (San'a) formed the Yemen Republic 1972)	Republic	SAN'A
6 BELIZE/BELICE (formerly British Honduras)	self-governing	BELMOPAN
BRUNEI (Negeri Brunei) (formerly Sarawak)	British protected sultanate (N. Borneo)	BANDAR SERI BEGAWAN
GUYANA (col. British Guiana)	Republic	GEORGETOWN
TAIWAN (formerly Formosa)	Republic	TAIPEI
8 SRI LANKA (formerly Ceylon)	Republic	COLOMBO
SURINAME (col. Dutch Guiana)	Republic	PARAMARIBO
9 IRIAN JAYA (Irian Barat, West Irian or West New Guinea) (formerly part of Dutch East Indies)	Province of Indonesia	DJAJAPURA
10 BANGLADESH (formerly East Pakistan)	People's Republic formed 1971	DACCA
KALIMANTAN (Indonesian name for Borneo) divided into West, Central, South & East Kalimantan	Provinces of Indonesia	PONTIANAK (W) PALANGKARAJA (C) BANDJARMASIN (S) SAMARINDRA (E)
PAPUA NEW GUINEA (formerly Australian Papua & UN Territory of New Guinea)	Australian territory admin. as part of Territory of Papua & New Guinea	PORT MORESBY
SARAWAK & **SABAH**	States of E. Malaysia on N. Borneo	KUCHING KOTA KINABULU
THE UNITED ARAB EMIRATES (formerly Trucial States or Trucial Oman) include:		
OMAN (Sultanat Uman) (formerly Muscat and Oman)	Sultanate	MUSCAT
DUBAI (Dubayy) (incl. exclave Hajarayn)	Emirate	DUBAYY (Dubai)
QATAR (Dawlat Qatar)	State of Qatar	ad-DAWHAH (Doha)
SHARJAH (Ash-Shariqah) (incl. exclaves Dibbah, Khwar al-Fakkan, Khwar al-Kalba)	Emirate	ash-SHARIQAH (Sharjah)
ABU DHABI (Abu Zaby)	Sultanate	ABU ZABY

Islands	Status	Capital or admin. headquarters
4 **FIJI** (borders on Melanesia) main islands: Viti Levu, Vanua Levu, Lau group	Independent	SUVA (on Viti Levu)
5 **SAMOA** main islands: Tutuila, Manu'a, Rose Island	Dependency of US	PAGO PAGO (on Tutuila)
TONGA or PULE'ANGA TONGA (Kingdom of Tonga, also called Friendly Islands) main islands: Tongatapu/Tongatabu, Vavau, Haapai	Independent 1970	NUKUALOFA (on Tongatapu/Tongatabu
6 **HAWAII** includes Mauna Kea, highest island in Polynesia	50th state of US	HONOLULU
TAHITI or OTAHEITE includes Tahiti Nui & Tahiti Iti; largest island of the the Windward Group (Society Islands)	French Polynesia	PAPEETE (on Tahiti, capital of French Polynesia)
TUBUAI ISLANDS (Austral Islands) main islands: Tubuai, Rurutu Raevavae, Rimatara, Rapa	French Polynesia	MATAURA (on Tubuai)
TUVALU (col. Ellice Islands) (formerly part of the British crown colony of Gilbert & Ellice islands) largest island: Vaitupu	Independent 1978, constitutional monarchy	FUNAFUTI (on Funafuti)
7 **EASTER ISLAND – RAPANUI** (Great Rapa) or **TE PITO TE HENUA** (Navel of the World) main islets: Motu-Nui, Motu-Iti, Motu-Kaokao	Dependency of Chile	HANGA-ROA (on Easter Island)
TOKELAU ISLANDS (Union Group) main islands: Nukunono, Atafu, Fakaofo	New Zealand territory	NUKUNONO (unofficial capital)
TUAMOTU ARCHIPELAGO or PAUMOTU main islands: NW = Rangiroa, Makemo, Raroia (Kon-Tiki!), centre: Anaa, Amanu, Hao, SE = Mururoa, Fagataufa, Tureia	French Polynesia	APATAKI (on Apataki)
MANGAREVA/MAGAREVA ISLANDS (Gambier Islands) main islands: Mangareva/ Magareva, Taravai, Aukeua, Akamaru	French Polynesia	RIKITEA (on Mangareva/ Magareva)
CLIPPERTON ISLANDS (uninhabited)	French Polynesia	

POLYNESIA

Islands	Status	Capital or admin. headquarters
NEW ZEALAND (North & South)	Independent	WELLINGTON (on North Island)
COOK ISLANDS S (Lower) Cooks: Rarotonga, Atiu Takutea, Mauke, Mitiaro, Manuae, N (Manuhiki) Cooks: Penrhyn, Manihiki, Danger (Pukapuka), Palmerston, Rakakanga, Suvorov, Nassau	Dependency of New Zealand	AVARUA (on Rarotonga)
WESTERN SAMOA main islands: Savaii, Upolu	Independent 1962	APIA (on Upolu)
SOCIETY ISLANDS Windward group: Tahiti, Moorea, Leeward group: Bora-Bora, Raiatea Motu-Iti, Huahine	French Polynesia	PAPEETE (on Tahiti)
MARQUESAS ISLANDS main islands: Hiva Ova (largest), Tahuata, Nuku Hiva/Nukahiva, Hatutu	French Polynesia	HAKAPEHI (TAI-O-HAE) (on Nuku Hiva/Nukahiva)

MELANESIA

Islands	Status	Capital or admin. headquarters
FIJI – see Polynesia		
LOYALTY ISLANDS main islands: Mare, Uvea, Lifou	French New Caledonia	TADINOU (on Mare)
VANUATU (col. New Hebrides) main islands: Espiritu Santo (largest), Efate, Banks, Ambrim	Republic	VILA (on Efate)
BISMARCK ARCHIPELAGO main islands: New Britain, New Ireland, the Admiralties, Mussau, Lavongai (New Hanover), Duke & York Islands, Vitu Islands	Papua New Guinea	RABAUL (on New Britain)
ADMIRALTY ISLANDS main islands: Manus (largest) Hermit & Ninigo groups	extension of Bismarck Archipelago	LORENGAU (on Manus)
NEW CALEDONIA main islands: New Caledonia, Belep, Pins, Walpole, Hunter, Huon	French Overseas Territory	NOUMEA (on New Caledonia)
D'ENTRECASTEAUX ISLANDS main islands: Normanby, Fergusson, Goodenough (Morata), Sanaroa (Welle), Dobu	Papua New Guinea	VIVIGANI (on Goodenough)

Islands	Status	Capital or admin. headquarters
GUAM (largest & southernmost of the Mariana Islands)	self-governing territory of US	AGANA
***BANABA** (col. Ocean Island)	Republic	Tapiwa?
NAOERO/NAURU (col. Ger. Marschall Islands protectorate: UN Trust Territory under Australia)	Republic	YAREN (on Naoero/Nauru)
MARIANA ISLANDS (North) main islands: Saipan, Tinian Agrihan (highest), Rota	UN Trust Territory under US jurisdiction	SAIPAN (on Saipan – also territorial capital)
CAROLINE ISLANDS main islands: Ponape, Yap, Truk, Kusaie, Nukuoro, Kapingamarangi	UN Trust Territory under US jurisdiction	SAIPAN
KIRIBATI (col. Gilbert Islands, or Kingsmill) stretching from Washington to Flint islands & Christmas atoll to Banaba; main islands: Tarawa Butaritari (Makin), Abemama, Abaiang (the former British crown colony included Ocean Island, Central & Southern Line Islands, Phoenix I.)	Independent 1979	TARAWA (on Tarawa)
MARSHALL ISLANDS main islands: Radak Chain (Sunrise): Mili, Majuro, Bikar, Utirik Ralik Chain (Sunset): Kwajalein, Jaluit, Bikini, Wotho, Eniwetok	UN Trust Territory under US jurisdiction	SAIPAN
THE TRUST TERRITORY OF THE UN under US jurisdiction includes: Mariana & Caroline Islands, Marshall Islands, the Federated States of Micronesia (Ponape, Kusaie, Truk & Yap) and the district of Palau	under US jurisdiction	

* Population resettled on Rambi/Fiji

Born	Rule	Name	Manner of Death
12/7 100 B.C.	60–44 B.C.	Gaius **JULIUS CAESAR** (wife CORNELIA)	murdered 15/3
23/9 63 B.C.	27 B.C.– 14 A.D.	Caesar **AUGUSTUS** (Octavian/Gaius Octavius/Gaius Julius Caesar Octavius) (wife **LIVIA**)	old age (77) on 19/8
16/11 42 B.C. in Rome	14–37 A.D.	**TIBERIUS** (Claudius Nero Caesar Augustus) (wife **JULIA**)	natural 16/3 on Capri
31/8 12 B.C. in Antium/Anzio/Italy	37–41	**CALIGULA** (Gaius Caesar) (wife **CAESONIA**)	murdered 24/1
1/8 10 A.D. in Lugdunum/Lyon	41–54	**CLAUDIUS I** (Tiberius Claudius Drusus Nero Germanicus) (wife & niece **AGRIPPINA**)	poisoned 13/10
15/12 37 in Rome	54–68	**NERO** (Lucius Domitius Achenobarbus) (wife: a) **OCTAVIA**, b) **POPPAEA SABINA**, first wife of Otho)	suicide

End of Caesar's line

Born	Rule	Name	Manner of Death
24/12 3 B.C.	68–69	**GALBA** (Servius Sulpicius)	murdered 15/1
28/4 32 A.D.	69–69	**OTHO** (Marcus Salvius Otho) (wife **POPPAEA SABINA**)	suicide 16/4
15 A.D.	69–69	**VITELLIUS** (Aulus)	murdered 20/12

Flavian House

Born	Rule	Name	Manner of Death
9 A.D.	69–79	**VESPASIAN** (Titus Flavius Vespasianus)	natural 24/6
30/12 39 A.D.	79–81	**TITUS** (Titus Flavius Vespasianus) (wife **AGRIPPA II BERENICE**, wife of Herod)	murdered? 13/9
24/10 51 A.D.	81–96	**DOMITIAN** (Titus Flavius Domitianus)	murdered 18/9

End of Flavian line & the 12 Caesars

"FIVE GOOD EMPERORS"

Born	Rule	Name	Manner of Death
c. 30 A.D.	96–98	**NERVA** (Marcus Cocceius Nerva)	natural
15/9 53 in Italica (Santiponce/Spain)	98–117	**TRAJAN** (Marcus Ulpius Traianus, Germanicus) (wife **PLOTINA**)	natural 8/8 in Selinus/Selindi (TR)
24/1 76 in Rome?	117–138	**HADRIAN** (Publius Aelius Hadrianus) (wife **VIBIA SABINA**)	natural 10/7
19/9 86 Lanuvium	138–161	**ANTONINUS PIUS** (Titus Aurelius Fulvius Boinonius Arrius Antoninus) (wife **FAUSTINA**)	natural 7/3
15/12 130	161–169	**LUCIUS VERUS** (Lucius Aurelius)	natural

ROMAN EMPERORS

Born	Rule	Name	Manner of Death
26/4 121 A.D.	169–180	**MARCUS AURELIUS** (Antoninus) (co-ruler with Antoninus Pius & Lucius Verus 140s–169)	natural 17/3
31/8 161 in Rome	180–192	**COMMODUS** (Lucius Aelius Aurelius) (mistress **MARCIA**)	murdered 31/12
1/8 126 (Liguria)	193–193	**PERTINAX** (Publius Helvius)	murdered 28/3

Born	Rule	Name	Manner of Death
c. 135 in Milan	193–193	**MARCUS DIDIUS** (Julianus)	murdered 1/6
146 in Leptis Magna, Libya	193–211	***SEPTIMIUS SEVERUS** (Severus Lucius Septimius) (wife **JULIA DOMNA**)	illness Febr. in Eburacum/York, Engl.

* 198–211 Septimius Severus ruled with his son Caracalla

189 in Milan	209–212	**GETA** (Publius Septimius) (together with his father Septimus Severus & brother Caracalla)	murdered Febr.
4/4 188 in Lugdunum/Lyon	198–217	**CARACALLA** (Marcus Aurelius Antoninus) sole ruler 212–217 (wife **FULVIA PLAUTILLA**)	murdered 8/4 in Carrhae (Harran/ TR)
c. 164 (Caesarea/ Algeria)	217–218	**MACRINUS** (Marcus Opellius)	executed June (TR)
204 (Emesa/Homs)	218–222	**ELAGABALUS (HELIOGABALUS)** (Varius Avitus Bassianus)	murdered
208 (Phoenicia/ Lebanon)	222–235	**SEVERUS ALEXANDER** (Marcus Aurelius Severus Alexander)	murdered in Gaul
	235–238	**MAXIMINUS/MAXIMIN** (Caius Julius Verus Maximinius)	murdered March
c. 157	238 for 3 weeks	**GORDIAN I** (Marcus Antonius Gordianus) together with his son **GORDIAN II**	suicide Apr. killed in battle
225	Aug. 238– 244	***GORDIAN III** (Marcus Antonius Gordianus)	murdered in Zaitha

* May 238–Aug. 238 GORDIAN III ruled with the elderly senators Maximus and Balbinus, both murdered

	244–249	**PHILIP THE ARABIAN** (Marcus Julius Philippus)	murdered
c. 201 (Budalia/ Pannonia/Yu)	249–251	**DECIUS** (Gaius Messius Quintus Trajanus)	killed in battle
	251–253	**GALLUS** (Gaius Vibius Trebonianus) co-rulers: Hostilian (son of Decius, died early) & Volusianus (his own son)	murdered
Mauretania/Africa	253–253	**AEMILIAN** (Marcus Aemilius Aemilianus) ruled 3 months	murdered
	253–260	**VALERIAN** (Publius Licinus Valerianus); his son Gallienus ruled the West	in Persian captivity
	260–268	***GALLIENUS** (Italy & the Balkans only); fought usurper **AUREOLUS**	murdered

* While GALLIENUS ruled Italy & the Balkans POSTUMUS (258–268) was independent emperor in Gaul; he was succeeded by VICTORINUS

May 214 (Dardania Yu)	268–270	**CLAUDIUS II GOTHICUS** (Marcus Aurelius Claudius)	of plague
	270 for 3 months	**QUINTILLUS** (brother of Claudius II)	murdered?
c. 215	270–275	***AURELIAN** (Lucius Domitius Aurelianus)	murdered in Caenophrurium (TR)

* TETRICUS ruled Spain, Gaul & Britain, but went over to Aurelian's side

Born	Rule	Name	Manner of Death
	275 for 6 months	**ULPIA SEVERINA** (widow of Aurelian)	natural
c. 200	275–276	**TACITUS** (Marcus Claudius)	murdered Apr. in Tyana/Cappadocia
	276–276	**FLORIAN** (Florianus) half-brother of Tacitus	murdered June
	276–282	**PROBUS** (Marcus Aurelius Probus)	murdered Nov.
245 (Dalmatia)	284–305	**DIOCLETIAN** (Gaius Aurelius Valerius Diocletianus) in the East; co-emperor in the West:	abdicated 1/5; died 313 or 316
	286–305	**MAXIMIAN** (Marcus Aurelius Valerius Maximanus)	abdicated 1/5; murdered or suicide 308
	305–306	**CONSTANTIUS I CHLORUS** (Aurelius Valerius Constantius) of the West (wife: a) HELEN b) THEODORA, stepdaughter of Maximian), father of Constantine the Great	natural
Sardica/Sofia	305–311	**GALERIUS** (Gaius Valerius Maximianus) of the East	disease
	306–306	**FLAVIUS VALERIUS SEVERUS** declared emperor in West by Galerius (his friend)	murdered by Maxentius, son of Maximian
	306–312	**MAXENTIUS** (Marcus Aurelius Valerius) proclaimed Augustus of the West 28/10 306	killed by Constantine in battle
	308–313	**MAXIMINUS** (Gaius Galerius Valerius) nephew & friend of Galerius who proclaimed him Augustus of the East 308; died in Tarsus/TR shortly after having invaded dominion of Licinius & been defeated	disease
	308–324	**LICINIUS** (Valerius Licinianus Licinius) 11/11 308 Galerius declared Maxentius a usurper & appointed Licinius Augustus of the West; Constantine defeated Licinius at Adrinople 324	executed 325
27/2 late 280s	324–337	**CONSTANTINE THE GREAT** (emperor of the West from 312; Licinius emperor of the East 308–324); declared Constantinople the capital of the East Roman Empire (wife **FAUSTA**, daughter of Maximian)	natural 22/5
7/8 317 (Sirmium, Yu)	337–361	**CONSTANTIUS II** (Flavius Julius Constantius) co-emperor with his brothers, **CONSTANTINE II** (murdered 340) and **CONSTANT I** (murdered 350); sole ruler 353–361	illness
331/332	361–363	**JULIAN THE APOSTATE** (Flavius Claudius Julianus)	died in battle June

Born	Rule	Name	Manner of Death
c. 331 (Singidunum/ Belgrade)	363–364	**JOVIAN** (Flavius Jovianus)	natural 17/2
321	364–375 (West)	**VALENTINIAN I** (Flavius Valentinianus) (wife/2nd **JUSTINA**) 28/3 he appointed his younger brother Valens as co-ruler (East)	illness March
c. 328	364–378 (East)	*VALENS (uncle of Gratian)	killed in battle 9/8

* The pagan PROCOPIUS proclaimed himself Emperor in Constantinople in September 365, but he was killed by Valens on 27/5 366.

Born	Rule	Name	Manner of Death
359 (Sirmium, Yu)	367–383 (West)	**GRATIAN** (Flavius Gratianus) proclaimed co-emperor on 24/8 367 by his father Valentinian I and from that date also shared his office with his uncle Valens till 378	
371 (Treveri/Trier)	375–392 (West)	**VALENTINIAN II** (Flavius Valentinianus) half-brother of Gratian and son of **JUSTINA & VALENTINIAN I**; recognized as co-ruler of West (Italy, Africa, Illyrium) by Gratian; 387–388 in exile in Thessalonica; a caesar compared to Theodosius I	murdered?
11/1 347 (Cauca/ Coca/Spain)	379–395 (East & West)	**THEODOSIUS (I) THE GREAT** (son of Valentinian I's general Theodosius) one of the last to reign over both East & West Roman Empire; appointed his sons Honorius (West) & Arcadius (East) to succeed him	illness 17/1
	383–388 (West)	**MAGNUS MAXIMUS** Spanish usurper who ruled Britain, Gaul & Spain; he and his son **FLAVIUS VICTOR** as co-ruler recognized for a short time as coemperor by Theodosius I & Valentinian II	executed by Theodosius
9/9 384	393–423 (West)	*HONORIUS FLAVIUS, co-ruler with his father Theodosius I 23/1 393– 17/1 395 then sole ruler until 409 and again from 411–423; (wives: 1) **MARIA**, 2) her sister **THERMANTIA**)	natural

* ATTALUS (Priscus Attalus), a usurper elevated to emperor by the Visigothic leaders Alaric & Ataulphus (409–410 & 414), was exiled by Honorius

Born	Rule	Name	Manner of Death
377	383–408 (East)	**ARCADIUS**, ruled jointly with his father Theodosius I 383–395, solely 395–402, together with his own son Theodosius II 402–408; (wife **EUDOXIA**)	natural

Born	Rule	Name	Manner of Death
	407–411	**CONSTANTINE III** (Flavius Claudius Constantinus) usurping emperor of Britain & Gaul, recognized by Honorius 409 as joint ruler but threatened Italy; had made his son **CONSTANS** caesar 407	executed by Honorius' generals
	421–421 (West)	**CONSTANTIUS III**, Honorius' master of the soldiers who helped to overthrow Constantine III; in 417 married **PLACIDIA**, half-sister of Honorius; appointed co-emperor 8/2 421 but died soon afterwards, still unrecognized by the Eastern Emperor	natural
2/7 419 in Ravenna	425–455 (West)	***VALENTINIAN III** (Flavius Valentinianus) son of Constantius III and Placidia who controlled the government till 437; married **LICINIA EUDOXIA** 29/10 437 (daughter of Theodosius II)	murdered 16/3

* JOHN, a usurper, ruled briefly in the West (423–425) on death of Honorius

Born	Rule	Name	Manner of Death
396	455–455 (West)	**MAXIMUS PETRONIUS**, proclaimed Western Emperor 17/3 455 and forced Valentinian's widow **EUDOXIA** to marry him	killed by the people 31/5
10/4 401	408–450 (East)	**THEODOSIUS II**, son of Arcadius who made him co-emperor 402; (wife: **EUDOCIA**)	of injuries from hunting accident
396	450–457 (East)	**MARCIAN**, ruled together with his nominal wife Empress **PULCHERIA** (d. 453), sister of Theodosius II	natural
	455–456 (West)	**AVITUS** (Eparchius Aritus) proclaimed Emperor by the Goths of Toulouse, but forced to abdicate by the "kingmaker" Ricimer on 17/10 456	
	457–461 (West)	**MAJORIAN** (Julius Majorianus) helped to overthrow emperor Avitus (455–456)	executed 7/8
	457–474 (East)	**LEO I**, a Thracian who recognized Majorian in the West 457, but not his successor Libius Severus in 461; vacant throne in the West for 2 years until he installed Anthemius 467 as West Roman Emperor	natural
	461–465 (West)	**LIBIUS SEVERUS**, installed by the "kingmaker" Ricimer, but never recognized by Leo I	natural 15/8
	467–472 (West)	**ANTHEMIUS**, son-in-law of Eastern Emperor Marcian; (wife **EUPHEMIA**) his daughter **ALYPIA** married to Ricimer	beheaded 11/7

Born	Rule	Name	Manner of Death
	472–472 (West)	**OLYBRIUS**, installed by Ricimer and emperor from April to Nov.; (wife: **PLACIDIA**, daughter of Valentinian III)	natural 2/11
	473–474 (West)	**GLYCERIUS**, installed as emperor 5/3 473 by Gundobad (nephew of Ricimer); never recognized by Leo I who sent a fleet commanded by **JULIUS NEPOS** against him	natural
	474–475 (West)	**JULIUS NEPOS**, proclaimed himself emperor on landing in Italy; Glycerius surrendered without a struggle	murdered
Isauria	475–491 (East)	**ZENO**, father of Leo II (474–474 who died 7 years old); in exile 475–Aug. 476 when **BASILISCUS** (brother-in-law of Leo I) ruled in Constantinople; appointed Theodoric to replace Odoacer as king of Italy (489)	natural
	475–476	**ROMULUS AUGUSTULUS**, usurper and last of the Western Roman Emperors; installed on the throne 31/10 475 after his father Orestes (who ruled Italy in his young son's name) had deposed Julius Nepos; German warrior **ODOACER** captured & executed Orestes 28/8 476	unknown

End of Western Roman Empire

38

CLASSICAL MISCELLANY

THE SEVENS

The Seven Wonders of the World

1 The **PYRAMIDS** of Egypt
2 The **TOMB of MAUSOLOS in Bodrum**
3 The **COLOSSUS** at Rhodes
4 The **HANGING GARDENS** of Babylon
5 The **TEMPLE OF ARTEMIS** at Ephesus
6 The **STATUE OF ZEUS** by Phidias
7 The **PHAROS of Alexandria** or
  The **PALACE OF CYRUS** cemented with gold

The Seven Deadly Sins

ENVY
LUST
ANGER
PRIDE
SLOTH
GLUTTONY
COVETOUSNESS

The Seven Sleepers of Ephesus

Western tradition
JOHN
DENIS
MALCHUS
MARCIAN
MAXIMIAN
SERAPION
CONSTANTINE

The Seven Wise Men
(according to Plato)

BIAS
MYSON
SOLON
CHILON
THALES
PITTACUS
CLEOBOLUS

The Seven Against Thebes

The seven military leaders in the civil war between Oedipus' twin sons Eteocles and Polyneices
TYDEUS
CAPANEUS
ETEOCLUS
AMPHIBRAUS
POLYNEICES (or ADRASTUS)
HIPPOMEDON (or ADRASTUS)
PARTHENOPAEUS

The Seven Hills of Rome

CAELIAN
VIMINAL
AVENTINE
PALATINE
ESQUILINE
QUITRINAL
CAPITOLINE

The Seven Senses

SIGHT
SMELL
TASTE
SPEECH
FEELING
HEARING
UNDERSTANDING

Eastern tradition
JOHN
MARTIN
ANTONIUS
DIONYSIUS
JAMBLICHUS
MAXIMILIAN
CONSTANTINE

The Seven Pleiades (stars)

Daughters of Atlas & Pleione
MAIA
MEROPE
TAYGETE
ALCYONE (brightest)
CELAENO
ELECTRA
ASTEROPE (faintest)

The Seven Epigoni

The seven sons of the seven chieftains against Thebes

ALCMAEON
DIOMEDES
EURYALUS
AEGIALEUS
PROMACHOS
STHENELUS
AMPHILOCHUS

THE THREES AND FOURS

THE FOUR PRIMARY DIVINE BEINGS

from whom Erebus (the dark void) and Night were born.

CHAOS	Space
GAIA/GE	Earth
TARTARUS	Hell
EROS	Love

THE GREEK FATES

CLOTHO	spins the thread of life	The Spinner
LACHESIS	controls its destiny	The Disposer of Lots
ATROPOS	cuts it off	The Inflexible One

THE FURIES

Avenging deities – ERINYES or EUMENIDES – sent from Tartarus to avenge wrong and punish crime.

ALECTO	Unceasing in Anger
MEGAERA	Jealous
TISIPHONE	Avenger of Murder

THE HARPIES

Malignant monsters with birds' wings and claws who snatched away the souls of the dead.

AELLO	Stormswift
OCYPETE	Swiftwing
CELAENO	Dark one
PODARGE	Swiftfoot

THE SEASONS (HORAE)

Three daughters of Zeus and Themis or of Helios (sun) and Selene (moon).

DIKE	Justice
EIRENE	Peace
EUNOMIA	Good Order

THE CYCLOPS

Three round-eyed sons of Uranus & Gaia who forged the thunderbolts for Zeus; one-eyed cannibal giants (Homer) who built walls of ancient cities.

ARGES	Bright
BRONTES	Thunderous
STEROPES	Lightener

THE PYRAMIDS OF EGYPT

CHEOPS
KHAFRE
HENKAURA
ZOSER

THE THREE GRACES

Goddesses of fertility and charm, associated with Aphrodite; daughters of Zeus by Hera or Eurynome (daughter of Oceanus) or of Helios and Aegle.

AGLAIA	Brightness
THALIA	Bloom
EUPHROSYNE	Joyfulness

THE THREE GORGONS

Winged female creatures with hair of snakes; daughters of Phorcys and his sister-wife Ceto who were children of Gaia and Pontus, the sea.

MEDUSA	The Queen
EURYALE	The Far Springer
STHENNO	The Mighty

THE THREE GORGON SISTERS

with only a single eye between them

DINO
ENYO
PEMPHREDO

THE HECATONCHEIRES

Hundred-handed giants, children of Uranus and Gaia/Ge.

GYES   COTTUS   BRIAREUS

SIXTEEN NYMPHS

4 ECHO — repulses Pan

5 THETIS — mother of Achilles

6 AEGINA — wife of Zeus
CALYCE — mother of Endymion
DAPHNE — of a mountain
MEROPE — wife of river god Asopos
RHODAS — mated with the sun Helios
THOOSA — mother of Polyphemus

7 ASTERIA — mother of Hecate
CLYMENE — wife of Helios,
    mother of Phaethon

GALATEA — of the sea
8 ARETHUSA — one of the Hesperides
CASTALIA — excited Apollo
ECHENAIS — loved by Daphnis
PENELOPE — mother of Pan,
    wife of Odysseus,
    wife of Hermes

PERIBOCA — mother of Penelope

THE NINE MUSES

4 CLIO — History

5 ERATO — Erotic Poetry

6 THALIA — Comedy
URANIA — Astronomy

7 EUTERPE — Lyric Poetry

8 CALLIOPE — Epic Song

9 MELPOMENE — Tragedy

10 POLYHYMNIA — Hymns

11 TERPSICHORE — Dance

THE 12 TITANS

(Children of Heaven/Uranus &
Earth/Ge/Gaia)

4 RHEA
THEA
5 COIUS
CRIUS
6 CRONUS
PHOEBE

6 TETHYS
THEMIS
7 IAPETUS
OCEANUS
8 HYPERION

9 MNEMOSYNE

GROUPS OF NYMPHS BY HABITAT

6 DRYADS — of the trees
NAIADS — of caves and springs
7 NEREIDS — of the sea

10 HAMADRYADS — of trees

THE HESPERIDES

Guardians of Golden Apples; variously
daughters of Erebus & Night,
Atlas & Hesperis, or Phorcys & Ceto

5 AEGLE

8 ARETHUSA
ERYTHEIA

8 HESPERIS or

12 HESPERETHUSA

THE SIX WIVES OF HERMES

5 HERSE — son of Cephalus, a hero!

6 CHIONE — son Autolycus

8 AGLAUCUS — son Ceryx, first high priest of Eleusis

8 PENELOPE — son Pan

9 DEIANOIRA

10 PERSEPHONE — son Eleusis, eponymous hero

41

OFFSPRING OF ZEUS

(the son of Cronus & Rhea)

3 **ATE** (d) evil; evicted from Olympus by Zeus

ARES (s) god of war; warlike spirit; mother: Hera

4 **HEBE** (d) mother: Hera; goddess of youth; married Heracles

5 **AEGLE** (d) wife of Helios (sun god); sometimes claimed as mother of the Three Graces

ARCAS (s) mother: Callisto; ancestor of the Arcadians

BELUS (s) mother: Io; father of Danaus & Aegyptus

HELEN (d) mother: Leda of Sparta; wife of Tyndareus

MINOS (s) mother: Europa; King of Crete

6 **AEACUS** (s) mother: nymph Aegina

AGLAIA (d) one of the Three Graces

APOLLO (s) mother: Leto; god of divine distance, crops & herds; Averter of Evil (Alexikakos); common to Greece & Rome

ATHENE (d) mother: Metis; virgin goddess of war & good counsel

CLOTHO (d) one of the Three Fates

HERMES (s) mother: Maia; fertility & messenger god born in a cave

POLLUX (s) mother: Leda; twin-brother of Castor (the Dioscuri)

6 **THALIA** (d) one of the Three Graces

ZETHUS (s) mother: Antiope

7 **AMPHION** (s) mother: Antiope

ARTEMIS (d) mother: Leto; goddess of wild nature; sister of Apollo

PERSEUS (s) mother: Danae; founder of Mycenae; King of Argos

ZAGREUS (s) mother: Persephone; killed as a child by the Titans

8 **DARDANUS** (s) mother: Electra; founder of Troy; grandfather of Tros

DIONYSUS (s) mother: Semele; wine god

ENDYMION (s) mother: nymph Calyce; King of Elis

HERACLES (s) mother: Alcmene; of the 12 Labours

LACHESIS (d) one of the Three Fates

SARPEDON (s) mother: Europa; leader of Lycian forces in Trojan War

TANTALUS (s) punished by eternal thirst & hunger; ancestor of Pelopids

10 **HEPHAESTUS** (s) mother: Hera; smith god

PERSEPHONE (d) mother: Demeter; wife of Hades; as Kore, grain goddess

11 **EUPHROSTYNE** (d) one of the Three Graces

12 **RHADAMANTHUS** (s) mother: Europa; King of the Cyclades islands

CONSORTS OF ZEUS

2 **IO** daughter of Inachus (river god of Argos); priestess Callithyia

4 **HERA** sister & wife of Zeus; Queen of Heaven; as Eileithyia, birth goddess

LEDA daughter of Thestius (King of Aetolia); Zeus swanned around and so she leda-'n-egg hatching Helen & Pollux

LETO daughter of Coeus & Phoebe (Titans); goddess of fertility

MAIA eldest of the 7 daughters of Titan Atlas (the Pleiades) by Pleione

5 **DANAE** daughter of Acrisius, King of Argos

METIS (wise counsel); Zeus mated with Metis by mouth and Athene was his brainchild

6 **AEGINA** daughter of river god Asopus & nymph Merope

CALYCE a nymph; mother of Endymion who was loved by moon goddess Selene

EUROPA daughter of Phoenix who rose from the ashes to take Zeus, the bull, by the horns to Crete

SEMELE daughter of Cadmus (founder of Thebes) and Harmonia; niece of Europa

6 **SELENE** moon goddess; daughter of Eos

THEMIS steadfast daughter of Gaia; prophetess; mother of the Seasons & the Fates

7 **ALCMENE** daughter of Electryon, king of Mycenae; wife of Amphitryon who killed his uncle Electryon

*ANTIOPE daughter of Nycteus (one of the Spartoi) raped by Zeus in the guise of a satyr

DEMETER sister & consort of Zeus; goddess of agriculture, health, birth & marriage & divinity of the underworld

**ELECTRA daughter of Atlas & Pleione; mother of the Cabeiri (Cabiri), protectors of seafarers & promoters of fertility

*not to be confused with the daughter of Ares, god of war, or a queen of the Amazones.

**not to be confused with the mother of the Harpies Aello & Okypete, or the daughter of Agamemnon and Clytemnestra.

CONSORTS OF ZEUS

8 CALLISTO handmaiden of Artemis who changed her into a she-bear; later, by courtesy of Zeus, she stars as Ursa Major and her son (Arcas) as Arcturus

EURYNOME daughter of Oceanus; together with Hera & Aegle variously regarded as mother of the Three Graces

8 GANYMEDE son of Tros (or Laomedon), King of Troy; Latin Catamitus; kidnapped by Zeus in the guise of an eagle

10 PERSEPHONE daughter & consort of Zeus; as Persephassa goddess of the dead

BROTHERS & SISTERS OF ZEUS

4 HERA Queen of Olympus; mother of Ares (god of war), Hebe (goddess of youth & cupbearer to the gods), Hephaestus

5 HADES ruled the underworld together with his queen Persephone

7 DEMETER goddess of agriculture; bore Plutus (Wealth) by her consort Iason, and Persephone by Zeus; also known as Ioulo

8 POSEIDON god of sea, water, earthquakes; also worshipped as "Hippios" (of horses); divine ancestor of rulers of Thessaly & Messenia

OFFSPRING OF POSEIDON

(brother of Zeus)

5 ARION/AREION by DEMETER; swift horse who saved the life of Adrastus,King of Argos

ORION son by EURYALE, one of the Gorgons

6 NELEUS son of TYRO; father of Nestor, Pero, etc.

PELIAS brother of Neleus

TRITON son by AMPHITRITE; minor sea god

7 ANCAEUS son by TEGEA; King of the Leleges of Samos

ANTAEUS son by GAIA; wrestling giant of Libya, crushed by Heracles

BUSIRIS son by LYSSIANASSA; King of Egypt (Usire/Osiris); killed by Heracles

*GLAUCUS gleaming son, in love with sea god Melicertes; merman covered with shells and seaweed; sea god

PEGASUS by the monster MEDUSA; winged horse

8 EUMOLPUS sweet-singing son by CHIONE, daughter of Boreas (North Wind); King of Thrace

NAUPLIUS son by AMYMONE, one of Danaus' 50 daughters

10 AMPHIMARUS son; father by Linus (the musician killed by Apollo) by the Muse Urania

POLYPHEMUS son by the nymph THOOSA; sea god and one of the Cyclopes; made Odysseus his prisoner

*not to be confused with a) son of Sisyphus (King of Corinth) by Merope: father of Bellerophon; b) the honeyed son of King Minos (Crete) and Pasiphae; c) "gold for bronze" Lycian prince, ally of Priam in the Trojan War; grandson of Bellerophon

TROJAN WAR

Besiegers of Troy and ancestors & offspring

4 AJAX – colossal son of Telamon (king of Salamis); took on Hector single-handed; rescued body of Achilles from the Trojans

AJAX – small son of Oileus (king-of Locri); violated Cassandra; drowned by Poseidon

5 CREON – father of Lycomedes of Scyros who hosted Achilles, and killed Theseus, Attic hero

6 ATREUS – father of Agamemnon & Menelaus by Aerope; son of Pelops; later

6 married Pelopia; daughter & wife of Thyestes

DANAOI – besiegers of Troy

MOPSUS – seer and son of Manto by Carian king Rhacius (or Apollo); challenged Calchas after fall of Troy

NESTOR – son of Neleus (brother of Pelias, son of Poseidon by Tyro); Achaean leader; sailed home after the war

PELEUS – father of Achilles; husband of Thetis (one of the Nereids)

43

TROJAN WAR

Besiegers of Troy and ancestors & offspring

TEUCER – half-brother of Ajax; famous archer; defended Achaean camp; founded city of Salamis on Cyprus

7
ARGEIOI – besiegers of Troy

CALCHAS – seer of the Achaean forces; son of Thestor; priest of Apollo

ORESTES – son of Agamemnon & Clytemnestra

PROTEUS – helped Menelaus to reach Sparta; assistant of Poseidon

8
ACHAEANS – besieged Troy together with the Danaoi & Argeioi

ACHILLES – son of Peleus (king of the Myrmidons) & Thetis; handsome warrior of Agamemnon's army; killed Hector

DIOMEDES – commander of 80 Argive ships and important leader; son of Tydeus (one of seven against Thebes); wounded Aphrodite; took the Trojan Palladium

MENELAUS – brother of Agamemnon; husband of Helen

ODYSSEUS – captured Troy by means of the wooden horse; suitor of Helen; king

8 of Ithaca and son of Laertes & Anticleia; father by Penelope of Telemachus

TELEPHUS – wounded by Achilles; guided Achaean fleet to Troy; son of Heracles & Ange

9
AGAMEMNON – commander-in-chief of the forces against Troy; brother of Menelaus; kin of Mycenae or Argos and son of Atreus and Aerope; husband of Clytemnestra (daughter of Tyndareus, king of Sparta); murdered by their son Orestes; his daughters: Iphigeneia/Iphianassa (sacrificed to Artemis), Electra/Laodice, Chrysothemis

PATROCLUS – cousin of Achilles and allowed to impersonate him; killed by Hector

10
ANTILOCHUS – son of Nestor; killed by Memnon

TELEMACHUS – son of Odysseus by Penelope; welcomed by Nestor when searching for his father Odysseus

Defenders of Troy and ancestors & offspring

4
ILUS – ancestor of Priam; one of the three sons of Tros

TROS – grandson of Dardanus; father of Ilus, Ganymede & Arsaracus

5
HELEN – daughter of Zeus by Leda or Nemesis; sister of Clytemnestra; wife of Menelaus of Sparta; after death of Paris wife of his brother Dephobus whom she betrayed; indirect cause of the war

PARIS – son of Priam; stole Helen and caused the Trojan War

PRIAM – King of Troy (VII) son of Laomedon; also known as Podarces; father of Hector, Paris, Cassandra, Polyxena, Helenus, Polydorus, Troilus

6
AENEAS – cousin of Hector; leader of Trojan survivors; founder of Rome; son of Trojan Anchises by Aphrodite

HECTOR – chief Trojan warrior; eldest son of Priam

HECUBA – wife of Priam

MEMNON – hero and brother of Priam; son of Eos (dawn); King of Ethiopia; killed Antilochus and was killed by Achilles

7
ANTENOR – elder of the city of Troy; advises the Trojans to return Helen to Menelaus, and Agamemnon to give up girl he stole from Achilles

GLAUCUS – ally of Troy; leader of the Lycian forces

7
HELENUS – son of Priam and Hecuba

HESIONE – daughter of Laomedon

TROILUS – son of Priam; killed early by Achilles

8
ANCHISES – father of Aeneas by Aphrodite; king of Dardanus on Mt Ida

ASTYANAX – son of Hector

DARDANUS – founder of Troy; grandfather of Tros; son of Zeus & Electra; father of Erichtonius

GANYMEDE – one of the three sons of Tros

LAOMEDON – father of Priam and Hesione; refused to pay Apollo and Poseidon for building the walls of Troy; he and all his sons (except Priam) killed by Heracles

POLYXENA – daughter of Priam and Hecuba

SARPEDON – ally of Priam; leader of the Lycian forces

TITHONUS – son of Laomedon, king of Troy, and brother of Priam; father of Memnon by Eos; made immortal but not ageless by Zeus

9
ARSARACUS – one of the three sons of Tros

POLYDORUS – son of Priam and Hecuba

ANDROMACHE – wife of Hector

3 **INO** — second wife of ATHAMAS who hated his children by NEPHELE and wanted PHRIXUS sacrificed

5 **AESON** — father of JASON deprived of the throne of Iolcos by his half-brother PELIAS

CIRCE — witch-goddess & sister of the king of Colchis; (or daughter of HELIOS, the sun god & the nymph PERSE); freed MEDEA & JASON from the guilt of murdering ABSYRTUS

CREON — king of Corinth whose daughter caught JASON's fancy and drove MEDEA mad with rage

HELLE — daughter of JASON's uncle ATHAMAS by NEPHELE, the cloud goddess; tried to escape by sea with her brother PHRIXUS on the ram with the golden fleece; drowned in the Helle-spont

JASON — son of AESON who had been told by his uncle PELIAS to fetch the Golden Fleece of Colchis if he wanted to regain the throne of Iolcos, his rightful inheritance; assembled fifty heroes on board "Argo" and set sail to find this fleece washed in a gold-carrying stream of the Caucasus; met MEDEA and married her on the return voyage

MEDEA — enchantress of JASON who escaped with him and the Golden Fleece from Colchis; killed PELIAS on their return and turned murderous in jealousy towards the daughter of CREON, killing both, and her own children by JASON; later became Queen to AEGEUS of Athens and when attempting to poison her stepson THESEUS was exiled; eventually reached Colchis and restored her father AEETES as king; by some accounts her Athenian son MEDUS later gave his name to the country of the Medes (Media) who later joined with the Persians

TALOS — rock-throwing bronze giant; a creation of the god Hephaestus; invulnerable to fire, but made drunk by MEDEA who by prising out the bronze nail in his foot killed him

6 **AEETES** — King of Colchis and father of MEDEA; refused to give up the Golden Fleece and placed many obstacles in the way of JASON & MEDEA

AEGEUS — king of Athens who received the refugee MEDEA and married her

AMYCUS — ruler in Bithynia of the savage Bebryces; killed by POLYDEUCES

CHIRON — king of the CENTAURS (half man half horse); educator of JASON,

6 ACHILLES & ASCLEPIUS (god of medicine, son of APOLLO and the nymph CORONIS)

MOPSUS — seer (one of two); sailed on "Argo"; died of snake bite in Libya

PELIAS — king of Iolcos and uncle of JASON; usurper

SIRENS — daughters of the river god ARCHELOUS; spurned by the Argonauts

TIPHYS — navigator of the Argonauts

TRITON — minor sea god, son of POSEIDON by AMPHITRITE; assisted JASON

7 **ANCAEUS** — navigator of the Argonauts after TIPHYS

ATHAMAS — uncle of JASON; king of the MINYANS in Boeotian city of Orchomenus; father of PHRIXUS & HELLE by NEPHELE; later consort of jealous INO

CYANEAN — ROCKS (the Symplegades) two moving cliffs at the mouth of the Bosphorus that crushed whatever sought to pass

CYZICUS — king of the DOLIONES who was killed by JASON

HARPIES — supernatural winged beings; tormentors of king PHINEUS

MINYANS — the tribe of JASON whose most prominent members took part in the expedition

NEPHELE — first wife and cloud goddess of ATHAMAS who bore him HELLE and PHRIXUS

ORPHEUS — musician and husband of EURYDICE, a dryad

PHINEUS — aged and blind king whose food was spoilt by the HARPIES; he told the Argonauts the course to Colchis and how to clear the CYANEAN ROCKS

PHRIXUS — son of ATHAMAS and brother of HELLE who escaped to Colchis on the ram with the Golden Fleece; on arrival he killed the ram and hung up the fleece in the grove of ARES there to be guarded by a dragon which MEDEA later put to sleep

8 **ABSYRTUS** — son of AEETES and younger brother of MEDEA

ALCIMEDE — perhaps the wife of AESON and mother of JASON

DOLIONES — the tribe ruled by CYZICUS

10 **POLYDEUCES** — one of the Argonauts who defeated the Bithynian king AMYCUS in a fist fight

A

AA	volcanic lava; river (Scand.)	**gl, go**
AB	a Hebrew month	
AD	a short advertisement	
AE	one (Sc.)	
AF	of (Sc.)	
AH	exclamation of satisfaction	
AI	South American three-toed sloth	**zo**
AL	'the' in Arabic	
AM	part of verb 'be'	
AN	if; ornate box	
AP	son of (Welsh)	
AS	Roman pound; Roman bronze coin	**me, mn**
AS	an integer; ridge (Scand.)	**ma, go**
AT	preposition of place	
AW	interjection	
AX	axe	**to**
AY	yes; yea; more so	

B

BA	the soul (Egypt)	**rl**
BE	Japanese bread-winner; 2nd letter	
BE	exist; Chinese dialect	
BI-	bisexual; both of; double; two	**cf**
BO	sacred tree of Buddha	**bt**
BY	preposition of agent	

C

CA'	ca' canny (Sc.)
CE	letter 'C'
CO	company

D

DA	father; knife	
DE	musical note	**mu**
DI-	of both	**cf**
DO	ditto; act; perform	
DO	1st note	**mu**
DY	lake-bottom plant detritus; element dysprosium	**ec, ch**

E

EA	Chaldean fish god	**rl**
EA	an inlet; drainage canal in Fens	**go**
EE	eye (Sc.)	
EF	the letter 'F'	
EH	exclamation	

EL	'the' in Spanish (masc. sing.); the letter 'L'	
'EM	them	
EM	printing unit of space; the letter 'M'	**me**
EN	half the width of an em	**me**
EP-	outside; extra; above	**cf**
ER	interjection	
ES	the letter 'S'	
EX	late; out of	
EX-	formerly	**cf**

F

FA	4th note (major key)	**mu**
FE	4th note (minor key)	**mu**
FO	Chinese Buddha	**rl**
FU	Chinese prefecture; food vessel (bronze age)	
FY	fie; denoting disgust	

G

GE	Mother-Earth (Gr.)	
GI	judo, karate garment	
GO	proceed; depart; fare	
GU	violin	**mu**

H

HA	exclamation
HE	male pronoun
HI	exclamation
HM	hum, perhaps, disbelief
HO	exclamation
HU	bronze-age wine store vessel (China)

I

ID	} fish (carp); hedonist (Fr.)	**zo**
IDE		
IE	pine tree	**bt**
IF	supposing that	
IL	male pronoun, definite article (It.)	
I'M	I am	
IN	within, inside	
IO	triumphal cry	
IO	beloved of Jupiter	
IS	being, existing	
-IS	of abnormal condition, disease (Gr.)	**cf**
IT	personality; sex appeal; thing in general	

J

JO	a sweetheart (Sc.)

K

KA	jackdaw (Sc.); spirit	zo
KA	ethereal double (Egypt); tropical tree	bt
KO	knock out	
KY	kye; kine; cattle (Sc.)	

L

LA	'the' (Fr., It., Sp.: fem.); 6th note	mu
LE	'the' (Fr. masc.)	
LI	Chinese mile (1.6 km); bronze-age food vessel (China)	me
LO	behold	

M

MA	Goddess of Right (Egypt); mother (slang)	rl
ME	1st-person pronoun	
MI	third musical note in sol-fa scale	mu
MO	(half-a-mo); Medical Officer	md
MP	a legislator; a politician	
MS	abbr. for Mrs or Miss	
MU	Greek letter	
MY	of me	

N

NA	}	
NE	} negative reply	
NO	}	
NU	letter of Greek alphabet	

O

OB	objection	lw
OD	magnetic force	
OE	grandchild	
OF	preposition of possession	
OG	King of Basan (Old Test.)	
OH	exclamation	
OK	all correct	
OM	Hindu mantra chant	mu, rl
ON	preposition of location	
OP	a short work; opus	
OR	alternatively; heraldic gold	
OS	bone; mouth; ridge (Scand.)	pl, gl, go
OT-	} of the ear (Gr.)	pl, cf
OTO-	}	
OU	} exclamation of pain	
OW	}	
OX	a male of cattle	zo

P

PA	Maori fort	
PH	acid/alkaline content value	me
PI	mixed type (printing)	
PI	ritual jade (China)	
PO	chamber-pot	

R

RA	hawk-headed sun-god (Egypt); musical note	rl, mu
RE	concerning	
RE	ra, 2nd note	mu
RH	rhesus blood type	md

S

SE	musical note	mu
SI	7th note	mu
SO	thus, therefore, then; 5th note	mu
ST	street; saint (abbreviation)	

T

TA	thanks	
TE	musical note	mu
TI	tree-lily (Polynesia)	bt
TM	measure of glucose in man	md
TO	preposition of direction	
TV	(television)	

U

UG	disgust; a surfeit	
UH	}	
UM	} exclamation	
UN-	negative, not	cf
UP	preposition, adverb of direction	
UR	of the Chaldees; prehistoric, original, primitive (Ger.)	cf
US	objective of 'we'	
UT	1st note	mu

V

VA	go on	mu
VE	brother of Odin	rl
VO	a creek	

W

WA	exclamation; outrigger canoe, Pacific	nt

WE plural pronoun
WO whoa! stop

Y

YA exclamation
YE you; the (obs.)
YI Chinese philosophy

YO exclamation
YU precious jade; wine vessel (China)

Z

ZO image (Jap.); Himalyan cattle   zo
ZZ slumber

49

A

AAH	the Moon-God of Egypt	rl
AAM	30–35 gallons (136–159 litres), Dutch liquid	me
ABA	Eastern camel-hair fabric	
ABB	yarn for the warp	
ABC	a railway guide; alphabet	
ABP	abbr. for Archbishop	
ABU	father (Arabic)	
ABY	atone; pay penalty; retribution	
ACE	aviator; particle; (cards)	
ACT	deed in writing; do; perform	lw, pc
ADD	join; tag; annex; append; tot	
ADO	stir; fuss; commotion; hubbub	
ADS.	advertisements	
ADZ	adze; wood-shaping; tilling	to, ag
AFT	abaft; astern	nt
AGA ⎫	oriental title; (Khan) Ismaili	
AGHA ⎬	spiritual leader	rl
AGE	era; period; epoch; senility	
AGO	past; gone	
AHA!	exclamation of discovery	
AID	succour; help; subsidy; assistant	
AIK	oak (Sc.)	bt
AIL	suffer; pain; peak; pine	
AIM	object; direct; intend; purpose	
AIN	own (Sc.)	
AIR	mien; ventilate; display; tune	
AIT	river or lake islet; eyot	
AKE	ache (obs.)	
ALA	wing or side petal of blossom	bt
ALB	white linen clerical vestment	rl
ALE	mead; beer	
ALK	resin from turpentine tree	
ALL	entirely; whole	
ALP	pasture land; (high mountain)	go
ALS	also (Sc.); serum	md
ALT	high notes in the scale	mu
AMA	holy wine or vessel	rl
AMP	electrical unit (abbr. for ampère)	me
ANA	miscellaneous facts; Celtic goddess	
ANA	equal parts	md
AND	the ampersand; &	pr
AND	logic element; binaries	cp
ANE	one (Sc.)	
ANN	annat (Sc.)	lw
ANT	emmet; pismire; termite	zo
ANU	Celtic goddess; Babylonian sea-god	
ANY	some (in questions, negatives)	
APE	imitate; copy; mimic; monkey	zo
APT	appropriate; pertinent; prone	
ARC	luminous bridge; curve; (lamp)	el, ma
ARE	hectare (2.5 acres)	me
ARG	abbreviation for chemical silver	
ARK	chest; coffer; place of refuge; floating zoo	rl, nt
ARM	equip; limb; estuary	
ARN	elder tree	bt

ART	skill; dexterity; craft	
ARY	any (Sc.)	
ASA	gum; Norse God (Valhalla)	bt, rl
ASA	colour system	pg
ASE	Peer Gynt's mother	
ASH	cinder; forest tree; wood; volcanic	bt, gl, go
ASK	interrogate; invite; sue	
ASP	poisonous snake (Cleopatra)	zo
ASS	moke; burro; donkey	zo
ATE	Goddess of Mischief	
AUF	fool; oaf; simpleton	
AUK	flightless sea bird; garefowl	zo
AVA	kava; Hawaiian palm-lily drink	
AVE	prayer; hail	rl
AWA'	away (Sc.)	
AWE	reverential veneration	
AWL	the cobbler's tool; bradawl	to
AWN	beard in chaff	bt
AXE	to cut down; hatchet	to
AXO-	of nerve fibre projection (Gr.)	cf
AYE	yea; for ever	
AZO	azobenzene derivative	ch

B

BAA	to bleat	
BAB	fishing bob	
BAC	ferry; brewing tub	
BAD	depraved; detrimental; evil; baneful	
BAG	sack; wallet; pouch; steal; baseball	bd, ga
BAH!	a derogatory exclamation	
BAM	bamboozle; hoax	
BAN	muslin; bar; interdict; outlaw	
BAP	small soft bread loaf (Scotland)	
BAR	ban; prohibit; hinder; stop; ingot	
BAR	division in musical notation	mu
BAR	(sand-); pub; glazing; law; rod	nv, go, lw
-BAR-	of weight, pressure (Gr.)	cf
BAT	spree; batsman; vampire	
BAT	striker; brick-; lead wedge	bd
BAY	bark; laurel; wing; mill-dam; (sick-); cove; bight	bt, bd, go
BBC	(broadcasting)	
BED	couch; berth; layer; plant; back	
BEE	emblem of the French Empire; insect	zo
BEG	crave; implore; entreat; petition	
BEL	Baal; a Babylonian god; circuit amplifier	rl, tc
BEL	logarithmic unit	ma
BEN	(Big Ben); mountain; within (Sc.)	
BEN	winged seed of ben-tree	bt
BET	lay; wager; stake; gamble; pledge	
BEY ⎫	a Turkish title	
BEG ⎬		

BIB	feeder; sip; tipple; whiting pout; (fencing)	**zo, ga**
BID	order; charge; direct; offer; invite; tender	
BIG	huge; swollen; pregnant; barley	**bt**
BIN	a receptacle for wine, corn, etc.	
BIO-	organic, of life (Gr.)	**cf, bl**
BIS	encore	
BIT	(horse's bit); piece; fragment; lathe; harness; binary digit	**cp, to**
BOA	snake; fur collar	**zo**
BOB	style of hairdressing	
BOB	sleigh; shilling (5 pence); bob-sled downhill run racing	**ga**
BOG	sog; morass; swamp; marsh	
BOK	a South African deer	**zo**
BOM	boma; boa; snake	**zo**
BOO	cry down; decry; hoot; execrate	
BOT	the larva of the bot-fly	**zo**
BOW	arc; bob; bend; a tie; prow; squash shot; horsehair stick on stringed instruments; archery	**ga, mu**
BOX	(theatre); (compass); driver's seat; rugby scrum	
BOX	flowchart, signal, connection, container; close-rank (cycling); abdomen protector (cricket) (baseball)	**cp, ga**
BOX	case; chest; encase; shrub	**bt**
BOX	cuff; buffet; spar; fight	
BOY	lad; page; stripling; Champagne	
BOZ	Charles Dickens' nom-de-plume	
BRA	woman's garment	
BUB	yeast; strong drink; boy (USA, Ger.)	
BUD	sprout; blossom; graft	**bt**
BUD	chum (Am.)	
BUG	insect; bedbug; bugbear; secret mike	**zo**
BUM	bailiff; loafer; backside	
BUN	style of coiffure; a confection	
BUR	burr; rough edge; chestnut shell; drill bit	**bt, to**
BUS	omnibus; trunk route for signals	**cp**
BUT	yet; except; nevertheless; unless	
BUY	purchase; bribe; corrupt	
BYE	(cricket); (golf); (tournament draw)	**ga**

CEE	a shape of spring	
CHI	Greek letter; -square	**ma**
CID	Spanish chief; poem	
CIG	cigarette, fag	
CIT	citizen	
CLY	to steal	
COB	pony; male swan; spider	**zo**
COB	a head; spike of maize; nut	**bt, ck**
COB	harbour; clay; basket; dollar	**nm**
COD	pod; husk; deceive; codfish	**zo**
C.O.D.	cash on delivery	
COG	small boat	**nt**
COG	coax; wheedle; cheat; wooden bowl	
COG	nib (roof tile); tenon (cocking joint); toothed wheel	**bd, cr**
COL	mountain pass; neck	
CON	study; memorize; steer; a knock; swindle	
COO	(dove)	
COP	hill; head; tuft	
COP	policeman; arrest; (ice hockey)	
COR	heart; horn	**mu**
COS	lettuce	**bt**
COT	cottage; crib; small boat	**nt**
COW	browbeat; intimidate; depress	**zo**
COX	coxswain; steersman (rowers)	**ga**
COY	shy; bashful; demure; diffident	
COZ	cousin	
CRI	the crackle of pewter	
CRU	proposed int'n'l monetary unit	
CRU	yield; produce; grape-juice (Fr.)	**ck**
CRY	sob; yell; bawl; blazon	
CUB	enclosure for cattle; young animal	**zo**
CUD	food for re-chewing	
CUE	(billiards); (acting); signal; stimulus; shuffleboard	
CUP	to bleed; a beverage; (drink); prize; warp in plank	**bd**
CUR	mongrel; pariah; dog	**zo**
CUT	incision; gash; wound; channel	
CUT	chop; sever; carve; avoid; shorten	
CWM	steep rounded hollow (Welsh)	
CWT	a hundredweight (50 kg)	**me**
-CYT	} of the cells	**cf**
-CYTE	}	

C

CAB	cabriolet; 3 pints (1.7 litres) (Heb.)	**me**
CAC-	degenerate; diseased (cacophony)	**cf**
CAD	a vulgarian	
CAM	(machinery); oval wheel	
CAN	able to; preserve (food); pannikin	
CAP	to out-do; headgear; roof of windmill	**ar**
CAP	detonate	
CAR	vehicle	
CAT	tackle; whip; rig; puss; mouser	**nt, zo**
CAW	also kaw	
CAY	kay; key; shoal; reef; islet	

D

DAB	fish; expert; trial effort; touch ground (motorcycling)	**ck, zo**
DAD	a blow; to thrash; to scatter; father	
DAG	shred; cut	
DAG	dagger; pistol	
DAH	dhar; Burmese curved knife	
DAK	post; bungalow (Ind.)	**ar**
DAL	lentil	**bt**
DAM	Indian coin; barrier; brood mare with foals	**nm**
DAN	tub, a title; martial arts expert	

DAP	to fish with a may-fly	
DAR	dace	zo
DAW	dawn; jackdaw	zo
DAY	epoch; era; time	
DEB	a debutante	
DEE	die (Sc.)	
DEL	nabla; differential operator	nc, me
DEN	cave; haunt; snuggery	
DEW	an aqueous precipitation	
DEY	dairymaid	
DIB	dip; make holes	
DID	diddled; performed	
DIE	stamp; (dice); perish; metal block; (death); pedestal dado	ar, pr
DIG	appreciate, like (slang)	
DIG	delve; scoop; excavate; (volleyball)	ga
DIK	trouble	
DIM	obscure; vague; tarnish	
DIN	clamour; row; paper size	pt, me
DIN	colour system	pg
DIP	dop; duck; douse; souse; gradient; magnetic angle; (fondue)	ce
DIS	to fail; Pluto; the underworld	
DIT	a ditty (Spens.)	
DIV	evil spirit (Persian)	rl
DOD	clip; poll; lop	
DOE	female of fallow-deer, hare, rabbit	zo
DOG	follow; trail; track; canine; (firedogs); dressing iron; nippers; spike	zo, to
DOH	first note of tonic sol-fa scale	mu
DOL	pain intensity unit	
DOM	a Portuguese title	
DON	put on; assume; a Spanish title	
DOP	to dip; duck	
DOP	Cape brandy	
DOR	befool; mock; mockery; bedim	
DOR	dorr; dung-beetle; drone	zo
DOT	dowry; point; stop; speck; staccato or lengthened note	mu
DOW	fit and able	
DRY	sere; parch; desiccate	
DUB	to name; substitute sound	cn
DUB	to smooth; rub; confer knighthood	
DUD	worthless; defective	
DUE	owing; proper; becoming	
DUG	udder; nudged; exhumed; excavated	
DUM	North Sea fishing boat (Dutch)	nt
DUN	mound; drab colour; gloomy	
DUN	to cure fish; to demand payment	
DUO	song in two parts	mu
DUO	microcopying film process	
DUP	to open	
DUR	Ger. major key	mu
DUX	a leader	
DYE	colour; tinge; stain	
DYS-	failure; impairment	cf, md

E

EAN	to produce	
EAR	plough or till; lug; heed; hearing organ	pl
EAT	chew; consume; devour; erode	
EAU	-de-Cologne; anti-odour	
EBB	recede; wane; subside	
ECU	five-franc piece	nm
EEL	snake-like fish	zo
EEN	eyes (Sc.)	
E'EN	even	
E'ER	ever	
EFT	a newt; forthwith (obs.)	zo
EGG	incite; impel; stimulate	
EGO	} the self-conscious subject	cf
EGO-		
EIK	eke; add; addition (Sc.)	
EKE	increase; likewise; in addition	
ELD	old age; olden times; decrepitude	
ELF	sprite; gnome; imp; pixy; fairy	
ELK	moose; the whooper swan	zo
ELL	45 inches (114 cm) (cloth); pipe-fitting; elbow	me
ELM	stately tree	bt
EMU	Australian bird, cassowary type	zo
END	kill; close; conclude; terminate; aim	
ENE	once (Sc.)	
ENG	durable dark Burmese wood	fr
ENS	entity	
EON	eternity; perfection; an age; aeon	
EOS	Dawn Goddess	rl
EPI-	outside; above; extra	cf
ERA	age; period; epoch; cycle	
ERE	before; sooner than	
ERF	small garden in S. Africa	
ERG	unit of work; 1 dyne; force; purpose; sand dune desert (Arab)	me, pc, go
ERN	sea eagle	zo
ERR	offend; sin; wander; trespass	
ERS	vetch	bt
ESS	the letter 'S'	
ETC	et cetera, and so forth	
EVE	evening; the day before an event	
EWE	a female sheep	zo
EXO-	outside of	cf
EYE	observe; watch; view; bud	bt
EYE	(needle); visual organ	zo

F

FAD	whim; craze; crochet; hobby	
FAD	flavinco-enzyme	
FAG	knot; end; cigarette	
FAG	drudge; fatigue; a bore; pupil servant	
FAH	spoken sol-fa note	mu
FAM	the hand (slang)	

52

FAN	a votary; agitate; inflame; admirer; blower; alluvial	**gl**
FAN	spread out (football); winnower; (baseball); (Amer. football)	**ga**
FAN	air cooler; winnower scaffold floor; belt	**bd**
FAP	drunk; fuddled (Shak.)	
FAR	distant; remote; buck-wheat	**bt, ck**
FAT	printing term; vat; obese	
FAW	gypsy	
FAX	electronic facsimile transmission	**tc**
FAY	fairy; elf; fit closely	
FAY	fey; to clean out	
FEB	a short month	
FED	ate; subsisted; supplied	
FEE	remuneration; pay; reward; toll	
FEN	marsh lands; (Chinese) money	**nm**
FET	get; fetch (obs.)	
FEU	tenure; to rent, lease	
FEW	scant; rare; scarce	
FEY	fay; spiritual exaltation; fated	
FEZ	cap with tassel	
FIB	petty falsehood	
FID	a wedge	**nt**
FIE!	exclamation of disgust	
FIG	excrescence; tobacco; a fruit	**bt**
FIL	(Iraq), (Jordan)	**nm**
FIN	an organ of locomotion (fishes); end (Fr.)	**zo, mu**
FIR	a cone-bearing tree	**bt**
FIT	appropriate; qualified; spasm	**md**
FIX	quandary; dilemma; hitch; tie; (position); ground control	**ce, nv**
		md
FLU	influenza	
FLY	vehicle; sly; observant; abscond; coastal sailboat (Dutch)	**nt**
FLY	printing term; flee; decamp; insect	**me, zo**
FOB	watch pocket; impose; delude	
FOE	antagonist; opponent; enemy	
FOG	moss; rank grass; thick mist	**bt**
FOH	Buddha (Chinese)	
FOO	Chinese department	
FOP	a dandy; a nut; beau; coxcomb	
FOR	on this account	
FOU	tipsy; full; a bushel (Sc.)	**me**
FOX	deceive; to stain; reynard	**zo**
FOY	parting feast; assistance boat	**nv**
FRA	brother; (Fra Anselmo) (It.)	**rl**
FRO	from; away; back	
FRY	cook; swarm; smolt (fish)	**ck, zo**
FUB	fat man; cheat	
FUD	hare's tail	**zo**
FUG	frowsty warmth	
FUM	Chinese phoenix	
FUN	merriment; jollification	
FUR	incrustation; a pelt	**zo**

G

GAB	talk; a hook	
GAD	gauntlet spike; wedge	**to**
GAD	rod; goad; to rove	
GAE	go (Sc.)	
GAG	a wheeze; to silence	
GAL	unit of gravity; girl	**me**
GAM	gossip; talk; school of whales	**zo**
GAM	mouth; leg	
GAP	fissure; rift; cranny; chink	
GAR	to compel (Sc.); a marine fish	**zo**
GAS	to gab; ether; gasoline; chat	**ch**
GAT	pistol; a strait; a gap	
GAY	gey, lively, merry; homosexual	
GED	pike or luce	**zo**
GEE	turn; go faster	
GEL	viscous colloidal	
GEM	jewel; treasure; a leaf-bud	**bt**
GEN	detailed information; manna (Heb.)	
GEO	gio; creek; voe; vae; firth; frith	
GET	obtain; breed; divorce (Jew.); return of ball	**rl, ga**
GEY	gay; fairly; rather (Sc.)	
GIB	a cat; the Rock; iron or steel packing band, cotters	**zo, cr**
GID	sheep-disease; sturdy	
GIE	give (Sc.)	
GIF	if (Sc.)	
GIG	whirl; cloth machine; vehicle	
GIM	neat	
GIN	machine; snare; schnapps	
GIN	native woman (Aust.)	
GIP	clean herrings	
GNU	buffalo (S. Africa)	**zo**
GOA	Tibetan antelope	**zo**
GOB	mouthful; refuse coal	
GOB	worked out mine	
GOD	Deity; idol; image	
GOG	and Magog	
GOT	seized; procured; achieved	
GOY	gentile, Christian (Jew.)	
GRU	ice	
GUE	Shetland violin	**mu**
GUF	} reed ships	**nt**
GUFA		
GOPHER		
GUG	inclined mine road	**mn**
GUL	sail; outrigger; dugout (Papua)	**nt**
GUM	stick; mucilage; resin	**bt**
GUN	a revolver or pistol	
GUP	idle chatter; rumour	
GUT	narrow channel; intestine; intuition	**md, pl**
GUY	rope; effigy; burlesque; man	**nt**
GYM	gymnastics	
GYN	timber-loading device	**fr**
GYP	college servant; bedmaker	

H

HAD	befooled; caught; kept; owned	
HAE	have (Sc.)	
HAG	parasite fish; virago; beldam	zo
HAH!	exclamation	
HAM	Noah's second son	
HAM	a heavy actor; amateur radio operator	
HAN	plural of have (Spens.); inn (Turk.)	
HAP	chance; luck; accident; fortuity	
HAS	owns; possesses; acquires	
HAT	dignity of Cardinal; bonnet	
HAW	hawthorn berry	bt
HAW	hedge; boundary	
HAY	cut grass; hedge; fence	
HEL	Goddess of Death (Scand.)	
HEM	a cough; to sew; to edge	
HEN	a fowl	zo
HEP	hip; berry of the dog-rose	bt
HER	of a female	
HET	hot and bothered	
HET	heterosexual	
HEW	chop; hack; fell; cut	
HEX	concerning six items (Gr.)	cf
HEY!	exclamation to call attention	
HIC!	a small hiccup	
HID	secreted; cached; concealed	
HIE	a cry; to hasten	
HIM	objective of 'he'	
HIN	6 quarts (6.8 litres) (Heb.)	me
HIP	rafter; berry; hep	ar, bt
HIP	-hurray	
HIS	belonging to him	
HIT	strike; success; computer-made answer|	mu, cp
HIT	identifiable data record	cp
HOA!	ahoy	
HOB	part of grate; hub; peg or stake, target for quoits	
HOB	a rustic; a fairy	
HOD	(for bricks); a coal-scuttle	
HOE	a promontory; to weed	to
HOG	scrubbing broom; boar; pig	zo
HOG	to cut hair; bend; short run of curling stone; act selfishly	ga
HOO!	hold! stop!	
HOP	small dance; plant	bt
HOT	violent; acrid; fervid; ardent	
HOT	highly radioactive (atomic)	nc
HOW	glen; dell; low hill	
HOX	to hamstring	
HOY	small ship	nt
HOY!	ahoy; hoa!; sailing coaster, smack, sloop	nt
HUB	hilt; a boss; a centre; wheel-cover; (quoits); socket for plug	cp
HUE	and cry; tint	
HUG	embrace; enfold; clasp	
HUH!	exclamation	

HUM	bee song; tuneful noise; Pooh-song; note of industry; stale odour; (doubt)	mu
HUM	extraneous elements from other circuits in amplifier	el
HUM	limestone outcrops (karst)	gl
HUN	Tartar; savage nomadic Asiatic race	
HUP!	a horse hastener	
HUT	hovel; shed; cabin; cot	
HUX	method of fishing	
HYP	depression; hip	

I

IBO	native of East Nigeria	
ICE	to cover with sugar; frozen water	
ICH	(Ich Dien) Prince of Wales' motto	
ICY	frigid; cold; chilling; frosty	
IDE	kind of carp	zo
IDO	artificial language	
ILK	clan, category	
ILL	ailing; evil; badly; sick	
IMP	extend; strengthen; graft; sprite	
INK	writing, printing fluid	
INN	caravanserai; tavern; hostelry	
ION	electrically charged particle	el
I.O.U.	a note of hand; (I owe you) debt agreement	
IRE	rage; fury; resentment; passion	
IRK	weary; trouble; distress	
ISE	I shall (Sc.)	
ISH	exit; issue (Sc.)	
ISM	ideological prejudice	
ISO-	equal; same (Gr.)	cf
ITS	belonging to it	
IVY	a creeper sacred to Bacchus	bt

J

JAB	prod; poke; stab; a thrust; injection; fast punch (boxing); stroke (hockey)	ga
JAD	a quarrying cut	
JAG	a notch; a binge; to stab	
JAH	Jehovah	
JAK	bread-fruit tree	bt
JAM	child's garment; squeeze; a conserve; congested (traffic)	
JAM	(Am. football) impede; (baseball) pitch inside	ga
JAP	Japanese	
JAR	discord; jolt; jangle; gallipot	
JAT	Indo-Aryan	
JAW	lecture; the mouth; to splash; corner (billiards)	pl
JAY	bird; nitwit	zo
JEE	to move; to budge (Sc.)	
JET	spray; black variety of lignite	mn

JEU	a game (Fr.)	
JEW	Hebrew, Israeli	
JIB	to balk; to shy; a sail; lifting arm, boom (crane)	nt
JIG	tune; dance; mechanical guide	to
JOB	stab; profession; work; unit of runs	cp
JOE	a sweetheart (Sc.)	
JOG	rog; push; nudge; remind; trot	
JOT	an iota; a tittle; to note	
JOW	to toll; a stroke of a bell (Sc.)	
JOY	rapture; ecstasy; bliss; glee	
JUD	a mass of coal	me
JUG	incarcerate; a ewer; to stew	
JUR	earth-nut	bt
JUT	protrude; project; to collide	

K

KAA	the rock python	zo
KAE	jackdaw (Sc.)	zo
KAF	fountain conferring immortality	
KAM	crooked (Shak.)	
KAS	} Dutch wardrobe; chest	
KAST		
KAT	Egyptian weight	me
KAW	caw	
KAY	shoal; cay; key; reef	
KEA	parrot that kills sheep (NZ)	zo
KEB	ewe; sheep louse	zo
KEF	drugged stupor	
KEG	small cask or barrel	
KEN	know; recognise; knowledge	
KEP	shaft-hoist stop; to catch (Sc.)	
KET	carrion; matted wool; a fleece (Sc.)	
KEV	1,000 electron-volts	me
KEX	fool's parsley; dried stalks	bt
KEY	code; crib; solution; legend; wedge; clamp; (lock); -board music; quay; signal; identification digit; penalty area (baseball)	cp, to, mu, me
KID	faggot; bundle of sticks	
KID	tub; deceive; hoax; young goat	zo
KIF	Indian hemp	
KIN	relationship; affinity; kindred	
KIP	1000-lb (454-kg) force unit; nap	eg
KIP	small untanned hide	le
KIT	tub; bottle; violin; gear	mu
KOA	acacia (Sandwich Islands)	bt
KOB	water antelope; target (quoits)	zo
KOP	hill (S. Africa)	
KRI	Hebrew marginal direction	
KRU	Kroo; a Liberian	
KYA	native hut (S. Africa)	
KYE	kine (Sc.)	zo

L

LAC	dye; shellac; transparent resin	mn

LAD	youngster; stripling; boy	
LAG	convict; dawdle; loiter; dally	
LAG	delay; insulate; cover; wrap	
LAH	spoken sol-fa note	mu
LAI	} ballad, poem	mu
LAY		
LAM	to thrash; weaving device; Arabic letter	
LAP	fold; wrap; polish; circuit; drink	
LAR	Roman Household God	rl
LAR	white-handed gibbon	zo
LAT	inscribed pillar (India)	
LAT	Latvian money	nm
LAV	a word (Gypsy)	
LAW	an allowance; edict; statute; canon	
LAX	slack; loose; remiss	
LAY	} ballad; exorcise; put down	
LAI		
LAY	non-clerical; laic; inexpert	
LAZ	las, Black Sea Turks	
LBW	leg before wicket	
LEA	measure of yarn; meadow	me
LEA	lay; open land; pasture	
LED	induced; helped; conducted	
LEE	sheltered; lea; meadow	
LEG	lower limb; stage, tack in sailing	nt, nv
LEG	section of route; path in routine walk	cp
LEG	square- (cricket); division of turns (skittles)	ga
LEI	garland	
LEK	bird courtship; coin	zo
LEO	lion; 5th sign of Zodiac	
LET	permit; allow; lease; hire; (badminton, tennis)	ga
LET	hindrance; prevent; delay	
LEU	} Romanian money	nm
LEI		
LEV	} Bulgarian money	nm
LEY		
LEW	luke-warm; tepid	
LEX	an enactment	lw
LEY	lea; pasture; common pewter	
LIB	ad lib.	
LID	top; cover; coverlet	
LIE	falsehood; rest; recline; repose	
LIE	shape of landscape; situation of ball (golf)	ga
LIN	a waterfall; to cease	
LIP	touch the edge; rim; mouth	
LIS	litigation	lw
LIS	fleur-de-lis; heraldic lily	bt, hd
LIT	lighted; kindled; ignited	
LOB	clumsy; worm; underarm throw (cricket) (badminton)	zo, ga
LOG	record; tree-trunk	nt
LOG	¾ pint (0.4 litre) (Hebrew)	me
LOG	diary; record; tree section	cp, nt
LOG	logarithmic mathematics	ma
LOO	toilet; card game	
LOP	truncate; amputate; dock	

55

LOT	to catalogue; fate; portion; unit of weight	**me**
LOW	base; vile; abject; depressed	
LOW	bellow; moo; to flame; to blaze (Sc.)	
LOW	first of group jump (parachuting)	
LOY	narrow spade	
LSD	money, (Libra; Solidus; Denarius)	
LSD	hallucination drug	**md**
LUD	King Lud patron of anti-automation	
LUE	to sift	
LUG	ear; tug; haul; drag; handle; (sail)	**nt**
LUM	chimney (Sc.)	
LUR	Scand. prehistoric bronze horn	**mu**
LUX	unit of light	**me**
LUZ	a legendary bone	
LYE	alkaline solution	**ch**
LYM	dog on leash	**zo**

M

MAB	the queen of the fairies	
MAC	son of (Sc.)	
MAD	crazy; demented; raving; insane	
MAG	chatter; steal; magpie	**zo**
MAG	halfpenny	**nm**
MAL-	faulty; wrong; imperfect	**cf**
MAM	Madame; ma'am	
MAN	employee; husband; mankind	**nt**
MAO	the peacock	**zo**
MAP	delineate; chart; draw	
MAR	spoil; deface; impair; disfigure	
MAT	dull surface; weave; interlace; twist	**pg**
MAT	carpet; raft; slab; reinforcement; site of bout (wrestling)	**ga**
MAW	craw; crop stomach	
MAX	a kind of gin	
MAY	have permission, possibility	
MAY	hawthorn blossom; 5th month	**bt**
MEL **MALL** **MELL**	honey; unit of pitch; leafy bower; promenade	**me, mu**
MEN	humanity	
MET	Metropolitan; a bushel (36 litres)	**me**
MEV	million electron-volts	**me**
MEW	sea-gull; moult	**zo**
MEW	cage; confine; a cat-call	
MHO	electrical unit of conductivity	**me**
MID	central; amid; middle	
MIL	one-thousandth of an inch (2.5 cm)	**me**
MIM	prim; demure; precise	
MIR	Russian commune	
MIS-	hatred of (Gr.)	**cf**
MIX	blend; combine; jumble; mingle	
MNA	mina; 50 shekels	**nm**
MOA	extinct bird, emu type (NZ)	**zo**
MOB	cap; rabble; populace; crowd	
MOD	assembly; meeting	
MOD	modern; Gaelic choral contest	**mu**
MOE	mow; grimace; mop	

MOG	move away	
MON	Cambodian language; canoe (Solomon Islands)	**nt**
MOO	cow noise	
MOP	swab; a hiring-fair; a grimace	
MOR	type of humus layer	**fr**
MOT	bon mot; witticism	
MOW	stack; heap; pile of hay; cut down	
MOW	facial expression; moe	
MRS	mistress	
MUD	mire; sludge; slime	
MUG	fool; face; cup	
MUM	silence; a special brew of beer	
MUN	man (dialect)	
MUX	to spoil; a mess	
MYA	shellfish	**zo**

N

NAB	seize; nap; grab; a knoll	
NAE	none (Sc.)	
NAF	unfashionable; unsuitable	
NAG	harass; pester; horse	**zo**
NAM	distraint (obs.)	**lw**
NAP	doze, forty winks	
NAP	a card game; a racing tip	
NAY	contrariwise	
N.C.O.	non-commissioned officer	
NEB	beak; nose; nib; a point	
NEE	born (Fr.)	
NEF	silver model ship; cadenas; casket; salt cellar	**nt**
NEK	a pass (S. Africa); a col	
NEO-	new style; revived; recent (Gr.)	**cf**
NEP	catmint; knot in cotton fibre	**bt**
NET	neat; nett; snare; capture	
NEW	novel; recent; fresh; modern	
NIB	beak; point; neb	
NIL	nihil; zero; nothing	
NIM	steal; margosa oil	
NIP	squeeze; pinch; sip; a dram	
NIS	not so; imp; hobgoblin; mix	
NIT	egg of louse; light unit	**zo, me**
NIX	water elf; nothing	
NOB	aristocrat; knave at cribbage; head	
NOD	bow; beck; drowse	
NOG	small pot; tree nail	
NOG	wooden brick; peg; noggin; ale	
NOM	de plume	
NON-	negative; not; without (Lat.)	**cf**
NOR	logic	
NOT	negating; Boolean logic of false and true	**cp**
NOW	at this time	
NOX	illumination measurement unit	**lt, me**
NOX	Nyx; personification of night	
NOY	unit of perceived noisiness	**ac, me**
NUB	shove; hang; knob; gist	
NUN	a religeuse; a sister	**rl**

NUR	knot in wood
NUT	a dandy; screwed bolt end; eccentric person
NUT	boss on anchor; single-seeded fruit in shell; ridge holding violin etc strings above sound box **nt, bt, mu**
NUX	(vomica) **md, bt**
NYE	brood of pheasants **zo**
NYS	none is (Spens.)
NYX	Goddess of Night, daughter of Chaos

O

OAF	changeling; fool; dolt; idiot
OAK	outer door (university); hardwood tree **bt**
OAR	to row; an oarsman **nt**
OAT	a grain; a pan-pipe **bt, mu**
OBI	oby; magic; a fetish (West Indies)
OBI	Japanese sash; karate belt
OCA	potato (S. Amer.); palm-leaf book (Sri Lanka)
OCH!	oh! or ah! (Sc. & Ir.)
ODD	singular; peculiar; quaint; droll
ODE	poem or song set to music
ODO	Bishop of Bayeux, A.D.1066
O'ER	poetical over
OES	O's; circlets
OFF	away; gone
OFT	often; frequently; repeatedly
OHM	electrical resistance **me**
OHO!	exclamation
-OID	of resemblance, similarity (Gr.) **cf**
OIL	anoint; lubricate; a lubricant
OKE	Turkish weight, 2¾ lb (1.2 kg) **me**
OLD	antique; archaic; pristine; aged
OLM	a blind lizard **zo**
ONE	individual; unity; undivided
OOF	money
OOM	uncle (Cape Dutch)
OPE	open
OPO-	derived from juice **cf, bt, ck**
OPS	Goddess of Wealth; wife of Saturn
OPT	to choose; elect; pick
-OPY **OPIA**	} of visual defect (Gr.) **cf**
ORA	mouths, orifices (Lat.) **pl**
ORB	globe; circle
ORC	whale; grampus; an ogre **zo**
ORD	edge; beginning
ORE	mineral-bearing earth; coin (Scand.) **mn, nm**
ORT	a bit; refuse; a crumb
OUR	three-quarters of an hour
OUT	without; beyond; get out!
OVA	eggs **zo**
OWE	run up an account
OWL	night bird; to smuggle **zo**
OWN	possess; admit; concede

OXO	organic compound radical **ch**
OZS	ounces

P

PAD	cushion; stuff; paw; data; packet; assembly **tc, zo**
PAD	attenuator; electrical network; bed **el**
PAH!	exclamation of disgust
PAH	stockade (New Zealand)
PAL	staunch friend; palooka; mate
PAM	knave of clubs at loo (card game)
PAN	forest god; small pool; (frying); (gold)
PAN-	all, everywhere, everything (Gr.) **cf**
PAP	conical hill; nipple
PAR	equality; (golf)
PAR	parr; young salmon **zo**
PAS	pace, ballet step
PAT	dab; tap; rap; caress; aptly
PAU	bustard (S. Africa) **zo**
PAW	pad; handle roughly
PAX	era of peace
PAX	kiss of peace; an osculatory **rl**
PAY	to cover with pitch; stipend; wages
PEA	(thimble-rigging) **bt**
PED	pack-saddle; basket
PED	small pack-saddle; pedal **mu**
PEE	to urinate
PEG	short drink; spigot; wooden nail (tent); (croquet); rod; dowel; spike
PEG	secure; fasten; (tent, violin, prices); a scale
PEN	pound; enclosure; mountain; indite
PEN	female swan; quill **zo**
PEP	energy; drive (USA)
PER	by
PES	hind-limb podium **zo**
PET	temper; fondle; a favourite **zo**
PEW	a seat in church **rl**
PHI	binary listing **ma**
PIA	arrowroot (Polynesian) **bt**
PIE	magpie; pye **zo**
PIE	prayer-book; pi; mixed print
PIG	earthen vessel; to guzzle; hog; (lead); (iron) **zo, ml**
-PIK	high lob (pelota) **ga**
PIN	half a firkin; transfix; wedge; pile (wrestling); tip **ga, me**
PIN	peg; nail; to fasten; dowel; dovetail tenon **jn**
PIP	to black-ball; chirp; a depression
PIP	disease of fowls; melancholy **vt**
PIT	set; match; mine; abyss; (theatre); oppose; (cock) (motor racing) **ga**
PIU	more (It.)
PIX	holy box; coin box; pyx
PLY	fold; layer; bias; veneer; roofing felt; to ferry **nt**
POA	a genus of grass **bt**

POD	husk; to swell; unit in a group; room	**bt**
POD	a shoal of whales or seals	**zo**
POE	or parson-bird (New Zealand)	**zo**
POH!	exclamation	
POI	Polynesian taro paste	
POM	Pomeranian dog; Englishman in Australia	
POP	burst; explode; pawn; hit music	**mu**
POT	to shoot; tankard; poteen, home distilled; cannabis marijuana; (bowls)	**bt, ck, ch**
POW	poll; head (Sc.)	
POX	small-pox; syphilis; cow-pox	**md**
POY	balancing-pole; a grant	
POZ	positive; certain	
PRE-	before (pre-war) (Lat.)	**cf**
PRO	for; professional	
PRO-	in favour of (on account of) (Gr.)	**cf**
PRY	peer; snoop; examine	
PSI	} Greek letter	
PSY		
PUB	licensed public drinking house	
PUD	paw; pad; pudding	**zo**
PUG	dog; fox or monkey; pugilist	**zo**
PUN	a form of humour; a paronomasia	
PUP	to whelp; young dog or seal	**zo**
PUR	purr; curr; (owl or cat noise)	
PUS	discharge from infection	**md**
PUT	to steer; bud; game at cards; rustic; (throwing the weight/shot)	
PUT	wanton woman; signal of distress	
PUY	volcanic formation	
PYA	Burmese money	**nm**
PYE	rule for determining Easter date	**rl**
PYE	pie; magpie	**zo**
PYX	pix; holy box; coin box at the Mint	

Q

QUA	as (Lat.)	
QUI	who (Lat.)	
QUO	whither (Lat.); status quo: as it is	

R

RAD	radical; afraid (Sc.)	
RAD	unit of radiation dose	**me**
RAG	a famous club; to torment; garment; ragtime music; Hindi scale; melodic pattern	**mu**
RAI	one-third acre (Siam)	**me**
RAJ	power (India)	
RAM	engine; prow; butt; cram	**zo**
RAN	raced; scurried; flowed; melted	
RAP	snatch; tap	
RAP	counterfeit Irish halfpenny	**nm**
RAS	vizier (Abyssinia)	
RAT	to desert; a rodent	**zo**

RAW	bleak; crude; uncooked; unprocessed data	**cp**
RAX	reach; strain (Sc.)	
RAY	part of flower; a beam	**bt**
RAY	the skate; sheep scab; spoken sol-fa note	**zo, mu**
RED	to disentangle; revolutionary	
REE	hen-bird of ruff	**zo**
REE	riddle; tipsy; Portuguese coin	**nm**
REF	referee	
REG	gravel, desert plain (Arab.)	
REH	saline efflorescence (India)	
REI	Portuguese money of account	**nm**
REM	ionizing radiation dosage	
REN	the kidney	**md**
REP	debauchee; rip	
REP	fabric; repetition; repertory (theatre)	
RES	a thing; a point	**lw**
RET	to rot flax; hemp or jute	
REV	to speed up; Reverend	**rl**
REV	to increase revolutions, accelerate	
REV	revise, revision; revert, reverse	
REX	a king	
RIA	inlet of the sea	
RIB	bone; watercress; petiole; ridge; edge; projecting band; (spare) (frame)	**bt, ar, mo**
RID	to free; clear; expel; destroy	
RIE	rye	**bt**
RIG	wanton; manipulate	**nt, zo**
RIM	brim; border; edge	
RIO	ounce (28 grams) (Japan); a tael	**me**
RIP	to saw with the grain; (winkle) seaward current (surfing); rest in peace	**ga**
RIP	fish-basket; tear; rend; a Lothario	
RIT	strike; tear (Sc.); ritardando, repeat	**mu**
ROB	rook; fleece; strip; fruit syrup	
ROC	fabulous bird; rok	**zo**
ROD	pole or perch ($5\frac{1}{2}$ yd/5 metres); cane, metal bar (piston); twig; gun (Amer.); angling; retinal nerve	**nc, me**
ROE	deer; edible gonads	**zo**
ROG	to jog; to shake	
ROK	roc; fabulous bird	**zo**
ROM	gipsy; a Romany	
RON	King Arthur's ebony spear	
ROO	a kangaroo	**zo**
ROT	to decay; putrefy; nonsense	
ROW	line; brawl; din; (oars); quarrel	
ROW	cards; punched cards	**cp**
ROY	a king (obs.)	
RUA	storage pit (NZ)	
RUB	chafe; abrade; dilemma	
RUC	rok; roc; a fabulous bird	**zo**
RUD	rub; polish; flush; ochre	
RUE	lament; regret; suffer; sorrow	
RUE	herb of grace	**bt**
RUG	mat; coverlet; a drink; shaggy dog	
RUM	grog; queer; quaint; odd; fantastic	

RUN	unit of scoring in baseball, cricket, stoolball; chicken coop	ga
RUN	hurry; speed; propel; tour; demand	
RUN	manage; sequence; performance	cp
RUT	wheel track; groove; desire	
RUT	mating season; deep piste (skiing); monotony of routine	
RYE	rie; (whisky)	bt
RYE	a bird disease	

S

SAB	sob (Sc.)	
SAC	bag, often fluid-containing	md
SAD	sorry; downcast; gloomy; dismal	
SAE	so (Sc.); stamped addressed envelope	
SAG	droop; settle; bend; sink	
SAI	Brazilian monkey	zo
SAL	Indian timber tree	bt
SAL	salt	ch
SAM	together; to collect; to curdle	
SAP	undermine; juice; a worker; moisture (stone)	bt
SAT	seated; perched; settled	
SAW	a saying; an adage; seen	to
SAX	a knife; slate-cutter's hammer	to
SAY	tell; declare; utter; allege	
SAZ	guitar (Turk.)	
SEA	basin; an ocean; wave surge	
SEC	dry (flavour)	
SED	(fish-hook); a fillet	
SEE	watch; descry; heed; a throne	rl
SEG	sedge; a bullock	bt, zo
SEL	self (Sc.)	
SEN	(Jap.) (Indonesian)	nm
SEP	sepal; leaf	bt
SET	a twist; squared block; firm; fixed; ready	
SET	group of waves; tennis rallies, scores; (surfing); badger's den	ga
SET	clique; social clan; group	
SET	water flow direction; bend; (pile driving)	
SET } god of darkness (Egypt)		rl
SETH }		
SEW	stitch; baste	
SEX	gender	
SHA	shapo; wild sheep	zo
SHE	feminine pronoun	
SHY	coy; bashful; diffident; wary	
SIB } akin to (sibling) brother, sister		
SYB }		
SIC	as written	
SIK	to seek (Sc.)	
SIL	ochre pigment	
SIM	a Simeonite; low churchman	rl
SIN	transgress; wickedness; iniquity	
SIP	sup	
SIR	sire; master	
SIS	girl; sweetheart; sister	

-SIS	condition, state (of health) (Gr.)	cf
SIT	brood; incubate; rest; repose	
SIX	sax (Sc.)	
SKI	(winter sport); slender plank for gliding, jumping on snow	ga
SKY	to loft; heavens; the weather; raise oarblade too high (rowing)	ae, ga
SLY	artful; wily; astute; fly	
SNY	upward curve	
SOB	cry; blubber; weep; snivel	
SOC	privilege; sac	lw
SOD	turf; sward; lawn; grass	
SOG	a bog; morass; marsh; to saturate	
SOH	spoken form of 5th note of sol-fa scale	mu
SOL	old French halfpenny (Peru)	nm
SOL	the sun; gold; 5th note of sol-fa scale	mu
SON	offspring; a disciple	
SON	sound (Fr.)	mu
SOP	to soak; to steep; a bribe	
SOS	help!	
SOT	drunkard	
SOU	French mite; sol	nm
SOW	disseminate; plant; broadcast; fem pig	zo
SOX	haberdashery	
SOY	bean, sauce; oriental footwear	bt, ck
SPA	spring; health resort; hydro	
SPY	espy; behold; detect; observe	
STY } pig pen; eye ailment		md
STYE }		
SUB	subaltern; substitute	
SUB-	beneath, inferior, under (Lat.)	cf
SUE	prosecute; plead	lw
SUG	a kind of worm	zo
SUM	total; amount; addend plus augend	ma, cp
SUN	Phoebus Apollo; Sol; Helios; centre of solar system	as
SUP	to take supper; imbibe	
SUS	arrest on suspicion	lw
SYB } akin to		
SIB }		
SUP	to imbibe	
SYN	syne; since (Sc.)	
SYN-	joined, together, along with (Gr.)	cf

T

TAB	flap; tally; check; leather, finger protector for bow (theatre) (archery)	
TAD	street boy (USA)	
TAG	catchword; touch; label; game; wedge; append	ga
TAG	identification symbols, digits; expel (baseball)	cp, ga
TAI	Japanese bream	zo
TAJ	Mahal; headdress (Ind.)	

TAN	to beat; brown colour	
TAP	rap; pat; knock; broach	
TAP	faucet; screw; stopcock	to, pb
TAR	sailor; pitch; bitumen; incite	nt
TAT	needlework; pony	
TAT	native cloth	
TAU	bug; toad-fish	zo
TAU	Egyptian or St Anthony's cross	rl
TAW	a marble; game	
TAX	accuse; strain; tariff; levy	
TEA	beverage; bohea	bt, ck
TEC	teck; detective	
TED	spread	
TEE	(golf); Chinese umbrella; hinge; 7th note	mu
TEG	deer; sheep; tag	zo
TEN	a net drawn up	
TER	thrice	
TEW	gear; iron chain; scourge	
THE	definite article	
THO'	though	
THY	of thee; thine	
TIB	a courtesan	
TIC	nervous twitch; spasm	md
TIE	dead-heat; bind; link; unite	
TIG	a game; a cup	
TIN	can; preserve; receptacle; money; metal; wall strip (squash)	mn, ga
TIP	gratuity; vails; cant; tilt; incline	
TIR	shooting contest (Fr.)	
'TIS	it is	
TIT	small bird; pony	zo
TOD	28 lb of wool	me
TOD	bush; fox	bt, zo
TOE	extremity	
TOG	to dress; a garment	
TOK	a nesting place of capercaillies	zo
TOL	take away	
TOM	male cat	zo
TON	fashion; 20 cwt (1 tonne)	me
TON	hundred runs, century (cricket)	ga
TOO	more than enough	
TOP	a toy; vertex; zenith; acme; excel	
TOR	granite outcrop on a hill	
TOT	to add; child	me
TOW	flax; hemp; haul	bt
TOY	to trifle; plaything; light instrument; lute	mu
TRI-	of three together (Gr.)	cf
TRY	4 points at Rugby football	ga
TRY	test; essay; attempt; endeavour	
TUB	basin; container; a boat	nt
TUG	towing (-ship) or aircraft (gliding)	nt
TUI	parson-bird (NZ)	zo
TUN	barrel; large cask	me
TUP	ram; to butt; hammer	zo
TUR	Caucasian goat	zo
TUT!	deprecating exclamation	
TUT	piece-work; a hassock	
TWA	two (Sc.)	
TWO	a pair; brace; couple; deuce	
TYE	ore washing buddle; tie	
TYG	tall china cup	
TYR	a son of Odin	rl

U

UDA	purplish brown glaze	
UDO	Japanese vegetable	bt
UDO	universal language	
UGH!	exclamation of disgust	
ULE	gum (Mexico)	bt
ULT	ultimo	
UMA	wife of Siva	rl
UNA	cat-boat having a centreboard	nt
UNI-	treat as one, singular	cf
UNO	United Nations Organisation	
UPS	peak occasions; (downs)	
URE	practice; wont; work; exercise	
URE	wild ox; aurochs	zo
URF	stunted child (Sc.)	
URN	jar; vase; receptacle	
URY	hazy (Sc.)	
USE	usage; avail; employ; apply; usury	
UTA	American lizard	zo
UTU	blood-money; requital (NZ)	
UVA	a bunch	bt

V

VAC	vacation	
V.A.D.	war worker; (Women's) Voluntary Aid Detachment	
VAE	voe; gio; creek; firth; frith; fiord	
VAG	peat (Sc.)	
VAN	fan; forefront; vehicle; vane	
VAR	unit of reactive power of A/C	el, me
VAS	blood vessel; vesicle, glandular tubes	pl
VAT	fat; vessel; tank; value-added tax	
VEL	unit of size; airborne	me
VEO	unit for perceived weight	me
VET	horse doctor; examine	
VEX	plague; harass; fret; chafe	
VIA	by way of	
VIE	strive; contend; contest	
VIF	lively (Fr.)	mu
VIM	force	
VIS	power	
VIZ	namely	
VLY	vlei; pool (S. Africa)	
VOE	vae; geo; gio; fiord; estuary; firth	
VOL	two wings conjoined at base; crest	hd
VOR	navigational ranging system	nv
VOW	pledge; dedicate; consecrate; oath	
VOX	voice; song part	mu
VUG	rock cavity (Cornish)	
VUM	vow (Amer.)	

W

WAD	manganese ore; mass of paper	mn
WAE	woe (Sc.)	
WAG	vibrate; wit; jester; humorist	
WAN	pale; sickly; languid	
WAP	whop; a bundle; swat; wrap; copulate; beat	
WAR	strife; enmity; discord; contend	
WAS	past of 'be' (sing.)	
WAT	hare; drunken (Sc.)	zo
WAX	increase; grow; beeswax	
WAY	route; passage; track; usage	
WEB	a textile fabric; cobweb	
WED	a pledge; to marry	
WEE	diminutive; urinate (sl.)	
WEN	(London); tumour; wart	md
WET	humid; moist; watery; drench	
WEY	various weights, salt, corn, etc	me
WHO	which person?	
WHY	for what reason?	
WIG	vallancy; toupee; periwig; peruke	
WIG	berate; scold; lecture; upbraid	
WIN	gain; procure; acquire; achieved	
WIS } **WIT**	know (obs.)	
WIT	wag; humour; reason; facetiousness	
WOE	affliction; sorrow; grief; anguish	
WON	to dwell; an abode (Korea)	nm
WON	earned; got; swayed; persuaded	
WOO	to court	
WOP	whop; whip; Italian	
WOT	know	
WOW	event; sound change	
WOX	waxed (Spens.)	
WRY	awry; askew; crooked; distorted	
WYE	a person (Sc.)	
WYE	Y-branched pipe	pb

Y

YAB	jabber (Sc.)	
YAH!	exclamation of derision	
YAK	Tibetan ox	zo
YAM	sweet potato	bt, ck
YAO	pottery ware (China)	
YAP	yell; cry; bark	
YAW	deviate; sideways heaving; head movement of horse (gliding)	nt
YEA	ay; aye; yes; truly; verily	
YEN	a gold or silver Japanese coin	nm
YEP	yeh; yes (Amer.)	
YES	yea; aye; ay	
YET	a gate (Sc.)	
YET	still; further; besides; however	
YEW	wood for the bow	bt
YEX	hiccough	
YID	a Jew (Yiddish)	
YIP	pert forward girl (Sc.)	
YOD	phonetic sound 'y'	
YON	yonder	
YOU	2nd-person pronoun	
YOW	ewe (Sc.)	zo
YUG	an age of the world (Hind.)	

Z

ZAK	Kashmir raft	nt
ZAX	slate cutter; sax	to
ZEA	maize	bt
ZED } **ZEE**	the letter Z (English; Amer.)	
ZEL	cymbal	mu
ZHO	zobo; hybrid yak and cow	zo
ZIP	liveliness; a ping; a fastening	
ZOO	zoological gardens	
ZOO-	of animal classification (Gr.)	cf
ZUZ	an ancient Jewish coin	nm

A

ABBA	Chaldean or Coptic divine; father	rl
ABBE	French abbot; priest	rl
ABED	in bed	
ABER	river mouth (Celtic)	
ABET	aid; incite; favour; countenance	
ABIB	1st month of the Jewish year	
ABLE	skilful; adroit; expert; competent	
ABLY	masterly; powerfully; cleverly	
A-BOX	opposite bracing of yards	nt
ABUT	meet; adjoin; rest; terminate	
ABYE	aby; atone; pay the penalty (obs.)	
ACER	the maple-tree	bt
ACES	(spot); dice game	
ACHE	pain; pang; agony; anguish	
ACID	sour; tart; bitter; vitriolic	
ACME	zenith; apex; pinnacle; pitch	
ACNE	a skin disease	md
ACOP	atop; on high (obs.)	
ACOR	acidity	md
ACOY	accoy; to soothe (obs.)	
ACRE	4840 square yards = 4046 sq m =	
	0.405 hectares = 4 roods	me
ACRO-	topmost; first (Gr.)	cf
ACTA	proceedings in a court	lw
ACYL	carboxylic acid radical	ch
ADAM	the first man; a gaoler	
ADAR	12th month of the Jewish year	
ADDS	overall quantities, extras	bd
ADIT	opening or passage; entrance	
ADRY	athirst	
ADZE	adz; a mattock	to
AEON	an age; era; cycle; period; eon	
AERO-	air or gas	cf
AERY	eyry; ayry; an eagle's nest	zo
AERY	ethereal; visionary	
AFAR	away; distant; remote; aloof	
AFER	the South-West wind	
AFFY	to betroth; trust; confide (obs.)	
AGAR	ploughman of playing fields, Eton	
AGAR	seaweed; mucilage; gel	bl, ck, md
AGED	elderly; ancient; antiquated	
AGEE	awry; askew; asquint; ajee	
AGEN	again	
AGHA	} ruler of sect; estates owner	rl
AGA		
AGIO	premium; discount; brokerage	
AGNI	Hindu fire-god and protector	
AGOG	astir; eager; excited	
AGON	sardine-like Alpine fish	ck
AGON	contest; struggle; (antagonist) (Gr.)	ga
AGUA	South American toad	zo
AGUE	malarial fever; chilliness	md
AHEM!	exclamation	
AHOY!	exclamation (nautical)	nt
AIDE	helper; assistant; coadjutor	
AIDS	acquired immune deficiency syndrome	md

AIDS	last three fingers of sword hand (fencing)	ga
AINE	elder son; cadet	
AIN'T	(are not)	
AINU	aboriginal (Jap.)	
AIRA	hair-grass	bt
AIRE	an altar; Irish freeman	
AIRT	direction; quarter (Sc.)	
AIRY	blythe; breezy; ethereal; spacious	
AJAR	slightly opened	
AJEE	agee; ajar; askew	
AJOG	jogging along	
AKEE	West Indian fruit tree	bt
AKIN	sib; agnate; similar; related	
ALAR	winged, pertaining to wings	
ALAS	alack; welladay	
ALBE	albeit; even though	
ALCA	sea-auk genus	zo
ALEE	on the lee-side	nt
ALEW	halloo (obs.)	
ALFA	esparto grass	bt
ALGA	seaweed	bt
ALGO-	pain	cf, md
ALIF	1st letter Arabic alphabet	pr
ALLA	in the manner of	me
ALLY	alley; a marble of real alabaster	
ALLY	unite; marry; confederate; friend	
ALMA	} Egyptian dancing girl	
ALME		
ALMS	oblations; gifts; bounty	
ALOD	allod; freehold	
ALOE	a large genus of bitter herbs	bt
ALOW	below; ablaze (Sc.)	nt
ALPS	European high mountains; pasture land	go
ALSO	in like manner; further	
ALTO	male voice of highest pitch	mu
ALUM	mordant mineral salt	ch
AMAH	ayah; Indian nurse	
AMBE	ancient surgical instrument	md
AMBO	high reading desk	
AMEN	Egyptian deity of the dead	rl
AMIA	bow-fin or mud-fish (N. Amer.)	zo
AMIC	ammoniac	ch
AMID	betwixt; between; amongst	
AMIN	ammoniate	ch
AMIR	} arab ruler	
EMIR		
AMMA	a truss; Syrian abbess	rl
AMMO	ammunition	
AMOK	amuck; frenzy (Malay)	
AMOR	Roman cupid; Eros	
AMOY	language (Formosa)	
AMYL	a tar product	ch
ANAK	a giant of Palestine	
ANAL	of the anus	pl, zo
ANER	male ant	zo
ANEW	again; freshly; repeatedly	
ANGI-	of blood vessels	cf, md
ANIL	the indigo plant	bt

ANKH	life symbol (Egypt)	
ANNA	16 annas to the rupee	nm
ANOA	wild ox of Celebes	zo
ANON	at once; then again	
ANSA	decorated vase-handle	
ANTA	a pilaster	
ANTE	a stake at poker	
ANTE-	before	cf
ANUS	excremental orifice	pl
APAY	to satisfy; to repay (obs.)	
APED	copied; imitated; mimicked	
APER	an impersonator	
APEX	acme; zenith; pinnacle; point	
APIS	sacred bull (Egypt)	
APOD	fish without ventral fins	zo
APSE	polygonal recess	rl
AQUA	water; solution	rl
ARAB	Saracen; Moor	
ARAF	Mohammedan purgatory	
ARAK	oriental palm sap spirit; areca nut	bt
ARAR	North African timber tree	bt
ARBA	covered wagon (Tartar)	
ARCA	chest or coffer	rl
ARCH	roguish; cunning; shrewd portal	ar
ARCO	bow of stringed instrument	mu
AREA	yard; enclosure; region; district; memory; field	cp, el
ARES	Mars, the God of War	
ARGO	the Argonauts' ship	nt
ARIA	air; tune; melody	mu
ARID	dry; parched; sterile; barren	
ARIL	outer seed cover	bt
ARMS	armorial emblems	
ARMY	host; array; throng; force	
AROW	successively; in a row	
ARPA	harp (It.)	mu
'ARRY }		
HARRY }	jovial Cockney name	
ARSE	backside; tail of block	nt
ARTS	crafts; guiles	
ARTY	spuriously aesthetic	
ARUM	lily genus	bt
ARYL	aromatic hydrocarbon radical	ch
ASAR	eskar; gravel ridges	
ASCI	bags of spores	bt
ASHY	ashen; wan; pallid; hueless	
ASIA	largest continent	
ATKA	type of mackerel	zo
ATLI	a Norse king (Atle)	
ATOM	jot; tittle; whit; particle	
ATOP	acop; on top (obs.)	
ATTO	one million million millionth 10^{-18}	cp, ma
AUDI-	of hearing	cf
AULA	a hall; a court	
AULD	old (Sc.)	
AUNT	(Aunt Sally)	
AURA	a zephyr; emanation	nm
AUTO	da fe; autocar	
AVAL	an endorsement on a bill	

AVEL	an awn of barley	bt
AVEN	subterranean; sinkhole	go, gl
AVER	avouch; confirm; authenticate	
AVES	birds collectively	zo
AVID	eager; greedy; voracious	
AVON	river (Celt.)	
AVOW	own; aver; admit; confess	
AWAY	afar; distant; abroad; absent	
AWED	inspired by reverence; cowed	
AWNY	bearded	bt
AWRY	askew; oblique; crooked	
AXAL	axial (obs.)	
AXED	discharged; sacked; cut down	
AXEL	freestyle jump (ice skating); (optional)	
AXIL	angle between branch and trunk	bt
AXIN	cochineal ointment	
AXIS	the chital; Indian spotted deer	zo
AXLE	axis; spindle; shaft	
AXON	nerve cell impulse-carrying process	zo
AYAH	amah; Indian nurse	
AYES	supporting votes	
AYRE	old English song, verse	
AYRY	eyry; eyrie; an eagle's nest	zo
AZAN	polychrome microanalytical	
AZER	native of Central Asia	
AZOL	developer	pt

B

BAAL	Phoenician god; false god; idol	
BAAS	the boss; master (Cape Dutch)	
BABA	Papa, Pope, Patriarch; rum- (cake)	rl
BABE	infant; suckling	
BABU	Hindu clerk	
BACK	help; support; wager; retreat; trim sails to windward (sailing); reverse; (-pay); fall; (wrestling) (football); extrados of arch; posterior	nt, ar
BADE	(bid); commanded	
BAFF	biff; smite; buff	
BAFT	abaft; an oriental fabric	
BAHT	Thai monetary unit	nm
BAIL	(cricket); hoop; handle; surety	lw
BAIT	worry; badger; a lure; refreshment	
BAIU	plum rains; Japan	go
BAKE	harden; parch	
BALD	bare; hairless; prosaic; unadorned	
BALE	bane; harm; misery; bundle	
BALK }		
BAUK }	impede; refuse; timber; (baseball)	
BAULK }		ga
BALL	party; rout; globe; bullet	
BALM	salve; unguent; fragrance	
BANC	bench (obs.)	lw
BAND	bond; unite; a troupe; a coterie; musicians; brace; (elastic); magnetic; zone; wave length	lw, mu, bd, el, cp
BANE	poison; ruin; sheep-rot	ch, bt, zo

BANG	explosion; a fringe of hair	
BANG	bhang; the assassin's drug	
BANG	a drink; beer, cider, nutmeg, ginger	
BANI	Romanian monetary unit	**nm**
BANK	bench of rowers; deposit; loan office; tilt ridge; obstacle; (jump)	**cp**
BANT	adopt a slimming diet	
BARB	to shave; (fish-hook); horse	**zo**
BARD	wandering minstrel; a poet	
BARE	naked; nude; exposed; bleak	
BARI-	} low (baritone) (Gr.)	**cf**
BARY-		
BARK	cortex; yelp; yap; a ship; cork	**bt, nt**
BARM	yeast; ferment; leaven	
BARN	granary; store; out-building; (-dance)	
BARN	nuclear cross-section unit 10^{-18} metres	**me**
BARO-	of weight, pressure (barometer)	**cf**
BART	Bartholomew, baronet	
BARU	fluffy fibre	**bt**
BASE	basis; abject; vile; sordid; foundation; data; radix; baseball	**cp**
BASH	smite; baff; biff; wallop; buffet	
BASI-	} depth (bassoon) (Gr.)	**cf**
BASO-		
BASK	luxuriate; revel	
BASS	(ale); low; deep; grave	**mu**
BASS	American linden tree; perch	**bt, zo**
BAST	bass; fibre of that tree	**bt**
BAST	cat-headed Egyptian goddess	**rl**
BATE	abate; decrease; lessen; curtail	
BATH	6 gallons (27 litres), Jewish liquid	**me**
BAUD	telegraphic transmission; pulse rate (modulation)	**me, cp, tc, rd**
BAUK	} beam; ridge; hinder	
BALK		
BAULK		
BAWD	whore; hare	**zo**
BAWL	howl; yawl; yell; shout	
BAWN	fort; cattle-pen	
BAYA	the Indian weaver bird	**zo**
BAYS	laurels of distinction	**bt**
BEAD	bubble; globule; a moulding; module	**cp**
BEAK	magistrate; prow; bill; mandible	
BEAM	rafter; ray; shine; emit; smile; plank (gymn.) (fencing) (baseball)	**ga**
BEAM	radio directional system; width	**nt**
BEAN	leguminous plant	**bt**
BEAR	carry; uphold; suffer; produce	**zo**
BEAT	spent; exhausted; batter; throb; rhythm; notation	**mu**
BEAT	a policeman's perambulation; patrol route; sail to windward	**nt**
BEAU	fop; dandy; gallant; coxcomb	
BECK	beckon; a small stream	
BEEF	grumble (USA); strength	
BEEN	the vina; Indian guitar	**mu**
BEEP	telephonic signal	
BEER	ale; lager; swipes	

BEET	the beetroot	**bt**
BEIN	comfortable; well-found (Sc.)	
BEJA	triba (Africa)	
BELL	model of soundness; to bellow; resonant musical instrument (church)	**mu**
BELT	zone; girdle; band; thrash	
BEMA	judge's seat; pulpit	**rl**
BEND	deflect; stoop; incline; a spree	
BEND	diagonal band on a shield; cause ball to swerve in flight (soccer)	**hd, ga**
BENE	the oil-plant	**bt**
BENT	curved; crooked; withered grass	
BERE	bear; barley (Sc.)	**bt**
BERG	mountain; iceberg	
BERM	a ledge; slanting bank	
BEST	worst; defeat; overcome	
BETA	ray; function; 2nd letter of Gr. alphabet	**nc**
BEVY	swarm; flock; throng	
BHEL	Bengal quince	**bt**
BHIL	a Dravidian race (Ind.)	
BIAS	prejudice; (bowls); error; partiality	**cp**
BIAS	voltage applied to determine characteristics of device	**el, ps**
BIBS	part of netball uniform	
BICE	pale blue or green	
BIDE	await; tarry; stay; dwell	
BIER	a conveyance for the dead	
BIFF	baff; buff; smite; crash	
BIGA	two-horsed Roman chariot	
BIGG	bere; a kind of barley (Sc.)	
BIKE	bicycle; wasp's nest; a swarm	**zo**
BIKH	aconitine (Hindu)	
BILE	bitter liver secretion	**md**
BILE	ill-humour	
BILK	balk; cheat; deceive; thwart	
BILL	fondle; account; placard; poster; narrow headland; peninsula	**go**
BIND	tie; fasten; restrain; secure	
BIND	seizing prey in flight (falconry); (fencing)	**ga**
BINE	hop-stems, etc.	**bt**
BING	a heap of corn or alum	
BINK	bench; bank; shelf (Sc.)	
BINT	a girl (Arabic)	
BION	plant capable of separate life	**bt**
BIOS	yeast-growth promoter	**ch**
BIRD	(get the bird); a fowl; shuttlecock (badminton)	**zo, ga**
BIRK	the birch-tree	**bt**
BIRL	spin; whirl (Sc.)	
BIRR	impetus; violent thrust; a whirr	
BIRT	the turbot	**zo**
BISE	cold dry wind (Swiss)	
BISK	bisque; soup; pottery	**ck**
BITE	a nibble; etch; nip; grip; grasp	
BITT	(to bitt a cable)	**nt**
BLAB	divulge; disclose; tell tales	
BLAD	fragment; lump; stain; batter (Sc.)	

BLAE	blue (Sc.)	
BLAY	} a river fish; the bleak	**zo**
BLEY		
BLEA	inner bark of tree	**bt**
BLEB	transparent blister; bubble	**md**
BLED	past tense of bleed	
BLEE	complexion; colour	
BLET	spot on decayed fruit; to rot	**bt**
BLEW	sounded, puffed; panted	
BLIP	radar reflection spot	**rd**
BLOB	viscous globule	
BLOC	political/economic grouping	
BLOT	blur; mar; tarnish; erase	
BLOW	sound (horn); puff; pant; (baseball); (bowling); strike (boxing)	**ga, mu**
BLUB	sob; cry; blubber; blistering (USA); hole in plastercast	**bd**
BLUE	navy; cobalt; ultramarine; glum	
BLUE	azure; sapphire; (Oxford)	
BLUR	dim; sully; obscure; blot	
BOAR	male hog	**zo**
BOAT	craft; bark; skiff; vessel	**nt**
BOCK	light beer	
BODE	portend; presage; augur	
BODY	corpse; carcass; substance; torso; horse (gymn.)	
BOER	Afrikaaner	
BOGU	kendo armour of Kendoka	**ga**
BOGY	bogey; bugbear; hobgoblin	
BOIL	seethe; rage; fume	
BOKO	nasal organ (sl.)	
BOLD	brave; valiant; daring; doughty	
BOLE	a tree-trunk; recess	**bt**
BOLL	pod; capsule	**bt**
BOLO	Filipino knife; uppercut blow (boxing)	**ga**
BOLT	abscond; gulp; missile; fasten; sift; lock (door)	
BOMA	boa; anaconda	**zo**
BOMB	petard; block-buster; bombard; success	
BOMB	(basketball); (lacrosse); (surfing); (Am. football)	**ga**
BOND	link; band; contract; (bricks)	
BONE	steal; (china); skeletal	**zo**
BONK	knock; extreme fatigue (cycling)	**sp**
BONT	many coloured (S. Africa)	
BONY	full of bones; strong; stout	
BOOB	booby; dunce; blockhead	
BOOH!	a derisive interjection	
BOOK	tome; volume; manual	
BOOM	boost; resound; barrier; spar attached to mast; dhow	**nt**
BOON	benefit; merry; jovial	
BOOR	clodhopper; lout; lubber	
BOOT	gain; to eject; luggage recess; facing brickwork base	**ar**
BORA	cold Adriatic wind	
BORD	coal face (mining)	
BORE	tidal wave; tire; calibre; drill	

BORN	née; begotten	
BORT	} low quality diamond for drills	**to**
BOART		
BOSA	a Persian liquor	
BOSH	tosh; inane chatter; bunkum	
BOSK	bosket; thicket; grove	
BOSS	foreman; stud; protuberance; keystone; boxwood cone; hole plug; coiled straw target (archery); dome of rock	**pb gl**
BOTE	compensation; reparation	**lw**
BOTH	all of two	
BOTS	botts; the larvae of the botfly	**zo**
BOUD	insect in grain; weevil	**zo**
BOUN	to dress; prepare; set out (Sc.)	
BOUT	contest; conflict; turn	
BOVO	Genoese fishing boat	**nt**
BOWK	large iron barrel; kibble	**mn**
BOWL	beaker; goblet; (cricket); dish; (pipe); heavy ball, stadium, show centre (Am. football); throw	**ga**
BOWS	the fore-end of a ship	**nt**
BRAD	small nail	
BRAE	hill overlooking valley	**go**
BRAG	boast; vaunt; a game of cards	
BRAN	refuse of grain	**bt**
BRAT	urchin; gamin; child	
BRAW	fine; brave; showy (Sc.)	
BRAY	braise; pound; clamour; blare	
BRED	reared; raised; nurtured	
BREE	eyebrow; liquor	
BREN	sub-machine gun	
BRER	brother; (brer-rabbit)	
BRET	a fish of the turbot kind	**zo**
BREW	concoct; devise; plot	
BRIE	a cream cheese	
BRIG	two-masted square-rigged ship	**nt**
BRIL	unit of brightness	**me**
BRIM	verge; marge; border; to coast	
BRIN	a fan-stick	
BRIO	vivacity	**mu**
BRIT	whitebait, etc.	**zo**
BROB	a wooden wedge	
BROC	pewter wine measure	
BROG	an awl; to pierce	**to**
BROW	rim; edge; brink; forehead	
BUBO	the eagle owl	**zo**
BUCK	talk; jump; deer; dollar	**zo, nm**
BUDE	a gas burner	
BUFF	baff; biff; strike; yellow; devotee	
BUFF	pliant leather; the bare skin	
BUHL	brass and tortoiseshell inlay	
BUHR	burr-stone; a millstone	**mn**
BULB	(electric); corm; tuber	**bt**
BULK	mass; volume; magnitude; storage	**cp**
BULL	(papal); (Irish); walrus; centre of target (rifle shooting); deck game; male bovine, deer	**ga, zo**
BUMP	fall; the call of the bittern; noise of rocks; volleyball pass	**zo, ga**

BUND	league; embankment; quay	
BUNG	barrel-stopper; large cork	
BUNK	depart; sleeping berth	**nt**
BUNT	butt; part of a sail; (baseball)	**nt, ga**
BUOY	cheer; sustain; float	**nt**
BURG	bury; borough; burgh	
BURK	burke; murder; smother; hush up	
BURL	a knot in thread or wood	
BURN	a brook; parch; char; glow	
BURN	combustion; (sun); (bowls); (Am. football)	**ga**
BURR	rough edge; the burdock; growth on tree-trunk, root;	**bt**
BURT	flat-fish, turbot type	**zo**
BURY	burgh; clump of trees; inter	
BUSH	thimble; (bearings); a shrub; (-baby)	**bt, zo**
BUSH	outback; wild scrubland	**go**
BUSK	to act in the street	
BUSS	to kiss; a fishing boat	**nt**
BUST	bosom; sculpture; broken	
BUSY	sedulous; officious; industrious	
BUTT	log end; meet exactly; abut	
BUTT	thrust; a mound; bottom; fag-end; (rifle); bum	
BUZZ	rumour; a whispered report	
BYRE	a cow-house	
BYTE	data or data transfer unit	**cp**

C

CABA	cabas; work-basket; pannier	
CACO-	degenerate; diseased; (cacophony)	**cf**
CADE	cask of herrings; pet lamb	**zo**
CADI	kadi; Turkish judge	
CAER	camp; fort (Celt.)	
CAFE	coffee-house; restaurant	
CAGE	crib; cabin; confine; mew; lift (mine); goal poles	**ga**
CAIC CAIQUE }	Turkish skiff	**nt**
CAID	alcayde; Arab judge	
CAIN	kain; rent in kind; a weasel	**zo**
CAKE	solidify; harden; a tablet	
CAKY	encrusted	
CALF	part of leg; (Golden)	**zo**
CALK	caulk; spike; calkin	**nt**
CALL	dub; term; summon; visit; conversation time unit	**cp, me, tc**
CALM	still; unflurried; peaceful; without wind	
CALP	shale bed (Irish)	**mn**
CALX	chalk or lime	**mn**
CAMA	South African hartebeest	**zo**
CAME	arrived; reached; attained; lead for lights fixing	**bd**
CAMP	encamp; pitch a tent	
CAMP	exaggeratedly stylized	
CAMP	temporary outdoor dwelling place	
CANE	rattan; bamboo; beat	**bt**

CANG	Chinese pillory	
CANT	incline; thieves' patter; hypocrisy; tilt	
CANT	to cut waste from a log	**bd**
CANY	made of cane	
CAPA	Spanish cloak	
CAPE	capa; cope; headland; ness	
CAPO	device on guitar fingerboard	**mu**
CARD	woolcomb; personality; game; (wool); (credit); (punched); (score)	**cp**
CARE	tend; concern; worry; heed	
CARK	care; trouble; fret; anxiety	
CARL	churl; clown	
CARP	cavil; censure; goldfish	**zo**
CARR	reclaimed bog land	
CART	van; wagon; transport	
CASE	box; enclose; plight; facing (brick); patient; law	
CASH	specie; money; small Chinese coin	**nm**
CASK	casque; helmet; barrel; tub; cade	
CAST	mien; shed; toss; mould; tint; throw; direct, arrange, performers; (eye); (angling)	
CAST	swift, clean-shooting bow (archery)	**ga**
CATA- KATA- }	from; against (catapult); down	**cf**
CATE	dainty food	
CAUF	live fish box	
CAUK	sulphate of baryta	**mn**
CAUL	net; membrane; aluminium or plywood sheet	**bd**
CAVE	cavern; grotto; den; beware!	
CAVY	genus of rodents; guinea-pig	**zo**
CAWK	heavy spar	**mn**
CEDE	yield; relinquish; apportion; forego	
CEIL	ciel; roof; ceiling	
CELL	cavity; dungeon; nucleus + protoplasm	**el, bl**
CELO	unit of acceleration	**me**
CELT	Kelt; early Aryan	
CENT	10 cents make one dime	**nm**
CERE	to wax; to wrap in cerecloth	
CERT	alleged certainty; a snip	
CESS	sess; to tax; a local rate	
CEST	cestus; a belt or girdle	
CHAC	Central American rain gods	
CHAD	shad; sea-bream; punched hole	**zo, cp**
CHAI	gipsy girl	
CHAL	gipsy man	
CHAM	King of Tartary; Mogul khan	
CHAP	jaw; cleft; fellow; guy; chapman	
CHAR	a lake fish; to scorch; to burn	**zo**
CHAT	talk; gossip; warbler; wheatear	**zo**
CHAW	chew; masticate; champ	
CHAY	shay; chaise; open carriage	
CHEF	expert cook	
CHEW	ruminate; munch	
CHIC	charmingly correct	
CHID	scolded; rated; rebuked	

CHIG	to chew; a quid; chaw
CHIN	part of face
CHIP	fruit basket; cut; to chaff; stake; golf shot **ga**
CHIP	(potato); semi-conductor; (microchip data); **ck, cp**
CHIR-	the hand (chiromancy, palmistry) **cf**
CHOP	the jaw; veer; vary; change
CHOP	cut; meat; strike; (cricket); (table tennis) **ga**
CHOU	ornamental ribbon
CHOW	Chinese dog **zo**
CHOY	Indian madder **bt**
CHUB	the cheven; a freshwater carp **zo**
CHUG	a fussy engine noise
CHUI	Judo referee's rebuke
CHUM	pal; palooka; buddy; messmate
CHUT	a peevish cry
CIEL	ceil; plaster; wainscot
CILL	} wall, window frame base **ar**
SILL	
CIMA	cyma; ogee moulding of cornice
CIRC	prehistoric stone circle
CIRE	polished silk fabric (Fr.)
CIRL	a species of bunting **zo**
CIST	cyst; stone chest; tomb
CITE	quote; summon; adduce **lw**
CITY	cathedral town
CIVE	chive; onion **bt**
CLAD	garbed; dressed; clothed
CLAG	clog; bemire (Sc.)
CLAM	bivalve shellfish; to clog **zo**
CLAN	family; coterie; clique; set
CLAP	beak of hawk; applaud; cheer **zo**
CLAW	tear; scratch; lacerate; talon; nail extractor **cr**
CLAY	alumina; fine grained earth; (ceramics) **mn**
CLEF	key **mu**
CLEG	horse-fly
CLEM	to starve
CLEW	clue; trace; brail; truss; aft corner of windsail **nt**
CLIO	Muse of History; molluscs **zo**
CLIP	cut; trim; prune; curtail; embrace
CLIP	fasten; (film); speed; club; (Am. football) **ga**
CLIP	coloured marker (croquet)
CLOD	sod; turf; lump; yokel; rustic
CLOG	obstruct; hamper; trammel
CLOT	curdle; thicken; coagulate **md**
CLOU	the essential point
CLOY	glut; pall; satiate; surfeit
CLUB	cudgel; bludgeon; combine; set
CLUE	clew; hint; guide; ball of string
COAK	a dowel-pin; metal bush
COAL	mineral fuel **mn**
COAT	cover; lay; spread; vesture
COAX	cajole; allure; wheedle
COCA	the cocaine plant (Peru) **bt**

COCH	coach (Spens.)
COCK	rooster; cockerel; chanticleer **zo**
COCK	haycock; chief; arrow-notch; stopcock (water, gas); buddy **bd**
COCO	coconut palm **bt**
CODA	finale **mu**
CODE	digest of laws, rules; cypher; (genetic) **lw, cp**
CODY	trampoline somersault
CO-ED	mixed school
COFF	to buy (Sc.)
COFT	bought (Sc.)
COHO	acronym; coherent oscillator **rd**
COIF	headdress; judge's black cap **lw**
COIL	trouble; bustle; curl; wind
COIN	counterfeit; invent; quoin; wedge
COIR	cordage; coconut fibre **nv**
COIX	a grass; Job's tears **bt**
COKE	slang for cocaine
COLD	icy; polar; gelid; passionless
COLE	kale; cabbages generally **bt**
COLL	fondle; embrace
COLT	young horse; camel or ass **zo**
COLT	gun; young cricketer
COMA	stupor; drowsiness **md**
COMA	tuft of follicles; (comet) **bt**
COMB	cock's comb; crest; wave; (bees)
COMB	combe; coomb; dell; valley
COME	reach; attain; ensue; arrive
COME	as, like; (come prima); as at first **mu**
COMS	malt-dust
COND	to navigate **nt**
CONE	(fir-cone); buoy; navigation mark; doubles badminton **bt, nt**
CONK	the nose
CONN	con; cond; steer; navigate **nt**
CONS	arguments against; cf. pros
CONY	coney; hyrax; rock-rabbit **zo**
COOF	silly coon (Sc.)
COOK	cuckoo-noise; chef; falsify
COOL	calm; collected; allay; indifferent
COOM	soot; axle dirt; coal-dust
COON	nigger; sly fellow; raccoon **zo**
CO-OP	co-operative stores
COOP	hen-coop; cask; cage; confine
COOT	the ankle (Sc.); a water-fowl **zo**
COPE	vie; contend; struggle; cloak; wall ridge; mouldings **rl, bd**
COPT	Egyptian Christian
COPY	model; ape; mimic; transcribe
CORB	} iron coal basket; alms-basket
CORF	
CORD	line; rope; braid; cut wood
CORD	(vocal); (spinal); (umbilical) **pl**
CORE	centre; heart; kernel; (solid) base; (steel) brick) **bd**
CORK	a stopper; bung; bark of cork oak **bt**
CORM	a kind of bulb **bt**
CORN	preserve; an excrescence; grain **bt**
COSE	to make one's self cosy (Sc.)

COSH	to slug; to smite; cosy
COSS	about 1¾ miles (2.8 km) (Ind.) **me**
COST	price; charge; outlay; detriment
COSY	tea-pot cover; cozy; snug
COTE	sheepfold; pass by; outstrip
COUP	exploit; stroke; barter; overturn
COVE	bay; bight; harbour; a fellow; moulding **bd**
COWL	a monk's hood; chimney-pot
COXA	the hip-joint; leg of insect **pl, zo**
COXY	cocksure; bumptious
COZE	to chat; a talk
COZY	cosy; snug; comfortable
CRAB	bitter apple; peevish person **bt**
CRAB	a portable winch; crustacean **zo**
CRAG	steep, ragged, rockface **gl, mo**
CRAM	ram; stuff; glut; study
CRAN	about 750 herrings **me**
CRAW	maw; crop; fowl's stomach
CRAX	S. American bird; curassow **zo**
CREE	to soften grain
CREW	mob; gang; crowd; crowed **nt**
CREX	the white bullace **bt**
CRIB	manger; cot; coop; copy; grillage; (Xmas) **ce, rl**
CRIS	creese; Malay knife; kris
CROP	reap; an ox-hide; whip; craw
CROW	brag; vaunt; crowbar; croak **zo**
CROY	embankment; fish-trap
CRUD	hardening crust of snow (skiing)
CRUP	the buttocks; brittle
CRUT	a dwarf; shaggy oak-bark **bt**
CRUX	the crucial point; mountaineering
CUBE	the third power
CUCA	coca; cocaine shrub **bt**
CUFF	sleeve-end; buffet; slap; a stroke
CUIR	leather
CULL	pick; pluck; choose
CULM	coal-dust; corn or grass stalk **bt**
CULT	ritual; worship; system; ism
CURB	check; restraint; kerb
CURD	coagulated milk
CURE	remedy; antidote; panacea; heal
CURE	care of souls, priest (Fr.) **rl**
CURL	wind; wave; ringlet; ripple; (Am. football); wave-top (surfing) **ga**
CURR	purr; snore like a barn-owl
CURT	abrupt; terse; brief; laconic
CUSK	burbot, an eel-like fish **zo**
CUSP	a kink in a curve
CUSS	a curse; cross-grained fellow
CUTE	shrewd; clever; adroit; chic
CWYM	rounded valley
CYAR	the ear-hole **pl**
CYMA	moulding of a cornice; ogee
CYME	young; shoot; inflorescence **bt**
CYST	water-bag; bladder; growth **pl**
-CYTE	} (cytology = of cells) **cf**
CYTO-	
CZAR	Tsar; Tzar (Rus.)

D

DACE	small river fish; dare; dart **zo**
DADA	anarchic artistic non-style
DADE	hold child by leading-strings
DADO	decorative skirting
DAFF	to play the fool (Sc.)
DAFT	idiotic; absurd; ridiculous
DAGO	a Southern European; lateen, felucca (Naples) (California) **nt**
DAIL	Irish Parliament
DAIS	raised platform; a canopy
DAKS	sports trousers
DALE	vale; valley; dingle
DALI	Brazilian timber-tree **bt**
DALL	incised tile; cow-dung fuel
DALT	a foster-child
DAME	the wife of a baronet
DAMN	doom; condemn; ruin
DAMP	dank; humid; depress; discourage
DANE	great dane dog **zo**
DANG	elegant form of damn
DANK	moist; clammy; humid; damp
DANT	soft or fine coal **pl**
DARE	defy; venture; challenge; presume
DARG	a day's work; a task (Sc.)
DARI	Indian millet **bt**
DARK	ebon; murky; Cimmerian
DARN	to mend by stitching
DART	rush; run; hurl; a missile
DASH	throw; onset; elan; frustrate
DATA	accepted inferences; premises; facts
DATA	available coded information **cp, tc**
DATE	period; epoch; age; a fruit **bt**
DAUB	smear; sully; smirch; plaster
DAUD	dawd; thump; knock; a lump (Sc.)
DAUK	a flaw in timber
DAUR	to dare (Sc.)
DAUW	Burchell's zebra **zo**
DAVY	safety-lamp; affidavit
DAWK	dak; mail carried by relays (Ind.)
DAWM	a fortieth of a rupee (Ind.) **nm**
DAWN	cock-crow; dayspring; gleam
DAZE	stun; amaze; astound; confuse
D-DAY	invasion day
DEAD	exactly; directly; defunct; late
DEAF	heedless; inattentive; (no kernel)
DEAL	pinewood; allot; treat; bargain
DEAN	guild president; church dignitary **rl**
DEAR	beloved; costly; expensive
DEBT	liability; arrears; obligation
DECA-	ten times (decade) **cf**
DECI-	one tenth (decilitre) **cf**
DECK	adorn; array; (cards); floor, sound centre; (surfing) **nt, cp, tc**
DEED	feat; exploit; document **lw**
DEEM	opine; judge; imagine; believe
DEEP	the ocean; profound; recondite
DEER	a solid-horned ungulate **zo**

DEEV	evil spirit (Persia)	
DEFT	dextrous; adroit; handy; skilful	
DEFY	flout; spurn; brave; dare	
DEIL	the devil; scrat; Old Scratch (Sc.)	
DELE	delete; erase; efface; obliterate	
DELF	delftware; pottery; a drain	
DELI	(delicatessen) food shop	ck
DELL	dale; dene; dingle; vale	
DEME	possible interbreeders	bl
DEME	Greek township; tribal division	
DEMO	demonstration (political)	
DEMY	a size of paper	
DENE	dell; dune; sandhill	
DENT	niche; notch; dint; indentation	
DENY	contradict; gainsay; refute	
DERM	the skin	md
DERN	durn; secret; dreadful; gatepost	
DERV	diesel oil	
DESI	(designated) baseball hitter	ga
DESK	writing table; a lectern	
DEVA	a benign spirit (Hindu)	rl
DEVI	the wife of Siva (Hindu)	rl
DEWY	spangled with dew	
DHAI	midwife, wet-nurse (Hindu)	
DHAK	East Indian timber-tree	bt
DHAL	pulse porridge (Ind.)	ck
DHAR	Burmese curved knife	
DHOW	Arab ship; lateen sail	nt
DIAD	divalent atom; social (dyad)	ch
DIAL	(telephone); face; indicator disc	
DICE	sometimes loaded	
DICK	sworn declaration; detective	lw
DIDO	antic; caper; queen of Carthage	
DIEB	North African jackal	zo
DIED	perished; expired; departed	
DIES	(dies non); (screw-taps)	to
DIET	assembly; viands; sustenance	
DIGS	lodgings	
DIKA	West African mango	bt
DIKE	ditch; rine; rhine; mortarless wall	
DILL	medicinal herb; condiment	bt, md, ck
DIME	a ten-cent piece (USA)	nm
DINE	give a dinner to; eat	
DING	ring; urge; enforce; dash; sea-damage to surfboard	
DINK	braw; neat; trim (Sc.); hit (tennis) (volleyball)	ga
DINT	dent; power; blow; stroke	
DIOL	dihydric alcohol	ch
DIRE	awful; disastrous; calamitous	
DIRK	dagger; poniard (Sc.); dark (obs.)	
DIRL	to tingle; vibrate (Sc.)	
DIRT	mud; mire; dust; muck; grime; soil	
DISA	S. African orchid	bt
DISC	disk; record; flat round plate; recording plate (gramophone)	cp, tc
DISH	a culinary conception; frustrate	
DISK	disc; any flat round growth; magnetic computer storage device	bt, cp
DISS	an Algerian grass	bt
DIVA	a prima donna	mu
DIVE	plunge; descend; a gambling hell	
DOAB	alluvial land (India)	
DOAT }	admire; defect, timber	
DOTE }		
DOCK	curtail; lessen; deduct; a weed	bt
DOCK	basin for shipping; (law court)	nv, lw
DODD	cut off; clip; poll; a mound	
DODO	extinct bird (Mauritius)	zo
DOER	agent; executive; performer	
DOFF	daff; take off; divest	
DOGE	Venetian magistrate	
DOHL	pulse; (dried peas)	bt
DOIT	Dutch or Scotch half-farthing	nm
DOJO	martial arts centre	
DOKE	a dint; a dimple	
DOLE	an allowance; dispense; pain; grief	
DOLL	to dress up; a toy	
DOLT	dunce; booby; dullard	
DOME	a cupola; round roof; similar rock formation	gl
DONE	ended; finished; transacted	
DONG	Vietnamese monetary unit	nm
DON'T	prelude to a prohibition	
DOOB	an Indian grass	bt
DOOD	camel or dromedary	zo
DOOK	a bung; a bathe (Sc.)	
DOOL	dole; gloom; sorrow (Sc.)	
DOOM	kismet; condemn; last judgment.	
DOOR	portal; entrance; access; egress	
DOPA	source of adrenalin	ch
DOPE	drug; narcotic; doctor; varnish	
DOPO	after(wards)	mu
DORA	Defence of the Realm Act	
DORN	the thorn-back skate	zo
DORP	burg; town; village	
DORR	the dor-beetle	zo
DORY	golden coloured fish; skiff; dinghy	zo, nt
DOSE	draught; drench; physic	
DOSS	a shake-down; a hassock	
DOST	thou doest	
DOTE	love tenderly; talk trash; (infatuation)	
DOTH	a poetical 'do'	
DOTS	grains, insulating material	
DOTY	decayed; half-rotten	
DOUC	a highly coloured monkey	zo
DOUM	the doom-palm	bt
DOUP	weaving half-heald	tx
DOUR	stern; grim; relentless; obstinate	
DOUT	extinguish	
DOUX	sweet (Fr.); also billet doux love notes	mu
DOVE	emblem of peace	zo
DOWD	woman's nightcap; scruffy	
DOWF	dull; heavy; spiritless (Sc.)	
DOWN	fluff; pasture; hill; prone	
DOXY	loose woman; moll	
DOZE	nap; slumber; forty winks	

DOZY }	drowsy; sleepy; dreamy;	
DOSY }	date; timber, decay	
DRAB	khaki colour; a cloth; a trull	
DRAD	dread; dreaded (Spens.)	
DRAG	(billiards); (snooker); (coaching); (net)	ga
DRAG	a hunt; haul; pull; steel plate smoother; linger	bd
DRAG	uneven painting; men got up as women	
DRAM	drachm; a tot of spirits	me
DRAT	a mild expletive	
DRAW	limn; allure; attract; (chimney); lottery; tie; weighted stone (curling); sails	ga, nt
DRAY	strong cart for heavy goods	
DREE	endure; bear; suffer (Sc.)	
DREW	drafted; depicted; extracted	
DREY	a squirrel's nest	zo
DRIB	purloin small pieces; inveigle	
DRIP	ooze; dribble; trickle; percolate; cornice projection	ar
DROP	globule; bead; sink; quit; lower newel stair-post projection; overtake; discontinue	ar
DROW	trow; troll; cave elf (Shetland)	
DRUB	maul; thrash; beat; pound	
DRUG	drudge; a narcotic	md
DRUM	ridge of hills; tambour	mu
DRUM	base of dome; recording centre	cp
DUAD	union of two	
DUAL	twofold	
DUAN	a division of a poem; a canto	
DUCE	leader, dictator (It.)	
DUCK	cloth; dive; dip; underplay; bird; zero score (cricket)	zo, ga
DUCT	tube; canal; pipe; conduit	
DUDE	a dandy; fop; nut	
DUDS	clothing; rags; useless ones	
DUEL	single combat	
DUET	composition for two voices	mu
DUFF	low-calory fine-grain coal	mn
DUFF	muff; a pudding; refurbish; useless	
DUKE	(strawberry leaves); peer	
DUKW	amphibious army vehicle	
DULE	woe (Sc.)	
DULL	benumb; blunt; abate; stolid	
DULY	properly; regularly; exactly	
DUMA	Russian Parliament (Tsarist)	
DUMB	mute; inarticulate; soundless; lighter	nt
DUMP	(bawling); (drag racing); (trotting); (ice hockey); (Am. football)	ga
DUMP	unload; rubbish-heap; storage program; slovenly place	
DUNE	dene; sandy waste	
DUNG	manure; compost; soil	
DUNK	dipping bread into soup, etc.	ck
DUNT	staggering affection; heavy blow	
DUPE	gull; delude; outwit; hoodwink	

DURA	an Indian grass	bt
DURE	endure; harden; severe	
DURN	dern; a door-post	
DUSE	deuce; demon; evil spirit	
DUSH	to throw down (Sc.)	
DUSK	eventide; twilight; eve	
DUST	pulverulence; a disturbance	
DUTY	obligation; excise; tariff	
DWAM	swoon; qualm; faint (Sc.)	
DYAD	cf. monad; 2-person group	ch
DYAK	a native of Borneo	
DYED	stained; tinted; tinged	
DYER	dye-worker	
DYKE	dike; ditch; fosse; dry walling (Sc.); lesbian	bd
DYNE	the unit of force	me

E

EACH	both; every one	
EARL }	lord; peer	
JARL }		
EARN	win; gain; merit; acquire	
EASE	allay; still; assuage; relief	
EAST	a cardinal point	
EASY	facile; affluent; flowing	
EAVE	roof overhang; (eaves' dropping)	ar
EBON	of ebony; black	
ECAD	habitat-adapted plant form	bt
ECHE	to eke out; augment (Sc.)	
ECHO	repeat; resound; reverberate	
ECHO	delayed reflected sound	tc
ECRU	pale yellowish brown	
ECTO-	external	cf
EDAM	spherical Dutch cheese	
EDDA	Scandinavian saga	
EDDY	ripple; swirl; vortex	
EDEN	garden of delight	
EDGE	brink; fringe; zest; sharpness	
EDGY	on edge; nervous	
EDIT	revise; annotate; arrange data	cp
EGAD	a refined expletive	
EGAL	equal (Shak.)	
EGER	eagre; bore; tidal wave	
EGIS	aegis; a shield	
EIGH	exclamation of surprise	
EILD	dry; not giving milk (Sc.)	
EIRE	Republic of Ireland	
EJOO	the sago palm	bt
EKED	existed on small pittance	
ELAN	dash; impetuosity; vivacity	
ELIA	Charles Lamb	
ELMO	Elmo's fire; electrical flame	
ELMY	abounding with elms	bt
ELSE	other; otherwise; besides	
ELUL	12th month of the Jewish year	
EMIR	amir; Eastern title	
EMIT	vent; eject; exhale; discharge	
EMYS	terrapin genus	zo

ENDO-	internal (Gr.)	cf
ENEW	drive back; pursue (obs.)	
ENOW	enough; just now; soon (Sc.)	
ENSA	forces entertainment organisation	
ENTE	heraldic engraftment	
ENTO-	internal (Gr.)	cf
ENVY	ill-will; malice; covet; grudge	
EOAN	dawning; eastern	
EPEE	foil; rapier (Fr.)	
EPHA	ephah; Hebrew bushel	me
EPIC	heroic; lofty; a rhapsody	
EPOS	epic poem; Homeric narrative	
ERGO	therefore	
ERGO-	of work (Gr.)	cf
ERIC	eriach; blood-money (Irish Law)	
ERIN	the Green Isle	
ERNE	the sea-eagle	zo
EROS	God of Love; Cupid	
ERSE	the Gaelic language	
ERSH	stubble	bt
ERST	formerly; whilom	
ESOX	the pike	zo
ESPY	discover; observe; perceive; notice	
ESSE	mere existence	
ETCH	engrave; draw; cropped ground	
ETEM	chemical fungicide	ch
ETNA	volcano (Sicily)	
ETON	a returnable note	
ETUI	needle case; container; etwee	
EUGE	bravo; well done	
EUGH	obsolete form of yew	bt
EVEN	level; uniform; steady; impartial	
EVER	aye; always; eternally	
EVET	eft; newt; ewft	zo
EVIL	harm; malice; baneful; malign	
EVOE	a Bacchanalian cry	
EWER	pitcher; jug with handle	
EWFT	eft; newt; evet (obs.)	zo
EWRY	scullery; place of ewers, pots	
EXAM	examination	
EXES	expenses	
EXIT	way out; a stage departure	
EXON	an officer; Yeoman of the Guard	
EXPO	exposition; exhibition	
EXUL	an exile (Spens.)	
EYAS	nyas; young hawk	zo
EYED	observed; watched; espied	
EYER	a watcher	
EYES	visual organs; discs on bowls	
EYNE	eyes (Sc.)	
EYOT	ait; river or lake islet	
EYRA	S. American cat	zo
EYRE	journey; circuit; court	lw
EYRY	eyrie; ayry; eagle's nest	zo

F

FAAM	Indian orchid	bt
FAAP	the garfish	zo

FABA	broad Windsor bean; purée	bt, ck
FACE	defy; dare; surface; confront; dial; forward side of stick; wave; (hockey); (surfing)	ga
FACT	incident; actuality; occurrence	
FACY	impudent	
FADE	wither; dwindle; insipid; ball off course; loose colour	
FADO	lament of the heart (Port.)	mu
FAEX	dregs	
FAIK	to abate; to excuse (Sc.)	
FAIL	wane; flag; decline; neglect	
FAIN	willingly; gladly; readily	
FAIR	market; just; equitable; blond	
FAIX	by my faith	
FAJA	coloured sash (pelota)	ga
FAKE	a cable coil; counterfeit; pretence	ʃ
FALA	old madrigal	mu
FALL	autumn; the Fall; drop; cascade; part of halyard sail	nt
FALX	a membrane	md
FAMA	the goddess of rumour	
FAME	renown; repute; lustre; celebrity	
FANE	vane; temple; church	rl
FANG	tooth; claw; talon	
FANK	sheepfold (Sc.)	
FARD	face-paint	
FARE	manage; victuals; passenger	
FARL	Scottish oatcake	ck
FARM	ferm; till; cultivate; lease	
FARO	card game; sour beer	ck
FART	puff of wind; flatus	
FASH	to bother; trouble; annoy (Sc.)	
FAST	firm; rapid; fleet; dissolute; stand-fast; order to desist (archery)	
FATA	Morgana; a mirage; perfect knight	
FATE	kismet; doom; destiny; lot	
FAUN	woodland deity; Pan	
FAUX	pas; offensive false step	
FAVA	faba; bean puree	ck
FAWN	cringe; a colour; fallow-deer	zo
FAZE	disconcert; worry	
FEAL	faithful; constant; loyal	
FEAR	awe; alarm; dread; anxiety	
FEAT	exploit; deed; trick	
FECK	efficacy; strength (Sc.)	
FEED	cater; sustain; provender	
FEED	thickening paint; (-pipe); consume; (cattle-)	
FEEL	sense; touch; experience	
FEER	} companion	
FERE	}	
FEET	paws, hoofs	
FELL	hew; cut; tumbled; barren hill	
FELL	cruel; deadly; spirited; skin	
FELO	de se; suicide	lw
FELT	fabric; sensed; handled; touched	
FEME	a woman	
FEND	parry; ward off; make shift	
FEOD	feud; fief (obs.)	

FERM	a farm; abode; lodging (Spens.)		
FERN	vascular cryptogamous plant	bt	
FESS	fesse; broad heraldic band	hd	
FETE	gala; festival; carnival; holiday		
FEUD	clan warfare; strife; a fief		
FIAR	freeholder, not a life-renter	lw	
FIAT	decree; command; ukase		
FICO	a snap of the fingers; a fig	bt	
FIEF	land held on feudal tenure	lw	
FIFE	a variety of flute	mu	
FIKE	fidget; trivial detail		
FIKY	fussy (Sc.)		
FILE	list; dossier; smoothing tool; data set to	cp	
FILE	arrange in order; available stored information	tc	
FILL	sate; glut; replenish; earthwork	bd	
FILM	thin skin; scum; thread; pellicle		
FIND	discover; discovery; decide		
FINE	forfeit; delicate; tenuous; exact; end (It.)	mu	
FINN	a Finlander		
FINS	stabilisers on ships, aircraft (surfing)		
FIRE	discharge; kindle; ignite; blaze		
FIRK	whip; beat; rouse (Sc.)		
FIRM	fast; tight; compact; a company		
FIRN	neve; granular glacier snow		
FISC	state treasury; revenue; purse		
FISH	to angle; search by sweeping	zo	
FISK	to frisk; to move briskly (obs.)		
FIST	neif; the clenched hand; to punch		
FIST	calligraphy		
FITT	fitte; fytte; song (obs.)		
FITZ	son of		
FIVE	the pentad		
FIZZ	hiss; champagne		
FLAG	banner; ensign; to signal	nt	
FLAG	droop; weary; a stone; a plant	bt	
FLAK	anti-aircraft gunfire (German)		
FLAM	whim; fancy; falsehood; impose		
FLAM	2 note side drum flourish	mu	
FLAN	open tart; savoury quiche	ck	
FLAP	flop; wave; vibrate; cover; pastry	ck	
FLAT	smooth; level; insipid; residence		
FLAT	level; (platform); sandbar; lowered pitch	mu	
FLAW	blemish; defect; crevice; a gust		
FLAX	linum; the linen plant	bt	
FLAY	skin; excoriate; strip; criticise		
FLEA	pulex irritans	zo	
FLED	ran; bolted; retreated		
FLEE	escape; abscond; decamp		
FLEW	fled; the chap of a hound		
FLEX	to bend; an electric lead		
FLEY	flay; frighten; cause to fly		
FLIP	a joy ride; (egg-flip)		
FLIT	fly; dart; flicker; migrate		
FLIX	fur; beaver-down	zo	
FLOC	accumulation of solids in liquid		
FLOE	an icefield		
FLOG	lash; thrash; scourge; whip		
FLOP	flap; a failure; a fiasco; high jump		
FLOT	stratified ore		
FLOW	run; emanate; abound; circulate		
FLUE	smoke pipe; light down; fluff		
FLUX	flow; mutation; change; (soldering)		
FOAL	colt or filly	zo	
FOAM	spume; froth; spray; rage; lightweight concrete	bd	
FOHN	warm mountain wind (N. Alpine)		
FOIE	liver (Fr.)		
FOIL	track of game; baffle; outwit; (table tennis)	ga	
FOIL	thin metal; fencing rapier	ga	
FOIN	a thrust with spear or sword		
FOLD	lap; wrap; furl; double; envelop; bend in rock strata; (sheep)	gl	
FOLK	kindred; relations; people		
FOND	loving; attached; archive unit	pr	
FONE	foes (Spens.)		
FONT	fount; source; spring; type	rl, pr	
FOOD	viands; victuals; rations		
FOOL	gull; beguile; hoodwink; ninny		
FOOT	pay; discharge; settle; walking base of body; lower edge; measure of pitch	pl, me, mu	
FORD	wade; a river crossing		
FORE	a warning cry at golf		
FORK	branch; divide; divaricate		
FORM	bench; formula; mould; fashion		
FORM	bed of hare; mode; ceremony		
FORS	force; fortitude; fortune (Ruskin)		
FORT	keep; citadel; fastness		
FOSS	ditch or moat		
FOUD	magistrate or bailiff (Orkney)		
FOUL	noisome; ribald; unfair; sullied		
FOUL	infringement of rules in games, sports	ga	
FOUR	4; cricket boundary worth four runs score; (petit)	ga, ck	
FOWL	poultry	zo	
FOXY	sly; wily; sour; a colour		
FOZY	spongy (Sc.)		
FRAB	to worry		
FRAP	to bind; to strike		
FRAU	a German married woman		
FRAY	rub; brush; quarrel; skirmish		
FREE	rid; loose; clear; informal; wind from the beam or abaft; available; unmarked player (netball)	nv	
FRET	fray; fume; chafe; abrade; grieve		
FRET	(saw); (work); geometrical ornament; wood slats for fingers on guitar-like instruments	cr, mu	
FRIT	glass material; a wheat-fly	zo	
FRIZ	frizz; to curl; to crisp		
FROE	woodcutter's cleaver	to	
FROG	a batrachian; horse's foot; rail crossings	zo, rw	

72

FROG	cloak or coat button or tassel; brick indentation	**bd**	
FROM	preposition of source		
FROW	tool for lathe splitting	**to**	
FROW	a loose woman; a slut		
FUAR	feuar; landholder (Sc.)		
FUEL	combustibles		
FUFF	puff; a burst of anger (Sc.)		
FUGA			
FUGE }	contrapuntal composition	**mu**	
FUGUE			
FUGH	exclamation of abhorrence		
FULL	replete; copious; ample; thicken		
FUME	smoke; vapour; exhalation; reek		
FUMY	vaporous; fumous; fussy		
FUND	reserve; store; supply; capital		
FUNG	mythical Chinese pheasant	**zo**	
FUNK	terror; fear; shirk; touchwood		
FUOR	decayed-rafter strengthener	**cr**	
FURL	fold; roll; stow; wrap		
FURY	frenzy; rage; turbulence; shrew		
FUSE }	melt; liquefy; blend;		
FUZE }	quickmatch; a timing device		
FUSS	ado; stir; fume; fidget; fret		
FUST	shaft of column; musty smell		
FUZZ	fluff; light particles; police		
FYKE	bagnet for fishing		
FYRD	pre-Conquest Saxon military array		

G

GABY	a simpleton; nitwit		
GADE	gaid; gad; goad; graver	**to**	
GAEL	Celtic		
GAFF	low theatre; a hook; a spar	**nt**	
GAGE	a pledge; stake; wager; plum	**bt**	
GAID	gade; gad; spike on gauntlet	**to**	
GAIN	get; win; acquire; profit		
GAIN	increase of message signal power; mortise; notch	**tc, cr**	
GAIR	gore (Sc.)		
GAIT	walk; bearing; step; pace		
GAIT	pasturage; charge; sheaf of corn	**bt**	
GALA	festival; festivity; pomp; show		
GALE	high wind; rent; a bog plant	**bt**	
GALL	vex; torment; provoke; rancour		
GALL	bile; malignity; glass scum		
GALT	gault; clay; marl; brick-earth		
GAMB	leg; shank		
GAME	lame; plucky; dauntless; pastime		
GAMO-	marital, sexual union	**cf**	
GAMP	an umbrella		
GAMY	high in flavour		
GANG	crew; band; horde; coterie	**hd**	
GANT	to yawn (Sc.); glove, basket (pelota)		
GAOL	jail; prison; objective		
GAPE	stare; to yawn		
GARB	dress; costume; heraldic sheaf		
GARE	greedy (Sc.); beware; look out		

GARI	Indian carriage		
GASH	slash; score; slit; wound		
GASP	pant; puff		
GAST	to terrify (Shak.)		
GATA	tropical Atlantic shark	**zo**	
GATE	(slalom); (canoeing); (skiing); (water skiing)	**ga**	
GATE	entrance; barrier; attendance; ban		
GATE	goal; portal; electrical switch	**ga, cp**	
GATE	(flood-); (valve); (lock)		
GAUB	an Indian tree; guy-rope	**bt, nt**	
GAUD	a gewgaw; showy ornament; gawd		
GAUL	old France; hollow in a finishing coat	**pt**	
GAUM	to smear; to daub		
GAUN	going (Sc.)		
GAUP	gawp; gape		
GAUR	a wild Indian ox	**zo**	
GAVE	presented; granted; yielded		
GAWD	gaud; a piece of finery		
GAWK	gowk; simpleton; a cuckoo	**zo**	
GAWN	small tub; a ladle		
GAZE	stare; view; regard; contemplate		
GEAL	to congeal; pert. to earth		
GEAN	wild cherry	**bt**	
GEAR	tackle; harness; dress; mechanism		
GEAT	hole for metal casting		
GECK	dupe; mock; simpleton		
GEDD	the pike	**zo**	
GEED	went faster		
GEEZ	archaic Semitic dialect		
GEGG	a hoax; a trick (Sc.)		
GELD	gold; tribute; castrate; spay		
GELT	geld; gilt; money; emasculated		
GENA	the cheek	**md**	
GENE	heredity factor	**md**	
GENS	Roman class; patrineal kin, sib		
GENT	a would-be gentleman		
GENU	nerve-tract bend		
-GENY	of origin; cause; generation	**cf, bl**	
GERM	ovule; nucleus; a bacillus	**md**	
GEST	an exploit; feat; bearing		
GEUM	avens and herb-bennet genus	**bt**	
GHAT	Indian mountain; landing-stair		
GHEE	Indian oil or butter		
GIBE	jibe; sneer; deride; taunt	**nt**	
GIFT	boon; bounty; gratuity; faculty		
GIGA	one thousand million 10^9; jig (It.), folkloric dance form	**ma, mu**	
GIGO	garbage in, garbage out; data unreliability	**cp**	
GILD	guild; trade's union; add lustre		
GILL	a flirt; a ravine; ground ivy; mountain stream	**bt, go**	
GILL	breathing organ; $\frac{1}{4}$ pint	**zo, me**	
GILT	gilded; aureate; a young sow	**zo**	
GIMP	smart; spruce; a trimming		
GING	gang or company		
GINN	jinn; djinn; demon; spirit		
GIRD	bind; reproach; gibe; spasm		

GIRL	young roe-buck; young woman	zo
GIRN	grin; snarl (Sc.)	
GIRO	payment transfer system	
GIRR	a hoop (Sc.)	
GIRT	tightly moored; bound; girth	nt
GIRT	surround rail; beam	cr
GIST	essential point; pith	
GITE	bed or an abode (Fr.); (mountaineering)	ga
GIVE	yield; confer; grant; present	
GIZZ	phiz; face (Sc.)	
GLAD	(eye); joyous; elated; delectable	
GLEE	hilarity; merriment; mirth	
GLEE	squint; part song	mu
GLEG	clever; apt; sharp (Sc.)	
GLEN	vale; dale; dell; dingle; valley	
GLEY	to squint; to glance (Sc.)	
GLIA	supportive cells (neuroglia)	bl
GLIB	voluble; fluent; ready; facile	
GLIM	a light; a glimmer	
GLOW	fervour; shine; burn; gleam	
GLUE	cement; an adhesive	
GLUM	grum; crestfallen; downcast	
GLUT	surfeit; surplus; cloy; satiate	
G-MAN	gun-man; bandit	
GNAR	knar; yarr; snarl	
GNAT	insect	zo
GNAW	bite; corrode; erode; champ	
GOAD	spur; rouse; incite; an ankus	
GOAF	worked-out mine; slag	
GOAL	end; aim; ambition; object; score-portal	ga
GOAN	Indian; E. African Indian	
GOAT	Capricornus; horned animal	zo
GOBO	sound-absorbing panel	cn
GO-BY	evasion	
GOBY	fish having nests of seaweed	zo
GODS	lofty theatrical supporters	
GOEL	an avenger of blood (Heb.)	
GOER	a mover; a go-between	
GOLA	a cyma; cyme; a moulding	
GOLD	or; money wealth; bull at archery	
GOLF	goff; gowf; for 9, 18 or 19 holes	ga
GOME	black cart-grease	
GONA-	} of genitals, offspring, seed	
GONO-		
GOND	native Indian tribe	
GONE	hied; wended; fared; left; parted	
GONE	group of 4 nuclei or cells	cy
GONG	prelude to a meal; percussion instrument, oriental	mu
GOOD	weal; virtuous; upright; proper	
GOOF	simpleton; silly cuckoo	
GOOR	coarse sugar from the date-palm	
GORE	clotted blood; wedge of cloth	
GORM	sheen; shine of varnish	
GORY	sanguinary; ensanguined	
GOSH	an ejaculation	
GOTH	Teutonic barbarian	

GOUL	} howl; yowl	
GOWL		
GOUM	native Algerian soldier (Fr.)	
GOUT	a drop; taste; relish	
GOUT	paroxysmal form of arthritis	md
GOWD	gold (Sc.)	
GOWF	golf; goff	
GOWK	gouk; simpleton; oaf; cuckoo	zo
GOWN	robe; garment	
GRAB	snatch; seize; grip; a card game	
GRAB	two-masted vessel (Malabar)	nt
GRAF	German title; a count	
GRAM	misery; chick pea; weight	bt, me
-GRAM	written; drawn; result	cf
GRAY	grey; ash-coloured	
GREE	a step; degree; goodwill	
GREW	thrived; raised; progressed	
GREY	gray; a neutral tint	
GRID	frame; network; box layout of lines	el
GRIG	sand-eel; grasshopper; cricket	zo
GRIM	stern; dire; hideous; grisly	
GRIN	girn; smirk; a snare	
GRIP	clutch; handbag; small ditch	
GRIT	endurance; courage; quartz-rock (sand)	gl
GROG	rum and water	
GROS	silken fabric	
GROT	a grotto	
GROW	wax; develop; expand; raise	
GRUB	caterpillar; food; (cricket); root out	zo
GRUM	glum; surly; morose; guttural	
GUAG	space left by mineral extraction	mn
GUAN	Brazilian game bird	zo
GUDE	good (Sc.)	
GUFA	Tigris ferry boat	nt
GUHR	loose earth found in rocks	mn
GUIB	the harnessed antelope	zo
GULF	chasm; abyss; bight; bay	
GULL	beguile; hoax; deceive; sea-bird	zo
GULP	as many bytes as digits; swallow; choke	cp
GULY	coloured red in heraldry	hd
GUNK	semi-solid material from synthesis	
GURU	Hindu teacher	
GUSH	rush; spout; stream; an outburst	
GUST	squall; burst of passion; relish; taste unit	pc
GYAL	gayal; E. Indian ox	zo
GYBE	gibe; sneer	nt
GYLE	to ferment; a brew	
GYNE	ant	zo
GYNE-	} of females	cf
GYNO-		
-GYNY		
GYRA	embroidered border	
GYRE	a circular motion	
GYRO	a gyroscope	
GYTE	crazy; mad; a child (Sc.)	
GYVE	fetter; shackle; handcuff; bond	

H

HAAF	deep-sea fishing ground (Shetland)
HAAK	sailing lighter (North sea)
HAAR	harr; a cold sea mist
HACK	notch; gash; kick; chopper **to**
HACK	literary drudge; sorry; jade (horse) **zo**
HACK	mattock; blow; foothold (curling) **ga**
HADE	slope of mineral vein or fault; hole in the ice
HADJ	} a pilgrimage to Mecca
HAJJ	
HAEM	iron pigment in haemoglobin **md**
HAET	} a whit (Sc.)
HAIT	
HAFF	river mouth, lagoon (Ger.)
HAFT	heft; hilt; handle; to haggle
HA-HA	haw-haw; sunken fence; laughter
HAIK	hyke; haick; an Arab wrap
HAIL	health; greeting; frozen rain
HAIN	save; preserve; spare (Sc.)
HAIR	jot; iota; quality; character
HAKA	native dance (New Zealand)
HAKE	a pot-hook; loiter; sea fish **zo**
HALD	hold (Sc.)
HALE	haul; drag; healthy; robust
HALF	a moiety; a half-back; draw (tie); golf; term (netball) **ga**
HALL	manor house; a college; aula **ar**
HALM	} corn-stalk; stubble
HAUM	
HAULM	
HALO	a saintly aura; solar, lunar ring of light **rl, as**
HALT	to stop; to limp; crippled; waver
HAME	bar for trace attachment
HAND	manual labour; assistance
HAND	proffer; (cards); 4 in (horses); serve (badminton) **me**
HANG	suspend; hover; slope; drift; long jump technique
HANK	skein; coil; hoop; ring **nt**
HARD	firm; compact; arduous
HARE	to speed; puss **zo**
HARK	hear; listen; attend (nostalgia)
HARL	fibres of flax; troll for fish; rough cast (Sc.) **bt**
HARM	hurt; scathe; wrong; injury
HARN	coarse linen fabric (Sc.) **tx**
HARO	an appeal (Channel Islands) **lw**
HARP	reiterate; lyre, plucked instrument **mu**
HARR	haar; a storm; an eagre
HART	male red-deer **zo**
HASH	chop; mangle; mince; a jumble; mess-up; unwanted data **ck, cp**
HASP	clasp or fastening; staple; clip **jn**
HAST	(thou) havest
HATE	abhor; loathe; enmity; odium
HATH	has

HAUL	tug; pull; drag; draw; heave
HAUM	} stem of crop, stubble **bt, ag**
HALM	
HAULM	
HAVE	own; possess; hold; contain
HAWK	rapacious bird or person **zo**
HAWK	intentional cough; to peddle
HAWK	plasterer's mortar board **to**
HAWM	to lounge about
HAZE	fog; mist; pall; miasma; to bully
HAZY	vague; obscure; indistinct; murky
HEAD	top; chief; steer; (bowls); (beer)
HEAD	acme; (black-); electromagnetic **cp, tc**
HEAL	cure; remedy; assuage; compose
HEAP	pile; mound; amass; collect; jack and live bowls
HEAR	heed; hark; try judicially **lw**
HEAT	rage; passion; ardour; excite; qualifying round in sports; to warm **ga**
HEBE	an Olympian cup-bearer
HECK	fish-weir; a rack; river bend
HEED	mind; mark; obey; regard; caution
HEEL	submit; low fellow; twerp; underfoot; spur **jn**
HEFT	hilt; handle; heaved
HEIR	inheritor; offspring
HELD	grasped; adhered; restrained
HELE	to conceal; to hide (obs.)
HELL	Hades, Gehenna; gambling house
HELM	tiller; steering gear; steer **nt**
HELM	helmet; crown; top; guide; direct
HELP	aid; abet; back; second; relieve
HEMA-	} of blood (Gr.) **cf, pl**
HEMO-	
HEMP	rope-fibre; a plant **bt**
HEND	to seize; to apprehend (obs.)
HERA	(Juno), wife of Zeus
HERB	a simple; an annual plant **bt**
HERD	drove; rabble; tend; collect
HERE	at this place
HERL	harl; barb of feather
HERM	(Hermes') head or bust on decorative pillar **ar, rl**
HERN	heron (obs.) **zo**
HERO	a priestess of Aphrodite
HERR	German gent
HERS	} of her
HERN	
HEST	behest; command (Shak.)
HEWN	cut; felled; chiselled
HICK	bucolic; country cousin (USA)
HIDE	about 100 acres (41 hectares) **me**
HIDE	a skin; pelt; secrete; cache
HIED	set off
HI-FI	high-fidelity sound
HIGH	eminent; lofty; arrogant; shrill; pressure; drug-induced state
HIKE	to carry; to ramble; long distance walk; (price rise) (Am. football)

HILA	the eyes of beans	bt
HILL	to earth up plants; midget mountain; (mole-)	bt, go
HILT	haft; heft; handle	
HIND	a rustic; backward; a deer	zo
HINK	a reaping hook	to
HINT	imply; insinuate; innuendo	
HIRE	rent; charter; lease; salary	
HISK	to breathe with difficulty	
HISS	also HISH and HIZZ	
HIST!	hush!	
HIVE	to collect; store up; a skep	
HOAR	hoary; rime; venerable	
HOAX	gammon; spoof; dupe; delude	
HOBO	a tramp; a vagrant (USA)	
HOCK	Rhenish wine; a joint; the hough	
HOED	weeded	
HOER	manipulator of a hoe	
HOGG	hog; a two-year old sheep	zo
HOIK	hike; an upward turn	
HOIT	to leap; to caper	
HOLD	grasp; contain; keep; cargo space; order a hall	cp, nt
HOLE	cavity; lair; burrow; pierce; (golf)	
HOLE	orifice; punched-card system	cp
HOLM	evergreen oak; holly	
HOLM	flat land; an islet (Scand.)	bt
HOLT	woodland; a copse; a burrow	
HOLY	sanctified; consecrated; divine	
HOME	habitat; seat; institution; residence	
HOMO-	of same; alike; (homosexual) (Gr.)	cf
HOMY	homelike	
HONE	to pine; to moan; a whetstone	
HONG	Chinese factory	
HONK	to hoot	
HOOD	cowl; cover; to blind	
HOOF	horse's foot; to walk	
HOOK	promontory; snare; sickle	zo
HOOK	to bend; to steal; seize; connect; strike; curved device; to hit (boxing) (bowls) (baseball) (rugby) (football) (cricket); (rug making); hold	to
HOOP	a whoop; a band; a toy; (baseball)	
HOOP	the basket and its rim (basketball)	
HOOT	honk; boo; decry; execrate	
HOPE	expect; anticipate; confidence	
HOPS	beer flavouring	bt
HORN	cornucopia; drinking cup; wind instrument; antler; phallus; pyramidal mountain peak	go, pl, zo, mu
HORS	out of; beyond (hors-de-combat)	
HOSE	stockings; hosiery; to sprinkle	
HOSH	courtyard of Arab house	
HOST	multitude; consecrated water	
HOUR	always passing	
HOVA	a Malagasi; from Madagascar	
HOVE	to heave; to raise; to loiter	
HOWE	how; hollow; glen; dell (Sc.)	
HOWK	dig; burrow; extract (Sc.)	

HOWL	gowl; yowl; wail; yell; squall	
HOYA	genus of climbing plants	
HUAN	jade Chinese ritual object	rl
HUCK	a German trout	zo
HUED	coloured; tinted	
HUEL	a wheal; a Cornish mine	
HUER	fish-scout watching for shoals	
HUFF	swell; bluster; anger; (draughts)	
HUGE	vast; colossal; gigantic; immense	
HUIA	New Zealand starling	zo
HULK	old ship used as store, prison, etc.	nt
HULL	husk; pod; to pierce; ship	bt, nt
HUMP	hillock; to carry; depression	
HUNG	dangled; draped; hovered	pc
HUNK	chunk; lump; large slice	
HUNT	pursue; hound; search; chase	
HURL	cast; pitch; fling; whirl	
HURT	pain; offend; mar; an injury	
HUSH	quiet; calm; still; silence	
HUSK	hull; rind; coating	
HUSO	the great sturgeon	bt
HUTU	native of Rwanda (Africa)	zo
HWAN	(Korea)	
HWYC	emotional fervour; intonation (Welsh)	nm
HYKE	haik; loose Arab garment	
HYMN	panegyric; paean; song of praise	mu
HYPE	a wrestling throw	
HYPO	diluted; syringe (sl.); injection	ch, md
HYPO-	of lesser, smaller (Gr.)	cf

I

IBEX	chamois; mountain wild goat	zo
IBID	in the same place (Lat.)	
IBIS	a wading bird, sacred in Egypt	zo
ICED	frozen; congealed	
ICON	} sacred picture; image	rl
IKON		
IDEA	notion; fantasy; conceit; insight; scheme; plan; vision	
IDEM	the same	lw
IDEO-	of mental image; idea	cf
IDES	Roman date	
IDIO-	personal; self produced; distinct	cf
IDLE	inert; lazy; inactive; unused	
IDLY	indolently	
IDOL	hero; pet; image	
IDYL	idyll; pastoral poem	
IGEL	squat tumbler glass (Ger.)	
IKAT	pattern dye and weave technique (Indonesia)	wv
ILEX	evergreen oak	bt
ILKA	each (Sc.)	
IMAM	Mohammedan priest	rl
IMAN	Moslem faith	rl
IMPI	Zulu regiment	
INBY	inbye; inwards (Sc.)	
INCA	ancient king or prince of Peru	
INCA	an Indian of Peru	

INCH	creep forward; isle (Sc.)	**me**
INFO	information (centre)	
INGO	include; entry; jamb of window; fireplace (Sc.)	**ar**
INKY	black; blotted	
INLY	inward; secret	
INRO	Japanese comfit box	
INTO	preposition of direction	
IOTA	a jot; tittle; whit; particle	
IPSA-	} one's own, or of self (Gr.)	**cf**
IPSO-		
IRIS	Rainbow Goddess, messenger of Zeus; eye membrane	**pl**
IRON	golf club; metal; to smoothe	**mn**
IRON	gyve, fetter; strength	
ISCA	excrescence on oak or hazel	**bt**
ISIS	Moon Goddess; mother of Horus	
ISLE	ait; eyot; islet	
ITCH	constant teasing desire	**md**
ITEM	detail; entry; innuendo	
ITER	canal or duct	**zo**
ITIS	undiagnosed disease	**md**
IWAN	Islamic vaulted hall	**ar**
IWIS	ywis; certainly	
IXIA	South African iridaceous plants	**bt**
IZBA	log hut (Rus.)	

J

JACA	the bread-fruit tree	**bt**
JACK	(cards); flag; lifter (car); pike	**zo, nt**
JACK	appliance; sailor; (bowls); plug	**nt, cp**
JACK	harpsichord plucking device	**mu**
JADE	sorry nag; mean woman	**zo**
JADE	to fatigue; Chinese gemstone	**mn**
JAIL	gaol; to imprison	
JAIN	Indian religious sect	
JAMB	a door-post; to wedge; stick	
JANE	jean; twilled cloth; Genoese	**nm**
JANN	jinn; Moslem demon	
JANT	jaunt; ramble	
JAPE	jibe; joke; jest; quip	
JARL	earl (Norse)	
JAUP	to bespatter (Sc.)	
JAWY	with jaws	
JAZZ	rag-time music	**mu**
JEAN	jane; twilled cloth	
JEEP	American general purposes vehicle	
JEER	mock; scoff; taunt; deride	
JEFF	dicing with quadrants; circus rope	
JEHU	a coachman	
JERK	yerk; jolt; pluck; twitch; a good-for-nothing; (weight-lifting)	
JESS	a leg-strap in falconry	
JEST	jape; quirk; raillery; banter	
JETE	leap from one foot to another (gymn.)	
JHOW	Indian grass	**bt**
JIFF	a jiffy; a moment	

JILL	a flirt; Jack's girl friend	
JILT	deceive; delude; to discard	
JIMP	neat; slender; elegant (Sc.)	
JINK	a sharp turn; to dodge	
JINN	ginn; djinn; Moslem demon	
JINX	bad joss	
JIVE	jazz dance (swing)	
JOCK	a Scotsman; college athlete (USA); -strap (genital support)	
JOEY	small kangaroo	**zo**
JOEY	small drinking glass; 4d. piece	**nm**
JOHN	a variety of pink	**bt**
JOIN	link together; associate	
JOKE	jest; banter; witticism	
JOLE	jowl; jaw; jolt	
JOLT	jar; jog; jerk; shake	
JOSH	to rag; ridicule	
JOSS	Chinese idol; luck; incense; perfume (wooden stick)	
JOTA	(Sp.) dance, with castanets	
JOUK	jook; duck; dodge; bow (Sc.); perched hawk (falconry)	
JOVE	Jupiter; alchemist's tin	
JOWL	dewlap; the cheek	
JUBA	negro dance	
JUBE	rood-loft	**rl**
JUDO	advanced form of Jap. wrestling	
JUDY	Mr Punch's wife	
JUGA	leaflets in a pinnate leaf	**bt**
JU-JU	W. African black magic	
JUKE	a head movement; -box (gramophone); feint (Am. football)	
JULY	seventh month	
JUMP	leap; skip; bound; purloin; escape; recoil of guns; sprint (cycling)	
JUNE	sixth month	
JUNK	scrap-metal; trash; Chinese ship	**nt**
JUNO	Queen of Heaven	
JURY	twelve persons; makeshift	**lw**
JUST	true; exact; impartial; barely	
JUTE	sack and twine fibre	**bt**

K

KABA	sacred stone of Mecca and Islam	**rl**
KADI	cadi; Moslem judge	
KAEP	dugout canoe (sail) (Philippines)	**nt**
KAGO	Japanese palanquin	
KAGU	crane of New Caledonia	**zo**
KAIF	keif; drugged stupor	
KAIK	} small sailing vessel (Med.)	**nt**
CAIQUE		
KAIL	a ninepin	
KAIN	cain; tribute in kind	
KAKA	New Zealand parrot	**zo**
KAKI	the Chinese date-plum; persimmon fruit	**bt, ck**
KALA	time; destiny; death (Sanskrit)	
KALE	kail; colewort; curly cabbage	**bt**

KALI	prickly saltwort or glasswort	**bt**	KING	monarch; sovereign; ruler; a card
KALI	wife of Siva; goddess of destruction		KINK	bend; knot; curl; loop; whim
KAMA	Hindu cupid		KINO	a mixture of gums; catechu
KAME	glacier-outwash mound	**gl**	KIPE	basket for catching fish
KAMI	Japanese god or title		KIRI	knobkerrie; Kaffir throwing stick
KANA	Japanese handwriting		KIRK	a church (Sc.)	**rl**
KANG	Chinese water-jar		KIRN	kern; last sheaf; harvest image
KANS	Indian sugar-cane grass	**bt**	KISH	wicker turf basket; impure graphite
KAON	1 of class of mesons		KISS	buss; touch gently; (billiards)
KART	midget racing car		KIST	chest; coffer
KAST			KITE	accommodation bill; a toy; a bird	**zo**
KAS	} Dutch wardrobe		KITH	kindred; acquaintances; friends
KATA	Tibetan cloth or scarf		KIVE	a mashing vat
KATA-			KIWI	apteryx, NZ flightless bird; fruit	**zo, bt**
CATA-	} against, down (Gr.)	**cf**	KNAB	to bite; to gnaw
KAVA	ava; Polynesian drink; plant	**bt**	KNAG	knot in wood; peg; a wart
KECK	to retch; dried hemlock	**bt**	KNAP	to snap; a swelling; a hillock
KEEK	to peep (Sc.)		KNAR	gnar; snarl; growl; a knarl
KEEL	ruddle; flat-bottomed barge (coal)		KNEE	leg-joint; graphic curve	**pl, ma**
KEEL	undermost part of ship; projecting fin;		KNEW	understood; perceived
	capsize; main frame of airship;		KNIT	draw together; weave; wrinkle
	(balancer)	**nt**	KNOB	a bunch; boss; door-handle
KEEN	acute; eager; sharp		KNOP	knob; hilltop (S.A.); button
KEEN	funeral song (Irish)	**mu**	KNOT	knag; small sandpiper; 1 sea mile (200
KEEP	stronghold; provender; retain			yards, 1.85 km) per hour	**go, nv, zo**
KEIF	kaif; drugged stupor		KNOW	comprehend; discern; approve
KEIR	bleaching-vat		KNUB	knob; a small lump
KELK	a blow; to beat; large stone		KNUR	knar; gnarl; wooden ball
KELL	caul; cobweb; film; network		KNUT	a nut; a dandy
KELP	kilp; seaweed; wrack		KOBA	kob; African water antelope	**zo**
KELT	Celt; salmon; woollen cloth	**zo, tx**	KOEL	Indian cuckoo	**zo**
KEMB	to comb		KOFF	Dutch sailing vessel	**nt**
KEMP	coarse rough hairs of wool		KOHL	black antimony eye pigment
KENT	pole; pike; bugle with keys	**mu**	KOLA	African nut tree; a beverage	**bt**
KEPI	military cap (Fr.)		KOOK	novice surfer; inept person
KEPT	held; stored; retained; endured		KORO	fear of penis retraction	**pc**
KERB	curb; edge of pavement		KOTH	volcanic mud (S. America)	**mn**
KERF	a saw-cut; a swath		KOTO	Japanese stringed instrument	**mu**
KERN			KRIS	creese; Malay dagger
QUERN	} a hand-mill; to granulate		KROO	an African race
KERN			KUDU	a large African antelope	**zo**
KIRN	} Irish foot-soldier		KUEI	food vessel; bronze age; (China)
KETA	a caviare fish	**zo**	KUFI	calligraphy (Mid. East)
KHAN	Oriental ruler		KUNA	Panamanian Indian
KHEL	a clan (Afghanistan)		KURD	native of Near East
KHOR	wadi-like riverbed (Sudan)		KVAS	rye beer (Rus.)	**ck**
KHUD	Indian ravine		KYAT	(Burma) monetary unit	**nm**
KIBE	chilblain	**md**	KYLE	narrow strait or sound (Sc.)
KIBY	affected with chilblains			
KICK	resist; rebel; spurn; boot; punt			
KIEF	keif; kef; stupor; drowsiness		**L**	
KIER	keir; bleaching-vat			
KILL	slay; destroy; despatch; consume		LACE	tie; fasten; beat; intermix
KILN	furnace; oven		LACK	want; need; deficiency
KILO	unit of 1000 (metric system) 10^3	**me**	LACY	lace-like texture
KILP	kelp; calcined ashes of seaweed		LADE	load; burden; ladle; bale
KILT	a philibeg; pleated skirt; tuck up		LADY	a gentlewoman
KIND	class; type; genus; benign; gentle		LAIC	a layman
KINE	cows	**zo**	LAID	deposited; ribbed; prostrate
KINE-	of moving; movies; cinema (Gr.)	**cf**	LAIN	rested; reclined; reposed

LAIR	den; form; burrow; quagmire
LAIS	a courtesan
LAKE	mere; pool; crimson colour; inland water **pt**
LAKH	lac; 100,000 rupees **nm**
LAKY	resembling a lake
LAMA	Tibetan priest
LAMB	to yean **zo**
LAME	halt; crippled; feeble; imperfect
LAME	gold- or silver-threaded material
LAMP	lantern; to shine
LANA	the genipap tree of Demerara **bt**
LAND	realm; tract; debark; (fish); (bowls) **ae**
LANE	narrow way; passage; by-road; subdivision of track (running); (traffic)
LANG	long (Sc.)
LANK	lax; loose; languid; drooping; thin
LANX	Roman platter
LAPP	a Laplander; Sami
LARD	bacon fat; smear; flatter
LARE	Roman household god **rl**
LARK	frolic; prank; spree; skylark **zo**
LASH	whip; scourge; satirize; a stripe
LASS	girl; a sweetheart
LAST	final; boot-maker's anvil **to**
LAST	continue; endure; a cargo
LATE	overdue; past; recent; deceased
LATH	a narrow strip of wood; batten
LAUD	extol; praise; eulogy; panegyric
LAVA	plutonic rock matter; magma **mn, gl**
LAVE	to wash; bathe; bath
LAWN	fine linen or cambric; greensward (garden)
LAZE	to idle
LAZY	inert; torpid; slothful; sluggish
LEAD	surpass; guide; precede; plummet; conductor, plumbing metal; bullets; (swing the) **el, pb, nt**
LEAF	thin plate; lamina; page of book
LEAK	ooze; drip; percolate; rift
LEAL	loyal; true; faithful
LEAN	rest; rely; depend; incline; lank
LEAP	clear; spring; caper; frisk
LEAR	to learn; learning (Spens.)
LEAT	watercourse to a mill
LEDA	beloved of Zeus; disguised as swan **rl**
LEEK	an emblem of Wales; onion, genus **hd, bt**
LEER	ogle; smirk
LEES	the dregs; open lands (park)
LEET	court of record; list of candidates **lw**
LEFT	sinister; abandoned; bequeathed
LEHR	glass annealing oven
LEND	advance; loan; furnish; grant
LENE	unaspirated
LENO	a fabric like muslin **tx**
LENS	optical glass (camera) (spectacles) (tele-, micro-scope)
LENT	loaned; inclined; a fast; slow music pace (It.) **rl, mu**
LESS	smaller; inferior; minor
LEST	for fear that
LETO	mother of Apollo and Artemis
LETT	Baltic people of Latvia, Lettland
LEUD	Frankish vassal
LEVY	tribute; exact; muster; impose
LEWD	licentious; rude; pornographic
LIAR	an economiser of the truth
LIAS	argillaceous limestone **mn**
LICE	insect carriers of typhus; bedbugs; skin, hair parasites; ticks **zo**
LICH / **LYCH**	dead body; corpse; funeral gate
LICK	to lap; defeat; overcome
LIDO	a bathing pool with sunbathing area
LIED	stated falsely; German ballad
LIEF	gladly; willingly; beloved
LIEN	right of retention; cylindrical bronze vessel (China) **lw**
LIEU	place; stead
LIFE	vitality; duration; memoir; existence; -style; -sentence
LIFT	exalt; raise; elevate; steal; underarm stroke (badminton); thermal current (gliding); hitchhiking; serenity and elevation after drugtaking
LIKE	prefer; enjoy; cognate; match
LILT	cheerful song or air; ditty **mu**
LILY	fleur-de-lis **bt**
LIMB	edge; border; an imp; branch; extension to torso **bt, zo**
LIME	to ensnare; citrus fruit **bt**
LIMN	to paint; draw; illuminate
LIMP	walk lamely; slack; flaccid
LIMY	glutinous; viscous
LINE	ancestry; business; the Equator; rope; link; (air-); note; life- **ro**
LING	small bronze bell (China)
LING	sea-fish; common heather **zo, bt**
LINK	torch; nexus; tie; connect; chain, circuit (route); (missing-); 7.92 in (20 cm) **me**
LINN	pool; waterfall
LINO	linoleum
LINT	surgical linen; loose fibre dust **md**
LINY	streaky; wrinkled
LION	cat; predator, King of Jungle, symbol of power **zo**
LIPP	a crimson fish **zo**
LIRA / **LIRE**	Italian, Turkish, money **nm**
LIRE / **LYRE**	harp **mu**
LIRK	a fold; to hang in creases (Sc.)
LISI	canoe, S. Pacific **nt**
LISP	make th of s
LIST	enlist; register; roll; elect; wish
LITH	joint; segment

LIVE	exist; survive; active; alive; dwell; appearing in person; mortal
LOAD	lade; cumber; charge; incubus
LOAF	lounge; dawdle; (bread)
LOAM	rich mould; sand-clay mix (with humus); soil **ag**
LOAN	lend; advance; imprest
LOBE	projecting part of ear; a cotyledon; arc of skating **pl, bt, ga**
LOCH	lake; arm of the sea
LOCK	close; seal; bolt; hug; ringlet (hair); entwine; adding resource to process **cp**
LOCO	locomotive; stand-in; playing at a certain pitch (It.) **rw, mu**
LODE	vein in ore; drain; open ditch
LOFT	upper room; attic; to glide; striking angle (golf)
LOGE	a box in a theatre
LOGO	symbol for services, organisations
-LOGY	science of, knowledge; speech **cf**
LOIN	pubic, genital zone; groin; crutch; -cloth **pl**
LOKE	grassy road (East Anglia)
LOKI	Norse god of evil or mischief, lightning and destruction **rl**
LOLL	sprawl; lounge
LOMA	lobe; fringe
LOMP	the lump fish **zo**
LONE	isolated; solitary; secluded
LONG	prolix; lengthy; crave; aspire
LONK	north-Engl. mountain wool **tx**
LOOF	the palm of the hand
LOOK	scan; gaze; peer; seem; mien
LOOM	approach menacingly; weaving device; lighthouse rays; midpoint of oar (rowing)
LOON	Great Northern Diver (water bird); rascal, loafer **zo**
LOOP	bight; bend; loophole; closed circuit feedback; continous tape; flank of horse **cp, zo**
LOOS	laus; praise (Spens.)
LOOT	booty; plunder; sack; ransack
LOPE	run with easy strides
LOPH	molar cusp crest **zo**
LORD	dominate; master; ruler; a peer
LORE	wisdom; erudition; doctrine
LORN	forlorn; lost; forsaken; undone
LORY	Australian parrot **zo**
LOSE	mislay; waste; squander; fail
LOSS	defeat; reverse; deprivation; reduction of power; lose out; bereavement **cp, el, tc**
LOST	missing; astray; vicious; dreamy
LOTE	lotus; water-lily **bt**
LOTH	averse; unwilling; allergic
LOTO	lotto; a game
LOUD	stentorian; clamorous; noisy
LOUP	loop; to leap

LOUR	scowl; frown; glower
LOUT	boor; clod; booby; yokel
LOVE	adore; affection; courtship (-birds); zero score (lawn tennis)
LOWN	sheltered; tranquil (Sc.)
LUAU	traditional roast-pig feast (Hawaii) **ck**
LUCE	full grown pike **zo**
LUCK	hap; fate; hazard; fortune; chance
LUDI	
LUDUS	} public games (Rome)
LUDO	a game (dice and counters)
LUES	poison; plague; disease
LUFF	the weather-gauge; leading edge of a sail **nt**
LUGE	toboggan
LULL	calm; assuage; an interim
LUMP	chunk; projection; hunk
LUNA	the moon; heraldic argent **hd**
LUNE	half-moon shape
LUNG	respiratory organ **md**
LUNT	a light; a slow-match
LURE	entice; decoy; bait; recall (falconry)
LURE	dummy bird (falconry); mechanical hare, rabbit (greyhounds)
LURK	skulk; lie in wait
LUSH	juicy; luscious; richly verdant **bt**
LUSK	a sluggard; to laze
LUST	desire; cupidity; covet
LUTE	tenacious composition; guitar **mu**
LUTH	lute (Fr.) **mu**
LUTZ	jump (ice skating) technique
LUXE	luxuriousness (Fr.)
LYAM	leam; dog-leash
LYME	a coarse grass **bt**
LYNX	sharp-eyed cat **zo**
LYON	Heraldic Court (Sc.) **hd**
LYRA	a constellation
LYRA	brain psalterium in mammals **zo**
LYRE	
LYRA	} early harp (It.) **mu**
LYSE	make undergo lysis

M

MA'AM	marm; madame
MAAR	a crater
MACE	staff of authority; spice **bt**
MACH	supersonic speed
MACK	
MAIK	} make (Sc.)
MADE	formed; fashioned; compelled
MAGE	a magician
MAGI	wise men of the East
MAID	lass; lassie; damsel
MAIL	the post; chain-armour
MAIM	cripple; mutilate; disable
MAIN	at dice or cockfighting; essential
MAIN	the ocean; might; power; pipe
MAKE	do; gain; form; cause; reach

MAKI	a Malagasy lemur	zo
MAKO	Australasian shark	zo
MALA	maxilla lobe in insects	zo
MALE	masculine gender	
MALL	mallet; to bruise; public walk	
MALM	calcareous loam	mn
MALT	steeped grain	
MAMA	mamma; mammy	
MANA	magical influence (Maori)	
MANE	neck hair on lions, horses	zo
MANX	curtailed (cat); of Isle of Man	
MANY	sundry; divers; manifold	
MARC	oil-cake refuse	
MARE	female horse	zo
MARK	(letters of); brand; stigma; coin (Ger.); catch (football); strike (bowls)	nm
MARK	(post); symbol; character; code pulse	cp
MARL	mixture of clay, sand and lime	
MARM	ma'am; madame	
MARS	God of War; a planet	
MART	market; bazaar; emporium; hammer (Sc.)	
MASH	mix; crush; knead; compound	
MASK	veil; cloak; revel; disguise; visor	
MASK	(gas-); conceal; isolating bits	cp
MASS	bulk; size; whole; heap	rl
MAST	beech-nuts, etc.; supporter of sails, aerials, airships	ae, bt, nt
MATE	comrade; checkmate; tea plant	bt, ck
MATH	a mowing	
MATT	roughened; glass; non-glossy photographs, paint	pg, pt
MAUD	shepherd's woollen plaid (Sc.)	tx
MAUL	mall; hammer; to molest; melée (rugby football); tear (flesh)	to
MAWK	a maggot	zo
MAXI	larger than standard	
MAYA	language; Hindu mythology	
MAZE	daze; bewilder; a labyrinth	
MAZY	winding; intricate	
MEAD	spiced ale; meadow; field	
MEAL	a repast; ground grain	
MEAN	middle; average; intend; signify	
MEAT	food; flesh	
MEDE	a native of Media	
MEED	reward; recompense; guerdon	
MEEK	mild; lowly; pacific; unassuming	
MEER	mere; pool; lake (obs.)	
MEET	fit; proper; encounter; join; competition (athletics); (hunting) start	
MEGA-	one million times	cf, ma, me
MEIO-	decrease in size or numbers (Gr.)	cf
MELD	fuse; merge; face-up (cards)	
MELT	fuse; thaw; soften; dissolve	
MEMO	memorandum; note; jotting	
MEND	repair; patch; amend; correct	
MENO	less tempo; slower (It.)	mu
MENU	bill of fare; optional facilities	ck, cp
MERE	pool; lake; marsh; boundary	
MERE	unmixed; simply; alone; only	
MERI	Maori war club	
MERK	an old Scots silver coin	nm
MERV	silk dress material	tx
MESA	broad; flat; rocky; tableland (Sp.)	
MESH	ensnare; net-work; brewery grains	
MESO-	middle; intermediate secondary (Gr.)	cf
MESS	muddle; jumble; dish of food; eat	
META	Roman racing pylon; half-speed (tempo) (It.)	mu
META-	between; beyond; change (Gr.)	cf
METE	measure; limit; boundary	
MEUM	and tuum (liturgical me or thee)	rl
MEWL	to squall	
MEWS	stables; cages for hawks	
MEZE	hors d'oeuvres (Turk.)	
MIAN	Ind. title of respect	
MIAU	a cat-call	
MICA	a silicate used as glass	mn
MICE	small rodents	zo
MICH	lie hid; skulk; sneak; play truant	
MICO	vegetable butter or solid oil	bt
MIDA	the larva of the bean-fly	zo
MIEN	air; bearing; deportment; aspect	
MIFF	annoyance; resentment	
MIKE	shirk; loiter; microphone	
MILD	suave; bland; placid; soothing	
MILE	1760 yards (1.609 km)	me
MILK	cat-lap	
MILL	grind; factory; fight	nm
MILO	the strongman of Crotona	
MILT	the spleen; roe; spawn	zo
MIME	mimic; ape; copy; a farce	
MINA	50 shekels; Indian bird	zo
MIND	mark; heed; dislike; intention	
MINE	pit; colliery; sap; of me	
MING	Chinese porcelain; dynasty	
MINI-	small; of compact size	cf
MINK	furry animal, weasel type	zo
MINO	Japanese raincoat	
MINT	coin factory; unused, fresh	nm
MINT	aromatic plant; to invent	bt
MINX	pert selfish girl; she-puppy	zo
MINY	subterraneous	
MIRE	mud; ooze; slime; swampy ground; bog (Swed.)	go
MIRK	murk; gloom; dark	
MIRY	muddy; marshy; soggy	
MISE	cost; expense; a treaty	lw
MISS	fail; want; need; spinster	
MIST	fog; haze; obscurity	
MISY	mysy; impure iron ore	mn
MITE	widow's donation; insect	nm, zo
MITT	mitten; a covering for the wrist	
MITY	full of insects	zo
MIXT	mixed; mingled; blended	
MOAN	bewail; lament; deplore	
MOAT	protective ditch	

MOCK	taunt; flaunt; deride; imitate	
MOCO	the rock cavy	zo
MODE	style; form; way; vogue; fashion	
MODE	method; wave frequency	el
MODI	methods; (modus)	
MODO	style of playing required (It.)	mu
MODO	system of major, minor scales	mu
MODS	first B.A. examination, Oxford	
MOFF	Caucasian silk fabric	tx
MOGI-	effort, difficulty, defect (Gr.)	cf
MOHO	earth crust/mantle boundary	gl, go
MOHR	West African gazelle	zo
MOIL	toil; soil; daub	
MOKE	ass; donkey; burro	zo
MOKO	Maori tattooing	
MOLD	mould	
MOLE	jetty; a blemish; artificial harbour	
MOLE	the gentleman in velveteens	zo
MOLE	unit of substance, betrayer of secrets; birthmark	
MOLL	courtesan; gangster's sweetheart; minor key (Ger.)	mu
MOLT	melt; moult (obs.)	
MOLY	a countercharm; garlic	bt
MOME	a dullard; buffoon	
MONK	an ink-stain in printing; friar	rl
MONO	single transmission path	el
MOOD	disposition; humour; temper; vein	
MOON	wander aimlessly; a satellite	
MOOP	to nibble; to browse (Sc.)	
MOOR	fasten; berth; heath; (Othello)	
MOOT	an assembly; debate; discuss	
MOPE	to be dull and listless	
MOPS	a pug-dog	zo
MOPY	downcast; dejected; sad	
MORA	finger game; tree; short syllable	bt
MORE	additional; further; again	
MORN	morning; tomorrow	
MORT	death tune; a quantity	
MOSS	a cryptogamic plant	bt
MOST	more than more	
MOTE	mite; particle; speck; blemish	
MOTE	moot; assembly; to debate (obs.)	
MOTH	large-winged insect	zo
MÓTO-	of creating; movement (Gr.) (It.)	cf, mu
MOUE	a pout; a grimace (Fr.)	
MOUL	mool; mouldy (Sc.)	
MOVE	stir; shift; budge; propose	
MOWN	scythed; cut	
MOXA	a cauterizer	bt, md
MOYA	volcanic mud	mn
MOZE	to raise the nap on cloth	
MUCH	plenteous; greatly; largely	
MUCK	refuse; dirt	
MUFF	a duffer; hand-warmer	
MUID	hogshead; dry measure for corn	
MUIR	moor (Sc.)	
MULE	slipper; machine; a hybrid	zo
MULL	snuff-box; headland; mistake	

MULL	to heat wine, punch; to ponder, err	
MULL	cotton book-cover	pr
MULT	multure; fee for grinding corn	
MUMM	to mask; act; masquerade	
MUMP	nibble; grin; deceive; beg	
MUON	heaviest known lepton	nc
MURE	immure; a wall	
MURK	mirk; darkness; obscurity	
MUSA	banana genus	bt
MUSE	meditate; ponder; contemplate	
MUSH	pulp; travel by dog-sled	
MUSK	a scent; a deer	zo
MUSS	a mess; scramble; disarrange	
MUST	obliged; necessitated	
MUST	mould; unfermented grape juice	
MUST	elephant frenzy	
MUTA	change style of playing (It.)	mu
MUTE	dumb; still; a sordine	mu
MUTT	a fool	
MUXY	gloomy; dirty	
MYNA	the Indian starling	zo
MYTH	legend; fable; invention	
MYXA	beak extremities	zo

N

NABK	a plant in the crown of thorns	bt
NAGA	sacred Hindu snakes	zo
NAIB	Indian law officer	
NAIF	naive; artless; ingenuous	
NAIK	Indian corporal	
NAIL	to spike; secure; $2\frac{1}{4}$ inches (57 mm)	me
NAJA	venomous snake; a cobra	zo
NAME	call; term; nominate; renown	
NANA	benteak skill	
NAND	logic; NOT-AND (Boolean)	cp
NANO-	one thousand millionth 10^{-9}	ma
NANO-	second, and light advances one foot	me
NAOS	a shrine (Greek)	
NAPE	the back of the neck	
NAPO	(ne plus); finish	
NAPU	the musk-deer of Java	zo
NARD	spikenard; an unguent; Arab backgammon	nt
NARE	nostril	zo
NARK	police spy; a squealer	
NARY	neither; nor any	
NASO-	nasal, of the nose	cf
NATE	buttock	md
NAVE	(wheel); hub; main aisle	rl
NAVY	fleet of ships	nt
NAZE	cape; mull; headland; ness	
NAZI	German national socialist	
NEAL	anneal; to temper	
NEAP	a small-measure tide	nv
NEAR	nigh; close; stingy; miserly	
NEAT	trim; tidy; simple; cattle	zo

NECK	col; an isthmus	
NEED	want; lack; require; poverty	
NEEM	margosa oil	
NEEP	a turnip	bt
NE'ER	never	
NEMO	nobody	
NEON	a gas	ch
NEPE	flannel footwear	
NERD	untidy, good-for-nothing, person	
NERF	car bump (motor racing)	
NERO	a tyrant; imperial fiddler (Rome)	
NESH	soft; crumbly; tender	
NESS	naze; cape; promontory	
NEST	abode; resort	
NETT	without discount	
NEUM	neume; a musical phrase	mu
NEVE	glacial snow; firn	
NEWS	tidings; word; report; advice	
NEWT	an eft; amphibian	zo
NEXT	close to; bordering	
NIAS	nyas; eyas; a young hawk	zo
NIBS	His Nibs; home ruler	
NICE	precise; fine; finical; pleasant	
NICK	notch; reckoning; winning throw	
NICK	prison; Satan; shot (squash)	ga
NIDE	a brood of pheasants	zo
NIGH	near; impending; almost	
NIKE	Greek goddess of victory	
NILE	reactivity unit	nc
NILL	unwilling; incandescent sparks	
NINE	one over the eight	
NIPA	Indian palm tree; toddy	bt
NISI	prius; unless previously	lw
NIXY	nixie; malignant water-spirit	
NIZY	dunce; simpleton	
NOCK	the notch of an arrow	
NODE	knot; knob; information site; junction (stem)	bt, cp
NODE	drama plot; difficulty; retransmission; border-point of sound	tc, mu
NOEL	Xmas; Yule	
NOES	opposition votes	
NOIL	a knot of combed wool	
NOLL	} the head; poll; the crown	
NOUL		
NOWL	}	
NOMA	mouth gangrene	md
NOME	tract of land in Egypt or Greece	
NONE	not one	
NOOK	cranny; corner; recess; arbour	
NOON	mid-day; height; meridional	
NO-OP	do nothing instruction	cp
NOPE	American negation	
NORM	rule; model; standard; output; behaviour	
NORN	one of the three Norse fates	
NOSE	sagacity; scent; pry; projection	
NOSY	nosey; inquisitive	
NOTE	heed; mark; record; letter; fame	
NOTE	single musical sound; ultimatum	

NOUN	a substantive	
NOUS	talent, sharp wit, intellect	
NOUT	neat; cattle (Sc.)	zo
NOVA	a new star	
NOWT	cattle (Sc.)	
NOWY	knotted	hd
NUDE	bare; naked; undraped; stark	
NULL	void; invalid; nugatory	
NULL	ineffectual; no-op	cp
NUMB	torpid; deadened; paralysed	
NUNG	a bale of cloves	
NURL	to mill; to indent	
NYAS	nias; eyas; young hawk	zo

O

OAKS	a race for fillies at Epsom	
OAKY	hard; tough; strong	
OAST	hop-kiln	
OATH	vow; pledge; curse; expletive	
OBEX	a barrier; an obstacle	
OBEY	heed; mind; comply; submit	
OBIT	R. C. funeral service	rl
OBOE	the hautboy	mu
OBOL	Charon's ferry fee over Styx	nm
OBUS	projectile (Fr.)	
ODAL	udal; absolute tenure in land	lw
ODDS	chances; probabilities	
ODIC	odylic force	
ODIN	Norse father of heaven	
ODOR	} stink, smell	
ODOUR		
ODYL	magnetic force	
OFFA	King of Mercia	
OGAM	ogham; ancient Irish writing	
OGEE	a double curve in architecture	
OGLE	side glance; leer; smicker	
OGPU	Soviet police	
OGRE	monster; giant	
OILY	greasy; unctuous; oleaginous	
OKAY	perfectly correct	
OKRA	gumbo vegetable; mallow	bt, ck
OKTA	⅛ of sky area	mt
OLEO	oleomargarine; oleograph	
OLID	evil-smelling	
OLIO	mess; medley; mixture; stew	
OLLA	olio; jar; urn; cooking pot	
OLPE	Grecian jug	
OMAR	Khayyam, the tentmaker	
OMEN	sign; portent; presage; augury	
OMER	a Hebrew unit of capacity	me
OMIT	miss; skip; exclude; neglect	
ONCE	also onst	
ONCO-	of mass; swelling; tumour (Gr.)	cf
ONDE	fabric using shades for effect	tx
ONDY	wavy	hd
ONER	singular; a single; an adept	
ONLY	sole; alone; singly; barely; but	
ONST	once	

ONTO-	of origin; development (Gr.)	**cf**
ONUS	burden; load; responsibility	
ONYM	species or zoological group	**zo**
ONYX	agate streaked with chalcedony	
OOCH	illegal mooring method (yachting)	
OOFY	wealthy; opulent; plutocratic	
OOID	egg-shaped	
OOZE	slime; mire; exude; leak; drip	
OOZY	viscous; slimy	
OPAH	the king-fish or sunfish	**zo**
OPAL	iridescent precious stone	**mn**
OPEN	overt; candid; undo; begin; start	
-OPIA }		
-OPY }	sight defect (Gr.)	**cf, md**
O-PIP	observing station	
OPUS	a composition; a work	**mu**
ORAL	by word of mouth	
ORCA	the whale genus	**zo**
ORFE	a gold fish; ide	**zo**
ORGY	sensual, sexual excess; drunken revelry; orge	
ORLE	fillet under an ovolo	**ar**
OROU	trading vessel; canoe (Papua)	**nt**
ORRA	odd; worthless (Sc.)	
ORYX	antelope; legendary unicorn	**zo**
-OSIS	of pathology, diseased (Gr.)	**cf, md**
OSMO-	liquid balance pressures	**cf**
OTEZ	remove! (usually the mutes) (Fr.)	**mu**
OTIC	receptor cells in ear	**pl**
OTTI	attar; an essential oil; perfume	
OUCH	a jewel socket	
OURS }		
OURN }	belonging to us	
OUSE	bark for tanning	
OUST	evict; eject; expel; dislodge	
OUZO	aniseed spirits (Gr.)	
OVAL	elliptical	
OVEN	kiln	
OVER	(cricket); above; besides; very	
OVID	horned ruminant	**zo**
OVUM	egg, female reproductive cell	**md, zo**
OWED	due; outstanding; indebted	
OWRE	the wild ox	**zo**
OWSE	tan vat liquor	
OXEN	kine; cattle; neat	**zo**
OXER	a stiff fence	
OYER	judicial authority to hold courts	**'lw**
OYES }		
OYEZ }	the call of the public crier	

P

PACA	South American rodent	**zo**
PACE	rate; speed; step; walk; peace	
PACK	stow; crowd; bale; load; (cards)	
PACK	group (cubs, wolves, forwards) Rugby; secret influence; store data	**cp**
PACO	the alpaca; Peruvian sheep	**zo**
PACT	bond; agreement; contract	

PADS	body protection (cricket)	
PAFF	piff-paff; jargon	
PAGE	bell-hop; attendant (boy); wooden wedge; leaf; screen display; paginate	**ce, cp, tc**
PAID	requited; defrayed; settled; met	
PAIK	a beating (Sc.)	
PAIL	bucket	
PAIN	vex; fret; rack; torment; injure	
PAIR	two; twain; brace; couple	
PAIS	a jury list	**lw**
PALA	South African antelope	**zo**
PALE	wan; sallow; paling; district	
PALE	a vertical division	**hd**
PALI	Buddhist sacred language	**rl**
PALL	mantle; cloak; cloy; sate; surfeit; funerary cloth cover	
PALM	to conceal; a token of victory	**bt**
PALP	jointed feeler	**zo**
PALT	rubbish (Dutch)	
PALY	ashen; divided vertically	**hd**
PAND	narrow curtain over a bed (Sc.)	
PANE	window glass; a patch	
PANG	throe; paroxysm; to cram	
PANT	gasp; puff; blow; palpitate	
PAPA	Greek parish priest; a bishop	**rl**
PARA	paragraph; old Ottoman money	**nm**
PARA	Brazilian rubber	**bt**
PARA-	irregular; beyond (Gr.)	**cf**
-PARA	bring forth; (parent) (Gr.)	**cf**
PARD	the leopard; a partner	**zo**
PARE	cut; peel; skive; lessen; diminish	
PARK	train of artillery; an enclosure; (cars); public garden; sportsfield (Sc.)	
PARR	young salmon	**zo**
PART	sever; allot; parcel; divide; quit	
PASS	exceed; overstep; ignore; enact; mountain route via col; discharge; narrow way; satisfy examiners; length of inviting gesture; (time); water ski course; (football)	
PAST	gone; done; over; former; bygone	
PATE	top of head; pie, patty, meat paste	
PATH	way; track; trail; channel; access	
PATH	route (transmission); sequence	**cp**
PAUL }		
PAWL }	a check stop	**nt**
PAUW	the South African bustard	**zo**
PAVE	smooth; prepare; facilitate	
PAVE	the cobbled roads of France	
PAVO	peacock; southern constellation	**zo**
PAWK	trick; a cunning device (Sc.)	
PAWN	pledge; hypothecate; a chessman	
PAYA	Honduran Indian	
PAYE	pay as you earn	
PEAK	top; acme; apex; zenith; upper aft corner (sail)	**mo**
PEAL	clang; echo; resound; thunder	
PEAN	paean; song of triumph	
PEAR	a fruity	**bt**

PEAS	fine gravel for parachuters' landings	
PEAT	turf used for fuel	
PEBA	armadillo; the black tatou	zo
PECH	} to pant (Sc.)	
PEGH		
PECK	strike with beak; 2 gal. (9 litres)	me
PEDI-	of the feet (Gr.)	cf, md
PEDO-	} of children, infants (Gr.)	cf
PAEDO-		
PEEK	to peep (Sc.)	
PEEL	skin; pare; rind; bark; flay; fall; (croquet) (jumping)	mo
PEEL	a shovel; a fort; to pillage	
PEEN	mason's hammer with cutting face	to
PEEP	a sly look; the cry of a chicken	
PEER	to peep; to appear; a nobleman; equal status group	
PEKE	a Pekinese dog	zo
PELA	white wax from a scale-insect	
PELF	money; riches; filthy lucre	
PELL	skin; hide; parchment	
PELT	raw hide; throw; rain heavily	
PEND	hang; impend; an enclosure	
PENT	enclosed; confined; shut up	
PEON	day-labourer; bondsman; police	
PEON	foot-soldier; serf (Mex.); messenger	
PEPO	a fruit of the gourd type	bt
PERI	fairy excluded from paradise	
PERK	smarten up; trim; spruce	
PERM	a permanent wave	
PERN	the honey-buzzard	zo
PERT	saucy; forward; impertinent	
PESO	(Philippines); dollar	nm
PEST	plague; pestilence; scourge	
PHEW!	exclamation of exertion	
PHIZ	face; visage: physiognomy	
PHON	a decibel; unit of loudness	me
PHOT	unit of illumination	me
PIAL	spinal cord membrane	md
PIAT	anti-tank gun	
PICA	magpie; size of type	pr
PICA	depraved appetite	md
PICE	Indian (Nepalese)	nm
PICK	cull; select; choice; peck; charge forward (basketball)	to
PICO-	one million millionth 10^{-12}	cf, ma
PICT	early Scottish race	
PIDE	unleavened bread (Turk.)	ck
PIED	spotted	
PIER	jetty; mole; pillar	
PIET	the magpie; dipper; water-ousel	zo
PIFA	piffero; rustic shawm (It.)	mu
PIKA	small rodent; guinea-pig type	zo
PIKE	peak; a turnpike; a weapon; fish; posture	zo
PILA	Roman javelin; pile column	bd
PILE	nap; heap; mass; stake; projecting carpet threads (velvet, knots)	el, wv
PILI	hairs on bacteria	zo
PILL	to rod; plunder; blackball	md

PILO-	of body hair (Gr.)	cf
PIMP	procurer for immoral purposes	
PINE	to wilt; pine-apple; fir-tree	bt
PING	the noise of a bullet	
PINK	to pierce; to knock; a flower; mast-carrying sail ship	bt, nt
PINT	measure of capacity; 4 gills (0.5 1)	me
PINY	full of pines	bt
PIPE	exchequer roll; long tube; calumet	
PIPE	to call; cask; bosun's whistle; gravel filled water run-off	mu
PIPI	pods for tanning	
PIPY	tubular	
PIRN	reel; bobbin; thread on a reel	
PISE	rammed clay	
PISH!	exclamation of contempt	
PITH	quintessence; gist; marrow	bt
PITS	(coal); cell cavities; scars	
PITS	service (motor racing); sunken floor	
PITY	ruth; condolence; compassion	
PIXY	pixie; a small fairy	
PIZE	term used in execration	
PLAN	plot; scheme; design; sketch	
PLAP	plop; plash; splash	
PLAT	to plait; piece of ground; dish	
PLAX	flat platelike structure	zo
PLAY	act; romp; game; frolic; farce; match; umpire's command	ga
PLEA	excuse; prayer; claim; argument	
PLED	pleaded; argued; disputed	
PLIM	to swell	
PLOD	jog along; toil; moil; drudge	
PLOP	to fall into water	
PLOT	plan; concoct; outline; allotment	
PLOW	a plough	
PLOY	employment; a frolic (Sc.)	
PLUG	a stopple; stop; plod; peg; pipe-fitting; repeat (tv) (angling)	
PLUM	£100,000; a fruit	bt
PLUS	in addition; more	
PNYX	Athenian meeting place	
POCH	card game (half pack) (4 persons)	ga
POCK	a pustule	md
POCO	little; rather (It.); slightly	mu, md
POEM	ode; lyric; elegy	
POET	bard; balladmonger	
POGO	a pastime	
POKE	bag; bonnet; nudge; prod	
POKY	small; cramped; confined; stupid	
POLE	a mast; $5\frac{1}{2}$ yd (5 m); Polish man; (magnetic)	me, ps, nv
POLK	to dance the polka	
POLL	clip; lop; election; head; parrot	zo
POLO	4-a side mounted game (ball and sticks); Sp. dance with song	ga, mu
POLT	a blow; a hard knock; a club; (bolt)	
POLY-	of many (Gr.)	cf
POME	an apple; a ball of dominion	bt
POMP	pageantry; ceremony; display	
POND	pool; mere; to ponder	

PONE	bread made from Indian corn	**ck**
PONE	who cuts dealt cards	
PONK	a nocturnal spirit (Shak.)	
PONS	medical link or bridge	**md**
PONY	£25; nag; tit; palfrey	**zo**
POOD	Russian weight, 36 lb (16 kg)	**me**
POOH!	exclamation of contempt; bearish	
POOL	mere; pond; tarn; merge; combine; billiards	**ga**
POON	East Indian tree; wood for spars	**bt**
POOP	nincompoop; stern of ship	**nt**
POOR	scant; meagre; sterile; needy	
POPE	the Bishop of Rome	**rl**
POPO	outrigger, sail dugout	**nt**
PORE	con; study; small orifice	**md**
PORK	swine flesh	
PORN	pornography	
PORT	bagpipe music; mien; bearing	**mu**
PORT	wine; haven; entry; larboard	**nt**
PORT	gateway for information retrieval	**cp, tc**
PORY	porous; pervious	
POSE	puzzle; nonplus; feign; a posture	
POSH	very superior	
POST	size of paper; mail; station; record	
POST	passing (Am. football); (basketball); settlement; (last)	**mu**
POST	appoint (job); pillar; file information	**cp**
POST-	after, later, behind (Gr.)	**cf**
POSY	motto or verse; nosegay	**bt**
POTT	size of hand-cut paper	**pp**
POUF	pouffe; large cushion; gauze	
POUR	rush; gush; flow; emit; stream	
POUT	to register pique; whiting	**zo**
PRAD	a horse (slang)	
PRAM	perambulator; Baltic coasting vessel; dinghy with transoms	**nt**
PRAO }	vessel of East Indies	**nt**
PRAU }		
PRAY	beg; crave; implore; entreat	
PREE	to prove; to taste (Sc.)	
PREP	preparation; preparatory	
PREX	college president (USA)	
PREY	despoil; pillage; devour; quarry	
PRIG	pilfer; a coxcomb; a fop	
PRIM	formal; precise; privet shrub	**bt**
PROA	Malay sailing canoe	**nt**
PROD	goad; poke; nudge; prick	
PROG	proctor	
PROM	promenade concert	**mu**
PROP	support; uphold; buttress	
PROS	arguments for; cf. cons	
PROW	the cutwater	**nt**
PROX	proximo	
PRYS	price (Spens.)	
PSHA!	pshaw	
PTAH	Egyptian God, the Creator	
PUCE	flea-colour	
PUCK	ice hockey ball; an imp	
PUDU	a small deer of the Andes	**zo**
PUFF	fuff; pant; blow; flatter; a whiff	

PUGH	interjection of disgust	
PUJA	Hindu ritual; obeisance	
PUKE	to vomit	
PUKU	Central African antelope	**zo**
PULE	to whine; to cry	
PULK	Laplander's sledge	
PULL	draw; drag; haul; pluck; pick; handle (sash lift) sidestroke (polo)	
PULP	any soft uniform mass	
PULS	Afghan monetary unit	**nm**
PULT	Germ. orchestral music stand	
PULU	Hawaiian tree-fern fibre	**bt**
PUMA	Peruvian lion	**zo**
PUMP	raise water; interrogate; inflate; dance shoes; compressor; (angling)	
PUMY	pumice-stone	**mn**
PUNA	Andean plateau	
PUNK	tinder; dud; worthless	
PUNT	gamble; kick; flat-boat	**nt**
PUNY	tiny; weak; petty; Lilliputian	
PUPA }	a chrysalis	**zo**
PUPE }		
PURE	chaste; unsullied; unmixed; neat	
PURL	knit; row; ripple; mulled ale; fine wire worked round silk thread	
PURR	curr; (a cat or pigeon noise)	
PUSH	a gang; urge; jostle; press; badminton	
PUSS	hare or cat	**zo**
PUTT	an endeavour to hole the ball (golf)	
PUXI	North Amer. edible caterpillar	**zo**
PYES	calendar for calculating Easter	**rl**
PYIC	discharging pus	**md**
PYRE	a funeral pile for cremation (Hindu)	**rl**
PYRO	pyrogallic acid	**ch**

Q

QUAB	quob; tremble (obs.)	
QUAD	quadrangle; quadruped; prison	**zo**
QUAG	quagmire; morass; swamp	
QUAT	a nonentity; a twerp	
QUAY	wharf; landing place	
QUEY	a young cow or heifer (Sc.)	**zo**
QUIB	quip; jibe; jest	
QUID	£1; a chew of tobacco	**nm**
QUIN	a kind of scallop	**zo**
QUIP	sally; retort; taunt; quirk	
QUIT	leave; desert; retire; release	
QUIZ	puzzle; chaff; ridicule; an enquiry	
QUOB	quab; tremble	
QUOD	prison	
QUOP	quap; throb	

R

RAAD	South African parliament	
RABI	the grain crop of Hindustan	
RACA	a term of contempt	

RACE	tidal high seas by headlands; compete; current (mill) rapids; human, run, (horse); groove (ball)	
		ga, nv
RACH	dog; pointer or setter	**zo**
RACK	torture; stretch; anguish; harass	
RACK	a grating; wrack; cloud; to amble	
RACK	(torture) toothed rail (cog); shelf	
RACY	spirited; piquant; pungent	
RAFF	riff-raff; rabble; rubbish	
RAFT	a floating framework	**nt**
RAGE	rave; fume; fury; storm; craze	
RAGG	ragstone; siliceous sandstone	**mn**
RAGI	species of millet	**bt**
RAHU	the dark planet in Hindu Myth	
RAID	foray; inroad; invasion; irruption	
RAIL	fence; scold; genus of birds	**zo**
RAIL	sleeping on sleepers	**rw**
RAIN	pitter-patter; a downpour	
RAIS	Arab chief, captain	
RAJA	rajah	
RAKE	roué; inclination; gardening; non-vertical angle of mast, funnel etc.	
		to, nt
RAKI	Levant; aniseed brandy	
RAKU	tea ceremony pottery Japan	
RALE	rattling sound in the lungs	**md**
RALL	rallentando, slow down (It.)	**mu**
RAMA	heroic incarnation of Vishnu	**rl**
RAMI	appendage ends in collembola	**zo**
RAMP	a slope; a swindle; climb; spring	
RANA	amphibian genus, frogs, etc.	**zo**
RANA	a Rajput prince or chief	
RAND	mountain; S. African monetary unit	
		nm
RAND	edge; border; margin; inner sole	
RANG	past tense of ring	
RANI	ranee; the wife of a rajah	
RANK	row; grade; foul; musty; nasty; set of organ pipes	
RANT	rave; orate; spout; declaim	
RANT	corranto, dances	**mu**
RANZ	alphorn for cowherds	**mu**
RAPE	land division in Sussex; oil-seed	**bt**
RAPE	ravish; violate; outrage	
RAPT	enthralled; absorbed; fascinated	
RARE	choice; unusual; precious; raw	
RASE	raze; erase; expunge; level	
RASH	hasty; headlong; to slice	**md**
RASP	to file; abrade; raspberry	**to, bt**
RATA	a New Zealand ironwood tree	**bt**
RATE	scold; assess; appraise; speed	
RATH	Burmese state carriage	
RATH	rathe; early; soon; Irish fort	
RAVE	rant; fume; storm; drive	
RAZE	rase; gut; demolish; overthrow	
READ	peruse; decipher; study; erudite; understand (radio); evaluate conditions (curling)	
REAL	true; genuine; a Spanish coin	**nm**

REAM	to enlarge; to froth; 20 quires	
REAN	rine; rone; rune; a ditch	
REAP	gain; crop; gather; harvest	
REAR	raise; breed; erect; end; behind	
RECK	to care for; regard; heed	
REDD	to tidy; to arrange; to clear	
REDE	counsel; advise; advice	
REED	rush; aquatic grass	
REED	to thatch; a pipe	**mu**
REEF	rocky ledge; shoal; lode	**nt**
REEK	smoke; vapour; fume; stink	
REEL	sway; whirl; totter; a bobbin; a quick pattern-dance	**mu**
REEM	the unicorn of the Bible	**zo**
REFT	bereft; left destitute	
REIM	riem; raw-hide thong (S. Africa)	
REIN	govern; restrain; check; curb	
REIS	Brazilian or Portuguese money	**nm**
RELY	depend; lean; confide; trust	
REND	rip; tear; sunder; sever; rupture	
RENT	hire; let; lease; schism; tear	
REPP	ribbed fabric	
RESP	a sheep disease	
REST	repose; lean; recline; respite	
RETE	a plexus; network of vessels	**md**
REUS	a defendant; debtor	**lw**
REVE	dream; reverie (obs.)	
RHEA	the South American ostrich	**zo**
RHEA	Hellenic nature-goddess	**rl**
RHEA	the ramie plant or fibre	**bt**
-RHEA **RHEO-** }	flowing, fluidity (Gr.)	**cf, md**
RHOM	parallelogram brick	
RHUS	cashew-nut genus	**bt**
RIAL	ryal (Iran); English gold	**nm**
RICE	a wedding cereal	**bt**
RICH	opulent; wealthy; fertile; luscious	
RICK	stack; wrench; sprain	
RIDE	domineer; control; a district	
RIEL	(Cambodia)	**nm**
RIEM	reim; leather rope (S. Africa)	
RIFE	ryfe; prevalent; current; abundant	
RIFF	a moroccan	
RIFT	fissure; cleft; gap; split; chink	
RIGA	deal; balsam; hemp from Riga	**bt**
RILE	vex; anger; provoke; irritate	
RILL	rivulet; brook; streamlet	
RIMA	narrow cleft	**pl**
RIME	hoar-frost; rhyme; poem	
RIND	peel; bark; external cover	**bt**
RINE	rind; to touch	
RINE	rone; rune; rean; water-course	
RING	encircle; hoop; arena; combine	
RINK	a sheet of ice for curling, ice hockey, skating	**ga**
RIOT	orgy; broil; uproar; tumult	
RIPE	mature; ready; mellow; fit	
RIPT	ripped; torn	
RISE	soar; mount; tower; rebel	
RISK	chance; hazard; peril; speculate	

RISP	to rasp; branch of green stalks	bt
RITE	form; usage; observance	
RIVA	rift; cleft	
RIVE	a bank; tear; rend; pierce	
RIVO	a drinking cry (Shak.)	
RIXY	quarrelsome; the sea-swallow	zo
ROAD	route; thoroughfare; highway	
ROAM	rove; ramble; meander; saunter	
ROAN	a colour; sheepskin binding	
ROAR	yell; shout; bellow; howl	
ROBE	clothe; invest; drape; dress	
ROCK	a distaff; oscillate; sweetmeat; part of hard earth-crust; 'Rock 'n roll' popular music	gl, mu
RODE	travelled; a raid; a roadstead	
RODS	retinal receptors (eye); (reactors)	pl, nc
ROER	elephant gun	
ROIL	rile; to stir up; to vex	
ROIN	royne; whisper; mutter	
ROKE	reek; smoke; mist	
ROKY	foggy; reeky; smokey	
ROLE	part; function; character	
ROLL	reel; lurch; enfold; scroll; tilting movement (gliding); mini-loaf sandwich; stroke (croquet); rapid drum notes	ga, mu, nt
ROME	Vatican Catholicism	rl
ROMP	sport; frisk; caper; gambol	
RONE	rine; rune; rean; gutter; Rhone	
RONG	rung; tolled (obs.)	
RONT	runt; stunted; a stump	
ROOD	The Cross	rl
ROOD	a quarter of an acre	me
ROOF	cover; canopy; shelter; overhang	ar, mo
ROOK	cheat; defraud; gregarious bird; chariot (Arab); castle (chess)	zo
ROOL	to ruffle; to raggle	
ROOM	chamber; stead; space; scope	
ROOM	roum; a deep-blue dye	
ROON	rim; border (Sc.)	
ROOP	to roar; hoarseness (obs.)	
ROOT	fix; implant; origin; radix	bt
ROOT	lowest note of a chord; tenon; (square, cubic)	ma, cr
ROPE	tie; secure; bind; tether	
ROPY	stringy; viscous; adhesive	
ROSE	arose; colour; (ceiling); (bit); flower; sound vent of lute	mu
ROSS	the refuse of plants (Sc.)	
ROSY	roseate; blooming; blushing	
ROTA	roster; R.C. court; wheel of life; perpetual musical round, canon	rl, mu
ROTE	mechanical repetition	
ROTI	the joint (Fr.)	
ROTL	a 12 oz (350 g) Arab weight	me
ROUE	rake; debauchee; libertine	
ROUM	room; a deep-blue dye	

ROUP	a fowl disease; an auction (Sc.)	
ROUT	vanquish; defeat; disorder; cut a groove	
ROUT	social fuction; soirée	
ROUX	sauce of melted butter, flour	ck
ROVE	roam; ramble; stray; range	
RUBE	a rustic (USA)	
RUBY	a size of type; a gem	mn
RUCK	wrinkle; fold; crease; sprain; 3 players in football	ga
RUDD	freshwater fish; the red-eye	zo
RUDE	boorish; churlish; rough; raw	
RUED	regretted; repented	
RUFF	a frill; to trump; a bird	zo
RUGA	fold; corrugation	
RUIN	wreck; demolish; subvert	
RUKH	the jungle (India)	
RULE	control; sway; precept; custom; straight rule	rl
RUMP	the Parliament of 1648	
RUNE	incised writing of the Norsemen	
RUNG	a ladder step; tolled	
RUNN	low-lying land in India	
RUNT	ront; dwarf; stump; a pigeon	zo
RUSA	Indian deer, the sambar	zo
RUSA	Indian grass; (geranium oil)	bt
RUSE	wile; trick; artifice; stratagem	
RUSH	dash; fly; career; sally; a reed	bt
RUSK	a biscuit	
RUSS	a Russian	
RUST	fust; must; corrosion	
RUTA	genus of plants; rue	bt
RUTH	mercy; pity; sorrow; misery	
RYAL	rial; rose-noble, old English	nm
RYKE	to reach (Sc.)	
RYND	iron millstone support	
RYOT	Indian cultivator	
RYPE	the Norwegian ptarmigan	zo
RYVE	rive; to pierce (Spens.)	

S

SACK	wine; garment; pillage; pouch	
SACK	dismiss; container (wool)	
SADR	the lote-bush	bt
SAFE	sure; secure; reliable; certain	
SAFE	strongbox; guaranteed	
SAGA	heroic Norse legends	
SAGE	a Solomon; genus salvia	bt
SAGO	edible palm pith	bt
SAGY	seasoned with sage	
SAIC	Levantine ketch	nt
SAID	stated; declared; alleged	
SAIL	cruise; glide; depart	nt
SAIN	to consecrate (Sc.)	
SAIR	to serve; to satisfy; sore (Sc.)	
SAKE	cause; regard; reason	
SAKI	Japanese wine from rice	ck
SAKI	South American monkey genus	zo

SALE	auction; market; vendition	
SALP	swimming tunicate	zo
SALT	mariner; wit; pungent; salacious	
SALT	sodium chloride	ch
SAME	ditto; identical; exactly similar	
SAMP	porridge made from Indian corn	
SAND	grit; force of character	mn
SANE	rational; sound; normal; lucid	
SANG	chanted; blood red	hd
SANK	foundered; subsided; dug	
SANS	without (Shak.)	
SAPO	the toad-fish	zo
SARD	a precious stone; agate	mn
SARE	pelota game	
SARI	Indian garment; scarf	
SARK	a shirt or chemise	
SARN	a pavement	
SASH	window frame; a scarf	
SASS	impudence; sauce	
SATE	cloy; glut; gratify; surfeit	
SATI	suttee; self-immolation (India)	
SAUL	Indian tree; an oratorio	bt, mu
SAUT	salt (Sc.)	
SAVE	except; rescue; to husband; retain	
SAWN	cut with a saw	
SAXE	a kind of paper; light blue	
SCAB	a blackleg; a sore	md
SCAD	horse-mackerel	zo
SCAN	view; examine; scrutinize; poetic meter	
SCAN	check records; test communication channels	cp
SCAR	mark; blemish; steep rock	
SCAT	a tax; scare away; be off	
SCAW	skaw; a promontory	
SCON	scun; skim; skip	
SCOT	a Scotsman; a tax	
SCOW	flat-bottomed boat; dumb-barge	nt
SCRY	descry; espy	
SCUD	rack; wrack; hasten; bustle; small low clouds	mt
SCUG	skug; shelter; expiate	
SCUM	dross; froth; refuse; scoria	
SCUN	scon; skim	
SCUP	a swing; the porgy fish	zo
SCUR	graze; jerk; a stunted horn (Sc.)	
SCUT	a short tail	
SCYE	armhole of a garment	
SEAH	Jewish dry measure, 14 pt	me
SEAL	fasten; a pinniped; drainwater; seadog	zo, pb
SEAM	joint; vein; stratum	
SEAN	seine; a drag-net	
SEAR	burn; scorch; a pawl; dry; sere	
SEAT	chair; site; residence; abode	
SEAX	Celtic sword	
SECT	faction; schism; party	
SEED	germ; embryo; progeny; selected player (tennis)	bt, zo
SEEK	try; ask; hunt; search; court	
SEEL	to close the eyelids; good fortune	
SEEM	appear; look; pretend	
SEEN	observed; regarded; perceived	
SEEP	to ooze; to trickle; to sipe	
SEER	augur; prophet; soothsayer	
SEER	Indian kilogram	me
SEGO	an American plant	bt
SEID	a descendant of Mohammed	
SEIL	sile; strain; a sieve (Sc.)	
SELF	particular; simple; selfishness	
SELF-	of one's own effort, single	cf
SELL	vend; barter; hawk; betray	
SEME	heraldic printing design detail; strewn with stars, etc.	pr, hd
SEMI	demi; hemi; a prefix	
SEND	transmit; propel; eject	
SENS	since (Spens.)	
SENT	forwarded; despatched; flung	
SEPS	reptile gems; lizards	zo
SEPT	a clan in Ireland	
SERA	a lock of any kind; pl. of serum	md
SERB	native of Serbia	
SERE	sear; withered; parched; dry	
SERE	succession of plant communities	bt
SERF	thrall; villein; slave; helot	
SESS	cess; tax	
SETA	bristle; prickle	
SETH	god of death (Egypt)	
SET		
SETT	squared block; packing piece; pile driving	
SETT	badger's home; (mining)	
SEVE	wine's distinctive bouquet (Fr.)	
SEWN	stitched	
SEXT	musical interval	mu
SHAD	a fish of the herring type	zo
SHAG	tobacco; green cormorant	zo
SHAG	coarse hair; roughen; deform	
SHAH	Persian monarch	
SHAM	deceive; substitute	
SHAN	Burmese borderer	
SHAW	a grove; a thicket	
SHAY	chaise; a vehicle	
SHEA	African butter-tree	bt
SHED	emit; diffuse; cot; shack	
SHET	free from; be rid of	
SHEW	show; exhibit; parade	
SHIM	brake-plate; to wedge up; packing tool	
SHIN	to climb; tramp; trudge; fishplate (track)	rw
SHIP	to export; seagoing vessel	nt
SHIR	shirr; to pucker	
SHIT	to defecate; faeces; nonsense; insult	
SHOD	provided with shoes	
SHOE	footwear; pick-up; fitting; socket; (horn)	rw
SHOG	shake; jog; a shock	
SHOO!	begone; scare away	
SHOP	emporium; store; imprison	

SHOT	a reckoning; a marksman; pellets; report; injection; dose; attempt winner (bowls) **ga**
SHOT	putting the weight/shot (throwing)
SHOW	flaunt; blazon; expound; pomp
SHUG	to shrug; to crawl
SHUN	avoid; evade; eschew; elude
SHUT	bar; lock; close; slam; secure
SIAL	granitic earth shell **gl**
SICE	the six at dice
SICE	syce; groom (India)
SICK	to incite; poorly; ailing; disgusted
SIDA	genus of mallows **bt**
SIDE	verge; border; cause; behalf; face
SIDI	Afr. Moslem title of respect
SIDY	aloof and pretentious
SIFT	separate; examine; sort
SIGH	mourn; repine; lament
SIGN	beckon; endorse; emblem; portent
SIGN	arithmetical or instructional pointer **cp, ma**
SIKE	syke; Arctic stream
SIKH	a Punjab soldier
SILE	a sieve; a colander
SILK	cocoon thread; Queen's Counsel; eggshell gloss **tx, lw, pt**
SILL	doorstep; window frame (lock) igneous rock plate **bd, gl**
SILO	fodder storage; ensilage
SILT	sediment; ooze; percolate
SIMA	basaltic earth shell **gl**
SIMP	a simpleton; a mutt
SIND **SYND**	} to rinse (Sc.)
SINE	syne; since; then (Sc.)
SING	relate in verse; chant; squeal
SINK	flag; droop; subside; founder; descending air mass (gliding)
SINK	point where lines of flux end; (kitchen) **el**
SINN	Fein (Irish party)
SIPE	to ooze; to seep; to percolate
SIRE	Your Majesty; progenitor
SIST	summon; delay; stay (Sc.) **lw**
SITE	location; place; position; spot
SIUM	the water parsnip **bt**
SIVA	the Destroyer in Hindu religion **rl**
SIZE	glue; varnish; bulk; volume
SIZY	sticky; viscous
SKAT	a card game **ga**
SKAW	scaw; a promontory
SKEE	ski; a winter sport
SKEG	stump; branch; wild plum **bt**
SKEG	fin-keel of surfboard; rudder fastening (yachting)
SKEP	beehive; wicker basket
SKEW **SKUE**	} awry; oblique; a squint
SKID	heavy timber; drag shoe; side-slip
SKIM	graze; touch; skirt; brush

SKIN	peel; pare; flay; hide; pelt; caul; veneer; film
SKIO **SKEO**	} a hut in the Orkneys
SKIP	skipper; large tub; omit; leap; kibble
SKIP	(-rope); jump to next instruction **cp**
SKIP	captain of team; rink (ice sports)
SKIT	a lampoon; burlesque
SKOT	unit of low-intensity lighting
SKUA	the pirate gull **zo**
SKUG	a squirrel **zo**
SKUG	scug; shelter; expiate
SKYE	terrier **zo**
SKYR	curds (Iceland)
SLAB	chunk; block; thick; mud
SLAB	pitcher's mound (baseball); flat rock shelf **mo**
SLAE	sloe (Sc.); blackthorn **bt**
SLAG	scoria; debris; mine waste
SLAM	bang; shut with violence; (cards); illegal lift (wrestling) **ga**
SLAP	spank; a cleft; a gap in a fence
SLAT	strip; lath; slate; sharp blow
SLAV	European ethnic grouping
SLAW	sliced cabbage used as salad
SLAY	kill; destroy; despatch; murder
SLED	sledge; sleigh; vehicle on runners on snow
SLEW	slue; to twist; turn round; killed
SLEY	the reed of a weaver's loom
SLIC	Selecting Listing in Combination
SLID	slipped; skidded; glided; tripped
SLIM	slight; slender; lithe; crafty
SLIP	trip; fall; scion; twig; cutting **bt**
SLIP	carriage; ring; escape; let go; garment; mistake **el, ps**
SLIP	launch (way); (factor); (scraper); paint
SLIP	ceramic decor base; fielding position (cricket)
SLIT	rip; rend; tear; slash; sever
SLOB	muddy ground
SLOE	slae; blackthorn **bt**
SLOG	smite; swipe; work doggedly
SLOP	a policeman; a mess; a spill
SLOT	track of deer; slit; groove; fixture
SLOT	ideal place on wave (surfing); reserved future; tackle; (timetable); machine (Am. football)
SLOW	tardy; dilatory; dull; inactive; (-down)
SLOW	timescale greater than physical time units **cp**
SLUB	to twist whilst spinning
SLUD	sludge; ooze; mud
SLUE	slew; to revolve
SLUG	sluggard; a pellet **zo**
SLUG	pound, unit of acceleration of mass; typecast; gastropod; strike; token coin **me, pr, zo**
SLUM	a purlieu; squalid neighbourhood
SLUR	stigma; stain; aspersion; sully **mu**

90

SLUT	a slattern; a jade	
SMEE	widgeon; pintail	zo
SMEW	migratory sea duck	zo
SMIT	to infect; a stain; infection	
SMOG	smoky fog	
SMUG	self-satisfied; to confiscate	
SMUR	fine misty rain; to drizzle (Sc.)	
SMUT	soot; a plant disease	
SNAG	projecting stump; an obstacle	
SNAP	bite; nip; snip; crack; break	
SNAP	a snap-shot; a photo; (cards); bite; (Am. football); break; grab; sudden action; (dragon)	bt
SNAR	to snarl (Spens.)	
SNEB	snib; snub; check; reprimand	
SNEE	a large knife (Dutch)	
SNIG	to cut; an eel	zo
SNIP	clip; piece; snippet; a certainty (horse-racing)	
SNOB	shoemaker; tuft-hunter	
SNOD	neat; trim; sleek (Sc.)	
SNOW	frozen vapour flakes; (cocaine)	mt
SNUB	snib; check; slight	
SNUG	cosy; compact; sheltered	
SOAK	steep; drench; saturate	
SOAP	to flatter; washing agent; (box); (opera)	
SOAR	rise; mount; tower; aspire	
SOCK	plough-share; hose	
SODA	an alkali	ch
SOFA	couch; divan; ottoman	
SOFI / **SUFI**	Moslem mystic; dervish	rl
SOFT	pliable; plastic; yielding; dulcet	
SOHO	a sportsman's halloo (Shak.)	
SOIL	loam; stain; sully; tarnish	
SOKE	soc; privilege; (East Anglian)	lw
SOLA	hat-plant; sponge-wood; pith	bt
SOLD	retailed; peddled; taken in	
SOLE	only; unique; solitary; under-surface of shoe, ski, golf club, curling stone; fish	ck, zo
SOLI	the plural of solo	mu
SOLO	a card game	mu
SOMA	an intoxicating drink	ck
SOMA	animal body	zo
SOMA- / **SOME-**	somatic of the body (Gr.)	cf
SOME	distinctive; several; indefinite	
SONE	unit of loudness	ac
SONG	lay; carol; ballad; lullaby	mu
SOON	anon; early; willingly; lief	
SOOP	to sweep (Sc.)	
SOOT	sout; grime	
SOPH	sophomore; a student	
SORA	Carolina rail	zo
SORB	mountain ash; service tree	bt
SORE	raw; tender; grievous; painful	
SORI	fern spore-cases	bt
SORN	to cadge board and lodgings	

SORT	arrange; classify; kind; race; character	
SORY	sulphate of iron	ch
SO-SO	indifferent; moderate	
SOSS	a mess; a puddle; plump	
SOUK	bazaar; Eastern market	
SOUL	spirit; fervour; essence	
SOUM	sowm; pasturage (Sc.)	
SOUP	broth; consommé; muddle; mix-up; broken wave foam surfing; laboratory medium for cultures	ch
SOUR	tart; acid; rancid; caustic; bitter	
SOUT	soot; grime (obs.)	
SOWL	to pull by the ears (Shak.)	
SOWN	disseminated; scattered; strewn	
SOYA	Japanese bean	bt
SPAD / **SPUD**	potato; surveyor's nail (USA)	
SPAE	spay; foretell; divine	
SPAM	spiced ham	
SPAN	a yoke; to bridge; wholly; (spick)	me
SPAN	interval; difference in value range	cp, mu
SPAR	to box; rafter; pole	nt, mn
SPAT	the spawn of shellfish; a slap	zo
SPAY	to render unfertile; geld	
SPEC	speculation	
SPED	fled; hurried; hastened	
SPER	to bolt; to shut (obs.)	
SPET	to spit (obs.)	
SPEW	spue; vomit	
SPIE	a keen glance; spy (obs.)	
SPIN	turn; twist; twirl; prolong	
SPIT	a shoal; an iron prong; barbecue; spittle	
SPIT	depth of spade blade, shallows, barbecue	me, to
SPIV	felonious speculating parasite	
SPOT	blot; stain; patch; mark; site	
SPOT	hand punch (cards); treated carbon paper	
SPOT	aiming point; billiard balls; (leopard); observe	
SPRY	alert; brisk; nimble; lively	
SPUD	narrow spade; potato; plumb bob nail; weight; dowel	bt, jn
SPUE	spew; eject; vomit	
SPUN	whirled; woven; extended	
SPUR	goad; urge; impel; prick; groyne; post	
SPUR	siding; wing dam; griffe (decor); (dyke)	
STAB	pierce; spear; gore; thrust	
STAG	male deer; share pusher; (men only)	zo
STAM	to confound; confusion	
STAR	an asterisk; a heavenly body	
STAW	to stand still; a surfeit (Sc.)	
STAY	stop; check; curb; tarry; abide	lw
STAY	support (rope, wire); remain; (put); stamina	nt
STEM	dam; hold; resist; stock; stalk	bt

STEM	pillar in bow, also for rudder of vessel	**nt**		
STEN	a tommy-gun			
STEP	pace; tread; rung; stage			
STEP	fixture for securing base of movable mast	**nt**		
STET	let it stand (Lat.), instruction to printers			
STEW	ragout; simmer; fishpond			
STIE	to ascend (Spens.)			
STIR	spur; stimulate; tumult; prison			
STOA	covered colonnade	**ar**		
STOB	stub; stump; wedge			
STOG	to stir up mud			
STOP	block; impede; cease; desist			
STOT	young ox; steer	**zo**		
STOW	pack; arrange; place			
STUB	stump; to extirpate; a counterfoil			
STUC	stucco; stone-like plaster coat	**bd**		
STUD	knob; nail; breeding place; collar fastener; headless bolt (gun) weld			
STUG	a thorn (Sc.)			
STUM	unfermented wine; must			
STUN	bewilder; amaze; dumbfound			
STYE	an inflamed eyelid	**md**		
STYX	river in Hades; (see **Obol**)			
SUCH	sich; so; like; similar			
SUCK	imbibe; absorb; engulf			
SUDD	flood debris, dense mat of aquatic vegetation (Nile)			
SUDS	soapsuds	**nt**		
SUED	entreated; prosecuted; high and dry			
SUER	a plaintiff	**lw**		
SUET	fatty tissue			
SUEZ	canal; (Lesseps, the engineer)			
SUFI	Islamic mystic; Moslem sect			
SUIT	gratify; beseem; action; case			
SULK	glower; be sullen			
SUMA	Nicaraguan Indian			
SUMO	Japanese wrestling and martial art			
SUMP	pit; morass			
SUNG	chanted			
SUNK	immersed; engulfed; dug			
SUNN	Indian plant; its fibre	**bt**		
SUPE	a supernumerary; a toady			
SURA	a chapter of the Koran			
SURA	the sap of the coco-palm	**bt**		
SURD	an irrational number			
SURE	certain; secure; reliable; safe			
SURF	foaming waters			
SWAB	swob; mop up			
SWAD	pod; podgy person; clump			
SWAG	plunder; festoon; sag			
SWAM	swim (past tense)			
SWAN	the Swan of Avon, Shakespeare	**zo**		
SWAP	swop; a blow; a stroke; to barter			
SWAT	a fly-killer; a smart blow			
SWAY	rock; roll; reel; influence; power; (thatching)	**bd**		
SWIG	gulp down; pulley gear			
SWIM	float; overflow; be dizzy			
SWIN	sea river or channel			
SWOB	swab; mop			
SWOP	swap; exchange; barter			
SWOT	swat; an earnest student			
SWUM	swim (past participle)			
SYBO	cibol; onion	**bt**		
SYCE	sice; chauffeur; groom (India)			
SYKE	sike; rill; rivulet (Sc.)			
SYNE	sine; since (Sc.)			

T

TAAL	Cape Dutch dialect			
TABU	taboo; ban; veto; prohibit; hide			
TACE	be silent	**mu**		
TACK	a nail; hard food; hasten; change course (zigzag) sailing	**nt**		
TACO	fried tortilla/salad dish (Mex.)	**ck**		
TACT	diplomacy; finesse			
TAEL	money of account	**nm**		
TAEL	Chinese ounce	**me**		
TA'EN	taken			
TAFT	a plumbing joint			
TAHA	African weaver-bird	**zo**		
TAHR	Himalayan goat	**zo**		
TAIC	Indo-Chinese; their language, Thaic			
TAIL	extremity; queue; trail; entail			
TAIN	mirror silver			
TAIT	tate; fibre; lock of hair (Sc.)			
TAKE	grasp; seize; adopt; carry			
TALC	mica	**mn**		
TALE	story; fable; narration			
TALK	parley; prate; palaver; speech; lecture; (small)			
TALL	towering; elevated			
TAME	docile; dull; insipid; domesticate			
TAMP	pack earth solidly; thump; pun			
TANA	Indian police station			
TANE	ta'en; taken			
TANG	point; twang; seaweed; flavour; scent			
TANK	cistern; reservoir; refuel; armoured vehicle			
TANK	(think); mercury delay line	**cp**		
TANT	small scarlet spider	**zo**		
TAPA	Polynesian fibre cloth; side tidbits in a bar (Sp.)	**ck, wv**		
TAPE	to bind; ribbon; to measure; (red)			
TAPE	magnetic strip for recording data	**cp**		
TAPU	tabu; taboo; bar; veto			
TARA	old Irish Convocation			
TARA	an edible New Zealand fern	**bt**		
TARE	gross weight; a weed	**bt**		
TARN	mountain pool; a marsh			
TARO	edible plant of the arum type	**bt**		
TART	sharp; bitter; pungent; small pie			
TASH	Indian silk fabric with gold thread			
TASK	toil; drudgery; labour			
TASS	a drinking-cup; a heap			

TASS	pouch; thigh-armour	
TA-TA	good-bye; a short walk	
TATE	a London Picture Gallery	
TATH	cattle dung; to manure	
TATU	tatou; peba; armadillo	zo
TAUT	tense; strained; stressed	
TAWA	N. Zealand hardwood	
TAWS	tawse; a leather strap (Sc.)	
TAXI	motor-cab; move on runway	ae
TAYO	apronlike garment (S. America)	
T-BAR	drag ski-lift	
TEAK	hardwood tree; the wood	bt
TEAL	small waterfowl; a duck	zo
TEAM	side; group; draught animals	zo
TEAN	sorrow; vex; tease (Sc.)	
TEAR	rip; rend; lacerate; (sob)	
TEAT	a nipple	
TECK	detective	
TEDE	tead; torch; flambeau	
TEED	ball mounted for driving off (golf)	
TEEM	swarm; to abound; be prolific	
TEEM	pour molten glass	gs
TEEN	grief; affliction; allot (obs.)	
TEER	to stir; to sieve	
TEFF	Abyssinian cereal grass	bt
TEIL	the lime tree	bt
TEIL	part of book, volume of series	
TELA	weblike tissue	zo
TELD	told (Spens.)	
TELE-	of far, distant, ends (Gk.)	cf
TELL	recite; divulge; blab; reckon	
TEND	incline; verge; mind; nurture	
TENT	lint; probe; a pavilion	
TENT	sacramental wine	rl
TERM	} dub; entitle; phrase; period;	
HERM	} a pedestal supporting a bust	ar
TERN	threefold; sea-bird; gull-type	zo
TERN	a prize in a lottery	
TEST	refining vessel; essay; assay	
TEST	attest; proof; ordeal; criterion	
TEST	probe; examine; check data element; competition	cp
TETE	head; head-dress (Fr.)	
TETT	a plait (obs.)	
TETT	theme; subject; thesis; treatise	
TEXT	writing; (-book); theme; sermon	
TEXT	the message for transmission	tc
THAI	(Siamese); language; people	
THAN	conjunction of comparison	
THAR	goat-antelope of Nepal	zo
THAT	demons. adj.; pronoun	
THAW	run; fuse; melt; liquefy	
THEA	the tea plant	bt
THEE	objective of thou	
THEM	objective of they	
THEN	adverb of past time	
THEW	muscle; sinew; strength	
THEY	Kipling's pronoun; the bosses who decide	

THIG	to beg; to beseech; to sorn	
THIN	lean; fine; lank; spare; sparse	
THIS	demons. adj.; pronoun	
THOR	the God of Thunder	rl
THOU	treat with familiarity	
THRO	} through	
THRU	}	
THUD	a dull sound	
THUG	Indian strangler or poisoner	
THUS	frankincense; a form of resin	bt
TIAO	Chinese money of account	nm
TIBU	Saharan tribe	
TICE	entice; a decoy	
TICK	credit; bed fabric; mark; (clock); bug	zo
TICK	blood-sucking, cattle disease carrier	zo
TIDE	season; course; current	
TIDY	neat; spruce; trim; orderly	
TIED	united; constrained; fastened	
TIER	row; rank; mountain range; mainsail to boom canvas link	nt
TIFF	} quarrel; peevishness	
TIFT	}	
TIFF	quaff; a short drink; adorn	
TIGE	the shaft of a column	ar
TIKE	tyke; dog; cur; Yorkshireman	zo
TIKI	Maori charm or amulet	
TILE	roofing material; a hat	
TILL	cash drawer; cultivate; tillite; boulder clay; moraine boulders	mn, gl
TILT	tent; a covering; a hood; ship with awning	nt
TILT	to hammer; incline; lean; slant	
TIME	era; epoch; term; spell; date; (switch)	
TIME	single channel with multiplex signals	cp
TINE	point of antler; spike; to enclose	
TING	food vessel, bronze; China	
TING	} ring; tinkle	
TINK	}	
TINT	hue; dye; stain; tinge	
TINY	pygmy; wee; puny; minute	
TIRE	tyre; iron hoop; attire; headdress	
TIRE	weary; harass; vex; fatigue	
TIRL	quiver; vibrate; twirl (Sc.)	
TIRO	tyro; novice; beginner	
TIRR	tear; strip off (Sc.)	
TITI	South Amer. squirrel monkey	zo
TIVY	with speed; tantivy	
TOAD	an amphibious batrachian	zo
TOAT	handle of bench plane	cr
TOBY	beer-mug; Punch's pet dog	zo
TOCO	toko; punishment	
TO-DO	ado; bustle; excitement	
TODY	green humming bird	zo
TOED	of obliquely fastened timber	cr
TOED	trod; toed the line	
TOFF	fop; dandy; swell	
TOFT	grove; messuage	lw
TOFU	soya curd (Chin.)	ck

TOGA	Roman raiment	
TOGE	a robe (Shak.)	
TOGS	ceremonial garments	
TOHO	a dog-call	
TOIL	moil; snare; travail; pains; strive	
TOIT	a cushion	
TOKO	toco; a drubbing	
TOLA	Indian weight; 180 grains troy	
TOLD	narrated; related; recounted	
TOLE	toll; entice; attract	
TOLL	tribute; (funeral bell); telephone	
TOLT	old English writ	**lw**
TOLU	oleo-resin; balsam	**bt**
TOMB	grave; sepulchre; mausoleum	
TOME	book; volume; work	
-TOMY	of surgery, removal (Gr.)	**cf, md**
TONE	cadence; inflection; tint	
TONG	the tongue of a buckle (Spens.)	
TONK	a mighty smite	
TONY	a simpleton; genteel; posh; sailing canoe, Bombay	**nt**
TOOK	grabbed; gained; captured	
TOOL	cat's-paw; drive a coach	
TOOM	empty; rubbish-heap	
TOON	Indian cedar	**bt**
TOOT	a wastrel; the devil; honk	
TOPE	shark known as the penny-dog	**zo**
TOPE	Buddhist monument	
TOPE	clump of trees; to booze	
TOPO	fishing boat, (Venice)	
-TOPY	of location, habitat (Gr.)	**cf**
TORE	dead winter grass	**bt**
TORE	rent; split; a torus; a moulding	
TORI	mouldings at the base of columns	
TORN	lacerated; ript	
TORR	unit of low pressure	**ps**
TORT	redress of wrongs	**lw**
TORY	a Conservative	
TOSE	to tease (obs.)	
TOSH	bosh; twaddle; boloney	
TOSS	pitch; hurl; cast; throw of coin (matches/sport)	
TOST	flung; writhed	
TOSY	teased; soft (obs.)	
TOTE	to carry; totalisator	
TOTY	Ind. odd-job man	
TOUR	trip; round; jaunt; ramble	
TOUT	paid agent; tipster; to pout	
TOWN	a city; London	
TOWY	like tow; hempen	
TOYE	lute music	**mu**
TOZE	to pluck; pull by the ears	
TRAM	a beam; tramcar	
TRAP	U-shaped bend (pipe); bunker (golf); igneous rock	**mn**
TRAP	adorn; drape; ambush; ensnare; gin; pony carriage; switch	**el, mn**
TRAP	automatic branch operation for emergencies	**cp**
TRAY	salver; trez; third; shallow sink	

TREE	the Cross; decoder; family	**cp**
TREK	travel by ox-wagons (S. Africa)	
TREK	blue, black outlines on tin glazed earthenware (Holland)	**-**
TRET	a trade allowance	
TREY	a three at cards or dice	
TREZ	third; the third tine of antler	
TRIG	trim; tight; secure; a dandy	
TRIG	wedge; skid; boundary line	
TRIM	neat; tidy; clip; adjust; edging, skirtings	**bd**
TRIM	correct level of vessel in water; speeds of surfing; balance (gliding)	
TRIO	composition in three parts	**mu**
TRIP	tour; err; slip; stumble; dance; 'high' period of drug influence	
TROD	trampled; walked	
TRON	ancient beam balance (Sc.)	
TROT	to run; an old woman (Shak.); gait of a horse	
TROW	to trust; believe; suppose	
TROY	weights used for gold, etc.	**me**
TRUE	loyal; staunch; straight; exact	
TRUG	hod for mortar; gardening basket	
TSAR	Czar; Ksar; Tzar; Zsar; ruler of Russia	
TSUN	Chinese inch	**me**
TSUN	ritual jade (China)	
TUAN	title of respect (China and Malay)	
TUBA	bass trumpet; transmitter	**mu**
TUBE	pipe; telescope; Underground; cathode (television); (follicle); hollow part of wave (surfing)	**rw**
TUCK	rapier; fold; net; pull; thrust	
TUCK	beat of drum; food; to cram; body posture (athletic)	
TUFA	inexpensive cheroot	
TUFA	calcareous deposit; volcanic dust	**mn, gl**
TUFF	volcanic rock-debris	**mn**
TUFT	knot; bunch; clump; tuffet	
TULE	Californian bulrush	**bt**
TUMP	hillock; to earth up	
TUNA	the prickly pear	**bt**
TUNA	the great tunny fish	**zo**
TUNE	air; melody; strain; harmony	
TURF	sod; sward; earth; peat; racing	
TURK	Ottoman; citizen of Turkey; (young Turk, zealot)	
TURM	a troop (obs.)	
TURN	spin; bend; divert; curdle; hinge; act; output	**cp**
TURR	three-stringed Burmese violin	**mu**
TUSH!	pshaw; tush (Shak.)	
TUSK	pointed tooth; sea-fish cod type	**zo**
TUTU	short ballet skirt; shrub (NZ)	**bt**
TUUM	(meum and tuum); thine (Latin)	
TUZA	tucan; Mexican pouched rat	**zo**
TWAL	twelve (Sc.)	
TWAS	it was	
TWAY	twain; two (Sc.)	

TWEE	precious, overly cute	
TWIG	observe; understand; sprig	**bt**
TWIN	double; duplex	
TWIT	taunt; ridicule; upbraid; ass	
TYKE	tike; Yorkshireman; dog; cur	**zo**
TYMP	mouth of blast furnace's hearth	
TYNE	anxiety; disappear; perish (obs.)	
TYPE	kind; sort; class; species; emblem	
TYPO	a compositor	
TYRE	tire; attire; dress	
TYRO	tiro; novice; recruit; neophyte	
TZAR	Tsar; Czar; Ksar; Zsar (Rus.)	

U

UBAC	shadeside of mountain (Fr.)	
UCHE	2 mast, passenger canoe	**nt**
UDAL	odal; freehold estate	**lw**
UGLY	hideous; unsightly; hateful	
ULEX	furze genus	**bt**
ULNA	an arm-bone	**md**
UMBO	boss of a shield; a knob	
UMBO	the point of a bivalve shell	**zo**
UNAU	S. American two-toed sloth	**zo**
UNBE	undo; destroy (obs.)	
UNCO	uncommon (Sc.)	
UNDE	wavy	**hd**
UNDO	open; untie; nullify	
UNIO	genus of freshwater mussels	**zo**
UNIT	a standard quantity	**me**
UNTO	preposition of direction	
UPAS	the deadly antiar tree	**bt**
UPBY	further up (Sc.)	
UPON	on	
URAO	American soda	**mn**
URDE	pointed, variated	**hd**
URDU	a language much used in India	
UREA	a crystalline compound	**md**
URGE	push; drive; impel; incite; spur	
URIA	a genus of sea-birds, guillemots	**zo**
URIC	an acid	**md**
URRY	blue clay near a coal seam	**mn**
URSA	a constellation	
URUS	the European wild ox	**zo**
URVA	an ichneumon (India)	**zo**
USED	habituated; employed; worn	
USER	consumer; expender; subscriber; controller	**cp, tc**
USUS	act, right of making use of something	
UTAS	} festivity, season	
UTIS		
UTIE	wall tie (USA)	
UVAE	grapes, raisins, etc.	**bt**
UVEA	part of the iris of the eye	**md**

V

VADE	fade (Shak.)	

VAIL	veil; tip; gratuity; submission	
VAIN	empty; conceited; unavailing	
VAIR	heraldic fur	**hd**
VAKA	outrigger, sailing canoe	**nt**
VAKE	to be vacant (Sc.)	
VALE	dale; valley; recede; farewell	
VALI	provincial governor (Turk.)	
VAMP	boot-uppers; to patch	
VAMP	cinema character	
VAMP	improvise accompaniment	**mu**
VANE	weathercock; nag; blade; fane; feather-fletching of arrow (archery)	
VANG	peak steadying brace	**nt**
VARA	S. Amer. yd of 33 in (84 cm)	**me**
VARE	a wand of authority	
VARI	monkey (Madagascar)	**zo**
VARY	alter; change; alternate; differ	
VASE	urn	
VASO-	of canal, duct, blood-vessel	**cf, md**
VAST	huge; spacious; colossal	
V-CUT	wedge cut, tunnelling technique	**ce**
VEAL	dinner for prodigal son; calf flesh	**ck, pl**
VEDA	sacred Hindu books	**rl**
VEER	vary; turn; shift	
VEGA	single-crop irrigated land (Sp.); star	**as, pl**
VEIL	mask; cloak; screen; cover	
VEIN	lode; seam; ledge; mood; humour	
VEIN	blood vessel; (vascular) bundle (leaf)	**bt**
VELD	} (South Africa) high grazing	
-VELDT	} land (Transvaal) weald	
VELE	veil (Spens.)	
VELL	rennet; to cut turf	
VELO	speed of 1 ft (30 cm) per sec.	**me**
VENA	a vein	**md**
VEND	sell; hawk; peddle	
VENT	utter; discharge; orifice; sale; wind	
VERB	part of speech	
VERT	the greenery of the forest	**lw**
VERT	convert; pervert; heraldic green	**hd**
VERY	a signal light	
VEST	endow; endue; clothe; a garment	
VETO	ban; forbid; taboo; embargo	
VETU	lozenge	**hd**
VIAL	phial; ampulla; level tube, bubble	
VICE	vise; a screw-press	**to**
VICE	iniquity; defect; sin; in place of	
VIDE	see (Lat.)	
VIED	contested; competed; strove	
VIEW	eye; scan; survey; vista; prospect	
VILE	base; ignoble; paltry; cheap	
VILL	villa; suburban seat	
VINA	East Indian banjo	**mu**
VINE	climbing plant	**bt**
VINT	Russian card game; to make wine	
VINY	producing grapes or vines	
VIOL	antique violin	**mu**
VIRE	crossbow-bolt; heraldic amulet	**hd**

VISA	vise; stamp; permit; authorization
VISE	official endorsement
VIVA-	} of being alive (Lat.) **cf**
VIVI-	
VIVA	long live! (It.) (Sp.) (Ptg.)
VIVE	long live! (Fr.)
VIVO	lively; with animation **mu**
VLEI	artificial lake (S. Africa) **go**
VOCE	the voice; (sotto-voce) (It.)
VOID	null; invalid; empty; vacant; emit
VOLA	rapid series of notes **mu**
VOLE	a grand slam
VOLE	genus of rodents, water-rats, etc. **zo**
VOLT	electrical unit **me**
VOLT	a turn; sudden leap; (fencing)
VOTE	suffrage; ballot; elect; poll
VOYA	anchor cable **nt**
VRIL	force
VULN	to wound (heraldic) **hd**
VYSE	spiral staircase **ar, bd**

W

WADD	manganese ore **mn**
WADE	to ford
WADI	} often dry river bed (Arab.)
WADY	
WAFD	Egyptian nationalist party
WAFF	yaff; to bark; weak; paltry (Sc.)
WAFT	float; convey; beckon; ventilate
WAGA	outrigger sail canoe (Papua) **nt**
WAGE	pay; hire; stipend; salary
WAIF	a stray; vagabond; ownerless
WAIL	cry; weep; deplore; plaint
WAIN	wagon; constellation
WAIR	a plank
WAIT	bide; tarry; linger; serve; minister; carol singer; medieval musician; shawm **mu**
WAKA	Maori canoe **nt**
WAKE	funeral vigil; rouse; trail; wash
WALD	weld; mignonette (Sc.) **bt**
WALE	weal; raised streak; ridge; bruise
WALK	hike; saunter; gait; career; beat; baseball
WALL	dividing construction; rock face; alignment of players (soccer); obstacle (jumping) **bd**
WALT	cranky; tottering
WALY	beautiful; alas (Sc.)
WAME	the belly (Sc.)
WAND	rod; twig; staff; baton; (magic); target (archery) **ga**
WANE	ebb; fail; decline; droop; (moon); bark **bt**
WANG	cheek-bone; shoe-lace
WANT	need; crave; wish; penury
WAPP	shroud-tightener; yachting **nt**

WARD	fend; repel; custody; a minor
WARD	hospital dormitory; bailey, courtyard **ar**
WARE	a caution; goods; seaweed **bt**
WARK	bulwark; work (obs.)
WARM	ardent; fervid; keen; zealous
WARN	caution; admonish; notify
WARP	twist; haul; carpet thread base **nt, tx**
WART	a verruca; an excrescence **md**
WARY	canny; cautious; vigilant
WASE	straw head-pad
WASH	wake; lave; rinse; cleanse
WASP	stinging insect **zo**
WAST	preterite of 'to be'
WATT	unit of work **me**
WAUL	wawl; caterwaul
WAVE	sway; beckon; brandish; ripple
WAVE	swell; billow; comber; roller
WAVY	curly; sinuous; billowy
WAWE	a wave (Spens.)
WAWL	waul; to howl; caterwaul
WAXY	pliant; yielding; wrathful
WEAK	frail; insipid; watery; fragile
WEAL	prosperity; state; wale; stripe
WEAN	alienate; detach
WEAR	bear; don; sport; impair; alter course with stern on to wind **nv**
WEED	a cigar; to root out; eradicate **bt**
WEEK	7 days
WEEL	fish-trap; whirlpool; well (Sc.)
WEEM	underground abode (Sc.)
WEEN	to think; consider; guess; judge
WEEP	sob; bewail; lament
WEFT	threads crossing warp; waif **tx**
WEIR	wear; a low dam across a river
WEKA	Maori hen **zo**
WELD	join together; mignonette **bt**
WELK	wither; shrivel; wrinkle
WELL	fount; source; origin; hale; staircase area **ar, bd**
WELT	shoe-edging; to flog; metal roofing seam **bd**
WEND	wander; a Slavonic race
WENT	left; departed; decamped
WEPT	cried; lamented; sobbed
WERE	} past of 'to be'
WERT	
WEST	cardinal direction
WHAP	whop; whip; defeat
WHAT	interrogative
WHEN	adverb of time
WHET	sharpen; heighten; rouse
WHEW	exclamation of exertion
WHEY	skimmed milk
WHID	to whisk; a lie; a quarrel (Sc.)
WHIG	Liberal; sour whey
WHIM	caprice; crotchet; notion
WHIN	doleritic igneous rock **gl**
WHIN	gorse; furse **bt**

WHIP	quirt; flog; driver; coachman; V-shaped woodwind instrument; official, controlling group (MPs and cyclists)	mu
WHIR	whirl; spin; twirl	
WHIT	jot; iota; speck; scintilla	
WHIZ	whizz; a noise	
WHOA!	exclamation to halt	
WHOM	objective of who	
WHOP	whap; whip; defeat	
WHOT	hot (Spens.)	
WHUR	a noise	
WICK	(candle); creek; quick; alive; stone against stone (curling)	ga
WIDE	spacious; rife; distant; (cricket)	
WIEP	fascine; part of Dutch mattress	
WIFE	spouse	
WILD	rash; disorderly; savage	
WILE	ruse; stratagem; dodge; chicanery	
WILL	wish; desire; bequeath; testament	
WILT	to droop; to wither	
WILY	sly; artful; crafty; insidious	
WIND	coil; twist; turn; breeze; blow	
WINE	fermented fruit juice	
WING	to fly; to wound; aerofoil; stage; (chair); flank	
WING	flanker (football) fielder (baseball, lacrosse); annexe	ga
WINK	to nictitate	
WINY	having the flavour of wine	
WIPE	rub; clean; handkerchief	
WIRE	bind; snare; telegram	
WIRY	flexible and strong	
WISE	sagacious; sage; sapient; method	
WISH	will; want; desire; behest	
WISP	(of snipe); small broom; a whisk	
WISS	to wish (Sc.)	
WIST	knew	
WITE	to blame; to reproach (Spens.)	
WITH	withe; a twig; in company	
WIVE	to marry	
WOAD	plant yielding a blue dye	bt
WOLD	wood; a down; a weald	
WOLF	devour; wild canine; jarring howl sound	zo
WOMB	uterus	
WONT	habit; custom; practice; use	
WOOD	timber; grove; forest	bt
WOOF	the weft	
WOOL	fleece; a staple product	
WOOM	beaver fur	
WOON	governor of a Burmese province	
WORD	term; news; advice; pledge; (pass-)	
WORD	remark; rumour; data units	cp
WORE	bore; sported; donned; lasted	
WORK	toil; operate; endeavour	
WORM	a groveller; to insinuate	zo
WORN	rather the worse for wear	
WORT	malt after mashing; a plant	bt
WOVE	intertwined; matted; knitted	

WOWF	crazy (Sc.)	
WRAP	wind; swathe; enfold; muffle	
WREN	member of WRNS; a bird	zo
WRIT	summons; formal document	lw
WROT	wrought timber abbrev.	me
WULL	will (Spens.)	
WYND	a lane; narrow alley	

X

XEMA	genus of gulls	zo
XENO-	being strange, foreign (Gr.)	cf
XERO-	of being dry (Gr.)	cf
XMAS	Noel; Yule; Christmas	
X-RAY	Roentgen ray; tactical move (chess)	md, ga
XYST	gymnasium	

Y

YAFF	waff; to bark (Sc.)	
YALD	yauld; active; supple (Sc.)	
YAMA	Hindu Pluto	
YANK	an American; to heave; hoik; extract with a twist	
YAPP	limp leather binding	
YARD	36 in (91 cm); enclosed area	me
YARD	(Scotland); a court; spar with sail, gaff of lugsail	nt
YARE	dexterous; quick; prompt	
YARN	spun thread; sailor's story	
YARR	to snarl; the spurrey plant	bt
YAUD	a jade (Sc.)	
YAUP	yelp; hungry; blue titmouse	zo
YAWL	yowl; howl; fishing-boat	nt
YAWN	gape	
YAWS	tropical disease	md
YEAH	yes (USA)	
YEAN	yeen; to lamb	
YEAR	12 months	
YEEN	yean; to produce; to lamb	
YEGG	hobo; cracksman; safe-breaker	
YELD	barren, not giving milk	
YELK	yolk	
YELL	bawl; scream; screech	
YELP	yap; cry of pain; bark	
YERK	jerk; rouse; excite	
YEST	yeast	
YETI	abominable snowman	zo
YETT	yate; a gate (Sc.)	
YILL	ale (Sc.)	
YIPS	nervousness (golf)	
YITE	the yellow bunting	zo
YLEM	theoretical neutron substance	nc
YMIR	the Frost Giant (Scand.)	
YOGA	Hindu philosophy	
YOGI	ascetic yoga practitioner (Ind.)	
YO-HO	exclamation	

YOIT	the yellow bunting	zo
YOKE	team together; enslave; restrain	
YOKE	shoulder crosspiece harness, also of rudder	
YOKO	Japanese wood block	
YOLK	} wool oil	
YOLKY		
YELK		
YOND	beyond; yonder; mad (Spens.)	
YOOP	an onomatopoetic sob	
YORE	in olden time	
YOTE	board-game (West Africa)	
YOUR	of you	
YOWL	howl; yawl; gowl; bawl	
YO-YO	a toy; a bandalore	
YUAN	(China)	nm
YUCK	to itch; the itch	
YUGA	one of the Hindu ages of the world	
YUKO	score in judo	
YULE	Xmas; Noel; winter solstice	rl
YUMP	bump or collision (motor racing)	
YUNX	the wryneck bird	zo
YURT	a Siberian house or tent	
Y-WIS	i'wis; truly	

Z

ZAIM	Turkish military chief	
ZANY	buffoon; merry-andrew; mimic	
ZARF	zurf; metal coffee-cup holder	
ZATI	an Indian parrot	zo
ZAWN	cavern	mn
Z-BAR	building fixture	
ZEAL	fervour; intensity; enthusiasm	
ZEBU	humped domestic ox (India)	zo

ZEIN	zeine; a protein found in maize	bt
ZEND	a Persian dialect	
ZENO-	of strangeness, foreign (Gr.)	cf
ZEPP	zeppelin; airship	
ZERO	cipher; naught; nothing	
ZEST	peel-flavouring; gusto; relish	
ZETA	the Greek Z	
ZETA	sexton's room over porch	rl
ZEUS	Olympian deity	
ZIMB	Abyssinian tse-tse fly	zo
ZINC	a metallic element	ch
ZING	pep (USA)	
ZION	a hill in Jerusalem	
ZOAR	a place of refuge	
ZOBO	zhobo; dsomo; hybrid yak-cow	zo
ZOEA	crustaceans in a larval stage	zo
ZOIC	pertaining to life	
ZOID	zoospore	bt
ZOLA	Borax hardener	ch
ZOLL	German toll or custom-duty	
ZONA	zone; belt	
ZONA	patch; strip; area	zo
ZONE	belt; girdle; district; describe an area	cp
ZOOM	aerobatic manoeuvre	
ZOON	the product of a fertilized ovum	
ZOOP	extraneous noise	ac
ZOOT	fashionable; gaudy	
ZSAR	Czar; Ksar; Tsar; Tzar (Rus.)	
ZULU	African nation	
ZUNA	Angola sheep	zo
ZUNI	Mexican Indians	
ZUPA	Serbian village confederation	
ZURF	zarf; metal coffee-pot holder	
ZYME	a ferment; a disease germ	md

A

AAZIZ	Queen of Sheba; also Balkis	
ABACA	Manila hemp	bt
ABACI	counting frames	
ABACI	crowns of columns	ar
ABACK	aft; behind; backwards; sail position when wind is on wrong side	nv
ABAFT	aft; astern	nt
ABASE	lower; reduce; disgrace	
ABASH	awe; confound; disconcert	
ABASK	basking in the sun	
ABATE	wane; diminish; lessen	
ABBEY	a monastery	rl
ABBOT	the head of an abbey	rl
ABCEE	an abc; an alphabet	
ABEAM	abreast; on the beam	nt
ABEAR	to bear; endure; tolerate	
ABELE	the hoary poplar	bt
ABHAL	the fruit of the cypress	bt
ABHOR	hate; loathe; abominate; detest	
ABIDE	lodge; tarry; tolerate; sojourn	
ABIES	the fir genus	bt
ABLEN	a freshwater fish; the bleak	zo
ABLER	more competent; more expert	
ABLET	ablen; the bleak	zo
ABODE	house; dwelling; home; lived	
ABOHM	electro-magnetic unit	me
ABOIL	on the boil; boiling	
ABOMA	boa-constrictor (S. Amer.)	zo
A-BOMB	nuclear weapon	
ABORT	to miscarry; sterile; break off	cp, md
ABOUT	almost; around; anent; near	
ABOVE	aloft; over; before; exceeding	
ABRAY	rouse; startle; waken (obs.)	
ABRIN	toxic protein	ch
ABUSE	misuse; defame; traduce; revile	
ABUZZ	buzzing; humming	
ABYSM }	chasm; bottomless pit;	
ABYSS }	gulf; gorge; gap; fissure	
ACARI	mites and ticks	zo
ACCRA	Caribbean batter fritters	ck
ACERA	bubble-shell genus	zo
ACERB	sour; bitter; acid; harsh	
ACHAR	acid pickles; salt relishes (Pers.)	
ACHED	pained; sorrowed; grieved	
ACHOR	dandruff	md
ACINI	granulations; berries	md, bt
ACKEE	Jamaican fruit	bt
ACLIS	spiked club; javelin	
ACOCK	jaunty; defiantly	
ACOLD	chilly	
ACONE	insects' coneless compound eyes	zo
ACORN	oak seed; cord-end	bt
ACRED	lavishly landed	
ACRID	sour; pungent; bitter; mordant	

ACRON	head of embryonic insect	zo
ACTED	performed; simulated; deputized	
ACTIN	muscle protein	bl
ACTON	padded jerkin	
ACTOR	player; trouper; histrion	
ACUTE	keen; sharp; accent (illness)	md
ADAGE	proverb; dictum; maxim; saw	
ADAPT	adjust; accommodate	
ADAYS	nowadays	
ADDAX	African antelope	zo
ADDED	affixed; subjoined; appended	
ADDER	viper; snake; asp; calculator	cp, zo
ADDLE	confuse; putrid; muddled	
ADEEM	to revoke a legacy	lw
ADEPS	fatty tissue	md
ADEPT	adroit; expert; proficient	
AD-HOC	for a set purpose	
ADIEU	farewell; goodbye	
ADIOS	farewell (Sp.)	
AD-LIB	extemporise; natural body weight	md, mu
ADMAN	advertising pundit	
ADMIT	acknowledge; concede; own	
ADMIX	infuse; blend; mingle	
ADOBE	sun dried brick	
ADOBO	braised stew (Philippines)	ck
ADOPT	accept; assume; espouse; father	
ADORE	worship; revere; idolize; love	
ADORN	decorate; deck; enrich; garnish	
ADOWN	downward	
ADOXY	a tolerant belief	
ADSUM	(present at a roll-call)	
ADULT	a grown-up; mature; ripe	
ADUST	incinerated; pulverized	
ADYTA	chancels	rl
AEGER	sick; ill	md
AEGIS	Minerva's shield; protection	
AERIE	eyrie; eagle's nest	zo
AESOP	a fabulist; parable teller	
AFEAR	affear; to terrify (obs.)	
AFFIX	add; fasten; subjoin; attach	
AFIRE	aflame; blazing	
AFLAT	level with the ground	
AFOAM	foaming	
AFOOT	astir; happening	
AFORE	previously; before	
AFOUL	entangled; in collision with	
AFRIC	African	
AFRIT	afreet; evil demon; jinn (Arab)	
AFTER	later; in imitation of	
AGAIN	anew; afresh; moreover	
AGAIT	astir; afoot (Sc.)	
AGAMA	genus of lizards; saurians	zo
AGAMI	game bird, edible when young (S. Amer.)	zo, ck
AGAPE	staring; a love feast	
AGATA	shaded coloured glass (N. Amer.)	
AGATE	a quartz; ruby type	mn
AGATE	type printing measure	pr
AGATY	like an agate	

AGAVE	American aloe	**bt**
AGAVE	daughter of Cadmus	
AGAVE	succulent cactus; drink; peyote drug	
AGAZE	gazing	
AGENT	doer; factor; deputy; proxy	**lw**
AGGER	a mound; rampart	
AGILE	nimble; spry; alert; brisk	
AGING	} growing old	
AGEING		
AGIST	pasture rate	**lw**
AGLEE	} asquint; askew; awry; off the	
AGLEY	} line (Sc.)	
AGLET	a pendant; braided tag	
AGLOW	glowing; gleaming; shining	
AGNEL	French gold coin (lamb)	**nm**
AGNUS	Dei; pascal lamb	**rl, zo**
AGONE	ago; past; since; a line	
AGONY	pangs; anguish; torment; throe	
AGOOD	in earnest	
AGORA	Greek, Roman market place	
AGRAS	sweet Algerian drink	
AGREE	accede; engage; conform; concur	
AGRIN	grinning	
AGROM	an Indian tongue disease	**md**
AGUED	fevered; shivering	
AHEAD	leading; onward; in front	
AHEAP	trembling with fear	
AHIGH	on high	
AHOLD	close to the wind	**nt**
AHULL	hove to	**nt**
AIDED	abetted; seconded; succoured	
AIDER	helper; assistant; acolyte	
AIERY	aerie; eyrie; eagle's nest	**zo**
AIGRE	eagre; bore; high tidal wave	
AILED	afflicted; peaked; pined	
AIMED	directed; pointed; trained	
AIMER	purposeful person	
AIRED	ventilated; spread abroad	
AIRER	dryer; ventilator	
AISLE	passage; walk	**rl**
AITCH	(h); aitch-bone	
AJUGA	bugle genus of plants	**bt**
AKALI	Sikh fanatic	
AKELA	Kipling's lone wolf	**zo**
ALACK	alas; lackaday; woe is me	
ALAND	landed	
ALANT	heraldic mastiff	**hd**
ALARM	fear; scare; dismay; a tocsin	
ALARY	alar; having wings	**zo**
ALATE	winged; of late; lately	
ALBIN	an opaque white mineral	**mn**
ALBUM	book for photos or stamps	
ALCES	the elk; moose (N. America)	**zo**
ALDER	a hardwood tree	**bt**
ALERT	wary; watchful; vigilant	
ALGAE	the seaweeds	**bt**
ALGID	cold; chilly	**md**
ALGIN	seaweed extract for iodine	
ALGOL	a star; language-data	**cp**

ALGOR	unusual coldness	**md**
ALGUM	almug; sandal-wood	**bt**
ALIAS	otherwise; an assumed name	
ALIBI	proof of absence	**lw**
ALIEN	strange; exotic; remote; foreign	
ALIGN	} adjust; rectify; arrange;	
ALINE	} regulate; conform	
ALIKE	similar; analogous; equal	
ALISH	resembling beer	
ALITE	ground clinker from sintering	**ch**
ALIVE	vital; quick; alert; brisk	
ALKYD	glyptal resins; polyesters	
ALKYL	aliphatic radicals	**ch**
ALLAH	Moslem word for the Deity	**rl**
ALLAY	lull; calm; relieve; repress	
ALLEY	large marble; taw; passage	
ALL-IN	(policy) comprehensive	
ALL-IN	exhausted	
ALLIS	the allice shad; a fish	**zo**
ALLOD	freehold estate	
ALLOO	halloo	
ALLOT	distribute; apportion; assign	
ALLOW	admit; own; concede; grant	
ALLOY	a base admixture	
ALLYL	organic radicle	**ch**
ALMAH	} an Egyptian dancing girl	
ALMEH		
ALMRY	almonry; cupboard	
ALMUG	algum; sandal-wood	**bt**
ALOED	} tinctured with aloes;	
ALOID	} resembling aloes; bitter aloe	
ALOIN	} extract	**md**
ALOES	bitter purgative drug	**bt**
ALOFT	above; overhead; skyward	
ALONE	only; sole; single; isolated	
ALONG	by; beside; together	
ALOOF	apart; away; distant	
ALOSE	allis; shad-fish	**zo**
ALOUD	audibly; loudly; clamorously	
ALPEN	Alpine	
ALPHA	the first or beginning (Gr. letter)	
ALPIA	bird-seed	**bt**
ALTAR	shrine; sanctuary; receding step in drydock	**nt, rl**
ALTER	vary; change; turn; transform	
ALULA	bastard wing	**zo**
ALURE	cloister; gallery (obs.)	
ALUTA	leather treated with alum	
ALWAY	ever; always; regularly	
AMAIN	forcibly; suddenly; violently	
AMASS	heap; gather; accumulate; pile	
AMATE	subdue; daunt; stupefy (obs.)	
AMATI	violin (Cremona)	**mu**
AMAZE	daze; astound; perplex	
AMBER	fossilized resin	**mn**
AMBIT	precinct; extent; compass	
AMBLE	dawdle; saunter; stroll	
AMBLY-	dysfunction (Gr.)	**cf, md**
AMBON	lectern; pulpit	**rl**
AMBRY	alms-box; niche; almonry	**rl**

AMEER	} Afghan king; emir; prince	
AMERE		
AMEND	emend; better; rectify; correct	
AMENT	a catkin	bt
AMICE	pilgrim's cloak; linen gown	
AMICT	amice; cape or hood	rl
AMIDE	} an ammonia compound	ch
AMINE		
AMISS	wrong; faulty; erroneously	
AMITY	friendship; fellowship; harmony	
AMMON	Tibetan sheep	zo
AMONG	emong; amidst; amongst	
AMORT	halfdead; dejected; spiritless	
AMOUR	an affair; a love intrigue	
AMOVE	stir up; to affect	
AMPHI-	both	cf
AMPLE	ointment-box; wide; capacious	
AMPLY	plentifully; bountifully	
AMPUL	ample; oil-jar; flask	
AMSEL	} blackbird	zo
AMZEL		
AMUCK	madly; in murderous frenzy	
AMUSE	entertain; cheer; charm; divert	
ANANA	the pineapple	bt
ANCLE	also ANKLE; foot-leg joint	pl
ANCON	the elbow; a console	md
ANDRO-	male	cf
ANEAL	anele; to anoint	rl
ANEAR	near; nigh	
ANELE	extreme unction	rl
ANENT	concerning	
ANGEL	divine messenger; fish	zo, nm
ANGER	ire; rage; choler; passion	
ANGIO-	of blood vessels	cf
ANGLE	a corner; to entice; to fish; (tennis)	ga
ANGOR	acute pain or anxiety	
ANGRY	irate; wroth; piqued; riled	
ANGST	anxiety; anguish; pain (Ge.)	pc
ANIGH	nigh; near by	
ANILE	old womanish; imbecile	
ANIMA	female part of personality; soul	pc
ANIME	resin; fiery	bt
ANION	electro-negative ion	
ANISE	plant furnishing aniseed	bt
ANISO	unequal	
ANKER	European liquid measure	me
ANKLE	also ANCLE; foot-leg joint	pl
ANKUS	elephant goad	
ANNAL	a Mass	rl
ANNAT	an Ecclesiastical levy	rl
ANNET	the kittiwake	zo
ANNEX	add; append; join; unite	
ANNOY	badger; worry; affront; molest	
ANNUL	cancel; quash; revoke	
ANODE	positive electrical pole	el
ANOIA	idiocy; anoesia	pc
ANOMY	urban isolation syndrome	pc
ANOMY	lawlessness; miracle	
ANONA	custard-apple genus	bt

ANTIC	fantastic; prank; lark; caper	
ANTRE	a cave; a cavern	
ANURA	frogs, toads; batrachians	ze
ANVIL	ossicle, ear bone for sound	zo, md
ANVIL	blacksmith's forge block; operatic percussion	mu
ANZAC	Australian, NZ, Army Corps	
AOGAI	lacquer inlaid with mother-of-pearl (Haliotis), Japan	
AORTA	the great artery; coronary	pl
APACE	rapidly; swiftly; at speed	
APART	aloof; asunder; separately	
APEAK	} anchor aweigh	
APEEK		
APERT	open; public (obs.)	
APERY	monkey-house	zo
APHID	} green-fly; ant-cows	zo
APHIS		zo
APIAN	relating to bees	zo
APING	copying; mimicking; imitating	
APISH	ape-like	zo
APIUM	the celery genus	bt
APNEA	cessation of breathing	md
APODA	eels, etc.	zo
APODE	limbless creature	zo
A-POLE	wooden A frame	ce
APOOP	astern	nt
APORT	to port	nt
APPAL	scare; daunt; shock; astound	
APPAY	apay; to satisfy (obs.)	
APPEL	stop-call (fencing); appeal	ga
APPLE	the award of Paris; fruit; (Adam's); ball (baseball); orb; big city	bt, ga
APPLY	bestow; use; employ; refer	
APPUI	} support; reciprocal action	
APPUY		
APRIL	4th month	
APRON	short cassock; protective garment	rl
APRON	wedge; lathe; sea defence	to
APRON	aircraft parking area	
APRON	lead sheet dam slope; panel	ar
APSIS	extreme point in an orbit	
APTLY	fittingly; appositely; apropos	
ARABA	Turkish ox-cart; vehicle	
ARABY	Arabia	
ARACK	arrack; fermented palm juice	
ARBOR	tree genus; bower	bt
ARBOR	spindle; axis	
ARDEA	the heron genus	zo
ARDES	$5\frac{1}{2}$ bushels, Egyptian	me
ARDIL	fibre from groundnuts	bt
AREAD	} to divine; counsel; explain; interpret; solve	
AREDE		
AREED		
AREAL	(area); superficial	
AREAR	in the rear; to raise; uplift	
ARECA	betel-nut palm	bt
AREFY	dry up; shrivel; wither	
ARENA	ring; stage; battlefield	

ARENG	the sago palm	**bt**
ARETE	knife-edge mountain ridge (Swiss)	
ARGAL	crude tartar	**ch**
ARGIL	potter's earth	**mn**
ARGOL	argal; crude tartar	**ch**
ARGON	a light gas	**ch**
ARGOT	slang; jargon (Fr.)	
ARGUE	plead; dispute; reason; debate	
ARGUS	watchful; a pheasant	**zo**
ARIAN	heretic sect (Christian)	**rl**
ARIEL	a sprite; a gazelle	**zo**
ARIES	the Ram of the Zodiac	
ARIOT	riotously; uproariously	
ARISE	ascend; soar; emerge; rebel	
ARLES	earnest money on engagement	
ARMED	equipped; protected	
ARMET	medieval helmet	
ARMIL	insignia of royalty	
ARNEE	Indian buffalo	
ARNOT	pig-nut; earth-nut	**bt**
AROAR	uproariously; ariot	
AROID	a plant allied to the arum	**bt**
AROMA	scent; perfume; fragrance; odour	
AROSE	got up; began; sprang; revolted	
ARRAH	Indian lentil; Irish expletive	**bt, ck**
ARRAS	tapestry; hangings	
ARRAY	range; marshal; contents	**cp**
ARRET	decree; arrest	**lw**
ARRIS	sharp edge; arete	
ARROW	bolt; shaft; dart; reed	
ARSIS	vocal inflection; emphasis	
ARSON	fire-raising; pyromania	**lw**
ARTEL	a Russian guild	
ARYAN	Indo-European	
ASADO	Argentine barbecue	**ck**
ASCII	dwellers on the equator	
ASCOT	fashionable race meeting	
ASCUS	spore case	**bt**
ASDIC	submarine-detector	**nt**
ASHEN	wan; pale; hueless; pallid	
ASHES	results of cricket on the hearth	**ga**
ASHET	a serving dish (Sc.)	
ASHUR	Assyrian god	
ASIAN	Asiatic	
ASIDE	apart; away; aloof; laterally	
ASKED	invited; demanded; requested	
ASKER	a newt; petitioner; suitor	**zo**
ASKEW	awry; aslant; askance; oblique	
ASOAK	sodden	
ASPEN	the trembling poplar	**bt**
ASPER	a small silver Turkish coin	**nm**
ASPIC	savoury meat jelly; sap	**ck**
ASPIC	12 pounder cannon; lavender	**bt**
ASSAI	enough; very	**mu**
ASSAY	essay; test; try; analysis	
ASSER	rafter; thin lath	
ASSES	mokes; donkeys; burros	
ASSET	a possession	
ASSOT	besot; infatuate (Spens.)	
ASTAY	a cable direction	**nt**

ASTEL	a dam; a splinter	
ASTER	flowering plant	**bt**
ASTIR	alert; awake; agog; excited	
ASTON	astun; astonished (obs.)	
ASWAY	swinging; oscillating	
ASWIM	afloat	
ATAXY	functional disorder	**md**
ATCHI	Caucasian ibex	**zo**
ATELO-	incomplete; imperfect	**cf**
ATILT	on edge; slanting	
ATIMY	dishonour; disgrace	
ATLAS	a Titan; a moth; a bound collection of maps	**zo**
ATMAN	the Buddhist ego	
ATOLL	coral island	
ATOMY	atom; skeleton; a pygmy	
ATONE	expiate; satisfy; propitiate	
ATONY	debility; off colour	**md**
ATRIP	anchor clear; aweigh	**nt**
ATTAR	otto; fragrant rose oil	
ATTIC	Athenian; (salt); garret; loft	
ATTLE	refuse from mines; rubbish	
AUBIN	Canterbury gallop	
AUDIO-	related to hearing	**cf, tc**
AUDIT	examine accounts; review of patients; record	**cp**
AUFIN	bishop (chess)	**ga**
AUGER	a drill	**to**
AUGET	explosive charge for mines	
AUGHT	zero; ought; naught; 0	
AUGUR	seer; soothsayer; portend	
AULAE	Roman halls or courts	
AULIC	(royal court)	
AULOS	ancient Gr. oboe-like instrument	**mu**
AUMIL	amildar; Indian tax collector	
AUNTY	auntie	
AURAL	(exhalation); (ear)	
AURIC	golden	
AURIN	golden red dye	**ch**
AURUM	gold; chemical element	**ch**
AUXIN	growth-affecting substance	**ch**
AVAIL	benefit; help; suffice; use	
AVAST	stop; stay; cease	**nt**
AVENS	the herb bennet	**bt**
AVERT	avoid; divert; forfend; parry	
AVETE	greetings, welcome	
AVGAS	aviation spirit	**ae**
AVIAN	bird-like	**zo**
AVINE	pertaining to birds	**zo**
AVION	aeroplane (Fr.)	
AVISO	a dispatch boat (Sp.)	**nt**
AVOID	shun; elude; forsake; eschew	
AVOUE	French lawyer; advocate	**lw**
AWAIT	tarry; bide; stay; pause	
AWAKE	alert; ready; alive; vigilant	
AWARD	give; grant; adjudge; prize	
AWARE	mindful; conscious	
AWASH	nearly submerged	**nt**
AWAVE	waving; fluttering	
AWEEK	per week	

AWFUL	dire; dread; fearful; imposing	
AWHIR	whirring; spinning	
AWING	on the wing; flying; cowing	
AWNED	bearded like barley	**bt**
AWNER	grain separator	
AWOKE	bestirred; roused; incited	
AWORK	at work	
AXIAL	} on the same axis	
AXILE		
AXIOM	truism; assumed truth	
AXION	brain/spinal cord	**pl**
AXITE	a propellant	
AXLED	having a spindle	
AXMAN	chainman (USA)	
AXOID	axoidean	
AYELP	yelping; howling	
AZIDE	hydrazoic acid salt	**ch**
AZOIC	devoid of life	
AZOTE	nitrogen	**ch**
AZOTH	the alchemist cure-all; panacea	
AZOXY	potash/nitro-affected	**ch**
AZTEC	extinct Mexican-Indian	
AZURE	} sky-blue; the sky; the vault of	
AZURN	} heaven	
AZURY	blue; cerulean	
AZUSA	missile tracking system	**ro**
AZYME	unleavened bread	

B

BABEL	tower; din; jargon; clamour	
BABOO	babu; Indian clerk	
BABUL	gum-arabic tree	
BACCA	a berry	**bt**
BACCY	bacco; tobacco	**bt**
BACKS	defending players, dorsals; (football); Cam. University feature	**ar, ga, pl**
BACON	something to be saved; back-gammon	**ck**
BADAN	Adeni dhow	**nt**
BADGE	mark; emblem; recognition signal	**cp**
BADLY	corruptly; wickedly; imperfectly	
BAFFY	an old golf club	
BAGEL	hard glazed doughnut roll (Jew.)	**ck**
BAGGY	loose fitting; bulging	
BAHAR	3½ cwt (197 kg), East Indian	**me**
BAIRN	a child (Sc.)	
BAIZE	bayze; a coarse cloth	**tx**
BAJAK	sailship of Borneo Dyaks	**nt**
BAJAN	bejan; a freshman (Sc.)	
BAKAL	oriental shopkeeper	
BAKED	parched; hardened; dried up	
BAKER	bread/pastry maker	**ck**
BALAS	orange ruby	**mn**
BALED	in bundles	**ae**
BALER	a bowl; scoop	
BALKY	apt to stop suddenly	

BALMY	fragrant; soothing	
BALOO	the Bear	**as**
BALSA	Peruvian raft; a tree	**bt, nt**
BALUN	balance/unbalance transformer	**tc**
BAMBI	faun	**zo**
BANAK	American tree	**bt**
BANAL	commonplace; trivial; trite	
BANAT	Transylvanian district	
BANCA	outrigger sail canoe (Philippines)	**nt**
BANCO	bench; bank money	**lw**
BANDY	ice hockey; crooked; dispute	**ga**
BANJO	job an octaroon would like; 5 string fretted, plucked, stringed instrument	**mu**
BANNS	public notice of marriage	**lw, rl**
BANNY	a minnow	**zo**
BANTU	Negroid African tribe	
BARBE	war-horse armour; nun's kerchief	
BARBS	jagged tip of feathers	**zo**
BARED	naked; unadorned; stripped	
BARET	a biretta; cardinal's cap	**rl**
BARGE	shove; jostle	
BARGE	} cargo craft; large surfing board	
BARCA	}	**nt**
BARIA	baryta	**mn**
BARIC	pert. to weight/barium; barometric	
BARKY	of bark	
BARMY	(yeast); crazy; insane	
BARON	(of beef); a title	
BARRE	single finger chord on guitar	**mu**
BARRY	divided by horizontal bars	**hd**
BARYE	unit of pressure dynes	**me**
BASAL	basic; fundamental source	
BASED	founded on	
BASEL	tanned skin	**le**
BASIC	basal; fundamental source	**cp**
BASIL	chisel edge; a herb	**bt, ck**
BASIN	pond; dock; reservoir; bowl; trough	**ga, pl**
BASIS	ground work; first principle	
BASON	a basin	
BASSE	bass; fish like a perch	**zo**
BASSO	a bass singer (It.)	**mu**
BASTA	stop! enough (It.)	**mu**
BASTE	cook; sew; stitch; thrash	
BASTO	ace of clubs (cards)	**ga**
BATAK	Mayo-Polynesian language	
BATAK	people in Sumatra	
BATCH	lot; amount; crowd; series	**cp**
BATED	restrained; repressed; reduced	
BATEY	gold and silver embroidery	
BATHE	immerse	
BATHY-	deep (bathysphere)	**cf**
BATIK	method of dyeing (Ind.)	**tx**
BATIS	wattle-eye flycatcher	**zo**
BATON	staff; wand; sceptre; rod; (relay) athletics; truncheon; bread	**mu, ck, ga**
BATTA	Indian grant	
BATTY	bat-like; dotty	

BAUGE	cloth; drugget	**tx**
BAULK	deliberate fault (badminton); hinder; refuse (horse-jumping)	**ga**
BAULK	timber beam; thwart (billiards)	**ga**
BAVIN	faggot of brushwood	**bt, nt**
BAWDY	lewd; immoral	
BAYED	recessed; howled like a dog	
BAYOU	channel, outlet of river/lake	
BAZAR	bazaar; mart; souk; exchange	
BEACH	shore; strand; sands; margin	
BEADS	a rosary	**rl**
BEADY	small and bright	
BE-ALL	sum and substance; ultimate	
BEAMY	shining; radiant; broad	
BEANO	jamboree; beanfeast; spree	
BEARD	defy; oppose; confront	
BEAST	brute; ruffian; animal	
BEATS	(heart); (drum); fluctuations in sound intensity; strokes	**mu, pl, ps**
BEAUX	gallants (Fr.)	
BEBOP	dissonant jazz	**mu**
BECHE	drill extractor	**to**
BECKE	of microscope juncture light	**lt**
BEDADI	Irish interjection	
BEDEL	beadle (obs.)	
BEDEW	sprinkle; moisten	
BEDIM	obscure; cloud; darken	
BEECH	a hardwood tree	**bt**
BEEFY	stolid; powerful	
BEELD	shelter (Sc.)	
BEELE	pickaxe	**to**
BEERY	maudlin; fuddled	
BEFIT	suit; become	
BEFOG	confuse; obfuscate	
BEFUR	cover with fur or scale	
BEGADI	exclamation of surprise	
BEGAN	started; initiated; originated	
BEGAT	bred; sired; engendered	
BEGEM	bejewel	
BEGET	produce; generate	
BEGIN	start; initiate; commence	
BEGOT	procreated; gave rise to	
BEGUM	Moslem princess	
BEGUN	originated; opened	
BEHEN	sea-lavender	**bt**
BEIGE	fabric; yellowish grey	
BEING	existence; actuality	
BEISA	oryx; unicorn	**zo**
BEJAN	bajan; freshman (Sc.)	
BEKAH	half shekel (Hebrew)	**nm**
BEKER	S. African cup	
BELAY	fasten; hold	**nt**
BELCH	eructate; discharge; emit	
BELEE	on the lee side	
BELGA	Belgian currency	
BELIE	falsify; contradict; slander	
BELIT	rekindled; illuminated	
BELLE	a beauteous damsel	
BELLY	stomach; abdomen	

BELLY	upper side of stringed instrument; foul play (Am. football); (dance); part of bow (archery); to swell; underside of surfboard; (laugh)	**ga, mu**
BELOW	under; beneath; in Hades	
BEMAD	madden	
BENCH	seat; form; court; tribunal; form of quarry	**ce**
BENDS	cramps, pains (deepsea divers)	**md**
BENDY	divided into bends	**hd**
BENET	to ensnare; an exorcist	
BENJY	a straw hat	
BENNE	bene; an oil plant	**bt**
BENTH	ground ivy	**bt**
BENTY	covered with dry grass	
BEPAT	pat or tap repeatedly	
BERET	Basque cap	
BEROB	rob; plunder; pillage	
BEROE	luminous medusa	**zo**
BERRY	mound; barrow; fruit	**bt**
BERTH	bed; post; situation	**nt**
BERYL	a gem	**mn**
BERYX	perch-like sea fish	**zo**
BESAN	Indian lentil flour	**ck**
BESET	assail; encircle; surround	
BESIT	besiege	
BESOM	a broom of twigs, for ice sweeping (curling)	
BESOT	assot; get fuddled, or drunk	
BETEL	nut of the areca palm	**bt**
BETON	a kind of concrete	
BETSO	a small Venetian coin	**nm**
BETTY	flask; jemmy; sweet pastry	**ck**
BEVEL	} technique for glass, gem border; slant; to incline	**to**
BEZEL		
BEWET	to wet; to moisten	
BEWIG	to don a wig	
BEWIT	leather strap in falconry	
BEZAN	Bengali cotton cloth	**tx**
BEZAN	}	
BIZAN	} small ketch	**nt**
BEZAAN	}	
BEZEL	setting; groove	
BEZIL	} groove; metal setting for glass	
BEVEL	} or stone, door, gem in clock	
BHANG	hashish; Indian hemp	**bt**
BHYLE	Indian ox	**zo**
BIBBS	wooden brackets	**nt**
BIBLE	The Scriptures	**rl**
BIDDY	a fowl; a chicken	**zo**
BIDET	sitz bath; pack-pony	**zo**
BIDON	about 5 qt (5.6 litres)	**me**
BIDRI	Indian metal-ware	
BIELD	shelter; protection	
BIFER	twice-yearly flowering/fruiting	**bt**
BIFID	two-clefted	
BIGHT	cove; bay; coil; loop	**nt**
BIGLY	ostentatiously	
BIGOT	zealot; fanatic; dogmatist	

BIJOU	small; pretty; gem; trinket	
BILBO	Spanish rapier	
BILGE	bulging part of a cask; nonsense; hull space below waterline; curve of hull	nt
BILIN	bile	md
BILLI	giga; one thousand million 10⁹	cp
BILLY	Australian cooking can, goat (male)	zo
BINAC	Binary Automatic Computer	
BINAL	twin, double	
BINGE	a carousal	
BINGO	brandy; gambling pastime	
BINNY	a Nile fish	zo
BIOME	largest land community area	ec
BIOTA	a region's fauna/flora	ec
BIPED	two-footed animal	zo
BIPOD	(c.f. tripod) two-legged	
BIRCH	to flog; forest tree	bt
BIRLE	to carouse (Sc.)	
BIRSE	bristle; to bruise	
BIRSY	stubbly	
BIRTH	genesis; nativity; origin	
BISON	American buffalo	zo
BITCH	female dog; wolf; disagreeable woman; spike	ce
BITER	nibbler; cheat	
BITTS	a cable attachment	nt
BITTY	incomplete; fragmentary	
BIWAR	Japanese lute-form	mu
BIXIN	annatto	ch
BLACK	ebon; inky; dusky; sombre	
BLADE	roisterer; leaf; flat edge (bat, club, (golf), knife, oar, sword)	bt
BLAES	hardened shale	mn
BLAIN	blister; blotch	md
BLAME	chide; rebuke; reproach	
BLAND	soft; suave; mild; benign	
BLANK	lacuna; vacant; empty; void; (cartridge); no score	
BLARE	blazon; proclaim; clangour	
BLASE	cloyed; surfeited (Fr.)	
BLASE	immune to novelty or impressions	
BLASH	watery stuff (Sc.)	
BLAST	gust; explode; (shrivel); cell; noise	
BLAST	release memory areas	cp
BLATE	shy; bashful (Sc.)	
BLAZE	(horse); flame; proclaim	
BLAZE	a mark on trees	
BLEAK	drear; desolate; river-fish	zo
BLEAR	dim; rheumy; watery	
BLEAT	the cry of a sheep	
BLECK	coal-fish	zo
BLEED	exude; secrete; impoverish	
BLEEP	radio signal	
BLEND	mix; unite; knead; coalesce	
BLENT	blended; amalgamated	
BLESS	laud; exalt; praise; extol	
BLEST	endowed with blessings	
BLIMP	small airship; (Colonel)	
BLIND	ruse; feint; curtain; sightless	
BLINK	glance; flicker; ignore	
BLIRT	blore; squall; gust	nt
BLISS	ecstasy; rapture; felicity	
BLITE	the plant Good King Henry	bt
BLITZ	sudden total bombardment; lightning war (Ge.)	
BLIVE	soon; speedily (Sc.)	
BLOAT	blote; dry by smoke; dilate	
BLOCK	bar; obstruct; mass; (tackle) building; hoist;	cr, nt
BLOCK	unit of data	cp, me, tc
BLOCK	foul (badminton); (Am. football); (basketball)	ga
BLOKE	a fellow; a man	
BLOND	fair; flaxen	
BLOOD	cruor; gore; kindred; lineage	
BLOOM	bud; blossom; prime; thrive; film on old paint, iron, steel block	ce, bt, pt
BLOOP	sound-track joint thud	cn
BLORE	blirt; violent gust	
BLOTE	bloat; dry by smoke	
BLOWN	winded; trumpeted	
BLOWY	breezy; gusty; windy	
BLUED	tempered; squandered	
BLUER	more blue; gloomier	
BLUES	Royal Horse Guards; sad American-negro songs	mu
BLUEY	blanket; bundle (Australia)	
BLUFF	sheer; brusque; spoof; headland; cliff	go
BLUNT	blont; dull; abrupt	
BLURB	recommendation; description (bk. cover)	
BLURT	utter hastily	
BLUSH	flush; colour; redden	
BOARD	embark; victuals; council non-gem diamond drill;	
BOART }	square-sawn timber;	
BORT }	pressed wood; (squash) platform; stage; plank	to
BOAST	brag; crow; vaunt; angle stroke (squash)	ga
BOBBY	policeman	
BOCAL	glass beaker	
BOCHE	a Hun, also a German	
BODED	portended; presaged; augured	
BODGE	botch; mess up; fail	
BODHI	Buddhist sacred tree	bt
BODLE	farthing (Sc.)	nm
BOGAZ	karst chasm, canyon (Bosphorus)	gl, go
BOGEY	min. golf score; hobgoblin	ga
BOGGY	soggy; swampy; marshy	
BOGIE	railway axle; truck	rw
BOGLE	bugbear; scarecrow	
BOGUS	sham; spurious; false	
BOHEA	inferior tea	bt
BOIAR	boyar; Russian nobleman	

BOITE	night-club, disco	
BOLAR	pertaining to clay	
BOLAS	S. American missile	
BOLIN	bowline	nt
BOLUS	large pill	md
BOMBE	swollen Rococo style decor	
BONCE	marble game; head (slang)	ga
BONED	seized; stole; purloined	
BONER	sharp blow; mistake (baseball) (sl.)	
		ga
BONES	bobbins	mu
BONGO	African antelope; percussion single	
	small drum; head injury from fall	
	(skateboarding)	mu
BONNE	French nurse	
BONNY	bonnie; ore pocket	ml
BONUS	award; premium; subsidy	
BONZE	Buddhist priest	rl
BOOBY	looby; dunce; simpleton	
BOOBY	water bird	zo
BOODY	to sulk; to mope	
BOOED	hooted; noisily objected	
BOOER	vociferous interrupter	
BOOPS	humpbacked whale	zo
BOORT	(diamond polishing)	
BOOSE	booze; drink; swill	
BOOST	boom; push; eulogize	
BOOSY	boozy; tipsy; fuddled	
BOOTH	market stall	
BOOTS	last joined; shoe cleaner	
BOOTY	loot; spoil; plunder	
BORAK	banter; chaff (Australia)	
BORAX	tincal; borate of soda	ch
BORED	drilled; wearied	
BOREE	French peasants' dance	
BORER	an insect; seaworm	zo
BORIC	boracic	ch
BORNE	narrow-minded; carried	
BORON	a non-metallic element	ch
BOSCH	wood, bush (S. Afr.)	go
BOSKY	busky; shady; thickly wooded	
BOSOM	breast; confidential	
BOSON }	boatswain	nt
BO'SUN }		
BOSON	elementary particle (photons,	
	mesons)	nc
BOSSY	dictatorial; domineering	
BOTCH	to patch; worthless	
BOTHY	hut; cottage (Sc.)	
BOTTS	larvae; worms	zo
BOUCH	to bush; to debouch	
BOUGH	branch; limb; offshoot	bt
BOULE	(buhl); inlay work; hardwood log	
BOULE	Greek Parliament; roulette; French	
	bowls	ga
BOUND	limit; pale; leap; spring	
BOURG	a town; burgh; borough	
BOURN	bourne; stream; bound; border	
BOUSE	boose; booze; bowze; swill	
BOUSY	tipsy; drunken; crapulous	

BOVEY	a kind of coal	mn
BOWED	bent; curved; subdued	
BOWEL	rectum	pl
BOWER	arbour; shelter; anchor	nt
BOWER	the knave at euchre (cards)	ga
BOWET	young hawk	zo
BOWIE	a large knife	
BOWLS	skittles; a game	ga
BOWSE	to heave; bouse	nt
BOW-TO	to face the wind	nt
BOXED	crated	
BOXEN	made of boxwood	
BOXER	a pugilist	
BOX-IN	surrounding type with rule	pr
BOXTY	Halloween dish (Ir.)	ck
BOX-UP	mistake; error	
BOYAR	boiar; Russian nobleman	
BOYAU	ditch; trench (Fr.)	
BOYER	Flemish sloop	nt
BRACE	pair; couple; stiffen; anti-capsize	
	stroke (canoeing); stirrup-stand	
	(polo); support; tauten; string a	
	bow (archery)	ga, to
BRACH	bitch-hound	zo
BRACK	a flaw in cloth	
BRACT	specialized leaf	bt
BRADY-	slow	cf
BRAID	brede; broid; weave; entwine	
BRAIL	(falconry); to furl sails	ga, nt
BRAIN	cerebellum; intellect	
BRAIT	rough diamond	mn
BRAKE	thicket; harrow; wagonette	
BRAKY	overgrown with ferns	bt
BRAND	brond; stigma; mark; torch	
BRANK	buckwheat	bt
BRANK	bridle for scolds	
BRANT	a goose	zo
BRASH	hasty; brittle; loose rock	
BRASS	(top) money; impudence;	
	effrontery; alloy of copper and	
	zinc; metal wind instrument	ml,
		mu
BRAST	burst (Spens.)	
BRAUL	striped cloth	tx
BRAVE	to dare; heroic; valiant	
BRAVO	well done!; an assassin (It.)	
BRAWL	wrangle; bicker; quarrel	
BRAWN	muscular strength	
BRAXY	splenetic sheep disease	
BRAZE	to solder	
BREAD	food; fare; aliment	ck
BREAK	interval; smash; shatter; successful	
	sequence; separate; sprint;	
	voice-change; tone quality; short	
	solo	mu
BREAM	a fish; to clean	zo
BREED	beget; race; progeny	
BREEM }	stern; fiery (Spens.); cléar;	
BREME }	raging; celebrated	

BREER	} to sprout (Sc.)	
BRERE		
BRENT	lofty; smooth; a goose	zo
BREST	breast	
BREVE	a long note	mu
BRIAR	a pipe; wild rose	bt
BRIBE	suborn; graft; an inducement	bt
BRICK	a stout-hearted fellow	
BRIDE	(betrothed) banned but beloved	
BRIEF	short; concise; a writ	lw
BRIER	briar; wild rose	bt
BRILL	prill; type of turbot	zo
BRINE	salt water; the sea; tears	
BRING	fetch; convoy; produce	
BRINK	brim; brow; verge; marge	
BRINY	the sea; salty	
BRISK	agile; alert; nimble	
BRITE	over-ripe	
BRIZA	totter-grass	bt
BRIZE	the gadfly	zo
BROAD	wide; spacious; liberal; stretch of fresh water (inland); woman (Am.)	go
BROCH	early stone hut	
BROCK	badger; a brocket	zo
BROGH	burgh (Sc.)	
BROGH	prehistoric stone fort (Scand.)	
BROID	braid; to interweave	
BROIL	brawl; quarrel; affray	
BROKE	ruined; penniless	
BROMA	prepared chocolate	ck
BROME	a grass	bt
BROND	brand	
BRONX	a cocktail	
BROOD	incubate; progeny; meditate	
BROOK	beck; rill; tolerate; allow	
BROOL	a deep murmur	
BROOM	a besom; a shrub	bt
BROSE	Scotch porridge	
BROTH	soup; a concoction	ck
BROWN	tan; ecru; russet; sorrel	
BRUIN	a bear	zo
BRUIT	to noise abroad; a rumour	
BRUME	fog; mist; vapour	
BRUNT	shock; impulse	
BRUSH.	skirmish; scrap; sweep; conductor; grooming; touch lightly	
BRUTE	savage; senseless; rough	
BUCCO	puff-bird genus	zo
BUCHU	African medicinal plant	bt
BUCKO	a bully (USA)	
BUDDY	a partner; blooming	
BUDGE	lambskin fur; pompous; to stir	
BUFFA	comic opera (It.)	mu
BUFFO	comic actor	
BUFFS	a famous regiment	
BUFFY	buff colour	
BUGGY	a gig; a vehicle	
BUGLE	jet bead; horn	mu
BUGLE	genus of flowering plants	bt

BUILD	erect; construct; raise	
BUILT	fabricated; established	
BUIST	to mark sheep or cattle (Sc.)	
BULBY	bulbous	
BULGE	swell; belly	
BULGY	protuberant	
BULKY	vast; massive; voluminous	
BULLA	Papal seal; edict; mollusc	rl, zo
BULLA	bone cover of ear	pl
BULLY	hector; intimidate; splendid; salt beef; race off (hockey)	ga
BULSE	a bag of diamonds	
BUMBO	rumbo; a drink	
BUMPS	Cambridge and Oxford rowing event	
BUMPY	uneven	
BUNCH	set; lot; lump; batch; group of people (associated interest)	
BUNIA	Indian trader or banker	
BUNKO	bunco; a trick; swindle	
BUNNY	a rabbit	zo
BUNTY	wheat disease; purge	
BURAN	or **purga** westerly tundra wind (Siberia)	mt
BURGH	town; borough	
BURIN	engraving tool	to
BURKE	murder; hush up	
BURLY	stout; lusty; portly	
BURNT	charred; parched; tanned	
BURRO	donkey; moke	zo
BURRY	having burs; prickly	bt
BURSA	a sac; a pouch	md
BURSE	purse; bourse	
BURST	split; exploded; rent asunder	
BUSBY	bearskin headdress	
BUSES	vehicles	
BUSHI	kerido; samurai (Japanese knight)	
BUSHY	overgrown; bosky (tail)	
BUSKY	bosky; woody; shady	
BUTTE	hill with flat top; ridge	go
BUTTS	rifle range	
BUTTY	mining partner; deputy; barge	
BUTYL	butter extract	ch
BUXOM	(of females) comely; lively; jolly	
BUYER	purchaser; shopper	
BUZZY	muzzy; dazed	
BWANA	master; boss (Swahili)	
BYARD	miner's hauling strap	
BYATT	walkway, timber support	ce
BY-END	subsidiary aim	
BY-LAW	municipal bye-law	lw
BYOUS	extraordinary (Sc.)	
BY-WAY	(indirect route) by-path	lw

C

CAABA	Kaaba; shrine in Mecca	rl
CABAL	clique; junto; set	
CABAS	rush-basket	

107

CABBY	a cab-driver	
CABER	tossing the (Sc.); pole (trunk)	**ga**
CABIN	hut; shed; room in ship	**nt**
CABIR	nature worship (Lemnos)	
CABLE	wire; 100 fathoms	**me, nt**
CABOB	} dish of meat	**ck**
KEBAB		
CABRE	aero-stunt	
CACAO	the chocolate-tree	**bt**
CACHE	a hide; secret store	
CADDY	porter (golf); tea container	
CADET	younger son; trainee	
CADGE	peddle; sponge; portable perch (falconry)	
CADGY	frolicsome; wanton	
CADRE	nucleus; framework	
CAGED	captive; mewed	
CAGEY	cautious; irritable; secretive	
CAGOT	Pyrenees pariah race	
CA-IRA	'on with it' (Fr.)	
CAIRD	tinker; gipsy	
CAIRN	heap of stones; terrier	**zo**
CAKED	clotted; plastered	
CALID	hot; fiery; ardent; glowing	
CALIF	Caliph; Kalif; ruler (moslem)	**rl**
CALIN	a Chinese alloy	
CALIX	calyx; cup	**bt**
CALLA	bog-arum	**bt**
CALLE	caul; callet; network cap	
CALMY	calm; quiet; pacific	
CALPA	Kalpa; a day of Brahma	**rl**
CALVE	give birth	**zo**
CALYX	flower's outer whorl, calix	**bt**
CAMAN	shinty stick (Sc.)	
CAMEL	a Bactrian; caisson	**zo**
CAMEO	opposite to intaglio; 2-layered coloured gem-stone	
CAMIS	chemise; loose garment	
CAMPO	Savanna (Brazil)	**go**
CANAL	channel; duct; waterway	
CANAS	form of jousting	**ga**
CANDY	a sweetmeat; to crystallize	
CANED	thrashed; tanned	
CANEY	with unduly narrow growth rings	**fr**
CANNA	arrowroot; thickening starch	**bt, ck**
CANNE	walking cane; quarter staff (fencing)	
CANNY	shrewd; cautious; knowing	
CANOE	} a dugout	**nt**
CANOA		
CANON	precept; rule	**rl**
CANTO	a division of a poem, contrapuntal composition, song, solo song adding contrapuntal variation	**mu**
CANTY	cheerful; talkative	
CAPEL	caple; composite stone	**zo, mn**
CAPER	dance; gambol; a plant	**bt**
CAPER	Dutch privateer	**nt**
CAPLE	capel; capul; a horse	**zo**
CAPOC	kapok; Indian cotton	**bt**
CAPON	fish; letter; fowl	**zo**

CAPOT	to win all tricks at piquet	**ga**
CAPRA	she-goat	**zo**
CAPUL	caple	**zo**
CAPUT	distal-end swelling; head	**md**
CARAT	a weight for gold (carob seed)	**me**
CARED	heeded; recked; minded	
CARET	the mark ‸	
CAREX	sedge; reed; grass	**bt**
CARGO	load; freight	**nt**
CARIB	a Caribbean	
CARLE	rude strong man	
CARNY	blarney; flattery	
CAROB	locust or algaroba tree, bean	**bt**
CAROL	lay; ditty; warble; hymn	**mu**
CAROM	cannon in French billiards	**ga**
CARRY	convey; urge; accomplish; transfer (sound, golf); sustain	
CARSE	low-lying land	**go**
CARTE	(fencing score); card	**ga**
CARUS	unconsciousness	**md**
CARVE	cut; hack; slice; engrave	
CARVY	caraway plant	**bt**
CASAL	belonging to a case (grammar)	
CASCO	Manila barge	**nt**
CASED	boxed; packed; enveloped	
CASSE	broken paper	
CASTE	class; rank; lineage	
CATCH	latch; clutch; ensnare; seize; crab (rowing); a round (song); canon	**mu**
CATER	provide food, etc.	
CATES	viands; dainties	
CATTY	feline; spiteful	
CAULD	dam; weir (Sc.)	
CAULK	make water-tight	**nt**
CAUSE	reason; object; source	
CAVED	collapsed; fallen	
CAVES	grottoes; caverns	**gl, go**
CAVES	darts; table quoits (East Anglia)	
CAVIE	hen-coop or cage	
CAVIL	carp; censure; criticize	
CAVIN	covered approach	
CAWED	crowed	
CAWKY	of baryta; of barium oxide	**ch**
CAXON	hairy wig	
CEASE	cesse; end; stop; desist	
CEBUS	S. American monkey	**zo**
CEDAR	a Lebanon tree	**bt**
CEDED	granted; allotted; yielded	
CEDEZ	restrain the tempo (Fr.)	**mu**
CELLA	central body of temple	
CELLO	violoncello	**mu**
CENSE	burn incense	**rl**
CENTI-	100th; (centimetre)	**cf**
CENTO	a medley	**mu**
CEORL	churl; a freeman	
CERED	covered with wax	
CERES	harvest goddess	**rl**
CERGE	altar candle	**rl**
CERIC	wax-like	

CERIN	a constituent of wax	**ch**
CERTY	certainly (Sc.)	
CESTA	curved basket (pelota)	**ga**
CETIC	(spermaceti)	**zo**
CETYL	a radical in spermaceti	
CHACK	the toss of a horse's head	
CHAFE	rub; heat; vex; gall	
CHAFF	husks; deride; raillery	
CHAFT	chaps; the jaw (Sc.)	
CHAIN	parallel mountain ranges; line of islands; measure of distances; 22 yards = 20 metres; fetter, links; input; tether; necklace; series of consequences (-stores)	**go, me, cp**
CHAIR	seat; professorship; to preside; rail binding	**rw**
CHAKO	shako; a headdress	
CHALK	to record; touch-mark (bowls); white, ex-marine, soft limestone	**mn, go, gl**
CHAMA	large oyster	**zo**
CHAMP	(horses); chew; crunch	
CHAMP	potato dish (N. Ire.)	
CHANK	species of conch-shell	**zo**
CHANT	intone; carol	**mu**
CHAOS	anarchy; disorder; confusion	
CHAPE	the catch of a buckle	
CHAPS	the jaws; chops; cold-sores	**ck, md**
CHAPS	cowboy breeches	
CHARD	kale-like vegetable	**bt, ck**
CHARE	chore; daily work	
CHARE	narrow street or court	
CHARK	char; charcoal	
CHARM	spell; allure; amulet	
CHARM	nuclear behaviour	
CHARR	char; (trout)	**zo**
CHART	sea-map; weather map, graph, diagram	**nt**
CHARY	frugal; circumspect; wary	
CHASE	pursue; hunt; follow; race; forest; (baseball)	**ga**
CHASE	engrave; frame; type-case	
CHASM	gap; cleft; rift; abyss	
CHAUS	Ind./Afr. wild cat	**zo**
CHEAP	mean; common; paltry	
CHEAT	dupe; fraud; swindle; deceive (skating) (surfing)	**lw, ga**
CHECK	curb; stay; bridle; control; to examine; (chess king shahk)	**ga**
CHEEK	insolence; sauce; mortise; tenon lock; dormer side; jaw	**bd, cr, pl**
CHEEP	pipe; chirp; churr	
CHEER	gaiety; hearten; encourage	
CHELA	lobster claw	**zo**
CHELA	a Buddhist disciple	**rl**
CHEMO-	chemical action	**cf**
CHENG	Chinese reed instrument	**mu**
CHERI	darling (masc., Fr.)	
CHERT	flint; hornstone	**nt**

CHESS	a matey game	
CHEST	coffer; coffin; breast; set of 6 viols	**mu**
CHEVY	chivy; chase; scamper	
CHIAN	of Chios	
CHICA	orange-red dye; liquor; girl (Sp.)	**ck**
CHICH	a dwarf pea; lentil	**bt**
CHICK	to sprout; child; chicken	**zo**
CHICK	bamboo screen	
CHICO	youth (Sp.)	
CHIDE	scold; rebuke; reprove	
CHIEF	boss; head; prime; principal	
CHIEL	child; lad (Sc.)	
CHILD	babe; nursling; offspring	
CHILI	pod of cayenne pepper; hot southerly sirocco wind (Tunisia)	**bt, ck, mt**
CHILL	cold; frigid; depress	
CHIMB	edge of cask	
CHIME	harmonize; strike; agree	
CHINA	porcelain; Celestial Empire	
CHINE	cleft; ravine; backbone	**md, go**
CHINK	gap; rift; cranny; clink	
CHIPS	a carpenter (potato) software	**ck, cp**
CHIRK	chirp; cheep; cheerful	
CHIRM	bird noises	
CHIRO-	hand; (chiromancy, palmistry)	**cf**
CHIRP	chirr; chirl; to trill; bird call	
CHIRT	to squeeze	
CHIVE	a type of onion	**bt, ck**
CHIVY	chevy; chase; pursue	
CHOCK	wedge; block; a log	
CHODE	scolded; rated; upbraided	
CHOIR	the chancel	**rl**
CHOKE	gag; stifle; burke; strangle; stutter	
CHOKE	(carburettor); waveguide groove; inductor	**el**
CHOKY	prison (slang)	
CHOPS	chaps; the jaws	
CHORD	harmonious sound combination; wing-width (hang-gliding)	**mu**
CHORE	chare; household toil	
CHOSE	selected; picked; culled	
CHOSS	scree or shale climb	**mo**
CHOUT	blackmail; extortion (Hindu)	
CHROM-	colour (chromatic)	**cf**
CHUBB	patent lock; a safe	
CHUCK	jerk; throw; cluck; instrument	**to**
CHUCK	no ball (cricket) (Am football)	**ga**
CHUET	a pie of minced meat	**ck**
CHUFF } SHUFF }	cracked bricks; clown; boor	
CHULA	rebound from wall (pelota)	**ga**
CHUMP	lump of wood; blockhead	
CHUNK	lump or bit (marmalade)	**ck**
CHURL	ceorl; freeman; clodhopper	
CHURN	foam; jostle; agitate	
CHURR	chirp; chirk	

CHUTE	waterfall; sloping channel; start of race (sport)	
CHYAK	tease; chaff (Aust.)	
CHYLE	milky fluid	md
CHYME	partially digested food	md
CHYND	cleft to the chine (obs.)	
CIBOL	variety of onion; shallot	bt
CICER	chick-pea	bt
CIDER	cyder; fermented apple-juice	ck
CIGAR	a Havana	
CILIA	filaments; eye-lashes	md
CIMAR	cymar; simar; scarf	
CIMEX	bed-bug	zo
CINCH	girth; a certainty	
CIRCA	about, approximately (Lat.)	
CIRCE	a glamorous Syren	
CIRRI	tendrils; clouds	
CISCO	American char	zo
CISSY	effeminate youth	
CITAL	summons; accusation	lw
CITED	quoted; adduced; mentioned	
CIVET	cat; perfume; fur	
CIVIC	municipal; corporate	
CIVIL	polite; courteous; suave	
CIVVY	a civilian	
CLACK	click; clink; clatter; prate	
CLAES	clothes (Sc.)	
CLAIK	the barnacle goose	zo
CLAIM	right; privilege; usurp	
CLAMP	clump; fasten; cramp; joining device	cr, to
CLAMS	pincers; vice; seafood	ck, to, zo
CLANG	clank; clash	
CLANK	clatter; clangour	
CLARE	a nun of St. Clare	rl
CLARO	mild in taste (cigars)	
CLARY	sweet-herb	bt
CLASH	jar; differ; contend; collide	
CLASP	hasp; catch; grip	
CLASS	set; grade; category	
CLATS	slops; (mud wall) (Sc.)	
CLAUT	rake; scratch (Sc.)	
CLAVA	club-shaped swelling; fungi	zo, bt
CLAVE	clove; cleft; clung	
CLEAN	immaculate; pure; scour; innocent; penalty free (contests, events) (insurance)	
CLEAR	serene; free; lucid; to empty	cp
CLEAT	a wedge; slat; T-shaped fitting for rope	nt
CLEEK	golf club; hook; peg	
CLEFT	clift; split; rift; cranny	
CLEPE	to name; (yclept)	
CLERK	scribe; scrivener; recorder	
CLEVE	a cliff; a valley	
CLEVY	draught-iron of a plough	
CLICK	klick; tick; a latch	
CLIDE	burweed	bt
CLITE		
CLIFF	crag; headland; precipice	

CLIFT	cleft; fissure; breach	
CLIMB	scale; ascend; surmount	
CLIME	region; place; climate	
CLINE	ecological life assessment	bt, zo
CLING	hold; cleave; embrace	
CLINK	prison; chink; jingle	
CLINT	ridge of limestone between	
KLINT	fissures	gl
CLOAK	cover; pretext; mask	
CLOAM	earthenware	
CLOCK	chronometer; horologe; timepiece	nt
CLOFF	cleft; a weight allowance	
CLONE	plant stock; pure line	bt
CLONE	asexually produced individual; moron	zo
CLOOM	cloam; clay	
CLOOP	pop! (interjection)	
CLOOT	cloven hoof (Sc.)	
CLOSE	estop; end; grapple; cadence; shut; near; familiar	rl, mu
CLOSH	skittles	ga
CLOTH	woven fabric; the clergy	rl, tx
CLOUD	haze; vapour; obscure; billowy aerial mass; gloom	
CLOUR	to knock; a bump	
CLOUT	dish-cloth; nail; buffet; clothing; influence	
CLOVE	a spice; a weight	bt, me
CLOWN	jester; fool; buffoon; dunce	
CLUBS	suit (cards); (juggling); apparatus (gymnastics)	ga
CLUCK	the call of a hen	
CLUMP	cluster; group; patch	
CLUNG	clasped; adhered; held	
CLUNK	a gurgle	
CLUNY	pillow-lace	
CLUSE	narrow gorge in mountains (Jura) (Fr.)	go
CNIDA	stinging thread; jellyfish	zo
COACH	teach; trainer; vehicle	
CO-ACT	co-operate; aid; abet	
CO-AID	helper; assistant	
COALY	resembling coal	
COARB	bishop or abbot	rl
COAST	shore; strand; seaside	
COATI	American racoon	zo
COBBY	stout; brisk	
COBLE	fishing boat	nt
COBRA	hamadryad snake	zo
COCKY	conceited	
COCOA	beverage from cacao	bt, ck
COCUS	green ebony	bt
CODAN	carrier-operated-device-anti-noise	
CODED	in code; in cipher	
CODEX	ancient manuscript	
CODLE	coddle; pamper; caress	
CODON	triplet DNA bases fixing genetic codes	md, pl
COGUE	wooden milk bowl (Sc.)	

COIGN	corner-stone; quoin; wedge	
COKED	converted into coke	
COLIC	flatulence	md
COLIN	American partridge	zo
COLLY	coal-smut	
COLON	punctuation; money	
COLON	large intestine	pl
COLOR	colour; hue; tint; pigment	pt
COLZA	cabbage; rape oil	bt
COMBE		
COOMB }	hollow in hillside	go
COOMBE		
COMBO	small jazz/dance band	
COMER	an arrival	
COMET	card game; nebulous body	as, ga
COMFY	comfortable	
COMIC	droll; farcical; ludicrous	
COMMA	a butterfly; punctuation mark; posture (skiing)	zo
COMPO	plaster; stucco; soldier's ration	
COMPT	to count (obs.)	
COMUS	God of Revelry; a masque	
CONCH	seashell; trumpet; semicircular niche	mu, rl, ar
CONED	tapering	
CONES	fine flour; retina; pigments (eye)	
CONEY	cony; bunny	zo
CONGA	dance (Afro-Cuban)	mu
CONGE	leave; dismissal (Fr.)	
CONGO	black tea	bt
CONIA	hemlock	bt
CONIC	conical; tapering	
CONIN	conine; hemlock	bt
CONNE	conn; con; study; steer	
CONSY	consolation; motor race	
CONTO	money of account (Portugal)	
COOED	made love	
COOEE	cooey; Australian bush-call	
COOKY	a cook; a small cake	ck
COOLY	coolie (Hindu)	
COOMB	hollow in hillside; 4 bushels	go, me
CO-OPT	to select extra committee	
COPAL	a resin; a varnish	rl
COPEC	kopeck; a Russian copper	nm
COPED	vied; contended; overcame	
COPER	dealer	
COPOS	lassitude	
COPRA	dried coconut kernels	bt
COPSE	coppice; grove; thicket	
COPSY	covered with undergrowth	
CORAL	lobster roe; language	zo, cp
CORAL	marine growth reef; gem	bt, mn
CORDA	string; soft pedal (It.)	mu
CORED	centre removed, bored	
CORER	fruit/earth-sample cutting device	
CORGI	small breed of dog (Wales)	zo
CORKY	lively; skittish	
CORNO	French horn	mu
CORNU	a horn	zo
CORNY	horny; (humour) trite (slang)	

CORPS	staff; contingent; troops	
CORSE	a corpse (obs.)	
CORVE	tram used in mines	mn
COSEY	cosy; snug; teapot-cover	
COSTS	expenses	lw
COTTA	a surplice	rl
COUCH	sofa; divan; squat; grass	bt
COUGH	tussis; a cold	md
COULD	was able (past of can)	
COULE	a thrust (fencing)	ga
COUNT	compute; number; reckon; lord	
COUPE	closed car	
COURB	to stoop; bent (obs.)	
COURT	woo; invite; homage; tribunal	lw
COURT	(yard), rectangular enclosed play area; (cards)	
COURT	seat of king and counsellors; palace; (favour) (judge)	ga, lw
COUTH	familiar; agreeable	
COVED	arched over	
COVEN	a muster of witches	
COVER	wrap; cloak; shroud; invest	
COVET	desire; hanker after	
COVEY	a brood; a bevy	zo
COVIN	collusive fraudulence	lw
COWAN	uninitiated mason	
COWED	daunted; overawed; abashed	
COWER	fawn; quail; cringe; shrink	
COWLE	written agreement (Ang.-Ind.)	
COWRY	small shell used as money	
COXAE	hip-joints	md
COXED	commanded; steered	
COYLY	bashfully; demurely; shyly	
COYPU	nutria; S. American rodent	zo
COZEN	cheat; deceive; sponge	
CRACK	gap; rift; rent; crevice	
CRAFT	skill; dexterity; guile; vessel	nt
CRAIG	crag; the neck (Sc.)	gl
CRAKE	the corncrake	zo
CRAME	booth; covered stall	
CRAMP	a spasm; hinder; impede; joining device; metal; tool	bd
CRANE	hoisting machine; wader	zo
CRANK	handle; bend; twist; quirk	
CRAPE	transparent gauze; to curl	
CRAPS	a dice game (gambling)	ga
CRAPY	resembling crape	
CRARE	trading vessel	nt
CRASH	coarse cloth; shatter; smash	
CRASS	gross; dense; stupid	
CRATE	hamper; packing case	
CRAVE	beg; yearn; implore	
CRAWL	fish-pen; creep; abase	
CRAZE	mania; insane passion; fad	
CRAZY	mad; idiotic; rickety	
CREAK	grate	
CREAM	to mantle; top of milk	
CRECK	the corncrake	zo
CREDO	the creed	rl
CREED	belief; tenet; dogma	rl

CREEK	bay; cove inlet; bight
CREEL	fish-basket
CREEP	crawl; cringe; grovel; heat stress expansion/shrinkage of steel/ concrete **ce**
CREME	cream-like substance **ck**
CRENA	a furrow; a notch
CREPE	wrinkled fabric; rubber; pancake **ck**
CREPT	crawled; fawned; glided
CRESS	watercress, etc. **bt**
CREST	top; apex; summit; device (archery)
CREUX	the reverse of relief
CREWE	cruse; earthenware pot
CRICK	cramp; spasm; convulsion
CRIED	wept; sobbed; lamented
CRIER	proclaimer; howler
CRIES	yells; shrieks; shouts
CRIME	felony; enormity; misdeed
CRIMP	corrugate; decoy
CRINE	shrink; shrivel (Sc.)
CRISP	curl; brittle; friable
CRITH	unit weight of a gas **me**
CROAK	grumble; complain; die
CROAT	(Yugoslavian)
CROCK	soot; jar; pitcher; shard
CROFT	a small farm; a pasture; small writing table
CROMA	crome; a quaver **mu**
CROME	cromb; crook; hook
CRONE	old woman; a ewe
CRONY	familiar friend
CROOK	crome; bend; crosier; detachable section of horn **rl, mu**
CROOL	to mutter
CROOM	a pitchfork **to**
CROON	low moan
CROPE	a finial; the top
CRORE	100 lacs of rupees **nm**
CROSS	crusty; sullen; thwart
CROSS	hybrid; symbol; burden **rl**
CROUD	Welsh violin **mu**
CROUP	rump; throat disease **md**
CROUP	pommel or side-horse (gymn)
CROUT	pickled cabbage **ck**
CROWD	mob; throng; herd; swarm
CROWN	diadem; garland; 5 shillings (25p) **nm**
CROZE	cooper's tool; groove **to**
CRUCK	medieval oaken roof; crossbeam **ar**
CRUDE	raw; tough; immature
CRUEL	fell; dire; brutal; inhuman
CRUET	eucharistic flagon with stopper **rl**
CRUMB	soft part of a loaf **ck**
CRUMP	crooked; wrinkled; a bang
CRUNT	a blow on the head (Sc.)
CRUOR	coagulated blood; gore **md**
CRUSE	vial; small bottle
CRUSH	squeeze; subdue; pulverize
CRUST	incrustation; coating
CRWTH	Welsh violin **mu**

CRYPT	vault; tomb; catacomb
CRYPT-	secret; hidden (cryptic, coded) **cf**
CUBAN	a native of Cuba
CUBEB	dried pepper-berry **bt, ck**
CUBED	raised to third power
CUBIC	volumetric **me**
CUBIT	length of 18 or 22 in (45 or 55 cm) **me**
CUDDY	cabin; rent; donkey **zo**
CUFIC	an Arabic script
CUISH	cuisse; thigh-armour
CULCH	rubbish
CULET	lower facet of a diamond
CULEX	a gnat genus **zo**
CULLS	brick or timber rejects (USA)
CULLY	silly dupe; to deceive
CUMEN	one cubic metre per second **me**
CUMIN	cummin; caraway; spice **bt, ck**
CUPEL	assaying vessel
CUPID	Eros; the god of love
CURCH	a kerchief
CURDY	coagulated
CURED	healed; remedied; preserved
CURER	a fish-drier
CURIA	Senate house; court
CURIE	unit of radiation **me**
CURIO	rare bric-à-brac
CURLY	wavy; sinuous; twisty
CURRE	golden-eye duck **zo**
CURRY	to dress leather; thrash
CURRY	Indian spiced dish **ck**
CURSE	anathema; execrate; maledict
CURST	tormented; plagued
CURVE	turn; bend; inflect
CUSEC	cubic flow per second **me**
CUSHY	easy and well-paid
CUTCH	catechu; couch grass **bt**
CUTER	more cunning; sharper
CUTIN	in plant cuticle **bt**
CUT-IN	football; motoring; intrude **ga**
CUTIS	true skin **md**
CUTTO	cuttoe; large knife **to**
CUTTY	short; curtailed; clay pipe
CUT-UP	carved out; criticised adversely; distressed; (rough); high spin- shot (golf)
CUVEE	blend of wine (Fr.)
CYCAD	a palm **bt**
CYCLE	period; age; era; circle
CYCLE	series of repeating sequences **cp**
CYMRY	Cymric; Welsh
CYNIC	misanthrope; captious; morose
CZECH	Bohemian

D

DACHA	weekend villa (Rus.)
DADDY	dadda; papa; father; (sugar-)

DAFFY	stunt (riding 2 boards) (freestyle aerial skiing)	**ga**
DAGON	Philistine Fish-God	
DAILY	diurnal; quotidian	
DAIRI	(Japan) Mikado's palace	
DAIRY	milkshop; creamery	
DAISY	sometimes ox-eyed	**bt**
DAKER	corncrake; crake	**zo**
DAKIR	daker; dicker; half-a-score	
DALAI	Lama; Tibetan Priest-King	**rl**
DALER	a dalesman; coin dollar (Sw.)	**nm**
DALLY	sport; wanton; toy; dawdle	
DAMAN	coney; Syrian hyrax	**zo**
DAMAR	dammar; resin	**bt**
DAMON	and Pythias	
DAMPS	exhalations	
DAMPY	dejected; moist; humid	
DANCE	hop; caper; prance; pirouette	
DANDY	fop; beau; swell; coxcomb; ketch or yawl; sailship	**nt**
DANTY	broken coal	**mn**
DANZA	dance (It., Sp.)	**mu**
DARAF	elastance unit	**el**
DARBY	plasterer's float	**to**
DARCY	permeability coefficients unit	
DARED	braved; ventured; presumed	
DARIC	gold coin of Darius	**nm**
DARKY	darkey; negro; lantern	
DAROO	sycamore	**bt**
DARTS	target game (mini-javelins) (blow)	**ga**
DASHY	showy; ostentatious; gaudy	
DATED	of an era	
DATUM	something given	**cp**
DAUBE	braised meat in wine (Fr.)	**ck**
DAUBY	sticky; viscous; glutinous	
DAUNT	cow; appal; scare; intimidate	
DAVIT	ship's crane for lifeboats	**nt**
DAYAK	} Borneo, river people	
DYAK		
DAZED	mazed; dazzled; bewildered	
DEADS	ore débris	
DEALT	(cards); trafficked; traded	
DEARN	mournful; lonely; solitary	
DEARY	a dear	
DEATH	demise; decease	
DEAVE	to deafen (Sc.)	
DEBAG	remove trousers forcibly	
DEBAR	ban; deny; prevent; stop	
DEBEL	to conquer; subdue	
DEBIT	due; arrears; liability	
DEBUG	de-program; error removal	**cp**
DEBUG	cleansing of vermin, microphone	**cp**
DEBUS	get off a bus	
DEBUT	first appearance	
DEBYE	unit of dipole moment	**ps**
DECAD	decade; a group of ten years	**me**
DECAY	rot; putrify; wither	
DECAY	decline, decompose, disintegrate	
DECAY	decrease of voltage	**cp**

DECAY	transformation of radioactive nuclide	**nc**
DECEM	ten; (a prefix)	
DECOR	scheme of decoration	
DECOY	lure; ensnare; inveigle	
DECRY	censure; vilify; disparage	
DEDAL	daedal; intricate	
DEEDY	illustrious; active	
DEFER	delay; adjourn; postpone	
DEIFY	idolize; apotheosize	
DEIGN	condescend; vouchsafe	
DEISM	belief in a god	**rl**
DEIST	a free-thinking believer	
DEITY	god; divine providence	**rl**
DEKKO	reconnoitring look (Ind.)	
DEKLE	deckle; ragged	
DELAY	dally; retard; impede	
DELFT	glazed earthenware (from Holland)	
DELPH	delf; pottery	
DELTA	multiple river mouth; 4th letter (Gr.)	**go**
DELTA	(wing) alluvial deposits	**ae, gl**
DELVE	dig; scoop; excavate	
DEMIT	rèlease; resign	
DEMOB	demobilize	
DEMON	imp; goblin; devil; troll	
DEMOS	the proletariat	
DEMPT	deemed; judged (Spens.)	
DEMUR	pause; object; waver	
DENAY	deny; denial (obs.)	
DENIM	twilled cotton goods	
DENSE	compact; close; solid	
DEPOT	depository; storehouse	
DEPTH	profundity; abyss	
DERAY	to disarrange	
DERBY	a race; a hat	
DERIC	pertaining to skin	
DERMA-	of the skin	**cf, md, pl**
DERRY	a prejudice (Aust.)	
DETER	prevent; restrain; dissuade	
DEUCE	the Devil; score; two; (cards) (tennis)	**ga**
DEVIL	imp; to drudge; Lucifer	
DEWAN	Indian fiscal officer	
DEWED	bedewed	
DHOBI	Indian washerman	
DHOLE	Indian wild dog	**zo**
DHOTI	loin cloth (Hindu)	
DIAMB	2-iambi verse foot	
DIANA	moon-goddess; Artemis	**rl**
DIARY	journal; chronicle; record	
DIAZO	reproduction process paper	**pr**
DIBIT	2 binary units of information	**tc**
DICED	cut in cubes; bookbinding decoration	**ck**
DICER	dice-player	
DICHO-	combining in two parts	**cf, bt, pl**
DICHT	to wipe (Sc.)	
DICKY	open back-seat; apron; shirt-front	
DICTA	pronouncements	

DIDOT	typographical measurement	**go**
DIDST	(thou) did	
DIDUS	the dodo genus	**zo**
DIENE	unsaturated hydrocarbons	**ch, ps**
DIGHT	adorned; arrayed	
DIGIT	finger; toe; integer; data symbol	**cp, ma, pl**
DIGUE	water-advance-prevention seawall	
DIKED	banked; ditched	
DILDO	artificial penis	
DILLY	native bag (Australia)	
DILLY	diligence; the daffodil	**bt**
DILSH	inferior-coal layer	**mn**
DIMER	2-like-molecule-based species	**ch**
DIMLY	obscurely; vaguely	
DINAR	coin (Iran, Jordan, Yugoslavia)	**nm**
DINED	postprandially replete	
DINER	restaurant car	
DINGO	Australian dog	**zo**
DINGY	dull; sullied; squalid	
DINIC	dizzy; vertiginous	
DINKY	elegant	
DIODE	thermionic valve; one way circuit	**el**
DIOTA	two-handled jar	
DIPPY	a little insane	
DIPUS	the jerboa	
DIRGE	elegy; requiem; lament	
DIRTY	foul; sordid; mean; paltry	
DISCO	recorded-music dancehall, discotheque	
DISME	a tithe; a tenth; a dime	
DITAL	guitar tuning key	**mu**
DITCH	moat; trench; rine; drain	
DITTO	the same again	
DITTY	refrain; sonnet; ode; lilt	
DIVAN	council; saloon; sofa; couch	
DIVED	plunged; fathomed; explored	
DIVER	a sea-bird; underwater descendant	**zo**
DIVES	the rich man in the Bible	
DIVOT	a piece of turf	
DIVVY	share; divide	
DIXIE	camp-kettle; Southern USA	
DIZEN	to dress gaudily	
DJINN	genie; demon; afrit	
DO-ALL	factotum	
DOBBY	a dotard; part of a loom	
DOBOS	choc. torte with caramel topping	**ck**
DODDY	hornless cow	**zo**
DODGE	evade; avoid; shuffle	
DODGY	artful; tricky	
DOGAL	(doge of Venice)	
DOGGO	concealed	
DOGGY	fond of dogs	
DOGMA	tenet; doctrine; maxim	
DOGRA	a Kashmiri	
DOILT	crazy; daft (Sc.)	
DOILY	ornamented napkin	
DOING	performing; swindling	
DOLCE	softly, sweetly	**mu**

DOLED	bestowed sparingly	
DOLLY	camera carriage; grommet (washer); hardwood block; corn-; tee marker (curling)	**tv, ce**
DOLMA	rice-filled leaf	**ck**
DOLOR	dolour; grief; sorrow	
DOMAL	relating to a house	
DOMED	vaulted	
DOMRA	Russian plucked instrument	**mu**
DOMUS	patrician's house (Roman)	**ar**
DONAH	coster's sweetheart	
DONAT	donet; grammar-book; primer	
DONEE	the recipient	
DONGA	S. African ravine	**go**
DONNA	donya; a lady don (Sp.)	
DONOR	giver; bestower; (blood); semi-conductor	**ps**
DONYA	Spanish lady	
DOOLE	dole; gloom (obs.)	
DOOLY	Indian litter	
DOORN	S. African briar	**bt**
DOPED	drugged; covered with varnish	
DOPER	dauber; horse-coper	
DOPEY	slow-witted; dull	
DORAN	missile-tracking system	**rd**
DOREE	dory; golden-yellow fish	**zo**
DORIC	Greek architecture	**ar**
DORMY	unbeatable at golf	
DORSE	Baltic cod; coal-fish	**zo**
DORSE	reverse side	
DORTY	pettish; delicate (Sc.)	
DOSED	physicked; drenched	
DOSEH	religious ceremony (Cairo)	
DOSEL	dossal; tapestry	**rl**
DOSER	dossel; coloured cloths	**tx**
DOTAL	referring to a dowry	
DOTED	loved; drivelled	
DOTTY	barmy; silly; deranged	
DOUAR	dowar; Arab camp	
DOUAY	a Bible edition	
DOUBT	distrust; indecision; demur	
DOUCE	dulce; sweet	
DOUGH	money; the kneadful	
DOURA	millet	**bt**
DOUSE	dowse; slacken suddenly; drench	
DOVER	doze; slumber; a powder	**md**
DOWDY	slovenly; untidy; slatternly	
DOWEL	a wooden pin; steel rod (stairs); slate; cramp	**bd**
DOWER	dowry; dot; bequest	
DOWLE	fluff; down fibre	
DOWNY	filamentous; knowing	
DOWRY	dower; dot; endowment	
DOWSE	lower; close; put out	**nt**
DOYEN	senior member	
DOZED	snoozed; drowsed; slumbered	
DOZEN	apostolic number	
DOZER	nap taker	
DOZER	earth-moving tractor blade	
DRACO	a constellation	

DRAFF	dregs; residue	
DRAFT	outline; sketch; prepare	
DRAIL	to trail; to draggle	
DRAIN	empty; tap; a gutter, sewer; (brain-); transistor electrode	el
DRAKE	male duck	zo
DRAMA	histrionic art; play	
DRANK	quaffed; caroused; imbibed	
DRANT	to drone; to drawl	
DRAPE	cover; array; deck	
DRAWL	lag; drag; drone	
DRAWN	hauled; sketched; eviscerated	
DREAD	awe; fear; apprehension	
DREAM	reverie; hallucination	
DREAR	bleak; dismal; gloomy	
DREGS	less; draff; sediment	
DRENT	drenched (obs.)	
DRESS	garb; guise; apparel	
DREST	attired; arrayed	
DREUL	drool; dribble	
DRIED	aerified; parched; desiccated	
DRIER	desiccator; dryer	
DRIFT	wander; intention; surface water; glacial; continental; meaning; float; (archery) (motor-racing)	to, ga, gl, go
DRILL	cloth; ape; bore	zo, to
DRILY	dryly; sarcastically	
D-RING	'D'-shaped ring	to
DRINK	potion; draught; absorb	
DRIVE	urge; impel; coerce; motivate; private access road; hit	
DRIVE	operate; pulsating circuit	cp
DRIVE	mechanical power transmitter	
DROIL	ca' canny; drudgery	
DROIT	right; title	
DROLL	odd; rummy; whimsical	
DROME	racecourse; aerodrome	
DRONE	idler; hum; dawdle	
DRONE	bagpipes tone; male bee	mu, zo
DROOK	to drench; to duck (Sc.)	
DROOL	dreul; slaver; drivel	
DROOP	sag; fade; wilt; languish	
DROPS	small doses; gouts; pastilles(sweets); (rain) (ear/eye); guttae carvings; globular earrings	md, ae
DROSS	scum; dregs; scoria	
DROUK	drook; to duck (Sc.)	
DROVE	(cattle); forced; actuated; (road); driven; boaster (Sc.)	
DROWN	swamp; flood; deluge	
DRUID	bard	
DRUNK	crapulos; tipsy; quaffed	
DRUPE	a stone fruit	bt
DRUSE	mining cavity; a sect	mn, rl
DRUSY	having cavities	mn
DRUXY	partly decayed timber	
DRYAD	wood-nymph	

DRYAS	mountain avens	bt
DRYER	drier	
DRYLY	drily; insipidly; aridly	
DSOMO	zhomo; a hybrid	zo
DUCAL	with strawberry leaves; duke's	
DUCAT	Italian gold or silver	nm
DUCHY	a dukedom; duke's holiday	
DUDDY	ragged; in tatters	
DUKEY	wheeled platform; inclined-road train	
DULCE	soft; sweet; douce	
DULIA	angel adoration (RC)	rl
DULLY	stupidly; inertly; languidly	
DULSE	edible seaweed	bt
DUMBA	fat-tailed sheep	zo
DUMKA	} Rus., Cz., Ukrainian laments,	
DUMKY	} folksongs	mu
DUMMY	doll; (bridge); model for practice	cp
DUMMY	mallet head; mason's hammer	pb, to
DUMPS	low spirits; dejection	
DUMPY	short and thick	
DUNCE	dolt; dullard; booby	
DUNCH	punch; jolt; to gore	
DUNNE	the knot-sandpiper	zo
DUNNY	deaf; dull of apprehension	
DUOMO	Italian cathedral	rl, ar
DUPED	deluded; gulled; hoaxed	
DUPER	trickster; dodger; sharper	
DUPLE	double; twofold	
DUPPY	W. Indian ghost	
DURED	endured (obs.)	
DURGA	wife of Siva	rl
DURGY	undersized; dwarf	
DURIO	Malay tree; (durian fruit)	bt
DUROY	corduroy; figured serge	
DURRA	molasses/sugar-source sorghum grass	bt
DURRA	semi-tropical grain sorghum	bt
DURST	dared	
DURUM	hard wheat for pasta	bt, ck
DUSKY	swarthy; shady; dark; dim	
DUSTY	powdery	
DUTCH	a coster's wife; courage; treat	
DUVET	eiderdown; for bed or jacket	
DWALE	heretic; heraldic sable	hd
DWALE	the deadly nightshade	bt
DWALM	dwaum; swoon; sicken	
DWAMY	faint; languid; sickly (Sc.)	
DWANG	a crowbar; strutting (floor joists) (Sc.)	to
DWARF	imp; pygmy; midget; stunted	
DWELL	abide; reside; linger	
DWELT	stayed; tarried; sojourned	
DWINE	to pine; to fade	
DYING	moribund; expiring; demise	
DYKER	drywalling mason (Sc.)	
DYNAM	the unit of work	me

E

EAGER	keen; ardent; avid; zealous	
EAGLE	(golf); 10 dollar gold piece	nm
EAGLE	lectern; standard; erne; bird	zo
EAGRE	aigre; tidal wave; bore	
EARED	having lugs	
EARLY	rathe; forward; betimes	
EARST	erst; formerly	
EARTH	world; soil; humus; ground; base; end of flow	el
EASED	allayed; soothed; assuaged	
EASEL	canvas carrier	
EASLE	hot ashes (Sc.)	
EATEN	masticated; corroded	
EATER	consumer; devourer	
EAVES	overhanging roof-edges	ar
EBBED	waned; receded; declined	
EBLIS	a djinn; evil spirit	
EBONY	black wood	bt
ECHAL	synagogue cupboard for ark, law	rl
ECLAT	splendour; brilliance; panache	
ECTAL	ectad; outer; external	
EDDER	top binding of a hedge	
EDEMA	} dropsy, body swelling with	
OEDEMA	} waterlogged cells	md
EDGED	keen; bordered; fringed	
EDGES	curving, skating technique	
EDICT	ukase; decree; order	
EDIFY	uplift; enlighten; instruct	
EDILE	Roman magistrate	
EDUCE	elicit; draw; extract	
EDUCT	deduction	
EERIE	eirie; uncanny; weird	
EGEST	throw out; eject; cast	
EGGAR	egger; silkworm moth	zo
EGGED	incited; urged; impelled	
EGGER	an egg collector	
EGRET	aigrette; heron	zo
EIDER	sea-duck	zo
EIGHT	twice four; figurative (ice-skating)	
EIGNE	eldest son; first born	
EIGNE	entailed and inalienable	lw
EIKON	ikon; likeness (on wood or metal)	rl
EIRIE	eerie; weird; unaccountable	
EISEL	vinegar	ch
EJECT	evict; expel; oust; emit	
EKING	prolonging	
ELAIN	clarified oil or fat	
ELAND	antelope (S. Africa)	zo
ELAPS	venomous coral snake	zo
ELATE	exult; rouse; animate	
ELBOW	jostle; nudge; a bend; pipe-fitting, gate-joint	pb
ELCHI	Turkish envoy	
ELDER	older; ancestor	bt
ELECT	cull; select; chosen	
ELEGY	dirge; threnody; lament	
ELEMI	resin; chewing gum	bt

ELEOT	species of apple	bt
ELERS	designer of china-ware	
ELEVE	pupil (Fr.)	
ELFIN	small elf; puckish; pixy	
ELGIN	(marbles)	
ELIDE	contract; curtail	
ELITE	the elect; very select	
ELMEN	made of elm	bt
ELOGE	funeral oration	
ELOGY	panegyric; eulogy; encomium	
ELOIN	banish; remove (obs.)	
ELOPE	run away; abscond; decamp	
ELOPS	herring genus	zo
ELSIN	an awl (Sc.)	to
ELSSE	missile-tracking system	el
ELUDE	evade; baffle; escape	
ELUTE	cleanse; purify by washing	
ELVAN	Cornish rock; elvish	mn
ELVAS	prune; plum (Port.)	bt
ELVER	young eel	zo
EMAGE	area of text block in square ems	
EMBAR	prevent; bar; shut; stop	
EMBAY	to shelter; to landlock	
EMBED	imbed; set firmly	
EMBER	glowing fuel	
EMBOG	engulf	
EMBOW	to arch; to vault	
EMBOX	encase; pack	
EMBUS	to put in a bus	
EMEER	Ameer; Emir	
EMEND	amend; rectify; correct	
EMERY	carborundum	mn
EMMER	bucket; pail (S. Africa)	
EMMET	an ant; a pismire	zo
EMMEW	enmew; immew; confine	
EMOTE	register emotion	
EMPTY	void; vacant; vacuous; inane	
EMURE	immure (obs.)	
ENACT	ordain; decree; authorize	
ENATE	growing out	
ENDED	finished; concluded; ceased	
ENDER	a finale; a cropper	
END-ON	abutting	
ENDOR	home of a witch	
ENDOW	endue; indue; endew	
ENDUE	to invest; provide	
ENEID	epic poem	
ENEMA	a clyster; rectal douche	md
ENEMY	foe; rival; antagonist	
ENGLE	Angle; early English	
ENJOY	relish; appreciate	
ENMEW	emmew; immew; confine	
ENNUI	weariness; boredom (Fr.)	
ENODE	jointless; knotless	
ENORM	enormous (obs.)	
ENROL	list; enlist; chronicle	
ENSKY	to place in the sky (Shak.)	
ENSOR	levers net	tx
ENSUE	pursue; result; follow	
ENTAL	internal	

ENTER	invade; record; insert	
ENTRY	adit; inlet; portal; note	
ENURE	inure; accustom	
ENVOI }	diplomatic agent; legate;	
ENVOY }	postscript	
ENZYM	a ferment; yeast	**ch**
EOLIC	Eolian; Aeolian	
EOLUS	God of the Winds	
EOSIN	red dye or ink	**ch**
EPACT	moon's age at new year	
EPHAH	Hebrew bushel	**me**
EPHOD	vestment; surplice	**rl**
EPHOR	Greek magistrate	
EPOCH	era; cycle; remarkable period	
EPODE	part of an ode	
EPOPT	an Eleusinian initiate	
EPOXY	oxygen fixed to 2 different atoms; epoxide resin	
EPSOM	salts	**md**
EPURE	large working plan (Fr.)	
EQUAL	peer; competent; equable	
EQUES	Roman Knight	
EQUIP	rig; arm; accoutre; array	
EQUUS	the horse genus	**zo**
ERASE	delete; cancel; use null data	**cp**
ERATO	Muse of lyric poetry	
ERECT	build; upright; vertical	
-ERGIC	of work, function, purpose	**cf, pc**
-ERGIC	purposive; of innate drive	**pc**
ERGON	quantum of oscillator energy	**el**
ERGOT	parasitical fungus	**bt**
ERICA	the heath genus	**bt**
ERICK	a blood-fine (Irish)	**lw**
ERODE	eat away; corrode; consume	
EROSE	gnawed-looking (of leaves)	**bt**
EROTO-	of sexual love	**cf**
ERRED	strayed; sinned; wandered	
ERROR	mistake; fault; fallacy	**cp**
ERUCA	the salad plant; a larva	**bt, zo**
ERUPT	eject; eruct; burst forth	
ERVUM	the lentil	**bt, ck**
ESCAR }		
ESKAR }	glacial gravel ridge	
ESKER }		
ESCOT	scot; an ancient tax	
ESSAY	assay; attempt; trial; paper	
ESTER	ethereal salt	**ch**
ESTOC	short cavalry sword (Fr.)	
ESTOP	stop; bar; impede	**lw**
ETANG	lake amid sanddunes (Fr.)	**go**
ETAPE	stage point, esp. cycle races	
ETERN	eternal; endless	
ETHAL	(spermaceti)	**ch**
ETHER	upper air; volatile gas	**ch**
ETHIC	ethical; moral	
ETHOS	guiding spirit of a group or nation	
ETHYL	alcohol radical	**ch**
ETTLE	intend; guess (Sc.)	
ETUDE	a composition (Fr.)	**mu**
ETWEE	etui; pocket-case	

EULER	jump (ice-skating); card-game	**ga**
EUPAD	(antiseptic)	**ch**
EURUS	the East wind	**mt**
EUSOL	(antiseptic)	**ch**
EVADE	elude; avoid; foil; dodge	
EVENS	fifty-fifty	
EVENT	incident; outcome; occurrence	**cp**
EVERT	turn inside out	
EVERY	all; each	
EVICT	eject; dislodge; dispossess	
EVITE	evade; avoid; shun	
EVOKE	arouse; excite; summon	
EWEST	near (Sc.)	
EWHOW	alas! (Sc.)	
EXACT	precise; extort; mulct	
EXALT	raise; extol; magnify	
EXCEL	outvie; surpass; exceed	
EXEAT	a short leave	
EXEME	exempt (Sc.)	
EXERT	strive; try; endeavour	
EXIES	ecstasy; hysterics (Sc.)	
EXILE	refugee; banish; proscribe	
EXINE	outer pollen-grain wall layer	**bt**
EXIST	be; live; endure; last	
EXITE	limb-lobe in arthropoda	**zo**
EX-LEX	outlaw	**lw**
EXODE	dramatic climax	
EXPEL	eject; dislodge; oust	
EXTOL	exalt; laud; glorify	
EXTRA	supernumerary; additional	
EXTRA- }		
EXTRO- }	outside of; beyond	**cf, pc**
EXUDE	ooze; percolate; sweat	
EXULT	crow; gloat; triumph	
EYING	watching; observing	
EYRIE	aerie; eagle's nest	

F

FABLE	myth; legend; allegory	
FACED	defied; confronted; covered	
FACER	a blow	
FACET	small polished surface	
FACIA	control panel; shop name-board	
FADDY	crotchety; particular	
FADGE	suit; prosper; burden	
FAERY	fairy	
FAGIN	beech mast; a Jew (Dickens)	**bt**
FAGOT	faggot; bundle of sticks; bassoon	**mu**
FAGUS	the beech tree	**bt**
FAHAM	Indian orchid	**bt**
FAINT	swoon; dim; indistinct	
FAIRY	faery; peri; elf; pixie	
FAITH	tenet; dogma; belief	
FAKED	spurious; counterfeit	
FAKER	forger; cheat; swindler	
FAKIR	monkish mendicant; magician	
FALSE	sham; erroneous; untrue	

FAMED	illustrious; renowned	
FANAL	lighthouse; beacon	
FANAM	Madras money of account	**nm**
FANCY	pugilism; whim; idea; caprice	
FANGO	radio-active mud	**md**
FAN-IN	convergence; inputs to circuit	**el**
FANNY	messdeck kettle; underparts	**nt**
FANON	napkin; scarf	**rl**
FARAD	unit of electrical capacity	
FARCE	} forcemeat	**ck**
FARSI		
FARCE	comedy; travesty; parody	
FARCI	stuffed, filled	**ck**
FARCY	glanders; equine malady	
FARED	fed; travelled; prospered	
FARLE	oatcake (Sc.)	
FARSE	a Bible extract	**rl**
FARSI	Parsi (Persian) language	
FASTI	Roman calendar of festivals	
FATAL	lethal; baneful; ruinous	
FATED	doomed; destined	
FATES	Clotho, Lachesis & Atropos	
FATLY	obesely; grossly	
FATTY	adipose; pudgy; plump	
FAULT	blemish; mistake; (blame)	
	misfunction (electric); tectonic	
	crust break; infringement of	
	rules; tennis, badminton	**cp, el,**
		ga, gl
FAUNA	animal life	**zo**
FAUST	a drama by Goethe	
FAVUS	scalp disease	**md**
FEAST	banquet; carousel; delight	
FEAZE	unravel	
FECIT	he (or she) made it (art)	
FED-UP	disgruntled; browned off	
FEEZE	to twist; worry	
FEIGN	pretend; simulate; assume	
FEINT	stratagem; artifice; trick; pretence;	
	capillary break (fencing)	**ga**
FELID	one of the cat tribe	**zo**
FELIS	the cat tribe	**zo**
FELIX	the cartoon cat	
FELLY	felloe; part of rim of wheel	
FELON	criminal; miscreant; outlaw	
FEMTO	one thousand million millionth	
	10^{-15}	
FEMUR	thigh bone	**md, pl**
FENCE	receiver of stolen goods, border;	
	palisade; duel	**bd**
FENDY	shifty	
FENKS	finks; blubber refuse	
FENNY	marshy; swamp; boggy	
FEOFF	a fief; grant of land	**lw**
FERAE	wild animals	**zo**
FERAL	wild; deadly; funereal	
FERLY	fearful; a wonder	
FERMI	very small length unit	**nc**
FERNY	fernlike, covered with fern	**bt**
FERRY	river transport	

FESSE	heraldic band	**hd**
FESTA	saint's-day carnival (It.)	
FETAL	} also embryonic	**md**
FOETAL		
FETCH	trick; ghost; bring; carry; free wind	
	distance of storm	**nv, go, mt**
FETED	honoured; lionized	
FETID	noxious; stinking; noisome	
FETOR	offensive odour	
FETUS	an embryo; the young	**md**
FETWA	a judgment (Arab)	**lw**
FEUAR	a lease-holder (Sc.)	
FEVER	ferment; passion; ardour	**md**
FEWER	rather less	
FIARS	the prices of grain (Sc.)	
FIBER	strand of tissue; neuron	**pl**
FIBRE	staple; filament; strand; toughness	
FICHE	chit, official note form	
FICHU	small lace or muslin shawl	
FICUS	the fig	**bt**
FIDGE	to fidget; to be eager (Sc.)	
FIELD	glebe; arable acre, (sports) (racing)	
FIELD	(magnetic) stored data	**cp**
FIEND	imp; demon; monster; wretch	
FIERI	facias; a writ	**lw**
FIERY	ardent; fierce; igneous	
FIFED	fluted	**mu**
FIFER	fife-player	
FIFIE	fishing boat (Fife, Scotland)	**nt**
FIFTH	ordinal of 5; harmonic interval	**mu**
FIFTY	L	
FIGHT	fray; brawl; combat; contest	
FILAR	threadlike; filamentous	
FILCH	steal; pilfer; purloin	
FILED	smooth; polished	
FILER	one who files; artful	
FILES	smoothing tools; archives	**to**
FILLY	girl; foal	**zo**
FILMY	diaphanous	
FILTH	dirt; muck; impurity	
FINAL	last; ultimate; terminal	
FINCH	a passerine	**zo**
FINED	mulcted; amersed	
FINER	refiner; keener; smaller	
FINES	mechanical analysis particles	
FINIS	the end; conclusion	
FINOS	merino wool	
FIORD	} arm of the sea (Scand.)	**go**
FJORD		
FIRED	discharged; kindled; sacked	
FIRER	an incendiary; igniter	
FIRRY	full of pines	**bt**
FIRST	chief; premier; primeval	
FIRTH	} wide inlet, estuary	
FRITH		
FISHY	questionable; unreliable	
FISTY	left-handed person (Sc.)	
FITCH	pole-cat; fur-brush	**zo**
FITCH	vetch; chick-pea	**bt**
FITLY	aptly; properly; seemly	

FITTE	fytte; ballad	
FIT-UP	casing shutter, form work	**cp**
FIVER	£5 bank note	**nm**
FIVES	wall ball game; horse disease	**ga, vt**
FIXED	secured; placed; settled	
FIXER	builder, mason, fraudster	
FLACK	to flap; to flick; (Sc.); to	
FLAFF	flutter; to pant	
FLAIL	a threshing implement	**to**
FLAIR	natural aptitude	
FLAKE	hurdle; hanging platform	
FLAKE	scale; lamina; to peel off; (corn-); (snow-) hook bait (angling); coil a rope serpentine fashion	**nt**
FLAKY	fissile	
FLAME	ardour; blaze; flare	
FLAMY	lambent	
FLANG	miner's pick	**to**
FLANK	side; border; touch (Am. football)	
FLARE	a signal light; glare	
FLARE	flame; dress spread; talent	
FLARY	flaming; flickering	
FLASH	glint; sparkle; showy; mark; display (electric)	**el**
FLASK	ampulla; vial; phial	
FLAWN	custard; pancake	
FLAWY	defective; gusty	
FLAXY	light in colour	
FLEAD	pork fat for lard	
FLEAK	a small lock	
FLEAM	surgical knife	**md**
FLECK	dapple; speckle; variegate	
FLECK	the flounder	**zo**
FLEER	to mock; to flout	
FLEET	a creek; swift; flotilla	**nt**
FLESH	mankind; to accustom	
FLEWS	bloodhound's chaps	
FLICK	flip; fleece; wound; lifting stroke (hockey); silent movie	**ga**
FLIER	flyer; aeronaut; rectangle, shoring posts for old houses	
FLIER	pilot; ball out of bounds	
FLYER	fast mover (high)	**ae, ga**
FLIES	stage screens; (angling)	**zo**
FLIMP	watch-snatching (slang)	
FLING	hurl; dance; escapade	
FLINT	variety of quartz	**mn**
FLIPE	to fold back (Sc.)	
FLIRT	philander; coquet; flip	
FLISK	a comb; frisk; caper	
FLITE	flyte; scold; brawl (Sc.)	
FLOAT	drift; raft; buoy; weft and warp technique; (parade); (cash); memory	**wv, cp**
FLOAT	waft; plastering tool; cystern ball valve; drain pipe	**to**
FLOCK	wool; swarm; herd	**wv, zo**
FLONG	stereotyping paper	

FLOOD	spate; downpour; deluge	
FLOOK	fluke	
FLOOR	to stump; nonplus	
FLORA	flowers collectively	**bt**
FLORY	fleury; boat	**bd, nt**
FLOSS	silky substance; slag	
FLOUR	meal	
FLOUT	scoff; mock; taunt; jeer	
FLOWN	swollen with insolence	
FLUEY	fluffy; downy	
FLUFF	nap; down; lint	
FLUID	liquid; unsettled; gaseous	
FLUKE	parasite worm; (whale)	**zo**
FLUKE	(anchor); fortunate shot	**nt**
FLUKE	unaverage	
FLUKY	accidentally good	
FLUME	a water-chute	
FLUMP	plump down	
FLUNG	tossed; hurled; pitched	
FLUOR	calcium spar	**mn**
FLUSH	blush; poker term; level, even; margin	**pr**
FLUSH	chase out, surge; (hot); (toilet)	
FLUTE	kind of boat; wind instrument	**nt, mu**
FLUTY	flutelike	
FLYER	flier; aviator	
FLYTE	flite; scold; brawl (obs.)	
FOAMY	frothy; spumy	
FOCAL	converging	
FOCUS	point of convergence	
FOEHN	a hot wind in the Alps	**mt**
FOGEY	old-fashioned person	
FOGGY	obscure; hazy; indistinct	
FOGLE	silk handkerchief (slang)	
FOISM	Chinese Buddhism	**rl**
FOIST	impose; thrust; palm	
FOLIC	acid in vitamin-B complex	**md**
FOLIO	a sheet of paper	
FOLLY	inanity; absurdity; fatuity	
FOMES	absorbent substance	
FONDU	colour blending in calico, cheese and wine blending in pot (Swiss)	**ck**
FONDU	high alumina cement	
FOOTS	refuse; sediment	
FORAY	raid; inroad; sally; invasion	
FORBY	adjacent	
FORCE	power; energy; army; coerce; intervene	**cp**
FORCE	fors; foss; waterfall (Scand.)	**gl, go**
FORDO	undo; ruin; destroy	
FOREL	heavy parchment book cover	**pr**
FORET	a drill	**to**
FORGE	smithy; falsify; fabricate	
FORGO	renounce; go without	
FORKY	branching	
FORME	bed of type	**pr**
FORTE	outstanding skill; loud; handguard of sword (fencing)	**mu, ga**

FORTH	forward; onward; ahead	
FORTY	two score	
FORUM	tribunal; court; market-place	
FORUM	open discussion; public-speaking	
FOSSA	Malagasy civet cat	**zo**
FOSSE	ditch; moat; canal	
FOUAT	an onion (Sc.); the house-leek	
FOUET		**bt**
FOUND	to cast; establish; start	
FOUNT	spring; well; source; type	**pr, cp**
FOUTH	fowth; abundance (Sc.)	
FOVEA	pit; a pock mark; centre of vision in retina	**md**
FOXED	baffled; deluded; yellow damp stain	
FOYER	lobby; fire grate	
FRACK	freck; eager; bold; hale	
FRAIL	weak; infirm; rush basket	
FRAME	fashion; concoct; mood	
FRAME	a game of snooker; unit of film; tv; display; (snooker) chassis surround; conspire; entrap; falsify	**ga, lw**
FRANC	100 centimes	**nm**
FRANK	candid; open; gannet	**zo**
FRASS	excrement; manure	**zo**
FRATE	friar	**rl**
FRATI	friars; brethren	**rl**
FRAUD	guilt; imposture; deception	
FREAK	monstrosity; quirk; vagary	
FRECK	frack; eager; hale (Sc.)	
FREED	emancipated; exempted	
FREER	deliverer; more lavish	
FREET	friet; superstition (Sc.)	
FREMD	strange; a stranger (Sc.)	
FRESH	novel; recent; unsalted	
FRETT	ore refuse	
FREYA	wife of Odin	**rl**
FRIAR	frier; frate; wandering monk	**rl**
FRIED	simmered	
FRILL	ruffle; border; mannerism	
FRISK	romp; search; flisk	
FRITH	firth; forest; peace	
FRITO	crisp tortilla chip (Mex.)	**ck**
FRITZ	a German	
FRIZZ	to curl; to crisp	
FROCK	smock; costume	
FROND	fern leaf	**bt**
FRONS	part of skull	**md**
FRONT	van; face; assurance; weather; cover; (war)	**mt**
FRORE	flory; frozen (Spens.)	
FROST	rime; iciness; a failure	
FROTH	spume; foam; effervesce	
FROWN	glower; scowl	
FROWY	rank; musty	
FROZE	became ice; stopped still; acted coldly	
FRUIT	produce; crop; issue (ripeness); off-spring; fellow; edible plant seed flesh coating	**bt, ck**

FRUMP	a joke; dowdy woman	
FRUSH	brittle; broken; thrush	
FRYER	a frying pan	
FUBBY	fat and squat; chubby	
FUBSY		
FUCUS	dye; disguise; seaweed	**bt**
FUDER	large wine cask (Moselle)	
FUDGE	fake; nonsense; sweetméat	**ck**
FUERO	statute; charter (Sp.)	**lw**
FUFFY	fluffy; soft; downy	
FUGAL	like a fugue	**mu**
FUGIE	a runaway; a coward (Sc.)	
FUGLE	to act as ringleader	
FUGUE	polyphonic composition; escape from sanity	**mu, pc**
FULLY	amply; entirely; completely	
FUMET	bone/veg. essence for sauce; deer dung	**mh**
FUMID	smoky; vaporous	
FUNDI	a West African grain	**bt**
FUNGI	mushrooms; toadstools, etc.	**bt**
FUNGO	pre match, training practice; (Am. football)	**ga**
FUNIS	umbilical cord	**md**
FUNKY	nervous; timid; cowardly	
FUNNY	droll; comical; boat	**nt**
FUOCO	with fire (It.)	**mu**
FURCA	forked structure	**zo**
FUROR	wave of enthusiasm	
FURRY	incrusted	
FURZE	gorse; whin	
FURZY	whinny	
FUSED	melted; merged; blended	
FUSEE	vesuvian; firelock fuzee	
FUSIL	fusible; a musket	
FUSSY	fidgety; bustling	
FUSTY	musty; rank; mouldy	
FUZED	provided with a fuze	
FUZEE	fusee	
FUZZY	woolly; shaggy; blurred	
FYTTE	fitte; song; ballad	

G

GABEL	excise duty; salt tax (Fr. obs.)	
GABLE	roof/window construction	**ar**
GADGE	instrument of torture	
GADUS	the cod genus	**zo**
GAFFE	a social solecism	
GAGED	pledged; pawned; engaged	
GAGER	gauger	
GAILY	gayly; blithely; lively	
GAIZE	friable sandstone	**bd**
GALAH	Australian cockatoo	**zo**
GALBE	elegant sweep; contour	**ar**
GALEA	helmet-shaped	**bt**
GALLY	like gall; scare; daze	
GALON	scalloped-edge narrow lace	**tx**

GALOP	} lively round dance; racing	
GALLOP	} horse	mu, ga
GAMBA	a viol	mu
GAMBE	leg (often animal)	zo
GAMED	gambled; hazarded; wagered	
GAMIC	sexual	
GAMIN	urchin (Fr.)	
GAMMA	letter (Gr.); radioactive ray	
GAMUT	range; scope; entire series; notes and scales	mu
GANAT	}	
KANAT	} tunnel system (irrigation)	
KHANAT	} (Iran)	av
QANAT	}	
GANCH	Ottoman form of execution	
GANIL	limestone	mn
GANJA	Indian drink made of hemp	
GANZA	a wild goose	zo
GAPED	wide open; yawned	
GAPPY	crannied	
GARNI	} with addition of vegetables to	
GARNISH	} a dish	ck
GARNI	bed and breakfast only (hotel)	
GARRY	Indian carriage	
GARTH	fish-weir; yard; garden	
GARUA	winter precipitation mist in W. Peru	mt, go
GARUM	fish sauce	
GASSY	gaseous; aerated	
GATED	confined	
GAUCY	gawsy; buxom; jolly (Sc.)	
GAUDY	garish; tawdry; flashy	
GAUGE	estimate; measure; track width; (rain)	to, rw, to
GAULT	clay	mn
GAUMY	dauby; smeary	
GAUNT	lean; lanky; emaciated	
GAUSS	unit of magnetic intensity	me
GAUZE	transparent fabric; bandage; mesh	tx
GAUZY	filmy	
GAVEL	mason's hammer; mallet	to
GAVEL	sheaf of corn	
GAVOT	gavotte; a dance	
GAWKY	awkward; ungainly; clumsy	
GAYAL	wild ox	zo
GAYER	merrier; brighter	
GAZED	looked intently	
GAZEL	gazelle	zo
GAZER	starer; rubber-neck	
GAZON	turf (Fr.)	
GEACH	a thief; to steal (slang)	
GECKO	lizard	zo
GECOM	automatic computer code	cp
GEESE	plural of goose	zo
GEEST	heath; sandy region (glaciated)	gl, go
GEIGE	fiddle, violin (Ger.)	mu
GEIST	mental drive	
GELID	cold; freezing	

GEMEL	twin; coupled vessels/bottles	
GEMMA	leaf-bud	bt
GEMMY	glittering	
GEMOT	moot; assembly (obs.)	
GENET	civet-cat fur	
-GENIC	genetic; caused by genes; focus or origin	cf
GENIE	jinee; Arabian sprite	
GENII	men of ingenuity	
GENIO	ingenious person (It.)	
GENOA	a cake; large jib-sail	ck, nt
GENOM	gamete nucleus chromosome content	gn
GENRE	specialty; type of painting	pt
GENRO	Japanese elder statesmen	
GENTY	graceful (Sc.)	
GENUS	group of a species	zo
GENYS	lower jaw in vertebrates	zo
GEODE	crystalline cavity	mn
GEOID	the figure of the earth	gl, go
GERAH	twentieth of a shekel	nm
GERBE	sheaf; firework (Fr.)	
GESSO	stucco; plaster	
GESTE	generous action	
GET-UP	style of dress	
GHAUT	Indian mountain pass	
GHAZI	Arab fanatic; conqueror	
GHOST	spook; spectre; phantom	
GHOUL	a gruesome fiend	
GHYLL	goyal; ravine; gully	
GIANT	Cyclops; colossus; huge	
GIANT	monitor; nozzle; water gun	ce
GIBBE	a worn-out animal (Shak.)	
GIBED	jibed; taunted; jeered	nt
GIBEL	Prussian carp	zo
GIBER	scoffer; joker; derider	
GIBLI	hot sirocco wind (Libya)	go, mt
GIBUS	an opera hat	
GIDDY	dizzy; fickle; mutable	
GIGOT	jigot; leg of mutton (Fr.)	
GIGUE	lively tune; (Fr.) jig, dance	mu
GILLY	gillie; keeper (Sc.)	
GILPY	a tom-boy (Sc.)	
GIMEL	}	
GYMEL	} vocal music	mu
GIMME	very short putt (golf)	ga
GIPSY	gypsy; zingaro; a Romany	
GIRTH	girdle; thong; cinch; tummy belt of horse, holds on saddle	
GISMO	gadget, thing (slang)	
GIUST	joust (Spens.)	
GIVEN	presented; conceded	
GIVER	bestower; donor; granter	
GIVES	gyves; fetters; bonds	
GLACE	polished; sugar-surfaced	
GLADE	woodland avenue	
GLAIK	trick (Sc.)	
GLAIR	white of egg; varnish	
GLAND	a secretory organ; seal; olive	pl, pb
GLANS	bulbous end of penis	pl

121

GLARE	glower; frown; glitter	
GLARY	dazzling; lustrous	
GLASS	mirror; telescope; tumbler	
GLAUM	to grasp eagerly (Sc.)	
GLAUR	glower (Sc.)	
GLAUX	sea milkwort	bt
GLAVE	glaive; kind of halbert	
GLAZE	lustre; burnish; (windows)	
GLAZY	shiny; filmy	
GLEAD	glede; buzzard; kite	zo
GLEAM	ray; beam; glimmer; shine	
GLEAN	cull; collect; harvest	
GLEBA	spore-bearing tissue in truffles	bt
GLEBE	sod; church land	rl
GLEBY	turfy; cloddy	
GLEDE	glead; buzzard; kite	zo
GLEED	glowing ember	
GLEEK	three-handed card game	ga
GLEET	ooze (Sc.); inflammation	md
GLIAL	of Glial supportive cells	md, pl
GLIFF	glift; an alarm (Sc.)	
GLIMA	ancient style, Icelandic wrestling	ga
GLINT	gleam; a flash	
GLISK	a glimpse (Sc.)	
GLIST	glimmer; mica	mn
GLOAM	to darken	
GLOAT	exult; crow; revel	
GLOBE	orb; sphere; ball; earth	
GLOBY	spherical	
GLOME	globular head of flowers	bt
GLOOM	sadness; depression; darkness	
GLORY	exult; honour; renown	
GLOSS	comment; polish; veil	
GLOUP	subterranean blowhole; cave	gl
GLOUT	to be sulky	
GLOVE	gauntlet; mitten	
GLOZE	wheedle; flattery; adulation	
GLUED	stuck together; adhered	
GLUER	a user of mucilage	
GLUEY	adhesive; viscous; glutinous	
GLUGG **GLOGG**	} mulled wine (Scand.)	ck
GLUME	husks	bt
GLUON	hypothetical particle binding two quarks	el
GLYPH	vertical fluting	ar
GNARL	snarl; growl; grumble	
GNARR	a knot in wood; a snag	
GNASH	to grind the teeth	
GNOME	dwarf; a maxim	
GOBBO	okra; a fruit	bt
GODET	small glass reel	
GODET	gore/gusset to make a dress flare; shallow, handled, cup; (medieval Eng., Fr.)	tx
GODLY	holy; pious; devout	rl
GOETY	black magic	
GOFER	gauffre; wafer	
GOING	wending; faring; elapsing; road conditions	

GOING	horizontal nosings (stairs); departure	
GOLDY	goldfinch	zo
GOLLY	exclamation	
GONAD	reproductive gland	pl
GONAL	forming a gonad	zo
GONER	irretrievably lost	
GOODS	chattels; effects	
GOODY	a sweet	
GOOFY	crazy stunt; goofy foot on skateboard (Disney dog)	
GOOSE	tailor's iron; poultry bird	to, zo
GO-OUT	sluice in embankment	
GORAL	Indian antelope	zo
GORED	run through (bull-fighting); (tailoring)	
GORGE	gulch; defile; gulp; cram; narrow canyon	go
GORSE	whin	bt
GORSY	abounding in gorse	
GOUDA	a Dutch cheese	
GOUGE	scoop; circular chisel	to
GOURA	a pigeon genus	zo
GOURD	drinking cup; (cucumber)	bt
GOUTY	swollen; boggy	md
GOWAN	a daisy	bt
GOYAL	ghyll; kloof; combe	
GRAAL	Holy Grail; sacred chalice	rl
GRACE	adorn; embellish; favour	
GRADE	step; rank; slope; degree	
GRAFF	graft; ditch; moat	
GRAFT	intrigue; swindle; engraft	
GRAIL	Holy Grail; sacred chalice	rl
GRAIN	corn; response; flow; grist	bt, me
GRAIP	dung-fork	to
GRAMA	pasture land (USA)	go
GRAME	gram; misery	
GRAND	lordly; 1,000 dollars	nm
GRAND	granolithic screed; jointless cement floor	
GRANT	cede; confer; gift; largess	
GRAPE	fruit of the vine	bt
GRAPH	a diagram showing related factors	ma
GRAPY	like a grape	
GRASP	clasp; clutch; hold; scope	
GRASS	herbage; pasture; to turf; to betray others	bt
GRATE	abrade; rasp; jar; fireplace	
GRAVE	solemn; engrave; tomb; slow tempo	mu
GRAVY	meat juice	ck
GRAZE	skim; browse; touch lightly; pre-attack (fencing)	ga
GREAT	eminent; bulky; huge	
GREBE	web-footed bird	zo
GRECE	grize; steps; staircase	
GREED	voracity; avidity; gluttony	
GREEK	Attic; Doric; Hellenic	
GREEN	raw; fresh; inexperienced; outdoor range (archery)	ga

GREEN	verdant; (village); (golf); (bowls); unbroken wave (surfing); ecology party supporter	**ga**
GREES	grece; steps; stairway	
GREET	cry; weep; lament (Sc.); hail	
GREIT	greet; weep; cry	
GREYS	cavalry regiment	
GRIAS	species of pear	**bt**
GRICE	young wild boar	**zo**
GRIDE	gryde; grate; pierce	
GRIEF	woe; anguish; mishap	
GRIKE	limestone-rock fissure	**gl**
GRILL	broil; grid-iron; question	
GRIME	dirt; soil; sully; befoul	
GRIMY	filthy; smutty; unclean	
GRIND	abrade; pulverize; sharpen	
GRIPE	grasp; squeeze; ditch	
GRIST	corn; provision	
GRITS	coarse oatmeal; porridge (Sc.) (USA)	**ck**
GRIZE	grece; grees; staircase	
GROAN	moan; complain; grumble	
GROAT	Joey; fourpenny piece	**nm**
GROCK	a kindly clown	
GROIN	breakwater; under abdomen; intersection edge (vault)	**ar, ce**
GROOM	syce; equerry; bridegroom	
GROPE	search by feeling	
GROSS	coarse; 12 dozen	**me**
GROUP	clump; cluster; arrange; index reference	**cp**
GROUP	multiple channels on one path	**tc**
GROUP	sequence of data storage stations	**cp**
GROUT	coarse meal; mortar	
GROVE	wood; thicket; spinney	
GROWL	snarl; grumble; complain	
GROWN	raised; waxed; extended	
GRUEL	thin porridge	**ck**
GRUFF	surly; rude; churlish	
GRUNT	snort like a pig	
GRYDE	gride; grate	
GUACO	plant; snake-bite antidote	**bt**
GUANA	American lizard	**zo**
GUANO	bird's manure	
GUARD	shield; watch; bulwark	
GUARD	fire-; safety barrier between circuits; protect; soldier; linesmen; vigilante	**cp**
GUAVA	pear-shaped fruit	**bt**
GUESS	surmise; conjecture; divine	
GUEST	visitor; lodger	
GUFAH	} reeds for boats	**nt**
GUFA	}	
GOPHER	pilot; signpost; control; -line; edge; information	
GUIDE	pilot; signpost; control; -line; edge; information	**cp**
GUILD	trade's union; fraternity	
GUILE	craft; duplicity; cunning	
GUILT	proof or sense of wrong	**lw**

GUIRD	Cuban instrument	**mu**
GUISE	garb; aspect; manner	**-**
GULAR	(throat)	
GULCH	gully; gorge; ravine	
GULES	heraldic red	**hd**
GULFY	full of whirlpools	
GULLY	water-worn channel; (cricket); rift between rocks (mountaineering)	
GUMBO	a stew; okra soup; muddy course; (horse racing)	**ck, ga**
GUMMY	viscous, sticky	
GUNGE	market, granary (Ind.)	
GUNNY	Bengal sacking	**tx**
GURGE	whirlpool (obs.)	
GURRY	fish-offal; Ind. fortress	
GUSLA	ancient Slavonic single-string viol	**mu**
GUSLI	Russian zither-type instrument	**mu**
GUSTO	zest; relish; enjoyment	
GUSTY	squally; stormy; puffy	
GUTSY	deep voice; of the intestine; greedy	
GUTTA	Doric ornament; drop	**ar**
GUTTY	old type golf ball	
GUYED	mocked; ridiculed; derided	
GUYOT	submarine mountain	**gl, go**
GYALL	gayal; jungle bull	**zo**
GYBED	(a sailing manoeuvre)	**nt**
GYGIS	tern genus (water birds)	**zo**
GYMEL	} 14th C. vocal music	**mu**
GIMEL	}	
GYPSY	gipsy; zingaro; Romany	
GYRAL	revolving; whirling	
GYRON	heraldic device	**hd**
GYRUS	convolution of the brain	**md**
GYVES	bonds; fetters; shackles	

H

HABIT	dress; usage; wont; custom	
HABLE	habile; able (Spens.)	
HADES	the abode of the dead	
HADJI	pilgrim (Arab); hajji	
HAEMA-	} of blood (Gr.)	**cf, pl**
HAEMO-	}	
HAFIZ	knowledge of the Koran	
HAICK	Arab wrap	
HAIKH	an Armenian	
HAILY	apt to hail; icy	
HAIRY	vairy; furry	
HAJIB	Moslem court chamberlain	
HAJJI	hadji; pilgrim (Arab)	
HAKIM	wise man; physician (Arab)	
HALED	hauled; dragged along	
HALFA	esparto grass	**bt**
HALLO!	hello! hillo!	
HALMA	a board game of leapfrogging	
HALVA	ground sesame sweetmeat	**ck**
HALVE	bisect; divide	
HAMAL	porter (Turk.)	

HAMAM	Turkish bath	
HANAP	pewter goblet	
HANCE	haunch	ar
HANCH	to snap	
HANDY	near; dexterous; adroit	
HANIF	orthodox Moslem	
HANKY	handkerchief	
HANSA	of North German mercantile league, Hanseatic	
HAPLO-	single; simple (Gr.)	cf
HAPLY	perchance; peradventure	
HAPPY	joyous; lucky; opportune	
HARAM	the inviolable, Islam	rl
HARAS	stud; breeding establishment	
HARDS	hurds; refuse of flax	
HARDY	bold; intrepid; robust	
HARED	sprinted; sped; ran	
HAREM	seraglio; zenana; ladies' quarters	bd
HARLE	harl; flax-fibre	bt, tx
HARPE	spinelike insect structure	zo
HARPY	fabulous monster; vulture	zo
HARPY	golden eagle; extortioner	zo
HARRY	harass; ravage; raid	
HARSH	raucous; strident; caustic	
HASTE	alacrity; speed; hustle	
HASTY	swift; reckless; headlong	
HATCH	to plot; doorway; to shade	
HATED	loathed; abominated	
HATER	abhorrer; detester	
HATHI	wild Indian elephants	zo
HATTO	bishop eaten by rats	
HAULM	halm; stubble (harvest); stem	bt
HAUNT	frequent; importune; resort	
HAURL	harl; rough-cast	
HAUSA	Northern Nigerian	
HAVEN	port; refuge; asylum	
HAVER	to drivel; blather	
HAVOC	waste; carnage; devastation	
HAWSE	bow anchor pipe	nt
HAZED	bullied; punished	
HAZEL	a colour; nut-tree; nut	bt, ck
HAZER	steer riding, wrestling for cowboys (rodeo)	ga
HAZRI	Indian breakfast	ck
HEADS	or tails; toilets (bows); chief; source; foam; endpoint; tool edge	nt
HEADY	rash; hasty; wilful; intoxicating	
HEALD	warp guide in a loom	
HEAPY	in piles	
HEARD	listened to; tried	
HEART	core; centre; spirit	
HEATH	heather- or ling-covered acid or scrubland	go
HEATS	qualifying rounds	
HEAVE	to raise; push; haul; lateral fault of rock strata	nt
HEAVY	weighty, serious, ponderous, of gravity, massive; (baseball)	

HECTO-	multiplied by 100; of units (Gr.)	cf, me
HEDGE	lay off; enclose; fence	
HEDGE	guarded reservation (speech)	pc
HEFTY	heavy; strong; powerful	
HEIGH!	exclamation	
HEKIM	judge (Arab.)	
HELIO	a heliograph	
HELIX	screwthread form; snail	zo
HELLO!	hallo! hillo! hollo!	
HELOT	Spartan slave; serf	
HELVE	axe-handle; haft	
HEMAL	haemal; (blood)	md
HE-MAN	butch; virile	
HEMPY	like hemp	
HENCE	henceforth; away; therefore	
HENCH	chimney shaft side	bd
HENNA	a dye; a shrub	bt
HENRY	electrical induction unit	me
HEPAR	a sulphur compound	ch
HERBY	herbaceous; herbous	
HEROD	a tyrant	
HERON	a wading bird	zo
HERSE	a portcullis	
HERTZ	unit of signals frequency	me, tc
HERUT	political party (Israel)	
HET-UP	hot and bothered, aroused	
HEVEA	rubber-tree	bt
HEWED	axed; hacked; fashioned	
HEWER	cutter; sculptor; miner	
HIDER	one who conceals	
HIGHT	hecht; to command; to call	
HIKED	tramped	
HIKER	rambler; pedestrian	
HILCH	to hobble; a limp (Sc.)	
HILLY	undulating	go
HILUM	the eye of a bean	bt
HINDI	Indian dialect	
HINDU	practiser of Ind. religion	rl
HINGE	depend; turn; hang	
HINNY	whinny; a mule	zo
HIPPO-	(horse) (of rivers)	cf, zo, go
HIRED	chartered; leased; rented	
HIRER	an employer of labour	
HISTO-	of tissue (Gr.)	cf, pl
HITCH	fasten; catch; obstacle; knot; (baseball)	
HITHE	hythe; haven; port	
HIVED	stored; gathered	
HIVER	an apiarist	
HIVES	the croup; nettle-rash	md
HOARD	amass; garner; save; secrete	
HOARY	venerable; ancient; silvery	
HOAST	a cough; to cough	
HOBBY	recreation; horse; falcon	zo
HOBIT	mortar; short gun	
HOBOY		
HAUTBOY	} woodwind	mu
HAUTBOIS		
OBOE		

HOCUS	to cheat; to drug	
HODAD	incompetent surfer	
HODGE	a rustic	
HOGAN	strong liquor	
HOIST	hoise; heave; elevate; pulley	**to**
HOLEY	holed; riddled	
HOLLY	an evergreen	**bt**
HOMEO-	of sameness (Gr.)	**cf**
HOMER	homing pigeon; boomerang	**zo**
HOMER	guide signal arrangement; home run (baseball)	
HONDO	sad Andalusian song (Sp.)	**mu**
HONED	whetted; sharpened	
HONEY	sweetness	
HOOCH	fire-water	
HOOEY }	balderdash	
HOO-HA }		
HOOKA	hookah; narghile; hubble-bubble pipe	
HOOKY	full of barbs	
HOOLY	carefully; softly (Sc.)	
HOOSH	a stew; a mixture	**ck**
HOOVE	a cattle disease	**vt**
HOPAK }	Russian folk dance	**mu**
GOPAK }		
HOPED	desired; anticipated	
HOPPO	Chinese overseer	
HOPPY	flavoured with hops	
HORAL	horary; hourly	
HORDE	clan; throng; gang; crew	
HORNY	callous; spikey; lustful	
HORSE	steed; palfrey; nag; cob	**zo**
HORSE	cavalry; flogging frame	
HORST	elevated rock between faults (Ger.)	**gl**
HORSY	horsey; equuscentric	
HORUS	son of Osiris (Egypt)	
HOSED	drenched; watered	
HOTEL	inn; tavern; hostel	
HOTLY	eagerly; ardently; fervidly	
HOUGH	hamstring; the ham	
HOUND	pursue; chase; hunting dog	**zo**
HOURI	a nymph of paradise; peri	
HOUSE	mansion; domicile; lineage; (curling)	
HOVEL	shelter; hut; cabin; shed	
HOVER	hang; vacillate; wave	
HOWDY	a midwife (Sc.); howdie	
HOWEL	cooper's tool	**to**
HOWFF	houff; a haunt; resort (Sc.)	
HOWSO	howsoever; although	
HUBBY	husband	
HUFFY	petulant; irritable	
HULCH	hunch; bump; bunch	
HULKY	unwieldy; clumsy	
HULLO!	hallo!	
HULLY	husky	
HUMAN	mortal; cosmic; rational	
HUMET	abbreviated fesse	**hd**
HUMIC	wet; dank; mouldy	
HUMID	damp; moist	

HUMOR	bodily fluid (eye)	**md**
HUMPHI	exclamation of dissatisfaction	
HUMPY	Australian native hut	
HUMUS	decomposed organic soil enrichment	
HUMUS	chick pea/garlic puree	**ck**
HUNCH	presentiment; hump; lump	
HUNKS	miser; niggard	
HUNKY	rugged masculine physique	
HUNYA	fighting rams	**zo**
HURDS	hards; flax refuse	
HURLY	confusion; flurry (-burly)	
HURRY	hasten; expedite; speed	
HURST	a grove; a wood	
HUSKY	Canadian sled-dog	**zo**
HUSKY	hoarse; raucous; guttural	
HUSSY	housewife; brazen girl	
HUTCH	coop; chest; bin	
HUTIA	West Indian hog-rat	**zo**
HUZZA	also hurra	
HYADS	hyades; cluster of stars	
HYDRA	water monster; source of trouble	
HYDRO	a spa; a hotel	
HYDRO-	of water; spa (Gr.)	**cf, md**
HYENA	hyen; a carnivore	
HYLAM	form of junk (Siam)	**nt**
HYLEG	ruling planet in horoscope	
HYLIC	materialistic	
HYMEN	God of Marriage	**rl**
HYMEN	maidenhead; vaginal membrane	**pl**
HYOID	tongue-bone	**md**
HYONG	kata part of Kendo (Jap. wrestling)	**ga**
HYPER-	above normal; excessive (Gr.)	**cf**
HYPHA	a fungus filament	
HYRAX	rock-rabbit; cony	**zo**
HYSON	green tea (China)	**bt**
HYTHE	hithe; haven; port	

I

-IASIS	abnormal; diseased (Gr.)	**cf, md**
-IATRO }	of healing (Gr.)	**cf, pc, md**
-IATRY }		
ICENI	Ancient British tribe	
ICHOR	a god's blood; a fluid	**md**
ICIER	colder	
ICILY	frigidly; frostily	
ICING	a sugar-coating	
ICKER	an ear of corn (Sc.)	**bt**
ICTAL-	of transitory emotions (Gr.)	**cf, pc**
ICTIC	abrupt; sudden	
ICTUS	a stroke; accentuation	
IDEAL	Utopian; fanciful; visionary	
ID-EGO-	single but divided entity (Gr.)	**cf, pc**
IDIOM	peculiarity of phraseology	
IDIOT	Gothamite; Bedlamite; moron; silly; foolish person	**pc**
IDIST	Ido linguist	

IDLED	slacked
IDLER	drone; lounger; trifler
IDOLA	fantasies; apparitions
IDOSE	monosaccharide
IDRIS	mythical Welsh giant; (water)
IDYLL	pastoral poem
IGLOO	Eskimo snow-hut
ILEAC	colicky; iliac	**md**
ILEUM	(intestine)	**md**
ILEUS	intestinal obstruction, colic	**md**
ILIAC	pertaining to loins
ILIAD	epic poem; (siege of Troy)
ILIUM	part of hip-bone	**md**
ILLAM	gem-bearing Sri L. gravel	**gl**
IMAGE	ikon; idol; copy; likeness (mirror)
	stored (public relations)	**cp**
IMAGO	perfect state of insect	**zo**
IMAUM	imam; Islamic priest
IMBAR	embar; exclude
IMBAT	cool Near-Eastern wind	**mt**
IMBED }	place securely; plant
EMBED }	(gardening)
IMBER	the great northern diver	**zo**
IMBOW	to arch
IMBUE	dye; steep; stain; permeate
IMIDE	acid anhydride compound	**ch**
IMMEW	emmew; to confine
IMMIT	inject
IMMIX	to mingle
IMPEL	urge; drive; incite; actuate
IMPEN	to pen; to write
IMPLY	mean; hint; signify; involve
IMPUT	input; charge	**el, tc**
INAJA	Brazilian palm	**bt**
INANE	fatuous; empty; void; vapid
INAPT	unfit; inapposite; clumsy
INARM	to encircle
INBYE	mine direction	**mn**
INCOG	incognito; disguised
INCUR	(debt); become liable for; arouse	**lw**
INCUS	ear-bone like an anvil	**md**
INCUT	inset; side note let into text	**pr**
INDEX	pointer; forefinger; exponent
INDRA	Hindu God of Rain
INDRI	babakoto; large lemur	**zo**
INDUE	endue; invest; endow
INEPT	inane; futile; pointless
INERM	without prickles	**bt**
INERT	slack; dull; torpid; inactive
INEYE	to graft
INFER	deduce; gather; surmise
INFIX	implant; ingraft; instil; notational
	graft	**cp**
INFRA-	below; inferior; (-red); (Gr.)	**cf**
INGLE	fireside; (nook); (seat)	**ar, bd**
INGOT	a mass of metal	**mn**
INION	the nape of the neck; occiput	**md, pl**
INKER	recording device
INKLE	broad linen tape

INKOS	Zulu chief
INLAW	cf. outlaw
INLAY	(buhl); tesselate
INLET	bay; bight; creek; entrance; intake
	opening; valve	**cp, el, go, ro**
INNER	interior; within; (mind); (soul);
	central
INPUT	capital investment; charge; work
	done	**tc, el**
INPUT	program; data signal fed in	**cp**
INRUN	pre-ski-jump run (skiing)	**cp**
INSET	an insertion; implant
INTER	bury; inhume; entomb
INUIT	Eskimo name of people
INULA	herb	**bt**
INURE	enure; harden; toughen; train
INURN	bury; entomb
INUUS	Barbary ape	**zo**
INVAR	an alloy of nickel and steel
INWIT	intuition; conscience
IODAL }	containing iodine	**ch**
IODIC }	
IONIC	(Ionia)
IRADE	Turkish written decree	**lw**
IRAQI }	dwellers in Iraq
IRAKI }	
IRATE	wroth; ireful; angry; incensed
IRENE	Roman goddess of peace
IRIAN	relating to the iris	**md**
IRISH	Hibernian
IRITE	an iridium compound	**mn**
IRKED	bored; wearied; jaded
IROKO	African utility timber	**fr**
IRONE	smell constituent of violets	**ch**
IRONS	gyves; golf clubs	**nt**
IRONY	satire; sarcasm; mockery
ISIAC	referring to Isis
ISLAM	(Mohammedanism) submission to
	Allah	**rl**
ISLET	isle; eyot; atoll
ISSUE	egress; vent; outcome; result
ISTLE }	aloe fibre	**bt**
IXTLE }	
ITCHY	scratchy; desirous; uneasy
IULUS	julus; catkin; wireworm	**bt, zo**
IVIED	ivyed; covered with ivy
IVORY	dentine; elephant tusk	**zo**
IVRIT	modernised Hebrew (language)
IXION	wheel-bound king; (Hell)
IZARD	Pyrenean ibex or chamois	**zo**

J

JABOT	lace frill; neck ruffle
JACKS	wooden wedges
JADED	weary; tired; fagged; exhausted
JADOO	artificial silk	**tx**
JAFFA	orange (type)	**bt, ck**
JAGER	the great skua; pirate gull	**zo**

JAGGY	uneven; serrated; notched	
JALAP	a cathartic root	**bt,md**
JAMBE	a part of leg armour	
JAMBU	rose-apple tree	**bt**
JAMES	a flunkey	
JAMMY	smothered in jam	
JANTU	Indian water-raising device	
JANTY	jaunty; airy; showy	
JANUS	god of doorways	
JAPAN	varnish; lacquer; enamel	
JARDE	tumour on a horse's leg	**vt**
JASEY	worsted wig	
JASPE	veined jaspar	**mn**
JAUNT	trip; outing; excursion	
JAWED	talked; lectured	
JEANS	overalls; denim trousers	**tx**
JEBEL	mountain (Arab) Gibraltar	
JABAL	(Jabal Tariq)	**go**
JIBAL		
JEDGE	gauge; dean's warrant (Sc.)	
JEHAD	Islamic Holy War	
JELLY	gelatin; aspic (-fish) (wobble)	**ck**
JEMMY	gemmy; spruce; lever	**to**
JENNY	spinning machine; billiard shot	
JERID	Turkish javelin	
JERKY	spasmodic; convulsive; irregular	
JERKY	beef biltong	**ck**
JERRY	a German	
JESSE	candlestick; stained window	**rl**
JETTY	jut; projection; a pier	**nt**
JEWEL	gem; trinket	
JEWRY	Judaea; the Jews	
JHEEL	Indian marsh	**go**
JHOOM	jungle cultivation	
JIBED	gibed; sneered; taunted	**nt**
JIFFY	a moment; an instant	
JIMMY	jemmy; a lever for break-ins	**to**
JIMPY	slender; elegant (Sc.)	
JINTY		
JINGO	ultra-militarist	
JINKS	high jinks; merry-making	
JIPPO	jupon; vest	
JOCKO	a chimpanzee	**zo**
JODEL	yodel; Tyrolese singing	**mu**
JOINT	splice; seam; united; concerted; (drug)	
JOIST	floor beam	
JOKED	bantered; rallied	
JOKER	jester; wag; humorist; a card	
JOLLY	a marine; mirthful; a boat	**nt**
JONAH	bad luck bringer	
JORAM	drinking bowl or its contents	
JORUM		
JORIA	East Indian wool	**tx**
JOTUN	Norse giant	
JOUGS	iron neck-ring; pillory	
JOULE	electrical unit of work	**me**
JOUST	giust; tilt; encounter; tournament	
JUDAS	traitor; spy-hole; tree	**bt**
JUDGE	decide; arbiter; critic	**lw**

JUGAL	malar; (cheek-bone)	**pl**
JUGUM	pair of opposite leaves	**bt**
JUICE	sap; fluid extract; petrol	
JUICY	succulent; moist; lush	
JULAP	cordial cocktail (Am.)	**ck**
JULEP		
JULIS	a wrasse; a small fish	**zo**
JULUS	catkin; wire-worm	**zo, bt**
IULUS		
JUMAR	movable clamp on rope	**mo**
JUMBO	elephant; locomotive; airliner (jet); drill carriage	**zo**
JUMPS	nervous apprehension; obstacle (horse racing)	
JUNCO	North American snow-bird	**zo**
JUNTA	cabal; govt. by rebel clique	
JUNTO	coterie; clique; faction	
JUPON	jippo; surcoat; petticoat	
JURAL	legal; lawful	**lw**
JURAT	an alderman; (affidavit)	**lw**
JUROR	a juryman	**lw**
JUSSI	Manila textile fabric	**tx**
JUTES	invaders from Jutland	
JUTTY	a jetty	
JUXTA	sclerotized support in lepidoptera	

K

KAABA	caaba; sacred stone at Mecca	
KAAMA	hartebeest; S. Afr. antelope	**zo**
KABOB	meat on skewer	**ck**
KEBAB		
KADIR	(cup for pig-sticking)	
KAFIR	Kaffir; Turkish/Greek lateen ship	**nt**
KALAN	sea otter of North Pacific	**zo**
KALIF	Calif; Caliph; ruler of Islam	**rl**
KALPA	calpa; a day of Brahma	**rl**
KAMES	glacial deposits	**mn, go, gl**
KAMIS	Eastern tunic	
KANAT	ancient tunnel network	
KHANAT	(irrigation)	
KANDY	candy; S. Indian weight	**me**
KANEH	caneh; 6 cubits (Hebrew)	**me**
KANYA	Afr. shea tree; its butter	**bt, ck**
KAPOK	fibre of silk-cotton tree	**bt, tx**
KAPUR	Indonesian wood	**fr**
KARMA	destiny based on each incarnation	
KAROB	24th part of a grain	**me**
KAROO	South African plateau	**go**
KARRI	dense Australian wood; tree	**fr**
KARST	limestone caves (Yugoslavia)	**gl, go**
KARYO-	nucleus (Gr.)	**cf, pl**
KASHA	dress material	**tx**
KASHA	cracked-buckwheat meal (Rus.)	**ck**
KASHI	enamelled Islamic tiles (Persia, India)	
KASSU	catechu made from betel-nut	**bt, ck**
KAURI	New Zealand fir tree	**bt**

KAYAK	covered seal-skin canoe	
KAIAK	(Eskimo)	nt
KAYLE	ninepin; skittle	ga
KAZOO	children's 'hum' instrument	mu
KEBAB	meat dish (Turk.)	ck
KECKS	fool's parsley	bt
KEDGE	small anchor; using anchor rope to	
	move boat (sailing)	nt
KEDGE	kidge; brisk; lively	
KEDGY	cadgy; happy; merry; wanton	
KEEPS	permanent possession	
KEESH	carburet of iron	mn
KEEVE	vat; fermenting tub	
KEFIR	fermented milk	
KELAT	short springy Asian wool	tx
KELLY	top pipe of drill string; Manxman	
		mn
KELPY	malignant water-sprite (Sc.)	
KELTY	a penalty drink (Sc.)	
KEMPO	martial art (China)	
KEMPS	the plantain	
KENDO	swordsmanship (Japan)	
KERMA	kinetic movement energy released	
	in matter	ps, nc
KERNE	Irish foot-soldier; boor	
KETCH	two-masted vessel	nt
KETEN	colourless gas	ch
KEVEL	belaying pin	nt
KEVEL	young gazelle	zo
KEYED	wedged; beam; (typewriter);	
	solvable; tensed	cr, jn
KEYER	frequency-change device	tc
KHAKI	olive-drab; army uniform colour	
KHEDA	elephant enclosure	
KHMER	people and language (Cambodia)	
KIANG	Tibetan wild horse	zo
KIBED	chapped with cold	
KIDDY	youngster; goatling	zo
KIDEL	kiddle; fish-trap	
KIDGE	kedge; brisk; pot-bellied	
KILEY	kyley; boomerang	
KILIM	woven carpet without pile (Turk.)	
KINGS	two Biblical books	
KININ	plant hormone; quinine	bc
KINKY	crotchety; entangled; bizarre;	
	unconventional	
KINSH	stone-mason's lever	to
KIOSK	covered stall; booth (telephone);	
	open pavilion (Moslem)	ar
KITTY	kitten; common cash; jack (bowls)	
		zo, ga
KLANG	complex musical tone	mu
KLICK	click	
KLONG	canal; waterway; floating market	
	(Thai)	
KLOOF	S. African ravine	go
KNACK	skill; dexterity; faculty	
KNARL	gnarl; a knot in wood	
KNAUR	swollen tree-trunk outgrowth	bt
KNAVE	rascal; rogue; caitiff	

KNEAD	mix; blend; incorporate	
KNEED	baggy	
KNEEL	bend knee, submit	
KNELL	toll; ring; sound	
KNEPH	an Egyptian deity	
KNIFE	to stab; to lance; blade (cut)	to
KNOCK	rap; beat; buffet	
KNOLL	knell; hillock; mound	
KNOSP	ornamental flower-bud	
KNOTE	(rope-making)	
KNOUD	the grey gurnard	zo
KNOUT	Russian whip	
KNOWN	understood; recognized	
KNUBS	waste silk	tx
KNURL	knob; milled edge	
KNURR	knot in wood	
KOALA	Australian bear	zo
KOBIL	cobble; small boat	nt
KOFTE	meat rissole	ck
KOFTA		
KOKOB	venomous serpent	zo
KOKRA	wood used for flutes	bt
KOLEH	racing canoe (Malay)	nt
KONDO	bronze-gilt finish	
KOPEC	kopek; Russian farthing	nm
KOPJE	S. African hillock	go
KORAN	Moslem Bible	rl
KOTIA	Indian dhow	nt
KOTOW	kow-tow; make obeisance	
KRAAL	native village	
KRAIT	venomous snake	zo
KRANG	kreng; whale flesh	
KRILL	plankton; whale food	zo
KRONE	Scandinavian coin	nm
KRUPP	a gun	
KUDOS	credit; prestige; fame	
KUFIC	early Arab alphabet	
KUKRI	Gurkha knife	
KULAK	Russian peasant proprietor	
KUNDA	lawyer-vine	bt
KUTCH	cutch; catechu	bt
KVASS	Russian beer	
KWELA	tin whistle (African)	
KYACK	American pack saddle	
KYLEY	kiley; boomerang	
KYLIN	Chinese or Japanese dragon	
KYLIX	Greek drinking vessel	
KYLOE	Hebridean cattle	zo
KYOTO	Japanese pottery	
KYPOO	extract of catechu	
KYRIE	(Mass)	rl, mu
KYUDO	mounted archers (Japan)	

L

LABEL	badge, adhesive sticker; address	
	tag	hd
LABEL	coded information signal	cp
LABIA	lips of orifice	bt, pl

LABIS	cochlear; eucharistic spoon	rl
LACED	twined; stiffened; (straight)	
LACED	fortified drink; final punched card	cp
LACET	lace-work	tx
LACIS	filet lace; network	
LADAS	a classic runner	
LADED	burdened; loaded	
LADEN	freighted	
LADIN	Swiss Latin	
LADLE	scoop; bale; dole	
LAGAN	ligan (flotsam)	lw
LAGER	beer; for storage; (light)	
LAHAR	volcanic mud avalanche	gl
LAINE	woollen fabric	tx
LAIRD	Scottish landowner	
LAITY	laymen	
LAKIN	ladykin; small damsel	
LAMED	crippled	
LAMIA	sorceress; witch	
LAMMY	sailor's quilted jumper	
LANCE	lancet; spear; pierce	
LANCH	} a ship's boat on a man of war	
LAUNCH		nt
LANDE	sterile tract (Fr.)	
LANKY	lean; tall; gaunt	
LANTY	lightbuoy to aid navigation	nt
LAPEL	upper folds on face of a coat	
LAPIS	stone; (calico-printing)	mn
LAPSE	slip; slide; indiscretion	
LARCH	genus of trees; softwood; tamarack (USA)	bt
LARDY	full of lard	
LARES	Roman household gods	
LARGE	massive; bulky; copious; longest note	mu
LARGO	slowly	mu
LARKY	sportive; frolicsome	
LARRY	lorry; truck	
LARRY	mortar-mixing tool	to
LARUM	alarm	
LARUS	aquatic bird	zo
LARVA	caterpillar; grub; maggot	zo
LASER	resin; searing ray	md
LASSO	rope with running noose	
LASSU	slow section of a csardas Hung. dance	mu
LATCH	catch; fasten (door); attach oneself; comprehend	jn
LATER	tardier; more recent	
LATEX	sap; untreated rubber	bt
LATHE	county division; machine	to
LATHI	bamboo cudgel	
LATHY	thin; long and slender	
LATIN	Roman; of Latinium; tongue	
LAUDA	} religious song, concert poems	
LAUDE	} of praise (It.)	mu
LAUDS	liturgical office after matins; praises	rl
LAUGH	deride; guffaw	
LAURA	a hermitage	

LAUTA	royal Inca badge	
LAVED	washed; bathed	
LAVER	brazen washing basin	
LAVER	edible seaweed	bt
LAXLY	loosely; slackly; remissly	
LAY-BY	halting place beside road	
LAYER	seam; stratum; bed; hen	zo
LAY-IN	maternity; extended sleep	
LAY-UP	shot near basket (b-ball)	ga
LAZAR	leper	
LAZED	tranquillized	
LEACH	to wash by percolation	
LEADY	leaden	
LEAFY	leavy; full of leaves	
LEAKY	not watertight; tattling	
LEANT	inclined; reposed; trusted	
LEAPT	jumped; sprang	
LEARN	acquire; hear; memorize	
LEARY	old mine-shaft	
LEASE	let; hire; tenure	
LEASH	three; bind; thong	
LEAST	smallest; minutest	
LEAVE	forsake; quit; depart	
LEAVY	leafy	
LEDGE	shelf; ridge; layer	
LEDGY	full of ridges	
LEECH	blood-sucker; hanger-on; (limpet); leecher (doctor); sail	nt, zo
LEECH	edge of a sail	nt
LEERY	sly	
LEGAL	lawful; licit; proper; correct	lw
LEGER	a race; light; small	
LEGGY	lanky	
LEG-IT	proceed on foot; walk; hike	
LEGNO	wood (It.), drumstick	mu
LEMAN	lover; gallant; paramour	
LEMMA	grass glume; subsidiary theorem	bt, ma
LEMMA	summary preceding a tome	
-LEMMA-	of subsidiary theorem; (true data logic)	cf
LEMON	citrus fruit; the answer	bt, ck
LEMUR	ghost; nocturnal monkey	zo
LENCA	Honduran Indian	
LENTO	slowly	mu
LEPER	lazar	md
LEPID	jocose; pleasant	
LEPIS	a scale	zo
LEPRA	leprosy	md
-LEPSI	of seizure, collapse (Gr.)	cf, md
LEPTA	(Greece)	nm
LEPTO-	small, thin, fine, weak (Gr.)	cf, md
LESTE	dry African South wind	mt
LETCH	to separate by percolation	
LETHE	the river of oblivion	
LET-IN	admission; note added to text	
LET-UP	an alleviation	
LEUKO-	white; (blood); colourless	cf, md
LEVAN	polymerized grass fructose	ch
LEVEE	embankment; reception	

LEVEL	raze; plane; even; flush; grade	
LEVER	a jemmy; prise	**to**
LEWIS	a grip for masonry	
LIANA	tropical climbing plant	**bt**
LIANE	woody jungle climber	**bt**
LIANG	Chinese ounce	**me**
LIART	liard; lyart; dapple-grey	
LIBEL	slander; defame; traduce	**lw**
LIBER	bast; inner bark; a book	
LIBRA	the Balance (Zodiac)	
LICIT	lawful; permissible	
LIDAR	cloud pattern detector	**mt**
LIEGE	one bound by oath	
LIFER	prisoner sentenced for life	
LIGAN	lagan; (flotsam)	**lw**
LIGHT	kindle; illume; buoyant, easy; featherweight; music	**mu**
LIGNE	watch-movement measure unit	**hr**
LIKED	enjoyed; relished	
LIKEN	to compare	
LIKIN	Chinese transport duty	
LILAC	a colour; a shrub	**bt**
LIMBO	hell; paradise of fools	
LIMED	cemented; ensnared; treated	
LIMEN	threshold	**pc**
LIMER	fibre brush for limewashing	
LIMIT	restraint; bound; border	
LIMMA	a semitone	**mu**
LINCH	ledge; projection; cliff	
LINED	care-worn; with lines	
LINEN	flax cloth; underwear; bed wear	
LINER	a shim; a vessel; layer of paint	**nt**
LINGO	speech; language	
LINGO	jacquard harness weight	**wv**
LINGY	active; limber; heathery	
LININ	(cell nucleus)	
LINKS	(cuff); golf course; chains; shackles; connections; back players (hockey)	**ga**
LIPID	living-tissue fat/wax	**ch, md**
LIPPY	half-a-gallon (Sc.)	**me**
LISLE	thread	**tx**
LISSE	warp threads in tapestry	
LISTS	the combat-ground	
LITAS	Lithuanian currency unit	**nm**
LITHE	lythe; active; supple; pliant;	
LITHY	pliable; easily bent; limber	
LITHO	a lithograph	
LITRE	nearly 1¾ pints	**me**
LIVED	dwelt; abode; survived	
LIVEN	enliven; animate; vivify	
LIVER	internal organ	**md**
LIVID	ghastly pale	
LIVRE	old French franc	**nm**
LLAMA	Peruvian camel	**zo**
LLANO	S. American plain	**go**
LOACH	loche; a river-fish	**zo**
LOAMY	of sand-clay mix tilth; soil	
LOATH	reluctant; unwilling	

LOBAR	} lobate	**bt, md**
LOBED		
LOBBY	passage; to seek votes; pressure group; tambour entry hall	**ar, bd**
LOCAL	an inn; topical; regional	
LOCHE	a loach; a river-fish	**zo**
LOCUM	locum tenens; a deputy	
LOCUS	locality; position; area	
LODAR	special loran system, radar	**nv**
LODGE	reside; sojourn; deposit; dwelling; masons' workshop	
LOESS	alluvial deposits	**gl**
LOFTY	stately; imposing; towering	
LOGAN	poised rock; a berry	**bt**
LOGGE	miller's thumb; small fish	**zo**
LOGIA	oracles; dicta	
-LOGIA	of speech	**cf**
LOGIC	reasoning; dialectics	
LOGIE	sham jewels	
LOGON	provision for new group to be added	
LOG-ON	check-in for new users of computers	**cp, tc**
LOGOS	the Divine Word	
LOKAL	tavern, club, assembly place	
LOKUM	Turkish delight (sweetmeat)	**ck**
LOLLY	lollipop; a lump; money	
LOLOS	aboriginal race (China)	
LOOFA	luffa; flesh-brush	**bt**
LOONY	mad; lunatic	
LOOPY	kinky; dotty	
LOOSE	liberate; slack; vague; lax; free; puck, ball (ice hockey); let fly (archery)	**ga**
LOPED	ran with easy strides	
LORAN	radio-navigation system	**nt, nv**
LORDS	cricket ground	
LORIS	Cingalese monkey	**zo**
LORRY	larry; truck; vehicle	
LORUM	mandibular plates in hemiptera	**zo**
LOSEL	worthless; scoundrel; ne'erdowell	
LOSER	also ran; (billiards)	
LOSSY	of energy-dissipating equipment	
LOTIC	of running water	**ec**
LOTTO	a game	**ga**
LOTUS	lotos; water lily	**bt**
LOUGH	loch; an arm of the sea; ria; or inland lake	**go**
LOUIS	obsolete French gold coin	**nm**
LOURE	French bagpipe; dance; technique applied to violin playing	**mu**
LOUSE	parasitic insect	**zo**
LOUSY	mean; louse infested	
LOVAT	close tweed	**tx**
LOVED	adored; liked; esteemed	
LOVER	a Romeo; admirer; swain	
LOWER	depress; degrade; frown	
LOWLY	meek; humble; modest	
LOXIA	cross-bill birds	**zo**
LOYAL	leal; true; devoted	

LUBRA	black woman (Australia)	
LUCID	clear; limpid; sane; pure	
LUCKY	fortunate; auspicious	
LUCRE	gain; profit; wealth	
LUDIC-	of play; make believe; primary behaviour (Gr.)	cf, pc
LUDIC-	common	cf
LUGER	automatic pistol	
LUGER	driver of a snow vehicle	
LUMEN	unit of luminous flux	me
LUMPY	coagulated	
LUNAR	of the moon	
LUNCH	luncheon; midday repast	ck
LUNGA } LONGO }	long notes (It.)	mu
LUNGE } LONGE }	thrust; (equitation) (fencing)	ga
LUNIK	artificial moon satellite	
LUPIN	a flower	bt
LUPPA	cloth of gold or silver	tx
LUPUS	skin disease	md
LURCH	stagger; sway; roll; toss	
LURED	enticed; decoyed; inveigled	
LURID	glowing; sensational	
LUSHY	tipsy	
LUSTY	robust; vigorous; sturdy	
LUSUS	a freak; an exception	
LUTED	sealed with luting	
LUTER	lute-player	mu
LYART	liart; liard; dapple-grey	
LYASE	double-bonding enzyme	
LYCEE	high school (Fr.)	
LYING	mendacious; recumbent	
LYMPH	a fluid; vaccine	md
LYNCH	mob law; kill	
LYRIC	a short poem; tuneful	
LYRID	meteor from Lyra	
LYRIE	Manx shearwater gull	zo
LYSIN	disintegratory antibody	md
LYSIS	recovery	md
LYSSA	hydrophobia; rabies	
LYTHE	the pollack	zo
LYTHE	lithe; flexible; agile	
LYTIC } -LYTTIC }	pertaining to lysis; opposing a form of action (drugs) (Gr.)	cf, pc, md
LYTTA	rod of tongue cartilage	zo

M

MACAW	parrot; palm	zo, bt
MACER	a court usher	lw
MACHE	materials for papier maché	
MACLE	double crystal	mn
MACON	French wine	
MACRO-	of major, large	cf
MADAM	madame	
MADGE	leaden hammer; magpie	zo
MADIA	the tar-weed; oil-plant	bt

MADID	moist; wet; damp	
MADLY	deliriously; insanely	
MAFIA	Sicilian secret society	
MAFIC	non-felsic material in igneous rock	gl
MAGAR	Indian crocodile	zo
MAGAS	stringed-instrument bridge	mu
MAGIC	witchery; sorcery; charm	
MAGMA	plutonic rock	mn
MAGOG	legendary figure; giant	
MAGOT	Barbary ape; previously depicted as grotesque oriental figure	zo
MAHDI	Moslem prophet (dervish)	rl
MAHWA	butter-tree	bt
MAIZE	Indian corn	bt
MAJOR	a rank; greater	
MAKER	creator; manufacturer	
MAKWA	Chinese jacket	md
MALAR	cheek-bone	
MALAX	soften by kneading/diluting	
MALAY	of Malaysia	
MALIC	(apples)	bt
MALIK	village headman (Ind.)	
MALTY	malt-flavoured	
MAMBA	S. African snake	zo
MAMBO	dance	mu
MAMMA	mother; mammary gland (lactation)	pl
MAMMY	negro nurse	
MANAL	pertaining to the hand	
MANEB	chemical fungicide	ch
MANED	having a mane	
MANEH	mina; 50 shekels	nm
MANES	ghosts; departed souls	
MANET	stage direction 'remain'	
MANGA	covering for a cross	
MANGE	parasitic disease	md
MANGO	a fruit	bt
MANGY	scabrous	
MANIA	frenzy; delirium; craziness	
MANIS	the scaly ant-eater	zo
MANLY	hardy; intrepid; bold	
MANNA	food; a form of sap	bt
MANOR	freehold estate	
MANSE	the minister's house (Sc.)	
MANTA	ox-ray; a sea-fish	zo
MANUS	the hand	md
MANUS	fore-limb; podium	zo
MAORI	native race (N. Zealand)	
MAPES	ice skating jump	
MAPLE	sugar-tree	bt
MAQUI	Chilean evergreen shrub	bt
MARAH	bitterness (Hebrew)	
MARAY	moray; muray; eel-like fish	zo
MARCH	border; advance; walk	
MARDY	spoilt; naughty	
MARGE	brink; brim; verge; edge	
MARIA	lunar seas	as
MARID	powerful jinn	
MARLY	clay-like	

MARRY	unite; wed; espouse; join	
MARSH	bog; swamp; fen; morass	**go**
MASAI	African tribe	
MASER	micro-wave amplifier	**el**
MASHY	mashie; a golf club	
MASON	stone-worker	
MASSA	master	
MASSE	a billiard stroke	**ga**
MASSY	massive; bulky	
MASTY	full of beech-mast	**bt**
MATCH	suit; tally; agree; lucifer; equivalence; contest; best of 3 games (tennis)	**cp, ga**
MATED	(chess); married; matched	
MATER	mother	
MATEY	friendly; chum	
MATIN	morning (Fr.)	
MATTE	crude black copper	**mn**
MATZO	thin unleavened Passover bread	**ck**
MAULS	marsh mallow	**bt**
MAUND	an Eastern weight	**me**
MAUVE	a mallow colour	
MAVIS	the thrush	**zo**
MAWKY	crotchety; maudlin	
MAXIM	gun; adage; saw; precept	
MAYAN	native of Honduras, Mexico	
MAYBE	perhaps	
MAYOR	town chief	
MAZDA	Supreme Deity (Zend-Avesta)	**rl**
MAZED	bewildered; dazed; astounded	
MAZER	goblet; bowl	
MEALY	farinaceous	
MEANS	mode; agency; method; wealth	
MEANT	signified; purposed	
MEASE	a group of 500	**me**
MEATY	fleshy	
MEBOS	salted apricots (S. Africa)	**ck**
MECCA	desired objective; heart of Islam	**rl**
MEDAL	decoration	
MEDIA	agencies	
MEDIC	clover, lucerne, etc	**bt**
MEDOC	a red French wine	
MEINY	a retinue (Shak.)	
MELEE	fray; brawl; scuffle; mixture	
MELES	badger genus	**zo**
MELIC	lyric; a grass	**bt**
MELLA	honey mixtures	**ck**
MELON	a gourd	**bt**
MENSA	tooth biting surface; genius, brain	**md**
MERCY	pity; lenity; clemency; grace	
MERGE	coalesce; immerse; submerge	
MERIT	desert; worth; credit; earn	
MERLE	the blackbird	**zo**
MERON	posterior of certain insects	**zo**
MEROS	triglyph channel surfaces	**ar**
MERRY	the English wild cherry	**bt**
MERRY	blithe; jocund; lively; too strong a stroke (golf) (bowls)	**ga**
MESAL	mesial; median; central	

MESHY	netted; reticulated	
MESNE	intermediate	**lw**
MESON	cosmic ray constituent	
MESSA	musical setting (It.)	**mu**
MESSE	mass (R.C.) (Fr.), (Ger.)	**rl**
MESSY	mussy; muddled; disordered	
MESTO	sadly (It.)	**mu**
METAL	bullion; courage; ore	
METAL	broken stone for roads	
METED	measured; apportioned	
METEL	thorn apple	**bt**
METER	a measuring instrument	**me**
METIC	alien; foreign resident; ex-slave (Gr.)	
METIF	octoroon; mixed caste	
METIS	American half-breed	
METOL	4-methylaminophenol	**ch, pg**
METRA	a measuring instrument	
METRE	(verse); 39.37 inches; rhythm and beats of prosody and music	**me, mu**
METRO	underground railway	**rw**
METRO-	of mother or chief (Gr.)	**cf**
MEUTE	mew; cage for hawks	
MEWED	(cats); moulted; confined	
MEZZO	middle	**mu**
MIAOW	miaul; caterwaul	
MIASM	miasma; effluvia	**md**
MICHE	hide; skulk; pilfer	
MICKY	Irish lad; young bull; microphone (sl)	**zo**
MICRO-	tiny; one millionth 10^{-6}	**cf, ma**
MIDAS	had a golden touch	
MIDDY	a midshipman	**nt**
MIDGE	dwarf; gnat	**zo**
MID-ON	(cricket) fielding position	**ga**
MIDST	among; middle	
MIGHT	force; power; main	
MILCH	giving milk	
MILER	a mile runner	
MILKY	lacteal; lactic	
MILLI-	one thousandth 10^{-3}	**cf, ma**
MIMED	mimicked; acted	
MIMIC	ape; copy; mime; mock	
MINCE	chop fine; palliate	
MINED	dug; undermined	
MINER	sapper	
MINIE	old type rifle	
MINIM	dwarf; single drop; note	**mu**
MINIM	down-stroke of pen	
MINIM	2 crotchets or $\frac{1}{2}$ semi-breve	**mu**
MINOR	petty; lesser; small	**mu**
MINOS	King of Crete	
MINUS	less; lacking; wanting	
MIRED	bogged; unit of colour temperature	**me**
MIRTH	glee; gaiety; hilarity	
MIRZA	a Persian title	
MIS-DO	err; sin; trespass	

MISER	skinflint; hoarder; niggard; handauger	**to**
MISLE	mizzle; rain in small drops	
MISLY	drizzly	
MISSY	sentimental; namby-pamby	
MISTY	dim; obscure; cloudy	
MITRA	Persian sun-god	**rl**
MITRE	angle of 45 degrees; cap	**lw**
MITTS	mittens	
MIXED	blended; mingled; confused; atypical	
MIXEN	midden	
MIXER	a good companion; kitchen; compatible; frequency changer	**ro**
MIX-UP	mêlée; scuffle; brawl; muddle	
MIZZY	bog; swamp; quagmire	
MNEME	effect of memory persistence	**pc**
MOBBY	fermented fruit juice	
MOBLE	wrap the head in a hood	
MOBUS	motor-bus	
MOCCA	} chocolate/coffee mixture	**ck**
MOCHA		
MOCHA	agate	**mn**
MOCHE	packet of spun silk	**tx**
MODAL	logic; music; grammar general structure	**mu**
MODEL	example; pattern; copy; miniature; design; art	
MODEM	varying speed links to transmission lines	**tc**
MODER	matrix of astrolabe	**nv**
MODUS	style; a method	**lv**
MOGUL	ex Mongolian empire builder in India; type of steam locomotive; mound on ski slope	**rw**
MOHUR	Indian gold coin	**nm**
MOIRE	watered silk	**tx**
MOIST	dark; clammy; humid	
MOLAR	grinding; tooth; holistic phenomena	
MOLAR	purposive behaviour; learning situations	**pc**
MOLAR	volume of unit of substance	**nc, ps**
MOLER	diatomaceous earth	**bd**
MOLLY	the wagtail bird	**zo**
MOLTO	very; much (It.)	**mu**
MOMUS	God of Ridicule	**rl**
MONAD	primitive organism; minimal matter units	**zo**
MONAL	a pheasant	**zo**
MONDE	society (Fr.)	
MONEL	an alloy	
MONEY	cash; coin; currency; wealth	
MONGO	(Mongolia)	**nm**
MONOX	the crowberry	**bt**
MONTE	gambling game like faro	**ga**
MONTH	lunar cycle	
MOOCH	slouch; loiter	
MOODY	sullen; morose; glum; captious	
MOOED	lowed	
MOOLA	mollah; Moslem judge	**lw**

MOONY	dreamy	
MOORE	movement in gymnastics	
MOORY	sterile; boggy	
MOOSE	the elk	**zo**
MOPED	pined; motorised bicycle	
MOPPY	tipsy; fuddled	
MOPSY	mopsey; untidy woman	
MOPUS	a mope; drone; money	
MORAL	ethical; virtuous; meaning	
MORAT	mulberry juice	
MORAY	maray; fish of eel-type	**zo**
MOREL	cherry; nightshade	**bt**
MORES	social norms, behaviour, standards	
MORIL	morel; mushroom	**bt**
MORMO	bugbear	
MORNE	blunt head of a lance	
MORON	mental defective; retarded; stupid	
MORSE	signalling (code); the walrus; cope or cloak clasp (metal)	**ro, zo, rl**
MORUS	mulberry	**bt**
MOSES	a law-giver	
MOSEY	saunter; walk slowly (Amer.)	
MOSSO	(It.) moving; animated; lively	**mu**
MOSSY	cryptogamous; lichenous	**bt**
MOTED	dusty	
MOTEL	motorists' hotel	
MOTET	sacred melody	**mu**
MOTHY	moth-eaten	
MOTIF	theme; feature	**mu, ar, hd, wv, le, cr**
MOTIF	repeated pattern in art, music	
MOTOR	automobile; engine; prime mover	**eg**
MOTOR	stimulator of movement	**pl**
MOTTE	(mote) castle mound	**ar**
MOTTO	pithy maxim; slogan; theme	
MOUCH	mooch; skulk; slouch	
MOULD	blight; create; shape; form; fungus	**bt**
MOULT	to cast feathers	
MOUND	knoll; tumulus; hillock	
MOUNT	climb; scale; ascend; tower	
MOURN	bewail; lament; deplore	
MOUSE	small rodent	**zo**
MOUSY	mouselike; quiet	
MOUTH	opening; orifice; declaim; (river); (utterance); pompous speech	
MOVED	shifted; budged; roused	
MOVER	proposer	
MOWED	scythed; cut	
MOWER	a mowing machine; (one man and)	
MOYEN	means; influence	
MPRET	Albanian ruler	
MTEPI	canoe dugout, sail (East Africa)	**nt**
MUCIC	an acid	**ch**
MUCID	musty; mouldy; slimy	
MUCIN	viscous proteins/carbohydrates	
MUCKY	dirty; filthy; muddy	
MUCOR	mould; fungus	**bt**
MUCRO	stiff sharp point	**bt**

MUCUS	slime	md
MUDAR	madar; medicinal herb	bt
MUDDY	turbid; impure; obscure	
MUDIR	Eastern governor	
MUFTI	Moslem priest or lawyer	rl
MUFTI	civilian clothing	
MUGGY	damp and warm	
MUGIL	the mullet fish	zo
MULCH	mulsh; litter; manure	
MULCT	fine; penalize	lw
MULEY	mooly; hornless	
MULGA	Australian acacia	bt
MULLA	mullah; fanatic	rl
MULSE	mulled wine	
MULSH	mulch; litter; manure	
MULTI-	many sided; of uses; much (Lat.)	cf
MUMMY	bituminous drug; (Egypt)	
MUMPS	epidemic parotitis	md
MUNCH	chew; crunch; masticate	
MUNGO	shoddy; inferior cloth	tx
MURAL	fixed to a wall	
MURAY	cf. moray; murry	zo
MURED	immured; pent	
MUREX	Tyrian dye; molluscs	zo
MURID	Moslem disciple	
MURKY	lurid; dark; lowering	
MURRA	fluorspar	mn
MURRE	razorbill or guillemot	zo
MURRY	also **moray**; eel-like fish	zo
MUSAL	pert. to poetry/Muses	
MUSCA	fly genus	zo
MUSCI	the mosses	bt
MUSED	pondered; contemplated	
MUSER	ruminator	
MUSET	a gap in a fence (Fr.)	
MUSHY	pulpy	
MUSIC	melody; harmony	mu
MUSKY	fragrant like musk	
MUSSY	messy; disordered	
MUSTY	mucid; fusty; mouldy	
MUTCH	a woman's cap (Sc.)	
MUTED	muffled; pianissimo	mu
MUTIC	lacking defensive parts	zo
MUTON	smallest mutable gene element	gn
MUZZY	dazed; confused	
MYALL	Australian hard-wood tree	bt
MYOID	like muscle	md
MYOMA	muscle-fibre tumour	md
MYOPE	myops; short-sighted person	
MYOPY	myopia; short-sight	md
MYRRH	scented resin	bt
MYSIS	the opposum shrimp	zo
MYXON	fish of mullet family	zo

N

NABAM	chemical fungicide	
NABBY	sailing skiff (Scotland)	nt
NABEE	aconite poison	md

NABIT	crushed candy	
NABLA	del; differential operator	ps
NABOB	} wealthy individual	
NAWAB		
NACRE	mother-of-pearl	
NADIR	opposite to zenith	
NAEVE	a birthmark	md
NAGGY	querulous; quarrelsome	
NAGOR	Senegal antelope	zo
NAIAD	water-nymph	
NAIVE	artless; ingenuous; candid	
NAKED	stark; open; bare; denuded	
NAKER	a kettle-drum	mu
NAKIR	examiner of the dead (Koran)	
NAMED	yclept; specified; dubbed	
NAMER	nominator	
NANDU	rhea; American ostrich	zo
NANNY	children's nurse; female goat	zo
NAPOO	(ne plus); finished	
NAPPE	mountain-chain structure	gl
NAPPE	normal surface overflow of dam	ce
NAPPY	drowsy; a dish	
NAPPY	napkin; baby's diaper; horse refusing orders	
NARCO-	of sleep, numbness, stupor (Gr.)	cf
NARES	nostrils	md
NARIS	nostril	md
NARRE	near (Spens.)	
NASAL	of the nose, phonetics, errhine	md
NASIL	conflict-inhibiting social signal	
NASTY	foul; loathsome; ribald	
NATAL	nascent; initial	
NATCH	notch; the rump	
NATTE	interlaced ornamentation	
NATTY	neat; spruce; matching; trim	
NAVAL	nautical; maritime; marine	
NAVEL	the centre	md
NAVEW	wild turnip	bt
NAWAB	} Eastern ruler	
NABOB		
NAZIR	Indian bailiff	
NEAPS	shortfall tides	nt
NEATH	beneath	
NEBBY	saucy (Sc.)	
NEBEL	the Jew's harp	mu
NECRO-	of the dead (Gr.)	cf
NEDDY	donkey; moke; burro	zo
NEEDS	perforce; necessarily	
NEEDY	poor; indigent; penniless	
NEELE	neeld; needle; sharp point	
NEESE	neeze; sneeze	
NEGRE	nigger-colour (Fr.)	
NEGRO	black (African)	
NEGUS	Abyssinian King	
NEGUS	a drink; hot punch	
NEIGH	to whinny	
NEIST	next	
NEMPT	named; yclept (Spens.)	
NEPER	power ratio unit	me

NERVE	brace; pluck; hardihood; neural fibres	**md, pl**
NERVY	vigorous; nervous; fearful	
NESKI	Arabic script	
NETTY	meshy; reticulated	
NEUME	a musical phrase (Gr.)	**mu**
NEURO-	of nerve, fibre, tissue (Gr.)	**cf, pl**
NEVEL	to punch (Sc.)	
NEVER	not at any time	
NEVUS	birthmark; discolouration of skin	**pl**
NEWEL	finial of a staircase	
NEWLY	recently; freshly	
NEWSY	chatty; gossipy	
NEXUS	interconnecting link of series; bond	**lw, tc**
NEXUS	interconnecting cluster of ideas	
NICER	more pleasant; more exact	
NICHE	nook; corner; recess	
NICOL	(polarizing light)	
NIDGE	to dress stones	
NIDOR	the smell of cooking	
NIDUS	nest; a breeding place	**md**
NIECE	daughter of brother or sister	
NIFFY	smelly	
NIFTY	classy; stylish	
NIGHT	darkness; obscurity	
NIHIL	nil; zero; nothing	
NIKAU	New Zealand palm	**bt**
NINES	elaborate party clothes	
NINES	complement representing negative values	**cp**
NINNY	simpleton; nitwit; palooka	
NINON	dress material	
NINTH	ordinal number; interval of nine scale steps	**mu**
NIOBE	a weeper	
NIPPY	a waitress; alert; parsimonious	
NISAN	Jewish April	
NISUS	an effort; an endeavour	
NITID	gleaming; shining	
NITON	gaseous element	**ch**
NITRE	saltpetre	**ch**
NITTY	full of nits; lice eggs	**zo**
NIVAL	nivose; niveous; snowy	
NIXIE	water-elf	
NIZAM	Indian prince	
NOBBY	smart; ornate	
NOBEL	invented dynamite; prize	
NOBLE	patrician; obsolete gold coin	**nm**
NOBLY	grandly; splendidly	
NODAL	knotty	**mu**
NODDY	fool; sea-mew	**zo**
NODUS	knotty point	
NO-HIT	noscore for striking games	**ga**
NOHOW	in no way	
NOILS	wool-combings	
NOINT	anoint (Shak.)	
NOIRE	(Fr.) quarter-note; crotchet	**mu**
NOISE	din; clamour; uproar; digit or mode in fixed point	**cp**

NOISY	blatant; vociferous; riotous	
NOKES	a boob	
NOMAD	a wanderer; vagrant	
NOMEN	name (Lat.)	
NOMIC	customary	
NOMOS	Greek province	
NONCE	the present; time; now	
NONES	(Roman calendar)	
NONET	piece for 9 singers	**mu**
NOOPS	the cloudberry	**bt**
NOOSE	loop; lasso; lariat	
NOPAL	Mexican cactus	**bt**
NORIA	Persian water-wheel	
NORMA	a rule; a model	
NORNS	Scandinavian Fates	
NORSE	Viking; early Scandinavian	
NORTE	northerly wind in Central America (Sp.)	**mt**
NORTH	septentrion (Shak.)	
NOSED	snooped	
NOSEY	inquisitive	
NOTAL	dorsal; of the back	**md, pl**
NOTCH	natch; dent; nick; incision	
NOTED	famous; recorded; remarked	
NOTUM	back of a bug	**zo**
NOTUS	southerly wind	**mt**
NOVEL	recent; new; book of fiction	
NOWAY	in no manner; nohow	
NOWED	tied in a knot; coiled	**hd**
NOWEL	foundry loam	**fd**
NOYAU	almond cordial	
NUCHA	nape of the neck	**md**
NUDGE	jog; jostle; elbow	
NULLO	a game	**ga**
NUQUE	nape; back of neck	**md**
NURSE	tend; sickbed attendant	
NUTTY	nut-like; -flavoured	**ck**
NYALA	African antelope	**zo**
NYLON	artificial fibre	**tx**
NYMPH	maiden; development stage of insect	**zo**
NYULA	parasite insect	**zo**

O

OAKEN	made of oak	**bt**
OAKUM	picked tarred rope	**nt**
OARED	rowed; oar-bearing	**nt**
OASIS	fertile spot in desert	
OATEN	made of oats	**ck**
OAVES	dolts; changelings	
OBANG	old Japanese gold coin	**nm**
OBEAH	obi; West African magic	
OBESE	abnormally fat; corpulent	
OBOLE	weight of 10 or 12 g	**me**
OCCUR	happen; befall; chance	
OCEAN	main; the deep sea; embracer of continents	**go**
OCHRE	ocher; yellow pigment	

OCHRY	yellowish-brown	
OCREA	armoured shin-guard	bt, zo
OCTAD	series of eight	
OCTAL	notation system based on 8	
OCTAN	happening every 8 days	
OCTET	group of eight; packet signal	mu, tc
OCTYL	organic radical	ch
OCUBA	vegetable wax	bt
OCULO-	of the eye (Gr.)	cf, pl
ODDLY	queerly; quaintly	
ODEON	} ancient Grecian music hall	mu
ODEUM		
ODIUM	obloquy; hatred; enmity	
ODOUR	scent; fragrance; perfume	
ODYLE	mesmerism	
OFBIT	devil's bit; a scabious	bt
OFFAL	edible entrails; garbage	
OFFER	bid; tender; proposal	
OFTEN	oft; frequently; repeatedly	
-OGAMY	of marital relationship	cf
OGHAM	Irish alphabet	
OGIVE	pointed arch	ar, gl
OGLED	leered	
OGLER	voyeur	
OILED	lubricated	
OILER	oilcan; oilman	
OKAPI	animal related to giraffe	zo
OLDEN	ancient; aged; antique	
OLDER	more elderly	
OLEIC	an acid	ch
OLEIN	oleic glycerine ester	ch
OLENT	fragrant	
OLEON	olein; fatty oil	ch
OLEUM	fuming sulphuric acid	ch
OLIGA-	} of the few (Gr.)	cf
OLIGO-		
OLIVE	emblem of peace	bt
OLLAM	Irish doctor	
-OLOGY	study, knowledge, or science of (Gr.)	cf
OMAHA	a Sioux Indian of Nebraska	
OMATI	a Mexican Indian	
OMBRE	a card game	ga
OMBRE	colour-shaded woven stripes	tx
OMEGA	last letter of Greek alphabet	
OMLAH	N. Ind. court officers	
OMRAH	Moslem court lord	
ONCER	he did not do it again	
ONION	a shallot	bt
ON-OFF	control and keying electron	
ONSET	assault; attack; storm	
ONTAL	pert. to reality/noumena	
-ONYMY	group nomenclature (Gr.)	cf
OOMPH	magnetic personality	
OOPAK	black tea	
OOZED	seeped; percolated	
OPACO	} shadow side of mountain	
OPAC	slope (It.)	go
OPERA	drama set to music, voices; works	mu
OPHIC	pertaining to snakes, serpents	zo
OPINE	suppose; surmise; ween	
OPIUM	a narcotic drug	bt, md
OPSIN	rhodopsin protein	bc
OPTED	chosen; elected	
OPTIC	optical; the eye	md
ORACH	a kind of spinach	bt
ORALE	Papal veil	rl
ORANG		
ORANG-UTAN	} primate of Indonesia	zo
ORANT	worshipper	
ORATE	spout; declaim; harangue	
ORBED	globular; spherical	
ORBIT	ambit; heavenly path; circuit	
ORBIT	the eye-socket	md
ORCIN	killer whale	zo
ORDER	group; decoration; bid; decree; enact; ukase	
ORDER	rank; (working); (purchasing); (tall) purpose	
OREAD	mountain nymph	
ORGAL	argal; crude tartar	ch
ORGAN	medium; means; instrument (govt); keyboard instrument with bellows	mu
ORGAN	differentiated, function structure	bl
ORIBI	South African antelope	zo
ORIEL	mullioned window	
ORION	a constellation	as
ORIYA	(Orissa, India) language	
ORLON	artificial textile fabric	tx
ORLOP	a ship's deck	nt
ORMER	ear-shell	zo
ORNIS	avifauna; a bird	zo
ORPIN	yellow pigment	
ORRIS	gold or silver lace	
ORRIS	astringent root	bt
ORTHO-	correct, straight (Gr.)	cf
ORTYX	American quail	zo
ORVAL	the herb clary	bt
ORYZA	grass genus; rice	bt
OSCAN	early Italic tribe	
OSCAR	film award	
OSHAC	gum-plant	bt
OSIER	a willow	bt
OSMIC	(osmium)	bt
OSONE	oxidation product of osazone	ch
OSRAM	osmium and wolfram	ch
OSSIA	alternative version (It.)	mu
OTARY	genus of seals	zo
OTHER	different	
OTTAR	attar; aromatic oil	
OTTER	fishing device; water weasel	zo
OUBIT	a hairy caterpillar	zo
OUGHT	aught; nought; a cipher	
OUIJA	planchette	
OUKUM	untwisted rope, hemp	bd
OUNCE	snow-leopard	me, zo
OUNDY	wavy; scalloped	

OUPHE	oaf; dolt; idiot (Shak.)	
OUSEL	ouzel; blackbird	**zo**
OUTBY	out of doors (Sc.)	
OUTDO	exceed; surpass; eclipse	
OUTED	ejected; thrown out; sacked	
OUTER	exterior; external; outside	
OUTRE	odd; bizarre; strange	
OUZEL	ousel; blackbird	**zo**
OVARY	seed-vessel; female reproductive organ	**bt, pl**
OVATE	oval; egg-shaped	
OVERT	open to view; apparent	
OVINE	sheep-like	**zo**
OVISM	ovum germ theory	**gn**
OVOID	oval; oviform	
OVOLO	a moulding; wide & convex	**ar**
OVULE	small seed	**bt**
OWCHE	ouch; jewel socket	
OWING	due; outstanding	
OWLER	smuggler of wool	
OWLET	young owl	**zo**
OWNED	admitted; confessed; allowed	
OWNER	the captain	**nt**
OWSEN	oxen	**zo**
OWSER	tan vat liquor	
OX-BOT	bot-fly	**zo**
OXBOW	part of yoke	
OX-BOW	lake; former meander of river	**go, gl**
OX-EYE	daisy; marguerite	**bt**
OX-FLY	bot-fly	**zo**
OXIDE	oxygen compound	**ch**
OXIME	aldehyde/ketone compound	**ch**
OXINE	metal analysis reagent	**ch**
OXLIP	species of primrose	**bt**
OXTER	armpit; to hug (Sc.)	
OZENA	an ulcer	**md**
OZONE	condensed oxygen	**ch**

P

PAAUW	African bustard	**zo**
PACED	stepped; walked; hurried	
PACER	speed setter; (heart ticker); runner; trotting horse; (bowls)	**ga**
PADAR	coarse flour meal	**ck**
PADDY	Irishman; temper; rice	**bt**
PADMA	lotus	**bt**
PADRA	black tea (China)	**bt**
PADRE	army chaplain; priest	**rl**
PAEAN	chant of praise, joy, triumph	
PAEDO-	of children, infants (Gr.)	**cf**
PAEON	a poetical foot	
PAGAN	paynim; heathen; idolator	
PAGED	found by the bell-hop	
PAGLE	paigle; cowslip	**bt**
PAGUS	county division (obs.)	
PAINS	meticulous care	

PAINT	depict; portray; pigment; colour medium (art)	**pt**
PAIRK	a park; a field (Sc.)	
PAIRS	couples; 2 person teams (tennis) (rowing) etc.	**ga**
PALAS	Punjab bean	**bt**
PALAY	ivory-tree	**bt**
PALEA	inner husk; chaff	**bt**
PALED	blanched; encompassed	
PALEO-	of ancient; prehistoric life (Gr.)	**cf, zo**
PALES	Goddess of cattle	
PALIN-	of repetitive, reverse (Gr.)	**cf**
PALIO	horse-race, in Italy	**ga**
PALKI	palanquin	
PALMY	flourishing; thriving	
PALPI	jointed feelers	**zo**
PALSY	paralysis; benumb	**md**
PAMPA	grassy plain (S. America)	**go**
PANAX	ginseng; medicinal plant	**bt**
PANCH	thick mat; fender	**nt**
PANDA	giant (bear) and lesser (raccoon)	**zo**
PANDY	a slap on the open hand	
PANED	variegated; glazed	
PANEL	list; board; schedule; wall carving	**lw**
PANIC	fear; fright; terror; alarm	
PANSY	flower; effeminate man	**bt**
PANTO-	of all, everything (pantomime) (Gr.)	**cf**
PANTS	undershorts; short breaths (panting)	
PAPAL	popish; pontifical	**rl**
PAPAW	a fruit tree	**bt**
PAPER	journal; sheet; essay	
PAPPY	succulent; juicy; easy	
PARCH	dry; scorch; shrivel	
PARDI	} perdy; pardieu; in truth	
PARDY	} (Spens.)	
PARED	cut; shaved	
PARER	trimmer	
PAREU	Polynesian wrap	**tx**
PARGE	to apply plaster; whitewash	
PARKA	Alaskan fur coat with hood	
PARKY	cold; chilly	
PAROL	oral; by word of mouth	
PARRY	avert; evade; prevent; move (fencing)	
PARSE	analyse grammatically	
PARSI	Parsee; Indo-Persian	
PARTI	eligible suitor	
PARTS	abilities; talents	
PARTY	set; clique; cabal; faction	
PASCH	Passover (Hebrew); Easter	
PASEO	leisurely stroll, promenade (Sp.)	
PASHA	Turkish governor	
PASHM	under-fur of Cashmere goat	
PASSE	faded; out of date; old fashioned (Fr.)	
PASSE	17 to 36 at roulette	**ga**
PASTE	to stick; an adhesive	

PASTY	glutinous; patty; a pie	
PATCH	cobble; botch; mend; small area; (eye) (ice-skating)	
PATCH	routine for correcting mistakes	**cp**
PATED	with a head	
PATEN	patin; eucharistic plate	
PATER	father	
PATHO-	suffering; diseased, abnormal (Gr.)	**cf**
-PATHY	ditto, also treatment	
PATIO	courtyard	
PATLY	aptly; fitly; apropos	
PATTE	sash-band (Fr.)	
PATTY	a small pie; dumpling shaped concoction	**ck**
PAUSE	delay; tarry; hesitate; concert	
PAUSA	interval; halt or rest; (It.)	**mu**
PAVAN		
PAVEN	a dance (Sp.); a dream, vision	
PAVIN		
PAVED	tesselated	
PAVER	pavier; pavement layer	
PAVID	timid	
PAVON	lance pennon	
PAVOR	nightmarish dream; terror	
PAVAN	fantasy	**pc**
PAWED	fingered; scraped	
PAWKY	sly; crafty; shrewd	
PAYED	coated with pitch	
PAYED		
PAID	remunerated	
PAYEE	receiver of payments	
PAYER	rewarder; liquidator	
PAYNE	decorative floral printing style	**pr**
PAYSE	paise; peise; poise	
PEACE	harmony; concord; repose	
PEACH	to divulge	**bt**
PEACH	fruit; sweetheart	**bt**
PEAKY	sickly	
PEARL	a gem (oyster); mother (shell); fall; wave for surfing; a size of type	**pr**
PEASE	peas as pudding	
PEATY	like peat	
PEAVY	lumberman's hook	**to**
PECAN	American nut	**bt**
PECUL	Chinese weight, 133 lb (60 kg)	**me**
PEDAL	to cycle	
PEDIA-	concerning children, infants (Gr.)	**cf**
PEDUM	shepherd's crook	
PEELS	equal shots, (curling); rounds of bells	**ga, mu**
PEERY	peg top	
PEGGY	a warbler; bird	**zo**
PEINE	(squeeze to death)	
PEKAN	the fisher-marten	**zo**
PEKOE	black tea (China)	**bt**
PELLS	records; rolls of parchment	
PELMA	sole of foot	**md**
PELTA	light shield or buckler	

PENAL	punitive; disciplinary	
PENCE	pennies; (Peter)	**nm**
PENIS	male reproductive organ; phallus	**pl**
PENNA	a feather	**zo**
PENNY	a denarius	**nm**
PEONY	piony; a plant	**bt**
PERCH	pole; 5½ yd (5 m)	**me**
PERCH	fish, roost; seat; fixation pause	**zo, bt, pc**
PERDU	lost (Fr.); hidden; ambush	
PERIL	risk; hazard; danger; jeopardy	
PERKY	smart; lively; brisk	
PERMO	lustre; dress fabric	**tx**
PERRY	fermented pear juice	
PERSE	dark blue; a cloth	**tx, wv**
PESKY	irksome; trying; vexatious	
PETAL	a flower leaf	**bt**
PETAR	firework (Shak.); Thames boat	
PETARD		**nt**
PETER	blue flag; rock (cards)	**nt, rl, ga**
PETIT	mignon; petty; trivial	
PETRE	saltpetre	**ch**
PETTY	trivial; mean	
PEWIT	lapwing	
PEEWIT		**zo**
PEZZO	part of musical work (It.)	
PIECE		**mu**
PHARE	pharos; lighthouse; beacon	
PHARO	faro; a game of chance	
PHASE	stage of development; (moon); aspect; guise; periodic operation quantity; electrical cyclic motion; conduct a planned series on scheduled basis	**cp, el**
PHEON	the broad arrow	
PHIAL	ampulla, small flask for potion	
VIAL	(Gr.)	
PHILO-	fond of; loving; friendly	
-PHILE	towards (Gr.)	**cf**
PHLOX	flowering plant	**bt**
-PHOBE	hater of; averse to; anti- (Gr.)	**cf**
PHOCA	genus of seals (seadogs)	**zo**
-PHONE	speech, sound (telephone); lingual factor (Gr.)	**tc, cf**
PHONO-	science of sound, speech, word phonetics (Gr.)	**cf**
-PHOTO	of light reactions, pictures,	
PHOTO-	transmission (Gr.)	**cf**
PHREN	the head, brain, mind; mentality; psychology	**pl**
PHYLA	classifications of kind, genus	
PHYLO-	(Gr.)	**cf**
PHYMA	tubercle	**md**
PIANO	softly; keyboard	**mu**
PICEA	spruce genus	**bt**
PICOT	little lace loop	
PICRA	powdered aloes	**md**
PICUL	pecul; Chinese weight	**me**
PICUS	woodpecker	**zo**
PIDAN	preserved duck egg	**ck**

PI-DOG	Indian pariah dog; stray; scavenger **zo**	
PIECE	unite; bit; part; scrap	
PIEND	hammer point; hip (roof) (Sc.);	
PHEAN	of church-bells **rl, mu**	
PIENO	all performing (It.) **mu**	
PIETA	holy picture **rl**	
PIETY	holiness; sanctity	
PIEZE	pressure unit **me**	
PIGMY	pygmy; dwarf; midget	
PIKED	pointed; sharp; spiked	
PIKER	a tramp	
PILAR	hairy; hirsute	
PILAU	savoury rice dish **ck**	
PILAV		
PILAFF		
PILCH	fur or flannel gown	
PILED	amassed; heaped; erected	
PILER	gatherer	
PILOT	guide; steer; direct; (-boat); croquet; experimental; effort; processing representative; sample **nt, nv, ga, cp**	
PILUM	heavy javelin	
PILUS	a botanical hair **bt**	
PINCH	squeeze; take **me**	
PINED	languished; drooped	
PINGO	frozen hill (tundra) (Eskimo) **go, gl**	
PINIC	an acid **ch**	
PINKY	small boat; dinghy **nt**	
PINNA	wing-like structure **zo**	
PINNA	bone in ear/nose **md**	
PINNY	pinafore	
PINTA	tropical Amer. skin disease **md**	
PINTO	spotted American bean; piebald horse **zo**	
PIN-UP	cut-out romantic wall picture	
PIONY	peony; a flowering plant **bt**	
PIOUS	devout; godly; religious	
PIPAL	pipul; sacred fig tree **bt**	
PIPED	hollow	
PIPER	(bagpipes) **mu**	
PIPIT	tit-lark **zo**	
PIQUE	vexation	
PISTE	track; footprint; ski-way	
PITCH	toss; hurl; locate; tar; emphasis; acoustics; voice **mu**	
PITCH	angle of inclination of axis in fold **gl**	
PITCH	heaving of ship in storm; camping **nt**	
PITCH	play area; sports ground (baseball); position of ball (croquet, fencing) **ga**	
PITHY	terse; concise; laconic	
PITON	iron spike for ropes (climbing); peak tapering to a point **mo**	
PITOT	tube recording air speed	
PIVOT	hinge; axle; axis; centre	
PIXIE	pixy; a fairy; elf	
PIZZA	Italian savoury 'pie' **ck**	

PLACE	. site; scene; post; assign; digit position in ordered set **cp**
PLAGE	spectroheliogram spot **as**
PLAGE	continental seaside resort
PLAID	a tartan; a maud; clothing (Sc.) **tx, wv**
PLAIN	prairie; obvious; simple; grass lands; steppes; unelaborate **go**
PLAIT	weave; twine; braid
PLANE	level; flat; smooth; a tree; slide specimen **to, bt**
PLANK	sawn timber; lay down
PLANT	inculcate; sow; machinery; place in reserve; evidence (frame-up) **bt**
PLASH	plesh; pool; weave; splash
PLASM	mould or matrix
PLATE	silver ware; to overlay; wrought silver & gold; electro-plated silver **ch**
PLATE	accumulator electrode; ceramic; window glass; dish
PLATE	competition prize (money); (quantity plateful)
PLATO	Greek philosopher
PLATT	ore dump
PLATY-	of broad, flat shape (platypus) (Gr.) **cf**
PLAYA	beach; dryable wetlands (Sp.) **go**
PLAZA	public square; market place
PLEAD	argue; reason; entreat
PLEAT	fold
PLEBS	common people; proletariat
PLEIN	full; organ stops mixed max (Fr.) **mu**
PLEIO-	of more; increase **cf**
PLEON	abdominal region in crustacea **zo**
PLESH	plash; splash
PLICA	a hair disease **md**
PLIED	folded; carried on; ferried
PLIES	(plural) ply, laminate (wood)
PLUCK	animal offal; pick; cull
PLUCK	valour; daring; mettle; courage
PLUFF	to puff
PLUMB	vertical; to fathom level
PLUME	feather; crest; to pride (nom de)
PLUMP	stout; chubby; corpulent
PLUMY	feathered
PLUSH	a material long-pile cut velvet **wv, tx**
PLYER	transport worker
PMEST	formula: personality: matter: energy: space: time **me**
POACH	(eggs); (game)
POCKY	pitted
PODEX	anal region **zo**
PODGE	a fat man; a puddle
PODGY	short and fat; pudgy
POESY	poetry; a posy
POGGE	armed bull-head fish **zo**
POILU	French soldier; unshaven

POIND	distrain	**lw**
POINT	aim; tip; apex; sharpen; remark; fixed, floating decimal; identify; pedal; organ; score	**cp, mu**
POISE	weigh; self-assured	
PAISE	deportment, bearing,	
PAYSE	balance; unit of dynamic	
PEISE	viscosity	**ps**
POKAL	a drinking cup; prize (Ger.)	
POKED	thrust; jabbed; prodded	
POKER	(cards); the pochard duck	**zo**
POLAR	opposite	
POLEY	polled; without horns	
POLIO	infantile paralysis	**md**
POLJE	large limestone depression	**gl**
POLKA	a dance (Polish); (Bohemian)	**mu**
POLLY	parrot	**zo**
POLYP	coral, sea; anemone; a growth in humans	**md, zo**
PONGO	orang-utan, primate of Indonesia	**zo**
PONOR	vertical downshaft in karst sink-hole caves	**gl**
POOJA	Hindu ritual; obeisance	**rl**
POORT	col or pass (S. Africa)	**go**
POPPY	(opium) flower	**bt**
PORCH	portico; entrance; stoa	
PORED	examined diligently	
PORER	student	
PORES	sweat excretion glands (skin); granular soil cavities	**pl, gl**
PORGY	porgie; a sea-fish (Bess)	**zo**
PORKY	fat (super piglet)	
PORTA	transverse fissure; liver	**md**
PORTE	(sublime) Ottoman government	
POSED	perplexed; masqueraded	
POSER	an attitudiniser	
POSIT	to affirm; postulate	
POSSE	power; force of constables	
POTCH	thrust (Spens.)	
POTIN	Roman coin metal	
POTTO	West African sloth	**zo**
POTTY	petty; small; dotty	
POUCE	cortex particles in flax roughing	
POUCH	bag; wallet; sack; steal	
POULP	a cephalopod	**zo**
POULT	a young bird	**zo**
POUND	to crush; strike repeatedly; enclosure; money; unit of weight	**zo, nm, me**
POUZE	refuse of crushed apples	
POWAN	Loch Lomond fish	**zo**
POWER	force; faculty; control	**zo**
POYOU	armadillo	**zo**
PRAAM	a barge; small cargo coaster, Northern Europe	**nt**
PRADO	art gallery, Madrid	
PRAHU	Malay boat	**nt**
PRANG	a crash landing; destroy	
PRANK	prink; bedizen; caper; frolic	
PRASE	green quartz	**mn**

PRATE	babble; chatter; jabber	
PRAWN	a crustacean	**zo**
PREDY	ready for action	**nt**
PREEN	to clean the feathers	
PRESS	crush; urge; crowd; hurry; burden; newspapers; linen; juice extractor; press-ups (gymn.) (fencing) basketball	
PREST	at hand; ready money; to loan	
PREXY	college president (USA)	
PRICE	cost; charge; rate; reward	
PRICK	perforate; mark; penis	**pl**
PRIDE	arrogance; hauteur; conceit	
PRIED	peeped; spied; snooped	
PRIER	pryer; a nosey parker	
PRILL	brill; a fish	**zo**
PRIMA	first; leading	
PRIMA	repeated, resumption mark	**pr**
PRIME	chief; principal; zenith; first quality; prepare by charging (oil stoves, explosives, gas lamps); pre-paint coating; prize cycling	**pt, ps**
PRIMO	leading part	**mu**
PRIMY	blooming	
PRINK	prank; to dress up	
PRINT	stamp; brand; impress	
PRIOR	previous; earlier; cf. abbot	**rl**
PRISE	to lever	
PRISM	refracting glass	
PRIVY	private; outdoor toilet; parts (genitals); councillor	
PRIZE	esteem; reward; booty (ship, -money); salvage; premium; sports cup; (boxing) (racing)	
PROBE	scrutinize; examine; prove	
PROEM	preface	
PRONE	face downwards; apt to; rifleman's firing position; with tendency to	
PRONG	the tine of a fork	**to**
PROOF	test; ordeal; impenetrable; evidence (whisky); (water-); study; first print; control	**lw, ck, cp, pr**
PROPS	theatrical properties	
PRORE	the prow of a ship	**nt**
PROSE	non verse writing	
PROSO-	of matters ahead; future (Gr.)	**cf**
PROSY	prolix; tedious; vapid	
PROTO-	of beginning, original, primitive (Gr.)	**cf**
PROUD	vain; imperious; stately	
PROVE	evince; verify; examine	
PROWL	prey; stalk; rove; slink	
PROXY	substitute; deputy; agent	
PRUDE	person of intolerant modesty	
PRUNE	dried plum	**ck**
PRUNT	applied glass badge mass	**gs**
PRYAN	felspathic clay	**mn**
PRYER	prier; snooper	
PSALM	sacred song sung to a harp	**mu**

PSHAW!	belittling exclamation	
PSOAS	tenderloin	md
PSORA	the itch	md
PTERE	an alate organ; a wing	zo
PUBES	genital zone of abdomen	pl
PUBIC	of genital/loin region	pl
PUBIS	pelvic bones	md
PUDGY	podgy; fat; fleshy	
PUFFY	tumid; swollen; bombastic	
PUGIL	a pinch of	
PUKKA	veritable; genuine (Hindu)	
PULED	whined	
PULER	a whimperer	
PULEX	the flea	zo
PULKA	Lapland sledge	
PULPY	soft; succulent	
PULSE	a lentil; to throb; beat, transient	
	disturbance **ck, md, bt, ps, el**	
PUMPS	evening shoes (dancing) (men's)	
PUNCH	pummel; pierce; horse; chisel; (Mr,	
	puppet)	to, zo
PUNGY	Chesapeake Bay schooner	nt
PUNIC	Carthaginian; faithless	
PUNKA	punkah; Indian fan	
PUNTA	with the point of the bow of violin	
	(It.)	mu
PUNTO	fencing; Cuban dance	ga, mu
PUNTY	glass blower's iron	to
PUPAL	in the chrysalis state	zo
PUPIL	learner; tyro; alumni; (eye);	
	alumnus	pl
PUPPY	whelp; novice	zo
PUREE	thick soup; strained pulp	ck
PURER	cleaner; more chaste	
PURGA	north-westerly tundra wind	
BURAN	(Siberia)	mt
PURGE	cleanse; absolve; shrive	
PURIM	Jewish feast	
PURRE	the dunlin bird	zo
PURSE	to wrinkle; money-bag	
PURSY	fat and asthmatic	
PUSSY	willow catkin; tame cat	bt, zo
PUTID	putrid; worthless	
PUTOO	nut-meal	ck
PUTTI	chubby Baroque child image	
PUTTY	cement with linseed oil	
PUT-UP	preconcerted	
PUTZI	Chinese game	ga
PUZTA	Pannonian plain (Hungary)	go
PYGAL	related to backsides	
PYGMY	pigmy; midget; Lilliputian	
PYLON	gateway; turning mark; tower; tow-	
	rope hitch (water-skiing)	
PYOID	pus-like	md
PYRAL	(funeral pyre)	
PYRAN	cyclic carbon/oxygen compound	ch
PYRUS	apple or pear genus	bt
PYXIS	pyx; sacred box	rl

Q

QANAT	} underground irrigation	
GANAT	system (Iran)	
KANAT		go
Q-BOAT	disguised, armed ship	nt
QIBLA	mihrab wall, mosque	ar
QUACK	charlatan; humbug; empiric; cry	
QUADS	quadruplets	
QUAFF	gulp; swallow; drink deep	
QUAID	quelled (Spens.)	
QUAIL	cower; flinch; small bird; toy	
	musical instrument with birdsong	
		mu, zo
QUAIR	quire; a book	me
QUAKE	tremble; quiver; rock	
QUAKY	unstable; shaky; trembling	
QUALE	having independent existence	
QUALM	scruple; pang; throe	
QUANT	punt or jumping pole	
QUARK	hypothetical sub-atomic entity	
QUARK	curd cheese (Ger.)	ck
QUARL	a segment of fireclay	
QUARL	jellyfish	zo
QUART	(cards); 2 pints (1.13 litres)	me
QUASH	nullify; annul; override	
QUASI	as it were; virtually; pretence; false	
QUASI	excess data	cp
QUASI-	seemingly; resembling (Gr.)	cf
QUASS	kvass; Russian beer	
QUEAN	a saucy girl (obs.)	
QUEEN	(cards); (chess); (royal); (bee); gay	
		ga
QUEER	odd; rummy; curious; strange; gay	
QUEET	an ankle; a gaiter (Sc.)	
QUELL	suppress; crush; quench	
QUERK	to throttle; to grunt	
QUERL	to twirl; a coil	
QUERN	primitive stone handmill	
QUERY	question; dispute; ask	
QUEST	search; pursuit; inquiry	
QUEUE	a hopeful tail	
QUICK	fleet; agile; brisk; alive	
QUIET	still; calm; lull; pacify	
QUIFF	a curly lock	
QUI-HI	Anglo-Indian	
QUILL	a feather; a pen	zo
QUILP	a hideous dwarf	
QUILT	twilt; counterpane	
QUINA	quinine	md
QUINS	a quintuplet	
QUINT	sequence of five; organ stop	mu
QUIPO	} mnemonic Inca language;	
QUIPU	coloured and knotted cords	
QUIRE	choir; 24 sheets	me
QUIRK	twist; subterfuge; evasion	
QUIRT	riding whip	
QUITE	fully; exactly; entirely	
QUITS	acquittance; clear of debt	

QUOAD	as far as	
QUOIF	coif; headdress	
QUOIN	wedge	
QUOIT	discus	
QUOOK	quaked (Spens.)	
QUOTA	share; portion; allotment	
QUOTE	cite; mention; adduce	
QUOTH	spake; said; remarked	
QURAN	Koran; Moslem Holy Book	rl

R

RABBI	Jewish teacher	
RABID	furious; violent; result of rabies bite	md, zo
RABOT	marble polisher	
RACED	ran; hurried; competed	
RACER	that races; competes	
RACON	remote-object identifying beacon	
RADAR	radio-location	
RADGE	rodge; grey duck; gadwall	zo
RADII	plural of radius	
RADIO	telegram; wireless (-active)	nc, ro
RADIX	(logarithms); a root	ma, bt
RADON	radioactive element	ch
RAFFE	three-cornered sail	nt
RAFTY	damp; musty	
RAGED	raved; fumed; stormed	
RAILS	safety fence; iron road; surrounds (surfing)	rw
RAINY	showery	
RAISE	erect; uplift; exalt; breed	
RAJAH	Indian prince	
RAKED	enfiladed; searched; combed	
RAKER	ransacker; scraper	
RAKER	inclined tubular scaffolding	bd
RALLY	banter; recover; gathering (sports etc.)	ga
RALPH	a mischievous raven	zo
RAMAL	branching	
RAMED	framed on the stocks	nt
RAMET	asexual offspring of clone	
RAMEX	hernia; rupture	md
RAMIE	ramee; rope fibre	nt
RAMIE	Chinese grass for banknotes, textiles	tx
RAMMY	strongly scented	
RAMUS	branch; twig; spray	bt
RANCE	a rocket trough	
RANCH	stock-farm; (dude); estate	
RANDY	sexually rampant	
RANDY	a virago; a romp; a beggar	
RANEE	rani; Indian queen	
RANGE	array; align; scope; roam; distance; habitat	
RANGE	variation limits; mountain chains; (kitchen)	
RANGY	long-limbed and slender	
RANTY	boisterous; vociferous	

RAPED	violated; outraged; ravished	
RAPHE	seam; rib; partition	
RAPID	fast; fleet; swift; hasty	
RAPIN	devouring animal	hd
RARER	scarcer; more uncommon	
RASCH	quick (Ger.)	mu
RASED	} erased; effaced; demolished;	
RAZED	} blotted out	
RASPY	rough; scratchy; abrasive	
RASSE	small civet	zo
RATAL	rate value	
RATAN	rattan; a cane	zo
RATCH	pawl; ratchet; rack	
RATED	assessed; chid; scolded; valued	
RATEE	a person being rated	
RATEL	honey-badger	zo
RATER	assessor; (yachting)	
RATHE	early; quickly; rapidly	
RATIO	proportion; rate; quota	
RATTY	irascible; irate; angry	
RAVED	raged; ranted; drivelled	
RAVEL	entangle; untwist	
RAVEN	large crow-like bird	zo
RAVER	a maniac	
RAVIN	raven; prey; plunder; rapine	
RAWLY	unskilfully; immaturely	
RAYAH	Ottoman non-Moslem	
RAYED	shone; arrayed	
RAYON	artificial silk	tx
RAZEE	to cut down; prune	nt
RAZOR	shaving device	
REACH	expanse; stretch; scope	
REACT	recoil; resist; repeat	
READY	prompt; alert; willing	
REALM	kingdom; domain	
REAMY	novelty yarn	tx
RE-ARM	re-equip (defense)	
REAST	to dry by smoke	
REATA	riata; lariat; lasso	
REAVE	to bereave; ravage	
REBEC	} fore-runner of violin; Moorish	
REBECK	} fiddle	mu
REBEL	revolt; rise; insurgent	
REBID	(auction)	
REBUS	a pictorial puzzle	
REBUT	confute; disprove; rebuff	
RECAP	redescribe briefly	
RECCE	reconnaissance	
RECIF	reef or bar (S. Africa)	go, nv
RECIT	swell of organ	mu
RECTO	right-hand page	
RECUR	reappear; revert; resort	
REDAN	earthwork; redoubt	
REDIA	large stage in trematoda	zo
REDLY	blushingly	
REDUX	re-appearance; return	
REEDY	a thin tone (woodwind)	mu
REEFY	full of rocks	nv
REEKY	smoky; vaporous	
REESK	rank grass; waste land (Sc.)	

REEST	resist; arrest; stop (Sc.)	
REEVE	steward; sheriff; rope	lw
REEVE	the female ruff; a bird	zo
REFEL	refute; disprove (Shak.)	
REFER	submit; relate; advert	
REFIT	repair; re-equip	
REGAL	royal; kingly; princely; a reed-organ, portable, for churches	mu
REGET	regain; recover	
REGIE	government monopoly	
REGMA	botanical capsule	bt
REICH	German realm	
REIFY	to materialize	
REIGN	rule; govern; control	
REIST	reest; to baulk; arrest	
REIVE	reave; to ravage	
RELAI	chain of inns	
RELAX	abate; slacken; loosen	
RELAY	team race; pass on	
RELET	to offer on hire again	
RELIC	memento; souvenir; keepsake; survival from past	
RELIT	rekindled; re-illuminated	
REMAN	get a fresh crew	ae, nt
REMEX	a flight feather	zo
REMIT	replace; diminish; re-lease	
RENAL }		
RENES }	(kidneys)	md
RENEW	renovate; refurbish, restore	
RENIN	kidney hormone	md
RENTE	annuity from French funds	
REPAY	refund; recompense; avenge	
REPEL	repulse; parry; withstand	
REPET	repeat; the same again	md
REPLY	echo; answer; respond	
REPOT	transplant	
RE-RUN	repeat; commence again; restart after error or fiasco	cp
RESAW	saw again; revisualized	
RESET	reprint with alterations; adjust	pr
RESIN	rosin; conifer gum	bt
RESOL	synthetic resin	ch
RESOW	to sow again	
RESTY	indolent; restive	
RETCH	reach; strain	
RETEX	to annul	
RETRO-	predated, from the past (Gr.)	cf
RETRY	try again	
REVEL	feast; carouse; luxuriate	
REVET	(revetment)	
REVIE	outdo; retort	
REVUE	variety entertainment	mu
REWET	part of a wheel-lock	
REWIN	regain	
-RHAGE	of bleeding; discharge (Gr.)	cf, md
RHEIC	(rhubarb)	bt
RHEIN	chrysophanic acid	ch
RHEMA	word, verb (Gr.)	
RHEUM	watery mucous discharge	md
RHINE	rine; a ditch; artificial gem	

RHINO-	of the nose (Gr.)	cf, pl, zo
RHOMB	a rhombohedron; geometrical shape	ma
RHONE }		
RONE }	eaves gutter	bd
RHUMB	vertical circle; (compass)	
RHYME	rime; poetry; metre	
RHYNE	Russian hemp	bt
RIANT	laughing; smiling (Fr.)	
RIATA	reata; lasso	
RIBES	currant genus	bt
RICER	machine for mincing food	ck
RICIN	castor bean albumin	ch
RIDER	horseman; added clause	!
RIDGE	ledge; crest; weal; range	go
RIDGY	furrowed; corrugated	
RIFLE	ransack; strip; to groove	
RIGEL	a star in Orion	
RIGHT	due; equity; privilege	
RIGID	staunch; unbending; strict	
RIGOL	a diadem; crown; coronet	
RIGOR	rigour; rigidity	md
RIGOR	shivering, chill (of death)	md
RILED	angered; annoyed	
RILLE	lunar valley	
RIMED	frosted	
RIMER	an enlarging tool	to
RINGE	heather whisk	
RINGS	pair for hanging gymnasts	
RINKS	fours (bowls); ice floors (skating)	ga
RINSE	lave; clean; wash	
RIOJA	Spanish wine	
RIPEN	mature; develop; perfect	
RIPER	further advanced	
RIPON	a spur	
RISEL	support for a vine	
RISEN	ascended; mounted; revolted	
RISER	rebel; stair-board; handle, centre of bow (archery); early bird	
RISHI	poet; Vedic seer	
RISKY	hazardous; speculative	
RISSA	kittiwake genus	zo
RITHE	small stream	go
RITZY	luxurious; presumptuously; sham	
RIVAL	vie; emulate; match; equal	
RIVEL	to wrinkle; shrivel	
RIVEN	rived; rent; split	
RIVER	stream; torrent; tributary	
RIVET	clinch; fasten	
RIYAL	Sudanese coin	nm
RIZOM	head of corn or oats	bt
ROACH	part of sail; a fish	nt, zo
ROAST	parch; chaff outrageously	
ROBED	garbed; attired; arrayed	
ROBIN	national bird; circular appeal	zo
ROBLE	Californian white oak	bt
ROBOT	an automaton	
ROCKY	stony; shaky; unsteady	
ROCTA	ancient violin	mu

RODEO	cattle round-up; competitive spectacle	
RODGE	radge; grey duck; gadwall	zo
ROGER	a ram; a rogue	zo
ROGUE	knave; scamp; rascal; wild; genetic variant, vicious exception; wave (surfing)	
ROHAN	red-wood mahogany tree	bt
ROIST	to bluster; to swagger	
ROKER	thornback ray; skate	zo
ROMAL	kerchief; raw hide whip	
ROMAN	type of type; of Rome	pr
ROMEO	a lover	
ROMER	(Rhineland) broad wine glass	
ROMIC	a phonetic notation	
ROMPU	heraldic fracture	hd
ROMPY	rampageous	
RONDE	round-hand type (Fr.)	
RONDE	circular dance	
RONDO	music in several strains	mu
RONIN	Japanese outcast	
ROODY	coarse; luxuriant	
ROOFY	having roofs	
ROOKY	rookery; new recruit	
ROOMY	spacious	
ROOPY	roupy; hoarse	
ROOSE	to extol (Sc.)	
ROOST	a fowl support; to perch	
ROOTY	radical; bread (India)	ck
ROPED	tied; lashed; bound	
ROQUE	a form of croquet (Fr.)	ga
RORAL	dewy; roscid	
RORIC	moist with dew	
RORTY	exuberant; rampageous	
ROSET	a red colour; rosin	
ROSIN	resin; conifer gum	bt
ROTAL	according to roster	
ROTON	quantum of rotational energy	ps
ROTOR	a machine; airfoil; wind turbulence (aeronautics)	
ROUGE	(Eton wall game); cosmetic; point for Can. football	ga
ROUGH	rugged; crude; coarse; long grass areas on golf course	
ROUND	convex; rotund; period (tour); canon; (visits); (a table)	mu
ROUND	shot; in a circle; (drinks); (contest); cut; series	
ROUPY	roopy; hoarse	
ROUSE	carouse; disturb; awaken	
ROUST	rouse; stir up; incite	
ROUSY	noisy; riotous	
ROUTE	way; course; itinerary	
ROUTH	plentiful; abundant (Sc.)	
ROVED	roamed; wandered; rambled	
ROVER	nomad; pirate; (croquet); (Australian football)	ga
ROWAN	mountain ash	bt
ROWDY	ruffian; rough; boisterous; drunk and disorderly; noisy	

ROWED	sculled; upbraided	
ROWEL	spurwheel (riding)	
ROWEN	second hay crop	
ROWER	oarsman	
ROYAL	regal; superb; august	
ROYLE	to rile; to salt fish	
ROYNE	to bite; to gnaw; whisper	
RUADE	parallel turn (skiing)	
RUATA	junklike craft (Siam)	nt
RUBIA	madder genus	bt
RUBLE	rouble; Russian silver coin	nm
RUBUS	bramble genus	bt
RUCHE	plaited trimming	
RUDAS	a hag; virago (Sc.)	
RUDDY	rubicund; red	
RUDER	coarser; cruder	
RUDGE	a partridge	zo
RUFFE	ruff; freshwater perch	zo
RUGBY	(football); (school)	ga
RUING	regretting; lamenting	
RULED	lined; governed; decided	
RULER	monarch; regent; dictator	
RUMAL	romal; shawl (Hindu)	
RUMBA	Cuban dance	mu
RUMBO	rum punch	
RUMEN	paunch of ruminant	
RUMEX	sorrel genus	bt
RUMMY	odd; queer; card game	ga
RUNCH	crunch; the wild charlock	bt
RUNER	bard	
RUNIC	ancient Scandinavian script	
RUN-IN	the finish in racing; to train a new motor; arrest (police); to merge paragraphs	me, lw, pr
RUNNY	liquid	
RUN-ON	process of continuing; unbroken	pr
RUN-UP	gold band, binding; approach run (jump); last preparations before event; sew a garment rapidly; hoist a flag; accumulate debts	pr
RUPEE	16 annas	nm
RUPIA	skin disease	md
RURAL	Arcadian; sylvan; pastoral	
RUSHY	full of rushes	
RUSMA	rhusma; a depilatory	md
RUSTY	corroded; out of practice	
RUTAL	} derived from rue	bt
RUTIC		
RUTTY	uneven; furrowed; grooved	
RUVID	rough	
RYBAT	in- or outband	bd
RYPER	ptarmigans (Scand.)	zo

S

SABAL	a fan palm genus	bt
SABER	cavalry sword	
SABIN	unit of acoustic absorption	ac
SABLE	antelope; marten; fur	zo

SABLE	black; dusky; sombre	hd
SABOT	wooden shoe	
SABRA	} native of Israel; cavalry sword	
SABRE		
SACRE	saker; falcon; cannon	zo
SADDA	abbreviated Zendavesta	rl
SADHU	Hindu ascetic	
SADLY	gloomily; dismally; mournfully	
SAFER	surer; more secure	
SAGAN	Jewish priest	rl
SAGER	wiser; cleverer	
SAGRA	bettle genus	zo
SAGUM	Roman cloak	
SAHIB	boss (white) (India)	
SAIGA	puff-nosed antelope	zo
SAILY	like a sail	nt
SAINT	to canonize; a godly venerated Christian	rl
SAITH	(says)	
SAIVA	votary of Siva	rl
SAJOU	American monkey	zo
SAKER	sacre; hawk; old gun	zo
SAKIA	Persian water-wheel	
SALAD	mixed cold dish	ck
SALAL	evergreen shrub	bt
SALDA	a bug genus	zo
SALEP	} dried orchis root; winter	
SALOP	beverage	bt, ck
SALIC	male succession; law	lw
SALIN	saline; a salt	ch
SALIX	willow genus	bt
SALLE	salon; hall (Fr.)	
SALLE	paper-sorting room	pr
SALLY	bell-rope tufting; outburst; wit	
SALLY	a stone-fly; a wren	zo
SALMI	hashed game	ck
SALMO	salmon genus	zo
SALON	saloon; hall	
SALOP	} dried orchis root; winter	
SALEP	beverage	bt, ck
SALPA	genus of sea-squirts	zo
SALSE	volcanic mud	gl, go
SALTS	saline draughts	md
SALTY	witty; briny; saline	
SALVE	save; rescue; heal; a remedy	
SALVO	an exception; a volley	
SAMBA	dance (S. America)	mu
SAMBO	a negro; official Fila-style (wrestling)	ga
SAMIA	silk-worm genus	zo
SAMMY	American Tommy; G.I., footsoldier (Amer.)	
SANDY	yellowish red	
SANER	less idiotic; more normal	
SANSA	tambourine	mu
SAPID	savoury; affected; palatable	
SAPOR	flavour; taste	
SAPPY	juicy; succulent; weak	
SARDA	mackerel; tunny genus	zo

SAROD	} Indian guitar	mu
SAROH		
SAROS	an astronomical cycle	as
SARSE	a fine sieve	
SARUM	Salisbury; (rotten borough)	
SASIA	pigmy woodpeckers (Ind.)	zo
SASIN	antelope; Indian blackbuck	zo
SASSE	Dutch weir with flood-gates	
SATAN	Devil; Lucifer; Beelzebub	rl
SATED	replete; surfeited; cloyed	
SATIN	glossy fabric	tx
SATIS	enough (Latin)	
SATYR	goat-like sylvan deity; Pan	rl
SAUCE	impudence; a condiment; relish	
SAUCH	} the willow (Sc.)	bt
SAUGH		
SAUCY	pert; bold; malapert; flippant	
SAUDI	gold sovereign (Arabia)	nm
SAULT	a rapid (Canadian)	go
SAUNA	Finnish steam-bath	
SAURY	skipper-fish	zo
SAUTE	fried in fat	ck
SAVED	rescued; freed; redeemed; kept	
SAVER	a hoarder; an economist	
SAVIN	evergreen conifer	bt
SAVOR	savour; taste; odour; relish	
SAVOY	curly cabbage	bt
SAVVY	commonsense; nous; gumption	
SAWED	cut with a saw; sawn	
SAWNY	} a Scotsman	
SAWNEY		
SAXIN	saccharin	ch
SAXON	of Saxony	
SAYER	a speaker; an assayer	
SAYON	medieval peasant's jacket	
SAY-SO	a dictum	
SCAFF	food of any kind (Sc.); scoff	
SCAIL	skail; scatter; disperse (Sc.)	
SCALA	a surgical instrument	md
SCALD	the dodder-plant; a burn	bt
SCALD	skald; Scandinavian bard	
SCALE	climb; balance; flake; lamina; (fish-); proportion and size; exact drawing; sol-fa application	zo, mu, md
SCALL	leprosy; a scab; mean	
SCALP	token of victory; trophy	
SCALY	encrusted; shabby; mean	
SCAMP	rogue; knave; stint	
SCANT	to stint; scarcely sufficient	
SCAPE	leafless peduncle bearing flowers	bt
SCAPE	shaft of column; a fault	
SCAPE	stem; escape; miss	
SCARD	shard; sherd; fragment	
SCARE	alarm; appal; dismay; daunt	
SCARF	neckerchief; a carpenter's joint	
SCARF	cormorant; scart; skart	zo
SCARP	heraldic scarf; rampart slope	hd
SCART	to scratch; scrape; a niggard	
SCARY	timid; frightened; windy	

SCATE	skate; a fish	zo
SCATH	scathe; damage; injury; harm	
SCATT	scat; tax (Shetland Is.)	
SCAUD	scald; scold (Sc.)	
SCAUP	a sea-duck	zo
SCAUR	river bank; rocky cliffs; scar	go
SCELP	skelp; iron for gun-barrels	
SCENA	stage of an ancient theatre; operatic unit of aria, duet etc	mu
SCEND	ascend; to heave upwards	
SCENE	show; pageant; sight; view	
SCENT	perfume; odour; redolence; trail	
SCHUT	cattle-pound (South Africa)	
SCION	offshoot; branch; descendant	
SCISE	to cut (obs.)	
SCOAT	scote; to scotch; to wedge	
SCOBS	shavings; sawdust; dross	
SCOBY	} the chaffinch	zo
SCOBBY		
SCOFF	(food); sneer; mock; deride	
SCOLD	rate; upbraid; censure; chide	
SCOMM	a buffoon (obs.)	
SCONE	coronation stone; a confection	ck
SCOON	skim along the water	
SCOOP	dig; hollow; excavate; a ladle; (badminton); glide up to a note (singing)	mu
SCOOT	decamp; bolt; run	
SCOPA	stiff hairs of moths	zo
SCOPE	room; space; liberty; object	
-SCOPE	viewing instrument (Gr.)	cf
SCOPS	screech-owl	zo
-SCOPI	} viewing scrutiny (Gr.)	cf
-SCOPY		
SCORE	record; mark; furrow; scratch; music in parts form, printed	mu
SCORN	spurn; scout; disdain; deride	
SCOTE	a scotch; a wedge; a prop	
SCOTO-	of darkness (Gr.)	cf
SCOTS	Scottish	
SCOUP	to run; to scamper (Sc.)	
SCOUR	scrub; scrape; purge	
SCOUT	contemn; spurn; reconnoitre	
SCOUT	the guillemot; razor-bill	zo
SCOVE	to tamp; to poise	
SCOVY	smeared; blotched	
SCOWL	frown; lower; glower	
SCRAB	crab-apple; to scratch; scrape	bt
SCRAG	to throttle; odd lean bit	
SCRAM!	clear off! get out!	
SCRAM	emergency plant shutdown	nc
SCRAN	skran; scraps of food	
SCRAP	bit; atom; particle; tussle	
SCRAT	a devil; a goblin; monster	
SCRAW	a turf; a sod (Irish)	
SCRAY	sea-swallow	zo
SCREE	} slope of loose rock face	gl,
TALUS		mo
SCREW	twist; distort; force; old horse	
SCRIM	strong muslin lining for walls	tx

SCRIP	wallet; purse; satchel	
SCRIP	(receipt for) share certificates	
SCROD	to shed; young codfish	zo
SCROG	stunted bush; thicket	go
SCRUB	clean; scour; maquis; stunted growth land	bt, go
SCRUM	(football)	ga
SCUBA	underwater breathing apparatus	
SCUDO	Italian silver dollar	nm
SCUFF	scurf; a scale; to shuffle	
SCUFT	the nape of the neck	
SCULK	skulk; lurk; slink	
SCULL	an oar; a cockboat; to row	nt
SCULL	skua-gull; a shoal of fish	zo
SCULP	to carve; to engrave; to flay	
SCURF	dandruff; scum; bull-trout	zo
SCUTE	a shield; scale of fish	zo
SEAMY	dark; sordid; nasty	
SEA-OX	the walrus	zo
SEAVE	a wick made of a rush	
SEAVY	overgrown with rushes	bt
SEBAT	5th month of the Jewish year	
SEBUM	sebaceous gland excretion	zo
SECCO	a fresco; unaccompanied	mu
SEDAN	carrying chair; a disaster	
SEDGE	flock of herons; reeds; grass	zo, bt
SEDGY	overgrown with sedge or rushes	
SEEDY	shabby; run to seed; unwell	
SEEGA	board game (Egypt, Somalia)	ga
SEGNO	repetition	mu
SEGUE	follow on at once (It.)	mu
SEINE	large fishing net	
SEISM	an earthquake	
SEITY	personality; selfhood	
SEIZE	grasp; clutch; grapple; impound	
SEKOS	Greek sanctuary	
SELAH	a pause in the Psalms	
SELVA	tropical rainforest (Brazil)	go
SEMEN	fluid containing spermatozoa	zo
SEMIC	pertaining to a sign	
SEMIS	Roman bronze coin, half an as	nm
SENAL	a landmark (South America)	
SENCH	to cause to founder	
SENEX	S. American hawk; a swift	zo
SENNA	dried cassia leaves	md
SENOR	Spanish title of address	
SENSE	wisdom; reason; receptive perception; detect; notice	pc
SENSE	(common); (intuition); perception system	cp
SENZA	without	mu
SEPAL	calyx segment	bt
SEPIA	genus of cuttlefish; pigment	zo
SEPIC	done in sepia	
SEPOY	native Indian soldier	
SERAC	glacial ice	gl, go
SERAI	caravanserai; a Persian inn	
SERGE	twilled fabric	tx
SERIC	Chinese; silken	
SERIF	short cross-line in typography	pr

SERIN	song-bird; canary	zo
SERIR	} gravel desert Libya (Arab)	gl,
REG		go
SERON	bale of exotic produce	
SEROW	Asiatic goat	zo
SERRA	a saw; sierra; mountain ridge (Ptg.)	gl, go
SERRE	tightened, with tension, speed	mu
SERRY	to crowd together	
SERUM	antibody for inoculation	md
SERVE	do; act; suit; aid; obey; attend	
SERVE	put ball into play (court games)	ga
SERVO	braking system; difference minimiser	au, cp
SESHA	Serpent-King (Hindu)	rl
SESIA	clear-wing moths	zo
SESSA	hurry! (Shak.)	
SETAE	bristles; cat's whiskers	bt, zo
SETON	a dressing	md
SET-TO	an affray	
SET-UP	scheme; plot; locate; unit	
SEVEN	cardinal number	
SEVER	cut; part; sunder; detach	
SEWED	stitched; threaded	
SEWEL	a scarecrow	
SEWEN	sewin; salmon type	zo
SEWER	drain	
SEXTE	sixth hour service	rl
SEXTO	a size of book	
S'FOOT	an imprecation	
SHACK	a shed; to tramp; a vagabond	
SHADE	hue; tint; veil; cover; screen	
SHADY	shadowy; obscure; doubtful	
SHAFT	arrow; missile; handle; pit	
SHAHI	Persian copper coin	nm
SHAKE	jar; jolt; agitate; quiver; dance; shudder; trill (ornamental)	mu
SHAKO	chako; military cap	
SHAKY	tottering; unstable; loose	
SHALE	shaly clay; husk	mn
SHALL	future auxiliary verb	
SHALM	} type of oboe	mu
SHAWM		
SHALT	future auxiliary verb	
SHALY	laminated and friable	
SHAMA	Indian song-bird; cereal	zo, bt
SHAME	abash; mortify; infamy	
SHAND	shame; base coin; worthless	
SHANK	(golf); the tibia	pl
SHAPE	mould; fashion; form; image	
SHAPO	wild sheep of Tibet	zo
SHAPS	chaps; cowboy breeches	
SHARD	sherd; fragment; wing case	zo
SHARE	quota; part; portion; divide	
SHARK	a cheat; artful greedy fellow; predatory fish; financier; (Am. football)	
SHARN	cow-dung (Sc.)	
SHARP	fine; thin; keen; caustic	mu
SHAVE	pare; clip; shear; skim; graze	

SHAWL	a wrap	
SHAWM	forerunner of oboe	mu
SHEAF	a bundle; a collection	
SHEAL	to shell; to husk	
SHEAL	shiel; shepherd's hut	
SHEAR	clip; cut; fleece; strip; force; retreat	
SHEEN	gloss; lustre; shine; polish	
SHEEP	a woolly ruminant	zo
SHEER	absolute; precipitous; turn aside	
SHEET	a bed-cloth; wide expanse; rope	tx
SHEIK	Arab chief	
SHELF	ledge; shoal; sandbank	
SHELL	case; husk; projectile; bombard; racing rowing boat (universities)	nt
SHEND	to disgrace (Spens.)	
SHEOL	pit; Hades (Heb.)	rl
SHERD	shard; fragment; scard	
SHETH	part of plough	
SHEVA	(Hebrew vowel point)	
SHEWN	displayed; revealed; taught	
SHIAH	Mohammedan sect	
SHIAI	tournament (judo)	ga
SHIED	(coconuts); (horses)	
SHIEL	shieling; shelter for sheep (Sc.)	
SHIER	shyer; more bashful	
SHIFT	chemise; vary; alter; trick; wile; change place; working hours; flexible arithmetic; realignment of forwards (Amer. football)	ma, cp, ga
SHIKO	prostrate veneration (Burma)	rl
SHILY	shyly; coyly; timidly	
SHINE	radiate; glitter; flash; gloss	
SHINY	the East; gleaming; polished	
SHIRE	county; draught-horse	
SHIRK	evade; avoid; neglect; malinger	
SHIRL	to slide	
SHIRR	to pucker; to wrinkle	
SHIRT	a blouse; distinctive garment	
SHIST	schist; crystalline rock	mn
SHIVE	a slice; a wooden bung	
SHOAD	fragments of ore	mn
SHOAL	swarm; throng; bank; bar; fishes	nv, nt, zo
SHOAT	young hog	zo
SHOCK	sheaf; onset; to disgust; stook; disturbance	ag, cp, el
SHOER	a farrier; blacksmith	
SHOGI	chess variant (Japan)	ga
SHOLA	a wood; a thicket (Ind.)	
SHOLE	ground plank	
SHONE	radiated; sparkled; flashed	
SHOOK	cask staves; trembled; quaked	
SHOOL	beg; grimace; shovel (Sc.)	
SHOON	shoes	
SHOOT	emit; dart; fire; sprout	bt
SHORE	prop; brace; strand; beach	go
SHORL	tourmaline	mn

SHORN	shaven; fleeced; clipped	
SHORT	terse; abrupt; laconic; pithy; wee	
SHOTT	} seasonal salt lake	**go**
CHOTT		
SHOUT	cry; cheer; call; bellow	
SHOVE	jostle; push; press; elbow	
SHOWN	presented; paraded; revealed	
SHOWY	gay; garish; loud; gaudy	
SHRAB	shrub; a drink (Arab)	
SHRED	scrap; tatter; atom; piece	
SHREW	vixen; virago; scold	**zo**
SHROF	Indian money-lender	
SHROW	shrew; small dormouse	**zo**
SHRUB	a cordial; dwarf tree	**bt**
SHRUG	to draw up; contract	
SHUCK	a husk; shell or pod	**bt**
SHUNT	divert; electrical device; reassemble train; damage to car (sl.)	**el, rw**
SHYLY	shily; coyly; bashfully	
SIBBE	sib; akin	
SIBYL	prophetess; witch; sorceress	
SICCA	newly coined; a rupee	**nm**
SIDED	flattened; biased	
SIDER	partisan; protagonist	
SIDLE	to go crabwise	
SIEGE	besiege; invest; a throne	
SIELD	ceiled; plastered (Spens.)	
SIEUR	title of respect (Fr.)	
SIEVE	to sift; to strain; a temse	
SIGHT	see; view; observe; scene; visual scan check	**cp**
SIGIL	signature; occult mark; seal	
SIGMA	a Greek letter; reactor circuit	
SILAL	high-silica cast iron	**ml**
SILEX	silica	**mn**
SILKY	silken	
SILLY	inane; inept; unwise; stupid	
SILVA	sylva; forest trees	**bt**
SIMAR	cymar; cimar; scarf; loose dress	**tx**
SIMIA	genus of apes	**zo**
SINAL	pertaining to sinus	**pl**
SINCE	after; subsequently; because	
SINEW	a tendon	**md, pl**
SINGE	sear; burn; scorch	
SINIC	Seric; Chinese	
SINTO	shinto; ancestor-worship (Jap.)	**rl**
SINUS	a cavity; a bay; nasal duct	**pl**
SIOUX	Dakota Indian	
SIPED	oozed; exuded; percolated	
SIRED	fathered; generated	
SIREN	syren; seducer; hooter	
SIRIH	betel-leaf (Malay)	**bt**
SIRUP	sorop; syrup	
SISAL	fibrous plant, (ropemaking)	**bt**
SISON	stone parsley	**bt**
SISSY	sweetheart; a weakling	
SITAR	Indian long-necked lute	**mu**
SITED	placed, situated	
SIT-IN	demonstration by occupying premises	

SITTA	the nut-hatch	**zo**
SIVAN	Jewish month	
SIXTH	ordinal number; harmonic interval	**mu**
SIXTY	cardinal number	
SIZAR	a rationed student	
SIZED	graded; glued	
SIZEL	scissel; metal clipping	
SIZER	sizing machine	
SKAIL	scail; disperse; scatter; empty; spill	
SKAIN	skein; coil of yarn	
SKALD	scald; Scandinavian bard	
SKARN	silicate-gangue mineral	**gl**
SKATE	scate; the ray; a roller-skate	**zo**
SKEAN	skene; a dagger; a dirk (Sc.)	
SKEEL	a milking-pail; a tub (Sc.)	
SKEET	the pollack; a long scoop	**zo**
SKEIN	tangle; wild geese flying	**zo**
SKEIN	length of yarn (thread); series of victories	**tx**
SKELP	a blow; a large portion (Sc.)	
SKELP	tube-steel strip	**ml**
SKENE	skean; dagger; dirk (Sc.)	
SKIDS	short planks; load-taking rail; unsinkable tube	**bd**
SKIED	skyed; lofted; elevated	
SKIER	a lofted shot at cricket	
SKIER	one who travels on skis	
SKIES	the firmament	
SKIFF	a light boat; to skim; sculling (university) boat	**nt**
SKILL	knack; address; art; facility	
SKIMP	stint; scamp; scanty	
SKINK	African lizard; a shin-bone	**zo**
SKIRL	a shrill cry or sound	
SKIRR	scurry; hasten; scour	
SKIRT	hem; border; skim; edge; part of target (archery); garment (ladies'); canvas cover of canoe; feathers on shuttle (badminton)	
SKISH	competition (angling)	
SKITE	skyte; to glide or slip (Sc.)	
SKITE	the yellow bunting	**zo**
SKIVE	pare; split; shirk (slang)	
SKOAL	Hail! a toast! (Scand.)	
SKRAN	scran; scraps; rubbish; refuse	
SKULK	lurk; slink; cower; sneak	
SKULL	the sconce; the noddle	
SKYEY	skiey; ethereal	
SKYTE	skite; glide; slip (Sc.)	
SLACK	lax; loose; lazy; sluggish	
SLACK	shallow dell; small coal	
SLADE	valley; spade; Art School	
SLAIE	weaver's reed	
SLAIN	killed; despatched; murdered	
SLAKE	quench; extinguish; allay	
SLANG	argot; to scold; to abuse	
SLANT	tilt; list; lean; slope	
SLASH	cut; gash; slit; swipe	

SLATE	reprimand (slang); dense clay stone roofing slabs **bd, mn**
SLATT	slat; a lath
SLATY	like slate
SLAVE	serf; thrall; drudge; menial
SLAVE	(-stations of signal network) **ro, tc**
SLEEK	smooth; soft; glossy; silken
SLEEP	doze; slumber; nap; siesta
SLEET	snow mingled with rain
SLEPT	drowsed; slumbered; rested
SLICE	fire-shovel; cut; sever; piece; dip oar too deep; cause a ball to spin (golf) (cricket)
SLICK	plausible; easily done; ore
SLICY	apt to slice
SLIDE	glide; skid; grace notes; transparency; microscope; trombone **mu, pg**
SLIDE	moveable oarsman's seat; favourable wave (surfing)
SLIER	slyer; more crafty
S'LIFE	an imprecation
SLILY	slyly; artfully; astutely
SLIME	mire; sludge; ooze; mud
SLIMY	viscid; viscous; clammy
SLING	a drink; hurl; hang; cast; climbing rope loop **mo**
SLINK	untimely beast; skulk; lurk
SLIPE	slype; mining skip
SLIPS	men's bathing trunks
SLIPS	(theatre); (shipbuilding)
SLISH	slice; slash; cut
SLIVE	to slide; to skulk
SLOAM	clay between coal-beds **mn**
SLOAT	slot; bar; bolt
SLOID	} handicrafts
SLOYD	
SLOOM	to slumber; to sleep
SLOOP	escort ship, yacht **nt**
SLOPE	slant; shelve; grade; a ramp; (ski-); sneak off
SLOPS	ready-made clothes; nightsoil (prison)
SLOSH	slush; sludge; sentimentality
SLOTH	torpor; tree bear; laziness **zo**
SLOYD	sloid; Swedish manual training
SLUED	turned round; tipsy
SLUGS	half-roasted ore
SLUMP	collapse; sudden fall; marsh
SLUNG	flung; thrown; suspended; cast
SLUNK	lurked; cowered; skulked
SLUSH	slosh; sludge; mire; bathos
SLYLY	slily; astutely; craftily
SLYNE	face of a jointed rock **gl**
SLYPE	narrow passage
SMACK	slap; flavour; spice; dash **nt**
SMALL	tiny; petty; trivial; minute
SMALT	blue glass; blue pigment
SMART	rankle; pungent; trim; witty
SMASH	crash; crack; disrupt; ruin

SMASH	hard strokes (badminton) (volleyball)
SMEAR	daub; plaster; sully; begrime
SMELL	scent; aroma; odour; perfume
SMELT	stank; melt ore; small fish **zo**
SMIFT	a fuse
SMILE	smirk; grin; simper
SMIRK	an affected smile
SMITE	hit; buffet; knock; chasten
SMITH	a metal worker; blacksmith
SMOCK	a chemise; pastoral garment
SMOKE	fume; reek; exhale; vapour; (baseball)
SMOKY	steamy; vaporous
SMOLT	young river salmon **zo**
SMOOT	journeyman printer; smout
SMORE	smother (Sc.)
SMOTE	struck; blasted; slew
SMOUT	smowt; speckled trout **zo**
SMUCK	a crowd of jellyfishes **zo**
SNACK	hasty light repast; a share
SNAIL	spiral cam; mollusc **zo**
SNAKE	serpent; reptile; currency link-up **zo**
SNAKY	sly; cunning; serpentine
SNAPE	to bevel
SNARE	gin; net; toil; wile; trap
SNARL	gnarl; growl at; entangle
SNARY	insidious; complicated
SNASH	insolence; abusive language (Sc.)
SNATH	curved handle of a scythe
SNEAD	snath; snathe; sned
SNEAK	lurk; slink; skulk; blab
SNEAP	check; rebuke; nip
SNECK	snick; cut; a latch
SNEER	gibe; mock; jeer; scoff
SNELL	keen; sharp; severe (Sc.)
SNICK	a notch; nick; (cricket)
SNIDE	spurious; dishonest; counterfeit
SNIFF	to smell; inhale; scent; snuff
SNIFT	snort; sniff
SNIPE	to shoot from ambush; bird **zo**
SNIRT	a smothered laugh; snigger
SNOEK	S. African fish; barracouta **zo**
SNOOD	hairnet; a fillet
SNOOK	lurk; snoop; derisive action
SNOOL	to cringe; a sniveller (Sc.)
SNOOP	to pry
SNORE	loud breathing during sleep
SNORT	loud exhalation through nostrils
SNOUK	snook; lurk; snoop
SNOUT	nose; nozzle; proboscis; taper-end of valley glacier (Sp.) **gl, go**
SNOWY	pure; unblemished; niveous
SNUFF	sniff; (tobacco)
SOAPY	unctuous; emollient; flattering
SOAVE	sweetly **mu**
SOBER	staid; sedate; steady; grave
SOBOL	the Russian sable **zo**
SOCIO-	of social; societal nature **cf**
SOCKS	a drubbing; foot covers
SOCLE	plinth

SODDY	covered with sod; turfy	
SOFAR	underwater navigation system	**nv**
SOFTA	Moslem student	
SOGER	a shirker	
SOGGY	boggy; marshy; wet; saturated	
SOKEN	socage district	
SOKOL	Czech organisation	
SOLAH	solar; sola; sponge-wood	**bt**
SOLAR	sunshine parlour; solarium	
SOLDO	Italian copper coin	**nm**
SOLEA	raised pathway	**ar**
SOLED	(boots)	
SOLEN	razor-fish genus	**zo**
SOL-FA	(singing)	**mu**
SOLID	hard; dense; stout; stable	
SOLID	(-state) electronic devices; door; floor, etc.	**cp, bd**
SOLON	wise legislator; wiseacre	**zo**
SOLUM	piece of ground; soil	
SOLUS	alone; sole right, agreement	**lw**
SOLVE	elucidate; unravel; interpret	
SOMAJ	a Hindu society	
SOMMA	} highest; utmost	**mu**
SOMMO		
SONAR	underwater sound ranging	**nt, nv**
SONDE	upper atmospheric probe; long tube	
SONIC	relating to sound; (super-)	**ae**
SONIC	acoustic delay line	**cp**
SONNY	term of endearment	
SONSY	soncy; buxom; jolly; cordial	
SONTY	sanctity (Shak.)	
SOOJA	soya bean	**bt**
SOOTE	sweetly (Spens.)	
SOOTH	truth; reality; true; indeed	
SOOTY	begrimed	
SOPHA	a sofa; seat of a king	
SOPHI	Persian king	
SOPOR	deep sleep; moral lethargy	
SOPPY	moist; wet; silly; weak-minded	
SOPRA	above	**mu**
SORAL	pertaining to sorus	
SORBO	porous rubber	
SORDA	damped with a mute	**mu**
SORDE	lips/teeth crust during fever	**md**
SOREL	a buck of the third year	**zo**
SORER	more grieved; tenderer	
SOREX	a genus including shrew-mice	**zo**
SORRA	not; never (Irish)	
SORRY	sad; dejected; regretful; abject	
SORUS	cluster of capsules on ferns	**bt**
SOUGH	low moan; whine; drain	
SOUND	probe; fathom; hale; valid	
SOUND	(music) audible waves, ethereally sent	**tc**
SOUND	narrow sea passage; inlet	**go, nt**
SOUPY	like soup	
SOUSE	pickle; sauce; douse; swoop	
SOUTH	the Southern regions	
SOWAR	Indian cavalryman	
SOWED	strewn; spread; cast	

SOWER	propagator; disseminator	
SOWLE	to pull by the ears (Shak.)	
SOWTH	to whistle softly (Sc.)	
SPACE	extent; capacity; duration; (universe); a blank	**cp**
SPACE	area; line conditions in a spiral	**cp**
SPADE	(cards); gelding; dig	**ga, to**
SPADO	spade; eunuch; a sword	
SPAER	a diviner (Sc.)	
SPAHI	Algerian cavalryman	
SPAKE	discoursed; declared; told	
SPALE	spail; a splinter (Sc.)	
SPALL	break; split; clip	
SPALT	a flux; brittle	
SPANE	spean; to wean (Sc.)	
SPANG	a spangle; to leap; to hurl	
SPANK	a blow; a slap on the bottom	
SPARE	save; hoard; store; frugal	
SPARE	full-pins score on 2 balls (bowling)	**ga**
SPARK	to flash; bright lad	
SPASM	tic; throe; twitch; paroxysm	
SPATE	spait; a sudden flood	
SPAVE	to geld; to spay	
SPAWL	to split; to slaver	
SPAWN	offspring; ova; sperm	**zo**
SPEAK	express; declare; talk	
SPEAR	a lance; to pierce	
SPEAR	male descent (cf. **DISTAFF**)	**hd**
SPECK	stain; blemish; blubber; lard	
SPECS	spectacles; reading glasses	
SPEED	haste; urge; celerity; rate	
SPEER	speir; to ask (Sc.)	
SPELD	chip; splinter	
SPELK	rod; switch	
SPELL	charm; cantrip; period	
SPELT	spelled; German wheat	**bt**
SPEND	lavish; disburse; exhaust	
SPENT	consumed; worn; wasted	
SPERE	screen of open hall	**ar**
SPERM	spawn; semen	**zo**
SPEWY	wet; boggy	
SPHEX	the wasp genus	**zo**
SPICA	spur; spike; bandage	**md**
SPICE	to season; flavour; relish	
SPICK	spike; nail; tidy; fresh	
SPICY	aromatic; piquant; racy	**ck**
SPIED	observed; beheld	
SPIES	secret agents	
SPIKE	large nail; lavender; disarm (gun); impale; peak; (fence); volleyball	**bt**
SPIKY	spiny; sharp; pointed	
SPILE	} woodpile; fireplace; shed	
SPILL		
SPILL	upset; shed; effuse; lighter	
SPILT	diffused; scattered; dropped	
SPINE	spina; spike; back-bohe; thickness of arrow (archery); axis of book	**md**

SPINK	chaffinch; primrose	**zo, bt**
SPINY	thorny; spiky; difficult	
SPIRE	steeple; a curl; sedge	**bt**
SPIRT	spurt; spout; gush; jet	
SPIRY	spiral	
SPITE	gall; pique; hatred; malice	
SPITZ	Pomeranian dog	**zo**
SPIZA	a finch genus	**zo**
SPLAT	part of a chair-back	
SPLAY	wide; to slant; to slope	
SPLIT	divulge; rent; cleave	
SPODE	china-ware	
SPOIL	mar; booty; snake's skin	**zo**
SPOKE	orated; spouted; said	
SPOLE	spool; a small wheel	
SPOOF	hoax; humbug; bamboozle	
SPOOK	phantom; ghost; spectre	
SPOOL	spole; small wheel; bobbin; reel; roll; tape mounting cine	**cp**
SPOOM	to scud down wind (sailing)	**nv**
SPOON	ladle; to court; metal lure (angling); golf club	
SPOOR	track or trail of an animal	
SPORE	reproductive cell	
SPORT	play; gambol; romp; frolic	
SPOSH	slush	
SPOTS	a leopard	**zo**
SPOUT	pawn; gush; issue; nozzle	
SPRAG	a check-stop; young salmon; pipe or timber wedge	**bd**
SPRAT	small sea-fish	**zo**
SPRAY	foam; spring; diffuse	
SPREE	a carousal	
SPRIG	shoot; twig; a brad	
SPRIT	a sprout; boom; spar	**nt**
SPROD	a second year salmon	**zo**
SPRUE	a disease	**md**
SPUME	froth; spray	
SPUMY	foaming	
SPUNK	pluck; courage; tinder; semen	
SPURN	scorn; scout; slight; disdain	
SPURT	spout; sprint; rush; speed; sudden increase; spray	
SQUAB	clumsy; curt; unfledged; coy; removable stuffed chair-cushion	
SQUAD	band; gang; crew; bevy	
SQUAT	crouch; cower; dumpy; stocky; occupy empty house; technique (weight-lifting)	
SQUAW	American Indian woman	
SQUIB	firework; skit; lampoon	
SQUID	cuttlefish; a calamary	**zo**
SRUTI	Hindu tradition	
STACK	to pile; chimney; (cards); store; (hay); data; rock (sea)	**cp, mo**
STADE	stadium; arena	
STAFF	rod; pole; stick; personnel; (stave) notation system	**mu**
STAGE	produce; present; platform; set up; so far; rig; (motor race)	

STAGY	theatrical; histrionic	
STAID	steady; grave; sedate	
STAIN	sully; taint; tarnish; soil	
STAIR	a step; a stairway	
STAKE	picket; wager; risk; hazard; target (horse-shoe pitching)	
STALE	musty; vapid; effete; trite	
STALK	hunt; strut; stride; stem; haulm	**bt, ag**
STALL	(flying); stop; halt; booth; carved seat (church)	**rl**
STAMP	impress; brand; mark; type	
STAND	sustain; tolerate; defence; cricket partnership; upright; lacrosse; football	**ga**
STANG	(wooden pole-to-throb)	
STANK	reeked; (corruption)	
STARE	gape; gaze; the starling	**zo**
STARK	(naked); scared; severe	
STARR	Jewish deed; bond	**lw, rl**
START	begin; entry point (races)	
STATE	nation; officialdom; condition; (control); status; declare; (of war, alert) period of time; (circumstances)	
STAVE	staff; stick; ladder rung; musical notation; (-church; Scand); -dance	**ar mu**
STAYS	abdominable supports; visits; struts (aircraft); guy ropes (sails, masts, boats)	**md, ae, nt**
STEAD	substitution; bed frame; use; help	
STEAK	thick slice of meat	**ck**
STEAL	(hearts); (shows); quick scores (cricket); rob; move silently; seize; gain	
STEAM	(power); (engines); light cookery; water vapour	**rw, ck, ps**
STEAN	} crockery	
STEEN		
STEED	warhorse; palfrey, mount	
STEEK	stitch, pierce, shut (Sc.)	
STEEL	blade; metal; brace; nerve; strength; hardness; determination; resolution	
STEEP	imbue; dip; soak; excessive	
STEER	guide; pilot; bullock	**zo**
STEIN	earthenware beer tankard (Ger.)	
STELA	} inscribed column; tablet; sap system	
STELE		
STEND	leap; walk with long strides	
STENT	to stint; restrain; limit	
STEPS	ladders; grades; stages; (dance-) (ice)	
STERE	cubic metre	**nt**
STERN	dour; grim; rigorous	**nt**
STEVE	to stow	
STICA	Saxon farthing	**nm**
STICH	stave; a verse	**mu**
STICH	a row of trees	

STICK	stab; fix; attach; adhere	
STICK	a lift of parachutist; punishment; lacrosse	
STIED	penned like pigs	
STIFF	stark; rigid; prim; starchy	
STIFF	a non-winner entry (horse-racing); corpse	
STILB	unit of luminance	me
STILE	the gnomon of a sundial	
STILE	steps in wall or fence (footpath)	
STILL	not sparkling; calm; distil	
STILP	to go on crutches (Sc.)	
STILT	a pole; a snipe	zo
STIME	styme; a glimmer; ray (Sc.)	
STIMY	stymie; (golf)	
STING	prick; wound; hurt; afflict	
STINK	stench; odour; smell	
STINT	allotted task; limit; scrimp	
STINT	sandpiper; dunlin	zo
STIPA	the feather grasses	bt
STIPE	stalk; stem	bt
STIRK	young ox or cow	zo
STIRP	line of descent	
STIVE	to stew	ck
STIVY	stuffy; close	
STOAK	to stop; to choke	me
STOAT	ermine; weasel	zo
STOCK	cravat; store; garner; fund	
STOCK	ski-stick; log	
STOCK	chest, cupboard, door, material to hand; (in trade); (shares); live-; anchor beam; procure; punishment seat	nt
STOEP	stoop; verandah (S. Afr.)	
STOIC	a disciple of Zeno; uncomplaining sufferer	
STOKE	replenish; refuel	
STOLA	Roman lady's dress; shawl	
STOLE	peculated; plagiarised	rl
STOLE	a stolon; a sucker	bt
STOMA	breathing pore	bt
STOMP	stamp; stump	
STONE	boulder; pelt; 14 lb (6.3 kg)	me
STONY	hard; flinty; obdurate; broke	
STOOD	allowed; brooked; bore	
STOOK	stouk; 12 sheaves	bt
STOOL	a seat without a back; ramify	
STOOM	stum; renew fermentation	
STOOP	flagon; condescend; yield	
STOOR	stour; dust; commotion	
STOPE	mining ledge; to excavate	
STOPS	projecting stones; (organ); delays, hindrances	bd, mu, lw
STORE	hoard; garner; stock; supply	cp
STORK	infant conveyor	zo
STORM	fume; rage; scold; turmoil	
STORY	narrative; recital; account	
STOSH	fish-offal; pomace	
STOUK	stook; sheaves of corn	bt
STOUP	stoop; flagon; tankard	
STOUR	stoor; tumult; paroxysm	
STOUT	resolute; robust; a drink	
STOVE	oven; kiln; to heat	
STOWN	stolen (Sc.)	
STRAD	a Stradivarius violin	mu
STRAE	straw (Sc.)	bt
STRAP	a strop; chastise; beat	
STRAW	strae (Sc.); valueless trifle; thatch; cereal stalk	bd, bt
STRAY	err; rove; wander; deviate	
STREW	scatter; spread; broadcast	
STRIA	stripe; streak; small channel	
STRIG	stalk; footstalk	bt
STRIP	peel; divest; dismantle; shred	
STRIX	screech-owl	zo
STROB	measure of angular velocity	
STROP	strap; sharpen; a rope	me
STROW	strew; scatter	
STRUB	to rob	
STRUM	thrum	mu
STRUT	support; brace; walk; swagger	
STUCK	set; fixed; adhered; stabbed	
STUDS	wall timber; collar fasteners; men	
STUDY	con; scan; reflect; learning; den	
STUFA	jet of steam	
STUFF	cram; pack; cloth; fabric	
STULL	cross-timber in a mine	mn
STULM	shaft used to drain a mine	mn
STULP	a stump	
STUMP	log; block; stub; nonplus	
STUNG	pricked; afflicted; had	
STUNK	stank; smelt	
STUNT	to dwarf; (arrested); breakneck risks	
STUNT	box in teleprinter controlling operation	cp
STUPA	Buddhist monument; a dagoba	
STUPE	hot bandage; fomentation	md
STURT	strife; wrath; vexation	
STUTZ	parallel bars swing (gymn.)	ga
STYCA	Saxon half-farthing	nm
STYLE	pen; dub; entitle; mode; distinction; (life-)	
STYLE	constant, recognisable script for viewing	cp
STYLO	a pen; a stylograph	
STYME	stime; stimie (golf)	ga
SUAGE	to assuage (Milton)	
SUAVE	bland; pleasant; polite	
SUBAH	province; viceroyship (Ind.)	
SUDAK	the pike-perch	zo
SUDRA	the lowest Hindu caste	
SUEDE	unglazed leather	le
SUENT	neat and tidy	
SUETY	of suet fat	ck
SUFIC	Islamic mysticism	rl
SUGAR	flattery	
SUING	legal prosecution	lw
SUINT	lanoline	
SUIST	self-seeker	

SUITE	retinue; series; train; apartment	
SUITE	sequence of interrelated programs	cp
SULKS	grumpiness	
SULKY	light vehicle; sullen; morose	
SULLY	soil; taint; stain; defame	
SUMAC	sumach; plant used in dyeing	bt
SUMPH	dunce; blockhead (Sc.)	
SUNNA	Moslem traditions	lw, rl
SUNNI	orthodox Moslem; member of sect	rl
SUNNY	bright; brilliant; unclouded	
SUN-UP	sunrise; dawn; cock-crow	
SUPER	a supernumerary; special	
SUPER-	superior, above, beyond	cf
SUPRA-	transcending; (supra-national)	cf
SURAH	Indian silk; chapter of Koran	tx, rl
SURAL	(calf of the leg)	md
SURAT	coarse Indian cotton	tx
SURER	more certain; safer	
SURFY	covered with surf	
SURGE	roll; swell; heave; a billow; advance	
SURGY	swirling; towering; surfy	
SURLY	churlish; morose; crusty; gruff	
SURMA	Ind. eyeshadow	
SURRA	Eastern horse disease	vt
SURYA	Hindu sun-god	rl
SUSHI	bean-curd rice dish (Jap.)	ck
SUTOR	a cobbler	
SUTRA	(Brahminical ritual)	rl
SWACK	active; nimble; to gulp (Sc.)	
SWAGE	assuage; soften; mitigate	to
SWAGE	drill-bit shaping tool	to
SWAIN	a peasant; a country lover	
SWALE	shady spot; a vale; melt; sweal	
SWAMI	religious instructor (Hindu)	rl
SWAMP	flood; inundate; fen; slough	
SWANG	swamp; greensward	
SWANK	brag; swagger	
SWAPE	handle; oar; sconce	
SWARD	turf; bacon rind	
SWARE	testified; deposed; cursed	
SWARF	to faint; to swoon; grit	
SWARM	throng; teem; cluster; bevy; (bees)	zo
SWART	swarthy; tawny; dusky	
SWASH	dash, splash, with flourish	pr
SWATH	swathe; the sweep of a scythe	
SWATS	new ale (Sc.)	
SWAZI	(Swaziland)	
SWEAL	scorch; melt; gutter; swale	
SWEAR	affirm; vow; vouch; blaspheme	
SWEAT	exude; ooze; perspire; (toil)	
SWEDE	a turnip	bt, ck
SWEEP	(chimney); brush; lottery	
SWEEP	a bend; scope; curve; oar	nt
SWEER	sweir; lazy; reluctant (Sc.)	
SWEET	luscious; honeyed; dulcet	
SWELL	expand; dilate; amplify; bulge; undulating sea	mu, nt

SWELT	to swelter (Spens.)	
SWEPT	brushed; scoured; scrubbed	
SWIFT	fleet; quick; sudden; prompt	zo
SWILL	boose; quaff; wash; rinse	
SWINE	pig	
SWING	sway; dangle; hang; turning movement; acrobatics (gymn.); ski-turn; pendulum; 1930s music; golf, cricket, strokes, boxing punch	mu, ga
SWINK	labour; to toil; to drudge	
SWIPE	smite; slog; steal; groom (horse-racing)	
SWIRE	a col; a hollow between 2 hills	go
SWIRL	whirl; gyrate; eddy	
SWISH	to birch; thrash; posh; fine	
SWISS	Helvetian	
SWITH	quickly; away! begone!	
SWOON	to faint	
SWOOP	rush; stoop; descent	
SWORD	hanger; rapier; cutlass; blade	
SWORE	sworn; testified	
SWORN	under oath; affirmed	
SWOTE	sweetly (Spens.)	
SWUNG	rocked; vacillated; dangled	
SYCEE	silver in small ingots (China)	
SYKER	surely (Spens.)	
SYLPH	an airy fairy; (Pope); Cupid's beloved	
SYLVA	silva; forest trees (Fr.)	
SYNOD	ecclesiastical Council	rl
SYREN	siren; enticer; hooter	
SYRUP	sirup; sirop; sweetened liquid	
SYTHE	scythe (obs.)	

T

TABAC	snuff-colour; (tobacco)	
TABBY	brindled; watered silk; a cat; earliest plain weave	tx, zo wv
TABES	emaciation; atrophy	md
TABID	consumptive; phthisical	md
TABLE	index; list; schedule; board; array of data	cp
TABOO	ban; bar; prohibit; interdict	
TABOR	camp; laager; small drum	mu
TACCA	tropical plant genus	bt
TACET	be silent!	mu
TACHE	a catch; stain; freckle; loop	
TACHY-	rapidity, speed (Gr.)	cf
TACIT	silent; implicit; inferred	
TACKY	viscous; gummy; sticky	
TAFFY	a Welshman; toffy; blarney	
TAFIA	Malay rum	
TAGAL	Filipino	
TAGMA	region of metameric animal	zo
TAHLI	Hindu gold ornament	
TAIGA	coniferous region (Siberia)	go
TAILS	evening dress (for men)	

TAINT	stain; tarnish; sully; defile	
TAIPO	taepo; vicious animal (NZ)	zo
TAKEN	seized; captured; won; assumed	
TAKER	grasper; acceptor	
TALBE	air/sea rescue system	ro
TALES	equals in kind; (jurors)	lw
TALLY	agree; correspond; match; count; score; (wag)	
TALLY	printout from adding machine	cp
TALMA	loose cloak	
TALON	claw; concave; moulding	
TALPA	the mole genus; a wen	zo, md
TALUK	Indian subdistrict	
TALUS	steep scree slope; knuckle bone, dice; earthwork; ankle bone	gl, md
TAMBU	tamboo; taboo; ostracism	
TAMED	docile; domesticated; curbed	
TAMER	subjugator; subduer	
TAMIL	a Dravidian language (Sri Lanka)	
TAMIN	glazed worsted stuff	
TAMIS	tammy; straining cloth	
TAMMY	tamis; a tam-o'-shanter	
TAMUS	black bryony	bt
TANGO	Argentine dance	mu
TANGY	piquant; sharp in taste	
TANIA	African farinaceous tuber	bt
TANKA	Canton boat population	
TANNA	tana; Indian police station	
TANSY	Easter cake; bitter herb	ck, bt
TANTO	so; so much	mu
TANTY	Hindu loom	
TAPAS	side-snacks in a bar (Sp.)	
TAPED	measured; sized up	
TAPEN	made of tape	
TAPER	wax-candle; slender and conical	
TAPET	tapestry; tapis	
TAPIR	related to pig (South Amer.)	zo
TAPIS	tapestry; carpet (Fr.)	
TAPIS	hidden; under consideration	
TAPPA	tapa; fibre for mats	bt
TARDO	slowly	mu
TARDY	late; sluggish; dilatory	
TARED	tare allowance recorded	
TARFA	tamarisk; (exudes manna)	bt
TARGE	target; shield or buckler	
TARIN	the siskin	zo
TAROC	pack of 78 cards used for	
TAROT	divination	
TARRY	stay; linger; sojourn; loiter	
TARSE	the tarsus; foot; ankle	md
TARSI	feet of insects	zo
TARUS	projection between roof surfaces	
TARVE	a curve; a bend	
TASSE	thigh armour	
TASTE	savour; smack; experience	
TASTO	It. finger board of stringed or keyboard instrument	mu
TASTY	piquant; savoury; appetising	
TATAR	Turkic native within USSR	

TATOU	tatu; peba; armadillo	zo
TAT-TA	goodbye; a stroll	
TATTA	Indian screen; of cuscus grass	bt
TATTY	tattered; worn out; shabby	
TAUNT	deride, revile; high-masted	nt
TAWED	treated with alum	
TAWER	a leather-dresser	
TAWIE	tame (Sc.)	
TAWNY	fulvous; fulvid; tanned	
TAWSE	taws; leather strap (Sc.)	
TAXED	burdened; accused	
TAXEL	N. American badger	zo
TAXER	inspector of taxes	
TAXIN	yew extract	bt
TAXIS	organism movement toward stimulus	cf
-TAXIS	tropism; species responses	
TAXUS	yew genus	bt
TAZZA	wine cup with shallow bowl	
TEACH	coach; edify; instruct	
TEASE	vex; annoy; plague; harass	
TEBAM	dais; rostrum in synagogue	ar, rl
TECHY	tetchy; touchy; testy; petulant	
TEDDY	a bear; Pooh's cousin	zo
TEENS	thirteen to nineteen	
TEENY	wee; tiny; minute	
TEETH	dentures; snowcomb (curling)	
TE-HEE	titter; snigger	
TEIAN	Ionian, (Anacreon)	
TEINT	colour; tinge; tint; hue	pt
TELAR	web-like; woven; spun	
TELEO-	far, distant, end (Gr.)	cf
TELEX	teleprinter universal system	tc
TELIC	final; conclusive	
TELUM	last abdominal somite in insects	zo
TEMPE	amusement park in Thessaly	
TEMPO	(cards); relative rapidity	mu
TEMPT	allure; lure; decoy; entice	
TEMSE	sieve; to sift	
TENCH	a fish	zo
TENET	rigid doctrine; dogma; belief	
TENIA	moulding on architrave	ar
TENNE	an orange-brown colour	
TENON	mortise projection	
TENOR	purport; trend; course; high male voice	mu
TENSE	taut; tight; intent; strained	
TENTH	a tithe; ordinal number	
TENTY	attentive; alert	
TEPAL	a perianth leaf	bt
TEPEE	tall Indian tent (N. Am.)	
TEPID	lukewarm; moderate	
TEPOR		
TERCE	about 42 gal (191 litres)	me
TEREK	a sandpiper	zo
TERES	a muscle	md
TERFA	edible fruit-body of terferia	bt
TERMA	terminal lamina of brain	md
TERNE	inferior tin-plate	
TERRA	earth	

154

TERRY	a fabric	**tx**
TERSE	abrupt	
TESLA	magnetic-flux density	**me**
TESTA	husk; integument	**bt**
TESTY	techy; fretful; irritable	
TETRA-	of four parts (Gr.)	**cf**
TEUCH	teugh; tough (Sc.)	
TEWEL	chimney flue	
THANE	} Anglo-Saxon title; lesser baron	
THEGN		
THANK	express gratitude	
THARM	twisted gut	
THAWY	inclined to thaw	
THECA	seed or spore case	**bt**
THEFT	larceny; robbery; pilfering	
THEIC	tea-pot devotee	
THEIN	tea	**bt**
THEIR	of them	
THEMA	subject for discussion	
THEME	melodic/topical motif repeated	**mu**
THERE	at that place	
THERM	thermal unit of gas	**me**
THESE	pl. of this	
THETA	a Greek letter	
THEWY	muscular; strong	
THICK	dense; solid; stupid; friendly	
THIEF	pickpocket; an Autolycus	
THIGH	upper part of leg	**pl**
THILK	the same	
THILL	shaft of a cart; fire-clay	
THINE	thy	
THING	object; article; entity	
THING	Scandinavian Parliament	
THINK	deem; muse; cogitate	
THIRD	ordinal number, 3rd; melodic interval	**mu**
THIRL	to cut through workings	**mn**
THIRL	a restriction; to pierce	
THOFT	a rowing bench	
THOLE	pin for an oar; to suffer	**nt**
THONG	lash of whip; strap	
THORN	prickle; spine	**bt**
THORP	homestead; hamlet; dorp	
THOSE	pl. of that	
THOTH	Egyptian god of wisdom	
THOUS	African jackal genus	**zo**
THOWL	thole; pin for an oar	**nt**
THRAP	to fasten	
THRAW	to wrench; to twist (Sc.)	
THREE	cardinal number; a leash	
THREW	flung; hurled; projected	
THRID	to thread	
THROB	beat; palpitate; quiver	
THROE	pang; agony; anguish	
THROW	cast; toss; fell; pitch; (dice); (fit); (party)	
THRUM	yarn; fringe; to strum	**mu**
THULE	Ultima Thule	
THUMB	finger clumsily	
THUMP	bang; whack; pommel	

THURL	thirl; passage in a mine	
THUYA	arbor vitae	**bt**
THYME	a genus of plants	**bt**
THYMO-	of emotion, temper, soul (Gr.)	**cf**
THYMY	fragrant	
TIARA	ornamental head-dress	
TIBBY	cat	**zo**
TIBET	heavy goat-hair fabric	**tx**
TIBIA	the large shinbone	**md**
TICAL	Siamese rupee	**nm**
TICED	enticed; decoyed	
TIDAL	of tides	
TIDDY	the wren	**zo**
TIDED	surmounted	
TIE-IN	tubular scaffolding, interior grip	
TIFFY	an artificer	
TIGER	diminutive groom; jungle cat	**zo**
TIGHT	taut; tense; close; compact; tipsy; scrum (rugby football)	
TIGNA	forward somersault (gymn.)	**ga**
TIKUL	Indian tree	**bt**
TILDE	diacritical mark;	
TILED	tessellated	
TILER	tyler; Masonic doorkeeper	
TILIA	lime-tree	**bt**
TILKA	Hindu caste mark	
TILTH	cultivation	
TIMED	measured, finite	
TIMER	time-fixed, -ing device	**cp**
TIMES	the newspaper	
TIMES	durations	
TIMID	shy; fearful; diffident	
TIMON	Athenian misanthrope	
TINEA	moth genus; ringworm	**zo, md**
TINED	pronged	
TINGE	hue; tint; stain; dye	
TINGI	Brazilian soap-tree	**bt**
TINNY	like tin; sharp in sound	
TINTY	crudely tinted	
TIPSY	tight; drunk; fuddled	
TIRAZ	Moorish silk fabric	**tx**
TIRED	weary; harassed; attired	
T'IRON	a webbed bar	
TISIC	consumptive (Shak.)	
TISRI	Hebrew month	
TITAN	giant; Cyclops; Goliath	
TITHE	a tenth; a tax	**rl**
TITLE	claim; right; (due); ownership; deeds; rank	**lw**
TITRE	quantity of antibody	**ba**
TITUP	tittup; skip; canter	
TIVER	ochre sheep dye	
TIZZY	a sixpence	**nm**
TOADY	a sycophant	
TOAST	scorch; health proposal	
TOBAS	S. American native race	
TOBIT	Apocryphal book	
TODAY	this day	
TODDE	28 lb weight (obs.)	**me**
TODDY	a cordial; mixed drink; night-cap	

TOE-IN	front-wheels adjustment	**au**
TOFFY	toffee; taffy	
TOGED	arrayed in a toga	
TOGUE	mackinaw; lake-trout	**zo**
TOILE	twill; linen-silk mixture	**tx**
TOILS	a snare	
TOISE	old French linear unit	**me**
TOKAY	Hungarian wine	
TOKEN	sign; symbol; mark; badge	
TOMAN	Persian gold coin	**nm**
TOMIN	a weight of 12 grains	**me**
TOMMY	Atkins; soldier; lever	**to**
TONAL	accented; harmonious notes	**mu**
TONDO	circular relief sculpture	
TONED	moderated; shaded; tinted	
TONER	organic dye	**pt**
TONGA	Eastern cart	
TONIC	key-note; bracing; (quinine);	
	(muscle) (spasm)	**mu, md**
TONKA	tree whose seeds contain coumarin	
		bt
TONUS	state of persistent excitation; minor	
	scale; Gregorian tone	**mu**
TOOTH	prong; fang; tusk (cog) (comb)	
	(dog-)	**bt, ar, pl**
TOPAU	rhinoceros-bird	**zo**
TOPAZ	a gem	**mn**
TOPEE	sun helmet	
TOPER	toss-pot; sot; tippler	
TOPET	crested titmouse	**zo**
TOPHI	ear cartilage nodules	**zo**
TOPIA	Roman mural decoration	
TOPIC	theme; subject; a remedy	**md**
TOPOS	cliché description	
TOQUE	woman's twisted silk turban	
TORAH	the Mosaic law	**lw**
TORAN	Buddhist porch	**rl**
TORCH	flambeau; link; fire-brand	
TORIC	type of lens	
TORII	Jap. gateway	**ar**
TORSE	heraldic wreath	**hd**
TORSK	a cod	**zo**
TORSO	body trunk	**md**
TORUS	an architectural moulding	**ar**
TOSSY	contemptuous	
TOSYL	toluene/sulphonyl compound	**ch**
TOTAL	all; sum; whole; gross	
TOTED	carried; borne; transported	
TOTEM	superstitious symbol	
TOUCH	handle; concern; effect	
TOUGH	tenacious; coriaceous	
TOUSE	tousle; haul; tease	
TOUSY	disarranged	
TOWED	hauled; dragged; tugged	
TOWEL	an altar cloth; (bathroom,	
	swimming)	**rl**
TOWER	soar; mount; turret	
TOWNY	a townsman	
TOXIC	toxicological	
TOXIN	poison; virus	**md**

TOYED	dallied; sported	
TOYER	trifler	
TRACE	vestige; trail; follow; remains;	
	copy; sketch; harness; figures	
	(skating); (elements)	**ch**
TRACK	spoor; pathway; race-course	
TRACT	region; pamphlet; homily; bundle of	
	nerve fibres	
TRADE	barter; traffic; craft	
TRAIK	to wander (Sc.)	
TRAIL	haul; tow; track; follow	
TRAIN	drill; school; retinue	
TRAIT	characteristic	
TRAMA	agaric-gill hyphae	**bt**
TRAMP	hike; trudge; vagrant; hobo	
TRANK	skin for glove cutting	
TRANT	to hawk; to peddle	
TRAPA	the water-chestnut	**bt**
TRAPE	traipse; tramp	
TRAPS	luggage	
TRASH	poor whites (USA); refuse;	
	worthless	
TRASS	volcanic earth	**mn**
TRAVE	beam; wooden frame	
TRAWL	a drag-net	
TREAD	trample; step; press	
TREAT	doctor; manage; deal	
TREED	cornered	
TREEN	wooden; collectors' term for	
	household objects	
TREND	tend; incline; lean	
TRESS	ringlet; lock of hair	
TREST	a beam; a stool (Sc.)	
TREWS	Scottish trousers	**tx**
TRIAC	silicon-controlled rectifier	**el, ps**
TRIAD	a trinity; 3-colour phosphor dot	
	pictures; chord	**tv, mu**
TRIAD	3 binary digits, symbols, data units	
		cp
TRIAL	test; ordeal; case	**lw**
TRIAS	sandstone	**mn**
TRIBE	clan; race; class; order	
TRICE	an instant; to haul	**nt**
TRICK	dupe; cheat; artifice; (cards); duty	
	turn; device	
TRIED	essayed; attempted	**lw**
TRIER	experimentalist	
TRIES	(Rugby football, 3 or 4 points)	**ga**
TRILL	warble; quaver; shake	**mu**
TRINE	triple; threefold; a triad; astrology	
		as
TRINE	favourable planet aspect	**as**
TRIOR	an examiner	**lw**
TRIPE	stomach offal; nonsense	**ck**
TRIST	sorrowful; sad	
TRITE	hackneyed; obvious; worn	
TROCO	a ball game	**ga**
TROIC	Trojan	
TROKE	exchange; small wares (Sc.)	
TROLL	to fish; sing; cave-elf	

TRONA	Egyptian soda	**mn**
TRONC	distribution of pooled tips	
TRONE	steelyard; a drain	**me**
TROOP	throng; crowd; cluster	
TROPE	a metaphor; figure of speech; 12	
	note technique	**mu**
TROTH	to plight; confidence; faith	
TROUT	fish of Salmo genus	**zo**
TROVE	treasure trove	
TRUCE	lull; respite; armistice	
TRUCK	a wheel; barter; a vehicle	
TRUCK	wagon; mast-head	**nt**
TRUER	more worthy of belief	
TRULL	vagrant; a drab	
TRULY	verily; exactly; veritably	
TRUMP	(the last trump); to ruff; leading suit	
	(cards) (bridge)	**ga**
TRUMP	a trumpet; Jew's harp	**mu**
TRUNK	torso; butt; stem; saratoga	
TRUNK	highway, interface channel	**cp**
TRUSS	bind; fasten; framework of timbers	
		md, ar
TRUST	credit; reliance; merger	
TRUTH	probity; fact; honesty; reality;	
	(Boolean)	**ma**
TRYMA	a stone fruit; a drupe	**bt**
TRY-ON	a bluff	
TRYST	'rendezvous; (Lutheran carol)	**mu, rl**
TSUBA	Japanese sword hilt	
TSUNG	ritual jade (China)	**rl**
TUBAL	tubar; tubular; hollow	
TUBBY	fat; obese; dull	
TUBED	piped	
TUBER	bulbous growth	**bt**
TUCAN	Mexican pouched rat	**zo**
TUCUM	S. American palm	**bt**
TUDEH	political party (Iran)	
TUDOR	a royal house	
TUFTY	feathery	
TUILE	tuille; armour plates	
TUISM	a curious theory	
TULIP	showy flower	**bt**
TULLE	a delicate fabric; tuille	**tx**
TUMBA	instrument S. Domingo	**mu**
TUMID	swollen; bombastic	
TUMPY	lumpy; uneven	
TUNED	attuned; harmonized; adapted	
TUNER	sound adjuster; channel selector	
		mu, ro, tv
TUNIC	surcoat; a membrane	**md**
TUNNY	large fish, mackerel type	**zo**
TUQUE	toque; Canadian knitted cap	
TURBA	chorus of the people in opera	**mu**
TURBO	whelk and winkle genus	**zo**
TURBO-	jet engine	**ae**
TURCO	Ottoman soldier	
TURFY	swardy; grassy; cespitose	
TURNS	rotation; artistes' acts; pirouettes;	
	virtuoso tricks (ice skating)	
	(water-skiing)	

TURPS	turpentine	
TUSKS	see **TUSSES**; elephants' long	
	teeth; (ivory)	**zo**
TUSKY	with long teeth	
TUSSE	wall-face projecting stone	**bd**
TUTOR	coach; instruct; guardian	
TUTSI	native of Burundi (Africa)	
TUTTI	all in (It.)	**mu**
TUTTY	impure oxide of zinc	**ch**
TUZZY	tuft; tuffet; cluster	
TWAIN	a couple; brace; pair	
TWAIT	species of shad	**zo**
TWANG	tang; flavour	
TWANK	twang; a nasal note	**mu**
TWEAK	pinch; twist; twitch	
TWEED	twilled cloth	**tx, wv**
TWEEN	between; twixt	
TWEER	twier; blast-furnace	
TWERE	it were	
TWERP	nasty nitwit	
TWICE	twofold; doubly; encore	
TWILL }		
TWEEL }	woven fabric	**tx, wv**
TWILT	a quilt (Sc.)	
TWINE	entwine; wind; cord; string	
TWINK	twinkle; twitter; chirp	
TWIRE	to gleam; twist; twirl	
TWIRK	a twitch (Sc.)	
TWIRL	whirl; rotate; revolve	
TWIST	writhe; hunger; (tobacco)	
TWITE	mountain linnet	**zo**
TWIXT	betwixt; between	
TWO-ON	doing 2 jobs at once	**pr**
TWO-UP	printing, processing twin series	**pr**
TWYER	tweer; blast furnace; jet	
TYCHE	Greek goddess of fortune	
TYING	fastening; shackling	
TYLER	tiler; Masonic doorkeeper	
TYLER	tight-line gorge system	**fr**
TYPAL	typical; representative	
TYPED	typewritten; given a classification	
		pr
TYPHA	bulrush	**bt**
TYPIC	emblematic; symbolic	
TYRED	wheeled, pneumatic	
TYTHE	tithe; a tenth; church tax	**rl**

U

U-BOAT	a submarine	**nt**
UDDER	mammary gland	**zo**
UDEMA	galley (Swedish)	**nt**
U-DUCT	gas heater ventilator	**bd**
UGRIC	Finns, Magyars, Turks, etc.	
UHLAN	Prussian cavalryman	
UHURU	freedom (Swahili)	
UKASE	Russian decree	
ULCER	open sore	**md**
ULEMA	Turkish hierarchy	

ULMIC	(elm exudations)	**bt**
ULMIN	humus; a brown pigment	
ULMUS	elm genus	**bt**
ULNAD	toward the ulna	**md**
ULNAR	(forearm bone)	**md**
ULOID	like a scar	**md**
-ULOUS	of tendency toward	**cf**
ULTOR	anode	**el**
ULTRA	extreme	
-ULTRA	of extreme, beyond excessive	**cf**
UMBEL	inflorescent flower	**bt**
UMBER	brown pigment	
UMBRA	a shadow; (total solar eclipse)	**as**
UMBRE	the grayling	**zo**
UMIAK	Eskimo boat	**nt**
UMWEG	detour to goal, round about (Ger.)	**pc**
UNAPT	inept; irrelevant	
UNARM	disarm	
UNARY	consisting of 1 component; monadic operation	**ch, cp**
UNBAR	open; permit	
UNBAY	to open up	
UNBED	arouse	
UNBID	uninvited; spontaneous	
UNBIT	not bitten	
UNBOW	to unbend	**ar**
UNBOX	uncase; unpack	
UNCAP	unhat; uncover; open	
UNCLE	pawnbroker; relation	
UNCLE	oom; Sam; Tom; Remus	
UNCUS	hook or claw	**zo**
UNCUT	untrimmed; book before guillotine process	
UNDAM	release	
UNDER	below; lower: subject to	
UNDID	untied; nullified	
UNDUE	excessive; inordinate	
UNFIT	unqualified; improper	
UNFIX	detach; undo; loosen	
UNGUM	unstick	
UNHAT	uncover; uncap	
UNIAT	Russian Christian	**rl**
UNIFY	unite; combine	
UNION	coalition; guild; league; joint organisation; junction of pipes; marital	**pb, lw**
UNITE	join; concert; bind	
UNITY	concord; harmony; accord	
UNKED	unkid; strange; ugly	
UNLAP	unfold	
UNLAY	untwist; unravel	
UNLED	without guidance	
UNLET	vacant; tenantless	
UNMAN	dishearten; unnerve	
UNMEW	release from confinement	
UNNUN	unfrock	
UNODE	a geometric conception	**ma**
UNOIL	free from oil	
UNPAY	make undone	
UNPEN	release	
UNRIG	dismantle	
UNRIP	rip open	
UNSAY	retract; disavow	
UNSET	unmounted; runny; sticky; for computers as reset	**cp**
UNSEX	geld; castrate; spay	**md, vt**
UNSON	disinherit	
UNTAX	remove a tax	
UNTIE	undo; unbind; unknot	
UNTIL	till; to such time as	
UNTIN	uncan	
UNWEB	unweave; unravel	
UNWED	unmarried	
UNZIP	undo patent fastening	
UP-BOW	violin bow position in play	**mu**
UP-END	tilt; place in vertical position	
UPHER	rough scaffolding pole	**bd**
UPLAY	to hoard	
UPPER	superior; higher; part of shoe above sole; (-works of ship)	**nt**
UPRUN	run up; ascend	
UPSEE	after the manner of	
UPSET	capsize; overturn; disconcert; spill; tear in wood fibre; (stomach)	**md**
UPUPA	hoopoe genus	**zo**
URATE	(uric acid)	**ch**
URBAN	of the city	
UREDO	fungus genus	**bt**
UREIC	pertaining to urea	
URENA	Indian mallow	**bt**
URGED	pleaded; drove; impelled	
URGER	inciter; prompter; agitator	
URIAL	Asiatic wild sheep	**zo**
URILE	cormorant	**zo**
URINE	liquid body waste	**md**
URITE	tail of insect	**zo**
URMAN	Siberian forest land	**go**
URNAL	urn-shaped	
URNED	(cremated)	
URSON	Canadian porcupine	**zo**
URSUS	the bear genus	**zo**
URUBU	American turkey-buzzard	**zo**
URVED	curved upward	
USAGE	habit; wont; custom	
USHAS	Hindu aurora	
USHER	herald; introduce; precede; court official	**lw**
USING	applying; employing	
USUAL	normal; ordinary; habitual	
USURP	arrogate; assume; seize	
USURY	usure; exorbitant; interest	
UTTER	declare; enunciate; total	
UVALA	depression in karst area (Serbo-Croat)	**gl, go**
UVULA	(soft palate)	**md**
UZBEG	} Turkish Tatar	
UZBEK		

V

VAGAL	of the vagus nerves	
VAGUE	dim; indistinct; indefinite	
VAGUS	a cranial nerve	md
VAILS	tip; gratuity; backsheesh	
VAIRE }	charged with heraldic fur	hd
VAIRY }		
VAKIL	Indian attorney	lw
VALED	lowered; receded	
VALES	vails; pourboire; douceur	
VALET	gentleman's gentleman	
VALID	cogent; substantial; strong	
VALSE	waltz; dance	mu
VALUE	worth; price; cost; utility	
VALVE	electron tube; regulator device; (heart); (horn); steam	el, pl, mu, rw
VAMPS	short hose	
VANED	having vanes or blades	
VANIR	three Norse deities	
VAPID	insipid; feeble; jejune	
VAPOR	vapour; miasma; steam	
VAREC	seaweed; kelp	bt
VARIA	miscellany	
VARIX	uneven dilation	md
VARUS	pigeon-toed	
VARVE	clay, silt sediments in lake or sea	gl, go
VASAL	(blood-vessel)	md
VASTY	spacious; immense; boundless	
VATIC	prophetic; oracular	
VAULT	leap; cell; tomb; crypt	
VAUNT	boast; exult; swagger	
VEALY	calflike; immature	
VEDAS	Hindu sacred writings	rl
VEDIC	according to the Vedas	
VEERY	American thrush	zo
VEGAN	total vegetarian	
VEHME	German secret society	
VEINY	full of veins	
VELAR	cupola or dome	ar
VELDT	grass lands (S. Africa)	
VELIA	water-bugs	zo
VELUM	soft palate	md
VENAL	mercenary; corrupt; sordid	
VENEW }	a thrust or hit in fencing	ga
VENEY }		
VENGE	avenge (Shak.)	
VENOM	virus; poison; rancour; gall	
VENUE	location of an event	
VENUS	Aphrodite	
VEREY	signal light	
VERGE	edge; staff; mace; margin (punched card)	cp, rl
VERSE	poetry; stanza; stich; stave	
VERSO	left-hand page	pr
VERST	Russian; ⅔ of a mile (1 km)	me
VERTU	virtu; rarity in art	

VERVE	energy; vigour; inspiration	
VESPA	wasp genus	zo
VESTA	goddess of the hearth	
VESTA	match; lucifer; taper	
VETCH	ers; the tare	bt
VEXED	troubled; bothered; piqued	
VEXER	provoker; annoyer	
VEXIL	a banner; a petal	bt
VIAND	food	
VIBEX	a blood spot	md
VICAR	parish parson	rl
VIDEO	recorded television film; visual display unit	cp
VIEWY	visionary; speculative	
VIFDA	vivda; dried meat	ck
VIGIA	charted rock (Sp.)	
VIGIL	watch; wake; eve	
VILER	more degraded	
VILLA	country residence (Roman)	ar
VILLI	small fibres	md, bt
VIMEN	slender shoot	bt
VINCA	periwinkle	bt
VINED	with tendrils	
VINIC	alcoholic	
VINYL	plastic fibre	
VIOLA	plant genus; stringed instrument	bt, mu
VIPER	adder; asp	zo
VIREO	American song-birds	zo
VIRGO	(Zodiac); a constellation; the Maiden	as
VIRID	green	
VIRTU	vertu; rarity in art	
VIRUS	poison; venom; toxin	md
VIRUS	transmitter of infection	md
VISIE	a searching glance (Sc.)	
VISIT	frequent; call; drop in	
VISON	American mink	zo
VISOR }	movable part of a helmet; a mask	
VIZOR }		
VISTA	view; scene; prospect	
VITAL	essential; animate; living	
VITEX	verbena	bt
VITIS	the vine	bt
VITTA	a headband; garland	
VITTA	stripe; oil cavity	bt
VIURE	heraldic ribbon (Fr.)	hd
VIVAT	(applause)	
VIVDA	vifda; dried meat	ck
VIVES	a disease of horses	vt
VIVID	intense; brilliant; graphic	
VIZEN	scold; shrew; termagant	zo
VIZIR	vizier; vezir; minister (Ottoman)	
VLACH	a Wallachian; (Romanian)	
VOCAL	articulate	
VODAS	echo-suppression device	tc
VODER	synthetic-speech device	ac
VODKA	Russian drink	
VOGAD	telephony	
VOGIE	vain; merry (Sc.)	

VOGUE	fashion; mode; practice	
VOICE	express; declare; utter; sound production; (vocal)	**mu**
VOICE	human speech as electrical signals	**tc**
VOIDS	ratio of solids to spaces occupied by air or water	
VOILE	gauzy material	**tx**
VOLAR	(palm of the hand)	**md**
VOLEE	rapid phrase	**mu**
VOLET	part of triptych	
VOLTA	an old dance; repeat	**mu**
VOLTE	old dances; turns	
VOLTE	full turn on the haunches (dressage) (horsemanship)	
VOLTI	turn over	**mu**
VOLVA	hypha sheath in agarics	
VOLVE	ponder; turn over (obs.)	
VOMER	ploughshare; nose-bone	**md**
VOMIT	spew; eject; disgorge	
VOTED	polled; balloted	
VOTER	elector	
VOUCH	guarantee; affirm; aver	
VOWED	swore; pledged; dedicated	
VOWEL	open speech sound	
VOWER	pledger; promiser; swearer	
VROUW	woman; wife (Dutch)	
VUGGY	full of cavities	
VULGO	vernacular; popular style	
VULVA	female genital; orifice	**pl**
VUOTA	} pause, interval (It.)	**mu**
VUOTO		
VYING	striving; competing	

W

WACKE	basalt; trap-rock	**mn**
WADDY	Australian war club	
WADED	forded	
WADER	long-legged bird	**zo**
WADEX	word/author index for computers	
WAFER	crisp cake	**ck**
WAGED	pledged; conducted; salaried	
WAGEL	black gull	**zo**
WAGER	bet; hazard; stake; gamble	
WAGES	stipend; remuneration	
WAGON	wain; lorry; truck	
WAHOO	cascara sagrada	**md, bt**
WAIST	bodice; corsage	
WAITS	Yule minstrels	
WAIVE	remit; forego; relinquish	
WAKED	kept vigil; stimulated	
WAKEN	awaken; excite; animate	
WALAN	amboyna tree	**bt**
WALAP	outrigger sail canoe (S. Pacific)	**nt**
WALED	striped	
WALER	Australian horse	**zo**
WALTY	unstable	**nt**
WALTZ	valse; dance	**mu**

WANDY	wandlike; flexible	
WANED	ebbed; decreased; declined	
WANLY	sickly; languidly	
WANTY	a loading strap	
WARES	merchandise; commodities	
WARTY	excrescent	
WASHY	watery; thin; feeble	
WASTE	dissipate; squander; fritter; industrial rubbish; (-land)	
WATCH	guard; tend; mark	**nt**
WATER	irrigate; moisten; sprinkle	
WAVED	fluctuated; brandished	
WAVER	sway; totter; vacillate	
WAVEY	the snow-goose	
WAXED	cered; grew; increased	
WAXEN	ceruminous	
WEALD	wold; woodland	**fr, go**
WEARY	jaded; spent; fatigue; tire	
WEAVE	plait; mat; entwine; interlace	**wv**
WEAVE	figure of 8 movement (basketball) (lacrosse) (football)	**ga**
WEBBY	filmy; reticulated	
WEBER	magnetic flux	**me**
WEDGE	coign; a scotch; golf club; blockers (Am. football) (gap forcer)	**ga**
WEEDS	widow's mourning apparel	
WEEDY	weak and lanky	**bt**
WEELY	wicker fish trap	
WEEPY	lacrimose; oozy	
WEIGH	balance; ponder; (anchor)	**nt**
WEIRD	eerie; uncanny; supernatural	
WEISM	excessive use of 'we'	
WELCH	Welsh; Cymric	
WELSH	Cymric; abscond	
WENCH	maid; damsel	
WENNY	(sebaceous cyst)	**md**
WERSH	tasteless; unsalted (Sc.)	
WHACK	thwack; defeat; smite	
WHALE	the orc; a cetacean	**zo**
WHALL	wall-eye	
WHAME	the burrel-fly	**zo**
WHANG	bang; whack; leather thong	
WHARE	Maori hut	
WHARF	quay; dock; pier	
WHAUP	curlew	**zo**
WHEAL	weal; bruise mark after blow	**pl**
WHEAL	mine (Cornish)	**mn**
WHEAT	a cereal	**bt**
WHEEL	turn; revolve; whirl; leg throw (judo) (drill)	**ga**
WHEEN	a small quantity (Sc.)	
WHEFT	a knotted flag	
WHELK	a gasteropod	**zo**
WHELM	overwhelm	
WHELP	puppy; cub; pup; to litter	**zo**
WHERE	the place concerned	
WHICH	the item concerned	
WHIFF	puff; outrigger boat; strike-out (baseball); smell; cigarette	**nt, ga**
WHIFT	a breath; a snatch; glimpse	

WHILE	pass the time	
WHILK	the scoter; sea duck	zo
WHINE	whimper; snivel; cry	
WHIPT	scourged; thrashed	
WHIRL	twirl; spin; gyrate; eddy	
WHISK	a brush; stir; hasten; rush	
WHIST	keep silence; (cards)	ga
WHITE	pale; wan; pallid; chalky	
WHIZZ	whiz; rush past; flash by; of fireworks (-king)	
WHOLE	entire; intact; total	
WHOOP	a shout of joy	
WHOOT	hoot	
WHORL	convolution; spiral; medieval furniture motif	
WHORT	whurt; whortleberry	bt
WHOSE	the owner of item concerned	
WHOSO	he who	
WICKY	mountain ash	bt
WIDDY	widow; withy; withe	bt
WIDEN	extend; enlarge	
WIDER	broader; more remote	
WIDOW	to bereave; (cards)	
WIDTH	span; amplitude; beam	
WIELD	control; exert; ply; brandish	
WIERY	wet; moist; miry (obs.)	
WIGAN	stiff canvas	tx
WIGHT	a creature; strong; nimble	
WILED	beguiled; hoaxed; cheated	
WILLY	wool cleaning machine	
WINCE	flinch; blench; shrink	
WINCH	hoisting machine	
WINDY	stormy; breezy; pneumatic (Sc.); afraid	
WINED	drank wine	
WINGS	boundary players (football) (bowls) (flying) (theatre)	ga
WINGY	rapid	
WINZE	ventilating shaft; a curse	
WIPED	rubbed; mopped; cleansed	
WIPER	mechanical device	
WIRED	telegraphed; snared	
WISER	sager; more expedient	
WISPY	flocculent; nebulous	
WITAN	Witenagemot (Anglo-Saxon); moot; council	
WITCH	hag; crone; sibyl	
WITHE	willow twig	bt
WITHY	species of willow	bt
WITTY	droll; facetious; humorous	
WIVES	spouses	
WIZEN	shrivelled; dried up	
WODEN	Odin; Wotan	rl
WOMAN	female human	
WOMBY	capacious (Shak.)	
WOMEN	pl. of woman	
WONGA	Australian pigeon	zo
WOODS	wooden-head clubs (golf)	
WOODY	sylvan; ligneous	
WOOED	courted	

WOOER	a lover; a swain	
WOOFS	variation in handicapping (golf)	ga
WOOFY	dense; close in texture	
WOOLD	to twist; dyer's weed	bt
WOONT	the mole	zo
WOOTZ	Bengal steel	
WORDY	verbose; prolix; garrulous	
WORLD	universe; globe; earth	
WORMY	vermigerous	zo
WORRY	fret; chafe; fidget; badger	
WORSE	comparative of bad	
WORST	best; defeat; conquer	
WORTH	value; cost; merit; desert	
WOTAN	Odin; Woden	rl
WOULD	conditional auxil. verb	
WOUND	harm; hurt; lacerate	
WOVEN	plaited; interlaced	
WRACK	ruin; seaweed	bt
WRANG	wrung; twisted and squeezed	
WRAPT	wrapped; hidden; enveloped	
WRATH	ire; rage; fury; passion	
WRAUL	wrawl; to caterwaul	
WREAK	avenge; inflict; indulge	
WRECK	ruin; blight; shatter	
WREST	twist; wrench; strain	
WRICK	to sprain	
WRIER	more contorted	
WRING	extort; wrest; writhe	
WRIST	hand/arm joint	
WRITE	indite; scrawl; scribble; (pen); transcribe data	cp
WRONG	injure; falsify; error; tort	
WROTE	inscribed; penned; engrossed	
WROTH	wrathful, angry; furious	
WRUNG	tormented; racked	
WRYLY	distorted; askew	
WYTHE	(with) (withier) willow twig	bt

X

XEBEC	Algerian pirate ship	nt
XENIA	pollen effect on young plant	bt
XENON	a gas	ch
XERIC	adapted to dry conditions	ec
X-MARK	face-mark	cr
X-RING	innermost target (shooting)	
X-UNIT	x-ray unit	md
XYLEM	woody tissue	
XYLIC	benzoic acid	ch
XYLOL	aromatic fluid	
XYLYL	xylene	ch

Y

YACCA	Jamaican tree	bt
YACHT	pleasure ship	nt
YACOU	guan; a game bird	zo
YAGER	Jaeger; light infantry	

YAGLI	traditional oiled wrestling (Turkey)	
		ga
YAHOO	hooligan	
YAMEN	} mandarin's house; Chinese	
YAMUN	} office	
YAPOK	S. American water-opossum	**zo**
YAPON	evergreen shrub; cassine	**bt**
YAQUI	Mexican Indians	
YASHT	Zend-Avesta prayer book	**rl**
YAWED	slithered in rough sea	**nt**
YEARN	crave; hanker; desire	
YEAST	leaven; balm; ferment	
YELEK	a long vest (Turk.)	
YERBA	Paraguay tea	**bt**
YESTY	yeasty	
YEWEN	made of yew	**bt**
YEXED	hiccupped	
YIELD	submit; render; supply	
YODEL	yodle; Tyrolese singing	
YOGIN	Hindu philosopher	
YOICK	to encourage	
YOJAN	about 5 miles (8 km) (E. Ind.)	**me**
YOKED	coupled; linked; paired	
YOKEL	rustic; churl; clodhopper	
YOLKY	egg-yolk consistency	
YORKY	slate with curved cleave	
YOSHI	order to continue judo contest	
YOUNG	boyish; juvenile; recent	
YOURS	of you	
YOUTH	lad; stripling; heyday	
YRNEH	unit of reciprocal inductance	**el, me**
YUCCA	lily genus	**bt**
YUCKY	itchy	
YULAN	Chinese magnolia	**bt**
YULOH	aft-oar for sculling	**nt**

Z

ZABRA	Spanish coasting vessel	**nt**
ZAMBO	cross-bred Indian	
ZAMIA	a palm genus	**bt**
ZANJE	irrigation canal (S. Amer.)	
ZANTE	satin-wood	**bt**
ZARUG	} Aden dhow	
ZARUK	}	**nt**
ZAYAT	Burmese inn	

ZEBEC	xebec; Algerian ship	**nt**
ZEBRA	an ungulate	**zo**
ZEBUS	Abyssinian tsetse-fly	**zo**
ZEINE	the gluten of maize	**bt**
ZEMNI	the blind mole-rat	**zo**
ZENER	semi-conductor current	
ZERDA	African fox	**zo**
ZHOBO	} hybrid, yak and cow	
ZHOMO	}	
ZIARA	Moslem shrine	**rl**
ZIBET	Asiatic civet	**zo**
ZIMBA	Am. Indian and Eskimo game	**ga**
ZIMBI	cowry used as money	**zo**
ZINCO	zincograph	
ZINKE	old type of cornet	**mu**
ZINKY	zincy; partly zinc	
ZIZEL	marmot; ground-squirrel	**zo**
ZLOTY	Polish money	**nm**
ZOAEA	} larval crustacean	
ZOOEA	}	**zo**
ZOCCO	}	
ZOCLE	} square base	
ZOEAL	early crustacean life	**zo**
ZOFRA	Moorish carpet	
ZOGAN	Japanese inlay work	
ZOHAR	sacred Jewish book	**rl**
ZOISM	theory of life origin	
ZOIST	a believer in zoism	
ZONAL	}	
ZONAR	}	
ZONIC	} like a girdle; regional	
ZONES	}	
ZONDA	the dry wind of the Andes	
ZONES	regions, climates, 5 belts of earth	
		go
ZOOID	polyp; polypide	**zo**
ZOOKS	gadzooks; exclamation	
ZOPPA	} limping syncopation	
ZOPPO	}	**mu**
ZORIL	African skunk	**zo**
ZORRA	American skunk	**zo**
ZORRO	S. American fox-wolf	**zo**
ZUPAN	Serbian rural council	
ZYGAL	like an 'H'	
ZYGON	connecting bar	
ZYMIC	relating to fermentation	
ZYMIN	ex-enzyme	**zo**

A

ABACOT	bycoket; hat of state (15th cent.)	
ABACUS	a counting device; slabstone on capital	**ar**
ABALYN	synthetic resin; lacquer	
ABASED	humbled; debased; sunk	
ABASIA	inco-ordination in walking	**md**
ABATED	mitigated; subsided	
ABATER	reducer; assuager	
ABATIS	abattis; obstacles	
ABATTE	heavy meat-flattening knife	**ck**
ABBACY	office of abbot	**rl**
ABBATE	a title	**rl**
ABBESS	head of nuns' abbey	**rl**
ABDALS	Moslem fanatics (Pers.)	
ABDEST	Mohammedan rite	
ABDIEL	the faithful seraph	
ABDUCE	separate; retract	
ABDUCT	remove; kidnap	
ABIDED	abode; sojourned; tarried	
ABIDER	dweller; settler	
ABIENT	avoidance reflex	**pc**
ABJECT	servile; base; ignoble	
ABJURE	renounce; recant; repudiate	
ABKARI	} Persian excise duty on wine	
ABKARY	}	
ABLAUT	(vowel change)	
ABLAZE	flaming; excited	
ABLEST	most competent; cleverest	
ABLINS	perhaps	
ABLOOM	thriving; flowering	**bt**
ABLUSH	blushing; flushing	
ABOARD	afloat; inside	**nt**
ABORAL	remote from the mouth	**pl**
ABOUND	flow; team; swarm	
ABRADE	scrape; grate	
ABRAYD	to awaken (Spens.)	
ABROAD	apart; far; widely	
ABROOK	endure	
ABRUPT	steep; hasty; brusque; curt	
ABSEIL	rapid twin rope descent technique	**mo**
ABSENT	away; left; distracted	
ABSORB	engulf; consume; swallow	
ABSURD	irrational; asinine	
ABULIA	atrophy of reasoning	**md, pc**
ABUSED	reviled; violated; traduced	
ABUSER	reviler; slanderer	
ACACIA	flowering shrub	**bt**
ACACIO	acajou; cashew nut	**bt**
ACADIA	Nova Scotia	
ACAJOU	gum; acacio	**bt**
ACARUS	insect genus	**zo**
ACATES	food	**ck**
ACCEDE	assent; agree; comply	
ACCEND	kindle (obs.)	
ACCENT	tone; stress; cadence	
ACCEPT	take; receive; admit	

ACCESS	entry; approach; retrieval	**cp**
ACCITE	to cite	**·**
ACCLOY	to cloy; satiate; surfeit	
ACCOIL	to collect (Spens.)	
ACCORD	concede; deign; tally	
ACCOST	confront; hail; greet	
ACCOUB	edible thistle	**ck**
ACCREW	} to result in; inure; proceed; accumulate	
ACCRUE	}	
ACCUSE	charge; cite; censure	
ACEDIA	torpor; fish	**md, zo**
ACERIC	(maple)	**bt**
ACETAL	plastic; cosmetic base	**:ch**
ACETIC	an acid in olive oil	**ch, ck**
ACETYL	radical of acetic acid	**ch**
ACHENE	seeded fruit	**bt**
ACHING	continued pain; sorrowing	
ACHIRA	edible canna; ginger, america herbs	**ck, bt**
ACHTEL	eighth note; quaver	**mu**
ACICLE	bristle; sharp crystal	**bt, mn**
ACIDIC	containing acid	**ch**
ACINUS	berry	**bt**
ACK-ACK	anti-aircraft	
ACLIDE	spiked club	
ACMITE	pyroxene rock	**mn**
ACNODE	in double point tangets	**ma**
ACOPIC	curative of fatigue	**md**
ACORIA	morbid appetite for food	**md**
ACORUS	sweet flag; calamus root	**bt**
ACQUIT	absolve; release; exonerate	
ACRACY	anarchy	
ACRISY	poor judgment	
ACRITA	sponges	**zo**
ACROSS	athwart; transversely	
ACTING	performing; pretending	
ACTION	deed; feat; gesture; (angling) function; momentum	**md, lw, ps**
ACTIVE	operational; alert; busy	
ACTUAL	real; true; absolute; definite	**cp**
ACUATE	pointed	
ACUITY	sharpness (perception)	
ACULEI	prickles; thorns	**bt, zo**
ACUMEN	keenness of perception	
ADAGIO	leisurely	**mu**
ADAMIC	pertaining to Adam	
ADDEEM	judge	
ADDEND	an increase	**cp, ma**
ADDICT	accustom; habituate; devote	
ADDING	totting; summing	
ADDLED	deranged; rotten	
ADDUCE	allege; assign; advance; cite	
ADDUCT	product of molecular reaction	**ch**
ADENIA	enlargement of glands	**md**
ADHERE	cohere; cling; cleave	
ADIENT	tending to expose to stimulus	
ADIEUS	} farewells	
ADIEUX	}	
ADIPIC	fatty; adipose	

163

ADJECT	to add to	
ADJOIN	abut; annex; touch; unite	
ADJURE	exhort; urge; beg; pray	
ADJUST	arrange; trim; rectify; fit	
ADMASS	common consumers; the masses	
ADMIRE	esteem; prize; revere; respect	
ADNATE	joined to another organ	
ADNEXA	appendages; close structures	zo
ADNOUN	an adjective	
ADONAI	lord (Hebrew)	
ADONIC	species of short verse	
ADONIS	bird's eye; pheasant's eye	bt
ADONIS	youth loved by Venus	
ADOORS	at the door	
ADORAL	adjacent to the mouth	zo
ADORED	worshipped; idolized; beloved	
ADORER	admirer; lover; venerator	
ADREAD	fearful; apprehensive	
ADRENO-	of adrenalin	cf
ADRIFT	afloat; distracted; loose	
ADROIT	expert; skilful; masterly	
ADSORB	to condense a gas	
ADVENE	accede	
ADVENT	arrival; approach; coming	rl
ADVERT	to notice; to regard	
ADVICE	counsel; warning; tidings; rede	
ADVIEW	to view (Spens.)	
ADVISE	urge; recommend; inform	
ADVISO	news; intelligence	
ADYTUM	chancel	rl
ADZUKI	red Japanese bean	ck
AECIAL	spore-producing part of fungi	bt
AEDILE	Roman magistrate	
AENEID	epic poem	
AEOLIC	Greek dialect	
AEOLUS	god of the winds	
AERATE	expose to air action	
AERIAL	etherial; empyreal; airy; transits	
	(leaps); antenna	ro tv
AERIFY	aerate	
AEROBE	an organic growth	md
AEROSE	coppery; brassy	
AERUGO	verdigris; patina; rust	
AETHER	ether	ch
AFEARD	affrighted	
AFFAIR	incident; concern; skirmish	
AFFEAR	to terrify	
AFFECT	assume; feign; influence; mood	
AFFEER	settle a price	lw
AFFINE	similar curves of variables	ma
AFFIRM	vouch; ratify; endorse; allege	
AFFLUX	to flow	
AFFORD	produce; impart; confer; spare	
AFFRAY	onset; brawl; strife; fracas	
AFFRET	effray; broil; startle; frighten	
AFFUSE	sprinkle; pour upon	
AFGHAN	of Afghanistan	
AFIELD	in the open; away from base	
AFLAME	blazing; afire	
AFLOAT	at sea; unfixed	

AFOCAL	without focal length	pg
AFRAID	timid; fearful; anxious	
A-FRAME	two sloping legs joined at top	ce
AFREET	evil spirit (Arab.)	
AFRESH	anew; again	
AFRIDI	(Afghan.)	
AFRONT	in front (obs.)	
AFTERS	sweet or dessert course	ck
AGALMA	impression of a seal	
AGAMAE	cryptogamic plants	bt
AGAMIC	asexual	
AGARIC	fungus; mushroom	bt
AGAZED	thunder-struck; amazed	
AGEING	maturing; mellowing (process)	
AGENCY	intervention; mediation	
AGENDA	items of business	
AGHAST	appalled; astounded	
AGNAIL	a whitlow	md
AGNAME	nickname	
AGNATE	(relationship) akin; allied	
AGNISE	acknowledge; confess	
AGNOSY	ignorance	
AGOING	current; topical	
AGONIC	zero declination	
AGOUTA	Haitian rat	zo
AGOUTI	} guinea-pig; S. American	
AGOUTY	} rodent	zo
AGRAFA	Greek cheese	ck
AGRAIL	narrow-gauge railway	
AGREED	reconciled; concerted; tallied	
AGUISE	to dress (Spens.)	
AGUISH	shivering; chilly	md
AHIMSA	sacredness of life (Hindu, Jain)	
AIDANT	assisting	
AIDFUL	helpful; co-operative	
AIDING	assisting; succouring	
AIGLET	aglet; pendant; young eagle	zo
AIGRET	aigrette; plume	
AIKIDO	ancient Japanese martial art	
AILING	sick; unwell; indisposed	
AIMING	pointing; endeavouring	
AINHUM	chronic Negro disease causing	
	digit loss	
AIR-ACE	super-airman	
AIR-BED	inflated mattress	
AIRDOX	coal-mining process using air	
AIR-DRY	dry to parity with atmosphere	
AIR-GUN	air-operated weapon	
AIRILY	buoyantly; gaily	
AIRING	stroll; ventilation	
AIR-LOG	linear travel recorder	
AIRMAN	aeronaut	
AIR-SAC	air-cell	
AIRWAY	flying lane; airline	
AISLED	having aisles (church)	ar
AJOURE	perforated metalwork	
AKIMBO	arched; bent arms	
ALALIA	loss of speech	md
ALALIA	decorative script (Sp.); Moresque	
	ceramic wares	

ALARUM	alarm clock; alarm	
ALATED	alate; winged	**bt**
ALBATA	an alloy	
ALBEDO	light reflective power	
ALBEIT	although	
ALBERT	a watch chain	
ALBIAN	cretaceous rock stage	**gl**
ALBINO	abnormally white	
ALBION	England (Morte D'Arthur)	
ALBITE	(felspar)	**mn**
ALBUGO	eye-trouble; fungus	**md, bt**
ALCADE	} judge; magistrate (Sp.)	
ALCAID		
ALCAIC	poetic metre	
ALCEDO	} kingfisher	**zo**
ALCYON		
ALCLAD	an aluminium alloy	
ALCOVE	a bower; arbour; recess	
ALDERN	made of alder	
ALDINE	16th century books by Aldus	
ALDRIN	naphthalene insecticide	**ch**
ALECTO	a Fury	
ALEGAR	sour ale	
ALEGER	lively; cheerful	
ALERCE	cedar wood	**bt**
ALETTE	pilaster	**ar**
ALEVIN	salmon fry	**zo**
ALEXIA	inability to read	**md**
ALEXIN	defensive protein	**md**
ALGATE	always; nevertheless	
ALGOID	(seaweeds)	**bt**
ALGOUS	(algoid)	**bt**
ALIBLE	nourishing	
ALIGHT	descend; ignited; flaming	
ALINED	} brought into line	
ALIGNED		
ALIPED	having winged feet	
ALKALI	opposite to acid	**ch**
ALKANE	methane series	**ch**
ALKENE	ethylene series	**ch**
ALLEGE	also alegge; assert; maintain	
ALLELE	alternative form of gene	**gn**
ALLICE	Severn shad; fish	**zo**
ALLIED	united; related; cognate; akin	
ALLIES	affinities; associates	
ALL-OUT	top speed	
ALLUDE	refer; imply; hint; insinuate	
ALLURE	tempt; decoy; seduce; cajole	
ALMAIN	}	
ALMAND	} German dance	**mu**
ALLEMANDE	}	
ALMIRA	storage furniture (Ind.)	
ALMNER	almoner; dispenser	
ALMOIN	alms; alms-chest (tenure)	
ALMOND	dessert nut	**bt**
ALMOST	well-nigh; nearly	
ALMUCE	amice or furred hood	
ALNAGE	measuring by the ell	**me**
ALNICO	permanent magnet alloy	
ALOGIA	mental deficiency speech defect	

ALPACA	llama; Peruvian camel (mohair)	**tx, zo**
ALPHUS	leprosy; psoriasis	**md**
ALPINE	of the Alps	
ALPINI	Italian mountain troops	
ALPIST	bird-seed	**bt**
ALSIKE	Swedish clover	**bt**
ALTERN	alternate	
ALTHEA	rose of Sharon	**bt**
ALUDEL	distilling apparatus	**ch**
ALUMNA	a woman graduate	
ALUMNI	collegiates; pupils; scholars	
ALVINE	pert. to belly, intestines	**md**
ALWAYS	age; evermore; eternally	
AMADOU	dried fungus; tinder	
AMATOL	explosive	**ch**
AMAZED	astounded, nonplussed	
AMAZIA	mammary non-development	**md**
AMAZON	female warrior; virago; shrew	
AMBAGE	circumlocution; subterfuge	
AMBERY	amber-like	
AMBIGU	French version of poker	**ga**
AMBLED	at an easy pace; strolled	
AMBLER	saunterer	
AMBURY	} a disease in turnips	**bt**
ANBURY		
AMBUSH	troops in waiting	
AMELIA	congenital limb absence	**md**
AMENDE	} reparation (Fr.) recompense;	
AMENDS	} compensation; apology	
AMENED	ratified	
AMENIA	amenorrhoea; menstrual disorders	**md**
AMENTA	catkins	**bt**
AMERCE	to fine arbitrarily	
AMIDIN	starch solution	**ch**
AMIDOL	developing agent	**pg**
AMIMIA	loss of sign ability	**pc, md**
AMINOL	an explosive	**ch**
AMNION	embryonic habitat	**md, zo**
AMNOIS	membrane	**md**
AMOEBA	protozoa	**zo**
AMOMUM	cardamom; aromatic shrub	**bt**
AMORAL	non-moral	
AMORCE	toy detonator; percussion cap	
AMORET	sweetheart; love knot	
AMORPH	animal decoration	**ar**
AMOUNT	sum; total; aggregate; attain	
AMPERE	unit of current intensity	**el, me**
AMPLER	more copious; fuller; richer	
AMREET	water of immortality	
AMRITA	nectar; ambrosia	
AMULET	charm; talisman; safeguard	
AMURCA	olive-oil extract	
AMUSED	diverted; beguiled; enlivened	
AMUSIA	loss of musicality	**md, pc**
AMYLIC	} starch	**ch**
AMYLUM		
AMYOUS	lacking muscle; muscular weakening	**md**

AMYTAL	hypnotic barbiturate	pm
ANABAS	tree climbing fish	zo
ANADEM	garland; chaplet	
ANALET	précis of an analysis	
ANALOG	system behaviour comparison	cp
ANANAS	pineapple	bt
ANANYM	name written backwards	
ANATTO	} orange-red dye used for	
ANOTTO	} cheeses	
ANCHOR	often dropped; (sheet); -bolt	bd, nt
ANCOME	a boil; a whitlow	md
ANCONA	a fowl	zo
ANDEAN	(Andes)	
ANDRON	men's meeting room (Gr.)	
ANDROS-	male (Gr.)	cf, pc
ANELED	anointed (extreme unction)	
ANEPIA	loss of power of speech	md
ANERGY	failure of energy; immunity	
ANESIS	tuning to lower pitch	mu
ANESIS	abatement of symptoms	md
ANGARY	angaria; war-rights	
ANGINA	quinsy (pectoris)	md
ANGLED	fished; schemed	
ANGLER	the fishing frog	zo
ANGLES	early East Anglian settlers	
ANGORA	cloth; mohair; cat; goat; rabbit	tx, zo
ANHIMA	horned screamer bird	zo
ANICUT	dam for irrigation (Ind.)	
ANIGHT	at night	
ANILIC	pert. to anil, indigo; dyes	ch, tx
ANIMAL	creature; beast; carnal	zo
ANIMUS	malice; animosity; spirit; male bias; illwill	pc
ANKLED	having ankles	
ANKLET	ornament or fetter	
ANKYLO	fusion; bent	cf, md
ANLACE	dagger	
ANNALS	historical records	
ANNATE	} first fruits	rl
ANNATS	}	
ANNEAL	to temper	
ANNEXE	an addition	
ANNONA	year's produce	
ANNUAL	yearly	
ANODAL	genetic spiral upward	bt
ANODIC	anodal; positively polar	
ANOINT	anele; consecrate	
ANOLIS	lizard genus (Amer.)	zo
ANOMIA	} inability to recall names	pc
ANOMIC	}	
ANOMIE	crash of social values	pc
ANONYM	pseudonym	
ANOPIA	defective vision	md
ANORAK	hooded windproofer	
ANOTIA	absence of ears	
ANOURA	frog genus	zo
ANOXIA	deficiency of oxygen	md
ANSATE	handled	

ANSWER	respond; reply; fulfil; refute; 2nd, similar phrase	mu
ANT-COW	an aphis	zo
ANTERO-	before; prior to	cf
ANTHEM	song of praise	mu
ANTHER	part of stamen	bt
ANTHUS	meadow pipit	
ANTIAR	upas tree	bt
ANTLER	a horn	zo
ANTLIA	proboscis of insects	zo
ANTRUM	cavity; cave; den	md
ANUBIS	jackal-headed Egyptian deity	rl
ANULUS	ring-shaped structure	md
ANURAL	tailless	zo
ANURIA	absence of urine secretion	md
ANYHOW	in any case; in any way	
ANYWAY	anyhow	
AONIAN	(Muses)	
AORIST	a past tense (Gr.)	
AORTAL	} arterial	md
AORTIC	}	
AOSMIC	free from odour	
APACHE	Parisian assassin; Red Indian	
APATHY	torpor; lethargy; dullness	
APEDOM	apishness	
APEPSY	poor digestion	md
APERCU	a précis; a summary	
APHONY	loss of voice; dumbness	md
APHTHA	thrush disease	md
APIARY	art of beekeeping	
APICAL	topmost	
APICES	culminations; highest points	
APIECE	to each	
APINCH	pinching	
APLITE	quartz-feldspar microgranite	gl
APLOMB	self-possession; poise	
APLOME	garnet	mn
APNOEA	breath cessation	md
APODAL	} footless; without feet or fins	
APODEL	}	zo
APOGEE	furthest point; apex	
APONIA	painlessness	
APORIA	rhetorical doubt	
APOSIA	absence of thirst feeling	md
APOZEM	a decoction	bt
APPEAL	entreat; implore; invoke	lw
APPEAR	seem; emerge; dawn; look	
APPEND	add; fasten; subjoin	
APPORT	object produced by medium	
APPOSE	to seal; superimpose	
APTERA	wingless insects	zo
APTOTE	indeclinable noun	
APULSE	pulsing	
AQUILA	lectern; eagle	rl, zo
AQUILO	N., N-E. wind (Lat.)	mt
ARABIC	language; race	
ARABIN	gum arabic	bt
ARABIS	rock-cress	bt
ARABLE	tillable; cultivable	
ARAISE	to raise from the dead	

ARANGO	cornelian	**mn**
ARBOUR	bower; recess; retreat; spindle	
ARBUTE	strawberry tree (arbutus)	**bt**
ARCADE	arched gallery	
ARCADY	pastoral district; (Sir Philip Sidney)	
ARCANA	mysteries	
ARCANE	secret	
ARCATE	shaped like a bow	
ARCHED	vaulted; concave	
ARCHER	a bowman; Zodiac sign	**as**
ARCHIL	violet dye	**bt**
ARCHLY	roguishly; merrily; shrewdly	
ARCHON	Greek magistrate	
ARCING	electrical leakage; diversion	**el**
ARCTIC	northern; boreal; cold	
ARDENT	fiery; fervent; intense	
ARDOUR	warmth; heat; passion; zeal	
AREOLA }	cell nucleus; small area;	
AREOLE }	interstitial space	**md, bt**
ARETTE	entrust (Spens.)	
ARGALA	adjutant bird (Hindu)	**zo**
ARGALI	wild sheep of Asia	**zo**
ARGAND	(burner); (diagram)	
ARGEMA	optical ulcer	**md**
ARGENT	silver	**hd**
ARGIVE	(Argos); Greek	
ARGOSY	richly laden vessel	**nt**
ARGUED	reasoned; implied; mooted	
ARGUER	disputed; debated; pleaded	
ARGUFY	wrangle	
ARGUTE	subtle; ingenious	
ARIDAS	East African taffeta	**tx**
ARIGHT	rightly	
ARIOSE }	melodious song-like recitation	
ARIOSO }		**mu**
ARISEN	appeared; cropped up	
ARISTA	beard of corn	**bt**
ARKITE	Noachian	
ARMADA	fleet; flotilla	**nt**
ARMING	preparing for war	
ARMLET	band; creek; (armour)	
ARMORY	armoury; heraldry	**hd**
ARMOUR	weapon-proof plating; knight clothes	
ARMOUR	protection (underwater) of structure	**ce**
ARMPIT	the axilla	**md**
ARMURE	embossed-appearing cloth	**tx**
ARNAUT	Albanian mountaineer	
ARNICA	a plant genus	**bt**
AROINT }	begone!	
AROYNT }		
AROUND	about; encompassing	
AROURA	100 square feet (Egyptian)	**me**
AROUSE	excite; stir; provoke	
ARPENT	100 square perches	**me**
ARRACH	plant; the orache	**bt**
ARRACK	fermented toddy	
ARRANT	errant; unmitigated	
ARREAR	backward	
ARRECT	erect; intent; alert	
ARREST	stem; curb; detain; capture	
ARRIDE	to please; to laugh at	
ARRIVE	reach; attain; land; come	
ARROBA	Spanish 25 lb (11 kg) weight	**me**
ARROWY	like an arrow	
ARROYO	ravine; gully (Sp.)	**go**
ARSHIN	30 in (76 cm) (Rus.)	**me**
ARSINE	poison gas	**ch**
ARTERY	blood vessel	**md**
ARTFUL	sly; wily; subtle; astute	
ARTHRO-	joint; articulation	**cf, md**
ARTIST	painter; master; adept	**pt**
ARUNDO	reed genus	**bt**
ASALTO	(assault) Fox, Geese (variant) game	
ASCEND	climb; scale; mount	
ASCENT	rise; elevation; eminence	
ASCIAN	equator dweller	
ASEITY	self-origination	
ASEMIA	symbol comprehension inability	**pc**
ASGARD	abode of Norse gods	
ASHAKE	ashiver; aquake	
ASHAME	to feel shame (obs.)	
ASHERY	ash-heap	
ASHIER	more ashen; paler	
ASHLAR }	hewn stones	
ASHLER }		**ar**
ASHORE	stranded; aground; on land	**nt**
ASH-PAN	dust-pan	
ASH-PIT	fire-refuse tip (locomotive)	**rw**
ASITIA	off one's oats	**md**
ASKANT	askance; obliquely	
ASKARI	African soldier	
ASKING	requesting; begging; inviting	
ASLAKE	to slake; to mitigate	
ASLANT	sloping; askew; awry	
ASLEEP	dormant; slumbering	
ASLOPE	obliquely; aslant; atilt	
ASNORT	snorting	
ASONIA	inability to distinguish pitch	
ASPECT	outlook; mien; bearing; view	
ASPICK	lavender; asp	**bt, zo**
ASPIRE	crave; soar; yearn; aim	
ASPORT	remove feloniously	
ASPOUT	spouting	
ASQUAT	squatting	
ASSAIL	attack; defame; asperse	
ASSART	to grub up trees, etc.	
ASSARY	ancient Roman coin	**nm**
ASSENT	concur; agree; accord	
ASSERT	declare; maintain; allege; aver	
ASSESS	compute; tax; rate; value	
ASSETS	possessions; effects	
ASSIGN	allot; appoint; adduce	
ASSIST	aid; help; succour; abet	
ASSIZE	to assess	**lw**
ASSOIL	to pardon; to soil	
ASSORT	group; arrange; classify	
ASSUME	feign; sham; arrogate	

ASSURE	aver; guarantee; warrant	
ASTARE	staring	
ASTART	suddenly	
ASTERN	aft; abaft; in reverse	nt
ASTERT	astart; suddenly (Spens.)	
ASTHMA	breathing disorder	md
ASTRAL	starry; stellar; sidereal	
ASTRAY	erring; wandering; missing	
ASTRUT	puffed up (obs.)	
ASTUTE	artful; subtle; wily	
ASWARM	swarming	
ASWING	asway	
ASWOON	in a swoon	
ASYLUM	a sanctuary; refuge	
ATABAL	Moorish drum	mu
ATAMAN	Cossack chief	
ATAVIC	inherent; hereditary	
ATAVUS	remote ancestor	
ATAXIA	paralysis	md
ATAXIC	irregular	md
ATELIA	retaining childish traits	pc
ATHENE	goddess of wisdom and war	rl
AT-HOME	a reception	
ATHROB	throbbing	
ATHYMY	melancholy	
ATKINS	British private soldier	
ATOCIA	female sterility	md
ATOMIC	minute	
ATONAL	lacking tone	mu
ATONED	reconciled; propitiated	
ATONER	an expiator	
ATONIC	unaccented; debilitated	md
ATOPIC	displaced; allergic	
ATRIAL	pertaining to atrium	
ATRIUM	Roman hall; cavity; sinus; fish gills	zo
ATROUS	jet black	
ATTACH	annex; adhere; cement	
ATTACK	storm; charge; assail; impugn	
ATTACK	sudden onset of battle or disease	
ATTAIN	acquire; achieve; reach; grasp	
ATTASK	to task	
ATTEND	serve; guard; hearken; heed	
ATTENT	intention; attentive (Spens.)	
ATTEST	ratify; confirm; endorse	
ATTIRE	garb; rig; accoutre; outfit	
ATTORN	transfer homage	lw
ATTRAP	array; adorn	
ATTUNE	harmonize; accord; adapt	
ATWAIN	in sunder	
ATWEEN	between	
ATWIXT	betwixt	
ATYPIC	unclassified; unusual	md
AUBADE	dawn; concert; morning song	
AUBURN	carroty; Titian	
AUDILE	who prefers auditory images to visuals	
AUDION	wireless amplifier	ro
AUGEAN	foul; arduous and toilsome	
AUGEND	sum to be added to	cp, ma

AUGITE	volcanic rock	mn
AUGURY	omen; portent; sign; presage	
AUGUST	majestic; venerable; imposing	
AULETE	flautist	mu
AUMBRY	ambry; cupboard	rl
AUMUCE	amice; furred hood	
AUNTIE	aunty; prude	
AURATE	having ears; gilded (design)	ar
AUREAT	gilded; golden; auric	
AUREUS	Roman gold coin	nm
AURIFY	change into gold	
AURIGA	a constellation; the Charioteer	
AURINE	dye-acid	
AURIST	ear specialist	md
AURORA	goddess of dawn; northern lights	
AUROUS	golden; aureate	
AUSPEX	seer; diviner; prophet	
AUSSIE	an Australian	
AUSTER	South wind	mt
AUSTIN	Augustine	
AUTHOR	writer; creator; cause; agent	
AUTISM	self-absorption	
AUTUMN	the fall	
AVALON	a western legendary isle	
AVANCE	avens; herb bennet	bt
AVANTI	forward (It.)	
AVATAR	incarnation of Brahma	rl
AVAUNT	begone	
AVENER	} master of the Horse in feudal	
AVENOR	} times	
AVENGE	retaliate; to take revenge	
AVENUE	entry; access; approach; fine road	
AVERSE	loath; allergic; reluctant	
AVIARY	a large bird-cage	zo
AVIATE	to fly (aircraft pilot)	
AVIDIN	protein in egg	ch
AVIDLY	voraciously; greedily; eagerly	
AVISED	hue; complexion	
AVITAL	hereditary; ancestral	
AVOCAT	advocate (Fr.)	lw
AVOCET	} wading birds	zo
AVOSET	}	
AVOUCH	maintain; guarantee	
AVOURE	confession; justification (Spens.)	
AVOWAL	frank admission; confession	
AVOWED	openly declared; owned	
AVOWEE	(advowson)	lw
AVOWRY	(replevin)	lw
AVULSE	to grab	
AWAKEN	rouse; stir up; kindle	
AWASTE	wasting	
AWATCH	watching; alert	
AWEARY	tired; faded; spent	
AWEIGH	atrip; apeak (raise anchors)	nt
AWHEEL	cycling	
AWHILE	sometime; briefly; soon	
AWNING	tilt; canopy; baldequin	
AWRACK	wrecked	
AXENIC	free from parasites	md
AXICLE	sheave; pulley wheel	

AXILLA	armpit	md
AXUNGE	hog's lard; wheel-grease	
AYE-AYE	squirrel-like lemur	zo
AZALEA	plant, rhododendron type	bt
AZARIN	brilliant crimson dye	ch
AZAZEL	Satan's standard-bearer	
AZMURE	cloth with embossed appearance	
		tx
AZONAL	recent formation (soil)	
AZONIC	not local	
AZOTIC	lifeless	
AZRAEL	destroying angel	
AZURED	colour of azure	
AZURIN	blue dye	ch
AZYGOS	occurring singly	

B

BAAING	bleating	
BAALIM	false gods (Baal)	
BABBIT	Babbit metal	
BABBLE	chatter; prattle; drivel	
BABIES	infants; twins; triplets	
BABISH	infantile; foolish	
BABLAH	acacia-rind	bt
BABOON	type of primate	zo
BACKED	retired; aided; abetted	
BACKER	supporter; partisan	
BACKET	coal-box	
BACK-UP	supporting service	cp
BADGER	pester; annoy; bait; tool; mammal	
		to, zo
BADIAN	tree with anise-flavoured fruit	bt
BAFFLE	balk; thwart; acoustics; slat; plate	
		bd, ce
BAFTAS	cotton; muslin	tx
BAGFUL	contents; capacity of a bag	
BAGGED	stolen; shot	
BAGGIT	salmon after spawning	zo
BAGMAN	commercial traveller	
BAGNIO	bath-house (It.)	bd
BAGUIO	tropical cyclone; Philippines	mt
BAGWIG	an 18th century wig	
BAHADA	} piedmont alluvial plains	go
BAJADA		
BAILED	released on security	lw
BAILEE	(trustee)	lw
BAILER	one who stands bail; sump water	
	or sand pump	lw, ce
BAILEY	castle wall; courtyard	
BAILIE	alderman (Sc.)	lw
BAILOR	bailee	
BAITED	badgered; lured; enticed	
BAJREE	Indian grass	bt
BAKERY	bake-house	
BAKING	cooking; drying under heat;	
	stoving (Amer.)	bd
BALAAM	unimportant newsprint	
BALASS	a ruby	mn

BALATA	rubberlike gum	bt
BALBOA	coin of Panama	nm
BALDER	less hirsute; nordic sungod	rl
BALDLY	inelegantly; plainly	
BALEEN	whalebone	zo
BALING	bundling; emptying	
BALIZE	a sea-mark	tv
BALKAN	of S.E. Europe (peninsular)	go
BALKED	refused; frustrated	
BALKER	fish-spotter	
BALKIS	Queen of Sheba; also Aaziz	
BALLAD	epic song	
BALLED	clogged	
BALLET	art dance	
BALLOT	vote; ticket; to elect	
BALSAM	aromatic balm	bt
BALTIC	shipping exchange (sea)	go
BAMBOO	tree-like grass	bt
BAMMIE	Caribbean cassava cake	ck
BANANA	fruit; (republic); (can split)	bt, ck
BANCOR	monetary unit	nm
BANDED	united; bound	
BANDIT	outlaw; brigand; footpad	
BANDLE	2 ft (60 cm) (Irish)	me
BANDOG	watch-dog	zo
BANGED	with hair cut square	
BANGHY	Ind. porter's shoulder-yoke	
BANGLE	bracelet; armlet; ring	
BANGUE	bhang; a narcotic	
BANG-UP	slap-up; stylish	
BANIAN	Hindu caste; fig-tree	bt
BANISH	exile; expel; eject	
BANKED	deposited; road; rail; dyke	bd, rw
BANKER	lender; pushing locomotive; cards	
		ga
BANKER	mason's table; fishing boat;	
	(gambling)	
BANKET	auriferous rock (Transvaal)	gl
BANNED	barred; tabooed; vetoed	
BANNER	petal; flag; standard	bt
BANTAM	carved work; small hen; (boxing)	
		zo
BANTER	twit; rally; deride; bandy	
BANYAN	Indian fig; banian	bt
BANZAI!	Japanese hurrah; drag-racing	ga
BAOBAB	African tree	bt
BARANI	} gymnast's somersault (It.)	ga
BARONI		
BARBED	bearded; hooked; pointed	
BARBEL	carp	zo
BARBER	hairdresser (men)	
BARBET	bird; dog	zo
BARCOO	grass (Aust.)	bt
BARDIC	poetic; epic	
BAREGE	fabric	tx
BARELY	only just	
BAREME	rules for show-jumping	ga
BAREST	bleakest; baldest; plainest	
BARGED	charged into; shoved	
BARGEE	bargeman	

BARING	uncovering; unsheathing	
BARISH	rather bare	
BARIUM	metallic element	ch
BARKED	grazed (shins); helped	
BARKEN	to become like bark	
BARKER	shop-tout	
BARLEY	a cereal	bt
BARMAN	pot-man; bar-tender	
BARNED	stored	
BARNEY	humbug; prize fight	
BARONY	a baron's holding	
BARQUE	} three-masted ship	nt
BARQUA		
BARK	}	
BARRAS	resin	bt
BARRED	banned; excluded; ostracized	
BARREL	36 gal (163.6 litres) cask; part of pipe; (gun); vaulting	ar, bd, me
BARREN	bare; sterile; unfertile	
BARRET	beret; cap	rl
BARROW	mound; tumulus; truck	
BARSAC	white wine (Fr.)	
BARTER	trade; exchange; traffic	
BARTON	domain lands; farmhouse	
BARYON	heavy subatomic particle	ps
BARYTA	barium oxide	ch
BASALT	igneous rock	mn
BASELY	spuriously; corruptly	
BASIAL	osculatory	
BASIFY	make into a salifiable salt	
BASING	founding; establishing	
BASKED	warmed by the sun	
BASKET	pannier; creal; punnet; trug; goal (basketball)	
BASNET	helmet; bassinet	
BASQUE	Biscayan	
BASSET	outcrop; (cards); hound	zo
BASTED	(sewing)	ck
BASTON	heraldic baton	hd
BASUTO	African	
BASYLE	radicle	ch
BATATA	sweet potato	bt
BATEAU	light boat	nt
BATELO	small dhow (Arabian coasts)	nt
BATHED	laved; suffused	
BATHER	swimmer; laver	
BATHIC	pertaining to sea depths	
BATHOS	anti-climax; bombast	
BATING	except; abating; deducting	
BATLET	linen-beater	
BATMAN	an officer's servant (valet)	
BATOON	baston; bar; staff; truncheon	
BATTED	(cricket)	ga
BATTEL	Oxford kitchen account	
BATTEN	grow fat; be parasitic	
BATTEN	a lath; strip of softwood; (sailing)	bd
BATTER	culinary mixture; smite; player with striker (baseball, cricket)	ck, ga
BATTLE	war; strive; contest; fight	
BATTON	batten; a slat	
BATTUE	a beat; slaughter	
BAUBEE	} halfpenny (Sc.)	
BAWBEE		
BAUBLE	showy finery; gee-gaw; jester's wand	
BAURUA	prototype rapid sailing outrigger (Polynesia)	nt
BAVIAN	poetaster; baboon	zo
BAWLED	clamoured; shouted; yelled	
BAWLER	a howler	
BAWLEY	Thames fishing-boat	nt
BAWSON	} a badger	zo
BAWSIN		
BAWTIE	a hare; a dog	zo
BAXTER	(prints)	
BAYARD	a famous steed	
BAYARD	a very perfect knight	
BAYEUX	famous for its tapestry	
BAYING	in full cry	
BAYRAM	Mohammedan festival	
BAY-RUM	hair lotion	
BAZAAR	mart; emporium; exchange	
BEACHY	pebbly (of shoreline)	gl
BEACON	signal-fire; lighthouse	
BEADED	strung together	
BEADLE	parish officer; servitor	
BEAGLE	a hound; jammer	ro, zo
BEAKED	sharp-pointed	
BEAKER	a cup; glass vessel	
BEAMED	(antlers); smiled	
BEAMER	head line bowling (cricket) (foul)	ga
BEARER	a carrier; (funerals); (joist); (cheque)	bd
BEATEN	defeated; hackneyed	
BEATER	striker; (game)	
BEAUNE	a French wine	
BEAUTY	grace; comeliness; fairness	
BEAVER	(dam); worker; (fur hat); rodent	zo
BECALL	miscall; vituperate	
BECALM	still; pacify; soothe	
BECAME	grew into; graced	
BECKED	nodded; signed	
BECKET	an eye in a knot	nt
BECKON	call; wave; signal; invite	
BECOME	suit; befit; grace; adorn	
BECURL	to curl	
BEDASH	bespatter	
BEDAUB	smear; befoul; stain; paint	
BED-BUG	cimex; (bed-louse)	zo
BEDDED	planted out	
BEDDER	millstone; a plant	bt
BEDECK	array; gild; adorn	
BED-KEY	bedstead tightener	to
BEDLAM	mad-house; uproar	
BEDRAL	a beadle	
BEDRID	bedridden	
BEDROP	sprinkle; to speckle	

170

BEDUCK	to plunge under water	
BEDUIN	a Bedouin Arab	
BEDUST	cover with dust	
BEENAH	marriage (Sri Lanka)	
BEEPER	remote controlled aircraft	ae
BEETLE	maul; heavy mallet	zo
BEEVES	oxen; kine	zo
BEFALL	betide; happen; chance	
BEFANA	Epiphany present; a fairy	
BEFOAM	bespatter with foam	
BEFOOL	dupe; hoodwink; hoax	
BEFORE	prior to; formerly; above	
BEFOUL	defoul; defile; sully	
BEGGAR	ruin; surpass; pauper	
BEGGED	entreated; cadged	
BEGIFT	to make a presentation	
BEGILD	gild; to add gilt (gold)	
BEGILT	gilt; to have been gilded	
BEGIRD	enclose; encircle; environ	
BEGNAW	to corrode	
BEGONE!	go away; avaunt!	
BEHALF	benefit; interest; advantage	
BEHAVE	act; comport; demean	
BEHEAD	decapitate; execute	
BEHELD	saw; surveyed; contemplated	
BEHEST	command; mandate; order	
BEHIND	abaft; following; buttocks	pl
BEHOLD	regard; discern; look	
BEHOOF	profit; advantage; benefit	
BEHOTE	promised; vowed (Spens.)	
BEHOVE	befit; suit; beseem	
BEHOWL	to howl at (Shak.)	
BEHUNG	draped; well-endowed	
BEJANT	bejan; freshman (Sc.)	
BEJUCO	a cane	bt
BEKISS	kiss intensively; osculate	
BELACE	adorn with lace; beat	
BELAMY	good friend (Spens.)	
BELATE	delay; retard; hinder	
BELAUD	overpraise; bepuff	
BELDAM	a hag; beldame	
BELFRY	bat habitat; bell-tower	
BELGIC	Belgian; of Belgium	
BELIAL	a low and profligate devil	
BELIED	falsified; counterfeited	
BELIEF	faith; creed; dogma; tenet	
BELIER	a confidence-man	
BELIKE	likely; perhaps; maybe	
BELIVE	speedily; ere long (Sc.)	
BELLED	bellowed	
BELLIS	the daisy	bt
BELLOW	lead colic	md
BELLOW	roar; bawl; clamour	
BELLUM	Iraqi long canoe	nt
BELOCK	to fasten; to lock	
BELONE	garfish	zo
BELONG	to appertain	
BELTED	girt; zoned; girdled	
BELUGA	sturgeon; source of caviare	zo, ck
BEMASK	to conceal	

BEMAUL	wound; disfigure; bruise	
BEMBEX	genus of sand-wasps	zo
BEMIRE	bedaub; soil; besmirch	
BEMOAN	lament; bewail; mourn	
BEMOCK	deride; jeer; flout	
BEMOIL	bemire; bedraggle	
BEMUSE	daze; bewilder	
BENDER	spree; a stretcher	
BENGAL	fabric; (Lancer)	tx
BENIGN	kindly; amiable; friendly	
BENITO	navigation system	nv
BENNET	herb	bt
BEN-NUT	oil-nut of horse-radish tree	bt
BENSHI	banshee; Irish fairy	
BENUMB	stupefy; deaden; blunt	
BENZOL	benzene	ch
BEPELT	pelt vigorously	
BEPITY	to sympathize	
BEPUFF	belaud; overpraise	
BERATE	rate; scold; chide; reprove	
BERBER	Moroccans of Atlas mountains	
BERBER	a Barbary language	
BEREAN	extinct Scottish sect	
BEREFT	stripped; deprived; destitute	
BERLIN	a vehicle; wool	
BERTHA	Hun gun (1st world war)	
BESANT	⎫ Byzantine gold; circlet	hd,
BEZANT	⎭	nm
BESEEM	behove; befit; suit; become	
BESEEN	comely	
BESIDE	near; close to; alongside	
BESIGH	to sigh	
BESING	celebrate in song	
BESMUT	begrime; blacken	
BESOIL	defile; besmirch	
BESORT	to fit; to become	
BESPAT	spat upon	
BESPED	helped on	
BESPIT	to spit upon	
BESPOT	to mark with spots	
BESTED	overwhelmed; worsted	
BESTIR	hasten; rouse; strive	
BESTOW	confer; grant; give; award	
BESTUD	to stud	
BETAIL	curtail	
BETAKE	remove or repair to	
BETEEM	produce; shed	
BETHEL	a chapel; sect	rl
BETIDE	befall; happen; chance	
BETIME	betide; befall	
BETISE	stupid act (Fr.)	
BETONY	a plant	bt
BETOOK	went away; left	
BETORN	torn to pieces	
BETOSS	agitate violently	
BETRAP	ensnare	
BETRAY	divulge; reveal; entrap	
BETRIM	arrange; to deck	
BETTED	wagered	
BETTER	superior; amend; rectify; gambler	

BETTOR	punter; wagerer	
BEVIES	flocks; crowds	
BEVILE	heraldic device	hd
BEWAIL	moan; lament; grieve; deplore	
BEWARE	achtung! heed; mind	
BEWEEP	bewail	
BEWEPT	disfigured by weeping	
BEWRAP	envelope; enclose	
BEWRAY	betray; accuse	
BEWTER	bittern	zo
BEYLIK	a Bey's province	
BEYOND	over; past; farther	
BEZAAN	} Dutch ketch	nt
BEZAN		
BEZANT	besant; Dutch ship	nt
BEZOAR	a stony concretion	
BHARAL	wild sheep (Tibet)	zo
BHISTI	Indian water-carrier	
BIACID	of a base	ch
BIASED	prejudiced	
BIAZAL	having two optical axes	
BIBBER	wine-bibber; toper	
BIBLUS	papyrus; paper-reed	bt
BICEPS	a muscle	md
BICKER	bowl; quarrel; nipple	
BICORN	having 2 horns	
BIDALE	a benefit	
BIDDED	(auction) offered	
BIDDER	tenderer	
BIDENT	two-pronged	
BIDING	pausing; awaiting	
BIDOUS	lasting 2 days	
BIFFED	coshed; bashed	
BIFFIN	apple-pie; dried apple	
BIFLEX	double curve	
BIFOIL	two-blade plant	bt
BIFOLD	two-fold; double	
BIFORM	having two shapes	
BI-FUEL	propelled with two fuels	
BIGAMY	plural marriage	
BIG-END	crank end of connecting rod	
BIGGEN	} child's cap; small wooden	
BIGGIN	} bowl	
BIGGER	larger; greater; bulkier	
BIGRID	double-control-grid thermionic	el
BIG-WIG	important person	
BIKING	cycling	
BIKINI	minimum two-piece garment	
BILBAO	wall mirror (N. Amer.)	
BILDAR	Indian camp servant	
BILGED	broad-bottomed	
BILGED	fractured in the bilge	
BILKED	defrauded	
BILKER	an absconder	
BILLED	advertised	
BILLET	a log; note; lodgings; ticket; romanesque moulding; thumbpiece on a tankard	ar
BILLIE	tin can; billy; male goat	zo
BILLON	an alloy	

BILLOT	gold or silver bar	
BILLOW	roll; heave; surge; swell; glider wing fullness	ae
BIMANA	bimane; two-handed	
BINARY	mathematical system; 2 digits	ma, cp
BINARY	sonata form in 2 keys	mu
BINATE	double; in pairs; twosome; twin	
BINDER	a bandage; (book-); mason; cement; stirrup rod	bd, ce
BINGHI	Australian aborigine	
BINGLE	base hit (baseball)	ga
BINODE	2-electrode thermionic tube	el
BINOUS	binate; double	
BIOPSY	tissue examination	md
BIOSIS	life; distinguishing organisms	zo
BIOTIC	biological	md
BIOTIN	B vitamin	
BIPACK	two-film colour photography	
BIPONT	bipontine	pr
BIRDED	snared	
BIRDER	bird catcher	
BIRDIE	one under bogey at golf	ga
BIREME	cf. trireme; 2-banked oared galley, (Mediterranean)	nt
BIRKEN	made of birch-wood	
BIRKIE	lively lad (Sc.)	
BIRLER	a carouser	
BIRSLE	to scorch; to toast (Sc.)	
BISECT	to halve	
BISHOP	a drink; dress; church dignitary; (chess); horse-faking	ga, rl
BISLEY	(rifle shooting)	
BISMAR	Orkney steel-yard	
BISQUE	croquet handicap; glazeless firing	
BISQUE	lobster soup; extra stroke (golf)	ck, ga
BISSON	blind; blinding (Shak.)	
BISTRE	} brown pigment; sombre	
BISTER		
BISTRO	small eating house (Fr.)	
BITING	mordant; champing	
BITTED	(horse's bit)	
BITTEN	tricked; corroded	
BITTER	acrimonious; sour; tart; (beer); severe; (grief); (pill)	
BITTLE	flat club; beetle	
BITTOR	the bittern	zo
BIURET	urea product	ch
BIZARD	carnation	
BLADED	having a blade	
BLAGUE	blarney; swagger	
BLAMED	reproached; censured	
BLANCH	bleach; whiten; fade	
BLARED	trumpeted; pealed	
BLASHY	watery	
BLAZED	proclaimed; (trees)	
BLAZER	bright coloured sports jacket	
BLAZON	} to display; blare; bear	
BLASON	} (crest); (mark)	hd

BLEACH	blanch; whiten	
BLEAKY	bleak; cheerless	
BLEARY	blear-eyed; tired-looking	
BLEBBY	blubby; blistered	
BLENCH	blink; shrink; flinch	
BLENDE	an ore of zinc	**mn**
BLENNY	fish	**zo**
BLEWIT	mushroom	**bt**
BLEYME	inflammation	
BLIGHT	mildew; wither; shrivel	
BLINDS	camouflage; screens; deceit	
BLINKS	chickweed	**bt**
BLINKY	blink-eyed	
BLITHE	merry; gay; vivacious; joyous	
BLONDE	silk lace; fair lady	
BLOODY	sanguinary	
BLOOMY	blooming	
BLOSME	bloom (Spens.)	
BLOTCH	a blemish; pustule	
BLOTTO	fuddled	
BLOUSE	loose outer garment	
BLOW-BY	piston-leakage gas	**au**
BLOWED	blasted; confounded	
BLOWER	a whale; telephone; voice pipe	**zo**
BLOWSE	see blouse	
BLOWTH	bloom; blossoms	
BLOWZE	coarse woman	
BLOWZY	fat; tawdry; unkempt	
BLUELY	} of blue colour	
BLUISH		
BLUEST	most blue; gloomiest; (films)	
BLUFFY	rather bluff	
BLUING	tempering steel	
BLUISM	(blue-stocking)	
BLUNGE	(clay mixing)	
BOARDS	theatre stage; ice rink wall	
BOATEL	botel; boating hotel afloat	
BOATER	straw hat	
BOBBED	(hair); (winter sports)	
BOBBIN	spool; reel; magnetic core	**cp**
BOBBLE	bauble; trinket; ripple; decoration	
BOBBLE	regain lost balance (water-skiing); fumble (baseball)	
BOBLET	2-man bob; sled	**ga**
BOBWIG	wig of short hair	
BOCAGE	boscage; leafy underwood; small fields and large hedges (Fr.)	**bt, ag**
BODEGA	wine-shop (Sp.)	
BODGER	pedlar; botcher	
BODICE	woman's upper body garment	
BODIED	embodied	
BODIES	organizations; corpses; torsos	**pl**
BODILY	corporeally	
BODING	an omen; portending	
BODKIN	dagger; needle for tape	
BODKIN	three people crowded up	
BOECKL	figure skating, jump and turn	
BOEIER	Dutch merchantman	**nt**
BOFFIN	back-room scientist	

BOGGLE	to waver; to dissemble	
BOGLET	a small bog	
BOG-OAK	near-fossil wood	**bt**
BOG-ORE	porous limonite found in marshes	**mn**
BOILED	seethed	
BOILER	hot-water heater	
BOIOBI	green snake	**zo**
BOLARY	clay-like	
BOLDEN	to make bold; embolden	
BOLDER	more daring; saucier	
BOLDLY	confidently; valiantly	
BOLERO	Spanish dance; rhythm	**mu**
BOLIDE	meteor	
BOLLED	} podded; swollen	
BOLLEN		
BOLSON	Mexican drainage basin	
BOLTED	barred; swallowed	
BOLTER	bran-machine	
BOMBAX	cotton-tree	**bt**
BOMBED	blitzed	
BOMBIC	} silkworm	**zo**
BOMBYX		
BON-BON	sugar-plum; Xmas cracker	
BONDED	(warehoused)	
BONDER	binding stone or brick	
BONGAR	poisonous Indian snake	**zo**
BONGOS	Conga twin drums	**mu**
BONING	levelling; removing bones	
BONITO	(tunny) (Sp.)	**zo**
BON-MOT	witticism	
BONNET	cap; (sail); bay window roof; chimney netting	**nt, bd**
BONNIE	blithe; fair; joyous; pretty	
BONTEN	woollen stuff	**tx**
BON-TON	chic; good style; fashionable	
BONXIE	skua-gull	**zo**
BONZER	lucky strike (Aust.)	
BOODLE	money; marigold; loot	**bt**
BOOHOO	weep aloud	
BOOING	noisily disapproving; hooting	
BOOKED	entered; recorded; reserved; (copped)	
BOOKIE	bookmaker (betting)	
BOOMED	advertised; resounded	
BOOMER	kangaroo; large unrideable heavy-breaking wave (surfing)	**zo**
BOOPIC	ox-eyed	
BOOSED	} drank, swilled	
BOOZED		
BOOTED	sacked	
BOOTEE	short boot	
BOOTES	constellation	
BO-PEEP	hide and seek	
BORAGE	a plant	**bt**
BORATE	boric oxide	**ch**
BORCER	rock-drill	**to**
BORDAR	cottage	
BORDEL	bawdy-house of prostitutes	
BORDER	margin; boundary; edge	

BOREAL	} of North wind	**mt**
BOREAS		
BOREEN	Irish lane or track	
BORING	tedious; drilling	
BORLEY	} Thames barge	**nt**
BAWLEY		
BORROW	copy; assume; feign; obtain a loan; linguistic absorption; (arithmetical device)	**ma**
BORZOI	Russian hound	**zo**
BOSCHE	a Hun; German soldier; contours of green (golf)	
BOSKET	a grove; small wood	**bt**
BOSSED	controlled; dominated	
BOSSET	rudimentary antler	**zo**
BOSTAL	hill road	
BOSTON	a dance	**mu**
BOTANY	Australian wool; of plants	**bt, tx**
BOTCHY	ill-done; clumsy	
BOT-FLY	gad-fly	**zo**
BOTHER	pother; pester; worry	
BOTHIE	a house; a hut (Sc.)	
BOTONE	heraldic budding	**hd**
BO-TREE	sacred tree; pipal	**bt**
BOTTER	sea yacht	**nt**
BOTTLE	bundle of hay; water vessel	
BOTTOM	basis; foot; foundation; buttocks; dell; ship's; alluvial plain	**nt, pl**
BOTTOM	unjumpable ditch (horse riding); last innings (baseball)	**ga**
BOTTOM	time a diver spends under water	
BOUCAN	dried meat	
BOUCHE	metal plug	
BOUCLE	billowy woven cloth	**wv, tx**
BOUFFE	farcical (Fr.)	
BOUGHT	purchased; bribed	**md**
BOUGIE	instrument; form of music	**mu**
BOULET	sloping pastern	
BOUNCE	dog-fish; rebound (bad cheque); of ball games	**zo, ga**
BOUNDS	(out of bounds)	
BOUNTY	gift; reward; liberality	
BOURNE	destination; burn (Sc.); intermittent stream (often dry)	**go**
BOURSE	exchange; money market	
BOUTON	axon arborization end	**cy**
BOVATE	peasant holding (20 acres; 8 hectares)	**me**
BOVINE	dull; stupid	
BOW-BOY	Cupid; Eros	
BOW-CAP	an extreme bow of airship	
BOW-DYE	scarlet	
BOWELS	entrails; (undermost)	**pl**
BOWERY	shady; (New York)	
BOWESS	a young hawk	**zo**
BOWFIN	mudfish (N. Amer.)	**zo**
BOWING	fiddling; submitting (respect)	
BOWLED	(cricket); (bowls)	**ga**
BOW-LEG	a crooked leg	

BOWLER	a hat; cricketer; ball thrower	**ga**
BOWMAN	archer	
BOW-NET	lobster-pot	
BOW-OAR	No. 1 of a racing crew	
BOW-PEN	a drawing instrument	
BOW-SAW	narrow saw	**to**
BOWSIE	cleat	**nt**
BOW-TIE	male neckwear	**tx**
BOW-WOW	jocular word for dog	**zo**
BOWYER	bowman (obs.)	
BOXCAR	data converter; goods truck	**cp, rw**
BOX-DAM	surrounding coffer-dam	**ce**
BOX-DAY	day for lodging papers	**lw**
BOXING	pugilism; packaging; cased frame (in window)	
BOXING	(Christmas box); stone ballast under/between sleepers; boarding	**ce, bd**
BOYISH	youthful; puerile; young	
BOYUNA	serpent	**zo**
BRACED	supported; propped	
BRACER	pick-me-up; support; protector; arm guard (archery)	
BRACHY-	short	**cf**
BRAGLY	braggingly; boastfully (Spens.)	
BRAHMA	lock	
BRAINY	intellectual; clever	
BRAIRD	germination	**bt**
BRAISE	to stew	**ck**
BRAIZE	red pandora fish	**zo**
BRAKED	put on the brake	
BRANCH	bough; off-shoot; agency; division	
BRANCH	change of direction; sequence	**cp**
BRANDY	cognac	
BRANKS	scold's bridle	
BRANKY	showy (Sc.)	
BRANLE	} dance movement (Fr.); gavotte	**mu**
BRANSLE		
BRANNY	like bran	
BRASEN	} made of brass; impudent	
BRAZEN		
BRASHY	fragmentary	
BRASIL	} Brazil wood; sappan tree	**bt**
BRAZIL		
BRASSE	perch	**zo**
BRASSY	brassie; a golf club	
BRAVED	dared; defied; challenged	
BRAVER	nobler; more daring	
BRAWLY	bravely; excellently	
BRAWNY	hefty; lusty; sturdy; robust	
BRAYED	ground in a mortar	
BRAYER	(printing) roller	**to**
BRAYLE	hawk leash	
BRAZED	soldered	
BREACH	rupture; crack; rift; quarrel	
BREAST	a torus; bosom; oppose; stem; projecting wall; face	**bd**
BREAST	riser of stairway; window wall	**bd**
BREATH	aroma; pause; exhalation	

BREECH	the hinder part of a gun (loader)	
BREEKS	trousers	
BREESE	} soft wind; even pace	
BREEZE	} (horses); cinder-brick; gad	
	fly	**bd, zo**
BREEZY	gusty; windy; hearty	
BREGMA	part of skull	**md**
BREHON	Irish judge	**lw**
BRETON	of Brittany	
BREVET	a patent; nominal rank	
BREVIS	short; mass setting	**mu, rl**
BREWED	plotted; concocted	
BREWER	a brewster; maltster	
BRIARY	} set with brambles	**bt**
BRIERY	}	
BRIBED	seduced; hired	
BRIBER	a corrupter	
BRICKY	of brick	
BRIDAL	nuptial; conjugal	
BRIDGE	card game; span; surmount; loan;	
	violin; billiards; (bowls); (gym);	
	(wrestling); transition; convert;	
	link between passages	**ce, ga,**
		mu
BRIDLE	curb; control; restrain; check;	
	harness; track, path (horses)	
BRIGHT	vivid; shining; gay; merry	
BRIGUE	intrigue; cabal; strife	
BRILLS	eye-lashes (horse)	
BRIONY	bryony; a plant	**bt**
BRIQUE	red-haired Negro half-caste	
BRISKY	brisk; effervescing	
BRITON	ancient British inhabitant	
BROACH	hint; suggest; tap; clasp; pointed	
	chisel	**to**
BROADS	waterways	**go, nv**
BROCHE	brocade; embroider	
BROGAN	leather shoe	
BROGUE	shoe; Irish accent	
BROKEN	fractured; snapped; smashed	
BROKER	dealer	
BROLLY	umbrella	
BROMAL	oily fluid	**ch**
BROMIC	containing bromine	**ch**
BRONCO	unbroken horse (Amer.)	**zo**
BRONZE	an alloy of copper and tin	
BRONZY	bronze-like	
BROOCH	(a painting); ornamental clasp	
BROODY	pensive; hen	
BROOKY	abounding with streams	
BROOMY	full of broom (gorse)	**bt**
BROUGH	town; burgh; borough	
BROWNY	of a brown colour	
BROWSE	nibble; crop; feed	
BRUANG	Malayan bear	**zo**
BRUCIA	a poison	**md**
BRUISE	batter; crush; contuse; wale	
BRUMAL	(wintry)	
BRUMBY	unbroken horse	**zo**
BRUNCH	combined breakfast-lunch	**ck**

BRUSHY	rough; shaggy	
BRUTAL	inhuman; ruthless; savage	
BRUTUS	a kind of wig	
BRUZZE	V-shaped woodturning tool	**to**
BRYONY	briony; a plant	**bt**
BUBBLE	gurgle; cheat; (bath); (south sea);	
	(blow); (air)	
BUBBLY	champagne; effervescent	
BUCCAL	(cheek); cavity; mouth	**pl**
BUCCAN	dried meat	**ck**
BUCKED	bleached; exhilarated	
BUCKET	goal (basketball); (rain); (mill	
	wheel)	
BUCKET	pail; ride furiously; data;	
	container; kibble; seat	**ce cp**
BUCKIE	large whelk	**zo**
BUCKLE	brooch; clasp; wrinkle; thatcher's	
	spar	
BUCKRA	white man	
BUDDED	grafted	
BUDDHA	founder of religion	**rl**
BUDDLE	(ore-washing)	
BUDGER	a stirrer; a mover	
BUDGET	package; batch; (finance); tiler's	
	pocket	
BUDLET	a little bud	**bt**
BUDZAT	ne'er-do-well (Ind.)	
BUFFED	buffeted; polished	
BUFFEL	an American duck	**zo**
BUFFER	concussion-force deadener; senile	
	old fool	**rw**
BUFFER	limited memory storage	**cp**
BUFFET	cuff; smite; sideboard	
BUGEYE	wide-angle; fishing boat (N.	
	Amer.)	**cn, nt**
BUGGER	active sodomite	
BUG-KEY	faster transmission key	**tc**
BUGLER	horn blower	**mu**
BUGLET	a small glass bead	
BUGONG	a moth	**zo**
BUKSHA	Yemeni coin	**nm**
BUKSHI	tip; percentage (Ind.)	
BULBAR	} bulbous; bulbiform; bulby;	
BULBED	} bulbaceous	**bt**
BULBIL	bud developing into a plant	**bt**
BULBUL	nightingale; Turkish sweet	**ck, zo**
BULBUS	a corm; a bulb	**bt**
BULGAR	Bulgarian	**ck**
BULGED	protruded	
BULGER	a golf club	
BULGUR	cracked wheat (Levant)	**ck**
BULIMY	morbid appetite; voracity	**md**
BULKED	in bulk	
BULKER	street thief	
BULLED	(Stock Exchange)	
BULLER	torrential turmoil	
BULLET	projectile; slug	
BUMKIN	short broom	**nt**
BUMMED	hummed	
BUMMEL	meander; cycle seat	

175

BUMMER	camp follower; loafer
BUMMLE	to blunder; an idler
BUMPED	thumped
BUMPER	buffer; full; generous; bouncer; (cricket)
BUNCHY	clustered; tufty
BUNDLE	parcel; package; packet; roll
BUNGED	closed up
BUNGLE	miss; fail; botch
BUNION	a swelling **md**
BUNKED	decamped
BUNKER	(golf); (coal); bin; crib
BUNKUM	blather; nonsense
BUNSEN	gas burner **ch**
BUNTED	butted
BUNTER	mottled sandstone **mn**
BUNYIP	Australian monster
BUOYED	sustained; upheld
BURBLE	confusion; trouble
BURBOT	eel-pout; fish **zo**
BURDEN	chorus; incubus; load; onus
BUREAU	office; department
BURGEE	pennant; flag; coal **nt, mn**
BURGLE	rob premises
BURGOO	savoury mess **ck**
BURHEL	Asiatic goat **zo**
BURIAL	interment
BURIED	interred; inhumed
BURKED	hushed up; smothered; hesitated
BURLAP	coarse canvas
BURLED	with knots removed
BURLER	cloth-dresser
BURMAN	native of Burma; Burmese
BURNED	(bowls); scorched; charred
BURNER	flame controller; (bunsen); (balloon gas heater); (blow-lamp)
BURNET	plant; moth **bt, zo**
BURN-UP	reactor fuel-rod consumption **nc**
BURRED	roughened
BURROW	tunnel; mine; excavate
BURSAL BURSAE	} cavity **md**
BURSAR	treasurer; cashier; (college)
BURSCH	German student
BURTON	a tackle **nt**
BURYAT	Central Asian Turkmens
BUS-BAR	metallic rod link; contact **el**
BUSHED	lost in the bush
BUSHEL	8 gallons (36 litres) **me**
BUSIED	actively employed
BUSIES	detectives (sl.)
BUSILY	diligently; assiduously
BUSKED	wearing a busk; corseted
BUSKER	tragedian; street actor
BUSKIN	kind of boot; cothurnus
BUSMEN	transport workers
BUSSED	kissed; osculated; conveyed
BUSTED	gone bust (sl.); bankrupt; caught
BUSTER	frolic; a roisterer
BUSTLE	stuffed pad; stir; tumult

BUST-UP	violent quarrel
BUTANE	a paraffin; bottled gas for cooking etc. **ch**
BUTLER	house steward
BUTTED	rammed; bunted
BUTTER	to flatter; milkfat (cup) **ck, bt, ck**
BUTTIE	sandwich **ck**
BUTTON	to fasten; small mushroom; small disc; (curling)
BUXINE	(alkaloid) **ch**
BUYING	bribing; corrupting
BUZZED	spread abroad; bruited
BUZZER	tatler; tell-tale; vibratory sound
BUZZER	electric sound signal device (intercom.) **el**
BY-BLOW	illegitimate child
BYE-BYE	(golf); adieu
BYE-LAW	subsidiary law
BY-FORM	a variant
BYGONE	past; of yore
BY-LANE	side road
BYLINA	Russian poem; song **mu**
BY-LINE	goal line (soccer)
BYNAME	nickname
BY-PASS	a shunt; avoidance road
BY-PAST	past; gone by
BY-PATH	hidden path
BY-PLAY	significant acting in dumb show
BY-PLOT	subsidiary plot
BY-ROAD	secondary road
BY-ROOM	small ante-chamber
BYSSUS	fine linen cloth **tx**
BYSSUS	a tuft of filaments **zo**
BY-TIME	leisure time
BY-VIEW	self-interest
BY-WALK	by-path
BY-WIPE	a sarcastic allusion
BY-WORD	taunt; saw; adage; maxim
BY-WORK	by-time work
BYZANT	bezant; coin **nm**

C

CABALA	Jewish traditional doctrine **rl**
CABANA	beach house; shack
CABANE	pyramidal strut system **ae**
CABBLE	smash into small pieces
CABECA	Indian silk **tx**
CABIRI	ancient Semitic divinities
CABLED	telegraphed **el, ro, tc**
CABLET	tow-rope
CABMAN	cabby
CABRIE CABRIT	} prong-horn antelope **zo**
CABURN	spun-yarn
CACCIA	the chase, hunt (It.); oboe form **mu**
CACHED	hidden; concealed
CACHET	a seal; distinctive stamp

CACHOU	a sweetmeat; cashew nut	**bt, ck**	
CACKLE	titter; snigger; chatter		
CACOON	bean	**bt**	
CACTAL	(cactus)		
CACTUS	prickly plant	**bt**	
CADDIE	caddy (golf); porter		
CADDIS	tape; a worm	**zo**	
CADENT	falling; dropping	**mu**	
CADGED	sponged; begged; importuned		
CADGER	huckster; beggar; mendicant		
CADION	chemical detection reagent	**ch**	
CADMIA	sulphide of cadmium	**ch**	
CAECUM	a blind sac	**md**	
CAESAR	an autocrat; tsar; shah		
CAFARD	Algerian desert; melancholia	**go**	
CAFFRE	Caffrarian; wild tabby cat	**zo**	
CAFTAN	kaftan; Persian vest		
CAGING	confining; mewing; penning		
CAGMAG	meat unfit for food		
CAHIER	book; report; an issue		
CAHOOT	partnership		
CAIMAN	alligator (S. Amer.)	**zo**	
CAIQUE	} a Turkish skiff	**nt**	
KAIK			
CAJOLE	coax; wheedle; beguile		
CAKING	clotting; precipitating; coagulating		
CALADE	(manege ground)		
CALASH	vehicle; hood		
CALCAR	glass furnace		
CALCED	wearing shoes; shod		
CALCIC	containing calcium	**ch**	
CALCIO	17th century football, Florence	**ga**	
CALICO	cotton cloth	**tx**	
CALIGO	dimness of sight	**md**	
CALINA	dusty haze in Med. region	**mt**	
CALIPH			
CALIF	} chief of Islam	**rl**	
KHALIF			
CALKED	} made watertight; stopped up		
CAULKED		**nt**	
CALKER	} part of horseshoe		
CALKIN			
CALLED	left cards; dubbed; named; (phone)		
CALLER	fresh; visitor		
CALLET	a scold		
CALLID	skilled; expert; shrewd		
CALL-IN	transfer control; main to sub		
CALLOW	unfledged; inexperienced		
CALL-UP	military induction		
CALLUS	wart; hardening (skin & bone, also in trees)	**bd, bt, mt**	
CALMED	quiescent; lulled; allayed		
CALMLY	sedately; serenely; placidly		
CALORY	caloric; thermal unit	**me**	
CALPAC	Eastern cap		
CALTHA	king-cup	**bt**	
CALVER	caller; fresh; cool		
CALVES	pl. of calf	**zo**	
CALYON	wall construction stone	**bd**	

CAMAIL	chain-mail		
CAMASS	lily (edible bulbs)	**bt**	
CAMATA	acorns	**bt**	
CAMBER	convexity; to arch; dock; slope; tie-beam; flexibility of ski	**ar**	
CAMERA	judge's room; image-recorder	**lw, pg**	
CAMESE			
CAMISE	} shirt	**tx**	
CAMISO			
CAMION	motor truck, waggon		
CAMLET	Angora goat hair fabric	**tx wv**	
CAMPER	who lives temporarily rough		
CAMPOS	Savannah (Brazil)	**go**	
CAMPUS	college grounds		
CANAPE	cocktail delicacy; sofa or settee	**ck**	
CANARD	a hoax; rumour		
CANARY	wine; bird; dance	**zo**	
CANCAN	a dance		
CANCEL	quash; annul; blot		
CANCER	the Crab (Zodiac); malignant cell growth	**as, md**	
CANCHA	court for playing pelota	**ga**	
CANDID	frank; honest; sincere		
CANDIE	500 lb (226 kg) (Ind.)	**me**	
CANDLE	light; taper		
CANGUE	Chinese criminal yoke		
CANINE	doggy		
CANING	thrashing		
CANKER	corrode; infect	**md**	
CANNED	preserved; drunk		
CANNEL	bituminous coal	**mn**	
CANNON	(artillery); (billiards); (croquet)		
CANNOT	unable to		
CANOPY	awning; tilt; firmament; umbrella part of parachute	**ae**	
CANTAB	Cambridge; university; (degree)		
CANTAR	about 1 cwt (50 kg) (Syrian)	**me**	
CANTED	atilt; splayed; bevelled; off-square-oblique		
CANTER	a horse pace		
CANTHI	corners of the eye	**md**	
CANTLE	(saddle); fragment		
CANTON	Swiss province		
CANTOR	a precentor; singer (It.); leader of music; singing in Lutheran church, synagogue	**mu, rl**	
CANTUS	chant	**mu**	
CANUCK	Canadian		
CANVAS	sails in general	**nt**	
CANVAS	tent (linen covering); winning length (rowing)		
CANVAS	} list voting intentions		
CANVASS			
CANYON	deep ravine; gulch		
CAPFUL	filling a cap		
CAPIAS	writ	**lw**	
CAPITE	royal tenant, feudal	**lw**	
CAPIVI	balsam; copaiva	**md**	
CAPLIN	small smelt	**zo**	

CAP-NUT	end-sealed nut	**eg**
CAPOTE	long cloak (Fr.)	
CAPPED	(international); (hunting)	
CAPRIC	acid	**ch**
CAPRID	goaty	
CAPRIN	an acid found in butter	
CAPTOR	capturer	
CARACK	cargo-boat	**nt**
CARACT	mark; sign; character	
CARAFE	glass water-jug	
CARANX	mackerel	**zo**
CARAPA	crab-wood tree (S. Amer.)	**bt**
CARBOL	(carbolic)	**ch**
CARBON	charcoal	**ch**
CARBOY	glass jar	
CARBRO	carbon/bromide printing	**pg**
CARCEL	French luminous-flux unit	**lt**
CARDED	combed (wool)	
CARDIO-	of the heart	**cf, md**
CARDOL	cashew-nut oil	**ck**
CAREEN	to heel over	
CAREER	rush; progress; race; life	
CARESS	fondle; wheedle; embrace; hug	
CARFAX	cross-roads	
CARFOX	carfax; four-forked	
CARICA	paw-paw tree	**bt**
CARIES	decay	**md**
CARINA	keel-like structure	**bt, zo**
CARING	tending; feeling	
CARKED	worried; perplexed	
CARLOT	churl; peasant	
CARMAN	van driver	
CARMEN	carriers; an opera; a song (It.)	
CARNAL	fleshy; sensual; sexual	
CARNET	motor passport	
CARNEY	horse-disease	
CARNOT	thermal-efficiency unit	**eg**
CARPAL	of the wrist	**pl**
CARPED	cavilled; grumbled	
CARPEL	seed vessel	**bt**
CARPER	censurer; critic	
CARPET	floor fabric	
CARPUS	the wrist	**md**
CARRAT	carat	**me**
CARREL	cross-bow arrow; quarry	
CARROT	root vegetable	**bt**
CARTED	removed	
CARTEL	price fixers' ring; truce or peace vessel (white flag)	**nt**
CARTER	wagoner	
CARTON	(bull's-eye); pasteboard box	
CAR-TOW	glider launch method	
CARVED	hewn; chiselled; engraved	
CARVEL	jellyfish; Mediterranean dhowlike vessel	**zo, nt**
CARVEN	cut; sliced; shaped	
CARVER	sculptor; a knife	
CASABA	yellow winter melon	**bt**
CASEIC	(cheese)	**ch**
CASEIN	milk protein	
CASERN	barracks	
CASEUM	caseine	**ch**
CASHED	converted into specie	
CASHEW	tropical nut	**bt**
CASHOO	catechu; an astringent	**bt**
CASING	boxing; packing; wrapping; lining	**bd**
CASINO	saloon; gaming-house; card game 15th century (Fr.)	**bd**
CASKET	jewel case; reliquary	
CASQUE	a helmet; morion	
CASSIA	plant; cinnamon	**bt**
CASTER	cruet; small wheel	
CASTLE	citadel; fortress; stronghold	**ar**
CASTLE	(chess move); wicket (stumps) (cricket); (home)	**ga**
CASTOR	beaver genus	**zo**
CASTOR	a hat; plant	**bt**
CAST-UP	vomit; job content	**pr**
CASUAL	accidental; fortuitous	
CASULA	a chasuble; vestment	**rl**
CATCHY	deceptive; infectious	
CATENA	a chain; a series	
CATENA	doctrinal writings	
CATGUT	cord; violin string	**zo**
CATHAY	China; (Marco Polo)	
CATION	electro-positive element cathode	**el**
CATKIN	pendulous inflorescence	**bt**
CAT-LAP	tame tipple	
CATLOG	catalogue	
CATNAP	forty winks; doze	
CATNIP	mint; catmint	**bt**
CATSUP	a relish; ketchup	**ck**
CATTED	anchor housed	
CATTLE	kine; oxen	**zo**
CAUCUS	political organization	
CAUDAD	towards the tail	**zo**
CAUDAL	tail-like; inferior	**zo**
CAUDEX	palm-stem	**bt**
CAUDLE	hot spiced wine	
CAUGHT	trapped; entangled	
CAUKED	} water-tight	**nt**
CAWKED		
CAUKER	} (caulking oakum); a dram; a	
CAWKER	} tall story	**nt**
CAULIS	stem	**bt**
CAUSAL	producing; resulting	
CAUSED	occasioned; created; effected	
CAUSER	instigator; prime mover	
CAUSEY	pavée; causeway (obs.)	
CAUTEL	craft; wariness (obs.)	
CAUTER	searing-iron	
CAVEAT	a warning	**lw**
CAVERN	cave; grotto; den	
CAVIAR	fish-roe of the sturgeon	**zo**
CAVIES	guinea-pig	**zo**
CAVING	giving way; mining method	**ce**
CAVITY	void; pocket; vacuum	
CAVORT	prance; buck; leap	

CAXTON	a book in black letter	
CAYMAN	alligator; caiman	zo
CAYUSE	Wild West bronco; nag	zo
CEASED	stopped; desisted; terminated	
CEBELL	old English gavotte	mu
CECILS	rissoles	ck
CECITY	blindness	md
CEDARN	made of cedar-wood; of	
CEDARY	cedar colour	bt
CEDING	yielding; resigning	
CEDRAT	citron	bt
CEDULA	S. American mortgage	lw
CELERY	crisp vegetable	bt
CELIAC	coeliac; abdominal	md
CELLAR	vault (wine); (bank vault); (prices); cold storage; underground; (low)	
CELLED	honeycombed; alveolate	
CELTIC	Keltic	
CELURE	decorated route; wagon roof	
CEMENT	adhere; cohese; bind; glue	
CENSED	redolent with incense	
CENSER	urn for burning incense	rl
CENSOR	critic; inspector; carper	
CENSUS	official enumeration	
CENTAL	100 lb (45 kg)	me
CENTRE	middle; midst; (football);	
CENTER	(headquarters)	
CEPHAL-	of the head (Gr.)	cf
CEPOLA	snake-fish	zo
CERAGO	pollen	bt
CERATE	an ointment	md
CERCAL	caudal, of the tail	
CEREAL	grain; corn	bt
CEREUS	a cactus genus	bt
CERINE	an ore of cerium	mn
CERING	covering with wax	
CERIPH	serif	pr
CERISE	cherry-colour	
CERITE	cerium silicate	ch
CERIUM	metallic element	ch
CERMET	metal-ceramic alloy	ml
CEROON	seroon; a bale	
CERRIS	the bitter oak	bt
CERTES	in sooth; certainly (Sc.)	
CERTIE		
CERUSE	white-lead	ch
CERVID	with antlers (deer)	zo
CERVIX	neck of womb	md
CERVUS	the stag genus	zo
CESSED	taxed	
CESSIO	an assignment	lw
CESTUI	a beneficiary	lw
CESTUS	a girdle; boxing glove	
CESURA	metrical pause; an	
CESURE	interruption	
CETINE	spermaceti	zo
CHABUK	Eastern ship	nt
CHACMA	baboon	zo
CHAFED	fretted by rubbing; galled	
CHAFER	a beetle; cockchafer	zo
CHAFFY	light; worthless; jovial	
CHAGAN	a Khan; oriental ruler	
CHAISE	vehicle; shay	
CHALET	Swiss cottage	
CHALKA	Zulu king	
CHALKY	of chalk, pasty	
CHANCE	happen; betide; fortune	
CHANCY	hazardous; risky; fortuitous	
CHANGE	alter; vary; shift; veer; printout	cp
CHANTY	sailor's song	nt
CHAPEL	a printer's association; (church)	rl
CHAPPY	cleft; chinky	
CHARET	a chariot (Spens.)	
CHARGE	command; bid; trust; (cavalry); fee; load; indict	lw
CHARGE	(battery); property of elemental particles	el, ps
CHARKA	small cup with silver handle (Rus.)	
CHARON	ferryman of Styx	
CHARRY	like charcoal	
CHASED	followed; tracked; engraved	
CHASER	hunter; pursuer; a neutralising drink; steeple-chasing horse	
CHASMY	gaping; yawning	
CHASSE	a liqueur; dance step (ice skating); (badminton)	
CHASTE	pure; incorrupt; virtuous	
CHATON	the head of a ring (Fr.)	
CHATRI	umbrella-shaped dome (Hindu)	ar
CHATTA	umbrella (Ind.)	
CHATTY	talkative; gossipy	
CHAWED	gnawed; crunched;	
CHEWED	masticated	
CHECKY	checkered	
CHEEKY	insolent; impudent	
CHEERY	buoyant; merry; blithe	
CHEESE	milk product	
CHEESY	chic	
CHEKOA	porcelain-clay	mn
CHENAR	oriental plane tree	bt
CHINAR		
CHEQUE	order to pay; (banking); (bouncer)	
CHERRY	ruddy; a fruit tree	bt
CHERTY	flinty	mn
CHERUB	angel; child	
CHERUP	chirp; to urge	
CHESIL	gravel; shingle	mn
CHESTY	low pitched	
CHEUCA	Argentine Indian's game like hockey	ga
CHEVAL	a frame	
CHEVEN	chevin; chub	zo
CHEVET	an apse	ar
CHEWET	chough; chatterer	zo
CHIASM	(optic nerve)	md
CHIAUS	chouse; a cheat (obs.)	
CHICHA	liquor from maize (S. Amer.)	ck
CHICHI	'precious'; over-decorated	
CHICLE	chewing gum	bt

CHICLY	fashionably; modishly	
CHICOT	jester to Henri III	
CHILDE	chylde; nobleman's son (Harold)	
CHILLI	} cayenne pepper	bt
CHILI		
CHILLY	bleak; frigid	
CHIMED	struck; (interrupted)	
CHIMER	bishop's robe	rl
CHIMES	bell tunes (clocks)	mu
CHINCH	grain insect; bed-bug; cimex	zo
CHINED	cleft to the back-bone	
CHINEE	a Chinaman	
CHINKY	gaping; chappy	
CHINSE	to caulk	nt
CHINTZ	floral cotton cloth	tx
CHIPPY	off colour	
CHIRAL	pertaining to the hand	pl
CHIRPY	chatty; cheerful; cheery	
CHISEL	to cheat	to
CHISIL	chesil; gravel	mn
CHITAL	spotted deer	zo
CHITIN	horny material	zo
CHITON	a mollusc; Greek tunic	zo
CHITTY	childish; infantile	
CHIUSO	closed horn notes (It.)	mu
CHIVES	onion-like salad plant	bt, ck
CHIVVY	hasten; nag; pester	
CHOICE	select; dainty; option; election	
CHOKED	stifled; throttled; suppressed	
CHOKER	a tie; a neckerchief	
CHOKEY	prison	
CHOKRA	office boy (Ind.)	
CHOLER	anger; ire; spleen; rage	
CHOLIC	(bile); bilious	md
CHOOSE	pick; elect; adopt; prefer	
CHOOSY	pernickety; fastidious	
CHOPIN	quart (Sc.)	me
CHOPPY	irregular	
CHORAL	chanted; sung	mu
CHOREA	St Vitus' dance; the shakes	md
CHOREA-	dance; (choreography)	cf
CHOREE	trochee; poetic metre	
CHORIA	external membranes	bt
CHORIC	of a choir	mu
CHORUS	group of voices	mu
CHOSEN	elected; selected; picked	
CHOUAN	Breton guerilla	
CHOUGH	a crow	zo
CHOUSE	to cheat; a trick	
CHOWRY	fly-whisk (Ind.)	
CHRISM	Holy oil	rl
CHROMA	purity of colour; scale (Gr.)	
CHROMA-	} (chromatic)	cf
CHROMO-		
CHROME	metal	ch
CHRONO-	time (chronometer)	cf
CHUBBY	plump; buxom	
CHUFFY	puffy; surly	
CHUKKA	period of play at polo	ga
CHUMMY	sociable; matey	

CHUNAM	lime; stucco (Ind.)	mn
CHUNKY	with lumps (marmalade)	
CHURCH	temple; kirk	rl
CHURLY	churlish; surly; sullen	
CHUTNY	chutney; fruity pickle	ck
CHYLDE	churlish; surley; sullen	
CHYMIC	chemical	ch
CHYPRE	a perfume	
CICADA	} a chirping insect	zo
CICALA		
CICELY	a genus of plants; myrrh	bt
CICERO	type fount; (orator)	pr
CICUTA	hemlock; cow-bane	bt
CIERGE	wax candle	rl
CIGALE	cigala; cicada	zo
CILERY	carving; carved foliage	ar
CILICE	hair-cloth	
CILIUM	whip-like hair	bt, zo
CIMBEX	the saw-fly	zo
CIMBIA	a fillet	ar
CIMIER	crest of helmet (Fr.)	
CIMISE	bed-bug; cimex	zo
CIMNEL	simnel; saffron cake	
CINDER	ember; ash	
CINEMA	kinema; movies; talkies	
CINGLE	surcingle; girth; cinch	
CINQUE	(cards or dice); (ports); (5)	ga
CINTRE	centering	ar
CIPHER	zero; dot; nought; device	
CIPPUS	funereal column	
CIRCAR	district (Hindu)	
CIRCLE	ring; compass; circuit; set	
CIRCUM-	around; (circumference)	cf
CIRCUS	round place	
CIRQUE	} deep, rounded glacier hollow	
CORRIE		gl, go
CIRRUS	tendril; cloud	bt
CISLEU	a Jewish month	
CISSUS	wild vine	bt
CISTED	in a cyst; entombed	
CISTIC	cystic	md
CISTIL	pewter box	
CISTUS	rock-rose	bt
CITESS	citizeness	
CITHER	zither (guitar)	mu
CITIED	with many cities	
CITING	quoting; summoning	
CITOLE	a dulcimer; psaltery	mu
CITRIC	(lemons)	ch
CITRIL	song bird; a finch	zo
CITRIN	vitamin P	
CITRON	a fruit; lemon	bt
CITRUL	the pumpkin	bt
CITRUS	plant genus	bt
CIVICS	science of citizenship	
CIVIES	mufti; civilian clothes	
CIVISM	good citizenship	
CLAGGY	sticky; cloggy; cledgy	
CLAMMY	dank; viscous; sticky	
CLAQUE	hired applause	

CLARET	a wine; a colour	**ck**
CLARTY	miry; muddy	
CLASSY	superior; high-toned	
CLATCH	botch; daub	
CLAUSE	paragraph; proviso; condition	
CLAVER	gossip (Sc.)	
CLAVES	Cuban percussion	**mu**
CLAVIS	a translation; a key	
CLAVUS	toga stripe; corn; callus	**md**
CLAWED	torn; scratched; lacerated	
CLAYES	hurdles; wattles	
CLAYEY	like clay; cledgy	
CLEATS	herb coltsfoot; hooks	**bt**
CLEAVE	cling; cohere; split; rend	
CLECHE	a cross voided	**hd**
CLEDGE	fuller's earth (clay)	**mn**
CLEDGY	clayey; tenacious	
CLENCH	clinch; secure; fasten; grapple	
CLERGY	the cloth; priesthood	**rl**
CLERIC	clerical; a clerk; church officer	**rl**
CLEUCH	clough (Sc.); ravine	
CLEVER	able; adroit; gifted; dexterous	
CLEVIS	draught-iron of plough	
CLEWED	coiled; trussed	**nt**
CLICHE	artist's proof; trite phrase	
CLIENT	customer; dependant	
CLIFFY	} craggy; broken	**gl**
CLIFTY		
CLIMAX	acme; zenith; height; top	**ec**
CLINCH	clench; clutch; catch; grasp (boxing) (fencing)	
CLINGY	adhesive; sticky	
CLINIC	(bedside); hospital	**md**
CLIONE	'whales' food'; small fish	**zo**
CLIQUE	coterie; junto; cabal; set	
CLOACA	a sewer; reproductive canal	**zo**
CLOCHE	bell-glass; (hat)	
CLOCHE	protective glass cover for plants	
CLODDY	clodly; earthy; gross; boorish	
CLOGGY	adhesive; clingy	
CLOKED	cloaked; concealed	
CLONIC	convulsive	
CLONUS	muscular spasm	**md**
CLOSED	united; grappled; shut	
CLOSER	closure; tighter	
CLOSET	small room; wardrobe	**ar**
CLOTHE	attire; drape; invest; robe	
CLOTTY	curdy	
CLOUDY	dim; overcast; gloomy; murky	
CLOUGH	ravine; cleft; chine	
CLOUGH	trade allowance	
CLOVEN	cleft; split asunder	
CLOVER	trifolium	**bt**
CLOYED	satiated; cumbered; surfeited	
CLUMPS	a numskull; nitwit; dullard	
CLUMPY	massive; shapeless	
CLUMSY	awkward; heavy-handed	
CLUNCH	marl; clay	**mn**
CLUPEA	sprat genus	**zo**
CLUTCH	(of eggs); grasp; clench; grip	
CLUTCH	(motoring); crucial situation in game	
COACHY	a coachman	
COAGEL	gel made by coagulation	**md**
COAITA	S. American monkey; coati	**zo**
COALED	stoked (stocked with coal)	
CO-ALLY	fellow-helper; partner	
COARSE	crude; impure; rough; rude	
COATED	spread; covered	
COATEE	coat with short tails	
COAXED	persuaded; allured; seduced	
COAXER	cajoler; flatterer; wheedler	
COBALT	element; blue	**mn**
COBBLE	a stone; to repair	**mn**
COBCAL	sandal	
COBNUT	hazel-nut	**bt**
COBRES	S. American indigo	**bt**
COBRIC	cobra-type	**zo**
COBURG	a twilled fabric	**tx**
COBWEB	flimsy fly-trap; spider's web	
COCCUS	seed-vessel; microbe	**md, bt**
COCCYX	terminal bone of spine	**md**
COCHIN	a fowl	**zo**
COCKAL	the game of knuckle-bones	
COCKED	erect; inebriated	
COCKER	to pamper; a spaniel	**zo**
COCKER	famous for his arithmetic	
COCKET	customs seal; a certificate	
COCKLE	a weed	**bt**
COCKLE	shellfish; to pucker	**zo**
COCKSY	bumptious; conceited	
COCK-UP	extend above normal level	
COCK-UP	obvious mistake	
COCOON	insect case	**zo**
CODBER	pillow-slip	
CODDED	in a pod; hoaxed	
CODDER	a gatherer of peas	
CODDLE	indulge; pamper; humour	
CODGER	an eccentric old man	
CODIFY	digest; regulate	
CODING	putting into cipher	
CODIST	summarist; arranger	
CODLIN	an apple	**bt**
COELOM	the body cavity	**md**
COERCE	force; impel; constrain	
COEVAL	contemporaneous	
COFFEE	beverage from Ethiopian berry	**bt**
COFFER	pane; chest; lock chamber	**ar, ce, nt**
COFFIN	a printing frame; (funeral)	**pr**
COFFLE	a slave gang	
COGENT	potent; urgent; forcible; convincing; persuasive	
COGGED	toothed; cheated	
COGGIE	small bowl	
COGGLE	small boat	**nt**
COGNAC	brandy	**ck**
COHEIR	joint heir	
COHERE	cleave; unite; join; stick	
COHORN	obsolete trench-mortar	

COHORT	tenth part of a legion; group, companion	
COHUNE	palm	bt
COIGNE	enforced billeting (Irish)	
COILED	spiral; wound	
COINED	invented; minted	
COINER	counterfeiter; inventor	
COITUS	sexual intercourse; mating; copulating	
CO-JOIN	join together; unite	
COKING	taking cocaine	
COLDER	chillier	
COLDLY	frigidly	
COLLAR	neckband; (clothing); harness; pipe joint cover; tie beam	ar
COLLED	embraced; hugged	
COLLET	collar; setting of a jewel	
COLLIE	colley; sheep-dog	zo
COLLOP	a slice of meat	ck
COLLUM	lowest part of stem	bt
COLMAR	pear	bt
COLMEY	the coal-fish	zo
COLONY	a settlement (dominion)	
COLOUR	tint; hue; dye; shade	
COLTER	ploughshare	
COLUGO	flying lemur	zo
COLUMN	pillar; row; line; file; (agony)	bd, pr, cp
COLURE	intersecting celestial circle	as
COMARB	abbot; coarb	rl
COMART	an agreement	
COMATE	comose; hairy; hirsute	
COMBAT	contest; war; resist; oppose	
COMBED	brushed, carded, straightened	
COMBER	foaming billow; searcher (beach)	
COMEDO	a blackhead	md
COMEDY	a play	
COMELY	seemly; graceful; shapely	
COMFIT	sweetmeat; confit	ck
COMFRY	comfrey; wild plant	bt
COMING	approach; future; expected	
COMITY	courtesy; civility	
COMMIS	waiter's assistant; deputy	
COMMIT	entrust; enact; consign	
COMMIX	to mix; mingle	
COMMON	public; ordinary; usual; shared; grazing land (village)	
COMODO	easily flowing, leisurely (It.)	mu
COMOPT	cine-film with optical soundtrack	
COMOSE	hairy; downy; comate	
COMPEL	coerce; oblige; make	
COMPLY	agree; submit; yield; conform	
COMPOT	a preserve	ck
CONCHA	ear-cavity; conch	md
CONCHY	conscientious objector	
CONCUR	agree; harmonize; help	
CONDED	} navigated; steered;	
CONNED	} memorized; studied	
CONDER	pilot; fish-scout	
CONDOM	protective sheath	md

CONDOR	vulture	zo
CONFAB	pow-wow; conference	
CONFER	bestow; grant; consult	
CONFIT	comfit; sweetmeat	ck
CONFIX	fasten; attach; append	
CONGEE	conjee; dismissal; farewell	
CONGER	eel	zo
CONGOU	black tea	bt
CONICS	geometry of the cone	
CONIES	} rabbits; pikas; hyrax genus	
CONEYS	}	zo
CONIIN	conin; hemlock extract	md
CONIMA	gum resin	bt
CONINE	an alkaloid	ch
CONIUM	hemlock	bt
CONJEE	congee; rice-water	ck
CONKED	petered out	
CONKER	chestnut	bt
CON-MAN	trickster; swindler	
CONNER	an inspector; look-out; submarine upperworks	nt
CONOID	pineal gland; a paraboloid	pl
CONSOL	long-range navigational system	nv
CONSOL	Brit. funded gov't security	
CONSUL	a government official	
CONTRA	against; opposite; contrasting	
CONTRA-	lower in pitch; anti-	cf, mu
CONVEX	protuberant	
CONVEY	carry; transport; transfer	
CONVOY	escort; guard; protect	
CONYZA	fleabane	bt
COOEED	(Australian bush call)	
COOING	and billing	
COOKED	done to a turn	ck
COOKER	cooking-range	ck
COOKIE	super-heavy bomb; a bun	ck
COOLED	calmed; allayed; moderated	
COOLER	a drink; colder	
COOLIE	labourer (China)	
COOLLY	calmly; placidly; impudently	
COOMBE	combe; rounded valley	
COONTY	arrowroot (Florida)	bt
COOPED	cabined and confined	
COOPER	a mixed drink; cask-maker	
COOTIE	feathered legs (Sc.)	
COPANG	Japanese gold coin	nm
COPECK	1/100th part of rouble	nm
COPIED	transcribed; aped	
COPIER	copyer; scribe; plagiarist	
COPIES	reduplications; imitations	
COPING	top course of a wall; striving	
COPPED	caught; run in; arrested	
COPPER	a policeman; a penny; metal; washbowl	ml, nm
COPPIN	ball of thread	
COPTIC	(Egyptian Christianity)	
COPULA	a link	
COQUET	to flirt	
CORBAN	} Moslem festival; sacrifice;	
KURBAN	} gifts	

CORBEL	stone bracket	**ar**
CORBIE	a raven; carrion crow	**zo**
CORCLE	embryo seed	**bt**
CORCUR	purple dye	
CORDED	ribbed; furrowed	
CORDON	a ribbon of honour; a guard	
COREAN	} (of Korea)	
KOREAN		
CORERS	geological specimen collectors (oil)	
		to
CORING	boring; drilling (oil-fields)	**to**
CORIUM	true skin	**md**
CORKED	sealed (bottle)	
CORKER	a poser; a finisher	
CORKIR	red or purple lichen dye	
CORMUS	stem	**bt**
CORNEA	eye-membrane	**md**
CORNED	preserved; granulated; salted	
CORNEL	dog-wood	**bt**
CORNER	bend; angle; nook; cranny; sideways move on wave (surfing); free throw (water polo); (football)	
CORNET	an officer; trumpet	**mu**
CORNUA	horns	**zo**
CORODY	an allowance; a pension	
CORONA	a halo; a crown; (solar); psychic aura; discharge	**el**
COROZO	vegetable ivory	**bt**
CORPSE	carcass; corse; remains	
CORPUS	a body; association	**md**
CORRAL	cattle-pen; to round up	
CORRIE	} a hollow; a valley (Sc.)	
CIRQUE		
CORSAC	} Central Asian fox	**zo**
CORSAK		
CORSET	a bodice; stays	
CORTES	Spanish Parliament	
CORTEX	treebark; covering; outer tissue; skin	**bt, pl**
CORTIN	extract of adrenaline	**pm**
CORVEE	forced levy (pre-1789 Fr.)	
CORVEE	recruitment for road service	
CORVET	curvet; leap; frolic	
CORVUS	a crow	**zo**
CORVUS	grappling iron	**nt**
CORYMB	a panicle; a raceme	**bt**
CORYZA	snuffly cold	**md**
COSHED	bashed; slugged	
COSHER	to pamper; to chat	
COSIER	a botcher; cozier; cobbler	
COSILY	snugly	
COSINE	sine of complement of angle	**ma**
COSMIC	cosmical; orderly	
COSMOS	universe; order	
COSSAS	Indian Muslims	**rl**
COSSET	a pet lamb; to pet	**zo**
COSTAL	(rib)	**md**
CO-STAR	actors cast together	
COSTER	costermonger; apple-seller	

COSTLY	dear; sumptuous; rich	
COTEAU	divide between valleys	
COTISE	a bendlet	**hd**
COTTAR	a cottager; cotter	
COTTER	wedge; pin	
COTTON	yarn; oil; (-on, learn)	**bt, tx**
COTYLA	a sucker	**zo**
COTYLE	bone-cavity; cup	**md**
COUCAL	cuckoo	**zo**
COUGAR	puma	**zo**
COULEE	ravine; couloir	
COUPED	bartered for; cut off	
COUPEE	an antic; a salute	
COUPER	a dealer	
COUPLE	pair; brace; connect	
COUPON	a voucher	
COURAP	disease (E. Ind.)	**md**
COURSE	circuit; orbit; progress; series; river bed; flow; direction; hunt; (golf); (horse racing); (marathon); (rowing); etc.	
COUSIN	a kinsman	
COUTER	£1 (sl.)	**nm**
COUTIL	strong cotton fabric	**tx**
COVENT	a convent	**rl**
COVERT	concealed; secret; thicket	
COVESS	female cove or chap	
COVING	(fireplace); (jutting out); moulding	**bd**
COWAGE	a leguminous plant	**bt**
COWARD	craven; dastard; recreant	
COW-BOY	cattle herder; erratic cyclist	
COWDIE	cowrie-pine	**bt**
COWING	intimidating; browbeating	
COWISH	like a cow	
COWLED	hooded	
COW-MAN	cow-herd	
COWPEA	herb, source of black-eye peas	**bt**
COW-POX	cow-teat disease	**vt**
COWRIE	sea-shell; cowry	**zo**
COYISH	coy; rather reserved	
COYOTE	prairie wolf	**zo**
COYPOU	coypu; rodent (S. Amer.)	**zo**
COZIER	tramp; cosier	
CRABBY	perplexing; peevish; nit-ridden	
CRABER	water-vole	**zo**
CRABRO	hornet genus	**zo**
CRADLE	crib; a frame; to compose; somersault (trampoline)	
CRADLE	(cat's); rocking the net; (lacrosse); (wrestling)	**ga**
CRAFTY	artful; deceitful; cunning	
CRAGGE	the neck	
CRAGGY	rugged; rough; jagged	
CRAMBO	a game; a rhyme	**ga**
CRAMPY	affected with cramp	
CRANCH	crunch; chew	
CRANED	with neck out-stretched	
CRANIA	skulls (cranium)	**md**
CRANKY	eccentric; crotchet	

CRANNY	chink; fissure; cleft; rift	
CRANSE	boom iron to take stay-sails	nt
CRANTS	funeral garlands	
CRAPED	curled	
CRASIS	temperament	md
CRATCH	hay-rack; manger	
CRATED	boxed; encased	
CRATER	bomb-hole; funnel of volcano	gl
CRAVAT	necktie; neckscarf	tx
CRAVED	entreated; desired	
CRAVEN	coward; recreant; dastard	
CRAVER	beggar; an addict	
CRAYER	small trading ship	nt
CRAYON	chalk pencil	
CRAZED	decrepit; loony; deranged	
CREACH	} foray (Sc.); booty; raid	
CREAGH		
CREAKY	crepitative	
CREAMY	like cream	
CREANT	forming; creative	
CREASE	Malay dagger; creese	
CREASE	a fold; wicket limit (cricket); goal area (ice hockey)	ga
CREASY	crumpled	
CREATE	cause; fashion; invent	
CRECHE	a day-nursery	
CREDIT	trust; loan; merit; belief	
CREEKY	winding	
CREEPY	} eerie; horrific	
CREEPS		
CREESE	Malay dagger; crease	
CREESH	grease (Sc.)	
CREMOR	creamy juice	
CRENEL	loophole or notch	
CRENIC	acid	
CREOLE	descendant of people of mixed races; West Indies cookery	ck
CREPON	crepe fabric	tx
CRESOL	tar product	ch
CRESOL	resin/plastic phenols	ch
CRESSY	like water-cress	bt
CRESTA	the ice-run at St. Moritz	
CRETIC	a metric foot	
CRETIN	deformed; idiot; moron	
CREVET	goldsmith; crucible	
CREWEL	embroidery	
CRIKEY	exclamation of surprise	
CRIMED	charged with (framed)	lw
CRIMPY	frizzy, waved	
CRINAL	comate; hirsute, hairy	
CRINGE	fawn; stoop; cower	
CRISES	decisive moments	
CRISIS	emergency; turning point	
CRISPY	curled; brittle	
CRISTA	a crest; balance organ in ear	pl
CRITIC	arbiter; reviewer; judge	
CROAKY	harsh; guttural	
CROATS	Croatia (Yugoslavia)	
CROCHE	eighth note, quaver (Fr.)	mu
CROCUS	the saffron	bt
CROISE	attack on blade; cross-swords (fencing)	ga
CRONET	horse-hoof hair	
CROOKS	tubular devices	mu
CROPPY	crop-eared	
CROSSE	lacrosse stick	
CROTCH	a crutch; a fork	
CROTON	oil plant	bt
CROUCH	cringe; stoop; cower	
CROUPY	affected with croup	md
CROUSE	lively; pert (Sc.)	
CROWDY	gruel (Sc.); thin porridge	ck
CROWED	exulted; boasted	
CRUCKS	tree trunk framework	ar
CRUDER	rougher; coarser; harsher	
CRUISE	ocean travel	
CRUIVE	fish trap	
CRUMBY	in crumbs; crummy	
CRUMMY	cow with crumpled horn	zo
CRUNCH	cranch; munch; bite	
CRURAL	leggy	
CRUSET	crucible; crevet	
CRUSIE	lamp with rush wick (Sc.)	
CRUSTA	engraved gem; a shell	
CRUSTY	surly; peevish; morose; crabby	
CRUTCH	to support	
CRYING	notorious; outcry; clamour	
CRYPTO-	hidden; secret; (cryptogram); coded	cf
CUBAGE	solid content	
CUBICA	shallon cloth	tx
CUBING	raising to third power	
CUBISM	modern artistic geometry	
CUBIST	geometrical daubist	
CUBOID	(cubical)	
CUBSHA	Indian drug	
CUCKOO	migratory bird; simpleton; (clock); toy (instrument)	zo, mu
CUDDIE	a donkey; a silly ass	zo
CUDDLE	hug; embrace; fondle	
CUDGEL	bludgeon; club; batter; boys' game (cat and dog)	ga
CUE-BID	(contract bridge)	ga
CUENCA	pottery tiles decoration technique (Sp.)	
CUE-OWL	scops-owl; a migrant owl	zo
CUERPO	querpo; undress; partial array	
CUESTA	ridge of sloping strata (Sp.)	gl
CUISSE	thigh-armour	
CUITER	fondle; pamper	
CULDEE	order of monks	rl
CULLED	picked; gathered	
CULLER	a selector	
CULLET	scrap-glass	
CULLIS	broth; jelly; gutter; groove	ck
CULMEN	summit; highest point	go
CULTCH	oyster-spawn	zo
CULTUR	Kultur; German culture	
CULTUS	a cult	
CULVER	pigeon; wood-pigeon	zo

CUMBER	hamper; impede; clog	
CUMBLY	harsh woollen cloth (Ind.)	**tx**
CUMMER	kimmer; godmother; gossip	
CUMMIN	} spice seed; anti-colic	**bt, ck**
CUMIN		
CUNEAL	wedge-shaped	
CUNNER	Chesapeake oyster boat	**nt**
CUPFUL	filling a cup	**me**
CUP-MAN	boon companion	
CUPOLA	dome; furnace	**ar, ml**
CUPPED	bled; hollowed	
CUPPER	cup-bearer	
CUPRIC	of copper	**ch, ml**
CUP-TIE	annual football competition	
CUPULA	acorn-cup; gelatinous crusta body	**bt, md**
CUPULE	filbert-husk; cupula	**bt**
CURACY	curate's job	**rl**
CURARA	} arrow poison used by South	
CURARE	American Indians	
CURARI		
CURATE	assistant to parish priest	**rl**
CURBED	restrained; held back	
CURCAS	a nut	**bt**
CURDLE	coagulate; congeal	
CURFEW	time to rake out the fires; metal fire cover; prohibition to be out at night	
CURIET	cuirass (Spens.)	
CURING	preserving; healing; remedying	
CURLED	rippled; waved; twisted	
CURLER	(ice); (hair)	
CURLEW	the whaup	**zo**
CURRED	purred; cooed	
CURRIE	quarry (obs.); Indian stew	**ck**
CURSED	anathematized; tormented	
CURSER	vituperator	
CURSOR	a slide-rule adjunct	
CURSUS	a course; curriculum	
CURTAL	docked; curt; early form of bassoon	**mu**
CURTER	more brusque; terser	
CURTLY	concisely; shortly; briefly	
CURTSY	curtesy; an obeisance	
CURULE	Roman chair	
CURVED	arched; bent; bowed	
CURVET	corvet; leap; frolic	
CUSCUS	} N. African millet dish	**bt, ck**
COUSCOUS		
CUSCUS	flying squirrel; fibre	**zo, bt**
CUSHAT	ring dove	**zo**
CUSPID	a canine tooth	**md**
CUSSED	cursed (sl.)	
CUSTOM	habit; usage; wont; tax	
CUSTOS	a keeper	
CUTCHA	temporary (Ind.)	
CUTEST	most cunning; slyest	
CUTLER	a dealer in knives	
CUTLET	meat sliced with bone; chop	**ck**

CUT-OFF	paper process; meandering river; (ox-bow lake)	**go**
CUT-OFF	temporary fuel cessation	**eg**
CUT-OUT	automatic process stoppage	
CUTTER	a tailor; seagoing vessel; rubbed brick	**nt, bd**
CUTTER	author's abbreviation marks system	
CUTTLE	squid	**zo**
CUTTOE	large knife (US)	
CYANIN	colouring of rose/cornflower	**bt**
CYCLED	repeated sequence of operations	
CYCLIC	periodic; closed loop data	**cp**
CYCLUS	a bicycle or tricycle	
CYESIS	pregnancy	
CYGNET	young swan	**zo**
CYGNUS	swan genus	**zo**
CYMBAL	metal clashing instrument	**mu**
CYMENE	(camphor)	**md**
CYMOID	having a waving profile	
CYMOSE	} (inflorescence definite or	
CYMOUS	centrifugal)	**bt**
CYMRIC	Welsh	
CYNARA	artichoke genus	**bt**
CYNICS	Athenian philosophical sect	
CYNOID	dog-like	
CYPHEL	flowering shrub	**bt**
CYPHER	cipher; naught; a nonentity	
CY-PRES	near	**lw**
CYPRIS	shrimp species	**zo**
CYPRUS	black fabric	**tx**
CYSTIC	} bladder	**md**
CYSTIS		
CYTASE	an enzyme	**md**
CYTOID	cell-like	
CYTULA	fertilized ovum; zygote	**zo**

D

DABBED	pecked; patted	
DABBER	an inking ball; dome-shaped brush	**bd**
DABBLE	mix; meddle; sprinkle	
DABOIA	venomous snake	**zo**
DABREY	latex collection tray	**fr**
DACKER	to saunter; to lounge (Sc.)	
DACOIT	pirate; robber (Burma)	
DACRON	polyester fibre	**tx**
DACTYL	finger or toe	
DADDLE	walk totteringly	
DAEDAL	intricate; mazy; complex	
DAEMON	friendly spirit	
DAFTLY	idiotically; crazily	
DAGGED	cut into slips	
DAGGER	dirk; stiletto; poniard; (decorative)	**ar**
DAGGLE	bedraggle; defile; sully	
DAGOBA	Buddhist shrine	**rl**
DAGOES	Spaniards and Italians	

DAHLIA	a flower genus	bt
DAIKER	to adorn; to deck	
DAIKON	Japanese radish	bt
DAIMIO	Japanese noble	
DAINTY	choice; exquisite; tasty; chic	
DAKOIT	pirate; robber; dacoit	
DALILA	Delilah; a betrayer	
DALLOP	a tuft of grass; a lump	bt
DALTON	1/16 of oxygen atom mass	
DAMAGE	mar; hurt; impair; injury	
DAMASK	linen fabric	tx
DAMIER	large-squared pattern	
DAMINE	like a fallow deer	
DAMMAR	resin; damar	bt
DAMMED	embanked; confined	
DAMNED	condemned; doomed	
DAMPED	moderated; deadened	
DAMPEN	moisten; discourage; depress	
DAMPER	(ironing); a regulator	
DAMPER	printing roller (lithography)	pr
DAMPLY	unenthusiastically	
DAMSEL	lass; maiden; girl	
DAMSON	small plum	bt
DANCED	capered; frisked; hopped	
DANCER	a ballerina; Pavlova; Salome	
DANDER	saunter; anger	
DANDIE	terrier	zo
DANDLE	pet; fondle; caress	
DANGER	risk; peril; hazard; jeopardy	
DANGLE	to fondle; swing; suspend	
DANIEL	a wise judge	
DANISH	of Denmark	
DANITE	(Mormon sect)	
DANTON	to daunt; to subdue (Sc.)	
DAPHNE	evergreens	bt
DAPPED	fished with a mayfly	
DAPPER	neat; nimble; sprightly	
DAPPLE	to variegate with spots (horse)	pt
DARGER	day-worker	
DARING	lark snaring; audacious	
DARKEN	darkle; cloud	
DARKEN	obscure; perplex	
DARKER	blacker; duskier	
DARKEY	} negro	
DARKIE		
DARKLE	to grow dark	
DARKLY	opaquely; mysteriously	
DARNED	repaired; mended; accursed	
DARNEL	rye grass; tares	bt
DARNER	a darning machine	
DARTED	sprang out; shot; flew	
DARTER	Brazilian pelican	zo
DARTLE	spring out	
DARTRE	skin-disease; herpes	md
DARWAN	doorkeeper (Ind.)	
DASEIN	being-in-the-world (Ger.)	pc
DASHED	cast; sped; rushed; shattered	
DASHER	plunger; (haber-)	
DASSIE	badger; hyrax	zo
DATARY	papal officer	

DATING	(carbon-14 test); courting; (postmark)	ps
DATION	act of giving	
DATIVE	a case	
DATURA	thorn-apple	bt
DAUBED	smeared; plastered	
DAUBER	inferior painter	
DAUBRY	the work of a dauber	
DAUCUS	the carrot	bt
DAUNER	dander; perambulate	
DAVINA	volcanic substance	mn
DAWDLE	lag; dally; idle; trifle	
DAWISH	like a jackdaw	
DAWNED	began to appear	
DAY-BED	a sofa; couch	
DAY-BOY	non-resident schoolboy	
DAY-FLY	an ephemeral insect	zo
DAZING	mazing; stunning	
DAZZLE	daze; confuse; bewilder	
DEACON	church official	rl
DEADEN	benumb; blunt; obtund	
DEADLY	fatal; mortal; baneful; lethal	
DEAFEN	confuse; stun	
DEAFLY	unhearingly	
DEALER	vendor; monger; trader	
DEARER	costlier; fonder	
DEARIE	term of endearment	
DEARLY	expensively	
DEARTH	scarcity; lack; shortage	
DEASIL	opp. to widdershins	
DEBARK	disembark; land	
DEBASE	degrade; lower; humble	
DEBATE	dispute; contest; argue	
DEBLAI	cf. remblai; excavated soil	
DEBOSH	debauch (obs.)	
DEBOUT	to expel	
DEBRIS	bits and pieces	
DEBTED	indebted; owed	
DEBTEE	the lender	lw
DEBTOR	the borrower	lw
DEBUNK	expose; unmask; reveal	
DECADE	ten of (years); data locations	cp
DECAMP	abscond; bolt; fly	
DECANI	deans-side; southside (choir) of cathedral	ar, rl, mu
DECANT	to pour gently	
DECARE	1000 sq. metres	me
DECEIT	guile; fraud; chicanery	
DECENT	proper; seemly; suitable (clean)	
DECERN	to judge; to decree	
DECIDE	settle; determine; resolve	
DECILE	aspect; deci-intervals (tenth)	as, ma
DECIMA	a tenth	mu
DECIME	a tenth of a franc	nm
DECKED	adorned; arrayed; layered	nt
DECKER	adorner	
DECKLE	paper gauge	
DECKLE	paper-making frame; paper edge	
DECOCT	to boil; to devise; digest	

DECODE	decipher	
DECREE	ordain; ukase; fiat; edict	
DECREW	to decrease (Spens.)	
DECURY	squad of ten (Roman)	
DEDANS	gallery (tennis)	**ga**
DEDUCE	infer; gather; conclude	
DEDUCT	subtract; withdraw	
DEEDED	conveyed by deed	**lw**
DEEMED	believed; determined; judged	
DEEPEN	darken; dredge; make obscure	
DEEPER	further down	
DEEPLY	profoundly	
DEFACE	disfigure; injure; sully	
DEFAME	asperse; vilify; traduce	
DEFEAT	rout; frustrate; overwhelm	
DEFECT	flaw; blemish; faul (traitor)	
DEFEND	ward; protect; guard	
DEFIED	challenged; braved	
DEFIER	scorner, challenger (opponent)	
DEFILE	violate; taint; vitiate; a gorge	
DEFINE	specify; explain; limit	
DEFLEX	bend down	
DEFLUX	a discharge	**md**
DEFORM	distort; deface; spoil	
DEFRAY	pay; meet; liquidate; bear	
DEFTLY	deftly (Spens.); adroitly	
DEGAGE	unconstrained (Fr.)	
DEGRAS	sheepskin fat	**ch**
DEGREE	grade; rank; class; order; units of measurements	**me**
DEGUST	to taste	
DEHORN	remove horns from cattle	
DEHORS	irrelevant (Fr.); melody intended to "stand out"	**mu**
DEHORT	dissuade	
DE-ICER	anti-wing-ice device	
DEIFIC	divine; godlike	
DEIXIS	linguistic context limits	
DEJADA	rebounding ball (pelota)	**ga**
DEJECT	cast down; depress; dishearten	
DELATE	to sneak; to inform	
DELETE	erase; obliterate; efface	
DELIAC	} (of Delas) a vase	
DELIAN		
DELICE	} fleur-de-lis	
DELUCE		
DELICT	an offence; crime	**lw**
DELOUL	fast Arabian riding camel	**zo**
DELUDE	dupe; beguile; trick; cozen	
DELUGE	flood; cataclysm; inundate	
DELVED	dug; excavated; searched	
DELVER	a digger	
DEMAIN	demesne; an estate (domain)	**lw**
DEMAND	claim; exact; require; request	**cp**
DEMEAN	behave; lower; degrade	
DEMENT	madden; derange	
DEMISE	a death; to bequeath	
DEMODE	old fashioned	
DEMOTH	prepare stored arms (war)	
DEMURE	modest; grave; discreet	

DENARY	ten	
DENGUE	a fever	**md**
DENIAL	dementi; refutation; refusal	
DENIED	refused; contradicted; refuted	
DENIER	disowner; gainsayer; silk; nylon quality	**wv, tx**
DENNET	light two-wheeled carriage	
DENOTE	signify; imply; indicate	
DENSER	more compact; thicker; closer	
DENTAL	of teeth	
DENTED	} notched; concussed	
DINTED		
DENTEL	} dog toothed	**ar**
DENTIL		
DENTEX	sea perch	**zo**
DENTIN	} tooth ivory	
DENTINE		
DENUDE	strip; bare; divest	
DEODAR	sacred tree	
DEPART	start; vanish; retire; die	
DEPEND	rely; hang; hinge; rest	
DEPICT	sketch; limn; portray; draw	
DEPLOY	open; expand; extend; unfold	
DEPONE	to testify under oath	**lw**
DEPORT	banish; expel; behave	
DEPOSE	oust; divest of office; depone	
DEPUTE	delegate; authorize; charge	
DEPUTY	envoy; proxy; agent	
DERAIL	upset; leave rail track	**rw**
DERAIN	vindicate; prove; justify	
DERATE	reduce; devalue; demote	
DERBIO	a green sea-fish	**zo**
DERHAM	dirhem; Moroccan coin	**nm**
DERIDE	ridicule; mock; lampoon; scorn	
DERIVE	obtain; draw; trace; receive	
DERMAL	dermic; relating to skin	**pl**
DERMIS	innermost skin (corium)	**pl**
DERNED	darned; damned	
DERNLY	secretly	
DERRIS	plant insecticide	
DESCRY	to espy; detect; discern	
DESERT	quit; abandon; forsake; merit	
DESERT	a Sahara; fruit, etc.	**ck**
DESIGN	plan; devise; concoct; scheme	
DESINE	denote (Spens.)	
DESIRE	covet; crave; want; passion	
DESIST	stay; stop; forbear; pause	
DESMAN	musk-rat	**zo**
DESMID	river-weed	**bt**
DESPOT	dictator; tyrant; autocrat	
DETACH	sever; divide; part; disengage	
DETAIL	delineate; recount; relate; item	
DETAIN	retain; keep; hold; confine	
DETECT	discover; reveal; unmask	
DETENT	a check-stop	
DETEST	hate; abhor; loathe	
DETORT	to pervert	**lw**
DETOUR	deviation; circumambulation	
DETUNE	adjust resonant circuit	**ro**
DEUCED	devilish; confounded	

DEUNME	Jew turned Moslem	rl
DEVALL	cease; a stop (Sc.)	
DEVICE	gadget; ruse; artifice; emblem	
DEVISE	scheme; plan; bequeath	lw
DEVOID	lacking; vacant; empty	
DEVOIR	politeness; duty	
DEVOTE	dedicate; give; resign	
DEVOUR	gorge; gobble; consume	
DEVOUT	pious; saintly; sincere	
DEWANI	a dewan's office	
DEWING	bedewing	
DEWITT	to lynch	
DEWLAP	pendulous neck-flesh	
DEXTER	on the right-hand side	
DEZINK	(zinc extraction)	ch
DHANUK	member of low Indian caste	
DHARMA	law of Buddha	rl
DHOBIE	Indian washerman	
DHOOLY	Indian litter	
DHURRA	millet	bt
DIADEM	crown; coronet; tiara	
DIAMYL	(amyl)	ch
DIAPER	a napkin for incontinent babies	tx
DIARCH	with 2 xylem strands	bt
DIATOM	a seaweed	bt
DIAXON	with 2 axes, in sponges	zo
DIBBED	(gardening)	
DIBBER	pointed tool	to
DIBBLE	dibber; to make holes	
DICAST	dikast; Athenian judge	
DICING	gaming	
DICKER	ten; to barter	
DICTUM	maxim	
DICTUM	precept; award	lw
DIDDER	to shiver	
DIDDLE	cheat; totter; dodder	
DIESEL	heavy oil engine	
DIESIS	printing mark	pr
DIETED		
DIETAL	} food regime	
DIETER		
DIFFER	deviate; vary; wrangle	
DIGAMY	second marriage	
DIGENY	sexual reproduction	
DIGEST	peptonise; summary of ideas/plot	lw
DIGGED	delved; dug	
DIGGER	Australian	
DIGLOT	bi-lingual	
DIGRAM	a digraph	
DIKAST	dicast; Athenian judge	
DIK-DIK	S. African antelope	zo
DIKING	ditching	
DIKKAH	tribune in a mosque	
DIKKOP	bustard (S. African)	zo
DIKTAT	enforced settlement	
DILATE	amplify; expand; enlarge (stimulate)	md
DILOGY	double-entendre	
DILUTE	water; thin; attenuate	

DIMITY	figured cloth; strong cotton	tx
DIMMED	obscured; clouded; dulled	
DIMMER	more indistinct; fainter	
DIMOUT	partial black-out	
DIMPLE	cheek depression	
DIMWIT	fool	
DIN-DIN	Indian cymbals	mu
DINDLE		
DINNLE	} to tingle (Sc.); a thrill	
DINFUL	clamorous; noisy	
DINGED	hurled; enforced; urged	
DINGER	home-run (baseball)	
DINGES	what's its name (S. African)	
DINGHY	dingey; open, ballasted sailing craft	nt
DINGLE	dell; dale; vale; glen	
DINGUS	gadget; contraption	
DINKUM	honest; genuine (Aust.)	
DINNED	persistently repeated	
DINNER	principal meal	
DIODON	globe fish genus	zo
DIONYM	name containing 2 terms	
DIOTIC	affecting both ears	md
DIOXAN	wax/resin solvent	ch
DIPLEX	simultaneous transmission	
DIPLOE	skull tissue	md
DIPNOI	fish with lungs and gills	zo
DIPODY	two-footed	pl
DIPOLE	type of radio aerial	el, ro
DIPPED	immersed; doused; soused	
DIPPER	water ousel; ladle	zo
DIP-ROD	oil gauge	me
DIPSAS	serpent	zo
DIPYRE	a silicate of alumina	mn
DIRDUM	uproar; a scolding (Sc.)	
DIRECT	straight; bid; order; address	
DIREST	most calamitous; cruellest	
DIRHAM	} ancient oriental weight; silver	
DIRHEM	} coin (Morocco)	me, nm
DIRKED	stabbed	
DIRZEE	Indian needlewoman	
DISARM	render harmless	
DISBAR	to expel	lw
DISBUD	remove buds	
DISCAL	(disc)	
DISCUS	quoit; (Greek Games)	ga
DISCUS	flower centre	bt
DISEUR	(diseuse) raconteur (Fr.)	
DISHED	frustrated	
DISMAL	dull; doleful; lugubrious	
DISMAN	unman	
DISMAY	appal; scare; daunt; alarm	
DISOWN	deny; disclaim; reject; ignore	
DISPEL	banish; scatter; dismiss	
DISTAL	terminal; furthest from axis	bt
DISTIL	vaporize; drip; emanate	
DISUSE	desuetude; neglect	
DITHER	didder; tremble; hesitate	
DITION	dominion; rule; power	
DITONE	an interval	mu

DITTAY	an indictment (Sc.)	lw
DITTOS	a mono-coloured suit	
DIURNA	insects; ephemerae (of a day)	zo
DIVALI	Feast of Lanterns (Hindu)	
DIVERS	diverse; different; sundry	
DIVERT	distract; amuse; relax; deflect	
DIVEST	devest; strip; denude; bare	
DIVIDE	sever; sunder; cleave; share; watershed; separate into parts (vote)	ma, me
DIVINE	predict; augur; angelic; sacred	
DIVING	plunging; penetrating; swooping	
DIVISI	separation of strings for part playing (It.)	mu
DIVOTO	solemnly	mu
DIZAIN	poem in ten stanzas	
DIZOIC	with 2 sporozoites	zo
DJIBBA	Eastern garment	
DOABLE	practical	
DOBBIE	a dotard; a brownie	
DOBBIN	old horse	zo
DOCENT	teaching	
DOCILE	pliant; amenable; compliant	
DOCITY	docility	
DOCKED	cut short; moved into harbour	nt
DOCKER	dock-labourer; stevedore	
DOCKET	doquet; a summary	lw
DOCTOR	a fish; medico; to falsify	zo
DODDED	hornless	
DODDER	parasitic plant; didder; shake	bt
DODDLE	a pollard	bt, zo
DODGED	evaded; quibbled; avoided	
DODGER	trickster; shifter; evader	
DODINE	chemical fungicide	
DODKIN	a doit	nm
DODMAN	a snail	zo
DOFFED	removed; took off	
DOFFER	carding mechanism	
DOGANA	custom-house (It.); from 'Divan' frontier control (Turk.)	
DOGATE	dignity of doge (Venice)	
DOG-BEE	a drone	zo
DOG-BOX	enclosure for dogs	
DOG-EAR	broken/damaged book corner	
DOG-FOX	renard	zo
DOGGAR	ironstone	mn
DOGGED	sullen; obstinate; determined	
DOGGER	fishing boat	nt
DOG-LEG	crooked hole shot (golf)	
DOG-MAD	rabid; crazy; insane	
DOIGTE	finger play (fencing)	
DOILED	doilt; crazy (Sc.)	
DOINGS	multifarious activities	
DOITED	crazy; stupid	
DOLENT	full of woe (obs.)	
DOLINE	} closed hollow in karst region	
DOLINA	}	gl
DOLING	distributing	
DOLIUM	molluscs	zo
DOLLAR	100 cents	nm

DOLLED	prinked up	
DOLLOP	viscous mass; helping	ck
DOLMAN	hussar's jacket	
DOLMEN	ancient grave; cromlech	
DOLOSE	fraudulent; deceitful	
DOLOUR	anguish; sorrow; pain	
DOMAIN	demesne; dominion; sway	lw
DOMAIN	borders of strong magnetic force on ferromagnetic crystals	ps
DOM-BOC	Saxon book (judgments)	
DOMETT	shroud fabric	tx
DOMIFY	(horoscope)	
DOMINO	priest's cape; cloak; game	ga, rl
DOMITE	variety of trachyte	mn
DONARY	a gift	rl
DONATE	present; give	
DONJON	the keep	
DONKEY	burro; moke; ass	zo
DONSIE	perverse (Sc.)	
DONZEL	budding knight; a page	
DOOCOT	dovecote (Sc.)	
DOODLE	a simpleton; a trifler; drawing	
DOOLIE	Indian litter	
DOOMED	destined; condemned	
DOPING	doctoring; varnishing	
DOPPER	Dutch baptist	
DOPPIO	increase speed to double (It.)	mu
DORADO	constellation; a dolphin	as, zo
DORBIE	the dunlin	zo
DORCAS	charitable society	
DORIAN	Doric decoration	ar
DORING	lark-catching	
DORISM	Doricism	
DORMER	window in the roof	ar
DORMIE	dormy; unbeatable at golf	
DORMIN	hormone controlling dormancy	bt
DORNIC	figured linen	tx
DORSAL	nerves of touch, limbs	pl
DORSAL	spinal, back fin	pl, zo
DORSEL	pannier	
DORTER	dormitory	rl
DOSAGE	} taking medicine	
DOSING	}	
DOSSAL	} altar cloth	
DOSSEL	}	rl
DOSSIL	pledget; slug	md
DOTAGE	senility	
DOTANT	a dotard	
DOTARD	imbecile; driveller (senile)	
DOTERY	drivel	
DOTING	madly fond	
DOTISH	daft; imbecile; demented	
DOTTED	stippled	
DOTTER	birds'-eyes graining brush	pt
DOTTLE	pipe-ash	
DOUANE	custom-house (Fr.)	
DOUBLE	dual; twofold; duplicate; score (in sports) (turn, trill)	mu
DOUCHE	shower (bath)	
DOUGHY	soft consistency like dough	ck

DOUKAR	dabchick	zo
DOURLY	grimly; sternly; obstinately	
DOUSED	} extinguished; struck;	
DOUTED	drenched	
DOWSED		
DOUTER	extinguisher	
DOWELL	metal pin; cramp	ar
DOWERY	dowry; dot	
DOWLAS	coarse cloth	tx
DOWNED	floored	
DOWSER	water-diviner	
DOYLEY	lace mat; a doily	
DOZING	somnolent; drowsy	
DRABBY	sluttish	
DRACHM	drachma; a dram	nm
DRAFFY	dreggy; waste; worthless	
DRAFTS	draughts; recruits; (sketches)	ga
DRAGEE	sweetmeat	
DRAGON	monstrous saurian	zo
DRAPED	dressed; robed; clothed	
DRAPER	haberdasher	
DRAPET	coverlet	
DRAPPY	a wee drop (Sc.)	
DRAWEE	(Bill of Exchange) payee	
DRAWER	cheque-payer; (chest of); artist	
DRAZEL	a slut	
DREAMT	imagined; fancied	
DREAMY	fanciful; visionary	
DREARY	dismal; lonely; dull; gloomy	
DREDGE	a drag-net; to sprinkle; deepen channel	
DREGGY	(dregs); muddy	
DREICH	tiresome (Sc.)	
DRENCH	(tenure); soak; imbrue	lw
DRESSY	dapper; dandified	
DRIEST	very dry	
DRIFTY	(snow-drifts)	
DRIVEL	twaddle; prate; balderdash	
DRIVEN	urged; compelled; overworked	
DRIVER	a golf club; chauffeur; (pile-); supply circuit	el
DROGER	a coaster; drogher	nt
DROGUE	sea anchor; sleeve target including pilot parachute	ae
DROLLY	droll; laughable	
DROMIC	(race-course)	
DROMON	medieval warship; galley	nt
DROMOS	Greek race-course	
DRONED	buzzed; drawled; idled	
DRONGO	king crow	zo
DROPAX	a depilatory	
DROP-IN	computer error; visit	cp
DROPSY	condition of retention of fluids	md
DROSKY	Russian horse-cab	
DROSSY	impure; foul; worthless	
DROUGE	harpoon drag	
DROUMY	troubled; muddy	
DROUTH	dryness; thirst	
DROVER	cattle-driver	
DROWSE	nap; slumber; doze	

DROWSY	lethargic; comatose; soporific	
DRUDGE	menial; scullion; toil; slave	
DRUIDS	a sacred order	rl
DRUMLY	turbid; muddy	
DRUPEL	a stone-fruit; a drupe	bt
DRUSED	crystalline	
DRUSES	Moslem sect	rl
DRY-BOB	non-rower (Eton)	
DRY-FLY	(fishing) (angling)	
DRYING	parching; desiccating	
DRYISH	somewhat sarcastic	
DRYITE	fossil wood	mn
DRY-ROT	wood decay	
DRY-RUB	nettoyage à sec	
DUALIN	an explosive	ch
DUBASH	interpreter; guide (Ind.)	
DUBBED	styled; greased	
DUBBER	Indian bottle; dupper	
DUBBIN	a leather grease; dubbing	
DUCKED	bobbed; immersed	
DUCKER	a plunger; bird	zo
DUDDER	to shake; to deafen	
DUDEEN	Irish clay pipe	
DUELLO	duelling (It.)	
DUENNA	chaperone	
DUETTO	a duet	mu
DUFFED	stole cattle (Aust.)	
DUFFEL	} coarse cloth with thick nap;	
DUFFLE	felt-like	tx
DUFFER	a pedlar; muff; stupid person	
DUGONG	sea-cow; halicore; manatee	zo
DUG-OUT	canoe; shelter; (baseball)	ga, nt
DUG-OUT	retired officer	
DUIKER	duyker; cormorant	zo
DUKERY	seat of a duke	
DUKKER	to tell fortunes	
DULCET	melodious; honeyed (sounds)	mu
DULCIN	super-sweet crystalline chemical	
DULLED	blunted; assuaged; softened	
DULLER	more listless	
DUMBLY	silently; mutely	
DUM-DUM	soft-nosed bullet	
DUMOSE	} abounding with bushes and	
DUMOUS	briars	
DUMPED	unloaded; deposited; heaped; fallen surfer	
DUMPER	truck with unloading chute gear; unmanageable wave (surfing)	
DUMPLE	to cook a dumpling	
DUN-COW	species of ray	zo
DUNDER	dregs; lees	
DUNITE	olivine igneous rock	gl
DUNKER	tunker; baptist	
DUNLIN	sandpiper	zo
DUNLOP	a cheese; -type	ck
DUNNED	importuned	
DUNNER	debt-collector	
DUNTER	monumental mason or polisher	bd
DUPERY	duping; chicanery	
DUPING	gulling; deceiving	

DUPION	double cocoon	zo
DUPLET	electrons bonding atoms; pair of notes with equal time-value	mu, ps
DUPLEX	two-fold paper; double	pp
DUPLEX	double photography emulsion paper; twin; both ways current; two rooms	pg, cp
DUPPER	Indian bottle; dubber	
DURAIN	type of coal	mn
DURANT	glazed fabric	
DURATE	harsh to the ear	mu
DURBAR	audience; festival	
DURDEN	a thicket; a copse	
DURDUM	dirdum; an uproar	
DURENE	a tetramethylbenzene	ch
DURESS	restraint; imprisonment	
DURGAH	Moslem saint's shrine (Ind.)	rl
DURGAN	dwarf	
DURHAM	breed of cattle	zo
DURIAN	Malay fruit	bt
DURING	throughout; pending	
DURION	see durian	bt
DURITY	hardness; firmness	
DURRIE	Indian cotton fabric	tx
DUSKEN	to grow dark	
DUSKLY	duskily; gloomily	
DUSTER	a cloth	
DUST-UP	quarrel; fisticuffs	
DUTIED	taxed	
DUTIES	obligations; excises	
DUYKER	duiker; African antelope	zo
DYADIC	(two); characteristic of things paired	ch
DYADIC	binary operation	cp
DYEING	colouring; staining	
DYNAMO	energy converter	el
DYNAST	a ruler; dynasty	
DYNODE	valve	el
DYVOUR	a bankrupt (Sc.)	lw
DZEREN DZERON	} Mongolian antelope	zo

E

EADISH	aftermath; second crop	
EAGLET	a young eagle	zo
EAR-BOB	an earring	
EAR-CAP	ear-muff	
EARFUL	a diatribe; (explosion of anger)	
EARING	ploughing; rope	nt
EARLAP	tip of ear	md
EARNED	merited; won; deserved	
EARNER	wage taker; breadwinner	
EARTHY	material; gross; unrefined	
EAR-WAX	cerumen	
EAR-WIG	informer; insect	zo
EASERS	relief holes (prior to tunnelling)	ce
EASIER	more tranquil; more pliant	

EASILY	tranquilly; calmly	
EASING	relieving; calming; soothing	
EASSEL	easterly (Sc.)	
EASTER	Christian festival; after Saxon goddess (Eostre)	rl
EATAGE	cattle food	
EATING	eroding; devouring	
EBBING	waning; declining; subsiding	
ECARTE	card game	ga
ECBOLE	a digression	
ECESIS	unviable-species invasion	bl
ECHARD	non-usable soil water	bt
ECHOED	repeated; resounded	
ECHOES	reverberations	
ECHOIC	aural copycat; mimic	
ECLAIR	a confection	
ECLEGM	oil and syrup	md
-ECTOMY	(surgical) removal	cf, md
ECTYPE	a cast; a copy	ar
ECURIE	stable (Fr.)	
ECZEMA	a skin disease	md
EDDIED	swirled; rippled	
EDDISH	eadish; aftermath	
EDDOES	W. Indian potatoes	bt
EDENIC	(Eden)	
EDGING	border; frill; rim	
EDIBLE	eatable; esculent	
EDITED	revised; emended	
EDITOR	corrector; reviser; annotator	
EDUCED	extracted; elicited; derived	
EEL-POT	an eel-trap	
EERILY	wierdly; uncannily	
EFFACE	erase; expunge; delete	
EFFECT	achieve; cause; create	
EFFEIR	effere; affair (Sc.)	
EFFETE	spent; worn; barren; abortive	
EFFIGY	image; statue; figure; likeness	
EFFLUX	flow; effusion; discharge	
EFFORM	to shape	
EFFORT	essay; trial; striving; strain	
EFFRAY	affray (Sc.)	
EFFUSE	emanate; issue; pour; spill	
EGENCE	exigence	
EGERAN	garnet	mn
EGERIA	spiritual adviser	
EGG-CUP	boiled-egg server	
EGGERY	nesting-place	
EGGING	inciting	
EGGLER	an egg-dealer	
EGG-NOG	a drink; egg and rum	ck
EGOISM	conceit; vanity; self-praise	pc
EGOIST	egotist; not an altruist	
EGOITY	identity; personality	
EGOTIC	essence of the ego	pc
EGRESS	exit; outlet; emergence	
EGROIT	a sour cherry	bt
EIDENT	diligent (Sc.)	
EIDOLA	apparitions	
EIFFEL	tower, 985 ft (300 metres) high	
EIGHTH	an interval	mu

EIGHTS	(boar-racing)	
EIGHTY	four-score	
EIRACK	young hen (Sc.)	zo
EITHER	one of two	
EKEING	eking; adding; stretching	
ELAEIS	African oil palm	bt
ELAINE	the lily-maid of Astolat	
ELANCE	throw out; launch	
ELANET	insectivorous kite	zo
ELAPSE	intervene; pass; slip	
ELATED	exalted; proud; excited	
ELATER	click-beetle genus	zo
ELATOR	a rouser	
ELCHEE	} Turkish ambassador; envoy	
ELTCHI		
ELDEST	oldest	
ELDING	fuel (dial.)	
ELEGIE	} song of lamentation (Fr.) **mu**	
ELEGY		
ELEGIT	writ	lw
ELEMIN	oil from resin	
ELENCH	a disproof; a refutation	
ELEVEN	a cricket team	
ELEVON	hinged wing-control surface	ae
ELFISH	puckish; impish; mischievous	
ELICIT	deduce; evoke; extract	
ELIDED	cut off a syllable	
ELISOR	(jury selection)	lw
ELIXIR	a cordial; quintessence	
ELK-NUT	oil-nut	bt
ELLECK	red gurnet	zo
ELLOPS	snake or fish (obs.)	zo
ELODES	sweating sickness	md
ELOHIM	the Creator (Hebrew)	rl
ELOIGN	to carry away	
ELOPED	bolted; absconded; disappeared	
ELTCHI	elchee; Turkish ambassador	
ELUDED	evaded; dodged; foiled	
ELVANS	felspar veins	mn
ELVISH	elfish; elf-like; tricksy; -pixie	
ELWAND	an ellwand	me
ELYSEE	French president's residence	
ELYTRA	chitinized forewings in coleoptera	
EMBACE	} to degrade (obs.);	
EMBASE	} depreciate; debase	
EMBALE	to pack; to bundle	
EMBALL	encircle; ensphere	
EMBALM	perfume; to preserve	
EMBANK	confine by banks	
EMBARK	} start; enter; board	nt
IMBARK		
EMBERS	live cinders	
EMBLEM	badge; token; device; symbol	
EMBODY	imbody; incorporate; include	
EMBOIL	imboil; boil with anger (Spens.)	
EMBOLY	pushing or growing in	zo
EMBOSS	conceal; cover	
EMBRUE	imbrue; soak; drench; steep	
EMBRYO	germ; nucleus; rudiment	
EMERGE	emanate; appear; issue	

EMESIS	vomiting	md
EMETIC	causing vomiting	md
EMETIN	an emetic	md
EMEUTE	riot; disorder; insurrection	
EMIGRE	French royalist abroad	
EMMESH	immesh; enmesh; entrap	
EMPALE	impale; to enclose	
EMPARK	to enclose; to fence	
EMPASM	a deodorant powder	
EMPAWN	pawn; impawn; pledge	
EMPERY	empire; power	
EMPIRE	rule; sway; dominion	
EMPLOY	use; engross; occupy	
EMPUSA	} spectre or goblin sent by	
EMPUSE	} Hecate	
EMUCID	mouldy	
ENABLE	allow; permit; empower	
ENAMEL	durable paint; crown cover (teeth)	md
ENCAGE	to coop; emmew; incage	
ENCAMP	camp; pitch; settle	
ENCASE	incase; enclose	
ENCASH	pay in cash	
ENCAVE	to cache; to store away	
ENCODE	convert into cyphers or symbols	cp, tc
ENCODE	data as digits for processing	cp
ENCOPE	an incision	md
ENCORE	call for repeat (theatre)	
ENCYST	put in a bag	
END-ALL	finish; conclusion; ultimate	
ENDEAR	captivate; charm; win	
ENDING	finale; closing; finis	
ENDITE	phyllopodium lobe in crustacea	zo
ENDIVE	species of chicory	bt
ENDOSS	endorse; sanction; ratify	
ENDROL	dugout canoe sailing outrigger (S.W. Pacific)	nt
END-SAC	coelomic vesicle in arthropoda	
ENDUED	indued; endowed; supplied	
ENDURE	abide; brook; tolerate	
ENECIA	fever	md
ENERGY	vigour; power; intensity	
ENESIS	vomiting	md
ENFACE	superscribe	
ENFEST	infest	
ENFOLD	infold; wrap up	
ENFORM	to fashion; to mould	
ENFREE	to release	
ENGAGE	contend; agree; promise	
ENGAOL	to put in prison; enjail	
ENGILD	to gild; brighten	
ENGINE	machine; device; method	
ENGIRD	surround; encircle	
ENGLUT	to swallow; to fill	
ENGLYN	4-line stanza (Welsh)	
ENGOBE	ceramic technique	
ENGORE	to gore; to wound	
ENGRAM	essence of memory	md
ENGULF	ingulf; overwhelm; surround	

ENHALO	surround with a halo
ENIGMA	puzzle; riddle; mystery; rebus
ENISLE	isolate; confine
ENJAIL	imprison; incarcerate
ENJOIN	bid; direct; command
ENKOMO	small Cuban drum **mu**
ENLACE	enfold; entwine
ENLARD	to baste
ENLINK	connect; concatenate (coupling)
ENLIST	engage; enrol; secure
ENLOCK	lock up
ENMESH	emmesh; entrap
ENMITY	animus; hatred; aversion
ENMURE	to immure; imprison
ENNEAD	group of nine
ENODAL	without knobs
ENOSIS	political union (Gr.)
ENOUGH	ample; adequate; sufficient
ENRACE	to enroot; implant
ENRAGE	incense; infuriate; madden
ENRAIL	entrain
ENRANK	place in order
ENRAPT	in an ecstasy
ENRICH	fertilize; endow; adorn
ENRING	encircle; surround
ENROBE	invest; attire; array
ENROLL	enlist
ENROOT	enrace; implant
ENSATE	sword-shaped **bt**
ENSEAL	seal up; impress
ENSEAM	to sew up
ENSEAR	to cauterize
ENSIGN	an officer; a flag
ENSILE	store in a pit
ENSPAN	to yoke up (S. Africa)
ENSUED	followed; resulted; accrued
ENSURE	insure; assure; secure; fix
ENTAIL	leave; bequeath; involve **lw**
ENTAME	to tame; domesticate
ENTENT	intention; design
ENTERA	intestines **md**
ENTICE	seduce; allure; decoy; cajole
ENTIRE	(stout); complete; perfect
ENTIRE	ungelded stallion (horse-racing)
ENTITY	being; essence; existence
ENTOIL	to ensnare
ENTOMB	bury; inter; inhume
ENTRAP	inveigle; ensnare; entangle
ENTREE	freedom of access; a dish; subdivision of an act **ck, mu**
ENTUNE	chant; sing; hum **mu**
ENURED	inured; hardened **lw**
ENVIED	grudged; coveted
ENVIER	rival
ENWALL	inwall; enclose
ENWIND	entwine; enlace
ENWOMB	to mate; make pregnant
ENWRAP	envelop; engross; perplex
ENZONE	to girdle; surround
ENZYME	ferment; catalyst leavening **bt, ch**

EOCENE	a geological period
EOLIAN	Aeolian; Eolic
EOLITH	prehistoric flint implement **to**
EONISM	transvestism (d'Eon) **pc**
EOSTRE	Saxon goddess; (Easter)
EOTHEN	from the East
EOZOIC	} rock containing fossilized;
EOZOON	} foraminifera **mn**
EPACME	vigorous period in a life-history
EPARCH	Greek governor
EPAULE	part of bastion **ar**
EPEIRA	genus of spiders **zo**
EPHEBE	young Athenian
EPHORI	Spartan magistrates
EPIGEE	perigee; astronomical point
EPIZOA	parasites **zo**
EPODIC	lyric
EPONYM	name derived from a person
EPOPEE	epic poem
EPULIS	gum disease **md**
EQUANT	imaginary circle
EQUATE	to equalize; to average
EQUINE	horsey
EQUITY	impartial justice
ERASED	expunged; cancelled; deleted
ERASER	a scraper; a mark remover
ERBIUM	rare metal **ml**
EREBUS	darkness; son of Chaos
EREMIC	pertaining to sandy desert
ERENOW	before this time
ERGATE	sterile female ant, worker **zo**
ERIACH	a fine; blood-money (Irish) **lw**
ERINGO	eryngo; sea-holly **bt**
ERINYS	one of the Furies
ERLANG	unit of telephone traffic flow **tc, me**
ERMINE	the stoat's winter coat
ERODED	corroded; eaten; consumed
EROTIC	amatory; sexual; libidinous
ERRAND	mission; charge; message
ERRANT	roving; rambling; wandering
ERRATA	errors; mistakes
ERRING	straying; mistaking
ERSATZ	German reserve; a substitute
ERYNGO	sea-holly genus **bt**
ESCAPE	shun; evade; elude; flee; (wrestling)
ESCAPE	a non-weed in wild **bt**
ESCARP	steep slope
ESCARS	gravel ridges
ESCHAR	burnt wounds; scab **md**
ESCHEW	to shun; avoid; miss
ESCORT	protect; guard; convoy
ESCROL	heraldic scroll **hd**
ESCROW	deed; escrol **lw**
ESCUDO	Portuguese coin **nm**
ESKIMO	an Innuit; arctic dweller
ESLOIN	eloign; to carry away
ESNECY	privilege of choice **lw**
ESODIC	afferent; carrying towards

ESPADA	bull-fighting sword	
ESPIAL	spying; discovery; notice	
ESPIED	discovered unexpectedly	
ESPIER	a spy; a watcher	
ESPRIT	wit; sprightliness	
ESSENE	ascetic Hebrew	rl
ESSERA	skin eruption	md
ESSOIN	excuse for absence	lw
ESTAIN	French pewter	ml
ESTATE	condition; rank; property	
ESTEEM	deem; consider; value	
ESTRAY	to stray; a stray	
ESTRUS	(oestrus) heat; rut	bl
ETALON	an interferometer	lt
ETCHED	engraved; corroded by acid	
ETCHER	an engraver	
ETERNE	eternal (obs.)	
ETHANE	odourless paraffin gas	ch
ETHICS	moral science	
ETHIOP	an Ethiopian	
ETHNIC	racial; ethnological	
ETNEAN	(Etna); volcanic	gl
ETRIER	portable stirrup	mo
ETYMON	derivation; meaning	
ETYPIC	unique	
EUCAIN	drug similar to cocaine	md
EUCHRE	card game	ga
EUCLID	a geometer	
EUCONE	of insect compound eyes	zo
EULITE	an orthopyroxene	mn
EULOGY	panegyric; encomium	
EUNOMY	good government	
EUNUCH	emasculated man	
EUONYM	a suitable name	
EUPION	vegetable oil	bt
EUPODA	beetles	zo
EUREKA	Found! (Archimedes)	
EURITE	a granite	mn
EUTAXY	regularity	
EUTONY	pleasantness of word sound	
EVADED	eluded; dodged; avoided	
EVADER	sidestepper of law, tax, etc.	
EVANID	faint; evanescent	
EVENER	leveller; roller; plane	to, cr
EVENLY	smoothly; fairly; uniformly	
EVILLY	wickedly; maliciously	
EVINCE	display; show; exhibit	
EVIPAN	soporific injection	md
EVOKED	reminded; recalled; reroused	
EVOLVE	unfold; unroll; develop	
EXAMEN	a disquisition; an enquiry	
EXARCH	a title; viceroy; Gr. bishop	rl
EXCEED	cap; outdo; surpass; transcend	
EXCEPT	bar; ban; exclude; omit	
EXCERN	to sweat; to perspire	
EXCESS	surplus; glut; balance	
EXCIDE	to cut off	
EXCISE	duty; impost; tax; (Walpole)	
EXCITE	wake; rouse; incite; kindle	
EXCUSE	acquit; pardon; exempt	

EXCUSS	to decipher; shake off	
EXCUSS	to seize and detain	lw
EXEDRA	a hall; a recess	ar, bd
EXEMPT	free; released; immune	
EXEQUY	funeral rites	
EXEUNT	all quit the stage	
EXHALE	emit; reek; emanate; breathe	
EXHORT	urge; encourage; counsel	
EXHUME	unearth; disinter	
EXILED	banished; outlawed	
EXILIC	(Jewish) exile	
EXITUS	yearly rent; issue	lw
EXODIC	(Exodus); migratory	
EXODUS	departure	
EXOGEN	a class of plant	bt
EXOMIS	Greek sleeveless tunic	
EXOTIC	not native; extraneous; foreign	
EXPAND	spread; dilate; swell; extend	
EXPECT	hope; await; forecast	
EXPEND	disburse; consume; exert	
EXPERT	apt; adroit; skilful; able	
EXPIRE	end; die; stop; finish	
EXPIRY	conclusion; extinction	
EXPORT	ship; produce; send; carry	
EXPOSE	an exposure; reveal; unmask	
EXPUGN	take by assault; conquer	
EXSECT	to cut away; cut out	
EXSERT	to protrude	
EXSULE	apterous life-cycle form in	
	hemiptera	zo
EXTANT	existent; current	
EXTASY	ecstasy; rapture; trance	
EXTEND	stretch; reach; expand	
EXTENT	amount; scope; range; field	
EXTERN	day-boy	
EXTERN	not inherent; external	
EXTINE	(pollen grain)	bt
EXTORT	exact; extract; wrench; elicit	
EXUDED	sweated; oozed; percolated	
EXUVIA	cast-off skins, shells	zo
EYE-CUP	(used for eye lotion)	md
EYEFUL	a glance	
EYEING	watching	
EYELET	loop-hole	
EYELID	eye skin cover	pl
EYEPIT	eye socket	pl
EYRANT	bird of prey on nest	zo

F

FABIAN	policy of patiently waiting for opportune moment	
FABLED	fabricated; fictional	
FABLER	an Aesop; parable teller	
FABRIC	structure; texture; web	
FACADE	front view; face; masking	ar
FACE-UP	confront; position of printing	cp
FACIAL	frontal; of the face	md
FACIES	external appearance; the face	lw

194

FACILE	easy; dexterous; pliant	
FACING	confronting; opposing; covering; forward looking; surface finish **ar, ce**	
FACTOR	broker; middleman	
FACTOR	agent or manager of estate	
FACTOR	causal influence; component **ma**	
FACTUM	memorandum; deed; point of controversy **lw**	
FACULA	sun-spot **as**	
FADDLE	to trifle; to play	
FADGED	suited; prospered	
FADING	diminishing; withering; reducing speed at end of race **ro**	
FAECES	human excrement	
FAERIE	fairy; fairyland; (Spens.)	
FAFFLE	to stammer	
FAG-END	butt (cigarette)	
FAGGED	tired	
FAGGOT	} bundle of sticks; bassoon; facing brick **bd, mu**	
FAGOT		
FASCINE		
FAIKES	shaly sandstone **mn**	
FAILED	did not succeed; missed (fiasco)	
FAILLE	nun's veiling	
FAINTY	feeble; languid	
FAIRER	more equitable	
FAIRLY	moderately; passably	
FAITOR	rogue; impostor; evil-doer	
FAKEER	Indian beggar	
FAKING	forging; doctoring; feinting; pretending; (boxing); (badminton)	
FALCON	hawk; missile **zo**	
FALLAL	finery; streamer **wx, tx**	
FALLEN	sunk; lapsed; ebbed	
FALLOW	untilled; idle; dormant	
FALSER	more fallacious	
FALTER	totter; waver; vacillate	
FALUNS	Miocene deposits **gl**	
FAMBLE	the hand (sl.) **pl**	
FAMILY	household; race; lineage	
FAMINE	dearth; scarcity; starvation	
FAMOUS	renowned; eminent	
FANGED	toothed; taloned	
FANGLE	a contraption; novelty	
FANGOT	a quantity of wares	
FANNED	inflamed	
FANNEL	} flag; banner; splint	
FANION		
FANNER	winnower	
FAN-OUT	multiple outputs from a circuit **ps, el**	
FANTAN	Chinese gambling game **ga**	
FANTOM	phantom; spook; ghost	
FAQUIR	religious mendicant	
FARCIN	glanders; farcy	
FARDEL	a bundle; burden; load	
FARFEL	kosher dumplings; dough grains **ck**	

FARINA	pollen; flour **bt, ck**	
FARING	experiencing; feeding	
FARMED	leased	
FARMER	tiller; cultivator	
FARROW	litter of pigs	
FASCES	Roman badge	
FASCIA	a band; name-board; connective tissue **ar, pl**	
FASHED	vexed; worried (Sc.)	
FASTED	abstained from food	
FASTEN	bind; secure; tie; latch	
FASTER	quicker; speedier	
FASTLY	firmly	
FAT-HEN	goose-foot **bt**	
FATHER	adopt; beget; sire	
FATHOM	6 ft (1.8 m); comprehend **nt**	
FATTED	fattened	
FATTEN	grow plump	
FATTER	more obese	
FAUCAL	throaty; guttural	
FAUCES	(mouth) **md**	
FAUCET	a tap; fosset	
FAULTY	defective; blameworthy	
FAUNAL	relating to animals **zo**	
FAUNUS	Pan	
FAUTOR	a supporter	
FAVOSE	honeycombed; cellular	
FAVOUR	gift; patronize; bias	
FAWNER	sycophant; clinger; parasite	
FAYING	fitting closely **nt**	
FEALTY	fidelity; loyalty; homage	
FEARED	apprehended; dreaded	
FEATLY	neatly; dexterously; adroitly	
FEAZED	untwisted; unravelled	
FECIAL	Roman priest; fetial **rl**	
FECKLY	effectually	
FECULA	(plants); starch **bt**	
FECUND	prolific; fertile; fruitful	
FEDARY	a confederate	
FEDORA	trilby hat (USA)	
FEEBLE	faint; frail; weak	
FEEBLY	languidly	
FEEDER	a bib; a channel	
FEED-IN	programming data **cp**	
FEEING	hiring; recompensing	
FEELER	organ of animals, plants	
FEELER	tentative suggestion	
FELINE	catty; spiteful	
FELLAH	an Egyptian peasant; ploughman; (Arab.)	
FELLER	wood-cutter	
FELLIC	(bile) **md**	
FELLOE	felly; rim of wheel	
FELLOW	peer; mate; equal	
FELONY	crime; misdemeanour **lw**	
FELTED	covered with felt	
FELTER	to mat together	
FELTRE	cuirass	
FEMALE	feminine	
FENCED	equivocated	

FENCER	hedger; prevaricator		**FILLET**	band; plain lines on book; tool **to**
FENDER	protective rope mat; firescreen		**FILL-IN**	shadow technique **~pg**
	(low)	**nt**	**FILLIP**	to flip; an incitement
FENIAN	an Irish conspirator		**FILOSE**	thread-like
FEN-MAN	fen-lander; (East Anglian)		**FILTER**	strain; separate; selective process
FENNEC	African fox	**zo**		**tc**
FENNEL	vegetable	**bt, ck**	**FILTER**	limited band network output **el**
FENSON	chemical insecticide		**FILTHY**	foul; dirty; corrupt
FEODAL	feudal		**FILTRE**	coffee-brewing method (Fr.) **ck**
FERASH	lowly servant (Ind.)		**FIMBLE**	hemp **bt**
FERBAM	chemical fungicide	**ch**	**FINALE**	climax; conclusion; finis; last
FERGIE	double-side kick (skiing)			movement **mu**
FERIAE	Roman holidays		**FINDER**	discoverer **;**
FERIAL	(holidays)		**FINDON**	dried haddock **ck**
FERINE	wild; savage; untamed; fierce		**FINEER**	(fraudulent credit)
FERITY	wildness		**FINELY**	excellently; delicately
FERRET	silk ribbon; polecat	**zo**	**FINERY**	splendour; trappings; fallals **wv,**
FERRIC	(iron)	**ch**		**tx**
FERULA	fennel	**bt**	**FINEST**	keenest; sharpest; purest
FERULE	a rod; cane		**FINGER**	digit; pilfer; touch
FERVID	fervent; eager; ardent		**FINIAL**	a pinnacle; decorative acorn, knob
FESCUE	a pointer; a grass	**bt**		**ar**
FESTAL	joyous; gay		**FINING**	refining
FESTER	rankle; rot; putrefy		**FINISH**	end; terminate; accomplish
FETIAL	fecial; Roman priest	**rl**	**FINISH**	final coat of paint; fixed joinery **bd**
FETISH	fetich; charm; amulet; talisman		**FINITE**	limited; restricted
FETRON	junction field-effect transistor	**el**	**FINLET**	small fin **zo**
FETTER	manacle; shackle; bond; gyve		**FINNAN**	findon haddock **zo**
FETTLE	good condition; fitness		**FINNED**	bearing fins
FEUDAL	vassal-lord polity		**FINNER**	fin-back whale; torqual **zo**
FIACRE	French cab		**FINNIC**	Finnish
FIANCE	betrothed man		**FINNOC**	white trout **zo**
FIASCO	total failure, breakdown; flask		**FIORIN**	bent-grass **bt**
FIBBER	a liar		**FIPPLE**	wood block in recorder
FIBRED	having fibres			mouthpiece **mu**
FIBRID	synthetic fibrous bonding particle		**FIRING**	igniting; kindling; expelling
FIBRIL	small fibre; slender thread		**FIRKIN**	9 imperial gallons **me**
FIBRIN	gluten; clot formative	**bt, md**	**FIRLOT**	a quarter boll **me**
FIBULA	ancient brooch; leg bone	**md**	**FIRMAN**	Ottoman decree; licence (Turk.)
FICKLE	volatile; mercurial; unstable		**FIRMED**	confirmed; established
FICTOR	a modeller		**FIRMLY**	steadily; compactly
FIDDLE	a railing; violin; ruse	**mu**	**FISCAL**	treasurer; monetary **lw**
FIDGET	fret; chafe; worry		**FISHED**	strengthened; caught (angled)
FIERCE	savage; cruel; violent			(compliments) **nt**
FIESTA	carnival; bullfight (Sp.)		**FISHER**	weasel; black fox **zo**
FIGARO	a schemer; French newspaper		**FISHES**	alternative pl. of fish **zo**
FIGGED	all dressed up		**FISSLE**	rustle; whistle (Sc.)
FIGURE	reckon; digit; diagram; (father-);		**FISTED**	struck with the fist
	ground; timber markings;		**FISTIC**	(boxing); pugilistic
	musical phrase	**bd, cp, mu**	**FITCHE**	} pointed **hd**
FIJIAN	(Fiji Islands)		**FITCHY**	}
FIKERY	fuss (Sc.)		**FITFUL**	irregular; unreliable
FILAGO	cudweed	**bt**	**FITTED**	apt; seemly; adjusted
FILFOT	fylfot; a swastika		**FITTER**	an artificer; more seemly; engine
FILIAL	as a son			assembler **ce**
FILING	particle; (documents)		**FIXING**	deciding; settling
FILLED	replete		**FIXITY**	permanence; fastness
FILLER	Hungarian coin; (complete); paste;		**FIXIVE**	gummy; adhesive; glutinous
	extenders	**nm, bd**	**FIXURE**	stability; firmness (Shak.)
FILLET	hair-ribbon; boneless fish/meat	**ck**	**FIZGIG**	fisgig; a flirt; damp squib

FIZZED	hissed; effervesced
FIZZER	a fast one
FIZZLE	a fiasco; splutter
FLABBY	tabid; flaccid; lax
FLACON	scent-bottle; small flask (Fr.)
FLAGGY	drooping; languishing
FLAGON	a flask; later beer tankard
FLAKED	peeled off
FLAMBE	ignited brandy dish; uneven pottery glaze (Fr.) **ck**
FLAMED	glazed; excited
FLAMEN	Roman official of rites
FLANCH	a flange
FLANGE	projecting rim (wheel); pipe disc; chord (girder) **rw, ce**
FLANKS	haunches (horse); sides; intrados of arch **bd**
FLARED	burnt unsteadily
FLASHE	a sluice
FLASHY	gaudy; impulsive; vapid
FLATLY	positively; plainly
FLATTY	a policeman (sl.) (flat-foot); (puncture)
FLATUS	puff of body-wind
FLAUNT	vaunt; parade; display
FLAUTO	modern traverse flute (It.) **mu**
FLAVIN	yellow dye
FLAVOR	flavour; taste; quality; relish
FLAWED	defective
FLAXEN	pale yellow
FLAYED	skinned
FLAYER	skinner
FLECHE	arrow; slender spire; running attack (fencing)
FLEDGE	grow feathers
FLEDGY	feathery; downy
FLEECE	to strip; plunder
FLEECH	flatter; coax (Sc.)
FLEECY	woolly; flocculent **tx**
FLENCH	} to cut up the blubber of a
FLENSE	} whale
FLESHY	carnal; corporeal
FLETCH	to feather an arrow (archery)
FLEURY	(fleur-de-lis); dilly-flower; lily (Fr.) **hd**
FLEWED	deep-mouthed
FLEXED	bent
FLEXOR	joint-bending muscle **pl**
FLICKS	movies
FLIGHT	retreat; exodus; rout; stairs; aerial journey; escape (high-diving) (badminton) **ar**
FLIMSY	frail; trivial; weak
FLINCH	wince; blench; quail
FLINTS	nodules of silica (fossil sponges); flocculation **gl**
FLINTY	obdurate; hard; miserly
FLISKY	frisky (Sc.)
FLITCH	a side of bacon; stack of veneer panels **bd**

FLITTY	flighty; unstable
FLOATS	(paddle-wheels); mobile platforms (processions); rafts (lifesaving) **nt**
FLOATY	buoyant; light
FLOCCI	woolly filaments
FLOCKS	waste wool **tx**
FLOCKY	downy
FLOPPY	flaccid; drooping
FLORAL	flowery
FLORAN	tin ore **mn**
FLORET	flowerlet; decoration for spacing **bt, pr, ar**
FLORID	ornate; meretricious
FLORIN	once coined at Florence **nm**
FLOSSY	silky
FLOURY	like flour
FLOUSE	} to turn the edge of a tool; to
FLOUSH	} splash (Sc.); (flush) **to**
FLOWER	blow; bloom; blossom **bt**
FLUATE	fluoride **ch**
FLUCAN	clay **mn**
FLUENT	flowing; voluble; fluid
FLUFFY	downy; fluey
FLUING	of splayed window jambs **bd**
FLUKED	was fortunate
FLUNKY	a lackey; snob
FLURRY	agitation; bustle; perturb
FLUSHY	reddish
FLUTED	channelled; grooved **mu, ar**
FLUTER	flutist; flautist **mu**
FLUXED	melted; purged
FLUXES	fusible substances for soldering
FLY-BOX	receptacle for bait (angling) **bd**
FLYING	aviation; fleeing; soaring
FLYMAN	cabman
FLY-NET	mosquito curtain
FLY-NUT	winged nut
FLY-ROD	fishing rod for flies (angling)
FOAMED	spumed; frothed
FOBBED	imposed on; tricked
FOCILE	a bone (arm or leg) **pl**
FOCOSO	spiritedly **mu**
FO'C'SLE	forecastle; bows **nt**
FODDER	a weight; animal food **me**
FOEMAN	foe; antagonist; enemy
FOETAL	} of the unborn (embryonic)
FETAL	}
FOETOR	a stench; offensive odour
FOETUS	life in embryo **md**
FOG-BOW	white rainbow
FOGGED	blurred; overcast
FOGRAM	antiquated; a fogey
FOIBLE	faible; weak point; defect
FOIBLE	sharp half of sword (fencing) **ga**
FOILED	baffled; thwarted; balked
FOILER	a frustrator
FOISON	plenty; autumn
FOLDED	doubled; wrapped; furled
FOLDER	paper jacket

FOLIAR	(leaves); laminar	
FOLIER	goldsmith's foil	
FOLIOT	goblin	
FOLIUM	striatum; thin stratum; brain cover	gl, pl
FOLKSY	imitation rustic	
FOLLIA	(composition)	mu
FOLLOW	succeed; chase; pursue; heed	
FOMENT	fan; excite; stimulate	
FONDER	tenderer; (preference) (love)	
FONDLE	pet; caress; dandle	
FONDLY	affectionately; foolishly	
FONDUE	melted cheese/wine dish (Swiss)	ck
FONDUS	calico-printing	
FONTAL	primary; baptismal	
FOOLED	duped; hoodwinked; hoaxed	
FOOLEN	(embankment)	
FOOTED	walked; paid; kicked	
FOOTER	football (sl.)	ga
FOOTLE	twaddle; bunkum	
FOOZLE	bungle; mishit	
FORAGE	fodder; search; pillage	
FORBID	ban; inhibit; taboo; veto	
FORBYE	besides; hard by	
FORCED	unnatural; compulsory	
FORCER	compeller	
FORDED	crossed by wading	
FORE-BY	besides (Sc.)	
FOREDO	to destroy; undo; overpower	
FOREGO	yield; resign; relinquish	
FOREST	woodland; grove; boscage	
FORFEX	scissors	to
FORGAT	forgot	
FORGED	fabricated; spurious; welded	
FORGER	falsifier; hammerman	
FORGET	overlook; slight	
FORGOT	neglected	
FORINT	Hungarian currency	nm
FORKED	bifurcated	
FORLAY	to ambush; lie in wait for	
FORMAL	precise; exact; stiff; set	
FORMAT	style; layout; size; (printing); data	cp, pr
FORMED	arranged; moulded; shaped	
FORMER	prior; previous; bygone	
FORMIC	(acid)	ch
FORMYL	organic radical	ch
FORNIX	(shell); (brain)	md
FORPET	} a fourth part; a quarter (Sc.)	
FORPIT		
FORREL	forel; parchment	
FORRIT	forward (Sc.)	
FORROW	not with calf (Sc.)	zo
FORSAY	forbid; renounce	
FORTED	guarded; castellated	
FOSSIL	petrified	mn
FOSTER	cherish; nourish; encourage	
FOTHER	leak-stopping	nt
FOTMAL	70 lb (31.7 kg) of lead	me

FOUDRE	large storage/transport wine cask	
FOUGHT	strove; contended; warred	
FOULED	polluted; sullied	
FOULLY	scurvily; unfairly; basely	
FOURBE	a cheat; trickster	
FOURTH	ordinal number; 4th; interval (harmonic)	mu
FOWLER	bird-shooter	
FOX-BAT	flying fox	zo
FOXING	deceiving; duping; deluding	
FOXISH	cunning; sly; shrewd	
FOYBLE	part of sword-blade	
FRACAS	an uproar; brawl; riot	
FRACID	overripe; rotten	
FRAGOR	a crash	
FRAISE	defence of pointed stakes	
FRAMED	constructed; devised	
FRAMER	contriver; frame-maker	
FRANCO	free of expense; in bond (storage); duty-free	nt
FRANZY	crotchety (dial.)	
FRAPPE	chilled with ice (Fr.)	
FRATCH	a quarrel; a brawl (dial.)	
FRATER	refectory; brother; friar	rl
FRAYED	worn; chafed; fretted	
FRAZIL	anchor-ice; spicular ice	
FREELY	unimpeded; willingly; readily	
FREEZE	chill; numb; congeal; (statues); (golf); (basketball)	
FRENCH	Gallic	
FRENUM	a ligament	pl
FRENZY	delirium; madness; fury	
FRESCO	drink; paint; refreshment	
FRESCO	coolness; wall painting; (al fresco: out of doors)	
FRETTA	increase the pace (It.)	mu
FRETTE	a strengthening band	ar
FRETTY	ornate	
FRIARY	monastery	
FRIDAY	(Robinson Crusoe); assistant	
FRIDGE	ice-box; refrigerator	
FRIEND	ally; chum; intimate	
FRIEZE	rough stuff; decorative border	ar
FRIGGA	wife of Odin	rl
FRIGHT	alarm; dismay; panic; dread	
FRIGID	icy; cold; formal	
FRILLY	fluted; overdressed	pg
FRINGE	border; edge	
FRINGY	adorned with fringes	
FRISKY	gay; lively; sportive	
FRIVOL	to trifle	
FRIZEL	(flint-lock)	
FROGGY	abounding in frogs	
FROISE	pancake; fraise (Fr.)	ck
FROLIC	romp; gambol; play; lark	
FRONDE	political party (Fr.) 17th cent.	
FROSTY	chilling; wintry	
FROTHY	empty; unsubstantial; foamy	
FROUZY	rank; musty; rancid	
FROWER	a cleaver	to

FROWST	stuffy and hot	
FROWSY	frowzy; unkempt; disorderly	
FROZEN	froren; frosty; iced	
FRUGAL	thrifty; saving; parsimonious	
FRUITY	fruitful; luscious	
FRUMPY	dowdy	
FRUTEX	a shrub	bt
FRYING	cooking with fat	
FUCATE	painted; a sham	ar
FUCOID	a fossil seaweed	mn
FUDDLE	muddle; inebriate	
FUDGED	cheated; faked; bungled	
FUFFED	puffed	
FUGATO	like a fugue	mu
FUGILE	ear trouble	md
FUGUES	memoryless wandering	pc
FUHRER	Hitler-type dictator; leader; guide; (Ger.)	
FULANI	tribe (South Sahara)	
FULFIL	meet; effect; satisfy	
FULGID	fulgent; flashing; steaming	
FULGOR	splendour	
FULHAM }	a die loaded at one; corner	
FULLAM }	to throw high	
FULLAN }		
FULICA	coot genus	zo
FULLED	scoured and thickened	
FULLER	hammer	to
FULMAR	sea-fowl; the petrel	zo
FULVID	tawny; yellow	
FUMADO }	smoked food (Sp.)	ck
AHUMADO }		
FUMAGE	chimney tax; hearth money	
FUMBLE	grope; bungle; stammer	
FUMILY	sulkily; smokily	
FUMING	ammonia process	pg
FUMMEL	funnel; mule	zo
FUMOUS	(fumes); vaporous	
FUNDED	endowed	
FUNDUQ	caravanserai fort (Arab.)	ar
FUNDUS	back part	
FUNEST	doleful; lamentable	
FUNGAL }	(fungi) mushrooms	bt
FUNGIN }		
FUNGIA	genus of corals	zo
FUNGUS	plant	bt
FUNKED	played the coward	
FUNKIA	a lily genus	bt
FUNNEL	fummel; smoke-stack	
FURFUR	dandruff	md
FURIES	avenging deities	
FURLED	closely rolled	
FURORE	outburst of excitement, anger	
FURRED	encrusted (pipes); (hard water)	bd
FURROW	rut; groove; seam; corrugate	
FURZEN	furzy; whinny	bt
FUSAIN	friable coal	mn
FUSEAU	macroconidium of dermatophytes	bt
FUSING	liquefaction	

FUSION	melting; amalgamation	
FUSOID	wide-middled and end-tapered	bt
FUSSED	worried; fretted; fidgeted	
FUSTED	mouldy; rancid; malodorous	
FUSTET	shrub; the sumac	bt
FUSTIC	tropical American tree	bt
FUSURE	smelting; fusion	
FUTILE	bootless; vain; useless	
FUTTAH }	rat-proof raised store-house	
FUTTER }	(NZ)	
FUTURE	hereafter; prospective	
FUZZED	ground to powder	
FUZZLE	intoxicate; fuddle	

G

GABBED	talked; prattled	
GABBLE	jabber; prate; chatter	
GABBRO	(felspar)	mn
GABION	net frame holder for rocks as wall	ce
GABLED	having gables	bd
GABLET	small gable	
GABOON	African mahogany-like wood	fr
GADDED	wandered about	
GADDER	a gadabout; a rover	
GADFLY	horse-fly	zo
GADGET	a cunning device; contraption	
GADINE	gadean; cod-type	zo
GADOID	codfish type	zo
GAELIC	Scottish-Highland dialect; Celtic	
GAFFED	(fishing)	
GAFFER	rustic; foreman	
GAFFLE	spur (cock-fight)	
GAGAKU	Japanese court orchestral music	mu
GAGGED	silenced; joked	
GAGGER	an interpolator	to
GAGGLE	a flock of geese	zo
GAGMAN	joke-writer; comic	
GAIETY	gayety; merriment; vivacity	
GAINED	acquired; reached; won	
GAINER	winner, beneficiary	
GAINLY	comely; conveniently	
GAINST	against	
GAITED	having a distinctive walk	
GAITER	gamash	
GALACT-	of milking	cf
GALAGE	galosh; golosh	
GALAGO	lemur (Madagascar)	zo
GALANT	courtly dance	mu
GALAXY	Milky Way; brilliant assembly	
GALBAN	a gum used in medicine	bt
GALEAS	galley	nt
GALEGA	goat's rue	bt
GALENA	lead sulphide	ch
GALIOT	brigantine	nt
GALIUM	bed-straw genus	bt
GALLED	chagrined; fretted; vexed	

GALLET	stone splinter	
GALLEY	ship; boat; cook-house	nt
GALLIC	French; an acid	ch
GALLIO	insouciance personified	
GALLON	4 quarts (4.5 litres)	me
GALLOP	a dance; full speed of a horse; fast canter	
GALLOW	to terrify	
GALLUP	poll (public opinion); voting system	
GALOON	galloon; silk fabric	tx
GALOOT	lout	
GALORE	golore; in abundance	
GALOSH	galage; overshoe	
GAMASH	gaiters	
GAMBET	a bird; red-shank	zo
GAMBIT	opening move (chess)	ga
GAMBLE	stake; hazard; risk; wager	
GAMBOL	frolic; romp; caper	
GAMELY	pluckily	
GAMETE	mature reproductive cell	pl, zo
GAMGEE	absorbent wool/gauze	tx
GAMING	gambling	
GAMMER	old woman	
GAMMON	(bacon); hoax; cozen	
GAMONT	gamete-bearing individual	zo
-GAMOUS	marital, sexual, union	cf
GANDER	a glance (USA); male goose	zo
GANESA	Hindu elephant god	rl
GANGER	foreman; overman	
GANGUE	veinstone	mn
GANNET	solan goose	zo
GANOID	sturgeon type of fish	zo
GANOIN	fish dermis secretion	zo
GANTRY	travelling crane; signal frame	rw
GAOLED	imprisoned; incarcerated	
GAOLER	jailer; prison warder	
GAPING	yawning; staring; gazing	
GAPPED	pentatonic scale	mu
GARAGE	motor shed; repair shop	
GARBED	clothed	
GARBLE	separate; pervert; misquote	
GARCON	waiter (Fr.)	
GARDEN	a pleasance; park; (horticult.); (flowering)	
GARDON	roach; ide (Fr.)	zo
GARGET	throat inflammation	
GARGIL	goose disease	vt
GARGLE	a mouth wash	
GARGOL	swine disease	vt
GARIAL	gavial; crocodile	zo
GARISH	gaudy; ornate; florid	
GARLIC	genus of plants	bt
GARNER	to store; collect; hoard	
GARNET	carbuncle; precious stone	mn
GAROUS	garum, a fish sauce	ck
GARRAN	horse; galloway (Sc.)	zo
GARRET	loft; attic	
GARRON	(see garran)	
GARROT	a tourniquet; execution; (-cord)	md

GARROT	ocean duck	zo
GARRYA	flowering evergreen	bt
GARTER	stocking supporter	
GARUDA	Hindu demi-god; birdlike	rl
GARVEY	small sailing boat (N. Amer.)	nt
GARVIE	the sprat	zo
GAS-BAG	a blimp; airship; chatterbox	
GASCON	of Gascony	
GASHED	severely wounded	
GASHLY	ghastly; frightful	
GASIFY	convert into gas	
GAS-JET	a burner; flame	
GASKET	leakproof joint (materials)	bd
GASKIN	cord for lashing sails to yards; hemp fibre	
GAS-MAN	gas company employee	
GASPED	panted; blew; puffed	
GASPER	cigarette; fag (sl.)	
GASSED	poisoned by gas	
GAS-TAR	coal-tar	
GASTER	hymenoptera abdomen	zo
GATEAU	cake (Fr.); layer cake	ck
GATHER	assemble; muster; fold	
GATING	a university restriction	
GATING	circuit switching; sensory intake	el
GATTEN	dogwood	bt
GAUCHE	boorish; clumsy (Fr.)	
GAUCHE	bad-mannered (Fr.)	
GAUCHO	cow-boy; shepherd (S. Amer.)	
GAUFRE	honey-cake; wafer (Fr.)	ck
GAUGED	measured; estimated	
GAUGER	excise officer; width, size checker	to
GAUPUS	a silly person	
GAVAGE	forced bird-feeding	vt
GAVIAL	garial; crocodile (Asia)	zo
GAWPUS	a silly person	
GAYEST	liveliest; merriest; blithest	
GAY-YOU	fishing boat (Annam.)	
GAZEBO	summer house; balcony	
GAZING	viewing; gaping; regarding	
GAZUMP	selling price rise	
GEARED	harnessed	
GEBBIE	the stomach (Sc.)	
GEEZER	man in charge; elder	
GEHAZI	dhow; Arab sailboat	nt
GEIGER	radio-activity counter	
GEISHA	mousmee; dancing girl (Jap.)	
GELDED	castrated; enfeebled	
GELERT	Llewellyn's faithful hound	zo
GELTER	one chemical to remove another	ch
GEMARA	(Talmud) (Heb.)	rl
GEMINI	Castor and Pollux; (Zodiac)	
GEMMAE	leaf-buds	bt
GEMMAN	gentleman	
GEMMED	jewelled; budded	
GEMMHO	inverse meg-ohm	me
GEMOTE	} witenagemot Saxon Council	
GEMOT		

GENDER	sex; (grammar)	
GENERA	plural of genus	
GENIAL	hearty; kindly; cordial	
GENIUS	adept; gift; talent; djinn	
GENNET	jennet; small Spanish horse	zo
GENOME	gamete nucleus chromosome	gn
-GENOUS	producing	cf
GENTLE	larva of fly; tender; mild; (angling)	zo
GENTLY	tenderly; gradually	
GENTOO	a Hindu; a penguin	zo
GENTRY	'the nobs'; 'the upper ten'	
GENUAL	(knee)	pl
GEODIC	(crystalline cavity)	mn
GEOGEN	environmental factor	
GEOMYS	rodents (USA)	zo
GEORGE	a jewel	nm
GERANT	gerent; manager	
GERBIL	a rodent	zo
GERMAN	related to; germane; teutonic	
GERMEN	} an ovary; a germ	bt
GERMIN		
GERUND	verbal noun	
GERVAO	West Indian shrub	bt
GERVAS	plant (W. Indies)	bt
GESTIC	legendary	
GETTER	a sire; obtainer; achiever; collector	
GEUSIS	tasting	ck
GEW-GAW	} bauble, trinket, gaud	
GEE-GAW		
GEYSER	hot spring; steam fountain (NZ, Iceland, USA)	gl
GHARRY	gharri; Indian cart	
GHAZAL	} a form of Persian verse; gazelle	
GHAZEL		zo
GHEBER	} Zoroastrian	rl
GHEBRE		
GUEBRE		
GHETTO	Jewish quarter	
GHOBUN	outrigger sail dugout (Papua)	nt
GHURKA	Gurkha; native of Nepal	
GHURRY	clock; time interval (Ind.)	
GIAOUR	unbeliever (Turk.)	
GIBBER	jabber; gabble; babble	
GIBBET	hanging post	
GIBBON	an ape	zo
GIB-CAT	wornout cat	
GIBING	scoffing; jibing	nt
GIBLET	internal part of a fowl	
GIFTED	intellectual; able; talented	
GIGGIT	to move rapidly (USA)	
GIGGLE	snigger; titter; cackle	
GIGLET	} a giddy girl; a wanton	
GIGLOT		
GIGLIO	trawler (sail) (Mediterranean)	nt
GIGMAN	would-be gent	
GIGOLO	dancing partner; kept man	
GILDED	gilt	
GILDER	a guilder	

GILLIE	attendant; game-keeper (Sc.)	
GILPEY	boisterous boy or girl (Sc.)	
GILPIN	the coal-fish	zo
GIMBAL	compass steadier	nt
GIMLET	a boring tool	to
GIMMAL	(machinery)	
GIMMER	2-year-old ewe	zo
GIMPED	crenate	bt
GINETE	Spanish trooper	
GINGAL	Indian musket; swivel gun	
GINGER	sandy; reddish; spice	bt, ck
GINGKO	} Chinese yew; maiden-hair tree	
GINKGO		bt
GINGLE	jingle; Irish car	
GINNED	snared; (cotton)	
GINNET	a nag; a jennet	zo
GIRDED	reproached; braced; surrounded	
GIRDER	a cross-beam (construction)	
GIRDLE	belt; zone; enclosure	
GIRKIN	gherkin (cucumber)	bt
GIRNEL	granary; meal-chest	
GITANA	Spanish gipsy woman	
GITANO	Spanish gipsy man	
GIUSTO	in time; regular (It.)	mu
GIVING	yielding; allowing	
GIZZEN	to wither; leaky	
GLACIS	gentle slope; parapet (fortress)	ar
GLADLY	with pleasure; joyously	.
GLAGOL	Slavonic alphabet	
GLAIRY	viscous	
GLAIVE	broadsword or falchion	
GLANCE	glimpse; look; ricochet	
GLARED	stared; glowered; frowned	
GLASSY	} vitrified; smooth, shiny or mirrorlike surface	
GLAZED		
GLAZER	polisher; calico-smoother	
GLEAMY	casting rays of light	
GLEDGE	cunning look; to squint	
GLEETY	limpid; ichorous	
GLIBLY	volubly; oily tongued	
GLIDED	skimmed; skated	
GLIDER	engineless aeroplane	
GLIOMA	nervous-tissue disease	md
GLITZY	glistery; showiness; sham	
GLOBAL	globular; world-wide	
GLOBIN	(haemoglobin)	md
GLOMUS	capillary-mass glomeruli	zo
GLOOMY	dim; dismal; obscure	
GLORIA	a hymn; halo	rl
GLOSSO-	of tongue; words	cf
GLOSSY	smooth; sheeny; bright	
GLOVED	wearing gloves	
GLOVER	glove-maker	
GLOWED	showed warmth; shone; gleamed	
GLOWER	scowl; frown; glare	
GLOZED	palliated; wheedled	
GLOZER	flatterer; sycophant	
GLUCIC	(glucose)	ch
GLUING	cementing; uniting	
GLUISH	(glue); sticky; viscous	

GLUMAL	of the husk	**bt**
GLUMLY	sulkily; sullenly	
GLUMPS	the sulks	
GLUTEN }	starch free; wheat gum	**ck**
GLUTIN }		
GLYCIN	gelatin-sugar	**ch**
GLYCOL	a liquid	**ch**
GNARLY }	knotted; crabbed; gnarled	
GNARRY }		
GNAWED	fretted; tormented	
GNAWER	a rodent; masticator	**zo**
GNEISS	laminated; metamorphic rocks	**mn**
GNETUM	plant (E. Indies)	**bt**
GNOMIC	didactic	
GNOMON	sundial; shadow-caster	
-GNOSIA	(of knowledge)	**cf**
GNOSIS	esoteric knowledge	
GOADED	impelled; spurred; stung	
GOALIE }	goalkeeper (ice hockey)	
GOALER }	(polo) (football)	**ga**
GOANNA	iguana (Aust.)	**zo**
GOATEE	a beard	
GO-BANG	a game	**ga**
GOBBET	lump; swallow; mouthful	
GOBBIN	coal refuse	
GOBBLE	to swallow; bolt; (turkey)	
GOBLET	tumbler; glass cup; rummer	
GOBLIN	sprite; gnome; spectre	
GO-CART	two-wheeled cart	
GO-DOWN	warehouse; kneel	
GODSON	protegé	
GODWIT	bird of passage	**zo**
GOETIC	(black magic)	
GOFFER	to plait; to crimp	
GOGGLE	to roll the eyes; eye piece (tv)	
GOGLET	porous vase	
GOIDEL	Celtic; Gael	
GOITER }	a tumour; bronchocele	**md**
GOITRE }		
GOLDEN	gilt; excellent; auric	
GOLFER	golf player	
GOLIAS	medieval nom de plume	
GOLLAR	to scold; speak loudly	
GOLORE	abundance; galore	
GOLOSH	overshoe	
GOMMER	soup ingredient	
GOMUTI }	sago palm; black fibre	**bt**
GOMUTO }		
GONGED	prelude to a fine	
GONION	angle (of lower jaw)	**md**
GOODLY	fair; comely; seemly	
GOOGLY	a strange delivery (bowling), (cricket)	**ga**
GOOGOL	10 to the 100th power	**el**
GOORAL	Asiatic goat	**zo**
GOOROO	Hindoo teacher; guru	**rl**
GOPACK }	Russian folkdance	
HOPAK }		
GOPHER	American rodent	**zo**
GOPHER	"timber" of the Ark, reeds and bitumen coracle (Tigris)	**bt, nt, zo**
GOPURA	Hindu temple tower	
GORAMY	gourami; fish	**ar, zo**
GORGED	glutted; stuffed	**hd**
GORGET	throat armour; lady's ruff	
GORGET	instrument	**md**
GORGIO	gipsy term for a non-gipsy	
GORGON	ugly monster (Gr. myth.)	
GORHEN	hen grouse	**zo**
GORIER	more blood-stained	
GORING	a pricking; puncture	
GOSHEN	land of plenty	
GOSPEL	glad tidings; (New Testament)	
GOSSAN }	ferruginous rock	**mn**
GOZZAN }		
GOSSIP	chatter; boon companion	
GOTHIC	language (story); style	**ar, pt**
GOTTEN	got; acquired	
GOUDIE }	goldfinch (Sc.); a jewel; gold lace	
GOWDIE }		
GOUGED	scooped out	
GOURDE	coin (Haiti)	**nm**
GOURDY	swelling (horse)	**vt**
GOUSTY	dreary (Sc.)	
GOVERN	rule; sway; control; restrain	
GOWANS	dandelion	**bt**
GOWNED	robed; arrayed	
GOWPEN	a handful (Sc.)	
GRABEN	land-subsidence structure	**gl**
GRACED	virtuous; chaste	
GRACES	the Greek Charities	
GRADED	classified; arranged	
GRADER	road making implement; blade; sorter	**ce**
GRADIN	raised step or seat	
GRADUS	dictionary of prosody	
GRAFIN	German countess	
GRAINS	malt husks; prongs; harpoons	
GRAINY	granulated	
GRAITH	accoutrements; equipment (Sc.)	
GRAKLE	starling	**zo**
GRAMME	weight (Fr.); (1 cu.cc. water)	**me**
GRANGE	manor house with farm	
GRANNY	knot	**nt**
GRANTH	Sikh Scriptures	**rl**
GRANUM	pigment globule	**bt**
GRAPHO-	of drawing; recording	**cf**
GRAPPA	strong spirit from wine	
GRASSY	green	
GRATER	kitchen implement; shredder	**to**
GRATHE	to repair coal-mine plant	**mn**
GRATIN	oven-browned (cheese topping)	**ck**
GRATIS	without payment	
GRAVED	cleaned; chiselled; cut	**nt**
GRAVEL	disease; embarrass; puzzle	**md**
GRAVEL	granular material (stones); fragmented rock	**ce**
GRAVEN	engraved; carved	

GRAVER	(engraver); more sedate	to
GRAVES	white wine (Fr.)	
GRAVES	melted tallow	
GRAVID	pregnant	
GRAZED	scratched; brushed	
GRAZER	browser	
GRAZIA	} elegantly; gracefully (It.)	mu
GRAZIOSO		
GREASE	lubricate; bribe	
GREASY	unctuous; sebaceous; slippery	
GREATS	final exam. in classics, Ox. B.A.	
GREAVE	} leg armour	
GREEVE		
GREECE	} flight of steps; staircase; a	
GREESE	degree	
GRIECE		
GREEDY	eager; voracious; grasping	
GREENS	vegetables	bt
GREENY	greenish	
GREEVE	} steward; a reeve	
GREAVE		
GREGAL	gregarious	
GRICER	train-locomotive-spotter, fan	rw
GRIDED	grated; pierced	
GRIEVE	} sadden; lament	
GREEVE		
GRIFFE	horizontal frame knives	wv
GRILLE	iron grating (tennis); gate	bd, ar
GRILSE	young salmon	zo
GRIMED	begrimed; foul	
GRIMLY	fiercely; dourly	
GRINGO	Yankee in S. America	
GRIPED	furrowed; trenched	
GRIPER	extortioner; oppressor	
GRIPPE	influenza (Fr.)	
GRISLY	grim; ferocious; fierce; dire	
GRISON	weasel (S. Amer.)	zo
GRITER	teasel spade	to
GRITTY	sandy	
GRIVET	Abyssinian monkey	zo
GRIZEL	meek patient wife	
GROATS	hulled oats	
GROCER	provisioner	
GROGGY	tipsy; staggering	
GROMEL	gromil; gromwell; a plant	bt
GROMET	a rope ring	nt
GROOVE	furrow; rut; cutting	
GROPED	searched; picked; sought	
GROSER	gooseberry	bt
GROSZY	Polish coin	nm
GROTTO	cavern; cave	
GROUND	earth; clod; domain; cause	
GROUSE	complaint	zo
GROUTS	coarse meal; groats	ck
GROUTY	thick; muddy; sulky	
GROVEL	crawl; cringe; fawn	
GROWER	husbandman	
GROWTH	increase; progress	
GROYNE	} (Amer.) anti-erosion	
GROIN	breakwater; sea wall	

GRUBBY	grimy; dirty	
GRUDGE	envy; covet; enmity; dislike	
GRU-GRU	edible insect	zo
GRUMLY	morosely; surlily	
GRUMPH	grunt (Sc.)	
GRUMPY	surly; sullen; churlish	
GRYFON	griffin (obs.)	hd, zo
GUACHE	style of painting	
GUANIN	} bird excrement	
GUANO		
GUDDLE	to tickle trout (Sc.)	
GUEBRE	Gueber; Parsee fire-worshipper	
GUELPH	German medieval faction	
GUENON	African monkey	zo
GUFFAW	boisterous laugh	
GUGGLE	to gurgle	
GUIDED	regulated; instructed; steered	
GUIDER	a director; leader; pilot	
GUIDON	flag; signal (Fr.)	
GUILED	beguiled; treacherous	
GUILLS	corn marigold	bt
GUILTY	criminal; culpable; sinful	
GUINEA	fowl; worm; pig; coin; stable	
	groom	nm, zo
GUISER	mummer	
GUITAR	type of lute	mu
GULDEN	florin (Dutch)	nm
GULLED	duped; tricked; hoaxed	
GULLER	a cheat; impostor	
GULLET	throat (of bird); trench	md
GULLEY	large knife (Sc.); earth cleft	
GULOSE	aldohexose monosaccharide	ch
GULPED	swallowed; bolted	
GUMLAC	resinous matter	
GUMMED	stuck; cemented	
GUNITE	fine cement concrete	eg
GUNMAN	armed bandit	
GUNMEN	gangsters; assassins	
GUNNEL	a blenny; butterfish	zo
GUNNEL	ship's side; gunwale	nt
GUNNER	artillery-man	
GUN-SHY	fearful of firearms	
GUNTER	emergency sail; instrument	nt
GUNYAH	Australian native hut	
GURGLE	purl; ripple; murmur	
GURHKA	a native of Nepal	
GURJUN	Indian balsam	bt
GURLET	type of pickaxe	bd
GURLEY	cylinder fall speed	el, me
GURNET	fish; gurnard	zo
GURRAH	Indian earthen jar	
GUSHED	rushed; spurted; spouted	
GUSHER	oil-well; voluble person	
GUSSET	an insertion	
GUTNIK	swallowable transistor radio	
GUTTAE	Doric ornamentation	ar
GUTTED	plundered; eviscerated	
GUTTEE	bedewed	hd
GUTTER	trough; drainage; run off	ar, bd
GUTTER	inner margins of book	pr

GUTTLE	to guzzle	
GUZZLE	swill; swallow greedily	
GYBING	jibing	nt
GYMNIC	gymnastic (obs.)	
GYPSUM	lime sulphate	ch
GYRATE	spiral; revolve; spin	
GYROSE	like a crook	bt

H

HABBLE	perplex; stutter (Sc.)	
HABOOB	Sudan line-squall	mt
HACHEL	a sloven (Sc.)	
HACKED	mangled; hired; kicked	
HACKEE	chipmunk; American squirrel	zo
HACKET	kittiwake	zo
HACKLE	cock's neck feathers	
HACKLE	fly (angling); comb	
HACKLY	rough	
HADDIE	haddock (Sc.)	
HADDIN	a holding; residence (Sc.)	
HADING	geological fault	gl
HADITH	Moslem oral tradition	rl
HADRON	elementary particle class	nc
HAEMAD	on same side as heart	pl
HAEMAL	} relating to blood	md
HAEMIC		
HAEMIN	hydrochloride of haematin	ch
HAFFET	the temples (Sc.)	
HAFFLE	to lie; prevaricate	
HAFTED	handled	
HAGBUT	arquebuse; hackbut (ancient gun)	
HAGDEN	shearwater gull	zo
HAGEEN	dromedary; camel	zo
HAGGED	ugly; lean; haggish	
HAGGIS	Scottish dish	ck
HAGGLE	to mangle; higgle; bargain	
HAGLET	shearwater gull	zo
HAIDUK	Hungarian yeoman	
HAILED	greeted; came from	
HAIQUE	Arab wrap	
HAIRDO	hairstyle; coiffure	
HAIRED	hairy; hirsute; comate	
HAIRST	harvest (Sc.)	
HAKEEM	physician (Arabic)	
HALFER	fallow deer	zo
HALIDE	compound of halogen and other radical	
HALING	hauling	
HALION	skipper fish	zo
HALLAN	a partition (Sc.)	
HALLEL	Passover hymn	rl
HALLOA	hallo!	
HALLOO	a hunting cry	
HALLOW	to reverence	
HALLUX	hind toe of bird	zo
HALOED	sainted	
HALOID	(salt)	ch
HALSED	embraced by the neck	

HALSER	hawser	nt
HALTED	limped; hesitated; stopped	
HALTER	rope; cord	
HALVED	bisected; fifty-fifty	
HALVES	moieties	
HAMATE	set with hooks	
HAMBLE	mutilate the foot	
HAMITE	fossil; native (E. Africa)	
HAMLET	cluster of cottages	
HAMMAL	} Turkish porter	
HAMAL		
HAMMAM	} Turkish bath	
HAMAM		
HAMMER	forge; a gavel	to
HAMMER	throwing (athletics); a shot (squash); bones in ear	ga, pl
HAMOSE	} hooked	bt
HAMOUS		
HAMPER	basket; impede; embarrass	
HANDED	served; conducted; led on; right- or left-; tool	bd
HANDLE	touch; feel; manipulate	
HANGAR	aircraft shed	
HANGED	dangled; depended	
HANGER	broadsword; wood on hill-side	
HANGER	(clothes); steel bar; stirrup strap; baseball	
HANG-UP	unexpected hiatus; breakdown	
HANJAR	Persian dagger	
HANKED	skeined; jibbed	nt
HANKER	desire; crave; yearn; want	
HANSEL	earnest penny; handsel	
HANSOM	a horse-cab	
HANTLE	considerable number (Sc.)	
HAPPEN	occur; betide; chance; befall	
HAPTIC	pert. to sense of touch	
HARASS	annoy; tire; vex; worry	
HARDEN	nerve; steel; brace; inure	
HARDER	stiffer; firmer	
HARDLY	barely; scarcely; narrowly	
HARD-UP	impecunious; indigent	
HARELD	sea-duck	zo
HARIER	a harrier	zo
HARING	speeding	
HARISH	like a hare	
HARKED	listened; hurried	
HARKEN	hearken; listen; attend	
HARLED	covered with rough-cast	
HARLOT	strumpet; moll; trollop	
HARMAN	policeman; a copper	
HARMED	damaged; injured	
HARMEL	Syrian rue	bt
HARPED	iterated; dwelt	mu
HARPER	lyrist; harpist	mu
HARRIS	a tweed	
HARROW	lacerate; tear	
HARTAL	Indian boycott	
HASHED	chopped; mixed	
HASLET	roasting meat; pig's fry	
HASTED	hastened; hurried	

HASTEN	hurry; speed; despatch; urge
HAT-BOX	for hat transport
HATFUL	maximum score in an end (bowls)
HATHOR	goddess of love (Egypt)
HATING	detesting; loathing; abhorring
HAT-PEG	place to hang hat
HAT-PIN	woman's hat fixer
HATRED	odium; enmity; rancour
HATTED	wearing a hat
HATTER	independent miner (Aust.) (hats) (mad)
HAULED	dragged; tugged; towed
HAULER	haulier; carter
HAUNCH	part of an arch; hip to thigh **ar, pl**
HAUSSA	West African race
HAUTIN	sea-fish in fresh water **zo**
HAUYNE	a silicate **mn**
HAVANA	(cigar)
HAVERS	twaddle; empty talk
HAVING	holding; possessing
HAWHAW	sunk fence; guffaw (haha) **ar**
HAWKED	peddled; streaked
HAWKER	pedlar; retailer; falconer
HAWKEY	} dark cow with white
HAWKIE	} streaked face (Sc.) **zo**
HAWSER	halser; cable **nt**
HAY-BOX	cooking method **ck**
HAYMOW	hay in barn
HAYSEL	hay-makers' festival
HAZARD	risk; chance; peril; jeopardy; old dicing game; (golf); (billiards) **ga**
HAZILY	obscurely; foggily; mistily
HAZING	bullying; brutal horse-play
HEADED	(cask); (football)
HEADER	(brick); (diving); headline; identity label **cp**
HEAD-ON	directly; straight (collision)
HEALED	cured; remedied
HEALER	doctor; restorer
HEALTH	soundness; hygiene; haleness
HEAPED	massed; accumulated; piled
HEARER	one of an audience
HEARSE	funeral car
HEARTH	fireplace; fireside; home
HEARTY	robust; sincere; cordial
HEATED	agitated; excited; hectic
HEATER	warmer
HEATHY	heathery **bt**
HEAUME	heavy helmet
HEAVED	hoisted; dilated; panted
HEAVEN	Elysium; Paradise; bliss
HEAVER	a lever; strong man
HEAVES	disease (horse); broken wind **vt**
HEBREW	a Jew; Semitic language
HECATE	goddess of witchcraft
HECKLE	to comb; to question
HECTIC	feverish; heated; hot
HECTOR	intimidate; bully; a swaggering
HEDDLE	heald shaft in handloom **wv**
HEDERA	ivy **bt**

HEDGED	skulked; (betting)
HEDGER	a trimmer of fences
HEEDED	attended; noticed
HEE-HAW	to bray (donkey)
HEELED	armed; equipped; leant
HEELER	hanger-on (USA)
HEGIRA	} Mohammed's flight from
HEJIRA	} Mecca to Medina, A.D.622
HEIFER	young cow **zo**
HEIGHT	altitude; acme; zenith
HELIAC	heliacal; (sun) **as**
HELION	virago; shrew; hell-cat
HELITE	an amalgam **ch**
HELIUM	a gaseous element **ch**
HELLAS	ancient Greece
HELLER	German copper coin **nm**
HELMED	with a helmet; directed
HELMET	part of retort; head armour
HELOMA	corn on foot **md**
HELPED	prevented; aided; succoured
HELPER	assistant; abettor; ally
HELVED	having a handle; hafted
HELVIN	mineral **mn**
HEMINA	about 10 oz (283 g) **me**
HEMMED	bordered; enclosed
HEMMER	a stitcher; a sewer
HEMPEN	made of hemp **bt**
HENBIT	dead nettle **bt**
HENISM	philosophical belief
HEPTAD	series of seven
HERALD	harbinger; crier; proclaim
HERBAL	book describing plants
HERDED	tended; massed
HEREAT	at this point
HEREBY	by this (means) (document) (moment)
HEREIN	in this (document) (situation)
HEREOF	of this (before-mentioned)
HEREON	on this (occasion)
HERESY	schism; heterodoxy; recusancy
HERETO	in addition
HERIFF	burweed **bt**
HERIOT	a fine **lw**
HERMAE	sculptured busts
HERMES	Mercury (Gr.) the messenger **rl**
HERMIT	anchorite; recluse
HERNIA	rupture **md**
HEROES	demi-gods
HEROIC	bold; intrepid; valiant
HEROIN	a drug **md**
HERPES	skin disease; shingles **md**
HERREN	gentlemen (Ger.)
HERSED	in harrow form **hd**
HESPER	evening star; vesper; prayer **rl**
HESVAN	} Jewish month
HESHVAN	}
HETERO-	of unlike, different (sex) (Gr.) **cf**
HETMAN	Cossack chief
HEWING	hacking; shaping
HEXADE	series of six

HEXANE	paraffin	**ch**
HEXODE	a thermionic valve	
HEXOSE	monosaccharide subgroup, a sugar	**ch**
HEYDAY	frolic; period of vigour; zenith	
HIATUS	a chasm; gap; lacuna	**md**
HICCUP	} temporary breakdown of	
HICCOUGH	} breathing	**md**
HICKEY	pipe-bending tool (Amer.)	**to, ce**
HIDAGE	a tax	**lw**
HIDDEN	latent; covert; recondite	
HIDING	a beating; screening; masking	
HIEING	going along; hiking	
HIEMAL	wintry; hyemal	
HIGGLE	to bargain; haggle	
HIGHER	superior; nobler (above)	
HIGHLY	eminently; loftily	
HI-JACK	kidnap; rob; armed take-over of transport	
HIJRAH	Hegira; flight from Mecca	
HIKING	walking; foot-slogging	
HILARY	Law Court session; Oxford term	**lw**
HILLED	earthed up	
HILSAH	fish (Ganges)	**zo**
HILTED	hafted; helved	
HINDEE	North Indian tongue	
HINDER	delay; interference with flat of ball (handball) (paddle ball)	
HINGED	depended on; swing on (door)	
HINTED	implied	
HINTER	suggester	
HIPPED	melancholic; roof	**ar**
HIPPIC	horsy; equine	
HIPPIE	unkempt wanderer	
HIPPUS	clonic spasm of iris	**md**
HIRAME	gold, silver leaf on lacquer (Jap.)	
HIRCIN	mutton suet	
HIRCUS	the goat	**zo**
HIRING	bribing; engaging	
HIRMOI	} hymns; ode (Gr. church)	**rl**
HIRMOS	}	
HIRSEL	} flock of sheep (Sc.); a	
HIRSLE	} throng; to slide	
HISPID	bristly	
HISSED	hizzed	
HISSER	disapprover	
HITCHY	catchy	
HITHER	to this place	
HIT-OUT	aim blows; verbal attack; aggressive action by players or fans (boxing); starting shot in hockey	**ga**
HITTER	smiter; slogger; striker	**ga**
HIVING	storing; clustering (bees)	
HOARSE	guttural; husky; raucous	
HOAXED	tricked; gulled; gammoned	
HOAXEE	the victim	
HOAXER	practical joker	

HOAZIN	(S. Amer.) pheasant	**zo**
HOBBER	touching the kob (quoits)	**ga**
HOBBIT	denizen of middle world; (Tolkien)	
HOBBLE	halt; limp; shackle; clog; leg harness (farm)	
HOBJOB	an odd job	
HOBNOB	to be familiar; associate; chat	
HOCKET	hiccup (Fr.); extra rests in vocal parts	**mu**
HOCKEY	11-a-side stick and ball game	**ga**
HOCKLE	to mow; hamstring	
HODDEN	grey cloth	**tx**
HODMAN	mason's labourer	
HOEING	weeding	
HOGGED	clipped; bent	
HOGGER	(whole)	
HOGGET	young sheep; colt or boar	**zo**
HOGGIE	fishing craft (Brighton)	
HOGGIN	sand and gravel mixture	
HOGPEN	hogsty (Am); pigsty	
HOG-PIT	waste paper stock pit	**pp**
HOGSTY	pig pen; pigsty	
HOIDEN	hoyden; a romp; rude; rustic	
HOLANI	early form of hockey (Turk.)	**ga**
HOLARD	whole of soil water	**bt**
HOLDER	a tenant; possessor (-stand) (-case)	**lw**
HOLD-UP	robbery under arms	
HOLIER	more sacred	
HOLILY	piously	
HOLISM	treatment of the body as one entity	
HOLLER	} shout (distress)	
HOLLOA	}	
HOLLOW	empty; void; cavity-wall; vacuum; dell	**bd**
HOLMIA	oxide of holmium	**ch**
HOLMIC	(holmium)	**ch**
HOMAGE	fealty; devotion; loyalty	
HOMELY	plain; simple; domestic	
HOMILY	sermon; address; discourse	
HOMING	(pigeons); aerial navigation; returning to base	**ae**
HOMINY	boiled maize	**ck**
HONEST	fair; just; trusty; sincere	
HONING	whetting	
HONKED	(cry of wild geese)	
HONOUR	exalt; dignify; fame; renown; first choice	
HOODED	cowled; cloaked	
HOODIE	carrion-crow (Sc.)	**zo**
HOODOO	} witchcraft; (W. Indies);	
VOODOO	} column of boulders and earth	**rl, gl**
HOOFED	ungulate	
HOOKAH	water smoking pipe; narghile (Turk.)	
HOOKED	(golf); hamate	

206

HOOKER	fishing boat; prostitute; scrum player (Rugby football) **nt, ga**	
HOOKUM	command; instructions (Ind.)	
HOOK-UP	radio connections; (-link) **cp, ro, tc, tv**	
HOOPED	encircled; whooped	
HOOPER	(tubs); a cooper	
HOOP-LA	game at fairs **ga**	
HOOPOE	} crested birds, horn-bill type	
HOOPOO	} **zo**	
HOOTCH	hooch; firewater (USA)	
HOOTED	honked	
HOOTER	a siren	
HOOVED	ungulate **zo**	
HOOVEN	(cattle-disease) **vt, zo**	
HOOVER	dust-removing appliance	
HOOVES	pl. of hoof; cleft feet **zo**	
HOPDOG	pale tussock moth **zo**	
HOP-FLY	plant louse **zo**	
HOPING	desiring; trusting	
HOPPED	danced; bounced	
HOPPER	wooden trough; hop-picker; lighter (dredging) **nt**	
HOPPER	locust; truck; punched card feeder **zo, cp**	
HOPPET	hand-basket **rw**	
HOPPIT	kibble; sinking bucket; skip **ce**	
HORARY	book of hours (prayers) **rl**	
HORNED	with horns; butted	
HORNER	dealer in horns; sand-eel **zo**	
HORNET	stinging insect **zo**	
HORNIE	the devil; old Nick	
HORRID	horrific; terrible; dreadful	
HORROR	terror; panic; alarm; dismay	
HORSED	mounted (rider)	
HOSIER	dealer in stockings	
HOSTEL	an inn; lodging house	
HOT-BED	earth-bed; breeding place **bt**	
HOT-DOG	sausage sandwich **ck**	
HOT-POT	meat-stew **ck**	
HOT-ROD	supercharged car	
HOTTER	more ardent; warmer	
HOUDAH	howdah; seat on an elephant	
HOUDAN	breed of fowls **zo**	
HOUNDS	(mast head) **nt**	
HOURLY	at every hour (trains)	
HOUSED	resided; sheltered; stored	
HOUSEL	the Eucharist **rl**	
HOUSTY	a sore throat (dial.)	
HOWDAH	houdah; seat on an elephant	
HOWDIE	midwife (Sc.)	
HOWKER	hooker; vessel (Dutch) **nt**	
HOWLED	yowled; cried; lamented	
HOWLER	(monkey); grievous error **zo**	
HOWLET	(owlet); fledgling owl (dial.) **zo**	
HOYDEN	hoiden; tomboy; romp	
HRAMSA	garlic-flavoured cheese (Sc.) **ck**	
HUBBLE	an uproar; hubbub	
HUBBLY	rowdy	
HUBBUB	disorder; noise; uproar; din	

HUCKLE	the hip; a haunch	
HUDDLE	crowd; confuse; jumble; counsel before line-up (Amer. football) **ga**	
HUDDUP	get up!; fertile, irrigated, 2 crops land **ag**	
HUFFED	blustered; (draughts) forfeited **ga**	
HUFFER	a bully; blusterer;	
HUGELY	enormously; immensely	
HULLED	pierced; husked	
HULLER	hulling machine	
HUMANE	kind; benign; merciful	
HUMBLE	degrade; abash; meek; lowly	
HUMBLY	unobtrusively	
HUMBUG	quackery; charlatan; peppermint	
HUMECT	} to moisten; to dampen	
HUMIFY	}	
HUMEFY	}	
HUMERI	bones of the upper arm **md**	
HUMETE	abbreviated fesse **hd**	
HUMHUM	coarse cloth (Ind.) **tx**	
HUMIAN	philosophy of David Hume	
HUMINE	black ground powder; humus	
HUMITE	limestone **mn**	
HUMMED	buzzed; droned	
HUMMEL	hornless; awnless	
HUMMER	a sledge-runner	
HUMMIE	small bulge	
HUMMUS	} chick-pea/garlic purée	
HUMMUZ	} (Mid. East) **ck**	
HUMOUS	}	
HUMOUR	indulge; pamper; wit **md**	
HUMPED	shouldered; hunchback	
HUMPEN	drinking glass (Ger.)	
HUMPER	meat-porter; carrier	
HUNGER	hanker; desire; crave	
HUNGRY	ravenous; famishing	
HUNKER	to squat down; old fogey	
HUNTED	searched; sought; hounded	
HUNTER	chaser; stalker **zo**	
HURBUR	burdock **bt**	
HURDLE	wattle fence	
HURLED	flung; heaved; slung; cast	
HURLER	a thrower; pitcher	
HURLEY	shinty; the stick used in hurling	
HURRAH	} shout of triumph	
HURRAY	}	
HURTER	a buffer plank	
HURTLE	to whirl; to crash	
HUSHED	quietened; calmed; stilled	
HUSKED	hulled	
HUSKER	a remover of husks	
HUSSAR	light cavalryman	
HUSSIF	(housewife); a holdall	
HUSTLE	bustle; jostle; elbow; rush	
HUTTED	in huts	
HUZOOR	Indian title of respect	
HYADES	5 stars in Taurus **as**	
HYAENA	hyena **zo**	

HYBRID	cross-bred; mongrel; analog; digital mix	**cp**
HYDRIA	Grecian water-vase	
HYDRIC	(hydrogen)	**ch**
HYDRID	hydrogen compound	**ch**
HYDROA	itching skin disease	**md**
HYDRON	dry/rigid, wet/soft plastic	
HYDRUS	constellation; water-snake	**as, zo**
HYEMAL	hiemal; wintry	
HYETAL	(rainfall)	
HYGEIA	Goddess of Health	
HYKSOS	Egyptian dynasty	
HYLISM	materialism	
HYMNAL	collection of hymns	
HYMNED	celebrated in song	
HYMNIC	of hymns	
HYPHAE	fungoid filaments	**bt**
HYPHEN	word-join stroke	
HYPNUM	a moss genus	**bt**
HYSSOP	aromatic herb	**bt**

I

IAMBIC	rhythmic	
IAMBUS	Greek satiric metre	
-IATRIC	of healing, medical (Gr.)	**cf, md**
IBERIS	candytuft	**bt**
IBEXES	wild goats (Alps)	**zo**
IBIDEM	in the same place	
ICARUS	an early aeronaut	
ICE-AGE	period of icing over	
ICE-AXE	ice-breaking, -cutting device	**to**
ICE-CAP	earth ice layer	
ICE-MAN	ice deliverer	
ICE-SAW	ice-cutting device	**to**
ICICLE	frozen water stalactite	
ICIEST	frostiest	
ICONIC	illustrative	
ICONIC	brief visual experience; of sacred portrayal	**pc, rl**
IDEATE	to fancy; project fantasy	**pc**
IDIASM	a peculiarity	
IDIOCY	lunacy; dementia; craziness	
IDLING	nothing doing	
IDOLUM	} mental picture	
IDOLON		
I'FAITH	indeed; truly; verily	
IF-THEN	conditional indication operation	**cp**
IGNAVY	laziness; idleness	
IGNITE	kindle; inflame; fire	
IGNORE	disregard; overlook; skip (agent)	**cp**
IGUANA	lizard; a saurian	**zo**
ILEXES	holm-oaks	**bt**
ILL-GOT	ill-gotten	
ILLISH	somewhat unwell	
ILLITE	monoclinic clay material	**mn**
ILLUDE	to deceive; delude	

ILLUME	illumine; brighten	
ILL-USE	mistreat	
IMAGED	imagined; fancied	
IMBALM	embalm	
IMBAND	form into band	
IMBANK	embank	
IMBARK	embark; board	
IMBIBE	absorb; assimilate; drink	
IMBODY	embody; incorporate	
IMBOIL	emboil; burn with anger	
IMBREX	pantile; curved roof-tile	
IMBRUE	to moisten; to drench	
IMBUED	dyed; inspired; steeped	
IMMANE	huge; savage (Shak.)	
IMMASK	to cover	
IMMESH	entangle; enmesh	
IMMUNE	secure against attack	
IMMURE	enclose; incarcerate; confine	
IMPACT	shock; stroke; collision	
IMPAGE	horizontal part of door-frame	**bd**
IMPAIR	mar; injure; harm; vitiate	
IMPALA	South African antelope	**zo**
IMPALE	transfix	
IMPALM	to grasp	
IMPARK	enclose	
IMPARL	to hold mutual discourse	
IMPARL	parley	
IMPART	bestow; confer; divulge	
IMPAVE	to pave	
IMPAWN	to pledge	
IMPEDE	obstruct; hinder; thwart	
IMPEND	threaten; hover; approach	
IMPEST	infect with plague	
IMPING	ekeing; extending; grafting	
IMPISH	puckish; mischievous	
IMPLEX	complicated	
IMPONE	to stake; to wager	
IMPORT	imply; purport; gist; drift	
IMPOSE	lay; inflict; charge; dictate	
IMPOST	a tax; a duty; a cess; bracket-like base for arches	**ar**
IMPUGN	attack; contradict; question	
IMPURE	unclean; sullied; tarnished	
IMPUTE	charge; ascribe; imply	
INARCH	to graft	
INBAND	header stone	**bd**
INBOND	brick-laying	**bd**
INBORN	innate; inherent; congenital	
INBRED	in-tribe parentage	
INCAGE	encage; confine	
INCARN	to incarnate	
INCASE	encase; enclose; enshrine	
INCASK	to put in a cask	
INCAST	a bonus; thrown in	
INCAVO	incised part of an intaglio	
INCEPT	to begin; to commence	
INCEST	prohibited co-habitation among close kin	
INCHED	advanced by inches	
INCISE	engrave; scribe	

INCITE	stir; goad; foment; rouse	
INCLIP	to grasp; enclose; surround	
INCOME	revenue; annual receipts	
INCONY	delicate; fine; pretty (Shak.)	
INCULT	uncultivated	
INCUSE	to stamp	
INCUSS	incuse; forge	
INDABA	native council	
INDART	to rush in (Shak.)	
INDEED	really; truly; verily; actually	
INDENE	liquid coal-tar hydrocarbon	ch
INDENT	to notch; order; make a deed; stonework design	ar, lw
INDIAN	of India; aboriginal Amer.	
INDICT	to charge in writing	lw
INDIGN	unworthy	
INDIGO	a blue dye	bt
INDITE	endite; write; pen; dictate	
INDIUM	metallic element	ch
INDOLE	benzpyrrole	ch
INDOOR	within the house	
INDUCE	urge; actuate; incite	
INDUCT	introduce; install; initiate	
INDUED	endued; invested with	
INDUNA	Zulu chief	
INEUNT	a cusp	
INFALL	an inroad	
INFAME	defame	
INFAMY	shame; obloquy; disgrace	
INFANT	babe; suckling; minor	
INFECT	corrupt; vitiate; taint	
INFEFF	} (land transfer)	lw
INFEFT		
INFELT	heart-felt	
INFEST	enfest; overrun; throng; beset	
INFIMA	end species in classification list	
INFIRM	frail; weak; decrepit	
INFLOW	that which flows in	
INFLUX	importation in abundance	
INFOLD	enfold; embrace	
INFORM	tell; notify; apprize	
INFULA	Roman priestly badge	rl
INFUSE	instil; inculcate; steep	
INGATE	aperture in a mould	
INGEST	absorb; swallow	
IN-GOAL	Rugby football	ga
INGULF	engulf; overwhelm	
INHALE	breathe in	
INHAUL	(a rope)	nt
INHERE	to be innate	
INHIVE	to hive (bees)	
INHOOP	to confine	
INHOUR	reactivity unit	nc
INHUME	to inter; to bury; entomb	
INJECT	interpolate; insert	
INJURE	harm; hurt; mar; impair	
INJURY	ill; detriment; wrong; damage	lw
INK-BAG	(cuttle-fish)	zo
INKING	marking with ink	
INKNIT	to knit in	

INKNOT	to knot	
INKOSI	Zulu chief, king	
INK-POT	ink container	
INK-SAC	(cuttle-fish)	zo
INLACE	to lace	
INLAID	fitted flush to surface	
INLAND	remote from the sea	
INLIER	geological formation	gl
INLINE	white-relieved black-letter print	pr
IN-LINE	(traffic) program instructions	cp
INLOCK	enlock	
INMATE	resident; guest; denizen	
INMOST	innermost; deepest	
INNATE	inherent; congenital; inborn	
INNING	harvest grain	
INNUIT	an Eskimo	
INRAIL	enclose with rails; fencing	nt
INROAD	raid; foray; incursion	
INROLL	enroll (obs.)	
INRUSH	invasion; irruption	
INSANE	mad; crazy; deranged	
INSEAM	mark with a seam	
INSECT	mean; contemptible	
INSECT	six-legged invertebrate	zo
INSERT	inject; introduce; infix	
INSHIP	embark; to ship	
INSIDE	inner; internal; interior	
INSIST	maintain; demand; urge	
INSOLE	inner sole	
INSPAN	to yoke	
INSTAL	install; induct; invest	
INSTAR	adorn with stars	
INSTEP	part of the foot	pl
INSTIL	infuse; ingraft; implant	
INSTOP	make fast; to stop	
INSULA	part of cortex (brain); island	pl
INSULA	middle-class house (Roman)	ar
INSULT	abuse; affront; ridicule	
INSURE	ensure; assure; guarantee	
INTACT	inviolate; integral; scatheless	
INTAKE	inlet of a pipe	
INTEND	mean; purpose; contemplate	
INTENT	set; bent; eager; attentive	
INTERN	confine; segregate	
INTIMA	innermost organ layer	zo
INTIME	private; home-like	
INTINE	inner coat of pollen grain	bt
INTOED	with toes turned in	
INTOMB	entomb; bury; inter	
INTONE	to chant	mu
INTORT	to twist; to wreathe; to wind	
INTRAP	entrap (obs.)	
IN-TURN	curved sliding shot (curling)	ga
INTUSE	a bruise (Spens.)	md
INULIN	vegetable base (elecampane)	bt, ck
INUNCT	anoint	
INURED	hardened; accustomed	lw
INVADE	raid; infringe; assault; violate	
INVENT	devise; contrive; create; make	

INVERT	reverse; upset; overturn	
INVEST	indue; bedeck; array; beset	
INVITE	ask; bid; call; request; solicit	
INVOKE	adjure; conjure; implicate	
INWALL	enclose; enwall	
INWARD	inside; inner; internal	
INWICK	curling cannon	
INWITH	within (Sc.)	
INWORK	work within	
INWORN	inwrought	
INWRAP	to perplex; enwrap	
INYALA	nyala; bushbuck	zo
IODATE	(iodic acid)	ch
IODIDE	salt of hydriodic acid	ch
IODINE	medicinal element	ch
IODISM	morbid state	
IODIZE	treat with iodine	
IOLITE	a translucent silicate	mn
IONIAN	(Ionia)	ar
IONISM	Ionic architecture	
IONIUM	(radium)	ch
IONIZE	convert into ions	ps
IONONE	terpene compound	ch
IRANIC	from Iran	
IREFUL	angry; wroth; incensed	
IRENIC	pacific; peaceful	
IRIDAL	prismatic; iridian	
IRIDIN	active principle of iris	
IRISED	like a rainbow	
IRITIC	(iritis); inflamed	md
IRITIS	(eye disease)	md
IRKING	irksome; tedious; wearying	
IRONED	in irons; smoothed	
IRONER	a laundry operative	
IRONIC	satirical; sarcastic	
IRRUPT	to interrupt; invade	
ISABEL	brownish yellow	
ISAGON	equi-angular figure	
ISATIC	woad-like	bt
ISATIN	an indigo product	ch
ISATIS	plant providing woad dye	bt
ISLAND	isle; to insulate	
ISOBAR	line of equal barometric pressure	
ISODIA	Jewish sacred feast	rl
ISOGAM	line of constant acceleration of free fall	ps, el
ISOGON	an isagon	
ISOHEL	sunshine comparison map	mt
ISOLUX	same-light-intensity line	lt
ISOMER	(similar substance)	ch
ISONYM	paronym	
ISOPIC	contemporaneously formed	gl
ISOPOD	(crustaceans)	zo
ISRAEL	Jacob and his offspring	
ISSUED	distributed; emitted; emerged	
ISSUER	publisher; utterer	
ITALIC	Italian; semi cursive script	pr
ITCHED	wanted to; craved; hankered	
ITSELF	reflexive pronoun	
IVIGAR	sea-urchin	zo

IZZARD	the letter Z	

J

JABBED	poked; prodded	
JABBER	much talk; prattle; gabble	
JABBLE	rough sea; splash (Sc.)	
JABIRI	Brazilian stork	zo
JACANA	wading bird	zo
JACENT	lying at length	
JACKAL	dog-like animal	zo
JACKED	lifted with a jack (motor car)	
JACKET	cover; jerkin; coat	
JADERY	tricks of a jade	
JADISH	vicious; unchaste	
JAEGER	gull; huntsman (Ger.)	zo
JAGGED	notched; ragged; serrated	
JAGGER	brass wheel; pastry	
JAGHIR	a reward (Hindu)	
JAGUAR	S. American leopard	zo
JAILED	gaoled; incarcerated	
JAILER	} gaoler; warder (prison)	
JAILOR		
JALEBI	saffron batter sweetmeat (Ind.)	ck
JAMBEE	a cane; walking-stick	
JAMBOK	sjambok; hide whip	
JAMBUL	Indian evergreen	bt
JAMMED	crushed; squeezed	
JAMMER	radio interferer; competitor blocking Roller Derby race	
JAMPAN	sedan chair (Ind.)	
JANGLE	wrangle; clash; bicker	
JANKER	log-transporter (Sc.)	
JARGON	nonsense; gibberish; palaver	
JAROOL	Indian blood-wood	bt
JARRAH	tree (W. Australia)	bt
JARRED	wrangled; grated	
JARVEY	jaunty driver (Irish)	
JASHER	lost Hebrew book	rl
JASMIN	climbing shrub	bt
JASPER	quartz	mn
JATAKA	nativity (Buddha)	rl
JAUNCE	to jolt; a jaunt (Shak.)	
JAUNTY	airy; sprightly; finical	
JAW-BOX	a sink (Sc.)	
JAWING	scolding	
JEAMES	a flunkey	
JEERED	mocked; derided; taunted	
JEERER	scoffer; sneerer	
JEJUNE	void of interest; meagre	
JENNET	gennet; small Spanish horse	zo
JERBOA	a jumping rodent	zo
JEREED	jerid; blunt javelin	
JERKED	twitched; flipped; jolted	
JERKER	underhand thrower	
JERKIN	a coat; jacket	
JERKIN	a hawk; gyrfalcon	zo
JERQUE	examine ship's papers	
JERSEY	cow; knitted garment	zo

JERVIN	alkaloid (hellebore)	**ch**
JESSED	heraldic ornamentation	**hd**
JESTED	joked; made merry; quizzed	
JESTER	joker; buffoon; wag; fool	
JET-LAG	disturbance of body time change	
JETSAM	} goods thrown overboard;	
JETSOM	} jetson; jettisoned	**lw, nt**
JETTEE	projection	**ar**
JETTON	metal counter	
JEWESS	female Jew	
JEWISH	Hebrew	
JEZAIL	Afghan rifle	
JIBBAH	jubbah; Eastern garment	**tx**
JIBBED	refused to go; baulked	
JIBBER	restive horse	**zo**
JIBING	sneering; quizzing; taunting	
JIBOYA	boa-constrictor; snake	**zo**
JIFFEY	an instant	
JIGGED	danced	**mu**
JIGGER	liquid measure; mechanical device	**me**
JIGGER	golf club; insect; chigger	**ga, zo**
JIGGLE	wriggle; joggle; jolt	
JIGJOG	jolting	
JIG-SAW	fret-saw; a puzzle (pictorial)	**ga**
JILLET	a flirt; a wanton	
JILTED	discarded	
JIMSON	thorn-apple	**bt**
JINGAL	Eastern cannon	
JINGLE	Irish covered car; tinkle; rhyme	
JINKER	dodged; eluded; turned sharply	
JINKER	timber-cart (Aust.)	
JINNEE	djinn; jinn; genie; periodic sound alternation	
JITTER	instability; fear	**el**
JITTER	cathode ray tube signals	**cp, el**
JOBBER	stockbroker; book stocker/dealer	
JOBBER	builder's handyman	**bd**
JOB-LOT	odds and ends (auction) (sale)	
JOCKEY	to cheat; rider of races	
JOCOSE	facetious; humorous; waggish	
JOCUND	sportive; merry; cheerful	
JOGGED	travelled slowly; shook	
JOGGER	jostler (runner)	
JOGGLE	a notch; to jar; to shake	
JOGGLE	agitate; punched cards	**cp**
JOHNNY	gay spark	
JOINED	united; coupled; connected	
JOINER	a carpenter	
JOISTS	floor-board supports	**ar**
JOKING	jesting; bantering; rallying	
JOKULL	glacial ice-cap	**gl, go**
JOLTED	jogged; shook; jounced	
JOLTER	hustler	
JORDAN	a river; chamber pot (Shak.)	
JOSEPH	riding habit; unsized paper	**pr**
JOSKIN	yokel; clown	
JOSSER	a fellow; a chap; a palooka	
JOSTLE	hustle; elbow; joggle; justle	
JOTTED	noted; recorded	

JOTTER	memorandum book	
JOUNCE	to jolt; shake	
JOVIAL	genial; convivial; blithe	
JOVIAN	(Jupiter) of Jove	
JOWDER	} fish hawker	
JOWTER	}	
JOWLER	hunting dog	**zo**
JOYFUL	happy; pleased; glad; blithe	
JOYOUS	gay; airy; merry; jocund	
JUBATE	maned; having a fringe	
JUBBAH	Eastern garment	**tx**
JUDAIC	Jewish; Hebrew; Israelitish	
JUDDER	shudder; jar; screen scan blurs	**cp**
JUDEAN	native of Judea	
JUDGED	considered; sentenced	
JUDGER	a judge; umpire; arbitrator	
JUDICA	Passion Sunday	**rl**
JUGATE	coupled; yoked	**bt**
JUGFUL	filling a jug	**me**
JUGGED	(hare); imprisoned	
JUGGLE	conjure; shuffle; swindle	
JUG-JUG	meat in aspic; nightingale's song	
JUICER	machine for extracting fruit juice	
JUJUBE	shrub; lozenge	**bt, ck**
JULIAN	calendar; system	
JUMART	hybrid animal (Fr.)	**zo**
JUMBAL	crisp sweet cake	**ck**
JUMBLE	confuse; mix; muddle	
JUMBUK	a sheep (Aust.)	**zo**
JUMENT	a mare	**zo**
JUMPED	bounded; grabbed; sprang; of wild horses fleeing	
JUMPER	chisel	**to**
JUMPER	religious sect; over-blouse	**rl**
JUNCUS	plants (rush)	**bt**
JUNGLE	the rukh (concréte)	**go**
JUNGLY	jungli; unsophisticated	
JUNIOR	younger; a son	
JUNIUS	anonymous writer	
JUNKER	Prussian landowner, aristocrat	
JUNKET	a sweetmeat; to feast; regale	**ck**
JUPATI	palm yielding raffia fibre	**bt**
JURANT	swearing	**lw**
JURIST	a lawyer	**lw**
JUSTER	more equitable	
JUSTLE	jostle; nudge; elbow	
JUSTLY	fairly; impartially; rightly	
JUTTED	projected; protruded	
JUZAIL	Afghan heavy rifle	
JYMOLD	gimmal; gimbal	

K

KABAKA	former ruler of Buganda (Uganda)	
KABALA	Moslem Holy of Holies	**rl**
KABOOK	iron-stone (Sri Lanka)	**mn**
KABOON	backward somersault (trampoline)	
KABUKI	realistic dramatic art (Jap.)	
KABYLE	Algerian Berber	

KACHIN	Burmese borderer	
KAFFIR	a Kafir	
KAFILA	caravan; train of camels	
KAFTAN	robe (Turk.)	tx
KAIROS	critical moment of decision for changes	pc
KAISER	German emperor	
KAKAPO	New Zealand parrot	zo
KALIUM	potassium	ch
KALMIA	American laurel	bt
KALONG	Malay fox-bat	zo
KALPIS	Grecian water-vase	
KAMEES	kamis; Eastern garment	
KAMELA	} orange dye (E. Indies)	bt
KAMILA		
KAMERA	camera; private room; secret	
KAMMER	(Ger.) salon; drawing room; chamber	mu
KAMSIN	a hot wind of the Sahara	mt
KANAKA	South Sea islander	
KANARA	Persian runner carpet in pairs	tx, wv
KANTEN	a seaweed	bt
KANUCK	a Canadian	
KAOLIN	China clay	
KARAKA	NZ food tree	bt
KARATE	open-handed fighting (Jap.)	ga
KARMIC	relating to Karma	
KAROSS	skin blanket (S. Africa)	tx
KARREN	grooved limestone (karst)	gl
KARROO	tableland (S. Africa)	go
KARYON	cell-nucleus	bl
KASBAH	Arab town, fort (N. Africa)	
KATION	cation	
KATIPO	Austr. venomous spider	zo
KAYLES	early form of skittles (English)	ga
KAYMAK	clotted cream (Turk.)	
KAYSER	wave-number unit	ps
KEBBIE	a cudgel (Sc.)	
KEBLAH	} towards Mecca	
KIBLAH		
KECKLE	cackle; (rope protection)	
KECKSY	dried stalks	bt
KEDDAH	kheda; elephant trap	
KEDGED	warped; towed into dock	nt
KEDGER	a kedge; small anchor	nt
KEEKER	mine inspector (Sc.)	
KEELED	carinated; navigated	nt, nv
KEELER	tub; bargee	nt
KEELIE	kestrel; street Arab (Sc.)	zo
KEENER	professional mourner	
KEENLY	sharply; acutely; astutely	
KEEPER	guard-ring; warden; latch-piece; zoo; armature; magnet	el
KEEVED	tubbed	
KELKEL	dried sole	ck
KELOID	of scar tissue	md
KELPIE	water spirit; seaweed gatherer (Sc.)	
KELSON	keelson; inner keel	nt

KELTIC	Celtic	
KELTIE	kittiwake gull	zo
KELVIN	thermo-dynamic temperature	me
KENCHI	ivory carving tool	to
KENNED	recognized; knew	
KENNEL	channel; gutter; a haunt	
KENTLE	100 lb (45 kg); quintal	me
KENYTE	fine-grained igneous rock	gl
KERION	hair disease	md
KERITE	insulating material	
KERMES	crimson dye; cochineal	zo
KERMIS	kermess; Dutch fair	
KERNED	letter with projecting face	pr
KERNEL	inner nut; heart; set of procedures	bt, cp
KERRIA	Japanese rose	bt
KERRIE	knob-kerrie	
KERSEY	woollen cloth	tx
KETENE	acetone-based compound	ch
KETONE	acetone	ch
KETOSE	ketonic monosaccharide	ch
KETTLE	water-boiling pot	
KEUPER	sandstone	mn
KEYAGE	quayage	
KEYING	signals by modulation	el
KEY-MEN	the indispensables	
KEYPAD	symbols and digit entry to computer	cp
KEY-PIN	key-pivot	
KEY-WAY	longitudinal key-slot cut	eg
KHALIF	Calif; Caliph; chief of Islam	
KHANAT	ancient hill tunnels for water supply	ar
KHILIM	} woven rug (Turk.)	tx
KILIM		
KIBBLE	cudgel; hand-mill; hound	zo
KIBBLE	iron-ore bucket; coal measure	me
KICKED	hacked; objected; punted	
KICKER	footballer; thrill-giver; (horse); rebel; base of wall, column	ga, ar, ce
KICKUP	small dance	
KIDDER	a corn cornerer; a carpet	tx
KIDDER	forestaller; huckster	
KIDDLE	weir	
KIDDOW	guillemot	zo
KID-FOX	young fox	zo
KIDNAP	abduct; capture; steal	
KIDNEY	kind; humour	md
KIEKIE	New Zealand shrub	bt
KIKUYU	tribe (Kenya)	
KILERG	1,000 ergs	me
KILHIG	tree-pushing pole	fr
KILLAS	slate	mn
KILLED	fascinated; neutralized	
KILLER	whale	zo
KILLOW	a black earth	mn
KILLUT	Indian robe of honour	tx
KILTED	wearing Scots kilt	tx
KILTIE	kilted soldier (Sc.)	

KIMMER	woman neighbour	
KIMONO	Japanese robe	**tx**
KINASE	activator of true enzymes	**bc**
KINATE	salt	**ch**
KINCOB	Indian thread work	**tx**
KINDER	more benevolent	
KINDLE	provoke; animate; ignite	
KINDLY	congenial; benevolent	
KINEMA	cinema; body movement linguistics	
KINETY	structure unit in protozoa	**zo**
KINGLY	regal; imperial; august	
KINKED	snarled; twisted	
KINKLE	a kink; twist; ruck	**wv**
KIPPER	a salmon after spawning	**zo**
KIPPER	smoked herring	**ck**
KIRBEH	Arab water-skin	
KIRKIN	(church attendance)	**rl**
KIRPAN	Sikh 3 ft (0.9 m) knife	
KIRSCH	wild cherry liqueur	**ck**
KIRTLE	a gown; a mantle	**tx**
KIRTLE	weight of flax	**me**
KISHKA	Yiddish/Polish sausage	**ck**
KISMET	fate; destiny	
KISSED	bussed; (billiards)	**ga**
KISSER	mouth (sl.); bow-string knot (archery)	
KIT-BAG	army barracks bag	
KIT-KAT	rounders for boys	**ga**
KITTEN	baby cat	**zo**
KITTLE	ticklish; intractable (Sc.)	
KITTLY	ticklish; sensitive	
KLAXON	a motor horn	
KLEPHT	Greek bandit	
K-MESON	} elementary particles	**ps**
KILO-MESON		
KNACKY	cunning	
KNAGGY	knotty; rough in temper	
KNARRY	knotty; rugged	
KNAWEL	a plant	**bt**
KNICKS	knickers; undergarment	
KNIFED	stabbed	
KNIGHT	a chess-man; a paladin	
KNITCH	faggot (dial.)	
KNOBBY	knotty; stubborn	
KNOTTY	intricate; difficult	
KNOWER	an erudite man	
KOBALT	cobalt	**ch**
KOBANG	old Japanese gold coin	**nm**
KOBOLD	goblin; gnome	
KOLVEN	club and ball game (Holland)	**ga**
KOODOO	antelope (S. Africa); kudu	**zo**
KOPECK	} Russian farthing	**nm**
KOPEK		
KOREAN	} (of Korea)	
COREAN		
KORKIR	corkir; purple dye	**bt**
KORUNA	crown (Czech)	**nm**
KOSHER	of food; ritually prepared (Jew.)	**ck**

KOSMOS	} universe	
COSMOS		
KOTWAL	Indian police officer	
KOUSSO	plant (Abys.)	**bt**
KOWHAI	Maori trees	**bt**
KOW-TOW	salutation; obeissance (China)	
KOZUKA	knife beside a sword (Jap.)	
KRAKEN	sea monster (Danish)	
KRANTZ	rocky summit (S. Africa); crown	**go**
KRASIS	Eucharistic wine with water	**rl**
KREESE	creese; Malay dagger	
K-THIBH	(Hebrew Scriptures)	**rl**
KUKANG	lemur or loris (Malay)	**zo**
KULICH	Orthodox Easter cake (Rus.)	**ck**
KULTUR	education; German culture	
KUMBAR	Indian coarse wood	**bt**
KUMBUK	E. Indian tree	**bt**
KUMISS	koumiss; drink (Tartar)	**ck**
KUMMEL	a liqueur	**ck**
KUNKUR	Indian limestone	**gl**
KURKEE	coarse blanket	
KURUSH	(Turkey) small coin	**nm**
KUSHTI	national wrestling (Iran)	**ga**
KUSKUS	} millet dish (Arab); fibre	
COUSCOUS	(Indian)	**bt, ck**
KUTTAR	short Indian dagger	
K-VALUE	thermal conductivity of material	
KWAART	clear lead glaze (Holland)	
KYBOSH	insurmountable obstruction	
KYLOES	Highland cattle	**zo**

L

LAAGER	Boer wagon encampment	
LABEFY	impair; weaken	
LABIAL	lip (sounds); labia (vagina)	**pl**
LABILE	unstable; liable to err	
LABIUM	a lip; fold; (vagina); lip sound	**bt, pl**
LABOUR	toil; drudge; industry	
LABRET	lip ornament	
LABRUM	upper lip	**pl**
LACCIC	(a resinous dye)	**ch**
LAC-DYE	(dye); shellac	
LACHES	negligence	**lw**
LACING	twining; beating; intermixing	**tx**
LACKED	short of; needed; wanted	
LACKER	one in want	
LACKEY	flunkey; footman; attendant	
LACMUS	litmus; lichen-dye	**ch**
LACTIC	acid, milk, products	**ch, ck**
LACUNA	a void; gap; blank; hiatus	
LADDER	rent in stockings; climbing aid; (snakes); (Jacob's); mud bucket	**ce**
LADDIE	youngster; lad; boy (Sc.)	
LA-DI-DA	affected manner	
LADIES	gentlewomen	

LADING	freight; cargo; burden	
LADINO	Spanish dialect	
LADKIN	} wooden tool to open leaded	
LATTERKIN	} panes	**to, bd**
LADLED	spooned; dispensed	
LAGENA	amphora; vase	
LAG-END	the bitter end	
LAGGED	loitered; apprehended	
LAGGEN	barrel projection (Sc.)	
LAGGER	laggard; loafer; idler	
LAGOON	} lake; nearly enclosed sea	
LAGUNE	} inlet (bayou) (atoll); pool	
		go
LAICAL	(laity)	
LAID-IN	note of inclusion of extra item	**pr**
LAIDLY	loathly; clumsy (dial.)	
LAID-ON	available, made ready for use	
LAID-UP	ill; out of action; (mothballs)	
LAITHE	pollack fish	**zo**
LAKIST	(Lake school of poetry)	
LALLAN	lowland (Sc.)	
LAMBDA	Gr. letter; warmth and energy;	
	gay symbol	
LAMBED	yeaned	
LAMBIE	small lamb (Sc.)	**zo**
LAMELY	haltingly	
LAMENT	deplore; wail; a jeremiad; dirge;	
	piece for bagpipes	**mu**
LAMINA	thin plate; ply (laminated)	
LAMING	crippling; disabling	
LAMISH	somewhat lame	
LAMMAS	1st August	
LAMMED	thrashed; drubbed	
LAMMER	amber (Sc.)	
LAMMIE	quilted jumper; lammy	**tx**
LAMPAS	swelling in horse's palate	**vt**
LAMPAS	heavier form of damask figured	
	cloth	**tx**
LAMPIC	(alcohol)	**ch**
LANARY	wool store	
LANATE	woolly	**tx**
LANCED	cut open; pierced	
LANCER	a cavalry-man	
LANCET	a cutting instrument	**md**
LANCET	window	**ar**
LANDAU	a carriage	
LANDED	disembarked; owning estates	
LANDER	a miner	
LANGET	coarse Dutch lace	**tx**
LANGUE	tongue (linguistics)	
LANGUR	Indian monkey	**zo**
LANKLY	ungracefully; clumsily	
LANNER	hawk; falcon	**zo**
LANUGO	prenatal hair in mammals	**zo**
LAPDOG	small pet dog	**zo**
LAPFUL	load in one's lap	
LAPIES	grooved limestone rock (karst)	**gl**
LAPPED	gem cutting; racing	
LAPPEL	lapel; folded flap	
LAPPER	folder	

LAPPET	loose flap; a lobe	
LAPSED	slipped; become void; (below par)	
LAPSUS	slip; memory failure; (of pen,	
	tongue) (Lat.); mistake; error	
LARDED	smeared with lard	**ck**
LARDER	storehouse	
LARDON	slice of bacon	**ck**
LARGER	bigger; wider; greater; bulkier	
LARIAT	lasso; rope with noose	
LAROID	pertaining to gulls	**zo**
LARRUP	to beat; to flog	
LARVAE	caterpillars; grubs; maggots	**zo**
LARVAL	(larva)	**zo**
LARYNX	throat; vocal cord	**pl**
LASCAR	East Indian sailor	
LASHED	secured; scourged, buffetted	
LASHER	rope; pool below a weir; whipper	
LASHES	thongs; eye-lashes; whip strokes	
LASKET	loop line in a sail	**nt**
LASQUE	flat diamond	**mn**
LASSIE	damsel; maid; lass; collie dog	**zo**
LASTED	endured; remained; continued	
LASTER	bootmaker; cobbler	
LASTLY	ultimately; finally; endwise	
LATEEN	triangular sail	**nt**
LATELY	recently; latterly	
LATENT	dormant; concealed; potential	
LATERO-	lateral, to the side, sideways on	
	(Gr.)	**cf**
LATEST	most up-to-date	
LATHEN	made of laths	
LATHER	soapy froth; foam	
LATISH	somewhat late	
LATRIA	highest kind of worship	**rl**
LATTEN	sheet brass	
LATTER	modern; recent; previous	
LAUDED	praised; extolled; magnified	
LAUDER	eulogist; ecomiast; panegyrist	
LAUNCE	a balance; an eel	**zo**
LAUNCH	hurl; inaugurate; start; float;	
	passenger tender; craft; lifeboat	
		nt
LAUREL	the bay-tree	**bt**
LAURIN	an extract from laurel	**ck**
LAVABO	ritualistic washing	**rl**
LAVAGE	washing	**md**
LAVING	bathing	
LAVISH	squander; dissipate; luxurious	
LAVOLT	medieval dance; lavolta	
LAW-DAY	day of open court	**lw**
LAWFUL	legal; legitimate; rightful	
LAWING	litigation; tavern-bill	**lw**
LAWYER	solicitor; counsel; advocate	
LAXIST	amoral philanderer	
LAXITY	slackness; latitude; neglect	
LAXMAN	lacrosse player	
LAY-DAY	a lading day	
LAYING	placing; betting; imputing	
LAYMAN	not a cleric; unprofessional	
LAY-OFF	dismissal (industrial)	

LAY-OUT	set out; plan	
LAZILY	slothfully; drowsily; supinely	
LAZING	idling	
LAZULI	blue spar	mn
LEADED	set in lead	
LEADEN	heavy; dull	
LEADER	head; chief; guide; director	
LEADER	(editorial); preceding signal	cp
LEAD-IN	wire connecting an aerial	
LEAFED	having leaves	bt
LEAGUE	combine; union; cabal	
LEAKED	oozed; percolated	
LEALTY	loyalty; fidelity	
LEAMER	dog on leam	zo
LEANED	relied; leant; inclined	
LEANER	thinner; skimpier	
LEANLY	lankly; slenderly; scantily	
LEAN-TO	a shed beside a wall	ar
LEAPED	sprang; skipped; gambolled	
LEAPER	jumper; vaulter; chaser	zo
LEASED	let out; hired; reserved for user	
		cp
LEASER	gleaner	
LEAVED	interleaved	bt
LEAVEN	yeast; balm; ferment; imbue	
LEAVER	a forsaker; quitter; deserter	
LECTIN	antibody-like substance	bc
LECTOR	reader	rl
LEDGER	scaffold; account book	ar
LEERED	ogled; gloated	
LEEWAY	arrears of work; sideways	
	movement of boat	nt
LEGACY	bequest; gift; devise	lw
LEGATE	ambassador; envoy; delegate	
LEGATO	smoothly	mu
LEG-BYE	(cricket); penalty	ga
LEGEND	myth; fable; fiction; caption	
LEGGED	dashed off	
LEGION	host; multitude; horde; army	
LEGIST	skilled in law; jurist	lw
LEGUME	seed vessel; pod; vegetable	bt
LEIGER	a resident ambassador (Shak.)	
LEIPOA	Australian game-bird	zo
LENDER	loaner	
LENGTH	extent; duration; reach	
LENIFY	assuage; mollify	
LENITY	clemency; leniency	
LENTEN	(Lent); sparing; during fast	rl
LENTIC	of standing water	ec
LENTIL	a bean; pulse	bt
LENTOR	slowness; tenacity; viscosity	
LENVOY	postscript	
LEONID	a meteor from Leo	as
LEPCHA	native of Sikkim	
LEPPER	} steeplechase horse	
LEAPER	}	
-LEPSIA	of seizure, epilepsy (Gr.)	cf
LEPTON	hundredth of a drachma	nm
LEPTON	nuclear particle	nc
LEPTUS	larval form of acarina	zo

LESENE	pilaster-strip moulding (Saxon)	ar
LESION	injury; wound	md
LESSEE	(lease); tenant	lw
LESSEN	reduce; mitigate; decrease	
LESSER	lower; minor; inferior	
LESSON	task; precept; warning; Bible	
	reading; short keyboard piece	
		mu, rl
LESSOR	lease holder	lw
LETHAL	fatal; deadly; mortal	
LET-OFF	a reprieve	
LET-OUT	release	
LETTER	note; epistle; missive; initial,	
	monogram	
LETTIC	Lettish; (Latvia)	
LEUCOL	coal-tar product	
LEVADA	descending irrigation channel	
	(Madeira)	ag
LEVADE	horse dressage movement	
LEVANT	to decamp; the East	
LEVIED	mustered; taxed	
LEVITE	Jewish tribe; priest	rl
LEVITY	frivolity; flippancy; giddiness	
LEVURE	flour water paste for sealing pot-	
	lids	ck
LEVYNE	zeolite	mn
LEWDLY	lustfully; indecently	
LEYDEN	electrical jar	el
LIABLE	accountable; likely; obnoxious	
LIAISE	to form a liaison; link-up	
LIBANT	sipping	
LIBATE	to make a libation	
LIBIDO	life force; sexual urge	
LIBYAN	(N. Africa)	
LICHEN	reindeer moss	bt
LICHEN	skin disease	md
LICKED	lapped; lammed; defeated	
LICTOR	Roman officer	
LIDDED	having lids	
LIEDER	German ballads	mu
LIENAL	of the spleen	pl
LIERNE	cross-rib	ar
LIFTED	elevated; stole; upraised	
LIFTER	weight-lifter (gymn.); (shop-) thief;	
	raiser	
LIGAND	outlying ion	ch
LIGASE	catalysing enzyme	ch
LIGATE	to tie up	md
LIGGER	thatch ridge stick; bedspread;	
	night-line	
LIGHTS	(ancient); (Northern); offal; lamps	
LIGNIN	wood-fibre	
LIGNUM	hardwood	bt
LIGULA	} grass; petal	
LIGULE	}	bt
LIGURE	precious stone	mn
LIKELY	probable; credible	
LIKING	love; fondness; regard	
LILIED	adorned with lilies	
LILITH	Adam's first wife	

LILTED	sung rhythmically	**mu**
LIMBEC	a still; a distilling vessel	
LIMBED	with limbs	
LIMBER	flexible; pliant; supple	
LIMBIC	bordering; marginal	**pr**
LIMBUS	limbo; paradise of fools	
LIMING	snaring; treating with lime	
LIMMER	mongrel; idler; jade	**zo**
LIMNED	painted; illuminated	
LIMNER	artist; delineator	
LIMOUS	muddy; slimy; sticky	
LIMPED	walked with disability	
LIMPER	a lame man	
LIMPET	univalve mollusc; leech caisson	
	(for docks); hanger on	**zo, ce**
LIMPID	clear; pellucid; pure	
LINAGE	(cost per line) advert rate	**pr**
LINDEN	lime tree	**bt**
LINEAL	in a direct line (graph) (diagram)	
LINEAR	slender; graph; key to	
	combinations	**cp**
LINE-UP	show of unity; order of batting	
	(cricket); horses at start of race;	
	wave break point (surfing);	
	football	**ga**
LINGAM	sacred symbol (Hindu)	**rl**
LINGEL	waxed thread (Sc.)	
LINGER	lag; loiter; dawdle; tarry	
LINGET	} an ingot; metal block	**ml**
LINGOT		
LINHAY	farm shed	
LINING	aligning; inner cover; first coating;	
	ease; painting defect	**bd**
LINKED	connected; united; coupled	
LINKED	subroutine, outside program path	
		cp
LINNET	bird; lintie	**zo**
LINSEY	mixed wool and linen cloth	**tx**
LINTEL	} joist beam over a doorway,	
LINTOL	window	**bd**
LINTER	cotton fibre	**tx**
LINTIE	linnet; a song-bird (Sc.)	**zo**
LINVAR	linear variometer resolver	**el**
LIONEL	} young lion	**zo**
LIONET		
LIPASE	enzyme	**ch**
LIPLET	little lip	
LIPOIC	an acid regulating oxidation	**ch**
LIPOID	fatty; sebaceous	**md**
LIPOMA	a fatty tumour	**md**
LIPPED	labiate; (golf)	
LIPPEN	to rely; to trust (Sc.)	
LIPPER	a rippling; surface roughness	
LIPPIE	quarter of a peck (Sc.)	**me**
LIQUID	fluid; fluent; melting; dulcet	
LIQUID	(cash); flowing speech sounds 'r'	
	and 'l'	
LIQUOR	spirits; drink	
LISBON	a Portuguese wine	
LISPED	couldn't pronounce 's' sounds	

LISPER	person who lisps	
LISSOM	lithe; agile; pliant; supple	
LISTED	enlisted; canted over; registered	
LISTEL	fillet	**ar**
LISTEN	hark; attend; eavesdrop	
LISTER	arranger; recorder	
LITANY	solemn supplication	**rl**
LITCHI	} fruit (China)	**bt**
LYCHEE		
LITHER	lazy; worthless; smooth	
LITHIA	oxide of lithium	**md**
LITHIC	(stone)	**ar.; md**
LITMUS	acid test dye	**ch**
LITTER	scatter; the newborn; bedding	**zo**
LITTLE	tiny; pygmy; brief; trivial	
LITUUS	augur's staff	
LIVEDO	blueness of skin from congestion	
LIVELY	joyful; active; vigorous; quick	
LIVERY	uniform; costume	**tx**
LIVERY	writ of possession	**lw**
LIVING	livelihood; animate	**rl**
LIZARD	saurian reptile	**zo**
LLANOS	plains of South America	**go**
LOADED	laden; filled; cumbered	
LOADER	one of the gun's crew; stacker	
LOADER	input memory routine	**cp**
LOAFED	lounged	
LOAFER	idler; vagrant; flaneur; drone	
LOANED	lent; advanced; borrowed	
LOATHE	hate; detest; abhor	
LOAVES	of bread	**ck**
LOBATE	(lobes)	
LOBBED	pitched; gently threw	
LOBING	gadrooning	
LOBOLA	wife-purchase (S. Africa)	
LOBOSE	lobate	**bt**
LOBULE	small lobe	
LOCALE	meeting place (hall) (Fr.)	
LOCATE	fix; place; settle; find	
LOCHAN	a pond; a loch (Sc.)	
LOCKED	grappled; embraced; clasped	
LOCKER	a cupboard; a drawer	
LOCKET	an ornament; a fastening	
LOCK-UP	jail-cell, garage with lock	
LOCULI	cells	**bt**
LOCUST	acacia tree; insect	**bt, zo**
LODGED	deposited; dwelt; harboured	
LODGER	temporary resident	
LODORE	a cataract	
LOFTED	skied	
LOFTER	(golf)	
LOGGAN	rocking stone; logan	
LOGGAT	} medieval ninepin; heavy	
LOGGET	wooden pole	
LOGGED	recorded	**nt**
LOGGER	lumberman; recorder of events	**cp**
LOGGIA	gallery or arcade (Italian)	**ar**
LOG-HUT	log-cabin	**bd**
LOG-LOG	logarithm of a logarithm	**ma**
LOGMAN	woodman; logger	

LOG-OFF	check-out	cp
LOGWAY	chute route beside dam	ce
LOHOCK	syrup	md
LOIMIC	(plague)	md
LOITER	linger; dawdle; delay; tarry	
LOLIGO	cuttle-fish; squid	zo
LOLIUM	genus of grass	bt
LOLLED	hung out; reclined	
LOLLER	lounger; flaneur	
LOLLOP	to lounge	
LOMENT	a type of legume	bt
LONELY	solitary; remote; forlorn	
LONGAN	Chinese fruit tree	bt
LONGED	craved; desired	
LONGER	more extensive; taller	
LOOFAH	sponge; skeleton; gourd	bt
LOOKED	examined; observed; glanced	
LOOKER	onlooker; spectator	
LOOK-IN	hasty visit; glance; short participation (Am. football)	
LOOK-UP	seek information; select data by key	cp
LOOMED	rose to view	
LOOPED	encircled; knotted	
LOOPER	a caterpillar; wave over surfer; short pass (Am. football)	zo
LOOSED	set free	
LOOSEN	slacken; release; untie; relax	
LOOTED	ransacked	
LOOTER	plunderer; pillager; despoiler	
LOP-EAR	a lop-eared rabbit	zo
LOPING	running easily	
LOPPED	trimmed; truncated	
LOPPER	to curdle; trimmer; a cutting	
LOQUAT	Chinese fruit	bt
LORATE	thong-shaped	
LORCHA	junk-rigged Portuguese ship	nt
LORDED	domineered	
LORDLY	noble; magnificent; arrogant	
LORICA	a cuirass	
LORING	learning (Spens.)	
LORIOT	golden oriole	zo
LOSING	mislaying; squandering; failing	
LOSSES	casualties; damages; privations	
LOTION	a wash	
LOUDER	noisier; more stentorian	
LOUDLY	uproariously; clamorously	
LOUNGE	loll; loaf; recline; idle	
LOURED	frowned; scowled	
LOUSED	infested with lice	
LOUVER	louvre; ventilator	
LOUVRE	open turret (Fr.)	ar
LOVAGE	genus of herb; angelica type	bt
LOVELY	beauteous; delectable	
LOVING	adoring; esteeming	
LOWBOY	low chest of drawers (N. Amer.)	
LOWERY	gloomy; overcast; murky	
LOWEST	most debased; deepest	
LOWING	bellowing; mooing	

LUBBER	heavy, clumsy fellow	
LUBRIC	slippery; lewd	
LUCAMA	fruit (Chile)	bt
LUCENT	bright; shining; clear	
LUCINA	Diana or Juno	
LUCKIE	elderly woman (Sc.)	
LUCUMO	Etruscan title	
LUETIC	pestilential	md
LUFFER	(see Louvre); open turret	ar
LUGGED	tugged; hauled; dragged	
LUGGER	small sailing ship	nt
LUGGIE	vase with ears	
LULLED	soothed; assuaged; calmed	
LUMBAL	} vertebrae	md
LUMBAR		
LUMBER	junk; rubbish; trash; refuse	
LUMERG	unit of luminous energy	lt, me
LUMPED	heaped up	
LUMPER	stevedore	
LUMPIA	oriental egg roll	ck
LUNACY	mania; dementia; craziness	
LUNARY	lunar; moonwort fern	bt
LUNATE	like a crescent-moon	
LUNGED	thrust	
LUNKAH	Indian cheroot	bt
LUNULA	} crescent-like; lunate	
LUNULE		
LUPINE	wolf-like; wolfish	
LUPINE	lupin; a fodder plant	bt
LURING	enticing; inveigling; decoying	
LURKED	hid; laid in wait	
LURKER	skulker	
LUSIAD	Portuguese epic poem	
LUSTED	eagerly desired	
LUSTIC	lusty; vigorous	
LUSTRA	periods of five years	
LUSTRE	Roman purification ceremony	
LUSTRE	gloss; splendour; glory	
LUTEAL	of the corpus luteum	zo
LUTEIN	egg yellow	ck
LUTINE	(Lloyd's bell) (marine disaster)	
LUTING	a composition; clay; joining clay pieces using slip	
LUTIST	lute player	mu
LUTOSE	miry	
LUXATE	dislocate	
LUXURY	epicurism; voluptuousness; super-comfort	
LUZULA	a rush genus	bt
LYCEUM	lecture hall	
LYCHEE	Chinese dessert fruit	ck
LYDIAN	effeminate	
LYDITE	black slate; touchstone	mn
LYMPHY	(lymph)	md
LYRATE	lyre-shaped	
LYRISM	playing the lyre	mu
LYRIST	lyrical writer	
LYSINE	diamino-caproic acid	ch

M

MABOLA	Philippine tree	bt
MACACO	a tropical tree	bt
MACHAN	platform for tiger-shooting	
MACIES	emaciation; wasting away	md
MACKLE	macule; a blur in printing	pr
MACKLE	spot, blotch, stain	
MACLED	spotted	
MACRON	a mark showing long vowel	
MACULA	retinal vision area (eye)	pl
MACULE	spot symptom (small-) (chicken-) pox	md
MADCAP	hair-brained; frolicsome	
MADDEN	enrage; infuriate	
MADDER	a plant; a red dye	bt
MADMAN	maniac; bedlamite	
MADRAS	bright kerchief; cotton fabric	tx
MAENAD	a frenzied woman	
MAFFIA	mafia; Sicilian secret society	
MAGGOT	worm; grub; larva; a whim	zo
MAGIAN	Wise Men of the East	
MAGILP	megilp; painters' varnish	pt
MAGISM	Persian philosophy	
MAGNET	lodestone; attraction; lure	
MAGNON	spin-wave energy quantum	nc
MAGNOX	magnesium alloy	ch
MAGNUM	2 quart (2.2 litre) bottle	me
MAGPIE	(target shooting) (nil); bird	zo
MAGUEY	Mexican aloe	bt
MAGYAR	Hungarian	
MAHOUN	mahound; evil spirit (Arabic)	
MAHOUT	elephant driver	
MAHSIR	mahseer; an Indian fish	zo
MAIDAN	Indian parade ground; a plain	
MAIDEN	lass; damsel; virgin; guillotine	
MAIDEN	untaken, non-winner (horse-racing); non-scoring (cricket)	
MAILED	posted; clad in armour	
MAIMED	crippled; disabled; mutilated	
MAINLY	chiefly; principally; largely	
MAINOR	stolen goods; theft	lw
MAJLIS	parliament of Iran, Egypt	
MAJOON	narcotic drug mixture (Hindu)	
MAKE-UP	fiction; facial embellishment	
MAKING	forcing; compelling; reaching	
MAKORE	African mahogany wood	bt
MALADY	ailment; disorder; complaint	
MALAGA	a Spanish wine	
MALATE	a salt of malic acid	ch
MALAWI	native of E. Africa	
MALAXE	to rub, knead plaster	
MALEIC	obtained from malic acid	ch
MALGRE	maugre; in spite of	
MALICE	spite; rancour; malevolence	
MALIGN	defame; slander; traduce	
MALISM	pessimistic belief	
MALKIN	scarecrow; mawkin	
MALLEE	Australian tree	bt

MALLET	maul; beetle; wooden hammer (croquet, polo)	ga, to, rw
MALLOW	plant (marsh)	bt
MALTED	malt added	br
MALTHA	petroleum	
MAMMAL	genus of breast-feeders	zo
MAMMEE	West Indian fruit	bt
MAMMER	stammer; hesitate; hover	
MAMMET	puppet; scarecrow	
MAMMON	god of riches; wealth	
MANAGE	contrive; control; regulate	
MANANA	tomorrow or perhaps later (Sp.)	
MANCHE	sleeve; the channel (Fr.)	hd
MANCHU	former ruling class in China	
MANDOM	humanity	
MANEGE	riding school; equitation	
MANFUL	virile; courageous; bold	
MANGAL	charcoal brazier (Turk.)	
MANGER	a trough	
MANGLE	mutilate; to calender (laundry)	
MANIAC	madman; lunatic; fiend	
MANILA	Manilla cheroot	bt
MANIOC	tapioca; cassava	bt
MANISM	belief in nature cult	
MANITO	Great Spirit (American Ind.)	rl
MANJAK	Barbados asphalt	
MANNAN	anhydride of mannose	ch
MANNED	provided a crew	
MANNER	behaviour; style; deportment	
MANQUE	1 to 18 in roulette; missed career	
MANTEL	a beam; mantel-shelf	
MANTIC	inspired; prophetic; vatic	
MANTID	pertaining to mantis	zo
MANTIS	a praying insect	zo
MANTLE	cloak; hood; covering; suffuse; rock layer between crust and core of earth; (-piece) (gas-)	gl
MANTON	Spanish shawl	
MANTRA	a Vedic hymn; meditational prayer, sound ritual	rl, pc
MANTUA	lady's cloak or gown	
MANUAL	handbook, organ key-board	mu
MANURE	compost; fertilizer; dressing	
MANWAY	underground ladderway	mn
MAOISM	ideas of Mao Tse Tung	
MAOIST	follower of Mao Tse Tung	
MAPPED	charted; drew; delineated	
MAQUIS	French Resistance force	
MAQUIS	rough scrub in Med.	bt
MARACA	Latin-American percussion	mu
MARAUD	raid; plunder; pillage	
MARBLE	decorative metamorphic rock; balls; famous friezes	gl, bd, mn
MARBLY	like marble	
MARCEL	a hair wave; style of coiffure	
MARCIA	a march (It.)	mu
MARCID	wasting	
MARCOR	marasmus; weight loss	md
MARGAY	American tiger-cat	zo
MARGED	bordered; edged	

MARGIN	verge; brim; brink; reserve	
MARGOT	fish (perch)	zo
MARIAN	concerning the Virgin Mary	
MARIAN	Virgin Mary (year)	rl
MARIET	violet campanula	bt
MARINA	yacht-mooring basin	nt
MARINE	nautical; naval; maritime	nt
MARISH	a marsh; swamp	
MARIST	sect, follower of Virgin Mary	
MARKAB	dhow, Egypt	nt
MARKED	unmistakable; notable	
MARKER	examiner; buoy; signpost	nt
MARKER	device for determining call paths	
		tc
MARKET	mart; emporium; sale; vend	
MARMOT	ground squirrel	zo
MAROON	claret-colour; firework (alarm signal)	
MAROON	runaway negro slave	
MARQUE	accredited; boundary; model	
MARRAM	sand dune; bent grass	bt
MARRED	disfigured; impaired	
MARRER	spoiler; bungler; botcher	
MARRON	chestnut (Fr.); hue, shade	bt, ck
MARROT	guillemot	zo
MARROW	medulla; essence; pith; (veg) (bone)	bt, pl ck
MARSHY	boggy; fenny; paludal	
MARTEN	(weasel)	zo
MARTIN	swallow	zo
MARTYR	victim; sacrifice; persecute	
MARVEL	wonder; prodigy; miracle	
MARVER	iron or stone block	
MARVER	glass blower's table	gs
MASCLE	heraldic lozenge	hd
MASCON	moon high-gravity region	as
MASCOT	charm; talisman; halidom	
MASHAQ	Persian goatskin water-bag	
MASHED	bruised; pulped; kneaded	
MASHER	fop; dandy; lady-killer	
MASHIE	a golf-club	
MASHVA	} mini-dhow (E. Afr.)	nt
MUCHVA		
MASJID	masjed; a mosque (Arabic)	rl
MASKED	disguised; cloaked; screened	
MASKER	masquerader; mummer	
MASLIN	rye-bread	ck
MASORA	Hebrew traditions	
MASQUE	mask; a play; revel	
MASSED	collected; heaped; lumped	
MASSES	the proletariat	
MASSIF	central mountain-mass (Fr.)	go
MASTAX	gizzard in rotifera	zo
MASTED	having masts	nt
MASTEL	maple tree	bt
MASTER	maestro; tutor; teacher; expert	
MASTIC	resin; coating with proofing; (pitch); (bitumastic)	bt, bd
MASTIC	liquorice-like flavour	ck
MATHES	may-weed	bt

MATICO	Peruvian astringent plant	bt
MATIES	herring; a wrasse; matjes (Dutch)	zo
MATING	pairing; check-mating	zo
MATINS	morning service	rl
MATRIX	original die; mould; cavity; array of items, numbers (discs)	pr, cp
MATRON	head nurse; dame	
MATTED	entangled; interlaced	
MATTER	signify; import; stuff; affair	
MATURE	ripen; mellow; full grown	
MAUDIT	one pursued by bad luck	
MAUGRE	in spite of	
MAULED	hammered; mangled; bruised	
MAUMAU	Kenyan nationalists	
MAUNDY	Thursday before Good Friday	
MAUSER	rifle	
MAWMET	maumet; mammet; puppet	
MAXIMA	highest or top limits	
MAXIXE	dance (Brazil)	mu
MAY-BUG	cockchafer	zo
MAYDAY	verbal distress call	tc
MAY-DEW	spring	
MAY-FLY	a species of ephemera	zo
MAYHAP	perhaps	
MAYHEM	criminal mutilation; maiming (Am.)	lw
MAYING	gathering may	
MAZARD	skull; cherry	bt
MAZDAH	supreme deity (Zend Avesta)	rl
MAZILY	confusedly; distractedly	
MAZING	bewildering; perplexing	
MAZOUT	petroleum extract	ch
MEABLE	easily penetrable	
MEADOW	mead; lea; sward; field	
MEAGER	} thin; skinny; lean; gaunt;	
MEAGRE	} lank; mean; emaciated	
MEAKER	a minnow	zo
MEALER	(out-boarder)	
MEALIE	maize dish (Africa)	ck, bt
MEANLY	ignobly; basely; sordidly	
MEASLY	stingy; miserly; meagre	
MEATHE	mead; a liquor	ck
MEATUS	passage in the body	pl
MEDDLE	muddle; intrude; interfere	
MEDIAD	} toward median axis	
MESIAD		
MEDIAL	average; mean; mediocre	
MEDIAN	traversal; a Mede	as
MEDICK	lucerne or clover	bt
MEDICO	doctor or student	md
MEDISM	Grecian treachery	
MEDIUM	moderate; means; psychic	
MEDIUS	the middle finger	pl
MEDLAR	fruit	bt
MEDLEY	farrago; jumble; olio	mu
MEDUSA	jellyfish; a gorgon	zo
MEEKEN	to humble; to abase	
MEEKLY	lowly; submissively	
MEETLY	fitly; suitably; correctly	

MEGALO-	of great size, power (Gr.)	cf
MEGASS	bagasse; cane refuse	
MEGERG	million ergs	me
MEGGER	insulation recorder	ps
MEGILP	magilp; linseed-oil and varnish	
MEGOHM	a million ohms	me
MEGRIM	neuralgic pain; migraine	md
MEGRIM	flat fish; witch/lemon sole	zo
MEHARI	racing dromedary; camel	zo
MEHTAR	Ind. house-servant, groom	
MEHTER	battle band (Turk.)	mu
MELINE	canary-yellow	
MELLAY	mêlée; affray; broil; brawl	
MELLEY	scuffle; contest; conflict	
MELLIT	a horse-scab	vt, zo
MELLOW	mature; ripe; genial; soften	
MELODY	air; tune; descant; theme	mu
MELTED	molten; dissolved; relaxed	
MELTER	liquefier	
MELTON	woollen cloth	tx
MEMBER	part; limb; component	
MEMNON	desert crier	
MEMOIR	life; biography; journal	
MEMORY	remembrance; recollection; access store	cp
MENACE	threat; alarm; intimidate	
MENAGE	housekeeping; household (group)	
MENALD	speckled	
MENDED	restored; rectified; improved	
MENDER	repairer; restorer	
MENHIR	obelisk; long grave stone	
MENIAL	slave; flunkey; degrading (chore)	
MENINX	a brain-membrane	pl
MENNAD	the minnow	zo
MENSAL	monthly	
MENSES	menstruation	pl
MENTAL	intellectual; psychical	
MENTOR	guide; monitor; counsellor	
MENURA	lyre-bird	zo
MERCER	a dealer in silks and cloths	
MERELY	simply; solely; only; purely	
MERESE	wine-glass stem flange	
MERGED	sunk; absorbed; immersed	
MERGER	an amalgamation	
MERINO	sheep; wool	tx, zo
MERISM	development of like members	bt
MERKIN	false hair; a mop	
MERLIN	falcon; small hawk	zo
MERLON	projecting part of battlement	ar
MERMAN	cf. mermaid	
MERONT	phase in neosporidia	zo
MEROPS	bird; bee-eater	zo
-MEROUS	of number of parts (Gr.)	cf
MERULA	thrush; blackbird	zo
MESAIL	vizor of helmet	
MESCAL	Mexican drink	
MESETA	tableland (Spain)	go
MESHED	reticulated; engaged	
MESIAL	} middle; median	
MESIAN		

MESLIN	maslin; mixed grain	bt
MESODE	part of an ode	
MESPOT	Mesopotamia	
MESSED	mussed; confused; ate together	
MESSIN	a mongrel (Sc.)	zo
MESTEE	half-caste; octoroon	
METAGE	measurement	me
METEOR	aerolite; shooting star	
METHAM	chemical insecticide, weedkiller	
METHER	vessel for mead	
METHOD	order; system; process	
METHYL	spirit	ch
METIER	role (Fr.); profession (vocational)	
METING	measuring	
METOPE	forehead; sculptural frieze	ar
METRIC	decimal system of weights and measures	
-METRIC	(isometric) of measure	cf
METTLE	courage; ardour; pluck	
MEWING	caterwauling; confining	
MEWLED	yowled; squalled	
MEWLER	a crying child	
MIASMA	bad air; exhalation	
MICHED	concealed; played truant	
MICHER	skulker; beggar; pilferer	
MICKLE	muckle; great; much	
MICMAC	an American Indian	
MICRON	millionth part of metre	me
MID-AGE	middle time of life	
MID-AIR	up in the air	
MIDDAY	noon; meridian	
MIDDEN	dunghill	
MIDDLE	centre; intermediate; medial	
MIDGET	sand-fly; dwarf	zo
MID-LEG	} (cricket) fielding position	ga
MID-OFF		
MIDRIB	largest leaf vein	bt
MID-SEA	at sea	nt
MIDWAY	halfway	
MIFFED	ruffled; annoyed	
MIGHTY	puissant; potent; dynamic	
MIGNON	dainty; pretty	
MIHRAB	mosque niche facing Mecca	rl
MIKADO	Emperor of Japan	
MILADY	my lady	
MILDEN	to mollify	
MILDER	calmer; softer; gentler	
MILDEW	mould; blight; rust; must	bt
MILDLY	leniently; placidly; suavely	
MILIEU	environment	
MILIUM	millet grass	bt
MILKED	emptied; taken advantage of	
MILKEN	milk-like	
MILKER	cow-man	
MILLED	ground; struggled; levigated	
MILLER	one who grinds corn	
MILLET	grain	
MILORD	my lord	
MILSEY	milk strainer	
MILTER	male fish	

MIMBAR	} pulpit in mosque	**ar, rl**
MIMBER		
MIMING	mimicking; aping; acting (theatre)	
MIMOSA	plant genus	**bt**
MINCED	affected; abbreviated	
MINCER	mincing machine	
MINDED	heeded; noted; objected	
MINDER	care-taker; attendant (nurse)	
MINGLE	blend; mix; join; jumble	
MINIFY	diminish; depreciate	
MINIMA	the lowest	
MINING	burrowing; sapping	
MINION	a favourite; sycophant	
MINISH	diminish; reduce; minify	
MINIUM	vermilion (colour)	**pt**
MINNIE	trench mortar	
MINNOW	meaker; mennad	**zo**
MINOAN	Cretan	
MINTED	coined; stamped; invented	
MINTER	inventor; creator	
MINTON	china ware	
MINUET	a dance (of symphony)	**mu**
MINUTE	small; tiny; minikin; record	
MIOMBO	woodland (Tanzania)	**fr**
MIOSIS	rhetorical understatement	
MIOTIC	eye-pupil contractor	**pl**
MIRAGE	optical illusion (oasis)	
MIRING	muddying; besmirching	
MIRROR	exemplar; reflector	
MISCUE	(billiards)	**ga**
MISDID	erred; blundered	
MISERE	(solo whist, no tricks) (cards)	**ga**
MISERY	distress; woe; grief; anguish	
MISFIT	square peg in round hole	
MISGET	obtain unjustly	
MISHAP	accident; ill chance	
MISHMI	vegetable drug	**md**
MISHNA	the text of the Talmud	**rl**
MISKEN	to ignore; be unaware (Sc.)	
MISKIN	a little bagpipe	**mu**
MISLAY	misplace; lose	
MISLED	(mislead); deluded; deceived	
MISSAL	Mass-book	**rl**
MISSAY	say wrongly; slander	
MISSED	failed; wanted; needed	
MISSEE	view erroneously	
MISSEL	thrush; storm cock	**zo**
MIS-SET	to arrange unfitly	
MISSIS	missus; mistress (Mrs)	
MISTER	ordinary title for man (Mr)	
MISTLE	missel-thrush	**zo**
MISUSE	abuse; profane; misapply	
MITHAN	Indian ox; gayal	**zo**
MITHRA	sun-god (Pers.) (later, Roman)	**rl**
MITRAL	like a mitre; somewhat conical	
MITRED	wearing mitre (Bishop)	**rl**
MITTEN	a boxing glove (fingerless)	
MIURUS	dactylic hexameter	
MIXING	mingling; jumbling	
MIZZEN	aft mast and sail	**nt**

MIZZLE	fine rain; to drizzle; decamp	
MIZZLY	misty	
-MNESIC	pertaining to memory	**pc**
MOANED	lamented; bewailed; deplored	
MOATED	surrounded with a ditch	
MOBBED	thronged; set about	
MOBCAP	a frilly cap	
MOBILE	volatile; mercurial; motile	
MOB-LAW	lynch-law	**lw**
MOCKED	derided; jeered; aped	
MOCKER	scorner; scoffer; taunter	
MOCK-UP	a non-working model	
MODENA	crimson	**pt**
MODERN	present; current; up-to-date	
MODEST	chaste; unassuming; diffident	
MODIFY	alter; change; vary; moderate	
MODISH	stylish; fashionable; chic	
MODIST	a follower of fashion	
MODIUS	2 gallons (Roman)	**me**
MODOCS	Oregon Indian tribe	
MODULE	model; proportion length; spacecraft	**ar, bd, me**
MODULE	hardware; self-contained unit, faculty behaviour; sputnik	**ae, cp**
MODULO	remaindering formula	**ma**
MOFFLE	bungle	
MOGOTE	conical hill (karst) (Sp.)	**gl, mn**
MOHAIR	hair of the Angora goat	**tx**
MOHAWK	ruffian; N. Amer. Indian; (ice-skating)	
MOHOLE	penetration of earth's crust	
MOIDER	to toil; confuse; spend (Sc.)	
MOIETY	a half; a share	
MOILED	drudged; toiled; soiled	
MOIRAE	the Fates	
MOLARS	grinder teeth of mammals	**pl**
MOLECH	} Phoenician god; Semitic deity; Australian lizard	**rl**
MOLOCH		**zo**
MOLEST	vex; harry; worry; pester	
MOLINE	mill-stone rynd	
MOLING	laying drains with mole plough	**ce**
MOLLAH	} judge; Moslem teacher; fanatic	
MOOLAH		**rl**
MULLAH		
MOLTEN	melted; liquefied; fused	
MOMENT	instant; trice; import	
MONDAY	Solomon Grundy's birthday	
MONERA	simple protozoans	**zo**
MONGER	deal; to deal in	
MONGOL	native of Mongolia (Downes Syndrome)	**md**
MONIAL	nun	**rl**
MONIED	rich; opulent	
MONIES	coins; means; specie	
MONISM	a doctrine of single reality	
MONIST	believer in monism	
MONKEY	a primate; bandar; rhesus	**zo**
MONKEY	£500; pile-driver; meddle	

221

MONODY	a dirge	**mu**
MONOID	(versification)	
MONOSY	abnormal condition	**bt**
MONTEM	Eton custom of money-raising	
MONTON	ore (Sp.)	**mn**
MONTRE	organ stop; ceramic	**mu**
MOO-COW	pet word for cow	**zo**
MOOING	lowing	
MOONED	wandered aimlessly	
MOONER	listless lounger	
MOONET	little moon	
MOORUK	Bennett's cassowary	**zo**
MOORVA	fibre; bowstring-hemp	**tx**
MOOTED	debated; discussed	
MOOTER	disputer	
MOPING	languishing	
MOPISH	gloomy; spiritless; despondent	
MOPOKE	Australian owl	**zo**
MOPPED	swabbed	
MOPPET	} puppet	
MOPSEY		
MORALE	courageous endurance	
MORASS	bog; fen; swamp; quagmire	
MORBID	diseased; vitiated; sickly	
MOREEN	watered woollen fabric	**tx**
MORGAY	shark; dog-fish	**zo**
MORGEN	about 2 acres (0.8 hectare)	**me**
MORGUE	mortuary (Fr.)	
MORIAN	a Moor; Moroccan	
MORION	open helmet	
MORKIN	dead beast	
MORLOP	jasper	**mn**
MORMON	member of sect (Utah)	**rl**
MORNED	blunted	**hd**
MORONE	a deep crimson colour	
MOROSE	sullen; surly; churlish	
MORRIS	folk dance style	
MORROW	the next day	
MORSAL	pert. to cutting edge	
MORSED	signalled by Morse	
MORSEL	titbit; piece; fragment	
MORTAL	human; deadly; fatal	
MORTAR	trench weapon; cement	
MORULA	button-scurvy	**md**
MOSAIC	law; inlaid ornamentation	**rl**
MOSAIC	green, symptoms of virus in plants	**lw, bt**
MOSLEM	Muslim; Mohammedan	**rl**
MOSQUE	temple; mesjid	**rl**
MOSTIC	maulstick	**pt**
MOSTLY	chiefly; mainly	
MOTHER	(liquors); dam; generatrix	
MOTILE	mobile; capable of movement	
MOTION	proposal; action; impulse	
MOTIVE	spur; incentive; reason	
MOTLEY	mixed; clown's costume	
MOT-MOT	American bird	**zo**
MOTORY	giving motion	
MOTTLE	to stain	
MOUJIK	muzhik; Russian peasant	

MOULDY	fusty; musty; rusty	
MOULIN	glacial crevasse; mill (Fr.) grinder	**ck**
MOUNTY	the rise of a hawk	
MOUSED	bound with spun-yarn	**nt**
MOUSER	capable cat	**zo**
MOUSSE	culinary confection	**ck**
MOUTAN	tree-peony	**bt**
MOUTHY	ranting; bombastic	
MOUTON	sheep; ancient French coin	**nm, zo**
MOVIES	moving pictures (cinema)	
MOVING	stirring; budging; touching	
MOWING	grass cutting	
MOZING	raising nap (cloth)	**tx**
MUCAGO	mucilage; mucus	
MUCATE	} mucic acid	**ch**
MUCITE		
MUCHLY	rather much	
MUCHVA	} mini-dhow (E. Afr.)	**nt**
MASHVA		
MUCKED	muddled; dirtied; spread dung	
MUCKER	a failure; a fall	
MUCKLE	much (Sc.)	
MUCOID	resembling mucus	**md**
MUCOSA	mucous membrane	
MUCOUS	mucoid; slimy; viscous	**md, ps**
MUDDER	muddy course, race-track (racing)	
MUDDLE	confuse; chaos; derange	
MUD-PIE	child's inedible confection	
MUFFED	fumbled and failed	
MUFFIN	a winter's delicacy	**ck**
MUFFLE	(furnace); deaden; shroud	
MUGGED	crammed up; beaten up	
MUGGER	Indian crocodile; assailant	**zo**
MUGUET	lily of the valley	**bt**
MULIER	wife	**lw**
MULISH	obstinate	
MULLAH	(see Mollah); teacher (Moslem)	**rl**
MULLED	hot; spiced (wine); pondered	**ck**
MULLEN	mullein plant	**bt**
MULLER	a miller (Sc.)	
MULLER	heating vessel; pestle	
MULLET	genus of fish	**zo**
MULLET	a star; a rowel	**hd**
MULLEY	mooly; a cow; hornless	**zo**
MULTUM	adulterant used in brewing	**br**
MUMBLE	mutter; chew	
MUMMER	masquerader; actor; histrion	
MUMPED	nibbled; grinned; chewed	
MUMPER	a beggar	
MUNDIC	iron pyrites	**mn**
MUNDIL	a turban	
MUNSHI	Eastern teacher	
MUNTIN	part of window, glass frame; mullion; Amer. centre of outdoor furniture	**ar**
MURAGE	money for town repairs (Fr.)	
MURDER	kill; assassinate; slaughter	
MURINE	(mice)	**zo**

MURING	immuring; walling up	
MURMUR	whisper; complain; repine	
MURPHY	potato (Irish)	bt
MURREN	a murrain (obs.)	gl
MURREY	dark red	
MUSANG	East Indian coffee-rat	zo
MUSCAL	(mosses)	bt
MUSCAT	a grape; a wine	bt
MUSCLE	thew; sinew	pl
MUSEUM	collection/treasure repository	
MUSHED	sledded (Alaska)	
MUSHER	snow traveller (Canada)	
MUSING	ruminating; reflecting	
MUSIVE	mosaic	
MUSKEG	swamp; marsh (Canada)	go
MUSKET	hawk; smooth-bore gun	zo
MUSK-OX	N. American arctic ox	zo
MUSLIM	Moslem; Mohammedan	
MUSLIN	soft cotton fabric	tx
MUSMON	moufflon; European sheep	zo
MUSNUD	Persian throne of state	
MUSSAL	Indian torch	
MUSSED	messed; disarranged	
MUSSEL	a shellfish	zo
MUSTAC	small tufted monkey	zo
MUSTEE	mestee; an octoroon	
MUSTER	parade; assemble; rally	
MUTAGE	(checking fermentation)	
MUTATE	to change	
MUTELY	dumbly; silently	
MUTING	guano; silencing; bribing	
MUTINY	riot; hijack by crew; riot; revolt	nt
MUTISM	dumbness; speechlessness	
MUTIVE	tending to alter	
MUTTER	murmur; grumble; maunder	
MUTTON	proverbially dead	
MUTUAL	reciprocal; correlative	
MUTULE	projection	ar
MUTUUM	loan contract	lw
MUZHIK	moujik; Russian peasant	
MUZZLE	jaw cover (dog)	
MUZZLE	gun mouth; censor	
MYCOID	fungus-like	
MYELIC	pertaining to spinal cord	
MYELIN	fatty material round nerve	zo
MYELON	spinal cord	pl
MYGALE	shrew mouse	zo
MYOGEN	water-soluble muscle albumin	ch
MYOPIA	near-sightedness	md
MYOPIC	short-sighted; purblind	md
MYOSIN		
MYOSIS	} disease of the eye	md
MYOTIC		
MYRIAD	countless; innumerable (stars)	
MYRTLE	genus of shrub	bt
MYRTUS	wax-myrtle; bay-berry	bt
MYSELF	reflexive pronoun	
MYSTIC	occult; recondite; enigmatic	
MYTHIC	legendary; fictitious; fanciful	
MYTHUS	a myth; a fable	

MYXINE	hag-fish	zo
MYXOID	mucoid	pl
MYXOMA	a tumour	md

N

NABBED	grabbed; arrested	
NABKET	snuff; small cake (Sc.)	ck
NAEVUS	birth-mark	md
NAGANA	tse-tse fly disease	md
NAGARI	Sanskrit script	
NAGGAR	cargo felucca boat	nt
NAGGED	scolded; upbraided; pestered	
NAGGER	a fault-finder	
NAHOOR	sheep (Nepal)	zo
NAIANT	(swimming)	hd, zo
NAILED	caught; secured; exposed	
NAILER	nail-maker	
NAKONG	water-koodoo (S. Africa)	zo
NAMELY	viz., specifically	
NAMING	christening; nominating	
NANDOO	S. American ostrich	zo
NANISM	dwarfishness	
NANKIN	nankeen; cotton cloth	tx
NANNAR	Chaldean moon-god	rl
NANOID	dwarf; pigmy	
NAPALM	flammable oil/soap gel (warfare)	ch
NAPERY	household linen	tx
NAPKIN	serviette; nappy; diaper (ring)	
NAPPAL	soaprock	mn
NAPPED	dozed; slumbered	
NARDOO	Australian plant	bt
NARDUS	mat-grass	bt
NARGIL	coconut tree; hubble-bubble	bt
NARIAL	} nasal	
NARINE	}	md
NARROW	strait; close; contracted (bowls)	
NARWAL	sea-unicorn; whale	zo
NASARD	organ stop	mu
NASION	part of nose	md
NASUTE	captious; critical	
NATANT	swimming; naiant	hd
NATION	people; race; country	
NATIVE	aboriginal; intrinsic; congenital	
NATRIX	genus of snakes	zo
NATRON	carbonate of soda	ch
NATTER	to nag (dial.); to chat, complain	
NATTES	surface decoration	ar
NATURE	universe; species; quality; character traits	
NAUGHT	0; zero; nought; nothing	me
NAUSEA	sea-sickness; disgust; qualm	
NAUTCH	dancing girl; a dance	
NAUTIC	nautical; naval; maritime	nt
NAZARD	3-f organ pitch	mu
NEANIC	of adolescent period	zo
NEAPED	aground at low tide	nv, nt
NEARBY	adjacent; nigh; at hand	

NEARED	approached; drew nigh	
NEARER	more adjacent	
NEARLY	closely; all but; almost	
NEATLY	smartly; featly; dexterously	
NEBBUK	(crown of thorns)	bt
NEB-NEB	acacia pods	bt
NEBRIS	fawn-skin worn by Bacchus	
NEBULA	heavy cloud; whirl (stars)	as
NEBULE	nebula; mist; fog	
NEBULY	wavy	
NECKED	embraced; hugged; beheaded	
NECRON	dead plant material	bt
NECTAR	ambrosia; honey-sap (juice)	ck
NEED-BE	a necessity	
NEEDED	wanted; lacked; necessitated	
NEEDER	requirer	
NEEDLE	critical	to
NEEDLY	thorny	
NEESED	} sneezed	
NEEZED		
NEGATE	deny; mollify	
NEKTON	swimming water organisms	bt, zo
NEMEAN	(lion killed by Hercules)	
NEOGEA	neotropical region	go
NEPALI	language (Nepal)	
NEPHEW	sibling's male child	
NEREID	sea-nymph	
NEREUS	sea-god	rl
NERINE	Guernsey lily	bt
NERITE	mollusc	zo
NERIUM	oleander	bt
NEROLI	oil from orange flowers	bt, ck
NERVAL	nervous; sinewy	
NERVED	fortified; plucky; courageous	
NESHEN	to soften	
NESHKI	Arabic script	
NESSUS	a Centaur	
NESTED	built a nest	
NESTLE	snuggle; rest; cherish	
NESTOR	genus of parrots (NZ)	zo
NETHER	lower; under	
NETRUM	minute spindle	cy
NETTED	reticulated; gained; trapped	
NETTLE	to irritate; fret	bt
NEURAD	dorsal	zo
NEURAL	(nerves)	md
NEURIC	nervous	
NEURIN	protein coating; membrane	
NEURON	nerve cell	md
NEUROT-	of the nerves (neurotic)	pc
NEUTER	neutral; non-partisan; sexless	
NEWING	yeast; barm	
NEWISH	somewhat novel	
NEW-SAD	recently bereaved (Shak.)	
NEWTON	gravity force	me
NIACIN	nicotinic acid; B Vitamin	ch
NIBBED	complete with nib	
NIBBLE	bite; gnaw	
NICELY	exactly; accurately; adroitly	
NICENE	(Nicaea) prayer-book creed (325)	rl

NICEST	daintiest; choicest	
NICETY	precision; delicacy	
NICHED	in a niche or recess	
NICHER	neigh; snigger	
NICKED	notched; stolen	
NICKEL	5 cent piece; metal; acoustic delay time	nm, mn
NICKER	a cheat; woodpecker; thief	zo
NICKEY	Manx fishing boat	nt
NIDDER	shiver; molest	
NIDGED	nudged (stone-cutting)	
NIDGET	a fool	
NID-NOD	nod repeatedly	
NIDOSE	olfactory	
NIELLO	engraving; ornamentation	
NIFFLE	pilfer; steal	
NIGGER	negro; black	
NIGGLE	trifle; to be finicky	
NIGHLY	nearly; adjacent	
NIGRIC	black	
NILGAI	Indian antelope	zo
NIMBLE	agile; lively; swift	
NIMBLY	alertly; briskly; quickly	
NIMBUS	a halo; rain cloud	mt
NIMROD	a mighty hunter	
NINETY	cardinal number	
NINGAL	Nannar's wife	
NIPPED	pinched; compressed; gripped	
NIPPER	tooth (horse); boy (slang); bed-bug	zo
NIPPLE	teat; dug; pap; mamilla	
NIPPON	Japan	
NIPTER	feet-washing ceremony	rl
NIRLES	herpes; shingles	md
NITRIC	(nitre); acid	ch
NITRON	reagent for nitric acid	ch
NITTER	bot-fly; body-louse	zo
NITWIT	numskull; idiot	
NIVOSE	4th French month (Revol.)	
NNGGAR	} cargo dhow (Nile)	nt
NUGGAR		
NO-BALL	(cricket) (penalty)	ga
NOBBLE	dope; lame; cheat	vt
NOBLER	more illustrious	
NOBODY	a nonentity; negative pronoun	
NOCAKE	parched corn	ck
NOCENT	hurtful; mischievous	
NOCTUA	large moth genus	zo
NODDED	bowed; acknowledged	
NODDER	a drowsy person	
NODDLE	the head	
NODOSE	knotted	
NODULE	small knot	
NOESIS	pure knowledge	
NOETIC	intellectual	
NOGGIN	small cup; $\frac{1}{4}$ pint (0.14 litres)	me
NO-GOOD	useless	
NOISED	reported; rumoured	
NO-LOAD	normal voltage, speed, but no output	el

224

NOMIAL	a single term in algebra	
NOMISM	moral law as basis of conduct	
NONAGE	immature; minority	
NONANE	paraffin hydrocarbon	ch
NONARY	group of nine	
NON-COM	an NCO; under-officer	
NON-CON	not content	
NON-EGO	(metaphysics)	
NONIUS	a graduating instrument	
NONOSE	monosaccharide group	ch
NOODLE	simpleton; form of pasta	ck
NOOSED	snared; caught; lassooed	
NORDIC	Scandinavian	
NORITE	coarse-grained igneous rock	gl
NORMAL	regular; conforming; without deviation; standard	
NORMAN	of Normandy	
NORROY	king at arms	hd
NOSEAN	a silicate	mn
NO-SIDE	end of a game of Rugby	ga
NOSING	snooping; blunt overhang of stair, sill, roof	ar, bd
NOSISM	speaking of self as regal 'we'	
NOSTOC	genus of seaweed	bt
NOTARY	official witness of documents	lw
NOTICE	see; remark; heed; intimation	
NOTIFY	warn; advise; apprise	
NOTING	recording; registering	
NOTION	idea; belief; theory; concept	
NOTOUR	notorious (Sc.)	
NOUGAT	a sweetmeat	ck
NOUGHT	0; naught; cypher; zero condition	cp
NOUNAL	(noun); of substantive	
NOUSLE	to nurse; nuzzle	
NOVENA	nine days' devotion	rl
NOVENE	by nines	
NOVICE	tyro; neophyte; probationer	
NOWAYS	in no way	
NOWISE	nohow	
NOWYED	heraldic branches	hd
NOYADE	execution by drowning (Fr.)	
NOZZLE	snout; projecting mouthpiece	
NUANCE	a subtle distinction	
NUBBIN	stunted maize	bt
NUBBLE	punch; small lump	
NUBBLY	bumpy; knotty	
NUBIAN	of Nubia; Sudanese	
NUBILE	marriageable	
NUCHAL	(nape of neck)	md
NUCLEI	cell-centres; cores; kernels	
NUCLEO-	of the nucleus (Gr.)	gr, cf
NUCULE	a little nut	
NUDELY	barely; nakedly	
NUDGED	jogged; poked; pushed	
NUDISM	} naked sun-worshipping	
NUDIST		
NUDITY	nakedness	
NUGGAR	mugger; alligator	zo

NUGGAR	} cargo dhow, Nile	nt
NNGGAR		
NUGGET	a lump of gold	mn
NULLAH	watercourse; ravine (Ind.)	go
NUMBED	torpid; paralysed; dazed	
NUMBER	count; compute; figure; identity; amount	
NUMBER	code address in network	tc
NUMBLY	in a frozen manner	
NUMNAH	saddle cloth	tx
NUNCIO	Papal representative	
NUNCLE	mine uncle (Shak.)	
NUNOME	mesh fabric	tx
NUPHAR	water-lily	bt
NUPPEN	surface droplets glass technique	
NURLED	milled like a coin	nm
NURSED	fostered; encouraged	
NURSER	tender; cherisher	
NUTANT	nodding	
NUT-MEG	an aromatic kernel	bt, ck
NUT-OIL	paint ingredient	bt
NUTRIA	the fur of the coypu	zo
NUTTER	a nut-gatherer	
NUZZER	a presentation (India)	
NUZZLE	nousle; fondle	
NYLGAU	nilgai; an Indian antelope	zo
NYMPHA	pupa; chrysalis	zo

O

OAFISH	idiotic; dull; doltish	
OARAGE	rowing	ga
OARING	sculling	ga
OARIUM	an ovary; ovarium	bt
OARLAP	a distinctive rabbit	zo
OBDUCE	draw over	
OBECHE	W. Afr. satinwood, Niger. whitewood	bt, fr
OBELUS	mark (†); obelisk	
OBERON	king of the fairies	
OBEYED	complied; yielded	
OBEYER	heeder; minder	
OBIISM	West Indian witchcraft	rl
OBITER	incidentally	
OBJECT	protest; demur; goal; intent	
OBJECT	purpose; thing; machine language	cp
OBJURE	to swear	
OBLATE	communion wafer-bread	rl
OBLIGE	compel; bind; favour; serve	
OBLONG	longer than broad	
OBOIST	oboe-player	mu
OBOLUS	Charon's ferry fee	nm
OBSESS	besiege; beset; haunt	
OBTAIN	get; win; acquire; attain	
OBTECT	of pupae unable to move	zo
OBTEST	to beseech; supplicate	
OBTUND	deaden; blunt	
OBTUSE	dull; stolid; stupid	

OBVERT	turn toward; to face	
OCCAMY	silvery alloy	
OCCULT	mystic; hidden; obscure	
OCCUPY	fill; possess; inhabit	
OCELLI	peacock's 'eyes'	zo
OCELOT	American leopard	zo
OCHREA	cup-shaped plant structure	bt
O'CLOCK	an indefinite time	
OCRACY	government	
OCTANE	petrol purification figure	ch
OCTANS	constellation (South Pole)	as
OCTANT	measuring instrument	me, nv
OCTAVE	ottava; consisting of eight	mu
OCTAVO	(eight leaves to the sheet)	pr
OCTILE	octant; eighth of a circle	
OCTODE	a thermionic valve	ps
OCTOSE	monosaccharide group	ch
OCTROI	monopoly, trade privilege (Fr.)	
OCULAR	visible	
OCULUS	circular orifice	ar
ODDITY	singularity; strangeness	
ODIOUS	hateful; detested; obnoxious	
ODYLIC	mesmeric	
OECIST	founder of Greek colony	
OEDEMA	localized dropsy; water retaining cells; obesity; swollen	md
OEUVRE	complete works; artist, writer	
OFF-DAY	unlucky occasion; free day	
OFFEND	affront; insult; trespass	
OFFICE	post; function; bureau; (holy); (telephone)	rl,tc
OFFING	outer sea; future	nt
OFFISH	haughty; snobbish	
OFF-LAP	strata conformation	gl
OFFSET	counter-balance; wall ledge; swan neck pipe; accounts; tax	bd
OFFSET	rubber-to-paper process	pr
OGAMIC	ancient Irish script	
OGDOAD	group of 8	
OGHAMS	ancient Irish alphabet	
OGIVAL	arched	ar
OGLING	an amorous advance (eyeing)	
OGRESS	a monstrous lady	
OGRISH	ogreish	
OH-HELL	card game like whist	ga
OIDIUM	fungus; vine-mildew	bt
OIL-BAG	oil gland	pl
OIL-CAN	oil applier	
OILERY	oilman's stock	
OIL-GAS	inflammable gas	ch
OILING	lubricating	
OIL-MAN	oil-dealer	
OIL-NUT	butternut	bt
OIL-RIG	boring apparatus for oil	
OLDEST	most senile; eldest	
OLDISH	somewhat ancient	
OLEATE	(oleic acid)	ch
OLEFIN	ethylene hydrocarbon	ch
OLEINE	liquid fat	
OLEOSE	oily; oleic	ps

OLERON	ancient code of sea laws	nt
OLIVER	small tilt-hammer; (Roland)	to
OLIVET	mock pearl	
OLIVIL	gum from the olive tree	
OLLAMH	ancient Irish doctor	md
OMASAL	(cow's stomach)	zo
OMASUM	ruminant's third stomach	
OMBROS	madder	
OMEDED	predicted; augured; presaged	
OMELET	omelette; beaten eggs	ck
OMNIFY	to render universal	
OMNIUM	(Stock Exchange)	
ONAGER	wild ass; ghorkhar	zo
ONCOME	deluge; approach	
ONCOST	extraneous mining charges	mn
ONDINE	undine; water-spirit	
ONDING	fall of rain or snow	mt
ONE-MAN	soloist	
ONE-TWO	successive punches (boxing)	
ONE-WAY	(traffic); single route	
ONEYER	(of uncertain origin)	
ONFALL	storm; attack; assault	
ONFLOW	gush; on stream	
ON-LINE	computer operation	cp
ON-LINE	on course; direct hit	mu
ONRUSH	onset; charge	
ON-SIDE	correct placing (football) (netball)	
ONWARD	forward; advancing	
ONYMAL	(technical group name)	zo
OOCYST	cyst round gametes in protozoa	zo
OOCYTE	cell in meiosis, forming ovum	zo
OODLES	quantities; heaps	
OOGAMY	union of un-like-sized gametes	bl
OOGENY	embryonic development	
OOIDAL	egg-shaped	
OOLITE	a limestone (ovulites)	mn
OOLITH	spherical concretion	gl
OOLOGY	the study of birds' eggs	
OOLONG	oulong; tea	bt, ck
OOMIAK	Eskimo boat	nt
OORIAL	wild sheep (India)	zo
OOTYPE	oviduct section	zo
OOZING	exuding; seeping; percolating	
OPAQUE	impermeable to light	
OPENED	undid; disclosed; revealed	
OPENER	beginner; cutter	
OPENLY	publicly; above-board	
OPERON	genes together in chromosome	gn
OPHITE	porphyry	mn
OPHITE	gnostic serpent-worshipper	rl
OPIANE	narcotine	ch
OPIATE	a sedative medicine	md
OPINED	supposed; thought; fancied	
OPPOSE	prevent; hinder; combat	
OPPUGN	oppose; obstruct; resist	
OPTANT	volunteer	
OPTICS	science of light and vision	
OPTIME	almost a wrangler	
OPTING	choosing; co-opting	

OPTION	choice; wish; selection; right to buy (Am. football)	
ORACHE	genus of plants; spinach	bt
ORACLE	wiseacre; ambiguous response	
ORALLY	by word of mouth	
ORANGE	Citrus aurantium	bt
ORATED	harangued; prated; spouted	
ORATOR	declaimer; spell-binder	
ORBATE	bereaved; fatherless	
ORBITA	eye-sockets	pl
ORCHIC	of the testis	zo
ORCHID	orchis	bt
ORCHIL	archil; purple dye; a lichen	bt
ORCHIO-	of the testicle (Gr.)	cf
ORCINE	lichen dye	
ORDAIN	prescribe; enjoin; appoint	
ORDEAL	test; trial; assay; scrutiny	
ORDERS	decorated columns	ar
ORDURE	excrement	
OREIDE	imitation gold	
OREXIS	appetite	md
ORGASM	sexual climax	md
OR-GATE	pulse circuit	el
ORGEAT	liquor (barley)	br
ORGIES	revels; carousals (sexual bouts)	
ORIENT	eastern; the east	
ORIGAN	marjoram (herb)	bt, ck
ORIGIN	fount; spring; source; root	
ORIHON	continued folded uncut sheet	pr
ORIOLE	a bird species	zo
ORISON	prayer; supplication	rl
ORMULU	} gilt brass	
ORMOLU		
ORMUZD	(Magian system)	
ORNATE	florid; embellished	
ORNERY	ordinary; mean; low	
OROIDE	alloy; oreide	mn
OROTIC	vitamin B-13; growth acid	ch
ORPHAN	child who has lost both parents	
ORPHIC	(Orpheus)	
ORPINE	a yellow plant	bt
ORRERY	model of solar system	
ORRICE	dried iris root	bt
ORTIVE	rising; eastern	
OSCINE	of a sub-order of birds	zo
OSCULE	small mouth	
OSELLA	Doge's medal (Venice)	
OSIERY	osier-bed	bt
OSIRIS	greatest Egyptian god	rl
OSMIUM	metallic element	mn
OSMOLE	unit of osmolic pressure	me
OSMOSE	(diffusion of fluids)	
OSOPHY	belief or doctrine	
OSPREY	sea-hawk; an egret plume	zo
OSSEIN	bone-cartilage	pl
OSSIFY	to become bone-like; harden to inflexible	
OSTEAL	pertaining to bone	
OSTENT	portent; show; appearance	
OSTIUM	an opening; mouth of river	go

OSTLER	stableman; groom	
OSTMEN	Danish settlers in Ireland	
OSTREA	oyster	zo
OTALGY	earache	md
OTARIA	genus of seals	zo
OTIANT	idle; resting	
OTIOSE	at ease; lazy; idle	
OTITIS	ear-trouble	md
OTTAVA	an octave (It.)	mu
OUSTED	deposed; ejected; thrown out	
OUSTER	ejection; dispossession	
OUTAGE	electrical failure	
OUTASK	ask for the last time	
OUTBAR	to shut out	
OUTBID	offer more	
OUTBYE	out of doors (Sc.)	
OUTCRY	hue; clamour; tumult; bruit	
OUTDID	excelled; surpassed; exceeded	
OUTFIT	equipment; clothing	
OUTING	expedition; trip; holiday	
OUTJET	exhaust vent	ae
OUTLAW	brigand; bandit; proscribe	
OUTLAY	expense; disbursement	
OUTLET	exit; vent; loophole	
OUTLIE	excel in lying	
OUTMAN	outnumber	
OUTPUT	production; resulting sound; signal	ro
OUTPUT	information from processor	cp
OUTRUN	outstrip; beat; surpass; flat, halting terrain, after ski-jump	
OUTSET	start; beginning; opening	
OUTSIT	sit longer than	
OUTSUM	outnumber	
OUTTOP	over-reach	
OUTVIE	surpass; out-rival; eclipse	
OUTWIT	dupe; overreach; circumvent	
OVALLY	elliptically	
OVERBY	adjacent	
OVERDO	carry too far	
OVERGO	exceed	
OVIBOS	musk-ox; buffalo-cow	zo
OVISAC	(ovary)	zo
OVULAR	embryonic	bt
OWLERY	haunt of owls	zo
OWLING	smuggling; especially wool	
OWLISH	as wise as an owl!	
OWNING	possessing; conceding	
OXALIC	an acid	ch
OXALIS	wood sorrel	bt
OXALYL	bivalent acid radical	ch
OXBIRD	the dunlin	zo
OXEOTE	rod-shaped	zo
OX-EYED	having large eyes	
OXFORD	(blue); (shoe); (movement)	
OXGALL	cleaning/painting agent	
OXGANG	} a bovate; about 15 ac. (6 ha)	
OXGATE	} of land; amount that could	
OXLAND	} be cultivated with one ox	
OXHEAD	block-head; dolt (Shak.)	

OX-HEEL	the setter-wort	**bt**
OX-HIDE	leather	
OXTAIL	(soup)	**ck**
OXYGEN	principal gas in atmosphere	**ch**
OXYGON	a triangle with 2 acute angles	
OXYMEL	honey and vinegar	
OYSTER	shell; pearl; (prairie)	**zo, ck**
OZALID	copy of engineering drawing	
OZOENA	chronic atrophic rhinitis	**md**
OZONIC	of ozone	

P

PACIFY	calm; appease; reconcile	
PACING	setting the pace; walking; measuring yards; giring against wind cycle	**nt**
PACKED	crowded; compressed; prearranged fraudulent voting	
PACKER	stower; inflatable rubber ring; washer	**ce**
PACKET	parcel; bale; a mail vessel	**nt**
PADANG	scrub heath (Malaya)	**go**
PADDED	travelled slowly; (cell); (protective)	
PADDER	foot-pad; highwayman	
PADDLE	} steamer; wade; canoe oar;	
PATTLE	} lever; seamphore	**nt**
PADNAG	ambling horse	**zo**
PADSAW	saw blade in toolholder kit	**to**
PADUAN	(Padua); the pavan	**mu**
PAEDIO-	of the feet (Gr.)	**cf**
PAELLA	rice-seafood-meat dish (Sp.)	**ck**
PAGING	marking pages; calling (persons); adding data; layout	**cp, pr**
PAGODA	pagode; temple; (Ind. coin)	**nm, rl**
PAID-UP	shares; capital; membership	**lw**
PAIGLE	cowslip	**bt**
PAINED	hurt; distressed; grieved	
PAINIM	(see Paynim); pagan	
PAIRED	coupled; yoked; mated; (voting)	
PAKEHA	white man (Maori)	
PALACE	(Crystal); ruler's residence	**ar**
PALAEO-	of ancient, prehistoric life (Gr.)	**cf, gl, zo**
PALAMA	toe-webbing	**zo**
PALATE	roof of mouth; taste-buds	**pl**
PALELY	wanly; ashy; pallidly	
PALING	a fence; blanching	
PALISH	wan; weak colour	**pt**
PALKEE	palanquin (Ind.)	
PALLAH	African antelope	**zo**
PALLAS	Athene, goddess of wisdom	**rl**
PALLED	cloaked; covered (coffin)	
PALLET	palette; small bed	
PALLID	pale; sallow; cadaverous	
PALLOR	pallidness	
PALMAR	(hand) palm, sole (hand/foot); volar	**pl**

PALMED	concealed; handled; conjured away; stolen	
PALMER	pilgrim (with palm leaf)	**rl**
PALMUS	palpitation; twitching	**md**
PALOLO	edible worm	**zo**
PALPAL	} (antennae-like feelers)	**zo**
PALPED	}	**zo**
PALPUS	feeler of an insect	**zo**
PALTER	dodge; shuffle; prevaricate	
PALTRY	mean; petty; despicable	
PAMPAS	treeless plains; grasses (S. Amer.)	**bt, go**
PAMPER	indulge; coddle; humour	
PANADA	bread pulp	**ck**
PANAMA	sun-hat	
PANARY	store-house for bread; pantry	
PANDER	a procurer; cater to (tastes)	
PANDIT	pundit; a learned man	
PANDUR	robber; Austrian soldier	
PANFRY	cook in frying pan	**ck**
PANFUL	filling a pan	**ck**
PANGED	emotionally upset	
PANISC	Pan as a satyr	
PANMUG	crockery; butter-pan	
PANNED	yielded	**mn**
PANNEL	rustic saddle	
PANNER	a nagger; faultfinder (gold)	
PANNUS	birthmark; a dressing	**md**
PANSER	belly-armour (obs.)	
PANSHI	sailing dugout (Bengal)	**nt**
PANTED	gasped; blew; palpitated	
PANTER	a snare; panther	**zo**
PANTON	a special kind of horseshoe	
PANTRY	food storage closet	
PANZER	armoured corps (Ger.); panser	
PAPACY	(pope); popery	**rl**
PAPAIN	digestive enzyme	**md**
PAPAYA	large sub-tropical fruit; pawpaw	**bt**
PAPERY	resembling paper	
PAPISH	characteristic of Popes	
PAPISM	papal doctrine; authority	**rl**
PAPIST	pro-Pope; Roman Catholic	
PAPPUS	hairy tuft	**bt**
PAPUAN	from New Guinea	
PAPULA	pimple	**md**
PAPYRI	scrolls of papyrus (Egypt)	
PARADE	show; display; flaunt	
PARAMO	wind-swept desert in Andes	**go**
PARANG	heavy Malay knife	
PARAPH	a flourish to a signature	
PARASE	movements (fencing)	
PARCAE	the Fates	
PARCEL	packet; bundle; piece; share; (land)	**lw**
PARDON	remit; condone; forgive	
PARDON	mercy	
PAREIL	an equal	
PARENT	author; producer; cause	
PAREVE	made without animal products	**ck**
PARFAY!	by or in faith!	

PARGET	rough plaster; gypsum	
PARIAH	outcast; mongrel	zo
PARIAN	(marble); (porcelain)	
PARINE	pertaining to titmouse (bird)	zo
PARING	rind; shaving; reducing	
PARISH	church district	rl
PARITY	equality; parage; check on transfer of data	cp
PARITY	space, reflection, symmetry	el
PARKED	(left); enclosed; assembled	au
PARKER	park-keeper; (nosey)	
PARKIN	perkin; Lancashire cake	ck
PARLAY	expand; exploit	
PARLEY	confer; discuss; talk	
PARODY	travesty; burlesque; caricature	
PAROLE	word of honour	
PAROUS	offspring liveborn (mammals)	zo
PARPEN	} transverse 2 faced stone in	
PARPEND	} wall	
PARPENT	}	ar
PARRAL	} collar to prevent spars from	
PARREL	} slipping from the mast	nt
PARROT	repeat by rote; talking bird	zo
PARSEC	interstellar distance unit	me
PARSED	analysed grammatically	
PARSEE	Persian living in India	
PARSON	vicar; clergyman	rl
PARTAN	crab (Sc.)	zo
PARTED	left; broke; separated	
PARTER	distributor; sharer	
PARTIM	in part	
PARTLY	not altogether	
PARURE	set of jewels	
PARVIS	court; portico	rl, ar
PASAKA	form of play (pelota)	ga
PASCAL	unit of pressure of newton unit	
PASSED	ignored; spent; elapsed	
PASSEE	faded (Fr.)	
PASSER	a passer-by	
PASSIM	here and there	
PASTED	basted; gummed	
PASTEL	crayon; chalk drawing	
PASTIL	medicated lozenge	md
PASTOR	shepherd; starling	rl, zo
PASTRY	confiserie	ck
PATCHY	unequal	
PATENT	spreading; open; copyright	lw
PATERA	shallow circular dish; ornament	
PATHAN	obs. for pashtum; Afghan/ Pakistani tribe	
PATHIC	(diseases)	md
PATHOS	deep emotion	
PATILE	Ganges barge, India	nt
PATINA	glow given by age; oxidised, lead, bronze effect	
PATINE	paten; eucharistic plate	rl
PATLID	stone at start (curling)	ga
PATOIS	dialect (Fr.)	
PATROL	mobile armed guard	
PATRON	customer; supporter; saint	rl

PATTED	tapped	
PATTEN	clog (Dutch wooden shoe)	
PATTER	high speed talk; sound (song) (feet) (raindrops)	
PATTLE	a paddle	
PAUNCH	the belly (obese)	pl
PAUPER	indigent person	
PAUSAL	ceasing; pausing	
PAUSED	hesitated; halted; tarried	
PAUSER	a deliberator; a demurrer	
PAVAGE	paving cost	
PAVANE	stately dirge; pavan; dream	mu
PAVIER	}	
PAVIOR	} paver; pavement layer	
PAVING	surfacing (crazy) (street)	
PAVISE	great shield	
PAWING	clawing; touching (rudely)	
PAWNED	pledged; risked; hazarded	
PAWNEE	N. American Indian tribe	
PAWNEE	pawnbroker	
PAWNER	a borrower on security (possessions)	
PAWPAW	papaw; a tropical fruit	bt
PAWWAW	powwow; a palaver	
PAXWAX	tendon; faxwax	zo
PAYANG	fishing boat (Malaya)	nt
PAY-BOX	public coin call box; telephone	
PAY-DAY	day when wages paid	
PAYING	gainful; punishing; tarring	
PAYNIM	painim; infidel; heathen	
PAY-OFF	payment; denouement; side-benefits; spin-off	nt, pc
PAYOLA	bribe to mention on media	
PEACHY	like a peach	
PEACOD	pea-pod	bt
PEAHEN	a peafowl	zo
PEAKED	looked ill; pointed	nt
PEALED	resounded; reverberated	
PEANUT	the ground-nut	bt
PEA-ORE	oxide of iron	mn
PEA-POD	pea seed envelope	bt
PEARLY	transparent; translucent	
PEBBLE	a stone; an agate	mn
PEBBLY	shingly	
PECKED	struck (birds); nagged (hen-)	
PECKER	woodpecker; courage; mouth	zo
PECKER	tape reader sensing device	cp
PECTEN	bivalve genus; scallop	zo
PECTEN	eye membrane of a bird	zo
PECTIC	congealing; gelatinizing	
PECTIN	(apple jelly)	
PECTUS	insect sclerite; vertebrate breast	zo
PEDALE	altar foot-cloth	rl
PEDANT	schoolmaster; precise person	
PEDATE	divided like a foot	bt
PEDDLE	to sell retail; to trifle; to hawk (drugs)	
PEDION	single-plane crystal	

PEDLAR	} hawker; vendor; bagman	
PEDLER		
PEECED	imperfect (Spens.)	
PEELED	stripped; skinned; pillaged	
PEELER	policeman (Sir Robert Peel); perfect wave (surfing); rind, skin remover	**ck**
PEENGE	whimper (Sc.)	
PEEPED	chirped; glimpsed; snooped	
PEEPER	(chicken); the eye	**zo**
PEEPUL	sacred tree; Indian bo-tree	**bt**
PEERER	a peeping Tom	
PEERIE	peg-top (Sc.)	
PEEVED	annoyed; fretful	
PEEWIT	green plover; lapwing	**zo**
PEGGED	fixed; toiled	
PEG-LEG	wooden leg	
PEG-TOP	a spinning top	
PELAGE	animal fur	**zo**
PELIKE	double-handled Greek vase	
PELION	and Ossa, mountains	
PELLET	small ball or shot; wood cover over screw	**jn**
PELMET	curtain housing	
PELOTA	} a Basque ball game	**ga**
PELOTE		
PILOTA		
PELTER	rainstorm; shower of missiles	
PELTRY	skins with fur on them	
PELVIC	(pelvis)	**pl**
PELVIS	a bony cavity	**pl**
PENCIL	light rays; small brush (graphite pen)	
PENDED	held up; balanced	
PENFUL	contents of a pen	
PENIAL	pertaining to penis; phallic	**pl**
PENMAN	scribe; author; clerk	
PENNAL	freshman (Ger.); student	
PENNED	wrote; indited; enclosed	
PENNER	writer; scribe	
PENNON	pennant; flag; streamer	**nt**
PENSEE	thought (Fr.) (literature)	
PENSUM	an imposition; examination	
PENTAD	set of five	
PENT-UP	confined; mewed	
PENULT	last but one	
PENURY	need; want; indigence	
PEOPLE	mob; rabble; populace; nation	
PEPITA	nugget of gold (Sp.)	
PEPLIS	water-purslane	**bt**
PEPLUM	} robe worn by Greek women	
PEPLUS		**tx**
PEPPER	pelt with shot; capsicum, (cayenne) condiment	**bt, ck**
PEPSIN	(gastric juice)	**md**
PEPTIC	digestive	
PERDIE!	pardieu!	
PERDUE	perdu; hidden; concealed	
PERIOD	age; era; term; epoch; stage	
PERISH	die; wither; expire; pass	

PERKED	smartened up; received extra benefits, encouraged	
PERKIN	perry; see parkin	
PERMIT	let; grant; sanction; tolerate	
PERNIS	honey-buzzard	**zo**
PERONE	fibula	
PERRON	external stairway	
PERSIC	Persian	
PERSON	individual; party; someone	
PERSUE	a track (Spens.)	
PERTLY	impudently; saucily	
PERUKE	a periwig; a vallancy	
PERUSE	read; scrutinize; observe	
PESADE	an equine evolution	
PESETA	Spanish money	**nm**
PESHWA	Mahratta chief (India)	
PESTER	vex; worry; harass; nettle	
PESTLE	a pulveriser	
PETARD	explosive machine; bomb	
PETARY	a peat-bog	
PETITE	small (Fr.); short and trim figure	
PETREL	sea-bird	**zo**
PETROL	gasoline	**ch**
PETTED	fondled; caressed; indulged	
PETTLE	indulge (Sc.)	
PEWTER	an alloy of tin and lead	
PEYOTE	cactus; source of mescalin	**bt**
PEZIZA	cup-shaped fungi	**bt**
PHANIC	visible; obvious	
PHAROS	lighthouse; world wonder (Gr.)	
PHASEL	French bean	**bt, ck**
PHASIS	} a stage of development	
PHASE		
PHASMA	leaf insects, etc.	**zo**
PHATIC	of speech as mood implement	
PHEESE	to beat; to worry (Sc.)	
PHENIC	carbolic	**ch**
PHENIX	fabulous bird; phoenix	**zo**
PHENOL	carbolic acid	
PHENYL	an organic radicle	**ch**
PHINOC	sea trout	**zo**
PHLEGM	calmness; indifference	
PHLEME	lancet	**md**
PHLEUM	cat's-tail grass, etc.	**bt**
PHLOEM	bast tissue	**bt**
PHOBIA	} morbid fear or aversion (Gr.)	
-PHOBIA		**md, cf**
PHOBOS	a satellite of Mars	
PHOCAL	(seal)	**zo**
PHOEBE	the moon-goddess	**rl**
PHOLAS	stone-boring molluscs	**zo**
PHONED	telephoned	
PHONEY	specious; sham; bogus	
-PHONIA	of vocal disorder (Gr.)	**cf**
PHONIC	phonetic	
PHONON	quantum of thermal energy	**me, ps**
PHORIA	lack of eye coordination	**md**
PHOSSY	caused by phosphorus	
-PHOTIC	concerning light (Gr.)	**cf**

PHOTON	unit of light energy	me
PHRASE	idiom; diction; style; theme; motif; melody	mu
PHYLON	} biological group	
PHYLUM		
PHYSIC	dose; drug; medicine	bt,md
PHYSIO-	of the physical, body (Gr.)	cf
PHYTIC	of a cereal acid	ch
PHYTON	bud	
PIACLE	sin, crime	
PIAFFE	a horse gait (Sp.)	
PIAZZA	square; market place (It.)	
PICARD	high shoe (Fr.)	
PICENE	coal-tar hydrocarbon	ch
PICKED	chose; culled; pilfered	
PICKER	selector; collector	
PICKET	sharp stake; guard; range-pole; striker at gate; railing (Am. football)	
PICKLE	preserve	
PICK-UP	(motoring)	ro
PICNIC	alfresco meal	
PICRIC	trinitro-phenol; lyddite	ch
PIDGIN	merged version made of two (or more) languages	
PIECED	mended; joined; augmented	
PIECER	patcher	
PIEDOG	a pariah; outcast; pye-dog	zo
PIELED	peeled; bare; bald (Shak.)	
PIEMAN	(Simple Simon)	
PIERCE	drill; bore; perforate	
PIERID	belonging to certain butterfly group	zo
PIFFLE	nonsense; worthless talk	
PIGEON	a town dove; tell tale; sneak	zo
PIGGIN	small bowl	
PIGLET	} a young porker	zo
PIGLING		
PIGNON	pine seed	bt
PIGNUT	carrot	bt, ck
PIG-STY	pig enclosure	
PILAFF	} rice dish; savoury	ck
PILAV		
PILARY	hairy; comate	pl
PILEUM	top of head in birds	zo
PILE-UP	crash (motoring)	
PILEUS	mushroom cap	bt
PILFER	purloin; filch; peculate; steal; rob	
PILING	amassing; stacking; heaping	
PILLAR	post; column; support; rock pinnacle	ar, mo
PILLED	black-balled	
PILLOW	a block; bearing; bed cushion	
PILOSE	} hairy; comate	
PILOUS		
PILOTA	} ball game (Basque)	ga
PELOTA		
PILULA	} a small pill	md
PILULE		
PI-MODE	multicavity magnetron operation	

PIMPLE	a pustule	md
PIMPLY	having pimples	
PINANG	betel nut	bt
PINARD	red Algerian wine	
PINCOP	weft in power loom	wv
PINDAR	Greek poet	
PINDER	pinner; impounder	
PINEAL	like a pine cone	bt
PINENE	terpene	ch
PINERY	hothouse	bt
PINGED	whistled by; bleeped (signalled)	ro
PINGLE	dawdle	
PINING	languishing; desiring	
PINION	feather; wheel; to shackle	
PINITE	(iolite)	mn
PINKED	pierced; pricked; stabbed	
PINNED	transfixed	
PINNER	pinmaker; pinder	
PINNET	pinnacle (Sc.)	
PINOLE	meal of sorts (USA)	
PINTLE	iron bolt	nt
PINXIT	he painted it (artist's mark)	
PIONED	full of peonies (Shak.)	
PIONER	a pioneer (Shak.)	
PIPAGE	pipe-distribution	
PIPING	boiling; shrill; feeble	
PIPKIN	boiler; small pot	
PIPPED	pilled; just defeated; de-stoned	ck
PIPPIN	apple	bt
PIQUED	offended; irritated	
PIQUET	card game; picket	ga
PIRACY	buccaneering; (copyright)	
PIRATE	freebooter; corsair; picaroon	
PIRAUA	} canoe, Atlantic coasts	nt
PIROGUE		
PIRNIE	night cap(Sc.)	
PISANG	plantain; banana	bt
PISCES	the fishes (Zodiac sign)	
PISTIL	part of flower	bt
PISTOL	a fire-arm	
PISTON	part of engine; valve (horn)	au, mu
PITAKA	Buddhist scriptures	rl
PITCHY	black; dark; tarry	
PITHED	central nervous system destroyed	
PITHOS	round Greek vase	
PITIED	commiserated	
PITIER	a compassionate party	
PITMAN	a miner	
PITSAW	large saw	to
PITTED	pock-marked; challenged; de-stoned	ck
PLACED	invested; ascribed; put	
PLACER	auriferous gravel	
PLACET	Latin affirmation; 'so be it'	
PLACID	serene; calm; even; tranquil	
PLAGAL	(Gregorian music)	mu
PLAGUE	pest; contagion; pester	
PLAGUY	vexatious; harassing	
PLAICE	plaise; fish	zo

PLAINT	lamentation; dirge; wail	**lw**
PLAISE	plaice	**zo**
PLANCH	to cover with planks	
PLANCK	unit of action, one joule second	**el, me**
PLANED	smoothed; (aeroplane)	
PLANER	planing machine	**to**
PLANET	a celestial body (solar system)	**as**
PLANTA	vertebrate foot sole	**zo**
PLAQUE	an ornament	
PLAQUE	destructive coating on teeth	**md**
PLASHY	sloppy	
PLASMA	ionised substance at solar gas state temperature for nuclear fusion purposes; blood liquids in cells	
PLASMA	quartz	**md**
PLATAN	plane tree	**bt**
PLATED	overlaid; armoured	
PLATEN	the roller of a typewriter; molten steel plates	**ce**
PLATER	race-horse	**zo**
PLATEY	flat	
PLAYED	sported; trifled; acted	
PLAYER	professional cricketer	**mu**
PLEACH	interweave	
PLEASE	like; prefer; delight; oblige	
PLEDGE	security; plight; pawn; toast	
PLEIAD	a star	**as**
PLEION	flat platelike structure	**zo**
PLENTY	abundance; profusion	
PLENUM	space; a full assembly	
PLEUGH	plough (Sc.)	
PLEURA	(lungs)	**md**
PLEVIN	assurance	**lw**
PLEXOR	hammer used with pleximeter	
PLEXUS	nerve centre	**md**
PLIANT	flexible; limber; lithe; facile	
PLIERS	plyers	**to**
PLIGHT	promise; dilemma; predicament	
PLINTH	pedestal	**ar**
PLISSE	pleated/woven cloth with shirred effect	**tx**
PLONGE	superior slope of parapet	
PLOUGH	plow; furrow; to pluck	
PLOVER	bird	**zo**
PLOWED	ploughed; failed (examination)	**ag**
PLUCKY	courageous; brave; bold	
PLUFFY	puffy (Sc.)	
PLUG-IN	connect; detachable unit	**el, ro, cp**
PLUMAE	stiff feathers	**zo**
PLUMED	took pride in	
PLUMPY	plump; fat; burly	
PLUNGE	dip; dive; sink; souse; (Am. football)	
PLURAL	} more than one	
PLUREL		
PLUSHY	like plush	**tx**
PLUTUS	the god of wealth	
PLYERS	pliers	**to**

PLYING	folding; touting; urging	
PNEUMA	breath; spirit; florid passage	**mu**
PNEUMA-	of air, respiration (lung) (Gr.)	**cf**
POACHY	set and soft	
POCKED	pitted	
POCKET	pouch; cavity; a poke; (air); stacker	**cp**
PODERE	country estate, farm (It.)	
PODGER	tightening wrench for tubular coupling	**to**
PODIAL	stalk-like	**bt**
PODITE	lobster's limb	**zo**
PODIUM	pedestal; rostrum; stylobate	**bt**
PODZOL	} leached subpolar strata (Russian)	**gl**
PODSOL		
POETIC	lyrical; metrical	
POETRY	poesy; verse	
POGROM	plunder and massacre (Rus.); persecution	**rl**
POINTE	tip of toes (ballet)	
POINTS	switch-point, features of horse; score; angles; of compass, 32	**nt, rw**
POISED	suspended in equilibrium	
POISER	a balancer	
POISON	venom; evil; kill (-gas) (-pen)	
POKING	thrusting	
POLACK	a Pole	
POLDER	reclaimed, drained land (Holland)	**ag, go**
POLICE	constabulary	
POLICY	statesmanship; strategy; plan	
POLING	scaffolding; punting	
POLISH	furbish; burnish; lustre	
POLITE	courtly; urbane; civil	
POLITY	the constitution	
POLLAM	jurisdiction of Ind. chief	**lw**
POLLAN	a salmon-type of Irish fish	**zo**
POLLED	cropped; lopped; voted	
POLLEN	flower seed; fine bran	**bt**
POLLER	voter; tree-trimmer	
POLLEX	thumb	**md**
POLLUX	twin brother of Castor	
POLONY	sausage	**ck**
POLYAD	polygamous element	**ch**
POLYPE	polyp; aquatic animal	**zo**
POMACE	crushed fruit	
POMADE	perfumed hair unguent	
POMELO	a citrus fruit; shaddock	**bt**
POMMEL	part of saddle; belabour	
POMMEL	flattener mallet (punner); knob; globular boss or knob; drum (Red Indians)	**to, bd**
POMMER	ancient bassoon (shawm)	**mu**
POMONA	goddess of fruit	
POM-POM	quick-firing gun battery	
POMPON	ornament; a tuft	
PONCHO	cloak (S. America)	
PONDER	weigh; meditate; ruminate	
PONENT	western	

232

PONGEE	soft woven silk	**tx**
PONGYI	Buddhist priest (Burma)	**rl**
PONTAC	claret	
PONTEE	pontil; punty	**gs, to**
PONTIC	(Black Sea)	
PONTIL	glass-maker's iron rod	**to**
PONTON	lighter; pontoon	
POODLE	curly-haired dog	**zo**
POOGYE	nose-flute (Ind.)	**mu**
POOLED	shared; amalgamated	
POOLER	leather worker	**le**
POONAC	pulp refuse	
POOPED	overtaken by a wave	
POORER	more impecunious; inferior	
POORLY	indisposed	
POPERY	Roman Catholicism	
POPGUN	an air gun of sorts	
POPISH	of Catholics; denigratory	
POPLAR	genus of trees; abele	**bt**
POPLIN	silk-cotton mix; shiny cotton (Fr.)	
		tx
POPPED	pawned; proposed; exploded	
POPPER	a pistol; popcorn; amyl nitrate, drug; plug; (angling)	
POPPET	puppet; head of a lathe	
POPPLE	to bob about	
PORGIE	bream fish	**zo**
PORING	sweating; brooding; studying	
PORISM	corollary	
PORITE	a species of coral	**mn**
PORKER	young pig	**zo**
PORKET	porker	**zo**
POROID	having obvious pores	**bt**
POROSE	of pore-pierced cell walls	**bt**
POROUS	porose; interstitial limestone	**gl**
PORRET	small onion; leek	**bt**
PORRON	wine bottle with descending spout	
PORTAL	gate; entry; entrance	
PORTED	conveyed	**nt**
PORTER	door-keeper; carrier	
PORTLY	burly; stout; imposing	
POSADA	a Spanish inn (hotel)	
POSEUR	poser; an affected person (Fr.)	
POSING	feigning; puzzling; posturing	
POSNET	small bowl	
POSSET	a bedtime drink; potion	**ck**
POSSUM	opossum	**zo**
POSTAL	(order); (Union); (mail)	
POSTEA	record of subsequent events	
POSTED	set; stationed; hastened	
POSTER	bill; placard; advertisement; ball against goal-post (Am. football)	
POSTIL	marginal note; a homily	
POT-ALE	distillery refuse	**br**
POTALE	grain refuse	**br**
POTASH	alkali; potassium	**ch**
POTATO	murphy; a tuber	**bt**
POTBOY	a junior tapster; barman; bottle-washer	
POTEEN	home-made spirits (Irish)	**ck**

POTENT	efficacious; powerful; cogent	
POTHER	bother; bristle; fuss; ado	
POTION	dose; draught; philter	
POT-LID	a cover; stone on tee (curling)	**ck**
POTMAN	barman; general factotum	
POTTAH	lease (Ind.)	
POTTED	preserved; abbreviated	
POTTER	clay craftsman	
POTTLE	4 pints (2.2 litres); a tankard	**me**
POTTLE	a small basket for fruit	
POUDRE	powdered (Fr.)	
POUFFE	a cushion (Fr.)	
POULPE	octopus; poulp	**zo**
POUNCE	jump suddenly; snatch; seize; prey	
POUNCE	claw of a bird of prey	**zo**
POUNCE	fine blotting powder	
POURED	uttered; flowed; gushed	
POURER	the lady of the tea-pot	
POUSSE	bitters added to a drink	
POUTED	registered displeasure	
POUTER	pigeon having an inflated breast	
POWTER		
POWDER	crush; pulverize; sprinkle; ideal light snow surface (skiing)	
POW-WOW	incantation; conference (Red Indian)	
PRAISE	laud; extol; eulogize; encomium	
PRANCE	to bound; to spring	
PRANZO	meal (It.)	**ck**
PRATED	orated; gabbled; talked	
PRATER	a chatter-box	
PRAXIS	use; practice; an example	
PRAYED	supplicated; craved; besought	
PRAYER	petition; entreaty; orison	
PREACH	teach; exhort; declare	
PRECIS	prayers	**rl**
PRECIS	summary; abstract	
PRECUT	ready-sliced; -shaped (portions)	
PREDAL	rapacious; voracious; ravenous	
PREFAB	a prefabricated house	**ar**
PREFER	pick; select; choose; promote	
PREFIX	appoint beforehand; word, code qualifier	
PREPAY	pay in advance	
PRESBY-	of old, aged (Gr.)	**cf**
PRESEE	foresee; anticipate; foretell	
PRESES	chairman (Sc.)	
PRESTO	quickly; (conjuror) (It.)	**mu**
PRETER-	beyond	**cf**
PRETOR	Roman judge	
PRAETOR		
PRETTY	neat; comely; pleasing; canning	
PRETTY	the fairway of a golf course	
PRE-WAR	from before a war	
PREYED	ravened; ravaged; despoiled	
PREYER	a plunderer; freebooter	
PRICED	appraised; valued	
PRICEY	expensive	
PRIDED	plumed; arrogated	

PRIEST	pastor; divine; minister	rl
PRIMAL	primary; main; first; original	
PRIMER	detonator; pre-paint; text-book	pt
PRIMER	prayer-book; type of type	pr
PRIMET	} shrub	bt
PRIVET		
PRIMLY	precisely; formally; demurely	
PRIMUS	bishop (Sc.); first	rl
PRINCE	sovereign; lord; ruler	
PRIORY	monastery	rl
PRISED	prized; levered	
PRISMY	prismatic	
PRISON	jail; gaol; quod; restrain	
PRIVET	genus of shrub; primet	bt
PRIZED	valued; esteemed	
PRIZER	an appraiser	
PROBAN	flameproof fabric finish	ch, tx
PROBUD	reproductive bodies in cyclo-myaria	
PROCES	law-suit (Fr.)	lw
PROFIT	gain; benefit; advantage	
PROJET	a proposal; draft	
PROKER	a poker (dial.)	
PROLAN	mammal pregnancy hormone	pl
PROLEG	a caterpillar's leg	zo
PROLIX	long-winded; verbose	
PROMPT	urge; incite; quick; apt	
PROMPT	message from system to operator; (theatre) (cues)	cp
PRONTO	precipitately; at once!	
PROPED	pseudo-leg	zo
PROPEL	hurl; cast; throw; impel	
PROPER	correct; accurate; seemly	
PROSED	conversed in lengthy periods	
PROSER	tedious speaker	
PROSITI	here's luck! a toast! (Germ.)	
PROTEA	S. African flowering shrubs	bt
PROTON	electrical nucleus	
PROVED	tested; verified; established	
PROVEN	proved; justified	
PROVER	demonstrator; assayer	
PRUINA	powdery bloom on plant surfaces	
PRUNED	trimmed; clipped; lopped	
PRUNUS	genus of trees and shrubs	bt
PRUTAH	Israeli coin	nm
PRYING	peeping; curious; inquisitive	
PSEUDO	false; spurious; imitation; a pre-machine code	cp
PSORIC	(psora); itchy	md
PSYCHE	maiden beloved by Cupid; soul; mind	
PSYCHO-	of mind; psyche; psychology (Gr.)	cf
PTERIC	of wing or shoulder	zo
PTERIS	fern genus	bt
PTERNA	heel-pad in birds	zo
PTERON	Greek portico	
PTISAN	barley water; tisane	ck
PTOSIS	(fallen eyelid)	md
PTYXIS	leaf-folding in bud	bt

PUBLIC	open; common; general	
PUCKER	wrinkle; crease; furrow	
PUDDER	tumult; pother	
PUDDLE	muddy pool; (iron)	
PUDDLY	dirty; foul	
PUDEUR	sexual modesty (Fr.)	
PUEBLO	S. American town or village (Sp.)	
PUENTE	carved trestle table (Spain)	
PUFFED	fuffed; blown	
PUFFER	globe-fish; coastal steam cargo vessel (Scot.) (loco)	zo, nt, rw
PUFFIN	bird; an auk	zo
PUG-DOG	a lap-dog	zo
PUGREE	Indian hat scarf	
PUISNE	inferior in rank	
PUKKHA	pucka; real (Ind.)	
PULING	whimpering; whining	
PULLED	drawn; hauled; extracted	
PULLER	hauler; an attraction	
PULLET	young hen	zo
PULLEY	grooved wheel; tackle (crane)	to
PULL-IN	} roadside halt	
PULL-UP		
PULL-ON	boxing gloves	
PULPED	} mashed, machine-shredded	
PULPER		
PULPIT	rostrum; ambo	rl
PULQUE	a Mexican beverage	ck
PULSAR	space radio-energy source	as
PULSED	throbbed; vibrated	
PULTUN	native infantry regiment (Ind.)	
PULVIL	scented powder	
PULVIN	dosseret, supercapital (Byzant.)	ar
PULWAR	sailing dugout, cargo, Ganges, India	nt
PUMELO	pomelo; shaddock; fruit	
PUMICE	spongy lava; powder (pounce) for stencils; -stone	bd, mn, gl
PUMPED	forced transfer of liquids, gas; interrogated (tyres) (-dry); exhausted	
PUMPER	cross-examiner; pump man	
PUNCHI	Kashmiri people	
PUNCHY	fat; stocky	
PUNCTO	point (fencing); punctual	ga
PUNDIT	savant; wiseacre; guru; authority	
PUNICA	pomegranate	bt
PUNIER	weaker; feebler	
PUNISH	correct; chasten; scourge	
PUNKAH	fan (Ind.)	
PUNNER	a ram; maul; word-joker	to
PUNNET	basket for fruit	
PUNTED	betted; kicked	
PUNTER	gambler	
PUPATE	from caterpillar to pupa	zo
PUPOID	like a chrysalis	zo
PUPPED	whelped; littered	
PUPPET	doll; marionette; pawn	
PURANA	sacred Sanskrit books	rl
PURDAH	curtain; seclusion	

PURELY	simply; clearly; really
PUREST	without blemish
PURFLE	embroider **tx**
PURFLY	wrinkled
PURGED	cleaned; purified; shriven
PURGER	an aperient; laxative
PURIFY	cleanse; clean
PURINE	uric acid compound, toxin **ch**
PURISM	precision; nicety; exactness
PURIST	stickler for style
PURITY	chastity; fineness; simplicity
PURLED	curled; swirled; knitted
PURLER	a fall; a cropper
PURLIN	a roof timber
PURPLE	colour; dye; mollusc; imperial; cardinalate **rl**
PURPLE	ornate (prose); rhetorical
PURRED	curred, (cats or pigeons)
PURSED	contracted; wrinkled
PURSER	paymaster; supply chief **nt**
PURSUE	follow; track; chase; practise
PURVEY	sell; cater; retail; procure
PUSHED	urged; impelled; jostled
PUSHER	type of plane; thruster
PUSH-IN	gatecrash; struggle; (hockey)
PUSHTU	Afghan tongue
PUSULE	small plant vacuole **bt**
PUTEAL	well-curb
PUTELI	Ganges boat **nt**
PUTLOG	short board; putlock
PUT-OUT	irritated; thwarted; laid; displayed; dismissed (cricket, baseball) **ga**
PUTRID	corrupt; rotten; decaying
PUTSCH	revolt attempt (Germ.)
PUTTED	took short green shot (golf) **ga**
PUTTEE	cloth legging; puttie (Ind.)
PUTTER	a golf club
PUTTOO	goat's-wool cloth **tx**
PUZZLE	bewilder; enigma; problem
PYCNID	(fungus' spores) **bt**
PYCNON	a semi-tone **mu**
PYEDOG	piedog; a pariah **zo**
PYEMIA	blood-poisoning **md**
PYEMIC	septicaemic **md**
PYGARG	antelope (Herodotus) **zo**
PYGARG	osprey or sea-eagle **zo**
PYKNIC	fat (of persons) **md**
PYLOME	opening in sarcodina **zo**
PYOSIS	formation of pus **md**
PYRENE	fruit stone **bt**
PYRENE	tar product **ch**
PYRITE	pyrites **mn**
PYROLA	wintergreen **md**
PYRONE	heterocyclic compound **ch**
PYROPE	garnet **mn**
PYTHIA	Delphic oracle priestess
PYTHON	serpent (slain by Apollo) **zo**
PYURIA	pus in urine **md**

Q

QUADRA	square frame or border
QUAERE	enquire; seek (Latin) (query)
QUAGGA	extinct zebra (S. Africa) **zo**
QUAGGY	boggy; marshy
QUAHOG	clam (N. America) **zo**
QUAICH	} drinking cup; tassie (Sc.)
QUAIGH	
QUAINT	droll; fantastic; curious; odd
QUAKED	shook; quivered; rocked
QUAKER	a Friend
QUANTA	(plural of Quantum) a quantity of anything
QUARRY	pit; prey; victim; an arrow
QUARTE	guard (fencing)
QUARTO	a size of book **pr**
QUARTZ	silica (double refracting) **mn**
QUARTZ	crystal with varying polarisation **ps, ch**
QUASAR	far-space radio-energy source **as**
QUATCH	squat; flat (Shak.)
QUAVER	quiver; tremble; vibrate; $\frac{1}{8}$ note **mu**
QUAYED	having a wharf; jettied **bd, nt**
QUBBAH	domed tomb (Arabic)
QUEASY	squeamish; fastidious
QUEEST	ring-dove **zo**
QUEINT	quaint (Spens.)
QUELCH	squelch
QUELEA	weaver-bird **zo**
QUENCH	extinguish (fire); slake (thirst)
QUERRY	equerry; groom; courtier
QUESAL	} resplendent trogon; brilliant green bird
QUEZAL	**zo**
QUEUED	lined up (waited turn)
QUHILK	whilk; which (Sc.)
QUICHE	egg flan with savoury filling **ck**
QUIDAM	somebody (Lat.)
QUIHYE	Anglo-Indian (Bengal)
QUIJAL	badge of Guatemala
QUILCH	couch grass **bt**
QUILLS	feather pens, porcupine spikes **zo**
QUINCE	fruit (jelly) **bt, ck**
QUINIC	(quinine) **md**
QUINOA	Mexican oats **bt**
QUINOL	reducing agent **pg**
QUINSY	tonsillitis **md**
QUINTA	manor, large farm (wine grower's) (Portugal)
QUINZE	card game (of 15) **ga**
QUIRED	in quires; sang in harmony **pr, mu**
QUIRKY	evasive; artful; illusive
QUITCH	couch grass **bt**
QUIVER	case for arrows; vibrate
QUODDY	open fishing boat (Maine, N. America) **nt**
QUOINS	dressed corner stones **ar, bd**
QUOITS	ring-throwing game (deck) **ga**

QUORUM	a valid executive	**lw**
QUOTED	referred; repeated; mentioned	
QUOTER	a citer	
QUOTHA	forsooth	
QUOTUM	share; proportion	
Q-VALUE	the amount of energy produced in nuclear reaction	

R

RABATE	beat down; abatement; rebate	
RABATO	turned-down collar; rebato (It.)	
RABBAN	super-rabbi	**rl**
RABBET	a groove in a plank	**cr**
RABBIN	Jewish lawyer or rabbi	
RABBIT	timid breeder and burrower; weak player; lesser person	**zo**
RABBLE	the mob; iron puddling bar	**me**
RABIES	canine (human) hydrophobia	**md, vt**
RACEME	a cluster	**bt**
RACHIS	backbone; spine	**bt, zo**
RACIAL	ethnic; colour judgement	
RACILY	piquantly; spicily; pungently	
RACING	contesting; competing (car)	**ga**
RACISM	ethnic or colour superiority attitude	
RACKED	strained; wrestled; stretched; (storage)	
RACKER	a torturer; storer	
RACKET	snow-shoe; clamour; (tennis) broad bat; fraud	
RACKLE	rattle; crackle	
RACK-UP	video information; lines ascending	**cp**
RADDLE	twist; red ochre	
RADEAU	scow defence ship (N. Amer.)	**nt**
RADIAL	like a ray	
RADIAN	an angle of 57.3 degrees	
RADISH	plant	**bt**
RADIUM	metal	**mn**
RADIUS	bone of forearm; half a diameter	**bt, md**
RADIUS	crane load formula based distance	
RADOUB	recaulking of ship's hull	**nt**
RADULA	mollusc's tongue	**zo**
RAFALE	burst of fire; squall	
RAFFED	swept; huddled together	
RAFFEE	} schooner sail	**nt**
RAFFIE		
RAFFIA	palm fibre	**bt**
RAFFLE	sweepstake; draw; lottery	
RAFTER	roof-timber; lumberman (river)	**bd, nt**
RAG DAY	students' carnival	
RAGBAG	odd scraps of fabric	**tx**
RAGGED	jagged; uneven; torn	
RAGGEE	Indian millet	**bt**
RAGGLE	notch irregularly; raglet	

RAGING	wroth; rabid; furious	
RAGLAN	} loose overcoat style	
RAGLIN		
RAGLET	narrow masonry groove	**ar, bd**
RAGMAN	rag-picker	
RAGOUT	stew; a spicy mixture	**ck**
RAG-TAG	riff-raff	
RAGULY	jagged	**hd**
RAIBLE	rabble (Sc.)	
RAIDER	invader; plunderer (sudden) (night) (cops)	
RAILER	scoffer; sneerer	
RAILEX	postal express service	
RAISER	producer	
RAISIN	a dried grape	**bt, ck**
RAJPUT	Royal Hindu	
RAKERY	debauchery	
RAKING	inclining; enfilading	
RAKISH	dissolute; licentious	
RALLUS	water-rails, etc.; birds	**zo**
RAMAGE	boughs of tree	**bt**
RAMARK	non-directional radio beacon	**nv**
RAMBLE	excursion; stroll; roam (on foot)	
RAM-CAT	tom-cat (male)	**zo**
RAMEAL	branching	**bt**
RAMENT	bristle-shaped leaflet	**bt**
RAMIFY	branch; divide; sub-divide	
RAMISM	system of logic	
RAMJET	open duct combustion	**ae**
RAMMED	butted; crammed	
RAMMEL	refuse wood	
RAMMER	sand-packing hand tool	**to**
RAMOON	mulberry (W. Indies)	**bt**
RAMOUS	} branched	
RAMOSE		
RAMPED	bounded; sprang; sloped	
RAMPER	race-course rough	
RAMROD	gun-bore stuffer	
RAMSON	hedgerow garlic	**bt**
RAMULE	small branch	**bt**
RANCHO	ranch; stock farm; ranche	
RANCID	sour; musty; fetid	
RANDAN	a row boat	**nt**
RANDLE	plate rack	
RANDOM	casual; haphazard; fortuitous	
RANDOM	numbers production	**cp**
RANGED	extended; disposed	
RANGER	forest guard (parks); commando; (free-) rover	**fr**
RANGIA	a bivalve genus	**zo**
RANINE	frog-like	**zo**
RANKER	fouler; officer from the ranks	
RANKLE	resent; remain bitter	
RANKLY	rampantly; excessively	
RANSOM	money to free a hostage	
RANTAN	clatter of pots and pans	
RANTER	spouter; boisterous preacher	
RANULA	frog-tongue	**md**
RAPHIA	raffia; palm fibre	**bt**
RAPHIS	crystal in plant cell	**bt**

RAPIDO	with rapidity; express	**mu, rw**
RAPIER	a thrusting sword	
RAPINE	pillage; spoliation; plunder	
RAPING	ravishing; violating	
RAPPED	tapped; struck	
RAPPEE	snuff	
RAPPEL	call to arms	
RAPPEN	Swiss centime (coin)	**nm**
RAPPER	knocker; arouser	
RAPTOR	a ravisher; a hawk	**zo**
RAPTUS	trance, seizure	
RAREFY	attenuate	
RARELY	seldom; infrequently	
RAREST	sparsest; thinnest; scarcest	
RARITY	scarcity; fewness; tenuity	
RASANT	flanking; raking	
RASCAL	rogue; scamp; knave; caitiff	
RASHER	thin slice; hastier	
RASHLY	audaciously; recklessly	
RASING	razing; levelling; demolishing	**bd**
RASION	rasure; an erasure	
RASPED	filed; abraded; grated	
RASPER	scraper; stiff fence	
RASTER	beam picture on screen, video signal	**tv**
RASURE	an erasure	**pr**
RATANY	Peruvian shrub	**bt**
RATEEN	ratteen; woollen fabric	**tx**
RATHER	sooner; preferably; slightly	
RATIFY	confirm; endorse; approve	
RATINE	rough-surface dress fabric	**tx**
RATING	tonnage; class; seaman; popularity scale; (rowing)	**nt**
RATION	share; quota; portion	
RATITE	flat-breasted	**zo**
RATLIN	(shrouds)	**nt, tx**
RATOON	sugarcane sprout	**bt**
RAT-PIT	no such thing	
RATRAC	snow compressor vehicle for clearing pistes (skiing)	
RATTAN	drum-beat; basketry	**bt**
RAT-TAT	postman's knock	
RATTED	deserted; informed upon	
RATTEN	stealing non-unionists' tools	
RATTER	rat-catcher	
RATTLE	chatter; vibrate; a herb; baby's toy; (snake); (rarely) percussion	**mu**
RAUCID	raucous; hoarse	
RAUCLE	rough; fearless (Sc.)	
RAVAGE	spoil; lay waste; ransack	
RAVINE	gulch; gulley; gorge; defile	**go**
RAVING	delirious; ranging; frenzied	
RAVISH	rape; violate; delight	
RAWISH	somewhat raw	
RAYING	radiating; shining	
RAY-OIL	ray-fish oil	**zo**
RAZING	overthrowing; rasing	
RAZURE	rasure; an erasure	**pr**
RAZZIA	a foray (Algerian); police raid	

READER	proof corrector; reading book	
REALIA	3-dimensional exhibits	
REALLY	truly; verily; actually	
REALTY	real estate	**lw**
REAMED	frothed; enlarged; edged	
REAMER	belling tool (drilled holes)	**to**
REAPED	acquired; cropped; obtained	
REAPER	harvester; a machine	**ag**
REARED	erected; educated	
REARER	up-bringer; guardian (foster-)	
REASON	logical, rational approach; motive; discuss; intelligence; excuse	
REASTY	rancid; rotting	
REAVED	bereaved; robbed	
REAVER	reiver; freebooter	
REAVOW	avow again; re-pledge	
RE-BACK	to repair spine of book	**pr**
REBATE	blunt; abatement; a rabbet	
REBATE	freestone; discount	**mn**
REBATO	a ruff; rabato	
REBECK	Moorish violin	**mu**
REBIND	refasten	
REBITE	engraving; acid process	**pr**
REBOIL	seethe again	**ck**
REBORE	worn-cylinder treatment	**au**
REBORN	re-incarnated	
REBOTE	(pelota)	**ga**
REBUFF	snub; repel; repulse	
REBUKE	upbraid; reprove; chide	
REBURY	inter again	
RECALL	revoke; rescind; retract	
RECANT	adjure; renounce; deny	
RECAST	compute again	
RECEDE	ebb; decrease; withdraw	
RECENT	modern; late; new; novel	
RECEPT }	having received; obtained	
RECEIPT }		
RECESS	niche; alcove; nook; interval; adjournment	
RECIPE	prescription; formula	**ck**
RECITE	tell; relate; repeat; recount	
RECKED	regarded; heeded	
RECKON	deem; calculate; estimate	
RECOAL	refuel	
RECOCT	reconcoct; vamp up	**ck**
RECOIL	kick; rebound; shrink	
RECOIN	remint	**nm**
RECORD	enter; note; achievement	
RECORD	achievement; (disc) evidence	**mu**
RECORD	archives; memory; filed data	**cp**
RECOUP	indemnify; make good	
RECTOR	academic leader; vicar	**rl**
RECTUM	section of intestine above anus	
RECTUS	equal-width muscle	**zo**
RECUIL }	recoil (Spens.)	
RECULE }		
RECUMB	to repose; lie down; rest	
RECURE	cure again	**md**
RECUSE	reject	**lw**
REDACT	to reduce; to edit	**pr**

REDBUD	Judas tree	**bt**
REDCAP	goldfinch; military policeman	**zo**
REDDED	tidied; arranged (Sc.)	
REDDEN	blush; red colour (rouge)	**pt**
REDDLE	raddle; red chalk	
RED-DOG	low-grade flour; (Am. football)	**ck**
REDEEM	ransom; free; retrieve; repay	**lw**
RED-EYE	rudd; carp	**zo**
RED-GUM	eucalyptus	**bt**
RED-HOT	extreme	
RED-LAC	Japanese wax-tree	**bt**
RED-OAK	N. American oak	**bt**
REDOUT	fort	
REDOWA	Bohemian dance	**mu**
REDRAW	redraft; copy	
RED-TOP	kind of grass	**bt**
REDUCE	degrade; curtail; abridge; decrease	
REDUCT	a diminution in size	
REDUIT	redoubt; redout; bastion; fort	
RED-WUD	stark mad (Sc.)	
REEBOK	rhebok; S. African antelope	**zo**
RE-ECHO	repeat; reverberate	
REECHY	smoked-stained (smoke-smog)	
REEDED	covered with reeds	
REEDEN	(reeds)	**bt**
RE-EDIT	compile new edition	
REEFER	wind-jacket; drugged cigarette	**nt**
REEFER	refrigerated ship	**nt**
REEKED	exhaled; fumed; smelt	
REEKIE	smokey (Sc.)	
REELED	staggered; spun; swayed	
REELER	the grasshopper warbler	**zo**
RE-FACE	redecoration (wall); reoppose (ice hockey)	**bd, pt**
REFAIT	a drawn game (Fr.)	**ga**
REFILL	replenish; film cassette	**pg**
RE-FIND	retrieve	
REFINE	clarify; purify; cleanse	
REFLET	iridescent glaze	
REFLEX	reactive; introspective; automatic reaction; wing structure	**ae**
REFLOW	re-issue	
REFLUX	ebb; return; redound	
REFOLD	replicate	
REFORM	make; remodel; betterment	**lw**
REFUEL	take in more fuel	
REFUGE	security; sanctuary; asylum; traffic 'island'	
REFUND	repay; return; restore	
REFUSE	veto; decline; deny; trash	
REFUTE	disprove; confute	
REGAIN	retrieve; recover; recapture	
REGALE	feast; entertain; gratify	
REGALO	a gift; a sumptuous repast (Sp.)	
REGARD	note; watch; repute	
REGENT	ruling; a ruler during minority	
REGIME	system; administration; government; diet regimen, rules	
REGINA	a queen	
REGION	province; tract; vicinity	
REGIUS	⎱ appointed by the Crown	
REGIUM	⎰	
REGIVE	restore	
REGLET	flat moulding	**pr**
REGLET	spacing block	**pr**
REGLOW	to recalesce; rekindle	
REGNAL	during the reign of	
REGNUM	badge of loyalty	
REGRET	rue; deplore; remorse	
REGULA	book of rules	**lw, rl**
REHASH	discuss again; rearrange	
REHEAD	head again	
RE-HEAL	to heal again	**md**
REIGLE	a channel or guide	
REINED	curbed	
REIVER	reaver; robber; freebooter	
REJECT	jilt; spurn; discard; repudiate	
REJOIN	reunite	
REJOLT	a new shock	
RELAID	(carpets)	
RELAIS	a rampart walk (Fr.)	
RELAND	land again	
RELATE	tell; recite; narrate; report	
RELENT	relax; yield; soften	
RELICT	a widow (obs.)	
RELIED	depended on; confided	
RELIEF	aid; redress; alleviation	
RELIER	a trusting person	
RELISH	appreciate; zest; gusto; taste	
RELIVE	revive	
RELOAD	recharge; refill; system recovery time	**cp**
RELUCT	to resist (obs.)	
RELUME	to rekindle	
REMADE	remanufacture; refashioned	
REMAIN	persist; tarry; stop; survive	
REMAKE	revamp	
REMAND	send back to custody	
REMARK	also re-mark; say; comment	
REMBLE	remove (dial.)	
REMEDY	cure; panacea	
REMIGE	large wing contour feather	**zo**
REMIND	call to remembrance	
REMISE	release; give back; renewed attack (fencing)	**lw**
REMISS	slack; dilatory; negligent	
REMORA	a sucking fish	**zo**
REMORD	strike with remorse (obs.)	
REMOTE	far; distant; secluded; slight; (control)	
REMOVE	dislodge; transport; eject	
REMPLI	heraldic colouring	**hd**
RENAME	rechristen; issue under new name	**lw**
RENARD	Reynard, a fox	**zo**
RENATE	renewed; born again	
RENDER	return; assign; supply; restore	
RENEGE	to revoke (cards); break oath or promise	

RENNET	enzyme for cheesemaking	**ck**
RENNIN	gastric juice ferment	**md**
RENOWN	fame; eminence; repute	
RENTAL	money paid for house, car, tv	
RENTED	hired (tenancy) (contract)	**lw**
RENTER	hires out flats, films, cars, tv	
RENTES	French Government securities	
RENULE	small kidney	**md**
RENVOY	return; dismissal (obs.)	
RE-OPEN	restart (file) (case)	**lw**
REPACE	retrace one's steps; re-measure	
		me
REPAID	requited; rewarded; liquidated	
REPAIR	patch; mend; restore; wend	
REPAND	bent back	
RE-PART	share; divide again	
REPAST	a meal; victuals; food	**ck**
REPEAL	annul; rescind; nullify	**lw**
REPEAT	iterate; renew; echo	
REPENT	beg forgiveness; apologise; rue; regret	
REPINE	fret; complain; murmur	
RE-PLAN	re-design; re-arrange	
REPONE	re-appoint	**lw**
REPORT	rumour; relate; bang	
REPOSE	lie; recline; rest	
REPOUR	re-issue	
REPPED	ribbed	
REPUGN	oppose (Shak.)	
REPUTE	reputation; renown; regard	
REQUIT	requited; repaid (Spens.)	
RESAIL	put to sea again	
RESALE	a second sale	
RESCUE	save; redeem; release	
RESEAT	repair-; change-seating	
RESEAU	a network (Fr.)	
RESECT	cut off	**md, sv**
RESEDA	mignonette genus	**bt**
RESELL	revend	
RESENT	dislike; repel; resist; hate	
RESIDE	live; dwell; lodge; sojourn	
RESIGN	also re-sign; forgo; yield	
RESILE	recede; start back	
RESINY	resinous; rosiny	
RESIST	oppose; thwart; withstand	
RESORB	swallow up	
RESORT	recourse; (holiday)	
RESTED	reposed; quieted; paused	
RESTEM	force back; recheck	
RESTIO	plant genus	**bt**
RESULT	ensue; outcome; sequel; end	
RESUME	renew; summarize; synopsis	
RETAIL	hawk; peddle; recount	
RETAIN	hold; keep; reserve; detain	
RETAKE	recapture	
RETARD	clog; hinder; impede; check	
RETENE	coal-tar constituent	**ch**
RETENT	retained; held back	
RE-TEST	try again; re-adjust; reset	

RETINA	a network of optic nerves; screen of sight	**pl**
RETINE	cancer cell growth inhibitor	**md**
RETIRE	recede; withdraw; shrink	
RETOLD	already narrated	
RETOOK	regained; recaptured	
RETORT	rejoinder; distilling vessel	
RETOSE	reticulated	**bt**
RETOSS	throw again	
RETOUR	return (Sc.)	
RETRAD	backward	
RETRAL	posterior; retrorse	
RETREE	paper refuse; wastage	**pr**
RETRIM	embellish; smarten up	
RETUND	to dull; to blunt	
RETURN	also re-turn; restore; recur	
RETUSE	blunt	
REVALE	of cornices completed in position	**ar, bd**
REVAMP	renovate; remake	
REVEAL	disclose; divulge; unveil; part of jamb	**ar**
REVERB	reverberate (Shak.)	
REVERE	adore; venerate; honour	
REVERS	revere; lapel (jacket)	
REVERT	return; reverse; relapse	
REVERY	reverie; dream; trance	
REVEST	revert; clothe again (obs.)	
REVIEW	survey; inspect; journal	
REVILE	asperse; traduce; defame	
REVISE	reconsider; improve; correct	
REVIVE	rouse; invigorate; quicken	
REVOKE	annul; cancel; quash	
REVOLT	rebel; nauseate; mutiny	
REVVED	rotated at speed (motor)	
REWARD	guerdon; repay; premium	
REWOOD	afforest	
REWORD	change the phraseology	
REXISM	} Royalist party, Belgium	
REXIST		
RHAGON	form of sponge	
RHAPIS	genus of Chinese palms	**bt**
RHESUS	bandar; Indian monkey	**zo**
RHEUMY	watery; rheumatic	**md**
RHEXIA	genus of flowering plants	**bt**
RHEXIS	rupture of bodily structure	**md**
RHINAE	shark genus	**zo**
RHINAL	nasal	**md**
RHIZIC	radical; root-like	**bt**
RHUSMA	a depilatory	**ch**
RHYMED	harmonized	
RHYMER	versifier	
RHYMIC	almost poetic	
RHYSSA	ichneumon flies	**zo**
RHYTHM	cadence; metre; symmetry	
RHYTON	Assyrian drinking vessel ceramic or metal	
RIALTO	a bridge in Venice	**ar**
RIANCY	gaiety; laughter	
RIBALD	coarse; rude; gross; lewd	

RIBAND	a ribbon; rail in palisade; (blue) **cr, nt**	
RIBBED	ridged; furrowed	
RIBBON	riband; strip; saw; hand apparatus (gymn) **cr**	
RIBIBE	rebec; old woman (obs.) **mu**	
RIBLET	rudimentary rib	
RIBOSE	pentose sugar in vitamin B-2 **ch**	
RICCIA	a plant genus **bt**	
RICHEN	enrich; enhance	
RICHER	wealthier	
RICHES	abundance; affluence	
RICHLY	opulently; sumptuously	
RICKED	piled; sprained	
RICKER	thin round timber **fr**	
RICKLE	small pile or rick (Sc.)	
RICTAL	gaping	
RICTUS	open mouth	
RIDDEL	altar-curtain **rl**	
RIDDEN	p. part. of ride; infested (lice-) (bed-)	
RIDDER	a remover	
RIDDLE	sieve; enigma; rebus (grate)	
RIDEAU	curtain (Fr.)	
RIDGED	ribbed; furrowed	
RIDGEL	} defective male **zo**	
RIDGIL		
RIGGOT		
RIGLAN		
RIDING	county sub-division	
RIEVER	reaver; robber; pirate	
RIFELY	abundantly	
RIFFLE	engraving tool; small shallow rapid (canoeing) **pr, to**	
RIFLED	pillaged; grooved	
RIFLER	robber; freebooter; plunderer; soldier	
RIFTED	cleft; split	
RIGGED	(the market) **nt**	
RIGGER	mechanic; fitter; long haired brush; (rowing) **to, pt**	
RIGGER	out-rigger (sailing); equipment (parachuting) **nt**	
RIGGLE	sand-eel **zo**	
RIGLET	(see reglet); flat piece of wood **cr**	
RIGOUR	rigidity; austerity; harshness	
RIG-OUT	complete outfit; uniform	
RILING	annoying; irritating	
RILLED	trilled; flowed	
RILLET	rivulet; stream **go**	
RIMIST	writer of doggerel	
RIMLET	thin rim	
RIMMED	bordered; edged	
RIMMER	pastry cutter **ck, to**	
RIMMON	Syrian god **rl**	
RIMOSE	} gnarled	
RIMOUS		
RIMPLE	wrinkle; rumple	
RIMSAW	edging saw **to**	
RIMULA	fossil limpets **mn**	

RINDED	peeled	
RINDLE	gutter; runnel; rine	
RINGED	encircled	
RINGER	expert shearer (Australia)	
RINKED	roller-skated	
RINSED	laved; cleansed; cleared	
RINSER	(washing machine)	
RIOTED	brawled; luxuriated	
RIOTER	disturber of the peace	
RIPECK	}	
REPECK	} punt pole for mooring	
RYPECK	}	
RIPELY	maturely	
RIPEST	mellowest	
RIPPED	torn; rent	
RIPPER	foghorn; cutter; saw; murderer **nt, to**	
RIPPLE	flax-comb; small wave; fiddleback (sycamore); finish **pt**	
RIPPLY	rippling	
RIPPON	a spur from Ripon	
RIPRAP	broken stone used for walls	
RIPSAW	a ripper **to**	
RISALA	troop of native cavalry	
RISBAN	defended ground	
RISERS	parachutists' webbing straps **ae**	
RISING	insurrection; towering	
RISKED	chanced; ventured (capital)	
RISKER	gambler; venturer	
RISLEY	an acrobat	
RISQUE	indelicate; audacious (Fr.)	
RITELY	with due rites	
RITTER	a knight (Ger.)	
RITUAL	rite; ceremony	
RIVAGE	the coast; shore; bank (Fr.) **go**	
RIVERY	riparian; of the shores	
RIVINA	the pokeweed genus **bt**	
RIVING	splitting; rending	
RIVOSE	tabby; furrowed	
RIZZER	dry in the sun (Sc.)	
RIZZER	a red currant (Sc.) **bt**	
RIZZLE	to creep; frizzle (dial.)	
ROAMED	ranged; rambled	
ROAMER	nomad; vagrant; stroller	
ROARED	bawled; guffawed	
ROARER	broken-winded horse **zo**	
ROBALO	a fish (USA) **zo**	
ROBBED	stole; despoiled; purloined	
ROBBER	brigand; bandit; burglar	
ROBBIN	spun-yarn	
ROBERD	chaffinch **zo**	
ROBING	attiring; dressing	
ROB-ROY	a canoe **nt**	
ROBUST	sturdy; vigorous; hale; hearty	
ROCCUS	striped bass fish **zo**	
ROCHEA	a plant genus **bt**	
ROCHET	fish; the roach **zo**	
ROCHET	bishop's surplice **rl**	
ROCKED	reeled; tottered	
ROCKEL	a woman's cloak	

ROCKER	mining cradle; (swivel chair); compulsory figure (ice skating)	
ROCKET	Stephenson's locomotive 1829	**rw**
ROCKET	firework; jet transport; alarm	**ae, sp**
ROCKIE	rock-linnet	**zo**
ROCOCO	florid style	**ar**
RODDIN	rowan-tree (Sc.)	**bt**
RODENT	gnawing; small mammal	**zo**
RODING	evening flight	
ROGGAN	logan; rocking stone	**gl**
ROGGLE	shake (dial.)	
ROILED	riled; vexed	
ROINEK	Boer name for British soldier	
ROLAND	legendary hero	
ROLLED	trundled; rotated; turned	
ROLLER	road levelling vehicle	
ROLLER	wave; blue crow; a sect	**zo**
ROLL-IN	hockey; to garage; activating process	**cp**
ROLL-ON	(ferry); copying file	**cp**
ROLOCK	brick on edge bond; oar-pivot	
ROWLOCK	on rowing boat	**bd, nt**
ROMAGE	tumult (Shak.)	
ROMAIC	modern Greek	
ROMANT	exaggerate; romance	
ROMANY	gipsy; gipsy language	
ROMERO	pilot-fish	**zo**
ROMIST	papist	**rl**
ROMPED	frolicked; gambolled; sported	
ROMPER	garment; overall suite	
RONDEL	poem, music cycle	**mu**
RONDEAU		
RONDLE	bastion turret	
RONION	mangy animal; leprous	
RONYON	lounger (Shak.)	**zo**
ROOFED	covered	
ROOFER	tiler	
ROOKED	cheated	
ROOKER	swindler	
ROOKIE	recruit	
ROOKLE	rootle	
ROOMED	lodged; housed; accommodated	
ROOMER	lodger (in bedsit or dormitory)	
ROOPIT	hoarse; roopy; roupy	
ROOTED	rootled; deep-set	
ROOTER	grubber; towed scarifier	
ROOTLE	rookle; poke about like a pig	
ROPERY	rope walk (factory)	
ROPING	lassoing	
ROQUET	(croquet)	**ga**
ROSARY	Catholic string of prayer beads	**rl**
ROSCID	dewy; roric	
ROSEAL	rose-like	
ROSERY	a rose garden	
ROSIED	adorned with roses	
ROSING	sprinkling	
ROSINY	resiny	
ROSSER	policeman (slang)	
ROSTEL	embryo root; radicle	**bt**
ROSTER	duty list; roll of names	
ROSULA	small rose	**bt**
ROTARY	rotatory	
ROTATE	spin; whirl; twirl; revolve (moon); (Am. football) (volleyball)	
ROTCHE	little auk	
ROT-GUT	bad liquor	
ROTHER	roaring; lowing (Shak.)	
ROTTED	disintegrated; decayed	
ROTTEN	corrupt; rank; moribund	
ROTTER	a pestilent person	
ROTULA	knee-cap	**md**
ROTUND	round; spherical	
ROTURE	plebeian rank (Fr.)	
ROUBLE	100 kopecks (Russian)	**nm**
ROUCOU	a dye (anotto)	
ROUGED	powdered (rosy cosmetic)	
ROUGET	swine-fever	
ROUNCE	a pulley; card game	**ga**
ROUNCY	a nag; a hack	**zo**
ROUSED	ruffled; agitated; provoked	
ROUSER	a stimulator; inciter	
ROUTED	fled in disorder; defeated	
ROUTER	sash-plane; message switching selector; plough	**cp, to**
ROUTLE	grub up; rootle	
ROVERY	roving; nomadism	
ROVING	rambling; ranging	
ROWING	sculling	
ROYALS	(family); of Western Red Cedar	**bt**
ROYENA	ebony	**bt**
RUA-PET	coastal vessel (Siam)	**nt**
RUBACE	rock crystal	**mn**
RUBATO	change of rhythm	**mu**
RUBBED	wiped; scoured; chafed; galled	
RUBBER	coagulated latex; set of 3 games (cards, sports)	**ga**
RUBBLE	undressed stone	
RUBBLY	broken	
RUBIAN	madder colour	
RUBIED	red as a ruby	
RUBIFY	to redden	
RUBIGO	mildew; rust (fungi) (rot)	**bt**
RUBINE	crimson dye; rubin	
RUB-OFF	incidental harm, side-effect of an action	
RUBRIC	a heading in red (prayerbook)	**pr, rl**
RUCKLE	wrinkle; pucker	
RUDDER	boat guiding device; trailing fin on aircraft	**nt, ae**
RUDDLE	red chalk or ochre	
RUDDOC	robin redbreast	**zo**
RUDDOCK		
RUDDOC	kind of apple; gold coin	**bt, nm**
RUDELY	boorishly; insolently; impolitely	
RUDEST	most savage; crudest	
RUEFUL	mournful; sad; melancholy	
RUELLE	a coterie	
RUFFED	trumped; finessed (Bridge)	**ga**

241

RUFFER	comb for flax	
RUFFIN	freshwater perch	zo
RUFFLE	a pleated border; disorder	
RUFOUS	ruddy; florid	
RUGATE	wrinkled; furrowed	
RUGGED	ragged; harsh; austere	
RUGGER	Rugby football	ga
RUGINE	surgeon's rasp	to
RUGOSA	corals	mn
RUGOSE	} wrinkled	
RUGOUS	}	
RUGATE	}	
RUINED	wrecked; destroyed; beggared	
RUINER	demolisher	
RULING	governing; ascendant	
RULLEY	a dray	
RUMBLE	carriage-seat; reverberate	
RUM-BUD	grog-blossom	
RUMKIN	tailless fowl	zo
RUMMEL	soakaway; dry well; pit	bd
RUMMER	drinking glass	
RUMOUR	report; bruit; hearsay	
RUMPLE	rimple; crumple; pucker	
RUMPUS	uproar; disturbance	
RUM-TUM	Thames sculling boat	nt
RUNDLE	a ladder-rung; a spoke	
RUNKLE	wrinkle	
RUNLET	} rivulet	nt
RUNNEL	}	
RUN-MAN	naval deserter	nt
RUNNER	rotating part of water wheel turbine; (coward); (plant gone to seed); (bean)	bt, ck
RUNNER	plough guide; timber joists; withies	
RUNNER	racer; messenger	
RUNNET	rennet for cheese making	ck
RUN-OFF	experimental, production-line method	
RUN-OFF	printing batch; drain; cattle stealing; abduct; compose rapidly; deviate from fixed route (horse racing); rainfall course	
RUNOFF	final contest; election; river floodwater	
RUN-OUT	rope length between mountaineers	
RUN-OUT	cricket; experiment	
RUNRIG	land tenure (Sc.)	
RUNWAY	track; airfield take-off path	ae, pb
RUPIAH	(Indonesia)	nm
RUPPIA	a grass genus	bt
RUSCUS	butcher's broom	bt
RUSHED	dashed; flew; ran; plunged	
RUSHEN	of rushes	bt
RUSHER	impetuous person; thruster	
RUSINE	of E. Ind. maned deer	zo
RUSSEL	woollen fabric; fox	tx, zo
RUSSET	homespun; apple	tx, bt
RUSSIA	leather	le

RUSTED	oxidized	
RUSTIC	rural; bucolic; pastoral	
RUSTLE	quiver; whisper (wind); steal	
RUSTRE	heraldic lozenge	hd
RUSURE	earth-slide	gl
RUTELA	beetle genus	zo
RUTILE	an oxide of titanium	ch
RUTTED	grooved; furrowed	
RUTTER	a chart; trooper	
RUTTLE	gurgle; rattle (dial.)	
RYBATE	rebate or jamb store	bd
RYPECK	ripeck; repeck; punt-pole	nt

S

SABALO	the tarpon; atlantic fish	zo
SABIAN	star worshipper	
SABINE	plant; the savin	bt
SABLED	darkened; furred	
SACBUT	sackbut; stringed instrument	mu
SACCOS	Oriental vestment	rl, tx
SACCUS	pouchlike structure	zo
SACHEL	} school-boys' book bag	
STACHEL	}	
SACHEM	Red Indian chief	
SACHET	scent bag; tea bag	
SACKED	plundered; dismissed	
SACKER	sack-filling machine	
SACRAL	(pelvic arch)	pl
SACRED	holy; divine; consecrated	
SACRUM	a pelvis bone	pl
SADDEN	to grieve; depress	
SADDLE	burden; clog; encumber; bolster; bug	
SADDLE	earth formation	go
SADDLE	odd piece; seat on a horse	
SADINA	sort of sardine	zo
SADISM	lustful cruelty	
SADIST	torturer; tormentor	
SAETER	} Norwegian mountain hut	
SETER	}	
SAFARI	caravan; expedition	
SAFELY	securely; surely; reliably	
SAFEST	surest	
SAFETY	security; protection; safeguard; (measure); score; snooker (Am. football)	
SAGELY	wisely; sagaciously	
SAGENE	fishing net; a network	
SAGENE	7 ft (2.1 m) (Russian)	me
SAGEST	wisest	
SAGGAR	sagger; fire-clay pot	
SAGGED	drooped; bent	
SAGGER	clay retort for stoneware	
SAGINA	pink genus	bt
SAGOIN	S. American monkey	zo
SAGUIN	capuchin monkey	zo
SAHARA	a desert (Africa)	go
SAILED	cruised	nt

SAILOR	A.B.; tar; seaman	nt
SAIQUE	} small trading ketch	nt
SAIC		
SAIRLY	sorely (Sc.)	
SAITHE	cod; ling, etc.	zo
SAKIEH	Persian water-wheel	
SALAAM	salutation (India)	
SALAMI	spiced sausage (It.)	ck
SALARY	pay; wages; stipend	
SALIAN	(Mars); salic; male heirs only	lw
SALIFY	to salten; add salt	ch, ck
SALINA	salt-marsh (Sp.)	
SALINA	salt from sea process	
SALINE	salty; briny	
SALITE	to season with salt	ck
SALITE	monoclinic pyroxene	mn
SALIVA	spittle	md
SALLAL	a fruit	bt
SALLET	light helmet	
SALLIE	} hired mourner (Sc.)	
SALUIE		
SALLOW	yellow; a willow	bt
SALMIS	ragout; salmi; a hash	ck
SALMON	highly prized fish	zo
SALOON	meeting room	
SALOOP	a decoction of sassafras	bt, ck
SALTED	preserved	
SALTEN	to preserve; made of salt	
SALTER	salt-seller	
SALTIE	a dab	zo
SALTUS	a mental jump	
SALUKI	hunting dog (Iran)	zo
SALUTE	hail; greet; accost	
SALVED	soothed; rescued	
SALVER	a tray	
SALVIA	sage	bt
SALVOR	a salvage expert	
SAMARA	winged fruit	bt
SAMARE	old-fashioned jacket	
SAMBAL	hot red-pepper paste	ck
SAMBAR	dhow	nt
SAMBOO	} Indian elk	zo
SAMBUR		
SAMELY	monotonous; unvaried	
SAMIAN	of Samos	
SAMIEL	Arabian/Saharan hot poison wind	
		mt
SAMIOT	native of Samos	
SAMITE	silk	tx
SAMLET	a parr; salmon	zo
SAMOAN	native of Samoa	
SAMPAN	sanpan; Chinese boat	nt
SAMPLE	try; taste; specimen	
SAMSHU	rice spirit (China)	ck
SAMYDA	West Indian birch	bt
SANCHO	negro guitar	mu
SANDAL	a Barbary vessel; footwear	nt
SANDIX	} red lead; vermilion	
SANDYX		

SANDUR	glacial outwash alluvial plain (Iceland)	go, gl
SANELY	rationally	
SANEST	most intelligent; soundest	
SANGAR	stone breastwork; masonry	bd
SANGHA	Buddhist church	rl
SANIES	discharge from ulcer	md
SANIFY	to restore to health	
SANITY	wisdom; normality; lucidity	
SANJAK	division of a vilayet (Turk.)	
SANNOP	} a brave; American Indian	
SANNUP		
SANTIR	} Eastern dulcimer	mu
SANTUR		
SANTON	Dervish priest	rl
SAPELE	silky-grained Afr. hardwood	fr
SAPFUL	juicy	bt
SAPIUM	gum-tree	bt
SAPOTA	sapodilla	bt
SAPOUR	flavour (savour)	
SAPPED	undermined (tunnels, explosives); weakened	
SAPPER	Royal Engineer	
SAPPHO	Greek poetess	
SAP-ROT	dry rot; fungal	bd
SAPYGA	digger-wasps	zo
SARCEL	pinion of a hawk's wing	zo
SARCEN	} Stonehenge sandstone; tin-worker; large sandstone boulder	
SARSEN		bd, gl, mn
SARDEL	herring type of fish	zo
SARGUS	fish of mullet type	zo
SARLAK	sarlac; the yak	zo
SARONG	Eastern skirt	
SARSIA	jellyfish	zo
SARTOR	one who dresses	
SASHES	window-framings; scarves	bd
SASINE	seizin (Sc.)	lw
SASTRA	sacred book (Hindu)	rl
SATANG	Thailand coin	nm
SATARA	lustred woollen cloth	tx
SATEEN	fabric	tx
SATINE	a hard wood	bt
SATING	satisfying; cloying	
SATINY	glossy	
SATIRE	irony; sarcasm; lampoon	
SATIVE	sown	
SATRAP	Persian provincial governor	
SATURN	planet; god of agriculture	
SAUCER	a piece of china-ware; flat canoe	nt
SAUGER	American pike	zo
SAUMUR	white wine	
SAUREL	the horse-mackerel	zo
SAURIA	reptile genus	zo
SAURUS	lizard-fish genus	zo
SAVAGE	barbaric; ferocious; brutal	
SAVANT	a scientist; professor	
SAVATE	French boxing	ga
SAVINE	medicinal shrub; red cedar	bt

SAVING	husbanding; excepting	
SAVORY	aromatic pot-herb	bt
SAVOUR	taste; flavour; odour	
SAVVEY	nous; commonsense	
SAW-CUT	groove, binder's sewing mark	pr
SAWDER	flattery	
SAW-FLY	plant-harmful insect	zo
SAW-NEB	sawbill	zo
SAWNEY	complete yarn breakage	tx
SAW-PIT	sawing location	
SAW-SET	tool for wrenching	to
SAWYER	plank-cutter	
SAXONY	flannel	tx
SAYING	saw; dictum; adage; proverb	
SAYNAY	a lamprey	zo
SBIRRO	Italian policeman	
S'BLOOD	an imprecation, exclamation	
SCABBY	rough; itchy; leprous	
SCAEAN	western (gate of Troy)	
SCAITH	harm; damage (Sc.)	
SCALAR	magnitude without direction	
SCALER	climber	
SCALER	instrument to register a count	to
SCALES	a balance; octaves	mu
SCALMA	a horse disease	vt
SCAMEL	bar-tailed godwit	zo
SCAMPI	prawns (It.)	ck, zo
SCANTY	meagre; niggardly; chary; see-through (clothing)	
SCAPHA	(helix of ear)	md
SCAPHO	sailing cargo ship (Greek)	nt
SCAPUS	shaft of column	
SCARAB	sacred sunbeetle; gem (Egypt)	rl
SCARCE	rare; infrequent; uncommon	
SCARED	affrightened; panic-stricken	
SCARPH	to scarf	cr
SCARRY	scarred; disfigured	
SCARUS	parrot fish	zo
SCATCH	a horse-bit	vt
SCATHE	injury; damage	
SCATHY	dangerous; mischievous (Sc.)	
SCATTY	showery; crazy	
SCAURY	gull (Shetlands)	zo
SCAZON	imperfect rhythm	
SCELIO	parasite insects	zo
SCENIC	dramatic; theatrical	
SCHANS	Zulu fort	
SCHEIK	sheik (Arabic)	
SCHELM	rascal (Boer)	
SCHEMA	diagrammatic representation; data base	cp
SCHEME	plan; plot; intrigue; devise	
SCHEMY	cunningly devised	
SCHENE	7½ miles (12 km) (Egyptian)	me
SCHISM	a split; discord; dissent	
SCHIST	slatey rock	mn
SCHIZO-	of split, separate, cleavage (Gr.)	cf, pc
SCHOOL	train; educate; academy	
SCHORL	tourmaline	mn

SCHUSS	unimpeded downhill ski run	ga
SCHUYT	ketch, sloop; (Dutch)	nt
SCIARA	gnats and midges	zo
SCIATH	Irish wicker shield	
SCIENT	knowing	
SCILLA	hyacinth	bt
SCLATE	slate (obs.)	
SCLAVE	a Slav; Slavonian	
SCLERA	hard coating	md
SCLERE	skeletal structure	zo
SCOBBY	chaffinch	zo
SCOGIE	a drudge (Sc.)	
SCOLEX	a worm	zo
SCOLIA	burrowing insects	zo
SCOLUS	thornlike process in larvae	zo
SCONCE	skull; bulwark	
SCONCE	to fine; wall candle with metal reflector	
-SCOPIA	viewing; scrutiny,	
-SCOPY	examination	md
SCOPIC	visual	
SCOPUS	genus of wading birds	zo
SCORCH	singe; char; parch; scar	
SCORED	registered; scratched	
SCORER	recorder	
SCORIA	dross; coarse pumice stone	mn
SCORSE	exchange (Sc.)	
SCORZA	variety of epidote	mn
SCOTCH	to cut; wedge	
SCOTER	a sea-duck	zo
SCOTIA	Scotland; a concave moulding	
SCOUSE	meat and vegetable broth	
SCOUTH	scope (Sc.)	
SCOUTS	boys' brigade; guides; talent spotters	
SCOVAN	tin lode (Cornish)	
SCOVED	smeared (dial.)	
SCOVEL	oven-mop	
SCRAMB	scrape together (dial.);	
SCRAMP	snatch	
SCRAPE	grate; abrade; rasp; difficulty	
SCRAWL	hasty writing (illegible)	
SCRAWM	to scratch (dial.)	
SCREAK	a screech; scream	
SCREAM	cry; yell; squall; shriek	
SCREED	tiresome harangue; a shred; wall-edging; jointless	
SCREEN	shroud; cloak; hide; sieve; scan; filter; (print); cinema; tv picture	tc
SCREES	stony debris	
SCREWS	divers' bends, caisson disease; fastening bolts, prison warders (sl.); propellers	nt, md
SCREWY	nefarious; underhand; exacting	
SCRIBE	writer; notary; scrivener	
SCRIKE	shriek (Spens.)	
SCRIME	to fence	ga
SCRIMP	to stint	
SCRINE	a shrine (Spens.)	

SCRIPT	handwriting; typescript; life-scenario; document; drama	**pc**
SCRIVE	scribe; engrave	
SCROBE	groove in mandible	**zo**
SCROLL	roll; list; register; flourish	
SCROOP	to grate; to crack	
SCRUFF	back of neck	**pl, zo**
SCRUNT	miser (Sc.)	
SCRUTO	theatrical trap	
SCRUZE	squeeze (Spens.)	
SCUFFY	shabby; seedy	
SCULPT	to sculpture; carve	
SCULSH	rubbish; lollypops	
SCUMMY	covered with scum	
SCURFF	bull-trout	**zo**
SCURFY	wasting disease; sores; (lack of Vit. C in diet)	
SCURVY	a race; scamper; show	
SCURRY	jumping	
SKURRY		
SCUTCH	to beat; to comb	
SCUTUM	Roman shield	**hd**
SCUTUM	middle notum sclerite in insects	
SCYLLA	six-headed monster; (Charybdis)	
SCYTHE	a reaping implement (death)	**ag, to**
S'DEATH	an imprecation	
SDEIGN	disdain (Spens.)	
SEA-APE	sea-otter	**zo**
SEA-BAR	tern	**zo**
SEA-BAT	flying fish	**zo**
SEA-BOY	sailor lad	**nt**
SEA-BUN	sea-urchin	**zo**
SEA-CAP	a sponge	**zo**
SEA-CAT	cat-fish	**zo**
SEA-COB	a gull	**zo**
SEA-COW	manatee; walrus	**zo**
SEA-DOG	common seal	**zo**
SEA-EAR	a mollusc; ormer shell	**zo**
SEA-EEL	conger	**zo**
SEA-EGG	sea-urchin	**zo**
SEA-FAN	a polyp	**zo**
SEA-FIR	another polyp	**zo**
SEA-FOX	thrasher shark	**zo**
SEA-GOD	Neptune	**rl**
SEA-HEN	guillemot	**zo**
SEA-HOG	porpoise	**zo**
SEALED	ratified; confirmed; shut	
SEALER	seal hunter; vessel	**nt**
SEAMAN	A.B.; tar; sailor	**nt**
SEA-MAT	polyzoa	**zo**
SEA-MAW	sea-mew	**zo**
SEAMED	united by sewing; lined	**tx**
SEAMER	seamster	
SEA-MEW	a gull	**zo**
SEA-MUD	ooze	
SEANCE	spiritualism session	
SEA-ORB	globe fish	**zo**
SEA-OWL	lump fish	**zo**
SEA-PAD	star-fish	**zo**
SEA-PEA	beach-pea	**bt**

SEA-PEN	quill zoophyte	**zo**
SEA-PIE	a seafowl	**zo**
SEA-PIG	the dugong	**zo**
SEA-RAT	herring-king; a fish	**zo**
SEARCE	to sift; a sieve (Sc.)	
SEARCH	scrutiny; seek; inquire; quest	
SEARCH	examine for specified conditions	**cp**
SEARED	cauterized; burnt; scorched	
SEA-ROD	a polyp	**zo**
SEASON	time; period; flavour	
SEATED	sited; established; accommodated	
SEA-WAY	steerage way	**nv**
SEBATE	a fatty compound	**ch**
SECALE	plant	**bt**
SECANT	(geometrical); cutting	**nv**
SECEDE	withdraw; segregate	
SECERN	secrete; discriminate	
SECESH	secessionist (USA)	
SECKEL	variety of pear	**bt**
SECOHM	electrical unit	**me**
SECOND	support; assist; inferior	**me**
SECOND	melodic interval; lower pitched part	**mu**
SECRET	covert; occult; privy; cryptic	
SECTOR	an area; a cutting; a zone	
SECTOR	part of recorded data block	**cp**
SECUND	unilateral	
SECURE	get; obtain; safe; firm	
SEDATE	staid; placid; serene; calm	
SEDENT	inactive; quiet; torpid	
SEDGED	flagged	**bt**
SEDILE	seat in chancel	**rl**
SEDUCE	decoy; tempt; entice; inveigle	
SEEDED	tournament-placed	
SEEDER	seed-drill	**to**
SEEING	observing; viewing; watching	
SEEKER	inquirer; seacher	
SEELDE	seldom (Spens.)	
SEELOS	series of three gates (slalom skiing)	
SEEMED	befitted; appeared	
SEEMER	pretentious person; pretender	
SEEMLY	proper; becoming; decorous	
SEEPED	oozed; percolated	
SEE-SAW	teeter-totter; unbalance; pastime	
SEE-SAW	sign reversing amplifier	**cp**
SEETHE	to boil; to soak	
SEGGAN	sedge (Sc.)	**bt**
SEGGAR	fire-clay pot; sagger	
SEGHOL	Hebrew vowel point	
SEICHE	change of water level (Fr.)	
SEINER	net-fisherman	**nt**
SEISED	possessed of	
SEISON	a parasite genus	**zo**
SEIZED	lashed; grasped; stuck fast	
SEIZER	grasper; snatcher; thief	
SEIZIN	possession	**lw**
SEISIN		**lw**
SEIZOR	bailiff	**lw**

SEJANT	sitting up	hd
SEJOIN	separate (obs.)	
SELDOM	rarely; hardly ever	
SELECT	pick; choose; prefer	
SELECT	courses of action after test	cp
SELENE	Greek Moon-goddess	rl
SELION	a ridge of land	
SELJUK	dynasty; art; empire (Turk.)	
SELLER	vendor; hawker; retailer	
SELVES	individualities	
SEMBLE	to dissemble (obs.)	
SEMELE	genus of bivalves	zo
SEMESE	half-eaten	
SEMITA	(sea-urchins)	zo
SEMITE	descendant of Shem	
SEMMIT	undershirt (Sc.)	
SEMPLE	simple (Sc.)	
SEMPRE	in the same style	mu
SENARY	six of	
SENATE	assembly; council	
SENDAL	thin linen	
SENDER	transmitter; despatcher; exchange control	cp
SENDER	signal transmission line	tc
SEND-UP	compliment; ridiculing	
SENEGA	snake-root; an antidote	bt
SENHOR	Portuguese senor	
SENILE	aged; doting; tottering; infirm	
SENIOR	elder; older; higher; superior	
SENNET	trumpet call (Shak.)	
SENNIT	braided cord; plaited straw	
SENORA	married lady (Sp.)	
SENSED	perceived, felt	
SENSEI	instructor (judo, karate)	ga
SENSOR	small-variation detection device	
SENSUM	sense datum	pc
SENTRY	sentinel; watchman; guardian	
SEPAWN	maize-meal	ck
SEPHEN	sting-ray	zo
SEPIUM	cuttle-bone	zo
SEPMAG	1-magnetic-soundtrack film	cn
SEPOPT	1-optical-soundtrack film	cn
SEPSIN	a ptomaine	md
SEPSIS	(blood poison); putrefaction	md
SEPTAL	partitional (Irish)	
SEPTAN	weekly	
SEPTET	seven part ensemble	mu
SEPTIC	rotten; putrid	md
SEPTON	(putrefaction)	
SEPTUM	a partition	bt
SEQUEL	consequence; upshot; result	
SEQUIN	a spangle; Venetian	nm
SERACS	postglacial ice pillars (Fr.)	
SERAIL	} seraglio; palace; seray;	
SARAY	} harem	
SERANG	Lascar boatswain	nt
SERAPE	zarafe; Mexican blanket	tx
SERAPH	six-winged angel	rl
SERDAB	secret chamber (Egypt)	
SEREIN	rain from a cloudless sky	mt

SERENA	damp evening air	mt
SERENE	calm; placid; tranquil; clear	
SERIAL	a periodical (instalments); identity number; in sequence	cp
SERIAN	Chinese; Seric	pr
SERICA	beetle genus	zo
SERIES	sequence; succession; order	
SERINE	acid from protein hydrolysis	ch
SERIPH	} (typesetting) (Sans Serif)	pr
SERIF	}	
SERMON	address; homily; discourse	
SEROON	package of drugs	me
SEROSA	chorium; connective-tissue membrane	pl
SEROUS	watery; thin	md
SERPET	basket (obs.)	
SERTAO	jungle wilderness (N.E. Brazil)	go
SERULA	red-breasted merganser	zo
SERVAL	small African leopard	zo
SERVED	ministered; acted; obeyed	
SERVER	salver; waiter; mass R.C.; beginner of volley (tennis) (squash) etc	rl
SESAME	plant having oily seeds	bt
SESBAN	a marsh plant	bt
SESELI	saxifrage	bt
SESTET	sextet; six part ensemble	mu
SESTON	tiny plankton organisms	oc, zo
SET-OFF	compensation; insulation	pr
SETOSE	} bristly	
SETOUS	}	
SET-OUT	display	
SETTEE	sofa; Mediterranean ship	nt
SETTER	sporting dog; tennis	ga, zo
SETTER	(type), (technician), (trend) (puzzle)	cp, pr, tv
SETTLE	wooden seat; colonize; pay	
SETULE	small bristle	bt
SEVERE	harsh; cruel; rigorous; plain	
SEVERY	part of vaulted ceiling	ar
SEVRES	porcelain (Fr.)	
SEWAGE	drainage; effluent; wastes	
SEWING	needlework	
SEXFID	six-cleft	bt
SEXISM	prejudice; sex discrimination	pc
SEXTAN	recurring every sixth day	
SEXTET	six part ensemble; team of 6 ice hockey players	mu, ga
SEXTIC	of the 6th degree	
SEXTON	gravedigger	rl
SEXUAL	of sex; sensual	
SHABBY	threadbare; paltry; beggarly	
SHADED	screened; obscured	
SHADOW	umbrage; dark; silhouette; eclipse; follow secretly	as
SHADUF	Nile water-raising device	
SHAGGY	rugged; rough; uneven	
SHAHPU	Tibetan wild sheep	zo
SHAIRL	Cashmere cloth	tx
SHAIRN	cow-dung (Sc.)	zo

SHAKAL	jackal	zo
SHAKEN	jarred; agitated; moved	
SHAKER	religious sect	rl
SHAKES	involuntary trembling; (deep sea divers) hand-split shingles	md
SHALLI	Indian cotton stuff	tx
SHALOT	(garlic); shallot	bt
SHAMAH	shama; Indian song-bird	zo
SHAMAL	Mesopotamian summer wind	mt
SHAMAN	animist; wizard (Siberia)	
SHAMED	abashed; disgraced	
SHAMMY	shamoy; chamois-leather	le
SHANNY	blenny fish	zo
SHANTY	hut; hovel; shack; sea chant	
SHAPED	moulded; formed; regulated	
SHAPER	metal-planing machine	to
SHARED	partook; divided; held in common; with joint access	
SHARER	participator	
SHARPY	oysterman's boat	nt
SHAVED	swindled; smooth-faced	
SHAVEN	without hair; shorn; bald	
SHAVER	a sharp dealer; a barber	
SHAVIE	a trick; a prank (Sc.)	
SHAYAK	coarse cloth (Tripoli)	tx
SHEAFY	(sheaves)	
SHEARS	cutters, scissors, (wool-)	to
SHEATH	scabbard; condom	md
SHEAVE	pulley-wheel	
SHEENY	bright; showy; a Jew	
SHEERS } SHEERLEGS }	a hoisting appliance; dipod portable crane	nt
SHEETS	sails; broad cloth; bedding (swaddling); paper	nt, pp, tx
SHEIKH	Arab chief; sheik	
SHEKEL	Jewish half-crown	me, nm
SHELFY	shelvy; shallow	
SHELLY	abounding with shells	
SHELLY	of shell-shake timber	fr
SHELTA	beggars' cant	
SHELTY	Shetland pony	zo
SHELVE	put aside; to incline	
SHELVY	sloping shallow	
SHE-OAK	Australian shrub	bt
SHEPPY	sheep-cote (-pen) (Aust.)	
SHERIF	shereef; Arab title	
SHERRY	a wine from (Jerez) (Sp.)	ck
SHEUCH } SHEUGH }	ditch; drain; trench; furrow (Sc.)	
SHEWEL	scarecrow	
SHICER	welsher (Australia)	
SHIELD	shelter; cover; screen; guard	
SHIFTY	tricky; resourceful; untrustworthy (eyes)	
SHIING	skiing; a winter sport	
SHIISM	Moslem schism (sect)	rl
SHIITE	believer in Shiism	
SHIKAR	big game hunting (Ind.)	
SHIMMY	chemise; a dance	

SHINDY	trouble; quarrel; spree; brawl	
SHINER	£1; a boot-black	nm
SHINNY } SHINTY } SHINDY }	bandy ball; West Highland hockey; turmoil; kicking sport	ga
SHINTO	Japanese ancestor worship	
SHIPOV	small sturgeon	zo
SHIPPO	Japanese enamel	
SHIPPY	ship-shape; in order; tidy	nt
SHIRAZ	a Persian drink	
SHIRES	the Shires; midland counties	
SHIRTY	indignant; wroth; angry	
SHIVER	tremble; quiver; slate	mn
SHOALY	shallow; shelfy; seabottom	nv
SHODDY	coarse cloth	tx
SHODER	goldbeater's packet	
SHOFAR	ram's horn trumpet (Heb.)	mu
SHOGUN	Japanese C. in C.	
SHONKY	shocking; twisting; dishonest	
SHOOED	drove away	
SHOPPY	commercial	
SHORAN	short-range navigation	nv, rd
SHORED	propped; buttressed; braced	bd
SHORER	a support	nt, bd
SHORTS	bran; pants	
SHOUGH	shaggy dog	zo
SHOULD	conditional auxil. verb	
SHOVED	obtruded; pushed; jostled	
SHOVEL	clergyman's hat; spade; upturned tip of ski	to
SHOVER	pusher	
SHOWER	distribute liberally; rain; douche	mt
SHRANK	contracted; recoiled	
SHREWD	astute; cunning; wise; canny	
SHRIEK	cry; scream; yell; screech	
SHRIFT	confession; absolution	rl
SHRIKE	butcher-bird	zo
SHRILL	high; sharp; piping (note)	mu
SHRIMP	a pink dwarf	zo
SHRINE	tomb; reliquary	rl
SHRINK	shrivel; wrinkle	
SHRITE	missel thrush; bird	zo
SHRIVE	to absolve; pardon	rl
SHROFF	Indian banker	
SHROUD	winding sheet	nt
SHROVE	pardoned; (Tuesday)	rl
SHRUFF	dross	tx
SHRUNK	contracted	
SHUCKS!	nonsense!	
SHUFTI	look! (Arab.)	
SHUNIS	herb; Scotch lovage	bt
SHYING	throwing; starting	
SIALIC	derivative of neuraminic acid	bc, ch
SICCAN	such (Sc.)	
SICCAR	sicker; sure (Sc.); certain	
SICKEN	(disgust); languish; become ill	
SICKLE	reaping hook	ag, to
SICKLY	faint; unhealthy; morbid	

SICSAC	crocodile bird	zo	**SINAIC**	(Mount Sinai)	
SICYOS	gourds	bt	**SIN-BIN**	bench for ice hockey offenders	**ga**
SIDDHA	} Buddhist who has attained		**SINDON**	a wrapper; winding sheet	
SIDDHI	} perfection	**rl**	**SINEWY**	strong; vigorous; muscular	
SIDDOW	soft; pulpy (dial.)		**SINFUL**	wrong; iniquitous; depraved	
SIDING	train storage track	**rw**	**SINGED**	scorched; slightly burnt	
SIDLED	moved furtively; sideways		**SINGER**	warbler; songster	**mu**
SIEMEN	unit of electrical conductance	**me**	**SINGLE**	choose; select; alone; celibate;	
SIENNA	yellow paint	**pt**		unit; score	**cp**
SIERRA	mountain range (Sp.)	**go**	**SINGLY**	uniquely; individually	
SIESTA	nap; forty winks; doze		**SINIAN**	Chinese rock formation	**mn**
SIFAKA	a lemur	**zo**	**SINISM**	Chinese custom	
SIFFLE	to whistle (Fr.)		**SINKER**	a plummet; weight for nets	
SIFTED	winnowed; bolted; separated	**ag**		(fishing)	
SIFTER	scrutinizer; separatist		**SINNED**	erred; transgressed	
SIGHED	breathed heavily, sadly		**SINNER**	transgressor	
SIGHER	repiner		**SINNET**	sennet; braided cordage	**nt**
SIGLUM	seal; mark; initials	**lw**	**SINTER**	a siliceous deposit	**mn**
SIGNAL	eminent; a sign; lamp; flag;		**SINTOC**	cinnamon bark	**bt**
	semaphore; traffic	**ae, nt, rw**	**SIOUAN**	Sioux; American Indian tribe	
SIGNAL	call (start or end) code	**tc**	**SIPAHI**	sepoy; colonial soldier	
SIGNED	signified; endorsed; agreed;		**SIPHON**	syphon; atmospheric pressure	
	autographed			pump (soda)	**ck, ce**
SIGNER	one who subscribes		**SIPING**	percolating; oozing; leaking	
SIGNET	a seal; ring with crest (Sc.)	**lw**	**SIPPED**	tasted	
SIGNOR	Mr. in Italian		**SIPPER**	drinker of small draughts	
SILAGE	ensilage; stored fodder		**SIPPET**	small sop	
SILANE	silicon hydride	**ch**	**SIPPLE**	to sup in sips	
SILENE	bladder-campion	**bt**	**SIRCAR**	sirkar; Hindu clerk	
SILENT	mute; dumb; taciturn		**SIRDAR**	Egyptian commander	
SILICA	flint; quartz; etc.	**mn**	**SIRENE**	a pitchpipe	**mu**
SILKED	repaired with silk backings (bks.)		**SIRING**	begetting	
SILKEN	delicate; tender	**tx**	**SIRIUS**	the Dog Star	**as**
SILLER	silver; money (Sc.)		**SIRRAH**	sir; sirree	
SILLON	a mound in a moat		**SIRUPY**	like syrup; syrupy	**ck**
SILPHA	carrion beetles	**zo**	**SISKIN**	bird; a finch	**zo**
SILTED	(waterway) choked with debris	**nv**	**SISSOO**	Indian timber-tree	**bt**
SILURE	cat-fish	**zo**	**SISTED**	summoned (Sc.)	**lw**
SILVAN	} woody; rustic	**fr**	**SISTER**	nun; nurse; sibling	
SYLVAN	}		**SITTER**	painter's patient model	
SILVER	money; bright	**nm**	**SITULA**	bucket-shaped vessel liturgical	**rl**
SIMBIL	African stork	**zo**	**SIWASH**	N. American Indian; Alaskan dog	
SIMIAL	} ape-like; monkey-like	**zo**			**zo**
SIMIAN	}		**SIZING**	size; weak glue; grading	
SIMILE	parable; comparison		**SIZZLE**	fry (frypan)	**ck**
SIMKIN	champagne (Ind.)		**SKATER**	one who skates (ice) (rollers)	
SIMMER	a gentle boil; stew	**ck**	**SKATHE**	scathe; injury; harm; damage	
SIMNEL	sweet fruit cake	**ck**	**SKEARY**	scary; scared	
SIMONY	buying preferment	**rl**	**SKEELY**	skilful (Sc.)	
SIMOOM	simoon	**mt**	**SKELIC**	pertaining to skeleton	**pl**
SIMOON	summer whirlwind Sahara (Arab.)		**SKELLY**	to squint (Sc.)	
		mt	**SKERRY**	rocky island	**go**
SIMORG	} fabulous Persian bird	**zo**	**SKETCH**	limn; portray; outline; draught	
SUMURG	}		**SKEWER**	to impale	
SIMOUS	snub-nosed; concave		**SKIING**	racing, jumping, on snow surfaces	
SIMPAI	Sumatra monkey	**zo**		on skis	
SIMPER	silly affected smile		**SKILLY**	thin gruel; (porridge)	**ck**
SIMPLE	naive; artless; frank; ingenuous		**SKILTS**	trews (Sc.)	
SIMPLY	merely; only; barely; solely		**SKIMPY**	scanty; meagre	
SIMSON	groundsel	**bt**	**SKINNY**	emaciated; lean; lank	

SKITTY	water-rail	zo
SKIVED	sliced; split	
SKIVER	split sheep-skin	
SKIVIE	askew (Sc.)	
SKLENT	to slant; to split (Sc.)	
SKRYER	a diviner	
SKURRY	scurry (Sc.); breeze; puff	mt
SKYISH	ethereal	
SLABBY	viscous; thick; sloppy	
SLACKS	women's trousers	
SLAGGY	(slag); scoriaceous	
SLAKED	quenched	
SLALOM	timed ski-race through 'gates' on snow	
SLANGY	colloquial	
SLAP-UP	posh; lavish	
SLASHY	muddy (Sc.)	
SLATCH	fair weather	nt
SLATED	abused; upbraided; chided	
SLATER	a wood louse	zo
SLAVED	drudged	
SLAVER	dribble; slave ship	nt
SLAVEY	serving wench; skivvy; kitchen maid	
SLAVIC	Slavonic	
SLAYER	murderer; killer	·
SLEAVE	unwrought silk; floss	tx
SLEAZY	decrepit; sordid; shabby; disreputable; worn out	
SLEDGE	heavy hammer; sled	to
SLEEKY	of smooth appearance	
SLEEPY	soporous; drowsy; somnolent	
SLEETY	wet and cold; wet snowfall	mt
SLEEVE	drogue; arm cover	
SLEEVE	metal pipe (joint); wind bag	bd, ce, ae
SLEIGH	sled; sledge; horse-drawn snow vehicle	
SLEUTH	detective; bloodhound	zo
SLEWED	swung askew; tipsy	
SLICED	(golf); chopped; pared	
SLICER	cutter	
SLICKS	(oil spill at sea); tread-less tyres (motor-racing)	
SLIDER	a moveable part	
SLIDER	hard curving throw (baseball)	
SLIEST	slyest; most artful; most crafty	
SLIGHT	scorn; ignore; disdain	
SLIMSY	flimsy; frail	
SLINKY	lean; furtive	
SLIP-ON	easily put on (clothing); condom	md
SLIPPY	nimble; unstable	
SLIP-UP	error; mistake	
SLITHY	lithe and slimy	
SLIVER	to cut; a splinter	
SLIVER	continuous fibre strand	tx
SLOGAN	war-cry (Sc.); curt phrase	
SLOKEN	quench; slocken	
SLOPED	decamped; at an angle	

SLOPPY	maudlin; slipshod	
SLOSHY	} muddy; boggy; watery; miry	
SLUSHY		
SLOUCH	a clown; depress; hang down	
SLOUGH	deep mud; morass; swamp	go
SLOUGH	a cast skin (snake's)	
SLOVAK	Slav of Slovakia	
SLOVEN	slattern; slut	
SLOVEN	splintered timber stump	fr
SLOWER	not so fast	
SLOWLY	gradually; tardily; sluggishly	
SLUDGE	mire; wet refuse	
SLUDGY	muddy	
SLUGGA	subterranean cavity	gl
SLUICE	floodgate; wash	
SLUICY	streaming	
SLUING	turning round	
SLUMPY	marshy	
SLURRY	to smear; to dirty; cement water mix; (trench)	ce
SLURVE	fast, curved throw (baseball)	ga
SLUSHY	swampy; muddy; miry	
SLUTCH	sediment; muck; mire	gl
SLYEST	sliest; most artful	
SMALLS	exams; underwear	
SMALTO	glass, enamel, mosiac fragment	
SMARMY	oily; ingratiating	
SMARTY	over-bright youth	
SMATCH	taste; tincture (Shak.)	
SMEARY	bedaubed; adhesive; glutinous	
SMEATH	aquatic bird; smew	zo
SMEECH	} smell of burning (dial.)	
SMITCH		
SMELLY	odoriferous	
SMIDDY	a smithy (Sc.); forget	
SMIGHT	smite (Spens.)	
SMILAX	sarsaparilla plant	bt, ck
SMILED	grinned; simpered	
SMILET	a little smile	
SMIRCH	depreciate; foul	
SMIRKY	smart; smiling	
SMITER	slogger; hitter	ga
SMITHY	} blacksmith's workshop, forge	
SMIDDY	(dial.)	
SMOKED	ridiculed; fumed; reeked	
SMOKER	a tobacco addict	
SMOKES	dry season mists, coast of Guinea	mt
SMOOTH	level; flatten; suave; bland	
SMOUCH	smack; to kiss	
SMOUSE	pedlar (S. Africa)	
SMUDGE	stain; blot; margin decoration (signwriting)	
SMUDGY	stained; smeary	
SMUGLY	primly; neatly; complacently	
SMURRY	misty (Sc.)	
SMUTCH	to blacken	
SMUTTY	sooty; lewd; dirty	
SNABBY	chaffinch (Sc.)	zo
SNACOT	pipe-fish	zo

SNAGGY	full of snags	
SNAKED	coiled; crept	nt
SNAPED	bevelled	
SNAPPY	abrupt; noticeable style	
SNARED	netted; caught	
SNARER	trapper; hunter; poacher	
SNATCH	grab; seize; grasp; fragment; (weight-lifting); (song)	mu
SNATHE	scythe-handle	to
SNEEZE	exhale violently	
SNIFFY	disdainful; proud	
SNIFTY	having a luscious smell	
SNIPER	concealed marksman; gunman	
SNIPPY	fragmentary; stingy	
SNITCH	nose	
SNIVEL	snuffle; blubber; whine	
SNOBBY	snobbish; bogus superiority	
SNOOTY	conceited snob	
SNOOZE	a nap; doze; siesta; drowse	
SNOTTY	midshipman	nt
SNOUTY	protuberant	
SNUBBY	somewhat snub; rather blunt	
SNUDGE	sneak; miser	
SNUFFY	irritable; peevish	
SNUGLY	cosily; comfortably	
SOAKED	sodden; drenched; steeped	
SOAKER	confirmed toper	
SOAKER	watertightness plug in roof	pb
SOAPED	lathered; shampooed	
SOARED	aspired; towered; ascended	
SOBBED	wept; cried	
SOBEIT	if it be so	lw
SOBOLE	budding/rooting stem	bt
SOCAGE	tenure of land by service	lw
SOCCER	association football	ga
SOCIAL	genial; civic; civil; festive	
SOCKED	biffed; whanged; coshed	
SOCKET	a cavity; (for a plug); pipe joint	cp, el, pb
SOCMAN	tenant by socage	lw
SODAIC	containing soda	
SODDED	turfed; grassed	bt
SODDEN	soaked; wet; drenched	
SODION	sodium ion	ch
SODIUM	metallic element	ch
SODOKU	rat-bite fever	md
SODOMY	anal intercourse (bestiality)	
SO-EVER	indefinite suffix	
SOFFET	small sofa	
SOFFIT	ceiling; underside of architectural element	ar
SOFISM	} form of Moslem belief	rl
SUFISM		
SOFTEN	enervate; relent; alleviate	
SOFTER	tenderer; milder	
SOFTLY	pliably; quietly; dulcetly	
SOGGED	saturated; sopped	
SOIGNE	well-decorated; carefully dressed	
SOILED	tarnished; smirched	
SOIREE	evening party (Fr.) (recital)	

SOLACE	consolation; cheer; relief	
SOLAND	the gannet	zo
SOLANO	} rainwind (Spain)	mt
LEVANTER		
SOLDER	fusible metallic cement	
SOLEIL	worsted dress fabric	tx
SOLELY	singly; alone; solitarily	
SOLEMN	august; grave; staid; serious	
SOLERA	cask; blending of sherry vintages	
SOLEUS	a leg muscle	pl
SOLING	large stones for road bed (pitching)	ce
SOLION	audio signal detector	el
SOLITO	in the usual manner	mu
SOLIVE	joist; cross-timber	ar
SOLLAR	} upper gallery; garret	
SOLLER		
SO-LONG	good-bye	
SOLUTE	loose; cheerful	
SOLVED	removed; resolved	
SOLVER	elucidator; interpreter; decoder	
SOMALI	native (Somalia)	
SOMALO	Somali currency	nm
SOMBRE	dismal; gloomy; lugubrious	
SOMITE	body segment	zo
SOMNUS	sleep personified	
SONANT	sounding; resonant	
SONATA	instrumental piece	mu
SONCIE	buxom; lucky	
SONERI	cloth of gold (Ind.)	tx
SONICS	study of mechanical vibrations	eg
SONNET	a poem of 14 lines	
SONORE	sonorously	mu
SONSIE	good natured (Sc.)	
SONTAG	knitted cap	
SOODRA	Hindu caste	
SOOJEE	} specially fine flour (Ind.)	ck
SOUJEE		
SUJEE		
SOONER	earlier; more readily	
SOORMA	an antimony cosmetic	
SOOSOO	river dolphin	zo
SOOTHE	calm; pacific; lull; palliate	
SOPHIC	teaching wisdom; wise	
SOPITE	to quash	
SOPPED	very wet; sogged	
SOPPER	wet feeder	
SORAGE	phase of hawk's life	zo
SORBET	water-ice; sherbet (Turk.)	ck
SORBIC	} vitamin C, acid	bt, ck
SORBIN		
SORBIN	mountain ash	bt
SORDES	sordor; dregs; filth	
SORDET	a mute for an instrument	mu
SORDID	base; vile; ignoble; foul	
SORELY	grievously; deeply; sadly	
SOREST	most grievous	
SORNER	gate-crasher; uninvited guest	
SOROSE	clustered	bt
SORREL	colour; buck	bt, zo

SORROW	woe; distress; affliction	
SORTED	grouped; suited	
SORTER	classifier; arranger; punched card machine	cp
SORTIE	sally; raid	
SOSSLE	dabble	
SOTHIC	dog-star	as
SOTNIA	Cossack troop	
SOTTED	besotted	
SOUARI	butter-nut tree of Guyana	bt
SOUCAR	Hindu banker/usurer	
SOUGHT	quested; hunted; tried	
SOULED	full of feeling	
SOUPER	(a convert) (drinker)	
SOUPLE	flail arm	
SOUPLE	sericin-content yarn/fabric	tx
SOURCE	fount; cause; spring; origin	
SOURCE	compiled object program language	cp
SOURER	more acid	
SOURLY	tartly; bitterly	
SOUSED	} pickled; rushed; struck	
SOWSED		
SOUTAR	} a cobbler; shoemaker	
SOUTER		
SOWTER		
SOVIET	Russian council committee	
SOVRAN	sovereign; monarch (obs.)	
SOWANS	} flummery from oat husks	ck
SOWENS		
SOW-BUG	a millipede	zo
SOWING	disseminating; propagating	
SOZZLE	sossle; muddle	
SOZZLY	sloppy	
SPACED	extended	
SPACER	distance piece	
SPADED	dug	
SPADER	clay spade	to
SPADIX	a spike; kind of inforescence	bt
SPAHEE	Algerian cavalryman	
SPALAX	mole-rats	zo
SPANDY	wholly; completely	
SPARED	saved; refrained; withheld	
SPARER	economiser	
SPARES	spare parts; duplicates	
SPARGE	to sprinkle	
SPARKE	battle-axe (Spens.)	
SPARKS	radio operator	
SPARRE	bolt; bar (Spens.)	
SPARRY	(spar); (crystalline)	mn
SPARSE	scanty; meagre; thin	
SPARTH	halberd; mace	
SPARVE	hedge-sparrow	zo
SPATHE	flower sheath	bt
SPAVIN	a swollen joint	vt, md
SPECIE	bullion; coin; cash	nm
SPECKY	speckled	
SPEECH	harangue; oration; palaver	
SPEEDY	prompt; fast; rapid; hasty	

SPEISE	cobalt/lead smelting product	mt
SPEISS	metallic dross	mn
SPELIN	form of Esperanto	
SPENCE	buttery; pantry	
SPETCH	strip of hide	le
SPEWED	spat; vomited	
SPHENE	titanite	mn
SPHERE	globe; orb; ball; domain	
SPHERY	spherical; round	
SPHINX	the Guinea baboon (man-lion)	zo
SPICAL	spiky	bt
SPICED	seasoned	ck
SPICER	spice-merchant	
SPIDER	a weaver of webs; Ariadne; cue support (billiards, snooker)	zo
SPIFFY	spruce; smart (slang)	
SPIGHT	spite (Spens.)	
SPIGOT	spile; peg for a cask	
SPIKED	pointed; put out of action	
SPIKES	outside nails; shoe grips for track events; grain	bt
SPILTH	anything spilt	
SPILUS	birth-mark; a naevus	md
SPINAL	(back-bone)	md
SPINED	thorny	
SPINEL	(corundum)	mn
SPINET	form of harpsichord	mu
SPINNY	a small copse	
SPIRAL	cork-screw; winding (Am. football) (skating) (parachuting)	
SPIRED	having a spire; sprouted	ar
SPIRIC	like an anchor-ring	nt
SPIRIT	zeal; soul; essence; spook	
SPITAL	hospital (obs.)	
SPITED	thwarted; vexed	
SPLASH	spatter; splurge; a sensation	
SPLEEN	anger; melancholy	md
SPLICE	to marry; a junction	
SPLINE	flexible ruler	
SPLINT	splent; support beside broken bone	md
SPLITS	with legs at angle of 180° (gymn.)	
SPLORE	a jollification (Sc.)	
SPOFFY	officious	
SPOKEN	told; articulated	
SPONGE	cadge; cake; marine creature	ck, zo
SPONGY	absorbent	
SPOOKY	eerie; ghostly	
SPOONY	weak-minded; amorous	
SPOSHY	slushy	
SPOT-ON	accurately placed	
SPOTTY	speckled	
SPOUSE	husband or wife	
SPRACK	sprightly; alert	
SPRAID	chapped with cold	
SPRAIN	strain; wrench	
SPRANG	jumped; leapt; bounded; tea	
SPRAWL	lounge; spread; straggle	

SPREAD	open; broadcast; scatter; savoury paste; banquet; extend; (show-jumping) **ck, ga, ro**	
SPRENT	sprinkled	
SPRING	well; fount; rise; emanate	
SPRINT	sprent; running race (spurt) (extra speed) **ga**	
SPRITE	elf; fay; pixy; fairy; hobgoblin	
SPRONG	sprung (Spens.)	
SPROUT	bud; germinate; shoot; spire	
SPRUCE	fir-tree; neat; trim; finical; furniture from the Baltic (Old English) **bt**	
SPRUIT	water-course (S. Africa)	
SPRUNG	tipsy; bent	
SPRUNT	leap; sprout	
SPRYER	more vigorous	
SPUDDY	chubby; podgy	
SPULYE	to spoil (Sc.)	
SPUNGE	sponge	
SPUNKY	mettlesome; spirited	
SPURGE	a plant **bt**	
SPURNE	to spur (Spens.)	
SPURRY	pink weed **bt**	
SPYING	spyism; coding; espionage; (agent)	
SQUAIL	a disc or counter	
SQUALL	blast; gust; yell; squeal	
SQUAMA	squame bract; scale **bt, zo**	
SQUARE	fair; just; bribe; adjust; straight; (rowing)	
SQUASH	a gourd; a game; crush **bt**	
SQUAWK	harsh utterance of protest	
SQUEAK	small creaking sound	
SQUEAL	to inform	
SQUILL	hyacinth; shrimp **bt, zo**	
SQUINT	a strabismus; glance **md**	
SQUIRE	escort; gallant	
SQUIRM	writhe; twist; wriggle	
SQUIRT	syringe; spout; eject	
STABLE	durable; fixed; constant; horse-house	
STABLY	firmly; steadfastly; securely	
STACTE	myrrh **bt**	
STADDA	comb-cutting saw **to**	
STADIA	a range-finder	
STAGED	performed; produced (dramatics)	
STAGER	old hand (theatre)	
STAGEY	melodramatic	
STAITH	coaling stage; staithe	
STAKED	(a claim); wagered	
STALAG	prisoners-of-war camp (Ger.)	
STALER	less fresh; older	
STAMEN	stamina; pollen container of flower **bt**	
STAMIN	harsh woollen stuff **tx**	
STANCE	position; attitude; station; (sport) (body)	
STANCH	staunch; firm; stop the flow	
STANZA	verse of poem	

STAPES	ear-bones **md**	
STAPLE	essentials; basic materials; needs; requirements	
STARCH	for stiffening clothes, etc. **tx**	
STARCH	feature of green plants; (stored sugar)	
STARED	gazed; glared; gaped	
STAREE	one who is stared at	
STARER	beholder	
STARRY	stellated (eyed)	
STARVE	famish; lack; deprive	
STASIS	static; stable; unchanging state **md**	
STATED	settled; regular; asserted	
STATER	ancient Greek gold coin **nm**	
STATHE	landing stage	
STATIC	motionless; in equilibrium; immobile	
STATIC	dump; rewriting at end of run **cp**	
STATOR	cf. rotor; circuit holder	
STATUA	an image (obs.)	
STATUE	image; figurine	
STATUS	rank; standing; position	
STATUS	situation warning of paper shortage **cp**	
STAVED	burst; delayed	
STAVES	(staff); rods; sticks	
STAXIS	haemorrhage; bleeding **md**	
STAYER	one with endurance; pacing rider	
STAY-IN	sit-in demonstration	
STAYNE	deface; stain (Spens.)	
STAYRE	a stair (Spens.)	
STEADY	equable; regular; uniform	
STEAMY	vaporous; humid; overshoot (golf)	
STEARE	a steer; an ox (Spens.) **zo**	
STEBOY!	go seek (dog talk)	
STEEDY	steady (Spens.)	
STEELY	hard; firm; obdurate	
STEELY	of glassy barley grains **br**	
STEEPY	precipitous	
STEEVE	to stow; pack closely	
STEGMA	small silica-filled cell **bt**	
STEMMA	pedigree; family tree	
STENCH	fetid; odour; effluent	
STEP-IN	take control; seize power	
STEPPE	Russian plain **go**	
STEREO	stereotype	
STEREO-	of three dimensions (Gr.) **cf**	
STERIC-	(atomic arrangement) **ch**	
STEROL	solid alcohol **ch**	
STERVE	starve (Spens.)	
STESSA	(It.) the same **mu**	
STEVEN	a clamour (Spens.)	
STEWED	simmered; seethed **ck**	
STHENE	unit of force	
STIBIC	(antimony) **ch**	
STICKS	to raise above shoulders; foul (hockey) (lacrosse) **ga**	
STICKY	gummy; adhesive; viscid	
STIDDY	a forge; smiddy; smithy	

STIFLE	suffocate; choke; smother	
STIGMA	} brand; mark; tarnish; a dot;	
STIGME	} disgrace	
STIGMA	eye spot of algae; spiracle of insect	**bt, zo**
STILAR	(sundial stile)	
STILLY	clam; tranquil; silent	
STILTY	stilted; high-hat	
STIMIE	stimy (golf) (balls in line)	**ga**
STINGO	strong ale	
STINGY	near; close; mean; parsimonious	
STINTY	stinted; limited	
STIPEL	stipule	**bt**
STIPES	stalk; stipe; stem	**bt**
STIRPS	progenitor; ancestor	
STITCH	sew; a twinge	
STITHY	anvil; forge	
STIVER	Dutch halfpenny coin	**nm**
STOCKY	sturdy; thick-set; robust	
STODGE	to cram	
STODGY	heavy; indigestible; starchy	**ck**
STOKED	fuelled	
STOKER	furnace operator (steamship, locomotive etc)	**nt, rw**
STOKES	kinematic viscosity symbol	**ps, me**
STOLEN	filched; purloined; taken	
STOLID	obtuse; phlegmatic	
STOLON	a runner	**bt**
STONED	lapidated (killed); drugged; drunk	
STONER	wall builder	
STOOGE	a butt; foil; foolish helper	**ro, tv**
STOORY	dusty	
STORAX	resinous balsam	**bt**
STORED	garnered; treasured	
STORER	hoarder; stocker	
STORES	an emporium; warehouse	
STOREY	(building); a floor	
STORGE	natural affection (Greek)	
STORMY	wild; rough; tempestuous	
STOUND	moment; mishap (Spens.)	
STOVED	dried; baked	**ck**
STOVER	fodder for cattle	
STOWED	packed; placed	
STOWER	stevedore; packer	
STRAFE	punish (Ger.); attack fiercely	
STRAIK	} a stroke (Sc.); tyre of wheel	
STRAKE	}	
STRAIN	exert; race; filter	**mu**
S-TRAIN	suburban train (Dan., Germ., etc.)	**rw**
STRAIT	narrows; distress; dilemma	**go**
STRAKE	(wheel); flanging	**nt**
STRAND	shore; beach; thread; fibre	
STRASS	flint glass	
STRATA	layers; beds	
STRATH	broad river valley (Sc.)	**go**
STRAWY	straw-like	
STREAK	stripe; line; run naked	
STREAM	flow; pour; brook; burn	
STREAM	data route from resource to controller	**cp**
STREET	roadway; avenue	
STRENE	race; strain (obs.)	
STRESS	accent; force; urgency; tension	
STREWN	strewed; scattered	
STRIAE	stripes; streaks	
STRICH	see strick (obs.)	
STRICK	screech-owl; flax	**zo**
STRIDE	stalk; step; gait	
STRIFE	discord; conflict; quarrel	
STRIGA	bristle; stripe	**bt**
STRIKE	buffet; clash; lock-out	
STRIKE	to hammer; work stoppage; hit a ball (golf); effect a blow; dismantle (camp); (drum)	**mu**
STRING	cord; twine; series	
STRIPE	band; line; stroke	
STRIPY	streaky	
STRIVE	vie; compete; attempt	
STROAM	to stroll; to roam (dial.)	
STROBE	waveform enlargement	**el**
STRODE	straddled; bestrode	
STROKE	blow; knock; caress; seizure; apoplexy; oarsman (stern seat); action of strike (golf); clock chime	
STROLL	ramble; rove; stray	
STROMA	tissue	**md**
STROMB	a gasteropod	**zo**
STROND	strand; beach (Shak.)	
STRONG	puissant; bold; lusty	
STROOK	struck (obs.)	
STROUP	spout; nozzle (Sc.)	
STROUT	strunt; to strut (obs.)	
STROVE	vied; toiled; tried; attempted	
STRUCK	smote; hit; collided; revolted	
STRUMA	goitre; scrofula	**md**
STRUNG	threaded; filed	
STUBBY	stocky; blunt; truncated	
STUCCO	plaster facing	**ar**
STUDIO	atelier; broadcasting chamber	
STUFFY	close; fusty; musty; angry	
STUGGY	thick-set; stumpy (dial.)	
STUMER	worthless cheque	
STUMPS	(cricket) wickets	**ga**
STUMPY	stubby; short and thick	
STUPID	witless; dull; idiotic; asinine	
STUPOR	torpor; coma; lethargy	
STURDY	robust; stalwart; vigorous	
STYING	penning	
STYLAR	pillar-like; pointed	
STYLED	designated; fashioned; described (character)	
STYLET	small pointed bristle	**bt**
STYLET	} dagger; poniard; high heel	
STILETTO	}	**md**
STYLUS	pen; style; needle (discs); sharp; light pen (torch)	**cp, tv**
STYMIE	(golf); stimy; balls in line	**ga**

STYRAX	gum plants; storax	**bt**
STYTHE	after-damp	
SUABLE	liable to be sued	**lw**
SUBDUE	quell; overpower; tame	
SUBFEU	(subinfeudation) (Sc.) tenancy	**lw**
SUBITO	quickly	**mu**
SUBLET	underlet	**lw**
SUBMIT	yield; capitulate; acquiesce	
SUBORN	to bribe; commit perjury	
SUBSET	subscriber's telephone apparatus;	
	part of larger grouping;	
	extension device for long	
	distance transmission boosting	
		ma, tc
SUBSET	part of maths 'set'	**ma**
SUBTIL	subtle; crafty	
SUBTLE	subtile; sly; crafty; clever	
SUBTLY	slyly; artfully; astutely	
SUBULA	sharp-pointed organ prolongation	
SUBURB	outskirt; neighbourhood	
SUBWAY	underground passage; metro	
SUCCIN	amber	
SUCCUS	juice; fruit sap fluid; electricity,	
	petrol (sl)	**bt, ck, me**
SUCKED	absorbed; imbibed	
SUCKEN	mill district (Sc.)	
SUCKER	a fish; a shoot; suction pad	**zo, bt**
SUCKER	gullible person	
SUCKET	sweetmeat	**ck**
SUCKLE	to wet-nurse	
SUDARY	a sweat-cloth	
SUDDEN	abrupt; quick; rapid; fleet	
SUDDER	chief; supreme (Ind.)	
SUEING	prosecuting; entreating	
SUFFER	brook; endure; allow; undergo	
SUFFIX	an affix	
SUFISM	Moslem doctrine	**rl**
SUGARY	sweet; honeyed; dulcet	
SUIDAE	pigs, hogs; etc.	**zo**
SUITED	contented; dressed	
SUITOR	wooer; admirer; litigant	
SUIVEZ	follow the soloist	**mu**
SUKAMA	native of Tanzania	
SULCUS	furrow; groove	
SULLEN	morose; sulky	
SULTAN	a fowl; a Moslem ruler, emperor	
		zo
SULTRY	stuffy; oppressive; stifling	
SUMACH	sumak; plant used in tanning	**bt**
SUMMED	counted; added	
SUMMER	season of year	
SUMMIT	top; acme; zenith; vertex	
SUMMON	bid; cite; invoke; prosecute	
SUMPIT	poisoned dart (Borneo)	
SUNBOW	rainbow	
SUNDAE	ice-cream with fruit and syrup	**ck**
SUNDAY	Christian holy day	
SUNDER	sleave; sever; disrupt; part	
SUN-DEW	a bog plant	**bt**
SUN-DOG	a parhelion; mock sun	**as**

SUNDRY	several; various; manifold	
SUN-GOD	Phoebus; Apollo; Re or Ra	**rl**
SUN-HAT	solar topee (panama)	
SUNKEN	submerged; engulfed	
SUNKET	an idler; food (Sc.)	
SUNLIT	illuminated by sun	
SUNNED	exposed to sun; sunbathed	
SUNSET	sundown	
SUN-TAN	brown skin from sun	
SUPAWN	Indian porridge	**ck**
SUPERB	magnificent; splendid	
SUPINE	indolent; torpid; inert	
SUPPER	evening meal	**ck**
SUPPLE	lithe; pliant; flexible	
SUPPLY	provide; furnish; grant	
SURBED	(stone-laying)	**bd**
SURCLE	little shoot; sucker	**bt**
SURELY	certainly; positively	
SUREST	safest; most certain	
SURETE	crim. investigation service (Fr.)	
SURETY	bond; guarantee; pledge	
SURGED	billowed; advanced in mass	
SURREY	a fowl; carriage (Amer.)	**zo**
SURTAX	an impost	
SURVEY	see; review; look; observe	
SUSLIK	marmot; ground squirrel	**zo**
SUSSED	arrested on suspicion	**lw**
SUTILE	wound stitching	**md**
SUTLER	camp follower; caterer	
SUTTEE	self-immolation	
SUTTLE	neat; (tare and tret)	
SUTURE	stitching thread	**bt, md**
SVELTE	lissom; slender	
SWADDY	militia-man (slang)	
SWAGED	mitigated; forged; burnt	
SWAGGY	bending	
SWALED	wasted; consumed	
SWAMPY	marshy; spongy	
SWANKY	swipes; boastful	
SWANNY	swan-like	
SWARAJ	home-rule (India)	
SWARDY	grassy	
SWARMY	oleaginous; unctuous	
SWARTH	tawny; apparition	
SWARVE	to swerve	
SWASHY	over-ripe	
SWATCH	a sample of cloth	**tx**
SWATHE	to bind; a bandage	
SWATHY	like a scythe-cut	
SWAYED	vacillated; tottered; wielded	
SWEATY	laborious	
SWEENY	emaciation; atrophy	**md**
SWEEPS	jeweller's dust/debris	
SWEEPY	strutting; wavy	
SWERVE	deviate; turn aside	
SWIM-UP	regroup in water for polo etc.	
SWINGE	to belabour; chastise	
SWINGY	ice conditions (curling)	
SWIPED	lashed out; slogged	
SWIPER	a smiter	

SWIPES	small beer	
SWIPEY	fuddled	
SWIRLY	curly	
SWITCH	twig; whip; bypass; shunt; control	
SWITCH	tap device for electrical circuit	**el**
SWIVEL	to turn; revolve; rowlock with pivot of oars (rowing)	
SWOUND	to swoon (obs.); faint	
SYCITE	fig-stone	**mn**
SYCOMA	tumour	**md**
SYLVAN	rustic; rural; woodland	**fr**
SYMBAL	cymbal	**mu**
SYMBOL	token; sign; badge; emblem; logo	**cp**
SYNDAW	a plant	**bt**
SYNDIC	magistrate; Andorran council	
SYNEMA	column of filaments	**bt**
SYNEPY	interjunction	
SYNTAX	grammatical sequence and structure	
SYNTAX	correct statements in source language	**cp**
SYNTOL	syntagmatic organisation lang.	
SYPHER	to join flush	
SYPHON	siphon; atmospheric pressure pump (soda)	
SYRIAC	} relating to Syria; the	
SYRIAN	} language	
SYRINX	vocal organ in birds; fistula	**zo**
SYRINX	Pan's pipes	**mu**
SYRTIC	like a quicksand	
SYRTIS	quicksand	
SYRUPY	sirupy; sugary	**ck**
SYSTEM	rule; method; order; plan (organised)	
SYSTEM	unit formed by interacting objects	**cp**
SYZYGY	astronomical conjunction	**as**

T

TABARD	} herald's coat; a tunic	**hd**
TABERD	}	
TABBED	having tabs; tagged; registered; listed	
TABEFY	to emaciate	
TABLED	catalogued; motion for discussion (bill)	
TABLER	boarder	
TABLES	for conversions; data; also indoor board-games	**ma, ga**
TABLET	flat monument	**md**
TABOUR	tabor; drum	**mu**
TABRET	small tabour or drum	**mu**
TABULA	calcareous partition in corals; backgammon, Roman board game	**ga**
TACKED	attached; stitched	
TACKER	he who tacks (nails)	

TACKET	hob-nail (Sc.)	
TACKLE	gear; implements; grapple; pulley; football challenge	**nt, ce, ga, to**
TACTIC	tactical; mode of operation; finesse	
TACTUS	sense of touch	
TAENIA	tape-worm; a fillet	**zo**
TAG-END	end of queue; list (last)	
TAGGED	tabbed; touched; fastened	
TAGGER	thin iron/tin sheet	**ml**
TAGGER	an appendage	
TAGLIA	a hoisting device; tackle (crane)	**ce**
TAG-RAG	and bobtail	
TAGUAN	Malayan flying squirrel	**zo**
TAHONA	ore crusher (Sp.)	
TAIGLE	entangle; delay; tarry	
TAILED	docked; followed	
TAILOR	clothes maker	
TAILYE	entail (Sc.)	**lw**
TAISCH	'second sight'; apparition (Sc.)	
TAJACU	Mexican wild pig; peccary	**zo**
TAKE-IN	a hoax	
TAKE-UP	tailoring	
TAKING	alluring; attractive; winning	
TAKRAW	7-a-side field game (S.E. Asia)	**ga**
TALBOT	unit of luminous energy	**lt, me**
TALBOT	sporting dog	**zo**
TALCKY	containing talc	**mn**
TALENT	genius; aptitude	**nm, me**
TALIAN	Bohemian dance	**mu**
TALION	retaliation	**lw**
TALKED	discoursed; prated; spoke	
TALKER	chatterbox; gossip	
TALLAT	} a hay-loft (dial.)	
TALLET	}	
TALLOT	}	
TALLER	sturdier; bolder; higher	
TALLOW	hard candle fat	
TALMUD	Hebrew Bible	**rl**
TALWEG	deep valley (Ger.)	**go**
TAMALE	Mexican corn meal-roll	**ck**
TAMANU	gamboge tree (Ɛ. Ind.)	**bt**
TAMARA	mixed spice	**ck**
TAMBAC	alloy; also aloes-wood	**mn, bt**
TAMBOO	taboo; tambu	
TAMBOR	globe-fish	**zo**
TAMELY	meekly; submissively	
TAMEST	flattest; dullest	
TAMINE	}	
TAMINY	} worsted stuff	**tx, wv**
TAMISE	}	
TAMROY	}	
TAMING	domesticating	
TAMKIN	tampion	
TAMMUZ	Syrian sun-god	**rl**
TAMPAN	South Afr. venomous tick	**zo**
TAMPED	packed with earth	
TAMPER	meddle; interfere; screed board	
TAMPIN	turning pins	
TAMPIN	boxwood pipe plug	**pb**

TAMPOE	an E. Indian fruit	**bt**
TAMPON	surgical plug	**md**
TAMTAM	gong of indefinite pitch	
TAN-BED	bark bed; sunray bed	
TANDEM	one behind the other	
TANDEM	master plus slave hardware units; bicycle for two; 2 horse coach	**cp**
TANGED	banged; twanged; flavoured	
TANGLE	Orcadian water-spirit	
TANGLE	mat; twist; involve; jumble	
TANGLY	complicated; intricate	
TANGUM	Tibetan piebald horse	**zo**
TANIST	land owner (Irish)	
TANITE	a cement	
TANJIB	} figured muslin (Ind.)	**tx**
TANZIB		
TANKED	stored; fuddled	
TANKER	oil-carrying ship (truck)	**nt**
TANKIA	boat population, (Canton)	
TANNED	browned off; leathered	
TANNER	sixpence; leather worker	**nm**
TANNIC	} an acid; astringent	**ch**
TANNIN		
TANNOY	amplified; loud speaker	
TANREC	} insect eater (Madagascar)	**zo**
TENREC		
TANTRA	Sanskrit holy book	**rl**
TAN-VAT	tub used in tanning	**le**
TAOISM	Chinese religion	**rl**
TAOIST	Chinese religionist	**rl**
TAO-TAI	Chinese official	
TAPETI	Brazilian hare	**zo**
TAPING	binding; measuring; recording	**to, tv**
TAPPED	screw-threaded; rapped	
TAPPER	rapper (wheels)	**rw**
TAPPET	(motor valves); small lever	**au**
TAPPIT	crested	
TARGET	shooting mark; production aims	
TARGET	aim; bid; mark; objective	
TARGUM	Bible in Chaldee	**rl**
TARIFF	tax; impost; schedule of charges; (customs); price system; points awarded (sport etc.)	
TARING	recording tare allowance	
TARMAC	road material	
TARNAL	eternal or infernal	
TARPAN	wild horse (Asia)	**zo**
TARPON	} the Jew-fish	**zo**
TARPUM		
TARRED	macadamised; asphalted	
TARSAL	(tarsus); (the ankle)	
TARSEL	hawk; tiercel	**zo**
TARSIA	marquetry	
TARSUS	instep; ankle	**pl**
TARTAN	chequered fabric (Sc.); ship	**nt, tx**
TARTAR	sediment (teeth) (wine casks); acid; argol; Asian Turkic peoples	**ch**

TARTLY	sharply; pungently; acidly	
TASCAL	informer's reward	
TASKED	employed; burdened	
TASKER	taskmaster; overseer	
TASLET	tasset; thigh armour	
TASSEL	a pendant	
TASSET	thigh armour	
TASSIE	drinking cup (Sc.)	
TASTED	experienced; savoured	
TASTER	food/wine sampler	
TATLER	a gossip; sandpiper	**zo**
TATTED	lace making	**tx**
TATTER	a rag	**tx**
TATTIE	Indian trellis; tatta	
TATTLE	prattle; gossip; babble	
TATTOO	army pageant; drum rhythms; skin picture	**mu**
TAUGHT	imparted; tutored; coached	
TAURUS	a sign of the Zodiac; the Bull	**as**
TAUTEN	stretch; strain	
TAUTER	tighter	
TAUTOG	N. American black-fish	**zo**
TAVERN	inn; hostel	
TAVERT	fuddled; muddled (Sc.)	
TAWDRY	gaudy; garish	
TAWERY	white leather factory	**le**
TAWING	leather dressing	**le**
TAWPIE	taupie (Sc.)	
TAWTOG	tautog	**zo**
TAXEME	linguistic selection	
TAXIED	(aeroplane on ground)	
TAXINE	alkaloid mixture	**ch**
TAXING	accusing; straining; costing	
TCHEKA	} first Soviet secret police	
CHEKA		
TCHICK	a click	
TEA-BAG	tea sachet; tisane	
TEA-CUP	tea-drinking vessel	
TEAGLE	a tackle; a hoist	
TEAGUE	an Irishman	
TEAMED	associated conjointly	
TEA-POT	vessel holding tea; (roller skating)	
TEA-POY	small table for teapot	
TEARER	render; ripper	
TEASED	combed; tantalized	
TEASEL	} plant with burs used for raising nap on cloth	
TEAZEL		
TEAZLE		**bt, tx**
TEAZE		
TEASER	a puzzle; aggravator	
TEA-SET	dishes for tea service	
TEATHE	(manure)	
TEA-URN	a samovar	
TEBBAD	Centr. Asian simoon wind	**mt**
TEBETH	Jewish month	
TECTUM	covering/roofing structure	**ar, bd**
TEDDED	spread (new-mown hay)	
TEDDER	a tether; hay-maker	
TEDDER	machine to loosen windrows	**ag**
TE DEUM	thanksgiving	**rl**

TEDIUM	boredom; ennui; monotony	
TEEING	(golf); ball-mounting for first drive per hole	
TEEMED	full of life; in myriads	
TEEMER	a producer	
TEEPEE	wigwam (N. Amer.)	
TEE-TEE	S. Amer. squirrel monkey	zo
TEETER	see-saw (USA)	
TEETHE	to grow teeth	
TEGMEN	inner seed coat	bt
TEGULA	sub-title; under-cover headline (Italian)	pr
TEINDS	tithes (Sc.)	
TELARY	web-like	
TELEDU	stinkard; Malayan badger	zo
TELEGA	Russian springless cart	
TELESM	amulet; charm	
TELFER	Telpher monorail; electric hoist	rw, ce
TELLER	bank cashier; tale-bearer; tally; scorer	
TELLUS	Goddess of Earth (Roman)	rl
TELSON	tail segment	zo
TELUGU	dialect (S. India)	
TEMOIN	column of earth	ce
TEMPER	anger; passion; spleen; tantrum	
TEMPER	mitigate; alleviate; anneal; reheating steel; temperament	ml
TEMPLE	Inns of court; place of worship	rl
TEMPLE	fane; part of head	
TENACE	(bridge)	ga
TENANT	lease-holder	lw
TENDED	cared for; contributed	
TENDER	mild; lenient; offer (loco) (boat) (bar-)	nt, rw
TENDON	a ligament	md
TENNER	£10 note	
TENNIS	net/ball game	ga
TENORA	Catalan instrument	mu
TENPIN	of bowling alley	ga
TENREC	hedgehog genus (Madagascar)	zo
TENSED	keyed up; taut; stretched	
TENSER	under greater strain	
TENSON	} tournament of song	mu
TENZON		
TENSOR	muscle	md
TENTED	probed	
TENTER	machine attendant	
TENTER	female cardroom operative	tx
TENUIS	voiceless stop consonant	
TENURE	possession; holding	
TENUTO	sustained	mu
TEPARY	hardy Amer. bean	bt
TEPEFY	to warm	
TEPHRA	erupted material; solids	gl
TERAPH	Hebrew household god	
TERBIC	containing terbium	ch
TERCEL	male falcon	zo
TERCET	triplet	mu

TEREDO	boring worm; ship-worm	zo
TERETE	cylindrical	
TERGAL	dorsal	
TERGUM	the back	
TERMED	terminated; designated	
TERMER	} holder of an estate for a	
TERMOR	} term of years	
TERMES	white ant genus	zo
TERMLY	term by term	
TERRAL	land breeze (coast) (Chile, Peru)	mt
TERREL	a spherical magnet	
TERRET	territ; harness pad ring	
TERROR	awe; dismay; dread; panic	
TESTED	proved; assayed	
TESTER	canopy; Henry VIII shilling; time trials inspector (cycling)	
TESTIS	male gonad; reproductive gland in scrotum	
TETANY	muscle spasm; lock-jaw	md
TETCHY	testy; peevish	
TETHER	tie; fasten; stake	
TETRAD	group of four	
TETRAO	capercaillie	zo
TETRYL	yellow detonating compound	ch
TETTER	a rash	md
TETTIX	cicada; tree-cricket	zo
TEUTON	ancient German	
TEWHIT	peewit; lapwing	zo
TEXTUS	authoritative version	
THAIRM	catgut (Sc.)	
THALER	German dollar	nm
THALIA	comic Muse	
THANKS	an expression of gratitude	
THATCH	roof with straw	
THAWED	melted	
THEAVE	ewe of the 1st year	zo
THEBAN	of Thebes	
THECAL	sac-like	bt
THECLA	hair-streak butterflies	zo
THEINE	tea alkaloid	ch
THEIRS	of them	
THEISM	belief in one God	
THEIST	believer in one God	
THEMIS	goddess of law	
THENAL	(palm or sole)	md
THENAR	palm or sole	md
THENCE	for that reason	
THEODY	hymn in praise of God	rl
THEORY	speculation; hypothesis; (idea)	
THERMO-	of heat (Gr.)	cf
THESIS	a theme; a dissertation; essay	
THETIC	dogmatic (thesis)	
THETIS	sea-nymph; the sea	
THEWED	trained; muscular	
THIBET	heavy woollen fabric	tx
THIBLE	a dibble	
THIEVE	filch; pilfer; purloin; rob	
T-HINGE	like a cross-garnet	jn
THINLY	scantily; sparsely	
THIRAM	chemical fungicide	

THIRDS	widows' rights	lw	TIDIER	neater	
THIRST	crave; yearn; hanker; desire		TIDILY	methodically; neatly	
THIRTY	cardinal number		TIED-UP	busy; ready for binding in cover	
THOLOS	beehive shaped chamber (Gr.)	ar	TIEING	binding; confining	
THOLUS	dome; cupola (Gr.)		TIE-PIN	ornament for a cravat	
THORAH	the Pentateuch	rl	TIERCE	42-gallon (190-litre) cask	me
THORAL	nuptial		TIERCE	5-f organ pitch	mu
THORAX	(chest)	md, pl	TIE-ROD	connecting rod (steam locomotive)	
THORNY	spiny; prickly; sharp				rw
THORON	thorium emanation	nc	TIE-WIG	court-wig	
THORPE	a homestead		TIFFIN	Indian lunch; superior snacks	ck
THOUGH	notwithstanding		TIGHTS	combined stockings and pantee	
THOWEL	thole-pin	nt	TIKKER	electrical make and break device	
THRALL	a slave; slavery				el
THRASH	drub; castigate; beat (punish)		TILERY	tilework; tile factory	
THRAVE	two stooks (Iceland)		TILING	roofing	bd
THRAWN	twisted (Sc.)		TILLED	cultivated; ploughed	ag
THREAD	cord; filament; drift; gist		TILLER	helm; drawer; cultivator; side	
THREAP	} contradict; urge; insist on			shoot (grass)	ag, nt
THREEP	} (Sc.)		TILMUS	floccillation	md
THREAT	menace; intimidation		TILTED	covered with awning; aslant	
THRENE	a lament (Gr.)		TILTER	tent-pegger; jouster (lancer)	
THRESH	thrash; drub; maul; trounce		TIMBAL	tymbal; kettledrum	mu
THRICE	three times; very		TIMBER	wood; lumber	
THRIFT	frugality; economy		TIMBRE	resonance; tone; quality	mu
THRIFT	the sea-pink	bt	TIMELY	opportune; punctual; apropos	
THRILL	excite; rouse; electrify		TIME-ON	extra time (sports matches etc.)	
THRIPS	corn-bugs	zo	TIMING	clocking; punctuality measuring	
THRIST	thirst (Spens.)			device	cp, me
THRIVE	wax; prosper; flourish		TIMIST	timekeeper (metronome)	mu
THROAT	the fauces	md	TINCAL	crude borax	mn
THRONE	sovereign power and dignity		TIN-CAN	food container	
THRONG	crowed; flock; congregate		TINDAL	Lascar bo'sun's mate	
THROVE	thrived; prospered		TINDER	touchwood (fire lighting)	bt
THROWN	cast; propelled; flung		TINEID	(small moths)	zo
THRUSH	horse disease	zo, vt	TINGAL	} crude borax	
THRUST	lunge; tilt; stab		TINKAL	}	mn
THUSLY	as follows		TINGED	tinkled; imbued; flavoured	
THWACK	belabour; whack; thump		TINGIS	an insect genus	zo
THWART	balk; frustrate; obstruct		TINGLE	thrill; small nail	
THYITE	pale green clay	mn	TINGUY	Brazilian soap-tree	bt
THYMOL	oil of thyme	md	TINIER	much smaller	
THYMUS	a gland	md	TINKED	tinged; tinkled	
THYRSE	panicle	bt	TINKER	bungler; a fish; rubbish man	
TIBIAL	bone; flute	pl, mu	TINKLE	make bell-like sound	mu
TICING	enticing; decoying; luring		TINMAN	a manufactuer; tinker	
TICKED	speckled; clicked; beat; marked		TINNED	preserved	
	(list)		TINNER	tin miner	
TICKEN	bed ticking; cloth	tx	TIN-POT	inferior	
TICKER	a watch; heart (sl.)	pl	TINSEL	finery; glittering; gaudy	
TICKET	voucher; coupon; pass		TINTED	tinged; imbued (coloured)	
TICKEY	coin (S. Africa)	mn	TINTER	colourist	
TICKLE	gratify; amuse; pleasurable touch		TIP-CAT	a children's game	ga
TICKLY	ticklish; risky; difficult		TIP-OFF	secret information; betrayal;	
TIC-TAC	bookie's signalling system			(basket-ball)	
TID-BIT	tit-bit; small snack (birds)		TIPPED	overturned; (racing)	
	(cocktails)	ck	TIPPET	garment; small cape	tx
TIDDER	to fondle		TIPPLE	drink	
TIDDLE	to potter; to trifle		TIP-TOE	walk on the toes	
TIDIED	cleared up; shipshape		TIP-TOP	first class	

TIPULA	insect genus; daddy-longlegs	zo
TIRADE	diatribe; invective; harangue	
TIRING	dressing; wearying	
TIRLED	vibrated; twisted	
TIRRET	handcuff; manacle; fetter	
TIRRIT	terror (Shak.)	zo
TIRWIT	lapwing	zo
TISANE	herbal drink	ck
TISSUE	web; fabric; series	md
TIT-BIT	tid-bit; morsel for birds or cocktails	ck
TITELY	quickly	
TITHED	taxed	
TITHER	tithe collector	
TITLED	yclept; inscribed; named	
TITLER	stickle-back	zo
TITLER	lettering screen	cn
TI-TREE	the manuka	bt
TITTER	giggle; snigger; laugh	
TITTLE	an iota; small particle	
TITTUP	canter (horse-riding)	
TMESIS	rhetorical intersection	
TOBINE	twilled silk	tx
TOCHER	dowry (Sc.)	
TOCSIN	an alarm; poisonous serum	zo
TODDLE	saunter	
TOE-CAP	boot-tip	
TOFFEE	chewy confection	ck
TOFORE	before; heretofore	
TOGGED	arrayed; dressed up	
TOGGLE	wooden pin; ski lift grip; safety rope device	nt, ae
TOGGLE	circuit based on stable state	cp
TOILED	moiled; strove	
TOILER	labourer; worker; striver	
TOILET	dress; attire; washroom (W.C.)	
TOISON	a fleece; sheepwool	tx
TOLEDO	sword-blade; gilded steel ornament (Sp.)	
TOLLED	rang church bells	mu
TOLLER	toll-gatherer (highway taxes) (tollgates)	
TOLLER	bell-ringer	
TOL-LOL	goodish	
TOLSEY	toll-booth; mart	
TOLTEC	early Mexican	
TOLTER	to flounder (dial.)	
TOLUIC	(benzene)	ch
TOLUOL	methylbenzene	ch
TOMAND	Arabian grain	me
TOMATO	red fruit-vegetable	bt
TOMAUN	Persian gold coin	nm
TOMBAC	copper-zinc alloy for gongs, bells; small boxes	
TOMBAK		
TOMBED	buried and exalted	
TOMBIC	like a tomb	
TOMBOC	Javanese weapon	
TOMBOY	a romping girl; hoyden	
TOM-CAT	male feline	zo
TOMCOD	a fish	zo

TOMIAL	cutting edge of a bird's bill	
TOMIUM		zo
TOMPON	inking pad	
TOMPOT	blenny fish	zo
TOM-TIT	blue tit	zo
TOMTOM	drum; (N. Amer. Indians)	mu
TONADA	tune, air (Sp.)	mu
TONAME	nickname; byname	
TONGAN	native of Tonga	
TONGUE	language; speech; scold; lick; (cross)	cr
TONING	intoning (recitative prayers)	rl
TONING	tinting; to suit (colours)	
TONISH	stylish; having 'ton'	
TONITE	an explosive	ch
TONSIL	throat appendage	pl
TOOART	Australian eucalyptus	bt
TOOLED	ornamented; drove	cr
TOOTED	hooted	
TOOTER	a piper	
TOOTHY	with teeth too apparent	
TOOTLE	play on the flute	mu
TOO-TOO	quite so; super	
TOPAZA	humming birds	zo
TOP-DOG	leader; victor	
TOPFUL	brimming	
TOP-HAT	topper	
TOPHET	place of torment (Hebrew)	
TOPHUS	(gout)	md
TOPMAE	insect labrum surface	zo
TOPMAN	top sawyer; dominant partner; demolisher	nt
TOPPED	surpassed; filled up; (golf)	
TOPPER	high hat	
TOPPLE	fall; tumble; collapse; totter	
TORERO	bull-fighter on foot	
TOROID	a symmetrical geometrical fig.	
TOROSE	swelling; protuberant	
TOROUS		
TORPID	inert; numb; lethargic	
TORPOR	apathy; dullness; dormancy	
TORQUE	twisting force (motors)	
TORQUE	collar; necklace	
TORRID	sultry; scorching; fiery	
TORSEL	twisted scroll	
TORULA	yeast plant	bt
TOSSED	thrown; pitched	
TOSSER	pitcher	
TOSS-UP	an even chance; spin a coin	
T'OTHER	the other	
TOTING	carrying; humping	
TOTTED	added up	
TOTTER	topple; reel; rock; stagger	
TOTTIE	a small tot (rum)	
TOUCAN	S. America bird	zo
TOUCHE	a palpable hit (fencing)	
TOUCHY	testy; irascible; petulant	
TOUPEE	a tuft; a curl; lock of false hair	
TOUPET		
TOURED	journeyed	

259

TOUSED	hauled; torn; rumpled	
TOUSER	a teaser; a worrit	
TOUSLE	to rumple; ruffle; derange	
TOUTED	canvassed	
TOUTER	a tout	
TOUTIE	petulant (Sc.)	
TOWAGE	haulage	
TOWARD	apt; docile; tractable	
TOWERY	lofty	
TOWHEE	America marsh robin	zo
TOWING	dragging; drawing	
TOW-NET	water-fauna sample net	oc
TOWSER	a dog	zo
TOXOID	detoxidified toxin	md
TOY-DOG	miniature dog	zo
TOYFUL	trifling	
TOYING	dallying; trifling	
TOYISH	playful; wanton	
TOY-MAN	a dealer in playthings	
TRABAL	beamy	ar
TRABEA	Roman consular robe	
TRACED	trailed; drawn; limned	
TRACER	investigator; (bullet); artificial isotop; monitor (drawings)	
TRADED	bartered; vended; sold	
TRADER	merchant; trafficker	
TRAGIC	shocking; calamitous	
TRAGUS	(ear portal)	md
TRANCE	coma; rapture; ecstasy	
TRANKA	juggler's box	
TRAPAN	to ensnare; stratagem	
TRAPES	a slut; a tramp	
TRAPPY	treacherous	
TRASHY	rubbishy; worthless	
TRAUMA	a shock; harsh experience	pc, md
TRAVEL	tour; trip; journey; move; deviation from spin (ice skating)	
TRAVIS	stable partition	
TREATY	pact; covenant; alliance	
TREBLE	triple; threefold; high voice	mu
TREBLY	triply	
TREFLE	trefoil; clover	bt
TREMEX	an insect genus	zo
TREMIE	underwater-concrete funnel	ce
TREMOR	shock; vibration	
TRENCH	cut; furrow; ditch; groove; (warfare)	
TREPAN	(skull cutting)	md
TREPAN	a cheat; ensnare; trapan	
TREPID	quaking; trembling; afraid	
TRESSY	curly	
TRIACT	having three rays	
TRIAGE	sorting, classifying state of wounded, injured	
TRIALS	performance tests; test cases	lw
TRIBAL	clannish	
TRICAR	motor-tricyle	
TRICHO-	of the hair (Gr.)	cf
TRICKY	intricate; difficult; troublesome	
TRICON	on-course signal system	nv

TRICOT	knitted fabric	tx
TRIFID	three-cleft	bt
TRIFLE	a sweet; gewgaw; dally	ck
TRIGLA	gurnards	zo
TRIGLY	dandified	
TRIGON	ancient harp; triangle	mu
TRILBY	a hat	
TRIMER	3-molecule substance	ch
TRIMLY	neatly; compactly; evenly balanced	
TRINAL	three-fold	
TRINGA	sandpiper genus	zo
TRIODE	thermionic valve	ro
TRIOSE	simplest monosaccharide	ck
TRIPLE	treble (darts); threesome; trinity; scores; baseball hit	ga
TRIPLY	threefold	
TRIPOD	three-legged stool or stand	
TRIPOS	Cambridge examination	
TRIPUS	1 of Weberian vesicles	zo
TRISTE	sad; sorrowful; gloomy	mu
TRITON	one of Neptune's trumpeters	
TRITON	genus of molluscs	zo
TRITON	nucleus of tritium atom	el, ps
TRITOR	tooth masticatory surface	zo
TRITYL	triphenylmethyl group	ch
TRIUNE	Trinity	rl
TRIVET	trevet; small hob; fireside	
TRIVIA	trivial matters (unimportant)	
TROCAR	surgical instrument	md
TROCHE	a lozenge; tabloid	
TROGGS	clothes (Sc.)	
TROGON	Central American bird	zo
TROIKA	Russian 3-horsed sleigh	
TROJAN	a champion; a plucky fellow	
TROLLY	small truck	
TROMBA	trumpet (It.)	mu
TROPHI	(insect's mouth)	zo
TROPHO-	of food nourishment (Gr.)	cf
TROPHY	prize; laurels; sculptured arms or armour	ar
TROPIC	(Cancer and Capricorn)	
-TROPIN	benefit of substance on organ	md
TROPPO	excessively; too much (It.)	mu
TROTYL	explosive	ch
TROUGH	groove; trench; furrow	
TROUPE	a company	
TROVER	(finding)	lw
TROWED	trusted; believed	
TROWEL	garden implement	to
TRUANT	vagrant; vagabond; shirker	
TRUDGE	tramp; plod; march	
TRUEST	exactest; most veracious	
TRUISM	axiom; platitude	
TRUITE	crackled (porcelain)	
TRUSTY	reliable; staunch; faithful	
TRYGON	sting-ray	zo
TRYING	irksome; difficult; arduous	
TRY-OUT	preliminary trial	
TSAMBA	black barley (Tibet)	bt

TSETSE	deadly fly (S. Africa)	zo
TSONGA	language (Mozambique)	
TSWANA	language (Africa)	
T-TOTUM	teetotum; teetotaller (sl.); abstainer	
TUAREG	tribe (Sahara)	
TUBAGE	inserting a tube	
TUBBED	bathed	
TUBFUL	the contents of a barrel	
TUB-GIG	Welsh open carriage	
TUBING	piping	
TUBULE	small tube	
TUCHUN	Chinese military governor	
TUCKED	stuffed; folded; pleated	
TUCKER	bib; frilling	
TUCKET	trumpet-call	mu
TUCK-IN	large meal; picnic	
TUFFET	Miss Muffet's seat; grass	
TUFTED	tufty; crested	
TUFTER	a stag-hound	zo
TUGGED	lugged	
TUGGER	a heaver; puller	
TUILLE	thigh armour	
TULWAR	Eastern sabre	
TUMBAK	coarse Persian tobacco	bt
TUMBLE	trip; stumble; somersault	
TUMBLY	uneven; unstable	
TUMEFY	to swell; distend; inflate	
TUMOUR	morbid swelling	md
TUMPED	hilled (gardening)	
TUM-TUM	W. Indian food; tomtom	ck
TUMULI	ancient mounds	
TUMULT	uproar; hubbub; turmoil	
TUNDRA	frozen subarctic plain	gl, go
TUNDUN	a toy; a bull-roarer	
TUNE-IN	find station on waveband	ro, tv
TUNGUS	Turanian tribe	
TUNING	syntonizing	ro
TUNKER	dunker; baptist; the great Dipper	
TUNNED	casked	
TUNNEL	funnel; passage; burrow	
TUPAIA	tree-shrew (Malay)	zo
TUPELO	gum-tree	bt
TUPPED	butted; rammed; served (ewes)	zo
TUPPER	ram; bricklayer's labourer	zo
TURACO	Afr. plantain-eating bird	zo
TURBAN	oriental head-dress (Sikh)	
TURBID	muddy; cloudy; confused	
TURBOT	} a flat-fish	zo
TURBIT		
TURDUS	the thrush	zo
TUREEN	a receptacle for soup	
TURFED	sodded; kicked out	
TURFEN	(turf); covered with sward	
TURGID	bloated; tumid; bombastic	
TURGOR	fullness	md
TURION	runner; underground shoot	bt
TURKEY	straight talk; poultry	zo, ck
TURKIS	turquoise	mn

TURMUT	turnip (dial.)	bt
TURNED	hinged; applied (lathe); revolved	cr
TURNER	lathe-worker; pigeon	zo
TURN-IN	part exchange deal; bed-time	
TURNIP	old-fashioned watch; root	bt
TURN-UP	an altercation; trumps	
TURNUS	swallow-tail butterfly	zo
TURREL	tool used by coopers	to
TURRET	minaret; small tower (castle)	ar
TURTLE	marine tortoise	zo
TURVES	plural of turf; sods (peat) (fuel)	
TUSCAN	a classic order of architecture	ar
TUSKAR	peat cutter	
TUSKED	tusky; toothy	
TUSKER	elephant	zo
TUSSAC	a tussock; cushion (grass)	bt
TUSSAH	wild silkworm fabric	tx
TUSSER	tussore silk	tx
TUSSIS	a cough	md
TUSSLE	scuffle; wrestle; contend	
TUTRIX	female guardian	
TUTSAN	a plant	bt
TU-WHIT	} owlish; night calls	
TU-WHOO		
TUXEDO	dinner jacket (USA)	
TUYERE	a pipe; twyer	
TWAITE	species of shad	zo
TWAITE	} arable land	
THWAITE		
TWEENY	maid; small cigar	
TWELVE	a dozen	
TWENTY	a score	
TWICER	compositor and pressman	
TWIGGY	abounding in shoots (skeletal)	bt
TWILLY	cotton-cleaning machine	tx
TWINED	twisted; meandered	tx
TWINER	climbing plant	bt
TWINGE	pang; twitch; spasm	
TWITCH	twinge; jerk	
TWITTY	yarns with twisted portions	tx
TWO-PLY	of 2 layers (wood, wool, etc.)	tx
T'WOULD	it would	
TWO-WAY	(a switch)	
TYBURN	(executions); (Marble Arch)	
TYCOON	Japanese prince; oil magnate (Am.)	
TYLOTE	sponge-spicule	zo
TYMBAL	kettledrum; timbal	mu
TYMPAN	printing frame	pr
TYPHON	evil genius (Egypt)	
TYPHUS	gaol fever	md
TYPIFY	exemplify; symbolize	
TYPIFY	categorizing of persons, objects; (typewriter)	pc
TYPIST	typewriter user	
TYRANT	autocrat; despot	
TYRIAN	purple	
TYRITE	a mineral	mn
TYSTIE	the black guillemot	zo
TZETZE	Abyssinian guitar	mu, zo

U

UAKARI	S. American monkeys	zo
UBERTY	fruitfulness	
UBIETY	local relation	
UBIQUE	everywhere	
UDMURT	native of Central Asia	
U-GAUGE	laboratory test tube of glass	
UGLIFY	to make hideous	
UGLILY	in an ungainly manner	
UGRIAN	Ugro-Finnic (Hungarian-Finnish-Turkic)	
UGSOME	hideous; gruesome	
UIGITE	a silicate of aluminium	mn
ULITIS	gum inflammation	md
ULLAGE	lack of fullness in a cask	
ULLING	ullage	
ULMOUS	(elm exudation)	bt
ULNARE	cuneiform bone	md
ULOSIS	cicatrisation	md
ULSTER	overcoat	
ULTIMO	last; in last month	
ULTION	revenge	
UMBERY	of umber colour	pt
UMBLES	entrails of deer	zo
UMBRAL	shady; darksome	
UMBRIL	umbrel; helmet vizor	
UMLAUT	vowel inflection (Ger.)	
UMPIRE	arbiter; referee; judge	
UMWELT	one's relationship with the environment	
UNABLE	powerless; impotent	
UNAWED	undismayed; undaunted; unimpressed	
UNBANK	(stoking)	
UNBEAR	to unharness; ungear	
UNBEND	to relax; undo; unknot	nt
UNBENT	relaxed; untied	
UNBIAS	to free from prejudice	
UNBIND	release; unfetter	
UNBITT	(release cable)	nt
UNBOLT	unfasten; unbar	
UNBONE	remove the bones	
UNBORN	non-existent; uncreated	
UNBRED	rude; underbred	
UNBURY	disinter; exhume	
UNCAGE	to free	
UNCALM	to disturb; agitate	
UNCAMP	dislodge	
UNCAPE	unhood	
UNCART	unload	
UNCASE	unpack; display; unsheath	
UNCATE	hooked	
UNCIAL	a script used in ancient MSS.	
UNCLAD	naked; nude	
UNCLEW	unwind	
UNCLOG	unhamper	
UNCOCK	(shooting); (hay-making)	
UNCOIF	remove cap	

UNCOIL	unwind	
UNCOIN	withdraw from currency	
UNCOLT	unhorse (Shak.)	
UNCORD	unbind	
UNCORK	open (bottles)	
UNCOWL	unveil	
UNCURL	untwist	
UNDATE	wavy; undose	
UNDEAF	to restore hearing	
UNDEAN	deprive of that office; unfrock	rl
UNDECK	divest of ornaments	
UNDERN	9 a.m.; the third hour	
UNDIES	underclothes	
UNDINE	water-nymph	
UNDOCK	to leave dock	nt
UNDOER	subversionary agent	
UNDONE	untied; awaiting performance	
UNDOSE	undulated; undate; wavy	
UNDRAW	draw aside	
UNDUKE	deprive of duke's rank	
UNDULL	sharpen; whet	
UNDULY	excessively; improperly	
UNEASE	mental unrest; anxiety	
UNEASY	restive; disturbed	
UNEATH	uneasily (Spens.)	
UNEDGE	unsharpen; blunten	
UNEVEN	rugged; rough; odd	
UNEYED	unnoticed; unobserved	
UNFACE	expose the character within	
UNFAIR	dishonest; foul; partial	
UNFAST	insecure	
UNFEED	without fee or salary	
UNFELT	unimpressed; callous	
UNFILE	remove from a file	
UNFINE	shabby	
UNFIRM	weak; unstable	
UNFIST	to release; unhand	
UNFOLD	open; expand; reveal	
UNFOOL	restore from folly; unhoax	
UNFORM	to destroy	
UNFREE	not free; tied; restricted	
UNFURL	display; unroll	
UNGAIN	ungainly; clumsy (obs.)	
UNGEAR	to unharness; unbear	
UNGILD	remove the gilding	
UNGILL	release from a gill-net	
UNGILT	not gilt	
UNGIRD	unbind	
UNGIRT	unconfined	
UNGLUE	ungum; unstick	
UNGOWN	disrobe	
UNGUAL	having claws, nails, etc.	
UNGUIS	claw; hoof	zo
UNGULA	instrument	md
UNGULA	section of a cylinder	
UNGYVE	unfetter	
UNHAIR	deprive of hair	
UNHAND	let go; release	
UNHANG	take off the line	
UNHASP	unfasten	

UNHEAD	behead; decapitate	
UNHEAL	} to uncover (Spens.)	
UNHELE		
UNHELM	remove helmet or rudder	**nt**
UNHEWN	rough	
UNHIVE	deprive of habitation	
UNHOLD	release	
UNHOLY	impious; profane; ungodly	
UNHOOK	disconnect	
UNHUNG	unhanged	
UNHURT	scatheless	
UNHUSK	to shell	
UNIATE	Greek Catholic sect	**rl**
UNIBLE	} unifiable	
UNIFIC		
UNIOLA	American grass genus	**bt**
UNIPED	single-footed	
UNIPOD	single support camera mount	**pg**
UNIQUE	peculiar; sole; unexampled	
UNISEX	for either, or both sexes together	
UNISON	harmony; concord; accord	**mu**
UNITAL	unique; singular	
UNITED	combined; coalesced	
UNITER	joiner; merger	
UNJUST	biased; partial	
UNKARD	} ugly; strange (dial.)	
UNKETH		
UNCOUTH		
UNKENT	unknown	
UNKEPT	discarded; rejected	
UNKIND	cruel; harsh; unfriendly	
UNKING	dethrone	
UNKNIT	unravel	
UNKNOT	untie; unfasten	**nt**
UNLACE	loose; loosen	
UNLADE	disburden; unload	
UNLAID	not allayed; untwisted	
UNLASH	let loose; unbind; untie	
UNLEAD	remove lead	**pr**
UNLEAL	unloyal	
UNLENT	not loaned	
UNLESS	if not; except	
UNLICH	unlike (Spens.)	
UNLIKE	dissimilar; heterogeneous	
UNLIME	extract the lime	
UNLINE	remove the lining	
UNLINK	unfasten	
UNLIVE	kill; dull; not electrified	
UNLOAD	relieve; lighten; unburden	
UNLOCK	unfasten	
UNLORD	deprive of that dignity	
UNLOVE	cease to love	
UNLUTE	unglue	
UNMADE	not manufactured	
UNMAKE	destroy; dismantle	
UNMASK	expose; denounce; reveal	
UNMEET	unworthy; unbecoming	
UNMIRY	not muddy	
UNMIXT	pure; unalloyed; sheer	
UNMOOR	to weigh anchor	**nt**

UNNAIL	extract the nails	
UNNEST	eject; evict	
UNNETH	uneath; not easily (Spens.)	
UNOWED	not due	
UNPACK	disburden; open; uncover possessions	
UNPACK	recover data from storage	**cp**
UNPAID	still owing; outstanding	
UNPICK	unravel; unknit	
UNPRAY	revoke a prayer	
UNPROP	remove a support	
UNPURE	impure; adulterated	
UNQUIT	not discharged	
UNREAD	not perused; ignorant	
UNREAL	fantastic; visionary; illusory	
UNREIN	slacken the rein	
UNRENT	untorn; unripped	
UNREST	disquiet; unease; fidgetiness	
UNRIPE	immature; crude; green	
UNROBE	undress	
UNROLL	open out; uncoil; evolve	
UNROOF	untile	
UNROOT	extirpate; eradicate	
UNROPE	untie; unlash	
UNRUDE	civil; complaisant	
UNRULY	riotous; turbulent	
UNSAFE	risky; hazardous; insecure	
UNSAID	unspoken	
UNSEAM	rip; cleave; unpick	
UNSEAT	unhorse; unsaddle	
UNSEEL	to open the eyes	
UNSEEN	invisible	
UNSELF	eliminate personality	
UNSENT	not despatched	
UNSEWN	unstitched	
UNSHED	retained; kept	
UNSHIP	remove; unload	**nt**
UNSHOD	barefoot	
UNSHOT	not discharged	
UNSHUT	open	
UNSOFT	not softly (Spens.)	
UNSOLD	not purchased	
UNSOUL	materialize; deaden	
UNSOWN	not propagated	
UNSPAR	remove spars	
UNSPED	undone	
UNSPIN	unravel	
UNSTEP	remove (a mast)	**nt**
UNSTOP	release	
UNSUNG	forgotten, neglected	
UNSURE	uncertain	
UNTACK	disjoin	
UNTAME	wild; undomesticated	
UNTELL	never to narrate	
UNTENT	uncover	
UNTIDY	slovenly; disorderly	
UNTIED	undone; unloosed	
UNTILE	unroof	
UNTOLD	uncounted; numberless	
UNTOMB	exhume	

263

UNTORN	unrent	
UNTRIM	disarray	
UNTROD	little frequented	
UNTRUE	false; fallacious; spurious	
UNTUCK	unfold	
UNTUNE	to disorder	
UNTURN	untwist; unscrew	
UNUSED	new; unaccustomed	
UNVEIL	uncover; reveal; unmask	
UNVOTE	out-vote	
UNWARM	chillsome	
UNWARY	rash; incautious; indiscreet	
UNWELL	ailing; stick; indisposed	
UNWEPT	not lamented	
UNWILY	lacking in craft	
UNWIND	uncoil; disentangle; unfurl; relax	
UNWIND	to show all instructions used	
UNWISE	indiscreet; imprudent	
UNWISH	wish not to be (Shak.)	
UNWOOF	unweave	
UNWORK	undo	
UNWORN	unimpaired	
UNWRAP	unfold; uncloak	
UNYOKE	separate; disjoin	
UPBEAR	sustain; elevate	
UPBEAT	unaccentuated rhythm	mu
UPBIND	confine	
UPCAST	uptoss	
UPCAST	upward strata displacement	gl
UPCOIL	to coil	
UPDATE	bring into line; modernise	cp
UPFILL	to fill	
UPFLOW	upgush	
UPGAZE	look upwards	
UPGROW	develop; evolve	
UPGUSH	upflow	
UPHAND	lift	
UPHEAP	pile up; amass	
UPHILL	toilsome; arduous; strenuous	
UPHOLD	advocate; maintain; champion	
UPHROE	awning support	nt
UPKEEP	maintenance	
UPLAND	highland	
UPLEAN	to incline upwards (Austral.)	
UPLIFT	upheaval; exaltation; upward force; morale raising	
UP-LINE	line to London (railway)	
UPLOCK	lock up	
UPLOOK	raise the eyes	
UPMAKE	column/page print arranging	pr
UPMOST	topmost	
UPPERS	of shoes (leather); stimulating drugs	
UP-PILE	accumulate; upheap	
UPPING	swan marking	
UPPISH	bumptious	
UP-PROP	to shore; support	
UPREAR	to raise the backside	
UPRISE	ascend; revolt	
UPRIST	up-risen; uprose	

UPROAR	riot; hubbub; turmoil	
UPROLL	furl	
UPROOT	eradicate; extirpate	
UPROSE	stood up; rebelled	
UPRUSH	surging up	
UPSEEK	seek above	
UPSEES	after the manner of	
UPSEND	throw up	
UPSHOT	outcome; issue; result	
UPSIDE	topside	
UPSOAR	zoom	
UPSTAY	sustain; support	
UPSWAY	swing up	
UPTAKE	mental agility	
UPTEAR	rend	
UPTILT	incline; tip	
UPTIME	serviceable time, normal	cp
UPTOSS	pitch	
UPTOWN	city centre (if north)	
UPTURN	overturn; overthrow	
UPWARD	ascending; uphill	
UPWAYS	upward	
UPWELL	upspring; gush	
UPWIND	to wind up	
URACIL	pyrimidine; nucleic acid	ch
URAEUM	tail-end of bird	zo
URAEUS	serpent emblem (Egypt)	
URAKEN	back fist blow (karate)	ga
URANIA	Muse of astronomy	
URANIC	(uranium); celestial	
URANIN	yellow dye	ch
URANUS	a planet; father of Saturn	
URANYL	chemical radical	ch
URATES	urine salts	md
URBANE	courteous; polite; affable	
URCEUS	single-handed jug; urn	
URCHIN	hedgehog; brat; gamin	zo
UREASE	enzyme	ch
UREIDE	acid derivative of urea	ch
URESIS	passing urine	
URETER	duct that carries urine	md
URETIC	a medicine	md
URGENT	pressing; imperative	
URGING	impelling; inciting	
URNING	consigning to an urn	
URONIC	of sugar oxidation compound	ch
UROPOD	abdominal limb	zo
URSINE	bear-like	zo
URTICA	nettle genus	bt
URVANT	turned up	hd
USABLE	employable; applicable	
USAGER	a religionist	rl
USANCE	usury	
USEFUL	helpful; beneficial	
USTION	combustion	
USURER	money-lender; a Shylock	
USWARD	towards us	
UTERUS	womb	
UTGARD	abode of Loki (Scand.)	
UTMOST	extreme; farthest	

264

UTOPIA	a political romance; an ideal society	
UVEOUS	grape-like	md
UVULAR	(uvula)	md

V

VACANT	void; empty; inane	
VACATE	quit; leave; annul; rescind	
VACHER	cow-keeper	
VACUNA	Roman goddess of horticulture	
VACUUM	void; vacuity; emptiness	
VADIUM	surety (Sc.)	lw
VAGARY	whim; crotchet; fancy	
VAGINA	sexual passage in female	zo
VAGOUS	wandering; erratic	
VAGUER	more indefinite; dimmer	
VAIDIC	Vedic; (philosophical)	
VAILED	submitted; tipped	
VAILER	a yielder	
VAINER	more conceited; falser	
VAINLY	ineffectually; proudly	
VAISYA	(Hindu caste)	
VAKASS	Armenian clerical vestment	rl
VAKEEL	Indian attorney	lw
VALETE	farewell	
VALGUS	knock-kneed man; club-foot	
VALINE	amino acid	ch
VALING	receding; lowering	
VALISE	portmanteau; holdall	
VALIUM	tranquilliser	ch, md
VALKYR	a Valkyrie; Walkyr	
VALKYR VALKYRIES	} Odin's messenger girls	
VALLAR	(rampart)	
VALLEY	dale; vale; dell; glen; dingle; (roof-edge) tile	bd
VALLUM	Roman rampart	
VALOUR	heroism; courage; prowess	
VALUED	esteemed; prized; treasured	
VALUER	appraiser	
VALVED	having valves	
VAMOSE	vamoose; to clear out	
VAMPED	improvised; patched; repaired	
VAMPER	a pianist; siren	mu
VANDAL	barbarian; destroyer	
VANISH	fade; disappear; depart	
VANITY	conceit; egotism; futility	
VAN-MAN	pantechnicon worker	
VANNER	light cart horse	zo
VAPORS	vapours; nervous dejection	md
VAPOUR	steam; reek; fume; to boast	
VARIED	diverse; motley; altered	
VARIER	an inconsistent person	
VARLET	scoundrel; rascal; knave	
VARMIN	vermin; varmint	zo
VARSAL	universal	
VARUNA	The Creator (Hindu Myth)	rl
VARZEA	Amazonian flood plain (Brazil)	go
VASSAL	retainer; dependant; bondman	

VASTER	on a grander scale	
VASTLY	spaciously; widely; immensely	
VASTUS	a thigh muscle	md
VAT-DYE	oxidation of textiles	tx
VATTED	mellowing; maturing	br
VAULTY	arched	
VAWARD	vanward; in the van	
V-BRICK	perforated instead of cavitied	bd
VEADER	Jewish intercalary month	
VECTOR	data display organism transmitting parasites	
VECTOR	force with thrust, direction, and magnitude	ma
VEDDAH	native Cingalese	
VEDUTA	painting of recognizable scene	
VEERED	changed course; shifted	nt
VEHMIC	(vehmgericht) (Austrian)	
VEILED	concealed; shrouded; glozed	
VEINED	streaked; variegated; venose	
VELARY	a sail or awning	
VELATE	enveloped; veiled	bt
VELETA	waltz	mu
VELITE	lightly armed Roman soldier	
VELLED	removed turf	
VELLET	velvet (Spens.)	
VELLON	Spanish money of account	
VELLUM	parchment from calf-skin	
VELLUS	downy foetal hair	zo
VELOCE	very quick	mu
VELOUR	velvet	
VELURE	velvet; smoothing pad	
VELVET	soft silky stuff	tx
VENDED	sold; peddled; hawked	
VENDEE	the buyer; purchaser	
VENDER VENDOR	} the seller	
VENDUE	an auction; roup	
VENEER	coating; layer; cover	
VENERY	sport; hunting	
VENEUR	head-keeper	
VENGER	an avenger (Spens.)	
VENIAL	excusable; pardonable	
VENITE	95th Psalm	
VENNEL	an alley-way (Sc.)	
VENOSE VENOUS	} veined	
VENTED	poured forth; uttered; emitted	
VENTER	the abdomen	md
VENTIL	(cornet valve)	mu
VENTRO-	ventral from the anterior, stomach, abdomen	cf
VENULE	blood vessel in chordata	zo
VERANO	dry season C. Amer. summer (Sp.)	
VERBAL	oral; by word of mouth	
VERDOY	charged with heraldic flowers	hd
VERDUN	antique rapier (Fr.)	
VERGED	sloped; inclined; bordered on	
VERGEE	about half acre	me
VERGER	church caretaker	rl
VERIFY	confirm; authenticate; identify	
VERILY	truly; really; certainly	

VERITE	realism, film documentary technique	cn
VERITY	actuality; fact; reality	
VERMES	worms	zo
VERMIL	vermilion colour	
VERMIN	noxious animal; rabble	zo
VERMIS	main part of cerebellum	zo
VERNAL	springlike	
VERREL	ferrule; see virole	
VERREY	vaire; furry	hd
VERSAL	universal (Shak.)	
VERSED	skilled; familiar; accomplished	
VERSER	versifier; poetaster	
VERSET	prelude	mu
VERSUS	against; opposing	
VERTEX	top; apex; acme; zenith	
VERVET	South African monkey	zo
VESICA	a bladder; a sac	md
VESPER	evening star, Venus	as
VESSEL	receptacle; utensil	nt
VESTAL	chaste (virgins)	
VESTED	fixed; legalized; established	
VESTRY	sacristy	rl
VETCHY	(vetch)	bt
VETOED	prohibited; banned; forbidden	
VETTED	carefully examined	
VETUST	ancient	
VEXING	annoying; tormenting; trying	
VIABLE	capable of existence	
VIANDS	food; provisions	
VIATIC	(journey)	
VIATOR	wayfarer	
VIBRIO	spiral bacillus	zo
VICARY	a vicarage	rl
VICTIM	a dupe; martyr; sacrifice	
VICTOR	conqueror; winner; champion	
VICUNA	the wild llama	zo
VIDAME	French noble	
VIDUAL	widowed	
VIELLE	antique viol (Fr.)	mu
VIEWED	beheld; surveyed; scanned	
VIEWER	examiner; inspector	
VIEWLY	striking	
VIGOUR	force; energy; manliness	
VIHARA	Buddhist temple	rl
VIKING	Norse sea-rover; longshipsman	nt
VILELY	basely; ignobly; malignantly	
VILEST	lowest; abject	
VILIFY	defame; traduce; disparage	
VILLUS	hair; wool	md
VILNED	wounded beast	hd
VIMANA	Indian temple	rl
VINAGE	wine doctoring	
VINERY	grape house	
VINNEY	a blue Dorset cheese	
VINOSE	} wine	
VINOUS	}	
VINTED	turned into wine	
VINTRY	wine shop; bodega; bistro	
VIOLAN	violet blue	mn
VIOLET	a colour; flower	bt

VIOLIN	fiddle; a kit	mu
VIRAGO	a termagant; vixen; shrew	
VIRENT	verdant; green; fresh	
VIRGIN	maiden; damsel; spinster; untouched; (city) fresh	
VIRILE	manly; robust; masculine	
VIRION	mature virus	zo
VIROLE	ferrule; hoop	hd
VIROSE	} poisonous	
VIROUS	}	
VIRTUE	integrity; probity; goodness	
VISAED	endorsed (passport)	
VISAGE	face; aspect; countenance	
VISCID	sticky; glutinous; tenacious	
VISCIN	mistletoe fruit substance	bt
VISCUM	mistletoe	bt
VISCUS	an entrail; singular form of viscera, innards	md
VISHNU	The Preserver (Hindu God)	rl
VISIER	} Ottoman minister	
VIZIER	}	
VISILE	who prefers visual images to auditory	
VISION	sight; dream; foresight; view; (video)	tv
VISIVE	visual	
VISUAL	visible; perceptible; data display unit	cp
VITALS	essential organs	
VITRIC	glassy	
VIVACE	lively	mu
VIVARY	small zoo; vivarium	zo
VIVERS	victuals (Sc.)	
VIVIFY	animate; enliven; quicken	
VIZARD	mask; visor	
VOCULE	a feeble cry	
VOICED	said; declared; uttered	
VOICER	spokesman	
VOIDED	evacuated; quitted; left	
VOIDER	shallow basket	
VOLANT	flying; nimble; active	hd
VOLATA	rapid phrase (It.)	mu
VOLENT	exercising will power	
VOLERY	flight of birds	
VOLLEY	salvo; shower; storm; strike with racquet (ball-games)	ga
VOLUME	book; tome; bulk; mass; magnetic storage; sound	cp
VOLUTE	spiral scroll	
VOLVOX	freshwater algae	bt
VOMICA	an abscess in the lungs	md
VOMITO	yellow fever	md
VOODOO	} witchcraft (Haiti)	
VOUDOU	}	rl
VAUDOO	}	
VORAGO	whirlpool; vortex; gulf	
VORANT	devouring	hd
VORTEX	whirlpool; whirlwind	
VOTARY	a fan; devotee; zealot	
VOTING	electing; polling	
VOTIVE	vowed; devoted	

VOULGE	ancient form of pike (Fr.)
VOWING	pledging; promising
VOYAGE	trip; cruise; passage
VOYANT	seer with psychic vision
VULCAN	god of fire
VULGAR	coarse; ordinary; vernacular

W

WABBLE	wobble; stand unsteadily	
WABBLY	insecure; unstable	
WADDED	stuffed; filled	
WADDIE	Australian war club	
WADDLE	walk like a duck	
WADING	fording	
WADMAL	thick woollen cloth	tx
WADSET	a mortgage	lw
WAEFUL	woeful; sorrowful (Sc.)	
WAFERY	wafer-like	
WAFFLE	a cake; a gauffre	
WAFTED	floated; waved; beckoned	
WAFTER	a fan	
WAGGED	shook; vibrated; swayed	
WAGGEL	great gull	zo
WAGGLE	vibrate; oscillate (golf)	
WAGGON	wagon; dray	
WAGING	betting; venturing; conducting	
WAG-WIT	a would-be wit	
WAHABI	Puritan Moslem	rl
WAHINE	Maori woman; female surfer (Am.)	
WAILED	bemoaned; lamented	
WAILER	howler; weeper	
WAITED	attended; tarried; lingered	
WAITER	attendant; servitor; garçon	
WAIVED	relinquished; forwent	
WAIVER	yielder; renouncer; relinquish; abandon	
WAKING	arousing; stimulating	
WALING	chastising	
WALING	trench-timbering plank	ce
WALKED	perambulated; strolled	
WALKER	hiker; pedestrian	
WALKYR	Valkyr; a Valkyrie	
WALLAH	an official (Ind.)	
WALLED	enclosed	
WALLER	a wall-builder	
WALLET	purse; scrip; pouch	
WALLEY	skating jump	
WALLOP	to boil; to beat; beer	br
WALLOW	welter; grovel; flounder	
WALNUT	commonest European nut	bt
WALRUS	the morse; sea-horse	zo
WAMBLE	to be queasy	
WAMMUS	knitted jacket (USA)	tx
WAMPEE	a Chinese fruit	
WAMPUM	beads used as cash (N.A. Ind.)	
WANDER	stroll; stray; roam	
WANDLE	supple; nimble (dial.)	
WANDOO	Australian white gum	bt
WANGLE	get by craft	

WANING	declining; ebbing; paling	
WANION	bad luck (Sc.)	
WANKLE	weak; unstable	
WANNED	made pale	
WANTED	needed; lacked; desired	
WANTER	a requirer; craver	
WANTON	sportive; frolicsome; frisky	
WAPITI	stag; American elk	zo
WAPPER	gudgeon; ball-on-string weapon	zo
WAPPET	yelping cur	zo
WARBLE	cattle tumour; quaver; sing	mu, vt
WAR-CRY	slogan	
WARDED	guarded; fended; parried	
WARDEN	guardian; protector; curator; custodian	
WARDER	turnkey; keeper; jailer	
WARELY	warily (Spens.)	
WARIER	more cautious	
WARILY	cautiously; carefully; cannily	
WARMAN	warrior; man-at-arms	
WARMER	hotter; keener	
WARMLY	earnestly; ardently; zealously	
WARMTH	heat; enthusiasm; fervency	
WARM-UP	loosening exercises, pre-match	
WARNED	cautioned; notified; apprised	
WARNER	an admonisher	
WARPED	distorted; perverted; biased	
WARPER	a weaver; a twister	tx, wv
WARRAY	to ravage by war (Spens.)	
WARREN	rabbit burrows; enclosure	
WAR-TAX	tax to help war	
WARTED	verrucose	md
WASABI	Jap. horseradish	ck
WASHED	laved; absterged; purged	
WASHER	metal ring; tap root	pb
WASH-IN	increase in angle of incidence	
WASH-UP	cleaning dishes	
WASTED	frittered; squandered	
WASTEL	a fine sort of bread	
WASTER	a cudgel; spendthrift; chisel; defective brick	
WATERY	aqueous; dilute; thin; insipid	
WATTLE	fowl's gills	zo
WATTLE	an acacia; a hurdle	bt
WAUCHT	} a deep draught; to quaff (Sc.)	
WAUGHT		
WAULED	} caterwauled	
WAWLED		
HOWLED		
WAVERY	unsteady; tremulous	
WAVING	undulating; swaying	
WAVURE	procrastination	
WAX-END	cobbler's thread	
WAXIER	more irate	
WAXING	growing; increasing; rising; application of wax weather-proofing to all soles and skis	
WAYLAY	to ambush; kidnap; mug; rob	
WAYOUT	advanced; unusual	
WEAKEN	impair; enfeeble; enervate	

WEAKER	more dilute; thinner; feebler	
WEAKLY	delicately; infirmly; frailly	
WEALTH	riches; opulence; abundance	
WEANED	alienated; withdrawn	
WEAPON	sometimes blunt	
WEARER	bearer; waster	
WEASEL	explosive carnivore	**zo**
WEAVER	bird	**zo**
WEAZEN	wizened; sharp; shrivelled (Sc.)	
WEBBED	arachnoid; woven (duck-foot)	**wv**
WEB-EYE	a disease of the cornea	**md**
WEB-FED	of printing paper by reel	**pr**
WEDDED	married; espoused; spliced	
WEDELN	S-course downhill ski technique	
WEDGED	scotched; compressed; ceramics	
WEEDED	hoed; eradicated; purged	
WEEDER	garden tool	**to**
WEEKLY	hebdomadary; a periodical	
WEENED	imagined; thought	
WEEPER	Niobe; a monkey	**zo**
WEEVER	sting-fish	**zo**
WEEVIL	a beetle	**zo**
WEIGHT	onus; incubus; load; burden; measure	**me**
WEIGHT	force needed to overcome inertia	
WELDED	united	
WELDER	Irish sub-tenant	
WELKIN	sky, clouds; universe (ring)	
WELLED	poured forth; spouted; gushed	
WELTED	edged; bordered	
WELTER	wallow; flounder; heavy	
WENDED	journeyed; wandered	
WENDIC	a Sorabian	
WESAND	}	
WEZAND	} wind-pipe	
WEAZAND	}	
WESTER	to turn westward	
WET-BOB	Eton aquatic sportsman	
WETHER	a castrated ram	**zo**
WETTER	damper; more showery	
WHALER	whale-boat	**nt**
WHALLY	having greenish-white eyes	
WHATEN	}	
WHATNA	} what kind of (Sc.)	
WHATSO	of whatever kind	
WHEELY	circular	
WHEEZE	puff; blow; ancient joke	
WHEEZY	asthmatic	
WHELKY	rounded; protuberant	
WHENAS	when; whereas (Shak.)	
WHENCE	wherefrom	
WHERRY	a liquor; sailing boat	**nt**
WHEUGH!	exclamation of surprise	
WHEWER	the widgeon; duck	**zo**
WHEYEY	whey-like	
WHILED	beguiled	
WHILES	meanwhile	
WHILLY	to cajole; to wheedle	
WHILOM	formerly	
WHILST	while	
WHIMSY	fad; caprice; fancy; crotchet	
WHINED	whimpered	
WHINER	sniveller	
WHINGE	to whine (Sc.)	
WHINNY	(horse); (gorse)	
WHIPPY	flexible; springy	
WHIRRY	to hurry off (Sc.)	
WHISHT!	hush!	
WHISKY	colour of Napoleon's white horse	
WHITEN	blanch; bleach; turn pale	
WHITER	purer; brighter	
WHITES	flannel trousers (cricket); (eyes); (eggs)	
WHOLLY	entirely; fully; utterly	
WHOMSO	every one whom	
WHYDAH	}	
WHIDAH	} African weaver bird	**zo**
WICKED	evil; sinful; ungodly; nefarious	
WICKEN	mountain ash	**bt**
WICKER	pliant twig; osier	**bt**
WICKET	small gate; (cricket)	
WICOPY	American basswood	**bt**
WIDELY	spaciously; extensively; rifely	
WIDEST	broadest; remotest	
WIELDY	manageable	
WIFELY	wively	
WIGEON	widgeon; duck	**zo**
WIGGED	berated; reproved; chid	
WIGGLE	wriggle; waggle	
WIGWAG	flag-wag; twist	
WIGWAM	Indian tent (tepee) (Amer.)	
WILDER	bewilder	
WILDLY	fiercely; recklessly; savagely	
WILFUL	wanton; perverse; obdurate	
WILIER	craftier; slyer	
WILILY	artfully; cunningly; insidiously	
WILING	beguiling; deceiving	
WILLED	resolved; bequeathed	**lw**
WILLER	one who wills	
WILLET	North American snipe	**zo**
WILLOW	a cricket bat tree	**bt**
WILTED	drooped; withered	
WIMBLE	to drill; gimlet	**to**
WIMBLE	nimble; active	
WIMPLE	a headdress; to ripple	
WINCED	flinched; quailed	
WINCER	a shrinker	
WINCEY	winsey; a fabric	**tx**
WINDED	blew; blown; caught scent	
WINDER	to fan; to winnow; a key	
WINDLE	a spindle; reel	
WINDOW	lattice; casement	
WIND-UP	alarm; trepidation; twisting force for throwing (sports)	
WINERY	where wine is bottled/stored	
WINGED	alate; rapid; wounded	
WINGER	chair; distant footballer	**ga**
WINKED	twinkled; flickered; acquiesced	
WINKER	horse's blinker	
WINKLE	periwinkle	**bt, zo**
WINNER	victor; conqueror; champion	
WINNOW	sift; examine; fan	

WINSEY	wincey; twilled cotton	**tx**
WINTER	hyemal, viernal; cold season	
WINTLE	stagger; writhe (Sc.)	
WINTRY	icy; frosty; cheerless	
WIPING	deterging; rubbing	
WIRIER	capable of greater strain	
WIRILY	vigorously; tenaciously	
WIRING	circuits; telegraphing	
WISARD	} sorcerer; necromancer	
WIZARD	}	
WISDOM	sagacity; knowledge	
WISELY	sagely; sensibly; sapiently	
WISEST	most learned and judicious	
WISHED	listed; wanted; longed for	
WISHER	desirer; yearner	
WISKET	a basket	
WISTLY	earnestly; attentively	
WITHAL	together with; likewise	
WITHED	bound with a withe	
WITHER	fade; pine; languish	
WITHIN	not exceeding; indoors	
WITH-IT	up to date; aware of trends	
WITTED	alert; wise	
WITWAL	popinjay; woodpecker	**zo**
WIVELY	wifely	
WIVERN	wyvern; winged dragon	**hd**
WOBBLE	wabble; oscillate; vibrate	**.**
WOBBLY	unstable; unsteady	
WOEFUL	waeful; tragic; grievous	
WOLFER	voracious feeder	
WOLVES	predacious animals	**zo**
WOMBAT	burrowing marsupial	**zo**
WONDER	marvel; miracle; prodigy; awe	
WONING	a dwelling	
WONTED	accustomed; usual	
WONTON	'Chinese ravioli', cooked in soup	
		ck
WOODED	afforested; timbered	**fr**
WOODEN	clumsy; impassive	
WOODIE	the gallows (Sc.)	
WOOFER	base loudspeaker	**ac**
WOOING	courting; courtship	
WOOLLY	lanate	**tx**
WORDED	expressed; phrased	
WORKED	moiled; strove; slaved	
WORKER	hand; toiler; operative	
WORK-UP	rehearsal; exercise; obtaining data, become heated	
WORMED	crept; insinuated; crawled	
WORMUL	} cow-maggot	**zo**
WORNIL	}	
WORREL	lizard (Egypt)	**zo**
WORRIT	an annoyance	
WORSEN	to defeat; to deteriorate	
WORSER	far worse	
WORTHY	exemplary; noble; meritorious	
WOUNDY	excessive; injurious	
WOU-WOU	silver gibbon; wow-wow (Java)	
WOWSER	kill-joy; fanatical Puritan	
WRAITH	apparition; ghost; spectre	
WRASSE	prickly fish	**zo**

WRATHY	apt to wrath; choleric	
WREATH	festoon; garland; chaplet	
WRENCH	strain; sprain; twist; spanner	**to**
WRETCH	villain; vagabond; miscreant	
WRIEST	most distorted	
WRIGHT	an artificer; mechanic	
WRITER	scribe; author; scribbler	
WRITHE	squirm; wriggle; contort	
WUTHER	to low (dial.)	
WUZZLE	to jumble (USA)	
WYVERN	wivern; heraldic dragon	**hd**

X

XANADU	Kubla Khan's country	
XANGTI	Zeus (Chinese)	
XANTHO-	of yellowness	**cf**
XENIAL	genial; friendly	
XENIUM	gift; picture of still life	
XENOPS	tree-creeper birds (S. Amer.)	**zo**
XERXES	Persian King; Ahasuerus	
X-GUIDE	transmission line	
XOANON	primitive Greek statue	
X-RAYED	(Rontgen rays)	**md**
XYLENE	a benzene derivative	**ch**
XYLITE	asbestos	**mn**
XYLOID	like wood	
XYLOMA	internally spore-forming body	**bt**
XYLOSE	wood sugar	**ch**
XYSTER	a bone scraper	**md**
XYSTOS	} covered portico used by	
XYSTUS	} athletes (Greek)	

Y

YABBER	speech (Australian)	
YAFFLE	the green woodpecker	**zo**
YAGGER	pedlar; hawker (Sc.)	
YAHVEH	Jahveh; Jehovah	**rl**
YAKSKA	Hindu gnome	
YAMMER	whine; blather; grumble	
YANKED	heaved	
YANKEE	Northern American	
YANKEE	a specially large jib	**nt**
YANKER	a big lie (Sc.)	
YAOURT	Turkish fermented milk	
YAPOCK	S. Amer. water-opossum	**zo**
YAPPED	yelped	
YAPPER	a yapping dog	**zo**
YARDED	confined	
YARNED	related; narrated	
YARPHA	peaty soil (Shetland)	
YARRAH	Australian red gum tree	**bt**
YARROW	the milfoil	**bt**
YARYAN	soda-recovery method	**pp**
YAUPED	yelped (USA)	**bt**
YAUPON	holly (used as tea)	
YAWING	deviating from course	**nt**
YAWLED	howled; cried	

YAWNED	gaped; oscitated	
YCLEPT	by name of; called	
YEANED	} brought forth	
YEENED		
YEARLY	annual	
YEASTY	turbid; frothy; foamy	
YELLED	bawled; howled; screamed	
YELLOW	cowardly	
YELPED	yauped; yapped; barked	
YELPER	yapper	
YEMENI	native of Yemen	
YENITE	a silicate of iron	mn
YEOMAN	a beefeater; farmer; tow-er	nt
YERKED	jerked	
YER-NUT	pig-nut	bt
YES-MAN	sycophant; ministerial	
YESTER	previous; last	
YEXING	hiccuping	
YOGISM	a Hindu philosophy	
YOICKS!	a hunting cry	
YOJANA	about 5 miles (8 km) (Indian)	me
YOKING	coupling; linking; harnessing; binding	
YOLKED	having a yolk; an eggy jolke	ck
YONDER	over there	
YONKER	a stripling	
YORKER	(cricket)	
YORUBA	tribe (South Sahara)	
YOUTHY	young; callow	
YOU-UNS	you, you ones	
YOWLED	howled; yelled	
YOWLEY	yellow bunting	zo
Y-TRACK	reversing lines for trains	rw
YTTRIA	oxide of yttrium	ch
YTTRIC	containing yttrium	ch
YUCKER	American woodpecker	zo

Z

ZABIAN	Sabian; non-Christian gnostic	
ZABISM	Sabianism	
ZABRUS	beetle genus	zo
ZACCAB	Yucatan wall plaster	
ZACCHO	the base of a pedestal	
ZAFFER	} cobalt ore	mn
ZAFFRE		
ZAMITE	fossil-plant	bt
ZANDER	sander; pike-perch	zo
ZANIES	clowns; buffoons	
ZANTHA	knitted fabric	tx
ZAPOTE	plums (Mexico)	bt
ZARAPE	serape; Mexican blanket	tx
ZAREBA	zeraba; zariba; fortified camp	
ZARNEC	orpiment	mn
ZEALOT	fanatic; bigot; partisan	
ZEATIN	adenine derivative	bc

ZEBECK	Algerian pirate-ship	nt
ZECHIN	sequin; Venetian gold	nm
ZEEKOE	hippopotamus (S. Africa)	zo
ZEETAK	red-coral (S. Africa)	
ZEMZEM	sacred fountain at Mecca	
ZENANA	women's quarter (Ind.)	
ZENDIK	Eastern heretic; magician	
ZENITH	acme; apex; climax; summit	
ZEPHYR	the west wind; soft breeze	mt
ZEREBA	zareba; thornbush stockade	
ZEUGEN	table-like masses of rock in deserts (Germ.)	gl, go
ZEUGMA	grammatical conjunction	
ZICSAC	sicsac; crocodile bird	zo
ZIG-ZAG	series of alternating turns (equestrian)	
ZILLAH	Indian district	
ZIMONE	(gluten)	
ZINCKY	like zinc	
ZINGEL	perch; Danube fish	zo
ZINNIA	a flower	bt
ZIPPED	whizzed; encoded	
ZIPPER	zip-fastener	
ZIRCON	a silicate	mn
ZITHER	the cithern	mu
ZIVOLA	yellow-hammer	zo
ZODIAC	a heavenly girdle; the ecliptic	
ZOETIC	vital	
ZOMBIE	moron; drugged person	
ZONARY	} resembling a girdle	
ZONOID		
ZONATE	belted	
ZONING	area allocation; planning	
ZONNAR	girdle worn in the Levant	
ZONULE	zonula; small zone	
ZONURE	lizard covered with spikes	zo
ZOONAL	embryonic	zo
ZOONIC	zoological	zo
ZOOSIS	animal-parasite-caused disease	
ZOO-ZOO	wood-pigeon	zo
ZOSTER	shingles	md
ZOUAVE	Algerian soldier	
ZOUNDS	'God's wounds'	
Z-SCORE	standard; sigma score (statistics)	
ZUFOLO	zuffolo; flageolet	mu
ZUMATE	} a salt of zymic acid	ch
ZYMATE		
ZUNIAN	Pueblo-Indian	
ZYGITE	an oarsman in a trireme	
ZYGOMA	the cheek-bone	md
ZYGOSE	(fertilization)	bt
ZYGOTE	a spore; a germ-cell	bt, zo
ZYMASE	a ferment; an enzyme	
ZYMITE	priest using leavened bread	rl
ZYMOID	like a ferment; yeasty	ch, ck
ZYMOME	insoluble gluten	
ZYTHUM	ancient type of beer	br

A

AARONIC	(Jewish priest-hood)	**rl**
ABACIST	an accountant	
ABACTOR	cattle thief; rustler	
ABADDON	Apollyon; bottomless pit	
ABALONE	mother-of-pearl	
ABANDON	joie-de-vivre; forsake; quit	
ABASHED	shamed; embarrassed	
ABASING	degrading; humbling	
ABATING	mitigating; stopping	
ABATTIS	military obstacles	
ABATURE	beast tracks	
ABAXIAL	oblique rays; outward from stem	**pg, bt**
ABBOZZO	preliminary sketch	
ABB-WOOL	warp-yarn	
ABDOMEN	the belly	**md**
ABDUCED	abducted; separated	
ABETTED	incited; aided; assisted	
ABETTER	an abettor; instigator	**lw**
ABEYANT	in abeyance	
ABIDING	residence; lasting; durable	
ABIETIC	(conifers)	**bt**
ABIETIN	(resin)	
ABIGAIL	serving-girl; Hebe; waitress	
ABIGEAT	cattle theft	**lw**
ABILITY	legal power; wealth; talent	
ABIOSIS	absence of life	
ABIOTIC	incompatible with life	
ABJUDGE	deprive by law	**lw**
ABJURED	recanted; repudiated	
ABJURER	forswearer	
ABLATOR	heat-protection material; instrument	**md**
ABLEPSY	blindness	**md**
ABLINGS	aiblins; perhaps	
ABLUENT	detergent	
ABOLISH	destroy; extirpate; annul	
ABOULIA	atrophy of reasoning	**pc, md**
ABRADED	scraped; worn away	
ABRAXAS	Gnostic god; amulet	
ABREAST	side by side	
ABRIDGE	curtail; epitomize; summarize	
ABROACH	tapped; afoot; astir	
ABSCESS	boil; ulcer	**md**
ABSCIND	cut off	
ABSCISS	a geometric line	
ABSCOND	decamp; bolt; quit; levant	
ABSENCE	lack; deficiency; non-presence	
ABSIDAL	apse-like	
ABSINTH	liqueur; wormwood	
ABSOLVE	release; exonerate; shrive	
ABSTAIN	refrain; desist; avoid	
ABUSING	perverting; violating	
ABUSION	deception; disparagement	
ABUSIVE	ribald; reviling; calumnious	
ABUTTAL	the boundary of lands	
ABUTTED	contiguous; bordered on	

ABUTTER	neighbour	**lw**
ABYSMAL	fathomless; profound	
ABYSSAL	bottomless	
ACADEMY	also academe; institution	
ACADIAN	Nova Scotian	
ACALEPH	jelly fish	
ACANTHA	prickly plant	**bt**
ACAPNIA	loss of CO_2 in blood	**md**
ACARDIA	heart-less	
ACARIDA	} mites; ticks	**zo**
ACARINA		
ACCABLE	overwhelm; crush (obs.)	
ACCEDED	assented; succeeded	
ACCEDER	one who concurs	
ACCIDIE	sloth; torpor (obs.)	
ACCLAIM	applaud; applause; proclaim	
ACCOAST	(low flying)	
ACCOLLE	collared	**hd**
ACCOMPT	account	
ACCOUNT	deem; reckon; recital; bill	
ACCOURT	to court (Spens.)	
ACCRETE	grow together	
ACCRUED	resulted; accumulated	
ACCURSE	curse; condemn; execrate	
ACCURST	accursed; damned; diabolical	
ACCUSAL	an accusation; indictment	
ACCUSED	defendant; arraigned	**lw**
ACCUSER	plaintiff	**lw**
ACERATE	(aceric acid)	**ch**
ACERBIC	sour; caustic; astringent	
ACEROLA	Amer. cherry-like fruit	**bt**
ACEROSE	acerous; prickly	**bt**
ACETARY	acid pulp	
ACETATE	(vinegar)	**ch**
ACETIFY	acidify	**ch**
ACETONE	liquid ketone; solvent	**ch**
ACETOUS	also acetose; sour	
ACHAEAN	of Archaia (Greek)	
ACHAENE	seeded fruit	**bt**
ACHATES	a true friend	
ACHERON	river of woe	
ACHIEVE	perform; perfect; attain	
ACHIOTE	red colouring matter from seeds	**ck**
ACHOLIA	lack of bile	**md**
ACHTUNG	beware!; look out! (Ger.)	
ACICULA	spiked crystals	
ACIDITY	sourness; tartness	
ACIDIZE	to add acid	
ACIDOID	potentially acid (soil)	
ACIFORM	needle-shaped	
ACINOUS	acinose; granular	
ACK-EMMA	a.m. (signalling)	
ACLINIC	no magnetic dip	
ACOLOGY	the healing art	**md**
ACOLYTE	also acolyth; assistant	**rl**
ACONITE	plant genus; monkshood	**bt**
ACONTIA	free threads of anthozoa	**zo**
ACOUCHY	guinea pig; agouti	**zo**
ACQUEST	acquisition	**lw**

ACQUIRE	get; gain; procure; win	
ACRASIA	inability of self-restraint	pc
ACRATIA	impotence	
ACREAGE	area in acres	
ACRISIA	therapeutic uncertainty	md
ACROBAT	a tumbler; funambulist	
ACROGEN	(club-moss); (tree-fern)	bt
ACRONIC	non-cosmical (astronomy)	
ACRONYM	word composed of initials	
ACRONYX	ingrowing nail	
ACROTER	pinnacle	ar
ACROTIC	superficial	md
ACRYLIC	acid, resins for plastics	ch
ACTABLE	performable	
ACTAMER	substance stopping bacteria growth	
ACTINIA	(sea-anemones)	zo
ACTINIC	chemical ray action (solar)	
ACTRESS	a lady of parts	
ACTUARY	statistical expert; registrar	
ACTUATE	impel; urge; instigate; incite	
ACULEUS	sting; prickle	zo, bt
ACUSHLA	darling (Irish)	
ACUTELY	keenly; intensely; poignantly	
ACYESIS	sterility of female	
ADACTYL	fingerless	
ADAGIAL	proverbial	
ADAMANT	the diamond	mn
ADAMITE	a nudist	
ADAPTED	conformed; attuned; adjusted	
ADAPTER	} fitment; joining device	
ADAPTOR		
ADAXIAL	axis-face of leaf	bt
ADDENDA	appendix; augmented matter	
ADDIBLE	addable	
ADDLING	going rotten; confusing	
ADDRESS	skill; accost; speech	
ADDRESS	stance over ball (golf); domicile; archery	
ADDUCED	cited; brt. forward; alleged	
ADDUCER	a deducer	
ADDULCE	to sweeten	
ADENINE	purine derivative	ch
ADENOID	growth in nasal pharynx	md
ADENOMA	glandular tumour	md
ADENOSE	} glandular	md
ADENOUS		
ADHERED	stuck; clung; held; cleaved	
ADHERER	partisan; ally; parasite	
ADHIBIT	attach; administer	
ADIPOMA	morbid obesity	md
ADIPOSE	fatty; adipous; sebaceous	
ADIPSIA	never thirsty	md
ADJOINT	united; connected	
ADJOURN	suspend; postpone; defer	
ADJUDGE	condemn; decree; ordain	
ADJUNCT	a concomitant	
ADJURED	charged on oath	
ADJURER	adjuror	
ADJUTOR	a helper; colleague; ally	

ADMIRAL	also ammiral	nt
ADMIRED	wondered; appreciated	
ADMIRER	a lover; adorer	
ADMIXED	adulterated; infused	
ADOLODE	distillation tester	
ADONAIS	Shelley's elegy on Keats	
ADONIZE	adonise; beautify	
ADOPTED	appropriated; fathered	
ADORING	worshipping; idolizing	
ADORNED	embellished; decked	
ADORSED	back to back	hd
ADRENAL	(kidneys); gland	md
ADULATE	flatter; cajole; belaud	
ADULLAM	(a cave of refuge)	
ADUSTED	sunburnt; parched	
ADVANCE	to extoll; loan; promote; move forward	
ADVENED	acceded	
ADVENER	an assentor	
ADVERSE	contrary; hostile; inimical	
ADVISED	notified; informed; apprised	
ADVISOR	adviser; counsellor	
ADVOWEE	a patron of a benefice	rl
ADYNAMY	weakness	md
AEOLIAN	aerial; deposits, sanddunes, caused by wind	mu, gl, go
AEOLIST	wind-bag	
AEONIAN	eternal	
AERATED	gassy	
AERATOR	soda-water machine	
AEROBAT	an aerial stunter	
AEROBIA	bacteria	md
AEROBIC	microbial; gymnastic dance	md
AEROBUS	passenger plane	
AEROGEL	gel containing gas	
AEROSOL	sprayed mist	ch
AERO-TOW	record heights achieved (gliding)	
AETATIS	at the age of	
AFFABLE	benign; gracious; sociable	
AFFABLY	cordially; courteously	
AFFICHE	notice; placard	
AFFINAL	akin; related	
AFFINED	united; allied; related	
AFFININ	insecticide from Mex. plant	
AFFIXED	attached; appended; annexed	
AFFLICT	distress; torment; chasten	
AFFORCE	reinforce	
AFFRONT	insult; outrage; abuse	
AFFUSED	spinkled	
AFFYING	betrothing	
AFGHANI	native (Afghanistan)	nm
AFLAUNT	flaunting	
AFRICAN	of Africa	
AGAINST	opposite; counter; despite	
AGALAXY	lack of milk	md
AGAMIST	matrimonial objector	
AGAMOUS	cryptogamic	
AGATINE	like agate	mn
AGATIZE	turn into agate	
AGELESS	timeless	

AGELONG	ancient; antiquated	
AGENDUM	a business item	
AGEUSIA	loss of taste	md
AGGRACE	to favour	
AGGRATE	to gratify	
AGGRESS	encroach; assault; intrude	
AGGROUP	group together	
AGILELY	quickly; actively	
AGILITY	nimbleness; readiness	
AGISTER	} grazing controller	
AGISTOR		
AGITATE	ruffle; perturb; confuse	
AGITATO	spasmodic; restless	mu
AGNAMED	known as	
AGNATHA	lampreys, hagfish	zo
AGNATIC	akin	
AGNOMEN	added surname	
AGNOSIA	perceptionlessness	md
AGONISE	} torture; suffer	
AGONIZE	} (after contest); wrestle	
	in the arena (Gr.)	ga
AGONISM	a competition	
AGONIST	a contestant; muscle	md
AGRAFFE	clasp for armour; a hook	
AGROUND	stranded	
AGYNOUS	non-reproductive	bt
AHRIMAN	evil spirit (Persian)	
AIBLINS	ablings; perhaps	
AIDANCE	help; succour; bounty	
AIDLESS	unsupported; unbacked; solo	
AIGULET	aglet; pendant	
AILANTO	tree of Heaven	bt
AILERON	wing lateral-control	ae
AILETTE	armoured epaulet	
AILMENT	malady; complaint; disorder	
AIMLESS	pointless; random; haphazard	
AIR BASE	strategic air supply point	
AIR GLOW	atmospheric luminosity	
AIR MAIL	post carried by air	
AIR MARK	par avion	
AIR RAID	attack by aeroplanes	
AIR-BATH	nudity for health	
AIR-BONE	hollow bone	
AIR-BUMP	sudden jolt during flight	ae
AIRCAST	sow seed from the air	
AIR-CORE	cable	tc
AIR-FLUE	hot air distributor	
AIRFOIL	aileron	
AIR-FUEL	gas-liquid ratio	eg
AIRHEAD	airport (forward supply); empty-headed	ae
AIR-HOLE	ventilator	
AIRLESS	stuffy	
AIRLIFT	aerial transportation	
AIRLINE	flight transport company	
AIR-LOCK	pump flow stoppage	
AIRPARK	fleet of aeroplanes	
AIRPORT	aeroplane landing area	
AIR-PUMP	vacuum maker	
AIR-SACS	quill vesicles	zo

AIR-SHED	a hangar	ae
AIRSHIP	dirigible; zeppelin	ae
AIRWAYS	airlines	ae
AJACINE	cycactonine acid ester	ch
AJUTAGE	vent pipe	
AKINETE	oil/food storage cell	bt
ALAMEDA	shaded promenade (Moorish)	ar
A-LA-MODE	stylish	
A-LA-MORT	till death	
ALANINE	amino acid	md
ALANTIN	starch	bt
ALARMED	shocked; appalled; daunted	
ALASKAN	(Alaska)	
ALASTOR	Nemesis	
ALBERIA	shield without arms	hd
ALBITIC	(felspar)	ch
ALBORAK	Mahomet's mount to heaven	
ALBUMEN	white of egg	
ALBUMIN	(endosperm)	md
ALCAICS	Alcaic verse	
ALCALDE	judge	
ALCANNA	henna	bt
ALCAZAR	Moorish palace	
ALCHEMY	alchymy; medieval chemistry	
ALCOHOL	pure wine spirit	ch
ALCYONE	star in Pleiades	as
ALECOST	costmary; ale flavouring	bt
ALE-GILL	medicated liquor	
ALEHOOF	ground ivy	bt
ALEMBIC	distilling retort	
ALENGTH	full length	
ALERTER	brisker; more wakeful	
ALERTLY	vigilantly; actively; warily	
ALETHIA	inability to forget	pc
ALETUDE	fatness; bulkiness	
ALEURON	albuminoid	bt
ALE-WIFE	kind of skad; mackerel	zo
ALFALFA	lucerne grass	bt
ALGAROT	antimony emetic	md
ALGATES	by all means; always	
ALGEBAR	the constellation, Orion	as
ALGEBRA	number-properties investigation	
ALGESIA	sensitiveness to pain	
ALGIFIC	producing cold	
ALHENNA	henna; alkenna; orange dye	
ALICANT	Spanish wine	
ALIDADE	surveyor's sight rule	sv
ALIENEE	transferee	
ALIENER	a parter	
ALIFORM	wing-like	
ALIGNED	adjusted; regulated; aimed	
ALIMENT	nutriment; sustenance; food	
ALIMONY	maintenance	lw
ALIQUOT	integral factor	
ALKANET	henna dye	bt
ALKORAN	alcoran; the Koran	rl
ALLALIA	loss of speech	md
ALLAYED	quieted; alleviated; pacified	
ALLEGED	averred; asserted; declared	

273

ALLEGRO	gaily; cheerful pace	**mu**
ALLERGY	distaste; repugnance	
ALLETTE	building wing; buttress	**ar**
ALL-GOOD	a plant	**bt**
ALL-HAIL	a greeting	
ALL-HEAL	a panacea; valerian, etc.	
ALLOBAR	non-natural-isotope form of element	**nc**
ALLONGE	added leaf; lunge	
ALLONYM	assumed name, pseudonym	
ALLOWED	abated; authorized	
ALLOXAN	cyclic ureide	**ch**
ALLOYED	debased; tempered	
ALL-PASS	phase-shift for any frequency	
ALLSEED	flax	**bt**
ALL-TIME	unprecedented occurrence	
ALLUDED	suggested; insinuated; hinted	
ALLURED	enticed; inveigled; decoyed	
ALLUVIA	waterborne deposit	
ALL-WATT	induction motor	**el**
ALL-WAVE	multi-wave	**ro**
ALL-WISE	of infinite wisdom	
ALLYING	betrothing; leaguing	
ALMADIE	bark canoe	**nt**
ALMANAC	calendar	
ALMOIGN	charitable endowment	
ALMONER	giver of alms	
ALMONRY	almsgiving place; cupboard	
ALMS-BOX	charity receptacle	
ALMS-FEE	Peter's pence	
ALMSMAN	receiver of alms	
ALNAGER	wool inspector	
ALODIUM	freehold	**lw**
ALOETIC	purgative	**md**
ALOGISM	illogical statement	
ALONGST	along with	
ALP-HORN	Swiss cow-horn	**mu**
ALREADY	before; previously	
ALSIRAT	bridge to paradise	
ALTERED	modified; transmuted	
ALTERNE	sudden plant-life change	**bt**
ALTHAEA	hollyhock genus	**bt**
ALTHING	Iceland Parliament	
ALT-HORN	saxhorn	**mu**
ALTRICE	bird hatching immature young	
ALTROSE	glucose stereoisomer	**ch**
ALUMINA	aluminium clay	**mn**
ALUMINE	oxide of aluminium	
ALUMING	impregnating with alum	
ALUMISH	resembling alum	
ALUMNUS	college student	
ALUNITE	alum-stone	**mn**
ALVEARY	hive; ear cavity	**pl**
ALVEATE	to hollow out	
ALVEOLA	small cavity	**bt**
ALVEOLE	tooth socket	**pl**
ALYSSUM	a rock plant	**bt**
AMALGAM	mercury alloy	**ch**
AMANDIN	(almonds)	**bt**
AMANOUS	lacking hands	

AMARANT	amaranth; a fadeless flower	**bt**
AMASSED	heaped; collected	
AMATEUR	not a professional	
AMATIVE	loving; lovesome	
AMATORY	ardent; erotic; passionate	
AMAZING	astounding; bewildering	
AMAZONE	riding habit	
AMBAGES	circumlocution; subterfuge	
AMBARIE	covered howdah	
AMBETTI	speck-containing glass	
AMBIENT	encompassing; enfolding	
AMBITAL	pertaining to skeletal parts	
AMBITUS	outer edge	
AMBLING	at an easy gait; sauntering	
AMBOYNA	a decorative wood	**bt**
AMBREIN	(ambergris)	
AMBROID	moulded amber	
AMBSACE	} double-ace (dice)	
AMESACE		
AMBULET	small ambulance	
AMELLUS	purple star-wort	**bt**
AMENAGE	domesticate; manage	
AMENDED	emended; ameliorated	
AMENING	ratifying; sanctioning	
AMENITY	pleasantness; agreeableness	
AMENTAL	bearing catkins	**bt**
AMENTIA	mental deficiency	**md**
AMENTUM	a catkin	**bt**
AMERCED	fined	
AMHARIC	language (Ethiopia)	
AMIABLE	lovable; benign; winsome	
AMIABLY	kindly; charmingly	
AMIDINE	wheat extract	
AMILDAR	Indian official	
AMMETER	ampere meter	**el**
AMMONAL	an explosive	**ch**
AMMONIA	pungent gas	**ch**
AMNESIA	loss of memory	**md, pc**
AMNESIC	loss of language ability	**md, pc**
AMNESTY	pardon; absolution; oblivion	
AMNIOTE	embryo sac classification	**zo**
AMOEBAN	pertaining to amoeba	
AMONGST	amid; between	
AMORIST	philanderer	
AMOROSA	} sweethearts; gallants	
AMOROSI		
AMOROSO	tenderly	**mu**
AMOROUS	amative; passionate	
AMORPHA	indigo	**bt**
AMOTION	deprivation	**lw**
AMPASSY	ampersand, the &	
AMPHORA	two-handled wine jar	
AMPLEST	most lavish; most copious	
AMPLIFY	expand; enlarge; augment	
AMPOULE	glass container for hypodermic dose	**md**
AMPULLA	small glass vial for oil, perfume, salts	
AMUSING	entertaining; droll; ludicrous	
AMUSIVE	amusing	

AMUTTER	muttering	
AMYLASE	starch-hydrolysing enzyme	ch
AMYLENE	(amyl)	ch
AMYLINE	starch cellulose	
AMYLOID	starchy	bt, ch
AMYLOSE	starch constituent	ch
ANABION	anabolism-dominated organism	
ANACARD	cashew-nut	bt
ANAEMIA	general debility	md
ANAEMIC	bloodless	md
ANAGOGE	} mindless interpretation	
ANAGOGY		
ANAGRAM	letter puzzle	
ANALECT	anthology	
ANALGIA	analgesia	
ANALITY	anal libidinous energy	md
ANALOGY	similarity; likeness	
ANALYSE	examine critically	
ANALYST	a resolver	
ANANICE	absolute necessity	
ANAPEST	poetic metre	
ANAPHIA	loss of sense of touch	
ANAPSID	having roofed skull	zo
ANARCHY	chaos; disorder; violence	
ANATASE	titanium oxide	ch
ANATOMY	a skeleton; dissection	md
ANATRON	glass scum	
ANAUDIA	loss of voice	
ANAXIAL	asymmetrical	zo
ANCHOVY	a small fish	zo
ANCHUSA	alkanet, red dye	bt
ANCIENT	antique; pristine ensign	
ANCONES	ornamental brackets	
ANCORAL	like an anchor; hooked	
ANCRESS	} female anchorite	
ANKRESS		
ANDANTE	rather slow	mu
ANDARAC	a red pigment	
ANDIRON	endiron; fire-dog	
ANDRASE	male-producing enzyme/ hormone	
ANDROID	automaton; robot; imitation man	
ANDVARI	a dwarf (Norse myth.)	
ANELACE	anlace; a broad dagger	
ANELING	annointing with oil	rl
ANEMONE	anemony; windflower	bt, zo
ANERGIA	lack of energy	md
ANEROID	a kind of barometer	
ANESONE	white anise liqueur	
ANETHOL	oil of anise	bt
ANEURIA	lack of nervous energy	
ANEURIN	B-group vitamin	
ANGARIA	war rights	
ANGELIC	seraphic; cherubic; heavenly	
ANGELOT	ancient lute; cheese	nm, mu, ck
ANGELUS	a prayer; (bell-ringing)	rl
ANGERED	exasperated; enraged; roused	
ANGERLY	angrily; wrathfully	
ANGEVIN	of Anjou	

ANGIOID	like blood/lymph vessel	
ANGIOMA	dilated-blood-vessel tumour	md
ANGLICE	in English	
ANGLIFY	to anglicize	
ANGLING	hopeful occupation	
ANGLIST	expert in English	
ANGRILY	wrathfully; irately	
ANGUINE	snake-like	
ANGUISH	agony; distress; rack; pang	
ANGULAR	sharp cornered	
ANIDIAN	shapeless	
ANILINE	indigo derivative	ch
ANILITY	dotage; senility; imbecility	
ANIMATE	actuate; vivify; excite	
ANIMATO	lively, animated	mu
ANIMISM	} religious theory that the	
ANIMIST	} soul is the vital principle	
ANISEED	the seed of the anise	bt
ANNATES	first fruits	rl, lw
ANNATTO	annotto; a reddish dye	bt
ANNELID	worm	zo
ANNEXED	affixed; subjoined; attached	
ANNOYED	harassed; pestered; molested	
ANNOYER	an irritator; teaser	
ANNUENT	nodding	
ANNUITY	a yearly payment	
ANNULAR	ring-like	
ANNULET	small fillet round a column	
ANNULUS	ring; ring-shaped; sphincter	pl, md
ANODERM	skinless	bt
ANODISE	dyeing aluminium	
ANODONT	a freshwater mussel	zo
ANODYNE	pain-killer; opiate; sedative	
ANOESIA	idiocy; comprehension failure	pc
ANOESIS	effortless reception of impressions	pc
ANOETIC	pertaining to anoesis	pc
ANOLINI	ravioli	ck
ANOLYTE	portion of electrolyte	el
ANOMALY	irregularity; eccentricity	
ANOPSIA	blindness; (cataract); squint	md
ANOREXY	lack of appetite	md
ANORMAL	abnormal	
ANOSMIA	loss of smell power	md
ANOTHER	one more	
ANSATED	with a handle	
ANTACID	a corrective; neutraliser	ch, md
ANTAPEX	point opposite to apex	as
ANT-BEAR	American ant-eater	zo
ANTE-ACT	an act preceding	
ANTEFIX	ornamental tiling	
ANT-EGGS	the pupae of ants	zo
ANTENNA	a feeler	ro, zo
ANT-HILL	a formicary	zo
ANTHOID	flower-like	bt
ANTHONY	saint; piglet	rl
ANTHRAX	wool-sorter's disease	md
ANTICAL	stem/leaf upper surface	bt
ANTICER	anti-icing means	ae

ANTICLY	oddly; fantastically; quaintly	
ANTICOR	animal disease	
ANTICUM	a front porch	
ANTI-GAS	for combating gas	
ANTIGEN	cause of antibodies	**md**
ANTILOG	anti-logarithm	**ma**
ANTIPYR	formalin	**ch**
ANTIQUA	printing type	**pr**
ANTIQUE	archaic; old; ancient	
ANTI-RED	anti-communist	
ANTISAG	preventing sagging	**ar**
ANT-LIKE	industrious	
ANT-LION	a neuropterous insect	**zo**
ANTONYM	the opposite of a synonym	
ANVILED	forged; wrought by a smith	
ANXIETY	concern; disquiet; uneasiness	
ANXIOUS	troubled; apprehensive	
ANYBODY	person unspecified	
ANYWAYS	anyhow	
ANYWHEN	any old time	
ANYWISE	somehow	
APAGOGE	} progressive argument;	
APAGOGY	} reductio ad absurdum	
APANAGE	natural attribute; perquisite	
APANDRY	male impotence	
APATITE	lime phosphate	**mn**
APAUMEE	open hand	**hd**
APE-HOOD	apishness	
APELIKE	imitative; simian	
APELLES	finished painter	
APEPSIA	poor digestion	**md**
APERTOR	eye-opener; muscle	**md**
APETALY	absence of petals	**bt**
APHACIA	lenslessness of eye	**md**
APHAGIA	inability to swallow, feed	**md,**
		zo
APHAKIA	lenslessness of eye	**md**
APHASIA	temporary dumbness	**md**
APHELIA	plural of aphelion	
APHEMIA	loss of speech	**md**
APHESIS	} vowel elision	
APHETIC	}	
APHIDES	plant-lice; ants' milchcows	**zo**
APHONIA	loss of voice	**md**
APHONIC	speechless	
APHORIA	sterility	
APHOTIC	able to grow without light	**bt**
APHRITE	carbonate of lime	**mn**
APHTHAE	ulceration of the mouth	**md**
APHYLLY	absence of leaves	**bt**
APICIAN	epicurean; gastronomic	
APIECES	in pieces (obs.)	
APINOID	clean	**md**
APISHLY	monkey-like	
A-PITPAT	palpitating	
APLANAT	lens lacking spherical aberration	
APLASIA	defective structural growth	**md**
APOCOPE	elision; verbal curtailment	
APOCYTE	cell-less protoplasm	**bt**
APODOUS	apodal, footless	

APOGAMY	sex function loss	**bt**
APOGEAN	culminating; climactic	
APOGENY	} sterility	
APOGYNY	}	**bt**
APOLOGY	excuse; explanation; plea	
APOLUNE	point in moon satellite orbit	**as**
APOPLEX	apoplexy (obs.)	
APOSTIL	marginal note; postscript	
APOSTLE	a divine messenger	
APOTOME	} mathematical difference; a	
APOTOMY	} major semitone	**mu**
APPAREL	equipment; attire; vesture	
APPEACH	impeach; censure (obs.)	
APPEASE	pacify; assuage; placate	
APPERIL	peril (Shak.)	
APPLAUD	praise; commend; extol	
APPLIED	referred; exercised; used	
APPOINT	nominate; prescribe; enjoin	
APPOSED	placed side by side	
APPOSER	an examiner; questioner	
APPRISE	inform; acquaint; warn	
APPRIZE	appreciate; appraise	
APPROOF	sanction; praise; trial	
APPROVE	ratify; assent; encourage	
APPULSE	rapprochement	
APRAXIA	loss of movement ability	**pc**
APRICOT	abricock	**bt**
APRICOT	brandy; fruit	**bt**
APRONED	wearing an apron	
APROPOS	pertinent; opportune; timely	
APROTIC	high-dielectric solvent	**ch**
APSIDAL	absidal; apse	
APSIDES	perigee and apogee	
APTERAL	wingless; end columns	**zo, ar**
APTERYX	kiwi-bird (New Zealand)	**zo**
APTHOUS	(thrush); ulcerous	**md**
APTNESS	suitability; felicity	
APTOTIC	indeclinable	
APYREXY	absence of fever	**md**
APYROUS	unchanged by heat	
AQUAFER	} permeable strata	
AQUIFER	}	**gl**
AQUARIA	(aquariums)	**zo**
AQUASOL	sulphonated castor oil	**ch**
AQUATIC	in/of water	
AQUEOUS	water; humid; damp	
AQUILON	the north wind	
ARABIAN	of Arabia	
ARABINE	gum arabic	**bt**
ARABISM	Arab idiom	
ARABIST	Arabic expert	
ARACHIS	peanut genus	**bt**
ARAMAIC	Syriac; Aramite	
ARAMEAN	Chaldaic; Chaldean	
ARATION	ploughing	
ARBITER	umpire; judge; referee	
ARBLAST	crossbow	
ARBORED	arboured	
ARBORET	shrub	**bt**
ARBUTUS	an evergreen	**bt**

ARCADED	having arcades	
ARCADIA	pastoral country	
ARCADIA	(Sir Philip Sidney)	
ARCANUM	a mystery; a secret	
ARCHAIC	Noachian; antiquated	
ARCHERY	a pastime	
ARCH-FOE	Satan	
ARCHING	curved; vaulting	
ARCHIVE	home for public documents; file	
ARCHLET	small arch	
ARCHWAY	gateway; gatehouse	
ARC-LAMP	carbon-pole-bridge lamp	
ARCTOID	like a bear	
ARCUATE	bow-shaped	
ARDENCY	passion; warmth; fire	
ARDUOUS	laborious; toilsome	
AREFIED	withered; arid; parched	
ARENOSE	sandy; arenaceous	
AREOLAR	areolic; cell nucleus	bt
ARGHOOL	Arab reed pipe	mu
ARGOTIC	slangy	
ARGUING	discussing; debating	
ARGYRIA	silver poisoning	md
ARGYROL	silver antiseptic	
ARICINA }	alkaloid drug	md
ARICINE }		
ARIDITY	dryness; aridness; sterility	
ARIETTA }	virtuoso operatic air	mu
ARIETTE }		
ARIGHTS	correctly	
ARILLED	having a husk	bt
ARILLUS	seed coating	bt
ARIPPLE	aglinting	
ARISING	emerging; originating	
ARMHOLE	clothing aperture for arm	tx
ARMIGER	an esquire; bearer of coat of arms	hd
ARMILLA	antique bracelet	
ARMLESS	lacking arms	
ARMOIRE	cupboard for coats of arms; aumbry	hd
ARMORIC	Breton dialect	
ARMOURY	arsenal; magazine	
ARNOTTO	annatto; orange dye	bt
AROUSAL	awakening; uprising	
AROUSED	excited; provoked	
ARRAIGN	accuse; summon	lw
ARRANGE	group; classify; dispose	
ARRAYED	marshalled; equipped	
ARREARS	payments overdue	
ARRIDED	pleased; gratified; scorned	
ARRIERE	rear; back; remote (Fr.); (pelota)	ar
ARRIVAL	advent; coming; newcomer	
ARRYISH	festive; jovial	
ARSENAL	armoury; depository	
ARSENIC	a metallic element	ch
ARTEMON	bowsail on merchantman of Rome	
ARTERIO-	of artery; arterial	cf

ARTICLE	essay; paper; indenture	
ARTISAN	artizan; workman; operative	
ARTISTE	a fine performer	
ARTLESS	simple; ingenuous; naive	
ARTSMAN	a craftsman	
ARTWORK	creative design	
ARUSPEX	soothsayer; seer; diviner	
ASARONE	form of camphor	
ASBOLIN	oil from soot	
ASCARID	parasite worm	zo
ASCESIS	self-discipline	rl
ASCETIC	austere; rigid; abstemious	
ASCIANS	equator dwellers	
ASCIDIA	molluscs	zo
ASCITES	peritoneal fluid collection	md
ASCITIC	dropsical	md
ASCRIBE	attribute; assign; impute	
ASEPSIS	sterilization	md
ASEPTIC	sterilized	
ASEXUAL	algamic; sexless	
ASHAMED	abashed; confused	
ASH-CAKE	pastry cooked in ashes	ck
ASH-FIRE	chemical operations fire	
ASH-HEAP	tip for ashes	
ASHIVER	atremble	
ASH-TRAY	cigarette butt tray	
ASH-WORT	a weed	bt
ASIARCH	Asiatic Proconsul	
ASIATIC	of Asia	
ASINEGO	a dolt; asinico	
ASININE	ass-like; idiotic; obstinate	
ASKANCE	obliquely; aslant; awry	
ASOCIAL	dropout from society	pc
ASPERGE	sprinkle	
ASPERSE	slander; vilify; traduce	
ASPHALT	bitumen	mn
ASPHYXY	suffocation	md
ASPIRED	soared; aimed high; yearned	
ASPIRER	aspirant; competitor	
ASPIRIN	a drug	md
ASPRAWL	sprawling	
ASPREAD	scattered	
ASPROUT	sprouting	
ASQUINT	obliquely; askew	
ASSAGAI	assegai; spear	
ASSAPAN	flying squirrel (N. Amer.)	zo
ASSAULT	onset; attack; storm; assail (fencing)	
ASSAYED	tested; tried; endeavoured	
ASSAYER	metallurgist; analyst	
ASSEGAI	assegay; Zulu spear	
ASSEVER	asseverate; allege; aver	
ASS-HEAD	blockhead	
ASSIEGE	to besiege	
ASSISTS	passes for goals (lacrosse)	
ASSIZER	inspector of weights	
ASSIZES	Courts of jurisdiction	lw
ASSIZOR	juror	lw
ASSUAGE	allay; pacify; mollify; quell	
ASSUMED	usurped; feigned; supposed	

ASSUMER	an arrogant person	
ASSURED	pledged; guaranteed	
ASSURER	} underwriter; insurer	lw
ASSUROR		
ASSWAGE	assuage (obs.)	
ASTABLE	free-running, self-sustaining	ro
ASTASIA	inability to keep erect	md
ASTATIC	unstable; lacking polarity	
ASTEISM	refined irony	
ASTERIA	(sapphire)	mn
ASTERID	star-fish	zo
ASTHORE	darling; acushla (Irish)	
ASTONED	astonished; confounded	
ASTOUND	amaze; daze; stupefy	
ASTRAEA	Goddess of Justice	
ASTRAND	stranded	
ASTRICT	restrict; bind	
ASTRIDE	astraddle	
ASTRITE	star-stone	mn
ASTROID	star-shaped	
ASTYLAR	without columns	
ASUDDEN	suddenly	
ASUNDER	apart; divided; divergent	
ATACTIC	of randomly arranged polymer constituents	ch
ATARAXY	impassiveness; coolness	
A-TAUNTO	tidy and shipshape	nv
ATAVISM	reversion to type	
ATAVIST	resembles his ancestors	
ATCHEEN	(banting), fast sail dugout (Malaya)	nt
ATEBRIN	anti-malarial drug	md
ATEKNIA	childlessness	
ATELENE	amorphous; imperfect	
ATELIER	studio; sculptor's workshop	
ATHALIA	saw-fly	
ATHANOR	alchemist's furnace	
ATHEISE	} proselytise unbelief	
ATHEIZE		
ATHEISM	disbelief	
ATHEIST	a nullifidian	
ATHIRST	eager; dry; thirsty	
ATHLETE	athleta; a contestant	
ATHRILL	thrilling	
ATHRONG	crowded	
ATHWART	across; askew; aslant	
ATHYMIA	lack of feeling	md
ATHYMIA	thymus gland deficiency	md
ATHYRIA	absence of thyroid gland	md
ATOBOMB	atomic bomb	
ATOKOUS	lacking offspring	
ATOMATE	covered by small particles	bt
ATOMISM	atomic theory	
ATOMIST	atomic theorist	
ATOMIZE	vaporize	
ATONING	expiating; reconciling	
ATRESIA	failure of opening development	
ATROPAL	not inverted; upturned	bt
ATROPHY	wasting away	md
ATROPIA	bella-donna	md

ATROPIN	deadly nightshade	bt
ATTABOY	a panegyric (USA)	
ATTACCA	continue without break (It.)	mu
ATTACHE	junior member of embassy; case	
ATTAGAS	a pheasant	zo
ATTAINT	corrupt; convicted	
ATTELET	ornamental meat skewer	ck
ATTEMPT	try; aim; endeavour; effort	
ATTICAL	classical	
ATTINGE	touch	
ATTIRED	garbed; dressed; arrayed	
ATTRACT	draw; allure; charm; decoy	
ATTRIST	to sadden	
ATTRITE	worn by friction; penitent	
ATTUNED	in harmony	
AUBERGE	an inn (Fr.)	
AUCTION	roup; vendue	
AUDIBLE	able to be heard	
AUDIBLY	spoken clearly	
AUDIENT	listening; attentive	
AUDILES	who prefer auditory images and stimuli	
AUDITED	examined; checked	
AUDITOR	examiner; accountant	
AUGITIC	(augite); (pyroxene)	mn
AUGMENT	amplify; increase; enhance	
AUGURAL	soothsaying; ominous	
AUGURED	portended; foretold	
AURALLY	(ear)	
AURATED	aureate; golden	
AUREATE	gilded	
AUREITY	the property of gold	
AURELIA	a chrysalis	zo
AUREOLA	aureole	
AUREOLE	golden halo	
AURICLE	ear; heart; leaf base	md, bt
AURIFIC	gold bearing	
AURITED	having ears	
AUROCHS	urus; wild ox; Eur. bison	zo
AURORAL	(dawn); eoan	
AUSLAUT	final syllable/word sound (Ger.)	
AUSONIA	Italy	
AUSPICE	augury; omen; portent	
AUSTERE	severely simple; ascetic	
AUSTRAL	southern	
AUTARCH	autocrat; tyrant	
AUTARKY	national self-sufficiency	
AUTOBUS	omnibus	
AUTOCAR	motor car	
AUTONYM	true name	
AUTOPSY	post-mortem exam.	md
AUTOSET	quick-levelling in surveying	
AUTO-VAC	vacuum	au
AUXESIS	hyperbole	
AUXETIC	amplifying	
AVAILED	answered the purpose; helped	
AVARICE	greed; rapacity; cupidity	
AVENAGE	barley-corn rent	lw
AVENGED	retaliated; revenged	

AVENGER	vindicator	
AVENOUS	lacking veins	**md**
AVERAGE	mean; moderate; ordinary	
AVERNUS	infernal regions	
AVERRED	affirmed; alleged; stated	
AVERTED	warded off; prevented	
AVERTER	preventer; diverter	
AVIATED	flew; planed	
AVIATOR	aeroplane pilot	
AVICIDE	killing of birds	
AVICULA	kind of pearl oyster	
AVIDITY	greed; voracity; eagerness	
AVIETTE	a glider	
AVIFORM	bird-shaped	
AVOCADO	alligator-pear	**bt, ck**
AVODIRE	African hard-wood	**bt**
AVOIDED	eschewed; annulled; eluded	
AVOIDER	dodger; shunner	
AVOWANT	defendant in replevin	**lw**
AVOWING	owning; admitting; averring	
AWAITED	eagerly expected; tarried	
AWAKING	rousing; bestirring	
AWARDED	bestowed; granted; allotted	
AWARDER	a judge; donor; giver	**lw**
AWAVING	fluttering	
AWELESS	without fear	
AWESOME	full of awe; fearsome	
AWFULLY	dreadfully; portentously	
AWKWARD	clumsy; ungainly; inapt	
AWL-BIRD	woodpecker	**zo**
AWL-WORT	an aquatic plant	**bt**
AWNLESS	beardless	**bt**
AXIALLY	from pole to pole	
AXIFORM	like a spindle or aborr	
AXILLAR	a feather	**zo, bt**
AXLE-BOX	automobile part	**au**
AXLE-PIN	linch-pin	
AXOLOTL	larval salamander	**zo**
AXOTOMY	severing of axon nerve	**md**
AZALINE	emulsion-sensitizing dye mixture	
AZAROLE	medlar	**bt**
AZELAIC	rancid-fat acid	**ch**
AZILIAN	pre-Neolithic	
AZIMUTH	arc of horizon and vertical angle; angular distances	**me, nv, as**
AZOTITE	nitrous acid	**ch**
AZOTIZE	to nitrogenise	
AZOTOUS	nitrous	
AZTECAN	Aztec	
AZULEJO	bright-coloured Iberian tile	
AZUREAN	sky-blue	
AZURINE	azure	
AZURITE	copper carbonate	**mn**
AZYGOUS	not in pairs	
AZYMITE	Armenian churchman	**rl**
AZYMOUS	unleavened; unfermented	

B

BAALISM	idolatry	
BAALITE	worshipper of Baal	
BABBING	catching eels (angling)	
BABBLED	chattered; jabbered	
BABBLER	tropical thrush	**zo**
BABIISM	Persian religion	
BABUINA	female baboon	**zo**
BABYISH	infantile	
BABYISM	infancy	
BACCARA	baccarat	
BACCARE	stand back!	
BACCATE	berry-shaped; pulpy	**bt**
BACCHIC	roistering; carousing	
BACCHUS	the god of Wine	
BACILLI	bacteria; microbes	**md**
BACK OFF	} retire, leave, retreat,	
BACK OUT	} withdraw	
BACK-CUT	tree-felling cut	**fr**
BACKERS	supporters; white background to targets	
BACKING	aiding; abetting; retiring; strengthening; (finance); anticlockwise (wind)	**nt**
BACK-LOG	delayed work	
BACK-OUT	reversal of missile drill	
BACK-SAW	thick-backed saw	**cr**
BACKSET	an eddy	
BACTRIS	peach-palm	**bt**
BADDISH	rather bad	
BADIAGA	small sponge	
BADIANE	bandian; aniseed	**bt**
BADNESS	depravity; evil; wickedness	
BAFFLED	foiled; checked; bewildered	
BAFFLER	thwarter; confounder	
BAGASSE	refuse sugar stalks	
BAGGAGE	luggage; belongings; traps	
BAGGALA	2-masted Arab vessel	**nt**
BAGGING	bag-cloth; pouching	
BAGPIPE	has 3 drones and a chanter	**mu**
BAGWORK	bagged concrete, gravel for sea wall	**ce**
BAHADUR	Indian title	
BAILAGE	ancient export duty	
BAILIFF	land steward; overseer	**lw**
BAILING	confining; releasing	
BAILLIE	a bailiff (Sc.)	
BAITING	victuals; badgering; harassing	
BAKE-OUT	electrode/valve pre-heating	**el**
BALANCE	poise; weigh; surplus	
BALANUS	crustacean; acorn-shell	**zo**
BALCONY	hanging porch	**bd**
BALDEST	barest; plainest	
BALDING	loss of hair	
BALDISH	somewhat bald	
BALDRIC	baudric; shoulder-belt	
BALEFUL	evil; noxious; pernicious	
BALISTA	large Roman catapult	
BALKING	} refusal at horse jump	
BAULKING	}	

BALLADE	} poetry with music	**mu**
BALLATA		
BALLAST	quasi-cargo; gravel; stability	**nt**
BALL-BOY	(tennis) (football)	**ga**
BALLETT	dance-like vocal composition	**mu**
BALLING	becoming clogged	
BALLISM	motor nerve disorder	**md**
BALLIUM	bulwark	
BALLOON	gas-filled envelope, skycraft	**ae**
BALLOON	vertical hit (cricket)	**ga**
BALMIER	sweeter; milder	
BALMILY	soothingly; fragrantly	
BALMING	assuaging; embalming	
BALNEAL	pertaining to bathing	
BALNEUM	a bath	**ch**
BALONEY	nonsense, something not to be believed	
BALSAMY	fragrant; aromatic	
BAMBINO	a child (It.)	
BAMMING	hoaxing; cheating	
BANABAN	Micronesian language	
BANBURY	a cake	**ck**
BANDAGE	ligament; ligature	
BANDANA	silk handkerchief	
BANDBOX	hat box, new-clothes box	
BANDEAU	brow-band	
BANDIAN	badiane; aniseed	**bt**
BANDIED	discussed; tossed; agitated	
BANDING	uniting together; decorative multiwood inlay, border	
BANDLET	bandelet; a flat moulding	
BANDORA	} ancient cittern	**mu**
PANDORA		
BANDORE	lute-like plucked continuo	**mu**
BANDROL	banderole; small flag	
BAND-SAW	saw over wheels	**to**
BANEFUL	baleful; deadly; venomous	
BANGING	overwhelming; clattering	
BANGLED	with bangles	
BANK-BAR	mine-shaft lining	**mn**
BANKING	relying; (financial); earthworks; tilting of aircraft	**ae**
BANKSIA	dwarf yellow climbing rose	**bt**
BANNING	cursing; proscribing; barring	
BANNOCK	oaten-cake (Sc.)	**ck**
BANQUET	feast; regalement	**ck**
BANSHEE	ghost (Irish)	
BANTENG	Malayan wild ox	
BANTERY	raillery	
BANTING	reducing the diet; slimming	
BANTING	wild ox (East. Ind.); atcheen, fast sail-dugout craft (Malaya)	**nt**
BANYULS	Pyrenean wine	
BAPTISM	immersion at christening	**rl**
BAPTIST	member of Protestant sect	
BAPTIZE	christen	
BARACAN	camel-hair cloth	**tx**
BARBARY	a Saracen country (N. Africa)	
BARBATE	bearded; awned	**bt**
BAR-BELL	dumb-bell; weight-lifting bar	

BARBING	shaving; trimming; piercing	
BARBOLA	modern gesso	
BARBULE	small beard	**bt**
BARCHAN	} windblown deposit	**gl**
BARCHANE		
BARDISH	bardic; (poetry)	
BARDISM	the lore of bards	
BARDLET	bardling; poetaster	
BAREBOW	without sighting or aiming (archery)	
BARGAIN	chaffer; haggle; compact	
BARGING	shoving; elbowing; jostling; intrusion of line (yachting)	
BARILLA	raw seaweed alkali	
BAR-IRON	malleable iron in bars	
BARK-BED	tanner's hot-bed	**le**
BARKERY	tan-house	**le**
BARKHAN	lone crescentic sandhill	**gl**
BARKING	peeling; (shins)	
BARK-PIT	tan-vat	**le**
BARMAID	Hebe; tavern server; sleeper	
BARMIER	fightier; more crazy	
BARMKIN	outer castle ward	
BARNABY	the apostle Barnabas	
BARNAGH	large welk	**zo**
BARNING	storing; garnering	
BARN-OWL	screech owl, night-bird	**zo**
BARONET	bart; hereditary title	
BAROQUE	17th Cent. style architecture, music	**mu**
BARRACE	lists (tournament)	
BARRACK	(booing)	
BARRAGE	embankment; barrier; dam; fencing	
BARRAGE	(artillery fire); barre chords on guitars	**mu**
BARRENS	elevated plateaux	
BARRICO	small keg (Sp.)	
BARRIER	hindrance; embargo; obstacle	
BARRING	excluding; banning	
BARRULY	heraldic division	**hd**
BAR-SHOE	special horseshoe	
BAR-SHOT	double connected shot	
BARTRAM	the plant pellitory	**bt**
BARWOOD	red dye-wood	**bt**
BARYTES	barium sulphate	**ch**
BARYTIC	(baryta)	
BARYTON	tenor-bass viol	**mu**
BASBLEU	blue stocking	
BASCULE	balanced drawbridge; perfect arc of horse jumping	
BASE-BOX	metal-plate measurement unit	**ml**
BASENET	bascinet; basnet; a helmet	
BASENJI	Congo barkless dog	**zo**
BASHFUL	strikingly modest; shy	
BASHING	coshing; slugging	
BASHLYK	Russian hood	
BASILAR	serving as a basis	
BASILIC	basilican style	
BASINED	in a basin	

BASINET	basnet; round helmet	
BASKING	luxuriating; revelling	
BASLARD	a small dagger	
BASSOCK	fibre mat	
BASSOON	bass oboe	mu
BASTARD	spurious; base-born; natural	
BASTILE	castle on wheels	
BASTING	coarse stitching	
BASTION	an out-work	
BATABLE	debatable; controversial	
BATATAS	sweet potatoes	bt
BAT-BOAT	sea-plane	ae, nt
BATEELE	} small dhow	nt
BATELO		
BATEFUL	contentious; disputable	
BATH BUN	a comestible	ck
BATHING	giving/having a bath	
BATHMAN	attendant	
BATH-MAT	thick bathroom carpet	
BATHYAL	pert. to deep-sea zone	
BATISTE	cambric	
BATSMAN	a cricketer	
BATTELS	provisions (Oxford)	
BATTERY	stored electricity; hens	el, zo
BATTERY	(assault); test group; (baseball)	
		lw
BATTERY	(artillery)	el
BATTING	quilting; cricket; angling	
BATTISH	bat-like	
BATTLED	battlemented; fought	
BATTLER	resident at Oxford	
BATTURE	raised sea/river bed	go
BATTUTA	3 bar rhythm beat (It.)	mu
BAUDRIC	shoulder sash	
BAULKED	shied; balked; jibbed	
BAUSOND	badger-like	zo
BAUXITE	(aluminium)	mn
BAWCOCK	fine fellow	
BAWDILY	lewdly; obscenely	
BAWDKIN	baldachin; canopy	rl
BAWLING	shouting; clamouring	
BAYONET	a weapon of offence	
BAY-SALT	evaporated sea-water	
BAY-TREE	the laurel	bt
BAYWOOD	mahogany	bt
BAY-YARN	woollen yarn	
BAZIGAR	nomadic Ind. gypsy	
BAZOOKA	anti-tank gun	
BEACHED	on the beach	
BEADING	narrow moulding	
BEADMAN	an almsman	
BEAKING	(cock-fighting)	
BEAMILY	broad on the beam	
BEAMING	radiant; gleaming; bright	
BEAN-FLY	a garden pest	zo
BEARDED	awned; defied; opposed	
BEARDIE	the whitethroat bird	zo
BEARING	(magnetic); (rein); (ball); wheel bearing	
BEARISH	uncouth; boorish; rude	
BEAR-PIT	enclosure for bears	

BEASTLY	brutal; sensual; bestial	
BEATIFY	(saint-hood); canonize	
BEATING	chastisement; battering	
BEATNIK	latter-day Bohemian	
BEAUISH	foppish	
BEBEERU	greenheart tree	bt
BECAUSE	owing to	
BECHARM	captivate; fascinate	
BECKING	nodding; bowing	
BECLOUD	obscure; darken; bedim	
BEDDING	planting out; bedclothes; foundation; gun mounting	bt
BEDEAUX	piece-work system	
BEDELRY	beadlery	
BEDEMAN	beadman	
BEDEVIL	bewitch	
BEDEWED	covered with dew; affused	
BEDEWER	a sprinkler	
BEDFAST	bed-ridden	
BED-GOWN	night gown	
BEDIGHT	adorned	
BEDIZEN	gaudily attired	
BED-MATE	bed-fellow	
BEDOUIN	nomadic Arab	
BED-POST	bedstead support	
BED-REST	recuperation	
BEDROCK	basic stratum	gl
BEDROOM	sleeping apartment	
BEDROPT	besprinkled; bedewed	
BEDSIDE	(table); (lamp); (manner)	
BED-SORE	sore from bed-lying	md
BED-TICK	cotton cloth	tx
BEDTIME	time to sleep	
BEDWARD	to bed	
BEDWARF	to belittle; to dwarf	
BEDWORK	easy toil	
BEE-BIRD	fly-catcher	zo
BEECHEN	of beech	
BEEF-TEA	meat-extract drink	
BEE-GLUE	beeswax	
BEE-HIVE	home for bees	
BEE-LINE	straight line	
BEE-MOTH	wax-moth	zo
BEESWAX	product of hives	
BEET-BUG	agricultural pest	zo
BEET-FLY	a dipterous insect	zo
BEETLED	jutted out; smote	
BEE-TREE	American linden	bt
BEFFANA	befana; Epiphany fairy	
BEGGARY	mendicancy; indigence	
BEGGING	soliciting; craving; imploring	
BEGHARD	beguine; religious order	rl
BEGLOOM	sadden	
BEGONIA	elephant's ear plant	bt
BEGORED	gory; ensanguined	
BEGRIME	(grime); sully; foul	
BEGROAN	lament; complain	
BEGUARD	a beghard; lay mendicant	
BEGUILE	pass pleasantly; amuse	
BEGUILE	deceive; delude; trick	
BEGUILE	soothe (obs.)	

BEGUINE	beghard; (religious order)	**rl**
BEHAVED	acted with propriety	
BEHENIC	of bean oil acid	**ch**
BEHONEY	sweeten	
BEHOOVE	to be necessary	
BEHOVED	was necessary; befitted	
BEINKED	smudged	
BEJEWEL	set with gems	
BEKNAVE	to call a knave	
BEKNOWN	known	
BELACED	adorned with lace	
BELATED	overdue; retarded	
BELAYED	fastened; held	**nt**
BELCHED	eructated	
BELCHER	coloured kerchief	
BELDAME	old hag	
BELEPER	infect with leprosy	
BELGARD	kind regard (obs.)	
BELGIAN	of Belgium	
BELIBEL	libel; traduce; slander	
BELIEVE	credit; opine; accept	
BELL-HOP	page boy	
BELLIED	dilated	
BELLING	full and ripe; bellowing; of deer in rut	**zo**
BELL-JAR	vacuum enclosure	
BELL-MAN	town crier	
BELLONA	goddess of War	
BELLOWS	(organ); wind producer	
BELOVED	dear; darling	
BELTANE	May Day fire festival	
BELTING	beating; a belt	
BELYING	calumniating; counterfeiting	
BEMAZED	astounded; stupefied; dazed	
BEMIRED	soiled; besmirched	
BEMOUTH	to mouth; declaim	
BEMUSED	dazed; bewildered; confused	
BENCHED	seated	
BENCHER	(inns of court)	**lw**
BENDING	curving; flexing; inclining	
BENDLET	small heraldic bend	**hd**
BENEATH	inferior; subordinate; under	
BENEFIC	favourable (astrol.)	
BENEFIT	boon; profit; gain; enrich	
BENELUX	Belgium, Netherlands and Luxemburg	
BENGALI	of Bengal	
BENIGHT	obscure; cloud	
BENISON	benediction	
BENOTED	amply annotated	
BENTEAK	Nana-wood	**bt**
BENTHOS	ocean-bed organisms	**zo**
BENZENE	cleaning solvent; paint	
BENZINE	remover	**ch**
BENZOIN	resinous incense	**bt**
BENZOLE	tar product	**ch**
BENZOYL	benzoic acid	**ch**
BEPAINT	paint; daub; smear	
BEPATCH	patch; cobble; mend	
BEPEARL	adorn with pearls	
BEPINCH	marked with pinches	

BEPLUME	feather	
BEPROSE	discuss tediously	
BEQUEST	legacy; inheritance	
BEQUOTE	quote frequently	
BERATED	scolded; nagged; chided	
BEREAVE	deprive; divest; despoil	
BERGYLT	red sea-fish	**zo**
BERHYME	to lampoon in verse	
BERLINE	berlin; a vehicle	
BERSERK	Norse warrior; in a fury	
BERTHED	moored; situated	**nt**
BERTHON	collapsible lifeboat	**nt**
BERTRAM	bastard pellitory	**bt**
BESAINT	beatify; canonize	**rl**
BESAYLE	great-grandfather	**lw**
BESEECH	implore; entreat; crave	
BESHAME	put to shame	
BESHINE	light up; illuminate	
BESHMET	grape pulp	
BESHONE	sparkled; glittered	
BESHREW	curse; execrate	
BESIDES	except; save; moreover	
BESIEGE	beset; invest; beleaguer	
BESLAVE	enthral; enslave	
BESLIME	to soil; besmirch; defile	
BESMEAR	to daub; dirty; begrime	
BESMOKE	blacken with smoke	
BESNUFF	foul with snuff	
BESOGNO	besonio; a beggar; Besonian	
BESPATE	spit upon	
BESPEAK	stipulate; betoken; order	
BESPEED	help along	
BESPICE	to season; to drug	
BESPIRT	to asperse; sprinkle	
BESPOKE	ordered	
BESPOUT	orate; declaim; harangue	
BESPURT	besputter	
BEST MAN	groomsman (weddings)	
BESTAIN	mark with spots	
BESTEAD	avail; help; relieve	
BESTIAL	brutal; live-stock (Sc.)	
BESTICK	to stick; prick	
BESTILL	to quiet	
BESTING	worsting; winning	
BESTORM	assail	
BESTREW	scatter; spread	
BESTRID	stepped across	
BESTUCK	transfixed	
BETAINE	beet alkaloid	**ch**
BETAKEN	departed; applied	
BETHANK	thank effusively	
BETHINK	recall to mind	
BETHRAL	enslave; captivate	
BETHUMB	crease	
BETHUMP	belabour; pommel	
BETIDED	happened; befell	
BETIMES	early; soon	
BETITLE	give a name to	
BETOKEN	indicate; foreshow	
BETREAD	step on	
BETROTH	affiance; plight	

BETTING	wagering; staking	
BETTONG	kangaroo rat	zo
BETULIN	birch camphor	
BETUTOR	instruct	
BETWEEN	amid	
BETWIXT	amidst	
BEVATON	proton synchrotron	
BEWARED	took care; heeded; minded	
BEWITCH	fascinate; enchant; charm	
BEZIQUE	card game	ga
BHANDAR	store; library (Hindu)	
BHISTEE	water-carrier (India)	
BIALATE	with 2 wings	
BIARCHY	rule by 2 persons	
BIASING	prejudicing; influencing	
BIAXIAL	with two axes	
BIBBING	tippling	
BIB-COCK	down-curving draw-off tap	eg
BIBELOT	personal trinket, snuffbox, etui etc.	
BIBLIST	a faithful one	
BI-CABLE	multi-line aerial ropeway	ce
BICHORD	doubly strung	mu
BICKERN	pointed anvil	to
BICOLOR	having 2 colours	
BICONIC	double-cone-shaped	bt
BICYCLE	bike; 2-wheeler	
BIDDERY	metal alloy	
BIDDING	enjoining; directing	
BIFFINS	dried apples	ck
BIFIDLY	cleft	
BIFILAR	double-threaded	
BIFOCAL	type of spectacles (twin lenses)	
BIFROST	Rainbow Bridge (Norse)	
BIG-BORE	larger rifles (8 mm) shooting	
BIGELOW	flexible sailing boom	nv
BIGENER	cross-breed	
BIGGEST	largest; greatest	
BIGGISH	somewhat massive	
BIG-HORN	wild sheep	zo
BIGNESS	of a size; bulkiness	
BIGOTED	dogmatic; intolerant	
BIGOTRY	zealotry; fanaticism	
BILBOES	bars and shackles	
BILGING	pumping	nt
BILIARY	} (bile)	md
BILIOUS		
BILKING	defrauding; eluding	
BILLING	invoicing (charging); petting	
BILLION	a large number	
BILL-MAN	hedger; pruning hook	
BILLOWY	roughish	
BILOBED	double-lobed	
BILSTED	mahogany substitute	cp
BILTONG	dried meat (S. Africa)	ck
BIMANAL	two-handed	
BIMETAL	of 2 different metals	el

BIMODAL	two similar frequencies	ma
BINDERY	bookbinding	
BINDING	obligatory; a fillet; fastening; (boot to ski); books	
BINDWEB	(nervous system)	md
BINNING	(wine)	
BINOCLE	double-telescope	
BINOTIC	binaural	
BIOCIDE	plant-life-destroying substance	
BIOGENY	life origin science	
BIOLITH	rock from living organisms	gl
BIOLOGY	science of life	bl
BIOMASS	population living weight	ec
BIONICS	study of functions of brains and computers	cp
BIORGAN	physiological organ	
BIOTAXY	grouping of organisms	zo
BIOTICS	living organisms (viruses, bacteria)	zo
BIOTINE	(alumina)	mn
BIOTITE	magnesia mica	mn
BIOTOMY	vivisection	
BIOTOPE	uniform habitat	
BIOTYPE	uniform genetic make-up	
BIPEDAL	having two feet	
BIPLANE	2-winged aeroplane	
BIPOLAR	with two poles	
BIPRISM	obtuse-angle prism	pg
BIRCHED	flogged	
BIRCHEN	of birch	
BIRDEYE	bird's eye	
BIRDING	snaring	
BIRDMAN	fowler; single flyer (hang-glider)	
BIRETTA	clerical cap	
BIRLING	whirling; spinning	
BIRLINN	Gaelic barge	
BIRYANI	type of pilaw (India)	
BISCUIT	thin dry cake	ck
BISMITE	bismuth-ochre	mn
BISMUTH	a metal	ch
BISSEXT	(leap year)	
BISTORT	snakeweed	bt
BITLESS	no bit	
BITTERN	also bittour	zo
BITTERN	brine	
BITTERS	spirituous liquor	
BITTILY	disjointedly	
BITTING	(horse)	
BITTOCK	small bit	
BITTOUR	the bittern	zo
BITUMED	bituminous	
BITUMEN	asphalt; pitch	mn
BIVALVE	a mollusc	zo
BIVIOUS	two ways	
BIVOUAC	make-do camp (army)	mo
BIZARRE	fantastic; whimsical; strange	

BIZONAL	under dual control	
BLABBED	babbled; told; revealed	
BLABBER	sneak; tell-tale; prattler	
BLACKED	inked; obscured	
BLACKEN	darken; defame; decry	
BLACKER	darker; more sullen	
BLACKEY	a negro	
BLACKLY	sombrely	
BLADDER	urine collection organ	md
BLADING	fitting a blade to	
BLAMING	censuring; reproaching	
BLANDLY	mildly; benign; affably	
BLANKET	the mullein	bt
BLANKET	cover (bed, snow); group usage; yacht; surrounder of nuclear reactor core	nc
BLANKLY	vacantly	
BLARING	strident	
BLARNEY	whimsical flattery	
BLARNEY	yellow Irish cheese	ck
BLASTED	withered; blighted; ruined	
BLASTER	froth-blower; golf	
BLATANT	obtrusively vulgar	
BLATHER	} also blether, to babble	
BLATTER		
BLAWORT	harebell	bt
BLAZING	flaming; proclaiming	
BLEAKER	more exposed; barer	
BLEAKLY	cheerlessly; drearily	
BLEEDER	haemophiliac; (baseball)	md
BLEMISH	defect	
BLENDED	mingled; blent; mixed	
BLENDER	mixing device; paint brush of badger hair; (tea)	ck, to
BLESBOK	S. African antelope	
BLESSED	extolled; glorified; adored	
BLETHER	blather	
BLETTED	decayed	
BLEWART	the germander speedwell	bt
BLEWITS	mushrooms	bt
BLIGHTY	England (soldiers' slang)	
BLINDED	shuttered; deceived	
BLINDER	more obtuse; a blinker	
BLINDLY	ignorantly; heedlessly	
BLINKED	twinkled; flickered; connived	
BLISTER	protective hull	nt
BLOATED	swollen; distended	
BLOATER	smoked herring	zo
BLOBBER	blubber	zo
BLOCKED	obstructed; jammed	
BLOCKER	headstone of column; offensive player (Am. football)	ar
BLOMARY	a forge	
BLONDIN	tight-rope walker	
BLOODED	(fox-hunting)	
BLOOMED	flowered; blossomed; throve	
BLOOMER	an error	
BLOSSOM	bloom; bud; flower	bt
BLOTCHY	patchy; smeary	
BLOTING	drying by smoke	
BLOTTED	stained; sullied	
BLOTTER	a blotting pad	
BLOWFLY	blue-bottle	zo
BLOW-GUN	blow-pipe	
BLOWING	puffing; disclosing; (glass); surface pits; hollows in sand, soil	gl, pb
BLOW-OUT	a spread; banquet; short work-out of horse (racing)	
BLOWZED	frowsy	
BLUBBER	wail; (whale)	
BLUCHER	a booting	
BLUE-CAP	tit-mouse; a Scot (Shak.)	zo
BLUE-CAT	Siberian cat	zo
BLUE-EYE	honey-eater bird	zo
BLUE-GUM	eucalyptus	bt
BLUEING	a metal finish; expanding	
BLUE-JAY	North American jay	zo
BLUFFED	concealed; spoofed	
BLUFFER	a deceiver; con-man	
BLUFFLY	bluntly; frankly; openly	
BLUNDER	gross mistake; howler	
BLUNGER	clay-mixer	
BLUNTED	took the edge off; dulled	
BLUNTER	more outspoken	
BLUNTLY	stolidly; obtusely	
BLURRED	dimmed; obscured	
BLURTED	uttered abruptly	
BLUSHED	flushed; coloured	
BLUSHET	a damsel	
BLUSTER	turbulence; swagger; storm	
BOARDED	lodged; embarked	nt
BOARDER	paying guest	
BOARISH	swinish; brutal	
BOASTED	vaunted; bragged; blustered	
BOASTER	a broad chisel; a vain proud fellow	to
BOAT-CAR	canal trolley	
BOAT-FLY	water-boatman	zo
BOATFUL	ship-load	nt
BOATING	an aquatic pastime	
BOATMAN	a rower; an oarsman	
BOBADIL	a swaggering captain	
BOBBERY	rampageous; uproar (Ind.)	
BOBBING	cheating; curtseying	
BOBBING	(winter sports); angling	
BOBBISH	hearty; energetic; uppish	
BOB-SLED	bob-sleigh	
BOBSTAY	bowsprit stay	nt
BOBTAIL	rabble; caudal abbreviation	
BOCLAND	feudal freehold	lw
BODEFUL	ominous	
BOG-BEAN	marsh plant	bt
BOGGARD	} bugbear; scarecrow;	
BOGGART	} hobgoblin; spectre	
BOGGLED	hesitated; vacillated	
BOGGLER	a waverer; demurrer; doubter	
BOG-LAND	fen; marsh; swamp	
BOG-MOSS	sphagnum	bt
BOG-RUSH	a sedge	bt

BOGYISM	dreadfulness	
BOHOROK	Föhn-like winds in Sumatra	mt
BOILING	enraged; seething	
BOLDEST	bravest; most valiant	
BOLETIC	fungoid extract	bt
BOLETUS	fungus genus	bt
BOLIVAR	Venezuelan currency unit	
BOLLARD	mooring post; kerb-post	nt
BOLLING	a pollard; a lopped tree	bt
BOLOGNA	sausage	ck
BOLONEY	phoney palaver	
BOLSTER	to support; prop; pillow	
BOLTING	sifting; swallowing	
BOMBARD	to pump with projectiles; (artillery); drop bombs	
BOMBARD	large leather water bottle, jug; larger shawm (bassoon)	mu
BOMBAST	fustian; rodomontade	
BOMBING	blitzing	
BOMBOUS	rounded, convex	
BONANZA	stroke of luck	
BONASUS	bison or wild ox	zo
BONDAGE	captivity; thraldom; helotry	
BONDING	(Customs); (bricklaying); pairing; linking	
BONDMAN	villein; peon	
BONE-ACE	card game	ga
BONE-ASH	burnt bones	
BONE-BED	strata with fossils	gl
BONETTA	tunny fish	zo
BONFIRE	a beacon	
BONNILY	handsomely	
BOOKFUL	theoretical	
BOOKING	reserving; buying; on record; (office)	
BOOKISH	studious	
BOOKLET	brochure; pamphlet	
BOOKMAN	scholar	
BOOLEAN	truth, algebra, and calculus system	cp
BOOMING	in demand; resounding	
BOOMKIN	short boom overhanging the stern	nt
BOONDER	Rhesus monkey	zo
BOORISH	mannerless; clumsy; lubberly	
BOOSING	tippling; bousing	
BOOSTED	advertised; eulogized	
BOOSTER	output or energy raising device; pump; compressor	bd
BOOTIED	laden with booty	
BOOTING	foot-wear; sacking	
BOOTLEG	sell prohibited goods; Am. football	ga
BOOZING	boosing; toping; getting drunk	
BORACIC	a boron derivative	ch
BORAZON	boron/nitrogen compound	ch
BORDAGE	feudal tenure	
BORDMAN	feudal tenant	
BORDURE	heraldic border	hd
BOREDOM	ennui; tedium; dullness	

BORNEOL	camphor-yielding chemical	ch
BORNITE	erubiscite; copper ore	mn
BOROUGH	electoral division; municipality	
BORSTAL	a reformatory for youth	
BOSCAGE	undergrowth; machia; scrubshrubs	
BOSHBOK	bush-buck	zo
BOSKAGE	woody thicket	
BOSOMED	embraced	
BOSQUET	an arbour	
BOSSAGE	(projecting stones)	
BOSSING	controlling; dominating; bullying	
BOSSISM	political dictatorship	
BOTANIC	botanical; floral	
BOTARGO	special sausage	ck
BOTARGO	grey-mullet roe	ck
BOTCHED	bungled; patched	
BOTCHER	incompetent worker	
BOTTINE	small boot	
BOTTLED	inebriated	
BOTTLER	one who puts liquids in bottles	
BOTTONY	heraldic cross	hd
BOUCHET	a pear	bt
BOUCHON	hollow watch plug	hr
BOUDOIR	a lady's private room	
BOUILLI	boiled meat	
BOULDER	bowlder; a large rock	
BOULIMY	morbid appetite	md
BOULTER	fishing line	
BOULTIN	convex moulding	
BOUNCED	rebounded; bluffed	
BOUNCER	chucker-out; bad cheque; (baseball); (cricket)	
BOUNDED	sprang; limited; bordered	
BOUNDER	inconsiderate ass	
BOUQUET	nosegay	bt
BOURBON	Kentucky corn whisky	
BOURDON	bass stop	mu
BOURDON	mule; pilgrim's staff	
BOURLAW	local jurisprudence	
BOURREE	lively dance (Fr., Sp.)	
BOW-BACK	crooked; hog-back	
BOW-BENT	bent as a bow	
BOW-HAND	left hand (archery)	
BOWLDER	a boulder	
BOWLESS	no bow	
BOWLINE	a rope; a non-slip knot	nt
BOWLING	(bowls); (cricket); trundling	
BOW-SHOT	about 80 yards (73 m) (archery)	
BOWSOCK	bow cover (archery)	
BOX-CALF	tanned calfskin	
BOX-COAT	heavy coat	
BOXHAUL	a luffing turn	nt
BOX-IRON	heater receptacle	
BOX-KITE	scientific kite	
BOX-LOOM	multiple-shuttle-box loom	tx
BOX-SLIP	boxwood planing face	cr
BOX-TOOL	single-point lathe cutter	eg
BOXWOOD	odiferous shrub; its wood	bt

BOYCOTT	ostracize; refuse to do business with	
BOYHOOD	puerility	
BRABBLE	squabble; a quarrel; broil	
BRACCIA	plural of braccio	
BRACCIO	Italian cubit	**me**
BRACING	fortifying; invigorating	**nt**
BRACKEN	brake-fern	**bt**
BRACKET	brace; corbel; a support; (figure-skating); small ornamental shelf	
BRACTED	(irregular leaf)	**bt**
BRADAWL	boring tool	**to**
BRAGGED	boasted; blustered	
BRAHMAN	} Hindu priest	**rl**
BRAHMIN		
BRAIDED	plaited; embroidered	
BRAILED	trussed	**nt**
BRAILLE	raised letters	
BRAINED	brainy; bashed	
BRAISED	stewed	**ck**
BRAKING	retarding	
BRAMBLE	brier-bush	**bt**
BRAMBLY	thorny; prickly	
BRANCHY	spreading; ramifying	
BRANDED	marked; disgraced	
BRANDLE	waver; shake	
BRANGLE	wrangle; a brawl	
BRANLIN	striped worm	**zo**
BRAN-NEW	brand-new	
BRANTLE	a dance	
BRASIER	}	
BRAZIER	} brass-worker; charcoal pan	
BRASERO	}	
BRASSET	casque or helmet	
BRASSIE	} golf club; a small fish (Sc.)	
BRASSEY	}	**zo**
BRATINA	loving cup (Russia)	
BRATTLE	clatter	
BRAVADO	arrogant bluster; showing off; dare-devil	
BRAVELY	gallantly; daringly	
BRAVERY	valour; heroism	
BRAVEST	most courageous	
BRAVING	defying; daring	
BRAVOES	hired assassins	
BRAVURA	florid virtuoso performance needed	**mu**
BRAWLED	wrangled; quarrelled	
BRAWLER	rowdy ruffian	
BRAWNER	boar-meat	**zo**
BRAYING	clamour; pounding	
BRAZIER	brasier	
BRAZING	soldering; capillary jointing (metals)	**ce**
BREACHY	unruly	
BREADTH	broadness; beaminess	
BREAKER	small water cask	
BREAKER	wave; circuit stop; gyratory or jaw (rocks, cask) (ice)	**el**

BREAK-IN	interruption; burglary	
BREAK-UP	disrupt; disillusion	
BREAMED	cleaned of barnacles	**nt**
BREATHE	respire; exhale; express	
BRECCIA	conglomerate	**mn**
BREEDER	begetter; sire	
BREVIER	a size of type	**pr**
BREVITY	terseness; conciseness	
BREVIUM	uranium	**ch**
BREWAGE	a brew	**br**
BREWERY	brewhouse	**br**
BREWING	plotting; hatching	
BRIABOT	angler-fish	**zo**
BRIBERY	palm-oil; graft	
BRIBING	illicit payments for illegal acts	
BRIBRIS	Costa Rican Indian	
BRICKED	blocked completely	
BRICKLE	brittle	
BRICOLE	rebound; bounce	
BRIDGED	spanned; traversed; linked; covered (loan)	
BRIDLED	curbed; checked	
BRIDLER	controller	
BRIDOON	snaffle bit	
BRIEFED	instructed	**lw**
BRIEFER	shorter; more concise	
BRIEFLY	curtly; pithily; in short	
BRIERED	set with briars	
BRIGADE	subdivision of army	
BRIGAND	bandit; outlaw; freebooter	**to**
BRIMFUL	almost overflowing	
BRIMMED	edged	
BRIMMER	a hat; a full glass	
BRINDLE	streaky-brown	
BRINING	salting	
BRINISH	salty; brackish	
BRINJAL	egg-plant (Indian)	**bt**
BRIOCHE	light cake (Fr.)	**ck**
BRISKER	sharper; quicker; sprier	
BRISKET	breast of meat	**ck**
BRISKLY	vivaciously	
BRISTLE	a stiff hair	
BRISTLY	rough and prickly	
BRISTOL	(glass); (china)	
BRISURE	rampart deviation	
BRITISH	of Britain	
BRITTLE	easily broken; fragile	
BRITZKA	} Polish carriage	
BRITSKA	}	
BROADEN	enlarge; extend; amplify	
BROADER	wider; more liberal	
BROADLY	tolerantly; spaciously	
BROCADE	woven silk	**tx**
BROCAGE	brokerage; brokery	
BROCARD	maxim or canon; wise words	
BROCART	cloth with gold, silver thread patterns	**tx**
BROCKED	black and white	
BROCKET	young red deer	**zo**
BRODKIN	a buskin; brodekin	

BROIDER	embroider	
BROILED	grilled	
BROILER	grid-iron; brawler; chicken for flame cooking	ck
BROKAGE	brokerage	
BROKERY	brokerage	
BROKING	bargaining; negotiating	
BROMATE	a salt of bromic acid	ch
BROMIDE	a sedative	ch
BROMINE	a liquid element	ch
BROMISM	state after overdose	md
BROMOIL	oil pigment prints	pt
BRONCHO	unbroken horse	zo
BRONZED	tanned	
BROODED	cherished; meditated	
BROOKED	allowed; enjoyed; endured	
BROOMED	swept	
BROTHEL	bawdy-house	
BROTHER	kinsman; comrade; friar	
BROUGHT	conducted; led; fetched	
BROWNED	bronzed; tanned	
BROWNER	more sunburnt	
BROWNIE	elf; young guide	
BROWSED	pastured; grazed	
BRUCHUS	pea-beetle	zo
BRUCINE	nux vomica	bt
BRUCITE	hydrate of magnesia	ch
BRUISED	injured; contused; pounded	
BRUISER	a boxer	
BRUITED	rumoured; noised abroad	
BRULZIE	broil; quarrel	
BRUMMER	large fly (S. Africa)	zo
BRUMOUS	foggy; wintry	
BRUNION	nectarine	bt
BRUSHED	swept; grazed	
BRUSQUE	abrupt; gruff; blunt	
BRUSTLE	rustle; bully	
BRUTIFY	brutalize	
BRUTISH	bestial; savage; crude cruelty	
BRUTISM	animalism	
BRUXISM	teeth-grinding	md
BRYOZOA	incrustations	zo
BUBALIS	antelope genus	zo
BUBALUS	buffalo	zo
BUBBLED	gurgled; burbled	
BUBBLER	a cheat	
BUBONIC	plague	md
BUBULUM	neat's-foot	ch
BUCCATE	with protruding cheeks	md
BUCCULA	double chin	
BUCEROS	rhinoceros horn-bill	zo
BUCHITE	clay/shale fusion rock	gl
BUCKEEN	Irish squireen	
BUCKEYE	horse-chestnut	bt
BUCKING	boasting; soaking	
BUCKISH	foppish; gay; dashing	
BUCKLED	bent; fastened	
BUCKLER	round shield	
BUCKRAM	stiffened cloth	
BUCKSAW	frame-saw	to

BUCOLIC	Arcadian; pastoral; rural	
BUCRANE	garlanded ox-skull frieze, Doric	ar
BUDDING	germinating; blossoming	bt
BUDGERO	Bengal boat	nt
BUDGING	shifting; stirring	
BUDLESS	barren; sterile	bt
BUFFALO	cattle-like animal	zo
BUFFING	polishing	
BUFFOON	a merry-andrew; jester	
BUGALET	square-rigger ship, Brittany	nt
BUGBEAR	bugaboo; hobgoblin; bogey	
BUGLOSS	borage	bt
BUGWORT	a plant	bt
BUHL-SAW	spaced-back frame-saw	to
BUILDED	built; erected; raised	
BUILDER	constructor	
BUILD-UP	favourable publicity	
BUILT-UP	urban area; compounded (timber) (interest)	
BUIRDLY	stalwart; burly (Sc.)	
BUKSHEE	paymaster (Indian)	
BULBING	bulging	
BULBLET	small bulb	bt
BULBOUS	bulb-shaped	bt
BULBULE	small bulb	
BULCHIN	bull-calf	zo
BULGING	protuberant; distended	
BULIMIA	rapid over-eating disorder	md
BULKIER	more massive	
BULKING	looming large; blending	
BULLACE	wild-plum	bt
BULLARY	(papal bulls)	
BULLATE	blistered	
BULL-BAT	night-hawk	zo
BULL-BEE	stag-beetle	zo
BULLDOG	college police	zo
BULL-FLY	gadfly	zo
BULLIED	blustered; hazed; (hockey)	
BULLIES	browbeaters; hectors	
BULLING	boosting	
BULLION	uncoined metal	
BULLISH	obstinate; mulish	
BULLOCK	steer	zo
BULLPEN	pitchers enclosure (baseball)	
BULL-PUP	young bulldog	zo
BULRUSH	the reed-mace	bt
BULWARK	ship's side	
BUMBAZE	bamboozle	
BUMBOAT	provision boat; formerly refuse remover	nt
BUMICKY	masonry repair cement	
BUMMALO	Bombay duck (dried fish)	
BUMMILY	preposteriously, protuberously	
BUMMING	humming	
BUMMOCK	ale	
BUMPERS	amateur flat race riders	
BUMPING	thumping; jarring; knocking	
BUMPKIN	short boom; rustic; swain	
BUNCHED	clustered; concentrated	

BUNDLED	wrapped	
BUNGEES	parachute openers	
BUNGLED	failed; mismanaged	
BUNGLER	muff; botcher	
BUNKAGE	coaling charge	nt
BUNKING	decamping; bolting	
BUNTING	bird; fabric	zo
BUOYAGE	placing buoys	nt
BUOYANT	light; floating	
BUOYING	sustaining	
BUPHAGA	beef-eater bird	zo
BURDASH	fringed sash	
BURDOCK	dock with prickly head	bt
BURETTE	graduated glass tube; phial	
BURGAGE	tenure in socage	
BURGEON	to bud; germinate	
BURGESS	borough freeman	
BURGHAL	of a borough	
BURGHER	inhabitant	
BURGLAR	house-breaker; cracksman	
BURGLED	stole; robbed	
BURIDDA	Ital. fish stew	ck
BURKING	smothering; concealing	
BURLACE	a variety of grape	bt
BURLIER	more robust; sturdier	
BURLING	removing knots	
BURMESE	(Burma)	
BURNING	vehement; ardent; fervent	
BURNISH	polish; furbish; brighten	
BURNOUS	Arab attire	
BURNOUT	excess-voltage change	el
BUR-REED	a plant	bt
BURRELL	pear; russet cloth	bt
BURRHEL	wild sheep of Tibet	zo
BURRING	raising a ridge	
BURROCK	small weir	
BURSARY	treasury	
BURSTER	eruptor; exploder; terrorist	
BURSTER	offline separation of output	cp
BURTHEN	burden	
BUR-WEED	a plant	bt
BURYING	burial; concealing; sepulture	
BUSH-CAT	the serval	zo
BUSHIDO	Japanese code of chivalry	
BUSHING	detachable lining	
BUSHMAN	aborigine	
BUSH-TIT	long tailed titmouse	zo
BUSKING	cruising; preparing	
BUSSING	kissing heartily	
BUS-STOP	here by request	
BUSTARD	a bird	zo
BUSTLED	hastened; fussed	
BUSTLER	booster; hustler	
BUSY-BEE	socially active person	
BUSYING	meddling; interfering	
BUTANOL	an alcohol	ch
BUTCHER	murder; slay; slaughter	
BUTLERY	pantry	
BUTMENT	an abutment	
BUTT-END	fag-end	

BUTTERY	store-room	
BUTTING	ramming; abutting	
BUTTOCK	stern; sit-upon; thigh	pl
BUTTONS	a page; tansy	bt
BUTTONY	adorned with buttons	
BUTYRIC	rancid	ch
BUVETTE	refreshment bar	
BUXEOUS	(box-tree)	bt
BUXOMLY	gaily; pliably	
BUYABLE	on sale	
BUZZARD	rapacious bird	zo
BUZZ-SAW	circular saw	to
BY-AND-BY	presently	
BYE-ROAD	secondary road	
BY-GOING	passing by	
BYNEMPT	by name	
BYOUSLY	outlandishly	
BY-PLACE	a quiet spot	
BYRONIC	cynical	
BYSSINE	of flax	
BYSSOID	fringed	
BY-THING	a minor detail	
BYWONER	squatter (S. Africa)	

C

CABARET	variety entertainment in tavern, night-club	
CABBAGE	to purloin; vegetable	bt
CABBALA	rabbinic mysticism	
CABBLED	fragmented	
CABEIRI	deities of Semitic origin	
CABESSE	Indian silk	tx
CAB-FARE	money for taxi ride	
CABINED	confined; cribbed	
CABINET	chamber; ministry	
CABINET	a show case	
CABIRIC	(nature worship)	
CABLING	telegraphing	
CABOOSE	ship's galley	nt
CAB-RANK	row of cars for hire	
CA'CANNY	work in slow time	
CACHEXY	morbid state	md
CACIMBO	heavy mists low cloud Angola	mt
CACIQUE	cazique; Mexican chieftain	
CACKLED	clacked	
CACKLER	a noisy fowl	zo
CACODYL	oily compound	ch
CACOEPY	false pronunciation	
CACOLET	mule-chair	
CACONYM	wrongly derived name	
CADAVER	corpse; dead body	
CADDICE	caddis-worm	zo
CADDISH	on the boundary line	
CADENAS	condiment casket	
CADENCE	modulated flow; tone; sequence; falling	mu
CADENCE	rhythmical movements	

CADENCY	regularity of movement	
CADENUS	Dean Swift	
CADENZA	a flourish	mu
CADGING	hawking; sponging; sorning	
CADMEAN	(Cadmus); moral victory	
CADMIUM	a metal	ch
CADRANS	(jewel cutting)	to
CAESIUM	a metal	ch
CAESURA	poetic pause	
CAFENET	Turkish inn	
CAFFEIC	(coffee)	
CAFFEIN	vegetable alkaloid	md
CAGOULE	waterproof hooded garment	mo
CAINITE	(Cain); a Gnostic	
CAISSON	floatable, sinkable wall for docks	nt
CAITIFF	knave; miscreant; churl	
CAJEPUT	cajuput; oil yielding tree	bt
CAJOLED	coaxed; inveigled	
CAJOLER	a wheedler; beguiler	
CAJUPUT	pungent oil	bt
CALABER	squirrel-fur	
CALAMAR	cuttle-fish	zo
CALAMUS	dragon's blood palm	bt
CALAMUS	antique Islamic reed pen	pr
CALANDO	diminuendo	mu
CALCIFY	turn to lime	
CALCINE	pulverize by heat	
CALCITE	calc-spar	mn
CALCIUM	a metallic element	ch
CALCULI	gall-stones	md
CALDERA	lava collapse crater; steep cliffs	gl
CALDRON	cauldron; boiler; kettle	
CALECHE	a vehicle; calash (Fr.)	
CALENDS	first of month	
CALIBAN	a tempestuous monster	
CALIBER	} diameter of bore gauge;	
CALIBRE	} capacity; faculty; talent	
CALICHE	sodium nitrate	ch
CALICLE	small cup	bt
CALIPEE	calipash; turtle fat	
CALIPER	measuring instrument	to
CALIVER	a musket	
CALKING	stopping stems	nt
CALLANT	a lad (Sc.)	
CALL-BOY	prompter's attendant	
CALLIER	photographic ratio	pg
CALLING	vocation; profession; trade; game-, dance instructions	
CALLOUS	insensitive; hard; obdurate	
CALLUNA	heather	bt
CALMANT	a sedative	md
CALMING	tranquillizing	
CALMUCK	Kalmuck; Mongolian	
CALOMEL	mercuric chloride	md
CALORIC	heating	
CALORIE	unit of heat	me
CALOTTE	skull-cap; dome	ar, rl
CALOYER	Greek monk	rl

CALTRAP	} spiked obstacle for use	
CALTROP	} against cavalry	
CALUMBA	climbing plant	bt
CALUMET	Indian peace-pipe	
CALUMNY	slander; aspersion; obloquy	
CALVARY	the place of skulls	rl
CALVING	bringing forth; (of cattle); iceberg detaching from main ice	zo oc
CALYCLE	coral-polyp	zo
CALYPSO	sea nymph; (Odysseus)	bt
CAMAIEU	cameo; a monochrome	
CAMARIN	chapel behind high altar (Sp)	ar, rl
CAMARON	freshwater prawn; Sp. shrimp	
CAMBIAL	pertaining to cambium	
CAMBISM	art of exchange; (cambio It.)	
CAMBIST	banker; financier	
CAMBIUM	cellular tissue	
CAMBLET	camel-hair cloth	tx
CAMBOGE	gamboge	bt
CAMBREL	meat-hook	
CAMBRIC	white linen	tx
CAMBUCA	pastoral staff	rl
CAMELOT	King Arthur's Court	
CAMELRY	camel corps	
CAMORRA	secret society (It.)	
CAMPANA	an anemone; bell (It.)	bt, mu
CAMPHOR	aromatic laurel	bt
CAMPING	encamping; struggling	
CAMPION	plant	bt
CAMSHIP	merchant ship with fighter aircraft	nt
CAMWOOD	a red wood	bt
CANAKIN	} small can	
CANIKEN	}	
CANARIE	triple time dance	mu
CANASTA	two-pack card game	ga
CAN-BUOY	conical buoy	
CANDELA	luminous intensity	me
CANDENT	incandescent; glowing	
CANDIED	sugary	
CANDIFY	preserve in sugar	
CANDOCK	yellow water-lily	bt
CANDOUR	frankness; openness	
CANELLA	West Indian tree	bt
CANHOOK	cask-hook	
CANKERY	cankered	
CANNELE	horizontally ribbed silk fabric	tx
CANNERY	factory	
CANNIER	more pawky (Sc.)	
CANNING	preserving; tinning	
CANNULA	surgical tube	md
CANONIC	canonical	rl
CANONRY	official residence of cathedral canon	rl
CANOPIC	(Canopic case)	
CANOPUS	star in Argo	as
CANTARO	drinking glass (Spain)	

CANTATA	sung piece with accompaniment, choral	mu
CANTEEN	cooking tin; cafeteria; box containing silver service cutlery etc.	ck
CANTHAL	pertaining to canthus	
CANTHUS	corner of the eye	mu
CANTING	hypocritical; sanctimonious; adjusting oblique edges for curves	rw
CANTION	a song (Spens.)	
CANTLET	fragment; cantle; a cutting	
CANTOON	cotton material	tx
CANTRED	hundred; county division	
CANTRIP	a witch's spell	
CANVASS	discuss; lobby	
CANZONE	song or melody	mu
CAPABLE	efficient; able	
CAPABLY	competently; skilfully	
CAP-A-PIE	from head to foot	
CAP-CASE	travelling case	
CAPELIN	small smelt fish	zo
CAPERED	frolicked; frisked; bounded	
CAPERER	a dancer	
CAP-IRON	cutting-iron stiffener	cr
CAPITAL	money; main; excellent	
CAPITAN	naval officer	nt
CAPITOL	Roman temple	
CAPORAL	shag tobacco	
CAPOTED	won all tricks at piquet	
CAPOUCH	monk's cowl	rl
CAPPING	topping; (hunt subscription)	
CAPRATE	a salt	ch
CAPRICE	whim; humour; light fugue style	mu
CAPRINE	like a goat	
CAPRINO	goat-milk cheese (Argentina)	ck
CAPROIC	goatish	
CAPRONE	flavouring oil	
CAPSIZE	upset; overturn	
CAPSTAN	windlass; tape-winder	nt, cp
CAPSULA	seed-vessel; a cap	bt
CAPSULE	soluble envelope	md
CAPSULE	detachable compartment	ae
CAPTAIN	leader; chief; master	nt
CAPTION	certificate; title; arrest	
CAPTIVE	prisoner	
CAPTURE	take; apprehend; catch	
CAPUCHE	a Capuchin's hood	rl
CAPULET	father of Romeo's Juliet	
CAPULIN	Mexican cherry	bt
CAR PARK	parking area	
CARACAL	Persian lynx	zo
CARACOL	snail; spiral shell; staircase	ar
CARACUL	Bukhara sheep	zo
CARAMEL	a sweetmeat; caromel	ck
CARANNA	aromatic resin (Amazon)	bt
CARAVAN	house on wheels	
CARAVEL	four-masted ship	nt
CARAWAY	seed; plant; spice	bt

CARBIDE	carburet	ch
CARBINE	short rifle	
CARCAKE	pancake	
CARCASE	body; bomb; framework	
CARCASS	a fire-work; shell arch	
CARDECU	French quarter-crown	nm
CARDIAC	(heart); cordial	md
CARDING	combing flax	
CARDOON	artichoke	bt
CARDUUS	thistle genus	bt
CAREFUL	meticulous; heedful; wary	
CARGOES	argosies	
CARIAMA	bird of prey	zo
CARIBOU	Arctic reindeer (N. Amer.)	zo
CARIOLE	light cart	
CARIOUS	decayed	
CARITAS	love of God and neighbour	rl
CARKING	anxious	
CARLINE	a witch; thistle genus	bt
CARLISM	} (Don Carlos) of Spain	
CARLIST		
CARLOCK	isinglass	
CARMINE	a pigment	
CARNAGE	slaughter; butchery	
CARNIFY	turn to flesh	
CARNOSE	} fleshy; meatlike	
CARNOUS		
CAROCHE	coach (Fr.)	
CAROLUS	sovereign of Charles I	nm
CAROSSE	sheepskin or fur rug (S. Africa)	
CAROTID	arterial	md
CAROTIN	carrot pigment, vitamin	md
CAROUSE	revel; feast; tipple	
CARPING	captious; cavilling; objecting	
CARPORT	open garage	
CARRACK	armed trading ship; argosy	nt
CARRIED	borne; upheld; transported	
CARRIER	transporter; conveyor	
CARRION	putrid meat	
CARROTY	rufous (rufus); colour of carrots	
CAR-SHED	carriage depot for buses, trains	rw
CARTAGE	conveyance	
CARTING	transporting	
CARTOON	topical sketch	
CARVING	slicing; cutting; engraving	
CARVIST	hawk on hand	zo
CARVONE	caraway oil ketone	ch
CARYOTA	fish-tail palms	bt
CASCADE	waterfall; collar	
CASCARA	herbal laxative	md
CASEASE	casein-decomposing enzyme	
CASEATE	(cheese)	
CASE-LAW	(a precedent)	lw
CASEMAN	compositor	
CASEOUS	like cheese	
CASHIER	discharge with ignominy	
CASHING	(cheques)	
CASSADA	tapioca	bt, ck
CASSAVA	tapioca	bt, ck

CASSINO	casino, card game	
CASSIUS	(purple)	
CASSOCK	a vestment	rl
CASSONE	bridal chest (It.)	
CASTING	rejecting; pitching; (mould); (spell); (roles); angling	
CASTLED	(chess)	
CASTLET	small castle	
CAST-OFF	laid aside	
CASTRAL	(camp)	
CASUIST	a quibbler; sophist	
CATALAN	Catalonian	
CATALLO	hybrid; buffalo and cow	zo
CATALOG	university calendar (USA)	
CATALPA	Shawnee-wood	bt
CATAPAN	Byzantine governor	
CATARRH	(inflammation)	
CATASTA	slave-block	
CATAWBA	Ohio grape	bt
CAT-BIRD	American thrush	zo
CAT-BOAT	boat with mast in bow	nt
CAT-CALL	derisive yell	
CATCHER	(base-ball)	
CATCHES	songs; (fish)	
CATCHUP	} tomato and spices sauce	
CATSUP	}	ck
KETCHUP	}	
CATCH-UP	draw level; chance-taking	
CATECHU	an astringent	md
CATERAN	freebooter (Sc.)	
CATERED	provided with food, etc.	
CATERER	purveyor	
CAT-EYED	(night vision)	
CAT-FALL	anchor rope	nt
CAT-FISH	wolf-fish; nurse-hound	zo
CATHEAD	anchor rest	
CATHECT	to direct feelings	
CATHODE	negative electrode	el, pc
CAT-HOLE	hawser hole	nt
CATHOOD	c.f. spinsterhood	
CATLIKE	feline character	
CATLING	small cat; cat-gut	zo
CAT-MINT	a species of Nepeta	bt
CAT-SALT	rough salt	
CAT'S-EYE	a quartz	mn
CAT'S-PAW	a dupe; a ripple	
CATTALO	hybrid; buffalo and cow	zo
CATTISH	spiteful	
CATWALK	narrow plank bridge	nt
CATWHIN	needle-gorse	bt
CAUDATE	with a tail	
CAULINE	stalky	bt
CAULKED	rendered watertight	
CAULKER	a dram; a whopper	
CAULOME	all organs of a shoot	bt
CAUSING	resulting in; occasioning	
CAUSTIC	corrosive; mordant	
CAUTERY	a searer	md
CAUTION	care; heed; warning	
CAVALRY	horse-soldiers	

CAVEMAN	a troglodyte; grotto-dweller	
CAVETTO	hollow moulding	
CAVIARE	sturgeon's roe	zo
CAYENNE	red pepper	bt
CAZIQUE	cacique; West Ind. chief	
CEASING	desisting; ending; stopping	
CEBIDAE	class of monkeys	zo
CEDARED	lots of cedars	
CEDILLA	'c' like 's'	
CEDRATE	the citron	bt
CEDRELA	a tropical cedar	bt
CEDRINE	a type of cedar	bt
CEILING	(aeroplane height); upper limit of room; high peak (prices)	ae, ar
CELADON	green, brown stoneware (China)	
CELESTA	keyboard; bell effects	mu
CELLASE	apricot-kernel enzyme	ch
CELLIST	violoncellist	mu
CELL-SAP	cell fluid constituents	cy
CELLULE	small cell	
CELSIUS	centigrade thermometer scale	ps
CEMBALO	It. clavichord, harpsichord	mu
CENACLE	supper-room	
CENSING	burning incense	
CENSION	assessment	
CENSUAL	(census)	
CENSURE	blame; rebuke; chide	
CENTAGE	percentage	
CENTAUR	mythological horse-man	
CENTAVO	Portuguese halfpenny	nm
CENTERS	temp. dome or arch supports	ar, bd
CENTILE	scores system below 100	ma
CENTIME	hundredth part of a franc	nm
CENTNER	foreign cwt	me
CENTRAD	one hundredth of a radian	nc, me
CENTRAL	mediate; middlemost	
CENTRED	concentrated; based; located	
CENTRIC	central	
CENTRON	neuron	zo
CENTRUM	part of spinal vertebra	pl
CENTURY	centenary; hundred; (runs, cricket score); (centurion, Roman)	
CERAMIC	(pottery)	
CERASIN	plum-gum	bt
CERATED	waxed	
CEREALS	breakfast food	
CEREOUS	} wax	
CERESIN	}	
CEROTIC	beeswax extract	
CERTAIN	assured; infallible; undeniable	
CERTIFY	avouch; attest; witness	
CERULIN	indigo	
CERUMEN	ear-wax	md
CERUSED	white-leaded	
CERVINE	(stags)	

CESIOUS	bluish-grey		**CHARGER**	platter; war horse	**zo**
CESSING	taxing		**CHARILY**	stingily; warily; reluctantly	
CESSION	relinquishment; surrender		**CHARING**	drudgery	
CESS-PIT	midden; cesspool; sewage tank		**CHARIOT**	state carriage	
		bd	**CHARISM**	miraculous power	
CESTODA	gutless tapeworms	**zo**	**CHARITY**	benevolence; alms	
CESTOID	tape-worm	**md**	**CHARLEY**	night-watchman	
CETACEA	whales, etc.	**zo**	**CHARLIE**	pointed beard	
CHABLIS	white wine		**CHARMED**	enchanted; fascinated	
CHABOUK	Eastern whip		**CHARMER**	a siren; beguiler	
CHACONY	} repeated theme slow		**CHARNEL**	mortuary; house of the dead	
CHACONNE	} dance	**mu**	**CHARPOY**	Indian bedstead	
CHAFERY	welding furnace		**CHARQUI**	dried beef (Peru)	
CHAFFED	bantered; scoffed; derided		**CHARRED**	scorched; seared; burnt	
CHAFFER	haggle; bargain		**CHARTED**	tabulated; recorded	**nt**
CHAFING	fretting; fuming; rubbing		**CHARTER**	right; privilege; hire	
CHAGRIN	vexation; irritation		**CHASING**	engraving; pursuing; hunting	
CHAINED	fettered; measured		**CHASSIS**	frame-work; base structure of	
CHAIRED	carried in triumph			vehicle	
CHAITYA	Indian Buddhist temple	**rl**	**CHASTEN**	correct; punish; humble	
CHALAZA	the base of an ovule	**bt**	**CHATEAU**	country seat	
CHALDEE	Chaldean		**CHATTAH**	Indian umbrella	
CHALDER	96 bushels	**me**	**CHATTED**	gossiped; prattled	
CHALICE	communion cup; goblet	**rl**	**CHATTEL**	movable property	**lw**
CHALKED	scored; recorded		**CHATTER**	talk; prate; tattle	
CHALLIS	fine silk	**tx**	**CHAUVIN**	French patriot; chauvinism	
CHALONE	an internal secretion	**md**		(excessive group loyalty)	
CHAMADE	invitation to a parley		**CHAWING**	chewing; munching	
CHAMBER	room; closet; hall; cavity		**CHAYOTE**	custard marrow	**ck**
CHAMFER	groove; polish		**CHEAPEN**	belittle; depreciate; reduce	
CHAMLET	camlet; camel-hair			price, quality	
CHAMOIS	leather	**zo**	**CHEAPER**	not so dear	
CHAMPAC	Indian tree; champak	**bt**	**CHEAPLY**	inexpensively	
CHAMPED	crunched; chewed; bit		**CHEATED**	bobbed; duped; gulled	
CHANCED	happened; befell; risked		**CHEATER**	trickster; swindler	
CHANCEL	clergy's area of church		**CHECHIA**	Arab skull-cap	
CHANDOO	prepared opium		**CHECKED**	restrained; hindered; verified	
CHANGED	altered; varied; shifted		**CHECKER**	chess board; to variegate;	
CHANGER	exchanger; shifter			section leader	**ce**
CHANNEL	canal; duct; strait; gutter	**cp, nt,**	**CHECK-IN**	arrival formality	
		tc	**CHEDDAR**	a cheese	**ck**
CHANSON	song (Fr.)	**mu**	**CHEEKED**	sauced; was impertinent	
CHANTED	(horse-coping); intoned		**CHEEPED**	chirped	
CHANTER	a precentor	**rl**	**CHEEPER**	young game bird	**zo**
CHANTER	(bagpipes)	**mu**	**CHEERED**	applauded; enlivened	
CHANTRY	chapel for mass	**rl**	**CHEERER**	vociferous supporter	
CHAOTIC	confused; disordered		**CHEERIO**	convivial salutation	
CHAPADA	tableland in Bahia, Brazil	**gl**	**CHEETAH**	hunting leopard	**zo**
CHAPATI	unleavened bread (India)	**ck**	**CHELATE**	(claw)	**zo**
CHAPEAU	a hat (Fr.)		**CHELONE**	tortoise; shell flower	**zo, bt**
CHAPLET	garland; wreath; coronal		**CHELSEA**	china porcelain; spiralled buns	
CHAPMAN	pedlar; hawker				**ck**
CHAPNET	} pewter salt-cellar		**CHEMISE**	shift; smock; slip	
CHAPNUT	}		**CHEMISM**	chemical action	**ch**
CHAPPED	seamed; cleft; cracked		**CHEMIST**	chymist; pharmacist; druggist	
CHAPPIE	ghost (Sc.)		**CHEMOSH**	a Moabite god	
CHAPTER	a decretal epistle	**rl**	**CHENILE**	fluffy cord	
CHARACT	a character (Shak.)		**CHEQUER**	checker; diversify	
CHARADE	dramatic enigma		**CHERGUI**	Saharan wind, Morocco	**mt**
CHARGED	loaded; accused		**CHERISH**	to foster; harbour; treasure	

CHERMES	} a crimson dye	
KERMES		
CHEROOT	Burmese or Manila cigar	
CHERVIL	culinary herb	bt
CHESNUT	a hoary jest	
CHESSEL	a cheese mould or vat	
CHESTED	boxed	
CHESTON	a species of plum	bt
CHETNIK	Yugoslav guerrilla	
CHEVIED	chased; pursued; hunted	
CHEVIOT	sheep bred on the Cheviots	zo
CHEVRON	zigzag badge	
CHEWING	chawing; munching	
CHIANTI	Italian red wine	
CHIASMA	nerve intersection	md
CHIBOUK	Turkish pipe; (chubuk)	
CHICANE	trick; artifice; (cards); evasion; diversion of circuit turns (motor cycling)	
CHICKED	sprouted; vegetated; hatched	
CHICKEN	young fowl; a child	zo
CHICORY	(often mixed with coffee)	bt
CHIDDEN	reproved; censured; rebuked	
CHIDING	rating; scolding; blaming	
CHIEFLY	principally; mainly; mostly	
CHIEFRY	rent; chief's lands	
CHIFFON	gauzy material	tx
CHIFFRE	denoting harmony (Fr.)	mu
CHIGGER	chigoe; West Indian flea	zo
CHIGNON	a coiffure	
CHIKARA	an Indian antelope	zo
CHIKARA	Indian guitar	mu
CHILDED	having a child (Shak.)	
CHILDLY	childishly	
CHILEAN	Chilian; native of Chile	
CHILIAD	a thousand years	
CHILLED	discouraged; depressed	
CHILLER	an iceberg or wet blanket	
CHILLUM	hookah	
CHILOMA	camel's lip	zo
CHIMERA	mythical monster; illusion	zo
CHIMERA	graft; hybrid; fish	zo
CHIMERE	bishop's robe	rl
CHIMNEY	funnel; smoke-stack; narrow rock cleft	mo, gl
CHINCHA	S. American rodent	zo
CHINDIT	Burmese guerilla	
CHINESE	Sinesian	
CHINGLE	shingle; gravel	mn
CHINING	cutting the backbone	
CHINKED	jingled; clinked	
CHINOOK	N. American Indian tribe; föhn wind by East Rocky mountains, Canada	mt
CHINSED	caulked	
CHINTHE	Burmese leogriff	
CHINWAG	chatty conversation	
CHIPAXE	light axe	to
CHIP-HAT	hat made of palm leaves	
CHIP-LOG	log-line attachment	nv

CHIPPED	chaffed; chopped	
CHIPPER	lively; twitter; potato cutter; sculptor	
CHIPPIE	holed shot (golf); (basket ball)	
CHIRPED	bird song	
CHIRPER	grasshopper	zo
CHIRRUP	bird noise	
CHISLEU	a Jewish month	
CHISLEY	gravelly	
CHITTER	shiver with cold	
CHITWAH	panda; red bear-cat	zo
CHLORAL	a narcotic	md
CHLORIC	chlorine derivative	ch
CHLORID	chloride	ch
CHOBDAR	servant to a rajah	
CHOCTAW	(skating); a tribe	
CHOIRED	in chorus	
CHOKING	stifling; strangling	
CHOLEIC	(bile)	md
CHOLERA	deadly infectious disase	md
CHOLINE	B vitamin; organic base	md
CHOLTRY	caravanserai; Eastern inn	
CHOOSER	a picker; a selector	
CHOPINE	clog or patten	
CHOPPED	cut; minced; changed	
CHOPPER	cleaver; axe; helicopter; pulsator	to, ae, cp
CHOPPER	high bouncing ball (baseball)	
CHORALE	choral composition	mu
CHORDAL	of chords	eg
CHORDED	strung	mu
CHOREUS	a trochee	
CHORION	a membrane	bt
CHORIST	chorister	rl
CHOROID	eye-membrane	md
CHORTLE	chuckle noisily; exult	
CHOWDER	dish of clams	ck
CHOWTER	grumble; croak	
CHRISOM	baptismal cloth	rl
CHROMAX	iron-based alloys	ml
CHROMIC	of chromium	ch
CHROMYL	chrome radical	ch
CHRONIC	long continuing; inveterate	
CHRONON	hypothetical particle of time	nc, ps
CHUCKED	pitched; tossed; thrown	
CHUCKIE	a chicken	zo
CHUCKLE	exult; crow	
CHUDDAH	chudder; cloak or cloth (Ind.)	tx
CHUFFED	proud; satisfied; steamed	rw
CHUKKUR	} period of play (polo)	
CHUKKA		
CHUMMED	roomed together	
CHUPATI	unleavened bread (Ind.)	ck
CHURCHY	pious; ritualistic	rl
CHURNED	agitated; jostled; upset	
CHURRED	made deep whirring sound	
CHURRUS	Indian resin	bt
CHUTNEE	chutney	bt
CHYAZIC	(hydro-cyanic)	ch

CHYMIFY	to digest	ch
CHYMIST	} pharmacist	
CHEMIST		
CIBORIA	canopies	rl
CICHLID	Tanganyika fish	zo
CICONIA	storks genus	zo
CIDARIS	sea-urchins	zo
CILIARY	(eyelashes)	md
CILIATE	with hairs	
CIMARRE	ceremonial wine vessel (2 handles) (Fr.)	
CIMBRIC	a language of Jutland-Germanic invaders of Imperial Rome	
CIMELIA	stored treasures	
CIMETER	scimitar	
CINDERY	full of cinders; ashy	
CINEOLE	eucalyptole	ch
CINEREA	nerve tissue	md
CIPOLIN	green marble	mn
CIRCEAN	fatefully fascinating	
CIRCLED	went round	
CIRCLER	circlet; small ring	
CIRCUIT	judical itinerary; round tour; racing track; electrical layout; water course; (cars, greyhounds), channel (radio, TV, telex); rotational route; golf; revolution (planetary); turn cp, el, lw, tc, ga	
CIRRATE	curly	
CIRROSE	} with tendrils; curls	bt
CIRROUS		
CISSING	retreat of paint from surface	pt
CISSOID	geometric curve	
CISTERN	wine-cooler	
CISTRON	gene (function)	md
CITABLE	quotable	
CITADEL	keep; stronghold; fortress	
CITADIN	alpine races for part-time skiers	
CITATOR	a summoner	lw
CITHARA	Greek lyre	mu
CITHERN	guitar	mu
CITIZEN	burgher; burgess; resident	
CITRATE	lemon salts	ch
CITRENE	oil of lemons	
CITRINE	a yellow	
CITTERN	cithern; zither	mu
CIVILLY	courteously; politely	
CIVVIES	mufti; civilian clothes	
CLABBER	thicken	
CLACHAN	small village (Sc.)	
CLACKED	clucked; clicked; jabbered	
CLACKER	clack-valve; football fan's rattle; twinstyle rachet	
CLADISM	evolutionary classification by common factor	
CLADODE	leaflike branch	bt
CLAIMED	demanded; insisted; usurped	
CLAIMER	claimant; appellant; horse when racing; challenger	

CLAMANT	crying; insistent	
CLAMBER	climb; scramble	
CLAMMED	clogged; smeared	
CLAMOUR	din; uproar; hubbub	
CLAMPED	clumped; held down	
CLAMPER	iron patch	
CLANGED	clashed; pranged	
CLANKED	clinked; clanged	
CLAP-NET	bird fowler's net	
CLAPPED	applauded; shut	
CLAPPER	tongue of a bell	
CLAQUER	claqueur; hired applauder	
CLARAIN	fine coal	
CLARIFY	make clear; strain; purify	
CLARINO	It. trumpet, horn parts; clarionet	mu
CLARION	a shrill trumpet	mu
CLARITY	clearness; distinctness	
CLARKIA	a flowering annual	bt
CLASHED	clattered; opposed	
CLASHEE	Ind. sailor; tent-erector	
CLASPED	grasped; gripped	
CLASPER	tendril; embracer	bt
CLASSED	ranked; grouped; ranged	
CLASSER	classificationist	
CLASSIC	first rate; standard; masterly	
CLASSIS	assembly or convention	rl
CLASTIC	fragmental; brittle	
CLATTER	clash; rattle; crash	
CLAUGHT	to snatch; catch (Sc.)	
CLAVATE	club-shaped	
CLAVIER	keyboard	mu
CLAWING	scratching; fawning	
CLAYING	puddling; purifying	
CLAYISH	clay-like	
CLAY-PIT	marl pit	
CLEANED	purified; washed; scoured	
CLEANER	dirt remover	
CLEANLY	spotlessly; adroitly	
CLEANSE	clear; purge; elutriate	
CLEAN-UP	a purge; cartoon technique; (baseball)	
CLEARED	acquitted; absolved	
CLEARER	more obvious; less opaque	
CLEARLY	distinctly; patently	
CLEAVED	split; parted; adhered	
CLEAVER	butcher's chopper	
CLEDDYO	Celtic sword	
CLEMENT	merciful; lenient; mild	
CLEMMED	starved; hungered	
CLEPING	naming (obs.)	
CLERISY	the clergy	rl
CLERKLY	learnedly; scholarly	
CLEWING	coiling; securing	nt
CLICKED	found favour; ticked	
CLICKER	cobbler; compositor	
CLICKET	knocker; door-latch	
CLIMATE	clime; weather	mt
CLIMBED	scaled; swarmed; ascended	
CLIMBER	a creeper; mountaineer	bt

CLINKED	clanked; jingled	
CLINKER	slag; (ship design)	
CLINOID	like a bed	
CLIPPED	shorn; pared; snipped; docked	
CLIPPER	schooner; cutter; trimmer	nt
CLIPPIE	bus-conductress	
CLISERE	climate changes and climaxes	
		ec, mt
CLITTER	clatter	
CLIVERS	goose-grass	bt
CLIVITY	slope; incline	
CLOAKED	disguised; concealed; hidden	
CLOBBER	clothing; cobbler's paste	
CLOCHER	belltower (Fr.)	ar, rl
CLOCKED	timed; clucked	
CLOCKER	time-keeper; clock-watcher	
CLODDED	clotted; mired	
CLOGGED	congested; coalesced	
CLOGGER	clog-maker	
CLOISON	partition (Fr.)	
CLOOTIE	cloven hoof; the Devil (Sc.)	
CLOSELY	intimately; accurately	
CLOSEST	nearest; densest	
CLOSE-UP	(movies)	
CLOSING	conclusion; sealing; clogging; deadline date; (horse-racing)	
CLOSURE	also cloture; enclosure	
CLOT-BUR	the burdock	bt
CLOTHED	attired; arrayed; draped	
CLOTHES	apparel	
CLOTTED	curdled	
CLOTTER	to coagulate	
CLOTURE	closure; conclusion	
CLOUDED	obscured; blended; dimmed	
CLOUTED	patched; buffeted	
CLOVATE	inverse taper	
CLOWNED	played the fool	
CLUBBED	coshed; bludgeoned	
CLUBBER	clubbist; club member	
CLUB-LAW	might is right	
CLUB-MAN	member of clubs	
CLUCKED	clocked; cackled	
CLUMBER	a spaniel	zo
CLUMPED	in clusters; mustered	
CLUMPER	to form clumps	
CLUNIAC	Benedictine monk	rl
CLUSTER	bunch; clump; assembly; adjacent notes played together	mu
CLUTTER	confused mass	
CLYPEAL	like a shield; scutate	
CLYPEUS	insect's forehead	zo
CLYSMIC	cleansing	
CLYSTER	an injection	md
COACHED	tutored; trained	
COACTED	compelled; concentrated	
COAGENT	an associate; colleague	
COAKING	dowelling	
COAL-BED	stratum of coal	
COAL-GAS	extraction from coal	

COALING	taking on coal fuel	nt
COALISE	form a coalition	
COALITE	a form of fuel	
COAL-PIT	mine	
COAL-TAR	extraction from bituminous coal	ch
COAL-TIT	a passerine bird	zo
COAMING	raised border surrounding cockpit of canoes	nt
CO-ANNEX	join jointly	
COARSEN	roughen	
COARSER	cruder; rougher; ruder	
COASTAL	littoral	
COASTED	free-wheeled	nt
COASTER	decanter stand	
COASTER	small ship	nt
COATING	layer; covering	
CO-AXIAL	having common axis	
COAXING	cajoling; wheedling	
COBBING	pulling the ears	
COBBLED	mended; tinkered; patched	
COBBLER	shoe repairer; botcher	
COBBLES	rounded stones for paving	ce
COBIRON	andiron; firedog	
COBLOAF	crusty loaf	
COB-SWAN	male swan	zo
COB-WALL	mud-wall	
COBWORK	log-house construction	ar
COCAINE	drug	md
COCALON	large cocoon	zo
COCHLEA	ear-cavity	md
COCINIC	cocoa extract	ch
COCKADE	hat badge	
COCKEYE	imperfect vision; a squint	
COCKING }	strutting; trigger-happy	jn
COGGING }		
COCKLED	puckered; wrinkled	
COCKLER	cockle merchant	
COCKNEY	true Londoner	
COCKPIT	cock-fighting arena; enclosure for pilot, canoeist; doling, sinkhole in karst areas	ae, nt, gl
COCK-SHY	a target; Aunt Sally	
COCONUT	cocoa-nut	bt
COCOTTE	light o'love (Fr.)	
COCTILE	baked	
COCTION	digestion; cooking	
CODDING	hoaxing	
CODDLED	pampered; simmered	
CODEINE	an alkaloid from opium	bt
CODETTA	rounding off passage (It.)	mu
CODFISH	esteemed food fish	zo
CODICES	manuscript books	
CODICIL	addition to a will	lw
CODILLA	coarse hemp	bt
CODILLE	card-term at ombre	
CODLING	young cod	zo
CODLING	codlin apple	bt
COELEBS	bachelor	

COELIAC	abdominal	md
COENURE	young tape-worm	zo
COEQUAL	a peer; a compeer	
COERCED	concussed; compelled	
COEXIST	be coeval	
COGENCE	convincing power; force	
COGENCY	urgency; potency	
COGGERY	trickery	
COGGING	cheating; initial hot rolling	ce
COGNATE	related; allied; akin; sib	
COGNIZE	to be aware of; recognize	
COG-WOOD	a Jamaican tree	bt
COHABIT	live together as married	lw
COHERED	adhered; cleaved; coalesced	
COHERER	early form of detector	ro
COHIBIT	restrain; hinder; prevent	
COIFFED	(hairdressing)	
COIGNED	billeted (Irish)	
COILING	entangling; winding up	
COINAGE	money; specie	
COINING	minting; conterfeiting	
COITION	sexual intercourse	
COJUROR	witness to credibility	lw
COLA-NUT	the kola-nut	bt
COLD-CUT	dissolving lacquers without heat	
COLDEST	iciest; frostiest	
COLDISH	chillsome	
COLD-PIG	cold douche	
COLIBRI	species of humming-bird	zo
COLICKY	with pains	
COLITIS	colic; colonic infection	md
COLLAGE	real objects on art forms	bt
COLLARD	cole-wort	
COLLATE	collect and compare	
COLLAUD	unite in praising	
COLLECT	a prayer; assemble; amass	
COLLEEN	Irish girl	
COLLEGE	academy; seminary; guild	
COLLIDE	crash; encounter; clash	
COLLIED	begrimed; coal-black (Shak.)	
COLLIER	miner; vessel	nt
COLLING	embracing; necking	
COLLOID	gelatinous	
COLLUDE	act in collusion; connive	
COLOBUS	a monkey genus	zo
COLONEL	highest regimental rank	
COLOSSI	gigantic statues	
COLOURS	(army); (awards)	
COLOURY	coloured	
COLTISH	frisky	
COLUBER	a snake genus	zo
COLUMBA	holy vessel; (Iona)	
COLUMEL	a small column	
COMBINE	unite; blend; coalesce	
COMBING	breaking into foam; smoothing; (hair); removing wet paint	
COMBUST	astrological term	as
COMETIC	(comets)	
COMFORT	console; solace; ease; cheer	
COMFREY	a plant	bt

COMICAL	droll; diverting; farcical	
COMITIA	assemblies	
COMMAND	govern; rule; enjoin; decree	
COMMARK	a frontier	
COMMEND	laud; praise; eulogize	
COMMENT	remark; note; criticize	
COMMERE	a gossip	
COMMODE	chest of drawers	
COMMONS	food; fare; non-nobility	ck
COMMOVE	agitate	
COMMUNE	converse; discourse	
COMMUNE	a self-sufficient group sharing family tasks	
COMMUTE	exchange; replace; travel	
COMPACT	united; a treaty; close	
COMPANY	party; group; society	
COMPARE	liken; assimilate	
COMPART	to divide	
COMPASS	to encircle; scope; limit; (magnet)	nt, nv
COMPEAR	appear in court (Sc.)	lw
COMPEER	equal; comrade; associate	
COMPEND	compendium; epitome	
COMPERE	the leader of a troupe	
COMPETE	strive; emulate; rival	
COMPILE	combine; arrange; amass	
COMPLEX	intricate; complicated	
COMPLEX	mental inhibition	pc
COMPLIN	evening service	rl
COMPLOT	conspiracy	
COMPOLE	auxiliary magnetic pole	nv, ps
COMPORT	behave fittingly; glass stand for syllabub glasses	
COMPOSE	create; calm; pacify	
COMPOST	a mixture	
COMPOTE	dish; fruit (Fr.)	ck
COMPTER	counter (obs.)	
COMPUTE	reckon; count; rate	
COMRADE	pal; mate; associate	
COMTISM	Positivism	
COMTIST	disciple of Comte	
CONACRE	sublet (Irish)	
CONATUS	volition; effort; impulse	
CONCAVE	hollow; scooped; turning inwards, converging	
CONCEAL	cloak; disguise; screen; cover; hide	
CONCEDE	yield; allow; grant	
CONCEIT	vanity; egotism; notion	
CONCENT	harmony; concord of sounds	
CONCEPT	general notion; fancy	
CONCERN	trouble; regard; firm	
CONCERT	devise; concoct	mu
CONCISE	terse; pithy; laconic	
CONCOCT	plot; hatch; brew	
CONCORD	harmony; amity; union	mu
CONCREW	to concrete (obs.)	
CONCUPY	a concubine (Shak.)	
CONCUSS	coerce; overawe; stun	
CONDEMN	doom; convict; blame	

CONDIGN	deserved; merited		
CONDING	navigating	**nt**	
CONDITE	to pickle; to preserve		
CONDOLE	console; sympathize		
CONDONE	pardon; overlook; forgive		
CONDUCE	lead to; tend; promote		
CONDUCT	guide; escort; deportment		
CONDUCT	direct a musical performance	**mu**	
CONDUIT	passage; pipe; channel		
CONDYLE	knuckle	**md**	
CONEINE	coniine; hemlock	**bt**	
CONFECT	a sweetmeat; to prepare	**ck**	
CONFESS	admit; own; disclose; avow		
CONFEST	confessed		
CONFIDE	rely; trust; depend		
CONFINE	limit; boundary; restrain		
CONFIRM	ratify; endorse; establish		
CONFLUX	confluence; a crowd		
CONFORM	comply; tally; adapt		
CONFUSE	confound; derange; perplex		
CONFUTE	disprove; refute		
CONGEAL	coagulate; benumb		
CONGEED	took leave		
CONGEST	to swell; accumulate		
CONGIES	vitamin-rich rice-cookery water		
CONGREE	to agree (obs.)		
CONGRUE	congree; agree; harmonize		
CONGRUE	to accord (obs.)·		
CONICAL	conic; tapering		
CONIFER	pine; fir; etc.	**bt**	
CONIINE	conine; hemlock	**bt**	
CONJECT	conjecture; guess (obs.)		
CONJOIN	unite; link; fasten		
CONJURE	invoke; juggle		
CONJURY	conjuring; legerdemain		
CONKERS	chestnuts (challenging game)		
CONNATE	congenital; innate; inherent		
CONNECT	couple; conjoin; hyphenate		
CONNING	steering; studying	**nt**	
CONNIVE	permit; wink at; abet		
CONNOTE	imply a sequence		
CONQUER	overpower; vanquish		
CONSENT	concur; agree; assent		
CONSIGN	despatch; send; transmit		
CONSIST	subsist; make up of		
CONSOLE	comfort; organ keyboard and stops; control table	**el, cp, tc**	
CONSOLS	funds		
CONSORT	compeer; fraternize; band; wife	**mu**	
CONSTAT	certificate of a record		
CONSULT	deliberate; confer		
CONSUME	devour; waste; expend		
CONSUTE	like stitching		
CONTACT	touch; juncture; taction		
CONTAIN	include; embody; comprise		
CONTEMN	despise; disregard; scorn		
CONTEND	strive; cope; vie; argue		
CONTENT	volume; satisfy; mollify		

CONTEST	struggle; contend; dispute		
CONTEXT	texture; firm; extract		
CONTORT	writhe; distort; twist		
CONTOUR	outline; height line; profile		
CONTROL	direct; sway; mastery; check	**cp, tc**	
CONTUND	contuse; bruise		
CONTUSE	bruise; crush		
CONVENE	assemble; muster; summon		
CONVENT	a nunnery	**rl**	
CONVERT	change; alter; transform; after-try (goal) rugby, Canadian football		
CONVICT	sentence; felon; lag		
CONVIVE	boon companion; a guest		
CONVOKE	convene; gather; summon		
COOKERY	cuisine		
COOKING	concocting; manipulating	**ck**	
COOLANT	temperature reducing fluid	**nc**	
COOLEST	most impudent		
COOLING	moderating		
COOLISH	somewhat cool		
COONCAN	card game		
COONTIE	arrowroot	**bt**	
COOPERY	barrel production		
COOPING	confining; penning		
CO-OPTED	elected		
COPAIBA	copaiva; balsam	**bt**	
COPEPOD	minute water organism	**zo**	
COPERTO	muffled covered drums	**mu**	
CO-PILOT	assistant aviator; partner	**ae, nt**	
COPIOUS	abundant; plenteous; ample		
COPLAND	angular piece of land		
COPPERY	like copper		
COPPICE	spinney		
COPPING	catching; arresting		
COPULAR	linking; of mating; coupling	**zo**	
COPULIN	vaginal secretion	**md**	
COPYCAT	apeing others' ideas		
COPYING	aping; transcribing		
COPYISM	copyist's work		
COPYIST	plagiarist; imitator		
COQUITO	palm with edible sap/seeds	**bt**	
CORACLE	wicker frame river boat,		
CURRAGH	Wales	**nt**	
CORANTO	dance; newsletter		
CORBEAU	raven-black		
CORBEIL	sculptured basket		
CORBITA	cargo vessel of Imperial Rome	**nt**	
CORCASS	Irish salt marsh		
CORCULE	an embryo	**bt**	
CORDAGE	rope		
CORDATE	heart-shaped	**bt**	
CORDIAL	cocktail; hearty; ardent		
CORDING	cordage; binding		
CORDITE	a propellant		
CORE-BOX	sand-moulding container	**fd**	
CORENZA	love (Cornish)		
CORINNE	gazelle	**zo**	

CORINTH	a currant	bt
CO-RIVAL	competitor	
CORKAGE	imposition at hotels; corking	
CORKING	stopping (bottles)	
CORK-LEG	artificial limb	
CORNAGE	(land tenure)	
CORN-COB	spike of maize	bt
CORNEAL	(eye-membrane)	md
CORNETT	woodwind 17th century	mu
CORN-FLY	destructive insect	zo
CORNICE	ledge of snow; a top moulding	mo, ar
CORNINE	quinine type	bt
CORNING	preserving; granulating	
CORNISH	(Cornwall)	
CORNIST	cornet blower	mu
CORN-LAW	regulating corn trade	lw
CORN-OIL	maize oil	ck
CORN-RIG	strip of growing corn	
CORNUAL	} horny	
CORNUTE		
CORN-VAN	winnowing machine	
COROLLA	floral whorl	bt
CORONAL	circlet; wreath	
CORONER	an inquirer	lw
CORONET	a moth; tiara	zo
CORONIS	elision; contraction	
CORRECT	O.K.; exact; precise; true	
CORRODE	gnaw; rust; canker	
CORRODY	allowance; pension	
CORRUPT	putrid; depraved; bribe	
CORSAGE	part of a dress	
CORSAIR	pirate; privateer; ottoman	nt
CORSITE	diorite	mn
CORSLET	sleeveless armour	
CORSNED	an ordeal	
CORTADA	reduced, hard low shot (pelota)	
CORTEGE	procession	
CORTICO-	of cortical (tissue)	cf
CORTILE	courtyard	
CORUBIN	aluminium oxide	ch
CORVINE	like a crow	
CORYDON	a rustic lover	
CORYLUS	hazel	bt
CORYPHA	fan-palm	bt
COSAQUE	cracker; bon-bon (Fr.)	
COSHERY	billeting (Irish)	
COSHING	bashing; slugging	
COSIEST	snuggest; coziest	
COSMISM	a philosophy	
COSMIST	a secularist	
COSSACK	Russian cavalryman	
COSTARD	apple	bt
COSTATE	ribbed	
COSTEAN	(prospecting)	
COSTING	accounting	
COSTIVE	obstructive; constipated	
COSTREL	pilgrim's bottle	
COSTUME	dress; uniform; livery	
COTERIE	social circle	

COT-FOLK	cottars (Sc.)	
COTHURN	buskin	
COTIDAL	contemporaneous tides	
COTINGA	chattering birds	zo
COTLAND	cottage land	
COTTAGE	cot; lodge; hut	
COTTICE	heraldic barulet	hd
COTTIER	Irish tenant	
COTTOID	fish genus; miller's thumb	zo
COTTONY	downy; nappy	
COUCHED	expressed; reclined	
COUCHEE	soirée; evening reception (Fr.)	
COUGHER	one having a tussis	
COULDST	(could)	
COULEUR	colour (Fr.)	
COULOIR	dredge; mountain cleft or erosion gully	mo
COULOMB	electrical unit of quantity	el
COULTER	fore-end of plough	
COUNCIL	ministry; assembly; diet	
COUNSEL	advice; barrister	lw
COUNTED	reckoned; relied; numbered	
COUNTER	contrary; adverse; opposed; small chest (Am. football) (curling)	
COUNTER	token; meter; table	cp
COUNTER-	being against (contra-) (ice-hockey)	cf
COUNTRY	region; nation; state	
COUPLED	paired; bracketed; joined	
COUPLER	connector; duplicated organ controls	mu
COUPLET	two lines; a pair with repetitive music	mu
COURAGE	pluck; valour; heroism	
COURANT	a disseminator	
COURIER	messenger; runner; dragoman	
COURLAN	S. American crane	zo
COURSED	hunted; pursued; chased	
COURSER	war-horse; plover	zo
COURSES	some sails	nt
COURTED	wooed; invited; solicited	
COURTER	a wooer; swain	
COURTLY	elegant; urbane; debonair	
COUTEAU	long knife	
COUTHIE	kindly; friendly (Sc.)	
COUTURE	(haute); clothes for the jet-set	
COUVADE	a curious custom	
COVELET	small bay	
COVERED	enveloped; veiled; spread	
COVERTS	certain feathers	zo
COVER-UP	boxing; concealment	
COVETED	longed for; desired	
COW-BANE	water-hemlock	bt
COW-BIRD	American cuckoo	zo
COW-CALF	female calf	zo
COWERED	cringed; shrank; crouched	
COWHAGE	a bean (Hindu)	
COW-HEEL	ox-foot stewed to a jelly	ck
COWHERD	a cow tender	

COWHIDE	leather	
COW-HORN	rustic, unvalved	mu
COW-ITCH	cowhage	bt
COWLICK	a lock of hair	
COWLIKE	ruminant; placid	
COWLING	hood	ae
COWSLIP	paigle	bt
COW-TREE	moraceous tree	bt
COW-WEED	herb	bt
COXCOMB	conceited fellow; dandy	
COYNESS	shyness; bashfulness	
COZENED	deceived; gulled	
COZENER	white collar bandit	
C-PARITY	charge parity (quantum)	me, ps
CRABBED	morose; surly; disparaged	
CRABBER	small open boat	nt
CRABITE	fossil crab	
CRAB-OIL	carap-oil	bt
CRACKED	crazy; snapped; split; broke	
CRACKER	cosaque; biscuit; firework	
CRACKLE	glazed fissures in china	
CRACK-UP	breakdown; crash	pc
CRACOWE	pointed shoe	
CRADLED	nurtured	
CRAGGED	rugged; jagged	
CRAKING	cawing	
CRAMBUS	grass moth	zo
CRAMESY	crimson	
CRAMMED	stuffed; studied	
CRAMMER	intensive teacher	
CRAMPED	confined; cabined	
CRAMPIT	curlers' stand	
CRAMPON	nippers; mountaineering	
CRAMPOON	spike	
CRANAGE	crane dues	
CRANIAL	skull	zo
CRANING	stretching the neck	
CRANIUM	a skull	md
CRANKED	bent; turned; wound	
CRANKLE	crinkle; wrinkle; a turn	
CRANNOG	lake dwelling	
CRAPING	curling	
CRAPNEL	grapnel; hook	
CRAPPIE	N. Amer. sunfish	zo
CRASHED	smashed; shattered; fell	
CRASHER	uninvited guest	
CRATING	boxing; encasing	
CRAUNCH	crunch; gnaw	
CRAVING	longing; yearning; desiring	
CRAWLED	crept; (swimming)	
CRAWLER	a reptile; a baby's overall	
CRAZIER	madder	
CRAZILY	daftly; distractedly	
CRAZING	weakening; breaking	ar
CREAKED	grated	
CREAMED	mantled; foamed	
CREANCE	hawk-leash line	
CREASED	folded; wrinkled; rugate	
CREATED	originated; produced	
CREATIN	muscular constituent	md
CREATOR	maker; originator; inventor	
CREDENT	credulous; trusting	
CREEING	softening grain	
CREEPER	crawler; ski-aid; plant; bird; larva of stonefly; bait (angling); low ball (cricket)	zo, bt, ga
CREEPIE	a cutty-stool (Sc.)	
CREMATE	reduce to ashes; incinerate	
CREMONA	a violin	mu
CRENATE	notched	bt
CRENAUX	loop-holes	
CREOSOL	(phenol)	ch
CREPANE	wound due to brushing	
CRESSET	beacon; torch	
CRESTED	surmounted	
CRETIFY	impregnate with lime	
CRETISM	a falsehood	
CRETOSE	chalky	
CREVICE	fissure; rift; breach	mo
CREWELS	embroidery	
CRIBBED	confined; plagiarized	
CRIBBLE	coarse sieve; a temse	
CRICKED	sprained	
CRICKET	a low stool; an insect; 11 a side bat and ball game	
CRICOID	ring-shaped	
CRIMINE	an interjection of surprise	
CRIMINI		
CRIMING	charging; accusing	
CRIMPED	plaited; shanghied	
CRIMPER	corrugating machine	
CRIMPLE	shrink; curl	
CRIMSON	cramesy	
CRINGED	cowered; fawned	
CRINGER	a yes-man; sycophant	
CRINGLE	eyelet in sail	nt
CRINITE	hairy; a fossil	
CRINKLE	crankle; wrinkle; crimp	
CRINOID	fossilized sea-lily	mn
CRINOSE	crinite; pilose; hairy	
CRIPPLE	disable; impair; hobble; bracket; jack rafter	bd
CRISPED	frizzled; made brittle	
CRISPER	curler; more friable	
CRISPIN	the cobblers' saint	
CRISPLY	briskly	
CRIZZEL	roughness on glass making	
CRIZZLE	it cloudy	
CROAKED	died; grumbled; decried	
CROAKER	a fish; a pessimist	zo
CROCHET	fancy-work	
CROCKED	blackened; broken down	
CROCKET	pinnacle adornment	ar
CROESUS	a wealthy man	
CROFTER	small farmer	
CROODLE	lie snug; cower	
CROOKED	tortuous; awry; bent	
CROONED	moaned; lamented	
CROONER	sentimental singer	

CROPFUL	satiated	
CROPPED	mowed; reaped; cut	
CROPPER	printing machine; heavy fall; steel bar cutter	**pr, ce**
CROQUET	up to date pall-mall	
CROSIER	crozier; bishop's crook	**rl**
CROSLET	crossed cross	**hd**
CROSSED	thwarted; interbred	
CROSSLY	peevishly; testily; petulantly	
CROTALO	Turkish cymbal	**mu**
CROTTLE	lichen-dye	
CROUTON	chopped fried bread	**ck**
CROWBAR	lever; jemmy	**to**
CROWDED	huddled; thronged	
CROWDER	Welsh fiddler	**mu**
CROWDIE	porridge (Sc.)	
CROWGER	striped wrasse, fish	**zo**
CROWING	exulting; rejoicing; boasting	
CROWNED	honoured; completed; (king)	
CROWNER	coroner (obs.)	
CROWNET	coronet (Shak.)	
CROW-TOE	the buttercup	**bt**
CROZIER	crosier; pastoral staff	**rl**
CRUCIAL	cross-like; critical; decisive	
CRUCIAN	goldfish; crusian	**zo**
CRUCIFY	mortify	
CRUCITE	red iron ore	**mn**
CRUDELY	unpolished; roughly	
CRUDEST	rawest; coarsest	
CRUDITY	rawness; immaturity	
CRUELER	more brutal; harsher	
CRUELTY	savagery; barbarity	
CRUISED	sailed	
CRUISER	reconnaissance warship; power yacht	**nt**
CRUISIE	primitive lamp	
CRULLER	a cake	**ck**
CRUMBED	fragmented	
CRUMBLE	pulverize; disintegrate	
CRUMBLY	friable	
CRUMPED	blasted; blown up	
CRUMPET	an indigestible comestible	
CRUMPLE	wrinkle; crunkle; ruffle	
CRUNKLE	crumple; crimp; crinkle	
CRUORIN	haemoglobin	**md**
CRUPPER	saddle-strap	
CRUSADE	idealistic campaign	
CRUSADO	Portuguese coin	**nm**
CRUSHED	overwhelmed; compressed	
CRUSHER	pulverizer	
CRUSIAN	crucian; carp; goldfish	**zo**
CRUSTED	encrusted; incrusted	
CRY-BABY	a weakling	
CRYOGEN	a freezing mixture	
CRYPTIC	hidden; occult; secret	
CRYPTON	krypton; a gas	**ch**
CRYSTAL	(Palace); (fortune-telling)	**mn**
CRYSTIC	pertaining to ice	
CSARISM	despotism	
CTENOID	comb-shaped	

CUADROS	frames; division lines (pelota); (Sp.)	
CUBBING	whelping; hunting	
CUBBISH	ill-mannered	
CUBEBIN	cubeb extract	**md**
CUBICAL	cubic	
CUBICLE	little bedroom	
CUBITAL	about 20 inches (50 cm)	
CUBITED	measured in cubits	
CUBITUS	a cubit	**me**
CUCKOLD	husband of loose wife	
CUCULUS	cuckoo	**zo**
CUDBEAR	a lichen; a purple dye	**bt**
CUDDLED	hugged; fondled; caressed	
CUDWEED	a plant	**bt**
CUE-BALL	(billiards)	
CUFFING	scuffling; buffeting	
CUINAGE	tin stamping	
CUIRASS	breastplate	
CUISINE	cookery	
CUITTLE	cajole; curry (Sc.)	
CUIVRES	brass band instruments (Fr.)	**mu**
CULETTE	hip-armour	
CULICID	mosquito	**zo**
CULLIED	duped; gulled; hoaxed	
CULLING	selecting; gathering; picking	
CULLION	bulbous root	**bt**
CULPRIT	delinquent; offender	
CULTIST	a pedant; dilettante	
CULTURE	refinement; education	
CULVERT	small bridge	
CUMBENT	recumbent; lying down	
CUMDACH	precious-book receptacle	
CUMQUAT	kumquat; Chinese fruit	**bt**
CUMSHAW	gift; tip; present (Ind.)	
CUMULUS	a heap; a large cloud with 'cauliflower' white heads	**mt**
CUNEATE	wedge-shaped	
CUNNING	crafty; sly; wily; astute	
CUP-FEED	seed drill system	**ag**
CUP-GALL	an oak-gall	**bt**
CUPHEAD	rivet shape	**ce**
CUP-MOSS	a lichen	**bt**
CUPPING	blood-letting	
CUPRITE	oxide of copper	**mn**
CUP-ROSE	poppy	**bt**
CUPROUS	copper compound	**ch**
CURABLE	remedial	
CURACAO	orange liqueur	
CURATOR	custodian; keeper; warden	
CURBING	repressing; restraining	
CURCUMA	(arrowroot, etc.)	**bt**
CURDING	coagulating	
CURDLED	congealed; thrilled	
CURE-ALL	panacea	
CURETTE	surgical scraper	**md**
CURIOSA	collection of exotic objects	
CURIOSO	virtuoso; a collector	
CURIOUS	rum; prying; unusual; queer	

CURLING	a pastime; coiling; bending; bowling round stones on ice rink (like bowls)	
CURRACH	} strong canvas seaboat, Aran, Ireland	
CURRAGH		
CORACLE		
CURRANT	ribes; a dried raisin	**bt**
CURRENT	accepted; present; tide; flow	
CURRIED	groomed	
CURRIER	leather-dresser	**le**
CURRING	purring; cooing	
CURRISH	snarling; spiteful; quarrelsome	
CURSING	swearing; execrating	
CURSIVE	flowing; running	
CURSORY	hasty; superficial; transient	
CURTAIL	abridge; contract; shorten	
CURTAIN	theatrical drapery	
CURTANA	sword of mercy, (Coron.)	
CURTATE	reduced; abbreviated; punched	**cp**
CURT-AXE	short broad-sword	
CURTEST	bluntest; briefest; shortest	
CURVATE	bent; curved	
CURVING	turning; inflecting	
CURVITY	regular bend	
CUSHION	pad; hassock; pouffe; buffering; (billiards)	
CUSSING	swearing (sl.)	
CUSTARD	baked milk pudding	**ck**
CUSTODE	a watchman; custodian	
CUSTODY	care; imprisonment; duress	
CUSTOMS	duties on merchandise	
CUSTREL	buckler-bearer; a costrel	
CUT-AWAY	(tailoring)	
CUT-AWAY	a style of coat or dress	
CUT-BACK	decrease production (industrial); retreat; manoeuvre	
CUT-DOWN	reduce; cheapen	
CUTICLE	outer-skin	**md**
CUTLASS	short broad sword	**nt**
CUTLERY	edged tools	
CUTLINE	across front wall (pelota)	
CUT-OVER	attack (fencing)	
CUT-RUSH	technique (croquet)	
CUTTING	satirical; sardonic; sarcastic	
CUTTING	trough; gap; sproutling	**bt, rw**
CUTTING	tailoring; escaping; ignoring	
CUT-WORK	type of embroidery	
CUT-WORM	caterpillar pest	**zo**
CUVETTE	crucible; trench; cunette	
CYANATE	cyanide	**ch**
CYANIDE	poison	**ch**
CYANINE	cyanite	**ch**
CYANITE	} silicate of aluminium	**mn**
KYANITE		
CYCLING	bicycle sport	
CYCLIST	bicycle rider	
CYCLOID	geometric curve	
CYCLONE	tornado; hurricane; typhoon; genus, waterfleas	**mt, zo**

CYCLOPS	one-eyed Sicilian giant	
CYCLORN	a cycle horn	
CYMBALO	the dulcimer	**mu**
CYNICAL	disparaging; ironical	
CYPERUS	a sedge	**bt**
CYPRESS	funereal tree	**bt**
CYPRIAN	licentious; (Cyprus)	
CYPRINE	(cypress); funereal	**bt**
CYPRIOT	courtesan; (Cyprus)	
CYSTINE	calculus growth	**md**
CYSTOID	} cystlike	**md**
CYSTOSE		**md**
CYSTOMA	tumour	**md**
CYTIDIN	nucleic acid	**ch**
CYTISUS	the broom genus	**bt**
CYTITIS	dermatitis	**md**
CZARDAS	Hungarian dance	**mu**
CZARINA	Tsarina	

D

DABBING	tapping; patting	
DABBLED	sprinkled; meddled; trifled	
DABBLER	dilettante; trifler	
DABSTER	an expert; adept	
DACOITY	dakoity; brigandage	
DADAISM	art movement	
DADDLED	tottered	
DADDOCK	the heart of a rotten tree	
DAFTEST	silliest; maddest; craziest	
DAGGING	wool clotted with dung, earth	
DAGGING	cutting into strips	
DAGGLED	befouled; smirched	
DAG-LOCK	hanging lock of wool	
DAGONET	King Arthur's fool	
DAGWOOD	dog-wood; sandwich	**bt**
DAHABIA	dhow for cargo, Nile	**nt**
DAHLINE	dahlia starch	**bt**
DAKOITY	dacoity	
DALLIED	trifled; dawdled; sported	
DALLIER	a trifler; flaneur	
DALRIAD	an Ulster Scot	
DAMAGED	marred; injured; hurt	
DAMBROD	a draught-board (Sc.)	
DAMMING	embanking	
DAMNIFY	to injure	
DAMNING	conclusive; condemning	
DAMOSEL	damozel; damsel	
DAMPFER	dampered; mute (Ger.)	**mu**
DAMPING	discouraging; moistening; lulling	
DAMPING	decreasing wave motion	**ro, el**
DAMPISH	moist; dank; humid	
DANAKIL	nomad fisher tribe	
DANCING	capering; pirouetting	
DANDIFY	smarten; beautify	
DANDLED	fondled	
DANELAW	Danelagh; Danish England	
DANGLED	suspended; swung; hung	
DANGLER	hanger-on	

DANKISH	damp and dark	
DANSKER	a Dane (Shak.)	
DANTEAN	sombre (Dante)	
DANTIST	a Dante scholar	
DAPHNAL	(laurels)	bt
DAPHNIA	water-fleas	zo
DAPHNIN	bay-extract	
DAPIFER	meat-bearer; royal steward	
DAPPING	may-fly fishing; sinking, a	
	housing, cement marks	cr
DAPPLED	variegated	
DAPSONE	sulphone leprosy specific	pm
DARBIES	handcuffs	
DARCALL	long-tailed duck	zo
DARCOCK	water-rail	zo
DARIOLE	rich cake	
DARKEST	most secret; blackest	
DARKISH	gloomy	
DARLING	beloved; dear; pet; idol	
DARNING	mending	
DARREIN	(benefice)	rl
DARTARS	sheep ulcers	
DARTING	casting; sprinting	
DASHING	rushing; impetuous; spirited	
DASHPOT	snubber	el
DASTARD	poltroon; coward; craven	
DASYPUS	armadillo genus	zo
DASYURE	Australian cat	zo
DATABLE	assignable to a period	
DATARIA	(papal chancery)	rl
DATISCA	hemp	bt
DATIVAL	(dative)	
DAUBERY	poor painting	
DAUBING	daubery; smearing	
DAUNTED	discouraged; cowed	
DAUPHIN	king's eldest son (Fr.)	
DAWDLED	lagged; dallied; tarried	
DAWDLER	time-waster; laggard	
DAWNING	day-break; day-spring	
DAY-BOOK	daily register	
DAY-COAL	(upper stratum)	mn
DAY-GIRL	non-resident schoolgirl	
DAY-LILY	the hemerocallis	bt
DAY-MAID	dairy-maid; daily girl	
DAY-PEEP	dawn	
DAY'S-MAN	umpire	
DAY-STAR	the morning star	
DAYSURE	a wolf genus	zo
DAY-TIME	not night	
DAYWORK	(paid daily)	
DAZOMET	chemical fungicide	
DAZZLED	dazed; bewildered; confused	
DEAD MEN	empty bottles	
DEAD-END	cul-de-sac	
DEAD-EYE	three-eyed naval block	nt
DEADISH	rather moribund; decaying	
DEADPAN	expressionless (facial)	
DEAD-PAY	(pay drawn; death concealed)	
DEAD-SET	determined effort	
DEAD-TOP	aboreal disease	bt

DEAF-AID	hearing device	
DEAF-NUT	(no kernel)	bt
DEALATE	divest of wings	
DEALING	negotiating; (cards)	
DEANERY	dean's premises	rl
DEAREST	most expensive; costliest	
DEARNLY	secretly; grievously	
DEASIUL	} opposite widder-shins	
DEASOIL		
DEATHLY	mortal; deadly; destructive	
DEBACLE	a rout; collapse; stampede	
DEBASED	adulterated; degraded	
DEBASER	contaminator	
DEBATED	deliberated; disputed	
DEBATER	arguer; controversialist	
DEBAUCH	carouse; corrupt; deprave	
DEBITED	charged with	
DEBITOR	debtor (Shak.)	
DEBOUCH	come into the open	
DECADAL	in tens	
DECADIC	pert. to decimal system	
DECAGON	ten-sided figure	
DECALIN	hydrogenized naphthalene	
	product	
DECANAL	(deanery)	rl
DECAPOD	having ten limbs; (lobster)	zo
DECARCH	commander over 10	
DECAYED	rotted; degenerated; wasted	
DECAYER	source of decay	
DECEASE	perish; die; expire; demise	
DECEIVE	beguile; mislead; overreach	
DECENCY	propriety; decorum	
DECHARM	disenchant	
DECIARE	tenth of an are (Fr.)	me
DECIBEL	unit of noise	me
DECIDED	resolute; firm; unwavering	
DECIDER	final heat	
DECIDUA	uterus membrane	pl
DECIMAL	a tenth	
DECKING	ornament; embellishment	
DECKLED	with edges uncut	
DECKLET	record, set of IBM cards	cp
DECLAIM	orate; harangue; rant; spout	
DECLARE	avouch; assert; proclaim	
DECLINE	refuse; decay; wane; languish	
DECODED	deciphered	
DECODER	info. locater/fetcher/solver	
DECORUM	seemliness; decency	
DECOYED	allured; snared; inveigled	
DECREED	ordered; resolved; enacted	
DECREET	announce court judgment	
DECRIAL	clamorous censure	
DECRIED	disparaged; traduced	
DECRIER	vilifier	
DECROWD	(slum clearance)	
DECROWN	discrown; dethrone	
DECUMAN	main gate; tenth; principal	
DECUPLE	tenfold	
DECURVE	straighten	
DEDIMUS	judicial commission	lw

DEDUCED	inferred; concluded; reasoned		DELUDER	deceiver; trickster; hoaxer
DEDUCTS	calculation (excluding doors windows etc) **bd**		DELUGED	flooded; inundated; swamped
			DELVING	digging; excavating
DEEDFUL	manful; doughty		DEMENTI	official denial (Fr.)
DEEDILY	valiantly		DEMERIT	a fault; defect
DEEDING	conveying by deed **lw**		DEMERSE	immerse; drown
DEEMING	opining; considering		DEMESNE	lord's farming land (feudal)
DEEPEST	most profound; lowest		DEMETON	chemical insecticide
DEEP-FRY	cooking method **ck**		DEMIGOD	almost worshipped person
DEEP-SEA	in deep ocean		DEMIREP	a lady of doubtful virtue
DEERITE	iron/manganese hydrous silicate		DEMISED	bequeathed; willed
DEFACED	disfigured; mutilated		DEMODED	old fashioned
DEFACER	spoiler		DEMONIC	fiendish; satanic; diabolical
DEFAMED	libelled; vilified		DEMONRY	devilry
DEFAMER	detractor; slandered		DEMONYM	pseudonym using pop. style ²
DEFAULT	to fail; failure; lapse		DEMOTIC	popular; common
DEFENCE	plea; excuse; protection		DENDRAL	living in trees
DEFIANT	provocative; contumacious		DENDRON	dendrite of nerve-cell
DEFICIT	shortage		DENIZEN	alien inhabitant; resident
DEFILED	polluted; vitiated		DENOTED	indicated; signified
DEFILER	contaminator; seducer		DENSELY	closely; thickly
DEFINED	accurately described; limited		DENSEST	thickest; closest
DEFINER	a clarifier **el**		DENSITY	compactness; stolidness
DEFLATE	release the air		DENTARY	(teeth); dermal bone **pl**
DEFLECT	divert; turn aside		DENTATE	toothed
DEFORCE	resist **lw**		DENTELS	toothed ornaments
DEFRAUD	trick; cheat; deceive		DENTINE	ivory tissue of teeth **pl**
DEFUNCT	deceased		DENTING	dinting; notching
DEFYING	challenging; flouting		DENTIST	tooth doctor **md**
DEGAUSS	antimagnetic device		DENTIZE	(dental work)
DEGLAZE	to clear thick gravy		DENTOID	tooth-like
DEGRADE	lower; humble; debase		DENTURE	false teeth
DEHISCE	to gape		DENUDED	stripped; bared; divested
DEICIDE	a god-destroyer		DENYING	controverting; refuting
DE-ICING	removing ice		DEODAND	a forfeit (obs.) **lw**
DEICTIC	clearly proving		DEODATE	heavenly gift
DEIFIED	exalted; idolized		DEPETER	stone-imitating plasterwork **bd**
DEIFORM	godlike		DEPLANE	cf. detrain
DEIGNED	condescended; vouchsafed		DEPLETE	to empty; exhaust; drain
DEISTIC	freethinking		DEPLORE	lament; grieve; bewail
DELAINE	all-wool dress fabric **tx**		DEPLUME	to pluck
DELATED	gave information; squealed; stretched; widened **lw, md**		DEPONED	testified **lw**
			DEPOSAL	dismissal; sacking
DELATOR	accuser; informer; relator; expander; widener **lw, md**		DEPOSED	bore witness; ousted
			DEPOSIT	store; lodge; intrust; part payment **cp**
DELAYED	procrastinated; deferred			
DELAYER	a cunctator; procrastinator		DEPRAVE	corrupt; debase; vitiate
DELEBLE	delible; erasable		DEPRESS	damp; dishearten; sadden
DELENDA	things to be erased		DEPRIVE	strip; rob; divest
DELETED	expunged; effaced		DEPUTED	delegated; authorized
DELIGHT	charm; ravish; joy; ecstasy		DERAIGN	darrain; justify (obs.)
DELILAH	a charming hairdresser		DERANGE	disturb; upset; ruffle
DELIMIT	fix limits		DERATED	freed from liability
DELIVER	cede; consign; rescue; save		DERBEND	Turkish guard house
DELOUSE	to remove lice		DERIDED	jeer; scorned; lampooned
DELPHIC	oracular		DERIDER	a mocker; scoffer
DELPHIN	classical edition		DERIVED	deduced; traced; obtained
DELTAIC	delta-like		DERMOID	like skin
DELTOID	a muscle **md**		DERNFUL	solitary; mournful
DELUDED	misled; beguiled; gulled		DERNIER	final; last (Fr.)

DERRICK	form of crane	**nt**
DERRING	daring	
DERVISH	Moslem monk	
DESCANT	comment freely; dilate	
DESCANT	part song; a commentary	
DESCEND	dismount; alight; drop; sink	
DESCENT	slope; decline; origin; raid	
DESERVE	earn; win; merit; justify	
DESIRED	wanted; solicited; coveted	
DESIRER	craver; yearner; fancier	
DESKILL	simplify industrial work	
DESMINE	stilbite; zeolitic mineral	**mn**
DESMOID	tufty	
DESPAIR	hopelessness; despondency	
DESPISE	disdain; contemn; scorn; scout	
DESPITE	in spite of; malice	
DESPOIL	rob; bereave; strip; rifle	
DESPOND	despair; dejectedness	
DESSERT	a fruit course; afters; table centre of bronze, porcelain (It.)	
DESTINE	to ordain; appoint	
DESTINY	fate; fortune; doom; Kismet	
DESTROY	devour; demolish; raze	
DETACHE	violin bowing technique (Fr.)	**mu**
DETENTE	relaxing political strain	
DETERGE	cleanse; wipe	
DETERMA	a useful wood from Guyana	**fr**
DETINUE	writ of distraint	**lw**
DETRACT	defame; disparage; traduce	
DETRAIN	alight from train	
DETRUDE	force down	
DETUNER	jet-engine noise-reduction structure	
DEUTZIA	a white flower	**bt**
DEVALUE	depreciate	
DEVELOP	grow; unfold; expand	
DEVIATE	swerve; turn; tack; digress	
DEVILED	stuffed; seasoned before frying	
DEVILET	small demon; imp	
DEVILRY	cruel mischief; diabolism	
DEVIOUS	wandering; erratic; tortuous	
DEVISED	contrived; willed; concocted	
DEVISEE	legatee	
DEVISER	inventor; schemer; planner	
DEVISOR	testator	
DEVOLVE	deliver; depute; impose	
DEVOTED	loving; ardent; attached	
DEVOTEE	an addict; a fan; zealot	
DEWANNY	office of dewan (India)	
DEW-CLAW	rudimentary claw	**zo**
DEW-DROP	drop of earth condensation	
DEW-FALL	aqueous precipitation	
DEWLAPT	with a dewlap	
DEW-POND	pond fed by condensation	
DEW-WORM	earthworm	**zo**
DEXTRAD	to the right side (body)	**md**
DEXTRAL	(not left)	
DEXTRAN	synthetic blood plasma	
DEXTRIN	starch gum	
DGHAISA	gondola	
DHAGOBA	Buddhist mound	**rl**
DHOOLIE	covered litter	
DHOOTIE	Indian loin-cloth fabric	**tx**
DHURRIE	Indian curtain	
DIABASE	variously defined rock type	**mn**
DIABOLO	game (devil on two sticks)	**ga**
DIACOPE	tmesis	
DIADROM	a beat; a vibration	
DIAGRAM	graph; sketch; drawing	
DIALECT	idiom; parlance	
DIALIST	dial-maker	
DIALIZE	separate	**ch**
DIALLED	rang up	
DIAMINE	2-amino-group compound	**ch**
DIAMOND	hard valuable stone; (cards); lozenge; baseball	**mn, hd, ga**
DIANDER	(two stamens)	**bt**
DIAPSID	condition of skulls	**zo**
DIARAIN	diarial; daily	
DIARCHY	dual monarchy	
DIARIAL	daily memoranda book	
DIARIES	daily records	
DIARISE	diarize; to record	
DIARIST	a chronicler	
DIASTER	stage in cell-division	**cy**
DIATOMS	seaweed	**bt**
DIATONI	face-dressed quoins	**bd**
DIAXONE	bipolar nerve cell	**zo**
DIBASIC	giving two salts	**ch**
DIBATAG	N. African gazelle	**zo**
DIBBING	dipping	
DIBBLED	made hole in the ground	
DIBBLER	planted	
DICE-BOX	dice holder	
DICEING	throwing dice	
DICERAS	clams	**zo**
DICHORD	lyre	**mu**
DICKITE	hydrated aluminium silicate	**mn**
DICLINY	state of sex separation	**bt**
DICTATE	enjoin; command; bid	
DICTION	style; speech; clear enunciation	
DIDACHE	apostolic teaching	
DIDDLED	out-witted; cajoled; cozened	
DIDDLER	a cheat; swindler; cajoler	
DIDIDAE	the dodo, etc.	**zo**
DIE-AWAY	languishing	
DIE-CAST	(condenser construction)	
DIEDRAL	dihedral	
DIE-HARD	last ditcher	
DIETARY	course of diet	
DIETING	banting; slimming	
DIETIST	dietitian	
DIE-WORK	die-cutting	
DIFFORM	irregular	
DIFFUSE	spread; copious; prolix	
DIGAMMA	obsolete Greek letter	
DIGGING	delving; grubbing; thrusting	
DIGHTLY	finely apparelled (obs.)	

DIGITAL	integral; decimal; binary; by finger	**ma**
DIGITAL	numeric system data	**el, cp**
DIGLYPH	grooved face	
DIGNIFY	ennoble; exalt; grace	
DIGNITY	majesty; decorum; rank	
DIGRAPH	(two letters)	
DIGRESS	deviate; wander; swerve	
DIGYNIA	curious plant; (two pistils)	**bt**
DIKETEN	ketene dimer	**ch**
DILATED	enlarged; expatiated	
DILATER	an expander; amplifier	
DILATOR	a muscle	**md**
DILEMMA	quandary; plight; strait	
DILLING	darling; weakling	
DILL-OIL	a carminative	**md**
DILUENT	a diluter; reducer	
DILUTED	watered; attenuated	
DILUTEE	unskilled worker (industrial)	
DILUTER	thinner	
DIMETER	(poetry)	
DIM-EYED	with weak vision; weepy	
DIMMING	blurring; clouding; dulling	
DIMMISH	somewhat obscure	
DIMNESS	vagueness; dinginess	
DIMPLED	showing dimples	
DINETTE	a dining compartment	
DINGING	ringing; urging; single coat stucco walls	**bd**
DINGOES	wild dogs of Australia	**zo**
DINMONT	shorn wether	**zo**
DINNING	advocating clamorously	
DINTING	denting; striking	
DIOCESE	a bishopric	**rl**
DIOCOEL	diencephalon lumen	**zo**
DIODONE	iodine x-ray preparation	
DIOECIA	genus of plants	**bt**
DIONAEA	Venus's fly-trap	**bt**
DIOPSIS	fly genus	**zo**
DIOPTER	optical measurement	**me**
DIOPTER	speculum; theodolite	
DIOPTRE	unit of lens power	**pg**
DIORAMA	panorama	
DIORISM	definition	
DIORITE	igneous rock	**mn**
DIOXIDE	oxygen-based oxide	**ch**
DIPHONE	a shorthand sign	
DIPLOID	twin chromosomes	**md**
DIPLOMA	a certificate	
DIPLONT	diploid-nuclei-bearing plant body	
DIPOLAR	with two poles	
DIPPING	dibbing; plunging; immersing	
DIPTERA	two-winged insect	
DIPTOTE	noun with 2 cases only	
DIP-TRAP	bend in a pipe	
DIPTYCH	pictorial altar-piece	**rl**
DIREFUL	calamitous; baleful; awful	
DIRKING	stabbing	
DIRT-BED	(quarrying)	
DIRTIED	soiled; sullied; begrimed	
DIRTIER	grubbier	
DIRTILY	filthily	
DIRT-PIE	mud-pie	
DISABLE	unfit; incapacitate; maim	
DISABLE	suppress an interrupt	**cp**
DISAGIO	money-exchange charge	
DISALLY	separate; sunder	
DISAVOW	repudiate; disown; deny	
DISBAND	disperse; disembody	
DISBARK	disembark	
DISBEND	unbend (obs.)	
DISCAGE	release; unmew	
DISCANT	descant; discourse	
DISCARD	cast; reject; abandon	
DISCASE	strip; unpack	
DISCEPT	debate; dispute	
DISCERN	espy; perceive; discriminate	
DISCERP	tear off; separate	
DISCOID	flat like a disc	
DISCORD	strife; brawl; animosity; dissonance	**mu**
DISCOUS	broad; flat	
DISCUSS	debate; argue; consume	
DISDAIN	spurn; contemn; ignore	
DISEASE	malady; complaint	**md**
DISEDGE	to blunt	
DISEUSE	woman reciter (Fr.)	
DISFAME	disrepute; evil reputation	
DISFORM	alter; deform; disfigure	
DISGOWN	unfrock	
DISGUST	nausea; aversion; loathing	
DISHELM	remove helmet	
DISHFUL	filling a dish	
DISHING	thwarting; frustrating	
DISHOME	evict	
DISHORN	remove horns	
DISJOIN	part; detach; sunder; sever	
DISJUNE	dejeuner; lunch (Sc.)	
DISLEAF	deprive of leaves	
DISLEAL	disloyal; dishonourable	
DISLIKE	hate; detest; antipathy	
DISLIMB	dismember	
DISLIMN	obliterate; efface (obs.)	
DISLINK	unlink; disjoin	
DISLOAD	unburden; unload	
DISMALS	mournings	
DISMASK	unmask; uncover; reveal	
DISMAST	remove masts	**nt**
DISMISS	cashier; discharge; sack	
DISNEST	eject	
DISOBEY	trangress; disregard; infringe	
DISOMUS	2-bodied monster	**md**
DISPAIR	separate; uncouple	
DISPARK	set at large	
DISPART	separate	
DISPEND	expend; disburse (obs.)	
DISPLAY	parade; flaunt; show; evince	
DISPLAY	reveal; put on screen	**cp, lw**
DISPONE	hand over	**lw**
DISPORT	sport; gambol; frolic; wanton	

DISPOSE	sell; transfer; arrange	
DISPOST	displace	
DISPUTE	argue; wrangle; bicker	
DISRANK	degrade	
DISRATE	reduce to lower rating	
DISROBE	unrobe; strip; divest; bare	
DISROOT	uproot; eradicate	
DISRUPT	break up; disintegrate	
DISSEAT	unseat	
DISSECT	anatomize; analyse; cut	
DISSENT	disagree; differ	
DISSERT	discourse; dissertation (obs.)	
DISTAFF	staff for holding unspun flax	
DISTAFF	the opposite of spear-side	
DISTAIN	sully; stain	
DISTANT	remote; far; aloof; reserved	
DISTEND	dilate; swell; expand; bloat	
DISTENT	distended (Spens.)	
DISTICH	rhyming couplet	
DISTOMA	genus of worms	**zo**
DISTORT	pervert; misrepresent	
DISTRIX	hair-end splitting	**md**
DISTUNE	put out of tune	
DISTURB	molest; confuse; vex; annoy	
DISTYLE	portico	
DISUSED	obsolete; neglected; abandoned	
DISWARN	dissuade	
DISWONT	deprive of wonted usage	
DISYOKE	unyoke	
DITCHED	fallen into the sea (RAF); discarded; failed examination	
DITCHER	ditch clearer	
DITHERY	nervous; agitated; tremulous	
DITTANY	candle plant	**bt**
DITTIED	sung	
DITTIES	sonnets; shanties	
DIURNAL	daily; quotidian; journal	
DIVERGE	fork; radiate; part	
DIVERSE	unlike; different; varied	
DIVIDED	severed; sundered; separated	
DIVIDER	distributor; apportioner	**cp, tc**
DIVINER	predictor; seer; magician	
DIVISOR	(arithmetic)	
DIVORCE	dissever; part; alienate	
DIVULGE	tell; reveal; disclose; impact	
DIVULSE	rend apart	
DIVVY-UP	divide	
DIZENED	bedecked	
DIZZARD	blockhead	
DIZZIED	dazed; bewildered; confused	
DIZZIER	giddier	
DIZZILY	confusedly	
DJEREED	} blunt Turkish javelin	
DJERRID	}	
DJIBBAH	} Eastern garment	
DJUBBAH	}	
DOBHASH	interpreter (Hindu)	
DOCETAE	an ungodly sect	
DOCETIC	heretical	
DOCIBLE	docile; tractable; amenable	

DOCIOUS	docile	
DOCKAGE	dock dues	
DOCKING	curtailing; clipping	**nt**
DOCKIZE	to convert into docks	
DOCQUET	docket; summary; list	
DODDART	hockey (obs.)	
DODDING	lopping; polling	
DODGERY	trickery; prevarication	
DODGING	evading; quibbling	
DOESKIN	soft leather	**le**
DOFFING	divesting; putting off	
DOG-BANE	plant with a bitter root	**bt**
DOG-BELT	part of dog harness	
DOG-BOLT	arrow; dog-meal	
DOG-CART	two-wheeled vehicle	
DOG-DAYS	(occur in July and August)	
DOGEATE	office of doge	
DOG-FISH	tope; small shark	**zo**
DOGGING	following closely; tailing	
DOGGISH	rather posh	
DOGGREL	doggerel; trashy verse	
DOGHEAD	gunlock hammer	
DOG-HOLE	not a luxurious abode	
DOGHOOD	cf. manhood	
DOGLIKE	having canine attributes	
DOG-NAIL	large nail	
DOG-ROSE	wild rose	**bt**
DOG'S-EAR	a fold in a page in a book	
DOGSHIP	personality of a dog	
DOG-SICK	sick as a dog	
DOGSKIN	glove leather	**le**
DOG'S-RUE	a plant; Scrophularia	**bt**
DOG-STAR	Sirius	**as**
DOG-TICK	a parasite	**zo**
DOGTROT	jog	
DOG-VANE	wind-vane	**nt**
DOGWOOD	flowering bush	**bt**
DOLABRA	Roman hatchet	
DOLEFUL	woe-begone; dismal; rueful	
DOLLIED	hammered; laundered	
DOLLIER	an ore-crusher	
DOLLMAN	Turkish robe	
DOLPHIN	fish; (pilot); a spar buoy	**zo, nt**
DOLTISH	stupid; stolid; witless	
DOMABLE	tamable; tractable	
DOMICAL	dome-shaped	
DOMINIE	schoolmaster (Sc.)	
DOMINUS	Master; Lord	
DONATOR	donor; presenter; giver	
DONNERD	donnert; stunned (Sc.)	
DONNING	putting on; assuming	
DONNISH	like a don	
DONNISM	self-importance	
DONSHIP	estate of being a don	
DOOMING	condemning; judging	
DOORING	door-case	
DOORMAT	boot-scraping mat	
DOORWAY	portico	
DOPPLER	change of frequency (colour, sound) (distance)	**ps**

DOPSKAL	font for baptism	**ar, rl**
DORHAWK	nightjar	**zo**
DORKING	a type of hen	**zo**
DORLACH	bundle; valise (Sc.)	
DORMANT	quiescent; latent	
DORMICE	sleepy rodents	**zo**
DORNICK	} figured linen	**tx**
DORNOCK		
DORTOUR	dorter; dormitory	**rl**
DOSSIER	file of papers; a brief (Fr.)	
DOTTARD	decayed tree	
DOTTIER	barmier; more foolish	
DOTTING	spotting; stippling	
DOTTREL	plover	**zo**
DOUBLED	turned; ran; repeated	
DOUBLER	duplicator; increaser	
DOUBLES	two teams of two against each other (golf, tennis, sculls)	
DOUBLET	jerkin; one of a pair	
DOUBTED	distrusted; suspected	
DOUBTER	an unbelieving Thomas	
DOUCELY	sweetly	
DOUCETS	} stones of deer	**zo**
DOWCETS		
DOUCEUR	tip; vail; gratuity	
DOUCHED	sprayed	
DOUCINE	ornamental moulding	
DOUGHTY	valiant; intrepid; dauntless	
DOUPION	double cocoon	**zo**
DOUREST	grimmest; staunchest	
DOURINE	breeding-horse infection	**vt**
DOUSING	} dipping; extinguishing;	
DOWSING	} water-divining	
DOUTING	extinguishing; quenching	
DOVECOT	dove-cote	**zo**
DOVEKIE	little auk (Sc.)	**zo**
DOVELET	young dove	**zo**
DOVERED	slumbered	
DOWABLE	endowable	
DOWAGER	widow with a jointure	
DOWDILY	untidily; slovenly	
DOWERED	gifted	
DOWN-BED	feather bed	
DOWN-BOW	playing motion (violin)	**mu**
DOWNING	felling; overcoming	
DOWSING	water-divining	
DOYENNE	senior lady	
DOZENTH	12th	
DRABBER	more dingy	
DRABBET	smocking	
DRABBLE	befoul; draggle	
DRABLER	additional sail	**nt**
DRACHMA	Greek silver coin	**me**
DRACINA	dragon's blood palm	**bt**
DRACINE	dracina; a dye	**bt**
DRACONE	nylon/rubber liquids container	
DRACULA	Bram Stoker's batman; vampiric	
DRAFTED	outlined; detached	
DRAFT-OX	draught-ox	**zo**
DRAG-BAR	draw-bar	

DRAGGED	tugged; hauled; lingered	
DRAGGLE	bemire; drabble	
DRAG-MAN	a fisherman	
DRAG-NET	his net	
DRAGOON	compel; coerce; cavalryman	
DRAINED	filtered; exhausted; emptied	
DRAINER	a colander	
DRAPERY	haberdashery	
DRAPIER	a Swift 'nom de plume'	
DRAPING	covering; dressing	
DRAPPIE	a wee drop (Sc.)	
DRASTIC	severe; forcible; efficacious	
DRATTED	confounded	
DRAUGHT	dose; breeze; outline	
DRAWBAR	connecting rod; train couplings; tractive force	**rw, me**
DRAWBOY	a weaving assistant	
DRAWING	pulling; sketch; plan	
DRAWLED	dawdled; droned	
DRAWLER	monotonous speaker	
DRAW-NET	bird net	
DRAWN-ON	printing technique	
DRAYAGE	charge for a dray	
DRAYMAN	dray-driver; brewer's driver	
DREADED	apprehended; feared	
DREADER	an alarmist	
DREAMED	dreamt; imagined	
DREAMER	visionary; idealist	
DREDGED	sprinkled	
DREDGER	tea cup with strainer lid; salt pot; vessel for deepening waterways	**nt**
DREEING	enduring; bearing (Sc.)	
DRESDEN	Meissen porcelain	
DRESSED	cooked; decked; arrayed in	
DRESSER	kitchen sideboard; (window-); (attendant)	
DRESSER	lead beater	**to**
DREULED	slavered; dribbled	
DRIBBED	inveigled; filched	
DRIBBLE	(football); trickle; drip; ooze	
DRIBLET	driplet; a small quantity	
DRIFTED	floated; enlarged	
DRIFTER	wanderer; fishing boat with drift net; amateur aimless wanderer; dilettante	**nt**
DRILLED	trained; perforated; pierced	
DRINKER	reveller; carouser; toper	
DRIP-DRY	non-iron fabric	
DRIPPED	dropped; oozed; trickled	
DRIP-TIP	a leaf-point	**bt**
DRIVE-IN	service for motorists	
DRIVING	dragooning; urging; forcing	
DRIZZLE	fine rain	
DRIZZLY	with fine rain	
DROGHER	coasting vessel	**nt**
DROGMAN	dragoman; interpreter	
DROGUET	ribbed fabric	
DROICHY	dwarfish (Gael.)	
DROILED	toiled tediously	

DROLLED	jested; clowned	
DROLLER	farceur; funnier; odder	
DROMOND	fast sailing ship	**nt**
DRONING	prosing; humming	
DRONISH	lazy	
DROOLED	slavered; dribbled	
DROOPED	withered; declined	
DROPLET	a drip; bead of moisture	
DROP-NET	a fishing-net	
DROP-OUT	computer error; failure (exams)	**cp**
DROP-OUT	social non-participant; (dropkick) (Rugby football)	
DROPPED	dripped; fell; quitted	
DROPPER	end fly of a cast	
DROSERA	sun-dew	**bt**
DROSHKY	Russian vehicle	
DROUGHT	aridity; dryness	
DROUTHY	thirsty; very dry	
DROWNED	overflowed; submerged	
DROWSED	dozed; slumbered; dovered	
DRUBBED	thrashed; thumped; mauled	
DRUBBER	a beater	
DRUDGED	plodded; toiled; slaved	
DRUDGER	toiler; menial; scullion	
DRUGGED	stupefied; physicked	**md**
DRUGGER	drogher; small ship	**nt**
DRUGGET	carpet covering	
DRUIDIC	(Druids)	
DRUMBLE	to drone	
DRUMLIN	long glacially-formed hill	**gl**
DRUMMED	expelled; tapped; played	
DRUMMER	salesman (USA); drum player	
DRUNKEN	inebriated; crapulous; tipsy	
DRUSIAN	Levantine sectarian (Moslem)	
DRYADES	wood nymphs; trees	**bt**
DRY-BEAT	(blows without blood)	
DRY-BONE	silicate of zinc	**mn**
DRY-CELL	type of battery	**el**
DRY-DOCK	ship repair stage	**nt**
DRY-EYED	tearless	
DRYNESS	aridity; drought; thirst	
DRY-PILE	voltaic battery	
DRY-RENT	(no distress)	**lw**
DRY-SALT	preserve; cure	
DRYSHOD	with shoes not wet	
DUALINE	dualin; form of dynamite	
DUALISM	a doctrine; Manichaeism	
DUALIST	(twofoldness in the universe)	
DUALITY	doubleness	
DUALIZE	split in twain	
DUARCHY	diarchy; dual control	
DUBBING	dubbin; grease; entitling	
DUBIATE	to doubt; to hesitate	
DUBIETY	doubtfulness; uncertainty	
DUBIOUS	undecided; vacillating	
DUCALLY	in ducal style	
DUCHESS	duke's wife	
DUCK-ANT	Jamaican termite	**zo**
DUCKING	a soaking; diving	**zo**

DUCTILE	tractile; malleable	
DUCTULE	narrow-lumen duct	**zo**
DUDDERY	rags; old clo' shop	
DUDGEON	dagger; sullenness	
DUE-BILL	accepted debt	
DUELIST	fighter	
DUELLED	fought a duel	
DUELLER	combatant in single fight	
DUENESS	fitness; propriety; seemliness	
DUFFING	sham; furbishing up	
DUKEDOM	duke's realm	
DULCIFY	sweeten	
DULCINE	manna-sugar; mannite	
DULCITE	saccharine	**ch**
DULCOSE	dulcine	
DULLARD	stupid fellow; blockhead	
DULLEST	bluntest; most obtuse	
DULLING	allaying; benumbing	
DULLISH	rather dull; somewhat inert	
DULNESS	dullness; stupidity; apathy	
DULOSIS	ant slavery	**zo**
DUMPING	heaping (exporting)	
DUMPISH	in the dumps	
DUN-BIRD	pochard duck	**zo**
DUNCERY	dulness; stupidity	
DUNCIAD	Pope's epic poem	
DUNCISH	not clever	
DUNEDIN	Edinburgh	
DUNFISH	cured cod-fish	**ck**
DUNGEON	dark prison; cell	
DUNKERS	Tunkers; triple baptists	
DUNKING	jumping to score (basketball)	
DUNNAGE	packing; baggage; timber	
DUNNING	debt collecting; fish curing	
DUNNISH	dirty brown	
DUNNOCK	hedge-sparrow	**zo**
DUODENA	ancient jury	**lw**
DUOTONE	two-colour half-tone printing	
DUO-TYPE	2 like plates for diff. colours	**pr**
DUPABLE	credulous; gullible	
DUPPING	opening as a door	
DURABLE	lasting; abiding; stable	
DURABLY	permanently; long lasting	
DURAMEN	heart-wood	**bt**
DURANCE	captivity; duress; restraint	
DURANTE	for life	
DUREFUL	long lasting	
DURESSE	severity; constraint (Fr.)	
DURIRON	acid-resistant iron alloy	**ml**
DURMAST	an oak	**bt**
DURSLEY	bloodless blows	**lw**
DUSKIER	more sable or swarthy	
DUSKILY	dimly; darkly	
DUSKISH	shadowy	
DUSTBIN	trash receptacle	
DUSTIER	more flocculent	
DUSTING	a beating	
DUSTMAN	garbage collector	
DUSTPAN	house cleaning implement	
DUTEOUS	obsequious; deferential	

DUTIFUL	obedient; respectful	
DUUMVIR	Roman magistrates	
DVORNIK	Russian concierge	
DWARFED	stunted; eclipsed	
DWELLED	sojourned; abode; inhabited	
DWELLER	resident; inmate; indigene	
DWINDLE	diminish; decrease; shrink	
DYARCHY	duarchy; dual control	
DYELINE	document-copying process	**pr**
DYE-WOOD	(various woods)	**bt**
DYE-WORK	dyeing establishment	
DYINGLY	deathly	
DYNAMIC	forceful; energetic; mobile	
DYNAMIC	influx message handling	**cp**
DYNASTY	family; succession; house	
DYPTICH	codex book between wood covers	
DYSLOGY	disapproval; disapprobation	
DYSNOMY	bad laws	
DYSOPSY	poor sight	**md**
DYSURIA	impaired urination	**md**
DYTICUS	water-beetles	**zo**
DYVOURY	bankruptcy	**lw**

E

EAGERLY	avidly; ardently; fervently	
EANLING	young lamb	**zo**
EARACHE	a pain in the ear	**md**
EARDROP	a pendant; earring	
EAR-DRUM	tympanum	**md**
EAR-HOLE	aural portal	
EARLDOM	the seignory of an earl	
EARLESS	reluctant to hear	
EARLIER	sooner	
EARLOCK	love-lock	
EARMARK	identity mark for sheep	
EARNEST	pledge; steady; persevering	
EARNING	winning; meriting; acquiring	
EAR-PICK	tool for cleaning ears	
EARRING	pendant; eardrop	
EARSHOT	hearing distance	
EARTHED	burrowed	**ro**
EARTHEN	of clay	
EARTHLY	carnal; mundane; terrestrial	
EASEFUL	restful; tranquil; contented	
EASIEST	least difficult; simplest	
EAST-END	east part of city	
EASTERN	oriental; auroral	
EASTING	east of any meridian	**nt**
EATABLE	edible; succulent; esculent	
EBB-TIDE	retrogression	
EBONIST	ebony worker	
EBONITE	vulcanite	
EBONIZE	ebonise	
EBRIETY	intoxication; intemperance	
EBRIOSE	fuddled; crapulous; tipsy	
EBRIOUS	fond of the bottle; temulent	

ECBASIS	} rhetorical treatment	
ECBATIC		
ECCRINE	cell-excretory glandular	**md**
ECDEMIC	foreign; not endemic	
ECDYSIS	moulting; sloughing	
ECHAPPE	(horse-breeding)	
ECHELLE	scale; ladder (Fr.)	
ECHELON	a ladder formation; cycling; to minimise crosswind	
ECHIDNA	Australian ant-eater, marsupial	**zo**
ECHIMYD	S. American dormouse	**zo**
ECHINUS	sea-urchin; moulding; egg and dart pattern; below capitals	**ar, zo**
ECHOING	resounding; repeating	
ECHOISM	onomatopoeia	
ECHOIST	a yes-man	
ECLIPSE	shroud; veil; surpass; obscuration of solar or lunar light by interpositions	**as**
ECLOGUE	pastoral poem	
ECOLOGY	biological geography of surroundings, environmental	
ECONOMY	care; thrift; providence	
ECOTONE	plant-community boundary	**bt, ec**
ECOTYPE	genetic-habitat-adapted plants	**bt, ec**
ECOUTES	listening posts (Fr.)	
ECSTASY	rapture; fervour; delight	
ECTASIS	mispronunciation	
ECTHYMA	a rash	**md**
ECTOPIA	dislocation	**md**
ECTOPIC	displaced	
ECTOZOA	parasites	**zo**
ECTYPAL	actual copy	
ECUELLE	two handled dish with cover	**ck**
EDACITY	greed; voracity; rapacity	
EDAPHON	soil community of living organisms	
EDDERED	bound by an edder	
EDDYING	swirling; whirling; vortical	
EDELITE	a silicate	**mn**
EDENTAL	toothless	
EDICTAL	laid down; ordered	
EDIFICE	a stylish building	
EDIFIED	benefited spiritually	
EDIFIER	an uplifter	
EDITING	revising; annotating	
EDITION	issue; number; impression	
EDUCATE	teach; tutor; school; train	
EDUCING	extracting; eliciting	
EDUCTOR	corkscrew	
EELBUCK	basket-net	
EEL-FARE	a young eel	**zo**
EEL-POUT	blenny	**zo**
EFFABLE	explicable; utterable	

EFFACED	erased; defaced	
EFFECTS	personal estate	
EFFENDI	Turkish title; gentleman; sir; master; (col.)	
EFFORCE	ravish; rape	
EFFULGE	gleam; glisten; coruscate	
EFFUSED	emanated; diffused	
EGALITY	parity; equality	
EGESTED	cast out; ejected	
EGG-BIRD	tern	zo
EGG-CELL	a zygote	zo
EGG-COSY	oval muff	
EGG-FLIP	a bracer; drink	
EGGHEAD	intellectual	
EGOTISM	self-sufficiency; vanity	
EGOTIST	egoist	
EGOTIZE	(excess of 'I')	
EGRETTE	spray of gems; aigrette	
EIDETIC	one having vivid mental pictures	pc
EIDOLON	apparition; phantom	
EIRENIC	irenic; peaceful	
EJECTED	threw out; dispossessed	
EJECTOR	chucker-out	
ELAIDIC	} oil products	ch
ELAIDIN		
ELANCED	threw; darted	
ELAPSED	intervened; slid away; passed.	
ELASTIC	resilient; springy	
ELASTIN	elastic	
ELATERY	elastic force; elasticity	
ELATINE	water-wort	bt
ELATING	crowning; exalting	
ELATION	gratification; exhilaration	
ELAULIC	with oil in pipes	hy
ELBAITE	tourmaline variety	mn
ELBOWED	thrust aside; nudged	
ELDERLY	getting on in years	
ELEATIC	philosophic	
ELECTED	chosen; picked; preferred	
ELECTOR	voter; German title	
ELECTRO-	(plate); (magnetic); electric	cf
ELEGANT	refined; graceful; tasteful	
ELEGIAC	a lament; dirge	
ELEGIST	plaintive writer	
ELEGIZE	lament in writing	
ELEIDIN	skin cells substance	zo
ELEMENT	part; component; ingredient	
ELEVATE	elate; raise; hoist; promote	
ELEVENS	an interim	
ELF-BOLT	elf-arrow	
ELF-LAND	fairy-land	
ELF-LOCK	tangled hair	
ELF-SHOT	flint arrow-head	
ELF-WORT	elecampane	bt
ELIDING	rebutting; shortening	
ELIMATE	to file; to polish	
ELISION	metric suppression	
ELK-WOOD	umbrella-tree	bt
ELLAGIC	of gall-nuts	bt
ELLIPSE	oval; orbit of a comet	ma, as
ELL-WAND	(a yard and a quarter)	
ELOGIST	orator at a funeral	
ELOGIUM	panegyric	
ELOHIST	Pentateuch author	
ELOINED	removed; separated; banished	
ELOPING	sloping; bolting; decamping	
ELUDING	dodging; evading; baffling	
ELUSION	evasion; avoidance	
ELUSIVE	illustory; deceptive; fugitive	
ELUSORY	hard to solve; intangible	
ELUTION	ablution	
ELUVIUM	detritus from rock weathering	
ELYSIAN	delightful; heavenly	
ELYSIUM	Greek paradise	
ELYTRAL	shield-like	zo
ELYTRON	} wing-sheath of beetles	zo
ELYTRUM		
ELZEVIR	edition of classics	
EMANANT	proceeding from	
EMANATE	originate; issue; flow	
EMARCID	wilted	
EMBALED	packed; bundled	
EMBARGO	a prohibition; veto	
EMBASSY	ambassadorial residence	
EMBATHE	to bathe	
EMBAYED	land-locked	
EMBLAZE	embellish; imblaze	
EMBLEMA	inlaid ornament	
EMBLICA	Indian tree	bt
EMBLOOM	bloom	
EMBOGUE	debouch; discharge	
EMBOLUS	wedge; a clot	md
EMBOSOM	to hug; embrace; enfold	
EMBOWER	imbower; to shelter	
EMBOXED	enclosed	
EMBRACE	clasp; welcome; include	
EMBRAID	to braid (obs.)	
EMBRAIL	brail; lash	
EMBRAVE	embellish; inspirit	
EMBREAD	embraid	
EMBROIL	implicate; start trouble	
EMBROWN	to brown	
EMBRUED	ensanguined heraldically	hd
EMBRUTE	to deteriorate; brutalize	
EMBRYON	an embryo	bt, zo
EMENDED	amended; corrected	
EMERALD	smaragdus; brilliant green	
EMERGED	resulted; emanated; arose	
EMERITI	honourably discharged	
EMETINE	ipecacuanha alkaloid	
EMICANT	sparkling; sparking	
EMINENT	exalted; prominent	
EMIRATE	the domain of emir	
EMITRON	early UK TV tube	
EMITTED	circulated; exhaled; gushed	
EMITTER	electrode; punched card signal	cp
EMMENIA	menstrual flow	md

EMMEWED	} confined; cooped up; also	
ENMEWED	} inmewed	
EMOTION	passion; agitation; feeling	
EMOTIVE	emotional; passionate	
EMPALED	impaled; transfixed; fenced	
EMPANEL	enrol	
EMPATHY	sympathetic reaction	
EMPERIL	endanger	
EMPEROR	head of an empire	
EMPIGHT	placed; fixed	
EMPIRIC	based on practical experience	
EMPIRIC	a quack; charlatan	
EMPLANE	cf. embark	
EMPLEAD	prosecute	lw
EMPLUME	to feather	
EMPOWER	authorize; warrant; allow	
EMPRESS	female ruler of empire	
EMPRISE	a dangerous enterprise	
EMPTIED	drained; depleted; discharged	
EMPTIER	more inane and vacuous	
EMPTION	purchase	
EMULATE	to vie; compete; rival	
EMULOUS	striving to equal	
EMULSIC	emulsive	md
EMULSIN	almond ferment	ch
EMU-WREN	an Australian bird	zo
ENABLED	authorized; allowed	
ENACTED	decreed; ordained	
ENACTOR	law-maker	lw
ENAMOUR	charm; fascinate; enslave	
ENARMED	with weapon	hd
ENATION	plant or leaf outgrowth	bt
ENCAGED	incaged; cooped	
ENCASED	incased; enclosed	
ENCAVED	cached in a cave	
ENCENIA	commemorations; festivals	
ENCHAFE	to rub warm	
ENCHAIN	bind; fetter; shackle	
ENCHANT	enamour; bewitch; captivate	
ENCHASE	set with jewels; engrave	
ENCHEER	heaten; exhilarate	
ENCHYMA	injection; infusion	md
ENCLASP	embrace; hug; enfold	
ENCLAVE	an inlier	
ENCLOSE	envelop; fence; wrap	
ENCLOUD	mystify	
ENCODER	a device converting data into	
	digits and signals	cp, tc
ENCOMIC	of kinky, woolly hair	
ENCORED	repeated by request	
ENCRATY	abstinence; self-control	
ENCRUST	coat; plaster	
ENDARCH	xylem strand characteristic	bt
ENDEMIC	local; indigenous	
ENDERON	true skin	md
ENDEWED	endowed (obs.)	
END-GAME	chess; final stage	
ENDIRON	andiron; firedog	
ENDLESS	eternal; interminable	
ENDLONG	not sideways	

END-MARK	code conclusion signal	cp
ENDMOST	uttermost	
END-NOTE	additional printed information	
ENDOGEN	botanical growth	bt
ENDORSE	indorse; assign; ratify	
ENDOWED	supplied; bequeathed	
ENDOWER	benefactor; donor	
END-SHIP	a village (obs.)	
ENDUING	induing; investing	
ENDURED	tolerated; brooked; bore	
ENDURER	stayer; patient sufferer	
ENDWAYS	on end; upright	
ENDWISE	endways; punched card feed-in	
		cp
ENDYSIS	development of new hair/skin	
ENERGIC	active; energetic	
ENFACED	opposite to endorsed	
ENFELON	make fierce (obs.)	
ENFEOFF	assignm...	
ENFILE		
ENFLES		
ENFORCE		
ENGAGED		
ENGAGER	employment a...	
ENGINED	powered; racked	
ENGLISH	of England; language	
ENGLOBE	inglobe; ensphere	
ENGLOOM	to depress	
ENGORGE	stuff with food; engulf	
ENGRACE	bring into favour	
ENGRAFT	insert; graft	
ENGRAIL	spot with dots	hd
ENGRAIN	dye; permeate	
ENGRASP	clutch; seize	
ENGRAVE	cut; chisel; carve	
ENGROSS	monopolize; absorb; copy	
ENGUARD	defend	
ENHANCE	to intensify; heighten	
ENISLED	isolated	
ENJOYED	relished; liked; fancied	
ENJOYER	appreciator; gourmet	
ENLACED	} entwined; spliced	
INLACED	}	
ENLARGE	amplify; extend; expand	
ENLIVEN	wake; arouse; quicken	
ENMURED	immured; imprisoned	
ENNICHE	to enshrine	
ENNOBLE	exalt; raise; aggrandize	
ENNUIED	bored stiff	
ENODING	unknotting	
ENOMOTY	Spartan band	
ENOUNCE	proclaim; announce	
ENPLANE	to board an aeroplane	
ENPRINT	small enlargement	pg
ENQUIRE	inquire; investigate; ask	
ENQUIRY	inquiry; question; search	
ENQUIRY	search address control to reach	
	terminal	tc
ENRACED	enrooted	
ENRAGED	exasperated; incensed	

ENRIDGE	to furrow	
ENRIPEN	to mellow; mature	
ENROBED	attired; invested	
ENROUGH	to roughen	
ENSILED	stored in a pit	
ENSKIED	raised to heaven	
ENSLAVE	enthral; captivate; subjugate	
ENSNARE	entrap; allure; inveigle	
ENSNARL	entangle; ravel	
ENSOBER	to calm down	
ENSTAMP	impress; imprint	
ENSTEEP	immerse; duck; souse	
ENSTYLE	to call; to name	
ENSUING	resulting; issuing; accruing	
ENSURED	insured; made certain	
ENSWEEP	pass over rapidly	
ENSWEPT	scoured	
ENTAMED	subdued; domesticated	

(several entries obscured)

	...corded; penetrated	
	entrant; competitor	
ENTERIC	typhoid fever	md
ENTERON	collenterata body cavity	zo
ENTHEAL	divinely inspired	
ENTHRAL	inthral; enslave	
ENTHUSE	to gush	
ENTICED	allured; attracted	
ENTICER	seducer; cajoler; wheedler	
ENTITLE	intitle; qualify; allow	
ENTOMIC	(insects)	zo
ENTONIC	of high tension	
ENTOTIC	(interior of ear)	md
ENTOZOA	internal parasites	zo
ENTRAIL	interweave; plait	
ENTRAIN	to board a train	
ENTRANT	intrant; competitor	
ENTREAT	beg; implore; importune	
ENTROPY	dissipation of energy	
ENTRUST	intrust; confide	
ENTUNED	chanted; sang	
ENTWINE	weave; interlace; twist	
ENTWIST	intwist; wring; contort	
ENURING	inuring; hardening	
ENVAULT	entomb	
ENVELOP	enwrap; enfold; encase	
ENVENOM	to poison	
ENVIOUS	jealous; invidious; grudging	
ENVIRON	envelop; encompass; engird	
ENVYING	grudging; coveting	
ENWHEEL	encircle; surround	
ENWOUND	entwined; woven	
ENWOVEN	interwoven	
ENZONED	girdled; belted	
EOAPHIC	soil-related	ag, gl
EOBIONT	stage in biopoiesis	bl
EPACRID	of heathlike shrubs	bt

EPAGOGE	figure of speech	
EPARCHY	prefecture	
EPAULET	shoulder-piece	
EPAXIAL	above the axis	
EPEEIST	duelling by sword (fencing)	
EPERGNE	ornamental stand	
EPHEBIC	adult; of optimum period	zo
EPHEBUS	young Greek citizen	
EPHELIS	freckle	md
EPIBOLY	overgrowth	zo
EPICARP	the rind	bt
EPICEDE	funeral ode	
EPICENE	common to both sexes	
EPICHIL	orchid labellum end	bt
EPICISM	sagas; heroic poems; etc	
EPICIST	epic writer	
EPICOLE	harmless ... animal	ec
EPI...URE		lw
	heraldic sword thrust	hd
	turn into flesh	
	compel; oblige; coerce	mn
	plighted; stipulated	
	... agent	bt
EPIGEIC	...face	bt
EPIGENE	mineral change	
EPIGONE	a descendant	
EPIGONE	spore-bag	bt
EPIGRAM	barbed wisdom	
EPIHYAL	hyoid arch element	zo
EPILATE	remove (hair)	
EPILOIA	development defect affliction	md
EPIMERE	mesothelial-wall zone in vert.'s	
EPIMYTH	moral of story	
EPIOTIC	a bone in vertebrate skull	zo
EPISODE	separate event within a narrative	
EPISOME	genetically active bacteria particle	
EPISTLE	lengthy letter	
EPITAPH	monumental inscription	
EPITAXY	crystal growth or deposition	
EPITHEM	lotion; poultice	
EPITHET	a disparaging, abusive description	
EPITOME	brief summary; abstract	
EPIZOAN		
EPIZOIC	} parasite, of animals	zo
EPIZOON		
EPOCHAL	remarkable; outstanding; memorable (of events and time)	
EPOXIDE	plastic resin	
EPULARY	festive	
EQUABLE	fair; serene; uniform; calm	
EQUABLY	uniformly; justly	
EQUALLY	evenly	
EQUATED	made equal; balanced	
EQUATOR	a great circle	
EQUERRY	mounted officer; gentleman-in-waiting; royal adjutant	

EQUINAL	horsy	
EQUINIA	glanders	md
EQUINOX	universal equality of day and night	
EQUINUS	foot deformity; hoof-like	md
EQUITES	Roman cavalry, knights (Lat.)	
ERASING	expunging; deleting	
ERASION	erasure; deletion; obliteration	
ERASURE	effacement; cancellation	
ERECTED	raised; constructed; uplifted	
ERECTER	a builder; prefabricator	
ERECTLY	uprightly; upstanding	
ERECTOR	erecting lens	
ERELONG	before long	
EREMITE	hermit; a solitary	
EREPSIN	an enzyme	
ERGODIC	probability theory	
ERGOTED	afflicted with fungus	bt
ERGUSIA	vitamin A	
ERICOID	with heather-like leaves	bt
ERINEUM	leafy excrescence	bt
ERINITE	arseniate of copper	mn
ERINOID	a plastic material (milk)	
ERINYES	the Furies	
ERISTIC	controversial	
ERITHRO-	of redness	cf
ERL-KING	northern epic; poem to music	mu
ERMELIN	ermine; the stoat	zo
ERMINED	adorned with fur	
ERMINES	white spots	hd
ERODENT	consuming; erosive	
ERODING	corroding; eating away	
EROSION	scour damage; weathering; denudation	gl
EROSIVE	gnawing; virulent; acid	
EROTEME	interrogation mark	
EROTICA	pornographic literature	
ERRABLE	fallible; aberrant	
ERRATIC	rambling; vagrant; capricious	
ERRATUM	an error; misprint; mistake	
ERRHINE	medical snuff	md
ERUDITE	scholarly; learned	
ERUGATE	smoothed	
ERUPTED	exploded; ejected	
ESCAPED	eluded; avoided; leaked	
ESCAPER	danger dodger	
ESCHARA	net-like coral	zo
ESCHEAT	forfeiture; confiscate	lw
ESCRIME	fencing; swordsmanship (Fr.)	
ESCROLL	heraldic scroll	hd
ESCUAGE	feudal tenure	
ESCULIN	alkaloid (horse chestnut)	ch
ESERINE	alkaloid (Calabar bean)	ch
ESKIMOS	inhabitants of Arctic America	
ESNECCA	royal yacht, medieval, English	
ESOPIAN	fabulous (Aesop)	
ESOTERY	mysticism; necromancy	
ESPADON	Spanish sword	
ESPARTO	grass (Spain & Algeria)	bt

ESPINEL	kind of ruby	mn
ESPOUSE	to marry; betroth	
ESPYING	observing; discovering	
ESQUIRE	originally a shield-bearer	
ESSAYED	assayed; tested; tried	
ESSAYER	essay writer	
ESSENCE	extract; quiddity	
ESSENES	Jewish fraternity	
ESSOIGN	essoin; excuse for absence	
ESTINTO	soft and lifeless (It.)	mu
ESTIVAL	(summer)	
ESTOILE	heraldic star	hd
ESTRADE	a dais (Fr.)	
ESTREAT	true extract	lw
ESTRIOL	} female hormone	md
ESTRONE		
ESTUARY	river mouth; firth; frith	
ESURINE	aperitif; a cocktail	
ETAERIO	berried fruit (strawberry)	bt
ETAGERE	set of shelves (Fr.)	
ETATISM	central control (government)	
ETCHANT	copper-removing chemical	ch
ETCHING	engraving; an impression	
ETERNAL	endless; perennial; immortal	
ETESIAN	Levant wind	
ETHERIA	river-oyster	zo
ETHICAL	moral	
ETHIOPS	dark-coloured	
ETHMOID	sieve-like; like a temse	
ETOILIN	yellow chlorophyll	ch
ETONIAN	of Eton (College)	
EUCHRED	outwitted (USA)	
EUCLASE	beryl	mn
EUCRITE	coarse-grained igneous rock	gl
EUDOXID	monogastric stage in siphonofora	
EUGAMIC	of maturity-period	zo
EUGENIA	a large genus of spices	bt
EUGENIC	(birth influence)	
EUGENIN	clove camphor	
EUGENOL	constituent of clove/cinnamon oil; (of flavour)	ck
EULALIA	an ornamental grass	
EULOGIA	praises; panegyrics	
EULOGIC	commendatory; laudatory	
EUPATHY	contentment/moderation	
EUPEPSY	hearty digestion	md
EUPHONY	melodious sound	
EUPHROE	ridge-pole	
EUPLOID	cell chromosome value	bl
EUPNOEA	free respiration	md
EURIPUS	strait having violent tides	
EURITIC	like granite	mn
EURYALE	water-lilies	bt
EUSTYLE	columnar building style	
EUTERPE	muse of music	
EUTONIA	firmness of tone	md
EUTROPY	variation in chem. compounds	
EVACUEE	a displaced person	
EVADING	eluding; dodging; foiling	

EVANGEL	the gospel; good news	
EVANISH	vanish; disappear	
EVASION	subterfuge; prevarication	
EVASIVE	elusive; elusory; slippery	
EVENING	eventide; night-fall; twilight	
EVERTED	turned inside out	
EVICTED	dispossessed; ejected	lw
EVICTOR	chucker-out	lw
EVIDENT	obvious; patent; manifest	
EVIL-EYE	a bewitching look	
EVINCED	manifested; proved	
EVIRATE	castrate; geld	
EVITATE	to avoid (Shak.)	
EVOCATE	to summon spirits	
EVOKING	rousing; exciting; eliciting	
EVOLUTE	geometric curve	
EVOLVED	unfolded; emitted; educed	
EWE-LAMB	poor man's only possession	
EXACTED	demanded; levied	
EXACTER	extortioner	
EXACTLY	just so; precisely; literally	
EXACTOR	a tax collector	
EXALTED	lofty; ennobled; elevated	
EXALTER	magnifier; extoller	
EXAMINE	inquire; scrutinize	
EXAMPLE	model; pattern; sample	
EXANGIA	blood-vessel	md
EXARATE	of pupae with free members	zo
EXARCHY	a vice-royalty	
EXCERPT	an extract; cutting; citation	
EXCHEAT	escheat; confiscate	lw
EXCIPLE	outer apothecium wall layer	bt
EXCISED	cut out; removed	
EXCITED	provoked; irritated; inflamed	
EXCITER	rouser; stimulant; agitator	
EXCITON	electron pair in semiconductor	
		el
EXCITOR	stimulating to activity	zo
EXCLAIM	vociferate; ejaculate	
EXCLAVE	opposite to enclave	
EXCLUDE	prohibit; debar; preclude	
EXCRETA	human or animal waste	md
EXCURSE	to digress; to wander	
EXCUSED	released; pardoned; condoned	
EXECUTE	accomplish; put to death	lw
EXEDRAE	halls; recesses	
EXEGETE	theological exponent	
EXERGUE	date space on coin	
EXERTED	strove; applied; used	
EXHALED	emitted; evaporated; breathed	
EXHAUST	drain; empty; expend; tire	
EXHIBIT	display; manifest; evince	
EXHUMED	disinterred; unearthed	
EXHUMER	a resurrectionist	
EXIGENT	urgent; critical; importunate	
EXILIAN	exiled Jew	
EXILING	banishing; proscribing	
EXILITY	tenuity; slenderness	
EXISTED	was; lasted; endured; subsisted	
EXITIAL	destructive to life	

EXOCONE	of insect compound eyes	zo
EXODERM	outer cell layer in porifera	zo
EXODIST	an emigrant	
EXOGAMY	outbreeding; beyond tribal group	
EXOMION	Greek sleeveless vest	
EXOTISM	(not indigenous)	
EXOTYPE	kind marked by non-heritability	
		zo
EXPANSE	stretch; extend; space	
EX-PARTE	prejudiced; biased	
EXPENSE	cost; outlay; charge; price	
EXPIATE	atone	
EXPIRED	exhaled; ended; stopped	
EXPLAIN	elucidate; interpret; expound	
EXPLODE	burst; detonate; discharge	
EXPLOIT	feat; deed; achievement	
EXPLORE	search; prospect; examine	
EXPORTS	outward bound, foreign paid, trade goods, services	
EXPOSAL	exposure; revelation	
EXPOSED	unmasked; debunked	
EXPOSER	revealer; nark	
EXPOUND	explain; unfold; interpret	
EXPRESS	explicit; exude; speedy	
EXPUNGE	erase; abrogate; cancel	
EXPURGE	purify; expurgate	
EXSCIND	cut out; exsect	
EXTATIC	ecstatic; rapturous	
EXTINCT	defunct; obsolete; quenched	
EXTRACT	decoction; essence; juice	
EXTRACT	extort; derive; select	
EXTREME	utmost; ultimate; excessive	
EXTRUDE	expel; eject; force out	
EXUDING	sweating; oozing; dripping	
EXULTED	crowed; triumphed; boasted	
EXUVIAE	cast-off skins, etc.	zo
EXUVIAL	(cast skins)	zo
EYE-BALL	eye orb	
EYE-BATH	eye basin	
EYE-BEAM	a glance	
EYE-BOLT	(for hooks)	nt
EYE-BROW	a hairy arch; dormer window	ar
EYE-DROP	a tear	
EYE-FLAP	blinker (horses)	
EYE-HOLE	peep-hole	
EYELASH	cilliary hair	
EYELESS	blind; unobservant	
EYELIAD	wanton glance	
EYESHOT	range of vision; by eye	
EYESORE	a hideosity	
EYESPOT	(peacock's feather); 'stigma' in algae	bl
EYEWASH	humbug; window dressing	
EYE-WINK	a wink (Shak.)	
EZEMENT	gymnast's performance	

F

F NUMBER	relative aperture; stop	pg

314

FABELLA	small sesamoid bone in mammals **zo**	
FABLIAU	12th cent. topical verse (Fr.)	
FABLING	romancing	
FABRILE	(handicraft)	
FABULAR	legendary; conversational tales (fable)	
FACE-OFF	putting ball in play (ice hockey, lacrosse, water polo)	
FACETED	having facets	
FACETIA	witty remarks, jokes, indecent writings	
FACETTE	listel; flat surface between flutes	
FACONNE	woven figurative design **wv**	
FACTICE	veg. oil vulcanisation product **ch**	
FACTION	cabal; clique; dissension	
FACTORY	works; mill; workshop	
FACTUAL	real; actual; authentic	
FACTURE	manufacture; workmanship	
FACULAE	large bright areas of sun photosphere	
FACULTY	knack; skill; dexterity	
FADAISE	trivial remark (Fr.)	
FADDING	shellac lacquering	
FADDISH	rather crotchety	
FADDIST	with-it person	
FADDLED	trifled; played	
FADEDLY	insipidly	
FADE-OUT	an evanescence; end of sequence; films, radio-drama; disappear gradually **cn**	
FADGING	suiting; prospering	
FAGGERY	drudgery	
FAGGING	enforced service	
FAGOTTO	bassoon **mu**	
FAHLERZ	copper crystal ore **mn**	
FAIENCE	fayence; glazed pottery	
FAILING	a foible; declining; miscarry	
FAILURE	fiasco; ruin; collapse	
FAILURE	disruption by defect **cp**	
FAINING	wishing; desiring	
FAINTED	swooned; languished	
FAINTER	weaker; paler; dimmer	
FAINTLY	dimly; indistinctly	
FAIREST	clearest; purest	
FAIRIES	enchantresses; pixies	
FAIRILY	like a fairy; elf-like	
FAIRING	a present; streamlining	
FAIRISH	reasonably fair; only moderately good; blonde-like	
FAIRWAY	(golf); navigable channel	
FAITOUR	impostor; scoundrel	
FALANGE	Spanish fascist party	
FALBALA	furbelow; puckered flounce	
FALCADE	(equitation); curvetting	
FALCATE	hooked; like a crescent	
FALCULA	claw **zo**	
FALDAGE	a farming privilege	
FALERNE	sweet white wine	

FALLACY	a sophism; chimera; untruth	
FALLALS	showy trifles	
FALLING	erring; tumbling; dropping	
FALLOUT	radioactive contamination; nuclear disagreement	
FALSELY	fallaciously; untruly	
FALSEST	most disloyal	
FALSIES	artificial bust	
FALSIFY	counterfeit; belie; fake	
FALSISH	somewhat erroneous	
FALSISM	obvious falsity	
FALSITY	fallacy; fabrication	
FAMULUS	magician's assistant	
FANATIC	bigot; zealot; visionary	
FANCIED	favoured; imagined; thought	
FANCIER	expert; breeder	
FANFARE	flourish of trumpets	
FANGLED	newly contrived	
FAN-MAIL	letters of adulation	
FANNING	extending; winnowing; (flames) cowboy's balance tactics	
FAN-PALM	the talipot palm **bt**	
FANTAIL	pigeon; a gas burner **zo**	
FANTASM	spook; phantasm	
FANTAST	visionary; enthusiast	
FANTASY	caprice; mental conception; free development **mu**	
FARADAY	unit of electrolysis	
FARADIC	inductive	
FARAWAY	distant; remote	
FARCEUR	satirical jester	
FARCIFY	to burlesque	
FARCING	edible stuffing; force-meat	
FARDAGE	dunnage; packing (Fr.) **nt**	
FARMERY	homestead	
FARMING	leasing of taxes	
FARMOST	uttermost; furthest	
FARNESS	remoteness	
FARRAGO	a medley; hodge-podge	
FARRIER	shoeing-smith; a vet	
FARRUCA	Andalusian dance **mu**	
FARTHEL	farl; oatcake	
FARTHER	besides; further; beyond	
FASCETS	glass-making tools **to**	
FASCIAE	fillets; name boards	
FASCIAL	(fasces)	
FASCINE	bound brushwood	
FASCISM	anti-socialism	
FASCIST	political party (Italy)	
FASHERY	annoyance; vexation	
FASHING	worrying; bothering	
FASHION	mode; vogue; style; mould	
FAST-DAY	non-eating day **rl**	
FASTEST	swiftest; fleetest; closest	
FASTING	abstaining from food	
FASTISH	rather dissipated	
FATALLY	mortally; calamitously	
FAT-BODY	fatty tissue in amphibians, insects **zo**	
FATEFUL	ominous; portentous	

FAT-HEAD	blockhead; moron; dunce	
FATIDIC	prophetic; oracular	
FATIGUE	tire; jade; lassitude	
FATLING	young fatted animal	zo
FATLUTE	luting	
FATNESS	obesity; corpulence; fertility	
FATTEST	most obese	
FATTING	fattening	
FATTISH	rather plump; adipose	
FATUITY	self-complacency; folly	
FATUOUS	illusory; imbecile; witless	
FAUCIAL	pertaining to fauces	
FAULTED	displaced; (tennis)	
FAULTER	defaulter	
FAUNIST	naturalist	
FAVOURS	party badges	
FAWNING	sycophantic; cringing	
FAYENCE	faience; pottery	
FEARFUL	dismayed; dire	
FEARING	dreading; revering; timid	
FEASTED	caroused; gratified	
FEASTER	a Lucullus	
FEATHER	adorn; quill; (oar)	zo
FEATURE	characteristic; aspect; trait	
FEAZING	unravelling	
FEBRILE	feverish	
FECULUM	starchy extract	
FEDERAL	confederated	
FEEDING	pasture; eating; subsisting; jelled paint	
FEE-FARM	tenure without fealty	
FEELING	sensibility; perception	
FEERING	first furrow (Sc.)	
FEE-TAIL	entailed estate	
FEEZING	twisting; unscrewing	
FEIGNED	simulated; shammed	
FEINTED	feigned	
FELIDAE	} the cat genus	zo
FELINAE		
FELLING	hewing; cutting down	
FELONRY	the convict class	
FELSITE	igneous rock	mn
FELSPAR	metamorphic rock	mn
FELTING	felt cloth	
FELUCCA	Mediterranean, Nile, sailboat	nt
FELWORT	mullein	bt
FEMINAL	womanly	
FEMORAL	(thigh)	md
FENCING	hedging; evading; sword duelling, sport	
FENDING	warding off; averting	
FEN-DUCK	shoveller-duck	zo
FEN-FIRE	will o' the wisp	
FENGITE	alabaster	mn
FENNISH	marshy; boggy; swampy	
FEODARY	feudal tenure	
FEOFFEE	receiver of a fief	
FEOFFOR	feoffer; fief-granter	
FERDWIT	a quittance; penalty	
FERINGI	European in India	

FERMATA	a pause	mu
FERMENT	inflame; commotion; yeast	
FERMION	generalized particle in statist. theory	
FERMIUM	man-made element	ch
FERNERY	fern garden	bt
FERN-OWL	night-jar	zo
FERRARA	a sword-blade (It.)	
FERRATE	an iron salt	ch
FERRIED	transported	
FERRIES	ferry-boats; air-lift transport	
FERRITE	ferro-magnetic (ceramics)	ch, cp
FERROUS	(iron)	ch
FERRUGO	plant-rust; fungus	bt
FERRULE	protecting cap; shaft of hunting horn	mu
FERTILE	inventive; prolific; fruitful	
FERULED	caned; punished	
FERVENT	zealous; ardent; glowing	
FERVOUR	eagerness; intensity; ardour	
FESTIVE	joyous; convivial; gay	
FESTOON	wreath; garland	
FESTUCA	grass genus	bt
FETCHED	brought; conveyed; reached	
FETCHER	collector; heaver	
FETLOCK	a tuft of hair	zo
FEUDARY	} medieval fee, rights	lw
FEODARY		
FEUDING	quarrelling (ice hockey)	
FEUDIST	writer on feudal law	lw
FEU-DUTY	annual payment (Sc.)	
FEVERED	agitated; febrile	
FEWNESS	paucity; scarcity; sparsity	
FEYNESS	otherworldliness	
FIANCEE	betrothed woman	
FIBBERY	mendacity	
FIBBING	prevaricating	
FIBROID	like fibre	
FIBROIN	cobweb material	
FIBROIN	tough elastic protein	bc
FIBROMA	fibrous tumour	md
FIBROSE	filamental	
FIBROUS	stringy	
FIBSTER	petty liar	
FIBULAR	(leg bone)	md
FICARIA	celandine	bt
FICTILE	plastic; mouldable	
FICTION	romance; fantasy; invention	
FICTIVE	imaginative; feigned	
FIDALGO	Portuguese hidalgo	
FIDDLED	trifled; meddled	
FIDDLER	a crab; violinist	zo
FIDDLEY	hatchway railing	nt
FIDGETY	restless; uneasy; impatient	
FIELDED	(cricket); (base-ball)	
FIELDER	not one of the batting side	
FIERCER	more violent	
FIERILY	vehemently; ardently	
FIFTEEN	a Rugby side	
FIG-CAKE	a sweetmeat	ck

FIGGERY	dressy ornament	
FIGGING	dressing up	
FIGHTER	combatant; warrior	
FIG-LEAF	early dress material	**bt**
FIGMENT	a fabrication	
FIG-TREE	Mediterranean plant	**bt**
FIGURAL	pictorial; figurate	
FIGURED	computed; depicted	
FIGWORT	a plant	**bt**
FILACER	} Law officer dealing with	
FILAZER	} writs and pleas	**lw**
FILARIA	parasitic worms	**zo**
FILBERT	hazel-nut	**bt**
FILCHED	purloined; stole	
FILCHER	pickpocket; pilferer	
FILEMOT	dead-leaf colour	
FILESET	magnetic disk; data system;	
	(manicure)	**cp**
FILIATE	affiliate; adopt	
FILIBEG	the kilt	
FILICAL	(ferns)	**bt**
FILICES	the ferns	**bt**
FILINGS	file fragments	
FILLING	satisfying; replenishing;	
	stuffing; bulk; ballast;	
	increased atmospheric	
	pressure in depression	**mt**
FILM-FAN	a devotee; star-worshipper	
FILMING	recording in celluloid	
FIMBRIA	fringe; brain neural fibre; bundle	
		pl
FIMETIC	foul in thought	
FINABLE	liable to a fine; amerceable	
FINALLY	ultimately; lastly; eventually	
FINANCE	money affairs; revenue	
FINBACK	rorqual whale	**zo**
FINCHED	striped; spotted	
FINDING	verdict; discovering	
FINECUT	chopped into small pieces	
FINESSE	subtlety; craft; artifice	
FIN-FISH	finback whale	**zo**
FIN-FOOT	tropical bird	**zo**
FINGENT	moulding	
FINICAL	fastidious; dainty; faddy	
FINICKY	niggling; meticulous	
FINIKIN	finicking; finicky	
FINLESS	having no flipper	
FINNACK	} white sea-trout	**zo**
FINNOCK	}	
FINNISH	of the Finns	
FIN-RAYS	bony fin supports (fish)	**zo**
FIN-TOED	web-footed	
FIORITE	volcanic residue	**mn**
FIRE-ARM	weapon	
FIRE-BAR	furnace bar	
FIRE-BOX	boiler fuel chamber	
FIRE-BUG	an incendiary	
FIREDOG	an andiron	
FIREFLY	a luminous beetle	**zo**

FIREMAN	fire fighter; relief pitcher	
	(baseball)	
FIRE-NEW	brand-new	
FIRE-PAN	brazier; priming pan	
FIRE-POT	tenant's rights	**lw**
FIRMARY	tenant's rights	**lw**
FIRMING	confirming; establishing	
FIRRING	wood strips for roof boarding	
	base	
FIRRING	} encrusting; lathing	
FURRING	}	**pb**
FISCITE	crystallized pyrargillite	**mn**
FISH-DAY	fast day	
FISHERY	fish-breeding station	
FISH-FAG	fish-wife	
FISH-FLY	a bait	**zo**
FISH-GIG	fishing appliance	
FISH-GOD	Dagon	
FISHIFY	to turn into a fish (Shak.)	
FISHILY	in a fishy manner	
FISHING	angling; piscatorial pursuit	
FISH-MAW	swimming bladder	
FISH-OIL	nutrient-rich oil	
FISHWAY	fish-ladder	
FISKERY	friskiness	
FISSILE	cleavable; laminate	
FISSION	fissure; rent; rift; fracture	
FISSIVE	fissile	
FISSURE	cleft; crevice; interstice	
FISTING	pommelling	
FIST-LAW	might is right	
FISTUCA	pile-driver	
FISTULA	ulcer; reed	**md**
FITCHED	pointed	**hd**
FITCHEE	fitched	
FITCHET	polecat; foumart	**zo**
FITMENT	a fitting	
FITNESS	aptness; decency; seemliness	
FITTAGE	brokerage	
FITTING	a fixture; appropriate	
FITWEED	anti-hysteric plant	**bt**
FIXABLE	securable	
FIXEDLY	firmly; steadfastly	
FIXINGS	fasteners holding joinery	**jn**
FIXTURE	apointment; engagement;	
	(match); building; fitment	
FIZZING	spluttering; hissing	
FIZZLED	failed; flopped	
FLACCID	flabby; tabid; loose; limp	
FLACKER	flutter like a bird	
FLACKET	flask; flasket	
FLACKIE	straw packing	
FLAFFER	to flutter (Sc.)	
FLAG-DAY	day when flags sold for charity	
FLAG-DAY	charity or national day	
FLAGGED	signalled; drooped	
FLAG-MAN	signaller	
FLAKING	crumbling; peeling; reed base	
	(thatching)	**bd**
FLAMING	blazing; burning; glowing	

FLAMMED	hoaxed	
FLAMMER	splitting knife	**to**
FLANEUR	an idling gossip	
FLANGED	having a raised edge	
FLANKED	bordered by; side by side	
FLANKER	that which lies beside; wingers and halfbacks (football)	
FLANNEL	woollen fabric; mullein genus	
FLAPPER	bird; girl	**zo**
FLARING	funnel-shaped; glaring	
FLASHED	glistened; sparkled; gleamed	
FLASHER	would-be-wit	
FLASKET	basket; flask	
FLATLET	a small flat	
FLATTED	flattened; depressed	
FLATTEN	level; lay low	
FLATTER	coax; cajole; compliment	
FLAUNTY	showy; gaudy	
FLAVEDO	yellowness	**bt**
FLAVIAN	(Flavius Vespasian)	
FLAVINE	a yellow dye	**bt**
FLAVONE	yellow plant pigment	**ch**
FLAVOUR	zest; savour; taste; relish; quality	
FLAWING	cracking; marring	
FLAYING	skinning; excoriating	
FLEABAG	sleeping bag	
FLEAPIT	shabby room; theatre	
FLEBILE	tearful; plaintive (It.)	**mu**
FLECKED	spotted	
FLECKER	to dapple	
FLEDGED	ready for flight	
FLEECED	clipped; shorn	
FLEECER	white collar bandit	
FLEEING	absconding; retreating	
FLEERED	mocked; scoffed	
FLEERER	a derider; flouter	
FLEETED	flitted; flew; sped	
FLEETLY	swiftly; nimbly; rapidly	
FLEMING	a native of Flanders	
FLEMISH	language of Flemings	
FLENSED	cut blubber	
FLESHED	satiated; glutted	
FLESHER	butcher; red-backed shrike	**zo**
FLESHLY	carnal; sensual; fat; obese	
FLETTON	pink/yellow indented brick	**bd**
FLEURET	floral decoration; fencing-foil	
FLEURON	type flower in printing	
FLEXILE	pliable; pliant; supple	
FLEXING	bending; turning	
FLEXION	inward inclination (bow and arrow)	
FLEXURE	bending; curvature	
FLICKED	flipped	
FLICKER	twinkle; scintillate; pulsating; (candle, movies)	
FLIFFIS	double somersault, trampoline	
FLIGHTY	volatile; mercurial; fickle	
FLINDER	splinter; fragment	
FLINGER	hurler	

FLIP-DOG	liquor heater	**zo**
FLIPPED	filliped; flicked	
FLIPPER	fore-limb of a cetacean	**zo**
FLIRTED	coquetted; flicked	
FLITTER	flutter; a tatter	
FLOATED	drifted; wafted	
FLOATER	voter; plasterer's float	
FLOCCUS	tuft of hair; down	
FLOCKED	crowded; swarmed; thronged	
FLOCKLY	like sheep	
FLOGGED	scourged; lashed	
FLOGGER	graining brush	**pt**
FLOODED	swamped; inundated; deluged	
FLOOKAN	slimy clay	
FLOORED	overthrown; baffled	
FLOORER	knockdown blow	
FLOPPED	failed; fizzled	
FLOPPER	faller; failure; splasher	
FLOREAL	8th month (Fr. Revolution)	
FLORIST	a nurseryman	
FLOROON	flower border	
FLORUIT	a life-time	
FLOTAGE	buoyancy	
FLOTSAM	recovered wreckage	
FLOUNCE	a jerky movement	
FLOURED	powdered	
FLOUTED	jeered; insulted	
FLOUTER	mocker; derider	
FLOWAGE	flow; current; discharge	
FLOWERY	florid; ornate; figurative	
FLOWING	fluent; copious; smooth	
FLUENCE	energy (f); particle (f-)	
FLUENCY	exuberance	
FLUEWAY	smoke and gas duct	
FLUFFED	bungled; foozled	
FLUIDAL	flowing; liquid	
FLUIDIC	fluid	
FLUIDLY	liquidly	
FLUKILY	by a fluke	
FLUKING	scoring by chance	
FLUMMOX	perplex; defeat	
FLUMPED	slumped	
FLUNKEY	footman; snob; toady	
FLUORIC	(fluorine)	**ch**
FLUSHED	blushed; roused; disturbed	
FLUSHER	lesser butcher-bird	**zo**
FLUSTER	agitation; disconcert; bustle	
FLUSTRA	sea-mat; polyzoa	**zo**
FLUTINA	accordion	**mu**
FLUTING	grooving	
FLUTIST	} flute-player	
FLAUTIST		
FLUTTER	speculation; palpitate; wave; undesirable modulation, scare	**ps, el**
FLUVIAL	(rivers); soil deposits, fluviatile	
FLUXIDE	fusible (welding)	
FLUXING	melting	
FLUXION	fusion; variation; change	

FLYAWAY	flighty; dismounting (gymnastics)	
FLYBACK	when scanner beam restarts cycle	**el, tc**
FLY-BILL	hand-bill	
FLY-BLOW	fly-larva	**zo**
FLY-BOAT	canal boat	
FLY-BOMB	pilotless aerial torpedo	
FLY-BOOK	(fishing)	
FLY-FLAP	fly-whisk	
FLY-HALF	(football)	
FLY-LEAF	blank page	
FLY-LINE	fishing line	
FLY-OVER	road or rail crossing	
FLY-PAST	flight by aircraft	
FLY-RAIL	table leaf support	
FLY-TRAP	an insectivorous plant	**bt**
FOALING	colt-birth	
FOAMING	raging; bubbling; creaming	
FOBBING	cheating; tricking	
FOCUSED	concentrated	
FODIENT	pertaining to digging	
FOE-LIKE	hostile; inimical; adverse	
FOG-BANK	accumulation of fog	
FOG-BELL	sea warning device	
FOG-DUST	cloud of groundbait (angling)	
FOGGAGE	coarse grass	**bt**
FOGGARA	underground irrigation channel (N. Africa, Arab.)	**go**
FOGGIER	murkier; more opaque	
FOGGILY	mistily	
FOGGING	obscuring	
FOGHORN	sea warning device	**nt**
FOGLAMP	penetrating headlight	
FOGLESS	clear	
FOG-RING	bank of fog	
FOGYISH	antiquated	
FOGYISM	dull notions	
FOILING	tracery; deer track	
FOILIST	fencer	
FOINING	thrusting; tilting	
FOISTED	falsified; thrust	
FOISTER	palmer; imposer; cheat	
FOLDAGE	sheep folding rights	
FOLDING	a fold; sheep penning	
FOLIAGE	leafage; boscage	
FOLIATE	a curve; laminate	
FOLINIC	acid constituent of folic acid	
FOLIOED	in folios or pages	
FOLIOLE	leaflet	**bt**
FOLIOSE	leafy	
FOLIOUS	thin; unsubstantial	
FOLLIES	imbecilities; inanities	
FOMITES	porous substances	**ch**
FONDANT	soft sweet; sugar icing (cakes, sweets)	**ck**
FONDEST	most affectionate	
FONDING	doting	
FONDLED	caressed; dandled	
FONDLER	sugar daddy	

FONDUTA	cheese/truffle fondue (N. Italy)	**ck**
FONTEIN	S. African spring	
FONTLET	small font	**rl**
FOODFUL	nourishing; nutritious	
FOOLERY	clowning; buffoonery	
FOOLING	hoodwinking; beguiling	
FOOLISH	doltish; stupid; irrational	
FOOT-BAR	aeroplane rudder control	**ae**
FOOTBOY	page; bell-hop	
FOOTHOT	hot-foot; immediately	
FOOTING	basis; entrance fee; condition of race course; touch ground twice	
FOOTLED	pottered	
FOOTMAN	flunkey; lackey; escort on coach; trivet (4 legs)	
FOOTPAD	highwayman; pickpocket; robber	
FOOT-ROT	disease of sheep	**vt**
FOOT-TON	a measure of work	**me**
FOOTWAY	footpath	
FOOZLED	footled; mishit	
FOOZLED	bungler	
FOPLING	young dandy	
FOPPERY	affectation; coxcombry	
FOPPISH	finical; dressy; effeminate (Restoration)	
FORAGED	plundered; pillaged	
FORAGER	ravager; a cap	
FORAMEN	a pore	**md**
FORAYED	invaded; raided	
FORAYER	marauder	
FORBADE	vetoed; banned; inhibited	
FORBEAR	ancestor; refrain; abstain	
FORBORE	desisted; withheld; shunned	
FORCEPS	pliers	**to**
FORCING	plant culture; coercing	
FORCITE	dynamite	
FORCQUE	fork; mine sump	**mn**
FORDING	crossing	
FORDONE	tired out	
FOREARM	lower part of arm	**pl**
FOREBAY	pipeline head reservoir	**hy**
FORE-BOW	front of saddle	
FORE-CAR	(motor-cycle)	
FOREDAY	forenoon	
FOREDID	overpowered; undid	
FORE-END	the front end	
FORE-GUT	part of animal alimentary canal	
FOREIGN	alien; exotic; strange	
FORELAY	ambush	
FORELEG	front leg	
FOREMAN	boss; overseer; ganger	**lw**
FORERAN	preceded; ushered	
FORERUN	herald	
FORESAW	foretold; forecast	
FORESAY	predict; presage; augar	
FORESEE	anticipate; forecast	
FORETOP	part of rigging	**nt**

FOREVER	everlasting; always	
FORFANG	an ancient felony	**lw**
FORFEIT	alienate; penalty; fine	
FORFEND	to avert; ward off	
FORGAVE	pardoned; absolved	
FORGERY	counterfeiting	
FORGING	shaping; hammering; smithing; counterfeiting	
FORGIVE	remit; excuse	
FORGONE	past; predetermined	
FORKFUL	fork-load	
FORKING	branching; dividing	
FORLANA	} old Italian dance	**mu**
FORLANE		
FORLORN	desolate; lost; hapless	
FORMANT	vowel pitch	
FORMATE	(formic acid)	**ch**
FORMFUL	imaginative; creative	
FORMICA	rigid laminated plastic material	
FORMING	shaping; moulding	
FORMOXY	organic radical	**ch**
FORMULA	set of symbols	
FORNENT	directly opposite (Sc.)	
FORPINE	waste away (obs.)	
FORSAKE	abandon; quit; desert	
FORSOOK	renounced; relinquished	
FORTIFY	strengthen; brace	
FORTLET	small redoubt	
FORTUNE	luck; Kismet; felicity	
FORWARD	bold; brazen; quicken; front-line footballer	
FORWENT	foregone	
FORWORN	tired out (obs.)	
FOSSICK	prospect; rummage	
FOSSWAY	Roman road	
FOUDRIE	jurisdiction (Sc.)	
FOUGADE	fougasse; mine	
FOULARD	silk	**tx**
FOULDER	to flame; gleam (obs.)	
FOULING	(gun-barrels); soiling	
FOUMART	the polecat; fitchew	**zo**
FOUNDED	started; established	
FOUNDER	collapsed; originator	
FOUNDRY	(metal-casting)	
FOURGON	baggage wagon	
FOVEATE	pitted	**bt**
FOVEOLA	dent; depression	**md**
FOVILLA	(pollen)	**bt**
FOWLING	falconry	
FOWLRUN	poultry yard	
FOX-CASE	fox-skin	
FOX-EVIL	baldness	**md**
FOXHOLE	defensive trench	
FOXHUNT	English diversion	
FOXLIKE	cunning	
FOXSHIP	craftiness	
FOXTAIL	a grass	**bt**
FOX-TRAP	a snare	
FOX-TROT	a dance	
FOYAITE	nepheline-syenite variety	**gl**

FRABBIT	peevish	
FRACHES	glass annealing trays	
FRACTED	broken	**hd**
FRAGILE	delicate; infirm; brittle	
FRAILLY	weakly; feebly	
FRAILTY	foible; weakness; infirmity	
FRAISED	defended by pointed stakes	
FRAKTUR	German black-letter type	
FRAME-UP	plot; conspiracy for entrapment	
FRAMING	forming; devising	
FRAMPEL	quarrelsome; peevish	
FRANCIC	Frankish	
FRANION	boon companion; paramour	
FRANKED	exempt; post paid	
FRANKLY	candidly; openly; unreserved	
FRANTIC	frenzied; raving; distracted	
FRAPPED	bound	**nt**
FRATCHY	quarrelsome	
FRATERY	refectory in monastery	**rl**
FRAUGHT	laden; pregnant; surcharged	
FRAYING	peel of deer's horn	
FRAZZLE	tatters; shreds	
FREAKED	streaked; checkered	
FRECKLE	macula	
FRECKLY	spotted	
FREEDOM	liberty; informality; scope	
FREEING	loosing; liberating	
FREEMAN	privileged citizen	
FREESIA	bulbous plant	**bt**
FREEWAY	by pass; motorway	
FREEZER	refrigerator	
F-REGION	} ionosphere	**ps**
F-LAYER		
FREIGHT	cargo; burden; burthen	
FREMLIN	beery, female gremlin	**ae**
FRENATE	bristly	**zo**
FRESHEN	refresh; invigorate; revive	
FRESHER	freshman; less faded	
FRESHES	a flood; a spate	
FRESHET	flooding of a river; clear stream	
FRESHLY	recently; briskly; newly	
FRESNEL	unit of optical frequency	
FRETFUL	petulant; testy; fractious	
FRET-SAW	woodworking tool	**to**
FRETTED	frayed; abraded; harassed	
FRETTEN	pock-pitted	
FRETTER	a worried woman	
FRIABLE	crumbly; powdery	
FRIAGEM	wintry cold spell in tropical campos, Brazil	
FRIARLY	unsophisticated	
FRIBBLE	frivolous; to trifle; totter	
FRIEZED	shaggy with nap; ornamented	
FRIGATE	a war-ship	**nt**
FRIJOLE	Mexican bean	**bt**
FRILLED	adorned like a ham	
FRINGED	bordered; edged	
FRINGES	alternate light and dark colours	
FRIPPER	old clothes merchant	
FRISEUR	hairdresser	

FRISIAN	Frieslander; cattle	**zo**
FRISKED	gambolled; searched	
FRISKER	a gad-about; a searcher	
FRISKET	a printing frame	
FRISLET	small ruffle	
FRISURE	a crisping of the hair	
FRITTED	fused; baked	
FRITTER	pancake; fragment; dissipate	
FRIZING	stripping grain surface	**le**
FRIZZED	curled	
FRIZZLE	to fry; to crisp; to splutter	
FRIZZLY	curly	
FROCKED	wearing a frock	
FROGBIT	acquatic plant	**bt**
FROGERY	a frog pool	**zo**
FROGGED	braided	
FROG-MAN	special type of diver	**nt**
FRONDED	leafy	**bt**
FRONTAL	a pediment; head on	
FRONTED	faced; encountered	
FRONTIS	front wall of court (pelota)	
FRONTON	a pelota ground (Sp.)	
FROSTED	roughened	
FROTHED	foamed	
FROUNCE	wrinkle; frown	
FROWARD	perverse; wayward	
FROWNED	scowled; glowered	
FROWSTY	foul and stuffy	
FRUCTED	bearing fruit	
FRUGGIN	oven stirring pole	
FRUITED	bore fruit	
FRUITER	fruit grower	
FRUMPED	jeered	
FRUMPER	scoffer; mocker	
FRUSTUM	a conic section	
FRUTIFY	fructify; team; produce	
FUBBERY	deception	
FUCATED	painted deceptively	
FUCHSIA	a flowering shrub	**bt**
FUCHSIN	red fuchsia dye	
FUDDLED	bemused; fuzzled	
FUDDLER	drunkard; toper	
FUDGING	faking	
FUEHRER	German leader	
FUELLER	stoker	
FUFFING	puffing	
FUGUIST	fugue composer	**mu**
FULCRUM	support for lever; raised end of bed	
FULGENT	dazzling; radiant; brilliant	
FULGORA	lantern fly	**zo**
FULGOUR	splendour	
FULLAGE	fuller's pay	
FULLERY	cloth works	
FULLEST	amplest; most exhaustive	
FULL-HOT	vehement; blazing	
FULLING	(cloth process)	
FULL-PAY	not docked	
FULMINE	fulminate	

FULNESS	repletion; plenty; plentitude	
FULSOME	obsequious; nauseous	
FULVOUS	tawny; fulvid	
FUMARIA	genus of plants	**bt**
FUMARIC	a vegetable extract	**bt**
FUMARIN	chemical rodenticide	
FUMBLED	bungled; groped	
FUMBLER	fozzler	
FUMETTE	smell of high game	
FUMITER	the fumitory plant	**bt**
FUN FAIR	amusement park	
FUNARIA	genus of mosses	**bt**
FUNCTOR	syntactic (words of function)	
FUNDING	forming a reserve	
FUNEBRE	funeral; march	**mu**
FUNERAL	sepulture; obsequies	
FUNGATE	(fungic acid)	**ch**
FUNGITE	fossil coral	**mn**
FUNGOID	fungus	**bt**
FUNGOUS	of fungi; behaving like fungus	
FUNICLE	ligature; ovule stalk	**pl, bt**
FUNKING	panicking; fearing	
FUNNILY	comically; humorously	
FUNNING	joking; diverting	
FURBISH	burnish; rub; polish	
FURCATE	forked	
FURCULA	the merrythought	**zo**
FURIANT	quick Czech dance	**mu**
FURIOSO	all out (It.)	**mu**
FURIOUS	frantic; raging; frenzied	
FURLANA	forlana; Venetian dance	
FURLING	wrapping; rolling	
FURLONG	220 yards (201 m); running; horse racing	**me**
FURMETY	frumenty; porridge	
FURNACE	firebox	
FURNISH	equip; supply; produce	
FURRIER	a dealer in furs	
FURRING	} (lathing); encrusting	**pb**
FIRRING		
FURROWY	in furrows	
FURTHER	farther; promote; encourage	
FURTIVE	stealthy; sly; clandestine	
FUSCINE	an oil extract	**ch**
FUSCOUS	swarthy	
FUSIBLE	able to be melted	
FUSSIER	more fidgety	
FUSSILY	restlessly	
FUSSING	making trouble	
FUSS-POT	anxious busy-body	
FUSTIAN	coarse cloth; bombastic	
FUSTIER	mouldier; mustier	
FUTCHEL	supporting bar	
FUTHORC	Runic alphabet	
FUTTOCK	ship's timber	
FUZZIER	curlier; more crinkled	
FUZZLED	fuddled; inebriated	
FYRDUNG	Saxon martial array	

G

GABBARD	gabbart; a barge	**nt**
GABBING	gossiping	
GABBLED	gaggled; chattered	
GABBLER	a babbler	
GABELLE	pre-Revolutionary salt-tax (Fr.)	
GABELER	salt tax collector	
GADDING	roving; wandering	
GADDISH	restless	
GADELLE	currant (Fr.)	**bt**
GADLING	gauntlet spike	
GADROON	ornamented edge	
GADSMAN	ploughman	
GADWALL	migratory duck	**zo**
GAEKWAR	Gaikwar; (Baroda)	
GAFFING	(fishing); gambling	
GAGGING	interpolation; silencing	
GAGGLED	gabbled	
GAHNITE	spinel-group mineral	**mn**
GAIASSA	cargo felucca, Nile	**nt**
GAINFUL	lucrative; beneficial	
GAINING	profiting; winning; acquiring	
GAINSAY	dispute; contradict	
GAIRISH	garish; gaudy	
GAITERS	gambadoes	
GALACTO-	of milk	**cf**
GALANTY'	(shadow pantomime)	
GALATEA	Pygmalion's statue	
GALATEA	cotton fabric	**tx**
GALEATE	crested	**zo**
GALEENY	guinea-fowl	**zo**
GALENIC	(lead)	
GALERIA	ancient Mexican water system	
GALETTE	a gateau	**ck**
GALILEE	West porch	**rl**
GALIPOT	pine-resin	**bt**
GALLANT	courtly; valiant; a beau	
GALLA-OX	Abyssinian ox	**zo**
GALLATE	(gallic acid)	**ch**
GALLEON	carrack; trader (Sp.)	**nt**
GALLERY	corridor; passage; balcony; (play to); tennis	
GALL-FLY	a pest	**zo**
GALLICE	in French	
GALLING	irritating; exasperating	
GALLIOT	galiot; brigantine; later, barge	**nt**
GALLIUM	a metallic element	**ch**
GALLIZE	(wine-making)	
GALL-NUT	a pestiferous growth	**bt**
GALLOON	woven fabric; lace	**tx**
GALLOWS	(Tyburn)	
GALOCHE	galosh; rubber over-shoe	
GALOPIN	kitchen-boy (Sc.)	
GALUMPH	bound exultingly	
GAMBADO	mud-gaiter; caper	
GAMBIAN	native of Gambia (W. Africa)	
GAMBIER	catechu; a dye	**bt**
GAMBIST	a viol player	**mu**
GAMBLED	staked; ventured; hazarded	
GAMBLER	speculator; wagerer	

GAMBOGE	also camboge	
GAMBREL	butcher's crook; roof	**ar**
GAME-BAG	hunter's bag	
GAME-EGG	a bad egg	**zo**
GAMEFUL	sportive; playful	
GAMELAN	Indonesian ensemble	**mu**
GAME-LEG	lameness	
GAMETAL	gametic; reproductive	
GAMETID	sporont-body bud cell	**zo**
GAMMOCK	sky-larking; gammon	
GAMPISH	bulging; slatternly	
GANCHED	(Turkish execution)	
GANGING	going (Sc.); joining	**el**
GANGLIA	nerve-centre	**md**
GANGREL	vagrant; vagabond	
GANG-SAW	multiple saw	**to**
GANGWAY	a passage (ships); scaffolding routes	**nt, bd**
GANGWAY	ledge of rock (mountaineering)	**mo**
GANOIDS	fish of sturgeon type	
GANOSIS	reducing shine on marble	
GANTLET	gauntler	
GANTREE	loom jacquard frame	**wv**
GAPPING	opening; cleaving	
GARBAGE	refuse; offal; litter; unwanted data	**cp**
GARBAGE	easy goal (basket ball), (ice hockey); soft shot (tennis)	
GARBLED	(suppressio veri)	
GARBLER	(suggestio falsi)	
GARBOIL	uproar; turmoil (Shak.)	
GARBURE	Pyrenean ragout/soup	**ck**
GARDANT	full-faced	**hd**
GARFISH	sea-fish; belone	**zo**
GARGLED	warbled	
GARLAND	wreath; chaplet; festoon; slide-slip while traversing slope (skiing)	
GARMENT	vesture; raiment; apparel	
GARNISH	adorn; pewter ware	
GAROTTE	garrotte; throttle; strangle with thread	
GARPIKE	the garfish	**zo**
GARUKHA	dhow	**nt**
GARVOCK	a sprat; garvie (Sc.)	**zo**
GAS-BUOY	marine device	**nt**
GAS-COAL	anthracite	
GAS-COKE	coal residuum	
GASEITY	gaseousness	
GASEOUS	containing gas	
GAS-FIRE	heating unit	
GASHFUL	mutilated; hideous	
GASHING	slicing; slitting	
GASKINS	leggings	
GAS-LAMP	Victorian lighting	
GAS-LIME	(gas filtration)	
GAS-MAIN	chief gas conduit	
GAS-MASK	war protection device	
GAS-OVEN	kitchen furniture	
GASPING	spasmodic breathing	

GAS-PIPE	gas conduit	
GAS-RING	cooker	
GASSING	loquacity	
GASSOUL	mineral soap (Morocco)	
GAS-TANK	gas storage receptacle	
GASTERO-	of the stomach	**cf, pl**
GASTRIC	gastral; (stomach)	**md**
GATEMAN	gate-keeper	
GATEWAY	entrance	
GATLING	a gun	
GAUDERY	finery; gew-gaws	
GAUDIED	embellished	
GAUDILY	ostentatiously	
GAUFFER	to crimp	
GAUFFRE	a batter cake	
GAUGING	mensuration; estimating; (width of rail)	**rw**
GAUGING	marking timber; rubbing bricks	
GAUGING	altering proportions in mortar or plaster mix	**bd**
GAULISH	(Gaul)	
GAULTER	gault or clay digger	
GAUMING	daubing; smearing	
GAUNTLY	lankily; leanly	
GAUNTRY	gantry; travelling crane	
GAVELET	land forfeiture	**lw**
GAVILAN	species of hawk	**zo**
GAVOTTE	a country dance	**mu**
GAYNESS	merriment; hilarity	
GAYSOME	blithe; vivacious; jolly	
GAZEFUL	regardant; contemplative	
GAZELLE	graceful animal	**zo**
GAZETTE	journal; newspaper; record	
GEAR-BOX	motor-engine	
GEARING	varying interconnected wheels; sliding seat (rowing)	
GEDRITE	orthorhombic amphibole	**mn**
GEGGERY	trickery (Sc.)	
GEHENNA	place of abomination	
GELABLE	congealable	
GELATIN	gelatine	
GELDING	castrated stallion	**zo**
GELIDLY	frigidity	
GELLING	conversion of liquid to jelly	**ck, pt**
GELLOCK	crowbar; gavelock	**to**
GEMMATE	budding	
GEMMERY	} collection of precious	
GEMMARY	} stones, mounted gems	
GEMMING	budding	
GEMMULE	small bud	**bt**
GEMSBOK	S. African antelope	**zo**
GENAPPE	worsted yarn	
GENERAL	vague; inexact; usual	
GENERIC	of general features classified	
GENESIS	starting point	
GENETIC	of origins; heredity; (chromosomes)	**bl**
GENETTE	genet; civit	**zo**
GENEVAN	of Geneva; Calvanist	**rl**
GENEVER	hollands; gin	

GENIPAP	orange-like fruit	**bt**
GENISTA	broom plant; (Plantagenet)	**bt**
GENITAL	of reproductive organs	**bl, pc**
GENITOR	creator	
GENOESE	of Genoa	
GENTEEL	elegant; polite; mincing	
GENTIAN	plant genus	**bt**
GENTILE	not a Jew	
GENTLER	milder; more kindly	
GENUINE	sincere; authentic; veritable	
GEOCOLE	periodically soil-dwelling organism	
GEODESY	(earth measurements)	
GEOGONY	(earth formations)	
GEOIDAL	earth-shaped	
GEOLOGY	study of rocks; composition, structure, history of our earth	**gl**
GEONOMY	physical geography	
GEORAMA	globular map	
GEORDIE	mine-lamp; guinea	**nm**
GEORGIC	rural poetry	
GEOTOME	soil-sample taker	**bt**
GEOXENE	accidentally soil-dwelling organism	
GERMANE	relevant; apposite; pertinent	
GERMULE	a small germ	**md**
GERVAIS	cream cheese (Fr.)	**ck**
GESTALT	total perception; art as unity	**pc**
GESTAPO	German secret police	
GESTATE	carry in womb	
GESTURE	sign; signal; action	
GETABLE	obtainable; procurable	
GET-AWAY	escape	
GETTING	acquisition; gaining; reaching	
G-FACTOR	energy level changes in magnetic field	**ps**
GHASTLY	fearsome; spectral; awful	
GHERKIN	small cucumber	**bt**
GHILGAI	Australian dewpond	
GHILLIE	game-keeper (Sc.)	
GHOSTLY	weird; spiritual; spectral	
GIANTLY	as gigantic-like, Cyclopean-like; of enormous strength	
GIANTRY	giants collectively	
GIBBOSE	humped	
GIBBOUS	convex	**as**
GIBLETS	kidneys and liver	
GIDDILY	vertiginously	
GIFTING	endowing; bestowing	
GIG-MILL	nap-raising device	
GILBERT	magnetic potential	
GILDING	painting gold	
GILLIAN	sweetheart	
GILLION	10 to the 9th power	**ma, me**
GILL-LID	gill covering	**zo**
GILVOUS	brownish	**bt**
GIMBALS	compass suspender	
GIMBLET	gimlet	**to**
GIMMICK	publicity trick	
GIN-FIZZ	a cocktail based on gin	

GINGALL	swivel gun	
GINGERY	hot-flavoured	
GINGHAM	umbrella; gamp; (material)	**tx**
GINGILI	sesame-oil	**bt, ck**
GINGING	mine-shaft lining	**mn**
GIN-MILL	off-licence (Amer.)	
GINNING	cotton making	
GINSENG	a Chinese pick-me-up; Chinese root for life-extending infusions	**ck**
GIN-SHOP	gin-palace	
GIN-TRAP	leg-trap; snare for poachers and animals	
GIOCOSO	jocund; playful (It.)	**mu**
GIPPING	gutting	
GIPSIES	Zingari	
GIRAFFE	the camelopard	**zo**
GIRASOL	fire-opal	**mn**
GIRDING	a covering; reproaching	
GIRDLED	zoned; belted	
GIRDLER	girdle maker	
GIRLISH	very young; lady-like	
GIRNING	grumbling (Sc.)	
GIRROCK	garfish	**zo**
GIRTHED	girdled; bound	
GISARME	battle-axe; bill; halberd	
GITTERN	cither; guitar	**mu**
GIZZARD	grinding organ of a bird	
GLACIAL	icy	
GLACIER	moving ice layer	
GLADDEN	delight; gratify; rejoice	
GLADDER	brighter; more cheerful	
GLAD-EYE	an invitation	
GLADIUS	swordfish	**zo**
GLADWYN	purple iris	**bt**
GLAIDIN	glutin; (wheat)	
GLAIKIT	giddy; foolish (Sc.)	
GLAIRED	varnished	
GLAMOUR	fascination; witchery	
GLANCED	glimpsed; ricocheted	
GLARING	refulgent; bare-faced	
GLASSES	specs	
GLAUCUS	genus of molluscs	**zo**
GLAZIER	pane-setter	
GLAZING	(windows); (pottery)	
GLEAMED	shone; flashed; glinted	
GLEANED	gathered; culled; harvested	
GLEANER	Ruth	
GLEBOUS	gleby; turfy	
GLEDGED	squinted	
GLEEFUL	gay; lively; hilarious	
GLEEMAN	minstrel	
GLENOID	cupped	**md**
GLEYING	squinting	
GLIADIN	gliadine; glutin	**ch**
GLIDING	flowing; skimming; sliding; parachuting	
GLIDING	unpowered flight using thermal currents	
GLIMMER	gleam; inkling	
GLIMPSE	glance; view; look	

GLINTED	gleamed; sparkled	
GLIOSIS	neuron replacement cells	**bl**
GLIRINE	rodent-like	
GLISTEN	shine; coruscate; scintillate	
GLISTER	glitter; lustre; sparkle	
GLITTER	glisten; brilliance; radiance	
GLOAMED	grew dark	
GLOATED	exulted; revelled	
GLOBARD	a glow-worm	**zo**
GLOBATE	spheroidal	
GLOBING	encircling	
GLOBOID	spherical	
GLOBOSE	round	
GLOBOUS	globular	
GLOBULE	corpuscle	
GLONOIN	trinitroglycerine alcohol solution	
GLOOMED	obscured; dimmed; moped	
GLORIED	exalted; took pride in	
GLORIFY	honour; magnify; extol; bless	
GLOSSAL	vocabulary; tongue	
GLOSSED	explained; palliated	
GLOSSER	polisher; commentator	
GLOSSIC	phonetic alphabet	
GLOTTAL	⎱ of vocal chords; phonetical	
GLOTTIC	⎰ stop	**md**
GLOTTIS	(larynx)	**md**
GLOWING	vehement, ardent; fervid	
GLOZING	specious representation	
GLUCIDE	saccharin, gluside	**ch**
GLUCINA	an oxide	**ch**
GLUCOSE	sugar	
GLUE-POT	gum receptacle	
GLUMMER	more dismal and dejected	
GLUMOUS	husky	**bt**
GLUTEUS	hind-limb muscle in vertebrates	
GLUTTED	gorged; surfeited; crammed	
GLUTTON	the wolverine	**zo**
GLYCINE	amino-acetic acid	**ch**
GLYOXOL	yellow dialdehyde liquid	**ch**
GLYPHIC	word picture; plastic model; ideogram; cartouche	
GLYPTIC	engraved; figured	
GMELINA	(verbena)	**bt**
GNARING	snarling; growling	
GNARLED	knotty; gnarred	
GNARRED	gnarled; knotty	
GNASHED	ground	
GNATHIC	(jaws); gnathal	**md**
GNATHOS	ventral sclerite in m. lepidoptera	
GNAT-NET	mosquito-net	
GNAWING	champing; eroding	
GNOCCHI	maize/potato dumplings (It.)	**ck**
GNOSTIC	speculative believer	
GOADING	inciting; annoying	
GO-AHEAD	enterprising	
GOATISH	lustful; satyr-like	
GOBBING	coal refuse	
GOBBLER	turkey-cock	**zo**
GOBBLER	gourmandizer	
GOBELIN	French tapestry	
GODDARD	pewter cup	

GODDESS	female deity	
GODETIA	a garden annual	**bt**
GO-DEVIL	concrete pipeline cleaner	**ce**
GODHEAD	divine nature	
GODHOOD	state of being god	
GODILLE	wavy ski-descent technique	
GODLESS	atheistic; irreligious; profane	
GODLIER	more righteous	
GODLIKE	deific	
GODLILY	devoutly	
GODLING	an inferior deity	
GODROON	gadroon; beading	
GODSEND	windfall; a crowning mercy	
GODSHIP	deification	
GODWARD	heavenward	
GOGGLED	lobster-eyed	
GOGGLES	eye-protectors	
GOITRED	afflicted with bronchocele	
GOLD-CUP	buttercup	**bt**
GOLDING	an apple; hops	**bt**
GOLDNEY	a bream	**zo**
GOLFING	mild sport	
GOLIARD	wandering jester	
GOLIATH	large beetle	**zo**
GOMBEEN	money-lending; usury (Irish)	
GOMELIN	cotton starch	
GOMERIL	a lout; stupid fellow (Sc.)	
GONAGRA	gout	**md**
GONDOLA	car of an airship; small cable car; galley (It.); canal pleasure boat, Venice	**ae, mo, nt**
GONGING	prelude to a fine	
GONIDIA	lichen-spores	**bt**
GONITIS	stifle joint inflammation	**vt**
GONOPOD	external insect-reproduction organ	**zo**
GOOD-BYE	adieu	
GOOD-DAY	conventional greeting	
GOOD-DEN }	good evening	
GOOD-E'EN }		
GOOD-EGGI	cordial approval	
GOODISH	not so bad	
GOODMAN	a husband	
GOOD-NOW	exclamation of wonder	
GOONDIE	Australian native hut	
GOOSERY	cf. swannery	**zo**
GOPURAN	Hindu gate tower	**ar**
GORCOCK	red grouse	**zo**
GOR-CROW	carrion crow	**zo**
GORDIAN	intricate; (knot)	
GORDIUS	hair-worm	**zo**
GORGING	cramming; stuffing	
GORILLA	largest anthropoid ape	**zo**
GORMAND	gourmand; glutton	
GORSEDD	Welsh bardic assembly	
GOSHAWK	short-winged hawk	**zo**
GOSLING	a young goose	**zo**
GOSNICK	small sea-fish; skipper	**zo**
GOSSIPY	chatty; loquacious	
GOSSOON	a boy (Irish)	
GOUACHE	(water-colour painting)	

GOUGING	scooping	
GOULARD	lead acetate	**ch**
GOULASH	a ragout; (cards)	**ck**
GOURAMI	tropical fish	**zo**
GOURMET	a dainty feeder; epicure	
GOURNET	gurnet	**zo**
GOWN-MAN	a divine, etc.	
G-PARITY	particle quantum number	**nc, ps**
GRAB-BAG	lucky-dip bag	
GRABBED	clutched; snatched	
GRABBER	gripper; pincher	
GRABBLE	sprawl; grope; paw	
GRACILE	slender	
GRACING	adorning; decking	
GRACKLE	Indian thrush	**zo**
GRADATE	to blend colour	
GRADELY	orderly; really good	
GRADINE	sculptor's chisel	**to**
GRADING	a decoration; classifying	
GRADUAL	step by step	
GRAFFER	notary; scrivener	**lw**
GRAFTED	incorporated	
GRAFTER	swindler	
GRAINED	(painted wood)	
GRAINER	grain-painter	
GRALLAE	wading birds	**zo**
GRALLIC	stilted	
GRAMARY	magic; wizardry	
GRAMMAR	a treatise; rules, inflections, syntax, lingual	
GRAMPUS	dolphin; killer whale	**zo**
GRANARY	grain-store	
GRANDAD	grandpa	
GRANDAM	a grannie	
GRANDEE	Spanish nobleman	
GRANDER	finer; superior; sublime	
GRANDLY	splendidly; superbly	
GRANDMA	grandam	
GRANGER	farm bailiff	
GRANITE	coarse, igneous, plutonic rock	**gl**
GRANNOM	grandam	
GRANTED	ceded; allotted; vouchsafed	
GRANTEE	the receiver	**lw**
GRANTER	the bestower	
GRANTOR	conveyor	**lw**
GRANULE	small particle	
GRAPERY	vinery	**bt**
GRAPHIC	pictorial; vivid; with dials, lights	**cp**
GRAPNEL	grappling-iron	
GRAPPLE	grasp; clutch; grip	
GRASPED	clasped; gripped; understood	
GRASPER	clasper; grabber	
GRASSED	brought down	
GRASSER	extra printing hand	
GRASSUM	a premium	
GRATIFY	please; humour; gladden	
GRATING	harsh; offensive; jarring; ventilator grill; manhole cover; distraction; scratching noise; rasping	**pc, ck**

GRAUNCH	unplanned error; machine's fault **cp**	
GRAUPEL	soft hail (Ger.)	
GRAVEDO	cold in the head	
GRAVELY	seriously; staidly; sober	
GRAVEST	most serious; very cogent	
GRAVIED	served with gravy	
GRAVING	engraving; scraping	
GRAVITA	gravely	
GRAVITY	enormity; importance; seriousness; falling force **lw, ps**	
GRAVURE	photogravure; printing technique **pr**	
GRAZIER	shepherd	
GRAZING	glancing; touching; browsing	
GREASED	lubricated; oiled	
GREASER	lubricator; a dago	
GREATEN	enhance; enlarge; augment	
GREATER	bulkier; bigger; larger	
GREATLY	vastly; notably; immensely	
GREAVES	leg-armour	
GREAVES	tallow refuse; cracklings	
GRECIAN	Greek or man of Greece (poet)	
GRECISM	Greek idiom	
GRECIZE	to Hellenize	
GRECQUE	coffee-machine	
GREENED	hoaxed; duped; gulled	
GREENER	more verdant	
GREENTH	verdure	
GREETED	accosted; welcomed	
GREGALE	NE winter wind,	
GREGAL	Mediterranean **mt**	
GREMIAL	bishops' pinafore **rl**	
GREMLIN	aerial imp; pilot's illusion; unskilled skateboardist	
GRENADE	hand-bomb	
GREY-HEN	stone bottle	
GREY-HEN	female grouse **zo**	
GREYISH	grayish	
GREYLAG	wild goose; grey goose **zo**	
GREY-OWL	tawny owl **zo**	
GRIBBLE	marine borer (crustacean) **zo**	
GRIDDED	marked in squares	
GRIDDLE	sieve; a grid	
GRIDING	grating; jarring	
GRIEVED	lamented; mourned	
GRIFFIN	greenhorn; a duenna	
GRIFFON	dragon-eagle **hd**	
GRIFFIN		
GRILLED	broiled; cross-examined	
GRIMACE	a moué; facial distortion	
GRIMING	fouling; soiling	
GRIMMER	dourer; fiercer; more grisly	
GRINDER	a molar; quern; peppermill; crusher	
GRINNED	smiled broadly	

GRIPING	grasping; trenching	
GRIPPED	seized; held; clutched	
GRIPPER	a bailiff	
GRIPPLE	usurious; tenacious	
GRIQUAS	Dutch half-castes	
GRISKIN	lean bacon	
GRISLED	grizzled; grey	
GRISTLE	a cartilage	
GRISTLY	cartilaginous	
GRITTED	grated; ground	
GRITTER	road, salt-spreading device	
GRIZZLE	whimper; gray	
GRIZZLY	grey; a bear **zo**	
GROANED	moaned; bewailed	
GROBIAN	clumsy lout	
GROCERY	provision shop	
GROGRAM	fabric of silk and mohair **tx**	
GROINED	arched	
GROLIER	(bookbinding)	
GROMMET	ring of rope	
GROOMED	soigné	
GROOVED	furrowed; scooped	
GROPING	seeking blindly; stumbling	
GROSSER	coarser; rougher	
GROSSLY	flagrantly; outrageously	
GROTIAN	(legal philosophy)	
GROUNDS	reasons; dregs; less	
GROUPED	graded; classified	
GROUPER	an arranger	
GROUSED	complained; murmured	
GROUSER	grumbler	
GROUTED	filled with cement	
GROWING	raising; waxing	
GROWLED	snarled	
GROWLER	a four-wheeled cab	
GROWN-UP	an adult	
GRUB-AXE	a hoe **to**	
GRUBBED	dug up	
GRUBBER	an investigator	
GRUBBLE	grope; grabble	
GRUDGED	envied; coveted	
GRUFFER	surlier; rougher	
GRUFFLY	churlishly; roughly; bluntly	
GRUMBLE	grouse; complain; repine	
GRUMMET	a grommet; a rope ring	
GRUMOSE	clustered	
GRUMOUS	clotted	
GRUNDEL	loach or rock-goby **zo**	
GRUNTER	a pig; a gurnet **zo**	
GRUYERE	a Swiss cheese **ck**	
GRYLLID	pertaining to crickets	
GRYPHON	heraldic dragon-eagle **hd**	
GRIFFIN		
GRYSBOK	S. African antelope **zo**	
GUAJIRA	peasant dance (Cuba)	
GUANACO	huanco; camel **zo**	

GUANINE	purine base in living tissues	bc
GUARANA	Brazil cocoa	bt
GUARANI	(Paraguay)	nm
GUARDED	wary; watchful; defended	
GUDGEON	an axle; a fish	zo
GUELDER	rose; snowball tree	bt
GUENONS	a monkey genus	zo
GUERDON	a reward; recompense	
GUEREZA	the Abyssinian monkey	zo
GUERITE	watch-tower	
GUESSED	divined; solved; supposed	
GUESSER	a conjecturer	
GUESTAN	to be a guest (Sc.)	
GUIACUM	lignum vitae	bt
GUICHET	small window as for tickets (Fr.)	
GUIDING	leading; directing; piloting	
GUILDER	Dutch golden coin	nm
GUILDRY	of guilds, collectively	
GUINEAN	(W. African)	
GUIPURE	a heavy lace	
GUISARD	a Christmas mummer	
GULLERY	imposture; deceitfulness; pretence	
GULLIED	water-worn; ravinous	
GULLIES	ravines; knives	
GULLING	greening; duping	
GUM-BOIL	inflamed swelling	md
GUM-BOOT	rubber shoe	
GUMDROP	a confection	
GUMMING	fruit-tree disease; cementing	bt
GUMMOUS	gummy; mucilaginous	
GUM-RASH	red gum; strophulus	md
GUM-THUS	resin from Amer. pine	bt
GUM-TREE	(quandary); (rubber)	bt
GUMWOOD	similar grain to rosewood	bt
GUNBOAT	small warship	nt
GUN-DECK	area of guns	nt
GUNDELO	cargo felucca, New	
GUNDELOW	England	nt
GUN-FIRE	time signal	
GUNLOCK	firing mechanism	
GUNNAGE	(number of guns)	nt
GUNNERY	the craft of the artillery	
GUNNING	shooting	
GUN-PORT	port-hole	nt
GUN-ROOM	a mess-room	nt
GUNSHOT	range	
GUN-SITE	location of gun	
GUNWALE	topmost plank	nt
GURGLED	purled; rippled	
GURNARD	gurnet fish	zo
GUSHING	spouting; flowing; effusive	
GUSTATE	to taste, consume	
GUSTILY	in gusts; fitfully; breezily	
GUTTATE	spotted	
GUTTING	gipping; eviscerating	
GUTTLED	gulped; swallowed	
GUTTULE	small drop	
GUTWORT	a tord-boyau	bt
GUZZLED	swilled; gorged; caroused	

GUZZLER	gourmand	
GWINIAD	freshwater salmon	zo
GWYNIAD	small white fish	zo
GYMNAST	athlete	
GYPLURE	moth sex attractant	zo
GYRATED	twirled; span; spun; rotated	
GYRATOR	component used at microwave frequencies	el
GYRINID	whirligig beetle	zo
GYRONNY	heraldic triangulation	hd
GYROSYN	flux-gate gyro compass	ae
GYTRASH	a ghost	

H

HABITAT	home; abode; natural environment of plant or animal	bt, zo
HABITED	dressed; attired	
HABITUE	a frequenter	
HACHURE	engraved line	
HACKBUT	an arquebus	
HACKERY	Bengal ox-cart	
HACKING	cutting; notching; kicking	
HACKLED	combed	
HACKLER	flax-comber	
HACKLES	feathers; imitation flies (angling)	
HACKLET	sea-bird; shearwater gull	zo
HACKLOG	chopping block	
HACKNEY	horse; cab; trite	zo
HACK-SAW	a saw for metal	to
HADDING	a holding on lease (Sc.)	
HADDOCK	a haddie (Sc.)	zo
HADROME	xylem conducting tissues	bt
HAEMONY	witch's bane plant	bt
HAFFETS	the temples (Sc.)	
HAFFLED	prevaricated	
HAFFLIN	half-grown (Sc.)	
HAFNIUM	metallic element	ch
HAFTING	fitting a handle	
HAGANAH	Jewish militia	
HAGBOAT	hull design of sailing vessels	nt
HAGDOWN	shearwater gull	zo
HAGFISH	parasite fish	zo
HAGGADA	Jewish commentary	
HAGGARD	stackyard; lean; hollow-eyed	
HAGGARD	adult bird from the wild (falconry)	
HAGGING	nagging; harassing	
HAGGISH	ugly; repulsive	
HAGGLED	mangled; bargained	
HAGGLER	higgler; bargainer	
HAGSEED	witch's offspring	
HAGSHIP	haggishness	
HAGWEED	broom	bt
HAILING	raining; greeting	
HAIRCUT	barber service	
HAIRNET	coiffure cover	
HAIR-OIL	hair dressing	

HAIRPIN	aid to coiffure	
HAITIAN	native of Haiti	
HALACHA	} Jewish oral laws and	
HALAKAH	} traditions	
HALBERD	} pike-like weapon	
HALBERT	}	
HALCYON	kingfisher; calm	zo
HALF-BED	stone laying term	bd
HALF-ONE	a golf handicap	
HALF-PAY	semi-retirement	
HALFWAY	intermediate position	
HALF-WIT	nitwit; moron	
HALIBUT	the largest flounder	zo
HALIDOM	mascot; sanctuary	
HALITUS	exhaled air	md
HALLAGE	market-hall dues	
HALLIER	bird net	
HALLING	Norw. acrobatic dance for men	
HALLION	hallyon; hallian; rascal	
HALOGAN	salt producer group	ch
HALOGEN	one of the 7th-group elements	
HALTERE	capitate thread in diptera	
HALTING	faltering; hesitating	
HALVANS	ore-mining refuse	mn
HALVING	tieing; bisecting	
HALYARD	halliard; running rope	nt
HAMBLED	mutilated the foot	
HAMBURG	domestic fowl	zo
HAMITIC	(Ham)	
HAMMING	overacting; radio hobby	tc
HAMMING	error checking code signal distance	cp
HAMMOCK	canvas hanging bed	nt
HAMSTER	a rodent	zo
HAMULAR	} small hook; hooked;	
HAMULUS	} hamate	
HANAPER	hamper; treasury	
HANBALI	traditional school of Islamic canonical law	rl, lw
HANDBAG	a reticule	
HANDFUL	gowpen (Sc.)	
HANDIER	more dexterous	
HANDILY	conveniently; adjacently	
HANDING	presenting; delivering	
HANDJAR	Persian dagger	
HANDLED	dealt with; manipulated	
HANDLER	dealer	
HAND-OFF	self-defence; fending off a tackle (rugby football)	
HANDOUT	prepared statement; sample; advertising material	
HANDSAW	carpenter's tool	to
HANDSEL	earnest money; a present	
HANDSET	telephone receiver and microphone (mouthpiece)	tc
HANGDOG	sullen; morose; abject	
HANGING	dangling; depending	
HANGMAN	topsman; public executioner	
HANG-NET	vertical net	
HANKIES	kerchiefs	tx

HANKING	making into skeins	
HANKLED	entangled; involved	
HANSARD	Parliamentary records	
HANSTER	a freeman of a guild	
HANUKAH	Jewish feast day	rl
HANUMAN	Hindu monkey-god	
HAPLESS	luckless	
HAPLOID	single chromosomes	
HAPLONT	special-nucleus-type plant	
HAP'ORTH	(halfpenny) (sl.)	nm
HAPPIER	more expert; luckier	
HAPPILY	joyously; blissfully; gaily	
HAPPING	happening	
HARBOUR	shelter; haven; asylum	
HARDEST	densest; firmest; harshest	
HARDIER	pluckier; braver; tougher	
HARDILY	stoutly; intrepidly; resolutely	
HARDISH	somewhat hard	
HARDOCK	harlock; burdock	
HARDPAN	bedrock; level of soil horizon	gl
HARD-RUN	greatly pressed	
HARDSET	beset by difficulty; hungry	
HARDTOP	fixed roof on a car	
HARD-WON	barely victorious	
HAREING	speeding	
HARELIP	fissured lip	md
HARICOT	French bean	bt
HARKING	listening; hurrying	
HARLING	process for protecting steel-clad houses	
HARMALA	wild rue	bt
HARMFUL	noxious; baneful; baleful	
HARMINE	wild rue extract	ch
HARMING	molesting; scathing	
HARMONY	unison; concord; amity; simultaneous sounding of concordant notes	mu
HARNESS	gear; tackle; equipment; hammock-like sling (horses) (gliders)	
HARPING	nagging; reiterating	mu
HARPIST	a harper	mu
HARPOON	barbed spear	
HARRIED	harassed; raided; ravaged	
HARRIER	hound; hawk; hare courser	zo
HARRIER	cross-country runner	
HARSHEN	stiffen; embitter	
HARSHER	rougher; severer; sterner	
HARSHLY	raucously; stridently	
HARTALL	orpiment	mn
HARTLEY	unit of information; bits	
HARTREE	atomic unit of energy	me, nc
HARVEST	crop; yield; produce	
HAS-BEEN	diminished fame	
HASHING	muddling; mangling	
HASHIRA	narrow print (Jap.)	
HASHISH	bhang; the assassin's drug	
HASLOCK	wool on sheep's throat	
HASSOCK	cushion; tuft; pouffe	
HASTATE	spear-shaped	

HASTIER	quicker; rasher; brisker	
HASTILY	rapidly; hurriedly; abruptly	
HASTING	ripening early; expediting	
HASTLER	turn-spit	
HATABLE	odious; obnoxious	
HATBAND	ribbon in hat	
HATCASE	bonnet-box	
HATCHED	shaded; incubated	
HATCHEL	to heckle; to tease	
HATCHER	plotter; conspirator	
HATCHES	coverings	nt
HATCHET	an axe	to
HATEFUL	detestable; execrable; odious	
HATLESS	bareheaded	
HAT-RACK	place to hang hat	
HAUBERK	coat of mail	
HAUGHTY	arrogant; proud	
HAULAGE	a charge for conveyance	
HAULIER	carter	
HAULING	tugging; drawing; dragging	
HAUNCHY	with full hips	
HAUNTED	frequented; followed	
HAUNTER	frequent visitor	
HAURLED	dragged; rough-cast	
HAUSTUS	adult medicine dose	
HAUTBOY	strawberry; oboe	bt, mu
HAUTEUR	disdian; arrogance; loftiness	
HAUTPAS	a dais	
HAVENOT	under-privileged	
HAW-BUCK	a clown	
HAWKBIT	a plant	bt
HAWKING	falconry; peddlary; touting	
HAWK-OWL	snowy owl	zo
HAYBAND	hay-rope	
HAYCOCK	gathered hay in stack	
HAYDITE	expanded clay (USA)	
HAYFORK	farm implement	to
HAYLOFT	part of barn	
HAYRICK	regular hay pile	
HAYSEED	hick, bumpkin	bt
HAY-TIER	hay bundler	
HAYWARD	a warden	
HAYWIRE	in confusion	
HAZELLY	light brown	
HAZIEST	foggiest; vaguest	
HEADILY	impetuously; precipitately	
HEADING	adit; headline; intercepting	
HEADMAN	chief; boss	
HEAD-PIN	no. 1 pin (bowling)	
HEADWAY	progress	
HEAL-ALL	valerian; a panacea	bt
HEALING	mollifying; remedying	
HEALTHY	hygienic; bracing; hale	
HEAPING	collecting; amassing	
HEARING	audition; trying	lw
HEARKEN	listen; attend; heed	
HEARSAY	rumour; report; gossip	
HEARSED	put in a hearse	
HEARTED	emboldened; cheered	
HEARTEN	encourage; rally; inspire	

HEATHEN	pagan; paynim; infidel	
HEATHER	ling; erica	bt
HEATING	warming; exciting	
HEAVERS	stevedores	
HEAVE-TO	storm tactics	nt
HEAVIER	weightier; denser	
HEAVILY	ponderously; onerously	
HEAVING	a rising; hoisting; throwing	
HEBAMIC	pert. to Socratic method	
HEBENON	hen-bane; poison	bt
HEBETIC	occurring at puberty	
HEBRAIC	Hebrew	
HECKLED	combed; questioned	
HECKLER	political enquirer	
HECTARE	100 ares	me
HECTOID	flushed; feverish; hectic	
HEDEOMA	penny-royal	bt
HEDERAL	of ivy	
HEDGING	guarding against loss	
HEDONIC	pleasure-seeking	
HEEDFUL	mindful; wary; cautious	
HEEDING	paying attention; regarding	
HEELING	(cock fighting); (football)	
HEFTIER	stronger; more vigorous	
HEFTILY	vigorously; powerfully	
HEGUMEN	Greek abbot	rl
HEIGH-HO	exclamation of complaisance	
HEINOUS	infamous; flagrant; atrocious	
HEIRDOM	succession	
HEIRESS	female inheritor	
HELCOID	ulcerous	md
HELIBUS }	helicopter bus/taxi	
HELICAB }		
HELICAL	spiral	
HELICES	circumvolutions; spirals	
HELICON	mount beloved by the Muses; tuba; sousaphone (USA)	
HELIOID	like the sun	
HELIXIN	an ivy extract	ch
HELL-BOX	receptacle for broken type	pr
HELL-CAT	malignant hag	
HELLENE	Greek	
HELL-HAG	author's invention	
HELLISH	diabolical; infernal; fiendish	
HELMAGE	guidance	
HELOSIS	condition of having corns	md
HELOTRY	serfdom; bondage; (Sparta)	
HELPFUL	assistant; useful; beneficial	
HELPING	share; aiding; abetting	
HELVING	hafting; fitting a handle	
HELVITE	beryllium silicate	mn
HEMIOLA }	rhythmic change (Gr.)	mu
HEMIOLIA }		
HEMIONE	half-ass; dziggetal	zo
HEMLOCK	conine; poison	bt
HEMMEMA	galley-man of war, Sweden	nt
HEMMING	edging; besetting; sewing	
HENBANE	narcotic plant	bt
HENCOOP	a fowl abode	
HENNAED	dyed with henna	

HENNERY	poultry farm	
HENOTIC	conciliatory	
HENPECK	nag; dominate	
HENTING	final furrow	
HENWIFE	chicken-girl	
HEPARIN	anticoagulant	
HEPATIC	liverish	md
HEPTADE	seven	
HEPTANE	petrol constituent	ch
HEPTODE	type of electric valve	
HEPTOSE	monosaccharide subgroup	ch
HERBAGE	pasture	
HERBARY	herb garden	
HERBIST	herbalist; collector of simples	
HERBLET	small herb	
HERBOUS	herbaceous; herbose	
HERDING	tending; crowding; group instinct; driving groups about	
HERDMAN	herdsman; ranchero	
HEREOUT	out of this	
HERETIC	unorthodox; schismatic	
HERISSE	bristled	
HERITOR	inheritor	
HERLING	young sea-trout	zo
HERNIAL	(rupture)	md
HEROINE	intrepid damsel	
HEROISM	valour; bravery; fortitude	
HEROIZE	lionize	
HERONRY	bird sanctuary	zo
HERRING	tasty fish	zo
HERSELF	reflexive pronoun	
HERSHIP	cattle-theft (Sc.)	
HESSIAN	jute fabric; burlage (USA)	
HESSITE	telluride of silver	mn
HETAIRA	Greek dancing girl	
HEXAGON	a six-sided figure	
HEXAPLA	a Bible edition	
HEXAPOD	with six feet	
HEXARCH	with 6 protoxylem strands	bt
HEXERIS	galley with 6 oar banks	
HEXONIC	chemical base	
HEYDUCK	Haiduk; Hungarian	
HEY-PASS	conjuror's command	
HIBACHI	charcoal brazier (Jap.)	
HICATEE	Central American tortoise	zo
HICKORY	American nut-bearing tree	bt
HICKWAY	small woodpecker	zo
HIDALGO	Spanish Don; asteroid	as
HIDEOUS	unshapely; monstrous; grisly	
HIDE-OUT	a cache	
HIEMATE	hiberbate; to winter	
HIGGLED	negotiated; peddled; chaffered	
HIGGLER	haggler; bargainer; hawker	
HIGHBOY	} pillar chest of drawers	
TALLBOY		
HIGHDAY	holiday	
HIGHEST	tallest; loftiest	
HIGHFED	pampered	
HIGH-HAT	high-brow	
HIGHLOW	sort of shoe	

HIGH-TOP	a masthead (Shak.)	
HIGHWAY	public road; trunk; signals; bus	cp
HIGHWAY	transmission canals for digitals	cp
HILDING	paltry; base; a deceiver	
HILLIER	steeper	
HILLING	earthing	
HILLMAN	a mountaineer	
HILLOCK	small hill	
HILLTOP	summit	
HIMSELF	reflexive pronoun	
HINDBOW	saddle cantle	
HIND-GUT	posterior of alimentary canal	zo
HINNIED	} cry of a horse	zo
WHINNIED		
HINTING	implying; suggesting	
HIP-BATH	portable sitting bath	
HIP-BELT	swordbelt	
HIP-GOUT	sciatica	md
HIP-KNOT	gable ornament	
HIP-LOCK	wrestling trick	
HIPPING	grieving; glooming	
HIPPOID	like a horse	
HIP-ROOF	a type of roof	
HIPSHOT	dislocated hip	
HIPSTER	clothes held by a belt	
HIRABLE	for hire; leasable	
HIRCINE	goatish	zo
HIRSUTE	hairy; rude	
HIRUDIN	anticoagulant chemical from leeches	
HISKING	breathing heavily	
HISSING	audible disapproval	
HISTONE	simple-protein group	ch
HISTORY	chronicle; annals; account	
HISTRIO	histrion; an actor	
HITCHED	caught; fastened; attached	
HITTING	smiting; striking; succeeding	
HITTITE	ancient Near-Eastern people	
HIVE-BEE	honey-bee	zo
HOARDED	garnered; amassed; secreted	
HOARDER	miser; husbandman	
HOATZIN	S. American bird	zo
HOAXING	duping; gammoning	
HOBBISH	clownish	
HOBBISM	a moral philosophy	
HOBBIST	follower of Hobbes	
HOBBLED	hoppled; tethered	
HOBBLER	horse-soldier	
HOBLIKE	boorish; clownish	
HOBNAIL	boot-nail	
HOBOISM	vagrancy (USA)	
HOCK-DAY	old English festival	
HOCKLED	houghed; hamstrung	
HODADDY	incompetent surf boarder	
HOE-CAKE	Indian meal cake	ck
HOE-DOWN	American folkdance	
HOGBACK	ridge; eskar	
HOGCOTE	pig-sty	

HOGGERS	miner's leg-wear	
HOGGING	bending	
HOGGISH	swinish; sordid; greedy	
HOG-HERD	swineherd	
HOG-MANE	clipped mane	
HOG-PLUM	tropical tree	bt
HOGSKIN	pigskin; leather	tx
HOGWASH	swill; pig food	
HOGWEED	cow parsnip	bt
HOISTED	raised; heaved	
HOISTER	an elevator; lift	
HOITING	capering	
HOLDALL	a pack; luggage	
HOLDING	tenure; retaining; grasping; asset; (company)	
HOLDING	grip (climbing); ground condition (horse racing)	
HOLIDAY	festival; vacation; non-working day	
HOLIEST	most sacred	
HOLLAND	coarse linen	tx
HOLMIUM	metallic element	ch
HOLM-OAK	evergreen oak	bt
HOLSTER	leather pistol case	
HOLY-DAY	feast day; sacred day	rl
HOMAGER	a vassal	
HOMBURG	gentleman's hat	
HOMELOT	home-plot	
HOMELYN	spotted ray	zo
HOMERIC	of Homer; grandiose	
HOMINID	man (ancient and modern)	
HOMONYM	equivocation	
HONESTY	best political creed	
HONEYED	flattering; sweet	
HONITON	centre for lace	
HONKING	(motoring); (geese)	
HONOURS	university degree; court cards; merit awards	
HOODING	covering; blinding	
HOODLUM	hooligan; rowdy; mobster	
HOODOCK	miserly (Sc.)	
HOOFING	walking	
HOOGAAR	cutter rigger pleasure boat Dutch	
HOOKING	ensnaring; bending; (polo)	
HOOKPIN	floor nail	
HOOP-ASH	nettle-tree	bt
HOOPING	binding; encircling	
HOOTING	decrying; booing	
HOP-BACK	brewer's vessel	
HOPBIND	} hop-vine	bt
HOPBINE	}	
HOPEFUL	eager; expectant; confident	
HOPEITE	hydrated zinc phosphate	mn
HOP-FLEA	a parasite	zo
HOPKILN	an oast	
HOPLITE	Greek heavy-armed soldier	
HOP-OAST	hop-kiln	
HOPPERS	a hopping game	

HOPPING	skipping; leaping; wrong in netball	
HOPPLED	hobbled; tethered	
HOPPLES	hobbles; rope shackles	
HOP-POLE	husbandry implement	
HOP-TREE	American shrub	bt
HOP-VINE	hopbind	bt
HOP-YARD	hop-garden	
HORDEIN	} barley starch/genus	bt
HORDEUM	}	
HORDING	crowding; herding; amassing	
HORIZON	where sea meets sky; limit of knowledge	
HORMONE	gland secretion	md
HORNBAR	crossbar	
HORN-BUG	stag beetle	zo
HORNING	debtor's summons	lw
HORNISH	ungual	
HORNITO	volcanic smoke-hole	
HORN-NUT	a water-plant	bt
HORN-OWL	tufted owl	zo
HORRENT	bristling	
HORRIFY	appal; terrify; alarm; shock	
HOSANNA	beatific invocation	rl
HOSEMAN	fireman	
HOSIERY	stock of stockings	
HOSPICE	home for terminally ill patients	
HOSTAGE	personal pledge	
HOSTESS	woman giving hospitality	
HOSTILE	inimical; adverse; opposed	
HOSTLER	ostler	
HOTFLUE	drying room	
HOT-FOOT	in haste	
HOT-HEAD	impetuous; rash	
HOTNESS	fieriness; ardency; fervency	
HOT-SPOT	internal combustion	
HOTSPUR	impetuous	
HOTTEST	most vehement	
HOT-TROD	Border pursuit	
HOT-WALL	(fruit culture)	
HOUARIO	pleasure sail boat Mediterranean	nt
HOUBARA	ruffed bustard	zo
HOUGHED	hockled; hamstrung	
HOUNDED	pursued; harassed; dogged	
HOUSAGE	storage fee	
HOUSING	saddle-cloth; sheltering; protective cover (machinery)	ce
HOVERED	vacillated; lingered	
HOVERER	waverer; flutterer	
HOWADJI	traveller; merchant (Arab)	
HOWBEIT	nevertheless	
HOWDY-DO	ado; fuss; commotion	
HOWEVER	notwithstanding	
HOWLING	dreary; lamenting; wailing	
HUANACO	} llama, Andes, S. America	
GUANACO	}	
HUDDLED	heaped; piled; mixed	
HUDDLER	bungler; confused cogitator	

HUELESS	colourless	
HUFFILY	petulantly; angrily; irritably	
HUFFING	puffing; swelling; (draughts)	
HUFFISH	hectoring; furious	
HUFFKIN	hot larded bread bun (Eng.)	ck
HUGGING	clasping; embracing; necking	
HULKING	big and clumsy	
HULLING	husking; shelling	
HUMANLY	ethically; rationally	
HUMBLED	abashed; humiliated	
HUMBLER	an abaser; mortifier	
HUMBUZZ	a bull-roarer	
HUMDRUM	commonplace; prosaic	
HUMERAL	Jewish veil	
HUMERUS	shoulder bone	pl
HUMETTE	heraldic fesse	hd
HUMIDLY	damply; dankly	
HUMMING	bumming; droning	
HUMMOCK	hommock; hillock	
HUMORAL	vapourish	
HUMULIN	} hop extract/genus	bt, ck
HUMULUS		
HUNCHED	bunched; crooked	
HUNDRED	cantred; county division	
HUNGRED	hungry; famished	
HUNKERS	the hams; haunches	
HUNTING	chasing; searching	
HUNTING	variation of thermostat-temperature	el
HURDLED	enclosed with a wattle fence	
HURDLER	racing jumper	
HURDLES	10 obstacles to overcome per event	
HURKARU	Hindu errand boy	
HURLING	casting; flinging; pitching	
HURLING	ancient form of hockey	
HURRIED	scurried; accelerated; ran	
HURRIED	cursory; superficial	
HURRIER	hastener; quickener; urger	
HURTFUL	noxious; baleful; detrimental	
HURTLED	whizzed; crashed	
HURTOIR	a bumper	
HUSBAND	male spouse; breadwinner	
HUSHABY	lullaby	
HUSHING	repressing; calming	
HUSHION	sort of sock (Sc.)	
HUSKIES	Eskimo dogs; toughs	zo
HUSKING	removing husks	
HUSSIES	worthless women	
HUSSITE	(John Huss); Moravian	
HUSTING	an assembly; a council	
HUSTLED	bustled; elbowed	
HUSTLER	energiser; jostler	
HUSWIFE	hussif; housewife	
HUTCHED	cooped; boxed; confined	
HUTMENT	a hut	
HUTTING	temporary building	
HYALINE	glassy	
HYALITE	clear opal	mn

HYALITH	dense black Bohemian glass; dark sealing wax	
HYALOID	vitreous	
HYDRANT	fire-plug	
HYDRATE	hydride; hydrous	ch
HYDRIAD	water-nymph	
HYDROID	hydra-like	
HYDROUS	containing water	
HYGEIAN	hygienic	
HYGIENE	sanitary science	
HYGROMA	fluid-filled swelling	vt
HYLOIST	materialist	
HYMNARY	hymn-book	
HYMNING	lauding	
HYMNIST	hymn-writer	
HYMNODY	hymn-singing	
HYODONT	pig-toothed	
HYPERON	cosmic-ray particle	nc
HYPNODY	larval resting period	zo
HYPNOID	resembling sleep	
HYPOGEA	cellars; basement	
HYPOPUS	development stage in cheesemites	
HYPPISH	hippish; depressing	
HYPURAL	below the tail	zo
HYSTRIX	the porcupine	zo

I

IAMBICS	classic verse	
IAMBISE	satirise; versify	
IBERIAN	Spanish and Portuguese	
ICARIAN	rash; headlong; adventurous	
ICEBELT	region of ice	
ICEBERG	floating ice mass	
ICEBIRD	little auk	zo
ICEBOAT	for travel on ice	
ICE-FALL	a glacier	
ICE-FERN	frosty incrustations	
ICE-FLOE	mass of ice chunks in sea	
ICE-FOOT	belt of ice; yacht on skates	nt
ICE-HILL	tobogganing slope	
ICEPACK	ice barrier at poles	
ICEPAIL	for chilling wine	
ICE-RINK	skating rink	
ICE-SPAR	ryacolite	mn
ICHABOD	calamity (Heb.)	
ICHNITE	fossil footprint	
ICHTHYS	Christian emblem	
ICINESS	frigidity	
ICTERIC	jaundiced	
ICTERUS	jaundice	md
ICTINUS	designer of the Parthenon	
IDALIAN	sacred to Venus	
IDEALLY	intellectually; mentally	
IDENTIC	identical	
IDIOTCY	imbecility; insanity	
IDIOTIC	fatuous; witless; inane	
IDLESSE	idleness	

IDOLISM	idolatry	
IDOLIST	idolater	
IDOLIZE	idolise; deify; adore; venerate	
IDYLIST	writer of idylls	
IDYLLIC	pastoral; poetic	
IGNEOUS	volcanic in origin	
IGNITED	lit; kindled; inflamed	
IGNITER	primer; detonator	
IGNITOR	electrode of ignition	
IGNOBLE	dishonourable; low; base	
IGNOBLY	infamously; unworthily	
IGNORED	disregarded; neglected	
IGOROTE	Filipino	
IJOLITE	coarse-grained igneous rock	**gl**
ILEITIS	ileum inflammation	**md**
ILLAPSE	glide; slip; a seizure	
ILL-BRED	poorly brought up	
ILLEGAL	unlawful; illegitimate; illicit	
ILLEISM	too much 'he'	
ILL-FAME	of bad repute	
ILLICIT	forbidden; banned; prohibited	
ILLNESS	malady; disease; ailment	
ILLOCAL	not local	
ILL-TIME	mistime	
ILL-TURN	unkindly act	
ILLUDED	deceived; deluded	
ILLUMED	elucidated; brightened	
ILL-USED	badly treated	
ILL-WILL	enmity; odium; spite; malice	
ILVAITE	hydrous iron silicate	**mn**
IMAGERY	fanciful concept	
IMAGINE	dream; think; suppose	
IMAGING	imagining	
IMAMATE	the parish of a moslem Imam (priest)	**rl**
IMBATHE	bathe	
IMBIBED	swallowed; absorbed	
IMBIBER	a toper; drunkard	
IMBLAZE	emblaze; illuminate	
IMBOSOM	embosom; caress	
IMBOUND	impound	
IMBOWED	embowed; arched	
IMBOWER	embower; shelter	
IMBREED	inbreed	
IMBREKE	houseleek	**bt**
IMBROWN	embrown; tan	
IMBRUED	drenched; soaked; stained	
IMBRUTE	to brutalize	
IMBUING	pervading; drenching	
IMBURSE	to finance	
IMITANT	counterfeit	
IMITATE	ape; copy; mimic; parody	
IMMENSE	titanic; colossal; boundless	
IMMERGE	} plunge into; souse; to	
IMMERSE	} engross; duck	
IMMIXED	mixed; blended	
IMMORAL	depraved; vicious	
IMMURED	shut up; imprisoned	
IMPAINT	to colour	
IMPALED	fenced in; spiked; transfixed	

IMPALSY	strike with palsy	
IMPANEL	empanel; enrol	
IMPASSE	deadlock	
IMPASTE	knead	
IMPASTO	thick colour	
IMPAVID	fearless; undaunted	
IMPEACH	call to account	
IMPEARL	decorate with pearls	
IMPEDED	hindered; obstructed	
IMPERIL	endanger; hazard; jeopardize	
IMPETUS	momentum	
IMPEYAN	Indian pheasant	**zo**
IMPFING	crystallisation technique	
IMPIETY	iniquity; profanity	
IMPINGE	to touch upon; infringe	
IMPIOUS	irreverent; ungodly	
IMPLANT	to graft; infuse; instil	
IMPLATE	to sheathe	
IMPLEAD	impeach; plead	
IMPLIED	understood; insinuated	
IMPLORE	entreat; crave; adjure	
IMPORTS	inward-bound trade goods	
IMPOSED	forced; misled	
IMPOSER	impostor; charlatan	
IMPOUND	confine; confiscate	
IMPREGN	impregnate	
IMPRESS	stamp; mark; imprint	
IMPREST	advanced cash	
IMPRINT	impress; fix on the mind	
IMPROVE	armed; ameliorate; raise	
IMPULSE	stimulus; urge to action; short signal	**cp**
IMPUTED	attributed; implied	
IMPUTER	ascriber	
IN-AND-IN	overly inbred	
INANELY	vapidly; stupidly	
INANITY	fatuity; emptiness	
INAPTLY	untimely; unsuitably	
INBEING	inherence	
INBOARD	within the ship (including motor); oar handle	
INBOUND	inward bound; ball thrown into play (basketball)	
INBREAK	inburst	
INBREED	mate with relative	
INBURST	irruption	
INCAGED	encaged; confined	
INCENSE	to inflame; madden; enrage	
INCHASE	enchase; engrave	
INCHEST	embox; encase	
INCHING	moving gradually	
INCHPIN	deer's sweetbread	
INCIPIT	here begins (Lat.); identifying reference with first bars	**mu**
INCISED	cut; engraved	
INCISOR	cutting tooth	
INCITED	roused; fomented; egged	
INCITER	agitator; agent provocateur	
INCIVIL	uncivil; impolite (obs.)	
INCLASP	embrace; enclasp	

INCLAVE	heraldic dovetail	**hd**
INCLINE	slope; tend; predispose	
INCLOSE	enclose; envelop; wrap	
INCLUDE	embody; comprise; contain	
INCOMER	new arrival	
INCRUST	encrust	
INCUBUS	incumbrance; dead weight; intercourse with devil	**pc, rl**
INCURVE	bend	
INCUSED	hammered; stamped	
INDICAN	a glucoside or acid	**ch**
INDICES	mathematical exponents; plural of index	**ma**
INDICIA	indications	
INDITED	scribbed; wrote; dictated	
INDITER	a writer; composer; penman	
INDOLES	inherent disposition	
INDOORS	within house	
INDORSE	endorse; countersign; ratify	
INDOXYL	isomer of oxindole	**ch**
INDRAFT	inflow; indraught	
INDRAWN	retracted	
INDUCED	impelled; prompted	
INDUCER	persuader; instigator	
INDUING	enduing; investing; endowing	
INDULGE	pamper; humour; gratify	
INDWELL	inhabit; occupy	
INEARTH	inter; bury; inhume	
INEPTLY	not aptly; pointlessly	
INERTIA	inertness; indolence	
INERTLY	sluggishly; torpidly	
INEXACT	unexact; incorrect; faulty	
INEYING	inoculating; grafting	
INFAMED	defamed; libelled; aspersed	
INFANCY	under 18	
INFANTA	Spanish princess	
INFANTE	Spanish prince	
INFARCT	blood-deprived necrotic tissue	**md**
INFARCT	coronary thombosis	**md**
INFAUST	unlucky; unfortunate	
INFERNO	hell	
INFIDEL	disbeliever; paynim; heathen	
INFIELD	cultivated ground	
INFIELD	cf. outfield (cricket); (baseball)	
INFIXED	fastened; clamped	
INFLAME	excite; fan; kindle; incense	
INFLATE	elate; expand; distend; bloat	
INFLECT	deflect; curve; bend	
INFLICT	impose; lay; punish	
INFULAE	priestly badges	**rl**
INFUSED	inspired; instilled; inculcated	
INFUSER	a coffee machine; tea-maker	
INGENER	a designer (Shak.)	
INGENUE	naïve girl	
INGESTA	food	**md**
INGLOBE	englobe; encircle; ensphere	
INGOING	direction entering; joining; enrolling	

INGOING	visible frame of door, window	**bd**
INGRAFT	engraft; instil; introduce	
INGRAIN	engrain; permeate	
INGRATE	ungrateful person (obs.)	
INGRESS	entrance; portal	
INGROSS	engross (obs.)	
IN-GROUP	elitist 'me-group'	
INHABIT	dwell; occupy	
INHALED	breathed	
INHALER	a respirator	
INHAUST	to drink in (obs.)	
INHERED	adhered; stuck	
INHERIT	acquire by bequest	
INHERSE	to bury (Shak.)	
INHIBIT	ban; prohibit; restrain; preventive signal	**cp**
INHUMAN	merciless; fell; ruthless	
INHUMED	interred; buried	
INITIAL	incipient; primary letter; as at entry	**cp**
INJELLY	gelatinise	
INJOINT	to joint (obs,.)	
INJURED	offended; marred; maltreated	
INJURER	abuser; impairer	
INKHORN	portable inkpot	
INKLING	hint; suggestion; innuendo	
INKNEED	knock-kneed	
INKWELL	ink-cup	
INLACED	enlaced; entwined	
INLAWED	cf. outlawed	
INLAYER	inlay worker	
INMEATS	the entrails	
INNERVE	invigorate; insinew	
INNINGS	reclaimed land; batting turn for team (cricket)	
INNUENT	significant	
IN-PHASE	(electrical)	
IN-PLANT	automatic data handling	**cp**
INQUEST	judicial inquiry	**lw**
INQUIRE	enquire; ask; interrogate	
INQUIRY	enquiry; examination; (information); access to programs	**cp**
INSCULP	engrave; carve (obs.)	
INSHELL	to hide as in a shell (obs.)	
INSHOOT	pitch to batter (baseball)	
INSHORE	close to the beach	
INSIDER	in the know	
INSIGHT	vision; perception	
INSINEW	innerve; invigorate	
INSIPID	tasteless; vapid; flat; tedious	
INSNARE	ensnare; entrap; inveigle	
INSOOTH	in truth	
INSPECT	supervise; investigate	
INSPIRE	animate; inflame; imbue	
INSTALL	instal; instate; induct; invest	
INSTANT	current; urgent; prompt	
INSTATE	install; inaugurate; introduce	
INSTEAD	in place of; in lieu	

334

INSTEEP	immerse; souse; duck	
INSTILL	instil; implant; inculcate	
INSTYLE	entitle; to name	
INSULAR	isolated; narrow-minded	
INSULIN	(diabetes treatment)	md
INSURED	ensured; guaranteed	
INSURER	underwriter	
INSWEPT	narrowed	
INTEGER	whole; a whole number	
INTENSE	acute; vehement; extreme	
INTERIM	a pause; in the meantime	
INTERNE	inmate; boarder	
INTHRAL	enthral; enslave; captivate	
INTITLE	entitle; intitule (obs.)	
INTONED	chanted	
INTONER	reciter in singing tone	
INTRADA	entry; prelimary piece (It.)	mu
INTRANT	entrant; entering; penetrating	
INTREAT	entreat; crave; importune	
INTROIT	opening anthem	rl
INTRUDE	obtrude; trespass; butt in	
INTRUST	entrust; commit; confide	
INTWINE	entwine; reticulate; weave	
INTWIST	entwist; ravel; interlace	
INULASE	an enzyme	md
INURING	enuring; habituating	
INUTILE	useless (Fr.)	
INVADED	violated; entered; occuped	
INVADER	aggressor; raider; attacker	
INVALID	null and void; infirm; weak	
INVEIGH	revile; reproach; upbraid	
INVERSE	reciprocal; inverted	
INVEXED	arched	hd
INVIOUS	impassable; untrodden	
INVITED	bid; bequested; asked	
INVITER	allurer; solicitor; enticer	
INVOICE	bill; schedule; inventory	
INVOKED	adjured; implored; besought	
INVOKER	summoner; conjuror	
INVOLVE	implicate; entangle; embrace	
INWARDS	internally	
INWEAVE	complicate; intwine	
INWHEEL	encircle; surround	
INWOVEN	intertwined	
IODIZED	treated with iodine	
IONIZED	electrified	
IPOMAEA	convolvulus	bt
IPSEITY	selfhood	
IRACUND	irascible; choleric; petulant	
IRANIAN	Persian	
IRENICS	pacific theology	
IRICISM	Irish bull	
IRIDEAE	iris plants	bt
IRIDISE	make iridescent	
IRIDIUM	metallic element	ch
IRISHRY	Irish people	
IRKSOME	wearisome; tiresome; tedious	
IRONIES	sarcastic censures	
IRONING	flattening	
IRONIST	ironical talker	

ISAGOGE	a treatise	
ISATINE	isatin; indigo; woad	ch
ISCHIUM	pelvic bone in tetrapods	zo
ISERINE	titanic steel	
ISHMAEL	an outcast	
ISIDIUM	excrescence on lichen	bt
ISLAMIC	Mohammedan; Moslem	
ISLEMAN	islander	
ISMATIC	faddish; fond of isms	
ISOBASE	land-depression line	gl
ISOBATH	under-sea contour	
ISODOMA	form of masonry	
ISODONT	uniform teeth	
ISOETES	quill-worts	bt
ISOGAMY	union of equal gametes	bt, zo
ISOGENY	similar origin	
ISOGRAM	map line linking like places	
ISOHYET	(seasonal) rainfall map	
ISOLATE	insulate; segregate; dissociate	
ISOMERS	same weight of molecular compounds	nc, ps
ISONEPH	equal-cloudiness line	mt
ISONETH	cloud map	mt
ISONOMY	equal rights	
ISONYMY	paronymy; equal	lw
ISOPODA	crustaceans	zo
ISOPYRE	impure opal	mn
ISOSPIN	quantum number isotopic spin	nc
ISOTACH	equal wind-speed line	mt
ISOTAXY	polymerization characteristic	
ISOTONE	stable nucleus (atom)	
ISOTOPE	allied element	ch
ISOTRON	isotope-separating device	nc
ISOTYPE	picture writing	
ISOZYME	like/unlike enzyme form	bc
ISRAELI	Jew (Israel)	
ISSUANT	issuing	hd
ISSUING	emanating; proceeding	
ISTHMUS	land joining larger masses	
ITACISM	Greek egotism	
ITALIAN	of Italy	
ITALICS	sloping letters	
ITALIOT	ancient city in S. Italy	
ITCHING	desirous	
ITEMIZE	itemize; particularize	
ITERACY	repetition	
ITERANT	repeating	
ITERATE	recapitulate	
IVORIED	provided with teeth	
IVY-BUSY	Bacchus's bush	bt
IXIODIC	infested with ticks	md, vt
IXOLITE	fossil resin	mn

J

JABBING	prodding; stabbing	
JACAMAR	tropical kingfisher	zo
JACCHUS	marmoset	zo

JACINTH	hyacinth; a gem	bt
JACKASS	male donkey; bird; schooner type	zo, nt
JACKBIT	blast-hole drill end	mn
JACKDAW	a daw	zo
JACKING	lifting; abandoning	
JACKPOT	(poker) winning hand takes all; total prize	
JACKSAW	goosander	zo
JACK-TAR	a sailor	nt
JACOBIN	revolutionary	
JACOBUS	James I sovereign	nm
JACONET	muslin	tx
JADEDLY	wearily	
JADEITE	a silicate	mn
JADOUBE	adjust chesspiece on square	
JAGGERY	palm sap sugar	
JAGGING	notching; carousing	
JAGHIRE	land revenues (Hindu)	
JAHVIST	scriptural writer	
JAI-ALAI	full-size court; merry festival (pelota)	
JAILING	gaoling; imprisoning	
JAINISM	an Indian religion	
JALAPIN	a purge	md
JALOUSE	to suspect (Sc.)	
JAMADAR	jemidar; Indian lieutenant	
JAMBONE	(cards on table at euchre)	
JAMDANI	flowery muslin	tx
JAMDARI	figured muslin	tx
JAMEWAR	goat hair cloth	tx
JAMMING	squeezing; pressing; packing tightly; rock climbing technique	mo
JAMMING	interference in radio reception	
JAMRACH	animal mart	
JAMSHID	King of the genii	
JANEITE	(Jane Austen)	
JANGADA	timber raft	
JANGLED	jingled; discordant	
JANGLER	wrangler	
JANITOR	doorkeeper	
JANIZAR	Janissary; Turkish soldier	
JANNOCK	bannock; a cake	ck
JANNOCK	straightforward	
JANTILY	jauntily; airily; finically	
JANTING	jaunting; rambling	
JANUARY	1st month	
JAP-SILK	a thin kind of silk	tx
JARGOON	a gem; zircon	mn
JARKMAN	begging letter writer	
JARRING	discordant; grating; clashing	
JASHAWK	young hawk	zo
JASMINE	fragrant flower	bt
JASPERY	like jasper	mn
JASPOID	jaspery	
JAUNDER	gossip (Sc.)	
JAUNTED	rambled; strolled	
JAUPING	spattering (Sc.)	

JAVELIN	} throwing spear; field event	
JUVELIN		
JAWBONE	Samson's lethal weapon	md
JAW-FALL	depression	
JAW-FOOT	maxilliped	zo
JAW-HOLE	a sink	
JAW-ROPE	sailing tackle	nt
JAYWALK	walk irresponsibly beside roadways	
JAZZING	dancing	mu
JEALOUS	envious; covetous; resentful	
JECORAL	pertaining to the liver	pl
JEDCOCK	jack snipe	zo
JEDDART	rough justice (Sc.)	
JEERING	derision; taunting; scoffing	
JEJUNUM	digestive organ	md
JELLIED	congealed	
JELLIFY	to become gelatinous	
JELLYBY	(a philanthropist)	
JEMIDAR	jamadar; Indian officer	
JEMIMAS	elastic-sided boots	
JENKINS	society reporter; toady	
JEOFAIL	an oversight	lw
JEOPARD	to hazard; to endanger	
JERKING	twitching; jolting	
JERVINE	white hellebore alkaloid	ch
JESSAMY	jasmine; a dandy	bt
JESSANT	heraldic uprising	hd
JESTFUL	humorous; witty; sportive	
JESTING	joking; quipping	
JETTIED	projected; jutted	
JETTING	spouting; emitting	
JEWELRY	gems; trinkets	
JEW'S-EAR	edible fungus	bt
JEZEBEL	a courtesan	
JEZHAIL	jezail; Afghan rifle	
JIBBING	balking; shying	
JIB-BOOM	part of rigging	nt
JIB-DOOR	flush door	
JIGAJOG	jig-jog; also jickajog	
JIGGERS	tropical foot complaint	md
JIGGING	sieving; dancing	
JIGGISH	frivolous; frolicsome	
JIGGLED	joggled; wriggled	
JILTING	discarding; rejecting	
JIMCROW	of black segregation (Amer.)	
JIM-JAMS	nervous apprehension	
JINGLED	jangled; tingled	
JINGLET	sleigh-bell clapper	
JINKING	dodging; twisting	
JITTERS	fear; distortion	el
JITTERY	nervy; agitated; dithery	
JOBBERY	intrigue	
JOBBING	doing small jobs	
JOBLESS	unemployed	
JOCULAR	jocose; facetious; droll	
JOGGING	stimulating; nudging; slow-running exercise; warming up	
JOGGLED	jostled; shook	
JOGGLES	stone jointing	

JOG-TROT	easy running pace	
JOHNIAN	(St. John's Col. Cam.)	
JOINDER	united action	**lw**
JOINERY	carpetry	
JOINING	uniting; linking; connecting	
JOINTED	articulated	
JOINTER	smoothing plane	**to**
JOINTLY	in concert; unitedly	
JOISTED	(floor-laying)	
JOLLIER	merrier; more genial	
JOLLIFY	celebrate; carouse	
JOLLILY	heartily; mirthfully	
JOLLITY	joviality; hilarity; frolic	
JOLTING	jerking; shaking	
JONGLER	a wandering minstrel	
JONQUIL	narcissus	**bt**
JOOKERY	jokery; trickery	
JOTTING	a memorandum	
JOUNCED	shook; jolted	
JOURNAL	diary; newspaper; log	
JOURNAL	spindle bearing; gazette	
JOURNEY	jaunt; excursion; travel	
JOUSTED	tilted	
JOYANCE	gaiety; festivity	
JOY-RIDE	riding vehicle for pleasure	
J-STROKE	to correct trim (canoeing)	
JUBILEE	fiftieth anniversary	
JUDAISE	practice Judaism	
JUDAISM	Jewish rites	
JUDAIST	follower of Jew. rites	
JUDAIZE	to enforce Judaism	
JUDCOCK	jack snipe	**zo**
JUDGING	trying; deeming; estimating	
JUFFERS	square timber	
JUGATED	coupled; yoked	
JUGGING	imprisoning; stewing	
JUGGINS	a simpleton	
JUGGLED	conjured; swindled	
JUGGLER	conjuror; wizard; marabout	
JUGLANS	walnut-genus	**bt**
JUGULAR	(vein)	**md**
JUGULUM	breast/neck region in birds	**zo**
JUJITSU	} Japanese wrestling	
JUJUTSU		
JUKE-BOX	electric gramophone; pay-sound rhythms	**el**
JUKSKEI	throwing the horse-shoe (S. Africa)	
JUMBLED	disordered; confused	
JUMBLER	a muddler	
JUMELLE	paired	
JUMPING	bounding; (claims); sudden change; (conclusions)	
JUMPING	leaping; also equestrian	
JUMP-OFF	high or long jump; also equestrian feat	
JUNCATE	junket; picnic; spree	
JUNCOUS	rush-like	
JUNIPER	coniferous tree; gin-berry	**bt**
JUNKING	coal-cutting process	**mn**

JUNKMAN	junk-dealer	
JUPETTE	short petticoat	
JUPITER	a planet	
JURALLY	lawfully; legally	**lw**
JURY-BOX	where jury sits	
JURY-MAN	juror	**lw**
JUSSIVE	imperative	
JUSTICE	equity; fairness; impartiality	
JUSTIFY	vindicate; exonerate; excuse; adjust text	**pr, cp**
JUTTING	projecting; beetling	
JUVELIN	} throwing spear; field event	
JAVELIN		
JUVENAL	a youth	
JUWANZA	camel-thorn	**bt**
JYNGINE	of wryneck bird family	**zo**

K

KABADDI	12-a-side field game (Far East)	
KABBALA	cabbala; shrine	
KABBALA	cabala; Jewish oral tradition	
KACHINA	doll (Amer. Indian)	
KADAYIF	Baklava-type pastry (Turk.)	**ck**
KADDISH	Jewish funeral prayer	**rl**
KAKAVIA	fish soup; cooking pot (Gr.)	**ck**
KAKODYL	cacodyl; noisome liquid	
KALENDS	1st day of Roman month	
KALMUCH	Calmuck; Mongolian	
KAMERAD	} 'I surrender' (Ger.)	
COMRADE		
KAMICHI	Brazilian tropical bird	**zo**
KAMPONG	(Malay) court-yard	
KANAGAI	lacquer work (Japan)	
KANDITE	kaolin minerals group	**mn**
KANTHAL	high-resistivity alloy	**ml**
KANTIAN	(Kant); Kantist	
KANTISM	a philosophy	
KAPITIA	lacquer (Sri Lanka)	
KARAGAN	Russian fox	**zo**
KARAITE	strict Jewish sect	**rl**
KARATAS	W. Indian pineapple	**bt**
KARTING	primitive, do it yourself, motor racing	
KASHGAR	white silky Asian wool	**tx**
KATHODE	negative electrode	
KATYDID	N. Amer. grasshopper	**zo**
KEATITE	synthetic silica form	**mn**
KEBBOCK	kebbuck; a cheese (Sc.)	
KECKLED	cackled	
KEDGING	warping	**nt**
KEDLACK	wild mustard	**bt**
KEEKING	peeping; prying	
KEELAGE	harbour duty	
KEELING	a codling; young codfish	**zo**
KEELMAN	bargee	
KEELSON	keel-plate	**nt**
KEENING	wailing; mourning	
KEEPING	lasting; retaining; observing	

KEEP-NET	aquarium for catch (angling)	
KEEVING	(fermentation)	
KEITLOA	S. African rhinoceros	zo
KELKING	beating; thrashing	
KENNICK	tinker jargon	
KENNING	range of vision; knowing	
KENOSIS	} divine abnegation	
KENOTIC		
KENTISH	of Kent	
KERASIN	brain-substance cerebroside	ch
KERATIN	(horn and hair)	md
KERFING	curving risers of bullnose steps	
		ar
KERMESS	Dutch fair	
KERNING	granulating	
KERNISH	clownish	
KERNITE	sodium borate	mn
KESTREL	a falcon	zo
KETCHUP	a sauce (tomato)	ck
KETOSIS	fat-metabolism toxaemia	md
KEYBOLT	part of lock	
KEYCOLD	cold as a key	
KEYED-UP	tense with suspense	
KEYHOLE	orifice for key	
KEYNOTE	which sets tone	mu
KEY-RING	key holder	
KEY-SEAT	a groove	
KEYWORD	word showing topic discussed	
KEYWORD	(code) retrieval; significant entry	
		cp
KHALIFA	khalif; calif; Mohammed's representative on earth	rl
KHAMSIN	hot wind of the Sahara	mt
KHANATE	khan's jurisdiction	
KHEDDAH	enclosure; (eleph. hunting)	
KHEDIVA	wife of a khedive	
KHEDIVE	chancellor-viceroy of Egypt, 19th C.	
KHOTBAH	} Mohammedan prayer and	
KHUTBAH	} service	rl
KIBBLED	fine-ground in a hand mill	
KIBBUTZ	communal farm (Israel)	
KIBITKA	Russian vehicle	
KICKING	spurning; punting	
KICK-OFF	start of play	
KIDDIES	youngsters	
KIDDING	bluffing; joking; replanting riverbanks	bt
KIDLING	a young kid	zo
KIDSKIN	goat leather	
KIKUMON	imperial crest of Japan	
KILLDEE	N. Amer. ring plover	zo
KILLICK	a small anchor (stone)	nt
KILLING	slaying; butchering; tiring	
KILL-JOY	a sourpuss	
KILLOCK	killick; small anchor	nt
KILN-DRY	desiccate; dry in kiln	
KILOVAR	volt-ampères unit	el
KILTING	trussing up (Sc.)	
KINDEST	most benevolent	

KINDLED	ignited; fired; incited	
KINDLER	an igniter	
KINDRED	relations; related; kin	
KINESIA	motion sickness	md
KINETIC	force in motion	
KINETIN	plant growth substance	bt
KINGCUP	marsh marigold	bt
KINGDOM	monarchy; realm; dominion	
KINGLET	golden-crested wren	zo
KING-PIN	head of organization	
KINKING	twisting; looping	
KINLESS	without kindred	
KINSHIP	relationship	
KINSMAN	a connection	
KIP-SHOP	house of ill-fame	
KIPSKIN	kip-leather	
KIRGHIZ	Central Asian	
KIRIMON	kikumon; a chrysanthemum	
KIRKTON	a village (Sc.)	
KIRTLED	with petticoat	
KIRUNDI	language of Burundi (Africa)	
KISSING	bussing; lips touching tenderly; bowl beside jack	
KITCHEN	cook-house; galley; area of the court (shuffleboard)	
KITHARA	ancient lyre (Gr.)	mu
KLICKED	clicked	
KLIPDAS	S. African rock-badger	zo
KLIPPEN	hill-top outliers	gl
KLISMOS	revived ancient chair (Gr.)	
KLODNIK	iced beetroot soup (Pol.)	ck
KNABBED	gnawed; bitten	
KNACKER	cat's meat purveyor; slaughterer of horses	
KNAPPED	snapped; nibbled	
KNAPPER	flint worker	
KNAPPLE	snap; nibble	
KNARRED	knotted	
KNAVERY	roguery; trickery; fraud	
KNAVISH	rascally; fraudulent	
KNEADED	massaged; mixed	
KNEADER	dough-mixer	
KNEECAP	knee-pan	md
KNEELER	prayer cushion, hassock	
KNEELER	pad-stone, kneestone, skew table, panel	bd
KNELLED	knolled; tolled	
KNESSET	Israeli Parliament	
KNIFING	stabbing	
KNITTED	contracted	
KNITTLE	a draw-thread	
KNOBBED	knobby	
KNOBBLE	small boss	
KNOBBLY	knobby; knotty	
KNOCKED	buffeted; rapped; hit	
KNOCKER	a rapper	
KNOCK-ON	ball falling forward (penalty scrum) (rugby football)	
KNOCK-UP	practice game (tennis)	
KNOLLED	knelled; tolled	

KNOLLER	bell-toller	
KNOPPER	gall-nut	bt
KNOTTED	tied; kinked; entangled	
KNOW-ALL	a wiseacre	
KNOW-HOW	technical expertise	
KNOWING	pawky; shrewd; astute	
KNUCKLE	(-under); submit; pinholes in hinge	bd
KNUCKLE	clenched fist; (-duster); threaten	pl
KOFTGAR	metal inlayer (Hindu)	
KOLA-NUT	cola-nut	bt
KOLKHOZ	Soviet collective farm	
KOLYTIC	inhibitory processes, hindering (Gr.)	pc
KOMATIC	long Eskimo sledge	
KORANIC	(Koran)	
KO-TOWED	made obeisance	
KOUMISS	fermented mare's milk	
KREATIN	creatin; muscle constituent	
KREMLIN	citadel (Moscow)	
KRIMMER	grey lambskin fur	
KRISHNA	an incarnation of Vishnu	
KRUPSIS	a theological doctrine	
KRYPTOL	electrical resistant	
KRYPTON	gaseous element	ch
KUH-HORN	Alpine horn	mu
KUMQUAT	Chinese citron	bt
KURBASH	Arab hippo-hide whip	
KURDISH	(Kurd)	
KURHAUS	spa pavilion (Ger.)	
KURSAAL	the pump-room of a spa	
KUWAITI	native of Kuwait	
KYANISE	rot-proofing of timber	
KYANITE	aluminium silicate	mn

L

LABARUM	symbolical banner	
LABIATE	lip-like	
LABROSE	thick-lipped	
LACCATE	as if varnished	bt
LACCINE	(shellac)	
LACEMAN	lace-dealer	
LACERTA	lizard genus	zo
LACINIA	leaf incision; maxilla lobe	bt, zo
LACK-ALL	destitute	
LACKING	needing; wanting	
LAC-LAKE	lac dye	
LACONIC	concise; pithy; curt; terse	
LACQUER	varnish	
LACQUEY	lackey; footman; flunkey	
LACTASE	lactose-dissolving enzyme	
LACTATE	(lactine); to suckle; milk salt	
LACTEAL	lactean; milky	
LACTONE	hydroxy acid anhydride	
LACTOSE	} sugar of milk	
LACTINE		
LACTUCA	lettuce genus	bt

LACUNAE	gaps; blanks; chasms	
LACUNAL	discontinuously	
LACUNAR	(panelled ceiling)	
LADANUM	resinous extract	md
LADINOS	Judeo-Spanish speaking Sephardim	
LADLING	spooning	
LADY-BUG	lady-fly	zo
LADY-COW	the ladybird	zo
LADY-DAY	March 25th	
LADYISH	genteel; affected	
LADYISM	gentility	
LAETARE	4th Sunday in Lent	
LAGGARD	lagging; sluggard	
LAGGING	hysteresis; dawdling; insulation covering	bd
LAGGING	deciding order of play (billiards)	
LAGOMYS	(tailless hares)	zo
LAGOPUS	grouse genus	zo
LAGOTIC	rabbit-eared	
LAICISE	} commit to laymen	
LAICIZE		
LAIRAGE	cattle depot; lair	
LAKATOI	large sailing raft (Papua)	nt
LAKELET	pool; mere; pond	
LAKSHMI	wife of Vishnu	rl
LALIQUE	artistic glassware	
LALLANS	Lowland Scots (dial)	
LALLING	repetition of a sound	
LAMAISM	Tibetan Buddhism	rl
LAMAIST	spirit-worshipper	rl
LAMB-ALE	shearing feast	
LAMBENT	softly radiant	
LAMBERT	unit of brightness	me
LAMBING	yeaning	
LAMBKIN	baby lamb	zo
LAMBOYS	armoured kilts	
LAMELLA	thin plate or scale	zo
LAMETER	} lamiter; a cripple	
LAMIGER		
LAMETTA	metal foil	
LAMINAR	laminal; in plates	
LAMMING	thrashing	
LAMPATE	a salt	ch
LAMPERN	lamprey	zo
LAMP-FLY	fire-fly	zo
LAMPING	ultraviolet detection	
LAMPION	fairy lamp	
LAMP-LIT	artificially illuminated	
LAMPOON	a satirical article	
LAMPREY	eel-like fish	zo
LANATED	woolly	
LANCERS	(cavalry); a dance	
LANCING	piercing; cutting	
LAND-ICE	fresh water, inland, ice	go
LANDING	disembarking; floor; (fish)	
LANDLER	Tyrolean waltz; folk song (Ger., Austrian)	mu
LANDMAN	landsman	

LANDTAG	governing body local parliament (Ger.)	
LAND-TAX	type of impost	
LANGAHA	snake (Madagascar)	zo
LANGITE	copper sulphate	mn
LANGLEY	unit of radiation	me
LANGREL	chain-shot	
LANGUED	heraldic tongue	hd
LANGUET	tongue-shaped	
LANGUID	feeble; listless; enervated	
LANGUOR	langure; lassitude	
LANIARY	slaughter house	
LANIARY	canine tooth	
LANIATE	tear in pieces	
LANKIER	taller and thinner	
LANOLIN	an ointment	md
LANTANA	verbena	bt
LANTERN	} turret windows crowning	
LANTHORN	} dome of church	ar, rl
LANYARD	laniard; short rope	
LAOCOON	(sculptured group)	
LAO-THAI	language of Laos	
LAOTIAN	native of Laos	
LAPILLI	volcanic stones; cinders	gl
LAPPING	polishing; wrapping; drinking; process for covering exposed copper	
LAPPISH	Laplandish; Lapp	
LAPSANG	for afternoon tea	ck
LAPSING	slipping; failing	
LAPUTAN	visionary	
LAPWING	peewit	zo
LAPWORK	overlapping work	
LARCENY	theft; pilfering	lw
LARCHES	conifers	bt
LARDING	smearing with lard	
LARD-OIL	a lubricant	
LARDOON	strip of bacon (lardon)	ck
LARGELY	greatly; abundantly	
LARGESS	bounty; alms; gift	
LARGEST	most capacious; biggest	
LARGISH	somewhat extensive	
LARIGOT	6-f organ pitch	mu
LARIKIN	larrikin; hooligan (Aust.)	
LARKING	sporting; on the spree	
LARMIER	drip-stone; corona	
LARNITE	orthosilicate of calcium	mn
LARVATE	larval; masked	zo
LASAGNA	flat pasta strip (It.)	ck
LASHING	scourging; upbraiding	
LASHKAR	N. Indian tribal force	
LASKETS	gaskets	nt
LASSOED	noosed	
LASSOES	lariats	
LASTAGE	ballast; fishing dues	
LASTING	abiding; enduring; durable	
LASTING	strong twill cloth	tx
LATAKIA	Syrian tobacco	bt
LATCHED	fastened; grasped; locked, secured	
LATCHES	door fastenings; lock systems; bolts	
LATCHET	shoe-fastening	
LATCHET	sapphirine gurnet	zo
LATEBRA	an egg cavity	zo
LATENCE	suspended activity	
LATENCY	force in suspense	
LATERAL	side by side	
-LATERAL	at the side of; beside; parallel irrigation channel or sewer	cp, ce
LATERAN	Roman cathedral	rl
LATHING	lath work	
LATRANT	barking	
LATRINE	camp privy; toilet	
LATROBE	a form of stove	
LATTICE	leaded window, network; grid; lacing style; records	cp
LATVIAN	Lettish; Baltic Sea	
LAUDING	extolling; praising	
LAUGHED	derided; expressed amusement; (sarcasm)	
LAUGHER	game won by a wide margin	
LAUNDER	wash; ore trough	
LAUNDRY	the wash	
LAURELS	bays of victory	bt
LAURITE	a sulphide	mn
LAUWINE	avalanche	
LAVOLTA	an old dance	
LAVROCK	lark	zo
LAW-BOOK	case book	lw
LAW-CALF	(bound in calf)	
LAWLESS	wild; rebellious; disorderly	
LAW-LORD	Lords' legal man	lw
LAW-LORE	Blackstone's	
LAW-SUIT	case in court	lw
LAXATOR	a muscle	md
LAXNESS	slackness; negligence	
LAYBACK	rock-climbing technique	mo
LAY-DAYS	(cargo lading)	
LAYERED	stratified	
LAYETTE	infant's outfit	
LAYLAND	pasture land	
LAYLOCK	lilac	bt
LAY-LORD	civil lord	nt
LAYOUTS	aerial somersaults (skiing)	
LAZARET	hospital	
LAZARLY	leprous	
LAZARUS	a poor man	
LAZIEST	most sluggish; idlest	
LAZY-BED	potato-bed	
L-DRIVER	learner driver	
LEACHED	strained through wood-ash	
LEADING	chief; principal; main	
LEAD-OFF	beginning of programme, concert etc; begin to depart	
LEAD-OUT	player about to receive ball (football)	
LEAFAGE	foliage; boscage	
LEAF-BED	gemma	bt

LEAF-FAT	fat in layers	
LEAFING	leaf-growth; (gold-); floating of metallic particles	**pt**
LEAFLET	handbill; small pamphlet	
LEAGUED	united; coalesced	
LEAGUER	camp; ally	
LEAKAGE	divulgence; percolation	
LEAKING	oozing; escaping	
LEANDER	channel swimmer	
LEANEST	thinnest; lankiest	
LEANING	penchant; bias; relying	
LEAPING	jumping; springing	
LEARNED	erudite; scholarly	
LEARNER	pupil; tyro; student	
LEASHED	bound; under control	
LEASING	falsehood; letting	
LEASOWE	a pasture	
LEATHER	tanned animal skin; to thrash	
LEAVING	desisting; bequeathing	
LECTERN	reading desk	**rl**
LECTION	a reading	
LECTUAL	necessitating bed-rest	
LECTURE	reproof; rebuke; discourse	
LEECHED	healed	**md**
LEECHEE	} Chinese fruit	**bt, ck**
LYCHEE		
LEEFANG	jib sheet	**nt**
LEEMOST	most leeward	**nv**
LEERILY	wideawake; sly; fly	
LEERING	ogling	
LEE-SIDE	} sheltered side	**nt**
LEEGAGE		
LEE-TIDE	tide with the wind	
LEEWARD	down wind	**nv**
LEFT-ARM	cricket	
LEGALLY	legitimately; licitly	
LEGATEE	inheritor of legacy, bequest	**lw**
LEG-BAIL	(absconding)	
LEGGATT	thatcher's wooden mallet	
LEGGERO	light and easy (lt.)	**mu**
LEGGERS	barge-pushers	
LEGGING	a gaiter	
LEGGISM	black-leggism	
LEGHORN	straw hat; fowl	**zo**
LEGIBLE	readable	
LEGIBLY	clearly written	
LEG-IRON	a fetter	
LEGITIM	Bairn's Part	**lw**
LEGLESS	apodal	
LEG-PULL	a draw; a joke; a hoax	
LEG-SIDE	right handed batsman's stand (cricket)	**ga**
LEG-SLIP	fielding position (cricket)	**ga**
LEGTRAP	(cricket)	
LEGUMEN	vegetable casein; pulse	**bt**
LEISTER	fishing spear (Ice.)	
LEISURE	restful ease	
LEMMATA	logical premises	
LEMMING	Arctic rodent	**zo**
LEMNIAN	(Lemnos)	

LEMPIRA	Honduras	**nm**
LEMURES	ghosts of evildoers	
LENDING	loaning; advancing	
LENGTHY	extended; protracted	
LENIENT	mild; clement; merciful	
LENTIGO	a rash; freckle	**md**
LENTISK	mastic tree	**bt**
LENTOID	lens-shaped	
LENTOUS	viscous; tenacious	
LEONERO	puma hunting dogs	**zo**
LEONIDS	meteor shower	**as**
LEONINE	like a lion	
LEOPARD	also libbard	**zo**
LEOTARD	one-piece, stretch costume	
LEPROMA	leprous swelling	**md**
LEPROSE	scurfy	**md**
LEPROSY	} dread disease	**md**
LEPROUS		**md**
LEPTOME	phloem elements	**bt**
LESBIAN	female homosexual	
LETCHED	percolated; filtered	
LET-DOWN	an avoidable failure	
LETHEAN	oblivious	
LETTERN	lectern; reading desk	
LETTING	preventing; hindering	
LETTISH	Latvian; Lettic	
LETTUCE	salad plant	**bt**
LEUCINE	(decomposition)	**md**
LEUCITE	volcanic rock	**mn**
LEUCOMA	wall-eye	**md**
LEUCOUS	albino	
LEVATOR	a muscle	**md**
LEVECHE	dry S.W. wind in Spain	**mt**
LEVELER	leveller	
LEVELLY	evenly; horizontally	
LEVERED	raised; lifted	
LEVERET	young hare	**zo**
LEVITIC	of Levites (Hebrew priests)	**rl**
LEVYING	collecting; exacting	
LEXICAL	alphabetically arranged	
LEXICON	dictionary	
LIAISON	co-ordination; intrigue	
LIANOID	ground-rooted climbing plant	**bt**
LIASSIC	geological formation	**gl**
LIBERAL	bounteous; generous	
LIBERTY	freedom; emancipation	
LIBRARY	a voluminous apartment; software; routes	**cp**
LIBRATE	to balance; poise; oscillate	
LICENCE	permission; excess; warrant	
LICENSE	to permit; allow; authorize	
LICH-OWL	screech-owl	**zo**
LICH-WAY	lych-way; funeral procession path in churchyard	
LICITLY	lawfully; legally; legitimately	
LICKING	a flogging; a thrashing	
LIE-ABED	a sluggard	
LIFT-BOY	} elevator operator (hotel, emporium)	
LIFTMAN		
LIFTING	elating; stealing; raising	

LIGATED	bandaged	**md**
LIGHTED	lit; ignited; illumined	
LIGHTEN	enlighten; alleviate; ease	
LIGHTER	barge; brighter; igniter	
LIGHTLY	buoyantly; airily; joyfully	
LIGNIFY	become woody	
LIGNINE	woody fibre	**bt**
LIGNITE	brown coal	**mn**
LIGNOSE	cellulose	
LIGROIN	paraffin	
LIGULAR	strap-shaped	**bt**
LIKABLE	attractive; lovable; amiable	
LIKENED	resembled; compared	
LILY-PAD	water-lily leaf	**bt**
LIMAÇON	heart-shaped curve	**ma**
LIMBATE	bordered; edged	
LIMBING	dismembering	
LIMBOUS	overlapping	**zo**
LIMBRIC	plain-weave cotton cloth	**tx**
LIME-LIT	illuminated	
LIME-PIT	limestone quarry	
LIMINAL	almost conscious	
LIMITED	restricted; circumscribed	
LIMITED	(liability company)	
LIMITER	restraining factor, agent; signal device	**cp**
LIMNING	water-colour painting	
LIMNITE	iron ore	**mn**
LIMOSIS	abnormal hunger	**md**
LIMPING	halting; walking lamely	
LIMPKIN	tropical crane	**zo**
LINCTUS	soothing syrup	**md**
LINEAGE	ancestry; extraction; race	
LINEATE	lined	
LINEMAN	railwayman, P.O. man; awaiting scrimmage (Am. football)	**el**
LINE-OUT	ball awaiting throw-in (Rugby football)	
LINGISM	Swedish drill	
LINGUAL	(tongue)	
LINKAGE	mechanical or cross cultural connections	
LINKAGE	mechanical or based on arithmetic or geometry	
LINKAGE	relation of genes in a chromosome	
LINKAGE	analog; magnetic flux in coil turns	**ps**
LINKBOY	torch bearer	
LINKING	connecting; joining	
LINKMAN	linkboy; mid-field player (soccer)	
LINNEAN	(Linnaeus, botanist)	
LINOXYN	dried film of linseed oil	**pt**
LINSANG	Indian civet	**zo**
LINSEED	flax-seed	**bt**
LIONCEL	small lion	**hd**
LION-CUB	baby lion	**zo**
LIONESS	lady lion	**zo**
LIONISM	tuft hunting	
LIONIZE	heroize	

LIP-BORN	hearsay; not genuine	
LIPIDIC	of lipid substance	
LIPPING	uttering; (golf); impudent remarking; golf stroke; opening	
LIQUATE	liquefy	
LIQUEFY	dissolve; melt; fuse	
LIQUEUR	a cordial	
LIRELLA	ridged apothecium	**bt**
LISPING	speaking with a lisp	
LISSOME	svelte; lissom; agile	
LISTFUL	attentive; heedful	
LISTING	tabulation; choosing	
LITERAL	au pied de la lettre	
LITHATE	(lithium)	**ch**
LITHELY	actively; pliantly	
LITHIUM	metallic element; salts; antipsychotic drugs	**ch, pc**
LITHOID	stone-like	
LITOTES	(figure of speech)	
LITTERY	covered with litter	
LITUATE	forked	
LITURGE	leader in public worship	**rl**
LITURGY	ritual	**rl**
LIVABLE	habitable	
LIVENED	cheered up; enlivened	
LIVE-OAK	American oak	**bt**
LIVERED	(lily-livered)	
LLANERO	S. American plain dweller	
LOADING	cargo; lading; charging	
LOADING	distancing circuits against power loss	**tc**
LOAFING	loitering; idling	
LOAMING	earthing	
LOANING	lending; advancing	
LOATHED	hated; detested	
LOATHER	an abhorrer	
LOATHLY	reluctant; unwilling; hateful	
LOBBIED	sought votes	
LOBBIES	vestibules	
LOBBING	pitching	**ga**
LOBCOCK	a lubber; a lubbard	
LOBELET	small lobe	
LOBELIA	a flower genus	**bt**
LOBIPED	having lobate feet	**zo**
LOBSTER	a decapod	**zo**
LOBULAR	lobed	
LOBULUS	small lobe	
LOBWORM	lug-worm	**zo**
LOCALLY	in the vicinity	
LOCATED	placed; fixed; found	
LOCATOR	finder	
LOCKAGE	canal dues; water losses	
LOCKIAN	(Locke's philosophy)	
LOCKING	grappling; securing	
LOCKIST	philosopher	
LOCK-JAW	tetanus	**md**
LOCK-MAN	under-sheriff (I. of M.)	
LOCK-OUT	(industrial) exclusion of employees	

LOCK-OUT	activation of hardware unit	**cp, el**
LOCKRAM	coarse linen	**tx**
LOCULAR	cell-like	
LOCULUS	small cell	
LOCUSTA	carob-tree	**bt**
LODGING	quarters; abode; harbour	
LOFTIER	of greater eminence	
LOFTILY	arrogantly	
LOFTING	raising; lifting	
LOGATOM	artificial testing word	**ac**
LOGBOOK	official record	**nt**
LOG-CHIP	log-line board	**nt**
LOGGATS	(ninepins)	**ga**
LOGGING	recording	**nt**
LOG-HEAD	a blockhead	
LOG-HEAP	log-pile; wood-pile	
LOGICAL	reasonable; deductive; sensible	
LOGICAL	entities as appearing to user	**cp**
LOGLINE	rope to log float	**nt**
LOGOGEN	using exact words for clear speech	
LOG-REEL	for puzzling sailors	**nt**
LOG-ROLL	pull strings	
LOG-SHIP	log-chip	**nt**
LOGWOOD	(red dye)	**bt**
LOLLARD	religious sect	**rl**
LOLLING	lounging; (tongue)	
LOMARIA	ferns	**bt**
LOMBARD	a banker; a money lender	
LONG-AGO	remote in time	
LONGBOW	medieval weapon	
LONGEST	most protracted	
LONG-HOP	(cricket)	**ga**
LONGING	eager desire; yearning	
LONGISH	somewhat long	
LONG-LEG	(cricket)	**ga**
LONG-OIL	high-oil-content varnish	**pt**
LONG-RUN	final issue	
LOOBILY	like a looby; clumsily	
LOOKING	search; watching; scanning	
LOOKING	a mirage; threatening	
LOOKOUT	sentinel; gazebo; view	
LOOK-SAY	word recognition	
LOOK-SEE	glance; hasty visit	
LOOMING	coming into sight, approaching	
LOONING	cry of the loon bird	**zo**
LOOPERS	(moth caterpillars)	**zo**
LOOPING	circling; knotting; coloured thread in glass technique	
LOOSELY	vaguely; diffusely; slackly	
LOOSING	relaxing; releasing	
LOOTING	pillaging; rifling	
LOPPING	amputating; curtailing	
LORDING	lordling	
LORELEI	a siren; rock on the Rhine	
LORETTE	a Delilah	
LORGNON	an eye-glass	
LORIMER LORINER}	bridle-maker	

LOSABLE	easily mislaid	
LOTTERY	game of chance	
LOTTING	cataloguing	
LOUDEST	showiest; noisiest	
LOUKOUM LOKUM}	Turkish delight	
LOUNDER	to beat; a blow (Sc.)	
LOUNGED	reclined; lolled	
LOUNGER	flaneur; loafer; idler	
LOURING	threatening; menacing	
LOUSILY	inferior word	
LOUTISH	clumsy; uncouth; oaflike	
LOVABLE	amiable; charming; winsome	
LOVE-ALL	no score tennis	
LOVE-DAY	settling day (Shak.)	
LOVEMAN	a plant	**bt**
LOVERED	having a lover	
LOVERLY	passionate; devoted	
LOW-BELL	(night-fowling)	
LOW-BORN	of humble birth	
LOW-BRED	poorly reared	
LOWBROW	unintellectual	
LOWDOWN	rascally	
LOWERED	threatened; frowned	
LOW-GEAR	low speed machine	**au**
LOWLAND	netherland	
LOW-LIFE	in poverty; degradation; crude	
LOWLILY	humbly; meekly	
LOWNESS	dejection; depression	
LOW-TIDE	when tide is out	
LOXOTIC	oblique; distorted	
LOYALLY	faithfully; devotedly	
LOYALTY	fealty; fidelity	
LOZENGE	a rhomb; a diamond shape, pastille	**hd, md**
LOZENGY	lozenged	**hd**
LUBBARD	a lubber	
LUCANUS	stag beetle	**zo**
LUCARNE	luthern; dormer window	
LUCENCE LUCENCY}	brightness; sheen; radiance; effulgence	
LUCERNE	plant for fodder	**bt**
LUCIDLY	clearly; limpidly; radiantly	
LUCIFER	Satan; a match	
LUCIGEN	powerful oil lamp	
LUCKIER	more fortunate	
LUCKILY	happily; fortunately	
LUFFING	turning toward wind	**nt**
LUGGAGE	baggage; impedimenta	
LUGGING	tugging; dragging; hauling	
LUGMARK	earmark	
LUGSAIL	4-cornered sail	**nt**
LUGWORM	lob-worm	**zo**
LUK-CHIN	hybrid Chinese	
LULLABY	soporific song	
LULLING	soothing; waning; subsiding	
LUMBAGO	muscular rheumatism	**md**
LUMINAL	narcotic drug	**md**
LUMPIER	bumpier; more awkward	

LUMPING	laying prefabricated sections of railway track	**rw**
LUMPISH	dull; heavy	
LUMP-SUM	cash down payment	
LUNATIC	maniac; crazy; insane	
LUNETTE	bastion; watch glass; half-moon window; figurative ornament	**ar, bd**
LUNULAR	crescent shaped	
LUNULET	lunular spot	
LUPULIN	hop extract	
LUPULUS	hop plant	**bt**
LURCHED	pitched; lurked; shifted	
LURCHER	a lurker; dog	**zo**
LURKING	skulking; awaiting	
LUSHING	swilling; toping	
LUSTFUL	lascivious	
LUSTIER	stronger; sturdier	
LUSTILY	vigorously	
LUSTING	desirous	
LUSTRAL	(purification)	
LUSTRUM	period of 5 years	
LUTCHET	mast-lowering, housing (frame) on deck	**nt**
LUTEOUS	fulvous; tawny	
LUTETIA	old name for Paris	
LUTHERN	lucarne; dormer-window	
LUTHIER	lutemaker (and viols) (Fr.)	**mu**
LUTRINE	(otter)	**zo**
LUXATED	dislocated	
LYCHNIC	(vespers, Greek church)	
LYCHNIS	campion plants	**bt**
LYCOPOD	a moss	**bt**
LYCOSID	wolf spider	**zo**
LYDDITE	a high explosive	
LYING-IN	awaiting birth; confinement (maternity)	**md**
LYINGLY	falsely; mendaciously	
LYMNATO	decorating by spray-gun technique	
LYMPHAD	sailing vessel (Sc.)	**nt**
LYNCEAN	lynx-eyed	**zo**
LYNCHED	summarily dealt with	
LYNCHET	unploughed strip	
LYRATED	lyre-shaped	
LYRICAL	musically poetic	

M

MACABRE	gruesome; grisly	
MACACUS	baboon	**zo**
MACADAM	road material	
MACAQUE	monkey	**zo**
MACCHIA }	low scrub Mediterranean; first undersketch of	
MAQUIS }	painting (It.) (Fr.)	
MACE-ALE	spiced ale	
MACERAL	elementary coal constituent	**mn**
MACHAIR	low-lying ground (Gael.)	

MACHETE	West Indian knife	
MACHINE	complicated device	
MACKITE	asbestos plaster	
MACRAME	fringe; corded edging; lace (Arabic)	**tx**
MACRONT	post-schizogony stage: neosporidia	
MACSHIP	merchant aircraft carrier (obs.)	**nt**
MACULAE	dark sun-spots	
MACULAR	of body tissue spots	
MAD-BRED	passionately conceived	
MADDEST	craziest	
MADDING	raging; distracted	
MADEIRA	a wine; a cake	
MADLING	a lunatic	
MADNESS	mania; delirium; frenzy	
MADONNA	Our Lady	
MADOQUA	Abyssinian antelope	**zo**
MADRIER	mine-plank	**mn**
MADRONA }	evergreen tree of California	
MADRONO }		**bt**
MADWEED	black horehound	**bt**
MADWORT	mugwort; cure for rabies	**bt**
MAESTRO	eminent conductor; N.W. wind (Mediterranean)	**mu**
MAFFICK	rejoice riotously	
MAFFLED	muddle-headed	
MAGENTA	purple aniline dye	
MAGGOTY	whimsical	
MAGICAL	talismanic; supernatural	
MAGINOT	French defensive line	
MAGNATE	wealthy, influential businessman	
MAGNETO	a generator	
MAGNETO-	drawing; recording (coated head); disks	
MAGNIFY	praise; enlarge; augment	
MAHALEB	cherry (Arab.)	**bt**
MAHATMA	adept in esoteric Buddhism	
MAHDISM	restoration of faith (Islam)	**rl**
MAHDIST	of Mahdism; Mahdi supporter	**rl**
MAHJONG	Chinese game	**ga**
MAHOUND	Moslem evil spirit	
MAHSEER	Indian river fish	**zo**
MAIL-BAG	post sack	
MAIL-CAR	postal van	
MAILING	posting	
MAIL-VAN	post vehicle	
MAIMING	mutilating; crippling	
MAINOUR	stolen property	**lw**
MAINTOP	part of rigging	**nt**
MAISTER	maestro; master	
MAIZENA	maize-meal	**bt**
MAJESTY	grandeur; magnificence	
MAJORAT	primogeniture (Fr.)	
MALACCA	cane	**bt**
MALACIA	pathological tissue softening	**md**
MALACON	variety of zircon	**mn**
MALAISE	unease; disquiet	
MALARIA	fever	**md**

MALAYAN	(Malay)	
MALEFIC	maleficent; baneful; noxious	
MALICHO	villainy	
MALISON	a curse; malediction	
MALLARD	wild duck	zo
MALLEIN	glanders inoculum	vt
MALLEUS	ear bone	md
MALLING	beating; mauling	
MALMSEY	canary wine	
MALTASE	an enzyme (glucose-splitting)	
		ch
MALTESE	native or language of Malta	
MALTING	brewing	br
MALTMAN	maltster	br
MALTOSE	enzyme, extracting sugar from	
	barley starch	ch
MALTOSE	starch sugar	ch
MAMELON	rounded mound	
MAMMARY	(breasts); (glands)	pl
MAMMATE	(mammals)	zo
MAMMOCK	shapeless mass; to mangle	
MAMMOSE	like a bosom	
MAMMOTH	elephantine; colossal	zo
MAMMULA	small protuberance	
MANACLE	handcuff; shackle; fetter	
MANAGED	contrived; administered	
MANAGER	controller; director	
MANAKIN	small bird; manikin	zo
MANATEE	sea-cow; dugong	zo
MANCHET	small French loaf	ck
MANCHOO	Chinese ruler	
MANDALA	mystic cosmos meditation	
	symbol	rl
MANDATE	command; charge; edict	
MANDIOC	cassava shrub	bt
MANDOLA	mandora; guitar	mu
MANDREL	lathe-head	
MANDRIL	mandrel; spindle	
MANETON	heavy gripping pinch-bolt	ae
MANGABY	monkey (Madagascar)	zo
MANGLED	calendered	
MANGLER	indifferent carver	
MANGOLD	mangel-wurzel	bt
MANHOLE	underground-channel exit	
MANHOOD	man's ideal	
MAN-HOUR	unit of work	me
MAN-HUNT	search for fugitive	
MANIHOC	} mandioc; tapioca; cassava	
MANIHOT	}	bt, ck
MANIKIN	manakin; dwarf; a bird	zo
MANILIO	arm-ring; copper coin	nm
MANILLA	cheroot; cigar	
MANILLE	a card value	ga
MANIPLE	handful; scarf	lw
MANITOU	Great Spirit	
MANKIND	blot on creation	
MANLIKE	as a man	
MAN-LOCK	air lock for pressure changes	
		mn, nt
MAN-MADE	hand-made	

MANNING	providing a crew	
MANNISH	masculine	
MANNITE	manna-sugar	bt
MANNOSE	a hexose	ch
MAN-ROPE	handrail	nt
MANSARD	(roof)	ar
MANSION	residence; house	
MANTLED	cloaked; disguised	
MANTLET	cloak; testudo	
MAN-TRAP	snare for trespassers	
MANUALE	case for papyrus rolled text	
MANUMIT	free from slavery	
MANURED	fertilized	
MANURER	cultivator	
MANX-CAT	tailless cat	zo
MAORMOR	royal steward (Sc.)	
MAPPERY	map-work	
MAPPING	surveying; delineating	
MAPPIST	cartographer	
MAQSURA	formerly concealment screen in	
	mosques (for royal box);	
	communal prayer area	ar, rl
MARABOU	adjutant stork	zo
MARACAN	parrot	zo
MARACAS	Cuban instrument	mu
MARATHI	Mahratta language	
MARBLED	veined (cheeses); stone veneer	
	effect; fat and lean (mixed)	
	meat	ck, ar
MARBLER	(decorator)	
MARBLES	friezes in stone; universal boys'	
	game with glass balls	
MARCATO	precisely as indicated (It.)	mu
MARCHED	bordered; advanced	
MARCHEN	folk-stories	
MARCHER	border-defender	
MARCHES	boundaries	
MAREMMA	marsh; malaria	md
MARGODE	bluish stone	mn
MARGOSA	Indian tree	bt
MARIKIN	marmoset	zo
MARIMBA	kind of xylophone	mu
MARINER	sailor; seafarer	nt
MARIPUT	civet	zo
MARITAL	(husband)	
MARKHOR	wild goat	zo
MARKING	branding; labelling	
MARLINE	rope	
MARLING	binding	nt
MARLITE	variety of marl	mn
MARLPIT	clay-pit	
MARMITE	cooking vessel	
MARMOSE	opossum	zo
MARPLOT	spoil-sport	
MARQUEE	large tent	
MARQUIS	French nobleman	
MARRANO	Jew converted to Christianity	
MARRIED	spliced; wedded	
MARRING	spoiling; interrupting	
MARROWY	full of marrow	

MARSALA	a light wine		
MARSHAL	arrange; harbinger; officer		
MARTEXT	careless preacher		
MARTIAL	warlike; military		
MARTINI	rifle; cocktail		
MARTITE	variety of haematite	mn	
MARTLET	house martin	hd, zo	
MARXIAN	a socialist		
MARXISM	communism		
MARXIST	communist		
MARYBUD	marigold	bt	
MASCARA	eye shading (cosmetics)		
MASCLED	net-like		
MASCULE }	lozenge-shaped	hd	
MASCULY }			
MASHING	mixing		
MASHLIN }	mashlum; mixed grain		
MASHLIM }			
MASH-TUB	where malt processed		
MASKING	revelling; disguising; (hiding); bit pattern	cp	
MASONIC	(freemasonry)		
MASONRY	stonework		
MASSAGE	friction	md	
MASSEUR	rubdown giver		
MASSING	accumulating; heaping		
MASSIVE	bulky; weighty; ponderous		
MASSORA	Biblical references		
MASTABA	Egyptian tomb		
MASTERY	skill; supremacy		
MASTFUL	full of beech-nuts		
MASTICH	gum; mastic	bt	
MASTIFF	large strong dog	zo	
MASTING	system of masts	nt	
MASTOID	nipple-shaped	md	
MASTOID	bone behind ear	md	
MATADOR	bull-fighter		
MATADOR	a domino game		
MATCHED	tallied; harmonized		
MATCHES	contests; lucifers		
MATCHET	machete; cutlass		
MATELOT	a sailor (Fr.)		
MATERIA	matter	md	
MATINAL	morning and early afternoon (performances)		
MATINEE	afternoon performance		
MATRASS	chemical retort		
MAT-REED	reed-mace	bt	
MATRICE	matrix; die		
MATROSS	assistant gunner		
MATTERY	purulent	md	
MATTING	mat-work; adding material surface onto silver (technique)		
MATTINS	daily service	rl	
MATTOCK	pick-adze for roots and stiff ground	to	
MATTOID	congenital idiot		
MATURED	mellow; ripened; payable		
MAUDLIN	drunk and whining		
MAULING	malling; hammering		

MAUNDER	mutter; to drivel		
MAURIST	a Benedictine	rl	
MAUTHER	mother (dialect)		
MAWASHI	silk cummerbund belt of sumo wrestler		
MAWKISH	squeamish		
MAW-SEED	poppy-seed	bt	
MAW-WORM	tape-worm	zo	
MAXILLA	upper jaw-bone	pl	
MAXIMAL	aphoristic		
MAXIMED	proverbial		
MAXIMUM	highest value		
MAXIMUS	senior of the name (school)		
MAXWELL	unit of magnetic flux	el	
MAY-BIRD	wood-thrush	zo	
MAY-DUKE	cherry	bt	
MAY-GAME	May-day sport		
MAY-LADY	May-queen		
MAY-LILY	spring flower	bt	
MAY-MORN	freshness		
MAYORAL	(mayor) of town's leading citizen, official		
MAY-POLE	flower-decked pole		
MAY-TIME	season of May		
MAY-WEED	camomile	bt	
MAZAGAN	bean	bt	
MAZARIN	deep blue		
MAZDEAN	godlike		
MAZEFUL	intricate; daedalian		
MAZURKA	Polish country dance; ice-skating jump	mu	
MAZZARD	skull; cherry		
MEADOWY	pasturable		
MEAL-ARK	meal-chest		
MEALMAN	grain merchant		
MEANDER	aimless wandering river course		
MEANING	purport; import; signifying		
MEASLED	spotted	md	
MEASLES	children's disease	md	
MEASURE	mete; gauge; value; degree; bar, metrical division	mu	
MEAT-FLY	blow-fly	zo	
MEAT-TEA	high tea		
MEAT-TUB	pickling tub		
MECCANO	constructional devices		
MECHLIN	lace		
MECONIC	(opium)	md	
MEDALET	small medal	rl	
MEDDLED	interfered; muddled		
MEDDLER	busybody		
MEDIACY	interposition; dispute-solving attempt		
MEDIANT	a tone	mu	
MEDIATE	negotiate settlement of claims		
MEDICAL	curative; sanatory	md	
MEDINAL	soporific drug	md	
MEDIOLA	bone in cochlea (ear)	pl	
MEDULLA	marrow; pith; inner core of organ	md	
MEDUSAE	Gorgons; hydrozoans	zo	

MEDUSAN	(petrifying)	
MEERKAT	mongoose (S. Africa)	zo
MEETING	encounter; concourse; duel	
MEGABIT	one million binary digits	cp
MEGAERA	one of the Furies	
MEGA-ERG	a million ergs	me
MEGAFOG	multiple foghorn	
MEGAPOD	having large feet	zo
MEGARON	ancient Gk. house	
MEGASSE	megass; cane residue	
MEGATON	measure of explosive force	me
MEGRIMS	giddiness; staggers	vt
MEIOSIS	hyperbole; cell division in gametes	
MEISSEN	(Dresden china)	
MELANGE	medley; farrago; jumble	
MELANIC	black	
MELANIN	black skin pigment	md
MELASMA	black spots	md
MELILOT	sweet-scented clover	bt
MELISMA	melodic ornamentation	mu
MELISSA	herb; balm	bt
MELLITE	honey-stone	mn
MELLOWY	mellow; soft; unctuous	
MELODIC	melodious; harmonious	mu
MELROSE	honey of roses	
MELTEMI	N. wind of East Med/Turk	mt
MELTING	fusing; softening; melting	
MEMBRAL	(limbs)	md
MEMENTO	keepsake; souvenir	
MENACED	alarmed; frightened	
MENACER	threatener; intimidator	
MENDING	repairing; amending	
MEN-FOLK	group of men	
MENGITE	anybody's guess	mn
MENINGE	brain tissue-envelope	zo
MENIVER	miniver; ermine & lambskin	
MENTHOL	peppermint camphor	ch
MENTION	remark; state; cite; declare	
MERANTI	Malayan hardwood	fr
MERCERY	haberdashery	
MERCIES	usually small	
MERCURY	planet; quicksilver	ch
MERCURY	Hermes; messenger; planet	
MERCURY	quicksilver; acoustic delay line	ch, cp
MERGING	absorbing; involving	
MERISIS	cell-division size increase	cy
MERITED	deserved; earned; incurred	
MERLING	the whiting	zo
MERMAID	woman with fish tail	
MERRIER	more cheerful	
MERRILY	joyously; blithely; happily	
MERSION	immersion	
MESALLY	centrally	
MESARCH	metal/protoxylem relationship	bt
MESEEMS	it seems to me	
MESHING	ensnaring; netting	
MESOBAR	region of normal atmosph. pressure	mt
MESODIC	(intermediate system)	
MESOPIC	night vision	
MESOPOD	central-stipe fungus fruit	bt
MESOTIC	paired cartilage in birds	zo
MESSAGE	despatch; missive; errand	
MESSAGE	information to be transmitted	tc
MESSIAH	also Messias	rl
MESSING	muddling; communal feeding	
MESS-TIN	a soldier's canteen food-dish	ck
MESTINO	} half-caste Spanish-Indian	
MESTIZO		
METAGON	cytoplasmic particle: paramecium	
METAZOA	multicellular animals	zo
METHANE	marsh-gas; firedamp	ch, mn
METHOIN	anticonvulsant chemical	pm
METOCHE	an architectural interval	
METONIC	lunar cycle of 19 years	as
METONYM	attribute representing a thing	
METOPIC	superficial	
METOPON	opium-based drug	md
METOTIC	behind auditory vesicle	zo
METOVUM	nutrition-surrounded ovum	zo
METRICS	versification; mensuration	
METRIFY	versify; poetise	
METRIST	a ballad-monger	
METTLED	high-spirited	
MEWLING	squalling	
MEXICAN	of Mexico	
MEZQUIT	} a Mexican tree	bt
MESQUIT		
MIASMAL	airborne infection	md
MIAUING	mewing	
MIAULED	caterwauled	
MICELLA	foundation structure of cell walls	
MICELLE	aggregate of molecules	ch
MICHING	pilfering	
MICROBE	germ; bacillus	md
MICROHM	electrical resistance	me
MIDDEST	middlemost	
MIDGARD	cf. Asgard (Scand.)	
MID-HOUR	crossword combination	
MID-IRON	golf-club	
MIDLAND	some way from the coast	
MID-LIFE	halfway to death	
MIDMOST	middlemost; central	
MID-NOON	midday	
MIDRASH	Jewish commentary	
MIDRIFF	diaphragm; garment	md
MIDSHIP	middle of ship	nt
MIDSPAN	between beam support	bd
MIDWIFE	birth assistant	
MIEMITE	limestone	mn
MIGRANT	nomad; wandering; roving	
MIGRATE	emigrate	
MILDEST	calmest; blandest	
MILDEWY	mouldy; musty; rusty	
MILEAGE	distance travelled	
MILFOIL	the yarrow	bt
MILIARY	a fever	md

MILIOLA	(fossil millet)	mn
MILITIA	citizen army	
MILK-BAR	snack bar	
MILKMAN	milk distributor	
MILK-RUN	routine round	
MILKSOP	effeminate fellow	
MILL-COG	water-wheel tooth	
MILL-DAM	mill reservoir	
MILLIAD	1000 years	
MILLIER	a thousand kilos (2204 lb)	me
MILLING	struggling; grinding	
MILLION	1,000,000	
MILLREA	} Portuguese and Brazilian	
MILREIS	} coins	nm
MILTING	spawning	
MILVINE	(kite family)	
MIMESIS	mimicry	
MIMETIC	imitative	
MIMICAL	mocking	
MIMICRY	impersonation; miming	
MIMULUS	musk plant	bt
MINARET	slender tower; (mosque)	rl
MINCING	affected; chopping; cutting	
MINDFUL	heedful; wary; attentive	
MINDING	marking; disliking; objecting	
MINERAL	earth substance	mn
MINERVA	Pallas Athene; (press); (novels)	
MINETTE	biotite-orthoclase lamprophyre	
MINEVER	} ermine and lambskin	
MINIVER	}	
MINGLED	joined; associated; jumbled	
MINGLER	a mixer; blender; compound	
MINIATE	to paint red	
MINIBUS	four-wheeled vehicle	
MINICAB	hired car	
MINIKIN	small pin; pet; favourite	
MINIMAL	smallest	
MINIMUM	least quantity	
MINIMUS	smallest; youngest	
MINIOUS	vermilion	
MINIVER	unspotted ermine fur	
MINORCA	a fowl	zo
MINSTER	cathedral; monastery church	rl
MINTAGE	coinage; mint dues	
MINTING	coining; inventing	
MINTMAN	coiner	
MINUEND	number to be diminished; subtraction	ma
MINUTED	briefly recorded	
MINUTIA	detailed detail (trivial)	
MIOCENE	geological period	
MIOLNIR	Thor's hammer	
MIRACLE	prodigy; supernatural event	
MIRADOR	balcony; viewpoint (Sp.)	
MIRATON	beef/onion stew (Fr.)	ck
MIRBANE	(bitter almonds)	
MIRIFIC	marvellous; wondrous	
MISBORN	born to misfortune	
MISCALL	revile; abuse	
MISCAST	wrong addition; in wrong role	

MISCITE	quote erroneously	
MISCOPY	copy amiss	
MISCUED	(billiards)	
MISDATE	put wrong date on	
MISDEAL	faulty card distribution	
MISDEED	fault; crime; trespass	
MISDEEM	judge wrongly	
MISDOER	delinquent; malefactor	
MISDONE	ill-done	
MISDRAW	draft badly	
MISERLY	parsimonious; niggardly	
MISFALL	mishap; misadventure	
MISFEED	hopper fault (punched cards)	cp
MISFIRE	fail to go off	
MISGAVE	filled with doubt	
MISGIVE	mistrust; doubt	
MISHNAH	} Jewish Oral Law	
MISHNIC	}	
MISKICK	football	
MISLAID	temporarily lost	
MISLEAD	dupe; delude; hoodwink	
MISLIKE	dislike; aversion	
MISLIVE	live a bad life	
MISLUCK	ill fortune; misfortune	
MISNAME	misterm; miscall	
MISPLAY	foozle	
MISRATE	rate erroneously	
MISREAD	read incorrectly	
MISRULE	anarchy; chaos; riot	
MISSAID	incorrectly stated	
MISSEEM	appear falsely	
MISSEND	} wrongly addressed	
MISSENT	}	
MISS-HIT	cricket	
MISSILE	bullet; projectile	
MISSING	lost; lacking; absent	
MISSION	trust; errand; embassy	
MISSISH	girlish; affected	
MISSIVE	missile; letter; message	
MISSTEP	a false step	
MISSUIT	not harmonize	
MISTAKE	err; error; fault; oversight	
MISTELL	misstate; misrepresent	
MISTERM	mischance; miscall	
MISTERY	a craft or trade	
MISTFUL	clouded; foggy	
MISTICO	coasting vessel	nt
MISTILY	hazily; obscurely	
MISTIME	judge occasion poorly	
MISTRAL	a cold N. or N.W. wind (Fr.)	mt
MISUSED	abused; squandered	
MISWEEN	judge wrongly	
MISWEND	wander; stray	
MISYOKE	yoke improperly	
MITHRAS	a Persian divinity	
MITOGEN	induces mitosis	
MITOSIS	complex cell division of somatic cells	
MITRATE	mitre-shaped	
MITRING	joining wood pieces at 90°	cr

MIXABLE	made-up word
MIXEDLY	confoundedly
MIXTION	gold-leaf fixative
MIXTURE	medley; hotch-potch; special organ stops **mu**
MIZMAZE	a labyrinth; a maze; amazed
MIZZLED	decamped
MJOLNIR	} Thor's hammer
MIOLNIR	
MOABITE	a tribe (in modern Jordan)
MOANFUL	mournful; grievous
MOANING	deploring; repining
MOBBING	crowding around
MOBBISH	tumultuous; disorderly
MOBILES	free-hanging ornaments
MOB-RULE	a form of democracy
MOBSMAN	well-dressed swindler
MOBSTER	gangster; hoodlam; ruffian
MOCKADO	ancient woollen fabric; tawdry
MOCKERY	scorn; derision; ridicule
MOCKING	taunting; jeering
MOCK-ORE	a zinc ore **mn**
MOCK-SUN	a parhelion
MODALLY	conditionally
MODESTY	chastity; propriety
MODICUM	small quantity
MODINHAR	Portuguese popular song **mu**
MODISTE	dressmaker
MODULAR	proportional
MODULOR	determinator of proportions of building units **bd**
MODULUS	factor of a function
MODWALL	bee-eater **zo**
MOEBIUS	freestyle aerial somersault (skiing)
MOELLON	masonry-filling
MOFETTE	(earth-fissures)
MOHICAN	Algonquin Indian
MOHSITE	titanite of iron **mn**
MOIDERT	bewildered (Sc.)
MOIDORE	Portuguese gold coin **nm**
MOILING	toiling; drudging
MOINEAU	bastion (Fr.)
MOISTEN	damp; add water
MOLASSE	sandstone **mn**
MOLE-RAT	a rodent **zo**
MOLETTA	} fishing boat (Portugal) **nt**
MULETTA	
MOLIMEN	strenuous effort
MOLLIFY	pacify; alleviate; soothe
MOLLINE	emollient base
MOLLUSC	} snails; gasteropods;
MOLLUSK	} cuttlefish; cephalopods **zo**
MOLOSSI	(3 long syllables)
MOMENTA	masses having velocity
MONACID	with one hydroxyl group **ch**
MONADIC	of elemental units; single operand process **ch, cp**
MONARCH	despot; king; ruler

MONAXON	of one axis only **zo**
MONEPIC	comprising one word
MONERAL	}
MONERAN	} protozoans
MONERON	}
MONEYED	rich; wealthy; opulent
MONEYER	coiner
MONGREL	mixed breed
MONIKER	nickname
MONITOR	mentor; advisor; lizard; big-gun naval ship; giant; debug **zo, nt, cp**
MONITOR	checker; deviation spotter; nozzle **cp**
MONKERY	monk-life
MONKEYS	primates **zo**
MONKISH	monastic
MONOCLE	eye-glass
MONODIC	monotonous and mournful
MONODON	narwhal **zo**
MONOGYN	type of plant **bt**
MONOMER	single-molecule substance **ch**
MONONYM	monomial name; single term (generic)
MONOPOD	carved single leg or foot support to wall chair or table Roman style
MONOTIC	affecting 1 ear only **md**
MONSOON	} Indian rainy season, S.W.,
MAVSIM	} NE winds **mt**
MONSTER	ogre; marvel; prodigy (Am. football)
MONTAGE	film editing
MONTANT	fencing term
MONTERO	horseman-cap (Sp.)
MONTHLY	menses
MONTOIR	mounting-stone (Fr.)
MONTURE	saddle-horse (Fr.) mount **zo**
MOOCHED	loitered; mouched
MOOCHER	thief; aimless wanderer
MOODILY	morosely; capriciously
MOOKTAR	Indian lawyer **lw**
MOOLVEE	doctor of Moslem law
MOONEYE	lake fish **zo**
MOONING	day-dreaming
MOONISH	fickle; variable
MOONLIT	visible in moonlight
MOON-MAD	moonstruck
MOON-SET	the setting of the moon
MOORAGE	anchorage
MOORHEN	water-hen **zo**
MOOR-ILL	cattle disease (Sc.) **vt**
MOORING	boat tie-up **nt**
MOORISH	Moresque; arabesque (Morocco) decor **ar, rl**
MOOTING	suggesting; debating
MOOTMEN	debating law students **lw**
MOPPING	dabbing; wiping
MORAINE	glacial debris
MORALER	moraliser (Shak.)

MORALLY	ethically; virtuously	
MORASSY	marshy; swampy; boggy	
MORBIDO	gentle, delicate (It.)	mu
MORBLEU	a French oath	
MORCEAU	morsel (Fr.)	ck
MORDANT	biting; caustic	
MORDENT	a trill	mu
MORELLA	} dark-red cherry	bt
MORELLO		
MORENDO	dying, slowing down (It.)	mu
MORESCO	arabesque; morisco	
MORGANA	(Fata)	
MORGLAY	claymore	
MORICHE	American palm	bt
MORINGA	Malay tree	bt
MORISCO	Moorish; moresco	
MORLING	dead sheep or its wool	
MORMOPS	repulsive looking bats	zo
MORNING	dayspring; daybreak	
MOROCCO	goatskin leather	
MOROSIS	feeble-mindedness	
MORPHEW	scurf	md
MORPHIA	opium extract	md
MORPHIC	morphological	
MORRHUA	(cod)	zo
MORRICE	Morris; Moorish	
MORRION	open helmet	
MORSURE	the act of biting	
MORTIDO	death wish; energy of Thanatos	
		pc
MORTIER	cap of state (Fr.)	
MORTIFY	putrefy; fester; corrupt	
MORTIFY	bodily self-denial; humiliate	
MORTISE	} a joint in carpentry	cr
MORTICE		
MOSAISM	(Moses)	
MOSCHUS	musk deer	zo
MOSELLE	light wine (Germany)	
MOSS-HAG	a slough in a bog	
MOTACIL	wag-tail	zo
MOTHERY	concreted; maternal	
MOTTLED	variegated; spotted	
MOTTLER	brush for graining, marbling	pt
MOTTOES	pithy maxims	
MOUCHER	skulker	
MOUFLON	wild sheep	zo
MOUILLE	liquid tone	
MOULAGE	casting footprints	
MOULDED	kneaded; shaped	
MOULDER	metal-caster; crumble	
MOULDIE	a torpedo	nt
MOULTED	shed	
MOULVIE	} Mahommedan priest; a	
MOULWEE	learned man	rl
MOUNDED	banked; fortified	
MOUNTED	on horseback; ascended	
MOUNTER	climber	
MOURNED	grieved; keened; wailed	
MOURNER	bewailer	
MOUSAKA	moussaka; Gr. dish	ck

MOUSING	cat-work; lashing	
MOUSMEE	geisha	
MOUTHED	orated; chewed	
MOUTHER	stump-orator; ranter	
MOVABLE	portable; mobile	
MOW-BURN	(hay)	
MOZARAB	(Christian Spaniard)	
MOZETTA	cardinal's cape	rl
MUCIGEN	chalice-cells substance	zo
MUCKING	muffing; muddling	
MUD-BATH	health measure	
MUD-BOAT	dredger	nt
MUD-CART	night-soil pick-up service	
MUD-CONE	mud volcano	
MUDDIED	fouled; dirtied; soiled	
MUDDING	smearing with mud	
MUDDLED	misused; confused; fuddled	
MUDDLER	mixer	
MUD-FISH	the bow-fin	zo
MUD-FLAT	low-tide bank	
MUD-HOLE	waterside residence	
MUD-LARK	a gamin	
MUDLINE	water/slurry division line	mn
MUD-SCOW	(dredging)	
MUD-SILL	tide mud level; soleplate	cr
MUD-WALL	soil embankment	
MUD-WORT	aquatic plant	bt
MUEDDIN	} Moslem prayer-caller	rl
MUEZZIN		
MUFFING	botching; fluffing	
MUFFLED	deadened; dulled	
MUFFLER	scarf	
MUFFLON	wild sheep	zo
MUGGARD	sullen; displeased	
MUGGENT	wild freshwater duck	zo
MUGGING	swotting; ruffianly attack	
MUGGINS	simpleton; a juggins	
MUGGISH	damp and warm	
MUGIENT	bellowing like cattle	
MUGWORT	wormwood plant	bt
MUGWUMP	independent politician	
MULATTO	offspring of black and white parentage	
MULCHED	} applied top dressing; soil	
MULSHED	cultivation	ag
MULCTED	fined; penalized; amerced	
MULETTE	Portuguese sailing vessel	
MULETTO	} fishing boat (Portugal)	
MOLETTA		nt
MULLEIN	yellow plant	bt
MULLING	warming and spicing	
MULLION	munnion; uprt. window bar	
MULLITE	aluminium silicate	mn
MULLOCK	rubbish; dirt	
MULTURE	grain grinding	
MUMBLED	muttered	
MUMBLER	indistinct articulator	
MU-MESON	elementary particle	nc
MUMMERY	masquerading; buffoonery	
MUMMIED	mummified	

MUMMIFY	embalm	
MUMMING	mummery; burlesquing	
MUMMOCK	ragged coat	
MUMPING	mockery; begging tricks	
MUMPISH	dull; sullen	
MUNCHED	crunched; chewed	
MUNCHER	a masticator	
MUNDANE	worldly; secular; temporal	
MUNDIFY	cleanse; purify	
MUNJEET	Siberian madder	bt
MUNNION	a mullion	
MUNTING	a door upright	
MUNTJAK	barking deer	zo
MUQARNA	stalactite ceiling decoration in mosques	rl
MURAENA	eel genus	zo
MUREXAN	purple dye	
MUREXES	} shellfish; Tyrian dye	zo
MURICES		
MURGEON	a wry face; grimace (Sc.)	
MURIATE	hydrochloric	ch
MURKIER	more overcast	
MURKILY	duskily; luridly; darkly	
MURRAIN	cattle disease	vt
MURRINE	fluorspar	mn
MURRION	morion; helmet	
MURTHER	murder	
MUSCARI	grape hyacinth	bt
MUSCITE	fossil moss	mn
MUSCLED	muscular	
MUSCOID	moss-like	bt
MUSEFUL	pensive; meditative	
MUSETTE	small bagpipe; satchel, haversack for refreshments (cycling)	mu
MUSHING	dog-sleighing	
MUSICAL	tuneful; harmonious	
MUSIMON	moufflon	zo
MUSK-BAG	perfume sachet	
MUSK-CAT	civet cat	zo
MUSKILY	like musk	
MUSK-RAT	the musquash	zo
MUSROLE	nose-band of a bridle	
MUSTANG	wild horse	zo
MUSTARD	sinapis	bt
MUSTELA	weasel	zo
MUSTILY	sourly; acridly; frowsily	
MUSTING	growing mouldy and rank	
MUTABLE	changeful; fickle; unstable	
MUTABLY	variably; inconstantly	
MUTAGEN	mutation producer	md
MUTANDA	things to be altered	
MUTTONY	resembling mutton	
MUZZILY	confusedly; dizzily	
MUZZLED	forcibly restrained	
MYALGIA	cramp	md
MYALGIC	tense; stiff	md
MYALISM	W. Ind. magic cult	
MYARIAN	(mussels)	zo
MYCELIA	mushroom spawn	bt

MYCETES	} howling monkeys	zo
MYCETIS		
MYCOSIS	} fungoid growth and infection; fungoid	md,
MYCOTIC		bt
MYELOID	marrow-like	
MYELOMA	bone-marrow malignancy	md
MYIASIS	parasitism by fly larvae	vt
MYLODON	extinct sloth	zo
MYOCELE	muscle hernia	md
MYOCOEL	coelomic space in myotome	zo
MYOCYTE	ectoplasm layer of protozoa	zo
MYODOME	eye-muscle chamber	zo
MYOGRAM	(muscular movement)	
MYOLOGY	(muscles)	md
MYOMERE	somite muscles	zo
MYONEME	ectoplasm fibril in protozoa	zo
MYOTOME	muscle merome	zo
MYOTOMY	dissection	md
MYOXINE	pertaining to dormice	
MYRINGA	ear-drum	
MYRRHIC	(myrrh)	bt
MYRRHIN	extract of myrrh	bt
MYRRHOL	myrrh-oil	bt
MYSTERY	mistery; a craft; enigma	
MYSTICS	a sect	
MYSTIFY	nonplus; perplex; bewilder	
MYTHIST	a recorder of legends	
MYTILUS	mollusc genus; mussels	zo
MYXOPOD	a protozoan	zo

N

NABBING	grabbing; seizing	
NACARAT	bright orange-red colour	
NACELLE	body of aeroplane	
NACODAH	Arab sea-captain	
NACRITE	pearl-like	mn
NACRITE	clay mineral	mn
NACROUS	pearly	
NAEVOID	(birthmark)	md
NAEVOUS	freckled	
NAGGING	incessant scolding	
NAIADES	water nymphs	
NAILERY	nail factory	
NAILING	spiking; fastening	
NAIL-ROD	nail material	
NAIVELY	artlessly; candidly	
NAIVETE	ingenuousness	
NAIVETY	unaffected simplicity	
NAKEDLY	starkly	
NAMABLE	nameable; nomenclatory	
NAMAQUA	African dove	zo
NANDINE	civet cat (W. Africa)	zo
NANKEEN	buff-coloured cloth (Nankin)	tx
NAOLOGY	study of church buildings	
NAPHTHA	rock-oil	mn
NAPLESS	threadbare	

NAPPING	dozing; snoozing; unalert; horse's refusal to continue exhibition etc	
NARCISM	} self love (Gr.)	
NARCISSISM		
NARCOMA	narcotics coma	md
NARCOUS	} stupor-inducing	
NARCOSE		
NARDINE	spikenard	bt
NARGILE	Eastern pipe; hubble-bubble	
NARRATE	chronicle; describe; report	
NARTHEX	porch with lean-to roof	rl
NARWHAL	sea-unicorn	zo
NASALIS	proboscis monkey	zo
NASALLY	through the nose	
NASARDE	organ stop	mu
NASCENT	natal; originating; incipient	
NASITIS	nasal inflammation	md
NASMYTH	inventor of steam hammer	
NASTIER	more disagreeable	
NASTILY	offensively; nauseously	
NATTERY	peevish; captious	
NATTIER	French blue; smarter	
NATTILY	neatly; sprucely	
NATURAL	an idiot; normal; inherent	
NATURED	temperamentally disposed	
NATUREL	unadulterated	
NAUGHTY	froward; perverse	
NAUPLII	crustaceans	zo
NAUTICS	art of navigation	nt
NAUTILI	cuttlefish	zo
NAVARCH	an admiral (Greek)	
NAVARHO	aircraft navigation system	
NAVARIN	mutton/vegetable stew	ck
NAVETTE	rape plant	bt
NAVVIES	labourers; canal diggers	
NAVY-CUT	rope-bound tobacco sliced	
NAYWORD	by-word; watch-word	
NAZIISM	German national socialism	
NEAD-END	show end	
NEALOGY	embryology	md
NEAREST	closest; stingiest	
NEARING	approaching, drawing nigh	
NEATEST	sprucest; tidiest; trimmest	
NEBULAE	gaseous matter	
NEBULAR	cloudy; vague; hazy	
NECKING	embracing; an annulet	ar
NECKLET	small necklace	
NECKTIE	cravat	
NECTARY	honey-gland	bt
NEEDFUL	essential; vital; requisite	
NEEDIER	rather worse off	
NEEDILY	necessitously	
NEEDING	wanting; lacking	
NEEDLED	pierced; embroidered	
NEEZING	} sneezing	
NEESING		
NEGATED	denied; mollified	
NEGATER	computer inverter	
NEGATON	negative electron	el
NEGATOR	NOT element; reversing binary	cp
NEGATUR	it is denied	lw
NEGLECT	disregard; omission	
NEGLIGE	loose attire; negligee	
NEGRESS	coloured woman	
NEGRITO	pygmy (Polynesia)	
NEGROID	negro-type	
NEGUNDO	box-elder	bt
NEHRUNG	spit at mouth of haff (lagoon) Ger. Baltic	go
NEIGHED	whinnied	
NEITHER	not either; not the one	
NELUMBO	water-lily; lotus	bt
NEMATIC	of substance with parallel orientation	ps
NEMESIC	retributive	
NEMESIS	goddess of vengeance	
NEMORAL	arboreal	
NEOCENE	geological formation	gl
NEOCENE	geological epoch; rock formation	gl
NEOLITE	silicate of aluminium	mn
NEOLITH	"stone-ager" epithet for today's dimwits	
NEOLOGY	(new terms); rationalism	
NEONATE	reborn with new ideas; immaturity	pc
NEORAMA	view of building interior	
NEOTENY	larval-character retention	zo
NEOTYPE	replacement of type within species	zo
NEOZOIC	geological system	
NEPHRIA	Bright's disease	md
NEPHRIC	of the kidney	pl
NEPHRON	excretory unit in kidney	pl
NEPOTIC	favouring the family	
NEPTUNE	sea-god; planet	as
NEREITE	fossil centipede	mn
NERITIC	of shallow coastal waters	
NERVATE	veined	bt
NERVINE	nerve tonic	md
NERVING	summoning resolution	
NERVOSE	having nerves	
NERVOUS	sensitive; timid; fearful; tense	
NERVOUS	neural system; neuronal	
NERVULE	} vein in leaf or insect's	
NERVURE	} wing	bt, zo
NESIOTE	living on an island	
NEST-EGG	cash savings	
NESTING	nidification; home-making; instructional loops	cp
NESTLED	cherished; lay close	
NESTLER	a snuggler; cuddler	
NET-BALL	a girls' game, 7-a-side; like basketball	ga
NET-CORD	(tennis)	ga
NET-FISH	caught trout	zo
NETSUKE	Japanese fastening	
NETTING	snaring	

NETTLED	stung; fretted; irritated	
NETTLER	a provoker	
NETWORK	reticulation; mesh; cord; fabric structure	
NETWORK	chain-series; data transmission system	**cp, tc**
NEURINE	nerve-matter	**md**
NEUROID	nerve-like	
NEUROMA	tumour	**md**
NEURONE	nerve cell	
NEUROSE	veined	
NEURULA	stage of embryo development	**zo**
NEUSTON	water-surface animals	**ec**
NEUTRAL	unbiased; indifferent	
NEUTRON	uncharged particle	**nc**
NEVADOS	(snow) katabatic mountain wind Andes, Ecuador	**mt**
NEW-BORN	just hatched	
NEWCOME	recently arrived	
NEW-LAID	fresh eggs	
NEW-MADE	novel; fresh; neoteric	
NEWNESS	novelty	
NEWSBOY	paper seller	
NEWSMAN	reporter	
NIAGARA	cataract; deluge; torrent	
NIBBLED	bit; pilfered; carped	
NIBBLER	dainty feeder	
NIBLICK	a golf club	
NICKING	stealing; notching	
NICTATE	wink	
NIDGING	stone dressing	
NIGELLA	love-in-a-mist	**bt**
NIGGARD	a miser; covetous; sparing	
NIGGERY	negroid	
NIGGLED	trifled	
NIGGLER	fuss-pot	
NIGHTED	benighted	
NIGHTIE	nightdress; robe de nuit	
NIGHTLY	every evening	
NIGRINE	an ore of titanium	**mn**
NIGRITE	insulating material	
NILLING	unwilling	
NILOTIC	of the river Nile	
NIMBLER	more agile; quicker; swifter	
NIMIETY	excessiveness	
NIMONIC	high-temperature-work alloy	**ml**
NINE-PIN	skittle	**ga**
NIOBEAN	(Niobe); lachrymose; tearful	
NIOBIUM	metallic element	**ch**
NIPBONE	herb comfrey	**bt**
NIPPERS	small pincers	**to**
NIPPIER	quicker; more agile	
NIPPIES	waitresses	
NIPPING	biting; pinching	
NIRVANA	unity with creation; liberation from desires; Buddhist aim	**rl**
NITENCY	effort; brightness	
NITHING	poltroon	
NITRATE	nitrite	**ch**

NITRIDE	metal/nitrogen compound	**ch**
NITRIFY	convert to nitre	**ch**
NITRILE	alkyl cyanide	**ch**
NITROUS	nitrose	**ch**
NIVEOUS	snowy	
NJORTHR	a Vanir (Norse)	
NOACHIC	of Noah's time	
NOBBLED	stole; tampered with a horse	
NOBBLER	confederate; doper	
NOBLESS	noblesse oblige; nobility attitudes	**pc**
NOBLEST	most illustrious	
NO-CLAIM	(insurance)	
NOCTUID	nocturnal moth	**zo**
NOCTULE	bat	**zo**
NOCTURN	a service of psalms; night; piece of music	**mu, rl**
NOCUOUS	harmful; noxious; baleful	
NODATED	knotted	
NODDING	(auction); unwary; nutation	
NODICAL	(ecliptic point)	**as**
NODULAR	(intersections)	
NODULED	knotted	
NODULUS	small knop	
NOEMICS	intellectual science	
NOETIAN	a dogmatic theologian	
NOGGING	brick and wood-work	
NOISILY	rowdily; loudly; uproariously	
NOISING	bruiting; rumouring	
NOISOME	noysome; disgusting	
NOMADIC	wandering; migratory	
NOMANCY	divination	
NOMARCH	Greek provincial governor	
NOMBLES	entrails of deer	
NOMBRIL	escutcheon centre	
NOMINAL	titular; ostensible	
NOMINEE	prospective candidate	
NON-ACID	alkali	
NON-AGED	under 18; minor (USA)	
NONAGON	nine-sided figure	
NONPLUS	perplex; astound; bewilder	
NON-SKID	steady grip tyres	
NONSTOP	uninterrupted (cinema); (chatter)	
NONSUCH	fodder plant	**bt**
NON-SUIT	no case	**lw**
NON-TERM	vacation	
NONUPLE	9-fold	
NOOLOGY	psychology	**pc**
NOONDAY	12 o'clock midday	
NOONING	siesta	
NOOSING	lassoing; snaring	
NORFOLK	loose jacket; turkey	
NOR-GATE	logic with binary digits	**cp**
NORIMON	Japanese palanquin	
NOR-LAND	north country	
NORTHER	north wind (USA)	**mt**
NORWICH	school of painting	
NOSE-BAG	horse's lunchbox	
NOSEGAY	bouquet	
NOSE-LED	befooled	

NOSTRIL	nose passage	
NOSTRUM	panacea; quack; medicine	
NOTABLE	signal; famous; memorable	
NOTABLY	conspicuously; notoriously	
NOTAEUM	bird's back	**zo**
NOTAGEA	Australian region	
NOTANDA	memoranda	
NOTCHED	scored; nicked	
NOTCHEL	to repudiate	
NOTCHER	scorer; flange stripping machine in steel fabrication	**ce**
NOTEDLY	markedly; particularly	
NOTELET	small note	
NOTE-ROW	} order of 12 note octave	**mu**
TONE-ROW		
NOTHING	nihil; zero; naught	
NOTHOUS	spurious; bastard	
NO-THROW	barely twisted silk thread	**tx**
NOTICED	observed; heeded; marked	
NOTITIA	a catalogue	
NOUMENA	opp. to phenomena	
NOURISH	cherish; foster; encourage	
NOURSLE	to bring up; to nurse	
NOVALIA	reclaimed land	
NOVELLA	supplemental decrees	
NOVELTY	newness	
NOVOLAK	phenol condensation product	**ch**
NOWHERE	address unknown	
NOXIOUS	hurtful; nocuous; baneful	
NOYADES	organised drownings (Fr.)	
NOYSOME	noisome; nauseating	
NUCLEAL	nuclear; (nucleus)	
NUCLEAR	central, like a kernel	
NUCLEIC	nucleoprotein non-protein part	**bc**
NUCLEIN	cell matter	
NUCLEON	proton; neutron; isospin	
NUCLEOR	nucleon core	**nc**
NUCLEUS	kernel; centre; head of comet	
NUCLIDE	atom-nucleus-distinguished isotope	
NUDGING	elbowing; jostling	
NULLIFY	annul; rescind; revoke; repeal	
NULLITY	invalidity; noughtiness	
NUMBERS	a biblical book	**rl**
NUMBING	deadening; paralysing	
NUMBLES	entrails of deer	
NUMERAL	digit; figure	
NUMERIC	numerical; character used as digit	**cp**
NUMMARY	numismatics	**nm**
NUNATAK	projecting rock (Eskimo)	
NUN-BUOY	conical buoy	
NUNDINE	market day (Roman)	
NUNHOOD	nunation	
NUNNERY	convent	**rl**
NUNNISH	sisterly; conventual	
NUPTIAL	conjugal; bridal; hymeneal	
NURAGHE	Sardinian fort	
NURLING	milling an edge	

NURSERY	(canons); training centre; plant and trees centre; children's place	
NURSERY	handicap race for 2-year-olds horseracing	
NURSING	fostering; developing	
NURTURE	upbringing; sustenance	
NUT-BUSH	hazel	**bt**
NUT-GALL	dyestuff source	**bt**
NUT-HOOK	crooked stick	
NUT-LOAF	} vegetarian	**ck**
NUT-MEAT		
NUT-MEAL	nut-flour rissole	**ck**
NUT-PINE	food-producing tree	**bt**
NUTTING	gathering nuts	
NUT-TREE	hazel	**bt**
NUT-WOOD	panel wood	**bt**
NUZZLED	nestled; cuddled	
NYCTALA	genus of owls	**zo**
NYLGHAU	antelope (Ind.)	**zo**
NYMPHAL	young and beautiful	
NYMPHLY	} girlish	
NYMPHIC		

O

OAFLIKE	doltish; stupid; idiotic	
OAK-BARK	could be cork	**bt**
OAK-FERN	3-branched polypody	**bt**
OAK-GALL	tree excrescence	**bt**
OAK-LEAF	colonel's decoration	**bt**
OAKLING	young oak	**bt**
OARFISH	ribbon-fish	
OARLOCK	rowlock	
OARSMAN	sculler	
OAT-CAKE	Gaelic delicacy	**ck**
OAT-MALT	malt from oats	
OATMEAL	rolled oats	
OBCONIC	funnel-shaped	
OBDUCED	drawn over; covered	
OBDURED	hardened; inured	
OBELION	part of skull	
OBELISK	printer's dagger (†); monolith, stone shaft	
OBELIZE	mark as spurious	
OBESITY	corpulence; fatness	
OBEYING	submitting; complying	
OBITUAL	funereal	
OBLIGED	gratified; forced; bound	
OBLIGEE	under bond	
OBLIGER	favourer	
OBLIGOR	bond giver	**lw**
OBLIQUE	askew; crooked; aslant	
OBLOQUY	calumny; censure; odium	
OBOLARY	poverty-stricken	
OBOVATE	} egg-shaped	
OBOVOID		
OBSCENE	repulsive; lewd	
OBSCURE	recondite; indistinct	

OBSEQUY	funeral rite	
OBSERVE	mark; notice; espy; remark	
OBTRUDE	intrude; thrust; interfere	
OBVERSE	head of coin	
OBVIATE	get round; preclude	
OBVIOUS	evident; patent; palpable	
OCARINA	instrument (Sicily); keyless, flutelike	mu
OCCIPUT	back of head	md
OCCLUDE	absorb; include	
OCEANIC	of oceans	
OCEANID	ocean nymph	
OCEANUS	ocean god	
OCELLAR	ocellate; with 'eyes'	zo
OCELLUS	single eye; a spot	
OCELOID	(big cat) of the leopard type	zo
OCHROID	pale yellow	
OCREATE	wearing boots/leggings	
OCTAGON	8-sided figure	
OCTAPLA	eight-fold text	
OCTAVUS	eighth (Latin)	
OCTETTE	group of eight; octet; (instruments)	mu
OCTOBER	10th month	
OCTOFID	eight segments	bt
OCTOPOD	eight-footed	zo
OCTOPUS	cuttlefish; squid	zo
OCTUPLE	eightfold	
OCTYLIC	(organic radicle)	ch
OCULATE	eyed	
OCULIST	eye doctor	md
OCYPETE	one of the Harpies	
ODALISK	houri; of the bedchamber; concubine (Turk.)	
ODD-EVEN	street numbering; parity check	cp
ODDMENT	remnant	
ODDNESS	oddity; eccentricity	
ODFORCE	mesmeric force	
ODONATA	dragonflies	zo
ODONTIC	pertaining to teeth	
ODORANT	odorous; fragrant	
ODORINE	a bone distillate	
ODOROUS	fragrant; redolent	
ODYSSEY	perilous journey	
OEDEMIA	surf-ducks	zo
OEDIPUS	a solver; King of Thebes	
OENOMEL	wine and honey	
OERSTED	magnetic field intensity	me
OESTRUM	frenzy; orgasm	
OESTRUS	gadfly; estrus; ovarian cycle; heat; rut	
OFF-BEAT	unusual, advanced	mu
OFFCOME	apology; pretext (Sc.)	
OFFENCE	crime; injury; assault	
OFFERED	proffered; tendered; essayed	
OFFERER	a bookie; volunteer	
OFFHAND	casual; impolite; (volleyball)	
OFFICER	person holding office; commission	

OFF-LINE	impromptu; off course; off centre	cp
OFFSCUM	offscouring	
OFFSIDE	right-hand side; football fault	
OFFWARD	leaning off	
OGHAMIC	(Irish script)	
OGREISH	like an ogre	
OGYGIAN	prehistoric; primeval	
OIL-BATH	bicycle accessory	
OIL-BIRD	the guacharo	zo
OIL-CAKE	cattle food	
OIL-GOLD	(gold leaf)	
OIL-MEAL	ground linseed cake	
OIL-MILL	oil factory	
OIL-PALM	oil source	bt
OIL-SHOP	lubricatorium	
OILSILK	oil-impregnated fabric	tx
OILSKIN	waterproof garment	
OIL-SUMP	drainage cavity in motor	
OIL-WELL	petroleum well	
OJIBWAY	Algonquin Indian	
OLDNESS	senility	
OLDSTER	middle-aged	
OLD-TIME	old fashioned; quondam	
OLEFINE	hydro-carbons	ch
OLIFANT	elephant	zo
OLIGIST	haematite	mn
OLITORY	(kitchen-garden)	
OLIVARY	olive shaped; oval	
OLIVINE	chrysolite	mn
OLYMPIC	of Olympus	
OLYMPUS	abode of the gods	
OMENING	auguring; presaging	
OMENTAL	} peritoneum	pl
OMENTUM		
OMICRON	Greek letter 'o'	
OMINOUS	portentous; inauspicious	
OMITTED	left out; neglected; dropped	
OMNEITY	state of including all things	
OMNIBUS	bus; compendium	
OMNIFIC	all-creating	
ONANISM	self-satisfaction	
ONCOSTS	overhead costs (Sc.)	
ONCOTIC	osmotic pressure of colloids	
ONDATRA	musk-rat	
ONE-EYED	limited in vision	
ONEFOLD	single	
ONEIRIC	pertaining to dream	pc
ONENESS	unity; concord	
ONERARY	operose; oppressive	
ONEROUS	burdensome; weighty	
ONESELF	me, you or anybody	
ONE-STEP	a dance	
ONE-TIME	former; previous	
ONGOING	event; developing; in progress regularly	pc
ONICOLO	cameo-onyx	mn
ONOCLEA	fern genus	bt
ONOLOGY	prattle	
ONSHORE	towards the land	

ONSTEAD	farmstead (Sc.)	
ONWARDS	forward; advancing	
ONYCHIA	a whitlow	**md**
ONYMISE	categorise	
ONYMOUS	not anonymous	
OOCYTIN	substance in spermatazoa	**bl**
OOECIUM	brood pouch	**zo**
OOGRAPH	egg drawing device	
OOLITIC	granular	
OOLOGIC	(birds' eggs)	**zo**
OOLYSIS	conversion to leaf	**bt**
OOMETRY	egg measurement	
OOPHYTE	gametophyte	**bt**
OOPLASM	central cytoplasm in oomycetes	
OOSPORE	fertilized ovum	**zo**
OOTHECA	egg-carrying structure	**zo**
OOZOOID	zooid arising from ovum	**zo**
OPACITY	opaqueness; obscurity	
OPACOUS	opaque; untransparent	
OPALINE	opalescent	
OPALIZE	opalise	
OPEN-AIR	out-door	
OPEN-END	radio; contract	
OPENING	aperture; breach; orifice; chance; vacancy	
OPENING	(ceremony); first move (gambit, chess)	
OPEN-JAW	air ticket (two way)	
OPERAND	quantity to be worked on	**cp, ma**
OPERANT	a worker; artisan; employee	
OPERATE	function; manipulate	**md**
OPEROSE	tedious	
OPEROUS	laborious; toilsome	
OPETIDE	spring-tide	
OPHIDIA	snakes	**zo**
OPHIURA	starfish	**zo**
OPIATED	drugged	
OPIATES	} class of drugs	
OPIOIDS		
OPINANT	of opinion	
OPINING	opinion; a notion; supposing	
OPINION	conception; idea; conjecture	
OPORICE	preserved fruit	
OPOSSUM	a marsupial	**zo**
OPPIDAN	town boy (Eton)	
OPPOSED	combatted; competed	
OPPOSER	rival; resister	
OPPRESS	persecute; crush; maltreat	
OPSONIC	} germ-resisting corpuscles	
OPSONIN		**md**
OPTICAL	of vision	
OPTICON	brain zone in insects	**zo**
OPTIMUM	best value	
OPULENT	wealthy; affluent	
OPUNTIA	cactus family	**bt**
OPUSCLE	opusculum; a small work	
ORAISON	orison; a prayer	**rl**
ORALITY	oral eroticism, oral disorder	
ORARIAN	coastal	

ORARION	} stole	**rl**
ORARIUM		
ORATING	spouting; declaiming	
ORATION	speech; harangue; address	
ORATORY	eloquence; chapel	**rl**
ORATRIX	lady speaker	
ORBIFIC	world-creating	
ORBITAL	revolutionary; elliptic; bony cavity (eye); molecular	**as, pl**
ORBLESS	without knobs	
ORBLIKE	globular	
ORCHARD	garden of fruit-trees	
ORCINOL	dihydric phenol	**ch**
ORDERED	regulated; commanded	
ORDERER	controller; manager	
ORDERLY	methodical; (military)	
ORDINAL	a number (of order); penalty in figurative ice-skating	
ORDINEE	young deacon	**rl**
OREADES	mountain nymphs	
ORECTIC	pert. to desires/satisfaction	
ORGANIC	vital; radical; fundamental	
ORGANON	} organised enquiry; dissertation	
ORGANUM		
ORGANRY	organ music	**mu**
ORGIAST	a Bacchanalian	
ORIENCY	brightness of colour	
ORIFICE	aperture; vent; pore	
ORIFORM	mouth-shaped	
ORIGAMI	paper cut-out, fold designs (Jap.)	
ORLEANS	cloth; plum	**bt**
OROGENY	(mountain formation)	
OROLOGY	mountain lore	
OROTUND	full voiced	
ORPHEAN	enchanting	
ORPHEUS	a maker of melodies	
ORPHISM	cult of Bacchus	
ORPHREY	embroidered border	
ORTHITE	allanite	**mn**
ORTHROS	morning service (Greek)	
ORTOLAN	garden bunting	**zo**
ORVIETO	a white wine	
OSAZONE	fraction of monosaccharide	**ch**
OSBORNE	convalescent home, I.O.W.	
OSCHEAL	scrotal	
OSCINES	singing birds	**zo**
OSCULAR	(kissing)	
OSCULUM	exhalant aperture in porifera	
OSIERED	with withes	
OSMANLI	a Turk; Ottoman dynasty	
OSMATIC	having olfactory organs	
OSMIOUS	containing osmium	**ch**
OSMOSIS	diffusion	**ch**
OSMOTIC	diffusible	
OSMUNDA	royal fern	**bt**
OSSELET	morbid growth	
OSSEOUS	bony	
OSSICLE	small bone	
OSSIFIC	bony	**md**
OSSUARY	charnel-house	

OSTEOID	like bone	
OSTERIA	hostelry (It.)	
OSTIARY	church janitor	rl
OSTIOLE	spore-door	bt
OSTIOMA	bone tumour	md
OSTITIS	inflammation	md
OSTRICH	also estrich	zo
OTALGIA	ear-ache	md
OTARINE	referring to seals	zo
OTIDINE	pertaining to bustards	zo
OTOCYST	auditory vesicle	md
OTOLITH	ear-stone	md
OTOLOGY	ear science	md
OTTOMAN	Turk; sofa; divan	
OURSELF	our kingly self	
OUSTING	ejecting; evicting; dislodging	
OUT-BACK	one from the interior (Australia)	
OUTBRAG	out-boast	
OUTBURN	burn away	
OUTCAST	pariah; exile	
OUTCOME	issue; sequel; upshot	
OUTCROP	geological fault	
OUTDARE	outventure	
OUTDONE	surpassed; eclipsed	
OUTDOOR	open air	
OUTEDGE	farthest extremity	
OUTFACE	to brave	
OUTFALL	the place of discharge	
OUTFLEW	L. Carroll-type word	
OUTFLOW	outlet	
OUTFOOT	out-pace; outsail	
OUTGATE	exit	
OUTGAZE	look longer than	
OUTGIVE	surpass in liberality	
OUTGOER	opposite of incomer	
OUTGONE	over-reached; went beyond	
OUTGROW	get too old for	
OUTGUSH	outpour; outwell	
OUTHAUL	a rope	nt
OUTHIRE	to let out	
OUTJEST	write dictionary definitions	
OUTLAND	foreign	
OUTLASH	sudden outburst	
OUTLAST	survive; outlive; outwear	
OUTLEAP	a sally	
OUTLIER	outcrop	
OUTLINE	draft; sketch; profile; synopsis; precis	
OUTLIVE	survive	
OUTLOOK	prospect; future; view	
OUTMATE	overmatch; checkmate	
OUTMOST	furthest outward	
OUTMOVE	out-manoeuvre	
OUTNAME	surpass in reputation	
OUTNESS	externality; objectiveness	
OUTPACE	outrun	
OUTPART	remote part	
OUTPEER	excel	
OUTPLAY	out-manoeuvre	
OUTPORT	branch port	

OUTPOST	detached fort	
OUTPOUR	stream; spout	
OUTPRAY	surpass in prayer	
OUTRAGE	wanton mischief; abuse	
OUTRANK	precede	
OUTRAZE	exterminate	
OUTRIDE	win horse race	
OUTROAD	a foray (Sc.)	
OUTROAR	an uproar	
OUTROOT	uproot; eradicate	
OUTRUSH	a raid; a foray	
OUTSAIL	win yacht race	
OUTSELL	succeed in America	
OUTSERT	extra outside binding leaf	pr
OUTSHOT	a projection	
OUTSIDE	external; exterior; superficial	
OUTSIZE	extra big	
OUTSOAR	word invented to fill space	
OUTSOLD	outvend	
OUTSOLE	outer sole	
OUTSPAN	to unyoke	
OUTSTAY	stay longer than	
OUTSTEP	overstep	
OUTTALK	over jabber	
OUTTURN	output; production; delivery throw (rugby football) (curling)	
OUTVIED	surpassed; exceeded	
OUTVOTE	get majority	
OUTWALK	outpace	
OUTWALL	outer wall	
OUTWARD	ostensible; apparent	
OUTWEAR	last longer; outlast	
OUTWELL	outgush	
OUTWENT	outstripped	
OUT-WICK	shot hitting another stone (curling)	
OUTWIND	extricate	
OUTWING	out-flank	
OUTWITH	beyond the scope of (Sc.)	
OUTWORE	lasted longer than	
OUTWORK	redoubt; ravelin	
OUTWORN	worn out; exhausted	
OUVRAGE	work (Fr.)	
OVARIAN	(ovary)	
OVATION	enthusiastic applause	
OVEN-TIT	willow-warbler	zo
OVERACT	act too much	
OVERALL	protective garment	
OVERARM	bowling (cricket)	
OVER-ATE	surfeited	
OVERAWE	intimidate; daunt; cow	
OVERBID	succeed at auction	
OVERBUY	buy too much	
OVERDUE	in arrears; outstanding; (debt)	
OVERDYE	dye too deeply	
OVEREAT	gourmandize	
OVEREYE	overlook	
OVERFAR	a bit much	
OVERFLY	soar beyond; fly over	

OVERLAP	lie partly over another; dialling faults	**tc**
OVERLAP	faulty transmission of facsimile scanning	**tc**
OVERLAY	overwhelm; bed cloth; multiple store program	**cp**
OVERLIE	to smother	
OVERMAN	foreman	
OVERMAN	mining manager; umpire	
OVERPAY	pay too much	
OVERPLY	over-exert	
OVERRAN	outran; invaded	
OVERRUN	swarm; infest; printing	**pr**
OVERSAW	superintended	
OVERSEA	foreign	
OVERSEE	superintend	
OVERSET	upset	
OVERSEW	stitch fit to burst	
OVERTAX	tax too highly	
OVERTLY	openly; publicly; patently	
OVERTOP	surpass	
OVICELL	brood-pouch in ectoprocta	**zo**
OVICIDE	killing of eggs/sheep	
OVIDIAN	(Ovid); verse form; narration; ideas	
OVIDUCT	ovary passage	**md**
OVIFORM	oval	
OVOIDAL	ovoid; egg-shaped	
OVOLOGY	egg-lore	
OVULARY	(seed)	**bt**
OVULITE	fossil egg	**mn**
OWENITE	(Robert Owen); cooperative idealist (reformist)	
OWL-EYED	with big orbs	
OWL-LIKE	fairly wise	
OWN-GOAL	to score for opponents; mistake	
OXALATE	of oxalic acid	**ch**
OXALITE	oxalate of iron	**mn**
OXAMIDE	oxalic acid amide	**ch**
OXHEART	kind of large sweet cherry	**bt**
OXIDANT	combustive agent	**ch**
OXIDASE	enzyme	**ch**
OXIDATE	} to rust	**ch**
OXIDIZE		**ch**
OXIMIDE	oxamic acid compound	**ch**
OXONIAN	of Oxford	
OX-STALL	home for non-bulls	
OXYACID	proton-giving hydroxide	**ch**
OXYDANT	oxygen component in rocket	**ae**
OXYNTIC	secreting acid (of stom. glands)	
OXYOPIA	acute vision	**md**
OXYSALT	containing oxygen	**ch**
OXYTONE	accented syllable	
OZONIDE	explosive organic compound	**ch**
OZONIZE	charge with ozone	
OZONOUS	ozonic	

P

PABULAR	yielding food	
PABULUM	aliment; fodder; nutriment	
PACABLE	appeasable	
PACATED	calmed; quieted; pacified	
PACEMAN	runner; fast bowler (cricket)	
PACHISI	pachesi; Indian backgammon	**ga**
PACHYMA	fungus genus	**bt**
PACIFIC	peaceful; tranquil; irenic	
PACKAGE	bale; bundle; parcel; (holiday)	
PACKAGE	generalised multipurpose program	**cp**
PACK-ICE	icy-sea barrier	
PACKING	crowding; stowing	
PACKMAN	peddler; hawker; tallyman	
PACKWAX	tendon in animals' necks	**zo**
PACKWAY	bridle path	
PACTION	a pact; covenant; bond	
PADDING	stuffing	
PADDLED	dabbled; propelled	
PADDLER	canoeist	
PADDOCK	frog or toad	**zo**
PADDOCK	puddock; field	
PADELLA	small lamp	
PADISHA	Persian title	
PADLOCK	heavy durable lock	
PADRONE	Italian employer	
PAD-TREE	harness frame	
PAENULA	chasuble	**rl**
PAEONIN	red colouring matter	
PAGEANT	spectacle; display; pompous	
PAGINAL	(pages)	
PAHLEVI	pehlevi; early Persian dialect	
PAILFUL	the contents of a bucket	
PAILLON	metal backing	
PAINFUL	grievous; vexatious; sore	
PAINING	afflicting; tormenting; aching	
PAINTED	limned; bedizened; daubed	
PAINTER	artist in colour; depictor	
PAINTER	R.A.; mooring rope	**nt**
PAIRING	mating; (voting)	
PAJAMAS	pyjamas; slumber wear	
PAKFONG	} German silver	
PAKTONG		
PALABRA	palaver (Sp.); (word)	
PALADIN	knight errant	
PALAMAE	toe-webbings	**zo**
PALATAL	(palate)	**md**
PALAVER	conference; pow-wow	
PALE-ALE	type of brew	**br**
PALEOUS	like chaff	
PALETOT	loose overcoat	
PALETTE	artist's board; (pelota)	
PALFREY	saddle-horse	**zo**
PALINAL	retrogressive	**md**
PALLIAL	(mantle of mollusc)	**zo**
PALLING	covering; surfeiting	
PALLIUM	archbishop's pall; cerebral cortex	**rl, pl**
PALLIUM	mantle-like brain/shell tissue	**pl**

PALLONE	Italian ball-game	**ga**
PALMARY	worthy; capital	
PALMATE	web-footed	**zo**
PALMERY	palm-house	**bt**
PALMING	concealing; handling	
PALMIST	fortune teller	
PALM-OIL	bribery	
PALMYRA	East Indian palm	**bt**
PALOOKA	guy; nitwit; simpleton; incompetent boxer	
PALPATE	to handle	
PALSHIP	comradeship	
PALSIED	paralysed	
PALUDAL	marshy; malarial; fenny	
PAMPERO	S.W. cold squall on pampas (Argentina)	**mt**
PANACEA	universal remedy	
PANACHE	plume; self-esteem	
PANAGIA	all holy; an ornament	**rl**
PANCAKE	aeroplane descent; thin cake fried in pan	**ae, ck**
PANDEAN	of Pan	
PANDECT	digest of Roman Law	
PANDION	osprey genus	**zo**
PANDORA **BANDORA**	plucked instruments, cittern; her fateful box; sea bream	**mu, zo**
PANDORE	a lute	**mu**
PANDOUR	Hungarian soldier; robber	
PANDURA	Neapolitan guitar	**mu**
PANEITY	state of being bread	**rl**
PANFISH	small non-commercial food fish	
PANGAEA	sial, great primeval single, continental landmass (Wegener's theory)	**gl**
PANGANI	East African ivory	
PANGING	paining; causing anguish	
PANICKY	jumpy; nervous; fearful	
PANICLE	a small web	**bt**
PANICUM	millet-grain	**bt**
PANIKIN	tin mug	
PANJANG	sampan, Malaysia	**nt**
PANNADE	curvetting	
PANNAGE	swine food	
PANNIER	(dress); basket; corbel	
PANNING	washing; yielding	
PANNOSE	like felt	
PANOCHA	coarse sugar (Mexico)	
PANOPLY	complete armour	
PAN-PIPE	mouth-organ	**mu**
PANSIED	with pansies	
PANTHER	leopard	**zo**
PANTHOS	Divinity made manifest	
PANTIES	undies	
PANTILE	pentile; curved tile	
PANTING	palpitating; desirous	
PANTLER	butler	
PANTOUM	Malayan quatrain	**mu**
PANURGE	a Rabelaisian rascal	
PANURGY	skill in work	
PAPALLY	popishly (ceremoniously)	**rl**

PAPBOAT	small feeding vessel for infants	
PAPERED	sand-papered	
PAPERER	paperhanger	
PAPHIAN	(worship of Venus)	
PAPILIO	butterfly	**zo**
PAPILLA	nerve extremity	**md**
PAPMEAT	soft food	
PAPOOSE	North American Indian infant	
PAPPING	feeding with pap	
PAPPOSE	pappous; downy	
PAPRIKA	red pepper (Hungarian)	**bt**
PAPULAE	dermal gills in echinodermata	
PAPULAR	pimply	**md**
PAPYRUS	sedge; scroll	**bt**
PARABLE	allegorical similitude	
PARACME	decline; decadence	
PARADED	displayed; vaunted	
PARADOS	rampart	
PARADOX	surprising statement	
PARAGON	model of perfection	
PARAMOS	semi-tundra (Andes)	
PARAPET	rampart	
PARASOL	sunshade	
PARBAKE	bake partially	**ck**
PARBOIL	boil partially	**ck**
PARCHED	scorched; dried; shrivelled	
PARDIEU	in truth	
PARDINE	like a leopard, spotted	
PAREIRA	drug (Brazilian plant)	**bt**
PARELLA **PARELLE** **PERELLE**	litmus lichen	**bt**
PARERGY	subsidiary work	
PARESIS	paralysis	**md**
PARETIC	partially paralysed	**md**
PARFAIT	cold egg/creme dessert	**ck**
PARGING	pargeting; external plaster work	
PARISON	intermediate glass shape	**gs**
PARITOR	beadle; apparitor	
PARKING	lodging; collecting	
PARLOUR	the Mayor's sanctum	
PARLOUS	perilous; difficult; precarious	
PARODIC	(parody); farcical	
PAROTIC	auricular	**md**
PAROTID **PAROTIS**	(salivary gland)	**md**
PARQUET	flooring; pit of theatre	
PARRIED	avoided; warded off; fended	
PARSING	grammatical exercise	
PARSLEY	a culinary herb	**bt**
PARSNIP	parsnep; a vegetable	**bt**
PARTAKE	to share; participate	
PARTIAL	biased; restricted; fond	
PARTIDO	15-point limit competition (pelota)	
PARTIES	sides; jamborees	
PARTING	division; separating; breaking	
PARTITA	suite, variations; notes	**mu**
PARTITE	partially parted	**bt**
PARTLET	a ruff; a collar; a hen	**zo**
PARTNER	colleague; associate; buddy	

PARULIS	gumboil	md
PARVENU	upstart	
PARVISE	porch; church garden	rl
PARVULE	tiny pill	
PASCHAL	(Easter)	
PASCUAL	grazing; pasturing	
PASGANG	striding technique (skiing)	
PASQUIL	} lampoon; satire	
PASQUIN		
PASSADE	} sword thrust; equestrian	
PASSADO	exercise	
PASSAGE	alley; clause; context; travel; law; extract of music, literature; slow trot	
PASSANT	walking	hd
PASSING	brief; transient; exceeding	
PASSION	ardour; fervour; wrath	
PASSIVE	patient; resigned; inert	
PASS-KEY	a master-key	
PASSMAN	(honours)	
PASSOUT	from behind opponents (ice skating)	
PASTE-IN	late correction, insert	pr
PASTERN	(fetlock); part of horse's foot	
PASTE-UP	extended arrangement of proof sheets	pr
PASTIES	patties; pies	ck
PASTIME	recreation; sport; diversion	
PASTING	cementing; gumming	
PASTOSE	painted thickly	
PASTURE	herbage; meadowland	
PATACHE	fishing boat from Malaysia	nt
PATAMAR	coasting vessel; dhow, India	nt
PATBALL	tennis of sorts	ga
PATCHED	repaired clumsily	
PATCHER	repairer; botcher	
PATELLA	limpet; kneecap	zo, pl
PATELLA	knee-cap; saucer	md
PATERAE	shallow dishes	
PATHWAY	footway; track; trail	
PATIENT	long-suffering	md
PATNESS	celerity in the uptake	
PATOLLI	Aztecs' board game	ga
PATONCE	heraldic curved cross	hd
PATRIAL	racial; national	
PATRICO	gipsy priest; patercove	
PATRIOT	staunch non-cosmopolitan	
PATRIST	a theologian	rl
PATROON	American proprietor	
PATTERN	model; exemplar; paragon	
PATTIES	pasties; pies	ck
PATTING	tapping	
PATTRAS	wooden wall-plug	
PATULIN	penicillium antibiotic	pm
PATURON	chelicerae segment in spiders	
PAUCITY	fewness; exiguity; lack	
PAULINE	(St Paul); sect	rl
PAUNCHY	obese; stout	
PAUSING	halting; wavering; tarrying	
PAVIAGE	road tax (Fr.)	
PAVIOUR	pavement layer	

PAWLATA	method of righting a kayak	
PAWNING	pledging; hypothecating	
PAXILLA	spine in asteroidea	zo
PAXIUBA	South American palm	bt
PAYABLE	due; profitable	
PAYBILL	order to pay	
PAYBOOK	record of payments	
PAYCOCK	vain husband of Juno	
PAYDIRT	alluvial deposit	
PAYLIST	payroll	
PAYLOAD	plane's cargo	
PAYMENT	recompense; reward	
PAYNISE	to preserve wood	
PAYROLL	paylist	
PAYSAGE	landscape (Fr.)	
PEACHED	divulged	
PEACHER	an informant	
PEA-COAT	pea-jacket	
PEACOCK	pavonine	zo
PEACRAB	small crustacean	zo
PEA-FOWL	a species of Pavo genus	zo
PEAKING	raising a yard obliquely; reaching full performance	nt
PEAKISH	off colour; sickly	
PEALING	ringing; resounding	
PEANISM	song of praise or triumph	
PEARLED	made success as oyster	
PEARLER	fishing boat (Japan)	nt
PEARLIN	lace made of silk thread	tx
PEASANT	a rustic; swain; hind	
PEASCOD	pea-pod; Tudor genital protector (mini)	bt
PEA-SOUP	London fog	
PEAT-BED	damp doss	
PEAT-BOG	Irish fuel source	
PEAT-HAG	peat-hole	
PEAVIES	lumbermen's levers	
PEBBLED	shingled	
PEBRINE	silk-worm disease	zo
PECCANT	sinning; guilty; criminal	
PECCARY	S. American pig	zo
PECCAVI	confession of error	
PECKING	picking up; striking	
PECKISH	hungry	
PECTASE	gel-forming plant enzyme	bt
PECTATE	pectose; gelatinous	
PECTINE	jelly from apple acid	ck, bt
PECTOSE	carbohydrate plant constituent	
PEDDLED	retailed; trifled	
PEDDLER	hawker; huckster	
PEDESIS	molecular vibration	
PEDICEL	} small stalk	bt
PEDICLE		
PEDLARY	hawking; (street) selling	
PEDOCAL	calcium rich zonal soil	gl, ag
PEDRAIL	tracked vehicle	
PEELING	excoriating; skinning	
PEELITE	follower of Sir R. Peel	
PEENING	hammer-blow metal-working	
PEEPING	snooping; peering	
PEERAGE	Debrett; rank of peer	

PEERESS	consort of a peer	
PEERING	prying; gazing; appearing	
PEEVERS	hop-scotch (Sc.)	
PEEVISH	querulous; snappish	
PEEWEEP	peewit; pewit	zo
PEGASUS	winged horse of the Muses	
PEGASUS	(fish); constellation	as, zo
PEGGING	fastening; (croquet)	
PEGWOOD	clock-hole cleaning sticks	
PEHLEVI	} early Persian dialect	
PAHLEVI		
PEISHWA	Mahratta prime minister	
PELAGIC	(deep sea)	
PELAMID	bonito; mackerel type	zo
PELASGI	Greek tribe	
PELICAN	genus of birds	zo
PELIOMA	livid spot	md
PELISSE	fur-coat	
PELLAGE	duty on skins	
PELOPID	a son of Pelops	
PELORIA	} abnormalism	md
PELORIC		
PELORUS	pivoted dial	nv
PELOTON	coiled hypha in fungi; bunch of racing cyclists	bt
PELTAST	soldier with buckler	
PELTATE	shield-like	
PELTING	pouring; throwing	
PENALLY	by way of punishment	
PENALTY	handicap; retribution; free kick or throw (matches)	
PENANCE	punishment; humiliation	
PENATES	Roman household gods	
PEN-CASE	pen-holder	
PENDANT	an ornament; pennant	
PENDENT	hanging; dangling	
PENDING	awaiting decision	
PENEIAN	(river Peneus in Vale of Tempe)	
PEN-FISH	sparoid fish	zo
PENFOLD	pinfold; enclosure for cattle	
PENGUIN	Antarctic sea-bird	zo
PENICIL	paint-brush	
PEN-NAME	pseudonym; nom de plume	
PENNANT	a long streamer	nt
PENNATE	winged; pinnate genus of birds	zo
PENNIED	having a cash asset	
PENNIES	pence	nm
PENNILL	stanza (Eisteddfod)	
PENNINE	magnesium/aluminium silicate	
PENNING	inditing; cooping	
PENSILE	pendulous; suspended	
PENSION	(boarding house); annuity; retirement income (social security)	
PENSIVE	meditative; thoughtful	
PENTACT	five-rayed	
PENTANE	(paraffin)	ch
PENTICE	pent-house; a sloping roof or weather cover	bd
PENTODE	pentone; wireless adjunct	

PENTOSE	a form of sugar	ch
PENTZIA	S. African shrub	bt
PENUCHE	type of fudge	ck
PENWORK	drawings, calligraphy, decoration on japanned lacquer furniture	
PEONAGE	} agricultural servitude	
PEONISM		
PEONIES	paeonies	bt
PEOPLED	inhabited	
PEPERIN	volcanic tufa	mn
PEPPERY	irascible; choleric	
PEP-PILL	stimulant	
PEPSINE	an enzyme	md
PEP-TALK	encouragement	
PEPTICS	digestion	md
PEPTIDE	protein-breakdown substance	ch
PEPTONE	digestive product	md
PER-ACID	hydrogen-peroxide/acid product	
PERBEND	bonding stone	
PERCALE	woven cambric	
PERCASE	perhaps	
PER-CENT	out of 100	
PERCEPT	that which is perceived	
PERCHED	roosted; settled	
PERCHER	candle; rooster	zo
PERCINE	like a perch; percoid	zo
PERCOCT	well cooked	
PERCOID	perch-like	zo
PERCUSS	strike; tap	
PERDURE	endure; persist	
PEREGAL	fully equal	
PEREION	thorax of crustacea	zo
PERELLE	} lichen	
PARELLE		bt
PARELLA		
PERFECT	to complete; faultless; intervals pitch	mu
PERFIDY	betrayal; treachery	
PERFORM	fulfil; act; execute; effect	
PERFUME	scent; aroma; fragrance	
PERFUSE	sprinkle; bedew; permeate	
PERGOLA	pergula; arbour	
PERHAPS	aiblins; peradventure	
PERIAPT	amulet; charm; talisman	
PERIDOT	green jewel; olivine	mn
PERIGEE	point nearest to earth of other orbits	
PERIKON	detector	ro
PERIQUE	Louisiana tobacco	
PERIWIG	peruke	
PERJURE	forswear	
PERJURY	false testimony	lw
PERKIER	more irrepressible	
PERKILY	saucily; jauntily; airily	
PERKING	peering, smartening up	
PERLITE	vitreous rock; aggregate in sandless gypsum plaster	mn, bd
PERMIAN	geological era	gl
PERMUTE	commute; change	
PEROPOD	rudimentary leg	zo

361

PERORAL	surrounding the mouth	zo
PEROSIS	slipped tendon	vt
PERPEND	ratiocinate; cogitate	
PERPEND	bonding stone	
PERPLEX	puzzle; nonplus; embarrass	
PERRIER	catapult; a table water	
PER-SALT	salt corresponding to per-acid	
PERSEID	a meteor from Perseus	
PERSEUS	slew Medusa; a constellation	
PERSIAN	Iranian	
PERSIST	persevere; continue; last	
PERSONA	(grata); actor's mask	
PERSPEX	a glazing material	
PERTAIN	to relate to; concern	
PERTURB	disturb; agitate; disquiet	
PERTUSE	riddled; bored	
PERUSAL	careful reading	
PERUSED	read; studied; examined	
PERUSER	a scrutineer of pages	pr
PERVADE	perfuse; impregnate; imbue	
PERVERT	deviate; lead astray	
PESHITO	Syriac Testament	rl
PESKILY	annoyingly	
PESTLED	pounded in a mortar	
PETALED	petalled; with petals	bt
PETASMA	curtainlike structure in prawns	
		zo
PETASUS	Mercury's winged cap	
PETERED	pottered; exhausted; (cards)	
PETEREL	petrel; Mother Carey's chick	zo
PETIOLE	leaf-stalk; pedicle	bt
PETRAIL	heavy framing beam	cr
PETRARY	catapult for stones	
PETREAN	stony	
PETRIFY	stupefy; dumbfound; stun	
PETRINE	according to St Peter	rl
PETROUS	rocklike	
PETTILY	meanly; trivially	
PETTING	fondling; canoodling	
PETTISH	peevish; fretful; querulous	
PETUNIA	a flower	bt
PETZITE	silver/gold telluride	mn
PEW-RENT	rent paid for use of pew	rl
PEWTERY	(pewter)	
PFENNIG	German copper coin	nm
PHACOID	lenticular	md
PHAETON	sky-hog; four-wheel carriage	
PHAETON	boatswain-bird	zo
PHALANX	compact body	
PHALLIC	Bacchanalian	
PHALLUS	symbol of procreation; penis	pl
PHANTOM	spectral; illusive; ghost	
PHARAOH	Egyptian title	
PHARATE	of development phase in insects	
PHARYNX	upper part of gullet	md
PHASING	correcting screen picture of facsimiles	tc, tv
PHELLEM	tissue external to phellogen	bt
PHENATE	(phenol)	ch
PHENOIC	carbolic	ch
PHIDIAS	Greek sculptor	

PHILTRE	philter; love potion	
PHINEAS	mascot of Univ. Coll. Hosp.	
PHLOEUM	phloem; bark-fibre	bt
PHOCINE	(seals)	zo
PHOEBUS	Apollo; the sun	
PHOENIX	date palm; fabulous bird	zo
PHONATE	to utter inarticulately	
PHONEME	relevant sound (linguistics)	
PHONICS	harmony; phonetics	
PHONING	telephoning	
PHONISM	synesthesia; noises off	
PHORESY	transport by clinging to animal	
		zo
PHORONE	acetone condensation product	
		ch
PHOTICS	science of light	
PHOTISM	colour sensation	
PHOTOMA	hallucinated flash of light	
PHRAGMA	septum or partition	zo
PHRASED	expressed; styled	
PHRASER	phrase-monger	
PHRATRY	tribal subdivision	
PHRENIC	diaphragmatic	md
PHRENSY	frenzy; madness; delirium	
PHYSICS	a science	
PHYTOID	plant-like	bt
PIACERE	at pleasure	mu
PIAFFER	a horse gait	
PIANINA	small piano	mu
PIANISM	musical technique	mu
PIANIST	an expert on the ivories	mu
PIANOLA	self-playing piano	mu
PIARIST	philanthropist, A.D. 1617	
PIASTRE	(Egypt)	nm
PIBROCH	a tune; bagpipe (Sc.)	mu
PICADOR	mounted bull-fighter	
PICAMAR	tar extract	
PICCAGE	pitch-money	lw
PICCOLO	small flute	mu
PICEOUS	pitch-black	
PICKAXE	pointed chopper	to
PICKING	petty larceny; choosing	
PICKLED	preserved	
PICK-OFF	automation device	
PICOTEE	carnation	bt
PICOTTE	little lace loop	
PICQUET	piquet; card game	
PICRATE	an explosive; lyddite	ch
PICRINE	foxglove extract	bt
PICRITE	olivine; peridot	mn
PICTISH	Celtic	
PICTURE	portrait; drawing; imagine	
PIDDOCK	mollusc	zo
PIEBALD	pyebald; motley	
PIECING	patching; uniting	
PIERAGE	pier tolls	
PIERCED	transfixed; impaled	
PIERCER	borer; gimlet; drill	
PIERIAN	(Muses); (Mount Pierus)	
PIERROT	an entertainer	
PIETISM	sanctimoniousness	

PIETIST	religious sect	rl
PIEWIFE	lapwing	zo
PIEZOID	piezo crystal blank	el
PIFFERO	oboe; organ-stop	mu
PIFFLED	chattered; drivelled	
PIG-DEER	invented animal	zo
PIGEYED	with small eyes	
PIGGERY	pig-sty	
PIGGING	living higgledy-piggledy	
PIGGISH	hoggish; swinish; messy	
PIGHTLE	small enclosure	
PIG-IRON	iron ingots	
PIG-LEAD	cast lead	
PIGMEAN	pygmean; Lilliputian	
PIGMENT	paint; colour; tincture	pt
PIGMIES	pygmies	
PIGNONS	fir-cone seeds	bt
PIGSKIN	(leather); (saddle)	le
PIGTAIL	plait of hair	
PIG-WASH	hog-wash	
PIKELET	} a crumpet; a tea-cake	
PIKELIN		
PIKEMAN	turnpike gatekeeper	
PIKRITE	igneous rock	mn
PILCHER	a scabbard	
PILEATE	cap-shaped	
PILFERY	petty theft; larceny	lw
PILGRIM	palmer; devotee; wayfarer	
PILKINS	pill-corn; oats	bt
PILLAGE	rifle; sack; ravage; loot	
PILLBOX	concrete emplacement; hat for ladies, pages, uniform	tx
PILLING	blackballing	
PILLION	padded saddle	
PILLORY	expose to ridicule	
PILLOWY	yielding; soft	
PILOTED	steered; conducted; guided	
PILOTIS	building on columns	ar
PILTOCK	coalfish	zo
PILULAR	(pills)	
PIMELIC	a fat product	ch
PIMENTA	} allspice; Jamaica pepper	
PIMENTO		bt, ck
PIMPLED	blotched	
PINACOL	tetra alkyl glycol	ch
PINBONE	hipbone of quadruped	zo
PIN-CASE	pin etui	
PINCERS	pliers	to
PINCHED	gripped; purloined	
PINCHER	sea fish	zo
PINCHES	nips	
PINDARI	Indian freebooter	
PINE-OIL	oil from resin	
PINETUM	plantation of pine-trees	bt
PIN-FIRE	(cartridge)	
PIN-FISH	a scaly fish; sailor's choice	zo
PINFOLD	cattle pound	

PINGING	like a bullet	
PINGUID	fat; greasy; unctuous	pt
PINHEAD	top of a pin; minute	
PIN-HOLD	pin-housing	
PINHOLE	tiny aperture	
PINK-EYE	a horse disease	vt
PINKING	scalloping; knocking	
PINKISH	somewhat pink	
PINNACE	a man-of-war's boat	nt
PINNATE	pennate; feathered	bt
PINNING	making fast	
PINNOCK	tom-tit	zo
PINNULA	} branchlet; small feather	
PINNULE		bt, zo
PINTADO	guinea-fowl; chintz; painted or printed calico 17th cent Sp.	zo, tx
PINTAIL	a duck	zo
PINT-POT	vessel holding pint	me
PIN-WORK	(flexing flax)	
PIONEER	forerunner; initiator, originator; 1st bowl as pilot	
PIONING	pioneering (Spens.)	
PIOUSLY	devoutly; religiously	
PIP-EMMA	p.m. (signalling)	
PIPERIC	peppery	
PIPETTE	graduated tube	
PIPLESS	seedless	bt
PIPPING	pilling; defeating; de-seeding	ck
PIQUANT	stimulating; caustic; tart	
PIQUING	irritating; nettling	
PIRAGUA	a dug-out canoe	nt
PIRATED	plundered; marauded	
PIRATIC	infringing; piratical	
PIROGUE	flat-bottomed boat (Sp.)	nt
PISCARY	fishing rights	
PISCINA	basin; fish-pond	rl
PISCINE	fishy; swimming pool (Fr.)	
PISMIRE	an ant; emmet	zo
PISTOLE	Spanish golden coin	nm
PITAPAT	in a flutter	
PITCHED	flung; tossed; planted; cast	
PITCHER	eared jug; the thrower (baseball); (horseshoe valiant)	
PITCOAL	coal from underground	mn
PITEOUS	woeful; sorry; compassionate	
PITFALL	a trap; snare; danger	
PIT-HEAD	top of coal mine	
PITHILY	tersely; concisely; briefly	
PITHING	extracting the marrow	
PITH-RAY	root or stem cell sheet	bt
PITIFUL	humane; lenient; wretched	
PIT-MIRK	dark as pitch (Sc.)	
PITTING	corrosion; striving; seed removal; pox marks	pb

PITTING	technique of plaster blowing; contesting	**bd**
PITTITE	playgoer	
PITUITA	} phlegm	**md**
PITUITE		
PITYING	commiserating; condoling	
PIVOTAL	axial	
PIVOTED	hinged; centred on	
PIXY-LED	bewildered	
PLACARD	bill; poster; notice	
PLACATE	pacify; conciliate; appease	
PLACEBO	imitation drug; prayer (R.C. mass)	**md, rl**
PLACING	identifying; assigning	
PLACKET	slit; pocket	
PLACODE	platelike structure	**zo**
PLACOID	scaly	
PLACULA	small plate; plaque	
PLAFOND	ceiling; a soffit	
PLAGIUM	kidnapping	**lw**
PLAGUED	distracted	
PLAGUER	a vexatious person	
PLAGULA	chitinous plate in solifugae	**zo**
PLAIDED	wearing a tartan	
PLAINER	clearer; more obvious	
PLAINLY	simply; clearly; candidly	
PLAITED	folded; woven	
PLAITER	an interlacer	
PLANARY	flat; level	
PLANCHE	body position (gymnastics)	
PLANCON	octagonally hewn log	**fr**
PLANING	smoothing; aeroplaning	
PLANISH	to hammer smooth	
PLANKED	laid down; floored	
PLANNED	sketched; schemed	
PLANNER	a projector; designer	
PLANTAR	(sole of foot)	
PLANTED	instilled; inculcated; sown	
PLANTER	settler; grower	
PLANULA	embryo protoplasm	**zo**
PLANXTY	Welsh lament	
PLASHED	splashed; dabbled	
PLASMIC	proto-plasmic	
PLASMID	changeable cytoplasm structure	**bl**
PLASMIN	fibrin-destroying blood substance	**ch**
PLASMON	flour-like food	
PLASTER	sinapism; daub; stucco	
PLASTIC	elastic; pliable; yielding	
PLASTID	living cell	**zo**
PLATANE	plane-tree	**bt**
PLATEAU	tableland; highland; ornamental stand on low plinth; shallow dish	
PLATEAU	flattened graphic curve; no reaction	**ma**
PLATINA	platinum	**ch**
PLATING	sheathing	

PLATOON	a squad (army); group of players (Am. football) (baseball)	
PLATTED	plaited; weaved	
PLATTER	wooden plate	
PLAUDIT	applause; approbation	
PLAY-BOX	theatre seat	
PLAYBOY	Lothario	
PLAY-DAY	holiday	
PLAYFUL	sportive; frolicsome	
PLAYING	acting; competing; romping	
PLAY-OFF	repeat match after a tie	**ga**
PLEADED	entreated; argued	**lw**
PLEADER	barrister; advocate	**lw**
PLEASED	delighted; contented; obliged	
PLEASER	charmer; gratifier	
PLEATED	platted; interlaced	
PLECTRE	plectrum; plectron	**mu**
PLEDGED	pawned; engaged	
PLEDGEE	pawnbroker	
PLEDGER	pawnbroker's customer	
PLEDGET	lint compress	**md**
PLEIADS	the Pleiades; 7 stars in Taurus	
PLENARY	in full; complete; entire	
PLENISH	provide; equip	
PLENIST	spacious materialist	
PLEOPOD	abdominal swimming appendage	**zo**
PLEROMA	abundance; fullness	
PLEROME	centre of apical meristem	**bt**
PLEURAL	(lungs)	**md**
PLEURON	shell extension	**zo**
PLEXURE	weaving; texture	
PLIABLE	limber; tractable; supple	
PLIABLY	flexibly; lithely	
PLIANCY	flexibility	
PLICATE	folded; plaited	
PLIFORM	in the form of a fold	
PLIMMED	swollen	
PLISKIE	plight (Sc.)	
PLODDED	toiled; drudged	
PLODDER	steady worker	
PLOPPED	plumped	
PLOSIVE	explosive (sound)	
PLOTFUL	full of schemes	
PLOTTED	planned; schemed; concocted	
PLOTTER	intriguer; conspirator	
PLOTTIE	mulled wine (Sc.)	
PLOUTER	to paddle or dabble	
PLOUTOS	plutonic wealth; riches	
PLOW-BOY	ploughboy	
PLOWING	ploughing	
PLOWMAN	ploughman, (lunch)	
PLUCKED	failed to pass; pulled	
PLUCKER	feather remover	
PLUGGED	plodded; shot; sealed	
PLUGGER	stopper	
PLUMAGE	plumery; feathers	
PLUMBED	measured; made vertical	
PLUMBER	lead-worker	

PLUMBUM	} lead	ch
PLUMBIC		
PLUMCOT	plum-apricot	bt
PLUMERY	display of plumes	
PLUMING	self-congratulation	
PLUMIST	feather-dresser	
PLUMMET	lead bob	
PLUMOSE	plumous; feathery	
PLUMPED	fell suddenly	
PLUMPER	chubbier; fatter; stouter	
PLUMPLY	roundly; fully	
PLUMULE	plumula; bud	bt
PLUNDER	loot; spoil; pillage; booty	
PLUNGED	dived; gambled heavily	
PLUNGER	part of a pump	
PLUNKET	blue colour	
PLUTEUS	pelagic larval form	zo
PLUVIAL	rainy; humid	
PLUVIUS	Jupiter	
PLY-WOOD	laminated wood	
POACEAE	the grasses	bt
POACHED	trespassed; stabbed; (eggs)	
POACHER	a toiler; setter of snares	
POCHARD	a duck	zo
POCHOIR	stencil colour process	pr
POCK-PIT	pock-mark	md
PODAGRA	gout	md
PODALIC	pertaining to feet	
PODDING	producing pods	
PODESTA	Italian magistrate	
PODITIC	(crab's leg)	zo
PODRIDA	Spanish stew	
POE-BIRD	tui; parson bird; (NZ)	zo
POEISIS	creation	
POETESS	lyrical lady	
POETICS	criticism of poetry	
POETIZE	poetise; versify	
POINDED	pounded; distrained	lw
POINTED	acute; sharp; keen; significant	
POINTEL	pencil; spike; style	
POINTER	fescue; indicator	zo
POISING	balancing; loading	
POITREL	horse-armour	
POLACCA	} Mediterranean sailing	
POLACRE	vessel	nt
POLACKA	polonaise (Polish dance)	mu
POLAIRE	ancient leather satchel for books	
POLARIS	guided missile	
POLARON	trapped electron	el
POLDERS	reclaimed land	
POLE-AXE	poll-axe	to
POLE-CAT	civet	zo
POLEMIC	controversial; contentious	
POLENTA	Italian maize porridge	
POLICED	regulated	
POLIGAR	S. Ind. village chieftain	
POLITER	more courteous or civil	
POLITIC	statesmanlike; discreet	
POLLACK	sea-fish, pollock, chub	zo
POLLARD	stag after casting his antlers	

POLLARD	lopped; bran; the chub	zo
POLL-AXE	pole-axe	to
POLLENT	strong; mighty; puissant	
POLLING	voting; lopping (trees);	
	multidrop network act	tc, bt
POLL-MAN	pass-man (Cam.)	
POLL-TAX	capitation tax	
POLLUTE	defile; profane; corrupt	
POLOIST	polo player	
POLONYM	joint-authorship name, work	
POLSTER	lichen moss on glacial rock	
	(Glacier Mouse) (Scand.)	bt
POLYACT	rayed	
POLYGON	angular figure	
POLYGYN	plant genus	bt
POLYMER	complex compound	ch
POLYOPY	multiple vision	
POLYOSE	polysaccharide	ch
POLYPOD	having all appendages	zo
POLYPUS	sea-anemone; coral	zo
POLYZOA	barnacles	zo
POMATUM	an unguent	
POMELOE	citron of shaddock kind	bt
POMEROY	the king-apple	bt
POMFRET	a fish	zo
POMMAGE	crushed apples	
POMMARD	a Burgundy wine	
POMPANO	edible fish (N. Amer.)	zo
POMPION	pumpkin	bt
POMPIRE	an apple	bt
POMPOSO	with due pomp	mu
POMPOUS	self-important; grandiose	
PONCEAU	poppy; poppy-coloured	bt
PONDAGE	water in a pond	
PONDING	collecting into a pond	
PONENTE	W. wind Mediterranean (It.)	mt
PONGIDS	long-armed anthropoid tailless	
	(gibbons) apes	zo
PONIARD	dagger	
PONTAGE	bridge toll	
PONTIFF	high priest; pope	rl
PONTINE	Roman marsh	
PONTOON	bridge of boats; card game	
POOH-BAH	a pluralist	
POOLING	merging; combining	
POOPING	(following sea)	
POOR-BOX	alms for the poor	
POOREST	most necessitous; neediest	
POOR-LAW	charity provisions	
POPCORN	parched maize	bt
POPEDOM	papality	rl
POP-EYED	with protruding eyes	
POPOVER	Amer. 'Yorkshire pudding'	ck
POPPIED	drowsy; slumbrous; narcotic	
POPPING	exploding; pawning; darting;	
	surface pitting; (champagne);	
	(eyes)	pb
POPPLED	rippled; bubbled	
POP-SHOP	pawn-shop	
POPULAR	familiar; prevailing; current	

POP-WEED	bladder-wort	bt
PORCATE	ridged	
PORCINE	piggy; swinish; suiform	zo
PORIFER	a sponge	
PORK-PIE	type of hat; meat in pastry	ck
POROSIS	bone formation	md
POROTIC	(porosis); callous	md
PORPHIN	pyrrole/methene nucleus group	
		ch
PORRECT	extended	
PORRIGO	dandruff	md
PORTAGE	porterage	
PORT-BAR	harbour bar	
PORTEND	foretell; augur; bode	
PORTENT	an evil omen; presage	
PORTICO	porch; stoa; colonnade	
PORTIFY	aggrandise	
PORTING	carrying; conveying	nt
PORTION	bit; part; share; division	
PORTRAY	paint; describe	
PORZANA	water-rail; crake	zo
POSAUNE	German trombone	mu
POSITED	postulated	
POSITIF	choir organ (Fr.)	
POSSESS	own; hold; keep; control	
POSTAGE	mail carriage fee	
POST-BAG	sack for letters	
POST-BOX	letter-box	
POST-BOY	mail collector	
POST-DAY	day for sending/getting mail	
POSTEEN	Kashmir sheepskin coat	
POSTERN	back-door; small gate	
POSTFIX	affix; suffix; append	
POSTING	mailing; recording	
POSTMAN	letter carrier	
POSTURE	pose; attitude; position	
POST-WAR	since hostilities ended	
POTABLE	drinkable; liquid	
POTAGER	porringer	
POTAMIC	pertaining to rivers	go
POTANCE	part of a watch	
POTARGO	a pickle	
POTASSA	potash	ch
POTATOR	an imbiber; toper	
POTCHER	paper-pulp machine	pp
POTENCE	heraldic gibbet	hd
POTENCE	inverted cock	hr
POTENCY	latent ability; power; effectiveness; strength	
POT-HEAD	dunderhead	
POTHEEN	Irish whiskey	
POT-HERB	cookery flavouring	
POT-HOLE	earth cavity	
POT-HOOK	fireplace hook	
POTICHE	porcelain vase	
POT-LIFE	period in pot before paint jells; also before food deteriorates	
		ck
POT-LUCK	makeshift meal; make-do	ck
POTOROO	rat kangaroo	zo

POT-SHOP	small inn	
POT-SHOT	random round	
POTTAGE	a mess; a stew	
POTTERY	earthenware	
POTTING	preserving; shooting	
POUCHED	bagged; marsupial	zo
POULARD	plump pullet	zo
POULTER	poulterer (Shak.)	
POULTRY	fattened fowls	zo
POUNCED	with claws; sprang; swooped	
POUNDAL	unit of force	me
POUNDED	confined; bruised	
POUNDER	pestle	
POURING	streaming; gushing	
POUTING	registering displeasure	
POVERTY	want; penury; indigence	
POWDERY	pulverous; floury; dusty	
POWERED	engined	
PRACTIC	deceitful; skilful (Shak.)	
PRAESES	academical disputers	
PRAETOR	Roman magistrate	
PRAIRIE	treeless grassy lands	go
PRAISED	lauded; glorified	
PRAISER	laudator; extoller; eulogizer	
PRAKARA	temple passage (India)	
PRAKRIT	Sanskrit and allied languages	
PRALINE	sweetmeat coated in chocolate, or sugar	ck
PRANCED	strutted; bounded	
PRANGED	bombed heavily; struck	
PRANKED	all dressed up; prinked	
PRANKER	practical joker; a dude	
PRATIES	potatoes (Irish)	bt
PRATING	babbling; boasting	
PRATTLE	idle chatter	
PRAYING	imploring; craving; begging	
PREACHY	tediously didactic	
PREBEND	canon's stipend	rl
PRECEDE	herald; usher; introduce	
PRECEPT	behest; maxim; rule; canon	
PRECIPE	writ	lw
PRECISE	exact; accurate; finical	
PREDATE	ante-date	
PREDIAL	(farm estate)	
PREDICT	presage; portend; foretell	
PREDONE	worn-out; exhausted	
PREDOOM	prejudge	
PRE-ECHO	prior sound from record defect	
PRE-EDIT	of input run of data for records	
		cp
PREEMPT	appropriate in advance	
PREENED	tidied up	
PREFACE	preamble; proem; prologue	
PREFECT	French magistrate; monitor	
PREFINE	limit; delimit	
PREFORM	form beforehand	
PREFORM	larger moulding composition	
PREHEAT	heat (oven) up for use	ck
PRELACY	episcopal church government	rl
PRELATE	church dignitary	rl

PRELECT	discourse; lecture; address	
PRELIMS	introductory features of book	
PRELIMS	examinations	
PRELUDE	preface; exordium	**mu**
PREMIAL	at a premium	
PREMIER	first; principal; P.M.	
PREMISE	antecedent proposition	
PREMISS	logical premise	
PREMIUM	bounty; fee; reward; bonus	
PRENDER	right of seizure	**lw**
PREORAL	in front of the jaw	
PREPAID	paid in advance	
PREPARE	make ready; manufacture	
PREPUCE	foreskin, penile cover	**md**
PREPUPA	insect stage before larval ecdysis	
PRERUPT	abrupt; steep	
PRESAGE	foretell; predict; prophesy	
PRESEEN	foreseen	
PRESELL	promote products in advance	
PRESENT	here; now; existing; current	
PRESENT	exhibit; proffer; gift	
PRESIDE	officiate; direct; control	
PRESSED	urged; crushed; encroached	
PRESSER	squeezer	
PRESSEZ	press-on, increase speed (Fr.)	**mu**
PRESSOR	causing arterial pressure rise	**zo**
PRESTER	mythical medieval priest	
PRESUME	assume; reckon; venture	
PRETEND	feign; simulate; claim	
PRETEST	pre-examine, check, control	
PRETEXT	excuse; plea; cloak	
PRETONE	(accented syllable)	
PRETZEL	crisp biscuit	
PREVAIL	dominate; win; succeed	
PREVENE	precede	
PREVENT	hinder; hamper; thwart	
PREVIEW	foresee	
PREVISE	forewarn; foresee	
PREWARN	give notice of	
PREYFUL	predatory	
PREYING	plundering; wasting; robbing	
PRIAPUS	god of procreation	
PRICING	costing; valuing; rating	
PRICKED	spurred; punctured; bored	
PRICKER	prickle; light horseman	
PRICKET	early candlestick	
PRICKET	a young buck	**zo**
PRICKET	stone-crop	**bt**
PRICKLE	to prick; a thorn	**bt**
PRICKLY	spinate; spicate	
PRIDIAN	of yesterday	
PRIDING	valuing; esteeming highly	
PRIDWIN	King Arthur's shield	
PRIGGED	filched; purloined; nabbed	
PRIGGER	thief; pincher	
PRIMACY	leading archbishopric	**rl**
PRIMAGE	a lading charge	
PRIMARY	main; first; pristine; initial	
PRIMATE	genus of apes; archbishop	**zo, rl**
PRIMELY	originally; excellently	
PRIMERO	card game	
PRIMEUR	early crop	
PRIMINE	outer husk	**bt**
PRIMING	(powder); first coat	**pt**
PRIMMED	formed precisely	
PRIMSIE	demure; prim (Sc.)	
PRIMULA	primrose genus	**bt**
PRINKED	pranked; all dressed up	
PRINKER	(dressed showily)	
PRINTED	published; pressed; issued	
PRINTER	typographer	
PRISAGE	a levy on wines	
PRISERE	primary succession	**bt**
PRISING	forcing open; levering	
PRISTIS	saw-fish	**zo**
PRITHEE	I pray thee	
PRIVACY	seclusion; solitude; retreat	
PRIVATE	soldier; personal; unofficial	
PRIVILY	privately, confidentially	
PRIVITY	secrecy; cognizance	
PRIZAGE	prisage; crown levy	
PRIZING	appreciating; valuing	
PROBANG	whalebone swab	**md**
PROBATE	proof of a will	**lw**
PROBING	scrutinizing; testing; sifting	
PROBITY	proved integrity; sincerity	
PROBLEM	enigma; query; conundrum	
PROCARP	female organ in rhodophyta	**bt**
PROCEED	advance; continue; act	
PROCESS	operation; course; progress	
PROCESS	method; patterning of data	**cp**
PROCTOR	university official	**lw**
PROCURE	get; obtain; induce	
PROCYON	lesser Dog-star	
PRODDED	goaded; shoved; poked	
PRODDER	inciter; stimulator	
PRODIFY	modify production car for motor racing	
PRODIGY	marvel; wonder; portent	
PRODUCE	engender; showed; bear	
PRODUCT	staple; yield; result of fabrication or multiplication	**cp, ck**
PROFACE	May it profit you!	
PROFANE	desecrate; secular	
PROFESS	own; aver; proclaim	
PROFFER	offer; tender; volunteer	
PROFILE	outline; side view; butter board (mortar board)	**bd**
PROFUSE	lavish; prodigal; copious	
PROGENY	offspring; issue; young	
PROGGED	begged; prodded; (proctored)	
PROGRAM	programme; syllabus	
PROJECT	propel; contrive; jut	
PROLATE	extended	
PROLEGS	legs of caterpillars	**zo**
PROLINE	protein cleavage product	**ch**
PROLONG	protract; lengthen; sustain	

PROMINE	cancer-cell growth stimulant **md**	
PROMISE	pledge; engage; stipulate	
PROMOTE	further; aid; elevate; organise; sponsor	
PRONAOS	temple porch	
PRONATE	face or palms downwards	
PRONELY	lying down	
PRONGED	fork-like; bifurcated	
PRONOTA	beetles' backs **zo**	
PRONOUN	word replacing noun	
PROOFED	tried; tested	
PROOTIC	an ear-bone **md**	
PROPALE	to disclose	
PROPANE	paraffin gas	
PROPEND	to favour; lean forward	
PROPENE	propyl alcohol **ch**	
PROPHET	seer; augur; preacher	
PROPINE	pledge; guarantee	
PROPINE	methyl acetylene **ch**	
PROPJET	a turbojet **ae**	
PROPOSE	suggest; intend; purpose	
PROPPED	shored; strutted; supported	
PROPUGN	vindicate; defend	
PRORATE	assess pro rata	
PRORSAD	prorsal; anterior **md**	
PROSAIC	unexciting; dull; humdrum	
PROSIFY	turn into prose	
PROSILY	unimaginatively	
PROSING	talking tediously	
PROSODY	(harmonious writing)	
PROSPER	thrive; flourish; succeed	
PROTEAN	in many guises	
PROTECT	shield; defend; ward	
PROTEGE	trusted nominee	
PROTEID	} complex substances in	
PROTEIN	} food, necessary for diet **ch**	
PROTEND	hold out; extend	
PROTEST	expostulate; exclaim; object	
PROTEUS	sea-god of Carpathian Sea	
PROTIUM	hydrogen isotope **ch**	
PROTYLE	hypothetical nucleus	
PROUDER	more arrogant and haughty	
PROUDLY	majestically; imperiously	
PROVAND	provision; provend (Shak.)	
PROVANT	of inferior quality	
PROVERB	saw; adage; epigram; maxim	
PROVIDE	supply; produce; survey	
PROVINE	(vine culture)	
PROVING	establishing; testing; trying; trial **lw**	
PROVING	fault testing program **cp**	
PROVISO	a condition	
PROVOKE	infuriate; enrage; rouse	
PROVOST	magistrate **rl**	
PROWESS	valour; skill; dexterity	
PROWEST	most valiant (obs.)	
PROWLED	slunk; roved; roamed	
PROWLER	stealthy stalker	
PROXIME	nearest	

PROXIMO	next month	
PRUDENT	wise; cautious; frugal	
PRUDERY	mock modesty	
PRUDISH	very formal; puritanical	
PRUNING	lopping; clipping; trimming	
PRURIGO	an itch **md**	
PRUSSIC	acid; a cyanide **ch**	
PRY-OVER	sideways movement for Canadian canoes	
PRYTANY	Athenian Council division	
PRYTHEE	I pray thee!	
PSALTER	psalm book; rosary	
PSCHENT	royal crown of ancient Egypt	
PSOATIC	(tenderloin) **md**	
PSYCHAL	spiritualistic	
PSYCHIC	not based on materialism	
PSYCHRO-	of coldness (Gr.) **cf**	
PTARMIC	sneezing mixture **md**	
PTERION	(craniology) **md**	
PTEROMA	Greek peridrome; side-wall	
PTEROPE	flying fox; fruit-bat **zo**	
PTOMAIN	} toxic matter	
PTOMAINE	} **md**	
PTYALIN	(saliva) **md**	
PUBERAL	of age	
PUBERTY	the generative age	
PUBLISH	announce; disclose; blazon	
PUCELLA	wine-glass top opener **gs**	
PUCELLE	Joan of Arc	
PUCERON	plant louse **zo**	
PUCKERY	wrinkled	
PUCKISH	impish; mischievous	
PUCK-OUT	free hit by defenders (hurling)	
PUDDING	fruity farinaceous food	
PUDDLED	stirred up the mud	
PUDDLER	iron-worker	
PUDENCY	modesty; bashfulness	
PUEBLAN	Mexican aborigine	
PUERILE	child-like, irresponsible, behaviour **pc**	
PUERING	skin-steeping/softening **le**	
PUFF-BOX	compact	
PUFFERY	} extravagant; advertisement	
PUFFING	}	
PUFFIER	more swollen	
PUFFILY	bombastically	
PUGAREE	puggree; puggery; Ind. scarf	
PUGGING	(sound prevention); ceramics	
PUGGREE	Indian scarf for topee	
PUGMILL	clay mill	
PUG-NOSE	retroussé	
PULIALL	herb pennyroyal **bt**	
PULLIES	pulley-wheels	
PULLING	extracting; wresting; towing; using only arms (swimming)	
PULLMAN	(railway carriage)	
PULL-OUT	extensible	
PULPIFY	mash	
PULPING	reducing to pulp	
PULPOUS	pulpy	

PULSATE	throb; palpitate; quiver	
PULSING	beating; vibrating; throbbing	
PULSION	propulsion	
PUMMAGE	crushed apples	
PUMPAGE	the amount pumped	
PUMPING	extracting information; syphoning liquids	
PUMPING	varying weight pressures in skateboarding	
PUMPKIN	pumpion; quashey; a gourd	**bt**
PUMP-ROD	part of engine	**au**
PUNCHED	perforated; struck	
PUNCHER	a bruiser; a drover	
PUNCH-UP	fist-fight (boxing)	
PUNCTUM	marking dot; tiny aperture	**zo**
PUNGENT	acrid; caustic; tart	
PUNJABI	an Indo-Aryan language	
PUNNAGE	punning	
PUNNING	quipping	
PUNSTER	a pun maker	
PUNT-GUN	for hijacking scull	
PUNTING	poling a punt forward; gambling against banker; (football)	
PUPATED	formed a chrysalis	**zo**
PURANIC	(Brahmin scriptures)	**rl**
PURBECK	Dorset stone	**mn**
PURFLED	decorated	**ar**
PURFLEW	wrought border	
PURGING	cleaning up; pruning	
PURITAN	religious bigot	
PURLIEU	slum; environs	
PURLINE	timber-work	
PURLING	rippling	
PURLOIN	steal; pilfer; filch	
PURPLED	dyed purple	
PURPLES	livid spots	**md**
PURPORT	signification; import	
PURPOSE	aim; intent; object	
PURPURA	Tyrian purple	**zo**
PURPURE	heraldic purple	**hd**
PURRING	curring; (feline felicitude)	
PURROCK	paddock	
PURSING	wrinkling	
PURSUED	continued; hunted; practised	
PURSUER	plaintiff (Sc.)	**lw**
PURSUIT	chase; search; calling; track cycling contests with equidistant starts	
PURVIEW	extent; scope; range	
PUSHFUL	enterprising; self-assertive	
PUSHING	vigorous; jostling; thrusting	
PUSH-OFF	leave hastily, forced departure	
PUSHPIN	a child's game	**ga**
PUSH-ROD	auto engine part	**au**
PUSTAKA	magic/divine book of bark strips (Indon.)	
PUSTULE	pimple	**md**
PUSZTAS	steppes, Hungary	
PUTAMEN	fruit-stone; husk	**bt**
PUTAMEN	lenticular nucleus	**md**

PUTLOGS	horizontal bearers of scaffolding	**bd**
PUTRIFY	rot; decay; decompose	
PUTTIED	fixed with putty	
PUTTIER	glazier	
PUTTIES	leg-wear; puttees	
PUTTING	(golf); (the weight)	
PUTTOCK	kite; buzzard	**zo**
PUTWITH	acknowledgement, addenda for book	
PUZZLED	perplexed; mystified	
PUZZLER	poser; riddler	
PYAEMIA	blood-poisoning	**md**
PYAEMIC	suffering from pyaemia	**md**
PYCNITE	topaz	**mn**
PYCNIUM	spermogonium in uredinales	**bt**
PYEBALD	piebald; of two colours	
PYE-BOOK	rules to determine Easter date	
PYGMEAN	pigmean; dwarfish	
PYGMIES	negrillos, negritas; 1.5 m. tall	
PYJAMAS	also pajamas; nightwear	
PYLORIC	of stomach-intestine entry	**zo**
PYLORUS	an outlet	**md**
PYRAMID	triangular on a square; tomb	**rl**
PYRENIN	paranuclein	**cy**
PYRETIC	fever-reducer	**md**
PYREXIA	fever	**md**
PYREXIC	feverish	**md**
PYRITES	an iron ore	
PYRITIC	(pyrites)	
PYROGEN	fever inducer	**md**
PYROSIS	indigestion; heartburn	**md**
PYROTIC	caustic; burning	**md**
PYRRHIC	war dance; costly	
PYRROLE	coal-tar constituent	**ch**
PYRUVIC	of an α-keto acid	**bc**
PYTHIAD	a period	
PYTHIAN	oracular	
PYXIDIA	capsules	**bt**

Q

Q-FACTOR	measure of efficiency of reactive electric circuit or of component	**el, nc**
QUABIRD	night heron	**zo**
QUACKED	boasted; practised quackery	
QUACKLE	croak; quack	
QUADRAT	filling piece in printing	**pr**
QUADREL	square tile	
QUADRIC	quadratic	
QUAFFED	tippled; swilled; caroused	
QUAFFER	deep drinker; soaker; toper	
QUAHAUG	American clam	**zo**
QUAILED	flinched; cowered; blenched	
QUAKERS	a sect	
QUAKERY	Quakerism	
QUAKING	shaking; quivering	
QUALIFY	entitle; regulate; dilute	

QUALITY	trait; attribute; grade	
QUAMASH	camass lily	bt
QUANACO	S. American llama	zo
QUANNET	flat file	to
QUANTAL	of small changes, amounts (Gr.)	cf
QUANTIC	algebraic function	
QUANTUM	a sufficiency; elemental unit of radiant energy; theory	el, nc
QUARREL	wrangle; brawl; bicker	
QUARREL	cross-bow bolt; diam. pane	
QUARTAN	every fourth day	
QUARTER	district; region; clemency	
QUARTET	quartette	mu
QUARTIC	of the fourth degree	
QUARTZY	(quartz)	
QUASARS	quasi-stellar radio sources	
QUASHED	rendered void; nullified	
QUASHEY	pumpkin; a gourd	bt
QUASSIA	bitter tonic	bt
QUASSIN	bitter extract	bt
QUATERN	a quarter; 4-pound loaf	
QUAVERY	tremulous; quivery; tottery	
QUAYAGE	quay dues	
QUEACHY	bog-like; unsteady; yielding	
QUEENED	played the queen	
QUEENLY	regal	
QUEERED	put at a disadvantage	
QUEERER	odder; rummier; stranger	
QUEERLY	quaintly; whimsically	
QUELLED	crushed; allayed; quenched	
QUELLER	subduer; represser	
QUERCUS	oak	bt
QUERELA	complaint	
QUERENT	inquirer; plaintiff	lw
QUERIED	doubted; challenged	
QUERIST	questioner; interrogator	
QUERLED	twirled	
QUERNAL	oaken	
QUESTED	sought; requested	
QUESTER	a seeker; searcher; candidate	
QUESTOR	Roman treasury official	
QUETZAL	resplendent trogon	nm, zo
QUIBBED	quipped; sneered	
QUIBBLE	prevaricate; cavil; trifle	
QUICKEN	revive; rouse; expedite	
QUICKER	faster; more swiftly	
QUICKIE	a fatuous film	
QUICKLY	rapidly; speedily; pronto	
QUIDDIT	a quibble	
QUIDDLE	to potter	
QUIETED	calmed; assuaged; mollified	
QUIETEN	lull; allay; pacify; soothe	
QUIETER	more placid or secluded	
QUIETLY	peacefully; serenely	
QUIETUS	discharge; death	
QUILLED	pleated; crimped	
QUILLET	a quibble; a furrow	
QUILLON	part of a sword-guard	
QUILTED	padded; tufted	

QUILTER	coverlet maker	
QUINARY	in fives; biquinary; (double binary)	
QUINATE	five-leafed	bt
QUININE	(cinchona)	md, bt
QUINNAT	king salmon	zo
QUINONE	(benzene)	ch
QUINTAD	pentad	
QUINTAL	a hundredweight	me
QUINTAL	100 lb or 100 kg	me
QUINTAN	recurring ague	md
QUINTAR	(Albania)	nm
QUINTET	5-part music	mu
QUINTIC	fifth degree	
QUINTUS	the fifth (Latin)	
QUIPPED	quibbled; taunted	
QUIRING	singing in unison	
QUISCHE	be still; calm; be silent	
QUITTAL	repayment; requital	
QUITTED	abandoned; forsook; left	
QUITTER	shirker; horse ulcer; deserter	vt
QUITTOR	chronic foot cartilage suppuration	vt
QUI-VIVE	alert	
QUIXOTE	a chivalrous Don	
QUIZZED	bantered; chaffed	
QUIZZER	a joker	
QUODLIN CODLIN	} cooking apple; boy	bt, ck
QUONDAM	former	
QUOTING	citing; pricing	
QUOTITY	quantity	

R

RABATED	beaten down; abated	
RABBANA	raffia matting (Madagascar)	
RABBITY	petty; rabbit-like	
RABBLER	puddler; iron-worker	
RABBONI	Jewish title	
RABIDLY	frantically; maniacally	
RABIFIC	causing hydrophobia	md
RABINET	ancient gun	
RABIOUS	raging mad	
RACCOON	N. American racoon	zo
RACE-CUP	a trophy	
RACEMED	clustered	bt
RACEMIC	acid from grapes	ch
RACEWAY	sluice	
RACKETS	racquet and ball game in court; (squash)	
RACKETT	woodwind, "sausage bassoon"	mu
RACKETY	bobbery; clamorous	
RACKING	decanting; straining	
RACQUET	racket	
RADDLED	interwoven; painted	
RADDOCK	ruddock; robin	zo
RADIALE	radiocarpal bone	md

RADIANT	beaming; effulgent; shining
RADIATE	sparkle; glitter; emit
RADICAL	essential; root; basic change, Liberal; molecular atoms
RADICAL	exacting skateboarding
RADICEL	small root of embryonic seedling **bt**
RADICLE	root; corm; rootlet
RADIOED	transmitted by wireless
RADULAR	rasping; rough
RAFFING	sweeping; snatching
RAFFISH	rakish; dissipated
RAFFLED	notched; (lottery)
RAFFLER	lottery organizer
RAFT-DOG	iron clamp
RAFTING	raft-work
RAG-BOLT	iron holdfast
RAG-BUSH	heathen shrine **bt**
RAG-DUST	rag refuse
RAGEFUL	angered; wroth; ireful
RAG-FAIR	old clothes sale
RAGGERY	rags collectively
RAGGING	plaguing; rampaging; deliberate slowing down of play (USA) **ga**
RAG-SHOP	ragpicker's emporium
RAGTIME	syncopation **mu**
RAGULED	jagged **hd**
RAG-WEED	ragwort **bt**
RAG-WOOL	shoddy
RAGWORK	mason's work using stones
RAGWORT	rag-weed **bt**
RAIDING	foraying; pillaging
RAILBUS	bus-engine railway coach **rw**
RAILCAR	self-propelled rail coach **rw**
RAILING	fencing; nagging; rating
RAILSAW	portable saw **to, rw**
RAILWAY	} iron road; train-track **rw**
RAILROAD	
RAIMENT	garb; vesture; apparel
RAINBOW	water-refracted sunlight
RAINING	pouring; showering
RAINMAP	weather chart
RAISING	erecting; levying; growing; ancient process of making hollow vessels from soft materials
RAKE-OFF	rebate
RAKSHAS	ghouls (Hindu mythology)
RALLIED	recovered; reformed
RALLIES	bouts; jamborees
RALLINE	(water-rails, etc.) **zo**
RAMADAN	} Mohammedan fast **rl**
RAMAZAN	
RAMBADE	boarding platform **nt**
RAMBLED	sauntered; maundered
RAMBLER	Dr Johnson's magazine
RAMBLER	a climbing rose **bt**
RAMEKIN	a cheese savoury **ck**
RAMENTA	scales on ferns **bt**

RAMEOUS	branching; ramulous
RAM-HEAD	iron lever; a cuckold
RAMLINE	guide line in ship-building
RAMMING	thrusting; forcing
RAMMISH	rank; strong-scented
RAMPAGE	frolic
RAMPANT	exuberant
RAMPART	rampire; fortified mound
RAMPICK	} dead-tree; tree-stump
RAMPIKE	
RAMPING	creeping; climbing; bounding
RAMPION	campanula **bt**
RAMPLER	a rover (Sc.)
RAMSKIN	cheese cake; ramekin **bt**
RAMSONS	garlic, broad-leaved **bt**
RAMSTAM	reckless; headlong (Sc.)
RAMULUS	small branch **bt**
RANCHED	(stock farming)
RANCHER	stock-breeder
RANCOUR	deep-seated enmity
RANGERS	riflemen
RANGIER	scythe (heraldic) **hd**
RANGING	ranking; roving; extending
RANIDAE	the frogs **zo**
RANKEST	coarsest; most rancid
RANKING	grading; ranging
RANKLED	festered; smouldered
RANSACK	rummage; pillage; plunder
RANTING	orating; declaiming; raving
RANTOCK	goosander **zo**
RAPE-OIL	cole-seed oil **bt**
RAPFULL	full of wind **nt**
RAPHAEL	an archangel; a painter
RAPHIDE	plant-cell crystal **bt**
RAPIDLY	speedily; swiftly; despatch
RAPLOCH	homespun (Sc.)
RAPPING	knocking; hitting; beating
RAPPING	mould pattern loosening **fd**
RAPPORT	harmony; consonance
RAPTURE	ecstasy; beatitude; bliss
RAREBIT	dainty morsel; (cheese on toast) Welsh **ck**
RASCONA	sail cargo boat, Venice **nt**
RASHING	thin layer of shale/poor coal **mn**
RASORES	gallinaceous birds **zo**
RASPING	grating; abrading
RASTRUM	a music-pen **mu**
RATABLE	taxable; assessable
RATABLY	by rate
RATAFIA	almond-flavoured biscuit
RATATAT	drumming **mu**
RATCHED	stretched; racked
RATCHEL	ratchil; loose stones
RATCHET	pawl; toothed bar
RAT-HOLE	retreat for rat
RATITAE	(ostriches, emus, kiwis) **zo**
RATLINE	} step of rigging ladder **nt**
RATLING	
RAT-RACE	career competition
RAT-TAIL	tapering

RATTEEN	twilled wool	**tx**
RATTERY	apostacy	
RATTING	quitting; abandoning	
RATTLED	clattered; shaken	
RATTLER	snake	**zo**
RATTOON	young sugar-cane	**bt**
RAT-TRAP	bicycle pedal	
RAUCITY	hoarseness	
RAUCOUS	harsh; roopy	
RAUNCHY	male ruggedness; strength	
RAVAGED	laid waste; devastated	
RAVAGER	despoiler; plunderer	
RAVELIN	part of a fort	
RAVENED	preyed; plundered	
RAVENER	ravager; devourer	
RAVINED	gullied	
RAVIOLI	meat-filled pasta cases (It.)	**ck**
RAWBONE	gaunt, lean person	
RAWCOLD	damp and cold (Shak.)	
RAWHEAD	bugaboo	
RAWHIDE	untanned skin	
RAWNESS	immaturity; callowness	
RAWPORT	porthole for an oar	**nt**
RAYLESS	dark	
REACHED	attained; arrived; stretched	
REACHER	stretcher	
REACTED	took violent action	
REACTOR	atomic power generator	**nc**
READIED	prepared	
READIER	prompter; more glib	
READILY	willingly; cheerfully	
READING	recital; version; studying	
READMIT	glove used when reading	
READ-OUT	transfer of data	**cp**
READ-OUT	data display on screen	
REAGENT	active agent	**ch**
REAGREE	reconcile	
REALGAR	red arsenic	**mn**
REALIEN	objects for study; teaching aids	
REALISM	naturalism (art); acceptance of limits to activity	
REALIST	a facer of facts	
REALITY	actuality; truth; verity	
REALIZE	realise; convert into cash	
REALLOT	re-assign	
REALTOR	estate agent (USA)	
REAMING	enlarging	
REANNEX	reunite	
REAPING	harvesting; gathering	
REAPPLY	try it again	
REARGUE	rehash	
REARING	breeding; lifting, raising	
REARISE	reascend	
REARMED	re-equipped	
RE-AROSE	got up again	
REAUMUR	scale of temperature	**ps**
REAVING	bereaving; ravaging	
REAWAKE	rouse again	
REBATED	blunted; diminished	
REBIRTH	renascence	

REBLOOM	impossible action	
REBOANT	resounding; reverberating	
REBORED	ennui resumed	
REBOUND	bounce; recoil; gain possession of ball (basketball)	
REBRACE	race by rebels	
REBUILD	re-edify	
REBUILT	re-erected	
REBUKED	chidden; upbraided	
REBUKER	reproacher	
REBURSE	repay	
RECARRY	carry anew	
RECEDED	retreated; withdrew	
RECEIPT	a recipe; formula; quittance	
RECEIVE	welcome; acquire; get	
RECENCY	newness	
RECHEAT	recall hounds	
RECITAL	concert; narration	
RECITED	narrated; rehearsed	
RECITER	relater	
RECKING	caring; heeding	
RECLAIM	rescue; salve; regain	
RECLAME	notoriety	
RECLASP	refasten	
RECLINE	lean; lie; rest; repose	
RECLOSE	fail to keep open	
RECLUSE	sequestered; a hermit	
RECOAST	coast back	
RECOUNT	tell; relate; enumerate	
RECOUPE	heraldic division	**hd**
RECOURE	recover (Spens.)	
RE-COVER	cover anew	
RECOVER	rally; revive; retrieve	
RECROSS	go back over	
RECRUIT	enlist; recuperate; novice	
RECTIFY	amend; correct; redress	
RECTION	grammatical influence	
RECTORY	rector's benefice	**rl**
RECTRIX	steering feather	**zo**
RECURVE	reflex	
RED-BIRD	bull-finch	**zo**
RED-BOOK	a register	
RED-CENT	copper cent	**nm**
RED-CLAY	raddle; reddle	
REDCOAT	a soldier	
REDCOCK	incendiary fire	
RED-CRAG	Pliocene rock	**mn**
RED-DEER	the common stag	**zo**
REDDEST	ultra-radical	
REDDING	arranging (Sc.)	
REDDISH	rubicund; Titian	
RED-DRUM	red-bass	**zo**
REDEYED	needing sleep	
RED-FISH	Pacific salmon	**zo**
RED-HAND	(Ulster)	
REDHEAD	a duck	**zo**
REDLEAD	minium	
REDLEGS	purple sandpiper	**zo**
REDNESS	ruddiness	
REDORSE	reverse of dorsal	

REDOUBT	fort	
REDOUND	conduce; lead; tend	
REDPOLL	linnet	zo
REDRAFT	revised copy	
REDRAWN	drawn again	
REDRESS	remedy; reparation	
REDRIVE	drive back	
RED-ROOT	buckthorn	bt
RED-SEAR	to break when too hot	
RED-SEED	small crustaceans	zo
REDSKIN	N. American Indian	
RED-TAIL	N. American buzzard	zo
REDTAPE	routine	
REDUCED	curtailed; abridged	
REDUCER	contractor	
RED-WEED	the poppy	
REDWING	fieldfare	zo
REDWOOD	sequoia	bt
RE-EDIFY	rebuild	
REEDING	moulding	ar
REEFING	shortening sail	nt
REEKING	fuming; smoking	
REELING	staggering; vacillating	
REEMING	caulking	nt
RE-ENTRY	regress; return	
RE-EQUIP	rearm	
RE-ERECT	rebuild	
REEVING	(passing a rope)	nt
REFEOFF	reinvest in a fief	
REFEREE	umpire; arbitrator; judge	
REFINED	highly cultivated	
REFINER	purifier; clarifier	
REFLAME	flare up again	
REFLECT	mirror; muse; meditate	
REFORGE	fashion anew	
REFRACT	to bend at an angle	
REFRAIN	chorus; forgo; abstain	
REFRESH	invigorate; revive; brace	
REFUGED	took sanctuary	
REFUGEE	a displaced person	
REFUSAL	declination; denial	
REFUSED	declined; denied; vetoed	
REFUSER	repudiator	
REFUTED	disproved; confuted	
REFUTER	rebutter	
REGALED	entertained sumptuously	
REGALIA	insignia of sovereignty	
REGALLY	royally	
REGATTA	series of races (rowing) (sailing) (powered boats)	nt
REGENCY	also regence	
REGIBLE	governable	
REGIMEN	regulation; diet	
REGNANT	ruling	
REGORGE	vomit	
REGRADE	re-assess	
REGRANT	grant again	
REGRATE	retail; treating hewn stone	bd
REGREDE	regrade (obs.)	
REGREET	welcome again	

REGRESS	return; re-entry	
REGULAR	steady; systematic; normal	
REGULON	enzyme-production gene group	gn
REGULUS	star in Leo	as
REGULUS	line set in ruled surface	ma
REIGNED	ruled; administered	
REINING	curbing; restraining	
REINTER	to bury again	
REIT-BOK	S. African buck	zo
REJOICE	revel; exult; gladden	
REJOINT	make a new joint	
REJOURN	adjourn; defer	
RELAPSE	delapse; backsliding; revert	
RELATED	akin; connected; recited	
RELATER	relator; delator	
RELATOR	informant	lw
RELAXED	loosened; slackened; abated	
RELAYED	transmitted	ro
RELEASE	set free; emancipate; liberate	
RE-LEASE	lease again	
RELIANT	confident; self-assured	
RELIEVE	release; allay; assuage	
RELIEVO	rilievo; in relief	
RELIGHT	rekindle; reignite	
RELIQUE	a relic (Fr.)	
RELIVED	lived again	
RELUMED	rekindled	
RELYING	depending; trusting	
REMAINS	(literary productions)	
REMANET	delayed lawsuit	lw
REMEANT	coming back (obs.)	
REMEGIA	a moth genus	zo
REMERCY	to thank (Spens.)	
REMERGE	merge again	
REMIGES	flight feathers	zo
REMIPED	oar-shaped feet	zo
REMISED	released; surrendered	lw
REMNANT	residue; odd lot; fragment	
REMODEL	refashion; remake; redesign	
REMORSE	anguish; compunction	
REMOTER	farther off	
REMOULD	shape anew	
REMOUNT	a fresh horse	zo
REMOVAL	euphemism for murder	
REMOVED	dislodged; abstracted	
REMOVER	shifter	
REMPHAN	Israelitish idol	
REMPLOY	} for disabled workers	
RE-EMPLOY		
RENAMED	rechristened	
RENDING	ripping; tearing; severing	
RENEGED	denied; revoked	
RENEWAL	refreshment; extension	
RENEWED	repeated; rejuvenated	
RENEWER	renovator	
RENT-DAY	time to pay or flit	
RENTIER	estate or fund holder	
RENTING	letting; leasing	
RENUENT	nodding	

373

RENVERS	half-pass in dressage (equestrian)	
REORDER	bid again; repeat request	
REPAINT	(a golf ball); a fresh coating	
REPAPER	(a palindrome)	
REPIANO	} full body of performers (It.)	
REPIENO	}	**mu**
REPINED	fretted; murmured; envied	
REPINER	plaintive person	
REPIQUE	(piquet)	
REPLACE	reinstate; refund	
REPLAIT	refold	
REPLETE	crammed; fraught	
REPLEVY	to bail	**lw**
REPLICA	a copy; duplicate; model	
REPLIED	answered; folded back	
REPLIER	respondent	
REPLUME	to preen	
REPOINT	sharpen; accentuate	
REPONED	replaced; relied	
REPOSAL	rest; sleep; ease	
REPOSED	settled; reclined	
REPOSER	slumberer	
REPOSIT	deposit	
REPRESS	crush; check; restrain	
REPRIEF	reproof (obs.)	
REPRINT	a subsequent edition	
REPRISE	repeat of music, song; estate charge; (fencing)	**lw**
REPRIVE	deprive (obs.)	
REPROOF	reprief; censure	
REPROVE	chide; upbraid	
REPTANT	creeping; reptilian	**zo**
REPTILE	snake; serpent	**zo**
REPULSE	rebuff; deter; reject	
REPUTED	alleged; deemed; reckoned	
REQUERE	request (Spens.)	
REQUEST	demand; entreat; solicit	
REQUIEM	a mass	**rl**
REQUIRE	want; lack; desire; need	
REQUITE	repay; reward; avenge	
REREDOS	altar screen	**rl**
RESCIND	revoke; quash; cancel	
RE-SCORE	try again	**mu**
RESCUED	freed; liberated	
RESCUER	deliverer; saviour	
RESEIZE	(legal confiscation)	**lw**
RESERVE	withhold; restraint	
RESHAPE	remould; remodel	
RESIANT	resident	**lw**
RESIDED	abode; inhered	
RESIDER	sojourner; dweller	
RESIDUE	remainder; dregs	
RESILED	started back; receded	
RESOLVE	determine; resolution	
RESOUND	reverberate; extol	
RE-SOUND	sound again; echo	
RESPEAK	repeat; reply	
RESPECT	revere; honour; esteem	
RESPIRE	breathe; inhale	

RESPITE	reprieve; pause; rest	
RE-SPOKE	reiterated; maintenance (bicycle)	
RESPOND	answer; accord; tally; react; pillar set under arch	**ar**
RESSAUT	a projection	**ar**
RESTANT	persistent; remaining	
RESTART	recommence re-run	**cp**
RESTATE	re-assert; recite	
RESTAUR	claim for indemnity	**lw**
REST-DAY	the Sabbath	
RESTFUL	tranquil; quiescent; irenic	
RESTIFF	restive (obs.)	
RESTILY	stubbornly; recalcitrantly	
RESTING	reposing; relaxing; leaning	
RESTIVE	refractory; obstinate	
RESTOCK	replenish	
RESTORE	reinstate; repair; heal	
RE-STORE	return to store	
RESUING	pre-mining technique	**mn**
RESUMED	renewed; continued	
RESURGE	rise again	**rl**
RETABLE	altar shelf for candles	
RETAKEN	recaptured	
RETAKER	recaptor	
RETENUE	self-control	
RETIARY	net-like, (gladiator)	
RETICLE	small net; reticule	
RETINAL	(retina) of the eye and sight (optic nerves)	**md**
RETINOL	resin oil; vitamin A	
RETINUE	suite; escort; bodyguard	
RETIPED	having veined feet	**zo**
RETIRAL	withdrawal; departure	
RETIRED	left; retreated; secluded	
RETOUCH	re-engrave; revise	
RETOURN	to turn back (obs.)	
RETRACE	return by the same road	
RETRACT	adjure; recant; revoke; withdraw	
RETRAIT	portrait; retired (Spens.)	
RETRATE	retreat (Spens.)	
RETREAD	repair of a tyre	
RETREAT	recede; asylum; refuse	
RETRIAL	repeating court case	**lw**
RETRUDE	to thrust back	
RETRUSE	abstruse; hidden; occult	
RETTERY	flax mill	
RETTING	prepared flax	
RETYRED	renewed wheel surfaces (motoring)	
REUNIFY	rejoin	
REUNION	social gathering	
REUNITE	reconcile; recombine	
REURGED	entreated again	
REUTTER	repeat; reiterate	
REVALUE	re-assess	
REVELRY	carousal; debauch; orgy	
REVENGE	requite; retaliate; vindicate	
REVENUE	income; return; reward	
REVENUE	(-man) (-cutter) ship	**nt**

REVERED	honoured; worshipped	
REVERER	venerator	
REVERIE	dreaminess; trance; vision	
REVERSE	misfortune; opposite; templet; template; backwards	
REVERSE	back spin; recovery (billiards) (putter)	
REVERSI	a counter-game	**ga**
REVERSO	left-hand page of a book	
REVESTU	heraldic squaring	**hd**
REVILED	aspersed; villified; abused	
REVILER	traducer; upbraider	
REVINCE	refute; disprove (obs.)	
REVISAL	revision; reviewal	
REVISED	amended; altered	
REVISER	also revisor; editor	
REVISIT	return to the same place	
REVIVAL	reawakening to life; (religious); repeat recall	
REVIVED	quickened; resuscitated	
REVIVER	invigorator; rouser	
REVIVOR	renewed action	**lw**
REVOKED	reneged; repealed; quashed	
REVOLVE	rotate; spin; whirl; circle	
REVOMIT	regorge	
REVVING	spinning at speed	
REWAKEN	re-arouse	
REWRITE	transcribe; return data to previous location; recall	**cp**
REYNARD	the fox	**zo**
RHABDOM	rodlike body in arthropoda eye	**zo**
RHABDOS	a straight spicule	**bt**
RHAETIC	Rhaetian	
RHAGADE	wet-skin crack	
RHAGOSE	spongy	
RHAMNUS	buckthorn, etc.	**bt**
RHATANY	Peruvian shrub	**bt**
RHEMISH	(Rheims)	
RHENISH	(Rhine)	
RHENIUM	metallic element	**ch**
RHESIAN	(Indian sacred monkey)	**zo**
RHIZINE **RHIZOID**	} rhizina; root-like	**bt**
RHIZOMA **RHIZOME**	} sucker-root	
RHIZOTA	small aquatic animals	**zo**
RHIZOTE	rooted	**bt**
RHODIAN	Rhodesian; (Rhodes)	
RHODIUM	hard white metal	**ch**
RHODORA	rhododendron	**bt**
RHOMBIS **RHOMBUS**	} oblique angled parallelogram	
RHONCUS	harsh bronchial-tube sound	**md**
RHOPODE	a marine invertebrate	**zo**
RHUBARB	pudding plant; statists' talk; rubbishy argument (baseball)	**bt, cp**
RHYMING	versifying	
RHYMIST	ballad-monger	
RHYNCHO	snouted	
RHYPHUS	genus of gnats	**zo**
RHYTINA	dugong; manatee, etc.	**zo**
RIB-BAND	(shipbuilding)	**nt**
RIBBING	lampooning; ridiculing; corrugation; frame; support	**nt, bd**
RIBBONS	driving reins	
RIBIBLE	rebec(k) forerunner of violin	**mu**
RIBLIKE	lying like slats	
RIBSTON	pippin; an apple	**bt**
RICASSO	part of rapier-blade	
RICE-HEN	American fowl	**zo**
RICINUS	castor-oil plant	**bt**
RICKERS	tree stems for spars	
RICKETS	softness of the bones	**md**
RICKETY	shaky; unstable; feeble	
RICKING	wrenching; spraining	
RICKSHA	jinricksha; carriage	
RICOTTA	bland creamy It. cheese	**ck**
RIDABLE	rideable	
RIDDING	freeing; banishing; clearing	
RIDDLED	full of holes	
RIDDLER	propounder of riddles	
RIDE-OFF	bumping and pushing (polo)	
RIDERED	stakes laid across bars	
RIDOTTO	musical entertainment (It.)	**mu**
RIETBOK	rietboc; reedbuck (S. Africa)	**zo**
RIFFLER	curved file	**to**
RIFLING	spiral grooving; ransacking	
RIFTING	riving; cleaving; splitting	**nt**
RIGAREE	broken design band; collar	**gs**
RIGGING	ropes and lines for masts, sails; tackle; fraudulent manipulation	**nt**
RIGGISH	wanton	
RIGGITE	jester; trickster (obs.)	
RIGHTED	redressed; rectified; adjusted	
RIGHTEN	set right; settle	
RIGHTER	redresser of wrongs	
RIGHTLY	properly; correctly	
RIGIDLY	inflexibly; staunchly	
RIGSDAG	Danish Parliament; now Folketing	
RIG-VEDA	Vedic doctrine	
RIKSDAG	Swedish Parliament	
RILIEVO	relievo; in relief	
RILLING	flowing; purling; rippling	
RIMFIRE	a cartridge	
RIMLESS	unframed	
RIMMING	making a border or edge	
RIMPLED	wrinkled; rumpled	
RINCEAU	carved and moulded vine foliage motif	**ar**
RINDING	peeling; excoriating	
RING-DOG	used for hauling timber	**fr**
RINGENT	irregular and gaping	
RINGHAL	spitting cobra	**zo**
RINGING	resounding	
RINGLET	circlet	

RINGMAN	third finger; Zulu chief	
RING-NET	butterfly-net	
RING-SAW	scroll-saw	**to**
RINKING	roller-skating	**ga**
RINSING	cleansing	
RIOLITE	silver selenide	**mn**
RIOTING	disorder; lawlessness	
RIOTISE	riot; extravagance (Spens.)	
RIOTOUS	turbulent; tumultuous	
RIPCORD	parachute release cord	
RIPIENO	supplementary	**mu**
RIPOSTE	lightning repartee; (fencing)	
RIPPING	splendid; tearing	
RIPPLED	purled; rilled	
RIPPLER	comb for flax	**to**
RIPPLET	tiny ripple	
RIPSACK	Californian whale	**zo**
RIPTIDE	fast flowing current	
RISBERM	glacis below jetties	
RISIBLE	laughable; droll; absurd	
RISIBLY	amusingly; farcically	
RISKIER	more hazardous	
RISKING	venturing; chancing; hazarding	
RISOTTO	Italian rice dish	**ck**
RISSOLE	an entrée	**ck**
RISTORI	woman's jacket	
RITTOCK	tern	**zo**
RIVALRY	emulation; competition	
RIVERET	small river; stream; rivulet	
RIVETED	fastened	
RIVETER	clincher	
RIVIERA	fashionable resort	
RIVIERE	a necklace of jewels	
RIVULET	stream; brook; riveret	
RIZOMED	heraldic grains	**hd**
ROADBED	road foundation	
ROADCAR	rural streetcar	
ROAD-HOG	a motor pest	
ROADING	team racing	
ROADMAN	road repairer	
ROAD-MAP	plan of road network	
ROADWAY	highway; turnpike; autobahn	
ROAMING	roving; wandering	
ROARING	bellowing; shouting; bawling	
ROASTED	parched; bantered	
ROASTER	gridiron	
ROBBERY	piracy; spoliation; pillage	
ROBBING	stealing; depriving; theft	
ROBINET	chaffinch	**zo**
ROBINIA	acacia	**bt**
ROCK-CAM	cam on rocking shaft	
ROCK-DOE	chamois	**zo**
ROCK-EEL	slippery customer	**zo**
ROCKERY	rock garden	
ROCKIER	more unstable	
ROCKILY	reeling; tottery	
ROCKING	lulling; staggering	
ROCK-OIL	petroleum; naphtha	**mn**
ROCKOON	balloon/rocket technique	**sp**
ROCK-TAR	petroleum	**mn**

RODDING	piping; drain-cleaning; levelling	**pb**
RODLIKE	cylindrical	
ROD-LINE	fishing line	
RODOMEL	roses and honey	
ROD-RING	(fishing-rod)	
RODSTER	an angler	
ROE-BUCK	male roe-deer	**zo**
ROE-DEER	small deer species	**zo**
ROGALLO	delta-shaped hang-glider	
ROGUERY	knavery; fraudulence	
ROGUISH	arch; wanton; puckish	
ROILING	rilling; angering	
ROINISH	roinous; mangy	
ROISTER	to bluster; swagger; bully	
ROKEAGE	parched Indian corn	
ROKELAY	short cloak; roguelaure	
ROLLICK	frolic	
ROLLING	trundling; wallowing; lurching	
ROLLMOP	cured spiced herring	**ck**
ROLLOCK	rowlock; also rullock	**nt**
ROLL-OFF	car ferry; primitive file	
ROLLWAY	an incline; a shoot	
ROMAIKA	modern Greek dance	
ROMAINE	cos; firm-leafed lettuce	
ROMALEA	a locust genus	**zo**
ROMANCE	historical fiction	
ROMANIC	derived from Latin	
ROMAUNT	a romance; exaggeration	
ROMEINE	(antimony and lime)	**mn**
ROMEITE	antimonite of calcium	**mn**
ROMMANY	gipsy language	
ROMPERS	children's overalls	
ROMPING	frolicking; capering	
ROMPISH	frisky; sportive; frolicsome	
RONCHIL	ronquil, a N. Pacific fish	**zo**
RONDEAU	verse with a refrain	**mu**
RONDENA	Andalusian serenade	**mu**
RONDEUR	rounded contour, shape	
RONGEUR	surgical forceps	**md**
RONQUIL	ronchil, sea-fish	**zo**
RONTGEN	(X-rays)	
ROOFING	materials for roof	
ROOFLET	small roof	
ROOINEK	an Englishman (S. Africa)	
ROOKERY	(rooks); (seals); (penguins)	**zo**
ROOKING	defrauding; fleecing	
ROOK-PIE	unsavoury dish	
ROOMAGE	stowage	
ROOMFUL	quantity of roses	
ROOMIER	more extensive	
ROOMILY	spaciously	
ROOMING	lodging	
ROOSTED	perched; slept	
ROOSTER	chanticleer	**zo**
ROOTAGE	manner of rooting	
ROOTCAP	tip at end of root	**bt**
ROOTERY	pile of stumps	
ROOTING	eradicating; implanting	
ROOTLED	rummaged; dug	

ROOTLET	radicle; a root fibre	**bt**
ROPALIC	club-shaped	
ROPEWAY	aerial transport	
RORQUAL	a whale	**zo**
ROSALIA	progressive melody	**mu**
ROSATED	crowned with roses	
ROSEATE	rosy; blushing	
ROSEBAY	willow-herb	**bt**
ROSE-BIT	(for countersinking)	**to**
ROSE-BOX	a plant	**bt**
ROSE-BUD	what Citizen Kane said	**bt**
ROSE-BUG	rose-chafer	**zo**
ROSE-CUT	(diamond-cutting)	
ROSE-HAW	} the fruit of the wild rose	
ROSE-HIP	}	**bt, ck**
ROSELET	ermine's summer fur	
ROSELLA	a parakeet	**zo**
ROSELLE	rose-mallow	**bt**
ROSEOLA	a rash	**md**
ROSE-RED	pretty pink	
ROSETTA	inscribed stone (Ptolemy V)	
ROSETTE	a favour; party election badge (coloured cloth)	**tx**
ROSIEST	most blushing	
ROSINED	resined; gingered up	
ROSLAND	moorland	
ROSOLIO	raisin brandy	
ROSSING	removing bark	
ROSTRAL	beak-like; underwater ramming beak in bow of Roman warship	**nt**
ROSTRUM	platform; pulpit; a beak	
ROSULAR	(leaves in clusters)	
ROTALIA	foraminifers	**zo**
ROTATED	revolved; spun; twirled	
ROTATOR	a rotor	
ROTCHET	red gurnard	**zo**
ROTCHIE	little auk; sea-dove	**zo**
ROTELLA	round shield	
ROTIFER	an animalcule	**zo**
ROTODIP	car-painting technique	
ROTONDE	ruff; cope (Fr.)	
ROTTING	decaying; fooling	
ROTTOLO	Levantine weight	**me**
ROTULAR	(patella)	**md**
ROTUNDA	circular building	
ROUCHED	puckered	
ROUELLE	wheel-like amulet	
ROUERIE	debauchery	
ROUGHED	rasped; (horse-shoes)	
ROUGHEN	scarify; coarsen	
ROUGHER	ruder; harsher; coarser	
ROUGHIE	dried heath (Sc.)	
ROUGHLY	boisterously; crudely	
ROUGH-UP	violent fight	
ROUGING	painting with rouge	
ROULADE	melodious passage	**mu**
ROULEAU	packet of coins	
ROUNDED	curved; turned	
ROUNDEL	a Norman shield; a ballad	
ROUNDER	more like a circle	
ROUNDLY	boldly; openly; plainly	
ROUND-UP	a rodeo	
ROUPING	selling by auction (Sc.)	
ROUSANT	starting up	**hd**
ROUSING	stimulating; brisk; lively	
ROUSTER	vagrant; vagabond	
ROUTHIE	plentiful; abundant (Sc.)	
ROUTIER	armed brigand (Fr.)	
ROUTINE	regularity; system; workstyle program	**cp**
ROUTING	rooting; defeating; combination of transmission paths	**cp**
ROUTISH	clamorous; disorderly	
ROWABLE	a truly oarful state	
ROWBOAT	pleasure vessel	**nt**
ROWDIER	more uproarious or rampant	
ROWDILY	turbulently; noisily	
ROWLOCK	}	
ROLLOCK	} support for oar in boat	**nt**
RULLOCK	}	
ROWPORT	oar-hole	
ROYALET	petty king; princelet	
ROYALLY	regally; imperially	
ROYALTY	author's perquisite	
ROYNISH	roinish; mangy	
ROYSTON	hooded crow	**zo**
ROYTISH	rowdy; wild (obs.)	
ROZELLE	hibiscus	**bt**
RUB-A-DUB	beat of drum	
RUBASSE	Ancona ruby	**mn**
RUBBING	chafing; tracing; scouring; sanding (stone)	**bd**
RUBBING	abrasion; brass tracing (tombs); massage	
RUBBISH	trash; litter; lumber	
RUB-DOWN	aphrodisiac	
RUBELLA	German measles	**md**
RUBIATE	madder	
RUBICAN	roan	
RUBICEL	variety of ruby	**mn**
RUBICON	boundary; fateful river	
RUBIFIC	making red	
RUBIOUS	ruby-red	
RUBYING	reddening	
RUCHING	a plaited frilling	
RUCKING	creasing; ruffling	
RUCKLED	wrinkled; rucked	
RUCTION	uproar; turmoil; disturbance	
RUDDIED	reddened	
RUDDIER	rosier; more rubicund	
RUDDILY	glowingly	
RUDDLED	interwoven; ochred	
RUDDOCK	robin; apple	**zo, bt**
RUDERAL	waste growth	**bt**
RUDESBY	uncivil fellow (Shak.)	
RUELLIA	a plant genus	**bt**
RUE-WORT	herb of grace	**bt**
RUFFIAN	desperado; apache; rascal	
RUFFING	trumping; ruffling	

RUFFLED	disordered; agitated	
RUFFLER	a bully	
RUGGING	heavy napped cloth	
RUINATE	demolish; destroy (Shak.)	
RUINING	wrecking; demolishing	
RUINOUS	pernicious; calamitous	
RULABLE	allowable; governable	
RULLION	veldt-shoe; virago	
RUMBLED	reverberated	
RUMBLER	tum	
RUMINAL	ruminant	**zo**
RUMMAGE	search; ransack	
RUMMIER	stranger; droller; quainter	
RUMMILY	oddly; whimsically	
RUMNESS	queerness; oddity	
RUMPLED	rimpled; crushed	
RUM-SHOP	a tavern	
RUNAWAY	fugitive; deserter; renegade	
RUNDALE	land tenure	
RUNDLED	rounded like a rung	
RUNDLET	small barrel; runlet	
RUNDOWN	caught between bases (baseball); detailed items	
RUN-DOWN	exhausted; weak; anaemic	
RUN-LINE	long straight rapidly painted line	
RUNNERS	timber sheet piles (excavation)	**ce**
RUNNING	in succession; careering; organizing; managing; moulding (decor); sailing downwind; jog trotting	**bd, nt**
RUN-OVER	continuation over page/body	
RUPTION	eruption	
RUPTIVE	ruptile; liable to snap	
RUPTURE	fracture; breach; rift	
RURALLY	rustically	
RUSALKA	water-nymph (Rus.)	
RUSHING	dashing; careering; flying	
RUSH-MAT	reed pad	
RUSH-NUT	edible tuber	**bt**
RUSSETY	reddish-brown	
RUSSIAN	of Russia	
RUSSIFY	to muscovate	
RUSSULA	red fungus	**bt**
RUSTFUL	rusty	
RUSTICA	ancient Rom. manuscript style	
RUSTIER	less practised	
RUSTILY	fustily; mustily	
RUSTING	oxidizing	
RUSTLED	stirred	
RUSTLER	cattle-thief	
RUSTRED	lozenge-shaped	**hd**
RUTHFUL	compassionate	
RUTTIER	routier, bearings chart	**nv**
RUTTING	grooving; furrowing; pairing	
RUTTISH	lustful; of mating season (deer)	
RYDBERG	atomic ionizing energy unit	**me, nc**
RYE-MOTH	a harvest pest	**zo**
RYE-WOLF	(German folk lore)	**zo**

RYE-WORM	larva of rye-moth	**zo**

S

SABAISM	} star worship, ancient	
SABEISM	} religion of Persia and Chaldea	
SABAOTH	armies (Heb.)	
SABBATH	day of rest	
SABELLA	sea-worms	**zo**
SABREUR	user of sabre (fencing)	
SABRING	cutting with a sabre	
SABURRA	grittiness of the tongue	
SACCADE	sudden check; rapid eye movement (dreams)	**mu**
SACCATA	molluscs	**zo**
SACCATE	sack-like	
SACCULE	small pouch	
SACELLA	altars; sanctuaries	
SACKAGE	pillage	
SACKBUT	} dulcimer, trombone	**mu**
SACBUT	}	
SACKFUL	bagful	
SACKING	looting; plundering	
SACODES	beetle genus	**zo**
SACRARY	a holy place (obs.)	
SACRING	consecration	**rl**
SACRIST	sacristan; a sexton	**rl**
SADDEST	most dismal and depressing	
SADDLED	loaded; hampered	
SADDLER	owner of wells	
SAD-EYED	mournful	
SADIRON	box-iron; flat-iron	
SADNESS	sorrowfulness; melancholy	
SADTREE	night jasmine	**bt**
SADWARE	term for pewter dishes, plates, etc.	**mn**
SAFFIAN	(tanned skins)	
SAFFRON	plant; a colour; flavour	**bt, ck**
SAGAMAN	a bard; narrator of sagas	
SAGATHY	woollen stuff	
SAGESSE	wisdom (Fr.)	
SAGGARD	box for baking porcelain	
SAGGING	bending; including	
SAGITTA	arrow; star in Great Bear constellation (Lat.)	**as**
SAGOUIN	capuchin monkey	**zo**
SAGUARO	giant cactus	**bt**
SAHLITE	augite	**mn**
SAIL-ARM	(windmill)	
SAILING	cruising	**nt**
SAIMIRI	squirrel monkey	**zo**
SAINTED	canonized	
SAINTLY	holy; devout; religious	
SAIRING	enough (Sc.)	
SAIVISM	worship of Siva	**rl**
SALABLE	saleable; vendible	
SALADIN	a Soldan; a Sultan	
SALAMBA	fishing device (Manila)	

SALAMIS	insect genus	**zo**
SALCHOW	skating jump	
SALIANT	salient; leaping; projecting	
SALICET	salicional soft tone organ stop	
		mu
SALICIN	willow extract	**ch**
SALIENT	Ypres; prominent	
SALIERE	salt-cellar (Fr.)	
SALIGOT	water caltrops	**bt**
SALIQUE	salic (male succession)	
SALIVAL	salivary	
SALLIED	dashed out	
SALLOWY	yellowish; jaundiced	
SALMIAC	sal-ammoniac	**ch**
SALMINE	fish-testicle protamine	**ch**
SALPIAN	ascidian	**zo**
SALPINX	Eustachian tube	**md**
SALSAFY	} oyster plant; purple goat's	
SALSIFY	} beard	**bt**
SALSOLA	glass-wort	**bt**
SALTANT	dancing; leaping	
SALTANT	suddenly developed variant	**bl**
SALTATE	to dance; leap; jump; skip	
SALT-BOX	salt cellar	
SALT-CAT	pigeon medicine	
SALTERN	salt factory	
SALTIER	saltire	
SALTING	sea-marsh; pickling; curing	
SALTIRE	St Andrew's cross	
SALTISH	brackish; briny	
SALT-PAN	evaporating pan	
SALT-PIT	open salt mine	
SALUTED	honoured; kissed; greeted	
SALUTER	that which salutes	
SALVAGE	rescue; compensation	
SALVETE	greetings to new members	
SALVING	healing; restoration	
SAMADHI	broken; mind/body link in yoga	
SAMBHUR	Indian stag	**zo**
SAMBUCA	ancient harp	**mu**
SAMBUKE	sambuca	**mu**
SAMIOTE	native of Samos	
SAMISEN	} Japanese lute	**mu**
SHAMISEN	}	
SAMNITE	Sabine tribe	
SAMOGON	illicitly distilled vodka (Rus.)	
SAMOLUS	primrose genus	**bt**
SAMOVAR	Russian tea-urn	
SAMOYED	sledge-dog	**zo**
SAMPLED	tried; tasted	
SAMPLER	needlework; pattern picture	
SAMPLER	soil, sand crusher for testing	**ce**
SAMSARA	transmigration; reincarnation	
SAMSHOO	rice spirit (China)	
SAMURAI	Japanese military class	
SANCTUM	a refuge; a shrine	**rl**
SANCTUS	a hymn	**rl**
SANDBAG	a convenient weapon	
SAND-BAR	estuarine barrier	
SANDBED	a mould	

SANDBOX	a caster of sand to dry wet ink; for slippery rails; W. Indian tree	**rw, bt**
SAND-BOY	proverbially a happy lad	
SANDBUG	digger-wasp	**zo**
SANDBUR	a weed	**bt**
SAND-DAB	plaice	**zo**
SAND-EEL	small fish	**zo**
SANDERS	red sandal-wood	**bt**
SAND-FLY	a biting midge	**zo**
SANDING	burying oysters; smoothing; flattening down	**jn, pt**
SANDISH	gritty; friable	
SANDJET	sand-blast	
SAND-LOB	lug-worm	**zo**
SANDMAN	children's sleep-giver	
SAND-PIT	source of sand	
SAND-RAT	the camass rat	**zo**
SANHITA	Vedic hymns	
SANICLE	healing plant	**bt**
SANKHYA	Hindu philosophy	
SAPAJOU	S. Amer. spider-monkey	**zo**
SAPERDA	boring beetles	**zo**
SAP-HEAD	(fortification)	
SAPHENA	prominent vein	**md**
SAPIENT	wise; sage; clever; astute	
SAPLESS	dry; not juicy	
SAPLING	young tree	**bt**
SAPLING	young grey-hound	**zo**
SAPONIN	soapwort extract	
SAPPHIC	(Sappho)	
SAPPING	undermining	
SAPPLES	soap-suds (Sc.)	
SAPROBE	plant growing in foul water	
SAPSAGO	a green Swiss cheese	**ck**
SAPWOOD	the alburnum	**bt**
SARACEN	Arab	
SARAFAN	Russian gala-dress	
SARAWAK	glossy yellow cane	
SARCASM	irony; satire; ridicule	
SARCELE	partly cut through	
SARCINA	fungoid plant	**bt**
SARCINE	(muscular tissue)	**md**
SARCODE	protoplasm	
SARCODY	conversion to fleshlike state	
SARCOID	flesh-like	
SARCOMA	tumour; skin cancer	**md**
SARCOUS	fleshy	
SARDANA	folk dance (Catalan)	**mu**
SARDINE	the young of the pilchard	**ck, zo**
SARDINE	boat West Europe	**nt**
SARDIUS	sard; a quartz	**mn**
SARGINA	mullet genus	**zo**
SARIGUE	opossum (Brazil)	**zo**
SARKING	roof sheathing	
SARMENT	a runner; filiform stem	**bt**
SARPLAR	sarpler; packing cloth	
SARSNET	fine woven silk	**tx**
SARTAGE	forest clearing	
SASHERY	sashes	

SASHING	window framing	
SASSABY	tsessebe; hartebeest	zo
SASSING	cheeking; saucing	
SATANIC	infernal; diabolical; devilish	
SATCHEL	small sack or container	
SATIATE	glutted; to cloy; to gorge	
SATIETY	a surfeit; excess; over gratification	
SATINET	thin satin	
SATIRIC	sarcastic; ironical; mordant	
SATISFY	gratify; requite; settle	
SATRAPY	Persian province	
SATSUMA	Japanese pottery; citrus fruit	bt
SATTARA	ribbed woollen material	tx
SATTEEN	ratteen; thick woollen fabric	tx
SATYRAL	} Satyr-like; lustful	
SATYRIC		
SATYRUS	orang-utan genus	zo
SAUCIER	ruder; more impudent	
SAUCILY	pertly; flippantly; pungently	
SAUCING	sassing; seasoning	
SAUNTER	dawdle; stroll; dally	
SAURIAN	lizard; reptile	zo
SAUROID	reptilian	
SAUSAGE	minced meat packed into skin	
		ck
SAUTOIR	diagonal ribbon	hd
SAVABLE	salvable	
SAVAGED	attacked brutally	
SAVANNA	treeless plain	go
SAVARIN	syrup-soaked yeast cake	ck
SAVE-ALL	an economizer	
SAVELOY	red smoked pork sausage	ck
SAVIGNY	red Burgundy wine	
SAVINGS	a nest-egg	
SAVIOUR	Messiah	rl
SAVOURY	of grateful savour	
SAW-BACK	a caterpillar	zo
SAWBILL	goosander; merganser	zo
SAWBUCK	sawhorse	
SAWDUST	carpentry by-product	
SAWFILE	triangular file	to
SAWFISH	serrated-proboscis fish	zo
SAWHORN	an insect	zo
SAWMILL	lumber factory	
SAWWHET	Acadian owl	zo
SAWWORT	a plant	bt
SAXHORN	brass wind-instrument	mu
SAXONIC	Saxon	
SAY-CAST	coarse part of wool, from tail	tx
SAYETTE	serge; woollen yarn	
SCABBED	mean; worthless	
SCABBLE	scapple; (stone-dressing)	
SCABIES	the itch	md
SCABRID	scabrous; rough; rugged	
SCADDLE	skaddle; hurtful; impish	
SCAGLIA	Italian calcareous rock	mn
SCALADE	} assault by escalade (Fr., It.)	
SCALADO		
SCALARY	stepped like a ladder	

SCALDED	immersed in boiling water	
SCALDER	Norse minstrel or bard	
SCALDIC	(Norse ballads)	
SCALENE	irregular triangle	
SCALING	removal of loosened rock	mn
SCALING	evaluation; measurement; (ladder)	
SCALING	fish scales; boiler cleaning	
SCALING	ornament of overlapping circles (fish scales); ladder for sieges	
SCALLED	scurfy; scabby	
SCALLOP	} shellfish; baking mould	zo
SCOLLOP		
SCALLOP	pilgrim badge; (border) (pattern)	
SCALOPS	American shrew-moles	zo
SCALPED	laid bare	
SCALPEL	dissecting knife	md
SCALPER	hair-raising savage	
SCAMBLE	shamble; scramble; mangle	
SCAMMEL	bar-tailed godwit	zo
SCAMMUM	geometrical figure	
SCAMPED	skimped	
SCAMPER	scurry; run; hasten	
SCANDAL	disgrace; infamy; discredit	
SCANDIX	Venus' comb	bt
SCANNED	scrutinized; perused	
SCANNER	television or radar beam	tv
SCANNER	(medical tests) sampling device	md, cp
SCANTED	limited; stinted	
SCANTLE	cut into small pieces	
SCANTLY	scantily; niggardly	
SCAPNET	minnow-net	
SCAPPLE	stone-dressing	
SCAPULA	shoulder blade	md
SCARCER	rarer; less plentiful	
SCARFED	(timber joint)	
SCARIFY	to scratch; to harrow	
SCARING	affrighting; daunting	
SCARLET	bright orangish red	
SCAROID	like parrot fish	
SCARPED	made precipitous	
SCARRED	disfigured	
SCARVES	kerchiefs; cravats	
SCATHED	injured; damaged; hurt	
SCATTER	disperse; strew; dispel; sow seed	
SCATTER	distributing data into areas of store	cp
SCAUPER	engraver's tool	to
SCAURIE	young gull (Sc.)	
SCENERY	prospect; view; landscape	
SCENTED	perfumed; smelt; suspected	
SCEPSIS	philosophic doubt	
SCEPTIC	skeptic, a doubter	
SCEPTRE	royal mace	
SCEPTRY	rather royal	
SCHAPPE	spun silk	tx
SCHELLY	white fish	zo
SCHEMED	plotted; planned; contrived	

SCHEMER	intriguer; plotter	
SCHEPEN	magistrate (Dutch)	
SCHERZO	playfully	**mu**
SCHESIS	habitude; wont	
SCHETIC	constitutional; habitual	
SCHINUS	mastic-tree	**bt**
S-CHISEL	well-boring cutter	**to**
SCHISMA	tonal difference	**mu**
SCHLICH	ore slime	
SCHLOSS	castle; ancient seat (Ger.)	
SCHMUCK	unsophisticated person; idiot (Jew.)	
SCHNAPS	schnapps; akvavit; eau de vie	
SCHOLAR	student; pupil; disciple	
SCHOLIA	marginal notes	
SCHORLY	tourmaline	**mn**
SCIATIC	affecting the hip	**md**
SCIBILE	knowable	
SCIENCE	knowledge; reduced to system	
SCINCUS	lizard; skink; a saurian	**zo**
SCIOLTO	with abandon	**mu**
SCIRPUS	bulrush genus	**bt**
SCISSEL	} metal clippings	
SCISSIL	}	
SCISSOR	to cut	
SCIURUS	squirrel genus	**zo**
SCLERAL	hard; ossified	**md**
SCLERIA	sedges	**bt**
SCOBINA	ends of grass	**bt**
SCOFFED	mocked; jeered; derided	
SCOFFER	a taunter; ridiculer	
SCOLDER	chided; nagged; rebuked	
SCOLDER	railer; upbraider	
SCOLITE	fossil worm	**mn**
SCOLLOP	scallop	**zo**
SCOMBER	mackerel genus	**zo**
SCOONED	skimmed; glided	
SCOONER	a schooner	**nt**
SCOOPED	hollowed out; dredged	
SCOOPER	a water-fowl; the avocet	**zo**
SCOOTED	bolted; squirted	
SCOOTER	ice-boat; toy; light motorcycle	
SCOPATE	brush-like	
SCOPTIC	bantering; jesting	
SCOPULA	small tuft of hairs	**zo**
SCORIAC	ashy	
SCORIAE	volcanic ashes	**mn**
SCORIFY	reduce to ashes	
SCORING	recording; scratching; counting points, runs, etc.	
SCORNED	disdained; spurned	
SCORNER	contemner; flouter	
SCORPER	a gouge	**to**
SCORPIO	(Zodiac); scorpion	**zo**
SCOTICE	in Scottish	**rl**
SCOTISM	doctrine of Duns Scotus	
SCOTIST	a theologian	**rl**
SCOTOMA	} blind spot; dizziness	**md**
SCOTOMY	}	
SCOURED	scurried; purged; rinsed	

SCOURER	scrubber; polisher; scraper	
SCOURGE	lash; chastise; plague	
SCOUTED	scorned; ridiculed	
SCOUTER	stone-flaker	
SCOWLED	registered displeasure	
SCRAGGY	lean and bony	
SCRANCH	scrunch; grind	
SCRANKY	scraggy; lank (Sc.)	
SCRANNY	lean; spare	
SCRAPED	erased; rubbed; rasped	
SCRAPER	miser; indifferent fiddler; scourer; plane	**to**
SCRAPIE	chronic nervous sheep disease	**vt**
SCRAPPY	fragmentary	
SCRATCH	lacerate; zero handicap	
SCRATCH	withdraw from contest; re-usable tape	**cp**
SCRAWLY	scribbled; ill-formed	
SCRAWNY	raw-boned	
SCREECH	scraich; scraigh	
SCREEVE	to write begging letters	
SCREWED	twisted; tipsy	
SCREWER	screw-driver; extortioner	
SCRIBAL	clerical	
SCRIBED	wrote; recorded; marked	
SCRIBER	engraving tool	**to**
SCRIEVE	glide swiftly (Sc.)	
SCRIMER	fencer (Shak.)	
SCRINGE	cringe; flinch; grate	
SCRITCH	screech; a thrush	**zo**
SCROGGY	having thick undergrowth	
SCROOGE	scrudge; squeeze	
SCROTAL	of the scrotum	
SCROTUM	testicle sac in mammals	**zo**
SCROUGE	squeeze; to crowd	
SCRUBBY	stunted; squabby	
SCRUFFY	scurfy; scaly; unkempt; untidy; uncouth	
SCRUNCH	crunch; crush	
SCRUPLE	20 grains, troy weight; honesty	**me**
SCRYING	crystal gazing	
SCUDDED	ran before the wind	**nt**
SCUDDLE	scuttle; skuttle	
SCUDLER	a scullion	
SCUFFLE	struggle; a hoe	**to**
SCULLED	rowed	**nt**
SCULLER	an oarsman	**nt**
SCULLER	rowed water taxi (London)	**nt**
SCULPIN	sea-fish; dragonet; bull-head	**zo**
SCUMBER	fox-dung	
SCUMBLE	overlay painting	
SCUMMER	a skimmer of scum	
SCUNNER	loathing; prejudice (Sc.)	
SCUPPER	vent; annihilate	
SCUPPET	scoppet; shovel	
SCURRIL	scurrilous; foul-mouthed	
SCURRIT	lesser tern	**zo**
SCURVEY	vitamin-deficiency disease	**md**

SCUTAGE	feudal tax	
SCUTATE	like a shield	
SCUTTER	scurry	
SCUTTLE	(coal); hatchway; sink	nt
SCYMNUS	ladybirds; sharks	zo
SCYPHUS	a large drinking-cup (Gr.)	
SCYPHUS	podetium end widening	bt
SCYTALE	secret message (Gr.)	
SCYTALE	coral snake	zo
SCYTHED	mowed; cut	
SCYTHIC	scythian	
SEA-BANK	protective bank	
SEA-BASS	marine fish	zo
SEA-BEAN	small univalve shell	bt, zo
SEA-BEAR	seal; polar bear	zo
SEA-BEAT	lashed by the waves	
SEA-BEET	rare vegetable	bt
SEA-BELT	fucus plant	bt
SEA-BIRD	aquatic bird	zo
SEA-BOAT	manageable at sea, stable, seaworthy	nt
SEA-BORN	produced by the sea	
SEA-CALF	common seal	zo
SEA-CARD	compass card	nt
SEA-CLAM	a bivalve	
SEA-COAL	cash	mn
SEA-COCK	gurnard; a valve	zo
SEA-COOK	marine father	nt
SEA-COOT	exotic ocean bird	zo
SEA-CORN	spawn	zo
SEA-CRAB	ocean crustacean	zo
SEA-CROW	cormorant	zo
SEA-DACE	bass	zo
SEA-DOVE	little auk	zo
SEA-DUCK	eider-duck	zo
SEA-FIRE	phosphorescence	
SEA-FISH	cod and others	zo
SEA-FOAM	meerschaum	mn
SEA-FOLK	sailors	
SEA-FOOD	fish as food	zo
SEA-GAGE	depth gauge	
SEA-GATE	harbour bar	
SEA-GIRT	insular	
SEA-GOWN	dress worn at sea	
SEAGULL	marine bird	zo
SEA-HAAR	sea-mist	
SEA-HALL	hall below the sea	
SEA-HARE	mollusc	zo
SEA-HAWK	a skua	zo
SEAHOLM	sea-holly	bt
SEAKALE	a cruciferous plant	bt
SEA-KING	a viking	
SEA-LACE	(seaweed)	bt
SEALANT	adhesive compound, plastic coating	ce
SEA-LARK	the dunlin	zo
SEA-LEGS	acclimatization to sailing	
SEALERY	seal-fishing station	
SEALIKE	unrivery	
SEA-LILY	sea-urchin	zo

SEA-LINE	horizon; sky-line	
SEALING	confirming; seal-hunting	
SEA-LION	large seal	zo
SEAL-OFF	closure	
SEA-LUCE	hake	zo
SEA-MAID	mermaid	
SEA-MALL	sea-gull	zo
SEA-MARK	land or sea-mark	
SEA-MILE	geographical mile; 6080 feet (1853 m)	
SEAMING	sewing together; scarring	
SEA-MINK	whiting	zo
SEA-MONK	monk-seal	zo
SEA-MOSS	seaweed	bt
SEAM-SET	tinman's punch	to
SEA-OOZE	soft mud	
SEA-PASS	passport	
SEA-PEAR	sea-squid	zo
SEA-PECK	the dunlin	zo
SEA-PERT	the opah fish	zo
SEA-PIKE	pike	zo
SEA-PINK	the thrift	bt
SEA-PORK	an ascidian	zo
SEAPORT	harbour for large ships	
SEA-REED	mat grass	bt
SEARING	cauterizing	
SEA-RISK	marine hazard	
SEA-ROLL	sea-cucumber	zo
SEA-ROOM	manoeuvre space	
SEA-ROSE	sea-anemone	zo
SEA-RUFF	sea-bream	zo
SEA-SALT	cookery condiment	mn
SEASICK	mal-de-mer	
SEASIDE	beach	
SEA-SLUG	a nudibranch	zo
SEASONS	climate and growth divisions of the year	
SEA-TANG	sea-tangle-weed	
SEATING	audience capacity; sitting places	
SEA-TOAD	angler fish	zo
SEA-TOST	common or garden tost	
SEA-TURN	a gale from the sea	
SEAVIEW	glimpse of the briny	
SEA-WALL	retaining wall	
SEA-WANE	wampum	
SEAWARD	toward the sea	
SEA-WARE	seaweed; sea-wrack	bt
SEAWEED	tangle; algae	bt
SEA-WHIP	a zoophyte	zo
SEA-WIFE	wrasse; mermaid	zo
SEA-WING	a sail	
SEA-WOLD	imaginary tract	
SEA-WOLF	wolf fish; pirate	zo
SEA-WORM	marine annelid	zo
SEBACIC	fatty acid	ch
SEBILLA	wooden bowl	
SEBUNDY	a sepoy	
SECANCY	intersection	
SECEDED	withdrew; separated	
SECEDER	separationist	

SECHIUM	genus of gourds **bt**	
SECLUDE	segregate; shut up	
SECONDO	bass of duet **mu**	
SECONDS	imperfect items; (stale); rejects	
SECONDS	assistants; endorses; time units (boxing) (duelling)	
SECRECY	privacy; stealth; reticence	
SECRETE	hide; conceal; cache; yield	
SECTANT	geometric figure	
SECTARY	sectarian	
SECTILE	sliceable	
SECTION	portion; division; segment; (cross-); leader	
SECTION	part of magnetic tape, block **cp**	
SECTIST	dissenter	
SECTIVE	divisible	
SECULAR	of the world; lay; temporal	
SECURED	obtained; ensured; fastened	
SECURER	protector; guardian; safer	
SEDILIA	altar seats **rl**	
SEDUCED	enticed; led astray	
SEDUCER	a libertine	
SEEABLE	visible	
SEE-CAWK	the American skunk **zo**	
SEED-BAG	germ-pouch	
SEED-BED	plantation	
SEED-BUD	germ of the fruit **bt**	
SEED-COD	seed-basket; husk	
SEEDFUL	promising; hopeful	
SEEDILY	shabbily	
SEEDING	(tournaments); sowing	
SEED-LAC	dried resin	
SEED-LOP	seed container **bt**	
SEED-OIL	linseed oil	
SEEKING	inquiring; questing	
SEELING	closing the eyelids	
SEEMING	specious; guise; apparent	
SEEPAGE	leakage; oozings	
SEETHED	boiled; soaked	
SEETHER	boiling pot	
SEGGROM	ragwort **bt**	
SEGMENT	a portion; section of a whole	
SEGMENT	redivide into chapters **cp**	
SEINING	netting fish	
SEISING	taking possession **lw**	
SEISMAL	seismic; (earthquake)	
SEISTAN	Persian summer north wind **mt**	
SEISURA	Australian fly-catchers **zo**	
SEIURUS	wagtail genus **zo**	
SEIZING	(ropes); grappling; binding	
SEIZURE	grasp; legal confiscation; stroke; attack, theft **md, lw**	
SEJEANT	sitting **hd**	
SELACHE	shark genus **zo**	
SELENIC	(selenium) **ch**	
SELFBOW	of single piece, yew **ar**	
SELF-FED	automatic	
SELFISH	egotistical; mean; ungenerous	
SELFISM	selfishness	
SELFIST	egoist	

SELINUM	milk-parsley **bt**	
SELLING	vending; hawking; betraying	
SELTZER	mineral water	
SELVAGE	selvedge; border	
SEMATIC	significant	
SEMEION	metrical mark	
SEMI-APE	a lemur **zo**	
SEMI-GOD	demi-god	
SEMILOR	imitation gold	
SEMINAL	rudimentary; original	
SEMINAR	teacher in a seminary; special study group	
SEMIPED	(prosody); a half-foot; meter (verse)	
SEMI-RAG	paper with some rag content	
SEMITIC	Jewish; Hebrew	
SENATOR	a counsellor	
SENATUS	governing body	
SENCION	} groundsel; ragwort **bt**	
SENECIO	}	
SENDING	despatching; forwarding	
SEND-OFF	farewell party	
SENECAN	style of philosophy of Seneca	
SENEGAL	African fire-bird **zo**	
SENIORY	council of elders	
SENSATE	sensible	
SENSILE	sensitive	
SENSING	understanding; feeling; perceptual awareness	
SENSION	perception	
SENSISM	sensualism	
SENSIST	sensationalist	
SENSORY	nerve system **md**	
SENSUAL	voluptuous	
SEPIARY	} referring to cuttlefish; (ink producers) **zo**	
SEPIOID	}	
SEPIOST	cuttle-bone **zo**	
SEPPUKU	hara-kiri (Jap.)	
SEPTATE	partitioned	
SEPTIME	fencing posture	
SEQUELA	a consequence; abnormal chronic condition **md**	
SEQUENT	following; succeeding	
SEQUOIA	Californian red-wood **bt**	
SERAPIS	Apis; goddess of fertility	
SERBIAN	of Serbia; Yugoslav	
SERENED	tranquillized	
SERENER	calmer; more placid	
SERENOA	dwarf-palms (Florida) **bt**	
SERFAGE	serfdom; slavery	
SERFDOM	villenage; thraldom	
SERIATE	in series; serial	
SERICIN	silk **tx**	
SERICON	alchemic red	
SERIEMA	cariama; (heron) **zo**	
SERIFIC	silk-producing	
SERINGA	flowering shrub **bt**	
SERINUS	canary genus **zo**	
SERIOLA	amber fish **zo**	
SERIOUS	grave; sedate; staid	

SERMENT	oath	
SERPENT	snake; reptile; (obs.) bassoon-like	**zo, mu**
SERPIGO	ring-worm	**md**
SERPULA	sea-worms	**zo**
SERRATE	serrous; notched	
SERRIED	at close interval	
SERRULA	comblike ridge on chelicerae	**zo**
SERTOLI	of seminiferous tubule cells	**zo**
SERTULE	collection of plants	**bt**
SERVAGE	servitude; enthralment	
SERVANT	retainer; henchman; menial	
SERVIAN	Serbian; Serb	
SERVICE	duty; performance; utility	
SERVICE	musical settings of anglican worship	**mu**
SERVICE	start of rally (squash) (tennis)	
SERVICE	maintenance; employment; (military); (public) (social) (tip)	**cp**
SERVILE	fawning; sycophantic; slave-like	
SERVING	ministering; (tennis)	**rl**
SERVITE	mendicant monk, 13th Cent.	
SESAMUM	sesame genus	**bt**
SESOTHO	Basuto language (S. Africa)	
SESSILE	(no stalk)	**bt**
SESSION	meeting; assize; sitting	**lw**
SESSION	period of open transmission	**cp, tc**
SESTINA	sestine; verse (Fr.)	
SESTOLE	sextuplet	
SETARIA	spiky grasses	**bt**
SET-BACK	check; reverse; recess	**ar**
SET-DOWN	a rebuff	
SETLESS	no score; tennis	**mu**
SETTIMA	⎫ the interval of a seventh	
SETTIMO	⎭ (It.)	**mu**
SETTING	appointing; congealing	
SETTLED	fixed; paid; sank; serene	
SETTLER	coloniser; arbitrator	
SETWALL	valerian	**bt**
SETWORK	(boat-building); (plaster)	
SEVENTH	ordinal number	
SEVENTY	cardinal number	
SEVERAL	sundry; diverse; various	
SEVERED	cut; rent; divided	
SEVERER	stricter; simple	
SEVRUGA	caviare-fish	**zo**
SEWED-UP	stranded	**nt**
SEXFOIL	six-leafed plant	**bt**
SEXLESS	of indeterminate gender	
SEXTAIN	(six lines)	
SEXTANS	Roman bronze coin	**nm**
SEXTANT	optical instrument	**nt**
SEXTERN	quire of 6 sheets	**pp**
SEXTILE	planet aspect	
SEXUALE	sexually-reproducing individual	**zo**
SHABASH	bravo! (Pers.)	
SHACKED	tramped; hibernated	

SHACKLE	manacle; gyve; bond; fetter	
SHADFLY	May-fly	**zo**
SHADIER	more dubious	
SHADILY	umbrageously	
SHADINE	American sardine	**zo**
SHADING	screening; tinting	
SHADOOF	water-raising device (Nile)	
SHADOWY	obscure; dim; gloomy	
SHAFTED	handled; hafted	
SHAGGED	shaggy; rough; rugged	
SHAHEEN	peregrine falcon	**zo**
SHAITAN	Satan (Arabic)	
SHAKE-UP	upheaval reorganisation	
SHAKILY	insecure; precariously	
SHAKING	quaking; jarring; jolting	
SHALLON	an edible fruit	**bt**
SHALLOP	rowing boat; skiff; gun-boat; fishing boat; tender	**nt**
SHALLOT	small type of onion	**bt**
SHALLOW	superficial; rudd-fish	**zo**
SHAMBLE	shuffle along	
SHAMING	humiliating; abasing	
SHAMMED	simulated; feigned	
SHAMMER	impostor; malingerer	
SHAMPOO	hair-washing	
SHANDRY	rickety conveyance (Irish)	
SHANGIE	shackle (Sc.)	
SHANGTI	Chinese for God	**rl**
SHANKED	(golf); shin; legged; (shanks's pony); stem	**zo, bt**
SHAPELY	finely formed	
SHAPING	moulding; fashioning	
SHARDED	beetle-winged	**zo**
SHARING	apportioning; dividing	
SHARKED	cheated; duped; gulled	
SHARKER	shark-hunter	
SHARPED	tricked; defrauded; duped	
SHARPEN	strop; point; whet	
SHARPER	a trickster; cheat; rogue	
SHARPIE	oysterman's boat; New England	**nt**
SHARPLY	keenly; acutely; tartly	
SHASTER	Hindu Bible	**rl**
SHASTRA	sacred Hindu book	**rl**
SHATTER	splinter; disrupt; smash	
SHAVIAN	(Bernard Shaw)	
SHAVING	slicing; paring; grazing	
SHEAFED	bundled in sheaves	
SHEARED	reaped; cut through	
SHEARER	clipper; reaper; cutter	
SHEATHE	encase; cover	
SHEATHY	like a scabbard	
SHEAVED	collected in sheaves	
SHEBANG	store; saloon	
SHEBECK	⎫ mixed rig boat	
CHEBECK	⎬	
XEBEC	⎭ Mediterranean, Russia	**nt**
SHEBEEN	Irish whiskey shop	
SHEDDER	emitter; diffuser	
SHEERED	moved away	

SHEETED	covered with sheets		**SHOPMAN**	shop/factory foreman	
SHELLAC	resin lac	**bt**	**SHOPPED**	imprisoned; framed	
SHELLED	bombarded; husked		**SHOPPER**	peripatetic buyer	
SHELLER	huller; shucker		**SHORAGE**	landing charge	
SHELTER	screen; asylum; refuge		**SHORING**	props; buttressing	
SHELTIE	Shetland pony	**zo**	**SHORTED**	circuit fault	**el**
SHELVED	put aside; pigeonholed		**SHORTEN**	abbreviate; abridge; curtail	
SHELVES	ledges		**SHORTER**	briefer; terser; curter	
SHEPPEY	sheep-cote		**SHOTGUN**	light sporting gun	
SHERBET	a cooling drink		**SHOT-PUT**	putting the weight (sport)	**ga**
SHEREEF	an amir; emir		**SHOTTED**	loaded	
SHERIAT	Islamic law	**lw**	**SHOTTEN**	dislocated; curdled	
SHERIFF	county officer	**lw**	**SHOULDS**	internalised demands on	
SHEWING	showing; demonstration			behaviour	**pc**
SHIFTED	changed; altered; quitted		**SHOUTED**	yelled; bawled; roared	
SHIFTER	remover; contriver		**SHOUTER**	crier; vociferator	
SHIITES	Persian sectarians		**SHOVING**	propelling; pushing; jostling	
SHIKARI	hunter (India)		**SHOW-BOX**	presentation carton	
SHILPIT	washy; feeble (Sc.)		**SHOW-END**	(roll of cloth)	
SHIMMED	wedged		**SHOWERY**	pluvial	
SHIMMER	gleam; glisten; glimmer		**SHOWILY**	ostentatiously; flashily	
SHINGLE	style of hair-cutting; loose		**SHOWING**	representation; displaying	
	pebbles on sea shore;		**SHOWMAN**	exhibitor; actor-manager; artiste	
	wooden roof tiles	**gl, bd**	**SHOW-OFF**	play for admiration; swank	
SHINGLY	pebbly		**SHREDDY**	ragged; fragmentary	
SHINING	resplendent; coruscating		**SHRILLY**	piercingly; sharply; high-toned	
SHINNED	climbed		**SHRINAL**	sacred; hallowed	
SHIP-BOY	sailor's solace	**nt**	**SHRINED**	enshrined	
SHIPFUL	boat-load		**SHRIVEL**	to dry up; parch	
SHIPLAP	rebate-cut sheathing boards	**cr**	**SHRIVEN**	given absolution	**rl**
SHIP-MAN	a sailor	**nt**	**SHRIVER**	a confessor; absolver	**rl**
SHIPPED	embarked; (oars)		**SHROUDS**	winding sheets; rigging from	
SHIPPEN	sheep-pen; stable			mast to ship's sides	**nt**
SHIPPER	exporter		**SHROUDY**	giving shelter	
SHIPTON	a prophetess		**SHRUBBY**	full of shrubs	**bt**
SHIP-WAY	(dry dock)		**SHUCKER**	husker; huller; sheller	
SHIRKED	evaded; avoided; scamped		**SHUDDER**	shake; quiver; shiver	
SHIRKER	malingerer; dodger		**SHUFFLE**	mix; cavil; quibble; (cards)	
SHIRLEY	bull-finch	**zo**	**SHUNNED**	avoided; eluded	
SHIRLEY	poppy	**bt**	**SHUNNER**	eschewer; evader	
SHIRRED	puckered		**SHUNTED**	turned aside	
SHIRTED	wearing a shirt		**SHUNTER**	a railway-man	
SHITTAH	} acacia; (Tabernacle wood)		**SHUT-EYE**	sleep; a nap	
SHITTIM	}	**bt**	**SHUT-OFF**	turn off (steam); stoppage;	
SHIVERY	brittle; chilly			isolated	
SHIZOKU	Japanese gentry		**SHUT-OUT**	no score for opponent (sport)	**ga**
SHOALED	became shallow		**SHUTTER**	window or aperture cover	
SHOALER	coasting-vessel	**nt**			**pg, bd**
SHOCKED	offended; surprised		**SHUTTLE**	sliding thread-holder	
SHOCKER	sensational novel		**SHYLOCK**	rapacious usurer	
SHOE-BOY	a shiner		**SHYNESS**	bashfulness; coyness	
SHOEING	farrier's work		**SHYSTER**	rascally lawyer	
SHOE-PEG	a nail		**SIAMANG**	Malay gibbon	**zo**
SHOE-TIE	shoe-lace		**SIAMESE**	(inseparables); joined before	
SHOGGED	jolted; jogged			birth (twins)	
SHOOING	scaring away		**SIBILUS**	sibilant rhoncus; (nasal)	
SHOOKED	packed			phonetics	
SHOOTER	marksman; sniper; goal scorer		**SIBLING**	one's brother or sister	
	(netball) (football)		**SIBSHIP**	all brothers and sisters of one	
SHOPBOY	assistant; errand boy			family	

SICCATE	dessicate; dry; parch	
SICCITY	aridity; dryness	
SICKBAY	hospital ward	nt
SICKBED	in-patient at home	md
SICKEST	very poorly	
SICKISH	unwell; out of sorts	
SICKLED	with sickle	
SICK-PAY	wages during illness	
SIC-LIKE	such like	
SIDEARM	sword or bayonet	
SIDEBOX	(theatre)	
SIDECAR	cocktail (motorcycle)	
SIDECUT	branch canal; not off the grand joint (butchers' meat)	
SIDE-OUT	losing a rally; loss on a service (tennis)	
SIDE-ROD	coupling rod (steam locomotive)	
SIDLING	edging away	
SIEMENS	unit of electrical conductance	el, me
SIENESE	of Sienna	
SIENITE	syenite; hornblende	mn
SIFFLED	whistled	
SIFFLET	small whistle	
SIFTING	scrutinizing; sorting; sieving; (basketball)	
SIGHFUL	grievous	
SIGHING	lamenting; repining	
SIGHTED	seen; viewed; glimpsed	
SIGHTER	a trial shot	
SIGHTLY	handsome	
SIGMATE	(sigma)	
SIGMOID	curve of beauty	
SIGNALS	warnings, lights, sounds; radio, flags, etc.	tc, nt
SIGNATE	designate	
SIGNIFY	indicate; betoken; portend	
SIGNING	subscribing; gesturing	
SIGNIOR	signor (It.)	
SIGNORA	an Italian lady	
SIGNORY	seigniory; overlordship	
SIKHARA	spire or tower of Indian temple	ar
SIKHISM	monotheistic sect	
SILENCE	quiescence; dumbness	
SILENUS	foster-father of Bacchus	
SILESIA	cotton fabric	tx
SILICIC	(silica)	ch
SILICLE	broad pod	bt
SILICON	an element	ch
SILIQUA	} seed vessel; carat	bt, me
SILIQUE		
SILKIER	more lustrous	
SILKING	silk chiffon application to books; lining (paint)	pt
SILKMAN	silk-mercer	
SILLAGO	a fish genus	zo
SILLERY	a white wine	
SILLIER	more witless	
SILLILY	inanely; foolishly; ineptly	

SILOXEN	polymerized silicon analogue	ch
SILTING	depositing mud	go
SILURUS	cat-fish	zo
SILVERN	of silver	
SILVERY	bright; clear; sweet	
SIMARRE	a cymar; a costume	
SIMILAR	alike; analogous; twin	
SIMILIA	similes; metaphors	
SIMILOR	semilor; imitation gold	
SIMIOUS	ape-like; simian	zo
SIMITAR	scimitar	
SIMPKIN	champagne	
SIMPLER	herbalist; plainer; easier	
SIMPLEX	one-way circuit flow	tc
SIMPLEX	centre shafted putter (golf)	
SIMPSON	groundsel	bt
SIMULAR	counterfeit; feigned	
SIMURGH	fabulous bird (Pers.)	
SINAPIS	sinapin; mustard	bt
SINBORN	illegitimate	
SINBRED	raised to vice	
SINCERE	true; genuine; honest	
SINEWED	powerful; vigorous	
SINGING	the vocal art; unwanted oscillation in transmission system	el
SINGLED	selected; separated	
SINGLES	tennis; reeled silk	
SINGLET	undervest	
SINGULT	a sob; a sigh	
SINICAL	(sine)	
SINKAGE	excess space for margins, headings	
SINKING	foundering; declining; enlarged cavity for screw	ju
SINLESS	innocent; blameless	
SINNING	transgressing	
SINOPIA	} red pigment; sinople;	
SINOPIS	} sinoper	
SINSICK	repentant	
SINSYNE	since (Sc.)	
SINUATE	insinuate; curved	
SINUOUS	sinuose; winding	
SINWORN	fabulous monster	
SIPPING	supping	
SIREDON	larval salamander	zo
SIRENIA	sea-cows	zo
SIRGANG	green jackdaw	zo
SIRLOIN	surloin	
SIROCCO	} hot desert wind from	
SCIROCCO	} North Africa	mt
SISTINE	} (Pope Sixtus) (Vatican,	
SIXTINE	} chapel)	rl
SISTING	summoning (Sc.)	lw
SISTRUM	holy rattle (Egypt)	mu
SITFAST	ulcer	md
SITHENS	since; after that	
SITTINE	(nut-hatches)	zo
SITTING	session; incubating; bent-knee stance (fencing)	

SITUATE	permanently fixed	
SIVAITE	follower of Sivia	rl
SIXFOLD	6 times as much	
SIXTEEN	age of sweetness	
SIZABLE	of a size; bulky	
SIZZLED	frizzled	
SJAMBOK	S. Afr. raw hide whip	
SKAFFIE	fishing lugger (Sc.)	nt
SKEETER	mosquito	zo
SKELDER	swindle	
SKELLUM	a rascal; scamp; scoundrel	
SKELTER	skedaddle	
SKEPFUL	basketful	
SKEPTIC	sceptic; doubting	
SKETCHY	vague; incomplete	
SKEWGEE	crooked; skewed	
SKIDDED	scotched; slipped	
SKIDLID	crash helmet	
SKID-PAN	motorists' training ground	
SKIFFLE	folk-song and jazz	mu
SKI-JUMP	skiing slide	
SKILFUL	dexterous; adept; expert	
SKI-LIFT	cable or funicular lift	
SKILLED	expert; artful; adroit	
SKILLET	iron cooking pot	
SKIMMED	glided; grazed	
SKIMMER	scoop; bird	zo
SKIMPED	stinted	
SKINFUL	amount of drunkenness	
SKINKER	tapster; barman	
SKINNED	peeled; fleeced	
SKINNER	a furrier	
SKIPPED	omitted; jumped	
SKIPPER	a fish; a captain	zo
SKIPPET	seal-box; boat	nt
SKIRLED	shrieked shrilly	
SKIRRET	water-parsnip	bt
SKIRTED	bordered	
SKIRTER	a dodger	
SKI-SUIT	winter costume	
SKITTER	glide; skim	
SKITTLE	bowl out; knock down	
SKIVING	leather splitting; work dodging	
SKULKED	lurked	
SKULKER	a shirker; malingerer	
SKULPIN	sea-fish	zo
SKYBLUE	azure	
SKYBORN	heaven-born	
SKYHIGH	excessively elevated	
SKYLARK	the laverock	zo
SKYLINE	horizon; sea-line	
SKYSAIL	sail above royal	nt
SKYTEEN	satin weave shirting	tx
SKYWARD	heading upward	
SLABBED	cut into thick slices	
SLABBER	slobber; dribble; slaver	
SLACKED	eased off	
SLACKEN	relax; mitigate; abate	
SLACKER	skulker; sluggard; idler	
SLACKLY	negligently; laxly	

SLAINTE!	Good health! (Irish)	
SLAKING	quenching; allaying	
SLAMKIN	a slut; loose gown	
SLAMMED	banged	
SLANDER	malign; traduce; obloquy	
SLANGED	abused; vituperated	
SLANKET	strip of land; slang	
SLANTED	sloped; tilted	
SLANTLY	slantwise; atilt; obliquely	
SLAPPED	smacked; spanked	
SLAPPER	slap-up affair	
SLASHED	gashed; cut	
SLASHER	cutting tool	to
SLATHER	lots of	
SLATING	roofing; reprimand; abusing	
SLATTER	to be wasteful; slovenly; slater; tile mason	bd
SLAVDOM	Slavs collectively	
SLAVERY	serfdom; thraldom; bondage	
SLAVING	drudging; moiling	
SLAVISH	servile; obsequious	
SLAYING	destroying; despatching	
SLEAVED	not spun; raw	
SLEAVED	separated; divided	
SLEDDED	on a sled	
SLEDGED	sledded; mushed	
SLEEKED	glided; smoothed	
SLEEKEN	to smooth	
SLEEKER	slicker	to
SLEEKIT	smooth-tongued (Sc.)	
SLEEKLY	fair spoken; glossily; silky	
SLEEPER	track bed; overnight (train); slumberer (bowling)	cr rw
SLEEPER	honeycomb wall; ear stud; valley; board (roof)	bd
SLEETED	rained and snowed	mt
SLEIDED	unwoven; sleaved	
SLEIGHT	dexterity; skill; adroitness	
SLENDER	frail; slim; slight	
SLEWING	rotatory roll of crane, ship, etc.	nt
SLEYING	swinging askew	
SLICING	severing; (golf)	
SLICKER	smarter; more deft	
SLIDDER	to slither; slip; slide	
SLIDING	a lapse; varying	
SLIMILY	viscously; muddily	
SLIMMER	more slender; lankier	
SLINGER	of slongs	
SLIPPED	conveyed secretly	
SLIPPER	steel cradle; mule	
SLIPWAY	(shipbuilding)	
SLITHER	slide about	
SLITTED	slashed; split	
SLITTER	a cutter	to
SLOBBER	slabber; dribble; slaver	
SLOCKEN	slake; quench	
SLOE-GIN	pleasant drink	
SLOGGED	hit hard	
SLOGGER	mighty smiter	

SLOPING	inclined; declinous; oblique		**SMUDGED**	blurred; blotted
SLOPPED	spilt		**SMUDGER**	plumber
SLOTTED	grooved		**SMUGGLE**	convey secretly; snuggle
SLOTTER	to foul; filth		**SMYTRIE**	a crowd of children (Sc.)
SLOUCHY	slackly		**SNABBLE**	snaffle; plunder; eat
SLOUGHY	swampy; miry; queachy		**SNAFFLE**	a bit; appropriate; filch
SLOVENE	language and people		**SNAGGED**	snaggy
	(Yugoslavia)		**SNAGGER**	a cutter	**to**
SLOWEST	dullest; tardiest		**SNAKING**	rope-winding	**nt**
SLOWING	delaying; retarding		**SNAKISH**	reptilian; serpentine
SLUBBER	to scamp; slabber		**SNAPING**	bevelling
SLUDGER	sewage dumping vessel; sand		**SNAPPED**	caught; broke; photographed
	pump; hole cleaner	**nt, to**	**SNAPPER**	a turtle	**zo**
SLUGGED	bashed; coshed		**SNARING**	entrapping; catching
SLUGGER	big hitter (baseball)		**SNARLED**	entangled; complicated
SLUICED	drenched; flushed		**SNARLER**	growler; grumbler
SLUMBER	sleep; repose; doze		**SNATCHY**	irregular
SLUMMER	slum visitor		**SNEAKER**	soft soled shoe
SLUMPED	fell heavily		**SNEAKER**	short drink
SLUNKEN	shrivelled		**SNECKED**	latched; fastened (Sc.)
SLURRED	sullied; disparaged	**mu**	**SNECK-UP**	go hang!
SLUSHER	scraper (USA)	**ce, mn**	**SNEDDEN**	sand-eel	**zo**
SLUTCHY	residual; mucky		**SNEERER**	derider; taunter
SLYNESS	sliness; craft; cunning		**SNEEZED**	snoze
SMACKED	slapped; spanked		**SNICKER**	snigger; giggle
SMACKER	a resounding kiss		**SNIFFED**	snuffed; inhaled
SMARAGD	the emerald	**mn**	**SNIFFLE**	snuffle
SMARTED	endured sharp pain		**SNIFTER**	dram; radio-detector
SMARTEN	brighten; quicken		**SNIGGER**	snicker; giggle
SMARTER	brisker; sprucer		**SNIGGLE**	ensnare
SMARTLY	promptly; readily; alertly		**SNIPING**	shooting from ambush
SMASHED	disrupted; broken; drunk		**SNIPPER**	a tailor
SMASHER	blow; fine thing; (argument)		**SNIPPET**	a cutting
SMASH-UP	a crash		**SNIRTLE**	snigger
SMATTER	slight superficial knowledge		**SNOODED**	wearing a fillet
SMEARED	daubed; contaminated		**SNOOKER**	potting game; (development of
SMEARER	overshoot-cancelling circuit	**tc**		billiards); pool
SMECTIC	with parallel-oriented atoms	**ps**	**SNOOPER**	a nosy Parker
SMEDDUM	energy; powder		**SNOOZER**	a daydreamer
SMELLED	had an odour; smelt		**SNORKEL**	breathing pipe (U-boat)	**nt**
SMELLER	the proboscis		**SNORTER**	a fast one (cricket)
SMELTER	ore-worker		**SNOTTER**	bowsprit housing	**nt**
SMERLIN	loach fish	**zo**	**SNOUTED**	with snout
SMICKER	to smirk; ogle; leer		**SNOW-BOX**	(stage snowstorm)
SMICKET	a smock		**SNOW-FED**	(streams)
SMICKLY	amorously		**SNOW-FLY**	a stone-fly	**zo**
SMIDGEN	a bittock; a trifle		**SNOW-ICE**	frozen slush
SMILING	smirking		**SNOW-MAN**	snowball in human form
SMIRKED	simpered		**SNOW-OWL**	the great white owl	**zo**
SMITING	striking; buffeting; hitting		**SNUBBED**	deliberately slighted
SMITTEN	afflicted; chastened		**SNUBBER**	shock absorber
SMITTLE	to infect		**SNUFFED**	sniffed
SMOKIER	reekier		**SNUFFER**	a snuff taker
SMOKILY	fumily		**SNUFFLE**	nasal catarrh	**md**
SMOKING	bloating; quizzing		**SNUGGLE**	smuggle; cuddle; fondle
SMOLDER	smoulder		**SNUGIFY**	to make cosy
SMOOTHE	palliate; flatter; flatten		**SNUZZLE**	nuzzle
SMOTHER	stifle; suppress (cricket) (ice		**SOAKAGE**	absorption
	hockey)		**SOAKING**	drenching; steeping; imbruing
SMOUSER	pedlar (S. Africa)		**SO-AND-SO**	a vague definition; (derogatory)

SOAP-BOX	orator's platform	
SOAPING	flattering; lathering	
SOAP-PAN	soap boiler	
SOARANT	heraldic flying	**hd**
SOARING	mental uplift; aspiring; at zenith; (eagle)	
SOARING	airborne on upward currents (gliding) (hang gliding)	
SOBBING	lamentation; ululation	
SOBERED	enjoyed morning after	
SOBERLY	staidly	
SOBOLES	botanical suckers	**bt**
SOCAGER	socage tenant	
SOCCAGE	land tenure	**lw**
SOCIETY	company; sodality; élite	
SOCKEYE	Pacific salmon	**zo**
SOCKING	beating; throwing	
SODA-ASH	impure sodium carbonate	**mn**
SODDING	turfing	
SOFA-BED	day-bed; divan; ottoman	
SOFTEST	gentlest; easiest	
SOFTISH	yielding; compliant	
SOGGING	saturating	
SOIGNEE	admirably turned out (Fr.)	
SOILING	staining; tarnishing; dirtying; replacing topsoil, (resoiling)	**ce, bt**
SOILURE	pollution	
SOJOURN	visit; tarry; remain; abide	
SOKEMAN	tenant by socage	**lw**
SOLACED	consoled; comforted	
SOLANUM	night-shade genus	**bt**
SOLDIER	warrior; man-at-arms; upright brick; vertical support	**bd, ar**
SOLENIA	enteron diverticula in hydroids	**zo**
SOLICIT	importune; canvass; crave	
SOLIDLY	compactly; firmly; densely	
SOLIDUM	complete sum	
SOLIDUS	's' for shilling	**nm**
SOLIPED	not cloven-hoofed	**zo**
SOLOIST	lone musician	**mu**
SOLOMON	wisdom personified; (seal)	**bt**
SOLONIC	wise like Solon	
SOLPUGA	a spider genus	**zo**
SOLUBLE	capable of solution	
SOLVEND	a substance to be dissolved	
SOLVENT	able to pay all debts	
SOLVING	elucidating; unravelling	
SOMATIC	corporeal; bodily	
SOMEHOW	in one way or another	
SOMEONE	unspecified person	
SOMNIAL	dreamy	
SONANCE	sonancy; a call (Shak.)	
SONCHUS	sow-thistle genus	**bt**
SONDELI	Indian musk-rat	**zo**
SONGFUL	full of glee	
SONGMAN	balladmonger	
SONLESS	defiliated	
SONNITE	Sunnite; orthodox Moslem	**rl**

SONSHIP	cf. daughterdom	
SOOPING	sweeping ice away (curling)	
SOOTHED	assuaged; pacified; cajoled	
SOOTHER	diplomatist; mollifier	
SOOTHLY	truly	
SOOTING	(sparking plugs)	
SOOTISH	like soot	
SOPHISM	a fallacy; specious argument	
SOPHIST	captious reasoner	
SOPHORA	pagoda tree	**bt**
SOPIENT	a soporific	
SOPPING	soaking; steeping	
SOPRANI	several sopranos	**mu**
SOPRANO	female treble	**mu**
SORBENT	an absorbent	
SORBIAN	} Slavonic race in Saxony	
SORBISH		
SORBILE	that can be sipped/drunk	
SORBINE	} sorbate; sweet berry	
SORBITE	} extract	**bt**
SORBOSE	keto hexose	**ch**
SORCERY	witchcraft; enchantment	
SORDINA	} damper pedal (piano)	**mu**
SORDINO		**mu**
SORDONO	(oboe)	**mu**
SOREHON	Irish tenure	
SORGHUM	sugar-cane	**bt**
SORICID	like a shrew	
SORITES	syllogistic argument	
SORNING	obtruding; sponging on	
SOROCHE	altitude sickness (Sp. Andes)	**md**
SORORAL	sisterly	
SOROSIS	mulberry type of fruit	**bt**
SOROSIS	woman's club	
SORRILY	meanly; pitiably	
SORTING	disposing; classifying; sequence; order	**cp**
SOSPIRO	a breathing rest	**mu**
SOSTRUM	life-saving reward (Gr.)	
SOTTING	tippling; toping; boozing	
SOTTISE	blundering act (Fr.)	
SOTTISH	besotted; foolish	
SOUBISE	onion sauce	**ck**
SOUCHET	boiled fish	**ck**
SOUFFLE	frothy egg-dish	**ck**
SOUFFLE	blowing sound over heart	**md**
SOULFUL	spiritually emotional	
SOUNDED	vibrated; tested	**nt**
SOUNDER	(Morse)	
SOUNDER	boar; herd of swine	**zo**
SOUNDEX	consonant-based coding system	
SOUNDLY	thoroughly; validly	
SOUPCON	a suspicion; a taste (Fr.)	
SOUREST	most acid; rankest	
SOURING	acidulating	
SOURISH	tart; acetous; acrid	
SOUROCK	sorrel	**bt**
SOURSOP	American custard apple	**bt**
SOUSING	pickling; drenching	

SOUTANE	cassock	**rl**
SOUTENU	sustained, smooth flow (Fr.)	**mu**
SOUTHER	south wind	
SOUTHLY	southerly	
SOU'WEST	S.W.	
SOVKHOZ	state-owned farm (Rus.)	
SOWBACK	gravel ridge	
SOYBEAN	oil-rich Asiatic legume	**bt, ck**
SOZZLED	sossled; tipsy; fuddled	
SPACIAL	extensive; commodious	
SPACING	arranging intervals	
SPADDLE	spittle; small spade	**to**
SPADING	digging	
SPADONE	double-handed sword	
SPAEMAN	diviner (Sc.)	
SPAIRGE	sparge; sprinkle	
SPALING	a bracing; cross-band	
SPALLED	chipped; splintered	
SPANCEL	cow-hobble	
SPANDAU	German light machine gun	
SPANGLE	glittering disc	
SPANGLY	sparkling	
SPANIEL	fawning; mean	**zo**
SPANISH	Iberian	
SPANKED	slapped; speeded	
SPANKER	a sail	**nt**
SPANNED	measured; embraced	
SPANNER	monkey-wrench	
SPAN-NEW	brand-new	
SPARELY	sparingly; charily	
SPARGED	sprinkled; sprayed	
SPARGER	sprinkler; diffuser	
SPARING	frugal; parsimonious	
SPARKED	played the gallant	
SPARKLE	coruscate; twinkle	
SPAROID	like sea bream	
SPARRED	disputed; wrangled; boxed	
SPARRER	boxing partner	
SPARROW	a small finch	**zo**
SPARSIM	here and there (Lat.)	
SPARTAN	austere; hardy; undaunted	
SPARVER	type of bed curtain	**tx**
SPASTIC	spasmodic	
SPATHED	ensheathed	
SPATHIC	laminated; foliated	
SPATIAL	spacial, wide; spacious	
SPATTER	asperse; besprinkle; splash	
SPATTLE	} saliva	
SPADDLE		
SPITTLE		
SPATULA	a blade; a small spade	**md**
SPATULE	(tail feather)	**zo**
SPAWLED	slavered	
SPAWNED	deposited eggs	
SPAWNER	female fish	**zo**
SPAYING	gelding	
SPEAKER	(House of Commons)	
SPEARED	lanced; pierced; impaled	
SPEARER	spearman	
SPECIAL	distinctive; particular	

SPECIES	group; genus; class; kind	
SPECIFY	definite; indicate; detail	
SPECKED	spotted; speckled	
SPECKLE	small speck or stain	
SPECTRA	(spectrum); images	
SPECTRE	apparition; spook; hobgoblin	
SPECULA	mirrors; reflectors	
SPEEDED	ran; hastened; executed	
SPEEDER	pace-maker	
SPEED-UP	accelerate	
SPELDER	a splinter; chip	
SPELEAN	troglodytic	
SPELLED	charmed; entranced; spelt	
SPELLER	spelling book	
SPELTER	soldering alloy; zinc compound	**ml**
SPENCER	butler; jacket	
SPENCER	gaff-sail	**nt**
SPENDER	prodigal; wastrel; waster	
SPERKET	spirket; harness hook	
SPEWING	vomiting	
SPHACEL	gangrene	**md**
SPHENIC	wedge-like	
SPHERAL	ball-like; globular	
SPHERED	englobed	
SPHERIC	spherical	
SPHYRNA	hammer-headed sharks	
SPICATE	} spicous; prickly; spinous;	
SPICOSE	} thorny; spinate	
SPICERY	(spices)	
SPICILY	pungently; piquantly	
SPICING	seasoning; varying	
SPICULE	} small pine; spike or ear	**bt**
SPICULA		
SPIDERY	very thin	
SPIEGEL	steel alloy	
SPIGNEL	baldmoney; a plant	**bt**
SPIKING	impaling; transfixing	
SPILING	building-piles	**bd**
SPILITE	fine-grained igneous rock	**gl**
SPILLED	spilt; wasted; slopped	
SPILLER	reefing rope; lucky strike; slow, even wave; (bowling); (surfing)	**nt**
SPILOMA	birthmark; a naevus	**md**
SPINACH	spinage	**bt**
SPINATE	spiky; spicate	**bt**
SPINDLE	axis; arbor	
SPINDLY	fusiform; slender	
SPINNER	a bait; textile operator	
SPINNEY	spinny; copse	
SPINODE	cusp in a curve	
SPIN-OFF	incidental by-product; side effect	
SPINOSE	spinous; thorny	**bt**
SPINULA	spicule	**bt**
SPINULE	small spine	**bt**
SPIRAEA	a plant genus	**bt**
SPIRANT	fricative consonant; a sibilant	
SPIRING	tapering; sprouting	

SPIRITO	} spirited	**mu**
SPIRITOSO		
SPIRITY	mettlesome; alcoholic	
SPIRKET	sperket; harness hook	
SPIRTED	spurted; spouted; gushed	
SPIRTLE	to spin; to spurt	
SPIRULA	cephalopods; cuttle-fish	**zo**
SPITBOX	a cuspidor	
SPITING	grudging; thwarting	
SPITTED	transfixed	**ck**
SPITTER	young deer	**zo**
SPITTLE	small spade; saliva	
SPIZINE	(buntings; finches)	**zo**
SPLASHY	wet and muddy	
SPLAYED	sloped; slanted	
SPLEENY	ill-humoured; fretful	
SPLEGET	a swab	**md**
SPLENIC	spleeny; fretful; melancholy	
SPLICED	interwoven; married; (main brace); hit	**nt**
SPLICER	joiner of ropes, tapes, etc.	**cp**
SPLINTS	surgical appliances	**md**
SPLODGE	daub; patch	
SPLODGY	stained; blotched	
SPLOTCH	smear; stain	
SPLURGE	rowdiness	
SPLURGY	boisterous; spend freely	
SPODIUM	ivory-black	
SPOFFLE	to bustle; to fuss	
SPOILED	pillaged; ruined; marred	
SPOILER	plunderer; bungler	
SPOLIUM	church property	**rl**
SPONDEE	poetic foot (2 long syllables)	
SPONDYL	a vertebra; a joint	**md**
SPONGED	deleted; purged; sorned	
SPONGER	a parasite; sorner	
SPONGIN	horny skeletal substance in porifera	**zo**
SPONSAL	(marriage)	
SPONSON	protecting bracket	**nt**
SPONSOR	guarantor; a surety	
SPOOFED	hoodwinked; hoaxed	
SPOOLED	wound on spools	
SPOOMED	scudded before the wind	
SPOONED	hit into the air; courted	
SPOONEY	love-sick	
SPOORER	tracker	
SPOROID	sporous; sporelike	**bt**
SPORONT	stage in protozoa life history	
SPORRAN	kilt-pouch	
SPORTED	wore; trifled; romped	
SPORTER	jester; player	
SPORULE	small spore	**bt**
SPOTTED	spied; detected; pied	
SPOTTER	sharp-sighted look-out; assistant to gymnast; (talent); (locomotive)	**rw**
SPOUSAL	nuptial; matrimonial	
SPOUTED	orated; spirted; pawned	
SPOUTER	declaimer; whale	**zo**

SPRAICH	shriek; cry (Sc.)	
SPRAYED	sprinkled; spumed; affused	
SPRAYER	water cart; town cleansing; flow aimer	
SPRAYEY	branching	
SPREAGH	plunder (Sc.)	
SPRIGGY	full of sprigs	
SPRIGHT	sprite; a spirit; a ghost	
SPRINGE	spring trap; a gin	
SPRINGY	vernal; elastic	
SPRINTS	bicycle wheels	
SPRUCED	smartened up; prinked	
SPRUNNY	spruce; a sweetheart	
SPRYEST	spriest; gayest; pertest	
SPUMING	spumous; frothy; foamy	
SPUMONE	ice-cream in varied layers (It.)	
SPUN-HAY	twisted hay	
SPUN-OUT	long drawn	
SPUR-DOG	a shark	**zo**
SPURIAE	bastard quills	**zo**
SPURNED	rejected; scouted; contemned	
SPURNER	a disdainer	
SPURRED	goaded; impelled; galloped	
SPURRER	inciter; instigator	
SPURREY	a plant	**bt**
SPURTED	spirted; gushed; sprinted	
SPURTLE	spurt; spirtle	
SPURWAY	bridle-path	
SPUTNIK	earth satellite (Rus.)	
SPUTTER	splutter	
SPY-BOAT	vessel for secret agents	**nt**
SPY-HOLE	peep-hole; Judas' hole	
SPYNDLE	unit of length of jute/flax yarn	
SQUABBY	squaddy; squat; tubby	
SQUACCO	crested heron	**zo**
SQUAILS	form of table bowls (19th Cent.)	
SQUALID	sordid; unclean; filthy	
SQUALLY	gusty; blustering	
SQUALOR	dirtiness; foulness	
SQUALUS	shark	**zo**
SQUARED	adjusted; tallied; bribed; position of oar blade in water (rowing)	
SQUASHY	pulpy; soft	
SQUATTY	squabby; clumsy	
SQUEASY	scrupulous; squeamish	
SQUEEZE	compress; crush; pinch; nip; block defensive lineman, score (Am. football) (baseball)	
SQUEEZY	congested; squashy	
SQUELCH	crush; suppress; quash	
SQUIFFY	tipsy; inebriated; sozzled	
SQUINCH	small stone arch; tight squeeze	
SQUINNY	to look asquint; meagre	
SQUIRED	escorted	
SQUITCH	quitch-grass	**bt**
SRADDHA	Hindu devotional offerings	**rl**
STABBED	wounded; pierced	
STABBER	awl; marlinspike	**to**
STABLED	stalled	

STABLER	stable-keeper	
STABLES	a trumpet call	**mu**
STACHYS	hedge-nettle genus	**bt**
STACKED	piled; (cards)	
STACKER	haymaker; washer-up; (kitchen) storeman	
STACKER	receptacle for punched cards	**cp**
STADDLE	crutch; support	
STADIUM	arena; running track	
STAFFED	manned by	
STAGERY	scenic exhibition	
STAGGER	astound; lurch; reel; sway; space out (hours)	
STAGING	a structure; producing	
STAIDLY	steadily; sedately; soberly	
STAINED	foxed; tarnished; sullied	
STAINER	a dyer	
STAITHE	coaling stage	
STAKING	hazarding; wagering	
STALDER	cask rack; horizontal bar exercise (gymn.)	
STALELY	mustily; effetely; insipidly	
STALEST	most trite	
STALKED	with peduncle	**bt**
STALKER	stealthy sportsman	
STALLED	fatted; lost speed	
STALLOY	silicon-content steel	**ml**
STAMINA	endurance; vitality; vigour	
STAMMEL	rough red cloth	**tx**
STAMMER	stutter	
STAMNOS	Greek urn	
STAMPED	impressed; crushed; branded	
STAMPER	ore crusher	
STAND-BY	a reserve	
STANDER	provider; candidate	
STAND-IN	deputy; substitute	
STAND-TO	military readiness	
STAND-UP	well fought	
STANIEL	} stanyel; kestrel; bird of prey; windhover	
STANNEL		
STANYEL		**zo**
STANINE	statistical unit	
STANNIC	(of tin)	
STANNUM	tin, metallic element	**ch**
STAPLED	connected together	
STAPLER	a dealer; clipping machine	
STARCHY	stiff; formal; precise	
STARDOM	film eminence	
STARING	glaring; gaping; prominent	
STARKEN	stiffen; make obstinate	
STARKLY	completely; absolutely	
STARLET	junior actress	
STAR-LIT	almost invisible	
STARRED	shone; bespangled	
STARTED	winced; roused; began	
STARTER	also ran (horse racing); motor; foretaste; beginner; (self); (races)	
STARTLE	alarm; frighten; surprise	
STARVED	famished; emaciated	

STASIMA	choral odes (Gr.)	
STATANT	standing	**hd**
STATELY	lofty; magnificent; imposing	
STATICE	sea-lavender	**bt**
STATICS	conditions for equilibrium	
STATING	narrating; affirming	
STATION	stock-farm; terminus; organisation; office; status	**rw**
STATION	location in network for computer, terminal	**cp**
STATISM	policy; art of government	
STATIST	statistical expert	
STATIVE	fixed; standing still	
STATOHM	obsolete electrostatic unit	**el, me**
STATUED	with statues	
STATURE	natural height	
STATUTE	an enactment; decree	**lw**
STAUNCH	stanch; trusty; steadfast	
STAVING	delaying; broaching	
STAYING	enduring; detaining; abiding	
STAY-PUT	semi-permanent	
STEALER	purloiner; peculator	
STEALTH	furtiveness; secrecy	
STEAMED	vaporized	
STEAMER	cooking vessel; ship	**nt**
STEARIC	of candle grease	**ch**
STEARIN	fat; wax; stearic acid	
STEELED	hardened; nerved	
STEEPED	soaked; drenched; imbrued	
STEEPEN	to make steep	
STEEPER	soaking vat	
STEEPLE	a spire	**rl**
STEEPLY	almost sheer; abruptly	
STEERED	conned; controlled; directed	
STEERER	pilot; guide; director	
STEEVED	packed closely	
STELENE	pillar-like; columnar	
STELLAR	astral; starry	
STEMLET	small stalk	
STEMMED	compressed	
STEMPLE	} cross-beam	
STEMPEL		
STEMSON	jointing timber	**nt**
STENCHY	odoriferous	
STENCIL	pattern plate	
STENGAH	whisky and soda (Malay)	
STENODE	supersonic heterodyne receiver	
STENTER	fabric-stretching machine	**tx**
STENTOR	a loud speaker	
STEP-INS	elastic-held shoes; underwear	
STEPNEY	spare-wheel; (born at sea)	
STEPPED	paced; walked; fixed	
STEPPER	horse with high action	
STEPSON	spouse's earlier product	
STERILE	barren; germ-free; acarpous	
STERLET	sturgeon	**zo**
STERNAL	(breast-bone)	**md**
STERNER	harsher; more austere	
STERNLY	severely; strictly; dourly	

STERN-TO	in reverse; backwards	**nt**
STERNUM	breast-bone	**md**
STEROID	sterol compound	**ch**
STEROLS	cholesterols in plants and animals	
STERTOR	noisy breathing	**md**
STETSON	a hat (USA)	
STEVING	stowing	**nt**
STEWARD	seneschal; bailiff	**nt**
STEWARD	(rally); (horse-racing); (ship); airline; purser; agent; waiter	**nt**
STEW-CAN	} cooking vessels	**ck**
STEW-PAN		
STEW-POT		
STEWING	simmering; worrying	
STHENIA	strength	**md**
STIBIAL	(antimony)	
STIBINE	antimony hydride	**ch**
STIBIUM	antimony	**ch**
STICHIC	rhythmic	
STICHOS	a line of verse	
STICKER	last ditcher; adherent	
STICKLE	a rapid in a stream	
STIFFEN	harden	
STIFFER	more rigid; harder; primmer	
STIFFLY	rigidly; firmly; starchy	
STIFLED	suffocated; smothered	
STILLED	hushed; calmed; distilled	
STILLER	pacifier; composer	
STILTED	pompous; bombastic	
STILTON	a cheese	**ck**
STIMIED	obstructed; (golf)	
STIMULI	incentives; spurs	
STINGER	"hot feet" of insects; wound pain; pontoon; lay barge	**mt, ce**
STINKER	despicable person	
STINTED	restricted; rationed	
STINTER	pincher; restrainer	
STIPATE	crowded	**bt**
STIPEND	salary; emolument	
STIPPLE	to make dots	
STIPTIC	astringent	**md**
STIPULA	} leaf appendage	**bt**
STIPULE		
STIRPES	forefathers; races	
STIRRED	roused; incited; bustled	
STIRRER	thriller; agitator; disturber	
STIRRUP	foot-holder for rider; pump; cup	
STIVING	stewing	
STOAKED	choked; stopped	**nt**
STOCKED	stored; saved; hoarded	
STOCKLI	movement on pommel horse (gymn.)	
STOICAL	passionless; unfeeling	
STOKING	adding fuel	
STOLLEN	sweet German yeast bread	**ck**
STOMACH	to brook; to resent; desire for; courage	**md**

STOMATA	breathing pore	**md**
STOMIUM	fern-sporangium-wall part	**bt**
STONIED	astonished; amazed	
STONILY	obdurately; unrelentingly	
STONING	pelting; (fruit)	
STOOGED	loitered; filled in time	
STOOKED	set up in sheaves	
STOOKER	harvest worker	
STOOMED	fermented	
STOOPED	condescended; swooped	
STOOPER	bender	
STOOTER	Dutch silver coin	**nm**
STOPGAP	locum tenens	
STOPING	series of ledges	
STOPPED	restrained; repressed; closed	
STOPPER	} restraint; a centre-back	
STOPPLE	(soccer)	
STORAGE	safe custody; space; (warehouse)	
STORAGE	accumulator cell; memory system	**el, cp**
STORIED	legendary; fabled	
STORIES	floors; tales	
STORING	garnering; hoarding	
STORMED	assaulted; raved; raged	
STORMER	blusterer	
STOTTER	rebound; a bounce (Sc.)	
STOUTEN	hearten; encheer	
STOUTER	more corpulent; braver	
STOUTLY	sturdily; stalwartly; robust	
STOVING	a heat treatment	
STOWAGE	packing; loading	
STOWING	arranging; packing	
STRAIKS	wheel-plates; strakes	
STRANGE	unfamiliar; abnormal; exotic	
STRAPPY	strong; fit; many straps	
STRATUM	rock formation	**gl**
STRATUS	cloud formation	**mt**
STRAWED	strewed	
STRAYED	erred; roved; deviated	
STRAYER	wandered; vagrant	
STRAYNE	strain; stress (Spens.)	
STREAKY	striped; bacon with lines of fat	**ck**
STREAMY	well watered	
STRELLI	movement on parallel bars (gymn.)	
STRETCH	reach; strain; expand; (baseball)	
STRETTO	quick and sharp (It.)	**mu**
STREULI	backward roll to handstand (gymn.)	**ga**
STREWED	strewn; scattered	
STRIATE	streaky; scratched	
STRIDOR	harsh noise; a jar	
STRIGES	the owl genus	**zo**
STRIGIL	skin-scraper	
STRIKER	(industrial action); blacksmith's assistant; attacking forwards (football); batsman (cricket) (baseball); firing pin	

STRINGS	viol family instruments	**mu**
STRINGY	filamentous	
STRIOLA	small/weak stria; scratch	
STRIPED	streaked	
STRIPES	a tiger	**zo**
STRIP-IN	recombining photo material	
STRIVEN	strove; struggled; tussled	
STRIVER	emulator; trier; competitor	
STROBIC	rate of turning; spinning	
STROCAL	glass-maker's shovel	
STROKED	rubbed gently; (rowing)	
STROKEN	struck (Spens.)	
STROKER	rubber; soother	
STROPHE	a stanza; verse; (Gr.)	
STRUDEL	Austrian thin-dough pastry	**ck**
STUBBED	blunted; obtuse; extirpated	
STUBBLE	corn stumps	**bt**
STUBBLY	like stubble; unshaven	
STUCKLE	clump of sheaves	
STUCK-UP	arrogant; pompous	
STUDDED	(shirts); (nails)	
STUDDLE	a trestle	
STUDENT	pupil; scholar; philomath	
STUDIED	conned; pondered; worked	
STUDIER	student; scrutinizer	
STUFFED	padded; crowded; rammed	
STUFFER	packer; crammer	
STUMBLE	trip; slip; blunder; lurch	
STUMBLY	apt to stumble	
STUMMED	fortified; doctored	
STUMMEL	tobacco pipe (Ger.)	
STUMPED	at a loss; (cricket)	
STUMPER	wicket-keeper; difficult problem; heavy walker; tree-cutter	
STUNNED	dumbfounded; amazed	
STUNNED	an astonisher; stupefier	
STUNTED	dwarfed; pygmean; runty	
STUPEFY	bemuse; dope; benumb	
STUPENT	struck with stupor	
STUPOSE	tufted; scaly; matted	
STURNUS	starling genus	**zo**
STUTTER	stammer; hesitant utterance	
STYGIAN	infernal; black; murky	
STYLATE	styloid; like a style or pen	
STYLING	naming; designating	
STYLISH	modish; chic; elegant	
STYLIST	fine writer	
STYLITE	pillar-dweller	
STYLIZE	to make conventional	
STYLOID	pen-like	
STYMIED	stimied; obstructed; (golf)	
STYPSIS	use of styptics	**md**
STYPTIC	stiptic; astringent	**md**
SUASIVE	urbane; agreeable	
SUASORY	convincing	
SUAVELY	pleasantly; blandly	
SUAVITY	affability; sweetness	
SUBACID	rather acid	
SUBADAR	Mogul governor	
SUBARID	slightly arid	

SUB-BASE	(submarines); road undersurface	**nt, ce**
SUBBASS	low organ note	**mu**
SUBBING	acting as substitute; subediting	
SUBCOXA	segment of primitive leg in insects	**zo**
SUBDEAN	under-dean	**rl**
SUBDUAL	conquest; subjugation	
SUBDUCE	withdraw	
SUBDUCT	subtract	
SUBDUED	piano; routed; worsted	
SUBDUER	queller; vanquisher	
SUBEDAR	native captain	
SUBEDIT	(edit)	
SUBERIC	of cork	
SUBERIN	cork-cell fatty mixture	**bt**
SUBFUSC	subfusk; dusky	
SUBGENS	sub-clan	
SUBGOAL	intermediary goal or achievement	
SUB-HEAD	sub-title	
SUBJECT	thesis; topic; subservient; conquer; impose; grammar; (fugue)	**lw, mu**
SUBJOIN	append; affix; postfix	
SUBLATE	carry off; take away	
SUBLIME	exalted; lofty; superb	
SUBNUDE	almost leafless	**bt**
SUBOVAL	almost ovate	
SUBPENA	subpoena; writ	**lw**
SUBRENT	sublet	
SUBSALT	below the salt	**ch**
SUBSIDE	sink; ebb; wane; abate	
SUBSIDY	a grant; dole; monetary aid	
SUBSIGN	undersign	
SUB-SILL	steel window-level wall covering	**bd**
SUBSIST	live; exist; endure	
SUBSOIL	the under-soil	
SUBSUME	include as comprehended	
SUBTACK	an under-lease (Sc.)	
SUBTEND	embrace; enfold	
SUBTILE	subtle; cunningly devised	
SUBTLER	wilier; craftier	
SUBTYPE	subdivision	
SUBURBS	outlying districts	
SUBVENE	aid; support	
SUBVERT	overthrow; ruin; corrupt	
SUCCADE	candied fruit	
SUCCEED	follow; prosper; win	
SUCCESS	prosperity; victory; triumph	
SUCCISE	ending below abruptly	**bt**
SUCCORY	chicory	**bt**
SUCCOSE	sappy	
SUCCOUR	aid; help; support; foster	
SUCCUBA	battering demons; spirits	
SUCCULA	capstan; winch	
SUCCUMB	yield; submit; die; capitulate	
SUCCUSS	to shake suddenly	
SUCKING	absorbing; imbibing	

SUCKLED	nursed	
SUCKLER	an infant; a suckling	
SUCROSE	cane sugar	
SUCTION	vacuum-filling	
SUDANIC	group of languages (Sudan)	
SUDORAL	sweaty; perspiring	
SUFFETE	Punic official	
SUFFICE	to content; be enough; avail	
SUFFUSE	diffuse; blush; overspread	
SUGARED	candied; sweetened	
SUGGEST	hint; insinuate; propose	
SUGGING	sea-rocked when stranded	**nt**
SUICIDE	felo-de-se; taking one's own life; self destruction	
SUIFORM	pig-like; swinish	
SUITING	pleasing; according	**tx**
SULCATE	grooved; furrowed	
SULKIER	more sullen	
SULKILY	morosely; sullenly; surlily	
SULKING	glowering	
SULLAGE	dross; scum	
SULLENS	morose; temper; the sulks	
SULLIED	tainted; tarnished; defamed	
SULPHUR	brimstone	**ch**
SULTANA	raisin; marsh bird	**bt, zo**
SUMATRA	Malaccan summer squall	**mt**
SUMLESS	beyond count	
SUMMARY	epitome; abstract; digest; report	**cp**
SUMMERY	summerlike; hot weather	
SUMMING	summary; adding; counting	
SUMMIST	writer of a compendium	
SUMMONS	writ; citation	**lw**
SUMPERS	cut holes (shaft sinking)	**mn**
SUMPTER	pack-horse	**zo**
SUN-BATH	outdoor near-nudity	
SUNBEAM	ray from the sun	
SUNBEAT	struck by the sun's rays	
SUNBIRD	humming bird	**zo**
SUNBURN	tan	
SUNCLAD	radiant	
SUNDARI	hardwood tree (Borneo)	**bt**
SUNDAWN	dawn-light	
SUNDIAL	stylish timepiece	
SUNDOWN	sunset	
SUNDROP	primrose (Amer.)	**bt**
SUNFISH	shark	**zo**
SUN-KIST.	kissed by the sun	
SUN-LAMP	ultra-violet ray	
SUNLESS	cloudy; overcast	
SUNLIKE	solar	
SUNMYTH	a solar myth	
SUNNING	sun-bathing	
SUNNITE	Sonnite; orthodox Muslim	
SUNRISE	dawn; cock-crow	
SUNROSE	sunflower	**bt**
SUNSPOT	solar phenomenon	**as**
SUNWARD	towards the sun	
SUNWISE	clock-wise	
SUPPING	eat evening meal	
SUPPLED	made pliant	
SUPPORT	prop; uphold; assist; position on arms (gymn)	
SUPPOSE	surmise; fancy; deem	
SUPREME	dominant; paramount	
SURANAL	above the anus	**zo**
SURBASE	cornice; base moulding	
SURCOAT	coat worn over chain mail	
SURDITY	lack of resonance; deafness	
SURFACE	exterior; superficies	
SURFARI	safari in search of good surfing	
SURFEIT	excess; plethora; cloy; gorge	
SURFING	to plane on forward portion of wave	
SURFMAN	skilled boatman	
SURGENT	swelling; heaving	
SURGEON	who treats people by operation	
SURGERY	cutting into bodies	**md**
SURGING	swirling; billowing; regular increases of power (Faradayism); running technique	
SURLIER	more churlish and crusty	
SURLILY	gruffly; sullenly; morosely	
SURLOIN	sirloin beef	**ck**
SURMISE	conjecture; suppose; imagine	
SURNAME	sirname; cognomen	
SURPASS	excel; exceed; outdo	
SURPLUS	residuum; balance; excess	
SURSIZE	feudal penalty	**lw**
SURTOUT	overcoat	
SURVIVE	outlive; endure; outlast	
SUSCEPT	parasite's host	
SUSPECT	doubtful; mistrust; distrust	
SUSPEND	hang; postpone; relieve	
SUSPIRE	sign; yearn; breathe	
SUSTAIN	uphold; bear; endure	
SUTLERY	sutler's occupation	
SUTLING	commissariat	
SUTURAL	sewn; seamy; stitched	
SUTURED	sewn together	
SWABBED	washed; mopped	
SWABBER	scrubber; mopper-up	
SWABIAN	(South German)	
SWADDLE	swathe; wrap; bind	
SWAGGED	sagged; leant	
SWAGGER	strut; ruffle; boast	
SWAGING	assuaging; mitigating	
SWAGING	metal-rod tapering	**mt**
SWAGMAN	burglar	
SWAHILI	East African language	
SWALING	wasting; consuming; burning	
SWALLET	underground stream	**go**
SWALLOW	voracity; engulf; absorb	**zo**
SWAMPED	overwhelmed; inundated	
SWANKED	boasted; bragged	
SWANKIE	swipes; thin beer	
SWANPAN	Chinese abacus	
SWAPPED	bartered; exchanged	
SWARAJI	home rule (India)	

SWARDED	grassy; turfy
SWARFED	fainted; swooned; dwalmed
SWARMED	thronged; teemed; clustered
SWARTHY	tawny; swart; dark
SWASHED	blustered; swanked
SWASHER	swash-buckler
SWATTED	hit with a fly swat
SWATTER	fly-killer
SWAYING	governing; oscillating
SWEALED	guttered like a candle
SWEARER	blasphemer
SWEATED	drudged; oozed; reeked
SWEATER	a pullover; jersey
SWEDISH	(Sweden)
SWEEPER	an artist of the brush; road cleaner
SWEEPER	defensive player (soccer) (hockey)
SWEETEN	to palliate; dulcify
SWEETER	more fragrant
SWEETIE	sweetmeat; confectionery
SWEETLY	dulcetly; fragrantly
SWELLED	inflated; heaved; bulged
SWELLEL	American squirrel **zo**
SWELLET	rush of water in a mine
SWELTER	perspire; sweat
SWELTRY	sultry; oppressive
SWERVED	deviated; turned aside
SWERVER	curve-swinger
SWIFTER	faster; nimbler; quicker
SWIFTLY	rapidly; promptly; suddenly
SWIGGED	drank deep; quaffed
SWILLED	rinsed; washed; boozed
SWILLER	copious absorber
SWIMMER	water-spider **zo**
SWINDLE	fraud; dupe; cheat
SWINERY	piggery
SWINGED	beaten up; punished
SWINGEL	
SWINGLE	} loose end of flail
SWIPPLE	
SWINGER	disco dancer; pendulum; trench bar; wife-swapper
SWINISH	hoggish; suiform
SWINKED	drudged; moiled; toiled
SWIPING	slogging; lashing out
SWIRLED	whirled; eddied
SWISHED	flogged
SWISHER	a wielder of the birch; shot for goal (basketball)
SWITHER	hesitate; doubt; fright
SWITZER	Swiss bodyguard; a Swiss
SWIZZLE	a mixed drink
SWOLLEN	distended; enlarged; bloated
SWOONED	fainted; swarfed; dwalmed
SWOOPED	caught on the wing
SWOPPED	swapped; bartered
SWOTTED	studied hard
SYBOTIC	pertaining to swineherd
SYCOSIS	barber's itch **md**

SYENITE	Egyptian granite	**· mn**
SYLPHID	small sylph; fairy	
SYLVINE	potassium chloride	**ch**
SYLVITE	potassium chloride	**ch**
SYMBION	symbiotic organism	**zo**
SYMPTOM	token; indication; sign	
SYNACMY	floral maturity	**bt**
SYNAPSE	nerve junction	**md**
SYNAPTE	Greek litany	**rl**
SYNAXIS	an assembly for worship	
SYNCARP	multiple fleshy fruit	**bt**
SYNCHRO	transformer for transmitting angular data	
SYNCOPE	contraction; collapse	
SYNERGY	co-operation	
SYNESIS	harmonious construction	
SYNNEMA	erect bunch of hyphae	**bt**
SYNOCHA	fever	**md**
SYNOCIL	a growth on sponges	
SYNODAL	bishop's benefit	**rl**
SYNODIC	(synod); conventional	
SYNONYM	a word of similar significance	
SYNOTUS	long-eared bat	**zo**
SYNOVIA	lubrication	**md**
SYNTONY	wireless tuning	
SYRINGA	mock-orange	**bt**
SYRINGE	a squirt; to spray	
SYSTOLE	contraction of the heart	**md**
SYSTYLE	a stylish portico	
SYSTYLE	type of colonnade	**ar**

T

TABANAC	French white wine	
TABANUS	horse-fly or gad-fly	**zo**
TABARET	satin striped silk	**tx**
TABELLA	lozenge	**md**
TABETIC	consumptive	**md**
TABIDLY	tabific; tabetic	
TABINET	curtain material	
TABLEAU	vivid picture (Fr.)	
TABLIER	apron; chess-board	
TABLING	setting down in order	
TABLOID	multum in parvo	**md**
TABOOED	banned; barred; accursed	
TABORER	drummer	**mu**
TABORET	small drum	**mu**
TABULAR	listed; tabulated; catalogued; program language	**cp**
TACHYON	fast-moving particle	**nc**
TACITLY	noiselessly implied	
TACKILY	stickily; adhesively	
TACKING	stitching; fastening; zigzag course against wind	**nt, nv**
TACKLED	seized; grappled with	
TACK-RAG	dust/grit remover	**pt**
TACTFUL	diplomatic and sensitive	
TACTICS	cunning moves	
TACTILE	tangible; perceptible	

TACTION	sense of touch; contact	
TACTOID	double-reflecting droplet	ch, ps
TACTUAL	tactile; palpable	
TADORNA	duck genus	zo
TADPOLE	embryonic frog; polliwog	zo
TADZHIK	Central Asian people	
TAENITE	iron-nickel solution	mn
TAFFETA	wavy fabric	tx
TAFFETY	taffeta; lustrous silk	tx
TAGALOG	language (Philippines)	
TAGETES	French marigolds	bt
TAGGERS	thin sheet iron	
TAGGING	following; tailing; tacking	
TAGMEME	smallest meaningful speech unit	
TAGSORE	sheep disease	vt
TAGTAIL	worm; parasite	vt
TAILAGE	entail	lw
TAILCAP	leather fold on book spine	
TAILEND	fag-end	
TAILING	following; a winter sport	
TAILZIE	deed of entail	lw
TAINTED	infected; stained; sullied	
TAIPING	Chinese rebel	
TAKE-OFF	a burlesque; ascent from earth; stroke (golf) (croquet)	ae
TAKE-OUT	withdraw; (insurance); courtship; (patents) (export)	lw
TAKINGS	cash receipts	
TAKOURA	golf-like game (Morocco)	
TAKSPAN	pine-roof shingles	ar
TALARIA	Mercury's winged sandals	
TALCITE	nacrite	mn
TALCOSE	talcous; a talc	
TALEFUL	newsy	
TALIPED	club footed	
TALIPES	slub-foot	md
TALIPOT	} talipat; fan-palm	bt
TALIPUT		
TALKIES	talking films	
TALKING	prating; discoursing	
TALLAGE	ancient tax	
TALLBOY	chest of drawers	
TALLEST	loftiest; highest	
TALLIED	agreed; correspond; fitted	
TALLIER	tally-keeper	
TALLISH	rather tall; of good height	
TALLITH	praying mantle (Heb.)	
TALLOWY	fatty	
TALLY-HO	hunting call	
TALONED	with claws	
TAMABLE	docile; tractable	
TAMANOA	ant-eater	zo
TAMARIN	S. American monkey	zo
TAMASHA	entertainment (India)	
TAMBOUR	drum; embroidery; vestibule; dome-(holding walls) tennis	mu, tx, ar
TAMBURA	} long Indian lute	mu
TANPURA		

TAMBURO	It. small snare drum	mu
TAMILIC	} Tamil; a dialect of Sri Lanka	
TAMULIC		
TAMMANY	political organisation, US	
TAMPING	(blasting)	
TAMPION	also tompion; a stopper	
TANADAR	Hindu police officer	
TANAGER	American finch	zo
TANAGRA	finches	zo
TANAGRA	terracotta ware	
TANGENT	meeting but not intersecting; clavichord, tongue	mu
TANGHIN	poison tree (Madagascar)	bt
TANGING	twanging; flavouring	
TANGLED	jumbled; matted; twisted	
TANGRAM	Chinese jigsaw	ga
TANKAGE	storage	
TANKARD	drinking vessel	
TANKCAR	tanker; oil-tank	
TANKING	waterproofing a basement	
TANLING	sun-bather	
TANNAGE	tanning materials	
TANNATE	a salt of tannic acid	ch
TANNERY	leather factory	le
TANNING	leathering	le
TANNINS	organic compounds used for ink and leather	ch
TANRIDE	riding school	
TANSPUD	bark-peeling tool	to
TANTARA	fanfare	mu
TANTITY	tantamount	
TANTIVY	at speed	
TANTONY	smallest pig in litter	zo
TANTRUM	temper; petulance	
TANYARD	tanning place	
TAPBOLT	screw bolt	
TAPERED	conical; pointed	
TAPETUM	(retina)	md
TAPIOCA	cassava	bt
TAPLASH	stale swipes	
TAPPING	broaching; screwcutting	
TAPROOM	bar	
TAPROOT	main sustenance root	bt
TAPSTER	} bartender	
TAPSMAN		
TARACEA	inlaid wood (Spanish style)	
TARAGOT	} Transylvanian clarinet	mu
TAROGOTA		
TARBUSH	tarboosh; fez	
TARDIER	slower; later; slacker	
TARDILY	slowly; reluctantly	
TARDIVE	tardiness; lateness	
TARNISH	sully; soil; stain	
TARRACE	volcanic earth	
TARRIED	loitered; lingered; sojourned	
TARRIER	dawdler; estate register	lw
TARRING	covering with bitumen	
TARROCK	arctic tern	zo
TARSIER	lemur; the malmag	zo
TARTANE	coastal trader Mediterranean	nt

TARTARY	Tartarus; nethermost hell	
TARTISH	somewhat sharp	
TARTLET	small tart	**ck**
TASHRIF	respect; compliment (Ind.)	
TASKING	taskwork; drudgery; toiling	
TASTIER	choicer; more succulent	
TASTILY	artistically	
TASTING	relishing; enjoying; gustation	
TATARIC	Mongolian, Turkish, etc.	
TATOUAY	armadillo; peba; tatou	**zo**
TATTERY	in rags	
TATTING	lace work	
TATTLED	gossiped; chatted; prated	
TATTLER	tale-bearer	
TAUNTED	derided; flouted; scorned	
TAUNTER	mocker; upbraider; reviler	
TAURIAN	(bulls)	
TAURIDS	meteoric shower	
TAURINE	ox extract; amino acid	**ch, md**
TAUTEST	tightest; tensest	
TAXABLE	rateable	
TAXCART	small farm cart	
TAXFREE	scot-free	
TAXICAB	hire car	
TAXI-ING	runway movements	**ae**
TAXI-MAN	cab driver	
TEA-CAKE	scone or bun for tea	**ck**
TEACHER	master; tutor; pedagogue	
TEACH-IN	active seminar discussion	
TEACHTA	member of parliament (Irish)	
TEA-COSY	pot warmer	
TEA-GOWN	long afternoon dress	
TEA-LEAD	(tea-chest linings)	
TEA-LEAF	blade of tea	**bt**
TEAMING	grouping; selecting	
TEARBAG	lachrymal gland	**md**
TEARFUL	maudlin; weeping; Niobean	
TEAR-GAS	riot repellant; eye irritant	**ch**
TEARING	rending; raving; raging	
TEA-ROSE	tea-scented rose	**bt**
TEARPIT	a lachrymal depression	
TEA-SHOP	shop serving tea	
TEASING	tantalizing; plaguing	
TEATHED	manured by livestock	
TEA-TIME	4/5 o'clock	
TEA-TRAY	on which tea carried	
TEA-TREE	Asian camellia; shrub	**bt**
TECHILY	fretfully; peevishly	
TECHNIC	technique; technical	
TECTRIX	a wing or tail feather	**zo**
TEDDING	spreading	
TEDESCO	German It.	
TEDIOUS	wearisome; hum-drum	
TEEBEAM	rolled steel shape; concrete flow	**ce**
TEEIRON	golf club (driver)	
TEEMFUL	prolific; swarming	
TEEMING	fruitful; abundant	
TEENAGE	thirteen to nineteen	
TEENING	troubling; provoking	

TEGULAR	(tiles)	
TEGUMEN	abdomen segment in lepidoptera	
TEKTITE	non-volcanic natural glass	**mn**
TELAMON	statue supporting masonry	
TELECAR	mobile telegraph office	
TELEOST	osseous	
TELERGY	telepathy	
TELESIA	sapphire	**mn**
TELLING	effective; informing	
TELPHER	} system of electric traction	
TELFER		
TEL-QUEL	exchange rate	
TELSTAR	television satellite	
TEMENOS	temple precinct (Gr.)	
TEMPEAN	delightful; (Vale of Tempe)	
TEMPERA	oilless paint; distemper	
TEMPEST	hurricane; typhoon; gale	
TEMPLAR	student of law	**lw**
TEMPLED	in a temple	
TEMPLET	template; jig	**to**
TEMPTED	allured; tried; solicited	
TEMPTER	a decoy; an enticer	
TENABLE	maintainable; rational	
TENANCY	tenure	
TENDING	tendentious; trending	
TENDRIL	twining shoot	**bt**
TENERAL	immature	**zo**
TENFOLD	decuple	
TENIOID	like tapeworms	**zo**
TENONED	mortised	
TENONER	tenon cutter	**to**
TEN-PINS	cf. nine-pins	
TENSELY	tautly; tightly	
TENSEST	stiffest; most emotional	
TENSILE	ductile	
TENSION	strain; stress; exigency	
TENSITY	tenseness; urgency	
TENSIVE	intensive	
TENTBED	canopied bed	
TENT-FLY	part of tent	
TENTFUL	tent fully occupied	
TENTGUY	tent-rope, not its occupant	
TENTING	probing; searching; camping	
TENTORY	the awning of a tent	
TENTPEG	} used to secure a tent	
TENTPIN		
TENTURE	wall hangings	
TENUATE	thin; attenuate	
TENUITY	rarity; thinness	
TENUOUS	diffused; slender	
TEPUKEI	large outrigger sail canoe S. Polynesia	**nt**
TEQUILA	fermented sap drink (Mex.)	
TERBIUM	a metallic element	**ch**
TERCINE	seed-coat	**bt**
TEREBIC	(turpentine)	**bt**
TEREBRA	Roman ram; ovipositor	**zo**
TEREKIA	sandpiper genus	**zo**
TERGANT	recursant	**hd**

TERGITE	back of an anthropod	zo
TERM-FEE	periodic payment	lw
TERMING	naming; denominating	
TERMINI	boundaries; extremities	
TERMITE	white ant	zo
TERNARY	in threes	
TERNATE	three-leafed	bt
TERNERY	tern breeding ground	
TERNION	(twelve pages)	
TERPENE	terebene	ch
TERRACE	raised level (vines); continuous house row; level promenade	ar
TERRAIN	geological features	
TERRANE	area covered by certain rock	gl
TERRAZO	Venetian mosaic	
TERRENE	terrestrial; earthy	
TERRIER	fine fighter	zo
TERRIER	tarrier; register	lw
TERRIFY	alarm; appal; dismay	
TERRINE	earthenware cooking dish	
TERSELY	concisely; briefly; laconically	
TERSION	wiping	
TERTIAL	wing feather	zo
TERTIAN	on alternate days	
TESSERA	mosaic block	
TESTACY	testate	lw
TESTATE	leaving a will	lw
TEST-BAN	nuclear weapons agreement	
TESTBED	for horticultural experiments	bt
TESTBED	software for program testing	cp
TESTERN	testril; a sixpence	nm
TESTIER	more irritable or irascible	
TESTIFY	affirm; avow; depose; depone	
TESTILY	peevishly; petulantly	
TESTING	proving; trying	
TESTOON	Henry VIII shilling	nm
TESTRIL	a tester; a sixpence	nm
TESTUDO	tortoise; early tank	zo
TETANIC	} lock-jaw; disease	md
TETANUS		
TETRACT	having four rays	
TETRODE	a thermionic valve	
TETROSE	monosaccharide	ch
TEXTILE	woven fabric	
TEXT-MAN	a quoter	
TEXTUAL	authoritative; written source; literal	rl
TEXTURA	medieval handwriting, Goth.; dark type	pr
TEXTURE	a web; structure; fabric	
THALIAN	comic	
THALLUS	a stem formation	
THALWEG	longitudinal river profile	gl
THAMMUZ	Osiris; Adonis	rl
THANAGE	thanedom (Sc.)	
THANATO-	of death (instinct) (Gr.)	cf
THANKED	gratefully acknowledged	
THAPSIA	plant genus	bt
THAWING	melting; dissolving	

THAYYAM	board game with sticks (Ind.)	
THEATRE	operations; drama	md
THEBAIA	} opium	md
THEBAIN		
THEBAIC	Theban	
THECATE	sheathed; encased	bt
THECIUM	spore-case	bt
THEORBO	lute with 11 strings	mu
THEOREM	logical proposition	
THERAPY	the curative art	md
THEREAT	on that account	
THEREBY	in consequence	
THEREIN	inside that	
THEREOF	about that	
THEREON	upon that	
THERETO	in addition	
THERIAC	alleged antidote	md
THERMAE	public steam baths (Roman)	
THERMAL	thermic; warm	
THERMIE	heat-calory unit (Fr.)	
THERMIT	incendiary mixture	
THERMOS	flask	
THEROID	animal-like	zo
THESEUS	slew Minotaur in Labyrinth	
THESPIS	founder of Greek drama	
THEURGY	miracle making	
THIAMIN	B vitamin	ch
THICKEN	condense; coagulate; curdle	
THICKER	closer; duller; muddier	
THICKET	underwood	
THICKLY	solidly; densely; closely	
THICKUN	£1; a sovereign	nm
THIEVED	stole; peculated; purloined	
THIGGED	cadged; begged	
THIGGER	threatening beggar; sorner	
THILLER	wheel-horse; shaft-horse	zo
THIMBLE	iron rope ring; fingertip sewing shield; sleeve piece	nt, tx
THINKER	cogitator; (Rodin)	
THINNED	attenuated; reduced	
THINNER	slimmer; slighter; (paint) solvents; (turpentine)	pt
THIRSTY	dry; parched; craving	
THISTLE	emblem of Scotland; weed	bt
THISTLY	overgrown with thistles	
THITHER	to there; yonder	
THOLING	enduring; yielding	
THOMISM	} doctrines of Thomas	
THOMIST	} Aquinas	rl
THORIDE	radioactive isotope	nc
THORITE	thorium silicate	mn
THORIUM	a metallic element	ch
THOUGHT	solicitude; concern; care; concept; consideration	
THOUING	treating with familiarity	
THRATCH	gasp for breath (Sc.)	
THREADY	filamentous	
THREAVE	24 sheaves	
THRIFTY	frugal; economical; thriving	
THRIVED	waxed; luxuriated	

THRIVEN	flourished; grown	
THRIVER	prosperer	
THROATY	guttural	
THRONAL	like a throne	
THRONED	exalted	
THROUGH	clear; unobstructed	
THROWER	caster; hurler; heaver	
THROW-IN	football	**ga**
THRUMMY	shaggy cloth; fringed	
THUGGEE	thug; assassin	
THULITE	Norwegian rock	**mn**
THULIUM	a metallic element	**ch**
THUMBED	beckoned for a lift	
THUMMIM	a perfect mystery	
THUMPED	struck heavily; drubbed	
THUMPER	whacker	
THUNDER	denounce; rumble	
THURIFY	to cense frankincense	
THWAITE	reclaimed land	
THYMINE	animal nucleoprotein constituent	**bc**
THYMOMA	tumour in thymus	**md**
THYRITE	voltage-rise limiting device	**el**
THYROID	shield-like gland	**md**
THYRSUS	ivy staff (Bacchus)	
THYRSUS	densely branched inflorescence	**bt**
THYSELF	reflexive pronoun	
TIARAED	wearing a tiara	
TIBETAN	of Tibet	
TIBICEN	flute player	**mu**
TICKING	bedding material; marking	
TICKLED	titillated; amused	
TICKLER	enlivener	
TIDDLER	small fry	**zo**
TIDERIP	rough water	
TIDEWAY	a channel	
TIDIEST	neatest; sprucest	
TIDINGS	news; intelligence; message	
TIE-BACK	window drape fastener	
TIE-BEAM	rafter retainer	
TIE-LINE	mooring rope; channel link	**nt, cp**
TIERCEL	male hawk	**zo**
TIERCET	triple rhyme	
TIFFANY	gauze; thin silk	**tx**
TIGELLA	short stem	**bt**
TIGHTEN	increase the strain	
TIGHTER	more compact; closer	
TIGHTLY	tautly; tensely	
TIGLINE	croton oil	**bt**
TIGRESS	fierce female tiger	**zo**
TIGRINE	marked like a tiger	
TIGRISH	fierce	
TIGROID	of nerve-cell granules	**cy**
TILBURY	dog-cart	
TILE-ORE	copper ore	**mn**
TILE-RED	brownish-red	
TILLAGE	cultivation	
TILLING	husbandry	

TILLITE	till; boulder clay	
TILSEED	seed of sesamum indicum	**bt**
TILTING	slanting; forging; jousting; twist throw (bowls)	
TIMBALE	a fowl dish; kettle-drum	**ck, mu**
TIMBREL	tambourine	**mu**
TIMEFUL	seasonable; timely	
TIME-GUN	parting shot	
TIME-LAG	an interim; delay	
TIME-OFF	leisure; break from work; free period	
TIME-OUT	entertainment; suspension of play (sport)	
TIMIDLY	fearfully; diffidently	
TIMOTHY	cat's tail grass	**bt**
TIMPANI	} kettle-drums	**mu**
TIMPANO		
TIMBALE		
TINAMOU	S. American quail	**zo**
TINCHEL	} deer battue	
TINCHIL		
TINDERY	inflammable	
TIN-FISH	torpedo	**nt**
TINFOIL	leaf aluminium	
TINGING	ringing; tinking	
TINGLED	thrilled; smarted	
TINIEST	smallest; puniest; microscopic	
TINKING	tinkling; ringing	
TINKLED	rang; clinked	
TINKLER	small bell	
TIN-MINE	Cornish hole	
TINNING	covering with tin	
TINNOCK	blue tit	**zo**
TINSICA	cartwheel with half-twist somersault (gymn.)	
TIN-TACK	tack off/for tin	
TINTAGE	colouring; shading	
TINTERS	stainers; dyers	**pt**
TINTIES	coloured films	
TINTING	tingeing	
TINTYPE	ferro-type	
TINWARE	tin pots	
TIN-ZINC	metal finish	**ml**
TIPCART	rubbish barrow	
TIPPING	(flute playing); hinting	**mu**
TIPPLED	drank deep	
TIPPLER	steady absorber	
TIPSIFY	inebriate	
TIPSILY	drunkenly	
TIPSTER	racing tout	
TIPTOED	walked warily	
TIQUEUR	person suffering from tic	**md**
TIRASSE	pedal coupling	**mu**
TIRLING	quivering; vibrating; twisting	
TISSUED	woven; variegated	
TITANIA	fairy queen	
TITANIC	gigantic; colossal	
TITHING	township	
TITLARK	meadow pipit	**zo**
TITLING	title pages	

TITLING	hedge sparrow	zo
TITMICE	tits	zo
TITOISM	political practice	
TITRATE	(volumetric analysis)	ch
TITTUPY	frisky	
TITULAR	nominal	
TIVERED	marked with ochre	
TOADIED	cringed; truckled; fawned	
TOADIES	sycophants	
TOASTED	dried; warmed	
TOASTER	bread burner	
TOBACCO	insidious narcotic	
TOBASCO	red pepper	
TOBOGAN	toboggan	
TOBYMAN	highwayman	
TOCCATA	a touchy composition	mu
TODDLED	strolled; meandered	
TODDLER	a tiny tot	
TOE-HOLD	foot grip for climber	
TOENAIL	horn on foot digits	
TOFTMAN	a cottager	
TOGGERY	raiment	
TOILFUL	wearisome	
TOILING	moiling; labouring; snaring	
TOKENED	spotted; marked	
TOLLAGE	dues	
TOLLBAR	toll-gate	
TOLLING	knelling; annulling	lw
TOLLMAN	toll-gatherer	
TOLUENE	methyl benzene	ch
TOMALLY	lobster liver	zo
TOMATIN	tomato antibiotic	ch
TOMBOLA	a form of lottery	ch
TOMBOLO	sand or shingle bar joining island to mainland (It.)	gl
TOMFOOL	buffoon	
TOMOSIS	disease of cotton plant	bt
TOMPION	inking pad; clockmaker	
TONGUED	possessing a tongue	
TO-NIGHT	night of this day	
TONNAGE	amount of tons	
TONNEAU	back-seat part of motor-car	au
TONSILE	clippable	
TONSURE	shaving; (shorn)	
TONTINE	co-operative loan	
TOOLBOX	container for implements; toolkit	bd, cr, jn
TOOLING	(bookbinding); driving	
TOOTHED	dentate; serrated edge; sawtooth; (dog)	ar
TOOTHER	projecting horizontal brick	bd
TOOTING	prying; hornblowing	
TOOTLED	played the flute	mu
TOPARCH	a Greek governor	
TOPBOOT	high-rising shoe	
TOPCOAT	light overcoat	
TOP-EDGE	smooth gilded upper book edge	
TOPFULL	brimming (Shak.)	
TOPHOLE	first-rate	
TOP-HUNG	of top-hinged window-sash	bd

TOPIARY	ornamental clipping	
TOPICAL	local; particular; allusive	
TOPKNOT	plume or crest of feathers	zo
TOPLESS	without a lid; bare-bosomed	
TOPMAST	elevated mast	nt
TOPMOST	highest	
TOPONYM	topographical name	
TOPPING	upper layer (decor); splendid	cr
TOPPING	beheading; hitting upper part of ball (golf, polo, cricket, etc.)	
TOPPLED	tumbled down	
TOPSAIL	part of rigging	nt
TOPSIDE	the upper part	
TOPSMAN	bailiff; public hangman	
TOPSOIL	planting earth	
TOPSPIN	rotary motion of ball (table-tennis)	
TORBITE	peat fuel	
TORCHER	torch-bearer; linkman	
TORCHON	geometric lace	
TORGOCH	a species of char	zo
TORMENT	rag; rack; plague; harry	
TORMINA	griping pains	md
TORNADO	cyclone; hurricane; typhoon	
TORNOTE	with blunt extremities	
TORPEDO	ray fish; the tin fish	zo, nt
TORPENT	torpid; inert	
TORPIFY	benumb	
TORQUED	wreathed	hd
TORREFY	parch; roast; scorch	
TORRENT	stream; flood; current	
TORSADE	twisted scroll	
TORSION	twisting force	
TORSIVE	spiral	
TORSTEN	an iron ore	mn
TORTEAU	red circlet	hd
TORTILE	coiled; wreathed	
TORTIVE	twisted; tortile; tortuous	
TORTRIX	a moth genus	zo
TORTURE	torment; agony; pang	
TORULUS	antenna socket	zo
TORVOUS	grim; stern in aspect	
TORYISM	Conservatism	
TOSSILY	perty	
TOSSING	(deciding); agitating; shaking; casting, coin or ball (netball)	
TOSS-POT	toper	
TOTALLY	wholly; entirely; completely	
TOTEMIC	(totems); emblematic	
TOTTERY	shaky; unsteady	
TOTTING	adding up	
TOUCHED	sympathetic; impinged	
TOUCHER	a close call; hitting the jack (bowls); confidence trickster	
TOUGHEN	indurate; harden	
TOUGHLY	stubbornly; tenaciously	
TOURACO	African bird	zo
TOURING	journeying	
TOURISM	co-ordinated travel	
TOURIST	tripper; excursionist	

TOURNEY	tournament	
TOUSING	teasing; worrying	
TOUSLED	unkempt; in disarray	
TOUTING	seeking custom	
TOWARDS	in direction of	
TOWBOAT	tug	**nt**
TOWERED	with towers	
TOWIRON	whaling toggle-iron	
TOWLINE	tow rope	
TOWNISH	urban	
TOWPATH	boat-haulage path	
TOWROPE	boat-haulage rope	
TOXEMIA	blood poisoning	**md**
TOXEMIC	septicaemic	**md**
TOXICAL	poisonous	
TOXODON	extinct rhinoceros	**zo**
TOYSHOP	plaything emporium	
TOYSOME	playful	
TOYWORT	shepherd's purse	**bt**
TRACERY	ornamental stonework	
TRACHEA	wind-pipe	**md**
TRACHLE	to draggle (Sc.)	
TRACING	a copy; traversing	
TRACKED	trailed; traversed	
TRACKER	a sleuth	
TRACTOR	agricultural, field, vehicle	
TRADE-IN	part exchange	
TRADING	commerce; barter	
TRADUCE	misrepresent; libel; slander	
TRAFFIC	intercourse; transport; trade; communications flow; unit of traffic (instantaneous conversations) Erlangs	**me, tc**
TRAGEDY	drama; calamity	
TRAIKET	worn out (Sc.)	
TRAILED	followed; dragged; dogged	
TRAILER	tracker; towed vehicle; preview (film); computer signal of filed data	**cp**
TRAINED	proficient; skilled	
TRAINEE	man under instruction	
TRAINER	a coach	
TRAIPSE	to tramp	
TRAITOR	quisling; betrayer	
TRAJECT	ferry; project	
TRAMCAR	passenger carriage on lines	
TRAMMEL	bird-net; compass; hamper	
TRAMPED	toured; walked; trudged	
TRAMPER	vagrant; stroller; hiker	
TRAMPLE	crush; spurn; squelch	
TRAMPOT	socket for a spindle	
TRAMWAY	street railway; light mineral line	**rw**
TRANCED	in a dream; enraptured	
TRANCHE	slice; book edge; portrayal of life	
TRANECT	ferry; traject	
TRANGLE	small band	**hd**
TRANKUM	a gew-gaw	
TRANNEL	wooden nail	

TRANSIT	conveyance; passage	
TRANSOM	cross-beam of window; stem of yacht	**bd, nt**
TRANTER	pedlar	
TRAPEZE	swinging cross-bar (circus) (gymnastics)	
TRAPPED	adorned; caught	
TRAPPER	setter of snares	
TRASHED	lopped; crushed; hindered	
TRAVAIL	toil; labour; affliction	
TRAVERS	dressage movement (equestrian)	
TRAWLED	fished	**nt**
TRAWLER	fishing boat	**nt**
TRAYLED	interwoven (Spens.)	
TREACLE	molasses; dark syrup	
TREACLY	viscous and sweet	
TREADER	trampler	
TREADLE	pedal	
TREASON	treachery; disloyalty	
TREATED	entertained; doctored	
TREATER	negotiator	
TREBLED	tripled; threefold	
TREDDLE	a treadle (obs.)	
TREEING	cornering	
TREFOIL	(clover)	**ar**
TREGOHM	million megohms	**el**
TREHALA	Turkish manna	**bt**
TREKKED	migrated	
TREKKER	(ox-wagons, S. Africa)	
TRELLIS	lattice work	
TREMBLE	quiver; shake; oscillate	
TREMBLY	tottery; unsteady	
TREMOLO TREMO-LANDO	} trembling; shaking	**mu**
TRENAIL	wooden nail	
TRENDED	tended; inclined; gravitated	
TRENDLE	a roller	
TRENTAL	30 masses	**rl**
TREPANG	sea-slug	**zo**
TRESSED	curled	
TRESSEL	trestle; a movable framework	
TRESTLE	a support; (table); (bridge); (ropeway); scaffold stand	**ce**
TREVISS	cross-beam	
TRIABLE	(jurisdiction)	**lw**
TRIADIC	trivalent	**ch**
TRIAENE	spicule in porifera	**zo**
TRIARCH	with 3 xylem strands in stele	**bt**
TRIATIC	jumper stay	**nt**
TRIAXON	with three axes	
TRIBBLE	paper drying frame	
TRIBLET	a goldsmith's mandril	**to**
TRIBUNE	Roman magistrate; platform	
TRIBUTE	tax; impost; toil; offering	
TRICEPS	extensor muscle	**md**
TRICHAS	American warblers	**zo**
TRICING	hauling; clewing	**nt**
TRICKED	defrauded; hoaxed	

TRICKER	trickster	
TRICKLE	drip; ooze; percolate	
TRICKLY	trickling	
TRICKSY	artful; deft	
TRICORN	three-cornered	
TRIDARN	having three tiers; Welsh drying cupboard (3 layers)	
TRIDENT	Neptune's sceptre	
TRIDUAN	every third day	
TRIDUUM	period of three days	
TRIFLED	dallied; toyed; played	
TRIFLER	philanderer; idler; fribbler	
TRIFOLY	trefoil	**bt**
TRIFORM	triple form	
TRIGAMY	cf. bigamy	
TRIGGED	skidded; obstructed	
TRIGGER	firing catch; (happy); activate; set off	
TRIGGER	switching device; bistable circuit	
TRIGLOT	in three languages	
TRIGONE	triangular area	
TRIGRAM	a triphthong; a trigraph; 3 letter sequence	
TRILABE	surgical fork	**md**
TRILITH	stone doorway	**ar**
TRILLED	warbled; quavered	
TRILOGY	a series of three books in literature	
TRIMERA	type of beetle	**zo**
TRIMMED	clipped; balanced; rebuked	
TRIMMER	fishing float; time-server; joists	**cr**
TRIMMER	shearer; trimming capacitator	**el**
TRINARY	ternary; threefold	
TRINDLE	trundle; trickle	
TRINGLE	curtain rod (Fr.)	
TRINITY	unit of 3	**rl**
TRINKET	small ornament	
TRINKLE	trickle or tinkle	
TRIOLET	poetic stanza	
TRIONAL	hypnotic drug	**md**
TRIONES	7 stars in Ursa Major	**as**
TRIPACK	3-emulsion-base process	**pg**
TRIPARA	woman giving birth 3 times	
TRIPERY	tripe-booth	
TRIPLED	trebled	
TRIPLES	series of midair jumps (skating)	
TRIPLET	three of a kind	**mu**
TRIPODY	verse measure of 3 feet	
TRIPOLI	polishing powder; diatomite	
TRIPOLY	Michaelmas daisy	**bt**
TRIPPED	erred; slipped; stumbled	
TRIPPER	excursionist; dancer	
TRIPSIS	shampooing; pulverizing	
TRIREME	a galley	**nt**
TRISECT	cut into three	
TRISEME	(tribrach)	
TRISMUS	lock-jaw; tetanus	**md**
TRISOMY	genetic basis of syndrome	**md**
TRISULA	Siva's trident	
TRITELY	jejunely; hackneyed	
TRITIUM	very rare isotope of hydrogen	
TRITOMA	red-hot poker	**bt**
TRITONE	dissonant interval	**mu**
TRIUMPH	exultation; success; ovation	
TRIVIAL	trifling; slight; paltry	
TRIVIUM	grammar; logic and rhetoric	
TROCHAL	wheel-shaped	**zo**
TROCHEE	long and short foot metre	
TROCHUS	gastropod genus	**zo**
TRODDEN	trampled	
TROGGIN	pedlary	
TROLAND	unit of illuminance (optics)	
TROLLED	sang; fished; rambled	
TROLLER	trolley; trolly	
TROLLEY	truck; metal pulley	
TROLLOL	sing; troll; trill	
TROLLOP	a slattern; a slut	
TROMLET	side horse movement (gymnastics)	
TROMMEL	mining sieve; rotary screen for coal	
TROMPIL	blast regulating device	
TRONAGE	wool-tax	
TROOPED	thronged; (the colours)	
TROOPER	mounted man; ship	**nt**
TROPHIC	(nutrition)	
TROPICS	(Cancer and Capricorn)	
TROPINE	constituent of atropine	**md**
TROPISM	enforced turning movement	
TROPIST	figurative speaker	
TROTTER	pig's foot; horse race with sulky, trotting	
TROUBLE	disturb; worry; trial; dolour	
TROUNCE	to larrup; castigate	
TROUPER	strolling player	
TROUSSE	set of instruments	**md**
TROWING	trusting; believing	
TRUANCY	vagrancy	
TRUCAGE	counterfeiting a picture	
TRUCKED	bartered; trafficked	
TRUCKER	exchange agent	
TRUCKLE	roller; yield; submit	
TRUDGED	walked wearily; tramped	
TRUDGEN	a swimming stroke	
TRUFFLE	an edible fungus	**bt**
TRUMEAU	part of a wall	
TRUMPED	deceived; ruffed	
TRUMPET	proclaim; blazon	**mu**
TRUNCAL	main; principal	
TRUNCUS	main blood vessel	**zo**
TRUNDLE	wheel; truck; to roll	
TRUNDLE	spool of golden thread	
TRUSSED	bound; tied up	
TRUSTED	credited; confided	
TRUSTEE	guardian; fiduciary	
TRUSTER	an optimist; creditor	
TRYABLE	triable	**lw**
TRYPETA	boring flies	**zo**
TRYPSIN	pepsin	**md**

TRYPTIC	peptic; digestive	md
TRY-SAIL	part of rigging	nt
TRYSTED	rendezvoused; appointed	
TRYSTER	tryst convener	
TSANTSA	head-shrinking technique	
TSARINA	Empress of Russia	
TSARISM	of the tzar (czar)	
TSARIST	Russian royalist	
T-SQUARE	draughtsman's tool	
TSUKPIN	Proa canoe, Micronesia	
TSUNAMI	seismic sea wave tremor, Japan	
TUATERA	tuatara; NZ lizard	zo
TUBBING	mine shaft lining; bathing	mn
TUBBISH	rotund	
TUB-FISH	sapphirine gurnard	zo
TUBICEN	trumpeter	mu
TUB-SIZE	strengthening dip for handmade paper	
TUBULAR	hollow; fistular; capillary	
TUCK-BOX	treats for schoolboys	
TUCKING	cramming; folding; gathering	
TUCK-OUT	tuck-in; blow-out	
TUEFALL	a pent-house	
TUESDAY	a weekday	
TUESITE	slate pencil material	mn
TUFTING	adorning with tufts	
TUGBOAT	small powerful boat	nt
TUGGING	lugging; pulling; hauling	
TUGHRIK	(Mongolia)	nm
TUITION	instruction; education	
TULCHAN	spoof calf	
TULLIAN	(Tullius Cicero)	
TUMBLED	rumpled; fallen; twigged	
TUMBLER	pigeon; glass; acrobat; lock system	zo
TUMBREL	tumbril; two-wheeled cart	
TUMIDLY	pompously; turgidly; puffily	
TUMPING	humping; carrying	
TUMULAR	heaped	
TUMULUS	burial mound	
TUNABLE	melodious; musical	
TUNABLY	harmoniously	
TUNDISH	wine funnel; flue; condensation collector	bd
TUNEFUL	musical; dulcet	
TUNG-OIL	wood-oil	bt
TUNICIN	animal cellulose	zo
TUNICLE	small tunic	
TUNMOOT	village council	
TUNNAGE	(and poundage) wine tax	
TUNNERY	tunny-netting area	
TUPPING	hammering; butting	
TURACIN	carmine	
TURAKOO	gaudy bird; plantain-eater	zo
TURBARY	turf digging rights	
TURBINE	rotary engine	
TURDINE	thrush-like	
TURFING	laying turf; swarding	
TURFITE	racing fan	
TURGENT	swelling; distended; tumid	

TURGITE	a form of haematite	mn
TURKISH	} (Turkestan)	
TURKMEN		
TURKOIS	turquoise	mn
TURMOIL	tumult; ado; hubbub	
TURNCAP	chimney cowl	
TURNERY	lathe work	
TURNING	flexure; spinning; fermenting	
TURNKEY	prison warder	
TURN-OUT	an equipage	
TURNPIN	} boxwood roller (U.S.A.)	
TAMPIN		
TURN-UPS	trouser leg folds	
TURPETH	purgative plant	bt
TURTLER	turtle-hunter	
TUSKING	projecting stones (toothing)	ar
TUSSIVE	afflicted with a cough	
TUSSLED	struggled; fought; battled	
TUSSOCK	tuffet; tuft	
TUSSORE	coarse silk	tx
TUTAMEN	a protection; a defence	
TUTANIA	Britannia metal; alloy of copper, calamine, antimony, tin (1770)	
TUTELAR	protective	
TUTENAG	a Chinese alloy; zinc	
TUTORED	taught; educated; instructed	
TUTULUS	Etruscan head-dress	
TUT-WORK	excavation piece-work	mn
TWADDLE	verbiage; balderdash; prattle (sl.)	
TWANGED	played the banjo	mu
TWANGLE	to twang	
TWANKAY	green tea	
TWANKED	twanged; twangled	
TWATTLE	gabble	
TWEAKED	twitched; pinched	
TWEEDLE	(fiddle); wheedle	
TWEELED	twiller (Sc.)	
TWEENIE	a maid	
TWEETER	loudspeaker	ac
TWELFTH	ordinal number; mutation stop organ	mu
TWIBILL	mattock; axe	to
TWIDDLE	twist; tweedle	
TWIGGED	understood; observed (sl.)	
TWIGGEN	of wicker	
TWINGED	twitched; pained	
TWINING	twisting; meandering; coiling	
TWINKLE	wink; glimmer; scintillate	
TWINNED	two at a time	
TWINSET	matching sweater and cardigan	
TWINTER	beast, two winters old	
TWIN-TOP	(motoring)	au
TWIRLED	span; rotated; whirled	
TWIRLER	spinner; twister	
TWISTED	spun; contorted; tangled	
TWISTER	a puzzle; perverter; tornado	
TWISTLE	twist; a wrench (Sc.)	
TWISTOR	computer memory device	
TWITTED	reproached; rallied; taunted	

TWITTEN	by-lane	
TWITTER	an upbraider; chirp; palpitate	
TWIZZLE	turn and twist; a step-dance on one spot; jig	
TWO-FOLD	twi-fold; double	
TWO-LINE	size of printing type; whip	**pr**
TWONESS	doubleness	
TWOSOME	a couple	
TWOSTEP	a dance	**mu**
TWO-TIME	double-cross	
TWO-WIRE	(AC or DC) transmit and receive channel	**tc**
TYCHISM	theory based on chance	
TYING-IN	tubular scaffolding, interior grip	**pt**
TYING-UP	mooring a vessel; securing	**nt**
TYING-UP	binding; setting book bands	**pr**
TYLARUS	padded hoof	**zo**
TYLOPOD	camel-footed	
TYLOSIS	eye-trouble	**md**
TYLOTIC	eye-inflammation	**md**
TYMPANA	ear-drums	**md**
TYMPANO	timpano; a drum	**mu**
TYMPANY	turgidity; flatulence	**md**
TYNWALD	parliament (Isle of Man)	
TYPE-BAR	a line of type	**pr**
TYPHOID	a fever	**md**
TYPHOON	cyclone; hurricane	**mt**
TYPHOUS	enteric	**md**
TYPICAL	emblematic; characteristic	
TYPONYM	type-name	
TYRANNY	despotism; iron rule	
TZARINA	Tsarina (Russia)	
TZIGANE	gipsy (Hungary)	

U

UBEROUS	fruitful	
UDALLER	odaller; freeholder	
UDARNIK	'shock' worker (Rus.)	
UKULELE	Hawaian guitar	**mu**
ULEXITE	hydrated sodium/calcium borate	**mn**
ULLALOO	Irish lament	
ULNARIA	arm-bones	**pl**
ULONCUS	swollen gums	**md**
ULULANT	wailing; sobbing	
ULULATE	howl; hoot	
ULYSSES	Odysseus; a wanderer	
UMBERED	tinged with umber	
UMBONAL	protuberant	
UMBONES	bosses on shields	
UMBONIC	humpy	
UMBRAGE	shade; resentment	
UMBRERE	helmet visor	
UMBRIAN	(Raphael)	
UMBRINE	dull darkish brown	**bt**
UMBRINE	a fish	**zo**
UMBROSE	shady; umbrageous	

UMPIRED	arbitrated; judged	
UMPTEEN	more than ten	
UNACTED	never staged	
UNAGING	immortal	
UNAIDED	single-handed	
UNAIRED	possibly damp; stuffy	
UNALIST	holding one benefice	**rl**
UNAPTLY	not à propos	
UNARMED	defenceless	
UNASKED	gratuitously	
UNAWARE	ignorant; uninformed	
UNBATED	unblunted; non-stop	
UNBAYED	opened up	
UNBEGUN	not started	
UNBLIND	restore vision	
UNBLOCK	to clear; (cards)	
UNBLOWN	not sounded; in the bud	
UNBORNE	not carried	
UNBOSOM	freely disclose	
UNBOUND	loose	
UNBOWED	unsubdued	
UNBRACE	relax; free from tension	
UNBRAID	disentangle	
UNBRUTE	domesticate; tame	
UNBUILT	not yet constructed	
UNBURNT	unconsumed	
UNCAGED	released; freed	
UNCANNY	eerie; weird; mysterious	
UNCARED	untended; unheeded	
UNCASED	taken out; displayed	
UNCEDED	not transferred or granted	
UNCHAIN	free; let loose; unfetter	
UNCHARM	unspell; exorcise	
UNCHARY	heedless; not frugal	
UNCINAL	hook-shaped	
UNCINUS	small hook	**md**
UNCIVIL	incivil; impolite	
UNCLASP	unfasten; disconnect	
UNCLEAN	foul; dirty; leprous	
UNCLEAR	confused; unintelligible	
UNCLING	unclasp; disengage	
UNCLOAK	disrobe; unveil; unmask	
UNCLOSE	open; babbling	
UNCLOUD	free from obscurity	
UNCOUTH	boorish; rustic; rough	
UNCOVER	lay open; disclose	
UNCROSS	straighten (the legs)	
UNCROWN	dethrone	
UNCTION	an anointing	**rl**
UNCULAR	avuncular	
UNDATED	waved	
UNDEIFY	remove a god	
UNDERDO	cook insufficiently	
UNDERGO	experience; bear; suffer	
UNDIGHT	to undress	
UNDOING	opening; unravelling; ruining	
UNDRAPE	strip; uncover	
UNDRAWN	not delineated	
UNDREAM	unimagined	
UNDRESS	not full parade uniform	

UNDRIED	wet; green	**UNITING**	combining; concerting
UNEARED	untilled (Shak.)	**UNITION**	conjunction
UNEARTH	disclose; reveal; discover	**UNITIVE**	harmonising
UNEATEN	not consumed	**UNITIZE**	to treat as one unit
UNEQUAL	varying; not uniform	**UNJOINT**	disconnect
UNEXACT	inexact; inaccurate	**UNKEMPT**	uncombed; rough
UNFADED	unwithered	**UNKNOWN**	nameless; anonymous
UNFAITH	infidelity	**UNLACED**	not done up; untied
UNFENCE	remove a hedge	**UNLADEN**	unladed; unloaded
UNFILED	unrasped; (papers)	**UNLATCH**	to open
UNFITLY	unsuitably; improperly	**UNLEARN**	to forget
UNFIXED	unsettled	**UNLEASH**	remove all constraint
UNFLESH	reduce to a skeleton	**UNLEAVE**	strip of leaves
UNFLUSH	lose colour	**UNLEVEL**	uneven; rough
UNFOUND	still lost; not met with	**UNLIMED**	freed from lime
UNFROCK	deprive of office **rl**	**UNLINED**	(paper); unruled
UNFUMED	not fumigated	**UNLIVED**	bereft of life (Shak.)
UNFUSED	not melted; not merged	**UNLOOSE**	unleash; unfasten
	together **gl**	**UNLOVED**	disliked
UNFUZED	(shells); not set for artillery firing	**UNLUCKY**	ill-starred; hapless
	mn	**UNLUSTY**	weak; infirm; sickly
UNGIVEN	not conceded	**UNLUTED**	unglued; uncemented
UNGLAZE	remove the glass	**UNMANLY**	effeminate; cowardly
UNGLOVE	bare the hand	**UNMARRY**	divorce
UNGLUED	unstuck	**UNMEANT**	not intended
UNGODLY	sinful; impious; profane	**UNMETED**	not measured
UNGRATE	ungrateful person	**UNMEWED**	set free; released
UNGUARD	leave defenceless	**UNMIXED**	pure; unadulterated
UNGUENT	an ointment **md**	**UNMOIST**	dehydrated; dry; arid
UNGULAR	(hoof; nails; etc.) **zo**	**UNMORAL**	immoral; licentious
UNGYVED	unfettered	**UNMOULD**	change the form of
UNHABLE	incapable (Spens.)	**UNMOVED**	impassive; serene; quiet
UNHANDY	awkward; clumsy	**UNNAMED**	anonymous
UNHAPPY	sad; grievous; sorrowful	**UNNERVE**	frighten; intimidate
UNHARDY	irresolute; delicate	**UNNOBLE**	ignoble (Spens.)
UNHASTY	slow; deliberate	**UNNOTED**	undistinguished
UNHEARD	inaudible; obscure	**UNOFTEN**	infrequently
UNHEART	to discourage (Shak.)	**UNOILED**	free from lubrication
UNHEEDY	careless; rash	**UNORDER**	countermand
UNHINGE	to unsettle; derange	**UNOWNED**	unacknowledged
UNHIRED	not engaged	**UNPAGED**	unnumbered (of prelim. pages)
UNHITCH	loosen; unfasten	**UNPAINT**	remove paint
UNHIVED	driven from shelter	**UNPANEL**	to unsaddle
UNHOARD	dissipate; spend	**UNPAVED**	uncobbled
UNHOPED	unexpected	**UNPENAL**	without penalty
UNHORSE	force to dismount	**UNPERCH**	dislodge; unroost
UNHOUSE	evict	**UNPLACE**	displace
UNIAXAL	uniaxial	**UNPLAIT**	unbraid; unravel
UNICITY	oneness; sameness	**UNPLUMB**	not vertical
UNICORN	a fabulous animal; oryx **zo**	**UNPLUME**	pluck
UNIDEAL	realistic; prosaic	**UNQUEEN**	dethrone
UNIFIED	united; merged	**UNQUIET**	unease; restless
UNIFIER	amalgamator; merger	**UNQUOTE**	end quotation
UNIFOIL	bearing only one leaf **bt**	**UNRAKED**	untilled
UNIFORM	consistent; steady	**UNRAVEL**	disentangle; solve
UNITAGE	measurement	**UNREADY**	irresolute; slow
UNITARY	monistic; integral	**UNREEVE**	withdraw a rope **nt**
UNITATE	remainder after division	**UNRIVET**	undo; loosen; detach
UNITERM	key-word graphic index system	**UNROBED**	undressed
UNITERM	information retrieval **cp**	**UNROUGH**	moderately smooth

UNROYAL	unkingly	
UNRULED	uncontrolled; unlined	
UNSATED	rapacious; not satisfied	
UNSCALY	having no scales	zo
UNSCREW	untwist; unfasten	
UNSENSE	to stun	
UNSEXED	lacking femininity	
UNSHELL	unhusk; release	
UNSHORN	unshaven; unclipped	
UNSHOWN	not exhibited	
UNSIGHT	cricket	
UNSIZED	not stiffened	
UNSLING	release from slings	
UNSLUNG	not projected	
UNSMOTE	unsmitten	
UNSNARL	disentangle; unravel	
UNSOLID	fluid; unsubstantial	
UNSOUND	erroneous; defective	
UNSPELL	uncharm; exorcise	
UNSPENT	unexhausted; still moving	
UNSPIED	unobserved; undetected	
UNSPIKE	pull out prickles	
UNSPILT	not shed; not slopped	
UNSPLIT	undivided	
UNSPOIL	restore	
UNSTACK	disperse; dishevel	
UNSTAID	unsteady; unstable	
UNSTATE	deprive of dignity	
UNSTEEL	soften; disarm	
UNSTICK	ungum; tear free	
UNSTRAP	loosen	
UNSTUCK	loosened; dished	
UNSTUNG	depierced	
UNSUNNY	dull; shady	
UNSWEAR	recall an oath	
UNSWEET	inharmonious; acid	
UNSWEPT	unbrushed	
UNSWORN	not on oath	
UNTAKEN	left; relinquished	
UNTAMED	savage; barbaric	
UNTAXED	not charged	
UNTHINK	dismiss from the mind	
UNTILED	detesselated	
UNTIRED	unwearied	
UNTOOTH	extract	
UNTRIED	inexperienced; new	
UNTRULY	falsely; erroneously	
UNTRUSS	take apart; dissect	
UNTRUTH	lie; imposture; error	
UNTUNED	not set to play	ro, mu
UNTWINE	untwist; unravel	
UNTWIST	disentangle	
UNTYING	unknotting	
UNURGED	unsolicited	
UNUSUAL	bizarre; queer; odd; rum	
UNVEXED	unharassed; untroubled	
UNVOWED	not bound by oath	
UNWAGED	unsalaried	
UNWAYED	trackless	
UNWEARY	unspent; unflagging	

UNWEAVE	unplait	
UNWHIPT	unbirched	
UNWIRED	unstrung	
UNWITCH	uncharm; unspell	
UNWITTY	lacking humour; prosaic	
UNWOOED	uncourted; unsolicited	
UNWOUND	untwined; uncoiled	
UNWOVEN	not made into cloth	
UNWRUNG	not galled	
UNYOKED	unrestrained (Shak.)	
UNZONED	unbelted	
UPBLAZE	to flare up	
UPBORNE	carried aloft	
UPBOUND	tied; restricted	
UPBRAID	rebuke; chide; taunt	
UPBREAK	shoot up	
UPBURST	outburst	
UPCHEER	encourage	
UPCLIMB	ascend	
UPENDED	stood on end	
UPFIELD	cricket	
UPGAZED	looked upwards	
UPGRADE	on the rise	
UPHEAVE	lift up; raise	
UPHOARD	secrete; amass; garner	
UPLYING	elevated	
UPPLUCK	gather up; uproot	
UPRAISE	to nurture; uplift	
UPRIGHT	vertical; honest; just; obstacle (show-jumping)	
UPRISEN	ascended	
UPROUSE	awaken	
UPSHIFT	change gear	
UPSHOOT	a sprout	bt
UPSIDES	horses exercising together	
UPSPEAR	shoot up straight	
UPSTAGE	(theatrical)	
UPSTAND	to stand up; to rise	
UPSTARE	upgaze	
UPSTART	parvenu; meadow saffron	bt
UPSURGE	upswell	
UPSWARM	opposite of downscool	
UPSWEEP	woman's coiffure; handing baton to relief runner; pole jumping	
UPSWELL	upsurge	
UPTHROW	an upheaval	
UPTIGHT	unduly inhibited	
UPTRACE	to trace	
UP-TRAIN	train to London	
UPTRILL	sing high	
UPWARDS	upward; upwardly	
URAEMIA	kidney disease	md
URALITE	fireproof material	mn
URA-NAGE	rear throw (judo)	
URANIAN	astronomical	
URANIDE	element beyond protactinium	ch
URANITE	a green uranium ore	mn
URANIUM	metallic element	ch
URANOUS	containing uranium	ch

URETHRA	urinary duct	zo
URGENCY	importunity; stress	
URICASE	uric acid salt	
URIDINE	crystalline nucleoside	ch
URINANT	bent fish	hd
URINARY	of the bladder/urine	md
URINATE	to pass body water	md
UROCYON	American grey fox	zo
UROCYST	the bladder	pl
URODELA	newts and salamanders	zo
UROLOGY	study of urinary tract	md
UROSOME	caudal segment	md
URSINAL	ursine; bearish	zo
URTICAL	(nettles)	bt
USELESS	vain; bootless; abortive	
USHERED	introduced; foreran; heralded	
USITATE	usually; customary	
USUALLY	normally; generally	
USURPED	arrogated; seized; assumed	
USURPER	a dictator	
UTENSIL	implement; vessel	
UTERINE	of the uterus	md
UTILISE	utilize; employ; apply	
UTILITY	usefulness	
UTOPIAN	imaginary; chimerical; ideal	
UTOPISM	unpractical hopefulness	
UTOPIST	optimist; visionary	
UTRICLE	small cell or bladder	md
UTTERED	issued; pronounced; said	
UTTERER	promulgator; (counterfeit)	
UTTERLY	absolutely; completely	
UVEITIS	eye congestion	md
UXORIAL	dotingly fond of a wife	

V

VACANCY	void; emptiness; listlessness	
VACATED	left; abandoned	
VACATOR	a quitter	
VACATUR	annulment	lw
VACCINE	lymph	md
VACHERY	cow-house; dairy	
VACUATE	make a vacuum	
VACUIST	vacant believer	
VACUITY	emptiness; a void	
VACUOLE	minute cavity	
VACUOUS	void; unfilled	
VAGITUS	cry of a new-born child	
VAGRANT	vagabond; nomad; tramp	
VAGUELY	dimly; indefinitely	
VAGUEST	most uncertain	
VAILING	veiling; tipping	
VAINEST	most conceited	
VALANCE	draped border	
VALENCE	} combining power;	
VALENCY	} compatibility of elements	
		ch
VALERIC	derived from valerian	bt
VALIANT	intrepid; gallant; doughty	

VALIDLY	with legal force	
VALINCH	cask tap	
VALLARY	(rampart)	
VALLATE	cup-shaped	
VALONIA	acorn-cup (Levant)	bt
VALSOID	with perithecia in circle	bt
VALUING	esteeming; appraising	
VALVATE	valvular	
VALVLET	valvula; small valve	
VALVULA	cerebellum process in fish	zo
VALVULE	valvula; small valve	
VAMOOSE	to retire	
VAMOSED	decamped	
VAMPING	patching; bewitching	mu
VAMPIRE	blood-sucker; a bat	zo
VAMPLET	spear buckler	
VANADIC	of vanadium	ch
VANADYL	electrolyte cation	ch
VANDYKE	lace collar	
VANESSA	butterfly genus (Swift)	zo
VAN-FOSS	a moat	
VANILLA	orchid; a flavour	bt
VANNING	mining operation	
VANSIRE	mongoose (Madagascar)	zo
VANTAGE	(tennis); advantage	
VANWARD	vanguard	
VAPIDLY	inertly; insipidly; languidly	
VAPOURS	nervous malady	md
VAPOURY	hypochondriac	
VAQUERO	S. American cow-puncher	
VARANUS	monitor lizard	zo
VAREUSE	seaman's jersey, jacket	
VARIANT	different; diverse	
VARIATE	to vary; alter	
VARICES	knotted veins	md
VARIETY	diversity; assortment	
VARIOLA	smallpox	md
VARIOLE	pitted	
VARIOUS	sundry; several; numerous	
VARMINT	vermin	zo
VARNISH	to gloss over; palliate	
VARSITY	university	
VARVELS	vervels; rings on a hawk	
VARYING	differing; deviating; altering	
VASTATE	make immune	
VASTEST	bulkiest; greatest	
VATICAN	papal power	
VATTING	mixing wines; customs	
VAUDOIS	Waldensian of Swiss canton	
VAULTED	arched; sprang	
VAULTER	bounder	
VAUNTED	boosted; bragged	
VAUNTER	braggart; boaster	
VAVASOR	titled landowner	
VECTION	porterage; convection	
VEDANGA	Veda commentary	
VEDANTA	Veda philosophy	
VEDETTE	vidette; mounted scout	
VEERING	shifting; changing; varying; wind moving clockwise	nt

VEGETAL	vegetable; plant	bt
VEHICLE	(painting); car; conveyance	
VEILING	veil material	
VEINAGE	vein system	bt, md
VEINING	ramification	
VEINLET	small vein	
VEINOUS	of the veins	
VEINULE	veinlet	
VELAMEN	a membrane	md
VELARIA	Roman amphitheatre awning	
VELIGER	larval stage of mollusca	zo
VELLING	cutting turf	
VELLUMY	like vellum	
VELOURS	plush fabric	tx
VELOUTE	creamy meat sauce	ck
VELVETY	smooth	
VENALLY	mercenary	
VENATIC	sporting	
VENDACE	a lake fish	zo
VENDING	selling; bartering	
VENERER	gamekeeper	
VENISON	deer meat	ck
VENOMED	poisoned	
VENTAGE	escape hole	
VENTAIL	helmet visor	
VENTING	releasing; uttering; emitting	
VENTOSE	windy; breezy	
VENTOSE	Republican month (Fr.)	
VENT-PEG	a spile; spigot	
VENTRAD	ventrally	zo
VENTRAL	abdominal	md
VENTRIC	ventral	
VENTURE	hazard; chance; dare	
VENTURI	convergent/divergent duct	ae
VERANDA	verandah; open portico	
VERBENA	vervain	bt
VERBIFY	verbalise	
VERBILE	person stimulated by words	pc
VERBOSE	wordy; prolix; loquacious	
VERDANT	unsophisticated; green	
VERDICT	decision; finding; judgment	
VERDITE	green S. Afr. rock	mn
VERDURE	green growth	
VERGENT	bordering; tending	
VERGING	inclining; adjacent to	
VERGLAS	thin ice or frost layer	
VERIEST	absolute; truest	
VERISMO	expressionist objectivity (art)	
VERITAS	French shipping bureau	
VERMEIL	a glaze; ormolu	
VERMIAN	wormlike	zo
VERMILY	vermilion	
VERMUTH	vermouth; absinth	
VERNANT	spring-like; vernal	
VERNATE	to flourish	
VERNIER	measuring device	
VERONAL	an opiate	md
VERRUCA	a wart; foot ailment	bt, md
VERSANT	conversant; familiar	
VERSENE	sodium versenate	ch

VERSIFY	relate in verse	
VERSINE	function of an angle	ma
VERSING	relating in rhyme	
VERSION	an account; interpretation	
VERSUAL	paragraphic	
VERSUTE	crafty; wily	
VERTIGO	dizziness; giddiness	md
VERULED	ringed	hd
VERULES	concentric rings	hd
VERVAIN	verbena	bt
VERVELS	varvels; rings on a hawk	
VESANIA	} insanity; psychoses	md, pc
VERSANIC		
VESICAL	} bladder-like cavity or cell	
VESICLE		md
VESPINE	wasplike	
VESPOID	wasplike	zo
VESTIGE	footprint; trace; mark	
VESTING	fabric for vests; investing	
VESTLET	a sea-anemone	zo
VESTRAL	(vestry)	
VESTURE	clothing; garment; dress	
VETERAN	experienced; seasoned; cars built before 1918	
VETIVER	a fragrant grass	bt
VETOING	prohibiting; barring; banning	
VETTING	examining; checking	
VETTURA	Italian cab	
VEXILLA	processional banners	
VIADUCT	raised road	
VIALFUL	a bottleful	
VIARIAN	wayfarer	
VIBICES	feverish spots	md
VIBRANT	resonant; undulous	
VIBRATE	oscillate; quiver; sway	
VIBRATO	tremolo	mu
VIBRION	mobile bacterium	md
VICEROY	king's deputy	
VICINAL	adjoining; near; neighbouring	
VICIOUS	depraved; sinful; defective	
VICTORY	success; mastery; triumph	
VICTRIX	a lady winner	
VICTUAL	provide provisions	
VIDENDA	things to be seen	
VIDETTE	vedette; mounted scout	
VIDIMUS	an inspection; summary	
VIDUAGE	} viduity; widowhood	
VIDUATE		
VIDUOUS	widowed	
VIEWING	surveying; scanning; eyeing	
VIGONIA	llama wool fabric	tx
VILAYET	Turkish province	
VILLAGE	hamlet; thorpe	
VILLAIN	miscreant; rascal; rogue	
VILLEIN	serf; villager	
VILLINO	small villa in a park	
VILLOSE	} shaggy; hairy	
VILLOUS		
VILUELA	ancient Spanish lute	mu
VIMINAL	of twigs	

VINALIA	Roman wine festival	
VINASSE	wine dregs	
VINCULA	brackets; several similarly treated terms	**ma**
VINEGAR	fermentation acid; sour wine	
VINGT-UN	card game	
VINTAGE	gathering of grapes; cars of 1919–1930	
VINTNER	wine-seller	
VIOLANE	violet-blue diopside	**mn**
VIOLATE	outrage; break; profane	
VIOLENT	fierce; vehement; furious	
VIOLINE	poisonous extract	**bt**
VIOLINO	ancient high-pitched viol (It.)	**mu**
VIOLIST	viola player	**mu**
VIOLONE	ancient double-bass (It.)	**mu**
VIRAZON	sea breeze, Chile, Peru	**mt**
VIRELAY	} medieval roundelay (Fr.)	
VIRELAI	}	**mu**
VIRGATE	wand-like; slender and straight	
VIRGATE	a quarter of a hide	**me**
VIRGULE	small rod; a comma	
VIROSIS	viral infection	**md**
VIRTUAL	potential; implicit; almost entirely; de facto	
VIRTUAL	environment for code and data	**cp**
VISAGED	envisaged	
VIS-A-VIS	face to face	
VISCERA	internal organs	**md**
VISCOUS	sticky; glutinous; tenacious	
VISEITE	zeolite	**mn**
VISIBLE	patent; evident; apparent	
VISIBLY	obviously; manifestly	
VISITED	stayed; chastised; afflicted	
VISITOR	visiter; a caller	
VISNOMY	physiognomy (Spens.)	
VISORED	masked	
VIS-VIVA	striking energy	
VITALLY	essentially	
VITAMIN	a food element	
VITIATE	to spoil; impair; debase	
VITRAIL	stained-glass window	
VITRAIN	a type of coal	**mn**
VITREUM	eye-fluid	**md**
VITRICS	glass-making	
VITRIFY	to glaze	
VITRINA	glass snails	**zo**
VITRINE	glass show case	
VITRIOL	sulphuric acid	**ch**
VITRITE	black glass	
VITTATE	with longitudinal stripes	**bt**
VITULAR	(calf); (veal)	
VIVENCY	existence	
VIVERRA	civet genus	**zo**
VIVIDLY	animatedly; brilliantly	
VIVIFIC	enlivening	
VIXENLY	snappish	
VOCABLE	a word; a name	
VOCALIC	containing vowels	

VOCALLY	by voice	
VOCODER	synthetic speech device	
VOCULAR	vocal	
VOETSAK	begone! (S. Africa)	
VOGLITE	uranium ore	**mn**
VOICING	expressing	
VOIDAGE	fractional quantity of voids	
VOIDING	ejecting; emptying	
VOIVODE	} Hungarian, Polish,	
VAIVODE	} Romanian governor	
VOLABLE	nimble-witted; volatile	
VOLANTE	Spanish vehicle; (It.) fast and light	**mu**
VOLAPUK	universal language	
VOLCANO	eruptive mountain	
VOLSUNG	Odin's grandson	
VOLTAGE	amount of volts	**el, me**
VOLTAIC	galvanic	
VOLUBLE	having the gift of the gab	
VOLUBLY	glibly; fluently	
VOLUMED	bulky	
VOLUMEN	rolled papyrus text	
VOLUSPA	song of the sybil (Scand.)	
VOLUTED	with spiral scroll	
VOMITUS	vomited matter	**md**
VORLAGE	forward leaning position (skiing)	
VOTABLE	enfranchised	
VOUCHED	warranted; attested	
VOUCHEE	warrantee	**lw**
VOUCHER	a witness; a pass	
VOWELLY	full of vowels	
VOYAGED	cruised; traversed	
VOYAGER	ocean traveller	
VULGATE	authentic Latin Bible	**rl**
VULPINE	foxy; cunning	
VULTURE	carrion-eating bird	**zo**
VULTURN	Australian turkey	**zo**

W

WABBLER	a wobbler	
WABSTER	webster; weaver	
WADABLE	fordable	
WADDING	stuffing	
WADDLED	walked like a duck	
WADDLER	wobbly walker	
WAD-HOOK	an extractor	**to**
WADMOLL	woollen cloth	**tx**
WADSETT	a mortgage	**lw**
WAENESS	sadness (Sc.)	
WAESOME	woesome; woeful; pitiful	
WAFERED	sealed; secured	
WAFTAGE	transportation	
WAFTING	floating; airing; beckoning	
WAFTURE	waftage; wavure	
WAGERED	hazarded; risked; staked	
WAGERER	a better	
WAGGERY	sportive merriment	
WAGGING	vibrating; stirring	

WAGGISH	droll; facetious; jocular	
WAGGLED	wiggled; swayed	
WAGONED	carted; transported	
WAGONER	cart-driver	
WAGSOME	whimsical; witty	
WAGTAIL	bird; joinery	**zo**
WAGWANT	totter-grass	**bt**
WAHABEE	primitive Moslem	**rl**
WAILFUL	mournful; sorrowful; grievous	
WAILING	bemoaning; lamenting	
WAINAGE	transport	
WAISTED	narrowed	
WAISTER	whaling greenhorn	
WAITING	attendance; biding; tarrying	
WAIVING	relinquishing; remitting	
WAIVODE	Polish governor	
WAKEFUL	alert; wary; vigilant	
WAKEMAN	watchman	
WAKENED	stimulated; excited	
WAKENER	a rouser; knocker-up	
WALKING	pedestrianism; hiking; rambling	
WALK-OUT	industrial strike; protest	
WALLABA	timber tree (Guyana)	**bt**
WALLABY	kangaroo-like animal	**zo**
WALLACH	Wallack; a Wallachian	
WALL-EYE	eye condition	**md**
WALLING	wall material	
WALLOON	Belgian (of French-speaking area)	
WALL-RUE	a fern	**bt**
WALTZED	cut a figure	
WALTZER	ballroom athlete	
WAMBLED	rumbled	
WAME-TOW	belly-band	
WAMPISH	to flourish; to brandish (Sc.)	
WAN-EYED	languid; sad	
WANGHEE	a cane; a stick	
WANGLED	acquired by craft	
WANHOPE	despair	
WANHORN	a plant	**bt**
WANNESS	pallor; paleness	
WANNISH	sickly	
WANTAGE	deficiency; lack	
WANTING	absent; desiring; needing	
WANTWIT	a numskull; nitwit	
WAPACUT	American snowy owl	**zo**
WARATAH	Australian shrub	**bt**
WARBLED	quavered; trilled; carolled	
WARBLER	a songster	**zo**
WARBLES	saddle-sores; tumours	
WARDAGE	watch-tax	
WARDIAN	botanist's case	
WARDING	repelling; fending; guarding	
WARD-WIT	warder's quittance	
WAREFUL	wary; cautious; vigilant	
WARFARE	strife; hostilities	
WARHEAD	explosive part of missile	
WARHOOP	war-cry; slogan	
WARIEST	most circumspect	
WARISON	a reward; a gift	

WARLIKE	belligerent; martial	
WARLOCK	wizard; a spell	
WARLORD	Junker militarist	
WARMEST	keenest; most ardent	
WARMING	heating	
WARNING	caution; notification; omen	
WARPATH	hostile expedition	
WARPING	twisting; distorting; wood expanding; dock	**nt**
WARPING	non-flatness in gramophone records	
WARRANT	authority; right; justify	
WARRING	contending; striving	
WARRIOR	veteran fighter	
WAR-RISK	(insurance)	
WAR-SCOT	war-tax; a levy	
WARSHIP	battleship, etc.	**nt**
WARSONG	song on martial theme	
WART-HOG	an African ungulate	**zo**
WARWOLF	military engine	
WARWORN	battle-weary	
WASH-DAY	laundry day	
WASHING	ablution; rinsing	
WASH-OUT	a failure; fiasco; all bowling pins standing	
WASHPOT	(Moab)	
WASHTUB	scrubbing vessel	
WASP-FLY	fly resembling wasp	**zo**
WASPISH	resentful; irritable	
WASSAIL	an occasion; punch	
WASTAGE	dissipation	
WASTING	emaciation	
WASTREL	waif; a dud	
WATCHED	guarded; tended; noted	
WATCHER	watchman	
WATCHET	light blue	
WATERED	wavy; moistened; sprinkled	
WATERER	irrigator	
WATTLED	(hurdles); (cocks-comb)	
WAULING	howling; caterwauling	
WAVELET	a ripple	
WAVERED	faltered; swayed	
WAVERER	hesitator	
WAVESON	flotsam	
WAVICLE	quantum mechanical entity	**ps**
WAX-BEAN	butter-bean	**bt**
WAXBILL	(weaver-bird)	**zo**
WAX-DOLL	poupée (Fr.)	
WAX-JACK	silver stand for sealing wax, taper	
WAX-MOTH	(a bee scourge)	**zo**
WAX-PALM	wax-producing tree	**bt**
WAX-TREE	American gamboge tree	**bt**
WAXWING	a crested bird	**zo**
WAXWORK	wax statue counterfeiting life	
WAYBILL	a list (transport)	
WAYFARE	to walk	
WAYGONE	exhausted; wayworn	
WAYLAND	a legendary smith	
WAYLESS	pathless; trackless	

WAY-MARK	direction pointer; sign	
WAY-POST	guide-post	
WAYSIDE	of the roadside	
WAYWARD	froward; wilful; unruly	
WAYWISE	directional capacity	
WAYWODE	waivode; Polish governor	
WAYWORN	exhausted; spent	
WEAKEST	puniest	
WEALDEN	(weald of Kent)	
WEALTHY	opulent; affluent; rich	
WEANING	alienating; detaching	
WEARIED	fatigued; jaded; careworn	
WEARIER	more jaded and tired	
WEARILY	tediously	
WEARING	exhausting	
WEARISH	withered; washy	
WEASAND	} windpipe; throat	**md**
WEAZAND		
WEATHER	climate; endure; overcome	
WEAVING	cloth-making; laying shingles	
	(roof tiles – wooden)	**bd**
WEBBING	hempen fabric	
WEB-EYED	filmy-eyed	**md**
WEB-FOOT	characteristic of aquatic birds	
WEBSTER	wabster; a weaver	
WEB-TOED	with webs between toes	
WEDDING	nuptials; espousal; marriage	
WEDGING	a timber joint; compressing;	
	doorstop	
WEDLOCK	matrimony	
WEEDERY	cf. fernery	
WEEDING	eliminating; purging	
WEE-FREE	Independent Liberal	
WEEKDAY	daily except Sunday; work day	
WEEKEND	Saturday and Sunday	
WEENING	thinking; imagining	
WEEPING	sobbing; crying; bewailing	
WEEVILY	full of weevils	**zo**
WEFTAGE	texture	
WE-GROUP	in-group; elitism	**pc**
WEIGHED	pondered; pressed; (anchor)	
WEIGHER	weighing machine	
WEIGH-IN	pre-contest weight check	
WEIGHTY	ponderous; onerous; grave	
WEIRDER	more fantastic	
WEIRDLY	eerily; uncannily	
WELAWAY	alas!	
WELCHER	welsher; absconding bookie	
WELCOME	salutation; greeting	
WELDING	welded joint	
WELFARE	comfort; prosperity; weal	
WELLING	springing; gushing	
WELL-MET	all hail! welcome!	
WELL-OFF	well-to-do; prosperous	
WELL-SET	firmly set	
WELL-WON	honestly gained	
WELSHED	decamped; absconded	
WELSHER	absconding bookie	
WELTING	shoe-edging	
WENDING	wandering; strolling	

WENDISH	the Wend dialect	
WENLOCK	limestone	**mn**
WENNISH	cyst-like	
WERGILD	} fine for murder; blood	
WERGOLD	} money	
WERWOLF	} wolf-man	
WEREWOLF		
WEST-END	fashionable; stylish	
WESTERN	occidental	
WESTING	westerly	
WET-DOCK	dock where ship can float	
WETNESS	dampness; humidity	
WET-SHOD	with wet feet	
WETTEST	supersaturated	
WET-TIME	wages for rainy days	
WETTING	moistening; drenching	
WETTISH	rather rainy	
WETWOOD	high-water-content wood	**fr**
WHACKED	beaten; defeated; smitten	
WHACKER	of large size; formidable	
WHAISLE	wheeze (Sc.)	
WHALERY	port & factory base for whaling	
	fleet	
WHALING	whale-fishing; thrashing	
WHANGEE	bamboo cane	**bt**
WHAPPED	struck; fluttered	
WHARFED	brought to shore	**nt**
WHARVES	quays; docks	
WHATNOT	small work table or stand with 3	
	or more shelves	
WHATTEN	what kind of (Sc.)	
WHEATEN	of wheat	**bt**
WHEEDLE	to coax; to cajole	
WHEELED	with wheels	
WHEELER	shaft-horse; cyclist	**zo**
WHEELER	wheelwright	
WHEEZED	breathed asthmatically	
WHEEZLE	whaizle; whaisle; obtain	
WHELKED	ridged; shell-like ornamentation	
WHELPED	littered; gave birth to brood	**zo**
WHEMMLE	an upset (Sc.)	
WHEREAS	in view of fact that	
WHEREAT	thereupon	
WHEREBY	through which	
WHEREIN	within which	
WHEREOF	whence	
WHEREON	upon which	
WHERESO	not actually a word	
WHERETO	to which	
WHERRET	to worrit; a blow	
WHETHER	if; in the case of	
WHETILE	woodpecker	**zo**
WHETTED	stimulated; urged	
WHETTER	a sharpener	
WHEWING	whistling with surprise	
WHEYISH	like whey	
WHEY-TUB	cream-tub	
WHIFFED	puffed	
WHIFFER	a puffer	
WHIFFET	whipper-snapper	

WHIFFLE	a flute; prevaricate	**mu**
WHILERE	recently	
WHILING	loitering; passing the time	
WHIMPER	whine; cry; moan	
WHIMPLE	wimple; head-dress	
WHIMSEY	whimsy; a caprice; crotchet	
WHINGER	dirk; hangar (Sc.)	
WHINING	complaining; snivelling	
WHIPCAT	a tailor	
WHIPPED	lashed; beaten; thrashed	
WHIPPER	a flagellant	
WHIPPET	greyhound; small tank	**zo**
WHIP-RAY	a sea-fish	**zo**
WHIPSAW	frame-held narrow saw	**to**
WHIP-TOP	whipping top	
WHIRLED	span; spun; revved	
WHIRLER	a whirligig	
WHIRRED	whurred; rotated	
WHIRRET	wherrit; vex; a blow	
WHISHED	whizzed	
WHISKER	hair of man's cheek	
WHISKET	a basket	
WHISKEY	whisky; a light dog-cart	
WHISPER	murmur; disclose	
WHISTLE	bosun's pipe; tin; police	**nt, mu**
WHISTLY	silently	
WHITELY	palely; pallidly	
WHITEST	purest; lightest	
WHITHER	to which place	
WHITING	whitewash; a fish	**zo**
WHITISH	near white	
WHITLOW	an abscess on finger or toe	**md**
WHITSUL	curds and whey	
WHITSUN	Whitsuntide; Pentecost	**rl**
WHITTAW	a saddler	
WHITTLE	shawl; to cut; pare	
WHIZZED	tore through the air	
WHIZZER	a fast one; form of arm lock (wrestling)	
WHOEVER	anyone at all	
WHOLISM	in entirety; as a whole	
WHOMMLE	confusion; overwhelm	
WHOOBUB	hubbub	
WHOOPED	hooted; yelled; shouted	
WHOOPEE	a joyous cry; a revel	
WHOOPER	the hooper swan	**zo**
WHOPPED	beat; defeated	
WHOPPER	whacker; very large	
WHORLED	spiral; convoluted	
WICKING	cannoning when curling; changing direction of bowl	
WICKIUP	shelter (Amer. Indian)	
WIDENED	extended; broadened	
WIDENER	an enlarger; a reamer	
WIDGEON	migratory duck	**zo**
WIDOWED	bereaved; viduous	
WIDOWER	bereaved husband	
WIELDED	handled; plied; governed	
WIELDER	a controller; user	
WIGGERS	dandelion	**bt**

WIGGERY	false hair	
WIGGING	a scolding; reprimand	
WIGGLED	waggled	
WIGGLER	a wriggler	
WIGHTLY	courageously; nimbly	
WIGLESS	deperuked	
WILD-ASS	the onager	**zo**
WILDCAT	speculative; strike (indust.)	**zo**
WILDEST	most turbulent and rash	
WILDING	growing wild; crab-apple	**bt**
WILDISH	rather wild	
WILD-OAT	youthful crop	**bt**
WILIEST	craftiest; pawkiest	
WILLING	devising; agreeing; consenting	
WILLOCK	young guillemot	**zo**
WILLOWY	slender; pliant	
WILSOME	wilful; stubborn; wayward	
WILTING	drooping; fading	
WIMBERY	whortleberry	**bt**
WIMBLED	drilled; bored	
WIMBREL	whimbrel; small curlew	**zo**
WIMPLED	puckered; wrinkled	
WINCHED	hoisted; hauled up	
WINDAGE	clearance	
WINDBAG	a would-be orator	
WIND-EGG	an addled egg	**zo**
WIND-GUN	air-gun	
WINDIER	breezier; more alarmed	
WINDIGO	Red Indian hunter syndrome	**pc**
WINDILY	breezily; panic-struck	
WINDING	tortuous; changing; scenting	
WINDROW	hay or peat in rows	
WINDSOR	Royal House	
WINEBAG	wine-skin; a tippler	
WINEFAT	a vat	
WINESAP	American winter apple	**bt**
WING-ICE	(ice on aircraft)	
WINGING	flying; wounding	
WINGLET	bastard wing	**zo**
WINKERS	flashing lights	**au**
WINKING	nictitating; conniving at	
WINNING	charming; acquiring; getting	
WINNOCK	windock; a window (Sc.)	
WINSOME	engaging; taking; seductive	
WINTERY	wintry; hyemal	
WIPE-OUT	intense interference	**tc**
WIPE-OUT	fall in wave (surfing); exterminate; slaughter	
WIREBAR	copper in tapered ingots	**ml**
WIREMAN	linesman	
WIREWAY	telpherage; aerial transport	
WIRIEST	leanest; toughest	
WISE-GUY	clever trickster; smart Alec	
WISHFUL	desirous; eager and anxious	
WISTFUL	pensive; meditative; yearning	
WISTITI	marmoset	**zo**
WITCHED	bewitched; charmed	
WITCHEN	mountain ash; rowan	**bt**
WITHERS	(horse's neck)	
WITHIES	willow twigs	**bt**

WITHOUT	outside; except; lacking
WITLESS	indiscreet; thoughtless
WITLOOF	chicory **bt**
WITNESS	attest; testimony; see
WITTIER	droller; more facetious
WITTILY	jocularly; humorously
WITTING	wotting; knowing
WITWALL	golden oriole **zo**
WIZENED	shrivelled; wimpled
WOBBLED	deviated
WOBBLER	wabbler; vacillator; erratic speed on course (curling)
WOESOME	woeful; waesome
WOLF-DOG	sheep-dog **zo**
WOLFISH	wolvish; rapacious; ravenous
WOLFKIN	young wolf
WOLF-MAN	wer-wolf (were-wolf)
WOLF-NET	large fishing net
WOLFRAM	tungsten **ch**
WOLSUNG	grandson of Odin
WOMANED	chaperoned
WOMANLY	feminine
WOMMERA	} spear; throwing stick
WOOMERA	} (Aust.)
WONGSHY	yellow dye (Chinese)
WOOD-ANT	the red ant **zo**
WOODCUT	a print from a wooden block
WOOD-GOD	sylvan deity
WOODMAN	a forester
WOODNUT	hazel-nut **bt**
WOOD-OIL	balsam **bt**
WOOD-OWL	brown owl **zo**
WOOD-TAR	a distillate **ch**
WOOD-TIN	tin-stone **mn**
WOOLDED	roped; lashed
WOOLDER	lashing stick
WOOLFAT	lanolin **zo**
WOOLLEN	of wool
WOOLMAN	wool dealer
WOOLSAW	evil spirit (C. American)
WOOLSEY	a dress material **tx**
WOORALI	}
WOURALI	} curare; arrow poison
WORRARA	}
WORDILY	verbose; prolix; garrulously
WORDING	phrasing; expressing
WORDISH	wordy; loquacious
WORKBAG	lady's sewing bag
WORKBOX	box of work materials
WORKDAY	M., T., W., Th., F.
WORKING	fermenting; drudging
WORKMAN	a toiler; operative
WORK-OUT	gymnastic exercise
WORKSHY	allergic to labour
WORLDLY	earthy; secular; mundane
WORMING	(rope); squirming
WORN-OUT	exhausted
WORRIED	harassed; bothered; troubled
WORRIER	a worrit; a hector
WORSHIP	adoration; idolize; venerate

WORSTED	wool yarn
WOULD-BE	aspiring
WOULDST	(thou) would
WOUNDED	injured; hurt; damaged
WOUNDER	a pain-giver
WRANGLE	brangle; bicker; brawl
WRAPPED	covered; swathed; wound
WRAPPER	envelope; scarf
WRAULED	} caterwauled; howled
WRAWLED	}
WREAKED	inflicted
WREAKER	an avenger
WREATHE	entwine; to garland
WREATHY	twisty; interlaced
WRECKED	shattered; ruined; destroyed
WRECKER	saboteur; blighter
WREN-TIT	Californian bird **zo**
WRESTED	wrenched; forced; pulled
WRESTER	a twister
WRESTLE	grapple; strive; contend
WRICKED	ricked; sprained
WRIGGLE	worm; squirm; writhe
WRIGGLY	tortuous; sinuous
WRINGER	a mangle
WRINKLE	crinkle; pucker; unglued area (of veneer) **bd**
WRINKLY	creased; rumpled
WRITE-UP	flattering notice
WRITHED	squirmed; wriggled
WRITHEN	contorted; coiled
WRITHLE	to wrinkle; to shrivel
WRITING	calligraphy; penmanship; literature; (desk); (paper)
WRITING	by electromagnet on tape, disk, drum **cp**
WRITTEN	inscribed; indited
WRONGED	maltreated; oppressed
WRONGER	a wrong-un; evil-doer
WRONGLY	falsely; unjustly
WROUGHT	worked; effected
WRYBILL	a New Zealand plover **zo**
WRYNECK	(woodpecker) **zo**
WRYNESS	crookedness
WUSTITE	cubic iron oxide **mn**
WUZZENT	wizened (Sc.)
WYANDOT	Iraquoian Indian; fowl **zo**
WYCH-ELM	witch-elm **bt**

X

XANTHIC	an acid; yellow **ch**
XANTHIN	yellow extract **bt**
XANTHOS	yellow colour given to Greek chariot horses
XENURUS	genus of armadillos **zo**
XERASIA	} hair disease; dryness of
XEROSIS	} the scalp **md**
XERODES	dry tumour **md**

XEROTES	} dryness of the body	**md**
XEROTIC		
XIPHIAS	sword-fish genus	**zo**
XIPHIAS	a Southern constellation	**as**
XIPHOID	ensiform	
XYLENOL	monohydric phenol	**ch**
XYLOLIN	wood pulp fabric	
XYLOPIA	bitter plants	**bt**

Y

YACHTED	cruised	
YACHTER	yachtsman	
YAHWISM	worship of Jehovah	**rl**
YAHWIST	Jehovist	**rl**
YAMADOU	nutmeg oil	**bt**
YANKING	jerking; heaving; hauling	
YAPPING	yelping; yauping	
YAPSTER	a yelper	
YARDAGE	yard dues; distance gained by player (Am. football); amount of sails; distance	**nt, me**
YARDAGE	yard-volume of excavation	**ce**
YARD-ARM	place for hanging	**nt**
YARDING	enclosing	
YARD-MAN	(farm); (railway)	
YARNING	narrating	
YARRING	snarling	
YARRISH	rough dry taste	
YASHMAK	Moslem woman's double veil	
YATAGAN	Turkish curved knife	
YAUPING	yelping	
YAWLING	howling; screaming	
YAWNING	gaping	
YEANING	} bringing forth young; lambing	
YEENING		
YEARNED	desirous; grieved	
YEGGMAN	criminal tramp (USA)	
YELDRIN	yellow bunting	**zo**
YELLING	howling	
YELLOCH	to yell; a yell (Sc.)	
YELLOWS	an animal disease	**vt**
YELLOWY	yellowish; sallowy	
YELPING	yauping; yapping	
YERKING	chucking; jerking	
YERKISH	lingo for chimpanzees	
YESTERN	(yesterday)	
YEW-TREE	(bow-wood)	**bt**
YEZIDIS	devil worshippers	
YIDDISH	Jewish dialect	
YIELDED	rendered; resigned; conceded	
YIELDER	capitulator; abdicator	
YODELER	Tyrolese singer	
YOGHURT	fermented milk	
YOICKED	} shouted Yoicks	
YORLING		
YOLDING	} yellow-hammer	**zo**
YOLDRIN		

YOLK-SAC	separating membrane within egg	**zo**
YORKIST	(War of Roses)	
YOUGHAL	needle-point lace	
YOUNGER	not so old	
YOUNGLY	inexperienced; juvenile	
YOUNKER	a stripling; youngster	
YOUTHLY	youthful; immature	
YOWLING	howling; bawling	
YPERITE	poison gas	**ch**
YTTRIUM	a metallic element	**ch**
YULE-LOG	Christmas fire	
YU-STONE	high-quality jade	**mn**

Z

ZABITAH	zabita; Turkish policeman	
ZADKIEL	(almanac)	
ZALACCA	dragon's blood palm	**bt**
ZAMARRA	sheepskin jacket (Sp.)	
ZAMOUSE	W. African ox	**zo**
ZANELLA	umbrella fabric	
ZANJERO	irrigation officer	
ZANONIA	cucumber	**bt, ck**
ZANSHIN	total awareness, alertness, thought (Jap.)	
ZANYING	fooling	
ZANYISM	buffoonery	
ZAPATEO	shoe dance (S. Amer.)	**mu**
ZAPHARA	sky blue dye used in pottery	
ZAREEBA	zareba; stockade	
ZARNICH	realgar; orpiment	**mn**
ZEALANT	a zealot; enthusiast; bigot	
ZEALFUL	zealous; enthusiastic; eager	
ZEALOUS	fervent; ardent; fervid	
ZEBRASS	a cross-breed; zebra and ass	**zo**
ZEBRINE	zebra type	**zo**
ZEBROID	zebra-like	**zo**
ZEBRULA	(zebra and horse)	**zo**
ZEDOARY	aromatic root	**bt**
ZEITNOT	clockbound administration; chess term (Ger.)	
ZEMSTVO	Russian local assembly	
ZEOLITE	aluminium silicate	**mn**
ZEROING	concentrating firepower	
ZEROIZE	to reset a meter to zero	**cp**
ZESTFUL	piquant; eager; keen	
ZESTING	flavouring; relishing	
ZETETIC	a seeker; a Pyrrhonist	
ZEUGITE	nuclear-fission cell	**nc**
ZEUXITE	a silicate of aluminium	**mn**
ZIMOCCA	bath-sponge	
ZINCALI	Spanish gipsies	
ZINCATE	zinc oxide	**ch**
ZINCIFY	coat with zinc	
ZINCITE	red zinc ore	**mn**
ZINCODE	} positive pole electrode; anode	
ZINCOID		
ZINCOUS	(zinc)	

ZINGARI	(cricket); gipsies (It.)	
ZINGARO	zingane; zingano (It.)	
ZIONISM	Jewish Nationalism	
ZIONIST	who supports free Israel	
ZIPCORD	parachute release cord	
ZIPHIUS	swordfish genus	**zo**
ZIPPING	pinging; whizzing; fastening	
ZITHERN	cithara	**mu**
ZITHERN	or zither	**mu**
ZIZANIA	aquatic grasses; (rice)	**bt**
ZOARIUM	polyzoan	**zo**
ZOCCOLO	square base	**ar**
ZOILEAN	supercritical	
ZOILISM	carping criticism	
ZOILIST	a caviller	
ZOISITE	a silicate; an epidote	**mn**
ZOLAISM	excessive naturalism	
ZONALLY	girdling	
ZONULAR	belted	
ZONULET	small girdle	
ZONURUS	saurian genus	**zo**
ZOOECIA	polyp cells	**zo**
ZOOGAMY	reproduction	
ZOOGENY ZOOGONY }	zoological origins	**zo**
ZOOIDAL	animal-like	**zo**

ZOOLITE ZOOLITH }	a fossil animal	**mn, zo**
ZOOLOGY	study of animals	**zo**
ZOOMING	flying low	
ZOONITE	articulated segment	
ZOONOMY	natural laws	
ZOOPERY	experimenting on lower animals	
ZOOTAXY	systematic zoology	
ZOOTOMY	animal anatomy	
ZOPISSA	pitch used medicinally	**md**
ZORGITE	a metallic ore	**mn**
ZORILLA ZORILLE ZORRINO }	American skunk	**zo**
ZOTHECA	alcove (Gr.)	
ZUFFOLO	Italian flute	**mu**
ZUNYITE	orthosilicate of aluminium	**mn**
ZURLITE	a Vesuvian mineral	**mn**
ZYGAENA	a shark genus	**zo**
ZYGOSIS ZYGOTIC }	conjugation of a zygote	**bt, zo**
ZYMOGEN	a fermentor	**ch**
ZYMOSIS	inflammation	**md**
ZYMOTIC	bacteriological	**md**
ZYMURGY	fermentation	**ch**

A

AARDVARK	ant-bear (S. Afr.)	zo
AARD-WOLF	African wolf	zo
AARONITE	Hebrew priest	rl
AASVOGEL	vulture (S. Afr.)	zo
ABACTION	cattle-theft; rustling	
ABACULUS	counting-frame; tablet	
ABAMPERE	absolute electromagnetic unit	
ABAMURUS	buttress	
ABAPICAL	distant from apex, apposite pole	
ABASHING	humiliating; shaming	
ABATABLE	reducible; alleviable	
ABAT-JOUR	skylight; reflector	
ABATTOIR	slaughter-house	
ABAT-VOIX	canopy over pulpit	rl
ABBATESS	abbess; Lady Superior	rl
ABBATIAL	under abbey control	rl
ABDALAVI	Egyptian musk melon	bt
ABDERIAN	given to laughter	
ABDERITE	a Thracian; Democrites	
ABDICANT	renouncing; an abdicator	
ABDICATE	resign; cede; renounce	
ABDITORY	secret repository	rl
ABDOCULE	shrine, opening between 2 columns	ar
ABDUCENS	outward movement	md, pc
ABDUCENT	retracting; separating	
ABDUCING	abducting; kidnapping	lw
ABDUCTED	removed; taken by fraud	lw
ABDUCTOR	kidnapper; a muscle	md
ABELIANS	} a sect practising marriage	
ABELITES	} chastity (Abel)	rl
ABELMOSK	Syrian mallow	bt
ABERDEEN	a terrier	zo
ABERRANT	abnormal; rambling	
ABERRATE	deviate; diverge; wander	
ABERRING	straying; digressing	
ABETMENT	aiding and abetting	lw
ABETTING	conniving; encouraging	
ABEYANCE	suspension; dormancy	
ABEYANCE	cessation; contemplation	
ABHORRED	hated; loathed; detested	
ABHORRER	Tory nickname, A.D. 1680	
ABIDANCE	abode; dwelling; habitation	
ABIETENE	} balsam	
ABIETINE	}	bt
ABIOGENY	spontaneous generation	
ABJECTLY	servilely; despicably	
ABJURING	apostacy; forswearing	
ABLATION	removal; attrition	md
ABLATIVE	the sixth case in Latin	
ABLEGATE	despatch; depute; delegate	
ABLEGATE	a Papal envoy	rl
ABLENESS	ability; skill, vigour	
ABLEPSIA	ablepsy; blindness	md
ABLOCATE	hire; lease; let	

ABLUTION	purification; baptism	rl
ABLUVION	water-deposited detritus	
ABNEGATE	deny; adjure; renounce	
ABNODATE	untie; remove the knots	
ABNORMAL	odd; irregular; monstrous	
ABOCOCKE	peaked cap of 15th century	
ABOMASUS	abomasum; cow's stomach	zo
ABORTING	miscarrying; frustrating	
ABORTION	a premature expulsion of a foetus; hideosity	md
ABORTIVE	premature; broken off	
ABRADANT	disintegrator; scraper	
ABRADING	grinding; abrasing; fraying	
ABRASION	surface wound; attrition	
ABRASIVE	scratchy; gritty; rough	
ABRASTOL	a preservative	ch
ABRIDGED	epitomized; curtailed	
ABROGATE	cancel; repeal; quash	
ABRUPTED	rent; torn asunder	
ABSCISSA	an axial line in geometry	
ABSENTED	played truant	
ABSENTEE	deliberate duty dodger	
ABSENTLY	dreamily; inattentively	
ABSINTHE	wormwood; French liqueur	bt
ABSOLUTE	pure; despotic; supreme	
ABSOLVED	acquitted; excused	
ABSOLVER	a pardoner; forgiver	
ABSONANT	irrational; discordant	
ABSONOUS	incongruous; out of tune	
ABSORBED	imbibed; preoccupied	
ABSTERGE	purge; wipe away	
ABSTRACT	detach, purloin, withdraw; copy; abstruse	lw
ABSTRACT	gist, summarise, intangible; epitomise; vague	pc
ABSTRUSE	recondite; occult; obscure	
ABSURDLY	irrationally; foolishly	
ABUNDANT	profuse; plentiful; copious	
ABUSABLE	violable; misapplicable	
ABUTILON	plant genus; the jute	bt
ABUTMENT	an arch support; adjacency	ar
ABUTTALS	estate boundaries	lw
ABUTTING	bordering; alongside	
ACADEMIC	scholastic; literary	
ACALEPHA	hydrozoa (jellyfish)	zo
ACANTHUS	a 'capital' plant	bt
ACARDIAC	heartless	
ACARIDAE	mites; ticks, etc	zo
ACARPOUS	sterile; barren	bt
ACAUDATE	tailless; acaudal	zo
ACAULOUS	acauline; stalkless	bt
ACCEDING	complying; consenting	
ACCENSOR	R.C. candle-trimmer	rl
ACCENTED	stressed; emphasized	
ACCENTOR	the hedge-sparrow	zo
ACCENTOR	leading singer	mu
ACCEPTED	admitted; acknowledged	

ACCEPTER ⎫ **ACCEPTOR** ⎭	the recipient of a Bill of Exchange; impedance (circuit); confirmed starter (horse racing) **lw, el, ga**	
ACCIDENT	mischance; fortuity; hap	
ACCLINAL	sloping; atilt	
ACCOLADE	(knighthood); an embrace	
ACCOLENT	neighbour; borderer	
ACCOLLED	collared	**hd**
ACCORDED	harmonized; granted	
ACCOSTED	hailed; greeted; addressed	
ACCOUNTS	recorded transactions	
ACCOUPLE	to link together	
ACCOUTRE	dress in military array	
ACCREDIT	authorize; empower; entrust	
ACCRETED	grew; increased	
ACCROACH	usurp; encroach	
ACCRUING	accumulating; resulting	
ACCURACY	precision; exactness; truth	
ACCURATE	correct; unerring	
ACCURSED	execrable; doomed	
ACCUSANT	informer; accuser	**lw**
ACCUSING	charging; impeaching	
ACCUSTOM	habituate; familiarize	
ACELDEMA	the field of blood (Hebrew)	
ACENTRIC	out of centre	
ACEPHALA	oyster genus	**zo**
ACERBATE	exasperate; embitter	
ACERBENT	caustic; astringent	
ACERBITY	bitterness; sour taste	
ACERVATE	clustered	
ACESCENT	turning sour	
ACETATED	(acetic acid)	**ch**
ACHENIUM	single-seeded fruit	**bt**
ACHERSET	8 bushel measure	**me**
ACHEWEED	gout-weed	**bt**
ACHIEVED	won; attained; perfected	
ACHIEVER	a performer; an executant	
ACHILOUS	lipless	**bt**
ACHIRITE	dioptase	**mn**
ACHROITE	tourmaline	**mn**
ACHROMAT	colour-blind individual; lens	
ACICULAE	spikes and prickles	**bt, zo**
ACICULAR	needle-shaped	
ACIDIFIC	producing acid	**ch**
ACIDNESS	bitterness; tartness	
ACIDOSIS	acidity	**md**
ACIERAGE	steel electro-plating	
ACIERATE	turn into steel	
ACNESTIS	part of spine	**zo**
ACOEMETI	religious community	
ACONITIC	(wolf's-bane, monk's-hood)	**bt**
ACORN-CUP	acorn top, case	**bt**
ACOUSTIC	relating to sound	**md**
ACQUAINT	notify; apprize; teach	**to**
ACQUIRED	scrounged; won; procured	
ACRIDIAN	locust	**zo**
ACRIDITY	pungency; harshness	
ACRIMONY	sharpness of temper	

ACRITUDE	corrosive quality	
ACROATIC	esoteric; (oral instruction)	
ACROLEIN	acryl aldehyde, propenal	**ch**
ACROLITH	statue with wooden body	
ACROMIUM	ventral process	
ACROSOME	head of sperm	**zo**
ACROSTIC	word puzzle in verse	
ACROTISM	lack of pulsation	**md**
ACTINISM	effect of light rays	
ACTINIUM	radio-active element	**ch**
ACTINOID	star-shaped	**zo**
ACTIVATE	to move to activity	
ACTIVELY	energetically; sedulously	
ACTIVISM	practical idealism	
ACTIVIST	production promoter (indust.)	
ACTIVITY	pastime; happening; movement	**cp, ps**
ACTUALLY	really; as a fact	
ACTUATED	influenced; set in motion	
ACUITION	accentuation	
ACULEATE	spiky; pointed	**bt**
ACUTANCE	clarity of enlargement	**pt**
ADAMITIC	Adamic; nudistic	
ADAPTING	adjusting; suiting	
ADAPTIVE	adaptable; conformable	
ADDEEMED	adjudged; considered	
ADDENDUM	adjunct; appendix	
ADDER-FLY	dragonfly	**zo**
ADDICTED	wont; prone; inclined	
ADDITION	accession; summation	**cp**
ADDITIVE	additional; adulterative	**ch, ck,** **ps**
ADDORSED	back to back	**hd**
ADDUCENT	retracting (muscles)	**md**
ADDUCING	citing; alleging	
ADDUCTOR	a muscle	**pl**
ADENOIDS ⎫ **ADENITIS** ⎭	inflammation of nasal glands	**md**
ADEPTION	attainment; perfection	
ADEQUACY	sufficiency; fitness	
ADEQUATE	suitable; condign	
ADFECTED	compounded	
ADHERENT	partisan; adhesive	
ADHERING	sticking to; supporting (of facts)	
ADHESION	coalescence; attachment	
ADHESIVE	tenacious; gummy	
ADIANTUM	maiden-hair fern	**bt**
ADIPOSIS	fat-deposit illness	**md**
ADJACENT	contiguous; close by	
ADJECTED	added to; joined	
ADJOINED	connected; neighbouring	
ADJUDGED	awarded; deemed	
ADJURING	charging on oath	**lw**
ADJUSTER	arranger; fitter	
ADJUTAGE	tubular connection	
ADJUTANT	assistant; regimental officer	
ADJUTANT	Indian scavenging stork	**zo**
ADJUTRIX	lady help	
ADJUVANT	helping; intensifier	**md**

ADLERIAN	of human inferiority	pc
ADMIRING	respecting; marvelling	
ADMITTED	included; conceded	
ADMIXING	mingling with	
ADMONISH	warn; reprove; exhort	
ADNATION	length attachment of organs	bt
ADOPTING	choosing; embracing	
ADOPTION	formal acceptance; (child)	
ADOPTIVE	selective	
ADORABLE	reverential; venerable	
ADORABLY	worshipfully; devotedly	
ADORNING	embellishing; decking	
ADRECTAL	adjacent to the rectum	md
ADROITLY	dexterously: adeptly	
ADSCRIPT	conscript; postscript	
ADSORBED	condensed	
ADULARIA	moonstone	mn
ADULATED	lauded; flattered	
ADULATOR	sycophant; yes-man	
ADULTERY	ex-marital cohabitation	
ADUNCATE	hooked	bt
ADUSTION	cauterization	md
ADVANCED	in the van; lent; progressed	
ADVANCER	promoter	
ADVENING	acceding	
ADVERTED	drew attention to	
ADVISING	counselling; notifying	
ADVISORY	hortative	
ADVOCAAT	brandy egg yolk liqueur (Dutch)	
ADVOCACY	defence; support	
ADVOCATE	barrister; recommend	lw
ADVOWSON	patronage of benefice	rl
ADYNAMIA	loss of vitality	md
ADYNAMIC	slack; lifeless; listless	
AEGROTAT	academic certificate	md
AERARIAN	voteless Roman freeman	
AERATING	charging with gas	
AERATION	gasification	
AERIALLY	ethereally	
AERIFIED	inflated	
AERIFORM	unsubstantial	
AEROBICS	gymnastics with music	
AEROCYST	seaweed air cell	bt
AERODART	dart dropped by airman	
AERODYNE	aircraft	ae
AEROFOIL	lifting surface (gliding)	
AEROGRAM	wireless message; letter	
AEROLITE	} meteoric stone;	
AEROLITH	} meteorite	mn
AEROLOGY	meteorology	
AERONAUT	airman; balloonist	
AEROSTAT	barrage balloon	
AESCULIN	horse-chestnut extract	bt
AESTHETE	professed beauty lover	
AESTIVAL	estival (summer)	
AFEBRILE	unaccompanied by fever	md
AFFECTED	moved; unnatural; insincere	
AFFEERED	fixed; confirmed	

AFFERENT	conducting inwards	md
AFFIANCE	confidence; betroth	
AFFINAGE	metal refining	
AFFINING	refining; purifying	
AFFINITY	relationship; attraction	
AFFIRMED	confirmed; ratified	
AFFIRMER	testifier; a Quaker	rl
AFFIXING	attaching; connecting	
AFFLATUS	inspiration; ecstasy	
AFFLUENT	a tributary; wealthy	
AFFORCED	ravished	
AFFORDED	yielded; bore the cost	
AFFOREST	convert into forest	
AFFRIGHT	sudden terror; frighten	
AFFRONTE	confronting	hd
AFFUSING	spraying; bedewing	rl
AFFUSION	baptismal sprinkling	rl
AFTER-ALL	in conclusion	
AFTER-WIT	wisdom after the event	
AGAL-WOOD	aloes-wood	bt
AGAR-AGAR	seaweed; edible gel	bt, ck
AGASTRIC	stomachless	zo
AGATIZED	turned into agate	
AGEDNESS	antiquity; senility	
AGENESIS	imperfect development	
AGENTIAL	acting through an agent	
AGERASIA	healthy-looking elder	
AGGRIEVE	give sorrow; injure	
AGIOTAGE	(stock jobbing)	
AGISTAGE	tax on pasturage	lw
AGITABLE	excitable; tremulous	
AGITATED	roused; instigated	
AGITATOR	agent provocateur	
AGLIMMER	shimmering	
AGLOSSAL	tongueless	zo
AGLOSSIA	tongueless; inarticulate	md
AGNATION	male descent	lw
AGNOSTIC	humanist; positivist	
AGONISED	tormented	
AGRAPHIA	inability to write	md
AGRARIAN	of farming, land, rural	
AGREEING	matching; tallying	
AGREMENT	adornment (Fr.)	mu
AGRESTAL	weedlike	bt
AGRESTIC	rustic; unpolished	
AGRIMONY	liverwort	bt
AGRONOMY	scientific farming	
AGRYPNIA	insomnia	md
AGUE-CAKE	a tumour	md
AGUE-TREE	sassafras tree	bt
AHEDONIA	depressive listlessness	md
A-HORIZON	podsol; uppermost of soil layers	ce, ag
AIGRETTE	egret's plume	zo
AIGUILLE	spire; peak; rock-drill	
AILERONS	wing brake flaps (gliding)	ae
AILLETTE	ailette; epaulet	
AIR-BORNE	no earthly connection	
AIR-BRAKE	brake operated by air	
AIR-BRICK	ventilating brick	

AIRBRUSH	fixative spray	
AIR-BUILT	chimerical; baseless	
AIRCRAFT	flying machines	
AIR-DRAIN	an airspace	**ar**
AIR-DRAWN	imaginary; visionary	
AIREDALE	terrier	**zo**
AIRFIELD	landing ground	
AIR-FLEET	unified collection of aeroplanes	
AIR-FLOAT	sand-shaking process	**mn**
AIRFRAME	fuselage	**zo**
AIRGRAPH	air mail letter; microfilm	
AIRINESS	lightness; gaiety	
AIR-LINER	commercial passenger plane	
AIR-PILOT	a flyer; a navigator	
AIRPLANE	aeroplane	
AIRPOISE	aneroid barometer	
AIR-POWER	air war potential	
AIRSCREW	propeller	
AIRSHAFT	ventilation shaft	
AIRSPACE	supra-construction; of territory	
AIRSPEED	rate relative to airflow (gliding)	
AIR-STOVE	heating apparatus	
AIRSTRIP	landing strip	
AIR-SWEPT	dry grinding process	**mn**
AIRTIGHT	impermeable to air	
AIRTRUNK	ventilating shaft	
AKINESIA	muscular weakness/paralysis	**md**
ALACRITY	briskness; agility; readiness	
ALARM-GUN	signal of distress	
ALARMING	calling to arms; ominous	
ALARMIST	Jeremiah; panic-monger	
ALBACORE	⎫ tunny-fish; species of	
ALBICORE	⎬ thynnus	**zo**
ALBANIAN	(Albania)	
ALBINESS	female albino	
ALBINISM	deficiency of pigment	
ALBORADA	folk music (Sp.)	**mu**
ALBUMESS	Lamb's album-keeper	
ALBURNUM	sap-wood	**bt**
ALCAHEST	alkahest; alchemists' solvent	
ALCATRAS	ocean birds; pelican	**zo**
ALCHEMIC	relating to alchemy	
ALDEHYDE	a volatile liquid	**ch**
ALDERMAN	a civic dignitary	
ALDOLASE	an enzyme	**ch**
ALEATORY	depending on dice	
ALEBENCH	alehouse bench	
ALEBERRY	hot ale with sops	
ALEHOUSE	(no spirit licence)	
ALEMBDAR	Sultan's standard-bearer	
ALE-STAKE	an alehouse sign	
ALEURONE	a protein in seeds	**bt**
ALFRESCO	in the open air	
ALGERINE	Algerian; pirate	
ALGIDITY	chilliness	
ALGOLOGY	the study of seaweeds	**bt**
ALGONKIN	Canadian Indian	
ALGORISM	the decimal system	

ALGRAPHY	aluminium printing	
ALHAMBRA	Moorish palace	
ALICANTE	Spanish red wine	
ALIENAGE	estrangement	
ALIENATE	transfer; estrange	
ALIENISM	study of insanity	**pc**
ALIENIST	mental specialist	**pc**
ALIGHTED	stepped off; descended	
ALIGNING	adjusting; dressing	
ALIQUANT	a remainder	
ALITRUNK	winged segment	**zo**
ALIZARIN	madder; synthetic dye	
ALKAHEST	⎫ solvent	
ALCAHEST	⎬	**ch**
ALKALIES	caustic bases	
ALKALIFY	⎫ neutralize an acid;	
ALKALIZE	⎬ alkalise	**ch**
ALKALINE	salty	**ch**
ALKALOID	active part of a drug	**md**
ALKERMES	a crimson cordial	
ALLANITE	cerium silicate	**ch**
ALLAYING	stilling; mitigating	
ALL-BURNT	rocket-fuel exhaustion moment	
ALL-CLEAR	end of danger	
ALLEGING	asserting as a fact	
ALLEGORY	parable; metaphor	
ALLELULA	alleluyah; halleluiah	
ALLERGIC	antipathetic	
ALLERION	heraldic beakless eagle	**hd**
ALLEY-WAY	narrow passage; board-game (E. Europe)	**ga**
ALL-FIRED	infernal; hell-fired	
ALL-FOURS	(cards); mode of progress	
ALLIANCE	union by treaty; coalition	
ALLIGATE	to bind together	
ALLOCATE	allot; assign; share	
ALLODIUM	freehold estate	**lw**
ALLODLAL	freehold; not feudal	
ALLOGAMY	cross-fertilization	**bt**
ALLOPATH	user of healing drugs	**md**
ALLOSOME	non-typical chromosome	**cy**
ALLOTTED	meted; assigned; dispensed	
ALLOTTEE	a sharer	
ALLOTYPE	varying type specimen	
ALL-OUTER	extremist; zealot	
ALLOWING	conceding; admitting	
ALLOYAGE	the alloying of metals	**ml**
ALLOYING	blending; debasing	
ALLSPICE	Jamaica pepper	**bt**
ALLUDING	hinting; insinuating	
ALLURING	enticing; tempting	
ALLUSION	hint; reference	
ALLUSIVE	relative; innuent	
ALLUSORY	symbolical; figurative	
ALLUVIAL	sedimentary	
ALLUVION	alluvial land	
ALLUVIUM	water-borne silt	
ALMAGEST	astronomical problems	**as**
ALMIGHTY	all-powerful; omnipotent	

ALMSDEED	act of charity	
ALMSGATE	(where alms were given)	
ALOMANCY	divination by salt	
ALOPECLA	baldness; fox-evil	md
ALPHABET	order or list of letters	
ALPHA-RAY	a radio-active ray	
ALPHENIC	white barley-sugar	ck
ALPINIST	mountaineer	
ALQUIFOU	Cornish lead ore	mn
ALSATIAN	sheep-dog; debauchee	zo
ALTARAGE	altar offerings	rl
ALTERANT	production of change	
ALTER-EGO	second self	
ALTERING	varying; changing	
ALTERITY	being otherwise	
ALTERNAT	precedence by rotation	
ALTHEINE	asparagine	bt
ALTHOUGH	notwithstanding	
ALTINCAR	unrefined borax	ch
ALTITUDE	height; eminence; (aircraft, gliders) data	ae
ALTO-CLEF	C on 3rd line of staff	mu
ALTRUISM	self-sacrifice	
ALTRUIST	philanthropist	
ALUMINIC	containing aluminium	mn
ALUMINUM	aluminium	ch
ALUNOGEN	aluminium sulphite	ch
ALVEATED	hollowed out; saucer-shape	
ALVEOLAR	speech sound; honeycomb-like	el
ALVEOLUS	alveole; tooth socket	
AMADAVAT	a weaver-bird	zo
AMANDINE	sweet almond ointment	
AMANDOLA	green marble	mn
AMANITIN	poison in fungi	ch
AMARACUS	marjoram	bt
AMARANTH	love-lies-bleeding	bt
AMASSING	piling up; accumulating	
AMAZEDLY	confusedly; dazedly	
AMBERITE	smokeless explosive	ch
AMBITION	desire; aspiration	
AMBIVERT	one turned both ways	pc
AMBLYGON	obtuse-angled	
AMBREADA	spurious amber	
AMBREATE	salt of ambreic acid	ch
AMBROSIN	Milanese coin	nm
AMBROSLA	food of the gods; bee-bread	
AMBULANT	peripatetic; hiking	
AMBULATE	saunter; walk; stroll; hike	
AMBUSHED	caught unaware	
AMENABLE	liable; pliant; subject	
AMENABLY	docilely; responsively	
AMENANCE	conduct; behaviour	
AMENDING	rectifying; correcting	
AMERCING	fining; mulcting	
AMERICAN	Yankee	
AMETHYST	anti-inebriation jewel	mn
AMIANTUS	fibrous asbestos	mn
AMICABLE	friendly; neighbourly	
AMICABLY	benignly; peacefully	

AMIDMOST	in the very centre	
AMISSING	lost; wanting	
AMITOSIS	constriction-division of nucleus	
AMITOTIC	characterized by amitosis	cy
AMMODYTE	sand-eel	zo
AMMONIAC	of nature of ammonia	ch
AMMONITE	explosive	
AMMONITE	spiral fossil	zo
AMMONIUM	base of ammonia	ch
AMNIOTIC	a membrane	md
AMOEBEAN	alternately answering	
AMOEBEUM	poetic dialogue	
AMOEBOID	} of simple structure; like	
AMOEBOUS	} a protozoon	zo
AMORETTO	cupid; a lover	
AMORTIZE	transfer property	lw
AMOUNTED	reached; rose; resulted	
AMPELITE	anti-pest earth	mn
AMPHIBIA	amphibians	zo
AMPHIGEN	a lichen-like plant	bt
AMPHIONT	a zygote; an egg-shell	zo
AMPHORAL	like a two-handled vase	
AMPHORIC	hollow sounding	md
AMPULLAR	like a two-handled flask	
AMPUTATE	lop; prune; sever	
AMULETIC	like an amulet; charming	
AMURCOUS	foul with dregs	
AMUSABLE	capable of enjoyment	
AMUSETTE	light field gun	
AMYGDALA	limbic system	pl
AMYLASES	diastase enzymes	ck
ANABASIS	epic of 10,000 mercenary Greeks (xenophone)	
ANABATIC	of hot-air convection winds	mt
ANABLEPS	a genus of fish	zo
ANABOLIC	body-building	md
ANACONDA	python (S. America)	zo
ANACUSIA	total deafness	md
ANAFRONT	frontal-zone warm-air rise	mt
ANAGLYPH	a cameo; stereoscopic	
ANAGOGIC	mystical; allegorical	
ANAGRAPH	catalogue; inventory	
ANALECTS	collection of lit'y fragments	
ANALEMMA	pedestal of sundial	
ANALEPSY	recurring epilepsy	md
ANALOGIC	analogous; alike; akin	
ANALOGON	} similarity; synonym; a	
ANALOGUE	} corresponding part	
ANALYSED	examined	
ANALYSER	scrutator; analyst	
ANALYSIS	opposite of synthesis	
ANALYTIC	inductive	
ANANDRIA	lack of maleness	md
ANANGIAN	lacking vascular system	pl
ANAPAEST	a reversed dactyl	
ANAPHASE	nuclear division stage	
ANAPHORA	rhetorical repetition	rl
ANARCHIC	lawless and turbulent	
ANASARCA	dropsy	md

421

ANATHEMA	excommunication	rl
ANATOMIC	internal	md
ANCESTOR	forefather; forebear	
ANCESTRY	lineage; descent	
ANCHORED	fixed securely	
ANCHORET	anchorite; hermit	rl
ANCONEAL	relating to the elbow	md
ANDERSON	a steel shelter	
ANDESINE	felspar; andes	mn
ANDESITE	igneous rock, Andes	mn
ANDIRONS	fire-dogs	
ANDORRAN	(Andorra)	
ANDROGEN	male hormone	bc
ANECDOTE	a chatty relation	
ANECHOIC	echoless	ac
ANEURISM }	dilated artery; abnormal	
ANEURYSM }	enlargement	md
ANGEL-BED	open bed without posts	
ANGELICA	plant; Californian wine	bt
ANGERING	inflaming; infuriating	
ANGLICAN	Church of England	rl
ANGLOMAN	anglo-maniac	
ANGRIEST	exceedingly irate	
ANGSTROM	light wave-length unit	lt, me
ANGULATE	angular	
ANHEDRAL	allotriomorphic	gl
ANHYPNIA	insomnia	md
ANICONIA	lack of mental energy	pc
ANIENTED	annulled	
ANIMALLY	beastly	
ANIMATED	enlivened	
ANIMATOR	a rouser	
ANIMETTA	cloth for chalice	rl
ANIRIDIA	absence of iris	md
ANISETTE	liqueur from aniseed	
ANISOPIA	unequal vision	md
ANNALISE	record historical events	
ANNALIST	writer of annals	
ANNAMITE	native of Annam, Vietnam	
ANNEALED	tempered	
ANNELIDA	worms	zo
ANNEXING	attaching; taking over	
ANNOTATE	add notes to; commentate	
ANNOUNCE	pronounce; proclaim	
ANNOYING	irritating; vexatious	
ANNUALLY	yearly; every year	
ANNULARY	ring bearing (fourth finger)	
ANNULATE	dividing into rings	
ANNULLED	rendered void; abolished	
ANNULLER	a voider	
ANNULOSE	annular; ringed	zo
ANODISED	treated electrically	
ANOINTED	consecrated; Messiah	rl
ANOPLURA	parasitic lice	zo
ANOREXIA	loss of appetite	md
ANORTHIC	oblique angled (crystal)	
ANOVULAR	eggless	pl
ANSERINE	gooselike; stupid; silly	
ANSWERED	solved; responded; refuted	
ANTALGIC	anodyne; pain-killer	md

ANT-EATER	ant-bear, etc.	zo
ANTECEDE	precede	
ANTEDATE	anticipate	
ANTEFIXA	ornamental tiling	
ANTELOPE	antilope	zo
ANTENATI	born before a given date	
ANTENNAE	feelers; aerials	zo
ANTENNAL	relating to the above	
ANTENODE	(maximum displacement)	el
ANTEPAST	antipasta; pre-meal appetizer	
ANTEPORT	outer gate or harbour	
ANTERIOR	prior; before	
ANTEROOM	antechamber	
ANTHELIA	luminous rings around sun	
ANTHELIX	antihelix; part of the ear	pl
ANTHEMIS	plant genus; camomile	bt
ANTHERAL	(pollen bearing anthers)	bt
ANTHESIS	full bloom	bt
ANTHOZOA	sea-anemones; corals	zo
ANTHROPO-	related to man	cf
ANTIACID	antacid medicine	md
ANTI-ARMY	pacifist	
ANTIBODY	a counteractive	md
ANTICIZE	to play antics	
ANTICOUS	centripetal	bt
ANTIDOTE	counter-measure	
ANTIDUNE	sandhill, dune	gl
ANTIGENY	sexual dimorphism	zo
ANTI-ICER	anti-freeze	
ANTILOGY	contradiction; antinomy	
ANTILOPE	antelope	zo
ANTIMASK	grotesque interlude	
ANTIMIST	preventing misting up	ch
ANTIMONY	stibium; a white metal	mn, ch
ANTINAZI	anti-Hitlerite	
ANTINODE	radio term	ro
ANTINOMY	legal contradiction	lw
ANTINOUS	ideal of youthful beauty	
ANTIPHON	anthem; alternate chanting	
ANTIPODE }	directly opposite; the	
ANTIPOLE }	opposite	
ANTIPOPE	opposition pope; (Avignon)	
ANTIQUED	simulated parchment (technique)	
ANTISERA	antibiotics	md
ANTISPIN	assisting recovery from spin	
ANTISTES	chief priest or prelate	rl
ANTI-TANK	(guns, mines, etc.)	
ANTITYPE	typical example	
ANTLERED	furnished with antlers	
ANTRORSE	up-turning	
ANYTHING	an unspecified object	
ANYWHERE	an undefined locality	
AORISTIC	indefinite as to time	
AORTITIS	inflammation of artery	md
APAGOGIC	reducing to an absurdity	
APELLOUS	without a skin	md
APERIENT	a laxative; an opening	md
APERITIF	a cocktail	
APERTURE	gap; hole; lens	pg

APEX-BEAT	heartbeat visibility point	**md, pl**
APHANITE	horn-blende, quartz, etc.	
APHELION	maximal distance of earth from sun	
APHIDIAN	(green-fly)	**zo**
APHLEBIA	lateral fern outgrowth	**bt**
APHONOUS	voiceless; dumb	**md**
APHORISM	a maxim; a saw	
APHORIST	a writer of adages	
APHORIZE	aphorise; define briefly	
APHRENIA	without mind	**pc**
APHTHOUS	ulcerous	**md**
APIARIAN	concerning bees	**zo**
APIARIST	a bee expert	
APICALLY	topmost: at the apex	
APLASTIC	not easily moulded	
APLUSTRE	ornament on stern	**nt**
APNEUSIS	state of maintained inspiration	
APOCONYM	name made by shortening word	
APOCRINE	of gland-cell breakdown	**md**
APODOSIS	consequent clause	
APOGAEIC	(apogees and aphelions)	
APOGRAPH	a copy; transcript	
APOLLYON	the destroying angel	
APOLOGIA	vindication; formal defence	
APOLOGIA	excuses	
APOLOGUE	moral fable; allegory	
APOPHYGE	base of column	**ar**
APOPLEXY	loss of mental control	**md**
APOSITIA	aversion to food	**md**
APOSTACY	} abandonment of	
APOSTASY	} principle; recantation	**rl**
APOSTATE	a renegade	
APOSTEME	apostume; an abscess	**md**
APOTHEGM	sententious maxim	
APPALLED	terrified; dismayed	
APPANAGE	territorial dependency	
APPARENT	obvious; evident; palpable	
APPEALED	implored; entreated	
APPEALER	a suppliant; invoker	
APPEARED	emerged; dawned; arrived	
APPEASED	soothed; allayed; mollified	
APPEASER	pacifier; tranquilliser	
APPELLEE	defendant in an appeal	**lw**
APPELLOR	prosecutor	
APPENDED	subjoined; attached	
APPENDIX	supplement; addendum	**md**
APPESTAT	appetite controller	
APPETENT	desirous; solicitous	
APPETITE	craving; longing; hunger	
APPETIZE	to create a desire	
APPLAUSE	praise; laudation	
APPLE-PIE	neat; orderly; bed	
APPLE-PIP	apple-seed	**bt**
APPLIQUE	applied work	
APPLYING	employing; requesting	
APPOSITE	fit; suitable; pertinent	
APPRAISE	set a value to; rate; survey	

APPRISED	informed; notified; told	
APPRIZED	appreciated; valued	
APPROACH	advance; resemble; avenue	
APPROVAL	approbation; sanction	
APPROVED	commended; ratified	
APPROVER	ratifier; king's evidence	
APPULSED	driven; struck; attacked	
APRES-SKI	clothes; party after snow sports	
APRON-MAN	a mechanic	
APTEROUS	wingless	**zo**
APTITUDE	natural ability; talent; faculty	
APYRETIC	feverless	**md**
APYREXIA	intermittent fever	**md**
AQUACADE	musical water show	
AQUALUNG	diver's oxygen pack	
AQUARIUM	tanks of aquatic animals	
AQUARIUS	water-carrier (zodiac)	
AQUASTAT	boiler temperature regulator	
AQUATINT	a print; (engrav. on copper)	
AQUATONE	photo printing process	**pg**
AQUEDUCT	artificial water channel	
AQUIFUGE	(clay strata) low permeability	
AQUILINE	like an eagle; hooked	
AQUITARD	slow permeability strata	**gl**
AQUOSITY	sloppiness	
ARACHNID	spider; mite or scorpion	**zo**
ARAINGEE	gallery of a mine	
ARAMAISM	an Aramaic idiom	
ARANEOUS	araneose; cobwebby	**zo**
ARAPUNGA	the bell-bird; campanero	**zo**
ARBALIST	arbalest; cross-bow	
ARBITRAL	arbitrational	
ARBOREAL	tree-like	**bt**
ARBORETA	shrubberies	
ARBORIST	tree expert; herbalist	
ARBOROUS	woody; arboreal	
ARBOURED	with shady bowers	
ARBUSCLE	dwarf tree	**bt**
ARBUSTUM	copse; shrubbery	**bt**
ARBUTEAN	(strawberry tree)	**bt**
ARCADIAN	pastoral; rustic	
ARCATURE	a small arcade	
ARCHAEAN	geologically remote	
ARCHAISM	an archaic expression	
ARCHAIZE	} use archaisms	
ARCHAISE	}	
ARCHDUKE	a princely title	
ARCHICAL	chief; primary	
ARCHIVAL	documentary	
ARCHIVES	record office; records	
ARCHLIKE	arcuate; iridian	
ARCHLUTE	double-stringed lute	**mu**
ARCH-MOCK	the height of mockery	
ARCHNESS	roguishness	
ARCHPOET	Poet Laureate	
ARCHWISE	bowed	
ARCTURUS	Bear-guard; star in Boötes	
ARCUATED	building dependent upon arches	**ar**

ARDENTLY	fiercely; zealously	
AREFYING	withering; desiccating	
ARENARIA	sandwort; chickweed	bt
AREOLATE	divided into small areas	
ARESCENT	drying	bt
ARGEMONE	silver-weed	bt
ARGENTAN	German silver	
ARGENTIC	argental; silvery	
ARGENTUM	silver; Ag	ch
ARGINASE	enzyme	pl
ARGONAUT	(golden fleece); cuttlefish	
ARGOSIES	richly laden vessels	
ARGUABLE	debatable	
ARGUFIED	wrangled	
ARGUMENT	discussion; an abstract	
ARGUTELY	keenly; shrewdly; piercing	
ARIANISE	convert to Arianism	rl
ARIANISM	doctrine of Arius	rl
ARIDNESS	dryness; sterility	
ARILLARY	(exterior coating of a seed)	bt
ARISINGS	replaced materials after refit	nv
ARISTATE	awned; bearded	bt
ARMAMENT	munitions; arms; guns	
ARMARIAN	monastic librarian	
ARMARIUM	scroll; book cupboard	
ARMATURE	armour; rotor of dynamo	
ARMCHAIR	chair with arm rests	
ARMENIAN	of Armenia; Christian sect	rl
ARMIGERO	esquire; armour-bearer	
ARMILLET	small bracelet; armlet	
ARMINIAN	(opposed to Calvinism)	rl
ARMORIAL	relating to coats-of-arms	hd
ARMORIST	expert in heraldry	hd
ARMOURED	plated	
ARMOURER	artificer; manufacturer	
ARMOZEEN	} taffeta or silk, used for	
ARMOZINE	} clerical gowns	tx
AROMATIC	fragrant; pungent	
AROUSING	stirring	
ARPEGGIO	harplike chord	mu
ARQUEBUS	heavy musket	
ARRANGED	settled; grouped	
ARRANGER	planner; orchestrator	
ARRANTLY	infamously; notoriously	
ARRASENE	Arras embroidery	
ARRAUGHT	taken by force	
ARRAYING	disposing; adorning	
ARRECTED	erect; upright	
ARRESTED	halted; seized; captured	
ARRESTER	an apprehender	lw
ARRETTED	accused	
ARRIDING	gratifying; pleasing	
ARRIMADA	front wall shot (pelota)	ga
ARRIVING	reaching; attaining; landing	
ARROGANT	haughty; overbearing	
ARROGATE	usurp; assume	
ARRONDEE	segmented heraldic cross	hd
ARROSION	corrosion; gnawing	

ARSENATE	} arsenical salts	ch
ARSENITE	}	
ARSONIST	} felon who deliberately	
ARSONITE	} sets fire to property	
ARTEFACT	man made, modified object	
ARTERIAL	(arteries); (roads)	md
ARTESIAN	(well with water-table pressure)	gl
ARTFULLY	craftily	
ARTICLED	bound by agreement	lw
ARTIFACT	product of primitive art	
ARTIFICE	stratagem; trick; device	
ARTISTIC	tasteful; aesthetic	
ARTISTRY	vocation; workmanship	
ARUSPICE	haruspex; soothsayer	
ARUSPICY	divination by augury	
ARVICOLA	vole genus	zo
ASBESTIC	made of asbestos	mn
ASBESTOS	incombustible material	
ASCENDED	rose; mounted	
ASCENDER	part of letters in printing	pr
ASCIDIUM	bottle-like appendage	bt
ASCORBIC	acid; vitamin C	ch
ASCRIBED	attributed; assigned	
ASEMASIA	inability to comprehend symbols	pc
ASHIKUBI	ankle kick (karate)	ga
ASHIWAZA	leg throwing (judo)	ga
ASH-LEACH	tub for washing wood-ash	
ASH-PLANT	ash sapling; walking stick	
ASH-STAND	ash-tray	
ASHY-GRAY	ashy in colour	
ASPARTIC	obtained from asparagus	bt
ASPERATE	to roughen	
ASPERGES	ceremonial sprinkling	rl
ASPERITY	harshness; sourness; acerbity	
ASPERSED	sprinkled; slandered; abused	
ASPHODEL	a lily; a daffodil	bt
ASPHYXIA	suffocation; pulse failure	md
ASPIRANT	suitor; candidate	
ASPIRATE	to emphasize the 'h' sound	
ASPIRING	longing; hoping; soaring	
ASPOROUS	without spores	bt
ASSAILED	assaulted; attacked; vilified	
ASSAILER	aggressor; invader; traducer	
ASSAMESE	native of Assam; (language)	
ASSARTED	grubbed up trees and bushes	
ASSASSIN	a thug primed with hashish	
ASSAYING	testing; analysing	
ASSEMBLE	convene; muster; congregate	
ASSEMBLY	meeting; company; parliament; synod	
ASSENTED	concurred; agreed; acquiesced	
ASSENTER	assentor; approver	
ASSERTED	maintained; averred	
ASSESSED	taxed; rated; appraised	
ASSESSOR	tax-master; valuer	lw
ASSIDENT	alongside; accompanying	

424

ASSIETTE	oblong dish; plate (Fr.)	
ASSIGNAT	paper currency, Fr. Rev.	nm
ASSIGNED	allotted; specified	
ASSIGNEE	a recipient	
ASSIGNOR	transferrer of an interest	
ASSINEGO	small donkey; fool; dolt	zo
ASSISTED	aided; abetted; sustained	
ASSIZING	assessing; regulating	
ASSONANT	harmonious; rhythmical	
ASSONATE	correspond in sound	mu
ASSORTED	mixed; varied; classified	
ASSUAGED	allayed; abated; appeased	
ASSUAGER	mitigator; alleviator	
ASSUMING	arrogant; presumptuous	
ASSURANT	holder of insurance policy	
ASSURING	affirming; pledging	
ASSYRIAN	a descendant of Shem	
ASTACIAN	shellfish, lobster type	zo
ASTERIAS	starfish genus	zo
ASTERISK	the mark ()	
ASTERISM	small cluster of stars	as
ASTERNAL	not joined to breastbone	
ASTEROID	minor planet; star-shaped	as
ASTHENIA	lack of vitality; debility	
ASTHENIC	feeble; weak	md
ASTOMATA	an order of infusoria	zo
ASTOMOUS	astomatous; mouthless	
ASTONIED	astounded; stunned; dazed	
ASTONISH	amaze; startle; surprise	
ASTRAGAL	bead, reel, moulding; glazing bar (Sc.)	bd
ASTRINGE	constrict; constrain	
ASTUNNED	astonished; mazed; dazed	
ASTUTELY	cunningly; craftily	
ASYSTOLE	heart failure	md
ATABRINE	quinine type	md
ATARAXIA	stoical indifference	
ATHEIZED	converted to disbelief	
ATHELING	Anglo-Saxon noble	
ATHENIAN	a Greek capitalist (Athens)	
ATHERINE	fish genus; mullets; smelts	zo
ATHEROMA	disease of arteries	md
ATHLETIC	strong; vigorous; sinewy	
ATLANTES	male supporting figures	
ATLANTIC	the herring pond; ocean	go
ATLANTIS	legendary island	
ATMOLOGY	science of vaporization	
ATOMICAL	atomic; minute	
ATOMIZED	vaporized	
ATOMIZER	a spray	
ATONABLE	expiable; amendable	
ATREMBLE	dithering	
ATROCITY	a cruel barbarous act	
ATROPHIC	emaciated; withered	
ATROPINE	bella-donna	md
ATROPISM	illness due to atropine	md
ATROPOUS	upturned; erect	bt
ATTACHED	fond; bound; arrested	lw
ATTACKED	assaulted; set about	
ATTACKER	assailant; invader; violator	

ATTAINED	achieved; secured; won	
ATTEMPER	placate; modify; temper (metal)	
ATTENDED	served; escorted; hearkened	
ATTENDER	attendant; close listener	
ATTENTAT	attempted assassination	
ATTESTED	invoked; endorsed	
ATTESTOR	attester; a witness	
ATTICISM	witty remark; Attic salt	
ATTICIZE	to use Athenian idioms	
ATTINGED	touched lightly; affected	
ATTIRING	arraying; adorning; robing	
ATTITUDE	pose; posture; bearing; opinion	
ATTORNED	transferred homage	
ATTORNEY	lawyer; solicitor	lw
ATTRITED	worn away; abraded; erased	
ATTRITUS	a grade of coal	mn
ATTUNING	harmonizing	mu
ATYPICAL	not conforming	
AUBUSSON	style of carpet	
AUCUPATE	to go bird-catching	
AUDACITY	boldness; effrontery; daring	
AUDIENCE	formal interview; listeners	
AUDITING	examining accounts	
AUDITION	vocal test; also sound tests	
AUDITIVE	audible	
AUDITORY	sense of hearing	md
AUGURATE	foretell by divination	
AUGURIAL	ominous	
AUGURIES	prognostications; portents	
AUGURING	presaging; prophesying	
AUGUSTAN	(Emperor Augustus)	
AUGUSTLY	majestically; imposingly	
AULARIAN	member of an Oxford Hall	
AURELIAN	(Emperor Aurelius); philosophy	
AUREOLED	in a halo	rl
AURICLED	eared	bt
AURICULA	the primula	bt
AURIFORM	ear-shaped	
AURILAVE	ear-washing instrument	md
AUROREAN	rosy; dawning	
AURULENT	golden	
AUSONIAN	Italian	
AUSTRIAN	of Austria	
AUTACOID	a hormone; a chalone	md
AUTARCHY	autocracy; absolutism	
AUTARKIC	self-sufficient	
AUTISTIC	withdrawn	pc
AUTOBAHN	fast motorway	
AUTOCADE	motor cavalcade	
AUTOCARP	self-fertilised fruit	bt
AUTOCODE	computer operation procedure	
AUTOCRAT	absolute ruler	rl
AUTOCYST	parasite-formed membrane	zo
AUTO-DA-FE	Inquisitional judgment	
AUTO-DYNE	frequency stabilizer	
AUTOGAMY	self-fertilization	bt
AUTOGENY	spontaneous generation	
AUTOGYRO	a type of aircraft	ae

AUTOLOGY	the study of self	
AUTOMATA	automatons: robots	
AUTOMATH	a self-taught man	
AUTONOMY	self-government	
AUTOPSIA	autopsy; post-mortem	md
AUTOPTIC	seen with one's own eyes	
AUTOSLED	snow vehicle	
AUTOSOME	non-sexual chromosome	cy
AUTOTOMY	amputation; cell division	
AUTOTYPE	} carbon copy process	
AUTOTYPY		
AUTUMNAL	peculiar to the autumn	
AUTUNITE	phosphate of uranium	ch
AUXILIAR	subsidiary; assisting	
AUXOCYTE	cell with meiosis	cy
AVAILING	profiting; sufficing; using	
AVELLANE	heraldic cross of filberts	hd
AVENGING	vindicating; retaliating	
AVENTAIL	visor; opening in a helmet	
AVENTURE	fatal accident	lw
AVERAGED	equated; proportional	
AVERCAKE	oatcake	ck
AVERMENT	affirmation	
AVERNIAN	Plutonic; infernal	
AVERRING	declaring; alleging	
AVERSANT	heraldic reversal	hd
AVERSELY	unwillingly; reluctantly	
AVERSION	dislike; hatred; allergy	
AVIARIST	keeper of caged birds	
AVIATING	flying	
AVIATION	travel by air	
AVIFAUNA	local birds	zo
AVISEFUL	wary; watchful; circumspect	
AVOIDING	eschewing; shunning	
AVOIDISM	trouble evasion	
AVOUCHED	guaranteed	
AVOWABLE	affirmable; declarable	
AVOWABLY	deposably; admittedly	
AVOWANCE	avowal; confession	
AVOWEDLY	openly; frankly	
AVULSION	forcible separation	
AWAITING	abiding; expecting	
AWAKABLE	not dead-asleep	
AWAKENED	spurred; stimulated	
AWAKENER	a rouser	
AWANTING	wanting; lacking; absent	
AWARDING	decreeing; bestowing	
AWEARIED	jaded; spent; worn	
AWEATHER	the weather-side	nt
AXE-HELVE	handle of an axe	
AXE-STONE	jade	mn
AXILLARY	(armpit); branch angle	bt
AXIOLOGY	theory of value	
AXIOTRON	value with controlled stream	
AXLETREE	spindle	
AXOIDEAN	axial	
AXOPLASM	material around axon	
AYENBITE	remorse	
AZOTIZED	nitrogenized	
AZULELOS	glazed blue-white tiles (Sp.)	

B

BABAKOTO	a large lemur	zo
BABBLING	prattling; gossiping	
BABELDOM	state of confusion	
BABIRUSA	pig deer of Sri Lanka	zo
BABISHLY	childishly	
BABOODOM	realm of red tape	
BABOOISM	plethora of verbiage	
BABOUCHE	oriental slipper	
BABY-FACE	term of endearment	
BABY-FARM	baby-boarding house	
BABYHOOD	state of infancy	
BACCARAT	a card game	ga
BACCHANT	bacchanalian	
BACHELOR	a degree-man; unmarried man	
BACILLAR	like baccili	md
BACILLUS	rod-like organism	md
BACKACHE	persistant pain near vertebrae	md
BACKAWAY	retreat; withdraw	
BACK-BAND	cart-saddle band	
BACKBEAR	poacher carrying off venison	lw
BACK-BITE	to speak evil; asperse	
BACK-BOND	conditional deed	
BACKBONE	reliability; spine	pl
BACKCAST	(angling) thrust; to heel (hunting)	
BACK-CHAT	impertinent rejoinder	
BACK-COCK	pendulum bracket	hr
BACKCOMB	reverse combing; coiffeure's technique	
BACKDATE	apply retrospectively (cheques)	
BACK-DOOR	clandestine; furtive	
BACKDOWN	retire; resign; withdraw	
BACK-DROP	drop scene	
BACK-DUTY	unpaid tax	lw
BACK-FALL	a wrestling throw	
BACKFIRE	a blow back; create unintended or reverse effect	
BACKFIST	a punch (karate)	
BACK-FLAP	folding shutter	
BACK-FLOW	reverse liquid flow	hy
BACK-FOLD	foldable part of shutter	jn
BACK-GEAR	lathe speed-reducer	eg
BACKHAND	(writing); negative compliment; (tennis stroke)	
BACK-HEEL	rugby football; wrestling throw	ga
BACKINGS	picture mounts; financial support; favourable data; furring strips on joints	bd
BACK-IRON	plane stiffening plate	cr
BACK-KICK	violent engine reversal; recoil of gun; bucking horse; angling	

BACKLASH	gear wear; political counter-reaction; whipping	
BACKMOST	hindermost	
BACKPACK	rucksack; snail's burden	
BACK-RAKE	surface/base relation	eg
BACK-RENT	dues	
BACK-REST	loom bar	tx
BACK-ROOM	behind the scenes	
BACKSEAT	furthest; rear place (bus, car, theatre)	
BACKSIDE	posterier; buttocks; behind	
BACKSPIN	backwards rotary motion of ball	ga
BACKSTAY	mast to stern, sides, rigging; support	
BACK-STEP	cycle mounting step	
BACKSTOP	armature-travel-limiting relay; manor fence; screen; (ice hockey) (baseball)	ga
BACK-VELD	back blocks (S. Africa)	
BACK-WALL	semi-conductor photovoltaic	eg
BACKWARD	hesitating; reluctant; retarded; unadvanced; in reverse	
BACKWASH	backward current; wake; after suction (air current); aftermath of event	
BACK-WAVE	spacing wave	tc
BACKWORK	non-mining colliery activity	
BACKWORM	filanders; hawk-disease	zo
BACONIAN	(Bacon); inductive	
BACTERIA	fungoid growths	md
BACTRIAN	two-humped camel	zo
BACULINE	rod-like	
BACULITE	fossil cuttlefish	mn
BADGERED	pestered; worried	
BADGERLY	grey like a badger	
BADIGEON	sculptor's cement	
BADINAGE	persiflage; chaff	
BADLANDS	arid, gullied, highland (Nevada)	
BAFFETAS	Indian muslin	tx
BAFFLING	defeating; hoodwinking	
BAGHEERA	the black panther (India)	zo
BAGPIPER	a piper	mu
BAGUETTE	round moulding; drumstick; crust bread (Fr.)	ar, ck
BAILABLE	able to be bailed	lw
BAIL-BALL	cricket ball bail high	
BAIL-BOND	security for appearance	
BAIL-DOCK	room at Old Bailey	lw
BAILMENT	delivery of goods in trust	lw
BAILSMAN	guarantor of bond	lw
BAKELITE	a plastic material	
BAKEMEAT	pastry; pies	ck
BAKSHISH	discount; commission; tip	
BALANCED	in equilibrium	
BALANCER	acrobat; tumbler	
BALANITE	fossil barnacle	mn
BALCONET	miniature balcony	
BALDCOOT	baldicoot; coot; monk	zo

BALDHEAD	no hair apparent	
BALDMONY	gentian	bt
BALDNESS	alopecia	md
BALD-PATE	species of wild duck	zo
BALDRICK	shoulder belt	
BALE-FIRE	signal-fire; funeral pyre	
BALESTRA	lunge (fencing)	
BALK-BACK	fibrous-back cloth	tx
BALK-LINE	baulk-line (billiards)	
BALLADER	ballad-monger	
BALLADRY	patriotic or epic verse	
BALL-CLAY	fine-textured detrital clay	gl
BALL-COCK	stopcock in a cistern	
BALLIAGE	an export duty	
BALLISTA	ancient catapult	
BALLONET	small balloon; gas bag	
BALLOTED	drew lots for; voted	
BALL-PANE	part flat, part globular	to
BALLROOM	location for stately measures	
BALLYHOO	bunkum; false fame	
BALLYRAG	bullyrag; torment	
BALMORAL	bonnet; boot; petticoat	
BALNEARY	a bathroom	
BALOTADE	an equine feat	
BALSAMIC	soothing; demulcent	
BALUSTER	supporting column	ar
BANALITY	triviality; triteness	
BANDAGED	surgically bound	
BANDANNA	Indian silk kerchief	
BANDEAUX	hair-bands or fillets	
BAND-EDGE	between 2 defined limits	el
BANDELET	bandlet	ar
BANDEROL	bannerol; small banner	
BANDFISH	long lean fish	zo
BANDITTI	bandits; robbers; outlaws	
BAND-PASS	freely passing specific currents	
BANDSMAN	a player	
BANDSTER	sheaf-binder	
BAND-STOP	attenuating specific currents	
BANDYING	tossing about	
BANEWORT	deadly nightshade	bt
BANG-BANG	servo control mechanism	am
BANGSTER	bragart; victor	
BANGTAIL	square-cut tail	
BANISHED	expelled; outlawed	
BANISTER	baluster; stair railings	
BANJOIST	fretful player	mu
BANKABLE	receivable at a bank	
BANK-BILL	note of exchange	
BANK-BOOK	depositor's account book	
BANK-NOTE	promissory note	
BANK-RATE	Bank of England rate	
BANKRUPT	insolvent; broke	
BANKSMAN	overseer at pit-mouth; crane-driver's helper	ce
BANLIEUE	environs of a town (Fr.)	
BANNERED	beflagged	
BANNERET	knighthood	
BANNEROL	banderol; small banner	

BANTERED	railed; chaffed	
BANTERER	joker; jester	
BANTLING	young child; bratling	
BANXRING	insect-eating squirrel	**zo**
BAPHOMET	Templar's idol	
BAPTIZED	baptised; immersed	**rl**
BARATHEA	woven fabric	**tx**
BARBACAN	barbican; outer defence	
BARBARED	shaved; shorn	
BARBARIC	foreign; savage; Hunnish	
BARBATED	bearded; awned	**bt**
BARBECUE	out-door cookery	
BARBERRY	thorny shrub; berberry	**bt**
BARBETTE	armoured defence	
BARBICAN	} gun-port in wall; outer	
BARBACAN	} defence of castle	**ar**
BARBITON	antique form of lyre	**mu**
BAR-CRAMP	plank-gluing bar	**to**
BARDLING	bardlet; poetaster; rhymster	
BAREBACK	unsaddled	
BAREBOAT	chartering contract	**lw**
BAREBONE	(Parliament); lean; thin	
BAREFOOT	bootless	
BARESARK	without shirt of mail	
BARGEMAN	barge owner; bargee	
BARGHEST	a dog-like goblin	
BARILLET	watch-spring case	
BARITONE	(between tenor and bass)	**mu**
BARKMILL	bark-crusher	
BARNABAS	cornflour	**bt**
BARNACLE	a twitch; cirriped; goose	**zo**
BARN-DOOR	a farm portal	
BARNEKIN	outermost castle ward	
BARNYARD	the rooster's realm	
BAROGRAM	record of atomospheric	
	pressure from barograph	**mt**
BAROLOGY	the science of weight	
BAROMETZ	a fern	**bt**
BARONAGE	cf. peerage	
BARONESS	wife or widow of baron	
BARONIAL	noble and spacious	
BAROSTAT	pressure device	**ps**
BAROUCHE	four-wheeled carriage	
BAR-POSTS	supports of field-gate	
BARRACAN	material of camel-hair	**tx**
BARRACKS	the soldier's home	
BARRANCO	barranca; deep gorge	
BARRATOR	encourager of litigation	**lw**
BARRATRY	traffic in church offices	**rl**
BARRENLY	sterilely; unfruitfully	
BARRULET	horizontal heraldic bar	**hd**
BAR-SHEAR	bar-cutter	**to**
BARTERED	exchanged commodities	
BARTERER	a dealer	
BARTIZAN	small overhanging turret	
BASALTIC	allied to basalt	**mn**
BASANITE	touchstone; flinty slate	**mn**
BASCINET	helmet of XVth century	
BASEBALL	national game (USA)	**ga**
BASEBAND	frequency modulation	
BASE-BORN	of low parentage	
BASE-BRED	of low breeding	
BASELESS	lacking any foundation	
BASE-LINE	a surveyor's base	**me**
BASEMENT	floor below ground level	
BASENESS	vileness; meanness	
BASE-PAIR	complementary acid bases	**bc**
BASE-RICH	iron-rich soil	
BASE-VIOL	bass-viol; violoncello	**mu**
BASHLESS	unashamed; undaunted	
BASICITY	ratio of acid to base	**ch**
BASIFIER	an alkali	**ch**
BASILIAN	monk of St. Basil	**rl**
BASILICA	church	**rl**
BASILICA	public hall (Roman)	
BASILING	grinding to an angle	
BASILISK	dragon; lizard; cannon	**zo**
BASINFUL	bowlful	
BASIPHIL	attracted to basic dyes	**zo**
BASKETED	hampered	
BASKETRY	wickerwork	
BASOPHIL	attracted to basic dyes	
BASQUINE	Basque outer petticoat	
BASS-DRUM	deep-noted drum	**mu**
BASSETTE	tenor or small bass viol	**mu**
BASS-HORN	deep-toned bassoon	**mu**
BASSINET	wickerwork perambulator	
BASS-TUBA	euphonium	**mu**
BASS-VIOL	base-viol; violoncello	**mu**
BASSWOOD	(N. Amer.)	**bt**
BASTAARD	Dutch half-breed (S. Afr.)	
BASTARDY	illegitimacy	
BASTERNA	mule-borne litter	
BASTILLE	old castle; state prison	
BATAVIAN	native of Batavi; (Indonesian)	
BATELESS	irrepressible	
BATHABLE	washable	
BATHETIC	anticlimatic; bombastic	
BATHMISM	inherent divergence	
BATHORSE	pack-horse	**zo**
BATH-RAIL	side-grip	
BATHROOM	balneary	
BATSWING	flat gas flame	
BATTELED	(Oxford University)	
BATTENED	grew fat; secured	
BATTERED	pounded; shattered	
BATTLING	striving; warring	
BATUCADA	batuque; dance (Brazil)	**mu**
BAUDEKIN	silk brocade; canopy	**rl**
BAUDRONS	Scottish name for the cat	
BAULKING	} checking; refusal (horse-	
BALKING	} jumping); jibbing	
BAVARIAN	of Bavaria	
BAWDRICK	baldrick; shoulder belt	
BAYADERE	Indian nautch girl	
BAYARDLY	blindly	
BAYBERRY	war-myrtle	**bt**
BDELLIUM	aromatic gum-resin	**bt**
BEACHING	running ashore; loose-graded	
	stones	**nt, ce**

BEACONED	lit up	
BEADLERY	beadle's jurisdiction	
BEAD-ROLL	names for masses	rl
BEADSMAN	almsman	
BEAD-TREE	the azedarac	bt
BEAD-WORK	ornamental work; coloured glass beads on cloth	tx
BEAGLING	hare-coursing on foot with dogs	
BEAK-HEAD	bow area; ship's WCs; ramming projection (Roman)	nt
BEAKIRON	bickern; anvil point	
BEAM-BIRD	spotted flycatcher	zo
BEAM-EDGE	searchlight angle	lt
BEAM-FLUX	total light flux	lt
BEAM-TRAP	electron beam-catching electrode	
BEAM-TREE	a hardwood tree	bt
BEAN-KING	king of the revels	
BEARABLE	tolerable; supportable	
BEARABLY	endurably; moderately	
BEARBIND	bearbine; bindweed	bt
BEARDING	meeting face to face	
BEAR-HERD	bear-keeper	
BEARINGS	sense of direction	
BEARLIKE	rude and rough; ursine	
BEAR'S-EAR	primula auricula	bt
BEARSKIN	headdress of the guards	
BEARWARD	bear-leader; Arcturus	
BEASTIES	small animals	zo
BEASTISH	brutal; animal	
BEATIFIC	ecstatic; rapturous	
BEAT-NOTE	rhythmic accentuation	
BEAUFREY	beam or joist	
BEAUPERE	father-in-law (Fr.)	
BEAUTIES	lovelies	
BEAUTIFY	adorn; array; garnish	
BEAVERED	covered with beaver fur	
BECALMED	motionless; tranquillized	
BECHAMEL	savoury sauce	
BECHANCE	befall; accidentally	
BECKONED	nodded; called; invited	
BECOMING	befitting; graceful	
BECUEING	scowing of an anchor on rocks	nt
BECURLED	with ringlets	
BEDABBLE	dabble; sprinkle	
BEDAGGLE	drag through the mire	
BEDARKEN	obscure; eclipse	
BEDASHED	bespattered	
BEDAUBED	smeared; plastered	
BED-CHAIR	bed back-rest	
BEDECKED	robed; embellished	
BEDEGUAR	a rose scourge	bt, zo
BEDESMAN	see beadsman	rl
BEDEWEEN	the birch tree	bt
BEDEWING	sprinkling	
BED-GOING	retiring	
BEDIMMED	blurred; tarnished; dulled	
BED-LINEN	sheets, etc.	
BEDMAKER	college servant	
BEDPLATE	foundation plate	
BEDPLATE	engine-frame base	eg
BED-QUILT	an overlay	
BEDRENCH	saturate; immerse; soak	
BEDSTAFF	cudgel, truncheon	
BEDSTEAD	a framework for a bed	
BEDSTOCK	part of bed	
BEDSTRAW	a plant	bt
BED-TABLE	table for use in bed	
BEDUCKED	soused	
BEDUSTED	smothered with dust	
BEDWARDS	on the way to bed	
BEE-BREAD	pollen collected by bees	bt
BEECH-OIL	beech nut oil	ck
BEE-EATER	a bird	zo
BEEFIEST	heftiest; lustiest	
BEEFWOOD	an Australian wood	bt
BEER-PUMP	beer-pull, spout	
BEERSHOP	inn; alehouse; tavern	
BEESWING	dregs of port	
BEETLING	overhanging; projecting	
BEETRAVE	beetroot	bt
BEETROOT	beetrave	bt
BEFITTED	suitable; becoming; worthy	
BEFLOWER	cover with flowers	
BEFOGGED	dimmed; confused	
BEFOOLED	deluded; hoaxed; gulled	
BEFOULED	polluted; begrimed	
BEFRIEND	favour; patronize; aid	
BEFRINGE	adorn with fringes	
BEFURRED	covered with fur	
BEGETTER	a sire	
BEGGABLE	borrowable	
BEGGARED	rendered penniless	
BEGGARLY	paltry; mean; abject	
BEGINNER	tyro; novice; neophyte	
BEGIRDED	belted	
BEGIRDLE	encompass; encircle	
BEGOTTEN	born; produced	
BEGREASE	lubricate	
BEGRIMED	soiled; grubby	
BEGRUDGE	envy	
BEGUILED	deluded; diverted	
BEGUILER	cheat; deceiver	
BEHAVING	comme il faut	
BEHAVIOR	(behaviour); conduct; response	pc
BEHEADAL	an execution	
BEHEADED	decapitated	
BEHEMOTH	Job's hippopotamus	zo
BEHOLDEN	grateful; indebted	
BEHOLDER	observer; surveyor	
BEHOVING	being necessary	
BEINNESS	comfort; well-being; acceptedness socially	pc
BEJESUIT	initiate in Jesuitism	rl
BEKISSED	smothered in kisses	
BELABOUR	to thrash; whack	

BELACING	adorning with lace	
BELAMOUR	a gallant; a fair lady	
BELATING	being late	
BELAUDED	eulogized	
BELAYING	fastening	nt
BELCHING	eructating	
BELFRIED	having belfries	
BELFRIES	steeples; watch-towers	rl
BELIEVED	credited; fancied	
BELIEVER	theist; devotee; pietist	
BELITTLE	disparage; deprecate	
BELLBIND	} bindweed	bt
BELL-BINE		
BELL-BIRD	New Zealand bird	zo
BELL-BUOY	the sailor's warning	nt
BELLCOTE	small belfry	
BELLOWED	roared; bawled	
BELL-PULL	bell-rope	
BELL-PUSH	push-button bell switch	el
BELL-ROPE	a ringer	
BELL-TENT	conical canvas tent	
BELLWORT	a campanula	bt
BELLYFUL	replete	
BELLY-GOD	greedy; epicure; gourmand	
BELLYING	swelling; billowing	
BELONGED	owned by; pertained	
BELOVING	loving; fond; doting	
BELT-FORK	belt-transfer prongs	eg
BELT-SLIP	pulley-face belt slippage	eg
BELZEBUB	Beelzebub; satan; the devil	
BEMASKED	wearing a mask	
BEMIRING	soiling	
BEMOANED	bewailed; lamented	
BEMUDDLE	mess up	
BEMUFFLE	wrap up	
BENCHING	extended benches; berm ledge above ditch	
BENCHING	concrete cast in manhole; iron plate	bd, ce
BENDABLE	not rigid	
BENEAPED	aground at low tide	nt
BENEDICK	} newly married man;	
BENEDICT	} learned saint	rl
BENEFICE	church living	
BENIGNLY	kindly; benevolently	
BENITIER	holy water vessel	
BENJAMIN	gum; overcoat	
BENOTING	noting fully	
BENT-TAIL	having a bent shank	eg
BENUMBED	torpid	
BENZOATE	a salt	ch
BEPEPPER	shoot repeatedly	
BEPESTER	annoy persistently	
BEPITIED	commiserated	
BEPLUMED	with plumes	
BEPOMMEL	belabour	
BEPOWDER	pulverize	
BEPRAISE	laud	
BEPUFFED	flattered	
BEQUADRO	natural (It.)	mu

BEQUEATH	entrust	
BERATING	scolding	
BERBERIN	barberry extract	ch
BERBERRY	the barberry	bt
BERCEUSE	cradle lullaby; song (Fr.)	
BERDACHE	Indian transvestite	
BEREAVED	bereft	bt
BERGAMOT	citron; perfume; pear	bt
BERGMEHL	crystalline earth	mn
BERGMOTE	a miner's court	
BERHYMED	celebrated in verse	
BERI-BERI	a tropical disease	md
BERNOUSE	burnouse; Arab mantle	
BERRYING	producing berries	
BERTHAGE	dock fees	
BERTHING	docking	nt
BESCRAWL	scribble	
BESCREAM	yell the house down	
BESCREEN	shelter	
BESEEMED	befitted	
BESEEMLY	becoming; fit; suitable	
BESETTER	an assailant	
BESHADOW	overshadow	
BESIDERY	variety of pear	bt
BESIEGED	beleaguered; encircled	
BESIEGER	an investor	
BESILVER	electro-plate	
BESLAVED	enslaved	
BESLAVER	slobber	
BESLIMED	bemired	
BESMIRCH	besmutch; beslime	
BESNOWED	snowed up	
BESOILED	defiled	
BESORTED	suited; fitted	
BESOTTED	drunk; crapulous; inebriated	
BESOUGHT	entreated; implored	
BESOULED	endowed with a soul	
BESPICED	highly seasoned	
BESPOKEN	made to order	
BESPREAD	broadcast; disseminate	
BESSEMER	a steel process	
BESTIARY	book about beasts	
BESTOWAL	gift; grant; distribution	
BESTOWED	gave; presented; awarded	
BESTOWER	donor; feoffer	
BESTREAK	mark with streaks	
BESTREWN	scattered; dispersed	
BESTRIDE	astride	
BESTRODE	traversed; mounted	
BETAFITE	hydrous uranium compound	mn
BETAKING	removing to; applying to	
BETA-RAYS	radium-rays	
BETATRON	electron speeding machine	
BETEARED	tearful; bedimmed	
BETEL-NUT	areca nut palm	bt
BETIDING	happening; befalling	
BETONGUE	scold; rail; nag	
BETOSSED	thrown about	
BETRAYAL	breach of trust	

BETRAYED	ensnared; beguiled; deceived	
BETRAYER	seducer; a Judas; traitor	
BETTERED	ameliorated; improved	
BETULINE	birch camphor	bt
BEVELING	rounded edge	
BEVELLED	basiled; on the slant	
BEVERAGE	drink; potion; potation	
BEVILLED	sloping lines	hd
BEWAILED	lamented	
BEWARING	minding; avoiding	
BEWIGGED	with wig; scolded	
BEWILDER	perplex; confuse	
BEWINTER	to chill	
BEWRAYED	disclosed	
BEWRAYER	betrayer	
BEZONIAN	beggar; rascal	
BHEESTIE	Hindu water-carrier	
B-HORIZON	lower level of soil	ag
BIANCONI	Irish car	
BIATHLON	skiing & shooting; running & swimming trophies	
BIBATION	tippling; a drink	ck
BIBLE-BOX	container for Bible	
BIBLICAL	scriptured	rl
BIBULOUS	absorbing	
BIB-VALVE	disc-closed draw-off tap	eg
BICAUDAL	with two tails	
BICKERED	squabbled	
BICOLOUR	of two colours	
BICONVEX	lens	ps
BICRURAL	two-legged	
BICUSPID	having two cusps	bt
BICYCLED	cycled	
BIDDABLE	worthy of being bid	
BIDENTAL	with two teeth	
BIENNIAL	once in two years	
BIER-BALK	right of way for funerals	
BIFACLAL	doublefaced	
BIFEROUS	two crops each year	bt
BIFIDATE	cleft in twain	bt
BIFORATE	having two pores	
BIGAMIST	husband of two or more wives	lw
BIGAMOUS	situation of plural marriage	lw
BIGAROON	white-heart cherry	bt
BIG-BONED	bony; osseous	
BIGGONET	cap; deerstalker	
BIGNONIA	plant genus	bt
BIG-SWOLN	ready to burst	
BIJOUTRY	bijouterie; trinkets	
BIJUGATE	twin	bt
BIJUGOUS	paired	
BIJWONER	squatter (S. Africa)	
BILABIAL	both lips; (phonetics)	
BILANDER	Dutch barge	nt
BILBERRY	whortleberry	bt
BILEDUCT	a canal	md
BILL-BOOK	account book	
BILLETED	quartered	
BILLETEE	person billeted	

BILLFISH	lake fish (N. Amer.)	zo
BILLHEAD	letterhead, printing	
BILLHOOK	hedge cutting tool	to
BILLIARD	(used for billiards)	
BILLOWED	surged; swelled	
BILLY-BOY	bluff-bowed ketch	nt
BILLY-CAN	bush teapot (Aust.)	
BILOBATE	with two lobes	
BIMANOUS	two-headed	
BIMANUAL	done with both hands	md
BIMARINE	between two seas	
BIMENSAL	six times in one year	
BIMESTER	two-monthly	
BIMIRROR	slightly inclined mirror pair	
BINABINA	canoe (S. Pacific)	nt
BINAURAL	adapted for two ears	
BINBASHI	Turkish army officer	
BINDWEED	bearbine; convolvulus	bt
BINNACLE	bittacle; compass box	nt
BINOMIAL	consisting of two terms	
BINOXIDE	a peroxide	oh
BIO-ASSAY	drug-power test on animals	pm
BIOBLAST	parturient protoplasm	
BIOCYTIN	vitamin in yeast	
BIOGENIC	produced by living organisms	
BIOGRAPH	bioscope; zoetrope	
BIOLYTIC	destructive to life	
BIOMETER	life-measuring instrument	bl
BIOMETRY	life mensuration	
BIONOMIC	ecological	bl
BIOPHORE	minute growth-capable particle	
BIOPLASM	protoplasm	zo
BIOSCOPE	early cinematograph	
BIOSOPHY	made of life	
BIPAROUS	twin-producing	
BIPENNIS	two-edged battle-axe	
BIQUARTZ	saccharimeter analyser	
BIRADIAL	part radial, part bilateral	zo
BIRAMOUS	double-branched	
BIRCHING	corporal punishment	
BIRD-BATH	garden ornament	
BIRD-BOLT	blunt arrow	
BIRD-CAGE	prison for birds; mini-aviary; a London Walk	
BIRD-CALL	bird whistle	
BIRD-EYED	quick-sighted; eagle-eyed	
BIRD-LICE	avian irritants	zo
BIRDLIKE	aviform	
BIRD-LIME	sticky stuff	
BIRD-SEED	not sown but cropped	
BIRD'S-EYE	seen from above; tobacco	
BIRD-SONG	warbling of birds	
BIRRETUM	judge's black cap	lw
BIRTHDAY	an anniversary	
BIRTHDOM	privilege of birth	
BISCAYAN	Basque	
BISCOTIN	sweet biscuit	
BISCROMA	demisemiquaver	mu
BISECTED	halved; split in twain	

431

BISECTOR	an equal divisor	
BISERIAL	in two series	
BISETOSE	double-bristled	**bt, zo**
BISEXUAL	hetero- and homosexual	
BISHOPED	horse coping	**vt, zo**
BISMATIC	with two nipples	**pl, zo**
BISQUINE	fishing lugger (Fr.)	**nt**
BISTABLE	with 2 stable states	**tc**
BISTATIC	transmitter/receiver apart	**rd**
BISTOURY	surgical knife	**md**
BITING-IN	(etching)	
BITINGLY	acidly; mordantly	
BITMAKER	lorimer; loriner	
BITMOUTH	bit of a bridle	
BITSTOCK	carpenter's brace	**to**
BITTACLE	compass housing	**nt**
BITTERED	soured	
BITTERLY	acrimoniously	
BIVALENT	diatomic valency	**ch**
BI-WEEKLY	periodically	
BIZCACHA	chinchilla, rodent	**zo**
BLABBING	telling; tatling	
BLACK-ART	necromancy	
BLACK-BOX	computer control unit; flight	
	recorder	**ae**
BLACKCAP	a warbler	**zo**
BLACK-FLY	turnip-flea	**zo**
BLACK-GUM	N. American tree	**bt**
BLACKING	a polish	
BLACKISH	somewhat dark	
BLACKLEG	strike-breaker	
BLACK-NEB	crow; crane, etc.	**zo**
BLACKOUT	loss of consciousness;	
	darkened city	
BLACKPOT	coarse ceramic	
BLACK-ROD	Usher to House of Lords	
BLACK-WAD	ore of manganese	**mn**
BLADDERY	vesicular	**md**
BLAMABLE	censurable	
BLAMABLY	reprehensibly	
BLAMEFUL	culpable	
BLANCARD	bleached woven cloth	
BLANCHED	deprived of colour	
BLANCHER	white-washer	
BLANDEST	smoothest; mildest	
BLANDISH	flatter; coax; cajole	
BLANKEST	most vacant	
BLANKING	frustrating	
BLASTEMA	an off-shoot	**bt**
BLASTING	detonating; cursing	
BLAST-OFF	launching of rocket	
BLASTULA	embryonic cell	**bl**
BLATANCY	obtrusive vulgarity	
BLAUWBOK	antelope (S. Africa)	**zo**
BLAZONED	embellished	
BLAZONER	a broadcaster	
BLAZONRY	heraldic painting	
BLEACHED	blanched	
BLEACHER	colour extractor	
BLEAKEST	coldest; barest; chilliest	

BLEAKISH	cold and cheerless	
BLEATING	blethering	
BLEEDING	blood-letting; gluing;	
	separation of liquids	
BLENCHED	flinched; paled	
BLENDING	intermingling; harmonizing	
BLENHEIM	spaniel; apple; plane	**zo, bt**
BLESSING	divine favour; boon; gain	
BLETTING	decaying	**rl**
BLIGHTED	mildewed	
BLIGHTER	pestilent fellow	
BLIMBING	a fruit	
BLIMPERY	blatant inefficiency	
BLINDAGE	camouflage	
BLINDERS	} eye-shades	
BLINKERS		
BLINDEST	most ignorant and heedless	
BLINDING	hoodwinking; (light); mat;	
	mathers; sight-losing	**ce**
BLINKARD	a blinker or winker	
BLINKERS	eye-shades	
BLINKING	ignoring; winking; gleaming	
BLISSFUL	rapturous; ecstatic	
BLISTERY	vesicated	
BLITHELY	joyously	
BLITHEST	merriest	
BLITZING	bombing	
BLIZZARD	violent snowstorm	
BLOATING	smoking; inflating; swelling	
BLOCKADE	hostile closure of ports as act	
	of war	**nt**
BLOCKING	obstructing; shaping; angling	
	tool	
BLOCKISH	like a blockhead	
BLOCK-OUT	defensive trick (basketball)	
BLOCK-TIN	pure tin	**pb**
BLODWYTE	fine for bloodshedding	
BLONCKET	gray	
BLOOD-HOT	98.6° F (37°C)	**md**
BLOODIED	stained with gore	
BLOODILY	sanguinely	
BLOODING	fox-hunting rite	
BLOOD-RED	a gory hue	
BLOOD-TAX	conscription	
BLOOD-WON	dearly bought	
BLOOMERS	garments; blunders	
BLOOMERY	forge for smelted iron	
BLOOMING	flourishing	
BLOSSOMY	full of blossom	
BLOTCHED	pimpled; maculose	
BLOTTING	obliterating	
BLOWBALL	dandelion head	**bt**
BLOWHOLE	a whale's nostril; vent in	
	cavern roof with fountain	
		zo, gl
BLOWLAMP	intense local-heat apparatus	
BLOWMILK	skim-milk	
BLOWPIPE	a tube; blow-gun	
BLUDGEON	truncheon; heavy stick	
BLUE-BACK	the field-fare	

BLUEBIRD	American warbler	zo	**BOLT-BOAT**	cobble	nt
BLUE-BOOK	Parliamentary report		**BOLT-HEAD**	a matrass	
BLUECOAT	Christ's Hospital schoolboy		**BOLT-HOLE**	escape hole	
BLUE-EYED	innocent; promising		**BOLT-ROPE**	rope round sail	nt
BLUE-FISH	mackerel	zo	**BOMBARDA**	a polacre brigantine (It.)	nt
BLUE-FUNK	alarm and despondency		**BOMBARDA**	euphonium (brass band)	mu
BLUEGILL	common Amer. sunfish		**BOMBARDE**	organ stop (16 ft.)	mu
BLUEGOWN	King's bedesman		**BOMB-FREE**	no raiders	
BLUEJOHN	decorative fluorspar	mn	**BOMBIATE**	a bombic salt	ch
BLUENESS	azureness		**BOM-PROOF**	book-club advance copy	pr
BLUENOSE	a Nova Scotian		**BONA-FIDE**	in good faith	
BLUE-PILL	mercurial pill	md	**BONDAGER**	helpful tenant	
BLUE-POLL	salmon type	zo	**BOND-DEBT**	bond-held debt	lw
BLUE-WING	a duck	zo	**BONDMAID**	slave	
BLUFFEST	most outspoken		**BONDSMAN**	surety; bondman	lw
BLUFFING	acting deceptively		**BONEACHE**	a pain	md
BLUISHLY	rather blue		**BONECAVE**	(prehistoric bones)	
BLUNGING	puddling clay		**BONEDUST**	manure	
BLUNTING	dulling; benumbing		**BONE-IDLE**	inert	
BLUNTISH	not sharp		**BONELACE**	bobbin-lace	
BLURRING	dimming; obscuring		**BONELESS**	spineless	
BLURTING	uttering hastily		**BONHOMIE**	geniality	
BLUSHFUL	modest		**BONIFACE**	an innkeeper	
BLUSHING	flushing; reddening, milky		**BONING-IN**	peg-lining	
	effect; lacquer		**BONNETED**	with hat or hood	
BLUSTERY	stormy		**BONSENSE**	opposite of nonsense	
BOARDING	embarking; lodging	nt	**BONSPIEL**	curling match	
BOARFISH	red and silver fish	zo	**BONTEBOK**	S. African antelope	zo
BOASTFUL	vaunting		**BOOBYHUT**	covered sleigh	
BOASTING	bragging; bucking; crowing;		**BOOBYISH**	dullish	
	stone surfacing		**BOOBYISM**	stupidity	
BOATABLE	navigable		**BOOHOOED**	lamented loudly	
BOATBILL	a heron	zo	**BOOKCASE**	shelved case	
BOATHOOK	aduncous adjunct		**BOOK-CLUB**	literary association	
BOATRACE	aquatic contest		**BOOK-DEBT**	outstanding account	
BOATROPE	a painter		**BOOKLESS**	unlearned	
BOBBINET	netted lace		**BOOKMARK**	book-marker	
BOBOLINK	the rice-bird	zo	**BOOKMATE**	schoolfellow	
BOB-WHITE	American partridge	zo	**BOOKNAME**	nonce name	
BOCK-BEER	lager beer		**BOOKOATH**	Bible oath	
BOCKELET	a hawk	zo	**BOOKPOST**	a postal facility (obs.)	
BOCKLAND	freehold land	lw	**BOOK-REST**	small lectern	
BODEMENT	a presentiment		**BOOKSHOP**	voluminous emporium	
BODILESS	incorporeal		**BOOKWORM**	avid reader	
BODLEIAN	(Oxford Library)		**BOOSTING**	advertising; pushing	
BODY-LINE	bowling at batsman; (penalty);		**BOOTHOSE**	spats	
	(cricket)		**BOOTIKIN**	leggings	
BODY-WALL	perivisceral cavity wall	zo	**BOOTJACK**	a boot remover	
BOG-BERRY	cranberry	bt	**BOOTLACE**	a latchet	
BOG-EARTH	peat	mn	**BOOTLAST**	last for boot-making	
BOGEYISM	frightfulness		**BOOTLESS**	unavailing	
BOGEYMAN	hobgoblin		**BOOTLICK**	a lickspittle	
BOGGLING	wavering; havering		**BOOT-TREE**	(for a shapely boot)	
BOG-WHORT	whortleberry	bt	**BORACHIO**	leather wine bag	
BOHEMIAN	unconventional		**BORACITE**	magnesium borate	ch
BOISERIE	wood panelling (Fr.)		**BORDEAUX**	claret	
BOLD-FACE	brazen		**BORDERED**	edged	
BOLDNESS	courage; audacity		**BORDERER**	border dweller	
BOLIVIAN	(Bolivia)		**BORDLAND**	reserved domain land	lw
BOLL-WORM	cotton-worm; weevil	zo	**BORD-LODE**	timber carrying	

BORECOLE	winter cabbage	**bt**
BOREHOLE	geological research site; (well); (irrigation); (oil)	
BOREWORM	teredo	**zo**
BORROWED	assumed; hypothecated	
BORROWER	cadger	
BORSTALL	hill road	
BOSTANCI	Turkish seraglio guards	
BOTANIST	plant studier	**bt**
BOTANIZE	pick flowers	
BOTCHERY	patchwork	
BOTCHING	clumsy repair work	
BOTHERED	plagued	
BOTRYOID	like a bunch of grapes	
BOTTLING	preserving	
BOTTOMED	fathomed	
BOTTOMRY	loan secured by ship	
BOTULISM	form of poisoning	**md**
BOUDERIE	pouting; petulance	
BOUDEUSE	sofa with adjustable back-rest	
BOUFFANT	puffed out	
BOUGHTEN	bought (archiac)	
BOUILLON	broth; soup	**ck**
BOUNCING	resilient; fraud (of cheques); playing ball down (netball)	
BOUNDARY	limit; (cricket)	
BOUNDING	leaping; bordering	
BOUNTREE	see bourtree	**bt**
BOURETTE	tufted waste-silk yarn	**tx**
BOURGEON	bud; sprout	
BOURTREE	the elder	**bt**
BOUTIQUE	trendy fashionable shop	
BOUZOUKI	Greek mandolin	**mu**
BOVIFORM	ox-like	
BOW-BRACE	archer's string-guard	
BOW-DRILL	rotary drill	
BOW-GRACE	a fender	**nt**
BOWINGLY	subserviently; courteously	
BOW-PIECE	bow-chaser; (gun)	**nt**
BOWSIGHT	adjustable aimer (archery)	
BOWSPRIT	a spar forward beyond the bows	**nt**
BOX-DRAIN	enclosed drain	
BOX-ELDER	ash-leaved maple	**bt**
BOX-FRAME	1-piece traction-motor frame	**el**
BOX-LOBBY	passage in theatre	
BOX-PLATE	web-plate steel	**bd**
BOX-PLEAT	a double fold	
BOX-THORN	a shrub	**bt**
BOYISHLY	puerilely	
BOY'S-PLAY	a prank; trifling	
BRACCATE	with feathered feet	**zo**
BRACELET	a handcuff; ornament	
BRACHIAL	belonging to the arm	
BRACKISH	somewhat salt	
BRACTEAL	leaf formation	**bt**
BRADBURY	£1 note (obs.)	
BRADSHAW	railway guide	
BRADYPOD	a sloth	**zo**

BRAGAGNA	felucca, Adriatic	**nt**
BRAGGART	boaster	
BRAGGING	vaunting	
BRAGOZZI	lugger, Venice	**nt**
BRAIDING	plaiting; (ribbon); (sword)	
BRAIDISM	hypnotism	
BRAILING	hauling in; trussing	**nt**
BRAIN-FAG	nervous exhaustion	
BRAINING	dashing out the brains	
BRAINISH	brain-sick; furious	
BRAINPAN	part of the skull	**md**
BRAISING	a form of cookery	**ck**
BRAKE-MAN	a controller; (bobsledding)	**rw**
BRAKE-VAN	the guard's domain	**rw**
BRAMBLED	overgrown	
BRANCARD	horse-borne litter; float; platform vehicle	
BRANCHED	forked; ramified	
BRANCHER	young bird	**zo**
BRANDIED	laced with brandy	
BRANDING	stigmatizing; marking	
BRANDISE	a trivet	
BRANDISH	flourish; wave; shake	
BRAND-NEW	bran-new; unused	
BRANGLED	wrangled	
BRANTAIL	the redstart; a warbler	**zo**
BRANT-FOX	a kind of small fox	**zo**
BRASSAGE	cost of mintage	
BRASSARD	an armlet	
BRASSART	arm armour	
BRASS-HAT	big-wig	
BRASSICA	the cabbage genus	**bt**
BRASSOCK	field mustard	**bt**
BRATLING	small brat	
BRATTICE	brettice; partition	
BRAUNITE	manganese oxide	**ch**
BRAWLING	wrangling	
BRAZENED	shameless	
BRAZENLY	impudently; boldly	
BRAZENRY	effrontery	
BRAZILIN	a red dye	**bt**
BREACHED	violated; tore open	
BREACHES	gaps; violations	
BREAD-NUT	a fruit	**bt**
BREAKAGE	rupture; fracture	
BREAKING	smashing; infinging	
BREAKMAN	brake's-man	
BREAK-OUT	violent escape; (molten metal); attack; (ice hockey); canoe off course	
BREAKVOW	a perjurer	
BREAMING	cleaning ship's bottom	
BREASTED	confronted	
BREATHED	exhaled; respired	
BREATHER	a respite	
BREECHED	put into trousers	
BREECHES	pantaloons	
BREEDING	lineage; begetting; nuclear transformation	**ps**
BREEZING	of unclear photo image	**cn**

BRELOGUE	watch-chain ornament	
BRENNAGE	an ancient tribute	
BREPHNIC	neanic, of adolescent period	**zo**
BRETHREN	brothers; kindred	
BRETTICE	brattice; partition	
BREVETCY	brevet rank	
BREVIARY	prayer-book, R.C.	**rl**
BREVIATE	epitome; a brief	**lw**
BREVIPED	short-legged	**zo**
BREVIPEN	short-winged	**zo**
BREWSTER	brewer; maltster	
BRIAREAN	many handed	
BRIBABLE	venal; corrupt	
BRICK-AXE	2-bladed brick-dressing axe	
BRICKBAT	half-a-brick	
BRICKING	building; wrecking	
BRICK-RED	dark orange-red	
BRICK-TEA	tea in blocks	
BRIDE-ALE	ale at a marriage	
BRIDE-BED	marriage-bed	
BRIDGING	joining up; loan; rock chimney climbing technique	**mo**
BRIDLING	controlling; scorning; ruffling	
BRIEFING	giving final instructions	
BRIEFMAN	brief compiler	
BRIGADED	combined	
BRIGHTEN	clarify	
BRIGHTLY	brilliantly	
BRIGUING	canvassing	
BRIMLESS	rimless	
BRIMMING	full; verging	
BRINDISI	It. toast; drinking song	**mu**
BRINDLED	streaky brown	
BRINEPAN	} salt extraction by	
BRINEPIT	} evaporation	
BRINGING	conveying; fetching	
BRISANCE	shattering effect	
BRISKING	quickening	
BRISKISH	rather spry	
BRISLING	small sardine or sprat	**zo**
BRISTLED	ruffled	
BRITTLED	(cooking venison)	
BRITZSKA	Polish carriage	
BROACHED	pierced	
BROACHER	first proposer	
BROAD-AXE	heavy axe	**to**
BROADEST	vastest; amplest	
BROADISH	rather broad	
BROCADED	embroidered	
BROCATEL	coarse brocade	
BROCCOLI	cultivated cabbage	**bt**
BROCHURE	pamphlet; leaflet	
BRODEKIN	buskin; half-boot	
BROIDERY	embroidery	
BROILING	grilling	
BROKENLY	disconnectedly	
BROKERLY	mean; low; servile	
BROMELIA	the pineapple	**bt**
BROMELIN	proteolytic enzyme	**ch**
BROMIDIC	dull; addict	**md**
BROMIZED	made to smell	**ch**
BRONCHIC	(windpipe)	**pl**
BRONZIFY	make into bronze	
BRONZING	metallic-lustre-giving	**pt**
BRONZITE	lustrous diallage	**mn**
BROODING	pondering; incubating	
BROOD-SAC	cockroach egg chamber	**zo**
BROOKING	bearing; enduring	
BROOKITE	crystalline titanium oxide	**mn**
BROOKLET	streamlet	
BROOMING	sweeping; breaming	
BROTHERS	male siblings; rope or chain sling	**ce**
BROUGHAM	one-horsed carriage	
BROUHAHA	fuss and bother	
BROWBEAT	bully; overbear; haze	
BROWLESS	shameless	
BROWNING	a process; a rifle; English; type variations on a song	**mu**
BROWNISH	somewhat sunburnt	
BROWNIST	congregationalist (now URC)	**rl**
BROW-POST	a main beam	
BROWSICK	dejected; melancholy	
BROWSING	pasturing	
BRUISING	contusing	
BRUMAIRE	November (Fr. Rev. cal.)	
BRUNETTE	dark hair and eyes	
BRUSH-BOX	brush-holder container	**el**
BRUSHING	sweeping; brisk	
BRUSH-OFF	curt rebuff; (lacrosse)	
BRUSSELS	(carpets); (sprouts)	
BRUSTLED	crackled; bullied	
BRUTALLY	ferociously; ruthlessly	
BRYOLOGY	study of mosses	
BRYONINE	extract of bryony	**ch**
BUBBLING	gurgling; cheating; surface film defect	
BUCCANED	(smoked meat)	
BUCCINAL	like a trumpet	
BUCCINUM	a whelk	**zo**
BUCHERON	Canadian forest worker	**fr**
BUCKBEAN	a water-plant	**bt**
BUCKETED	rode furiously	
BUCKHORN	buck's horn	**zo**
BUCK-JUMP	quick plunging leap	
BUCKLING	curling; fastening	
BUCKMAST	beech-mast	**bt**
BUCKRAKE	tractor transport attachment	**ag**
BUCKSHEE	gratuity; commission; free	
BUCKSHOT	large shot	
BUCKSKIN	soft yellow leather	
BUCRANIA	ornamental ox-skulls	
BUDDHISM	} religion founded by	
BUDDHIST	} Sakyamuni	**rl**
BUDDLING	ore washing	
BUDGEREE	good (Australian)	
BUDGETED	made provision	

BUFFCOAT	a soldier; a jacket	
BUFFERED	cushioned; shielded	
BUFFETED	struck; clouted	
BUFONITE	toadstone	mn
BUHL-WORK	inlaid tortoiseshell	
BUILDING	erecting; pile; structure	
BULGARIC	Bulgarian	
BULKHEAD	water-tight wall in ships; water tank cover	
BULK-TEST	radiation test sample	nc
BULL-BEEF	coarse beef	
BULL-CALF	male calf	zo
BULLDOSE	to haze; intimidate; coerce	
BULLDOZE	rase or level	
BULLETIN	official report	
BULL-FROG	North American frog	zo
BULLHEAD	miller's thumb (fish)	zo
BULLIRAG	to badger; ballyrag	
BULLNOSE	rounded edge	ar
BULLRING	Spanish arena	
BULL'S-EYE	glass window; sweet	
BULLWEED	knap-weed	bt
BULLWORT	bishop's-weed	bt
BULLYING	browbeating; threatening	
BULLYISM	hectoring; blustering	
BULLYRAG	abuse vehemently	
BULRUSHY	full of rushes	bt
BUMMALOE	Bombay duck (fish)	zo
BUMMAREE	fish-factor; money-lender	
BUMP-BALL	cricket	
BUNCHING	clustering; grouping; velocity modulation	nc
BUNDLING	hurrying; packaging; hospitality	
BUN-FIGHT	tea party	
BUNGALOW	one-storied house	
BUNGHOLE	hole in a cask	
BUNGLING	awkward; clumsy	
BUNGVENT	spile-hole in bung	
BUNKERED	coaled; in difficulties	
BUNODONT	a dental malady	md
BUNTLINE	a sheet	nt
BUOYANCY	specific lightness; floatability	nt
BURBERRY	a waterproof	
BURDENED	laden; overloaded	
BURGAMOT	bergamot; citron	bt
BURGANET	} Burgundian helmet;	
BURGONET	} helmet with visor	
BURGLARY	felony at night	
BURGLING	stealing; robbing	
BURGRAVE	German governor	
BURGUNDY	French wine	
BURINIST	engraver	
BURLETTA	burlesque; comic operetta	mu
BURNOOSE	Arab cloak	
BURNT-EAR	corn-disease	bt
BURROWED	excavated; tunnelled	
BURROWER	a rabbit	
BURR-PUMP	large pump	nt

BURSALIS	a muscle	md
BURSCHEN	German students	
BURSITIS	bursa inflammation	md
BURSTING	exploding; rending	
BUSH-BABY	night-ape (S. Africa)	zo
BUSH-BRED	reared in back country	
BUSHBUCK	antelope (S. Africa)	zo
BUSHELER	a clothes-repairer (USA)	
BUSH-ROPE	a liana; a creeper	bt
BUSH-VELD	bush country (S. Africa)	
BUSINESS	stage-craft; occupation	
BUSKINED	booted	
BUSYBODY	officious person	
BUSYLESS	being idle	
BUSYNESS	state of being busy	
BUTCHERY	slaughter; massacre	
BUTCHING	butchery (dialect)	
BUTTERED	missed	
BUTTERIS	farrier's knife	to
BUTTONED	fastened	
BUTTRESS	support; prop	
BUTTRICE	farrier's knife	to
BUTYRATE	salt of butyric acid	ch
BUTYROUS	buttery; oleaginous; greasy	ck
BUZKASHI	equestrian team game (Japan)	
BY-BIDDER	auction-bid encourager	
BYCOCKET	peaked cap (XVth cent.)	
BY-CORNER	odd corner	
BY-DESIGN	subsidiary purpose	
BY-LANDER	bilander; hoy	nt
BY-MATTER	something incidental	
BY-MOTIVE	unavowed motive	
BY-PASSED	avoided	
BYRONISM	Lord Byron's phrase	
BY-SPEECH	casual speech	
BY-STREET	side street	
BY-STROKE	sly stroke	
BY-THE-BYE	by the way	

C

CAATINGA	thorn forest of N.E. Brazil	
CABALISM	occultism; mystic science	
CABALIST	an adept	
CABALLED	plotted; conspired	
CABALLER	schemer; intriguer	
CABBAGED	filched; purloined; stole	
CABBLING	smashing into small pieces	
CABIN-BOY	waits on ship's passengers	
CABINING	confining; cooping up	
CABIRIAN	fire-worshipper (Lemnos)	
CABLE-WAY	blondin; tower-supported cables	
CABOCHED	} heraldic head without a	
CABOSHED	} neck	hd
CABOCHON	gem without facets	
CABOODLE	the whole lot	
CABOTAGE	coasting trade	
CABRIOLE	capriole; leap; (furniture)	

CAB-STAND	a rank	
CACHALOT	} the sperm whale	zo
CACHOLOT		
CACHEMIC	unhealthy	md
CACHEPOT	ornamental flower-pot cover	
CACHESEX	miniwear for beach	
CACHEXIA	severe emaciation	md
CACHUCHA	Spanish dance	mu
CACHUNDE	aromatic medicine	md
CACKEREL	a species of fish	zo
CACKLING	gossiping; chattering	
CACODOXY	erroneous opinion	
CACOLOGY	bad pronunciation	
CACOSMIA	aversion to smells	pc
CADASTRE	a survey of land	
CADENCED	modulated; rhythmical	
CADILLAC	a pear; motor car	bt
CADUCEUS	Mercury's wand	
CADUCITY	frailty; transitoriness	
CADUCOUS	early falling (leaves)	bt
CAERLEON	King Arthur's residence	
CAESIOUS	blue-grey	
CAESURAL	(metric pause)	
CAFFEINE	coffee alkaloid	ch
CAGELING	a bird in a cage	
CAILLACH	an old woman (Gael.)	
CAIMACAM	Turkish governor	
CAISSOON	caisson; watertight chest	
CAJOLERY	flattery; blandishment	
CAJOLING	wheedling; coaxing	
CAKESHOP	(confectionery)	
CAKE-WALK	pre-ragtime plantation dance (USA)	mu
CALABASH	gourd	bt
CALADIUM	plant genus	bt
CALAMARY	cuttlefish	zo
CALAMBAC	aloes-wood	bt
CALAMINE	zinc ore	mn
CALAMINT	aromatic plant	bt
CALAMITE	tremolite	mn
CALAMITY	disaster; affliction	
CALANDER	a lark	zo
CALANDRA	grain-weevil	zo
CALANGAY	white cockatoo	zo
CALATHUS	work-basket	
CALCEATE	shod; to shoe	
CALCEDON	opaline quartz	mn
CALCINED	reduced to quick-lime	
CALCINER	high-temperature heat device	
CALC-SPAR	calcite	mn
CALC-TUFF	a limestone	mn
CALCULON	size of brick	bd, me
CALCULUS	stone; (calculation)	md
CALENDAR	almanac; register; list	
CALENDER	hot-rolling machine	
CALFLESS	spindle-shanked	
CALF-LOVE	an early attachment	
CALF-SKIN	binding leather	
CALIBRED	bored; gauged	
CALIDITY	warmth; fervency; ardency	

CALIDUCT	a heating pipe	
CALIFATE	rulership of Islam	rl
CALIPASH	calipee; green turtle fat	
CALIPPIC	(Metonic cycles)	me
CALISAYA	Peruvian bark	bt
CALIXTIN	Hussite	rl
CALLAITE	turquoise	mn
CALL-BIRD	a decoy	zo
CALL-GIRL	prostitute	
CALLIOPE	muse of epic poetry; organ	mu
CALLIPER	a measuring device	to
CALL-LOAN	cash on demand	
CALL-NOTE	bird-call	
CALLOSUM	left-right brain link	pl
CALLOUSE	wart; hardening of skin, bone	md
CALL-OVER	a roll-call; betting odds on horses	
CALMNESS	placidity; tranquillity	
CALORIST	a heat theorist	
CALORIZE	aluminium-spray steel surfaces	ml
CALOTYPE	talbot-type	
CALTROPS	a plant	bt
CALUTRON	electromagnetic separator of images	ps
CALVERED	crimped; pickled	
CALVILLE	an apple	bt
CALYCINE	cuplike	bt
CALYCOID	like a calyx	
CALYMENE	trilobite genus	zo
CALYPTRA	a covering	bt
CAMASSIA	kind of hyacinth	bt
CAMATINA	acorns for tanning	
CAMBERED	slightly arched	
CAMBIATA	changed, device in counterpoint (It.)	mu
CAMBOGIA	gamboge gum	ch
CAMBRIAN	Welsh; era	gl
CAMELEER	camel driver	
CAMELEON	chameleon	zo
CAMELINE	camlet; camel hair	
CAMELISH	obstinate	
CAMELLIA	an evergreen	bt
CAMERATE	to build arch shape	ar
CAMISADE	} night attack with white shirts over armour	
CAMISADO		
CAMISOLE	a straightjacket	
CAMISTER	a clergyman	rl
CAMOMILE	a bitter plant	bt
CAMPAIGN	open country; crusade	
CAMP-FIRE	outdoor heating element	
CAMPHENE	camphine; camphor	ch
CAMP-SHOT	a pile revetment	
CAM-SHAFT	pan of machinery	au
CAMSTONE	whitening for doorsteps	
CAM-WHEEL	of centric mechanical item	
CANADIAN	Canuck	
CANAIGRE	Texan dock (plant)	bt

CANALIZE	make into a canal	
CANARESE	natives of Canara	
CANARIES	triple tune, old dance	mu
CANASTER	a kind of tobacco	bt
CANCELLI	} lattice-work in choir,	
CANCELLO	} chancel, of church	rl
CANCRINE	crab-like	zo
CANCROID	like cancer	md
CANDIDLY	frankly; sincerely; naively	
CANDYING	preserving in sugar	
CANE-HOLE	trench for sugar canes	
CANE-MILL	sugar crushing mill	
CANEPHOR	basket-bearing figure	
CANEWARE	yellowish stoneware dishes	
CANICULA	the dog-star; Sirius	
CANISTER	a tin; tea chest; case-shot	
CANITIES	whiteness of the hair	md
CANKERED	corroded; infected	
CANNABIN	cannabic extract	ch
CANNABIS	hemp; bhang	bt
CANNELON	mince-pie	
CANNIBAL	anthropophagite	
CANNIKIN	pannikin; a billy	
CANNONED	(billiards); collided	
CANNULAR	tubular	
CANOEIST	a paddler	
CANON-BIT	cannon-bit; (horse-bit)	
CANONESS	a beneficiary	rl
CANONIST	ecclesiastical expert	rl
CANONIZE	besaint	rl
CANON-LAW	diocesan digest	rl
CANOODLE	caress; fondle	
CANOPIED	with an awning	
CANOROUS	tuneful; musical; melodious	
CANSTICK	candlestick (Shak.)	
CANTERED	galloped easily	
CANTHOOK	lumberman's lever	to
CANTICLE	song or chant	
CANTICUM	a canticle	rl
CANTLING	brick-firing course	bd
CANTONAL	referring to a district	
CANTONED	divided into cantons	
CANTORIS	of the precentor	rl
CANZONET	air or song	
CAPACITY	volume; capability; faculty; motor power in terms of cylinder size	
CAPE-CART	two-wheeled vehicle (SA)	
CAPELINE	bandage; lady's wrap	md
CAPELLET	enlarged hock	
CAPERING	frolicsome frisking	
CAPER-TEA	black tea	bt
CAPIBARA	} Brazilian rodent allied to	
CAPYBARA	} the guinea-pig	zo
CAPITANO	a head-man	
CAPITATE	growing to a head	bt
CAPONIER	gallery in a fort	
CAPONISE	castrate; geld; emasculate	
CAPOTING	winning all tricks at piquet	
CAP-PAPER	wrapping or writing paper	
CAPRIFIG	pollinating inedible fig	bt
CAPRIOLE	equestrian jump	
CAPRIPED	goat-footed	
CAPROATE	a butric salt	ch
CAPRYLIC	normal; acidic	ch
CAP-SCREW	nutless screw-bolt	eg
CAPSICUM	red pepper; chilli	bt
CAPSTONE	fossil sea-urchin; a coping, wall ridge	mn, bd
CAPSULAR	in capsule form	
CAPTIOUS	hypercritical; censorious	
CAPTURED	caught; arrested	
CAPUCCIO	a hood or cowl	
CAPUCHIN	} monk; hooded cloak;	
CAPUCINE	} hooded monkey, pigeon	rl, zo
CARABINE	carbine; short rifle	
CARACARA	Brazilian carrion-hawk	zo
CARACOLE	spiral staircase	ar
CARACOLE	equestrian turn; shell	zo
CARACOLY	alloy of gold and silver	
CARACORE	patrol sail boat, Indonesia	nt
CARAPACE	tortoise shell; etc.	zo
CARAP-OIL	crab-wood oil	bt
CARAVELA	} part lateen, Atlantic,	
CARAVEL	} Spanish, Portuguese	nt
CARBOLIC	phenol	ch
CARBOLOY	carbide alloy for cutting tools	
CARBONIC	of carbon	ch
CARBONYL	metal/carbon-monoxide product	ch
CARBURET	impregnant with carbon	
CARCAJOU	wolverine or glutton	
CARCANET	collar of jewels	
CARDAMOM	aromatic spice (India)	bt
CARD-CASE	a receptacle	
CARDIACE	heart-shaped jewel	
CARDIGAN	knitted woollen jacket	
CARDINAL	short cloak; principal	rl
CARDIOID	heart-shaped curve	
CARDITIS	inflammation of heart	md
CAREENED	laid on one side	nt
CAREERED	raced; rushed; dashed	
CAREFREE	joyous	
CARELESS	heedless; remiss; incautious	
CARESSED	fondled; embraced; petted	
CAREWORN	grief-stricken	
CARGOOSE	crested grebe	zo
CARIACOU	Virginian deer	zo
CARIBBEE	a Caribbean	
CARICOUS	like a fig	bt
CARILLON	a ring of bells	
CARINATE	keel-shaped	bt
CARL-HEMP	female hemp plant	bt
CARNAGED	slaughtered; butchered	
CARNALLY	sensuously	
CARNAUBA	Brazilian palm	bt
CARNEOUS	fleshly	
CARNIFEX	public executioner	

CARNIVAL	revelry; masquerade	
CAROLINE	time of King Charles	
CAROLLED	warbled; sang	mu
CAROTEEL	East Indian weight	me
CAROTENE	vitamin A	
CAROUSAL	a jollification; orgies	
CAROUSED	held carnival; feasted	
CAROUSEL	tournament; tourney	
CAROUSER	a noisy reveller	
CARPETED	told off; rebuked	
CARRIAGE	cab; burden; behaviour	
CARRIERS	hauliers; (cableway);	
	containers; bags, baskets	
CARRIOLE	open carriage; sledge	
CARRITCH	catechism (Sc.)	
CARRYING	transporting; conveying	
CART-LOAD	a measure of capacity	
CARTOUCH	cartouche; hieroglyph	
CARUCAGE	tax on ploughs	
CARUCATE	(plough-land)	
CARUNCEL	fleshy excrescence	md
CARUNCLE	} wart; outgrowth on	
CARBUNCLE	} seeds	bt
CARYATIC	(Caryatides)	
CARYATID	a lady supporter	ar
CARYOKAR	butter-nut tree	bt
CASANOVA	type of salad	ck
CASCABEL	swell on cannon's mouth	
CASCADED	fell in torrents	
CASCALHO	diamond-bearing earth	
CASEMATE	armoured chamber	
CASEMENT	hinged window	
CASE-SHOT	short range ammunition	
CASE-WORM	caddis-worm	zo
CASHMERE	silky goat's hair	
CASKETED	enshrined; coffined	
CASSETTE	container	
CASS-WEED	shepherd's purse	bt
CASTANEA	chestnut-tree	bt
CASTANET	a clapper	mu
CASTAWAY	wrecked; rejected	
CAST-IRON	rigid; inflexible	
CASTLERY	feudal castle control	
CASTLING	(chess)	
CASTRATE	geld; emasculate	
CASTRATO	high voiced singer	mu
CASTWORK	moulded parts of a silver object	
CASUALLY	accidentally; fortuitously	
CASUALTY	killed or wounded	
CATACOMB	cave sepulchre	
CATALASE	hydrogen-peroxide-decomposing enzyme	ch
CATALYST	} (unchanged substance	
CATALYSE	} assisting chemical action)	
CATAPULT	a pellet projector	
CATARACT	waterfall; eye trouble	md
CAT-BLOCK	anchor-tackle	nt
CATCH-ALL	general jumble container	

CATCHFLY	certain plants	bt
CATCHING	infectious; charming	
CATCH-PIT	sump; matter-retaining catchment	
CATEGORY	order; class; division	
CATENARY	like a chain	
CATENATE	chain-like	bt
CATENOID	catenary revolution surface	ma
CATERESS	lady provider	
CATERING	food and entertainment	
CATHEDRA	bishop's throne	rl
CATHETUS	perpendicular line	
CATHEXIS	concentration of psychic energy	
CATHISMA	part of the psalter	
CATHODAL	negative electrode	el
CATHODIC	produced by cathode reaction	el
CATHOLIC	universal; liberal; tolerant	
CATILINE	daring conspirator	
CATODONT	teeth on lower jaw only	
CATOLYTE	electrolyte next to cathode	el
CATONIAN	resembling Cato; severe	
CATOPSIS	morbid keen-sightedness	
CAT'S-FOOT	ground ivy	bt
CAT'S-TAIL	the reed mace	bt
CAT-STICK	tip-cat's stick	
CAUDATED	having a tail; tailed	
CAUDICES	stems of trees	bt
CAUDICLE	an orchid stalk	bt
CAUDILLO	leader (Sp.)	
CAULCOLE	Corinthian cabbage	ar
CAULDRON	bowl-shaped boiler	
CAULICLE	caudicle; small stalk	bt
CAULKING	filling in cracks	nt
CAUSALLY	resultantly; productively	
CAUSERIE	gossip; small talk	
CAUSEUSE	settee for two	
CAUSEWAY	roadway over wet ground	
CAUTIOUS	wary; discreet; watchful	
CAVALIER	romantic; daring; royalist; beau; earth platform	
CAVATINA	short simple air	mu
CAVATION	excavation	
CAVEATED	warned	lw
CAVEATOR	caveat lodger	lw
CAVE-BEAR	extinct animal	zo
CAVERNED	hollowed out	
CAVESSON	horse-breaking appliance	
CAVICORN	hollow-horned	zo
CAVILLED	objected; carped; criticized	
CAVILLER	captious critic	
CAVORTED	pranced	
CELERIAC	turnip-rooted celery	bt
CELERITY	rapidity; swiftness; speed	
CELIBACY	the unmarried state	
CELIBATE	unwed	
CELLARER	wine steward; Simon	

CELLARET	small wine container; ornamented wooden chest
CELLULAR	honeycombed; alveolated
CEMENTED	glued; united; stuck
CEMETERY	burial ground; necropolis
CENATION	supping
CENOBITE	religious order **rl**
CENOTAPH	a monument; memorial
CENOZOIC	era of mammals **gl**
CENSORED	blue-pencilled
CENSURED	reprimanded; rebuked
CENTAURY	rose-pink flower **bt**
CENTERED	centred; localized
CENTESIS	puncturing a cavity **md**
CENTIARE	a square metre **me**
CENTIBAR	measurement of pressure **me**
CENTOISM	literary patchwork
CENTOIST	platitudinarian
CENTRING	football kick; centering; temp. dome or arch support **ce**
CENTROID	centre of gravity
CENTUPLE	a hundredfold
CENTURIA	division of 100 horsemen (Roman)
CEPHALGY	headache **md**
CEPHALIC	remedy for head-pains **md**
CEPHALIN	phosphatide substance in brain
CERAMICS	pottery
CERASINE	plum gum **bt**
CERASTES	a horned snake **zo**
CERATITE	species of ammonite **mn**
CERATODE	horny structure
CERATOID	ceratose; horny
CERBERUS	hell's watch-dog **zo**
CEREALIA	corn and grass **bt**
CEREALIN	a bran extract **ch**
CEREBRAL	brainy
CEREBRIC	cerebral **md**
CEREBRIN	something in the brain
CEREBRUM	part of the brain **md**
CEREMENT	shroud dipped in wax
CEREMONY	prescribed formality
CERESINE	refined ozocerite **el**
CERNUOUS	drooping **bt**
CERTINAL	a phenol developer **pg**
CERULEAN	sky-blue
CERULEIN	olive-green
CERUSITE	white lead **mn**
CERVELAT	saveloy; pork-brain sausage
CERVICAL	relating to the neck of womb **pl**
CESAREAN	childbirth operation; (Julius Caesar) **md**
CESSPOOL	drainage pit; midden
CESTODES	tapeworm **md**
CETACEAN	whale or dolphin **zo**
CETERACH	fern; cryptogam **bt**
CETOLOGY	natural history of cetaceans **zo**
CETRARIA	lichen; Iceland moss **bt**

CHACONNE	slow dance and music **mu**
CHADBAND	a canting hypocrite
CHAFEWAX	sealing-wax officer
CHAFFERY	haggling; bargaining
CHAFFING	bantering; scoffing
CHAFFRON	horse armour
CHAINAGE	measure of length or steel tape
CHAINING	restraining; fettering
CHAINLET	small chain
CHAINMAN	survey team a member; axeman (USA) **ag**
CHAIR-BED	convertible contraption
CHAIRING	carrying in triumph; (meeting)
CHAIRMAN	president or carrier
CHALDAIC	Babylonian
CHALDRON	25 cwt (l270 kg) of coal; portable cauldron; later truck-load in mines **me, mn**
CHALICED	cup-like
CHALKING	writing in chalk; break up of pigmented films **bd**
CHALKPIT	a quarry
CHALONIC	inhibitory, depressive **zo**
CHALOUPE	tender, gunboat (Fr.) **nt**
CHAMBREL	horse's hind leg joint
CHAMFRON	horse's head armour
CHAMORRO	native; language (Guam, Marianas)
CHAMPFER	bevelled angle on a surface
CHAMPING	chewing; gnawing; biting
CHAMPION	defender; hero; victor
CHANCERY	court of justice (civil); head lock **lw**
CHANCING	risking; happening
CHANDLER	candle-maker; dealer
CHANFRIN	fore-part of horse's head
CHANGE-UP	let-up; slow pitch throw (baseball)
CHANGING	altering; varying
CHANTING	intoning; reciting
CHAPATTY	flat unleavened bread (India)
CHAPBOOK	book hawked by chapmen
CHAPELET	stirrups and leathers
CHAPELRY	chapel district **rl**
CHAPERON	an escort; a cap
CHAPITER	capital of a column
CHAPLAIN	a sky-pilot; padre; priest to service groups **rl**
CHAPLASH	yellow-brown durable wood **fr**
CHAPLESS	without a lower jaw
CHAPPING	cleaving
CHAPTREL	arch-supporting capital
CHARCOAL	charred wood
CHARGING	rushing; costing; enjoining
CHARISMA	magnetic personality; grace
CHARLIES	night watchmen
CHARLOCK	wild mustard **bt**
CHARMING	fascinating; captivating
CHARRING	scorching; toasting

CHARTING	mapping; recording	
CHARTISM	} (universal suffrage)	
CHARTIST		
CHASSEUR	light-armed soldier; (hunter)	
CHASTELY	virtuously; modestly	
CHASTISE	flog; castigate; discipline	
CHASTITY	sexual abstinence	
CHASUBLE	vestment over alb	rl
CHATELET	small castle	
CHATONES	ornamental nailhead	
CHATTELS	miscellaneous property	
CHATTING	friendly conversation	
CHATWOOD	fuel; ducal mansion	
CHAUFFER	portable furnace; car driver	
CHAUNTER	chanter of bagpipes	mu
CHAUSSES	trunk-hose; leg-armour	
CHAY-ROOT	Indian red dye	bt
CHEATERY	fraud; deception	
CHEATING	knavery; duping; (card-sharper)	
CHEBACCO	fishing boat (N. America)	nt
CHECHAKO	tenderfoot (Alaska)	
CHECKBIT	binary check digit	cp
CHECKERS	a draughts game	
CHECKING	reproving; impeding	
CHECKOUT	departure formality	
CHEEKING	saucy behaviour	
CHEEPING	piping; chirping	
CHEERFUL	merry and bright	
CHEERILY	joyfully; gaily; blithely	
CHEERING	applause; comforting	
CHELIFER	book-scorpion	zo
CHELLEAN	early Palaeolithic	
CHELONIA	tortoises and turtles	zo
CHEMICAL	chymical	
CHEMOSIS	eye-disease symptom	md
CHEMURGY	applied organic chemistry	
CHENILLE	cord with short threads of silk, wool	
CHERUBIC	angelic	
CHERUBIM	a celestial spirit	
CHESHIRE	cheese; fading cat	zo
CHESIBLE	see chasuble	rl
CHESSMAN	a piece in chess	
CHESTING	encasing; boxing	
CHESTNUT	old joke; conker	bt
CHEVEREL	} kid-skin; flexible	
CHEVERIL		
CHEVERET	small table (English)	
CHEVILLE	bridge of a violin	mu
CHEVYING	chasing; pursuing	
CHIASMUS	inverse parallelism	
CHIASTIC	crossed	
CHICANED	cheated; tricked	
CHICANER	a swindler; artful dodger	
CHICCORY	chicory	bt
CHICKING	sprouting	
CHICK-PEA	edible pealike seed	bt
CHIEFAGE	capitation; poll tax	
CHIEFRIE	small feudal rent	lw

CHILD-BED	in labour; confinement	
CHILDISH	puerile; infantile	
CHILDREN	kids	
CHILIASM	doctrine of millennium	
CHILIAST	believer in that doctrine	
CHILLIER	cooler; colder	
CHILLING	discouraging; depressful; freezing; (damage)	
CHILTERN	(stewardship by the hundred)	
CHIMAERA	fabulous monster; illusion	
CHIMAERA	graft; hybrid; fish	zo
CHIMERIC	fanciful; delusive	
CHINAMAN	Chinese; left hander's googly (cricket)	
CHINAMPA	floating garden	
CHIN-CHIN	a toast	
CHINKING	jingling; tinkling sound	
CHINOITE	green mineral	
CHINREST	violin	
CHINSCAB	a sheep-disease	vt
CHINSING	caulking	
CHIPMUCK	} the ground-squirrel of North America	
CHIPMUNK		zo
CHIPPING	chaffing; chopping; fracturing	
CHIPSHOT	golf	
CHIRAGRA	gout in the hands	md
CHIRPING	cheeping	
CHIRRING	cooing; curring; purring	
CHIT-CHAT	small talk	
CHIVALRY	gallantry	
CHLOASMA	a skin disease	md
CHLORATE	salt of chloric acid	ch
CHLORIDE	compound of chlorine	ch
CHLORINE	a yellow gas	ch
CHLORITE	olive-green mineral	mn
CHLOROID	} pertaining to chlorine	
CHLOROUS		ch
CHOANATA	vertebrates; (nasal-oral)	zo
CHOANITE	fossil sponge	mn
CHOICELY	discriminately; exquisitely	
CHOIR-BOY	a sweet singer	rl
CHOIRING	singing in unison	
CHOLERIC	irascible; testy; petulant	
CHOLIAMB	iambic metre	
CHONDRAL	cartilaginous	md
CHONDRIN	gelatinous liquid	md
CHOOSING	selecting; picking	
CHOP-CHOP	hurry	
CHOPNESS	kind of spade	
CHOPPING	and changing; veering; cutting with axe; shortening stride (running)	
CHOP-SUEY	a succulent Chinese dish	ck
CHORAGIC	(musical production)	
CHORALLY	(choir or chorus)	
CHORDATA	vertebrates, etc.	zo
CHORDING	stringing; time-spaced tonal effect	mu
CHOREGUS	choragus	mu
CHORIAMB	iambic metre	

CHORISIS	separation	bt
C-HORIZON	soil level	ag
CHORTLED	chuckled loudly	
CHORUSED	concerted	
CHOUSING	swindling	
CHOW-CHOW	ginger chutney	
CHOW-MEIN	Chinese dish	ck
CHRESARD	plant water supply in earth	
CHRISMAL	(consecrated oil)	rl
CHRISTEN	baptize	rl
CHRISTIE	(christiania) change course (skiing)	
CHRISTIE	position for skateboard riding	
CHROMATE	salt of chromic acid	ch
CHROMIUM	a metallic element	ch
CHROMULE	colouring matter	bt
CHRYSENE	coal-tar component	ch
CHTHONIC	subterranean	
CHUCKIES	a game with pebbles	
CHUCKING	throwing; jerking; gripping	
CHUCKLED	exulted	
CHUFFILY	clownishly; churlishly	
CHUMMAGE	chamber-fellowship	
CHUMMERY	friendship; intimacy	
CHUMMING	messing together; comradeship; groundbait (angling)	
CHUMP-END	thick end	
CHUMSHIP	comradeship (Sc.)	
CHUPATTY	unleavened bread (Ind.)	ck
CHURINGA	Australian amulet	
CHURLISH	surly and sullen	
CHURNING	agitating; rotating; foaming	
CHUTZPAH	bold, impudent (Jew.)	
CHYLIFIC	producing chyle	md
CHYMICAL	chemical	
CHYMOSIN	gastric enzyme, rennin	ch
CIBATION	feeding	
CIBORIUM	eucharistic vessel	rl
CICATRIX	a scar	md
CICERONE	guide	
CICISBEI	sword-knots	
CICISBEO	philanderer	
CICURATE	to tame	
CIDER-CUP	a beverage	
CIDERIST	cider-maker	
CIDERKIN	inferior cider	
CILIATED	with eyelashes	
CILIFORM	(fine filaments)	bt
CIMBALOM	Hung. concert dulcimer	mu
CIMBORIO	lantern (Sp.)	ar
CIMBRIAN	a German tribe	
CIMOLITE	fuller's earth	mn
CINCHING	tightening roll of film	cn
CINCHONA	Peruvian bark	md
CINCTURE	girdle; belt	
CINDROUS	ashy	
CINEFILM	moving-picture film	cn
CINERAMA	wide screen film	cn
CINERARY	cindery	

CINEREAL	like ashes	
CINGULUM	band; zone; belt	
CINNABAR	dragon's blood	mn
CINNAMIC	cinnamon type	bt
CINNAMON	a spicy bark	bt
CIPHERED	written in code	
CIRCAEAN	infatuating (Circe)	
CIRCINUS	the Compasses (constellation)	as
CIRCLING	flying around	
CIRCUITY	indirect approach	
CIRCULAR	round; printed leaflet	
CIRRHOSE	terminating in a tendril or curl	
CIRRHOUS		bt
CIRRIPED	a barnacle	zo
CISELEUR	engraver; chaser	
CISELURE	chased metal-work	
CISTELLA	capsular shield	bt
CISTVAEN	stone tomb	
CITATION	mention in despatches	
CITATORY	citing; summoning	
CITREOUS	citric; lemon flavoured	
CITRININ	bacteriostat	
CITY-BRED	raised in town	
CIVET-CAT	polecat	zo
CIVETING	scenting with civet	
CIVILIAN	non-military	
CIVILIST	civil law expert	
CIVILITY	politeness; courtesy	
CIVILIZE	reclaim from barbarism	
CLACK-BOX	valve container	
CLACKING	clicking; jabbering	
CLADDING	metal-surfacing coins; extra wall or roof surfaces; siding (USA)	ar
CLADONIA	reindeer moss	bt
CLAGGING	adhesion of blacking	ml
CLAIMANT	assertor of claims	
CLAIMING	demanding; arrogating	
CLAMANCY	urgency; exigency	
CLAM-BAKE	seaside picnic (USA)	
CLAMMING	daubing; clogging	
CLAMPING	fastening; clumping	
CLANGING	resounding; clanking	
CLANGOUR	din; clamour	
CLANGOUS	resonant	
CLANKING	clanging; clashing	
CLANNISH	cliquish	
CLANSHIP	loyalty; sodality	
CLANSMAN	one of a clan	
CLAP-DISH	wooden platter	
CLAPOTIS	increasing pressure of larger waves breaking on sea wall	
CLAPPING	applauding; putting away	
CLAP-SILL	frame of lock-gates	
CLAP-TRAP	speciosity; theatrical	
CLAQUEUR	hired applauder	
CLARENCE	four-wheeled cab	
CLARINET	reed instrument	mu
CLARSACH	Gaelic small Celtic harp	mu

CLASHING	colliding; jarring; differing	
CLASPING	fastening; grasping; hugging	
CLASP-NUT	split/lathe nut	**eg**
CLASSIER	superior; loftier; finer	
CLASSIFY	arrange; tabulate	
CLASSING	grading; grouping; ranging	
CLASSMAN	a graduate	
CLASS-WAR	engineered strife	
CLAUDIAN	(Roman Emperors)	
CLAUSURE	closure; stoppage	
CLAVATED	with knobs on	
CLAVECIN	harpsichord	**mu**
CLAVIARY	index of keys	
CLAVICLE	collar-bone	**md**
CLAVIGER	clubman; key-man	
CLAWBACK	a sycophant	
CLAW-FOOT	foot deformity	**md**
CLAW-HAND	hand deformity	**md**
CLAWLESS	no claws	
CLAWSICK	foot-rot	
CLAY-COLD	lifeless	
CLAY-MARL	chalky clay	**mn**
CLAY-MILL	clay mixing mill	
CLAYMORE	Scottish broad-sword	
CLAYWEED	coltsfoot	**bt**
CLEADING	coffer dam; lock-gate boarding	**eg**
CLEANING	washing; purifying; clearing	
CLEANISH	rather clean	
CLEANSED	purged; purified	
CLEANSER	a detergent; purifier	
CLEARAGE	removal	
CLEAR-CUT	sharply outlined	
CLEAREST	plainest; purest	
CLEARING	(banking; woodcutting)	
CLEAVAGE	fracture; fissure; separation	
CLEAVERS	goose-grass	**bt**
CLEAVING	splitting; riving	
CLEAVING	clinging; uniting; adhering	
CLECKING	a brood; a clutch	**zo**
CLEMATIS	traveller's joy, etc.	**bt**
CLEMENCY	clemence; leniency; mercy	
CLENCHED	clinched; gripped	
CLERICAL	priestly	
CLERKAGE	clerical work	
CLERKDOM	baboonism	
CLERKERY	accountancy	
CLERKISH	somewhat learned	
CLEVEITE	Norwegian pitchblende	**mn**
CLEVERER	more astute; abler	
CLEVERLY	dexterously; adroitly	
CLICKING	progressing satisfactorily	
CLIENTAL	dependent	
CLIENTED	supplied with clients	
CLIMATIC	due to climate	
CLIMBERS	undersurfaces for skis for uphill	**mo**
CLIMBING	scrambling; scaling	
CLINCHED	clenched; held fast	
CLINCHER	decisive reply	

CLINGING	embracing; tenacious	
CLINICAL	bedside; casework, analytic, detached	**md**
CLINIQUE	nursing-home	**md**
CLINKANT	glittering	
CLINKING	jingling	
CLIPPERS	cutting tools	**to**
CLIPPING	shearing; trimming	
CLIQUISH	clannish	
CLIQUISM	exclusiveness	
CLISSERE	climate changes & climaxes	**ec, mt**
CLITELLA	bands of worms	**zo**
CLITHERS	burweed	**bt**
CLITHRAL	completely roofed	
CLITORIS	female erectile tissue	**pl**
CLOAKAGE	disguise; pretext	
CLOAK-BAG	portmanteau	
CLOAKING	hiding; veiling; screening	
CLOCHARD	tramp (Fr.)	
CLOCKING	checking in; timing	
CLODDING	clotting	
CLODDISH	boorish; rustic	
CLODPATE	dolt; blockhead	
CLODPOOL	dullard; clotpoll	
CLOGGING	coalescing; impeding	
CLOISTER	an ambulatory	**rl**
CLOSE-CUT	close-bodied; cropped	
CLOSEOUT	collapse of surfing wave	
CLOSETED	secluded	
CLOTHIER	cloth merchant; tailor	
CLOTHING	garments; dress; draping	
CLOTPOLL	clodpate	
CLOTTING	coagulating; curdling	
CLOUDAGE	cloudiness	
CLOUDERY	cloudage	
CLOUDILY	mistily	
CLOUDING	obscuring; dimming	
CLOUDLET	a little cloud	
CLOURING	chisel indentations on walls	**ar**
CLOUTING	patching; buffeting	
CLOVERED	in clover	
CLOWNERY	buffoonery; burlesque	
CLOWNING	playing the fool; jesting	
CLOWNISH	ungainly; rude; boorish	
CLOYLESS	insatiable	
CLOYMENT	a surfeit; a glut	
CLOYSOME	palling	
CLUBBING	combining; bludgeoning	
CLUBBISH	rustic; congenial	
CLUBBISM	the club system	
CLUBBIST	frequenter of clubs	
CLUB-FIST	large heavy fist	
CLUBFOOT	taliped	**md**
CLUBHAUL	tacking	**nt**
CLUB-LAND	(Pall Mall, etc.)	
CLUB-MOSS	lycopodium	**bt**
CLUB-ROOM	a meeting room	
CLUB-ROOT	a plant disease	**bt**
CLUB-RUSH	bulrush	**bt**

CLUCKING	hen-talk	
CLUELESS	without a trace	
CLUMPING	(bootmaking); bunching	
CLUMSIER	more awkward	
CLUMSILY	maladroitly	
CLUPEOID	like a herring	zo
CLUSTERY	in clusters or bunches	bt
CLUTCHED	caught; gripped; clasped	
CLYFAKER	a pickpocket	
CLYPEATE	like a shield; oscutate	
COACHBOX	driver's seat	
COACH-DOG	Dalmatian	zo
COACHFUL	full inside	
COACHING	tutoring; driving; training; racing	
COACHMAN	a coachee	
COACTING	alliance; working together	
COACTION	compulsion; coercion	
COACTIVE	working in unison	
COAGENCY	joint action	
COAGULUM	a blood clot	md
COALESCE	merge; unite; amalgamate	cp, tc
COALFISH	black-backed cod	zo
COAL-HOLE	small coal-cellar	
COAL-MINE	coal-pit	
COAL-SHIP	a collier	nt
COALWORK	a colliery	
COAMINGS	raised work	nt
COARSELY	crudely; churlishly	
COARSEST	roughest; grossest	
COARSISH	rather coarse	
CO-ASSUME	agree	
COASTING	(shipping, cycling)	nt
COAT-CARD	court-card	
COAT-LINK	two buttons and a link	
COBALTIC	rather blue	
COBBLING	shoe-repairing	
COBCOALS	cobbles	mn
CO-BISHOP	joint bishop	rl
COBSTONE	large rounded stone	mn
COBWEBBY	araneous	
COCCAGEE	cider apple	bt
COCCIDIA	parasites	md
COCCULUS	narcotic plant	bt
COCHLEAN	spiral	
COCHLEAR	twisted; spiral	
COCKADED	bearing a badge	
COCKATOO	crested parrot	zo
COCKAYNE	cocaigne; land of plenty	
COCK-BEAD	hanging decorative bead; moulding on edges of drawer fronts	
COCK-BILL	(anchor-dropping)	nt
COCK-BOAT	cog; lifeboat; tender	nt
COCK-CROW	dawn	
COCKERED	pampered	
COCKEREL	young cock	zo
COCK-EYED	asquint; crooked	md
COCKLING	puckering; wrinkling	

COCKLOFT	top loft	
COCK-SHOT	cock-shy; random round	
COCK-SHUT	eventide; twilight; curfew	
COCKSPUR	Virginian hawthorn	bt
COCKSURE	absolutely certain	
COCKTAIL	alcoholic drink; beetle	zo
COCOA-NUT	cokernut	bt
COCOBOLO	hard wood used for knife handles	
COCOYAMS	product of Ghana	bt, ck
COCTIBLE	able to be cooked	
CODDCELL	single electric cell	
CODDLING	pampering; indulging	
CODIFIED	systematized	
CODIFIER	a compiler; collator	
CODPIECE	Tudor, genitals protector	tx
CODSHEAD	type of yacht	nt
CO-EDITOR	joint editor	
COENZYME	a fellow enzyme	
COERCING	compelling; curbing	
COERCION	force; constraint	
COERCIVE	repressive; compulsive	
COESTATE	union of estates	
COEXPAND	dilate simultaneously	
COEXTEND	march together	
COFFERED	in a box	
COFFERER	a treasurer	
COFFINED	enclosed	
COGENTLY	forcibly; potently	
COGITATE	ponder; meditate; ruminate	
COGNIZEE	fine receiver	lw
COGNIZOR	exacter of a fine	lw
COGNOMEN	the surname	
COGNOSCE	give judgment	lw
COGNOVIT	acceptance of claim	lw
COGWHEEL	spur-wheel	
COHERENT	connected; consistent; logical; comprehensible	
COHERING	adhering; uniting	
COHESION	congruity; adhesion	
COHESIVE	sticky; gummy	
COHOBATE	distil	ch
COIFFEUR	hairdresser	
COIFFURE	a headdress	
COIGNING	extorting	
COINCIDE	happen simultaneously	
CO-INHERE	exist together	
COINLESS	impecunious; broke	
COISTRIL	a groom; see coystril	
COKE-OVEN	coal carbonization process	
COKERNUT	coconut	
COLANDER	perforated bowl	
COLATION	filtration	
COLATURE	straining	
COLDNESS	frigidity	
COLD-SETT	Smith's chisel	
COLDSHUT	casting imperfection	
COLD-TYPE	printing	
COLE-RAPE	the turnip	bt
COLESEED	cabbage seed	bt

COLESLAW	cabbage salad	
COLEWORT	young cabbage	**bt**
COLISEUM	Roman ruin	
COLLAGEN	gelatine	**ch**
COLLAPSE	breakdown; subside; faint; fall; tactic	**ga**
COLLARED	pressed; caught	
COLLARET	small collar	
COLLATED	collected; assembled	
COLLATOR	codifier; interpolator; verifier; assembler	**cp**
COLLEGER	Eton scholar	
COLLETIC	sticky; mucilaginous	
COLLIDED	crashed; encountered	
COLLIERY	coal-mine	
COLLOGUE	plot; confer	
COLLOIDS	the gummy sector of life (gelatin starch, paste); clay particles; smallest matter	
COLLOQUY	dialogue; conversation	
COLLUDED	acted in collusion	
COLLUDER	conspirator; plotter	
COLLYING	fouling	
COLONIAL	colonist	
COLONIST	a settler in the colonies	
COLONIZE	establish a colony	
COLOPEXY	abdominal operation	**md**
COLOPHON	publisher's tally mark	
COLORATE	coloured; dyed	
COLORINE	madder extract	**bt**
COLOSSAL	gigantic; herculean; titanic	
COLOSSUS	Apollo's statue	
COLOTOMY	colonic incision	**md**
COLOURED	specious; painted; tinged	
COLSTAFF	carrying pole	
COLUMBIC	containing niobium	**mn**
COLUMNAR	in columns	
COLUMNED	having pillars	
COMATOSE	lethargic; drowsy	
COMATOUS	sleepy; torpid	
COMBINED	united; coalesced	
COMBINER	a merger; blender	
COMBLESS	lacking comb or crest	
COME-BACK	repartee; return	
COMEDIAN	actor; player; performer	
COMEDIST	writer of comedy	
COME-DOWN	humiliation; anti-climax	
COMELILY	attractively; gracefully	
COMETARY	planetarium; orrery	
COMING-IN	entrance; income	
COMITIAL	relating to assemblies	
COMMANDO	a fighting force	
COMMATIC	staccato; concise	
COMMENCE	initiate; begin; originate	
COMMERCE	barter; trade; traffic	
COMMIXED	blended; combined	
COMMONED	held in common	
COMMONER	an M.P., not a nobleman	
COMMONEY	a playing-marble	
COMMONLY	usually; frequently	

COMMONTY	common land	
COMMOVED	agitated; disturbed	
COMMUNAL	public	
COMMUNED	held private converse	
COMMUTED	exchanged; altered; bussed	
COMMUTER	season ticket holder	
COMPAGES	a complex structure	
COMPARED	likened	
COMPESCE	to curb	
COMPETED	strove; emulated	
COMPILED	amassed; composed; set in order	
COMPILER	literary hack; editor; computer program	**cp**
COMPLAIN	grumble; grouse; repine	
COMPLECT	embrace	
COMPLETE	ended; perfect; fulfil	
COMPLICE	an accomplice	
COMPLIED	met; yielded; fulfilled	
COMPLIER	an active agent	
COMPLINE	evening service, R.C.	**rl**
COMPONED	heraldic squares	**hd**
COMPOSED	calm; invented; produced	
COMPOSER	a creator; writer	**mu**
COMPOSTO	compounded; medley	**mu**
COMPOUND	combine; agree; mingle	
COMPRESS	abridge; condense; bandage	
COMPRINT	pirate	**lw**
COMPRISE	include; embrace; contain	
COMPTOIR	cash-desk	
COMPUTED	calculated; rated	
COMPUTER	actuary; reckoner	
CONACRED	sub-let	
CONARIAL	} relating to the pineal	
CONARIUM	} gland	**md**
CONATION	volition	
CONATIVE	endeavouring	
CONCAUSE	secondary cause	
CONCAVED	hollowed	
CONCEDED	granted; allowed; yielded	
CONCEDER	a donor; relinquisher	
CONCEIVE	imagine; think; fancy; plan	
CONCEIVE	become pregnant	
CONCERTO	full accompaniment	**mu**
CONCETTO	a right merry conceit	
CONCHITE	fossil shell	**mn**
CONCHOID	shell-like curve	
CONCLAVE	synod; assembly; council	
CONCLUDE	close; terminate; infer	
CONCOURS	a gathering (Fr.)	
CONCRETE	not abstract; solid; cement	
CONDENSE	compress; solidify; shorten	
CONDITED	pickled; preserved	
CONDOLED	sympathized; commiserated	
CONDONED	pardoned; forgave	
CONDUCED	aided; led; promoted	
CONE-GEAR	variable-speed belt drive	
CONFALON	gonfalon; banneret	
CONFERVA	a seaweed	**bt**
CONFETTI	scraps of paper	

CONFETTI	(substitute for rice)	
CONFIDED	entrusted; hoped; relied	
CONFIDER	teller of secrets	
CONFINED	limited; shut-up; restrained	
CONFINER	borderer; neighbour	
CONFIXED	fastened	
CONFLATE	collect; assemble	
CONFLICT	combat; clash; discord	
CONFOUND	amaze; mystify	
CONFRERE	colleague; companion	
CONFRONT	face; beard; oppose	
CONFUSED	in disarray; flurried	
CONFUTED	disproved; overcame	
CONGENER	an affinity	
CONGIARY	Roman gift of wine	
CONGLOBE	to ball; ensphere	
CONGREET	salute mutually	
CONGRESS	representative assembly	
CONGREVE	lucifer; rocket	
CONICINE	hemlock	md
CONICITY	conicalness	
CONIFERS	(fir or pine) evergreens	bt
CONIFORM	conical	
CONJOINT	associated; connected	
CONJUGAL	matrimonial	
CONJUNCT	concurrent; united	
CONJURED	bound by oath; juggled	lw
CONJURER	} magician; juggler;	
CONJUROR	} wizard; marabout	
CONJUSTO	with gusto	mu
CONNIVED	overlooked; permitted	
CONNIVER	confidence man; accessory	
CONNOTED	included; implied	
CONOIDAL	almost conical	
CONOIDIC	conoidal	
CONQUEST	victory; subjugation	
CONSERVE	preserve; maintain	
CONSIDER	contemplate; regard; ponder	
CONSOLED	solaced; assuaged; cheered	
CONSOLER	a comforter; soother	
CONSOMME	clear soup	
CONSOUND	herb comfrey	bt
CONSPIRE	plot; intrigue; machinate	
CONSPUED	defamed; execrated	
CONSTANT	unchangeable; perpetual	
CONSTRUE	translate; interpret	
CONSULAR	Foreign Office service	
CONSULTA	council	
CONSUMED	dissipated; squandered	
CONSUMER	devourer; waster; eater	
CONSUMPT	quantity consumed	
CONTANGO	premium; discount	
CONTEMPT	disdain; scorn; derision;	
	(court)	lw
CONTENTS	the inside	
CONTERNO	contour; outline (It.)	
CONTINUE	endure; extend; persist	
CONTINUO	harmonised keyboard	
	accompaniment	mu
CONTLINE	intervening space	

CONTOURA	copying device	
CONTRACT	agreement; abridge	
CONTRAIL	condensation trail	mt
CONTRARY	otherwise; opposite	
CONTRAST	difference; clash; comparison	
		cp, el, pg
CONTRATE	opposed; mitred	
CONTRITE	penitent; repentant; humble	
CONTRIVE	bring about; scheme	
CONTUSED	bruised; crushed; knocked	
CONUSANT	knowing; cognizable	
CONVENED	called together; gathered	
CONVENER	summoner	
CONVERGE	approach; incline	
CONVERSE	talk; parley; reciprocal	
CONVEXED	vaulted	
CONVEXLY	in convex form	
CONVEYED	stolen; imparted	
CONVEYER	imposter; conveyancer	
CONVEYOR	transporter; carrier	
CONVINCE	persuade; satisfy; prove	
CONVOKED	convened; mustered	
CONVOLVE	roll together	
CONVOYED	escorted; guarded	
CONVULSE	writhe; agitate; perturb	
CONY-SKIN	rabbit-skin	
CONY-WOOL	rabbit's fur	
COOEEING	hailing in Australia	mt
COOK-ROOM	cook-house; caboose	
COOK-SHOP	eating-house	
COOLNESS	indifference; frigidity	
COOPERED	repaired; doctored	
CO-OPTING	electing	
CO-OPTION	adoption; election	
COPATAIN	high-crowned; pointed	
COPEPODA	water-boatmen; crustacea	zo
COPHOSIS	deafness	md
COPHOUSE	tool-house	
COPOPSIA	eye-strain	md
COPPERAS	sulphate of iron	ch
COPPERED	covered with copper	
COPULATE	unite; couple; mate	
COPYBOOK	exercise book; example	
COPYHOLD	not freehold	lw
COQUETRY	flirtation; philandering	
COQUETTE	a flirt; a jilt; courtesan	
COQUILLE	conch shaped guard of epée	
	(fencing)	
CORACITE	uraninite	mn
CORACOID	like a crow's beak	
CORANACH	coronach; a dirge	
CORDATED	heart-shaped	bt
CORDINER	cordwainer (Sp.); leather	
	worker	
CORDLESS	plug without flexible part	cp
CORDOVAN	cordwain; goatskin leather; of	
	Cordoba (Spain)	le
CORDUROY	ribbed cloth	tx
CORDWAIN	Spanish leather	le
CORD-WOOD	firewood	

CO-REGENT	joint ruler	
CORE-SAND	linseed moulding mixture	
CORK-SOLE	inner shoe-sole	
CORK-TREE	oak (quercus)	bt
CORKWING	a sea-fish	zo
CORKWOOD	balsawood (USA)	bt
CORN-BALL	pop-corn; maize	ck
CORN-BEEF	corned beef	
CORN-BIND	convulvulus	
CORNCAKE	Indian meal cake	ck
CORNEOUS	horny	
CORNERED	brought to bay; controlled	
CORNETCY	rank of a cornet	
CORNFLAG	gladiolus	bt
CORNICLE	a little horn	
CORNICLE	honey dew tube in aphids	zo
CORNIFIC	horn-producing	
CORNLAND	grain-land	
CORNLOFT	granary	
CORNMEAL	coarse maize flour	ck
CORN-MILL	a grinder; quern	
CORN-MINT	calamint	bt
CORN-MOTH	a pest	zo
CORN-PIPE	straw-pipe	
CORN-PONE	bread (Indian corn)	ck
CORN-RENT	rent paid in corn	
CORNUTED	with horns	
CORN-WAIN	farm-cart; (haywain)	
COROCORE	Malay boat	nt
COROLLET	a floret	bt
CORONACH	coranach; a lament	
CORONARY	crown-shaped, heart artery	md
CORONATE	crowned	
CORONIUM	gaseous element	ch
CORONOID	coracoid	
CORONULE	downy tuft on seeds	bt
CORPORAL	bodily; material; an N.C.O.	
CORPORAS	fine linen	rl
CORRIDOR	passage-way; gallery	
CORRIVAL	co-rival	
CORRODED	eaten away; rusted; eroded	
CORSELET	corslet; leather cuirass	
CORSICAN	(Napoleon)	
CORTICAL	outer tissue (brain), bark (tree)	md, bt
CORTISOL	adrenal hormone extract	pm
CORUNDUM	emerald; ruby; sapphire	
CORVETTE	sloop; convoy escort; naval	nt
CORYBANT	priest of Cybele	
CORYMBUS	top-knot	
CORYPHEE	ballet-dancer	mu
CORYSTES	masked crab	zo
COSECANT	an inverse sine	
COSENAGE	} cousinhood; a writ	lw
COSINAGE		
COSHERED	pampered; coddled	
COSHERER	(free board and lodgings)	
COSINESS	snugness	
COSMETIC	a beautifier	

COSMICAL	relating to the universe	
COSSETED	petted; fondled; caressed	
COSTATED	ribbed	
COST-BOOK	account book	
COST-FREE	free of charge	
COSTLESS	without price; free	
COSTLIER	more expensive; dearer	
COSTMARY	aromatic plant	bt
COST-PLUS	war contract price	
COSTUMED	garbed; dressed; robed	
COSTUMER	costumier; dressmaker	
CO-SURETY	joint security	
COTCHELL	privately-sold timber	
COTELINE	ribbed muslin	tx
CO-TENANT	joint tenant	
COTHOUSE	a cottar's house	
COTILLON	cotillion; round dance	mu
COTQUEAN	a womanly man	
COTSWOLD	sheep	zo
COTTABUS	wine throwing contest	
COTTAGED	covered with cottages	
COTTAGER	small holder	
COTTONED	attracted to; understood	
COTYLOID	cup-shaped	
COUCHANT	reclining	hd
COUCHING	removing cataract	md
COUGHING	a raucous noise	
COULISSE	theatrical side-scene	
COUMARIC	from Tonka beans	bt
COUMARIN	a scent	bt
COUNTESS	wife of earl or count	
COUNTING	reckoning; enumerating	
COUNT-OUT	adjournment; boxing	
COUPELET	cabriolet	
COUPLING	linking; a link	mu, rw
COURANTE	French dance; a paper	
COURANTO	musical paper	mu
COURSING	racing; chasing; pursuing	
COURT-DAY	sessions-day	lw
COURTESY	polished manners	
COURTIER	courtesy personified	
COURTING	wooing; soliciting; inviting	
COUSCOUS	semolina dish (N. Afr.)	ck
COUSINLY	friendly	
COUSINRY	kin; relations	
COUTILLE	material for corsets	
COVALENT	bond: 1 electron to 2 atoms	ch
COVENANT	contract; bond; pact	lw, rl
COVENTRY	ostracism	
COVERAGE	protection; insurance	
COVER-ALL	an overlay	
COVERCLE	a lid	
COVERING	protecting; including	
COVERLET	bed cover; counterpane	
COVERLID	coverlet	
COVERTLY	surreptitiously; insidiously	
COVETING	acquisitiveness	
COVETOUS	avaricious; rapacious	
COVINOUS	collusive; fraudulent	

COWARDLY	timidly; cravenly	
COWBELLS	alpine percussion	mu
COWBERRY	whortleberry	bt
COWERING	crouching; cringing	
COWGRASS	meadow trefoil	bt
COWHIDED	whipped	
COWHOUSE	a byre; milking-shed	
COW-LEECH	cow doctor (vetinerary)	
CO-WORKER	fellow toiler	
COWPILOT	West Indian fish	zo
COWPLANT	plant (Sri Lanka)	bt
COW-THIEF	a rustler	
COW-WHEAT	annual plant	bt
COXALGIA	hip disease	md
COXINESS	conceit; bumptiousness	
COXSWAIN	steersman; cox	nt
COYSTREL	} coistral; a groom; a	
COYSTRIL	} knave	
COZENAGE	deception; deceit; fraud	
COZENING	cheating; swindling	
CRABBING	peevish criticism; grousing	
CRABTREE	crab-apple	bt
CRABWOOD	S. American tree	bt
CRAB-YAWS	foot disease	md
CRACKING	distilling; splitting	
CRACK-JAW	difficult to pronounce	
CRACKLED	crepitated	
CRACKNEL	a biscuit	
CRACK-POT	a maniac; crazy	
CRACOWES	pointed shoes	
CRADLING	timber framework; goal pass (lacrosse)	
CRAFTIER	slyer; more cunning	
CRAFTILY	shrewdly; pawkily	
CRAGSMAN	rock-climber	
CRAM-FULL	no more room	
CRAMMING	stuffing; tutoring	
CRAMOISY	crimson; cremosin	
CRAMPING	restraining; impeding	
CRAMPONS	mountaineering spiked boots	
CRANE-FLY	daddy-longlegs	zo
CRANIATE	vertebrates with skull	zo
CRANKING	winding; turning; twisting	
CRANK-PIN	link; crank/connecting rod	eg
CRANNIED	full of chinks	
CRANNIES	nooks; fissures	
CRASHING	blundering; clashing	
CRATCHES	mangers; swollen pastern	
CRAVENLY	cowardly	
CRAW-CRAW	tropical skin disease	md
CRAWFISH	crayfish; langouste	zo
CRAWLING	on all fours; creeping; paint cracking, cissing	
CRAWLWAY	high duct, man-size	
CRAYFISH	crawfish	zo
CRAYONED	drawn with chalk	
CRAZIEST	maddest; most idiotic	
CREAKING	grating	
CREAMERY	milk-bar; dairy	
CREAMING	foaming; mantling	

CREAM-NUT	Brazil nut	
CREAM-POT	cosmetic container	
CREASING	folding	
CREASOTE	} tar product	ch, md
CREOSOTE	}	
CREATINE	} gristle on meat; chemical in muscle	ck,
KREATINE	}	md
CREATING	begetting; fashioning	
CREATION	the universe; cosmos	
CREATIVE	inventive; productive	
CREATRIX	a designing lady	
CREATURE	term of contempt	
CREDENCE	belief; credit; reliance; sacrament table	rl
CREDENDA	articles of faith	rl
CREDENZA	low cupboard on floor	
CREDIBLE	trustworthy; believable	
CREDIBLY	conceivably	
CREDITED	trusted; accepted	
CREDITOR	a lender; mortgagee	
CREEPING	crawling; cringing; stealing	
CREMATED	reduced to ashes	
CREMATOR	incinerator	
CREMORNE	French-window bolt	
CREMOSIN	crimson; cramoisy	
CRENATED	notched	
CRENELET	small loophole	
CRENELLE	loophole	
CREOLIAN	Creole	
CREOSOTE	coal-tar derivative	ch
CREPANCE	brushing (horse)	
CREPITUS	lung-rattle	md
CRESCENT	Turkish emblem	
CRESCIVE	growing; increasing	
CRESTING	topping; surfing; decorating; coloured identity of arrow (archery)	
CRETATED	chalked	
CRETONNE	patterned cloth	
CREUTZER	Austrian copper coin	nm
CREVASSE	fissure in glacier	
CREVICED	rent; cracked; flawed	
CRIBBAGE	card game	
CRIBBING	shift lining; copying	
CRIBBLED	sifted; riddled	
CRIBRATE	perforated	
CRIBROSE	full of holes	
CRIB-WORK	a form of structure; bridge foundation	ce
CRICETUS	genus of rodents	zo
CRIMEFUL	criminal; wicked; culpable	
CRIMINAL	felon; convict; illegal	lw
CRIMPAGE	press-gang work	
CRIMPING	plaiting; crisping	
CRIMPLED	curled	
CRINATED	hairy	
CRINGING	fawning; crouching; servile	
CRINKLED	wrinkled; corrugated	
CRIPPLED	disabled; impaired; maimed	

448

CRISPATE	curly	
CRISPING	crimping; twisting; waving	
CRISTATE	crested; tufted	
CRITERLA	standards of judgment	
CRITHMUM	the samphire	bt
CRITICAL	crucial; fault-finding; serious	
CRITICAL	nuclear transformation; chain reaction	nc
CRITIQUE	literary notice	
CROAKING	woeful; calamitous	
CROCEOUS	yellow; like saffron	
CROCKERY	earthenware	
CROCKING	blackening with soot	
CROCOITE	chromate of lead	mn
CROFTING	farming	
CROMLECH	ancient stone circle	
CROMORNA	organ-stop	mu
CROMSTER	} Elizabethan vessel, North	
CROMSTEREN	} Sea	
CROODLED	cowered	
CROOKING	bending; inflecting	
CROONING	moaning; lamenting	
CROPPING	harvesting; lopping; cutting	
CROP-SICK	sick of a surfeit	
CROSS-BAR	transverse bar	
CROSSBIT	cheated	
CROSS-BOW	a weapon	
CROSS-BUN	hot cross-bun	.
CROSS-CUT	short cut; large saw	to
CROSSING	a ford; traversing	
CROSSLET	small heraldic cross	hd
CROSS-PLY	standard flexible-tread	au
CROSS-ROW	the alphabet	
CROSS-SEA	choppy sea	
CROSS-TIE	railway sleeper	
CROSSWAY	by-way	
CROTALUM	castanet; small bell	mu
CROTCHED	forked	mu
CROTCHET	whimsey; fancy; conceit	
CROTONIC	(croton-oil)	bt
CROTTLES	lichens used for dyeing	bt
CROUCHED	cringed; fawned; truckled	
CROUPADE	equestrian feat	
CROUPIER	a raker of shekels	
CROUPOUS	croupy	md
CROW-BILL	forceps	md
CROWDING	urging; pressing; swarming	
CROWFOOT	ranunculus	bt
CROWMILL	crow-trap	
CROWNING	a coronation	
CROWNING	(mercy) completing	
CROWNLET	small crown	
CROWN-SAW	circular saw	to
CROW-SILK	aquatic plant	bt
CRUCIATE	cruciform	
CRUCIBLE	melting pot	
CRUCIFER	cross-bearer	
CRUCIFIX	religious emblem	rl
CRUDITES	raw-vegetable salad	ck
CRUELEST	most ruthless; harshest	
CRUISING	voyaging; sailing	
CRUMBING	covering with crumbs	
CRUMBLED	disintegrated; crushed	
CRUMENAL	a purse	
CRUMPLED	ruffled; rumpled; wrinkled	
CRUNCHED	munched	
CRUSADED	followed the cross	
CRUSADER	valiant enthusiast	
CRUSHING	subduing; overpowering	
CRUSTILY	morosely; sullenly	
CRUSTOSE	uninterrupted crust	bt
CRUTCHED	on crutches	
CRUTCHET	the perch, fish	zo
CRUZEIRO	Brazil currency unit	nm
CRYOLITE	a transparent stone	mn
CRYOSTAT	low-temperature thermostat	ps
CRYOTRON	small electronic switch	el
CUBATION	} determination of cubic	
CUBATURE	} contents	
CUBEBINE	a carminative	md
CUBIFORM	cubical	
CUBOIDAL	cube-like	
CUCHILLA	uplands (S. Amer.)	
CUCUMBER	a creeping plant	bt
CUCURBIT	distilling vessel	ch
CUDDLING	fondling; petting; hugging	
CUFFLINK	wrist adornment	
CUL-DE-SAC	dead-end; blind alley	
CULINARY	au cordon bleu	
CULLYING	imposing on	
CULLYISM	being a simpleton	
CULPABLE	censurable; blameworthy	
CULPABLY	guiltily; sinfully	
CULTRATE	knife-like	
CULTURAL	of group norms; of the arts	
CULTURED	intellectual; refined	
CULVERIN	a cannon	
CUMBERED	hampered; clogged	
CUMBRIAN	(Cumbria)	
CUMBROUS	unhandy; clumsy	
CUMULATE	a mass; collect	
CUMULOSE	heaped	
CUNABULA	a cradle; incunabula	
CUNABULA	books prior to A.D. 1500	
CUNARDER	a Cunard steamship	
CUNEATED	wedge-shaped; cuneiform	
CUNIFORM	Assyrian writing, etc.	
CUPBOARD	a repository	
CUP-CHUCK	bell-chuck on lathe	eg
CUPIDITY	covetousness; avarice; desire	
CUP-JOINT	male/female pipe joint	
CUPREOUS	like copper	
CURARINE	curari extract	ch
CURARISE	to poison with curari	
CURASSOW	S. American turkey	zo
CURATIVE	healing; restorative	
CURATORY	remedial; antidotal	
CURBLESS	without restraint	
CURB-ROOF	bent roof	

CURCULIO	corn-worm; weevil	**zo**
CURDLING	congealing; thickening	
CURLICUE	a fantastic curl; pig's tail	
CURLIWIG	a curved piece	
CURRENCY	coin; flow; circulation	
CURRICLE	two-wheeled chaise	
CURRYING	(food; leather; horse)	
CURSEDLY	execrably	
CURSITOR	Chancery writ writer	**lw**
CURSORES	running birds	**zo**
CURTLEAX	cutlass; curtal-ax	
CURTNESS	abruptness; terseness	
CURTSIED	made obeisance	
CURVATED	curved; bent	
CURVITAL	not straight	
CUSPIDAL	pointed	
CUSPIDOR	a spittoon	
CUSTOMED	wont; habituated	
CUSTOMER	purchaser; client; patron	
CUTCHERY	Indian court	**lw**
CUT-GLASS	art glassware	
CUTHBERT	Northumbrian apostle	**rl**
CUTIKINS	spats (Sc.)	
CUT-PRICE	cheap	
CUTPURSE	pickpocket	
CUT-UNDER	(fencing)	
CUTWATER	prow; wedge shape of stone piers; breakwater	**nt, ce**
CYANOGEN	poisonous gas	**ch**
CYANOSIS	skin disease	**md**
CYANOTIC	(blue jaundice)	**md**
CYCLAMEN	primrose family	**bt**
CYCLE-CAR	a combination	
CYCLICAL	circular; epic	
CYCLONIC	like a hurricane	**mt**
CYCLOPIA	one median eye (cyclops)	**zo**
CYCLOPIC	gigantic; monstrous	
CYCLOSIS	circulation; cell movement	
CYLINDER	closed tube (combustion) (expansion) (gas) (steam); data store	**cp**
CYLINDER	solid roller; monolith, bored piles	**ce**
CYMATIUM	cyme; a moulding	**ar**
CYNANCHE	sore throat	**md**
CYNICISM	misanthropy	
CYNOSURE	centre of attraction	
CYRENAIC	of Cyrene	
CYRILLIC	(Slavic alphabet)	
CYSTICLE	small cyst	**md**
CYSTITIS	inflammation of bladder	**md**
CYTISINE	laburnum alkaloid	
CYTOLOGY	study of cells	
CYTOSINE	nuclcic acid hydrolysis	**ch**
CYTOSOME	cell cytoplasm	**zo**
CYTOZOIC	intra-cellular; living in a cell	
CZECHISH	characteristic of Czechs	

D

DABBLING	meddling; trifling; ducks feeding	
DAB-CHICK	also dob-chick	**zo**
DACRYOMA	defective tear duct	**md**
DACRYOPS	eyelid cyst	**md**
DACTYLAR	(finger); (toe)	
DACTYLIC	(verse)	
DADDLING	tottering locomotion	
DADDLUMS	form of skittles	**ga**
DADO-RAIL	edge of border panelling	**ar**
DAEDALUS	human glider	
DAEMONIC	diabolical; satanic	
DAFFODIL	Lent lily	**bt**
DAFTNESS	lunacy; stupidity	
DAGGERED	stabbed	
DAGGLING	trapesing	
DAGO-BOAT	felucca, California and Naples	**nt**
DAG-SWAIN	coarse woollen fabric	**tx**
DAHABIAH }	state barge of Nile	**nt**
DAHABIEH		
DAINTILY	delicately; elegantly	
DAIQUIRI	rum drink	
DAIRYING	farming	**ag**
DAIRYMAN	dairy keeper; milkman	
DALESMAN	Lake District man	
DALLYING	trifling; delaying; fondling	
DALMAHOY	bushy bob-wig	
DALMATIC	long white vestment	**rl**
DAMAGING	injuring; impairing	
DAMASKED	variegated	
DAMASKIN	Damascus sword	
DAMASSIN	damask cloth	**tx**
DAMBOARD	draughtboard	
DAME-WORT	dame's violet	**bt**
DAMNABLE	pernicious; execrable	
DAMOCLES	his sword was a hanger	
DAMPENED	moistened; discouraged	
DAMPNESS	humidity	
DANALITE	iron/beryllium silicate	**mn**
DANCETTE	Norman zigzag moulding	**ar**
DANDERED	sauntered (Sc.)	
DANDIEST	neatest	
DANDLING	fondling; caressing	
DANDRUFF	scurf	**md**
DANDYISE	dress ostentatiously	
DANDYISH	foppish	
DANDYISM	elegance in attire	
DANE-GELD	tribute paid to Danes by Anglo-Saxons	
DANELAGH	Danish England (A.D. 878)	
DANE-WEED	a plant	**bt**
DANE-WORT	dwarf elder	**bt**
DANGLING	hanging by a thread	
DANSEUSE	ballerina	
DANUBIAN	(Danube)	
DAPEDIUS	ganoid fish	**zo**
DAPHNITE	iron-rich chlorite	**mn**
DAPPERLY	variegated	

DAPPLING	shading; spotting	
DARING-DO	derring-do; act of high daring, mischief	
DARINGLY	intrepidly; bravely	
DARKENED	obscured; clouded	
DARKLING	gloomy; sombre	
DARKNESS	ignorance; blindness	
DARK-ROOM	a developing locality	
DARKSOME	mysterious; dismal	
DASTARDY	cowardice; base timidity	
DASYURES	Australian marsupials	zo
DATELESS	immemorial; timeless	
DATE-LINE	where East meets West	
DATE-PALM	Biblical palm	bt, rl
DATE-PLUM	persimmon	bt
DATE-TREE	(many varieties)	bt
DATOLITE	a silicate	mn
DATURINE	thorn-apple alkaloid	ch
DAUBSTER	poor painter	
DAUGHTER	person's female child	
DAUNTING	intimidating; dismaying	
DAUPHINE	French princess	
DAVY-LAMP	miner's lamp	mn
DAWDLING	dallying; lagging; trifling	
DAYBREAK	dawn; dawning; day-spring	
DAY-DREAM	reverie; visionary scheme	
DAYDREAM	mental meandering	pc
DAYLIGHT	illumination	
DAYSHIFT	working period (industrial)	
DAY-SIGHT	night-blindness	
DAY-TO-DAY	ephemeral	
DAY-WOMAN	daily woman	
DAZZLING	bewildering; confusing	
DEAD-BEAT	exhausted	
DEAD-BORN	still-born	
DEADENED	retarded; benumbed	
DEAD-FALL	animal trap	
DEAD-FIRE	death omen	
DEAD-HEAD	(on the free list)	
DEAD-HEAT	bracketed	
DEADLIER	more malignant	
DEAD-LIFT	(no leverage or help)	
DEADLINE	a boundary; time-limit	
DEADLOCK	no compromise; impasse	
DEAD-LOSS	complete loss	
DEAD-MEAT	meat for market	
DEADNESS	inertness; inertia	
DEAD-PULL	dead-lift	
DEADRISE	design of rise from ship's bottom	nt
DEAD-ROPE	fixed rope in dead-eye	
DEAD-SHOT	unerring marksman	
DEAD-WALL	windowless wall	
DEAD-WIND	calm	mt
DEAD-WOOD	decayed or useless wood	
DEAD-WORK	unprofitable work	
DEAD-WORT	species of elder	bt
DEAFENED	stunned	
DEAF-MUTE	deaf and dumb	
DEAFNESS	hard of hearing	md
DEAL-FISH	a thin fish	zo
DEANSHIP	office of dean	rl
DEARNESS	costliness; tenderness	
DEARNFUL	solitary; mournful	
DEATH-BED	the passing place	
DEATHFUL	fateful; moribund	
DE-BANNED	freed; de-restricted	
DEBARKED	landed	
DEBARRED	excluded; prohibited	
DEBASING	degrading; vitiating	
DEBATING	discussing; disputing	
DEBILITY	functional weakness	
DEBITING	charging	
DEBONAIR	genial; cheerful; merry	
DEBOUCHE	an opening; a market	
DEBOUTED	expelled; ejected	
DEBTLESS	owing naught	
DEBUNKED	shown up	
DEBUTANT	a starter	
DECADENT	degenerate	
DECAGRAM	10 grams	me
DECALAGE	wing chords angle	ae
DECAMPED	sloped off; fled; bolted	
DECANTED	poured out	
DECANTER	glass wine bottle	
DECAPODA	prawns, lobsters, crabs	zo
DECAYING	rotting; declining; ebbing	
DECEASED	dead; departed; defunct	
DECEIVED	beguiled; duped; gulled	
DECEIVER	impostor; trickster	
DECEMBER	10th Roman month	
DECEMFID	ten-cleft	bt
DECEMVIR	Roman magistrate	
DECENTLY	comme il faut	
DECERNED	judged; decreed	
DECICAIN	local anaesthetic	pm
DECIDING	settling; resolving	
DECIDUAL	able to be cast off	
DECIGRAM	one-tenth of gram	me
DECIMATE	kill one in ten	
DECIPHER	decode	
DECISION	verdict; firmness; chosen action	cp
DECISIVE	final; conclusive	
DECISORY	determining	
DECK-GAME	(board-board, etc.)	
DECK-HAND	an A.B.	nt
DECK-LOAD	deck-cargo	
DECLARED	said; announced; averred	
DECLINAL	sloping downward	
DECLINED	pined; sank; shunned	
DECLINER	a refuser	
DECLUTCH	gear-changing (motoring)	
DECOCTED	cooked; digested	
DECODING	deciphering	
DECOLOUR	bleach	
DECORATE	deck; embellish; garnish	
DECOROUS	proper; befitting; seemly	
DECOYING	luring; enticing; inveigling	
DECREASE	minimize; reduce; curtail	
DECREPIT	broken down	
DECRETAL	a Papal decree	rl

DECRYING	disparaging; vilifying	
DECUPLED	tenfold	
DECURION	controller of ten	
DECURVED	bent down	**bt**
DEDENDUM	wheel/cylinder radial distance	
DEDICANT	dedicator	
DEDICATE	devote; consecrate; assign	
DEDITION	surrender	
DEDUCING	inferring; drawing; deriving	
DEDUCTED	subtracted; withdrawn	
DEEDLESS	inactive	
DEED-POLL	a legal instrument	**lw**
DEEMSTER	Manx judge	**lw**
DEEP-DYED	extreme; rascally	
DEEPENED	became more mysterious	
DEEP-LAID	cunning; intricate	
DEEP-MOST	uttermost	
DEEPNESS	profundity	
DEEP-READ	scholarly	
DEERFOOT	leathercraft	**to**
DEER-HAIR	heath club-rush	**bt**
DEER-HERD	a herd of deer	
DEER-LICK	salt lick	
DEER-NECK	scraggy	
DEER-PARK	paddock enclosure, zoo	
DEERSKIN	leather	
DEFACING	disfiguring; marring; spoiling	
DEFAMING	slandering; traducing	
DEFEATED	frustrated; overthrown	
DEFECATE	purge; empty bowels	
DEFECTOR	deserter; traitor	
DEFENCED	fortified; covered	
DEFENDED	warded off; shielded	
DEFENDER	protector; advocate	
DEFERENT	a conveyor; deferential	
DEFERRED	postponed; adjourned	
DEFERRER	a procrastinator	
DEFIANCE	a challenge; provocation	
DEFILADE	cf. enfilade	
DEFILING	polluting; corrupting	
DEFINING	explaining; specifying	
DEFINITE	precise; exact; certain	
DEFLATED	punctured	
DEFLEXED	bent	
DEFLEXOR	metal outrigger (hang gliding)	
DEFLOWER	deprive of virginity; rape	
DEFLUENT	flowing	
DEFORCED	resisted	**lw**
DEFOREST	clear of trees	
DEFORMED	disfigured; misshapen	
DEFORMER	destroyer of symmetry	
DEFRAYAL	payment	
DEFRAYED	met the cost; paid	
DEFRAYER	liquidator; settler	
DEFTNESS	adroitness; dexterity	
DEFUSION	breakup of balance	**pc**
DEGAUSSE	neutralize magnetic mine	
DEGRADED	reduced in rank	
DEGREASE	remove the grease	
DEHORNED	dodded (cattle)	
DEIFICAL	making divine	
DEIFYING	idolizing; exalting	
DEIGNING	condescending; vouchsafing	
DEISHEAL	clockwise	
DEJECTED	downcast; chapfallen	
DEJECTLY	gloomily; dolefully	
DEJEUNER	breakfast; lunch (Fr.)	
DEKATRON	cold cathode sealing tube	**ps**
DELATING	informing	
DELATION	informer's accusation	
DELAYING	retarding; hindering	
DELECTUS	classical anthology	
DELEGACY	representation	
DELEGATE	deputy; commissioner	
DELETING	obliterating; effacing	
DELETION	erasure; expunction	
DELETIVE	delible	
DELETORY	erasive; blotting	
DELIBATE	taste; sip	
DELICACY	consideration; tact; relish	
DELICATE	dainty; frail; slight	
DELIMING	hide lime-salt removal	
DELIRIUM	mental aberration; mania	
DELIVERY	rescue; distribution	
DELOUSED	cleared of vermin	
DELPHIAN	oracular	
DELPHINE	dauphin; dolphin	**zo**
DELUBRUM	shrine; sanctuary	
DELUDING	duping; gulling; misleading	
DELUGING	pouring; inundating	
DELUSION	fallacy; imposture	
DELUSIVE	deceptive; fallacious	
DELUSORY	illusory; deceitful	
DEMAGOGY	popular oration technique	
DEMANDED	queried; exacted; claimed	
DEMARCHE	ultimatum; counter-stroke	
DEMEANED	degraded; behaved	
DEMENTED	daft; crazy; deranged	
DEMENTIA	insanity; lunacy	**md**
DEMERARA	brown sugar	**bt**
DEMERSAL	near sea bottom	
DEMERSED	sub-aqueous	
DEMIBAIN	small bath	
DEMI-FOND	motor paced cycle race	
DEMIJOHN	bottle enclosed in wicker	
DEMILUNE	ravelin (fort.)	
DEMISING	bequeathing; devising	
DEMISSLY	humbly	
DEMISTER	windscreen condensation preventive	**au**
DEMI-TINT	a shade	
DEMI-TONE	a semitone	
DEMITTED	dismissed; resigned	
DEMIURGE	Plato's world-maker	
DEMI-VOLT	an equestrian trick	
DEMI-WOLF	progeny of dog and wolf	**zo**
DEMOBBED	demobilized; discharged	
DEMOCRAT	upholder of democracy	
DEMOLISH	destroy; raze; dismantle	
DEMOLOGY	social statistics	
DEMONESS	a diabolical lady	
DEMONIAC	possessed; infernal	

DEMONISM	Satanic cult	
DEMONIST	devil worshipper	
DEMONIZE	turn into a devil	
DEMONOMY	dominion of devils	
DEMPSTER	see deemster	
DEMURELY	gravely; sedately; modestly	
DEMURRED	hesitated; wavered; paused	
DEMURRER	a plea; objector	**lw**
DEMYSHIP	an Oxford scholarship	
DENARIUS	former English penny; d	**nm**
DENATURE	denaturalize	
DENDRITE	} receptor; neuron	**pl, bt**
DENDROID		
DENDROIT	tree-like fossil	**mn**
DENEGATE	deny; contradict; refute	
DENEHOLE	shaft cut in chalk	
DENIABLE	controvertible; refutable	
DENOTATE	denote; signify	
DENOTING	indicating; designating	
DENOUNCE	impeach; censure; threaten	
DENTAGRA	toothache	**md**
DENTATED	with teeth; notched	
DENTELLE	tooth-like decoration or edging	
DENTICLE	small projection; teeth in fish	
		zo
DENTIZED	toothed	
DENUDATE	strip bare; divest	
DENUDING	stripteasing	
DEPARTED	left; gone away; withdrew	
DEPARTER	metal refiner	
DEPENDED	relief; trusted; hung	
DEPICTED	described; limned; portrayed	
DEPICTOR	painter; artist	
DEPILATE	remove hair	
DEPLETED	emptied; drained	
DEPLORED	lamented; bewailed; grieved	
DEPLOYED	extended; unfolded	
DEPLUMED	plucked	
DEPONENT	a witness	**lw**
DEPONING	testifying under oath	**lw**
DEPORTED	expelled; banished	
DEPORTEE	reported; forcibly removed	
DEPOSING	ousting; removing	
DEPRAVED	corrupt; vicious; profligate	
DEPRAVER	vilifier; reprobate	
DEPRIVED	robbed; dispossessed	
DEPRIVER	a despoiler; brigand	
DEPURATE	cleanse; purify	
DEPUTING	authorizing; charging	
DEPUTIZE	delegate; act for another	
DERAILED	off the lines	**rw**
DERAILER	train-wrecker	**rw**
DERANGED	disordered; insane; mad	
DERATING	reducing liability	
DERATION	free from restriction	
DERBY-DAY	in June (horse race)	
DERBY-DOG	also ran	
DERBYITE	volunteer of 1915	
DERELICT	abandoned; deserted; left	

DERIDING	mocking; lampooning	
DERISION	laughing stock; mockery	
DERISIVE	scoffing; ridiculous	
DERISORY	scornful; contemptuous	
DERIVATE	a derivative	
DERIVING	deducing; tracing; obtaining	
DERMATIC	relating to the skin	**md**
DEROGATE	disparage; detract	
DESCRIBE	portray; narrate; tell	
DESCRIED	observed; espied; discerned	
DESERTED	forlorn; left; abandoned	
DESERTER	quitter; renegade; turncoat	
DESERVED	justified; merited; earned	
DESERVER	meritorious person	
DESIGNED	projected; invented; drew	
DESIGNER	schemer; contriver	
DESILVER	extract silver from	
DESIRING	craving; wanting	
DESIROUS	covetous; eager; longing	
DESISTED	stopped; ceased; forbore	
DESK-WORK	clerical work	
DESOLATE	solitary; deserted	
DESPATCH	dispatch; hasten; kill	
DESPISAL	contempt; scorn	
DESPISED	disdained; ignored; scouted	
DESPISER	scorner; contemner	
DESPITED	vexed; offended; teased	
DESPOTAT	territory under despot	
DESPOTIC	tyrannical; arbitrary	
DESTINED	ordained; fated	
DESTRIER	second charger	**zo**
DESTRUDO	desire for death, destruction	
		pc
DETACHED	isolated; disengaged	
DETAILED	particularized; recounted	
DETAILER	enumerator; narrator	
DETAINED	delayed; restrained; held	
DETAINER	withholder of goods	**lw**
DETECTED	found out; unmasked	
DETECTOR	detecter; discoverer	
DETERGED	cleansed; wiped	
DETERRED	prevented; hindered	
DETESTED	odious; abominated; loathed	
DETESTER	abhorrer	
DETHRONE	depose; discrown	
DETONATE	explode violently	
DETONIZE	fulminate	
DETRITAL	(detritus); residual	
DETRITED	worn down; eroded	
DETRITUS	disintegrated material	
DETRUDED	extruded; thrust	
DEUCE-ACE	a throw at dice	
DEUCEDLY	confoundedly	
DEUTERON	charged particle	**ch**
DEUTOVUM	development stage in acarina	
		zo
DEVALUED	depreciated	
DEVELOPE	evolve; unfold; amplify	

DEVESTED	divested; alienated	
DEVIANCE	differing from norms	**pc**
DEVIATED	swerved; strayed; veered	
DEVIATOR	a wanderer	
DEVILDOM	kingdom of hell	
DEVILESS	demoness	
DEVILISH	fiendish; malignant; diabolic	
DEVILISM	devil worship	
DEVILKIN	imp	
DEVILLED	highly seasoned; curried	
DEVILTRY	devilry; devilship	
DEVISING	scheming; bequeathing	
DEVOLUTE	transfer; depute	
DEVOLVED	handed over	
DEVONIAN	geological era	**gl, mn**
DEVOTING	dedicating; consecrating	
DEVOTION	zeal; piety; attachment	
DEVOURED	bolted; consumed; gobbled	
DEVOURER	absorber; destroyer	
DEVOUTLY	earnestly; piously; holily	
DEWBERRY	the bramble	**bt**
DEWINESS	precipitation	
DEW-POINT	a critical temperature	
DEWSTONE	a limestone	**mn**
DEXTRINE	starch gum	**ch**
DEXTRONE	synthetic blood	
DEXTROSE	glucose sugar	**ch**
DEXTROUS	dexterous; skilful	
DEZINKED	freed from zinc	
DIABASIC	greenstone type	**mn**
DIABETES	sugar sickness	**md**
DIABETIC	of diabetes	**md**
DIABLERY	diablerie; impishness	
DIABOLIC	satanic; demoniac; fiendish	
DIACETYL	colour/flavour constituent in butter	
DIACHYMA	cellular tissue	**bt**
DIACOELE	3rd brain ventricle in craniata	**zo**
DIACONAL	(deacon)	**rl**
DIACTINE	having two rays	
DIADELPH	twin	**bt**
DIADEMED	crowned	
DIADEXIS	disease mutation	**md**
DIADOCHI	ancient governors (Gr.)	
DIAGLYTH	an intaglio; carved gem	
DIAGNOSE	identify	**md**
DIAGONAL	cross-tie	
DIAGRAPH	drawing instrument	
DIALLAGE	monoclinic pyroxene	**mn**
DIALLAGE	rhetorical argument	
DIALLING	(telephoning)	
DIALOGIC	in dialogue form	
DIALOGUE	two talking; two-way exchange	**cp, tc**
DIALYSIS	filtration of body salts	**ch, md**
DIALYTIC	unbracing	
DIALYZED	} artificial kidney salts filter	
DIALYZER	}	**md, ch**
DIAMANTE	artificial glitter stones	

DIAMETER	an exact bisector	
DIANDRIA	two-stemmed plants	**bt**
DIANODAL	traversing a node	
DIANTHUS	carnations, pinks, etc.	**bt**
DIAPASON	concord of sounds	**mu**
DIAPAUSE	life-cycle stage in insects	**zo**
DIAPENTE	interval of a fifth	**mu**
DIAPERED	figured	
DIAPHANE	transparent woven silk	**tx**
DIAPHONE	electrical fog-signal	
DIAPHONY	part-writing based on plainsong	**mu**
DIARIZED	recorded in a diary	
DIASPORA	Jew dispersion	
DIASPORE	aluminium hydrate	**mn**
DIASTASE	malt sugar	
DIASTEMA	tooth-gap in jaw; stage of protoplasm	
DIASTOLE	heart dilatation	**md**
DIASTYLE	proportion in colonnades	**ar**
DIATOMIC	(two atoms)	**ch**
DIATONIC	natural scale	**mu**
DIATRIBE	stream of invective; tirade	
DIBBLING	planting	
DIBSTONE	stone used in a game	
DICARYON	simultaneously dividing nuclei	**cy**
DICE-COAL	small coal	**mn**
DICENTRA	bleeding-heart	**bt**
DICE-PLAY	dicing	
DICHLONE	chemical fungicide	**ch**
DICHOTIC	contrasting ear simulation	**md**
DICHOTIC	doubled; twinned	
DICHROIC	double refraction	
DICKERED	bargained	
DICLINIC	crystalline shape	
DICLORAN	chemical fungicide	**ch**
DICROTIC	double pulsation	**md**
DICTATED	bid; prescribed; ordained	
DICTATOR	autocrat; despot; tyrant	
DICYCLIC	with 2-whorled perianth	**bt**
DIDACTIC	instructive; moral; directive	
DIDACTYL	with all hind-foot toes separate	
DIDAPPER	dabchick	**zo**
DIDDERED	shivered	
DIDDLING	cheating; trifling; dawdling	
DIDYMATE	in pairs; twins	**bt, zo**
DIDYMIUM	a rare metal	**ch**
DIDYMOUS	growing in pairs	**bt**
DIEGESIS	explanation; narrative	
DIELYTRA	the bleeding-heart	**bt**
DIE-STOCK	die-holder	
DIETETIC	(food regime)	
DIFFERED	disagreed; diverged; varied	
DIFFRACT	break; refract	
DIFFUSED	disseminated; spread	
DIFFUSER	a spray; a damper for chimney or ducts	**bd**
DIGAMIST	married twice	

DIGENITE	cubic copper sulphide	**mn**
DIGESTED	classified; codified; arranged	
DIGESTER	a stock-pot	
DIGGABLE	suitable for spade work	
DIGGINGS	(gold); lodgings	
DIGITATE	having five leaflets	**bt**
DIGITRON	numerical read-out glow tube	
		el
DIGITULE	fingerlike process	**zo**
DIGONOUS	with two angles	**bt**
DIGYNIAN	⎫ flowers having cleft	
DIGYNOUS	⎭ styles	**bt**
DIHEDRAL	angle between planes	
DIHEDRON	geometric figures	
DIHEPTAL	of 14 in number	**el**
DIHYBRID	from parents different in 2	
	aspects	**gn**
DIKETONE	CO-group-containing	
	compound	**ch**
DILATANT	swelling; elastic	
DILATING	expanding; stretching	
DILATION	distention; amplification; by	
	stimulation	**md**
DILATIVE	expansive	
DILATORY	tardy; dallying; lagging	
DILIGENT	busy; industrious; assiduous	
DILLY-BAG	Australian rush-bag	
DILUTING	attenuating; weakening	
DILUTION	watering; reducing	
DILUVIAL	alluvial	
DILUVIUM	glacial or flood deposit	
DIMEDONE	alcohol-detecting reagent	**ch**
DIMEGALY	with different-sized	
	spermatozoa	**zo**
DIMERISM	duplex arrangement	
DIMEROUS	in two parts	
DIMETRIC	tetragonal	
DIMINISH	cut; abate; lessen; curtail	
DIMPLING	smiling	
DIMYARIA	molluscs	**zo**
DINAMODE	unit of work, metre-ton	
DINARCHY	dual control	
DINER-OUT	a table companion	
DING-DONG	hammer and tongs	
DINGHIES	small boats	**nt**
DINGIEST	dullest; dirtiest	
DINORNIS	moa-bird, N. Zealand	**zo**
DINOSAUR	extinct lizard	**zo**
DIOCESAN	a bishop	**rl**
DIOGENIC	(Diogenes); cynical outlook on	
	life	
DIOPSIDE	augite	**mn**
DIOPTASE	copper silicate	
DIOPTRIC	(refraction of light)	
DIORAMIC	(peep-show)	
DIORITIC	(igneous rock, diorite)	**mn**
DIOSCURI	Castor and Pollux	
DIPCHICK	dabchick	**zo**
DIPHASIC	in two phases	
DIPHENYL	coal-tar chemical	

DIPLEGIA	paralysis	**md**
DIPLEXER	two-way transmitter	**el**
DIPLOGEN	deuterium; heavy hydrogen	
DIPLOMAT	ambassador; envoy	
DIPLOPIA	double vision	**md**
DIPLOSIS	chromosome doubling	**cy**
DIPNOOUS	having lungs and gills	**zo**
DIPROTON	two-proton system	
DIPSACUS	the teasel	**bt**
DIPSOSIS	morbid-thirst	**md**
DIPTERAL	with two wings	**zo**
DIPTERAN	a fly	**zo**
DIPTEROS	(double peristyle)	**ar**
DIPTYCHA	writing tablets	
DIRECTED	addressed; enjoined	
DIRECTLY	expressly; soon; forthwith	
DIRECTOR	manager; controller	
DIRENESS	horror; calamity	
DIRHINIA	of both nostrils	**pl, md**
DIRIGENT	directing	
DIRTIEST	filthiest; most sordid	
DIRTYING	fouling; soiling	
DISABLED	incapacitated; crippled	
DISABUSE	enlighten; undeceive	
DISACRYL	acrolin polymer	**ch**
DISADORN	deprive of ornament	
DISAGREE	differ; vary; deviate	
DISALLOW	reject; forbid; disclaim	
DISANNEX	disunite; disjoin	
DISARMED	subdued; stripped	
DISARRAY	disorder; undress	
DISASTER	calamity; catastrophe	
DISBENCH	unseat	
DISBLOOM	disbud	
DISBOSOM	reveal	
DISBOWEL	disembowel	
DISBURSE	expend; spend	
DISCANDY	melt; dissolve	
DISCASED	undressed	
DISCHARM	disenchant	
DISCINCT	ungirded	
DISCIPLE	learner; follower; pupil	
DISCLAIM	disown; reject; renounce	
DISCLOSE	reveal; tell; betray	
DISCOUNT	allowance; forestall; deduct	
DISCOVER	detect; espy; divulge	
DISCRASE	a silver salt	**ch**
DISCREET	circumspect; prudent	
DISCRETE	separate; distinct	
DISCROWN	depose; dethrone	
DISCSEAL	form of valve	
DISEASED	indisposed; unhealthy; sickly	
DISEDGED	blunted	
DISEDIFY	scandalize	
DISENACT	repeal; annul	
DISENDOW	deprive of endowments	
DISENROL	cashier	
DISFLESH	disembody	
DISFROCK	expel from clergy	**rl**
DISGAVEL	a change in tenure	**lw**

DISGORGE	surrender; eject; vent
DISGRACE	ignominy; dishonour
DISGRADE	reduce in rank; disrate
DISGUISE	conceal; mask; cloak
DISHABIT	dislodge
DISHERIT	disinherit
DISHEVEL	disarray
DISHORSE	unhorse
DISINTER	exhume; unbury
DISINURE	render unfamiliar
DISIPPUS	an American butterfly **zo**
DISJOINT	dislocate
DISJUNCT	discontinuous
DISLEAVE	deprive of leaves
DISLIKED	detested; hated; loathed
DISLIKEN	made unlike
DISLODGE	evict; eject; oust
DISLOYAL	false; perfidious
DISMALLY	drearily; dolefully
DISMAYED	terror-struck; appalled
DISMOUNT	alight; descend; unhorse
DISORBED	thrown from its orbit
DISORDER	confusion; turbulence
DISOWNED	repudiated; denied
DISPATCH	despatch; expedite; send
DISPATHY	antipathy; allergy
DISPEACE	unrest; unease
DISPENSE	administer; dispence
DISPERSE	scatter; diffuse; dispel
DISPERSE	redistribute data **cp**
DISPIRIT	discourage; dishearten
DISPLACE	remove; discharge; oust
DISPLAIT	untwist; unravel
DISPLANT	uproot; eradicate
DISPLUME	pluck
DISPONED	disposed
DISPONEE	⎱ (conveyance of property
DISPONER	⎰ in legal form) **lw**
DISPONGE	dispunge; expunge
DISPOPED	deprived of popedom **rl**
DISPOSAL	right of bestowing
DISPOSED	inclined; arranged; biased
DISPOSER	administrator
DISPREAD	extend; expand
DISPRIZE	undervalue; belittle
DISPROOF	refutation; rebuttal
DISPROVE	confute; refute
DISPUNGE	disponge; expunge
DISPUTED	contested; wrangled
DISPUTER	arguer; debater
DISQUIET	to vex; unease; anxiety
DISRATED	reduced in rank; degraded
DISROBED	divested; denuded
DISROBER	raiment remover
DISSEIZE	dispossess **lw**
DISSERVE	to perform an ill turn
DISSEVER	cut in two; rend
DISSIGHT	an eye sore
DISSOLVE	loosen; liquefy; end
DISSUADE	deter; disincline

DISTALIA	5 bones in tetrapod limb **zo**
DISTALLY	remote
DISTANCE	interval; space; outstrip
DISTASTE	aversion; antipathy
DISTHENE	cyanite; kyanite **mn**
DISTINCT	definite; clear
DISTITLE	deprive of right
DISTOMUM	liver-fluke parasite **zo**
DISTRACT	divert; harass; bewilder
DISTRAIN	seize for debt **lw**
DISTRAIT	absent-minded
DISTREAM	overflow
DISTRESS	anguish; suffering; worry
DISTRICT	territory; region; quarter
DISTRUST	discredit; doubt; suspect
DISTUNED	put out of tune
DISUNION	breach of concord
DISUNITE	separate; disrupt
DISUNITY	isolation; dissension
DISUSAGE	disuse; desuetude
DISUSING	abandoning
DISVALUE	underrate; disprize
DISYOKED	untrammelled
DITCH-DOG	dead dog **zo**
DITCHING	excavating; clearing
DITHECAL	with two spore-cases **bt**
DITHEISM	⎱ co-existence of a good
DITHEIST	⎰ and an evil god
DITHERED	shivered; hesitated
DITOKOUS	having twins
DITROITE	coarse-grained alkali/syenite rock **mn**
DITTY-BAG	sailor's kit-bag
DITTY-BOX	sailor's treasure-box
DIURESIS	increased urination **md**
DIURETIC	urination stimulant **md**
DIVAGATE	digress; wander
DIVALENT	bivalent **ch**
DIVE-BOMB	aerial attack
DIVERGED	deviated; digressed; veered
DIVERTED	distracted; amused
DIVERTER	an entertainer
DIVESTED	stripped; deprived; bared
DIVIDEND	interest; share; profit
DIVIDERS	drawing, measuring instrument **ce, nv**
DIVIDING	cleaving; parting
DIVI-DIVI	pods used in tanning **bt**
DIVIDUAL	shared in common
DIVINELY	heavenly; exquisitely
DIVINIFY	treat as divine
DIVINITY	deity; theology **rl**
DIVINIZE	divinise; deify
DIVISION	category; army unit
DIVISIVE	dissentient; discordant
DIVORCED	forced assunder
DIVORCEE	person divorced
DIVORCER	divorcing person
DIVULGED	communicated; revealed
DIVULGER	betrayer of secrets

DIZENING	dressing gaudily	
DIZZYING	confusing	
DOCETISM	doctrine of a sect	**rl**
DOCETIST	a 2nd-century heretic	**rl**
DOCHMIAC	Greek metrical foot	
DOCILITY	pliance; tameness	
DOCIMACY	metallurgy	
DOCKIZED	erected docks	
DOCKYARD	naval establishment	**nt**
DOCTORAL	(doctor)	
DOCTORED	treated; doped	**md**
DOCTORLY	scholarly	
DOCTRINE	dogma; creed; tenet	
DOCUMENT	writing; record; writ; account	**lw**
DODDERED	quaked; tottered	
DODDERER	senile senior	
DODECANE	paraffin	**ch**
DODIPOLL	dolt; numbskull	
DODONIAN	oracular	
DOGBERRY	ignorant parish official	
DOG-BRIER	dog-rose	**bt**
DOG-CHEAP	bargain price	
DOG-EARED	crinkled corner	
DOGESHIP	Venetian office	
DOG-FACED	unprepossessing	
DOGGEDLY	obstinately; stolidly	
DOGGEREL	bad verse	
DOGGONED	confounded	
DOG-GRASS	couch grass	**bt**
DOG-HOUSE	kennel	
DOG-LATIN	barbarous Latin	
DOG-LEECH	a vet	
DOGMATIC	dictatorial; arbitrary	
DOG'S-BANE	a poisonous plant	**bt**
DOG'S-BODY	utility man	
DOG-SLEEP	cat-nap	
DOG'S-MEAT	offal	
DOG'S-NOSE	beer and gin	
DOG-TIRED	spent	
DOG-TOOTH	a Norman moulding	**ar**
DOG-TRICK	a currish wile	
DOG-WATCH	short ½ watch	**nt**
DOG-WEARY	exhausted	
DOG-WHEAT	dog-grass	**bt**
DOG-WHELK	kind of mollusc	**zo**
DOLDRUMS	calm zone; depression	
DOLERITE	medium-grain-size igneous rock	**gl**
DOLESOME	dismal; rueful	
DOLICHOS	hyacinth bean	**bt**
DO-LITTLE	lazy-bones	
DOLLARED	flush; wealthy	
DOLLED-UP	dressed showily	
DOLLHOOD	dollship	
DOLLY-MOP	handled mop	
DOLLY-TUB	washing tub	
DOLOMITE	magnesian limestone	**mn**
DOLOROSO	pathetically	**mu**
DOLOROUS	sorrowful; dolesome	

DOMAINAL	} (landed estate); (scope)	
DOMANIAL		
DOMELIKE	dome shaped	
DOMESMAN	judge; umpire	
DOMESTIC	household; maid	
DOMICILE	habitation; residence	
DOMIFIED	(horoscope)	
DOMINANT	prevailing; ruling; 5th note of scale	**mu**
DOMINATE	control; override	
DOMINEER	to hector; to sway	
DOMINION	sovereignty	
DOMINIUM	ownership	
DOMINOES	hooded capes; a game	
DONATING	giving; bestowing	
DONATION	presentation; offering; alms	
DONATISM	a Christian cult	**rl**
DONATIVE	gratuity; benefice; largesse	
DONATORY	recipient of land	**lw**
DONNERED	stunned (Sc.)	
DOOLTREE	duletree; the gallows	
DOOM-PALM	Egyptian palm	**bt**
DOOMSDAY	domesday (Book)	
DOOMSMAN	domesman; judge	
DOOR-BELL	a ringer	
DOOR-CASE	door framework	
DOOR-KNOB	a handle	
DOORLESS	without portal	
DOORNAIL	considered as dead	
DOOR-POST	regarded as deaf	
DOOR-SILL	lower framework	
DOOR-STEP	slice of bread (slang)	
DOOR-YARD	an enclosure	
DORICISM	Doric in expression	
DORMANCY	abeyance; latency	
DORMOUSE	somnolent rodent	**zo**
DORR-HAWK	night jar	**zo**
DORSALIS	dorsal organ artery	**zo**
DOSOLOGY	science of doses	**md**
DOTATION	donation; dowry	
DOTINGLY	stupidly; fondly	
DOTTEREL	a plover	**zo**
DOUANIER	custom-house officer (Fr.)	
DOUBLETS	(dice)	
DOUBLING	folding; running	
DOUBLOON	Spanish guinea	**nm**
DOUBLURE	book-binding	
DOUBTFUL	uncertain; ambiguous	
DOUBTING	distrusting; querying	
DOUBTIVE	questionable; dubious	
DOUCHING	spraying	
DOUGHBOY	American soldier	
DOUGHNUT	a confection	
DOUM-PALM	doom-palm	**bt**
DOURNESS	obstinacy; grimness	
DOVECOTE	pigeon house	
DOVE-EYED	meek-eyed	
DOVELIKE	gentle; innocent	
DOVERING	snoozing	
DOVESHIP	qualities of a dove	

DOVETAIL	a joint; synchronise	
DOWDYISH	rather slovenly	
DOWDYISM	shabbiness	
DOWELLED	pinned together	
DOWEL-PIN	a fastening	
DOWERING	endowing; bequeathing	
DOWFNESS	lethargy; dullness	
DOWNBEAR	depress	
DOWN-BEAT	descending stroke (conductor); gloomy; relaxed; informal	**mu**
DOWNBORE	discouraged	
DOWNCAST	dejected	
DOWNCOME	sudden fall	
DOWNFALL	debacle; ruin	
DOWNHAUL	a sheet	**nt**
DOWNHILL	a declivity	
DOWNLAND	hilly pasture land	
DOWN-LINE	(railways)	
DOWNPIPE	rainwater runaway	
DOWNPOUR	continuous heavy rain	
DOWNRUSH	downward draught	
DOWN-TIME	depression; machine inoperable	**pc, cp, tc**
DOWNTOWN	business centre	
DOWNTROD	trampled; tyrannised	
DOWNWARD	descending	
DOWNWEED	cotton weed	**bt**
DOXOLOGY	hymn of praise	**rl**
DOZINESS	drowsiness	
DRABBETT	} twilled linen used for	
DRABETTE	} smocks	
DRABBISH	slatternly; dowdy	
DRABBLED	fouled with mire	
DRABBLER	a sail extension	**nt**
DRACANTH	gum; tragacanth	**bt**
DRACONIC	(Draco); severe	
DRACONIN	dragon's blood	
DRAFFISH	dreggy; worthless	
DRAFT-BAR	swingle-tree	
DRAFTING	sketching; drawing up; conscripting; formulating	
DRAFTING	technique of cycling, driving	
DRAG-BOLT	draw-bar	
DRAGGING	tugging; tedious; forbidden footwork (netball); (motor racing)	
DRAGGLED	wet and dirty	
DRAG-HOOK	a connection	
DRAG-HUNT	foxing the hounds with a scented trail	
DRAGOMAN	guide; interpreter	
DRAGONET	small dragon; a fish	**zo**
DRAGONNE	heraldic lion-dragon	**hd**
DRAG-SHOE	a brake	
DRAGSMAN	coach-driver (horse-drawn)	
DRAILING	trailing; draggling	
DRAINAGE	sewage system	
DRAINING	emptying; exhausting	
DRAMATIC	theatrical; powerful voice	

DRAMBUIE	whisky liqueur	
DRAMMOCK	drummock; skilly; gruel	
DRAM-SHOP	shebeen; illicit bar	
DRAUGHTS	a game	
DRAUGHTY	inconveniently airy	
DRAWABLE	representable	
DRAWBACK	detriment; defect	
DRAWBOLT	coupling pin	
DRAWBORE	carpentry	
DRAWGATE	sluice gate	
DRAW-GEAR	harness; railway coupling	
DRAWLING	droning	
DRAW-LINK	a couple	
DRAW-WELL	deep well	
DREADFUL	frightful; dire; horrific	
DREADING	fearing; awing	
DREAMERY	reverie	
DREAMFUL	fanciful; dreamy	
DREAMILY	vaguely	
DREAMING	imagining	
DREARILY	gloomily; dismally	
DREDGING	deepening; sprinkling; underwater excavation	**ce**
DREGGISH	foul with lees	
DRENCHED	saturated; inundated	
DRENCHER	a soaker	
DRESSAGE	training of horses competition	
DRESSING	alignment; draping; binding; finishing stonework	**md, bd**
DRIBBLED	slavered	
DRIBBLER	(footballer)	
DRIBBLET	a small drop	
DRIFTAGE	leeway	**nt**
DRIFT-ICE	bits of iceberg	
DRIFTING	passively awaiting events	
DRIFT-NET	drifting herring net	
DRIFT-WAY	cattle-road; leeway	
DRILL-BOW	a boring device	**to**
DRILL-BOX	seed-box	
DRILLING	training; perforating	
DRINKING	imbibing; carousing	
DRIP-FLAP	part of balloon	**ae**
DRIPPING	(fat); (tap)	
DRIVABLE	conducible	
DRIVEWAY	} private access road (USA)	
DRIVE	}	
DRIZZLED	rained	
DROGHING	coastal trade, W. Indies	
DROILING	drudging; loitering	
DROLLERY	buffoonery; waggery	
DROLLING	jesting; clowning	
DROLLISH	fairly facetious	
DROMICAL	(race-course)	
DRONE-FLY	drone-bee	**zo**
DROOLING	slavering; slobbering	
DROOPING	withering; languishing	
DROP-DOWN	short first title in book	
DROP-GOAL	four points	
DROPHEAD	convertible automobile	**au**
DROPKICK	football	

DROPPING	flock of sheldrakes	**zo**
DROP-RIPE	ready to fall	
DROPSHOT	tennis	
DROP-SLIP	book stockist's order	
DROPWISE	in drops	
DROPWORT	meadow-sweet	**bt**
DROTCHEL	idle wench; slut	
DROUGHTY	thirsty; arid	
DROWNING	submerging; overwhelming	
DROWSILY	sleepily	
DROWSING	dozing	
DRUBBING	beating; mauling	
DRUDGERY	slavery; ignoble toil	
DRUDGING	moiling; plodding	
DRUDGISM	menial occupation	
DRUGFAST	drugproof; immune	**md**
DRUGGING	inducing stupor	
DRUGGIST	chemist; chymist	
DRUIDESS	lady soothsayer	
DRUIDISM	Celtic cult	
DRUMFIRE	continuous fire	
DRUMFISH	North American fish	**zo**
DRUMHEAD	(service; court-martial)	
DRUMMING	vibrating	
DRUNKARD	toper; dipsomaniac	
DRY-BIBLE	cattle-disease	**zo**
DRY-CLEAN	without using water	
DRY-FLIES	artificial gerats as bait (angling)	
DRY-GOODS	drapery	
DRY-PLATE	photographic plate	
DRY-POINT	engraving needle	
DRY-STEAM	(no unevaporated water)	
DRY-STONE	(no mortar used)	
DRY-STOVE	hot-house	
DUALIZED	halved; split in twain	
DUBITATE	to doubt; to vacillate	
DUCATOON	scudo; silver coin	**nm**
DUCHESSE	a table-cover	
DUCKBILL	platypus	**zo**
DUCK-DIVE	swimming-dive	
DUCK-FOOT	lowered inverted commas	
DUCK-HAWK	marsh-harrier	**zo**
DUCK-HOOK	very low stroke to left (golf)	
DUCKLING	young duck	**zo**
DUCK-MOLE	duckbill	**zo**
DUCKPINS	variation of ten pins alley	
DUCK'S-EGG	a zero (cricket)	
DUCK-SHOT	pellets for wild fowl	
DUCK-WEED	a water weed	**bt**
DUCTLESS	endocrine gland	**md**
DUELLING	} fighting in single combat	
DUELLIST		
DUELSOME	prone to duelling	
DUETTINO	short duet	**mu**
DUETTIST	a performer	**mu**
DUKELING	a petty duke	
DUKERIES	ducal country seats	
DUKESHIP	ducal rank	
DULCIANA	(It.) soft organ stop	**mu**

DULCIMER	stringed instrument; today the Cimbalom (Hung.)	**mu**
DULCITOR	saccharine	
DULE-TREE	dool-tree; the gallows	
DULL-EYED	lacking expression	
DULL-HEAD	a dolt	
DULLNESS	dulness; apathy	
DUMB-BELL	no ringing tone	
DUMB-CAKE	(baked on St. Mark's Eve)	
DUMB-CANE	(causing dumbness)	**bt**
DUMBNESS	muteness	
DUMB-SHOW	pantomime	
DUMMERER	bogus mute	
DUMOSITY	prickliness	
DUMPLING	pudding; abutment	**bd**
DUNCEDOM	the class of dunces	
DUN-DIVER	goosander	**zo**
DUNGAREE	Indian cloth; overalls	
DUNG-FORK	a gardening implement	
DUNG-HILL	cock's castle	
DUNG-MERE	} manure pit	
DUNG YARD		
DUODENAL	} the first of the small intestines	**md**
DUODENUM		
DUOLOGUE	conversation	
DUOPHASE	choke-use in valve circuit	**el**
DUPLEXER	two channel multiplexer (radar)	**ps**
DURATION	indefinite length of time	
DUSKNESS	twilight	
DUST-BALL	horse disease	
DUST-CART	rubbish conveyor	
DUST-COAT	light overcoat	
DUST-HOLE	ash-bin	
DUSTWELL	dust in glacial hollow	**gl**
DUTCHMAN	Hollander	
DUTIABLE	subject to customs	
DUTY-FREE	not customary	
DWARFING	stunting; overshadowing	
DWARFISH	pygmy; undersized; tiny	
DWARFISM	growth-hindering condition	**md**
DWELLING	domicile; habitat	
DWINDLED	declined; shrank	
DYE-HOUSE	where dyeing is done	
DYE-STUFF	dye material	
DYEWORKS	coloration factory	
DYNAMICS	masses in motion; gradations (loud & soft) in music	**ps** **mu**
DYNAMISM	} the theory of imminent energy	
DYNAMIST		
DYNAMITE	powerful explosive	
DYNASHIP	modern automaton sailing ship	**nt**
DYNASTIC	in succession	
DYNATRON	electrical oscillation	
DYSBASIA	walking difficulty	**md**
DYSCHROA	skin disease	**md**
DYSGENIC	detrimental to the race	
DYSLALIA	over-age baby talk	

DYSLEXIA	reading learning difficulty	
DYSLUITE	manganese ore	mn
DYSODILE	lignite	mn
DYSOPSIA	dimness of sight	md
DYSOREXY	depraved appetite	md
DYSPATHY	antipathy	
DYSPEPSY	indigestion	md
DYSPHONY	difficulty of speaking	
DYSPNOEA	difficulty in breathing	md
DYSTOCIA	difficult birth-labour	md
DYSTOMIC	(imperfect fracture)	mn
DYSTONIA	impaired muscle tone	md

E

EAGLE-OWL	great horned owl	zo
EAGLE-RAY	devil-fish	zo
EAR-BORED	(for ear-rings)	
EARPHONE	a receiver	
EAR-SHELL	a sea-shell	zo
EARTH-BAG	sandbag	
EARTH-FED	earthly contented	
EARTH-HOG	aardvark	zo
EARTHING	burrowing; burying	
EARTH-NUT	pig-nut; peanut	bt
EARTH-PEA	hog peanut	bt
EAR-TO-EAR	a definite distance	
EASELESS	non-stop; uneasy	
EASEMENT	relief; privilege; right of passage	lw
EASINESS	facility; comfort; quiet	
EASTERLY	oriental	
EASTLAND	the Orient	
EASTMOST	farthest east	
EASTWARD	toward the rising sun	
EASY-CARE	minimal-creasing fabrics	tx
EAU-DE-NIL	dull green colour (Nile)	
EAU-DE-VIE	brandy; akvavit	
EBENEZER	memorial stone; chapel	
EBIONISE	(Jewish Christian sect	
EBIONISM	that upheld the	
EBIONITE	Mosaic laws)	rl
EBLANINE	volatile crystal	ch
EBONIZED	blackened	
EBRIATED	intoxicated	
EBURNEAN	like ivory	
EBURNINE	like ivory	
ECAUDATE	tailless; Manx	zo
ECCLESIA	an assembly; a church	rl
ECCYESIS	external foetus development	
ECGONINE	coca-base alkaloid	ch
ECHINATE	prickly; bristled	
ECHINITE	fossil sea-urchin	mn
ECHINOID	like a sea-urchin	zo
ECHINOPS	globe thistle, etc.	bt
ECHIODON	sand-eel type	zo
ECHOLESS	no repetition	
ECLAMPSY	epilepsy	md
ECLECTIC	selected; picked	

ECLIPSED	obscured; disgraced	
ECLIPTIC	a great circle	
ECLOGITE	crystalline rock	mn
ECLOSION	emergence from egg case	zo
ECMNESIA	loss of short items of memory	pc
ECOCLINE	trans-habitat cline	ec
ECONOMIC	frugal; thrifty; careful	
ECOPHENE	physiologically habitat-affected type	
ECOSTATE	ribless	bt
ECPHASIS	explicit declaration	
ECPHORIA	establishing memory trace	pc
ECRASEUR	surgical instrument	md
ECSTATIC	rapturous; beatific	
ECTOCYST	outer cyst layer; exoskeleton	zo
ECTODERM	outer skin, also of embryo	md
ECTOGENY	pollen effect on female plant organs	bt
ECTOLOPH	mammalian tooth edge	zo
ECTOZOAN	an external parasite	zo
ECUMENIC	universal; catholic; general	
EDACIOUS	greedy; voracious	
EDDERING	making up fences	
EDDY-WIND	back draught	
EDENTATA	animal lacking front teeth	
EDENTATE		zo
EDGE-BONE	aitch bone; rump bone	
EDGELESS	blunt	
EDGE-RAIL	an iron rail	
EDGE-TOOL	cutting tool	to
EDGEWAYS	sideways	
EDGEWISE	sideways	
EDGINESS	angularity	
EDIFYING	enlightening; instructive	
EDITRESS	woman editor	
EDUCABLE	teachable	
EDUCATED	instructed; taught; literate	
EDUCATOR	tutor	
EDUCIBLE	deducible; extractible	
EDUCTION	extraction; deduction	
EEL-GRASS	grass-wrack	bt
EEL-SPEAR	fisherman's fork	
EELWORMS	plant-parasites; nematodes	zo
EERINESS	weirdness; creepiness	
EFFACING	expunging; deleting; erasing	
EFFECTED	accomplished; executed	
EFFECTOR	effecter; creator; doer; realiser	
EFFECTOR	active organ cells	pl
EFFERENT	conveying outward	
EFFICACY	production power	
EFFIGIAL	relating to images	
EFFIGIES	images; likenesses; guys	
EFFLUENT	a stream; outflow; with sewage	
EFFLUVIA	noxious exhalations	
EFFORCED	ravished; compelled	
EFFULGED	shone; beamed	

EFFUSING	shedding; pouring	
EFFUSION	emanation	
EFFUSIVE	demonstrative	
EFTSOONS	soon after; again	
EGESTING	discharging	
EGESTION	excretion	
EGG-APPLE	brinjal; aubergine	**bt**
EGG-DANCE	ancient blindfold hop	
EGG-GLAIR	pre-gilding eggwhite surface	**pt**
EGG-GLASS	sand-glass	
EGG-PLANT	brinjal; aubergine	**bt**
EGG-SHELL	thin porcelain; paint	
EGG-SLICE	frying spatula	**ck**
EGG-SPOON	small pointed spoon	
EGG-TOOTH	knob on chick's beak	
EGG-WHISK	wire brush	
EGLATERE	eglantine; sweetbriar	**bt**
EGO-ALIEN	refusal to accept self	**pc**
EGOISTIC	self-assertive; self-contained	
EGOMANIA	self-preoccupation	**pc**
EGOPATHY	aggressive; boasting	**pc**
EGOPHONY	a pleurisy symptom	**md**
EGOTIZED	self-conceited	
EGRESSED	departed; left	
EGYPTIAN	(Egypt); gipsy; tiny peg	
EIGHTEEN	$1\frac{1}{2}$ dozen	
EIGHTHLY	an ordinal number	
EJECTING	rejecting; cashiering	
EJECTION	discharge; dismissal	
EJECTIVE	expulsive; emissive	
ELAIDATE	} castor-oil derivative	**ch**
ELAIODIC		
ELANCING	darting; casting; launching	
ELAPHINE	like a stag	**zo**
ELAPSING	slipping away	
ELAPSION	lapse; interval	
ELASTICS	pack opening bands (parachuting)	
ELATEDLY	in high spirits	
ELATERIN	cucumber extract	**ch**
ELBOWING	jostling; nudging	
ELDER-GUN	pop-gun	
ELDORADO	land of fabulous wealth	
ELDRITCH	weird (Sc.)	
ELECTING	choosing; preferring	
ELECTION	freewill; choice; acceptance	
ELECTIVE	selective; preferential	
ELECTRET	permanently polarized material	**el**
ELECTRIC	stimulating	
ELECTRON	(negative electricity)	
ELECTRUM	silver and gold alloy	
ELEGANCE	refinement; taste; grace	
ELEGANCY	beauty of propriety	
ELEGANTE	lady of fashion	
ELEGIAST	sorrowful bard	
ELEGIZED	lamented in verse	
ELENCHIC	elenctic; refutatory	
ELENCHUS	a sophism	

ELEPHANT	size of paper; mammoth	**zo**
ELEUSINE	tropical grass	**bt**
ELEVATED	high; exalted; dignified	
ELEVATOR	a lift; animator; tail plane flap; (wrestling)	
ELEVENTH	ordinal number; (last hour)	
ELF-ARROW	flint arrow-head	
ELF-CHILD	a changeling	
ELICITED	deduced; extracted; evoked	
ELIDABLE	suppressible	
ELIGIBLE	fit; fully qualified	
ELIGIBLY	desirably; worthily	
ELIMATED	polished; smoothed	
ELINGUID	tongue-tied	
ELLIPSIS	gap; omission; hiatus	
ELLIPTIC	oval	
ELOCULAR	without partitions	
ELOINING	banishing	
ELONGATE	stretch; extend; lengthen	
ELOQUENT	fluent and impressive	
ELSEWISE	otherwise; differently	
ELUDIBLE	avoidable; escapable	
ELVANITE	crystalline rock	**mn**
ELVE-LOCK	elf-lock	
ELVISHLY	mischievously; impishly	
ELYDORIC	oil and water-colour	
ELYTRINE	(beetle wing material)	**zo**
EMACIATE	waste away; decline; pine	
EMANATED	derived from; originated	
EMBALING	bundling; packing	
EMBALMED	filled with sweet scent	
EMBALMER	preserver; mortician	
EMBANKED	mounded	
EMBARKED	ventured; undertook	
EMBARRED	encaged; shut in	
EMBATTLE	draw up for battle	
EMBAYING	enclosing in a bay	**nt**
EMBEDDED	firmly established	
EMBEZZLE	appropriate; peculate	
EMBITTER	exacerbate; exasperate	
EMBLAZED	displayed; bedecked	
EMBLAZON	blaze; adorn; embellish	
EMBODIED	incorporated; integrated	
EMBODIER	codifier; merger	
EMBOGGED	mired; bogged	
EMBOGUED	emptied; discharged; fell	
EMBOLDEN	encourage; reassure; impel	
EMBOLISM	intercalation; obstruction	**md**
EMBOLITE	a silver ore	**mn**
EMBOLIUM	narrow corium strip in hemiptera	
EMBORDER	adorn with a border	
EMBOSSED	ornamented in relief	
EMBOSSER	a craftsman	
EMBOTTLE	to bottle	
EMBOWING	arching; vaulting	
EMBRACED	embodied; clasped; hugged	
EMBRACER	corrupter of a jury	**lw**
EMBRAVED	inspired (obs.)	
EMBRONZE	fashion in bronze	

461

EMBRUTED	brutalized	
EMBRYOUS	inaugural	
EMBUSQUE	shirker in a cushy job (Fr.)	
EMBUSSED	loaded on a bus	
EMENDALS	repair-work	
EMENDATE	to correct; to rectify	
EMENDING	amending; reforming	
EMERGENT	pressing; urgent	
EMERGING	issuing; arising	
EMERITED	put on retired list	
EMERITUS	retired with honour	
EMERSION	reappearance; emergence	
EMETICAL	ejective	md
EMIGRANT	distant home seeker	
EMIGRATE	migrate; remove	
EMINENCE	distinction; celebrity	
EMINENCY	a title	
EMISSARY	envoy; spy; agent	
EMISSILE	capable of being emitted	
EMISSION	discharge; ejection	
EMISSIVE	emanative; expulsive	
EMISSORY	a duct; channel	md
EMITTING	issuing; delivering	
EMMANUEL	Immanuel; Messiah	rl
EMMARBLE	enmarble; petrify	
EMMEWING	confining; penning	
EMPACKET	to pack up	
EMPALING	transfixing	
EMPARKED	enclosed	
EMPATRON	patronise	
EMPAWNED	pledged	
EMPEOPLE	populate (obs.)	
EMPERISH	impair (obs.)	
EMPHASIS	stress; force; accent	
EMPHATIC	definite; positive; earnest	
EMPIERCE	pierce (obs.)	
EMPLANED	boarded an aeroplane	
EMPLOYED	at work; occupied	
EMPLOYEE	a wage earner; hand	
EMPLOYER	the boss	
EMPLUMED	plumed	
EMPLUNGE	plunge (obs.)	
EMPOISON	embitter; envenom	
EMPORIUM	large store; mart	
EMPTYING	exhausting; discharging	
EMPTYSIS	haemorrhage	md
EMPURPLE	to dye	
EMPUZZLE	mystify; bewilder; nonplus	
EMPYREAL	ethereal aerial; sublime	
EMPYREAN	highest; heaven	
EMULATED	vied; strove; competed	
EMULATOR	rival; copyist; bridging device	
		pc
EMULGENT	flowing; oozing	
EMULSIFY	liquate; blend	
EMULSINE	a fermented mixture	
EMULSION	milky liquid	
EMULSIVE	milk-like	
ENABLING	empowering; allowing	
ENACTING	decreeing; ordaining	

ENACTIVE	authoritative	
ENACTURE	purpose; action (Shak.)	
ENALLAGE	change of tense, etc.	
ENALURON	heraldic bordure	hd
ENARCHED	like a rainbow	
ENASCENT	being born	
ENAUNTER	lest by chance (obs.)	
ENCAENIA	festival; commemoration	
ENCAGING	confining; mewing	
ENCALLOW	brick claypit surface mould	bd
ENCAMPED	pitched; settled	
ENCARPUS	festoon of fruit	ar
ENCASHED	realized; cashed	
ENCASING	boxing; packing	
ENCASTRE	end-fixed, of a beam	bd
ENCAVING	hiding in a cave	
ENCEINTE	pregnant; main enclosure of a castle	ar
ENCHAFER	warmed up (obs.)	
ENCHARGE	to trust	
ENCHASED	decorated	
ENCHISEL	to chisel	
ENCHORIC	demotic	
ENCIRCLE	encompass; hem; environ	
ENCLISIS	} (grammatical	
ENCLITIC	} accentuation)	
ENCLOSED	wrapped; enveloped	
ENCLOSER	incloser	
ENCLOTHE	to clothe	
ENCOFFIN	prepare for burial	
ENCOLLAR	encircle	
ENCOLOUR	tinge	
ENCOLURE	horse's mane	
ENCOMIUM	panegyric; eulogy	
ENCORING	calling for a repeat	
ENCRADLE	lay in a cradle	
ENCRINAL	} (fossilized sea-lilies)	mn
ENCRINIC	}	
ENCROACH	trench; intrude; infringe	
ENCUMBER	burden; clog; obstruct	
ENCURLED	interlaced	
ENCYCLIC	circular	
ENCYSTED	enclosed in a wart or shell	md
ENDAMAGE	cause loss; spoil	
ENDANGER	hazard; imperil; jeopardize	
ENDEARED	beloved; made fond	
ENDEMIAL	locally prevalent	
ENDENIZE	naturalize	
ENDERMIC	(through the skin)	md
ENDOCARP	inner coat of fruit	bt
ENDOCYST	inner membrane	zo
ENDODERM	inner skin	zo
ENDOGAMY	tribal intermarriage	
END-ORGAN	receptor, motor nerve	pl
ENDORSED	ratified; approved	
ENDORSEE	the assignee	
ENDOSARC	endoplasm	bt
ENDOSOME	protozoa nuclei central mass	zo

ENDOWING	presenting; bequeathing	
ENDOZOIC	living inside animal	**bt**
ENDPAPER	link between cover & book	
END-PLATE	muscle motor-nerve ending	**zo**
END-PLATE	type of electrode	**el**
ENDRUDGE	enslave	
ENDURING	lasting; persisting	
ENERGICO	with vitality	**mu**
ENERGIZE	animate; excite; force	
ENERVATE	weaken; sap; relax	
ENFACING	(cf. endorsing)	
ENFAMISH	to famish	
ENFEEBLE	debilitate; paralyse	
ENFETTER	manacle; shackle	
ENFILADE	to rake; gunfire volley in	
	battle; doors in sequence	**ar**
ENFOLDED	clasped; enclosed	
ENFORCED	compelled; obliged	
ENFORCER	active agent; rules referee;	
	cop; pressurizer	
ENFOREST	afforest	**fr**
ENFORMED	fashioned	
ENFRAMED	placed in a frame	
ENGAGING	winning; charming	
ENGENDER	produce; beget	
ENGILDED	gilt	
ENGINEER	scheme; a sapper; (civil);	
	mechanic; fitter, contriver	
ENGINERY	implement of war	
ENGINING	contriving; racking	
ENGIRDED	encircled	
ENGIRDLE	encompass; encircle	
ENGLANTE	heraldic acorns, etc.	**hd**
ENGORGED	glutted	
ENGOULED	heraldic absorption	**hd**
ENGRAVED	scribed; chiselled; cut	
ENGRAVER	carver; sculptor	
ENGROOVE	cut a furrow	
ENGULFED	devoured; overwhelmed	
ENHANCED	heightened; raised	
ENHANCER	augmenter	
ENHARDEN	encourage; harden	
ENHUNGER	affamish	
ENHYDRIC	containing moisture	
ENJAILED	put in prison; jugged	
ENJOINED	commanded; directed	
ENJOINER	prohibiter	
ENJOYING	appreciating; delighting in	
ENKERNEL	put in a nutshell	
ENKINDLE	rouse; inflame; ignite	
ENLACING	encircling; entwining	
ENLARDED	basted	
ENLARGED	dilated; expanded	
ENLARGER	an amplifier	
ENLINKED	coupled; connected	
ENLISTED	enrolled; engaged	
ENLOCKED	enclosed; shut up	
ENMARBLE	emmarble; harden	
ENMESHED	entrapped; caught	
ENMOSSED	mossy	

ENMURING	immuring; imprisoning	
ENNEADIC	nine of	
ENNEAGON	nine-sided polygon	
ENNEATIC	ninth	
ENNOBLED	made illustrious	
ENORMITY	atrocity; depravity	
ENORMOUS	vast; monstrous; gigantic	
ENOUNCED	proclaimed; enunciated	
ENPLANED	(cf. entrained)	
ENQUIRED	inquired; investigated	
ENQUIRER	a snooper; questioner	
ENRAGING	maddening; exasperating	
ENRAVISH	enrapture; entrance	
ENRICHED	endowed; adorned	
ENRICHER	a fertilizer	
ENRIDGED	furrowed; corrugated	
ENRINGED	encircled	
ENROBING	dressing	
ENROLLED	registered; recorded	
ENROLLER	inscriber	
ENROOTED	firmly fixed; established	
ENSALADA	onion/tomato salad (Sp.)	**ck**
ENSAMPLE	a pattern; a model	
ENSCONCE	protect; hide; harbour	
ENSEALED	sealed up	
ENSEAMED	seamed	
ENSEARED	dried up	
ENSEMBLE	all together	**mu**
ENSHIELD	guard; screen	
ENSHRINE	treasure; cherish	
ENSHROUD	veil; mask; conceal	
ENSIFORM	like a sword	
ENSIGNCY	rank of ensign	
ENSIGNED	distinctively marked	
ENSILAGE	preservation of fodder	
ENSILING	storing in a pit	
ENSLAVED	in bondage; enthralled	
ENSLAVER	captor; subjugator	
ENSNARED	trapped; inveigled	
ENSOULED	animated	
ENSPHERE	englobe	
ENSTYLED	by name of	
ENSURING	assuring; safe-guarding	
ENSWATHE	bandage; wrap	
ENTACKLE	supply with gear	
ENTAILED	settled on heirs	
ENTAILER	a deviser	
ENTANGLE	mat; ravel; implicate	
ENTELLUS	sacred monkey	**zo**
ENTENDER	treat kindly	
ENTERING	penetrating; noting	
ENTHALPY	thermodynamic property	
ENTHRILL	to pierce (obs.)	
ENTHRONE	install; exalt; elevate	
ENTHUSED	became ardent	
ENTICING	alluring; coaxing	
ENTIRELY	fully; perfectly	
ENTIRETY	aggregate; completeness	
ENTITLED	styled; dubbed; empowered	
ENTOILED	snared; trapped	

463

ENTOMBED	buried; interred	
ENTOMOID	like an insect	zo
ENTOPTIC	inner vision	
ENTOZOIC }	referring to internal	
ENTOZOON }	parasites	zo
ENTR'ACTE	an interval	mu
ENTRAILS	internal parts; offal	md
ENTRANCE	entry; to ravish	
ENTREATY	urgent request; petition	
ENTREMET	sweet dish	ck
ENTRENCH	fortify; encroach	
ENTREPAS	an amble (Fr.)	
ENTREPOT	emporium; transit depot	
ENTRESOL	mezzanine storey	
ENTWINED	woven; plaited; twisted	
ENURESIS	incontinence	md, pc
ENVAPOUR	surround with vapour	
ENVASSAL	enslave; enthral	
ENVEIGLE	inveigle; lure; seduce	
ENVELOPE	a cover; surround; dirigible gasbag	
ENVELOPE	pre- and suffix data code signals	cp, tc
ENVIABLE	most desirable	
ENVIABLY	covetously; grudgingly	
ENVIRONS	suburbs; vicinity	
ENVISAGE	to face; to consider	
ENVOLUME	include	
ENZOOTIC	(localized disease)	zo
EOLIENNE	dress material; silk and wool	
EOLIPILE	experimental flask	
EOLITHIC	pre-paleolithic	gl
EPAGOGIC	inductive	
EPALPATE	no feelers	zo
EPANODOS	rhetorical recapitulation	
EPENDYMA	spinal cord epithelium in vertebrates	
EPENETIC	laudatory	
EPHEMERA	may-flies; etc.	zo
EPHESIAN	debauchee; (Ephesus)	
EPIBLAST	outer skin	md
EPICALEX	outer calyx	bt
EPICERIE	grocery; spices (Fr.)	
EPICOELE	cerebellum ventricle in craniata	zo
EPICOLIC	(abdomen over colon)	md
EPICOTYL	axis of feather or seedling	bt, zo
EPICRINE	type of secretion gland	cy
EPICYCLE	circulating circle	
EPIDEMIC	locally prevalent	md
EPIDOTIC	(vitreous ore)	mn
EPIGAMIC	appealing to opposite sex	zo
EPIGEOUS	low growing	bt
EPIGRAPH	motto; inscription	
EPILEPSY	fits	md
EPILOGIC	concluding	
EPILOGUE	farewell speech	
EPIMACUS	heraldic griffin	hd
EPIMERAL	(segment above joint)	zo
EPIMERON	posterior of sclerites in insects	
EPIMORPH	crystal natural cast	mn
EPINASTY	curvature	bt
EPINOSIC	advantage by illness	pc
EPIORNIS	extinct bird (Madagascar)	zo
EPIPHANY	January 6th	rl
EPIPHORA	streams of tears	md
EPIPHYTE	(mistletoe, orchids), non-parasitic cohabiting plant	bt
EPIPLASM	residual cytoplasm in ascus	bt
EPIPLOCE	rhetorical climax	
EPIPODIA	lateral foot lobes in gastropoda	zo
EPIPOLIC	fluorescent	
EPIPROCT	plate over insect anus	zo
EPIPUBIC	before or above pubis	zo
EPISCOPE	projection lantern	lt
EPISCOPY	superintendence; search	rl
EPISEMON	city badge (Gr.)	
EPISODAL	digressive; accidental	
EPISODIC	incidental; subordinate	
EPISPERM	outer seed cover	bt
EPISPORE	outside spore-wall layer	bt
EPISTLER	letter-writer; scribe	
EPISTOME	face/mouth region in various creatures	
EPISTYLE	the architrave	ar
EPITASIS	climax; culmination	
EPITHECA	diatom cell valve	bt
EPITONIC	overstrained	
EPITRITE	metrical foot	
EPITROPE	rhetorical concession	
EPIZOITE	sedentary attached animals	zo
EPIZOOTY	animal epidemic	zo
EPLICATE	unplaited	
EPONYMIC	yclept; named after	
EPOPOEIA	epic poetry	
EPSOMITE	Epsom salts	mn
EPULOTIC	cicatrizing	md
EQUALISE	equalize; even	
EQUALITY	uniformity; sameness	
EQUALLED	rivalled	
EQUATING	balancing	
EQUATION	allowance for inaccuracy	
EQUIFORM	of equal shape; similar	
EQUIPAGE	outfit; effects; train	
EQUIPPED	accoutred; armed	
EQUITANT	riding astraddle	
EQUIVOKE	an equivocation	
ERADIATE	emit; sparkle	
ERASABLE	effaceable	
ERASTIAN	follower of Erastus	
ERECTILE	capable of elevation	
ERECTING	raising; building	
ERECTION	structure; edifice; building; (penile)	bd
ERECTIVE	setting upright	
EREMETIC	secluded; solitary; hermetic	
EREPTION	snatching; wresting	

ERETHISM	acute irritation	md
EREWHILE	formerly	
ERGATOID	like a worker insect	zo
ERGONOMY	physiological distinction of functions	
ERGOSOME	unit of cell-protein synthesis	bl
ERGOTINE	} parasitical fungus	
ERGOTISE	} found in rye, etc.	
ERGOTISM	} of poisonous nature	bt
ERIGERON	flea-bane genus	bt
ERIONITE	uncommon zeolite	mn
ERMINOIS	heraldic fur	hd
EROTESIS	rhetorical question	
EROTETIC	interrogatory	
EROTICAL	amatory; amorous; (Eros)	
ERRANTLY	like knights of old	
ERRANTRY	rambling; roving	
ERRORIST	fallacious fellow	
ERUCTATE	belch	
ERUGATED	wrinkled; corrugated	
ERUMPENT	breaking out	bt
ERUPTING	casting out	
ERUPTION	outburst; volcanic; suppuration; boil	gl, md
ERUPTIVE	explosive	
ERYCINIA	insect genus	zo
ERYSIMUM	hare's ear, etc.	bt
ERYTHEMA	a skin disease	md
ERYTHRON	red blood cell	
ESCALADE	} attack by means of	
ESCALADO	} scaling ladders	
ESCALATE	increase in scope	
ESCALLOP	scallop; a bi-valve	zo
ESCALOPE	boneless meat slice	ck
ESCAPADE	prank; adventure; frolic	
ESCAPADO	desperado	
ESCAPING	evading; eluding	
ESCAPISM	} the quest of a mental	
ESCAPIST	} anodyne	
ESCARGOT	edible snail	ck
ESCAROLE	dark green salad plant	ck
ESCARPED	steeply sloped	
ESCHALOT	small onion; (shallot)	bt
ESCHEWED	shunned; avoided	
ESCHEWER	escapist	
ESCORTED	attended; conducted	
ESCOTTED	taxed; maintained	lw
ESCOUADE	a squad (Fr.)	
ESCULENT	edible	
ESOTERIC	secret; mysterious	
ESPALIER	trellised trees	
ESPARCET	sainfoin	bt
ESPECIAL	particular; special	
ESPIBAWN	ox-eye daisy	bt
ESPIOTTE	species of rye	bt
ESPOUSAL	betrothal	
ESPOUSED	married	
ESPOUSER	wooer	
ESPUNDIA	S. Amer. skin infection	md

ESQUIRED	escorted; protected	
ESSAYING	attempting; endeavouring	
ESSAYISH	experimental	
ESSAYIST	a scribe; writer	
ESSAYKIN	short essay	
ESSENCED	perfumed	
ESSENISM	Essene doctrine	
ESSEXITE	alkali-gabbro igneous rock	gl
ESSOINED	excused for absence	
ESSOINER	attendance excuser	lw
ESSONITE	yellow garnet	mn
ESSORANT	heraldic wings	hd
ESTAMPIE	Fr. instrumental, dance form	mu
ESTANCIA	cattle ranch, S. America	
ESTEEMED	held in high regard	
ESTEEMER	valuer; admirer	
ESTERASE	ester-hydrolising enzyme	ch
ESTHESIA	} sensitivity	
ESTHESIS	}	
-ESTHESIO	of sensibility	cf
ESTHETIC	aesthetic; perceptive	
ESTIMATE	appraise; calculate	
ESTIVAGE	method of ship loading	nt
ESTIVATE	pass the summer	
ESTONIAN	of Estonia (Baltic republic)	
ESTOPPED	impeded; barred	lw
ESTOPPEL	a plea	lw
ESTOVERS	timber supplies	lw
ESTRANGE	alienate; disaffect	
ESTRAYED	strayed	
ESTRIDGE	ostrich down	zo
ESTROGEN	female genital hormone	
ESURIENT	greedy; hungry	
ETA-MESON	zero spin elementary particle	ps
ETA-PATCH	balloon patch	
ETCETERA	etc; etc.	
ETEOSTIC	a chronogram	
ETERNITY	perpetuity	
ETERNIZE	eternise; immortalise	
ETHEREAL	airy; heavenly; celestial	
ETHERENE	etherine; a gas	ch
ETHERISM	effects of ether	
ETHERIZE	etherise; to gas	md
ETHEROLE	a light oil	ch
ETHICIST	moralist	
ETHIOPIC	Abyssinian; Ethiopian	
ETHNARCH	Greek governor	
ETHNICAL	racial; heathen; pagan	
ETHOGRAM	behaviour pattern	pc
ETHOLOGY	cultural customs; animal behaviour in wild	pc
ETHYLENE	carburetted hydrogen	ch
ETIOLATE	to blanch	
ETIOLOGY	study of causes	
ETOUFFEZ	(Fr.) stuff it down; dampen	mu
ETRURIAN	} native to Etruria	
ETRUSCAN	}	

ETYPICAL	exceptional; aberrant	
EUCALYPT	eucalyptus	bt
EUCARPIC	with vegetative & reproductive organs	
EUCHARIS	Amazon lilies, etc.	bt
EUCTICAL	supplicatory	
EUCYCLIC	made up of matching successive whorls	
EUGENICS	eugenism	
EUGENIST	(race culture)	
EUGUBINE	(bronze tablets)	
EUKARYON	higher-organism nucleus	bl
EULACHAN	candle-fish oil	
EULOGIST	panegyrist	
EULOGIUM	laudatory speech; encomium	
EULOGIZE	extol; applaud; flatter	
EUMERISM	aggregation of like parts	zo
EUMYDRIN	atropine-like medicament	md
EUNICEAE	a worm genus	zo
EUONYMIN	} an extract from the	
EUONYMUS	} spindle tree	bt
EUPATORY	hemp agrimony	bt
EUPATRID	Athenian aristocrat	
EUPEPSIA	good digestion	md
EUPEPTIC	highly digestible	
EUPHONIA	smooth enunciation	
EUPHONIC	harmonious; felicitous	
EUPHONON	harmonium	mu
EUPHORIA	satisfaction of the artist	
EUPHRASY	the eye-bright plant	md
EUPHUISM	bombastic diction	
EUPHUIST	affected speaker; pedant	
EUPHUIZE	over-emphasize	
EUPLOIDY	polyploidy involving exact haploid multiples	cy
EUPYRENE	typical, of spermatozoa	
EUPYRION	a quick-match, etc.	
EURASIAN	European-Asiatic	
EUROPIUM	metallic element	ch
EURYTHMY	symmetry; regularity	
EUSEBIAN	(Eusebius)	rl
EUSOCIAL	division of labour (insects)	zo
EUTECTIC	easily melted	
EUTHERIA	genus of mammals	zo
EUTHROPY	good digestion	
EUTHYMIA	tranquillity; relaxed state	pc
EUXENITE	uncommon rare-element mineral	mn
EVACUANT	purgative; laxative	pm
EVACUATE	quit; abandon; forsake; empty	
EVADIBLE	escapable; evasible	
EVANESCE	disappear; vanish	
EVASIBLE	avoidable; elusory	
EVECTION	convection	
EVEN-DOWN	downright	
EVENFALL	twilight	
EVENNESS	levelness; regularity	
EVENSONG	a service	rl
EVENTFUL	full of incident; stirring	
EVENTIDE	evenfall; evening	

EVENTUAL	last; ultimate; final	
EVERMORE	always; eternally	
EVERSION	turning inside-out	
EVERTING	overturning; upsetting	
EVERYDAY	usual; common; routine	
EVERYONE	everybody	
EVERYWAY	in all ways	
EVICTING	expelling; ousting	
EVICTION	dispossession	
EVIDENCE	testimony; witness	
EVILDOER	malefactor; criminal	
EVILNESS	malignity; depravity	
EVINCING	demonstrating; exhibiting	
EVINCIVE	indicative	
EVITABLE	avoidable; escapable	
EVOCATOR	a summoner	lw
EVOLATIC	volatile	
EVOLVENT	involute	
EVOLVING	unfolding	
EVULGATE	publish; divulge	
EVULSION	extraction	
EWIGKEIT	eternity (Ger.)	
EXACTING	enforcing; critical; rigid	
EXACTION	extortion; tribute	
EXALTING	extolling; honouring	
EXAMINED	inquired; studied	
EXAMINEE	candidate	
EXAMINER	scrutinizer; inspector	
EXAMPLAR	model; exemplar; pattern	
EXANTHEM	surface rash	md
EXCAVATE	delve; dig; scoop	
EXCEEDED	surpassed; capped; excelled	
EXCEEDER	outdoer; surpasser	
EXCEPTED	excluded; omitted	
EXCEPTOR	objector	
EXCERNED	excreted; exuded	
EXCESSED	exceeded	
EXCESSES	debaucheries	
EXCHANGE	barter; commute; transaction	cp
EXCISING	cutting out	
EXCISION	extirpation; amputation	
EXCITANT	a stimulant	
EXCITING	rousing; inciting; inflaming	
EXCITIVE	provocative	
EXCITRON	mercury-arc rectifier	el
EXCLUDED	banned; barred; vetoed	
EXCURSED	digressed; wandered	
EXCURSUS	supplemented treatise	
EXCUSING	remitting; condoning	
EXCUSSED	deciphered	
EXECRATE	curse; detest; abhor	
EXECUTED	beheaded; achieved	
EXECUTER	} testamentary agent;	lw
EXECUTOR	} deed drafter	
EXEGESIS	explanatory discourse	
EXEGETIC	elucidative	
EXEMPLAR	pattern; examplar; model	
EXEMPTED	excused; released	
EXEQUIAL	funereal	

EXEQUIES	burial rites	
EXERCISE	use; task; drill; exert	
EXERGUAL	date space on coin	
EXERTING	striving; wielding	
EXERTION	effort; strain; attempt	
EXERTIVE	labouring; toilsome	
EXHALANT	exhalent; evaporative	
EXHALING	breathing; emitting	
EXHORTED	encouraged; warned	
EXHORTER	incitor; adviser	
EXHUMATE	disinter; exhume	
EXHUMING	digging up	
EXIGEANT	exacting; importunate	
EXIGENCY	exigence; urgency	
EXIGIBLE	able to be levied	
EXIGUITY	scantiness; fineness	
EXIGUOUS	tiny; diminutive; minute	
EXIMIOUS	eminent; famous	
EXINTINE	floral membrane	bt
EXISTENT	extant; living	
EXISTING	being; continuing	
EXITANCE	(luminous), (radiant)	ps
EXITIOUS	deadly; malignant; noxious	
EX-LIBRIS	(book-plate)	
EXOCHITE	outer layer of fucales macrosporangium	
EXOCOELE	portion of coelenteron	zo
EXOCRINE	of gland secretion; duct-carried	zo
EXOGAMIC	of marriage outside social group	pc
EXOPHAGY	selective cannibalism	
EXORABLE	not relentless; lenient	
EXORCISM	} deliverance from evil	
EXORCIST	} spirits	
EXORCIZE	exorcise	
EXORDIAL	introductory	
EXORDIUM	the beginning; preamble	
EXOSMOSE	diffusion	
EXOSPORE	outer layer of spore wall	bt
EXOSTOME	part of ovule	bt
EXOTERIC	openly professed; superficial	
EXOTHERM	heat liberator	
EXOTOXIN	bacterium-released toxin	ba
EXPANDED	stretched; dilated	
EXPANDER	} with built in volume	
COMPANDOR	} compressor	el, cp
EXPECTED	awaited; forecast	
EXPEDITE	hasten; accelerate	
EXPELLEE	who got the boot	
EXPENDED	consumed; dissipated	
EXPERTLY	dexterously; adroitly	
EXPIABLE	atonable	
EXPIATED	made reparation	
EXPIATOR	indemnifier	
EXPIRANT	a dying person	
EX-PIRATE	retired free-booter	
EXPIRING	at death's door	
EXPLICIT	clearly stated; categorical	
EXPLODED	burst; repudiated	

EXPLODER	a machine	
EXPLORED	scrutinized; plumbed	
EXPLORER	investigator	
EXPONENT	an executant; idea supporter; power	ma
EXPORTED	shipped; sent abroad	
EXPORTER	foreign trader	
EXPOSING	exhibiting; revealing	
EXPOSURE	disclosure; revelation	
EXPUGNED	overcome; conquered	
EXPUNGED	erased; deleted	
EXSECTED	cut off	
EXSERTED	projecting; protruding	
EXTENDED	stretched; protracted	
EXTENDER	dilator; expander	
EXTENSOR	joint muscle	pl
EXTERIOR	outer; outward	
EXTERNAL	outer; foreign; exotic	
EXTERNAT	day school	
EXTOLLER	eulogizer	
EXTORTED	wrested; extracted	
EXTRADOS	convex surface of vault	
EXTRORSE	turned outward	
EXTRUDED	expelled; ejected	
EXULTANT	triumphant; jubilant	
EXULTING	crowing; rejoicing	
EXUVIATE	moult; shed a skin	
EYEGLASS	monocle	
EYEPIECE	telescope lens	
EYESALVE	eyewash; ointment	
EYESIGHT	vision	
EYE-STALK	eye-bearing stalk in crustacea	zo
EYESTONE	optical adjunct	md
EYE-TO-EYE	vis-à-vis; face to face	
EYETOOTH	a canine tooth	
EYEWATER	tear; lotion	

F

FABLIAUX	French metric poetry	
FABULIST	an Aesop	
FABULIZE	fabulise; romance	
FABULOUS	feigned; fictitious; unreal	
FABURDEN	plainsong with simple harmony	mu
FACE-ACHE	neuralgia	md
FACE-CARD	court card	
FACE-DOWN	submissive; of punch cards	cp
FACELESS	lacking a physiognomy	
FACE-PACK	cosmetic	
FACETIAE	witticisms; pleasantries	
FACETING	cutting facets	
FACIALLY	superficially; externally	
FACILITY	dexterity; readiness; address	
FACINGLY	oppositely	
FACTIOUS	turbulent; riotous	
FACTOTUM	general agent	

FACULOUS	spotted	
FADDLING	trifling; playing	
FADEAWAY	old soldier; screwball (baseball)	
FADELESS	imperishable; enduring	
FADINGLY	decreasingly; vapidly	
FAE-BERRY	fea-berry; gooseberry	**bt**
FAGGOTED	bundled	
FAGOTING	a kind of embroidery	
FAILDYKE	turf-wall (Sc.)	
FAIL-SAFE	automatic close-down device	**cp**
FAIL-SOFT	slowdown device	**cp**
FAINEANT	idler; do-nothing; sluggard	
FAINTEST	barely perceptible; dimmest	
FAINTING	swooning	
FAINTISH	giddy; languid	
FAIR-COPY	correct copy	
FAIR-HAND	freehand	
FAIRINGS	small porcelain ornament (Ger.)	
FAIR-LEAD	a rope-guide	**nt**
FAIRNESS	honest dealing; equity	
FAIR-PLAY	justice; impartiality	
FAIRYDOM	fairyland	
FAIRYISM	enchantment	
FAITHFUL	leal; loyal; steadfast	
FAKEMENT	makeshift; swindle	
FAKIRISM	mysticism; poverty	
FALCATED	like a sickle	
FALCHION	short curved sword	
FALCONER	a hawker	
FALCONET	small hawk; cannon	**zo**
FALCONRY	hawking	
FALDERAL	meaningless refrain	
FALDETTA	hood and cape (Malta)	
FALLABLE	unstable; depreciable	
FALL-AWAY	side or pass (basketball)	
FALL-BACK	reserve; retreat; (wrestling)	
FALL-DOWN	inadequacy; failure	
FALLIBLE	liable to error; deceptive	
FALLIBLY	erroneously	
FALLOWED	ploughed but not sown	
FALL-TRAP	a snare	
FALSETTE	} shrill and unnatural	
FALSETTO	} tone of voice	**mu**
FALSTAFF	fat face	**pr**
FALTERED	wavered; hesitated	
FAMELESS	undistinguished	
FAMILIAL	common to a family	
FAMILIAR	unceremonious; intimate	
FAMILIST	(16th century sect)	**rl**
FAMISHED	anhungered; starved	
FAMOUSLY	remarkably; eminently	
FAMULIST	magician's attendant	
FAN-BLAST	forced draught	
FANCIFUL	whimsical; capricious	
FANCYING	preferring; imagining	**mu**
FANDANGO	Spanish national dance	
FANFARON	swaggering bully; braggart	

FANGLESS	toothless	
FANLIGHT	window over front-door	
FANTASIA	musical medley	**mu**
FAN-WHEEL	ventilating device	
FARADAIC	} relating to a farad,	
FARADISE	} the practical unit of electrical	
FARADISM	} capacity	**me**
FARCICAL	ludicrous; absurd; droll	
FARCY-BUD	glanders	**vt**
FARDELED	in bundles	
FAREWELL	adieu; good-bye; parting	
FAR-FLUNG	widely disseminated	
FARINOSE	mealy; floury	
FARMABLE	cultivatable	
FARMYARD	rooster's realm	
FARRIERY	veterinary work	
FARROWED	littered	
FAR-SPENT	well advanced	
FARTHEST	ultimate; yondmost	
FARTHING	four a penny (d)	**nm**
FASCHING	German free-for-all carnival	
FASCICLE	a cluster	
FASCIOLA	narrow band of colour	**zo**
FASCIOLE	ciliated spines in spatangoidea	
FASCISTI	Italian fascists	
FASCISTS	opponents of socialism	
FASHIOUS	vexatious; provocative	
FASSAITE	monoclinic pyroxene	**mn**
FASTBALL	pitch at full speed (baseball)	
FASTENED	secured; bound; tied	
FASTNESS	a stronghold; security	
FATALISM	} (belief in the inevitable)	
FATALIST	}	
FATALITY	a calamity; disaster	
FATHERED	adopted; begat; sired	
FATHERLY	paternal; benign	
FATHOMED	comprehended; plumbed	
FATIGUED	weary; jaded; tired	
FATTENED	overfed	
FATTENER	a fat producer	
FATTRELS	ends of ribbon (Sc.)	
FAULTFUL	defective	
FAULTILY	imperfectly	
FAULTING	accusing	
FAUTEUIL	arm-chair; stall	
FAUVETTE	garden warbler	**zo**
FAVONIAN	(west wind)	
FAVOURED	encouraged; approved	
FAVOURER	patron; supporter	
FAYALITE	an iron ore	**mn**
FEABERRY	faeberry; gooseberry	**bt**
FEARLESS	intrepid; undaunted; heroic	
FEARSOME	dread; awe inspiring	
FEASIBLE	workable; achievable	
FEASIBLY	practicable; possibly	
FEAST-DAY	a festival	
FEASTFUL	sumptuous; luxurious	
FEASTING	banqueting; carousing	
FEAST-WON	bribed by feasting	

FEATEOUS	dexterous; deft	
FEATHERY	with plumes; golf-shot (raising soil); oar-stroke (spray)	
FEATNESS	adroitness; neatness	
FEATURED	impersonated	
FEBLESSE	feebleness; irresoluteness	
FEBRIFIC	causing fever	
FEBRUARY	month of expiation	
FECKLESS	inefficient; spiritless	
FECULENT	muddy; turbid; fetid	
FEDELINI	macaroni	
FEDERACY	confederacy; alliance	
FEDERARY	a confederate	
FEDERATE	league together	
FEEBLISH	weakish	
FEEDBACK	sound; energy phenomenon	**el**
FEED-BACK	reaction report	**cp**
FEED-HEAD	cistern of a boiler	
FEED-PIPE	water-pipe	
FEED-PUMP	a force-pump	
FEER-TYPE	positive process	**pg**
FEETLESS	footless; apodal	
FEIGNING	counterfeiting; shamming	
FEINTING	pretending; misleading	
FELDSPAR	felspar	**mn**
FELICIDE	cat-killing	
FELICITY	happiness; bliss; blessedness	
FELINITY	cattishness	
FELLABLE	capable of being felled	
FELLAHIN	Egyptian peasants	
FELLATIO	oral penis stimulation	
FELLNESS	ruthlessness; ferocity	
FELLOWED	matched	
FELLOWLY	companionable	
FELLSIDE	mountain side	
FELO-DE-SE	suicide	**lw**
FELSITIC	like porphyry	**mn**
FELSTONE	(quartz and felspar)	**mn**
FELTERED	matted together	
FELTMARK	imprint left in papermaking	
FELTSIDE	smooth side of roll of paper	
FELTWORT	the mullein	**bt**
FEMALITY	femininity	
FEMERELL	louvre or ventilator	
FEMICIDE	lady-killing	
FEMININE	female; effeminate; tender	
FEMINISM	(women's rights)	
FEMINIST	advocate of feminism	
FEMINITY	womanliness	
FEMINIZE	to make effeminate	
FENBERRY	cranberry	**bt**
FENCEFUL	affording defence	
FENCE-OFF	exclude; preliminary bout (fencing)	
FENCHONE	dicyclic ketone	**ch**
FENCIBLE	a home guard	
FENESTER	} a window	
FENESTRA		
FEN-GOOSE	greylag goose	**zo**

FENTHION	chemical insecticide	
FENUGREC	sort of clover	**bt**
FEOFFING	granting a fief	
FERACITY	fecundity; fruitfulness	
FERETORY	shrine for relics	**rl**
FERINELY	wildly; savagery	
FERN-SEED	spores	**bt**
FERNSHAW	a thicket of ferns	**bt**
FEROCITY	cruelty; savagery	
FERREOUS	of iron	
FERRETED	unearthed	
FERRETER	investigator	
FERRIAGE	ferry charge	
FERRITES	ferro magnetic materials (ceramics)	
FERRITIN	liver protein	
FERRULED	tipped	
FERRYING	transporting	
FERRY-MAN	Charon (river Styx)	
FERULING	caning	
FERVENCY	ardour; devotion; eagerness	
FERVIDLY	hotly; zealously; with heat	
FESTALLY	joyously; jovially; merrily	
FESTERED	rankled	
FESTIVAL	mirthful; an occasion	
FETCHING	attractive; bringing	
FETERITA	dwarf sorghum	**bt**
FETISHES	charms; talismans; amulets	
FETTERED	shackled; manacled	
FETTLING	conditioning	
FEVERFEW	a febrifuge	**bt**
FEVERING	agitating; heating	
FEVERISH	inconstant; sultry	
FEVEROUS	restless; excited	
FEWTRILS	trifles (dial.)	
FIBRILLA	a filament	**bt**
FIBROGEN	protein	
FIBROSIS	fibrous growth	
FIBROTIC	of fibrosis	**md**
FIBULATE	tell untruths; act as impostor (Sc.)	
FIBULATE	} (leg bones)	**md**
FIBULOUS		
FIDDLING	trifling; fidgeting; cheating **mu**	
FIDELITY	trust; staunchness	
FIDGETED	worried; fretted; chafed	
FIDICULA	small lute	**mu**
FIDUCIAL	confident; precise; exact	
FIELD-BED	camp-bed	
FIELD-DAY	tactical exercise	
FIELD-GUN	mobile gun	
FIELDING	cricket	
FIENDISH	malicious; devilish	
FIERCELY	zealously; vehemently	
FIERCEST	most ferocious	
FIERY-HOT	blazing; impetuous	
FIERY-NEW	brand-new	
FIFE-RAIL	belaying pin rack	**nt**
FIFTIETH	ordinal of fifty	
FIG-APPLE	a coreless apple	**bt**

FIG-EATER	garden warbler	**zo**
FIGHTING	contention; strife; faction	
FIG-SHELL	a univalve shell	**zo**
FIGULATE	moulded	
FIGULINE	potter's clay	**mn**
FIGURANT	male ballet dancer	
FIGURATE	of determinate form	
FIGURIAL	represented by a figure	
FIGURINE	small statuette (Fr.)	
FIGURING	calculating; symbolizing	
FIGURIST	one skilled in figures	
FILAGREE	filigree; metal lacework	
FILAMENT	slender thread	
FILATORY	spinning machine	
FILATURE	the reeling of silk	
FILCHING	pilfering; purloining	
FILE-FISH	a sea-fish	**zo**
FILIALLY	like a son or daughter	
FILIATED	adopted; amalgamated	
FILICORD	fern-like plant	**bt**
FILIFORM	thread-like	
FILIGREE	filagree; metallic lacework	
FILIOQUE	(clause in Nicene creed) concerning status of God's son	**rl**
FILIPINO	(Philippines)	
FILLETED	strung together	
FILLIBEG	a kilt (Sc.)	
FILLIPED	flipped	
FILMGOER	a frequenter of cinemas	
FILM-STAR	popular actor/actress	
FILOPINA	} philopina, a nut-game	
FILOPINO		
FILTERED	percolated; strained	
FILTHIER	grubbier	
FILTHILY	dirtily	
FILTRATE	filtered solution	
FINALISM	conclusiveness; purposeful, teleology (ends)	
FINALIST	in the last round	
FINALITY	kismet; eventuality	
FINANCED	capitalized	
FINDABLE	discoverable	
FINE-DRAW	invisible mending	
FINELESS	endless; unlimited	
FINENESS	purity	
FINE-SPUN	elaborated	
FINESSED	acted artfully	
FINESSER	crafty person	
FINGERED	handled	
FINGROMS	woollen cloth	
FINISHED	ended	
FINISHER	final blow	
FINITELY	within limits	
FINITUDE	limitation	
FINNIKIN	crested pigeon	**zo**
FINOCHIO	sweet fennel	**bt**
FINSCALE	rudd, fish	**zo**
FIN-WHALE	rorqual	**zo**
FIREARMS	offensive weapons	

FIREBACK	ornamental plate	
FIRE-BALL	incendiary weapon	
FIRE-BARS	furnace bars	
FIRE-BOAT	fire-fighting steamboat	
FIREBOMB	incendiary missile, grenade	
FIRECLAY	used for fire-bricks	**mn**
FIRECOCK	hydrant connexion	
FIREDAMP	explosive gas in mines	
FIRE-EYED	with fiery eyes	
FIREFLAG	flash of lightning	
FIRE-GIRL	woman fire fighter	
FIRE-HOOK	demolition hook	
FIRE-HOSE	portable piping	
FIRE-KILN	an oven	
FIRELESS	showing no flames	
FIRELOCK	antique musket	
FIRE-PLUG	valve in a water-main	
FIRESHIP	incendiary ship	**nt**
FIRESIDE	the hearth	
FIRE-STEP	firing step in trench	
FIRETAIL	the redstart	**zo**
FIRETRAP	(no means of escape)	
FIRE-WARD	fire-warden	
FIREWEED	a plant	**bt**
FIREWOOD	chopped sticks	
FIRMLESS	wavering; unstable	
FIRMNESS	solidity; resolution	
FIRST-AID	emergency help	
FISHABLE	capable of being fished	
FISH-BALL	fish-cake	
FISHBEAM	beam of special form	
FISH-CAKE	fish-ball	
FISH-COOP	box used for ice-fishing	
FISH-GLUE	an adhesive; isinglass	
FISH-HAWK	the osprey	**zo**
FISH-HOOK	barbed hook	
FISH-MEAL	fodder; fertilizer	
FISH-POND	fish storage tank	
FISH-ROOM	part of ship	
FISH-SKIN	fish epidermis	
FISHTAIL	a gas jet; jewelry	
FISH-WEIR	a fishgarth	
FISH-WIFE	fish vendor	
FISSIPED	cloven hoof	
FISSURED	cleft; cracked	
FISTIANA	boxing annals	
FISTINUT	pistachio nut	**bt**
FISTULAR	tubular	
FITFULLY	spasmodically; inconstantly	
FIVEFOLD	500%	
FIVELEAF	cinquefoil	
FIXATION	stability; firmness; obsessive behaviour; cast-iron attitudes	**pc**
FIXATIVE	a stabilizer; adhesive; gum	**pg**
FIXATURE	hair cream	
FIXIDITY	permanence; constancy	
FIZZLING	sizzling	
FLABBILY	limply	
FLAGGING	signalling; wilting	

FLAGRANT	notorious; glaring	
FLAG-SHIP	leading ship; with flag officer	**nt**
FLAG-WORM	green gentle	**zo**
FLAMBEAU	a lighted torch	
FLAMELET	small flame	
FLAMENCO	folk dance, music (Sp.)	**mu**
FLAMINGO	Amer. water bird	**zo**
FLAMMING	deluding	
FLAMMULE	pictorial Japanese flame	
FLANCHED	heraldic term; flanged	**hd**
FLANERIE	lounging (Fr.)	
FLANKING	bordering; touching	
FLAP-JACK	cookie; compact	**ck**
FLAPPING	flopping; waving; shaking	
FLASHILY	transiently; gaudily	
FLASHING	bursts of light; signals; burning bricks	
FLAT-BOAT	previous landing craft for invasions	**nt**
FLAT-FISH	flounder, sole, dab, plaice etc.	**zo**
FLAT-FOOT	flattie; policeman (slang)	
FLAT-HEAD	a N. American Indian	
FLAT-IRON	smoothing iron	
FLATNESS	monotony; depression	
FLAT-RACE	not a steeplechase	
FLATTERY	insincere compliment	
FLATTEST	dullest; lowest; very level	
FLATTING	a process	
FLATTISH	comparatively level	
FLATWISE	not edgewise	
FLAT-WORM	tape worm	**zo**
FLAUNTED	vaunted; paraded	
FLAUNTER	ostentatious person	
FLAUTATO	flute like effect from	
FLAUTANDO	violins (It.)	**mu**
FLAUTIST	flute player	
FLUTER		**mu**
FLAWLESS	perfect; without blemish	
FLAX-COMB	a heckle	
FLAX-LILY	New Zealand flax	**bt**
FLAX-MILL	a factory	
FLAX-SEED	linseed	**bt**
FLAX-TAIL	the reed-mace	**bt**
FLAX-WEED	plants of doubtful	
FLAX-WORT	provenance	**bt**
FLEA-BANE	flea-discouraging plant	**bt**
FLEA-BITE	an inconvenient trifle	
FLEAKING	reed covering under thatch	
FLEA-WORT	a plant	**bt**
FLECKING	dappling	
FLECTION	flexion; bending	
FLEECING	shearing; swindling	
FLEERING	mocking; taunting	
FLEETEST .	fastest; swiftest	
FLEETING	transient; passing; brief	
FLENCHED	flensed	
FLENSING	a whaling operation	
FLESH-FLY	blow-fly; bluebottle	**zo**

FLESHING	tights; scraping leather	
FLESHPOT	stock-pot; good living; night life	
FLETCHED	feathered (arrows)	
FLETCHER	arrow maker	
FLEXIBLE	pliant; tractable; lissom	
FLEXIBLY	sinuously; not rigidly	
FLEXUOSE	winding; wavering;	
FLEXUOUS	curving; elastic	
FLIC-FLAC	back handspring (gymnastics)	
FLICHTER	flutter; quiver (Sc.)	
FLICKING	flipping	
FLICORNO	brass band instruments including sax-like instrument (military) (It.)	**mu**
FLIGHTED	took wing	
FLIMFLAM	humbug; nonsense	
FLIMSIES	carbon copies	
FLIMSILY	unsubstantially	
FLINCHED	winced; shrank back	
FLINCHER	shrinker; coward	
FLINDERS	fragments; flitters	
FLINGING	hurling; casting; pitching	
FLINTIFY	turn into flint	
FLIPFLAP	an entertaining device; scenery, theatre	
FLIPFLOP	walking noise; two state circuit	**cp, el**
FLIPPANT	pert; saucy; glib	
FLIPPERS	swim fins of seal and surfer	
FLIPPING	flicking	
FLIRTING	philandering; (fan)	
FLIRTISH	somewhat coquettish	
FLITTERN	a young oak (dial.)	
FLITTERS	flinders; fragments; glitter	
FLITTING	migrating; hastening	
FLIXWEED	a hedge plant	**bt**
FLOATAGE	flotsam;	
FLOATSAM	shipwrecked goods	**lw**
FLOATERS	'flying flies' in the eye	**md**
FLOATERS	markers; inconstants, voters	
FLOATING	circulating; wafting	
FLOATING	sideways movement (basketball)	
FLOCCOSE	tufted	
FLOCCULE	small flock of wool	
FLOCK-BED	bed stuffed with flock	
FLOCK-GUN	dry spray for textile finishes	
FLOCKING	congregating; crowding	
FLOGGING	a chastisement	
FLOODING	inundating; swamping	
FLOOD-LIT	illuminated	
FLOOKING	cross vein or fissure	
FLOORAGE	floor space	
FLOORING	material for floors	
FLOORMAN	bookies' runner at races	
FLOPGATE	diverting materials moving gate	**mn**
FLOPPILY	limply; flaccidly	
FLOPPING	breaking down	

FLORALLY	with flowers	
FLORENCE	wine; cloth	tx
FLORIAGE	blossom	
FLORICAN	Indian bustard	zo
FLORIDLY	ornately; exuberantly	
FLORIGEN	hypothetical hormone	bt
FLOSCULE	a floret; a bloom	bt
FLOTILLA	small fleet	nt
FLOUNCED	threw oneself about	
FLOUNDER	struggle; a fish	zo
FLOURING	reducing to powder	
FLOURISH	prosper; wave; fanfare	mu
FLOUTING	mocking; jeering	
FLOWERED	blossomed	
FLOWERER	plant flowering periodically	
FLOW-LINE	production, transport diagram	cp
FLUENTLY	volubly; easily	
FLUE-PIPE	organ pipe (without reed)	mu
FLUFFING	muffing	
FLUIDICS	science of liquid tube flow	ps
FLUIDIFY	fluidise	
FLUIDITY	fluidism; liquidity	
FLUMMERY	a drink; humbug	
FLUORENE	coal tar product	mn
FLUORIDE	tooth protector	ch
FLUORINE	a gas	ch
FLUORITE	fluorspar	mn
FLUOROUS	derived from fluor	
FLURRIED	agitated; disconcerted	
FLUSHING	blushing; colouring	
FLUSTERY	confused; agitated	
FLUTTERY	flapping; oscillating; (pulse)	md
FLUXIBLE	fusible	
FLY-BLOWN	shopworn, stale, dated; mouldy	
FLY-BOARD	container for artificial flies (angling)	
FLY-MAKER	(fishing)	
FLYPAPER	a fly-trap	
FLY-SHEET	handbill; broadside	
FLY-WATER	an arsenical solution	
FLY-WHEEL	a conserver of momentum	
FOAL-FOOT	colt's foot	bt
FOCALIZE	focalise; converge	
FOCUSING	correcting perspectives	pg
FODDERER	cattle-feeder	
FOG-BOUND	wrapped in mist	
FOGEYDOM	senility	
FOGGIEST	most obscure; murkiest	
FOG-SMOKE	thick fog	
FOILABLE	able to be frustrated	
FOILPLAY	fencing	
FOILSMAN	fencer	
FOLDEROL	refrain of old song	
FOLDLESS	uncreased	
FOLD-YARD	cattle enclosure	
FOLIAGED	leafy	
FOLIATED	laminated	

FOLICOLE	living on leaves	bt
FOLKLAND	common land	lw
FOLK-LORE	legendary traditions	
FOLKMOTE	assembly of freemen	
FOLK-SONG	traditional song	mu
FOLK-TALE	fairy story	
FOLKWAYS	group tradition	
FOLLICLE	a pod; small secreting cavity	bt, pl
FOLLOWED	imitated; pursued	
FOLLOWER	partisan; adherent; copier	
FOLLOW-ON	giving second innings to opponents with lower score (cricket); strongly delivered bowl	
FOLLOW-UP	second stage support	
FOMENTED	excited; fanned	
FOMENTER	agent provocateur	
FONDLING	a beloved one	
FONDNESS	affection; predilection	
FONTANEL	a cavity	md
FONTANGE	wire cap-frame	
FOOD-CARD	a rational requirement	
FOODLESS	lacking sustenance	
FOOLSCAP	paper, $17 \times 13\frac{1}{2}$ inches	
FOOL-TRAP	snare for simpletons	
FOOTBALL	national sport	ga
FOOT-BATH	bath to ease feet	
FOOT-FALL	footstep; tread	
FOOTGEAR	shoes and stockings	
FOOT-HALT	a sheep disease	vt
FOOT-HILL	an underfeature	
FOOTHOLD	support niche	
FOOT-IRON	carriage step; fetter	
FOOTLESS	with nothing to stand on	
FOOTLING	trifling; trivial; trumpery	
FOOT-MARK	foot-print	
FOOT-MUFF	foot-warmer	
FOOT-NOTE	an addendum	
FOOT-PACE	slow rate of progression	
FOOTPATH	pedestrian way	
FOOT-POST	pedestrian messenger	
FOOT-RACE	running match	
FOOT-ROPE	rope along a yard	nt
FOOT-RULE	a 12-inch measure	me
FOOT-SLOG	march; walk; tramp; hike	
FOOTSORE	with aching feet	
FOOTSTEP	footfall	
FOOTWEAR	foot-gear	
FOOTWORK	movement (sport)	
FOOTWORN	worn by many feet	
FOOZLING	bungling	
FORAGING	ravaging; searching	
FORAMINA	openings; orifices	pl
FORAYING	plundering; raiding	
FORBORNE	refrained; spared	
FORCEDLY	compulsorily; unnaturally	
FORCEFUL	coercive	
FORCIBLE	cogent	
FORCIBLY	violently	

FORDABLE	crossable wetshod	
FORDOING	ruining; exhausting	
FOREBEAR	forbear; ancestor	
FOREBODE	prognosticate; portended	
FORE-BODY	foreward part of ship	nt
FORECAST	prediction; prognosis	
FOREDATE	antedate	
FOREDECK	in the bows	nt
FOREDONE	overpowered	
FOREDOOM	predestinate	
FOREDOOR	front door	
FORE-EDGE	front edge of book	
FOREFEEL	sense in anticipation	
FOREFELT	anticipated	
FOREFOOT	foremost end of keel	nt
FOREGIFT	lease premium	
FOREGOER	vor-trekker; precursor	
FOREGONE	already decided	
FOREHAND	cf. backhand	
FOREHEAD	brow; audacity; metope	
FORE-HOOK	strengthening piece	nt
FOREKNEW	foresaw	
FOREKNOW	know already	
FORELAID	previously arranged	
FORELAND	headland; bluff; cape	go
FORELEND	lend in anticipation	
FORELENT	previously loaned	
FORELOCK	sometimes a quiff	
FOREMAST	forward lower mast	nt
FOREMEAN	intend	
FOREMOST	in the van; leading	
FORENAME	Christian name	
FORENOON	from sunrise to noon	
FORENSAL	} concerning law-court	
FORENSIC	} procedure	lw
FOREPART	the beginning	
FOREPEAK	(in the bows)	nt
FOREPLAN	to scheme	
FOREPOLE	tunnel cutter	ce
FORE-RANK	front rank	
FORE-READ	prognosticate	
FORE-RENT	rent due before reaping	
FORESAID	previously mentioned	
FORESAIL	one of various sails	nt
FORESEEN	expected; anticipated	
FORESEER	prophet	
FORESHIP	fore-part of ship	nt
FORESHOW	introductory frolic; portend	
FORESIDE	front side	
FORESTAL	concerning forests	
FORESTAY	part of rigging	nt
FORESTER	woodsman	
FORESTRY	arboriculture	
FORETELL	predict; augur	
FORETIME	the past; days of yore	
FORETOLD	presaged; warned	
FOREWARD	the van; the front	
FOREWARN	caution; admonish; advise	
FOREWENT	foregone; by-gone	
FOREWIND	favouring breeze	
FOREWISH	look forward to	
FOREWORD	preface; prologue	
FOREYARD	(yard on foremast)	nt
FORFAIRN	down and out (Sc.)	
FORGEMAN	coach-smith	
FORGIVEN	condoned; absolved	
FORGIVER	pardoner; remitter	
FORGOING	preceding	
FORKEDLY	furcated	
FORKHEAD	(knuckle-joint)	
FORKLESS	not branching	
FORKTAIL	salmon; kite; crow	zo
FORMALIN	an antiseptic	ch
FORMALLY	precisely; ceremoniously	
FORMERET	wall rib in medieval vault	ar
FORMERLY	ci-devant; whilom	
FORMLESS	shapeless; chaotic	
FORMULAE	sets of symbols	
FORMULAR	prescribed; formal	
FORMWORK	shuttering (concrete mould)	ar
FORRADER	further forward (slang)	
FORSAKEN	left; abandoned; renounced	
FORSLACK	to relax (obs.)	
FORSOOTH	in truth; indeed	
FORSPEAK	forbid; bewitch	
FORSPEND	exhaust; squander	
FORSTALL	forestall (obs.)	
FORSWEAR	deny upon oath; abjure	
FORSWINK	exhaust; wear out	
FORSWORE	} pledged falsely;	
FORSWORN	} recanted	
FORSWUNK	over-laboured	
FORTHINK	regret (obs.)	
FORTRESS	fortalice; citadel	
FORTUIST	believer in chance	
FORTUITY	luck; accident	
FORTUNED	presaged	
FORWARDS	onward	
FORZANDO	emphatically (It.)	mu
FOSSDYKE	Roman earthwork (Lincs.)	
FOSSETTE	dimple	
FOSSORES	burrowers	zo
FOSTERED	brought up; cherished	
FOSTERER	a nurse	
FOSTRESS	foster-mother	
FOTHERED	stopped a leak	nt
FOUGASSE	land-mine	
FOUL-FISH	fish when spawning	zo
FOUL-HOOK	not hooked in gills	
FOULNESS	dirt; grossness; scurrility	
FOUL-PLAY	unfair action	
FOUNDERY	foundry	ml
FOUNDING	establishing; endowing	
FOUNTAIN	jet of water	
FOUNTFUL	full of springs	
FOURBALL	four singles match (golf)	
FOURCHEE	cross	hd
FOURFOLD	quadruple	
FOURLING	one of a quadruplet	
FOURNEAU	explosion chamber (Fr.)	

FOURSOME	(dance; game; golf)	
FOURTEEN	twice seven	
FOX-BRUSH	a trophy of the chase	
FOX-CHASE	hunting	
FOX-EARTH	reynard's home	
FOXGLOVE	digitalis	bt
FOXGRAPE	variety of grape	bt
FOXHOUND	hunt dog	zo
FOXINESS	craftiness; slyness	
FOX-SHARK	thresher shark	zo
FOX-SLEEP	pretended sleep	
FOZINESS	lack of spirit (Sc.)	
FRACTION	part; particle; fragment	
FRACTURE	break; rift; fissure	
FRAGARIA	the strawberry	bt
FRAGMENT	shard; scrap; remnant	
FRAGRANT	odoriferous; redolent	
FRAILISH	somewhat weak; delicate	
FRAMABLE	can be framed	
FRAME-SAW	Italian saw	to
FRANCATU	russetin apple	bt
FRANCIUM	heaviest alkali metal	ch
FRANK-FEE	tenure in fee-simple	lw
FRANKING	remitting postage	
FRANKISH	(Frank); proto-French	
FRANKLIN	old English freeholder	
FRAPPAGE	sharp slapping	
FRAPPING	binding; lashing	nt
FRASLING	the perch	zo
FRAUDFUL	dishonest; knavish	
FRAULEIN	German spinster	
FRAXININ	extract from ash bark	ch
FRAXINUS	ash-tree genus	bt
FREAKFUL	} capricious; whimsical;	
FREAKISH	} abnormal; erratic	
FRECKLED	maculate	
FREEBORN	not in vassalage	
FREE-CITY	independent town	
FREE-COST	cost free	
FREED-MAN	emancipated slave	
FREEHAND	without instrumental aid	
FREEHOLD	held in fee-simple	lw
FREE-LOVE	promiscuity	
FREENESS	freedom; liberty	
FREE-PORT	(duties not levied)	
FREE-REED	vibrating reed	mu
FREE-SHOT	legendary hunter	
FREE-SOIL	(no slavery)	
FREE-TRIP	tripping/closing mechanisms independent; gratis tour	
FREE-WILL	voluntary; spontaneous	
FREEZE-UP	immobility; infrozen	
FREEZING	congealing; chilling	
FREMITUS	palpable vibration	md
FRENETIC	frenzied; distracted	
FRENULUM	a butterfly's bristle	zo
FRENZIED	maddened; furious	
FREQUENT	oft repeated; recurrent	
FRESCADE	a cool walk	
FRESCOED	painted on plaster	
FRESCOER	a washy painter	
FRESHISH	almost fresh	
FRESHMAN	first year student	
FRESH-NEW	unpractised	
FRETTING	worrying; fuming; abrading	
FRETWORK	interlaced ornament	
FREUDIAN	psycho-analytic	
FRIATION	crumbling	
FRIBBLED	frivolled; tottered	
FRIBBLER	trifler	
FRICTION	attrition; abrasion; sliding; rolling	
FRICTION	kinetic, coefficient (dynamic, static)	ps
FRIENDED	befriended; well-disposed	
FRIENDLY	kind; favourable; amicable (society); (match)	
FRIESIAN	Frisian; (Friesland)	
FRIGHTED	affrighted; dismayed	
FRIGHTEN	alarm; scare; intimidate	
FRIGIDLY	coldly; icily	
FRILLING	edging material	
FRINGENT	} encircling; bordering;	
FRINGING	} tasselating	
FRIPPERY	fallals; old clothes	
FRISETTE	artificial curl	
FRISKFUL	lively; sportive	
FRISKILY	briskly; wantonly	
FRISKING	capering; skipping; romping	
FRITTING	pasty condition of powdered ore	gs, ml
FRIZETTE	see frisette	
FRIZZLED	curled; fried	
FRIZZLER	hairdresser; cloth-worker	tx
FROCKING	coarse jean	
FROG-FISH	angler-fish	zo
FROGGERY	an abode of frogs	
FROGLING	small frog	zo
FROG-SPIT	froth-fly	zo
FROMWARD	away from	
FRONDAGE	leafage	
FRONDENT	} leafy	
FRONDOSE	}	bt
FRONDOUS	}	
FRONTAGE	building line	
FRONTATE	widening like a leaf	
FRONTIER	boundary; border; march	
FRONTING	facing; opposing	
FRONTLET	fillet or browband	
FRONTOON	a pediment	ar
FROSTILY	frigidly; icily; freezingly	
FROSTING	icing	
FROTHERY	mere froth; foam	
FROTH-FLY	numerous parasites	zo
FROTHILY	verbosely	
FROTHING	bubbling	
FROTTAGE	coin-rubbing; erotic stimulation	
FROTTEUR	performer of frottage	
FROU-FROU	flounced petticoat	

FROUNCED	plaited; frowned	
FROWNING	glowering; scowling	
FRUCTIFY	to make fruitful; teem	
FRUCTOSE	fruit sugar	
FRUGALLY	economically; thriftily	
FRUITAGE	crop; harvest; produce	
FRUIT-BUD	flower to be fruit	bt
FRUITERY	fruit-loft	
FRUIT-FLY	a pest	zo
FRUITFUL	productive; fecund; prolific	
FRUITING	bearing fruit	
FRUITION	fulfilment; realization	
FRUITIVE	enjoying; gratifying	
FRUITLET	a small fruit	bt
FRUMENTY	porridge of sorts	
FRUMPING	insulting; flouting	
FRUMPISH	old-fashioned; ill-natured	
FRUSTULE	shell of a diatom	bt
FUCHSINE	magenta; rosaniline	
	hydrochloride; dye	ch
FUCHSITE	green muscovite	mn
FUDDLING	getting drunk	
FUELLING	stoking	
FUGACITY	instability; uncertainty	
FUGHETTA	(It.) a little fugue	mu
FUGITIVE	volatile; vagabond; refugee	
FUGLEMAN	exemplary soldier	
FULCRATE	with supports	bt
FULGENCY	effulgence; brilliance	
FULGURAL	(lightning); flashy	
FULL-AGED	of mature age	
FULL-BACK	(football)	
FULL-BUTT	head-on crash	
FULL-EYED	with prominent eyes	
FULL-FACE	cf. profile	
FULLNESS	fulness; repletion; profusion	
FULL-ROLL	swell and yawing; croquet	
	shot	nt
FULL-STOP	end of a period	
FULL-TIME	normal working hours	
FULL-WAGE	wireless rectifier	
FULMINED	fulminated; thundered	
FULMINIC	explosive; detonative	
FUMARASE	catalysing enzyme	
FUMAROLE	volcanic smoke hole	
FUMATORY	fumigating chamber	
FUMBLING	clumsy; groping	
FUMELESS	smokeless	
FUMEWORT	the fumitory plant	bt
FUMIGANT	fume-producing	
FUMIGATE	disinfect	
FUMITORY	fumewort	bt
FUMOSITY	smokiness; flatulence	
FUNCTION	duty; power; office	
FUNCTION	purpose; meeting; instruction	
		cp
FUNDABLE	able to be financed	
FUNDLESS	broke	
FUNEBRAL	}	
FUNEREAL	} sombre; woeful	

FUNERARY	mournful; dismal	
FUNGIBLE	interchangeable	
FUNK-HOLE	coward's corner	
FURBELOW	puckered flounce	
FURCATED	forked; branching	
FURCULAR	fork-shaped	
FURFURAL	fural solvent	ch
FURFUROL	organic liquid	ch
FURIBUND	raging; furious; frenzied	
FURLOUGH	leave of absence	
FURMENTY	see frumenty	
FURRIERY	the fur trade	
FURROWED	corrugated; ploughed	
FURTHEST	most distant; remotest	
FURUNCLE	a boil	md
FURY-LIKE	furious; violent; frantic	
FUSAROLE	a classic moulding	ar
FUSELAGE	body of aircraft	
FUSEL-OIL	malodorous spirit	
FUSIFORM	spindle-shaped	
FUSILEER	} armed with light	
FUSILIER	} flint-lock muskets	
FUSTERIC	a yellow dye	bt
FUSTILUG	fat unwieldy person	
FUTILELY	unavailingly; ineffectually	
FUTILITY	uselessness; vanity	
FUTURELY	in time to come	
FUTURISE	anticipate; antedate	
FUTURISM	art movement	
FUTURIST	(Biblical prophesies)	
FUTURITY	future time; the hereafter;	
	gamble on future	
	commodities	
FUZZ-BALL	puff-ball fungus	bt
FUZZLING	confusing; intoxicating	

G

GABARAGE	packing cloth	
GABBATHA	Pilate's judgment seat	
GABBLING	chattering; jabbering	
GABIONED	with gabions	
GABLE-END	part of house silhouette	ar
GADABOUT	roving busybody	
GADHELIC	Gaelic Celt language	
GADLINGS	steel spikes	
GADZOOKS	a mild expletive	
GAGGLING	noise of geese; cackling	
GAG-TOOTH	projecting tooth	
GAIEMENT	in lively style	mu
GAIETIES	vivacities; jollities	
GAINABLE	procurable; attainable	
GAINLESS	unprofitable; bootless	
GAINSAID	contradicted; denied	
GAIR-FOWL	gare-fowl; great auk	zo
GALACTAN	anhydride of galactose	ch
GALACTIA	excess of milk	md
GALACTIC	(the Milky Way)	as
GALACTIN	sap of cow tree	bt

GALALITH	material made from milk	
GALANGAL	spicy tropical plant	**bt**
GALATIAN	inhabitant of Galatia	
GALAXITE	rare form of spinel	**mn**
GALBANUM	a gum	**bt**
GALBULUS	fleshy-scaled strobilus	**bt**
GALEATED	floral helmet	
GALENISM	Dr Galen's principles	
GALENIST	one of his followers	
GALENITE	sulphide of lead	**mn**
GALENOID	(galenite)	
GALERITE	fossil sea-urchin	**mn**
GALILEAN	(Galileo; Galilee)	
GALL-DUCT	body channel	**md**
GALLEASS	} galley-galleon trader W	
GALLIASS	} Europe	**nt**
GALLIARD	gay fellow; brisk; a dance	
GALLICAN	(Gaul or France)	
GALLIPOT	a glazed pot; artist's pot; apothecary's pot	
GALLIVAT	Malay pirate ship	**nt**
GALLIZED	(wine production)	
GALLOPED	rode at a gallop	
GALLOPER	mounted orderly	
GALLOWAY	a hardy horse	**zo**
GALVANIC	variable pulsating current (Galvani)	**el**
GAMBESON	} doublet worn under	
GAMBISON	} armour	
GAMBLING	playing recklessly	
GAMBOGIC	(gamboge)	
GAMBROON	twilled linen cloth	**tx**
GAMEBIRD	bird to be shot at	
GAMECOCK	fighting cock	**zo**
GAME-LAWS	hunting regulations	**lw**
GAMENESS	courage; endurance	
GAMESOME	sportive; gay; playful	
GAMESTER	a gambler	
GAMMARUS	genus of crustaceans	**zo**
GAMMONED	pickled; bamboozled	
GAMMONER	practical joker	
GAMOBIUM	sexual generation in metagenesis	
GAMODEME	permitted close marriage	
GAMOGONY	sporogony; gamete formation	**zo**
GANG-DAYS	(Rogation week)	**rl**
GANGETIC	(River Ganges)	
GANGLAND	criminal resort	
GANGLIAC	ganglial; (ganglion)	
GANGLING	slender	
GANGLION	nerve centre	**md**
GANGRENE	mortification	**md**
GANGSMAN	foreman	
GANGSTER	desperado; ruffian	
GANGWEEK	(Rogation week)	**rl**
GANISTER	sandstone; fire-brick	**mn**
GANNETRY	haunt of solan geese	**zo**
GANTLINE	rope for sails/clothes	**nt**
GANYMEDE	cupbearer to Zeus	

GAOLBIRD	an old lag	
GAPINGLY	widely open	
GARBAGED	eviscerated	
GARBLING	distorted; perverting	
GARBOARD	plank next to keel	**nt**
GARCINIA	plant genus; mangosteen	**bt**
GARDENER	a cultivator	
GARDENIA	sub-tropical shrub; flower	**bt**
GARE-FOWL	gair-fowl; great auk	**zo**
GARGANEY	sea-duck	**zo**
GARGLING	warbling	
GARGOYLE	grotesque gutter-spout	
GARISHLY	gaudily; showily; tawdrily	
GARLICKY	like garlic	**bt**
GARNERED	harvested; stored	
GARRETED	with watch-towers	
GARRISON	an armed force	
GARROTTE	strangle; throttle	
GARRULUS	crow genus; jay	**zo**
GARTERED	with socks well up	
GASALIER	hanging pendant for gas	
GAS-BLACK	carbon-black pigment	**pt**
GASELIER	hanging pendant for gas	
GAS-GAUGE	(for testing pressure)	
GASIFORM	gaseous	
GAS-LIGHT	19th-cent. lighting	
GAS-METER	(for measuring volume)	
GAS-MOTOR	a gas engine	
GASOGENE	} aerating; apparatus	
GAZOGENE	}	
GASOLENE	} rectified petroleum;	
GASOLINE	} petrol	
GAS-STOVE	cooking stove	
GASTIGHT	air-tight	
GASTRAEA	primordial organism	**zo**
GASTRULA	embryonic cup	**zo**
GAS-WATER	(coal-gas purification)	
GAS-WORKS	a source of illumination	
GATE-BILL	record of fines	
GATE-FINE	fine when gated	
GATEFOLD	folded insert in a book	
GATELESS	without a gate	
GATE-POST	gate supporter	
GATE-VEIN	portal vein	**md**
GATHERED	collected; acquired	
GATHERER	gleaner; collector	
GAUDY-DAY	festival	
GAUDYING	making merry	
GAUNTLET	iron glove	
GAVELMAN	tenant in gavelkind	**lw**
GAVELOCK	crowbar; javelin	
GAWNTREE	barrel stand; gantry	
GAZETTED	published; recorded	
GAZOGENE	a gasogene	
GAZPACHO	Andalusian cold soup	**ck**
GAZUMPED	thwarted by gazumper (sl)	
GAZUMPER	raiser of agreed selling price	
GEAR-CASE	part of auto works	**au**
GEGENION	simple ion	**ch**
GELASTIC	risible	

GELATINE	an animal jelly
GELATION	solidification by cold
GELIDITY	extreme cold
GEMATRIA	a cabbalistic method
GEMINATE	in pairs **bt**
GEMINIDS	meteoric shower **as**
GEMINOUS	double
GEMMATED	budded **bt**
GEMMEOUS	gemlike
GEMSHORN	an organ stop **mu**
GENDARME	armed policeman (Fr.)
GENDERED	begat; sired; bred
GENE-FLOW	gene-mix within populations
GENERALE	general principle
GENERANT	a cause of production
GENERATE	originate; beget; produce
GENEROUS	munificent; liberal
GENESIAC	(Genesis)
GENETICS	study of heredity
GENETRIX	} a mother, female parent
GENITRIX	
GENEVESE	Genevan
GENIALLY	heartily; cordially; jovially
GENITALS	reproductive organs **zo**
GENITIVE	possessive case
GENITURE	birth; procreation
GENOCIDE	racial extermination
GENOMERE	hypothetical gene constituent **gn**
GENOSOME	chromosome part **cy**
GENOTYPE	individual's genetic constitution
GENTILIC	tribal; non-Jewish
GEOBIONT	soil organism **ec**
GEOCARPY	underground fruit ripening **bt**
GEOCLINE	cline across organism's range features
GEODESIC	} relating to
GEODETIC	measurements of the earth
GEOGNOST	student of geognosy
GEOGNOSY	petrography **gl**
GEOGONIC	(formation of the earth)
GEOLATRY	earth-worship
GEOMANCY	a form of divination
GEOMETER	a mathematician
GEOMETRY	mensuration
GEONASTY	groundward curvature **bt**
GEONOMIC	(physical laws)
GEOPHAGY	earth-eating
GEOPHONE	portable shock-wave recorder **gp**
GEOPHYTE	subterranean-budding plant **bt**
GEOPONIC	agricultural; husbandry
GEORDIES	Tynesiders
GEORGIAN	period; caucasian; (Georgia)
GEOSCOPY	observational knowledge
GEOTAXIS	gravity-stimulated movement response

GERANIOL	perfumery ester constituent **ch**
GERANIUM	showy pink flower **bt**
GERMANIC	Teutonic
GERMCELL	gamete
GERMINAL	sprouting; French month
GEROCOMY	regime for the aged **md**
GERONTIC	of individual's senescent period
GESTAGEN	hormone promoting pregnancy **ch**
GESTURAL	gesticulating
GESTURED	acted; posed; signalled
GHANAIAN	native of Ghana
GHETTOES	Jewish quarters
GHORKHAR	Asiatic wild ass; onager **zo**
GHOSTING	pattern staining; stand-in authorship
GHOULISH	gruesome; fiendish
GIANTESS	colossal lady
GIANTISM	hugeness
GIANTIZE	play the giant
GIBBSITE	aluminium-hydroxide constituent of bauxite **mn**
GIBINGLY	scornfully; mockingly
GIB-STAFF	water-gauge; pole
GIDDIEST	most thoughtless
GIDDYING	making dizzy
GIFTLING	a small present
GIGANTIC	enormous; elephantine
GIGGLING	tittering; sniggering
GIG-LAMPS	spectacles
GILLAROO	species of trout **zo**
GILLENIA	rose genus **bt**
GILL-FLAP	a membrane **zo**
GILT-EDGE	aureate; (securities)
GILT-HEAD	sea-bream **zo**
GILT-TAIL	species of worm **zo**
GIMCRACK	a gewgaw; jimcrack
GIMLETED	holed; bored
GINGERLY	cautiously; warily
GINGIVAL	relating to the gums **md**
GIN-HORSE	mill-horse **zo**
GIN-HOUSE	cotton factory
GIN-SLING	a short drink (Singapore cocktail) **ck**
GIPSYDOM	gipsy life
GIPSYISM	cheating; flattery
GIRASOLE	sunflower **bt**
GIRDLING	encompassing; surrounding
GIRLHOOD	juvenile femininity
GIRONDIN	moderate republican
GIRTHING	saddling; girdling
GIRT-LINE	rigging line **nt**
GIVEABLE	bestowable; presentable
GIVE-AWAY	unintended disclosure
GLABRATE	} smooth; without
GLABROUS	hair or down **bt**
GLACIATE	freeze; polish by ice
GLADDEST	very cheerful; merriest

GLADDING	rejoicing; delighting; elating	
GLADIATE	sword-shaped	
GLADIOLE	sword-lily	bt
GLADIOLI	plural of gladiolus	bt
GLADNESS	joy; joyfulness; cheer	
GLAD-RAGS	party frocks	
GLADSOME	pleasurable; pleasant	
GLAIRING	varnishing	
GLAIROUS	viscous	
GLANCING	glimpsing; ricocheting	
GLANDAGE	feeding on acorns	
GLANDERS	a horse disease	vt
GLANDULE	small gland	md
GLAREOUS	glairous; viscous	
GLASSEYE	a horse disease	
GLASSFUL	a measure of content	
GLASSILY	in a vitreous manner	
GLASSING	glazing	
GLASSITE	one of a Scottish sect	
GLASS-POT	(used for melting glass)	gs
GLAUCIUM	the yellow poppy	bt
GLAUCOMA	an eye-disease	md
GLAUCOUS	a sea-green colour	
GLEAMING	resplendent; radiating	
GLEANING	harvesting; culling; picking	
GLEDGING	squinting	
GLEESOME	frolicsome; hilarious; lively	
GLEISOIL	poor-drainage-influenced soil type	gl
GLIADINE	yellow extract	bt
GLIBNESS	gift of the gab	
GLIDDERY	slippery	
GLIMPSED	viewed hurriedly; glanced	
GLINTING	gleaming	
GLIOSOME	cytoplasmic granule	cy
GLISSADE	a glide on a glacier	
GLISSAUN	the coal-fish	zo
GLOAMING	dusk; twilight	
GLOATING	revelling; crowing; exulting	
GLOBATED	spherical	
GLOBULAR	spheric; round	
GLOBULET	round particle	
GLOBULIN	(a blood constituent)	md
GLOOMILY	despondently	
GLOOMING	obscuring; depressing	
GLORIANA	Queen Elizabeth	
GLORIOLE	a halo; saintly aura	rl
GLORIOSA	a lily	bt
GLORIOUS	illustrious; noble; eminent	
GLORYING	exulting; boasting	
GLORY-PEA	an Australian pea	bt
GLOSSARY	explanatory vocabulary	
GLOSSILY	smoothly; sleekly	
GLOSSINA	the tsetse fly	zo
GLOSSING	commenting; polishing	
GLOSSIST	annotator; glossarist	
GLOWERED	scowled; frowned	
GLOW-LAMP	incandescent lamp	
GLOW-WORM	a beetle	zo
GLOXINIA	flowering plant	bt

GLUCAGON	hormone increasing blood sugar	md
GLUCINUM	white metal; beryllium	
GLUCONIC	acid derived from glucose	ch
GLUCOSID	sugar compound	ch
GLUE-LINE	dielectric heating	
GLUMMEST	gloomiest; very morose	
GLUMNESS	sulkiness; depression	
GLUMPISH	sullen; splenetic; moody	
GLUTAEUS	posterior muscle	md
GLUTELIN	water-insoluble protein	ch
GLUTENIN	wheat glutelin protein	ch
GLUTTING	sating; saturating; cloying	
GLUTTONY	voracity; greed	
GLYCEROL	glycerine	ch
GLYCOGEN	animal starch	ch
GLYCONIC	kind of verse	
GLYPTICS	gem engraving	
GNARLING	gnawing	
GNARRING	snarling; growling	
GNASHING	grinding the teeth	
GNATHISM	(jaw measurement)	
GNATHITE	insect mouth-part	zo
GNATLING	small gnat	zo
GNAT-WORM	larva of gnat	zo
GNOMICAL	} relating to the art of	
GNOMONIC	} dialling	
GOA-CEDAR	a cypress	bt
GOAL-LINE	back-line (football)	
GOAL-POST	(football)	
GOATHERD	goat-minder	
GOATLING	small goat	zo
GOAT-MOTH	fabulous insect	zo
GOATSKIN	skin of goat	
GOAT'S-RUE	a plant	bt
GOBBLING	guzzling; turkey-noise	
GODCHILD	protegé	
GOD'S-ACRE	a graveyard	
GODSMITH	idol maker	
GOD-SPEED	a benediction	
GOETHITE	a hydrated iron oxide	mn
GOFFERED	crimped	
GO-GETTER	pushing person	
GOGGLING	rolling the eyes	
GOINGS-ON	queer happenings	
GOITERED	} afflicted with the goitre	
GOITROUS	}	md
GOLCONDA	diamond mine, Hyderabad	
GOLD-DUST	a plant	bt
GOLDENLY	splendidly; aureately	
GOLDFISH	a carp	zo
GOLD-FOIL	} thin gold	
GOLDLEAF	}	
GOLD-LACE	sumptuary decoration	
GOLDLESS	destitute of gold	
GOLD-LILY	the yellow lily	bt
GOLD-MINE	source of wealth	
GOLD-RUSH	prospector's scramble	
GOLD-SIZE	a varnish	
GOLD-WIRE	thread gold	

478

GOLD-WORK	mouth adornments	
GOLF-CLUB	tool for striking golf-ball	
GOLGOTHA	a charnel-house	
GOLLYWOG	grotesque doll	
GOLOSHES	galoshes; overshoes	
GOMARIST	opponent of Armenians	
GOMBROON	Persian pottery	
GONALGIA	pain in the knee	md
GONENESS	that sinking feeling	
GONFALON	a banner	
GONGYLUS	(seaweed)	bt
GONIMIUM	lichen thallus cell	bt
GONOCOEL	gonad cavity	zo
GONOCYTE	sexual cell in porifera	zo
GONODUCT	genital products duct	zo
GONOPORE	reproductive elements opening	
GONOSOME	repro. individuals in animal colony	zo
GONOTOME	embryo somite	zo
GOOD-DOER	benefactor; patron	
GOOD-FOLK	the fairies	
GOOD-LACK	expression of pity	
GOODLIER	more excellent; fairer	
GOODNESS	kindness; beneficence	
GOODWIFE	a term of respect	
GOODWILL	benevolence; an asset	
GOOGLIES	deceptive spheres	
GOOSE-CAP	a silly person	
GOOSE-EGG	a zero; a duck	zo
GORGEOUS	splendid and showy	
GORGONIA	corals	zo
GOSSAMER	filmy cobweb	
GOSSIPED	chatted; tattled	
GOSSIPRY	small talk; intimacy	
GOURMAND	glutton; epicurean	
GOUTWEED	goutwort	bt
GOVERNED	controlled; ruled; swayed	
GOVERNOR	regulator; guardian	
GOWNSMAN	cf. townsman (university)	
GRABBING	snatching; clutching	
GRABLINE	life-line on a lifeboat	nt
GRACE-CUP	loving cup	
GRACEFUL	elegant and easy	
GRACILIS	land-vertebrate thigh muscle	zo
GRACIOSO	Spanish clown	
GRACIOUS	affable; polite; benign	
GRADATED	graded; blended	
GRADATIM	step by step	
GRADIENT	slope; incline; variable quantity ratio	me, rw
GRADIENT	rate of change of potential in volts per metre	el
GRADUAND	about to be a graduate	
GRADUATE	pass; proportion; divide	
GRAECISM	a Greek idiom	
GRAECIZE	to turn into Greek	
GRAFFITI	ancient wall scribblings	
GRAFFITO	two colour plaster layers	

GRAFTING	bribing; (gardening)	
GRAINAGE	duties on grain	
GRAINING	imitating wood or marble using paints etc.; a fish	bd, zo
GRAIN-TIN	melted tin	
GRALLINE	(wading birds)	zo
GRALLOCK	entrails of deer	zo
GRAMARYE	necromancy; magic	
GRANDDAD	grandfather	
GRANDEST	most magnificent; noblest	
GRANDEUR	pomp; splendour; majesty	
GRANDSON	son's son	
GRANITIC	of granite	mn
GRANTING	conceding; conferring	
GRANULAR	in grains	
GRAPHICS	art of drawing	
GRAPHITE	blacklead	mn
GRAPHIUM	a style (for writing)	
GRAPPLED	seized; grasped; clutched	
GRASPING	gripping; avaricious	
GRASSING	turfing; laying low	
GRASS-OIL	an essential oil	bt
GRATEFUL	thankful; beholden	
GRATIOLA	hedge hyssop	bt
GRATUITY	tip; bonus; pourboire	
GRAVAMEN	principal charge	lw
GRAVELLY	full of gravel	
GRAVITAS	weight of dignity	
GRAVITON	quantum of gravitation (hypothetical)	ps
GRAY-EYED	grey-eyed	
GRAYLING	freshwater fish	zo
GRAZIOSO	gracefully	mu
GREASILY	unctuously	
GREASING	lubricating; corrupting	
GREATEST	largest; biggest; bulkiest	
GRECIZED	Hellenized	
GREEDILY	voraciously; eagerly	
GREENERY	verdure; foliage	
GREEN-FLY	a pest	zo
GREENING	hoaxing	
GREENISH	somewhat green	
GREEN-TEA	tea picked immature	bt
GREETING	welcoming; weeping (Sc.)	
GREFFIER	notary (Channel Isles)	lw
GREMLINS	malignant aerial imps	
GREYCING	greyhound racing	ga
GREYNESS	grayness	
GRID-BIAS	adjustment	ro
GRIDELIN	violet grey colour	
GRIDIRON	a grill; squared plan; map; traffic system	
GRIEVOUS	burdensome; heinous	
GRILLADE	grilled meat (Fr.)	ck
GRILLAGE	a cross-beam construction	
GRILLING	broiling; interrogating	
GRIMACED	smirked	
GRIMALDI	an old clown	
GRIMMEST	sternest; dourest	

479

GRIMNESS	fierceness; dourness	
GRIMOIRE	ancient handbook of black magic	
GRINDERY	shoemakers' materials	
GRINDING	pulverizing; crushing	
GRINNING	smiling broadly	
GRIPEFUL	distressing; colicky	
GRIPPING	holding tight; clutching	
GRISELDA	a very patient lady	
GRISEOUS	grey; grizzled	
GRITTING	grating; grinding; abrading	
GRIZZLED	grey; grumbled	
GROANFUL	mournful; lugubrious	
GROANING	moaning; complaining	
GROGGERY	a dram-shop	
GROGGING	(extracting spirit)	
GROG-SHOP	a pub	
GROINING	angular curves; pier-like bulwarks against the sea	**ar**
GROMWELL	a plant	**bt**
GROOMING	making neat and tidy; appearance	
GROOMING	(of horses); fur picking (animals)	
GROOVING	furrowing; scoring	
GROSBEAK	a finch	**zo**
GROSCHEN	Austrian coin	**nm**
GROTTOES	caves	
GROUNDED	on the ground	
GROUNDER	low ball at baseball	
GROUPING	arranging; disposing	
GROUSING	grumbling	
GROUTING	filling in with concrete	
GROWABLE	cultivatable	
GROWLERY	a private den	
GROWLING	grumbling; snarling	
GRUBBIER	dirtier	
GRUBBING	digging up	
GRUBBLED	groped	
GRUDGING	envying; coveting	
GRUESOME	horrible; grisly; grim	
GRUMBLED	complained; repined	
GRUMBLER	grouser	
GRUMNESS	surliness; dourness	
GRUMPHIE	a sow	**zo**
GRUNDSEL	groundsel	**bt**
GRYSBOCK	steinbock, (S. Africa)	**zo**
GUACHERO	oil-bird, (S. Amer.)	**zo**
GUAIACOL	an odorous liquid	**ch**
GUAIACUM	resinous lignum vitae	**bt**
GUANCHOS	natives of Canary Islands	
GUARACHA	a Cuban dance	**mu**
GUARANTY	basis of security	
GUARDANT	facing	**hd**
GUARDFUL	wary; cautious	
GUARDIAN	warden; protector	
GUARDING	watching; defending	
GUBBINGS	wild Devonians	
GUELPHIC	a royal family	

GUERILLA	guerrilla; an irregular (war)	
GUERNSEY	a garment; a cow	**zo**
GUESSING	imagining	
GUGGLING	gurgling	
GUICOWAR	Galkwar	
GUIDABLE	steerable	
GUIDANCE	direction; government	
GUILEFUL	crafty; insidious	
GUILTILY	criminally; culpably	
GUIMAUVE	marsh-mallow	**bt**
GUJARATI	language (Bombay)	
GULCHING	pre-rock-fall sound	**mn**
GULF-WEED	tropical seaweed	**bt**
GULLIBLE	easily deceived	
GULLIVER	swift traveller	
GULLYING	making a channel	
GULOSITY	voracity	
GUMPTION	shrewd sense; nous	
GUM-RESIN	gamboge	**bt**
GUNDALOW	weighted felucca sail barge New England	**nt**
GUN-LAYER	who prepares guns for firing	
GUNMETAL	alloy; copper and tin	
GUN-REACH	gunshot; range	
GUNSMITH	gun-maker	
GUNSTICK	ramrod	
GUNSTOCK	part of gun	
GUNSTONE	stone projectile	
GURGLING	purling; rippling	
GURKHALI	language (Nepal)	
GUSTABLE	tasty; savoury	
GUTTATED	sprinkled; bedewed	
GUTTERED	ran in drops	
GUTTLING	gorging; swallowing	
GUTTURAL	throaty	
GUYANESE	(Guyana, S. Amer.)	
GUZZLING	swilling; tippling; quaffing	
GVMNASIC	gymnastic	
GYMKHANA	equestrian competitions meeting	
GYMNICAL	athletic	
GYMNOTUS	electric eel	**zo**
GYNANDER	a plant	**bt**
GYNANDRY	male characteristics of the female	
GYNARCHY	female government	
GYNECIUM	women's quarters	
GYNERIUM	pampas grass	**bt**
GYPSEOUS	(gypsum)	**mn**
GYPSYISM	gipsyism	
GYRATING	spinning; rotating; whirling	
GYRATION	rotation; revolution	
GYRATORY	circling; revolutionary	
GYRODYNE	speedy helicopter	**ae**
GYROIDAL	spiral; winding	
GYROLITE	hydrated calcium silicate	**mn**
GYROPTER	helicopter	**ae**
GYROSTAT	gyroscope	

H

HABANERA	Cuban dance with singing	mu
HABENDUM	descriptive clause	lw
HABITANT	inhabitant; native	
HABITING	dressing; arraying	
HABITUAL	customary; usual; wonted	
HABITUDE	customary manner	
HACHURES	shaded height; indications by pen hatchings	pr
HACIENDA	estate or ranch (S. Amer.)	
HACKBOLT	great shearwater gull	zo
HACK-LINE	curling	
HACKLING	heckling; separating flax	
HAEMATIC	acting on the blood	
HAEMATIN	(haemoglobin)	md
HAGBERRY	bird-cherry	bt
HAGGADAH	} Rabinical commentary	
HAGGADIC	} on Old Testament	rl
HAGGLING	chaffering; bargaining	
HAGTAPER	the mullein	bt
HAILSHOT	small shot	
HAIRCORD	kind of carpet	tx
HAIR-LACE	hair ribbon	
HAIRLESS	bald	
HAIRLINE	a fine line	
HAIRPINS	colloquial: diminuendo and crescendo signs	mu
HAIR-SALT	epsomite	mn
HAIRWORK	work done with hair	
HAIRWORM	freshwater worm	zo
HALATION	photographic defect	pg
HALENESS	robustness; health	
HALF-BACK	(football)	
HALF-BOOT	(halfway to the knee)	
HALF-BRED	mongrel	
HALF-CELL	electrode with electrolyte contact	el
HALF-COCK	a safety position	
HALF-DEAD	almost dead	
HALF-DECK	half length deck	nt
HALF-DONE	incomplete; under-done	
HALF-FACE	the profile	
HALF-HALT	equestrian exercise	
HALF-INCH	map scale	
HALF-LIFE	radio-activity period	ps
HALF-LINE	light-shading technique	pr
HALFLING	a youth	
HALF-MARK	old coin, value 6s. 8d.	nm
HALFMAST	a sign of mourning (flag salute)	
HALF-MILE	athletics	
HALF-MOON	a semicircle; demilune	
HALF-NOTE	a semitone	
HALF-PASS	two-step for horses	
HALF-PAST	} clock time	
HALF-HOUR		
HALF-PIKE	short pike	
HALF-ROLL	light swell; croquet shot	nt

HALF-SEAS	halfway; half-drunk; half-storm	nt
HALF-SPAN	lean-to	ar
HALF-SUIT	body armour	
HALF-TIDE	neither in nor out	
HALF-TIME	an interval	
HALF-TINT	intermediate tint	
HALF-TONE	a printing process	pr
HALICORE	dugong; sea-cow	zo
HALIOTIS	mother-of-pearl shell	zo
HALL-DOOR	front door	
HALLIARD	} rigging ropes, lines for	
HALYARD	} sails	nt
HALL-MARK	a guarantee	
HALLOOED	shouted	
HALLOWED	reverenced; sanctified	
HALTERED	roped; tethered	
HALTERES	balancing wings	zo
HAMBLING	mutilating the foot	
HAMIFORM	hook-shaped	
HAMINDAS	egg/peppers/onion casserole (Jew.)	ck
HAMMERED	(Stock Exchange)	
HAMMERER	hammer-man; smith	
HAMPERED	impeded; packed; clogged	
HANDBALL	an old pastime; 11 a side field game	
HANDBELL	one rung by hand	mu
HANDBILL	anouncement; broadcast	
HANDBOOK	a manual	
HANDCART	transport to hell	
HANDCUFF	manacle; fetter; restrict in baseball	
HANDFAST	hold; custody; betroth	
HANDGEAR	(manual control)	
HANDGRIP	} climbing	
HANDHOLD		
HAND-HORN	with only harmonic series (valveless)	mu
HANDICAP	penalty; allowance	
HANDLESS	awkward	
HANDLINE	line without a rod	
HANDLING	manipulation	
HANDLIST	convenient list	
HANDLOOM	for home weaving	wv
HAND-MADE	product of home industry	
HANDMAID	an Abigail	
HANDMILL	a quern	
HANDPICK	select carefully	
HANDPOST	finger-post; guide	
HANDRAIL	support	
HAND-SALE	handshake deal	
HANDSOME	generous; good-looking	
HAND-WORK	sloid; sloyd	
HANDYMAN	jack-of-all-trades	
HANGABLE	dependable; suspensible	
HANGER-ON	parasite; retainer	
HANGFIRE	explosive-detonation delay	mn
HANGNAIL	agnail	md
HANGNEST	a bird	zo

HANG-OVER	after-party reaction	
HANKERED	coveted; longed; yearned	
HAPLODON	mountain beaver	zo
HAPLOSIS	chromosome halving	cy
HAPPENED	chanced; occurred; befell	
HAPTERON	of plant attachment organs	bt
HAQUETON	padded jacket	
HARA-KIRI	happy despatch; suicide (Jap.)	
HARANGUE	tirade; declaim	
HARASSED	wearied; persecuted	
HARASSER	a guerilla; annoyer; molester	
HARDBACK	book published in stiff covers	
HARDBAKE	toffee almond cake	ck
HARDBEAM	horn beam	bt
HARD-CASH	ready money	
HARD-CORE	unwavering resistance; stone fillers, essence of construction	bd
HARDENED	inured; obdurate	
HARDENER	toughener	ch
HARD-FERN	the northern fern	bt
HARD-HACK	steeple-bush	bt
HARDIEST	most robust; boldest	
HARDNESS	compactness; firmness	
HARDSHIP	injustice; tribulation	
HARDTACK	ship's biscuit	nt
HARDWARE	ironmongery; computers & equipment etc.	cp
HARDWOOD	close-grained timber	bt
HAREBELL	hairbell; campanula	bt
HAREFOOT	swift of foot	
HAREHUNE	horehound	bt
HAREPIPE	a snare	
HARE'S-EAR	a yellow flower	bt
HARLEIAN	a literary society	
HARLOTRY	wantonness	
HARMLESS	innocuous; inoffensive	
HARMONIC	concordant; consonant; tone	mu
HARMONIE	windband (Ger.)	
HARPINGS	battens	nt
HARRIDAN	gaunt old woman; vixen	
HARROWED	lacerated; tortured; torn	
HARROWER	sensationalist	
HARRYING	harassing; raiding; vexing	
HARTWORT	plant; seseli type	bt
HASTATED	spear-shaped	bt
HASTENED	expedited; urged	
HASTENER	urgent reminder	
HASTINGS	early peas	bt
HATBRUSH	brush for hats	
HATCHERY	incubator	
HATCHETY	sharp featured	
HATCHING	plotting; shading; breeding	
HATCHWAY	deck opening	nt
HATEABLE	odious; detestable	
HATSTAND	like a hatrack, but different	
HATTERIA	tuatara; lizard, (NZ)	zo
HAT-TRICK	3 times successful	
HAUNCHED	having haunches	

HAUNTING	frequenting; obsessing	
HAURIANT	(fish on end)	hd
HAURLING	dragging; trailing	
HAUSFRAU	housewife (Ger.)	
HAUTBOIS	(Fr.) 'loud-wood' Italianised as 'oboe'	mu
HAVANNAH	a cigar	
HAVELOCK	white cover for cap	
HAVILDAR	Warrant Officer (Ind.)	
HAVOCKED	devastated; wasted	
HAWAIIAN	(Hawaii)	
HAWFINCH	grosbeak	zo
HAWK-BELL	small bell on hawk's foot	
HAWK-EYED	lynx-eyed	
HAWK-MOTH	genus of moth	zo
HAWK-WEED	genus of weed	bt
HAWTHORN	the may	bt
HAY-FEVER	pollen allergy	md
HAY-FIELD	meadow	
HAY-KNIFE	stack-cutter	
HAY-MAKER	a swipe	
HAY-STACK	} hay storage; giant foam-topped wave (canoeing, surfing); pewter tavern measure (Irish)	me
HAY-COCK		
HAY-RICK		
HAZARDED	imperilled; ventured	
HAZARDER	a gambler; speculator	
HAZEL-HEN	ruffled grouse	zo
HAZEL-NUT	filbert	bt
HAZINESS	uncertainty; vagueness	
HEADACHE	occipital disorder	md
HEADACHY	off colour	
HEAD-BAND	book top; fillet	
HEAD-BOOM	jib-boom	nt
HEADFAST	mooring rope	nt
HEADGEAR	head-dress	
HEAD-HOLD	} (wrestling)	
HEAD-LOCK		
HEADIEST	most exhilarating	
HEADLAMP	(motor-car)	
HEADLAND	cape; promontory; ness	
HEADLESS	decapitated	
HEADLINE	newspaper superscripture	
HEAD-LOCK	wrestling hold	
HEADLONG	precipitately; steep; hasty	
HEAD-MAIN	main water supply	
HEAD-MARK	outstanding feature	
HEAD-MOLD	skull; a moulding	md
HEADMOST	most advanced	
HEAD-NOTE	introductory note	
HEAD-PUMP	latrines pump in bow of ship	nt
HEAD-RACE	lead to water-wheel	
HEAD-RENT	payment for use of a head	
HEAD-REST	a support	
HEAD-RING	Kaffir coiffure	
HEADROOM	ceiling clearance height	bd, me

HEADSAIL	set forward of mast (sailing)	
		nt
HEADSHIP	supreme authority	
HEAD-TIRE	head-dress	
HEAD-WIND	a contrary wind	
HEAD-WORD	title word	
HEAD-WORK	intellectual labour; sport	
HEALABLE	remediable; curable	
HEARABLE	audible	
HEARTILY	cordially; sincerely; warmly	
HEARTLET	small heart	
HEART-ROT	central decay	bt
HEATHERY	heathy; heath-clad	bt
HEATH-HEN	black grouse	zo
HEATH-PEA	legendary plant	bt
HEAT-SPOT	a freckle	
HEAT-UNIT	lot of hot air	me
HEAT-WAVE	calorific undulation	
HEAVENLY	celestial; seraphic	
HEAVIEST	most ponderous	
HEBDOMAD	a group of seven	
HEBETANT	making blunt; dulling	
HEBETATE	to dull; stupefy	
HEBETUDE	dullness; stupidity	
HEBRAIST	} concerned with	
HEBRAISM	} Hebrew customs	
HEBRAIZE	} and literature	
HECATOMB	sacrifice of 100	
HECKLING	hackling; combing	
HECKYMAL	blue tit	zo
HECTORED	boasted; swaggered	
HECTORER	brawler; bully; braggart	
HECTORLY	insolent; domineering	
HEDGEHOG	"Mr Prickles"	zo
HEDGEHOP	a low flight	
HEDGEPIG	young hedgehog	zo
HEDGEROW	bushy boundary	bt
HEDONICS	} doctrine that	
HEDONISM	} pleasure is the	
HEDONIST	} highest good	
HEEDLESS	regardless; rash	
HEELBALL	black wax	
HEEL-NICK	cut-out portion of movable	
	type	pr
HEFTIEST	sturdiest; beefiest	
HEGELIAN	(process of the spirit)	
HEGEMONY	leadership	
HEGUMENE	prior	rl
HEIGHTEN	enhance	
HEIRLESS	no heir	lw
HEIRLOOM	family jewel	
HEIRSHIP	inherent right	lw
HELCOSIS	ulceration	md
HELCOTIC	ulcerous	md
HELIACAL	(sunlight)	
HELICOID	spiral	
HELIODOR	S. Afr. yellow beryl	mn
HELIOSIS	sunstroke	md
HELIOZIA	protozoa	zo
HELIPORT	helicopter airfield	ae

HELLBENT	reckless	
HELLBORN	} of satanic origin	
HELLBRED	}	
HELLENIC	Grecian	
HELL-FIRE	Satan's illumination	
HELL-GATE	approach to inferno	
HELL-KITE	bird of ill-omen	zo
HELLWARD	devilish progress	
HELMETED	double-domed	
HELMINTH	a worm	zo
HELMLESS	rudderless	
HELMSMAN	steersman	
HELOTAGE	} slavery; bondage;	
HELOTISM	} servitude; serfdom	
HELPLESS	impotent; weak; powerless	
HELPMATE	wife; partner	
HELPMEET	helpmate; helper	
HELVETIA	Switzerland	
HELVETIC	Swiss	
HEMATITE	haematite	mn
HEMIGALE	Malayan civet	zo
HEMIOLIA	} change of rhythm in ratio	
HEMIOLA	} 2 to 3	mu
HEMIOLIC	}	
HEMIONUS	dziggetai	zo
HEMIOPIA	faulty vision	md
HEMIPODE	sort of quail	zo
HEMIPTER	cicada or bug	zo
HEMISOME	symmetrical half of animal	zo
HEMP-PALM	a pretend plant	bt
HEMP-SEED	gallow's bird (Shak.)	
HENCHMAN	servant; page; varlet	
HENEQUEN	} sisal hemp	
HENEQUIN	}	bt
HEN-HOUSE	coop	
HEN-HUSSY	a cotquean	
HEN-MOULD	black spongy soil	
HEN-PARTY	ladies' gossip group	
HEN-ROOST	poultry park	
HEN-WOMAN	hen-wife	
HEPATITE	barium sulphate	mn
HEPATIZE	hepatise; livery-work	
HEPATOMA	liver tumour	md
HEPTAGON	7 sided figure	
HEPTARCH	ruler of a heptarchy	
HERALDED	proclaimed; blazoned	
HERALDIC	} armorial bearings and	
HERALDRY	} ceremonial orders	hd
HERBAGED	grass covered	
HERBARIA	hortus siccus	bt
HERBELET	small herb	bt
HERBLESS	lacking vegetation	
HERCULES	labour member of Tiryns	
HERD-BOOK	cattle stud-book	
HERDSMAN	cow-puncher	
HEREAWAY	hereabouts	
HEREDITY	inherent propensity	
HEREINTO	into this	
HERESIES	schisms	
HEREUNTO	unto this	

HEREUPON	upon this; then	
HEREWITH	by saying this	
HERISSON	spiked obstruction	
HERITAGE	patrimony; legacy	
HERMETIC	air-tight; mystic; occult	
HERNIOID	ruptured; hernial	md
HERNSHAW	heronshaw; handsaw	zo
HEROICAL	intrepid; valiant; epic	
HEROICLY	dauntlessly; daringly	
HEROIZED	lionized; idealized	
HEROSHIP	heroism	
HERPETIC	shingly	md
HERTZIAN	(low frequency waves)	
HERTZITE	galena	mn
HESITANT	vacillating; doubtful	
HESITATE	pause; waver; demur	
HESPERUS	a wreck	
HEXAGRAM	Solomon's seal	
HEXAPLAR	sextuple	
HEY-GO-MAD	joyous interjection	
HIBERNAL	wintry	
HIBISCUS	tropical mallow	bt
HICCATEE	Cen. Amer. tortoise	zo
HICCOUGH	hiccup	
HICCUPED	belched politely	
HICKWALL	small woodpecker	zo
HIDDENLY	privily; furtively; covertly	
HIDE-ROPE	a reim (S. Afr.)	
HIDROSIS	sweat	md
HIELAMAN	native shield (Aust.)	
HIERARCH	chief priest	rl
HIERATIC	priestly	rl
HIERONYM	sacred name used as surname	
HIGGLING	haggling; chaffering	
HIGH-BALL	whisky and soda	
HIGHBORN	of noble birth	
HIGHBRED	not a hybrid	
HIGHBROW	so-called intellectual	
HIGH-HUNG	elevated	
HIGH-JUMP	athletics; dismissal	
HIGHLAND	where the heart is; (cattle)	
HIGH-LIFE	the jet set	
HIGH-MASS	special service	rl
HIGHMOST	topmost	
HIGHNESS	a rank; altitude	
HIGHROAD	thoroughfare	
HIGH-SPOT	climax	
HIGH-TIDE	floodtide	
HIGH-TIME	almost overdue	
HIGTAPER	the mullein	bt
HI-JACKED	transport passengers forcibly seized	
HI-JACKER	super-pirate	
HILARITY	gaiety; jollity; merriment	
HILL-FOLK	hillmen; Covenanters	
HILL-FORT	stronghold; fastness	
HILLOCKY	hummocky	
HILLSIDE	a declivity	
HINDERED	delayed; thwarted; impeded	

HINDERER	obstructionist; opposer	
HINDMOST	last; posterior	
HINDUISM	doctrine and rites	
HINGEING	depending on	
HIP-JOINT	with-it nightclub	
HIREABLE	on hire	
HIRELESS	wageless	
HIRELING	mercenary	
HIRPLING	running lamely	
HIRRIENT	trilling sound	
HIRUDINE	like a leech	
HISPANIC	Spanish	
HISTIOID	resembling tissue	md
HISTORIC	authentic; genuine; famous	
HISTRION	play-actor	
HITCHING	fastening; attaching	
HITHERTO	till now	
HIVELESS	not a single skep	
HIVE-NEST	multiple bird's nest	zo
HOACTZIN	hoatzin; S. Amer. bird	zo
HOARDING	storing; treasuring; fence	
HOARSELY	discordantly; raucously	
HOASTMAN	member of a guild	
HOBBLING	walking lamely; limping	
HOBBYISM	} cult of a favourite pursuit	
HOBBYIST	}	
HOCKCART	(last harvest load)	
HOCKHERB	a mallow	bt
HOCKLING	mowing	
HOCK-TIDE	a festival	
HOCUSSED	drugged; doped	
HOG-FRAME	(shipbuilding)	nt
HOGGEREL	sheep of second year	zo
HOGMANAY	Dec. 31st (Sc.)	
HOG-REEVE	medieval parish officer	
HOG'SBEAN	henbane	bt
HOG-SCORE	line on a curling rink	
HOGSHEAD	large cask	
HOGSTEER	wild boar	zo
HOHLRAUM	black-body radiator cavity	ac
HOISTING	raising; lifting; elevating	
HOISTWAY	trap-door	
HOLDBACK	check; retainer	
HOLDFAST	catch; grip; anchor spike with eye for joinery	bd
HOLDINGS	stock possessed by library	
HOLEWORT	moschatel	bt
HOLINESS	sanctity; devoutness	rl
HOLLANDS	geneva; schnapps	
HOLLOAED	shouted	
HOLLOWED	excavated; scooped	
HOLLOWLY	insincerely; vacantly	
HOLOGAMY	mature-cell fusion	bt
HOLOGRAM	laser optical imaging	ps
HOLOPTIC	side eyes meeting	zo
HOLOZOIC	eating other organisms	zo
HOLYROOD	holy cross	rl
HOLY-WEEK	the week before Easter	
HOLY-WRIT	the Scriptures	rl
HOMAGING	paying respects	

HOME-BIRD	stay-at-home	
HOMEBORN	native; domestic	
HOMEBRED	natural; unpolished	
HOME-FARM	nearest fields to farmhouse	
HOMEFELT	inward; private	
HOME-GOER	word rarely or never used	
HOMELAND	native land	
HOMELESS	on the streets	
HOMELIKE	not ornate	
HOMELILY	familiarly	
HOME-MADE	better-tasting	
HOME-RULE	autonomy	
HOMESICK	nostalgia	
HOMESPUN	rough worsted	
HOMEWARD	return journey	
HOMEWORK	out of school task	
HOMICIDE	man-slaughter	**lw**
HOMILIST	sermonizer	
HOMOBIUM	alga/fungus association	**bt**
HOMODONT	teeth all alike	**zo**
HOMODYNE	(wireless telephony)	**tc**
HOMOGAMY	hermaphroditism	**bt**
HOMOGENY	similarity of nature	
HOMOLOGY	affinity of structure	
HOMONYMY	(similar sounding words)	
HOMOSOTE	material for walls of huts	
HOMOTYPE	} structural affinity	
HOMOTYPY		
HONDURAN	(Honduras)	
HONESTLY	uprightly; sincerely	
HONE-WORT	herb parsley-piert	**bt**
HONEY-BAG	nectar sac of bee	**zo**
HONEY-BEE	nectar-sucker	**zo**
HONEYDEW	tobacco; melon	**bt**
HONEY-POT	a grape (S. Afr.)	**bt**
HONORARY	gratuitous; unpaid	
HONOURED	respected; revered	
HONOURER	venerator	
HOODWINK	befool; cheat; delude	
HOOFMARK	imprint; slot	
HOOK-WORM	a parasite	**zo**
HOOLIGAN	ruffian; rascal; bully	
HOOP-IRON	iron band	
HOOT-STOP	audible stop signal	**cp**
HOOT-TOOT	toot-toot!; motor horn signal	
HOPELESS	despairing; despondent	
HOPINGLY	thinking wishfully	
HOPPLING	hobbling	
HORATIAN	(Horace)	
HORMESIS	non-toxic organism stimulus	
		bt
HORNBEAK	garfish	**zo**
HORNBEAM	a tree	**bt**
HORNBILL	picarian bird	**zo**
HORNFISH	garfish	**zo**
HORNFOOT	hoofed	
HORNGATE	gate of dreams	
HORN-LEAD	chloride of lead	**mn**
HORNLESS	dodded	
HORNPIPE	air; dance; sailors'	**mu, nt**

HORNWORK	outer ramparts, bastions	**ar**
HORNWORT	water-plant	**bt**
HOROLOGY	works on clocks	
HOROPTER	normal combined vision	
HORRIBLE	revolting; fearful; dire	
HORRIBLY	hideously; appallingly	
HORRIDLY	foully; alarmingly	
HORRIFIC	terrific; awful; frightful	
HORSE-BOX	van	
HORSE-BOY	stable-boy	
HORSE-CAR	a carriage	
HORSE-FLY	large sucking fly	**zo**
HORSE-HOE	a harrow	
HORSEMAN	rider; equestrian	
HORSE-WAY	road or track	
HOSE-PIPE	a duct	
HOSE-REEL	firefighting equipment	
HOSPITAL	an almshouse	
HOSPODOR	Slav governor	
HOSTELRY	inn; tavern; local	
HOT-BLAST	pre-heated air	
HOTCHPOT	farrago; mixture; medley	
HOTELIER	hotel-keeper	
HOTHOUSE	greenhouse	
HOT-PLATE	a heating appliance	
HOT-PRESS	a machine	
HOT-SHORT	brittle	
HOTTONIA	water-violet	**bt**
HOT-WATER	trouble	
HOUGHING	ham stringing	
HOUNDING	pursuing; tracking; trailing	
HOUR-HAND	time indicator	
HOUSE-BOY	serving lad	
HOUSE-DOG	watch dog	**zo**
HOUSE-FLY	musca domestica	**zo**
HOUSE-TAX	a levy	**lw**
HOVELLED	meanly housed	
HOVELLER	longshoreman	
HOVERING	in suspense; maintaining a	
	fixed observation level	
	above earth	
HOWIEITE	triclinic hydrous silicate	**mn**
HOWITZER	short cannon	
HUCKSTER	an advertiser	
HUDDLING	cowering in mass	
HUDIBRAS	political satire by S. Butler	
HUGENESS	bulk; immensity; vastness	
HUGUENOT	French Protestant	**rl**
HUIA-BIRD	New Zealand bird	**zo**
HUMANELY	mercifully; benignly	
HUMANISM	} pragmatism;	
HUMANIST	human interests,	
HUMANITY	} grammar, rhetoric, etc.	
HUMANIZE	enlighten; civilize	
HUMATION	burial	
HUMBLING	abasing; shaming	
HUMEFIED	moistened	
HUMIDIFY	to dampen	
HUMIDITY	moisture	
HUMILITY	humbleness; meekness	

HUMMOCKY	hillocky	
HUMORISM	facetiousness; jocularity	
HUMORIST	jester; merryman	
HUMOROUS	witty; droll; comical	
HUMOURED	indulged; pampered	
HUMPBACK	a whale; road-bridge	**zo**
HUMPLESS	no depression here	
HUMSTRUM	humdrum; monotonous	
HUNG-BEEF	dried beef	
HUNGERED	famished; hankered	
HUNGRILY	cravingly	
HUNKERED	squatted	
HUNTRESS	a Diana	
HUNTSMAN	chasseur	
HURDLING	(athletics)	
HURLBONE	a horse bone	**zo**
HURLWIND	whirlwind	
HURRYING	urging; speeding	
HURTLESS	uninjured; innoxious	
HURTLING	whizzing	
HUSHED-UP	undisclosed	
HUSH-HUSH	very secret	
HUSH-MUSH	highly confidential	
HUSKIEST	very hoarse	
HUSTINGS	electioneering platform	
HUSTLING	bustling; jostling; elbowing	
HUTCHING	cooping	
HUZZAING	shouting with joy	
HYACINTH	a gem; flower	**mn, bt**
HYALITIS	optic inflammation	**md**
HYBODONT	irregular teeth	**md**
HYDATISM	a watery sound	**md**
HYDATOID	aqueous	
HYDRANTH	nutrition polyp	**zo**
HYDRATED	combined with water	
HYDROFIN	high speed motor-boat	
HYDROGEL	water soluble colloid	**ch**
HYDROGEN	gaseous element	**ch**
HYDROIDS	animal growths on seaweed	**zo**
HYDROMEL	watered honey	
HYDROMYS	water-rats, etc.	**zo**
HYDROPIC	thirsty	
HYDROPSY	dropsy	**md**
HYDROSOL	colloidal solution	
HYDROZOA	} jelly fish	**zo**
HYDROIDS		
HYDRURET	hybrid	**ch**
HYGIENC	salubrious; healthy	
HYLICISM	materialism	
HYLICIST	a philosopher	
HYLOBATE	a gibbon	**zo**
HYLOZOIC	materialistic	
HYMENEAL	conjugal; matrimonial	
HYMENEAN	nuptial; bridal	
HYMENIUM	part of fungus	**bt**
HYMN-BOOK	often A. & M.	**rl**
HYOIDEUS	nerve branch in vertebrates	**zo**
HYOSCINE	poisonous alkaloid	**md**
HYPALGIA	insusceptibility	

HYPAXIAL	below the axis	**zo**
HYPERGOL	rocket fuel	**sp**
HYPERION	a Titan	
HYPHAEMA	interior eye bleeding	**md**
HYPHENED	linked	
HYPHENIC	jointed	
HYPNOSIS	hypnotism	**md**
HYPNOTIC	mesmeric; sleep-inducing	
HYPOARIA	brain lobe in fish	**zo**
HYPOBOLE	form of argument	
HYPOCONE	molar cusp	**zo**
HYPODERM	cell layer under epidermis	**bt**
HYPOGEAL	underground	
HYPOGEAN	subterranean	
HYPOGENE	rock formation	**mn**
HYPOGEUM	underground gallery, vault, or mine	**ar, mn**
HYPOHYAL	hyoid arch element	**zo**
HYPOMERE	mesothelial wall zone	**zo**
HYPONOME	water escape funnel	**zo**
HYPOSMIA	diminished smell sensitivity	
HYPOTHEC	debt security	
HYPOZOAN	} below the limit of life	**gl**
HYPOZOIC		
HYSTERIA	nervous disorder	**md**
HYSTERIC	hysterical	

I

IANTHINA	purple sea-snails	**zo**
IATRICAL	medical	**md**
IBSENISM	(Henrik Ibsen); dramatic characterization; saying	
ICE-BLINK	a reflection; mirage	
ICE-BOUND	immobilized by ice	
ICE-BROOK	frozen brook	
ICE-CREAM	the content of a cornet	
ICE-FIELD	ice-floe	
ICE-FLOAT	ice-field	
ICE-HOUSE	building with ice in it	
ICE-LEDGE	much like any other ledge	
ICE-PLANT	frost flower	**bt**
ICE-SHEET	glacial ice	
ICE-WATER	Amer. national drink	
ICE-YACHT	boat for transport on ice	
ICHOROUS	like ichor	**md**
ICHTHINE	(fishes' eggs)	**zo**
ICHTHYIC	fishlike	
ICTERINE	yellow	
IDEALISM	transcendency	
IDEALIST	visionary	
IDEALITY	perfection	
IDEALIZE	idealise	
IDEATING	fancying	
IDEATION	conception	
IDEATIVE	imaginative	
IDENTIFY	recognize; integrate	
IDENTITY	individuality; sameness	

IDEOGRAM	ideograph; logo; picture word (cp Chinese)	
IDEOLOGY	metaphysics	
IDIOTISH	doltish; fatuous; inane	
IDIOTISM	imbecility; inanity	
IDIOTIZE	ridicule; befool	
IDLEHOOD	idleness	
IDLENESS	dolce far niente	
IDOCRASE	silicate of lime	**mn**
IDOLATER	a heretic	
IDOLATRY	image worship	
IDOLIZED	idolised	
IDOLIZER	a fan	
IGNATIAN	(St Ignatius)	**rl**
IGNITING	kindling; inflaming	
IGNITION	firing; lighting	
IGNITRON	mercury arc rectifier	**el**
IGNOMINY	public disgrace; obloquy	
IGNORANT	uninstructed; unaware	
IGNORING	disregarding; overlooking	
ILLAPSED	glided	
ILLATION	inference	
ILLATIVE	deducive; grammatical case (direction to)	
ILL-BLOOD	enmity; discord; rancour	
ILL-FATED	calamitous; unlucky	
ILL-FAURD	ill-favoured (Sc.)	
ILLINIUM	metallic element	**ch**
ILLIQUID	financial	
ILL-TIMED	ill-judged	
ILL-TREAT	maltreat	
ILLUDING	deceiving	
ILLUMINE	enlighten; irradiate	
ILLUMING	elucidating	
ILL-USAGE	harsh treatment	
ILLUSION	delusion dream; fantasy	
ILLUSIVE	} deceptive; fugitive;	
ILLUSORY	} hallucinatory	
ILLYRIAN	a Yugoslav	
ILMENITE	titanate of iron	**mn**
IMAGINAL	relating to an image	**zo**
IMAGINED	fancied; thought	
IMAGINER	dreamer	
IMBANDED	banded together	
IMBANKED	embanked	
IMBATHED	immersed	
IMBECILE	idiot; moron; Bedlamite	
IMBEDDED	firmly fixed	
IMBELLIC	pacific; unwarlike	
IMBIBING	absorbing; swallowing	
IMBITION	dye transfer	**pg**
IMBOWING	arching	
IMBRUING	drenching	
IMBRUTED	degenerated	
IMBUMENT	deep tincture	
IMBURSED	supplied with cash	
IMITABLE	easy to forge	
IMITANCY	mimicry	
IMITATED	parodied; aped	
IMITATOR	copy-cat; impersonator	

IMMANELY	savagely; brutally	
IMMANENT	inherent; innate	
IMMANITY	cruelty; inhumanity	
IMMANTLE	to cloak	
IMMASKED	disguised	
IMMATURE	unripe; crude; untimely; undeveloped	
IMMERGED	} submerged; soused;	
IMMERSED	} plunged; inundated	
IMMESHED	entangled; ensnared	
IMMINENT	impending; perilous	
IMMINGLE	mix; blend; amalgamate	
IMMITTED	injected; introduced	
IMMIXING	mingling; combining	
IMMOBILE	still; motionless; static	
IMMODEST	bold; indelicate; coarse	
IMMOLATE	sacrifice; surrender	
IMMORTAL	imperishable; deathless	
IMMUNITY	privilege; freedom	
IMMUNIZE	immunise; exempt	
IMPACTED	collided; struck	
IMPAIRED	enfeebled; blemished	
IMPAIRER	saboteur; marrer	
IMPALING	transfixing	
IMPALMED	grasped; handled	
IMPANATE	to sandwich	
IMPARITY	inequality; disproportion	
IMPARKED	enclosed	
IMPARLED	conversed; discussed	
IMPARTED	communicated; divulged	
IMPARTER	bestower; donator	
IMPASTED	kneaded	
IMPAWNED	pledged; mortgaged	
IMPEDING	obstructing; thwarting; personal foul in water polo	
IMPELLED	urged; induced; drove	
IMPELLER	instigator; inciter; centrifugal pump	
IMPENDED	threatened; hovered	
IMPENNED	enclosed; encompassed	
IMPERIAL	shorn beard; a goatee	
IMPERIUM	sovereignty	
IMPETIGO	an eruption	**md**
IMPIERCE	bore; drill; penetrate	
IMPINGER	dust-measuring device	**mn**
IMPISHLY	mischievously; wantonly	
IMPLATED	sheathed	
IMPLEACH	interweave	
IMPLEDGE	pawn; hypothecate	
IMPLICIT	tacit; implied; inferred	
IMPLORED	entreated; craved	
IMPLORER	supplicant; petitioner	
IMPLUMED	plucked	
IMPLUNGE	immerse; dive	
IMPLYING	indicating; connoting	
IMPOCKET	filch; steal	
IMPOISON	envenom; infect	
IMPOLDER	reclaim from sea (Holland)	
IMPOLICY	inexpedience	
IMPOLITE	positively rude; insolent	

IMPONENT	a backer; imposer; con-man	
IMPONING	wagering; betting	
IMPOROUS	gas-tight; impermeable	
IMPORTED	conveyed; denoted	
IMPORTER	foreign dealer	
IMPOSING	impressive; stately	
IMPOSTOR	trickster; charlatan	
IMPOTENT	helpless; incapable	
IMPRIMIS	in the first place	
IMPRISON	incarcerate; immure	
IMPROPER	unseemly; indelicate	
IMPROVED	bettered; amended	
IMPROVER	developer; rectifier	
IMPUDENT	saucy; shameless	
IMPUGNED	gainsaid; contradicted	
IMPUGNER	attacker; assailant	
IMPUNITY	exemption; immunity	
IMPURELY	unchastely; licentiously	
IMPURITY	an adulterant	
IMPURPLE	empurple; confer imperial honour and rank	
IMPUTING	charging; insinuating	
INACTION	inertia; sloth; indolence	
INACTIVE	idle; torpid; supine	
INAQUATE	turn into water	
INARABLE	unfit for tillage	
INASMUCH	because	
INAURATE	gild	
INBONDED	brick-laying technique	
INCAGING	confining; mewing	
INCANTON	merge into a canton	
INCARNED	incarnated	
INCASING	encasing; enclosing	
INCASKED	barrelled	
INCAVATE	hollow out	
INCENSED	inflamed; enraged	hd
INCENSOR	incense burner	
INCEPTOR	beginner; inaugurator	
INCERTUM	early rubble-filled masonry	bd
INCHMEAL	gradually	
INCHOATE	begun; immature; incipient	
INCIDENT	episode; event; fracas; breakdown	cp
INCIRCLE	encircle; encompass	
INCISELY	clear cut; acutely	
INCISING	scribing; engraving	
INCISION	cut; gash; slit	
INCISIVE	trenchant; sarcastic	
INCISORY	sharpness	
INCISURA	body notch; scar	
INCISURE	a cut; wound	pl
INCITANT	stimulant; provocative	
INCITING	goading; arousing; spurring	
INCIVISM	lack of communal spirit	
INCLINED	disposed; biased; tilted	
INCLINER	sloping dial	
INCLOSED	enclosed; penned; enfolded	
INCLOSER	a fencer of common land	
INCLUDED	contained; embodied	
INCOMING	entrance; arrival	

INCOMITY	incivility; rudeness	
INCORPSE	incorporate (obs.)	
INCREASE	aggravate; augment	
INCREATE	create within	
INCUBATE	hatch	
INCUBOUS	(leaf formation)	bt
INCUDATE	characteristic of rotifera	zo
INCUMBER	encumber; hinder	
INCURRED	contracted; ran into	
INCURVED	bent	
INCUSING	stamping	
INCUSSED	forged; struck	
INDAGATE	investigate	
INDAMINE	used in dye-making	ch
INDEBTED	under obligation	
INDECENT	unbecoming; coarse	
INDENTED	notched; toothed	
INDEVOTE	disloyal; unloving	
INDEVOUT	irreverent; impious	
INDEXING	compiling an index	
INDIAMAN	trading ship	nt
INDICANT	symptomatic	
INDICATE	show; suggest; denote	
INDICTED	impeached; charged	
INDICTEE	a defendant	
INDICTER	an accuser	
INDIGENE	a native; aboriginal	
INDIGENT	poor; needy; necessitous	
INDIRECT	devious; tortuous; oblique grammar (speech)	
INDITING	dictating; writing; penning	
INDOCILE	intractible; stubborn	
INDOLENT	lazy; sluggish; inert	
INDORSED	sanctioned; ratified	
INDORSEE	endorsee	
INDORSER	ratifier; confirmer	
INDRENCH	soak; saturate; steep	
INDUCING	actuating; urging; causing	
INDUCTED	invested; installed	rl
INDUCTOR	officiating minister	
INDULGED	gratified; humoured	
INDULGER	favourer	
INDULINE	a dye	ch
INDURATE	harden; inure	
INDUSIAL	(caterpillar skins)	zo
INDUSIUM	skin or cover	bt
INDUSTRY	trade; assiduity; diligence	
INDUVIAE	withered leaves	bt
INEDIBLE	uneatable	
INEDITED	unpublished	
INEQUITY	injustice; unfairness	
INERMOUS	no prickles	bt
INERTION	sluggishness; indolence	
INEXPERT	unskilled; unversed	
INFAMING	defaming; discrediting	
INFAMISE	} publicly brand with	
INFAMIZE	} infamy	
INFAMOUS	vile; notorious; heinous	
INFANTLY	childishly; infantile	
INFANTRY	foot-soldiers	

INFECTED	tainted; corrupted; disease-ridden	
INFECTER	carrier of disease	
INFECUND	sterile; barren; unprolific	
INFERIAE	Roman sacrifices	
INFERIOR	poor; subordinate; mediocre	
INFERNAL	diabolical; fiendish; satanic	
INFERRED	deduced; argued; surmised	
INFESTED	overrun; thronged; beset	
INFILTER	permeate; seep	
INFINITE	boundless; unlimited	
INFINITO	perpetual	**mu**
INFINITY	immensity	
INFIRMLY	irresolutely; feebly	
INFLAMED	exasperated; infuriated	
INFLAMER	agent provocateur	
INFLATED	distended; bloated; swollen	
INFLATOR	air-pump	
INFLATUS	inspiration	
INFLEXED	bent inwards	
INFLOWED	ran in	
INFLUENT	a tributary	
INFOLDED	embraced	
INFORMAL	unconventional; simple	
INFORMED	told; apprised; notified	
INFORMER	a sneak	
INFRA-DIG	beneath one's social standing	
INFRA-RED	beyond red in spectrum	
INFRINGE	violate; transgress	
INFRUGAL	prodigal; extravagant	
INFUMATE	to smoke	
INFUSING	inculcating; inspiring	
INFUSION	instillation; introduction	
INFUSIVE	penetrative	
INFUSORY	protozoic	**zo**
INGENIUM	bent of mind	
INGROOVE	engroove; furrow	
INGROWTH	opposite of outgrowth	
INGUINAL	(groin)	**md**
INGULFED	swallowed up	
INHALANT	a vapourizer	**md**
INHALING	breathing	
INHERENT	innate; congenital	
INHERING	sticking fast	
INHERSED	coffined	
INHESION	inherence	
INHOOPED	encaged; cooped	
INHUMING	burying; interring	
INIMICAL	allergic; hostile; contrary	
INIQUITY	vice; sinfulness; offence	
INITIATE	a novice; start; inaugurate	
INJECTED	forced in; introduced	
INJECTOR	kind of pump; syringe	**md**
INJURING	damaging; maltreating	
INKINESS	state of being inky	
INKMAKER	squid	
INKSTAND	ink-holder	
INK-STONE	sulphate of iron	**mn**
INLACING	enlacing	
INLANDER	not an islander	
INLAWING	clearing of attainder	
INLAYING	ornamenting	
INLOCATE	on ringside (gymnastics)	
INLOCKED	locked up	
INNATELY	instinctively; naturally	
INNERVED	invigorated	
INNOCENT	guileless; blameless; sinless	
INNOVATE	make changes; alter; new	
INNUENDO	an insinuation	
INORNATE	plain	
INOSITOL	yeast growth agent	**ch**
INQUIRED	asked; investigated	
INQUIRER	questioner; scrutineer	
INRAILED	enclosed	**nt**
INRIGGED	with rowlocks on gunwhale	**nt**
INSANELY	crazily; deliriously	
INSANITY	dementia; mania; lunacy	
INSCIENT	ignorant; illiterate; unread	
INSCONCE	ensconce; hide; lurk	
INSCRIBE	dedicate; engrave; imprint; rewrite data	**cp**
INSCROLL	write on a scroll	
INSEAMED	marked by a seam	
INSECTED	segmented	
INSECURE	uncertain; hazardous	
INSERTED	introduced; injected	
INSETTED	implanted	
INSHADED	tinted	
INSHRINE	enshrine; dedicate	
INSIGNIA	badges; emblems; tokens	
INSISTED	persisted; maintained; urged	
INSITION	ingraftment	
INSNARED	entangled; caught; ginned	
INSNARER	trapper	
INSOLATE	dry in the sun	
INSOLENT	contumacious; hubristic	
INSOMNIA	sleeplessness	**md**
INSOMUCH	so that	
INSPHERE	ensphere; englobe	
INSPIRED	inhaled; animated	
INSPIRER	spiritual leader	
INSPIRIT	enhearten; infuse	
INSTABLE	unstable; transient	
INSTANCE	specify; occurrence; incident	
INSTANCY	urgency; solicitation	
INSTATED	established	
INSTINCT	natural propensity	
INSTREAM	to flow	
INSTRUCT	edify; direct; enjoin; order	
INSTYLED	entitled; named; yclept	
INSUCKEN	milling restriction	**lw**
INSULATE	isolate; enisle	
INSULTED	affronted; outraged	
INSULTER	taunter; abuser; offender	
INSURANT	policy holder	
INSURING	assuring; underwriting	
INTAGLIO	opposite to cameo	
INTARSIA	pictorial inlay	
INTEGRAL	whole; entire; complete	
INTENDED	betrothed; meant; purposed	

INTENDER	contemplator	
INTENTLY	with fixed attention	
INTERACT	theatrical interval	
INTERCOM	two-way communication system	**tc**
INTEREST	concern; attention; discount	
INTERIOR	inside; inward; inner	
INTERLAY	insert	
INTERMIT	suspend	
INTERMIX	blend; commingle	
INTERNAL	domestic; within; inside	
INTERNED	confined; imprisoned	
INTERNEE	arrested alien	
INTERPOL	international criminal police	
INTERRED	buried; inhumed; entombed	
INTERREX	a regent; protector	
INTERTIE	connecting piece	
INTERVAL	gap; pause; (music); interim, specific time period **cp, mu, tc**	
INTER-WAR	of period between wars	
INTEXINE	pollen cover	**bt**
INTIMACY	} familiarity; friendship;	
INTIMATE	} near; close; declare	
INTIMITY	inwardness	
INTONATE	intone	
INTONING	chanting	
INTRADOS	lower surface of arch	
INTRENCH	encroach; infringe; trespass	
INTREPID	dauntless; doughty; daring	
INTRIGUE	cabal; interest; conspiracy	
INTROMIT	insert; admit	
INTRORSE	facing inwards	
INTRUDED	butted in; thrusted	
INTRUDER	trespasser; interloper	
INTUBATE	insert a tube	
INUNDANT	overflowing; overwhelming	
INUNDATE	flood; swamp; deluge	
INURBANE	rude; uncouth; discourteous	
INURNING	putting in an urn	
INUSTION	a branding	
INVADING	violating; raiding; entering	
INVARIED	set; constant; uniform	
INVASION	foray; attack; assault	
INVASIVE	aggressive; intrusive (tumours); (epidemic) **md**	
INVECKED	} scalloped	
INVECTED	}	
INVECTED	engrailed	**hd**
INVEIGLE	entice; wheedle; decoy; lure	
INVEILED	veiled	
INVENTED	devised; created; fabricated	
INVENTOR	innovator; contriver	
INVERTER	conversion device	**el**
INVERTER	sign reverser; negative binary signal	**cp**
INVESTED	arrayed; indued; beset	
INVESTOR	buyer; purchaser	
INVITING	attractive; alluring	
INVOCATE	adjure; invoke; beseech	

INVOICED	billed	
INVOKING	conjuring; summoning	
INVOLUTE	spiral	
INVOLVED	complicated; complex	
INWALLED	enclosed	
INWARDLY	privily; secretly	
INWORKED	inset	
IODAZIDE	iodine azide	**ch**
IODIZING	(iodine)	**md**
IODOFORM	an antiseptic	**md**
IODYRITE	iodide of silver	**ch**
IOLANTHE	a fairy; an opera	**mu**
IONICIZE	Grecianize	
IONIZING	electrolysing	
IOTACISM	excessive use of 'I'	
IPSATIVE	reflected, measured against self	**pc**
IREFULLY	angrily; furiously	
IRENICAL	tranquil; pacific	
IRENICON	peace propaganda	
IRIDITIS	eye inflammation	**md**
IRISATED	like a rainbow	
IRISCOPE	spectroscope	
IRISHISM	Celtic expression, humorous	
IRISHMAN	(Ireland)	
IRONBARK	eucalyptus	**bt**
IRONCLAD	metal-hulled warships	**nt**
IRON-CLAY	yellow iron ore	**mn**
IRONGREY	a colour	
IRONICAL	satirical; sarcastic; derisive	
IRON-SAND	firework mixture	**mn**
IRONSICK	rusty and leaky	
IRONSIDE	a Cromwellian	
IRONWARE	ironmongery	
IRONWOOD	tough timber	**bt**
IRONWORK	smithery	
IRRIGATE	supply with water; moisten	
IRRISION	derision; banter	
IRRITANT	annoying; exasperating	
IRRITATE	gall; nettle; provoke	
IRRORATE	as if dew-covered	**bt**
IRRUPTED	burst in; invaded; raided	
ISABELLE	yellowish grey	
ISAGOGIC	introductory	
ISENGRIM	a fabulous wolf	**zo**
ISLAMISM	Mohammedanism	**rl**
ISLAMITE	worshipper of Allah	**rl**
ISLAMIZE	proselytize	**rl**
ISLANDED	isolated	
ISLANDER	not an inlander	
ISLESMAN	(from the Hebrides)	
ISOBARIC	(equal barometric pressure)	**mt**
ISOCHEIM	line indicating equal winter temperatures	
ISOCHELA	equal-jointed chela	**zo**
ISOCHORE	gas pressure and temperature	
ISOCORIA	equal size of eye pupils	
ISOCRYME	line indicating equal winter temperatures	

ISODICON	short anthem	rl
ISODOMON	} masonry composed of	
ISODOMUM	} uniform blocks	
ISOGONAL	equi-angular	
ISOGONIC	(equal magnetic angles)	
ISOLATED	solitary; (fever epidemic); (sheltered); (prison); (hermit)	el
ISOLATOR	device for 2 way microwave flow	el
ISOLOGUE	like/unlike compound	ch
ISOMERIC	} different properties	
ISONYMIC	} of similar compounds	ch
ISOPATHY	homeopathy	md
ISOPLETH	map showing weather constituents	
ISOPRENE	synthetic rubber	ch
ISOSTASY	equal-pressure-caused equilibrium	
ISOSTERE	atmospheric volume line	mt
ISOTHERE	(equal summer heat)	
ISOTHERM	line of equal heat	
ISOTONIC	having equal tension	
ISOTOPES	nuclides of similar number but different mass	nc
ISOTOPIC	of isotopes	
ISSUABLE	distributable	
ISSUANCE	delivery	
ISTHMIAN	Corinthian	
ITALIOTE	a Greek colonist in Italy	
ITCH-MITE	burrowing insect	zo
ITERANCE	repetition	
ITERATED	repeated; recapitulated	
ITHURIEL	cherub; guardian angel	
IVORY-NUT	a palm-nut	bt

J

JABBERED	gabbled; chattered	
JABBERER	wind-bag	
JACKAROO	greenhorn squatter (Aust.)	
JACKETED	having a paper cover	
JACKFISH	pike	zo
JACK-FLAG	smaller than ensign	nt
JACK-FOOL	perfect fool	
JACK-HIGH	bowl level with jack	
JACKWOOD	jaca-tree	bt
JACKYARD	uppermost short extension to main-mast	nt
JACOBEAN	(James I)	
JACOBITE	partisan of James II	
JACQUARD	loom mechanism	wv
JACULATE	to throw; to dart	
JAGGEDLY	raggedly; unevenly	
JAILBIRD	old lag	
JALOUSIE	Venetian blind	
JAMAICAN	(Jamaica)	
JAMBEAUS	leggings	

JAMBOREE	Boy Scouts Rally, frolic, carousal	
JAMBOREE	hand with 5 highest trumps (cards)	
JAMPANEE	chair carrier	
JANGLING	wrangling	
JANICEPS	2-headed monstrosity	md
JANUFORM	double-faced	
JAPANESE	of Japan	
JAPANNED	varnished; enamelled	
JAPANNER	a shoeblack	
JAPAN-WAX	lacquer from sumac tree berries	
JAPHETIC	Armenian alphabet	
JAPONICA	Japanese quince	bt
JARARAKA	poisonous snake	zo
JAROSITE	iron-potassium sulphate	mn
JASPONYX	an onyx	mn
JAUNDICE	bile obstruction disorder	md
JAUNTIER	more sprightly	
JAUNTILY	debonairly	
JAUNTING	an outing	
JAVANESE	an Indonesian	
JAVELINA	wild boar	zo
JAW-LEVER	veterinary instrument	
JAW-TOOTH	a molar	pl
JEALOUSY	anxiety caused by rivals	
JEANETTE	coarse cloth	tx
JEBUSITE	a Canaanite	
JEHOVIST	Hebrew theologian	rl
JELLYBAG	a strainer	
JELUTONG	pale Malayan hardwood	fr
JENTLING	Danube chub	zo
JEOPARDY	danger; peril; hazard; risk	
JEREMIAD	lamentation	
JEROBOAM	super champagne bottle	
JERQUING	customs searching	nt
JERRICAN	5 gallon (22 litres) petrol tin	
JEST-BOOK	collection of jokes	
JESUITIC	} characteristics of Jesuits	
JESUITRY	}	
JET-BLACK	deepest black	
JET-CRAFT	} jet propelled aircraft	
JET-PLANE	}	
JETTISON	throw overboard	nt
JETTYING	projecting	
JEWELLED	set with gems	
JEWELLER	a craftsman with gems	
JEWISHLY	judaical	
JEW'S-HARP	small mouth instrument	mu
JICKAJOG	a shake; a push	
JIGGERED	flabbergasted	
JIGGLING	wriggling; joggling	
JIGMAKER	a tool-maker	
JINGLING	tinkling; rhyming	
JINGOISH	super-patriotic	
JINGOISM	ultra-patriotism	
JOBATION	a tedious scolding	
JOCKEYED	jostled; outwitted; deluded	
JOCOSELY	facetiously; joyously	

JOCOSITY	sportiveness; fun
JOCUNDLY	mirthfully; waggishly
JODHPURS	riding breeches
JOGGLING	shaking; jostling; elbowing
JOHANNES	old Portuguese gold coin **nm**
JOIN-HAND	connected script
JOINT-ILL	umbilicus disease **vt**
JOINTING	finishing joints between
	timbers/bricks **bd**
JOINT-OIL	synovia
JOINTURE	a settlement (estate) **lw**
JOISTING	fitting with laths
JOKINGLY	in jest; hilariously
JOLLIEST	very merry and bright
JOLT-HEAD	dunderhead
JONGLEUR	wandering minstrel; juggler
	mu
JORDANON	faintly varied breeding race **bt**
JOSTLING	pushing; hustling; crowding
JOUNCING	shaking; jolting (slang)
JOUSTING	a tourney; simulation of
	middle aged knights
JOVIALLY	festively; blithely
JOVIALTY	merriment; conviviality
JOYFULLY	rapturously; gladly
JOYOUSLY	blissfully; happily
JOYSTICK	aeroplane control lever **ae**
JUBILANT	triumphant; exulting
JUBILATE	celebrate; rejoice
JUDAICAL	Jewish **rl, lw**
JUDAIZED	conformed to Mosaic law
JUDAIZER	opponent of St Paul
JUDGMENT	sentence; decree; award
JUDICIAL	legal; legitimate; sagacious
JUGGLERY	manual dexterity
JUGGLING	conjuring; swindling
JUGO-SLAV	Yugoslav
JULIENNE	sliced vegetables (soup) **ck**
JUMBLING	confusing; mixing
JUMP-SEAT	collapsible seat
JUNCTION	union; coalition; coupling;
	(-pipe); (-box of circuits)
	(railway) **bd, rw**
JUNCTURE	exigency; moment of crisis;
	joined speech sounds
JUNKBALL	slow, breaking pitch (baseball)
JUNKETED	feasted; caroused
JUNK-RING	piston-packing
JUNONIAN	queenly
JURASSIC	geological period **gl**
JURATORY	comprising an oath
JURISTIC	legal jurisdictive
JURYMAST	temporary mast **nt**
JUSTLING	jostling; jolting
JUSTNESS	equity; impartiality
JUVENILE	young; puerile; adolescent

K

KAILWIFE	cabbage-seller; a scold (Sc.)
KAILYARD	kitchen-garden (Sc.)
KAKEMONO	Japanese picture
KAKOSMIA	abnormal reaction to smell **pc**
KALA-AZAR	black fever **md**
KALAMDAN	Persian writing case
KALAMKAR	Indian printed cotton **tx**
KALENDAR	calendar; almanac
KALERUNT	cabbage stalk **bt**
KALEVALA	Finnish epic
KALEYARD	kitchen-garden **bt**
KALINITE	alum **mn**
KALIYUGA	Hindu mythological era
KALOLOGY	science of beauty
KALOTYPE	early photograph
KAMADEVA	Indian Eros
KAMIKAZE	suicide bomb; plane (Jap.)
KANARESE	language (Mysore, India)
KANDAHAR	East Indian wool **tx**
KANGAROO	a marsupial **zo**
KANTIKOY	religious dance **rl, mu**
KARELIAN	Finno-Ugric in Ladoga region,
	USSR
KARYOTIN	nuclear reticulum substance
	cy
KASHMIRI	people and language (Kashmir)
KATABION	katabolic-predominant
	organism **bl**
KATAKANA	Japanese script
KAURI-GUM	a resin (Aust.) **bt**
KAYMAKAM	Turkish governor
KECKLING	binding rope **nt**
KEDGEREE	a breakfast-dish of rice, egg,
	fish **ck**
KEEL-BOAT	type of yacht **nt**
KEEL-HAUL	(punishment) **nt**
KEENNESS	acuity; astuteness
KEEPSAKE	memento; relic
KENETRON	large vacuum diode **el**
KENOTRON	wireless valve **ro**
KERASINE	} horn
KERATOSE	}
KERATOMA	skin tumour **md**
KERCHIEF	a head cover
KERMESSE	annual fair in Low Countries;
	also circuit road racing
	events
KERN-BABY	harvest image **bt**
KERNELLY	full of seeds **bt**
KEROSENE	paraffin **mn**
KETOXIME	ketone reaction product **ch**
KEYBLOCK	printing
KEYBOARD	clavier; (morse); type or digit
	encoder **mu, cp, tc**
KEYBOARD	systematic key selector **cp, tc**
KEY-BUGLE	Kent bugle **mu**
KEY-FRUIT	ash, sycamore, etc. **bt**
KEYING-IN	bonding a brick wall **bd**
KEY-MONEY	levy on a tenant

KEYPLATE	keyhole escutcheon	
KEYPUNCH	punch-card recording system	cp
KEYSTONE	main arch support	ar
KHOROVOD	Russian round dance with singing	mu
KIBITZER	critical observer (USA)	
KICKABLE	suitable for booting	
KICK-DOWN	switch	
KICKSHAW	a fallal	
KID-GLOVE	soft delicate glove	
KIEFEKIL	meerschaum	mn
KIELBASA	smoked Polish sausage	
KILL-CROP	a changeling	
KILLDEER	American plover	zo
KILLOGIE	a kiln (Sc.)	
KILL-TIME	a pastime	
KILN-HOLE	mouth of kiln	
KILOBITS	one thousand binary digits	me, cp
KILODYNE	1000 dynes; units of force	me
KILOGRAM	1000 grams weight	
KILOMEGA	one thousand million 10^9	
KILOWATT	1000 watts	me
KINDLESS	unnatural; merciless	
KINDLIER	more forbearing	
KINDLING	animating; tinder	
KINDNESS	benevolence; generosity	
KINEMICS	gestural expression	
KINESICS	gestural body movements	
KINETICS	dynamics	
KINGBIRD	American fly-catcher	zo
KING-CRAB	tropical crab	zo
KINGFISH	the opah	zo
KINGHOOD	sovereignty	
KINGLESS	republican	
KINGLIKE	truly regal	
KINGLING	ruler of petty state	
KINGPOST	principal strut and support for rigging (gliding/hang-)	
KINGSHIP	kingcraft	
KINGWANA	language	
KINGWOOD	ebony (S. Amer.)	bt
KINKAJOU	raccoon; honey-bear	zo
KINSFOLK	kindred; relations	
KIPPERED	cured	
KIRIKANE	gold foil application (Jap.)	
KIRKYARD	graveyard	rl
KIROUMBO	tropical bird	zo
KISS-CURL	a tempting lock	
KISTVAEN	stone sepulchre	
KITEFOOT	a tobacco plant	bt
KITTENED	had a kitty litter	
KITTLISH	ticklish	
KLYSTRON	electron converter	
KNABBING	gnawing	
KNACKISH	knavish	
KNAPPING	flint breaking	
KNAPSACK	haversack; rucksack	
KNAPWEED	bachelor's buttons	bt
KNEADING	dough work	

KNEE-DEEP	} nearly thigh high	
KNEE-HIGH		
KNEEHOLM	knee-holly	bt
KNEELING	kotowing	
KNEE-STOP	organ lever	mu
KNELLING	tolling	
KNICKERS	knickerbockers	
KNIFE-BOY	scullery lad	
KNIGHTED	now Sir	
KNIGHTLY	courtly	
KNIT-BONE	herb comfrey	bt
KNITTING	uniting; interlacing	
KNITWEAR	reticulated fabric	
KNOCKING	rapping; hitting; motoring	
KNOCK-OUT	K.O.; defeat of boxer; dealers' auction	
KNOLLING	knelling	
KNOTLESS	free from ties	
KNOTTIER	more intricate	
KNOTTING	securing; entangling; (carpets); (nauti-knots); dissolved shellac	tx, pt
KNOTWORK	ornamental work	
KNOUTING	scourging	
KNOWABLE	ascertainable; scibile	
KNOW-ALLS	wiseacres	
KNUCKLED	yielded; jointed	
KNULLING	fluting and reeding	ar
KOEMBANG	Fohn wind, Java	mt
KOFTGARI	} inlaying steel with gold	
KOFTWORK		
KOHELETH	Preacher (Solomon)	rl
KOHINOOR	famous diamond	mn
KOHLRABI	cole-turnip	bt
KOLINSKY	Siberian mink	zo
KOMITAJI	Balkan guerilla band	
KONISTRA	orchestra of a Greek theatre	
KOORBASH	} whip made from	
KOURBASH	} rhino hide	
KORFBALL	12 a-side field game (handball)	
KOTOWING	making obeisance	
KREASOTE	} tar by-product; wood	
CREOSOTE	} seasoning	bd, md, rw
KREUTZER	small Austrian copper coin	nm
KUKUKUKU	people (New Guinea)	
KURVEYOR	transport rider (S. Afr.)	
KUTTROLF	Waldglas vessel with curved neck (Ger.)	
KYANIZED	cyanized	ch
KYLOSSIS	club-foot	md
KYPHOSIS	vertebral deformity	md

L

LABDANUM	ladanum	ch
LABELLED	directed	
LABELLUM	lower petal	bt
LABIALLY	lipwise	
LABIATED	lipped	
LABILITY	quick emotional variations	pc

LABOURED	strove	
LABOURER	a toiler	
LABSKAUS	meat/vegetable stew (Scand.)	
		ck
LABURNIC	derived from laburnum	
LABURNUM	flowering tree	**bt**
LACE-BARK	bark of a tree	**bt**
LACE-BOOT	(no buttons)	
LACE-LEAF	aquatic plant	**bt**
LACERATE	tear	
LACEWING	an insect	**zo**
LACEWORK	decoration	
LACE-YOKE	needlework	
LACHESIS	one of the Fates	
LACING-IN	attaching end-boards to book body	
LACK-A-DAY	sorrowful exclamation	
LACKEYED	valeted	
LACONISM	brevity; pithiness	
LACROSSE	a Canadian game	**ga**
LACRYMAL	} tearful	
LACRIMAL	}	
LACHRYMAL	}	
LACTEOUS	milk-like	
LACTIFIC	milk producing	
LACTUCIC	(lettuce)	**bt**
LACUNOSE	pitted; furrowed	
LADDERED	(stockings)	
LADLEFUL	a measure	
LADYBACK	tandem cycle	
LADYBIRD	a helpful beetle	**zo**
LADY-FERN	tall slender fern	**bt**
LADY-HELP	distressed gentlewoman	
LADYHOOD	gentility	
LADYLIKE	well-bred; delicate	
LADYLOVE	a sweetheart	
LADYSHIP	a title for dame, wife of lord, knight	
LAGTHING	Norwegian Upper House (Parliament)	
LAICIZED	opened to the laity	
LAITANCE	milky mortar scum	**bd**
LAKE-LIKE	merely?	
LAMANTIN	the manatee	**zo**
LAMASERY	Tibetan monastery	**rl**
LAMBDOID	lambda-shaped (Gr.)	
LAMBENCY	play of light	
LAMBLIKE	gentle; meek	
LAMBLING	lambkin	**zo**
LAMBSKIN	soft fleece	
LAME-DUCK	a bankrupt	
LAMELLAR	of thin plates	
LAMENESS	halting; crippledness	
LAMENTED	deeply regretted	
LAMENTER	deplorer; bewailer	
LAMINARY	in thin plates	
LAMINATE	in layers	
LAMPHOLE	sewer lighting shaft	
LAMP-POST	support for drunk	
LANCEGAY	a kind of spear	
LANCELET	primitive vertebrate	**zo**

LANCHANG	lugger sailboat (Malaya)	**nt**
LAND-CRAB	land-dwelling crustacean	**zo**
LANDFALL	landslip	**nt**
LAND-FISH	fish out of water	
LAND-GIRL	wartime farm help	
LAND-HERD	a herd of animals	**zo**
LANDLADY	mine hostess	
LANDLESS	no holding	
LANDLINE	overhead cable	
LANDLOCK	protect from wind and sea	
LANDLORD	mine host; house or estate owner	
LANDMARK	notable event; conspicuous feature; boundary stone	
LANDMINE	parachuted bomb	
LANDNAMA	Domesday Book (Ice.)	
LANDRAIL	corncrake	**zo**
LAND-ROLL	clod-crusher	
LAND-SHIP	a tank	
LANDSLIP	landslide	
LANDSMAN	cf. seaman	
LAND-TURN	land-breeze	
LANDWARD	rural	
LANDWEHR	German militia	
LAND-WIND	off-shore wind	
LANGLAUF	cross-country skiing (Ger.)	
LANGRAGE	grape shot	
LANGSHAN	black Chinese hen	**zo**
LANGSYNE	time long past	
LANGUAGE	diction; vernacular; digital codes	**cp**
LANGUISH	pine; droop; decline	
LANIATED	torn to pieces	
LANKIEST	leanest	
LANKNESS	length without breadth	
LANNERET	small falcon	**zo**
LANOLINE	wool fat	
LANTHORN	hornsided lantern	
LAP-BOARD	board used by tailors	
LAPELLED	with lapels	
LAPIDARY	stone-cutter	
LAPIDATE	pelt with stones	
LAPIDIFY	turn into stone	
LAPIDIST	stone-worker	
LAPILLUS	fragment of lava	**mn**
LAP-JOINT	an overlapping joint	
LAPPETED	with flaps	
LAPSABLE	terminal; transient	
LAPSTONE	(used by a shoemaker)	
LARBOARD	port	**nt**
LARCENER	a thief; pilferer	
LARDERER	a store keeper	
LARGESSE	liberality; generosity	
LARKSPUR	a delphinium	**bt**
LARRIKIN	Australian hooligan	
LARVATED	masked	**zo**
LASER-RAY	searing ray	**md**
LASH-DOWN	secure firmly	**nt**
LASHINGS	an abundance; great quantity	
LASSLORN	jilted	
LAST-FOLD	last folded sheet in a book	

LATCH-KEY	domestic open sesame	
LATENESS	tardiness	
LATENTLY	secretly; apparently not	
LATERITE	brick-clay	**mn**
LATHERED	soapy; larruped	
LATHWORK	lath and plaster	
LATINISM	Latin idiom	
LATINIST	Latin scholar	
LATINITY	purity of Latin style	
LATINIZE	latinise	
LATITUDE	width; scope; laxity; North & South parallels	**go**
LATTERLY	more recently; lately	
LATTICED	cross-barred	
LAUDABLE	praiseworthy; honourable	
LAUDABLY	commendably	
LAUDANUM	an opiate	**md**
LAUGHING	riant	
LAUGHTER	convulsive merriment	
LAUNCHED	huried; began; initiated	
LAURASIA	primeval northern landmass	**gl**
LAUREATE	crowned with laurel	
LAVA-LIKE	hard and full of holes	
LAVATION	washing; purification	
LAVATORY	a wash-house	
LAVENDER	greyish blue	**bt**
LAVEROCK	skylark	**zo**
LAVISHED	spent; squandered	
LAVISHLY	prodigally; wastefully	
LAWFULLY	legally; justly; validly	
LAWGIVER	a legislator; a Solon	**lw**
LAWMAKER	an M.P.	
LAWYERLY	verbose	
LAXATION	relaxation; slackness	
LAXATIVE	opening mixture	**md**
LAY-ABOUT	lazy; good for nothing	
LAY-CLERK	a responder	**rl**
LAY-ELDER	Presbyterian elder	**l**
LAYERING	horticultural process	
LAYSTALL	byre	
LAYSTOOL	table for newly printed/clean paper	
LAZARIST	R.C. missionary	**rl**
LAZARONE	Neapolitan beggar	
LAZINESS	inertness; slackness	
LAZULITE	a blue stone	**mn**
LAZURITE	lapis lazuli constituent	**mn**
LEACHATE	extraction of salt in solution	**gl, mn**
LEACHING	making an alkali; rain-aided descent of soluble topsoil minerals	**gl**
LEAD-MILL	lapidary's plate	
LEADSMAN	a lead-swinger	**nt**
LEAF-LARD	leaf-fat lard	
LEAFLESS	destitute of leaves	
LEAFSCAR	a mark	**bt**
LEAGUING	confederating; coalescing	
LEANFACE	narrow-width type	**pr**
LEANNESS	thinness; gauntness	

LEAPFROG	play; overtaking; locational memory programs	**cp**
LEAP-YEAR	a year of 366 days	
LEARNING	scholarship; erudition	
LEASABLE	able to be let	
LEASHING	binding; securing	
LEATHERN	made of leather	
LEATHERS	protective paramilitary uniform (baseball); (hockey); (motor racing)	
LEATHERY	tough	
LEAVENED	modified; tempered	
LEAVINGS	residue; relics	
LEBANESE	a native of Lebanon	
LECANORA	lichen; manna	**bt**
LECITHIN	egg tissue	
LECTURED	reprimanded; chided	
LECTURER	an expositor	
LED-HORSE	spare horse	
LEE-BOARD	anti-drift device	**nt**
LEECHING	doctoring	**md**
LEEFANGE	sheet guide	**nt**
LEE-SHORE	windward shore	**nt**
LEFT-HAND	sinister	
LEFTWARD	to the left	
LEFT-WING	(politics)	
LEGACIES	bequests; gifts	
LEGALISE	authorise; sanction	
LEGALISM	adherence to law	**lw**
LEGALIST	stickler for law	
LEGALITY	lawfulness	
LEGALIZE	sanction; warrant	
LEGATARY	legatee	**lw**
LEGATINE	relating to a legate	
LEGATION	an embassy	
LEG-BREAK	crooked course bowling (cricket)	
LEGERITY	lightness	
LEGUMINA	pods	**bt**
LEGUMINE	nitrogenous proteid	**bt**
LEMONADE	a soft drink	
LEMUROID	} monkey-like	**zo**
LEMURINE		
LENDABLE	loanable	
LENGTHEN	extend; elongate; protract	
LENIENCE	} mildness; clemency; mercifulness; forbearance	
LENIENCY		
LENINISM	} follower of Lenin	
LENINIST		
LENITIVE	mitigating; sedative	
LENS-HOOD	light-shield	**pg**
LENTANDO	slowing up	**mu**
LENTICEL	cell-formation	**bt**
LENTICLE	lenslike mass; glass door of grandfather clock	**gl**
LENT-LILY	daffodil	**bt**
LEPALEPA	dugout outrigger sail canoe (New Guinea)	**nt**
LEPEROUS	leprous	**md**
LEPIDOID	ganoid; scaly	**zo**

LEPIDOTE	with scalelike hairs	**bt, zo**
LEPORINE	like a hare	**zo**
LESSENED	diminished; decreased	
LETHARGY	dullness; apathy; oblivion	
LETTERED	learned; printed	
LETTERER	sports award winner (USA)	
LEUCITIC	containing volcanic ore	**mn**
LEUCOSIS	pallor; albinism	**md**
LEVANTED	decamped; welshed	
LEVANTER	N. African wind	
LEVELING	} smoothing over;	
LEVELLING	reduction to intake capacity	
LEVELLED	flattened; raged; demolished	
LEVELLER	ultra-republican, 1649	
LEVERAGE	mechanical advantage	
LEVERING	exerting pressure	
LEVIABLE	taxable; imposable	
LEVIGATE	to smooth; to polish	
LEVIRATE	Hebrew marriage custom	
LEVITATE	cause to float	
LEVITIES	frivolities; flippancies	
LEVOLOSE	fruit sugar	
LEWDNESS	licentiousness	
LEWDSTER	a profligate	
LEWINIAN	field theory; life-space; group dynamics	**pc**
LEWISITE	poison gas	**ch**
LIBATION	a drink-offering	
LIBATORY	oblatory	
LIBELLED	slandered; defamed	
LIBELLER	lampooner; calumniator	
LIBERATE	set free; emancipate	
LIBERIAN	(Liberia)	
LIBRATED	balanced	
LIBRETTO	words of musical play	
LICENSED	authorized; allowed	
LICENSEE	holder of a license	
LICENSER	licence issuer	
LICHENIC	made from lichen	**bt**
LICHENIN	moss starch	
LICHGATE	lychgate	
LICHWAKE	likewake; death-watch	
LICKER-IN	toothed carding roller	**tx**
LICORICE	liquorice	**bt**
LIEGEMAN	vassal; henchman	
LIFEBELT	} marine lifesaving	
LIFEBOAT	} equipment	**nt**
LIFEBUOY	floating navigation marker	**nt**
LIFEHOLD	lease for life	**lw**
LIFELESS	dull; inanimate; extinct	
LIFELIKE	as if living	
LIFELINE	vital cord	
LIFELONG	till death	
LIFE-PEER	(not hereditary)	
LIFE-RAFT	(for shipwreck)	**nt**
LIFE-RATE	(life insurance)	
LIFE-RENT	rent during lifetime	**lw**

LIFE-SIZE	full scale	
LIFE-TIME	from birth to death, (actuarial); life-time of particle until recombination in a charge	
LIFE-WORK	reason for a career	
LIFTABLE	capable of elevation	
LIGAMENT	binder; tendon	
LIGASOID	gaseous/liquid colloidal system	**ps**
LIGATING	binding; bandaging	**md**
LIGATION	a fastening	
LIGATURE	bandage; band	**mu**
LIGHTFUL	cheery; happy; radiant	
LIGHTING	illuminating; kindling	
LIGHTISH	not heavy; fickle	
LIGHT-PEN	photo electric torch for screens	**tv, cp**
LIGNEOUS	wooden	
LIGNITIC	(lignite; brown coal)	**mn**
LIGULATE	straplike	
LIGURITE	pea-green gem	**mn**
LIKEABLE	pleasant enough	
LIKENESS	resemblance; similarity	
LIKENING	comparing	
LIKEWAKE	lichwake; death-watch	
LIKEWISE	also; moreover; besides	
LILACINE	extract of lilac	**bt**
LILLIPUT	miniature	
LILY-IRON	harpoon for swordfish	
LILY-STAR	feather-star	**bt**
LIMACOID	like a slug	**zo**
LIMATION	filing; polishing	
LIMATURE	filings	
LIMA-WOOD	Peruvian red-wood	**bt**
LIME-FREE	clear of calcium	
LIME-KILN	a furnace	
LIMERICK	verse often perverse	
LIME-SINK	a depression	
LIME-TREE	linden tree	**bt**
LIME-TWIG	a snare	
LIME-WASH	whitewash	
LIMEWORT	lychnis viscaria	**bt**
LIMITARY	finite; bounded	
LIMITING	confining; restricting	
LIMONITE	haematite ore	**mn**
LINAMENT	lint	**md**
LINARITE	a lead compound	**mn**
LINCHPIN	keeps the wheel on	
LINCTURE	linctus; medicine	**md**
LINEALLY	in a direct line	
LINEARLY	directly	
LINE-FEED	counting control device	**pr**
LINE-FISH	fish taken on a line	
LINELLAE	filament system in sarcodina	**zo**
LINESMAN	referee's assistant	
LING-BIRD	meadow-pipit	**zo**
LINGERED	lagged; delayed; tarried	

LINGERER	dawdler; loiterer; dallier	
LINGERIE	undies	
LINGUIST	seldom tongue-tied?	
LINIMENT	embrocation	
LINNAEAN	of Linnaeus; (botanical)	
LINOLEUM	lino; floorcloth	
LINOTYPE	type-setting machine	
LINSTOCK	flame-holder	
LIONIZED	heroized	
LIPAEMIA	fatty blood	md
LIPARITE	rhyolite; granitic lava rock	gl
LIPIODOL	X-ray-opaque substance	
LIPO-GRAM	(letter omission)	
LIPOSOME	fatty/oily globule	bt
LIPSTICK	a cosmetic	
LIQUABLE	fusible; fluent	
LIQUATED	liquified	
LIQUIDLY	smoothly; fluidal	
LIQUIDUS	solidification temperature line	ch
LIQUORED	in drink; tipsy	
LIRIPOOP	hood; trick; nincompoop	
LIROCONE	floury; powdery	
LISTENED	hearkened; attended; heard	
LISTENER	eavesdropper	
LISTLESS	languid; apathetic; torpid	
LITERACY	ability to read and write	
LITERARY	erudite; scholarly	
LITERATE	learned; studious	
LITERATI	men of letters	
LITEROSE	bookish	
LITHARGE	lead oxide	mn
LITHERLY	mischievous; lazy	
LITIGANT	engaged in a lawsuit	lw
LITIGATE	to go to law	lw
LITTERED	scattered; strewn; deranged	
LITTLE-GO	examination (Camb.)	
LITTORAL	a coastal strip	go
LITURATE	blurred; spotted	
LITURGIC	ritualistic	rl
LIVEABLE	habitable; residential	
LIVE-AXLE	driving axle	
LIVE-BAIT	sometimes a worm	
LIVELILY	vivaciously; briskly; alertly	
LIVELONG	lasting; the orpine	bt
LIVENING	cheering up; animating	
LIVE-RAIL	rail carrying current	
LIVERIED	in uniform	
LIVERIES	garbs; uniforms	
LIVERING	thickening of paints, varnish to unusable gel	pt
LIVERISH	bilious; testy	md
LIVE-WELL	kind of aquarium	
LIVE-WIRE	human dynamo	
LIVIDITY	discoloration	
LIVINGLY	lively; energetically; agilely	
LIXIVIAL	residual	ch
LIXIVIUM	lye; residuum	ch
LOAD-LINE	Plimsoll's mark	nt
LOANABLE	able to be lent	

LOAN-WORD	borrowed word	
LOATHFUL	abhorrent; detestable	
LOATHING	hating; antipathy	
LOBBYING	endeavouring to influence	
LOBBYIST	pressurist (parliamentary)	
LOBELINE	monoacidic alkaloid	ch
LOBLOLLY	gruel; lout; attendant	
LOBOTOMY	brain surgery	md
LOCALISM	provincialism	
LOCALITY	situation; district; spot	
LOCALIZE	assign to a place	
LOCATING	positioning; fixing	
LOCATION	film-setting; place; information storage site	cp
LOCATIVE	grammatical case	
LOCKFAST	firmly fastened	
LOCK-GATE	(on canal or river)	
LOCKLESS	without a lock	
LOCK-SILL	threshold of a lock	
LOCKSMAN	a turnkey	
LOCKSPIT	digging mark	
LOCK-WEIR	weir with lock	
LOCULATE	divided	
LOCULOSE	} internally	
LOCULOUS	} into cells	bt
LOCUTION	diction; phrase	
LOCUTORY	place for conversation	rl
LODESMAN	pilot	nt
LODESTAR	pole-star	as
LODGINGS	digs; accommodation	
LODGMENT	occupation; golf	
LODICULE	grass stamen scale	bt
LOG-BOARD	rough log	nt
LOG-CABIN	timber hut	
LOG-CANOE	dugout	nt
LOG-GLASS	timing device	nt
LOGICIAN	one skilled in logic	
LOGICIZE	deduce from reasoning	
LOGISTIC	logical	
LOGOGRAM	puzzle in verse	
LOGOTYPE	twin letters in printing	
LOG-SLATE	recording slate	nt
LOITERED	lingered; tarried	
LOITERER	an idler; flaneur	
LOKWEAVE	carpet-splice	
LOLLARDY	Lollard doctrine	rl
LOLLIPOP	sweet; (traffic sign)	
LOLLOPED	lounged; lurched	
LOMENTUM	branching fruit	bt
LOMONITE	a zeolite	mn
LONDONER	city slicker	
LONENESS	seclusion; solitude	
LONESOME	solitary	
LONGBOAT	naval lifeboat (sail), tender	nt
LONGERON	main spar of aeroplane	ae
LONGEVAL	long lived	
LONG-FIRM	swindling company	
LONGHAND	handwriting	
LONG-HAUL	lengthy; (transport)	
LONG-LEGS	daddy long-legs	zo

LONG-MOSS	tillandsia	**bt**
LONG-SHIP	Viking trader sail vessel	**nt**
LONG-SLIP	(cricket)	
LONGSOME	tiresome; tedious; irksome	
LONG-SPUN	protracted; extended	
LONG-STOP	(cricket)	
LONG-TAIL	not docked	
LONG-TERM	far seeing	
LONGUEUR	tedious patch, padding in lit.	
LONGWAYS	lengthways	
LONGWISE	in extenso	
LONICERA	honey-suckle genus	**bt**
LOOKER-ON	spectator; observer	
LOOM-GALE	minor gale	**mt**
LOOP-HOLE	an escape; gun port in a castle; legal evasion clause	**lw**
LOOP-LINE	alternative route	
LOOP-STOP	program stopper	**cp**
LOOSE-BOX	a stall	
LOOSENED	undone; relaxed; slackened	**md**
LOOSENER	a laxative	**md**
LOP-EARED	with drooping ears	
LOPOLITH	lens-shaped igneous intrusion	**gl**
LOP-SIDED	unbalanced; biased	
LORD-LIKE	haughty; imperious	
LORDLING	a would-be lord	
LORDOSIS	spinal curvature	**md**
LORD'S-DAY	Sunday	
LORDSHIP	sway; dominion; control	
LORICATE	to incrust	
LORIKEET	Australian parrot	**zo**
LOSINGLY	wastefully	
LOTHARIO	a libertine; a filly-buster	
LOUDNESS	uproar; clamour; resonance	
LOUNGING	reclining; lolling; idling	
LOVEBIRD	a budgerigar	**zo**
LOVEKNOT	a tangle	
LOVELACE	a libertine	
LOVELESS	passionless; frigid	
LOVELIES	beauteous damsels	
LOVE-LIFE	romance	
LOVELILY	delectably; enchantingly	
LOVELOCK	a manly curl	
LOVELORN	jilted	
LOVE-NEST	romantic abode	
LOVESICK	languishing	
LOVESOME	adorable	
LOVESUIT	courtship	
LOVINGLY	affectionately; fondly	
LOWERING	depressing; threatening	
LOW-WATER	at the ebb	
LOYALIST	patriot; faithful follower	
LUBBERLY	clumsily; maladroit	
LUCIDITY	clearness; luminosity	
LUCKIEST	most fortunate; happiest	
LUCKLESS	singularly unfortunate	

LUCKYBAG	} a bran tub	
LUCKYDIP	} with hidden gifts	
LUCULENT	translucent; lucid; clear	
LUCULLUS	an epicure	
LUGARITE	rare analcite-gabbro form	**gl**
LUKEWARM	tepid	
LUMBERED	rumbled along	
LUMBERER	woodman	
LUMINANT	shining; radiant	
LUMINARY	a heavenly body	
LUMINATE	illuminate; brighten	
LUMINOUS	phosphorescent; lucent	
LUMPFISH	a sea fish	**zo**
LUNARIAN	a moon observer	
LUNATION	a lunar month	
LUNCHEON	midday repast	
LUNCHING	eating in early afternoon	
LUNGEING	fencing; horse training	
LUNGFISH	queer fish	**zo**
LUNGLESS	not breathing	
LUNGWORT	a lichen	**bt**
LUNIFORM	moon-shaped	
LUNULATE	like a crescent	
LUPERCAL	Roman festival	
LUPININE	lupinus-seed alkaloid	**ch**
LUPINITE	a bitter extract	**bt**
LUPULONE	soft hops resin	**br**
LURCHING	stumbling; rolling; lurking	
LUSCIOUS	rich in flavour	
LUSTIEST	beefiest; heftiest; sexiest	
LUSTRATE	purify	
LUSTRING	silk cloth	**tx**
LUSTROUS	shining; luminous	
LUSTWORT	the sun-dew	**bt**
LUTANIST	a lute player	**mu**
LUTATION	sealing	
LUTECIUM	a metallic element	**ch**
LUTEOLIN	yellow dye	**bt**
LUTETIAN	of Paris	
LUTHERAN	Protestant	**rl**
LUTIDINE	bone-oil/coal-tar constituent	
LUXATING	displacing	
LUXATION	dislocation	
LUXMETER	illuminance measurement device	
LUXURIES	unnecessary pleasures	
LUXURIST	an indulger	
LYCHGATE	lichgate	**rl**
LYCOPODE	yellow powder	**bt**
LYMPHOID	like lymph	**md**
LYNCHING	mob law	
LYNCH-LAW	short-shrift	
LYNX-EYED	keen of vision	
LYOLYSIS	acid/base formation process	**ch**
LYRE-BIRD	Australian bird	**zo**
LYRICISM	lyric composition	
LYSERGIC	l.s.d. acid	**ch**
LYSOSOME	sac of hydrolytic enzymes	**bl**
LYSOZYME	bacteriolytic enzyme	**bl**

M

MACARIAN	blessed
MACARISM	a beatitude
MACARIZE	to bless
MACARONI	fop; food (pasta) **ck**
MACAROON	almond biscuit **ck**
MACASSAR	hair oil
MACERATE	harass; to steep; to rot
MACHINAL	mechanical
MACHINED	turned on a machine
MACHINER	operative
MACKEREL	scad; cloud pattern **zo**
MACRANER	large male ant **zo**
MACROPOD	long-legged **zo**
MACROPUS	kangaroo genus **zo**
MACULATE	to spot; to stain
MADDENED	infuriated; incensed
MADHOUSE	Bedlam; asylum
MADRIGAL	pastoral ditty **mu**
MAECENAS	rich art patron
MAENADIC	bacchanalian
MAESTOSO	majestically **mu**
MAFFLING	a simpleton
MAGAZINE	depot; store; periodical; feeder (gun) (slides)
MAGDALEN	home for repentants
MAGGIORE	It. major, greater **mu**
MAGICIAN	wizard; marabout
MAGIRICS	the culinary art
MAGISTER	master; doctor **md**
MAGNADUR	ceramic magnet/insulator material
MAGNESIA	a medicine **md**
MAGNESON	magnesium reagent **ch**
MAGNETIC	attractive; drawing
MAGNETON	constant of M, movement of an electron **el, ps**
MAGNIFIC	splendid; majestic
MAGNOLIA	a flowering tree **bt**
MAGOT-PIE	magpie **zo**
MAHADENA	Hindu god, Siva **rl**
MAHARAJA	Indian rajah
MAHOGANY	tropical tree **bt**
MAIDENLY	modest; demure; bashful
MAIDHOOD	girlhood; virginity
MAIEUTIC	delivering; evolving
MAILABLE	postable
MAIL-BOAT	a packet **nt**
MAIL-CART	post wagon
MAIL-CLAD	armour-plated
MAIL-DRAG	mail-coach
MAIN-BOOM	} parts of sailing
MAIN-DECK	} ship **nt**
MAINLAND	continent
MAINMAST	} chief
MAINSAIL	} rigging units **nt**
MAIN-PATH	main course; written routine **cp**

MAINSTAY	chief support; brace for mainmast **nt**
MAINTAIN	continue; assert; aver; hold
MAINYARD	part of rigging **nt**
MAJESTIC	imperial; august; regal
MAJOLICA	artificial pearls (Majorca)
MAJORATE	rank of major
MAJORITY	over 18
MAKEBATE	quarrel-maker
MAKELESS	matchless
MAKIMONO	Japanese picture
MALACOID	soft-bodied
MALADIES	disorders; ailments **md**
MALAGASH	} relating to
MALAGASY	} Madagascar
MALAMUTE	Arctic sledge dog **zo**
MALAPERT	saucy; impertinent; flippant
MALAPROP	of misuse of words
MALARIAL	(malaria) **md**
MALCHITE	diorite rock **gl**
MAL-DE-MER	sea-sickness **md**
MALE-FERN	common lowland fern **bt**
MALEFICE	evil deed; enchantment
MALENESS	having male physical characteristics
MALETOLT	} illegal exaction **lw**
MALETOTE	}
MALIGNED	traduced; slandered
MALIGNER	defamer; reviler; abuser
MALINGER	feign illness
MALLEATE	to hammer
MALLECHO	villainy; mischief (Shak.)
MALMROCK	sandstone **mn**
MALODOUR	a smell; stench
MALT-DUST	malt grains
MALTHENE	asphaltic bitumen constituent **ch**
MALT-KILN	} comprise malt factory
MALT-MILL	}
MALTREAT	abuse; hurt; harm; injure
MALTSTER	malt-maker
MALT-WORM	a tippler; weevil **zo**
MALUNION	improper bone-knitting **md**
MAMALIGA	maize-meal porridge **ck**
MAMBRINO	source of Don Quixote's helmet
MAMELUKE	Turkic military dynasty in Egypt; caucasian slave
MAMMALIA	suckers **zo**
MAMMARED	stammered
MAMMIFER	a mammal **zo**
MAMMILLA	a nipple **md**
MAMMODIS	Indian muslin **tx**
MANACLED	shackled; fettered
MANAGING	controlling; contriving
MAN-CHILD	a boy
MANCIPLE	a steward; purveyor
MANDAEAN	Babylonian sect
MANDAMUS	a writ **lw**
MANDARIN	official; orange; language **bt**

MANDATOR	commander; director	
MANDELIC	bitter almond extract	bt
MANDIBLE	a jaw of insect	zo
MANDINGO	tribe (South Sahara)	
MANDIOCA	cassava; manioc	bt
MANDOLIN	a guitar	mu
MANDORLA	oval panel	
MANDRAKE	white bryony	bt
MANDRILL	a baboon	zo
MAN-EATER	cannibal; tiger	zo
MANELESS	without a mane	
MANELIKE	like a mane	
MANEQUIN	manikin; artist's model	
MANFULLY	boldly; courageously	
MANGABEY	Malagasy monkey	zo
MANGANIN	copper-base alloy	
MANGCORN	mixed grain crop	
MANGLING	calendering; mutilating	
MANGONEL	a ballistic machine	
MANGROVE	a tree	bt
MAN-HATER	allergic to man	
MAN-HOURS	labour measure	
MANIACAL	raving; frenzied; lunatic	
MANICATE	hairy	bt
MANICHEE	a doctrinaire	
MANICURE	hand treatment	
MANIFEST	invoice of ship's cargo	nt
MANIFEST	evince; clear; obvious	
MANIFOLD	multiplied; numerous	
MANNERLY	of good address	
MANNIKIN	manikin; dwarf	
MANNITOL	hexahydric alcohol	ch
MANOCYST	receptive papilla in oomycetes	
		bt
MAN-OF-WAR	warship	nt
MANORIAL	referring to a manor	
MANOSTAT	pressure-constancy device	eg
MAN-POWER	male potential	
MAN-SIZED	adult dimensions	
MANSUETE	mild; gentle	
MANTELET	small cloak	
MANTIGER	heraldic term	hd
MANTILLA	hanging lace & comb hair style (Sp.)	
MANTISSA	decimal part of logarithm	
MANTISSA	number with floating point	cp,
		ma
MANTLING	blushing; flushing; suffusing	
MAN-TO-MAN	close, confidential; intimate; frank	
MANUALLY	by hand	
MANUCODE	bird of paradise	zo
MANURING	fertilizing	
MANUTYPE	hand-painted	
MAORI-HEN	the weka	zo
MAQUETTE	mock-up model, sketch (Fr.)	
MARABOUT	Indian stork	zo
MARABOUT	Moslem priest or wizard	rl
MARAGING	steel-hardening heat treatment	
		ml

MARASMUS	emaciation	
MARATHON	long distance race	
MARAUDED	roved; plundered; pillaged	
MARAUDER	raider; bandit; outlaw	
MARAVEDI	small Spanish copper	nm
MARBLING	form of decor	
MARCANDO	with precision	mu
MARCHING	bordering; foot slogging	
MARGARIC	pearly	
MARGARIN	ersatz butter	
MARGARON	a fatty substance	
MARGINAL	in the margin; slight amount	
MARGINED	edged; bordered	
MARGRAVE	German count	
MARIGOLD	orange flower	bt
MARIGRAM	tidal-height record	sv
MARINADE	steeping liquor	ck
MARINATE	steep in liquor; preserve	
MARITIME	marine; naval; nautical	
MARJORAM	aromatic plant	bt
MARKEDLY	unmistakably; eminently	
MARKETED	sold; vended	
MARKSMAN	crack shot	
MARLINED	twined with twine	nt
MARLITIC	(clay)	mn
MARMOSET	American monkey	zo
MAROCAIN	fine-rep dress fabric	tx
MARONITE	Jewish sect	
MAROONED	left on desert island	
MAROQUIN	morocco leather	
MARQUESS	a marquis	
MARQUISE	marchioness	
MARRIAGE	wedlock; espousal	
MARRYING	wedding; uniting	
MARSH-GAS	methane	ch
MARSH-HEN	moorhen	zo
MARSH-TIT	blackheaded tom-tit	zo
MARTAGON	turk's cap lily	bt
MARTELLO	circular tower	
MARTENOT	waves, keyboard, electronic piano	mu
MARTINET	a disciplinarian	
MARTYRED	victimized	
MARYGOLD	marigold	bt
MARY-SOLE	a flat-fish	zo
MARZIALE	martial (It.)	mu
MARZIPAN	a sweetmeat of almonds	ck
MASCARON	grotesque head as decoration	
MASORITE	a theologist	
MASSACRE	pogrom; carnage	
MASSAGED	kneaded; rubbed	
MASS-BELL	sacring-bell	
MASS-BOOK	R.C. missal	rl
MASSETER	a jaw muscle	pl
MASSEUSE	a manipulator	md
MASSICOT	lead oxide	mn
MASSORAH	Hebrew tradition	
MASTERED	conquered; overcame; learned; competent	
MASTERLY	expertly; dexterously	

MASTHEAD	newspaper main title; main top mast flag	**nt**
MASTITIS	breast inflammation	**md**
MASTLESS	dismasted; steam-diesel-powered vessels	**nt**
MASTODON	early mammoth	**zo**
MASTSHIP	masts, timber carrier vessel	**nt**
MASURIUM	a metallic element	**ch**
MATADORE	bull-fighter; domino game	
MATAMATA	S. Amer. river tortoise	**zo**
MATCHBOX	chez Lucifer	
MATCHING	equalling; suiting; comparing records; matchboard	**cp**
MATELOTE	fish/wine stew (Fr.)	**ck**
MATERIAL	stuff; essential; relevant	
MATERIEL	equipment (Fr.)	
MATERNAL	motherly	
MATESHIP	comradeship	
MAT-GRASS	weavable reeds	**bt**
MATHESIS	mathematics; learning	
MATHILDA	a tank	
MATRONAL	motherly; sedate	
MATRONLY	elderly	
MATTERED	signified; imported	
MATTRESS	stuffed, base of bed; concrete base (slab)	**ce**
MATURANT	a cataplasm	**md**
MATURATE	to poultice	**md**
MATURELY	deliberately; completely	
MATURING	ripening; mellowing	
MATURITY	readiness; fullness; ripeness; of age	
MAUNDRIL	a pick-axe	**to**
MAUVEINE	synthetic dyestuff	**ch**
MAVERICK	unbranded animal	
MAXIM-GUN	single-barrelled machine gun	
MAXIMIST	a dealer in old saws	
MAXIMIZE	raise to maximum	
MAY-APPLE	N. American fruit	**bt**
MAY-BLOBS	marsh marigold	**bt**
MAY-BLOOM	hawthorn	**bt**
MAYORESS	wife of mayor	
MAY-QUEEN	spring deity	
MAZARINE	deep blue; flat plate within a dish; cake	**ck**
MAZDAISM	Zoroastrianism	
MAZINESS	perplexity; haziness	
MAZOLOGY	a zoological science	**zo**
MAZOURKA	mazurka; Polish folk dance	**mu**
MEAGRELY	scantily; sparsely; meanly	
MEAL-POCK	} beggar's meal-bag	
MEAL-POKE		
MEALTIME	breakfast, lunch or dinner	
MEALWORM	one infesting flour	**zo**
MEAN-BORN	of humble origin	
MEANNESS	sordidness; paltriness	
MEANTIME	meanwhile	
MEASURED	meted; ascertained; steady	
MEASURER	computer; gauger	

MEAT-BALL	rissole, mini-hamburger	**ck**
MEATLESS	of vegetarian foods	**ck**
MEAT-RACK	hooked storage facilities	
MEAT-SAFE	storage cupboard	
MECHANIC	artisan; fitter	
MECONATE	} poppy-juice; opium; contents of foetal intestine	
MECONINE		
MECONIUM		**zo**
MEDALIST	a prize winner	
MEDALLIC	relating to medals	
MEDDLING	interfering; intruding	
MEDIATED	intervened; reconciled	
MEDIATOR	an intercessor; arbitrator	
MEDICATE	to doctor; to dose	
MEDICEAN	(Medici of Florence)	
MEDICINE	the curative art	**md**
MEDIEVAL	(Middle Ages)	
MEDIOCRE	middling; ordinary	
MEDITATE	ruminate; muse; intend	
MEDULLAR	pithy	**bt**
MEDULLIN	lilac cellulose	**bt**
MEEKENED	became gentle	
MEEKNESS	submissiveness; humility	
MEETNESS	fitness; propriety	
MEGALINE	magnetic flux unit	**el**
MEGALITH	stone monument	
MEGALOPS	last larval stage in crabs	**zo**
MEGAPODE	mound bird	**zo**
MEGATRON	light-house valve	
MEGAVOLT	million volts	
MEGAWATT	million watts	
MEIONITE	a silicate	**mn**
MEIOTAXY	whorl development failure	**bt**
MELAMINE	organic compound	**ch**
MELANISM	black coloration	
MELANITE	black garnet	**mn**
MELANOMA	pigmented mole	
MELANOUS	dark-visaged	
MELANURE	sea-bream	**zo**
MELIBEAN	alternately responsive	
MELILITE	complex mineral	**mn**
MELINITE	a high explosive	
MELLIFIC	honeyed	
MELLOWED	matured; ripened; enriched	
MELLOWLY	sweetly; melodiously	
MELODEON	harmonium	**mu**
MELODIST	composer	
MELODIZE	render harmonious	**mu**
MEMBERED	having limbs	
MEMBRANE	tissue wall; tent roof; film (surface)	**bt, zo**
MEMORIAL	relic; monument; memento	
MEMORIZE	learn by heart	
MEMPHIAN	} (Memphis)	
MEMPHITE		
MEMSAHIB	white lady (India)	
MENACING	threatening; intimidating	
MENDABLE	repairable	
MENHADEN	American herring	**zo**
MENILITE	brown opal	**mn**

MENINGES	brain membranes	**md**
MENISCAL	} crescent-shaped	
MENISCUS	} type of lens	
MENOLOGY	calendar of saints	
MENOPOME	mud-devil	**zo**
MENSURAL	measurable	
MENTALLY	intellectually	
MEPHISTO	diabolical chess automaton (Turk.)	
MEPHITIC	noxious; pestilential	
MEPHITIS	an exhalation; miasma	
MERCABLE	saleable; vendible	
MERCHAND	to traffic; to trade	
MERCHANT	trader; dealer; monger	
MERCIFUL	humane; clement; lenient	
MERCURIC	mercurial; quick witted; changeable	
MERCYISM	rumination; infantile regurgitation	
MERICARP	seed carpel	**bt**
MERIDIAN	great circle; noon	
MERINGUE	eggwhites and sugar cake	**ck**
MERIONES	Can. jumping mouse	**zo**
MERISTEM	formative tissue	
MERISTIC	segmented	**zo**
MERITING	deserving; earning	
MEROGAMY	individualized-gamete union	**bt**
MEROSMIA	smell sense deficiency	**md**
MEROSOME	a segment; a somite	**zo**
MEROXENE	biotite class	**mn**
MEROZOON	protozoon fragment	**zo**
MERRYMAN	mountebank; jester	
MESCALIN	alkaloid 'truth drug'	**md**
MESDAMES	ladies	
MESHWORK	network; reticulation	
MESITITE	a carbonate	**mn**
MESMEREE	one mesmerized	
MESMERIC	hypnotic	
MESOCARP	central carpel	**bt**
MESODERM	inner skin	**md**
MESOLITE	needlestone	**mn**
MESOMERE	muscle-plate zone in vertebrates	**zo**
MESOSOMA	abdomen division in arachnida	**zo**
MESOTRON	electron-directing device	
MESOTYPE	zeolitic mineral	**mn**
MESOZOIC	Triassic period	**gl**
MESQUITE	African thorn-bush	**bt**
MESSIDOR	June l9th–July 18th (Fr.)	
MESSMATE	table companion	
MESSROOM	forces' dining room	
MESSUAGE	premises and garden	
METACISM	excess of 'M'	
METACONE	cusp of mammal molar	**zo**
METADYNE	generator, converter	**el, ps**
METAIRIE	(produce sharing) Fr.	
METALLED	(roads); plated	
METALLIC	lustrous	
METALMAN	metal-worker	

METAMERE	similar body segment	**zo**
METAMICT	glassy amorphous state	**mn**
METAPHOR	allegory; image	
METASOMA	abdomen part in arachnida	**zo**
METASOME	mid-body of cyclops	**zo**
METATOME	an architectural space	
METAYAGE	see metairie	
METAZOAN	} multicellular	
METAZOIC	} construction of an	
METAZOON	} animal	**zo**
METECORN	a corn issue	
METEORIC	transient; dazzling; flashing	
METERAGE	measurement	
METEWAND	} yard-stick	
METEYARD	}	**me**
METHANOL	methyl alcohol	**ch**
METHINKS	I think	
METHODIC	systematic; orderly	
METHYLAL	chemical solvent	
METHYLIC	(methyl)	**ch**
METHYSIS	drunkenness	**md**
METONYMY	a trope	
ME-TOOISM	alsoiology	
METOPISM	(frontal suture)	**md**
METOPRYL	anaesthetic	**ch**
METRICAL	rhythmic	
MEZEREON	aromatic shrub	**bt**
MIASMATA	nauseous exhalations	
MICRANER	small male ant	**zo**
MICROBAR	unit of pressure	**ps**
MICROBIC	microbial	**zo**
MICROZOA	animalculae	**zo**
MICRURGY	cell-study technique	**bl**
MIDBRAIN	sight and hearing	**pl**
MIDDLING	mediocre; medium; average	
MIDFIELD	players (cricket, lacrosse)	
MIDNIGHT	24.00 hours	
MIDPOINT	} averages of extremes	
MIDRANGE	}	
MIDSHIPS	on bow-aft line, in the beam	**nt**
MIGHTFUL	powerful; dynamic	
MIGHTILY	vigorously; potently	
MIGRAINE	the vapours	**md**
MIGRATED	left; moved	
MIGRATOR	emigrant; nomad; rover	
MILANESE	(Milan)	
MILDEWED	mouldy; musty; rusty	
MILDNESS	gentleness; blandness	
MILEPOST	milestone	
MILESIAN	early Irish race	
MILITANT	eager to fight; warring	
MILITARY	martial; soldierly; warlike	
MILITATE	oppose; contend; fight	
MILK-MAID	dairy-maid	
MILK-TREE	the messaranduba	**bt**
MILK-WALK	(a district)	
MILK-WARM	tepid	
MILK-WEED	the sow-thistle	**bt**
MILK-WORT	flowering plant	**bt**

MILKY-WAY	a galaxy	
MILLEPED	ten centipedes in one	**zo**
MILL-HAND	factory operative	
MILLIARD	a thousand millions	
MILLIARE	thousandth of an are (Fr.)	
MILLIBAR	unit of barometric pressure	**me**
MILLIGAL	1000th of a gal	**gp**
MILLILUX	unit of illumination intensity	**lt**
MILLINER	bonnet-maker	
MILLIPED	milleped	**zo**
MILLPOND	mere quiescence?	
MILLRACE	actuating stream	
MILLTAIL	water past mill-wheel	
MILLWORK	mill machinery; prefabricated joinery	**jn**
MILTONIC	(Milton)	
MIMETITE	lead compound	**mn**
MIMICKED	aped; took off; imitated	
MIMICKER	impersonator; mime	
MINATORY	menacing; threatening	
MINCE-PIE	fruit-filled tart (Christmas)	**ck**
MINDLESS	stupid; heedless	
MINGLING	mixing; blending	
MINIATED	illuminated	
MINIBORE	(central heating); small bore piping	**bd**
MINIFIED	depreciated	
MINIMENT	muniment (obs.)	
MINIMIZE	treat slightingly	
MINISTER	servant; pastor; succour	
MINISTRY	agency; cabinet	
MINORITE	Franciscan friar	**rl**
MINORITY	the smaller number	
MINOTAUR	half man, half bull	
MINSTREL	ballad-monger	
MINTMARK	identification mark	**nm**
MINUETTO	} French, triple time dance	
MINUET	}	**mu**
MINUTELY	particularly; exactly	
MINUTEST	smallest; tiniest	
MINUTIAE	small details	
MINUTING	recording; noting	
MIRE-CROW	black-headed gull	**zo**
MIREPOIX	vegetable bed for braised meats	**ck**
MIRINESS	muddiness; swampiness	
MIRLITON	Fr. kazoo, hum-through toy	**mu**
MIRRORED	reflected	
MIRTHFUL	festive; jocund; vivacious	
MISAIMED	ill-directed	
MISAPPLY	pervert; misuse; abuse	
MISARRAY	disarray; disorder	
MISBEGOT	shapeless (Shak.)	
MISBOUND	in wrong order	**pr**
MISCARRY	to fail; be abortive	
MISCELLA	oil/solvent solution	**ch**
MISCHIEF	injury; harm; hurt; trouble	
MISCHOSE	made wrong choice	

MISCIBLE	mixable	
MISCLAIM	claim in error	
MISCOUNT	reckon wrongly	
MISCREED	false creed	
MISCUING	(billiards)	
MISDATED	forgot what day it was	
MISDEALT	(cards)	
MISDOING	wronging; offending	
MISDOUBT	suspicion; irresolution	
MISDRAWN	badly drawn	
MISDREAD	regard with dread	
MISENTER	to enter wrongly	
MISENTRY	erroneous record	
MISERERE	strangely decorated underseat brackets in choir stalls	**ar, rl**
MISFAITH	distrust; perfidy; catholic anthem	**rl, mu**
MISFEIGN	to disguise	
MISFIELD	cricket	
MISFIRED	did not go off	
MISGRAFF	} to graft amiss	
MISGRAFT	}	
MISGUIDE	lead astray	
MISHEARD	didn't get it	
MISHMASH	medley; hotch-potch; jumble	**mu, ck**
MISHNAIC	} (Jewish Oral Laws)	**rl, lw**
MISHNOTH	}	
MISINFER	deduce erroneously	
MISJUDGE	misconstrue; mistake	
MISLABEL	address incorrectly	
MISLAYER	untidy person	
MISLETOE	} parasitic plant	**bt**
MISTLETOE	}	
MISLIKED	disapproved; disliked	
MISMATCH	out-class	
MISNAMED	wrong appellation	
MISNOMER	incorrect appellation	
MISOGAMY	hatred of marriage	
MISOGYNY	hatred of women	
MISPLACE	displace; mislay	
MISPLEAD	win case for opponent	
MISPOINT	punctuate improperly	
MISPRINT	typographical error	
MISPRISE	to mistake	
MISPRIZE	slight; undervalue; belittle	
MISQUOTE	cite erroneously	
MISRATED	rated erroneously	
MISRULED	governed badly	
MISSABLE	not necessary or desirable to attain	
MISSERVE	serve unfaithfully	
MISSHAPE	to deform	
MISSPEAK	utter wrongly	
MISSPELL	write wrong	
MISSPELT	an error in orthography	
MISSPEND	squander; misuse	
MISSPENT	wasted; dissipated	
MISSTATE	state falsely	
MISTAKEN	in error; wrong; incorrect	

MISTEACH	teach wrongly	
MISTHINK	think ill of	
MISTIMED	chronologically erroneous	
MISTITLE	use wrong title	
MISTRAIN	to educate amiss	
MISTRESS	lady of the house	
MISTRIAL	(jury fail to agree)	lw
MISTRUST	want of confidence	
MISTRYST	to deceive (Sc.)	
MISTUNED	discordant	
MISTUTOR	to instruct amiss	
MISUSAGE	abuse; perversion	
MISUSING	misapplying; profaning	
MISVOUCH	to bear false witness	
MISWRITE	write incorrectly	
MISYOKED	mismatched	
MITCHELL	hewn Purbeck stone	
MITHRAIC	(Mithras)	
MITIGANT	alleviating; lenitive	
MITIGATE	lessen; allay; assuage	
MITTENED	wearing mitts	
MITTIMUS	a writ	lw
MIZZLING	clearing off; drizzling	
MNEMONIC	label chosen to aid memory	
MOBILITY	changeability; fickleness	
MOBILIZE	gather resources	
MOBOCRAT	demagogue	
MOCASSIN	} leather shoe;	
MOCCASIN	} venomous snake	zo
MOCKABLE	ridiculous; derisive	
MODALISM	Sabellian doctrine	
MODALIST	theorist	
MODALITY	logical custom; sensory system	
MODELLED	fashioned; designed	
MODELLER	copyist; plastic planner	
MODERATE	so-so; fair; pacify; mollify	
MODERATO	at moderate pace	mu
MODESTLY	decently; unobtrusively	
MODIFIED	altered; varied; changed	
MODIFIER	moderator	
MODINHAR	Portuguese popular song	mu
MODIOLAR	like a bushel measure	
MODIOLUS	central pillar of cochlea	zo
MODISHLY	foppishly; fashionable	
MODULATE	regulate; harmonize	
MOFUSSIL	rural districts (Hindu)	
MOHARRAM	Mohammedan fast	rl
MOIDERED	spent; toiled	
MOISTFUL	damp; humid	
MOISTURE	humidity	
MOLALITY	} mole/solvent solution	
MOLARITY	} ratio	ch
MOLASSES	treacle	
MOLE-CAST	a molehill	
MOLECULE	group of atoms	ch
MOLE-EYED	having small eyes	
MOLE-HILL	miniature mountain	
MOLE-SKIN	strong cotton fustian	tx
MOLESTED	troubled; pestered	

MOLESTER	an annoyer; harasser	
MOLINIST	a Jesuit	rl
MOLLIENT	assuaging; softening	
MOLLUSCA	invertebrates	zo
MOLYBDIC	(molybdenum)	ch
MOMENTLY	every moment	
MOMENTUM	impetus; impulsive weight	
MONACHAL	monastic	rl
MONANDRY	(one husband only)	
MONARCHO	fantastic person (Shak.)	
MONARCHY	a kingdom; an empire	
MONASTIC	a monk	rl
MONAURAL	uni-aural; one ear only	
MONAZITE	a phosphate	mn
MONDAINE	woman of fashion	
MONDAYNE	mundane (obs.)	
MONETARY	relating to money	
MONETIZE	to coin bullion	
MONEYBOX	cash-box	
MONGERED	dealt in	
MONGOOSE	mungoose	zo
MONIMENT	monument; image (Spens.)	
MONISTIC	single-minded	
MONITION	a summons	lw
MONITIVE	warning	
MONITORY	cautionary	
MONITRIX	woman instructor	
MONKEYED	played about with	
MONKFISH	angler-fish	zo
MONKHOOD	monastic state	rl
MONK-SEAL	kind of sea creature	zo
MONNIKER	sobriquet; nickname	
MONOBATH	developing/fixing solution; for single person only	pg
MONOBLOC	integral cylinder casting	au
MONOCARP	an annual plant	bt
MONOCLED	wearing an eye-glass	
MONOCRAT	autocrat	
MONOCULE	one-eyed animal	zo
MONOCYTE	uninuclear leucocyte	zo
MONODIST	writer of dirges	
MONODONT	having a single tooth	zo
MONOGAMY	(one wife)	
MONOGERM	seed-producing single seedling	bt
MONOGONY	asexual reproduction	
MONOGRAM	interwoven initials	
MONOGYNY	(one wife)	
MONOLITH	stone monument	
MONOLOGY	soliloquizing	
MONOLULU	Epsom Downs tipster	
MONOMARK	identification mark	
MONOMIAL	expressed by one term	
MONOPODE	single-footed	
MONOPOLY	exclusive privilege	
MONOPTIC	with one eye; monocular	
MONORAIL	single rail system	
MONOTINT	picture in one colour	
MONOTONE	unvaried tone	
MONOTONY	dull uniformity; tedium	

MONOTYPE	printing machine	
MONSIEUR	a Frenchman	
MONTANIC	mountainous	
MONTEITH	punch-bowl; kerchief	
MONTEURS	artificial flower makers	
MONTICLE	hillock; molehill	
MONUMENT	a memorial; cenotaph; beacon	
MOOCHING	loitering	
MOONBEAM	a lunar ray	
MOONCALF	monster; dolt	
MOON-EYED	purblind	
MOONFACE	a round face	
MOONFISH	opposite of sunfish	zo
MOONLESS	dark	
MOONLING	simpleton	
MOON-SAIL	a small sail	nt
MOONSEED	climbing plant	bt
MOONSHEE	Moslem linguist	
MOON-TYPE	embossed lettering	
MOONWORT	a fern	bt
MOON-YEAR	lunar year	
MOORCOCK	red grouse	zo
MOORFOWL	moorcock	zo
MOORGAME	grouse	zo
MOORHAWK	marsh harrier	zo
MOORLAND	moreland; peaty soil	go
MOORWHIN	a genista	bt
MOORWORT	marsh andromeda	bt
MOOTABLE	debatable; doubtful	
MOOT-CASE	a moot-point	
MOOT-HALL	judgment hall	
MOOT-HILL	a rendezvous	
MOPE-EYED	myopic; purblind	
MOPISHLY	gloomily; dejectedly	
MOQUETTE	a carpet (Fr.); of coarse wool & linen	
MORALIST	virtuous man	
MORALITY	ethics; virtue	
MORALIZE	philosophize	
MORATORY	delaying	
MORAVIAN	of Moravia; Hussite sect	rl
MORBIDLY	unhealthily	
MORBIFIC	causing disease	md
MORELAND	moorland	
MOREOVER	besides; also; likewise	
MORESQUE	arabesque	
MORIBUND	dying	
MORILLON	grape; duck	bt, zo
MORMYRUS	Egyptian pike	zo
MOROCCAN	(Morocco)	
MOROLOGY	foolish talk	
MOROSELY	sullenly; sourly	
MOROXITE	a phosphate	mn
MORPHEAN	sleepy; dreamy	
MORPHEMA	minimal meaningful linguistic unit	
MORPHEUS	god of sleep	
MORPHINE	morphia	md
MORTALLY	fatally; deadly	

MORTARED	(gun-fire; brickwork)	
MORTGAGE	pledge	lw
MORTISED	jointed	
MORTLAKE	ox-bow (ex-river) lake; Ox-bridge beer-lake	gl
MORTLING	morling; dead sheep	zo
MORTMAIN	inalienable property	lw
MORTUARY	charnel house; morgue	
MOSLINGS	curried leather	le
MOSQUITO	an insect	zo
MOSS-BACK	a Rip van Winkle	
MOSS-CLAD	mossy	
MOSSLAND	peat-land	go
MOSS-PINK	a phlox	bt
MOSS-ROSE	house plant	bt
MOSS-RUSH	bog plant	bt
MOTHBALL	naphthalene; anti-moth	
MOTHERED	adopted	
MOTHERLY	parental; tender	
MOTILITY	movement; mobility	
MOTIONAL	emotional	
MOTIONED	gestured; proposed	
MOTIONER	a mover	
MOTIVATE	actuate; impel; induce	
MOTIVITY	power of energizing	
MOTOR-BUS	coach	
MOTOR-CAR	automobile	
MOTORIAL	motory; giving motion	
MOTORING	travelling by car	
MOTORISE	equip with motors	
MOTORIST	car driver	
MOTORMAN	chauffeur; one-man-train driver	rw
MOTORWAY	fast main road	
MOTTLING	variegating	
MOUCHING	slouching; skulking	
MOUFFLON	wild sheep	zo
MOULD-BOX	box for casting	
MOULDING	shaping; fashioning	
MOULINET	drum of capstan	
MOULTING	shedding feathers	
MOUNDING	banking	
MOUNTAIN	a light wine	
MOUNTANT	photographic paste	
MOUNTIES	R. Can. Mounted Police	
MOUNTING	embellishment; ascending; the sword from guard to pommel	
MOURNFUL	lugubrious; grievous	
MOURNING	lamenting; sorrow	
MOUSE-EAR	a herb	bt
MOUSSAKA	mince-stuffed aubergine (Gr.)	ck
MOUSSEUX	sparkling frothy wine (Fr.)	
MOUTHFUL	pithy statement	
MOUTHING	con molto espressione	
MOVABLES	personal belongings; chattels, furniture	
MOVELESS	fixed; stationary	

MOVEMENT	agitation; crusade; section of musical work; speed indication	mu
MOVINGLY	affectingly; eloquently	
MOWBURNT	(hay)	
MUCCHERO	rose and violet infusion	
MUCEDINE	a fungus	bt
MUCHNESS	almost abundance	
MUCILAGE	gum	bt
MUCIVORA	insects	zo
MUCKERED	made a muck of	
MUCK-HEAP	midden	
MUCK-HILL	dung-hill	
MUCK-RAKE	dig up dirt	
MUCK-WEED	white goosefoot	bt
MUCK-WORM	a miser; a grub	zo
MUCOCELE	mucus accumulation	md
MUCOSITY	mouldiness	
MUCULENT	slimy; viscous	
MUDARINE	an extract	bt
MUDDLING	confusing; deranging	
MUDDYING	miring	
MUDGUARD	a screen	
MUDSTONE	argillaceous sedimentary rock	gl
MUD-VALVE	sediment valve	
MUFFLING	deadening; shrouding	
MUG-HOUSE	ale-house	
MUHARRAM	a Moslem month	
MULBERRY	a fruit-tree	bt
MULCHING	fertilizing	
MULCTING	fining; amercing	
MULE-DEER	N. American deer	zo
MULETEER	mule-driver	
MULEWORT	a fern	bt
MULISHLY	obstinately; stubbornly	
MULTEITY	multiplicity	
MULTIFID	many cleft	
MULTIPED	with many feet	
MULTIPLE	factor; combined units; parallelling	cp
MULTIPLY	increase; augment; spread	ma, cp
MULTI-PLY	more than 3 ply (-wood)	bd
MUMBLING	muttering	
MUMMYING	embalming	
MUNCHING	chewing; masticating	
MUNERARY	donative	
MUNGOOSE	mongoose	zo
MUNIMENT	title-deed; stronghold	
MUNITION	military stores; equipment	
MUNSHETS	} stick and hole field game	
MUNSHITS		
MURALLED	painted on a wall	
MURDERED	assassinated; slain	
MURDERER	a Cain	
MUREXIDE	a crystal	mn
MURIATED	soaked in brine	
MURIATIC	hydrochloric	ch
MURICATE	prickly; thorny; spiky	

MURIFORM	like a wall	
MURKSOME	darksome; obscure	
MURMURED	complained; repined	
MURMURER	grumbler; grouser	
MURRHINE	(fluor-spar)	mn
MUSCADEL	muscatel	bt
MUSCATEL	grape; wine	bt
MUSCULAR	brawny; sturdy; powerful	
MUSELESS	artless	
MUSHROOM	upstart; blewit; edible fungus	bt, ck
MUSICALE	private recital	mu
MUSICIAN	instrumentalist	mu
MUSINGLY	in contemplative fashion	
MUSK-BALL	perfumed sachet	
MUSK-CAVY	a rodent	zo
MUSK-DEER	Cent. Asian ruminant	zo
MUSK-DUCK	Muscovy duck	zo
MUSKETRY	rifle-shooting	
MUSK-PEAR	} odiferous fruits	bt
MUSK-PLUM		
MUSK-ROSE	rambling rose	bt
MUSK-WOOD	musky tree	bt
MUSLINET	coarse muslin	tx
MUSQUASH	musk-rat	zo
MUSQUITO	mosquito	zo
MUSTACHE	moustache	
MUSTAIBA	Brazilian hardwood	bt
MUSTERED	assembled; gathered	
MUTACISM	mytacism	
MUTATION	discontinuous variation	
MUTCHKIN	pint (Sc.)	me
MUTENESS	dumbness	
MUTICATE	without a point	bt
MUTICOUS	lacking defence structures	zo
MUTILATE	maim; dismember	
MUTINEER	insurgent	
MUTINIED	rebelled; revolted; struck	
MUTINOUS	seditious; unruly; turbulent	
MUTTERED	mumbled; whispered	
MUTTERER	grumbler; grouser	
MUTUALLY	reciprocally	
MUZZLING	restraining; silencing	
MYCELIUM	mushroom spawn	bt
MYCETOMA	a foot disease	md
MYCETOME	special insect organ	zo
MYCODERM	fungoid pellicle	md
MYCOLOGY	study of fungi	
MYELITIS	spinal disease	md
MYLODONT	(extinct sloth)	zo
MYLONITE	compact streaky rock	gl
MYOBLAST	embryonic-muscle cell	zo
MYOGENIC	of spontaneous muscle contraction	md
MYOGRAPH	recording machine	md
MYOMANCY	divination by mice	
MYONOSUS	} muscular disease	md
MYOPATHY		
MYOPHORE	muscle-connected structure	zo

MYOPLASM	contractile part of muscle cell	
		cy
MYOSITIC	} muscular inflammation	
MYOSITIS		md
MYOSOTIS	the forget-me-not	bt
MYOTASIS	muscular tension	pl
MYOTONIA	excessive muscle rigidity	pl
MYRIAPOD	centipede	zo
MYRIARCH	a commander	
MYRICINE	(bee's wax)	
MYRMIDON	desperate ruffian	
MYRRHINE	(myrrh)	bt
MYRTENOL	myrtle oil monoalcohol	ch
MYSTICAL	enigmatical; occult	
MYSTIQUE	reverence for cleverness/skills	
MYTACISM	excess of 'm' in speaking	
MYTHICAL	legendary; fabulous	
MYTILITE	fossil mussel	zo
MYTILOID	mussel-like	
MYXEDEMA	severe depression of nervous system activity	md
MYXOPODA	protozoans	zo

N

NACREOUS	pearly; iridescent	
NAILABLE	tolerates nails	bd
NAIL-FILE	manicurist's implement	
NAILHEAD	visible outer portion of nail	
NAILHEAD	early English embellishment	ar
NAIL-HOLE	surface depression after hammering	
NAILWORT	whitlow grass	bt
NAINSOOK	jaconet muslin	tx
NAISSANT	issuing	hd
NAMEABLE	identifiable	
NAMELESS	obscure; inglorious	
NAMESAKE	having identical name	
NANOSOMA	dwarfism	md
NAPHTHOL	coal-tar constituent	ch
NAPIFORM	turnip-shaped	
NAPOLEON	nap; 20 francs	nm
NAPOLITE	volcanic substance	mn
NARCEINE	opium extract	md
NARCISSI	flowers	bt
NARCOSIS	stupefaction; stupor	md
NARCOTIC	anodyne; sedative; opiate	
NARGHILE	hookah-pipe	
NARICORN	horny beak	zo
NARIFORM	beak-like	
NARRATED	recited; related; recounted	
NARRATOR	story-teller; historian	
NARROWED	contracted; cramped	
NARROWER	closer; nearer	
NARROWLY	nearly; barely; scarcely	
NASALITY	nosiness	
NASALIZE	enunciate nasally	
NASCENCY	growth; production	

NASICORN	horn-beaked	zo
NASIFORM	nose-shaped	
NATALITY	population's increase ability	ec
NATANTES	water-spiders	zo
NATANTLY	buoyantly	
NATATION	swimming	
NATATORY	of aquatic habits	
NATHLESS	nevertheless	
NATHMORE	never more	
NATIONAL	public; general; racial	
NATIVELY	by birth; naturally	
NATIVISM	doctrine of genetics versus experience	
NATIVITY	birth; a horoscope	
NATTERED	chatted	
NATTIEST	neatest; smartest	
NATURISM	nature worship	
NATURIST	practiser of nudism	
NAUMACHY	a sea-fight	
NAUPLIUS	larva of crustaceans	zo
NAUSCOPY	ship-sighting	
NAUSEANT	disgusting; revolting	
NAUSEATE	to sicken	
NAUSEOUS	offensive; repulsive	nt
NAUTICAL	marine; maritime; naval	
NAUTILUS	cuttlefish; diving bell	zo
NAVALISM	sea power	nt
NAVARCHY	admiralship	nt
NAVICERT	naval permit	nt
NAVICULA	incense-boat	
NAVIFORM	art; boat-like	nt
NAVIGATE	voyage; cruise; steer; pilot	nv
NAVY-BLUE	dark blue	nt
NAZARENE	of Nazareth	
NAZARITE	} a sect of early	
NAZIRITE	} Christians	rl
NAZIFIED	corrupted in thought	
NEALOGIC	adolescent	
NEARCTIC	N. of N. America	
NEARHAND	nigh; nearly	
NEARNESS	propinquity; closeness; togetherness	
NEAR-SIDE	left side looking forward	
NEATHERD	cow-herd	
NEATNESS	spick and span; dexterity	
NEBULIUM	questionable element	as
NEBULOSE	} nebular; cloudy; hazy;	
NEBULOUS	} misty; obscure	
NECKATEE	kerchief; scarf	
NECKBAND	collar	
NECKBEEF	coarse flesh	
NECKLACE	rivière; dog-collar	
NECKWEAR	scarves; ties; collars	
NECROPSY	post-mortem	
NECROSIS	mortification; death	md
NECROTIC	moribund	
NECTARED	honeyed	
NECTOPOD	swimming appendage	zo
NEED-FIRE	fire by friction	
NEEDLESS	unnecessary; superfluous	

NEEDLING	embroidering; sewing	
NEGATING	denying; disclaiming	
NEGATION	denial; refusal; confute; absence	
NEGATION	mirror-wise; reversal of digits	**cp**
NEGATIVE	right of veto; not; (photo)	**pg**
NEGATRON	thermionic tube	**el**
NEGLIGEE	loose apparel	
NEGRITOS	pygmies (Malay)	
NEGROISM	peculiarity of negro speech	
NEIGHING	whinnying	
NEMALINE	fibrous	
NEMALITE	hydrate of magnesia	**mn**
NEMATODA	eel worms	**zo**
NEMATOID	like a thread; internal parasite	**zo, md**
NEMERTEA	worms	**zo**
NEMOROSE	growing in groves	
NEMOROUS	woody	
NENUPHAR	water-lily	**bt**
NEOBLAST	large amoeboid cell	**zo**
NEOCRACY	rule by upstarts	
NEO-LATIN	modern Latin	
NEOLOGIC	(novel words)	
NEOMYCIN	antibiotic	**pm**
NEONATAL	of newborn infants	**md**
NEOPHRON	genus of vultures	**zo**
NEOPHYTE	novice; tyro; proselyte	
NEOPLASM	new tissue	
NEPALESE	a native of Nepal	
NEPENTHE	drug causing oblivion	**md**
NEPHRITE	jade	**mn**
NEPHROID	kidney-shaped	
NEPHROMA	kidney tumour	**md**
NEPIONIC	of embryonic period	**zo**
NEPOTISM	favouritism of family	
NEPOTIST	favours relatives	
NERONIAN	(Nero)	
NERVE-WAR	cold war	
NESCIENT	⎫ ignorant; unlettered;	
NESCIOUS	⎭ unaware; agnostic	
NESISTOR	bipolar-field-dependent transistor	
NESTLING	young bird	**zo**
NETHINIM	temple servants (Heb.)	
NETTLING	irritating; provoking	
NEURALGY	neuralgia	**md**
NEURAXIS	spinal cord-brain axis	
NEURITIS	nerve inflammation	**md**
NEURONAL	concerning the neuron	
NEUROPIL	brain nerve fibre maze	**zo**
NEUROSAL	neurotic; temperamental	
NEUROSIS	nervous disease	**md**
NEUROTIC	highly strung	
NEUTRINO	subatomic particle	**nc**
NEVADITE	rhyolite, acid lava	**gl**
NEWBLOWN	just blossoming	
NEWCOMER	late arrival	
NEW-MODEL	(Parliamentary Army)	

NEWS-HAWK	a reporter	
NEWS-REEL	topical film	
NEWS-ROOM	reading room	
NEXTNESS	proximity; propinquity	
NIBBLING	biting bit by bit	
NIBELUNG	mythical character	
NICENESS	precision; discrimination	
NICKELIC	of nickel	
NICKNACK	a trifle; gewgaw	
NICKNAME	a monniker; sobriquet	
NICKROME	alloy for electrical heating elements	**el, ps, ml**
NICOTINE	tobacco constituent	**ch**
NIDERING	rascal; coward	
NIDOROSE	⎫ smelling of cookery	**ck**
NIDOROUS	⎭	
NIDULANT	⎫ nestling, birdling	**zo**
NIDULATE	⎭	
NIELLURE	metal-work	
NIFFNAFF	a trifle; nicknack	
NIFLHEIM	region of mist (Teutonic)	
NIGERIAN	(Nigeria)	
NIGGLING	finicking; trifling	
NIGHNESS	nearness; proximity	
NIGHTCAP	cap or drink; horsehood (baseball)	
NIGHT-DOG	nocturnal venatic hound	
NIGHT-FLY	nocturnal moth	**zo**
NIGHT-HAG	a witch	
NIGHT-JAR	night-churr; goat-sucker	
NIGHT-MAN	scavenger	
NIGHT-OWL	who stays out late	
NIHILISM	extreme doctrine	
NIHILIST	Russian revolutionary	
NIHILITY	nothingness	
NINE-EDGE	feeding in punch cards	**cp**
NINE-EYES	lampreys	**zo**
NINEFOLD	9 times	
NINEPINS	skittles	
NINETEEN	cardinal number	
NINEVITE	of Nineveh	
NISBERRY	naseberry; medlar	**bt**
NITIDOUS	lustrous; shining; reflecting	**bt**
NITRATED	(nitric acid)	**ch**
NITROGEN	an inert gas	**ch**
NITROLIC	with nitro oxine group on same atom	
NITROXYL	halogen/metal-attached radical	
NIVATION	snow-caused erosion	
NOACHIAN	(Noah); archaic; bygone	
NOBBLING	doping; injuring; swindling	
NOBELIUM	man-made element	**ch**
NOBILITY	distinction; aristocracy	
NOBLEMAN	a peer	
NOBLESSE	the nobility	
NOCENTLY	guiltily; culpably	
NOCTILIO	bat-genus	**zo**
NOCTUARY	night record	
NOCTURNE	⎫ serenade; lyrical;	
NOTTURNO	⎭ (It.) night scene	**mu**

NODECUSP	a curve	
NODIFORM	knotted	
NODOSITY	an entanglement	
NODULOSE	knotty; nodulous	
NOEMATIC	} intellectual;	
NOETICAL	mental; thoughtful	
NOISETTE	hazelnut entrée	ck
NOMADISM	gipsy life	
NOMADIZE	wander with flocks	
NOMARCHY	provincial rule	
NOMINATE	designate; name; appoint	
NOMISTIC	lawful	
NOMOGENY	life origin	
NOMOGRAM	alignment chart; diagram	ce
NOMOLOGY	psychology	
NON-CLAIM	failure to claim	lw
NON-CREEP	smooth flow additive	ch
NON-ELECT	not of the elect	
NONESUCH	without parallel; paragon	
NON-JUROR	(Jacobite clergy)	rl
NONMETAL	negative-ion former	ch
NON-MORAL	amoral	
NON-NASAL	(phonetics)	
NON-PARTY	independent	
NON-RIGID	limp	
NONSENSE	balderdash; inanity; trash	
NON-TOXIC	not poisonous	md
NON-UNION	(trades union)	
NOONTIDE	midday	
NORMALCY	regularity; standard	
NORMALLY	usually; ordinary	
NORSEMAN	} (Viking) Scandinavian	
NORTHMAN		
NORTHERN	of the north	
NORTHING	distance northward	
NORWEYAN	Norwegian (Shak.)	
NOSEBAND	part of bridle	
NOSE-DIVE	a plunge	
NOSE-LEAF	a bat appendage	zo
NOSELESS	non-nasal	
NOSE-RING	bull's ornament	
NOSOLOGY	} classification	md
NOSONOMY	of diseases	
NOTALGIA	backache	md
NOTANDUM	a memorandum	
NOTARIAL	clerical	
NOTATION	system of figures	
NOTCHING	nicking; scoring	
NOTEBOOK	jotting pad	
NOTELESS	insignificant; petty; trivial	
NOTICING	observing; remarking	
NOTIFIED	made known; apprised	
NOTIONAL	fanciful; imaginative	
NOTORNIS	coot, (extinct) NZ	zo
NOTTURNO	} night serenade; lyrical	
NOCTURNE	(It.)	mu
NOTWHEAT	unbearded wheat	bt
NOUMENAL	not phenomenal	
NOUMENON	a definite conception	

NOVATIAN	puritanical sect	rl
NOVATION	debt transference	lw
NOVELESE	inferior-novel language style	
NOVELISH	resembling a novel	
NOVELIST	romancer; innovator	
NOVELIZE	to spin yarns	
NOVEMBER	eleventh month	
NOVENARY	nine collectively	
NOVERCAL	like a step-mother	
NOVERINT	a writ	lw
NOWADAYS	in these days; at present	
NUBECULA	cloudiness	md
NUBILITY	marriage	
NUBILOSE	} cloudy; overcast	
NUBILOUS		
NUCAMENT	a catkin	bt
NUCELLUS	nucleus of ovule	bt
NUCIFORM	nut-like	
NUCLEASE	nucleic-acid-hydrolysis enzyme	ch
NUCLEATE	having a nucleus	
NUCLEOLE	small nucleus	
NUCLEOME	protoplast's nuclear substance	bl
NUDATION	stripping area of plants	bt
NUDISTIC	scantily attired	
NUGATORY	ineffectual; futile; bootless	
NUISANCE	pest; annoyance; bother	
NUMBERED	reckoned; computed	
NUMBERER	counter; numerator	
NUMBNESS	torpor; stupefaction	
NUMERARY	not supernumerary	
NUMERATE	to number; to tell	
NUMEROUS	many; manifold; frequent	
NUMMULAR	numismatic	
NUMSKULL	blockhead; dunce	
NUNCHEON	luncheon	
NUNDINAL	(market day)	
NUPTIALS	a marriage	
NURIMONO	lacquer-ware (Jap.)	
NURSLING	an infant; child	
NURTURED	brought up; tended	
NUTARIAN	nut-eater	
NUTATION	nodding; Euler's angles showing position of body around a point	ma
NUT-BROWN	colour of ale	
NUTHATCH	small bird	zo
NUTHOUSE	lunatic asylum	
NUTMEGGY	like a nutmeg	
NUTRIENT	nourishing; alimental	
NUT-SCREW	monkey wrench	
NUTSHELL	receptacle for small amount	
NUZZLING	nestling	
NYMPHAEA	water-lilies	bt
NYMPHEAN	} maidenly;	
NYMPHISH	like a nymph	
NYSTATIN	antifungal antibiotic	

509

O

OAK-APPLE	wen on oak tree	bt
OAK-PAPER	a wall paper	
OAT-GRASS	sort of straw	bt
OATHABLE	capable of being sworn	
OBDUCING	enveloping; covering	
OBDURACY	stubbornness; callousness	
OBDURATE	harsh; hardened; inflexible	
OBEDIENT	dutiful; submissive	
OBEISANT	reverencing; respectful	
OBELIZED	marked as spurious, (†)	
OBERHAUS	upper house (Ger.)	
OBITUARY	list of the dead	
OBJECTED	protested; interposed	
OBJECTOR	opposer; heckler	
OBLATION	an offering; libation	
OBLATORY	donative; sacrificial	
OBLIGANT	bound by contract	lw
OBLIGATE	oblige; pledge; mortgage	
OBLIGATO	of special import	mu
OBLIGING	gratifying; constraining	
OBLIQUED	slanted	
OBLIQUUS	obliquely placed muscle	zo
OBLIVION	forgetfulness; (nepenthe)	
OBLONGUM	wing-vein cell coleoptera	zo
OBSCURED	eclipsed; clouded; dimmed	
OBSCURER	a concealer; hider	
OBSERVED	saw; remarked; obeyed	
OBSERVER	spectator; commentator	
OBSESSED	besieged; beset; haunted	
OBSIDIAN	volcanic rock	mn
OBSOLETE	discarded; archaic; effete	
OBSTACLE	hindrance; barrier; check	
OBSTRUCT	block; clog; impede; choke	
OBTAINED	got; won; earned; acquired	
OBTAINER	procurer; achiever	
OBTECTED	covered; hidden	
OBTEMPER	to comply with (Sc.)	lw
OBTESTED	besought; protested	
OBTRUDED	interfered; ejected	
OBTRUDER	intruder; gate-crasher	
OBTUNDED	blunted; deadened	
OBTURATE	to close up; seal; shut	
OBTUSELY	stolidly; stupidly	
OBTUSION	bluntness	
OBVERTED	faced; confronted	
OBVIATED	avoided; prevented	
OBVOLUTE	wavy; enfolded	bt
OCCAMISM	} doctrine of Occam	rl
OCCAMIST	}	
OCCASION	create; event; incident	
OCCIDENT	the west	
OCCLUDED	absorbed; shut up	
OCCLUSOR	a shutter; a valve	
OCCULTED	concealed; eclipsed	
OCCULTLY	secretly; reconditely	
OCCUPANT	holder; tenant; resident	
OCCUPIED	engaged; employed	

OCCUPIER	inhabiter	
OCCURRED	chanced; happened; befell	
OCEANIAN	(Oceania)	
OCEANITE	basaltic igneous rock	mn
OCELLARY	} with spots like eyes	
OCELLATE	} leopard-like genus	zo
OCHEROUS	yellow	
OCHIDORE	shore-crab	zo
OCHLESIS	} illness due to	
OCHLETIC	} overcrowding	md
OCHREATE	sheathing	bt
OCHREOUS	yellowish	
OCHROITE	cerite	mn
OCTAPODY	verse of 8 feet	
OCTARCHY	government by 8	
OCTOBASS	lower than double bass cello	mu
OCTONARY	referring to 8	
OCTOPODA	sub-order of molluscs	zo
OCTOROON	one-eighth negro blood	
OCTUPLET	(eight notes)	mu
OCULARLY	visibly; demonstrably	
ODIOUSLY	hatefully; offensively	
ODOGRAPH	distance and course meter	
ODOMETER	mileage recorder	
ODONTIST	dentist	md
ODONTOID	toothlike	
ODONTOMA	tooth tumour	md
OENANTHE	water dropwort	bt
OENOLOGY	study of wine	
OERLIKON	light A.A. gun	
OESTROUS	female reproductive cycle	
OFF-BREAK	(cricket)	
OFF-DRIVE	cricket stroke	
OFFENDED	violated; affronted	
OFFENDER	transgressor; delinquent	
OFFERING	tendering; proposing	
OFFICIAL	functional; authorized	
OFF-PRINT	a reprint	
OFF-SHOOT	branch	
OFFSHOOT	scion; branch; water-run off; roof gutter	bd
OFF-SHORE	near the land	
OFF-STAGE	off the record	
OFF-WHITE	pale cream	
OFT-TIMES	frequently; repeatedly	
OHMMETER	(resistance)	me
OILCLOTH	linoleum	
OIL-FIELD	oil well area	
OIL-FIRED	boiler; furnace	
OIL-GLAND	secreting gland	md
OILINESS	greasiness; lubricity	
OILING-IN	pre-painting surface preparation	
OIL-PAPER	transparent paper	
OIL-PRESS	olive squeezer	
OILSKINS	weatherproof garments	
OILSTONE	whetstone; sharpening stone; hone	
OINTMENT	an unguent	md

OITICICA	oil from nut tree (Brazil)	fr
OLD-TIMER	old-stager	
OLD-WORLD	antiquated	
OLEANDER	an evergreen	bt
OLEASTER	wild olive	bt
OLEFIANT	oil producing	
OLEOBROM	developing process	pg
OLEOCYST	oil-containing diverticulum	zo
OLEOSOME	cell fat inclusion	bt
OLFACTIE	odour intensity unit	me
OLIBANUM	frankincense	bt
OLIGARCH	one of power-sharing few	
OLIPHANT	elephant (obs.); cup made of ivory-tusk (medieval)	zo
OLIVE-OIL	perfect food	bt
OLIVETAN	a Benedictine	rl
OLYMPIAD	period of 4 years	
OLYMPIAN	godlike	
OLYMPICS	games	
OMADHAUN	madman (Irish)	
OMELETTE	beaten-egg dish	
OMISSION	oversight; failure; disregard	
OMISSIVE	exclusive; neglectful	
OMITTING	missing; skipping; dropping	
OMMATEUM	compound eye	zo
OMNIFORM	of all shapes; protean	
OMOHYOID	(shoulder-blade)	md
OMOIDEUM	pterygoid bone	md
OMOPLATE	shoulder-blade	md
OMPHALIC	(navel)	md
OMPHALOS	boss on a shield; hub	
ONCE-OVER	comprehensive glance	
ONCIDIUM	orchid genus	bt
ONCOLOGY	science of tumours	md
ONCOMING	approach; advance	
ONCOTOMY	cutting a tumour	md
ONE-HORSE	poorly equipped	
ONE-SIDED	partial; biased	
ONE-TRACK	single interest or file	
ONISCOID	like a woodlouse	zo
ONLINESS	loneliness	
ONLOOKER	spectator; observer	
ONOMANCY	divination	
ONRUSHES	onsets	
ONTOGENY	development during individual life history	
ONTOLOGY	metaphysics	
ONYCHIUM	pulvillus in insect	zo
ONYMATIC	generic	zo
OOGONIUM	algae/fungi female sex organ	bt
OOKINETE	vermiform stage in protozoa	zo
OOLOGIST	collector of bird's eggs	
OOSPHERE	an egg	zo
OOTOCOUS	oviparous	zo
OPALESCE	to be iridescent	
OPALIZED	make like an opal	
OPENCAST	outcrop; surface coal	mn

OPEN-EYED	watchful	
OPENNESS	frankness; sincerity	
OPEN-WELL	uncovered well	ar
OPEN-WORK	metal/lace pattern	
OPERA-HAT	a gibus	
OPERATED	performed; worked	md
OPERATIC	having to do with opera	
OPERATOR	workman; artisan; hand	
OPERETTA	short opera	mu
OPHIDIAN	reptilian	zo
OPHIDION	conger eel	zo
OPHIURAN	starfish	zo
OPIFICER	artificer	
OPINABLE	conjecturable	
OPIUM-DEN	centre for drug addicts	
OPOPONAX	a perfume; a gum	bt
OPPILATE	block up; obstruct	
OPPONENS	muscle related to digits	zo
OPPONENT	foe; rival; antagonist	
OPPOSING	resisting; withstanding	
OPPOSITE	contrary; adverse; inimical	
OPPUGNED	contested; fought	
OPPUGNER	adversary; competitor	
OPTATIVE	optional; elective; voluntary	
OPTICIAN	spectacle-maker	
OPTIMACY	the nobility	
OPTIMISM	hopefulness	
OPTIMIST	a sanguine person	
OPTIMIZE	take a bright view	
OPTIONAL	left to choice; discretional	
OPTOGRAM	image of object seen on retina	
OPULENCE	wealth; affluence; profusion	
OPULENCY	riches; possessions	
OPUSCULE	a small work	
ORACULAR	portentous; ominous	
ORANGERY	orange garden	
ORANGISM	(William of Orange)	
ORANGITE	thorium silicate	mn
ORATORIO	sacred musical drama	mu
ORATRESS	a woman orator	
ORCADIAN	(Orkney Islands)	
ORCHANET	alkanet	bt
ORCHESIS	art of dancing	
ORDAINED	bid; decreed; enjoined	
ORDAINER	assignor; prescriber	rl
ORDERING	disposing; directing	
ORDINAND	candidate for orders	rl
ORDINANT	a prelate	rl
ORDINARY	a dinner; usual; customary	
ORDINATE	methodical; orderly	
ORDINATE	vertical axis on two dimensional graph	
ORDNANCE	guns; cannon; artillery	
ORGANDIE	figured muslin	tx
ORGANIFY	add organic matter	
ORGANISM	living structure	
ORGANIST	a player	mu
ORGANIZE	frame; constitute; construct	
ORICHALC	imitation gold	
ORIENTAL	Eastern	

ORIENTED	lined up; on the beam	
ORIGINAL	primitive; primeval; novel	
ORILLION	a bastion	
ORINASAL	mouth and nose sound	
ORNAMENT	embellishment; decoration	
ORNATELY	elaborately; in florid style	
ORNITHIC	referring to birds	zo
ORONASAL	of mouth and nose	zo
ORPHANCY	orphanhood	
ORPHANED	parentless	
ORPIMENT	sulphurous yellow pigment; (arsenic sulphide)	ch
ORTHICON	type of camera tube	tv
ORTHODOX	true; conventional; correct	
ORTHOEPY	correct pronunciation	
ORYCTICS	fossils	mn
ORYZENIN	rice glutelin protein	ch
OSCINIAN	(singing birds)	zo
OSCITANT	drowsy; yawning	
OSCITATE	to gape	
OSCULANT	kissing	
OSCULATE	to buss	
OSETROVA	sturgeon; caviar	zo
OSMAZOME	meat extract	
OSNABURG	coarse linen	tx
OSOPHONE	headphone for the deaf	ac
OSSIANIC	(Ossian)	
OSSIFIED	turned into bone	
OSSOBUCO	stew of veal with bone, wine (It.)	ck
OSTEITIS	bone inflammation	md
OSTEOZOA	the vertebrata	md
OSTERICK	bistort plant	bt
OSTINATO	recurrent theme	mu
OSTIOLAR	cellular	
OSTRAKON	engraved pottery shard (Gr.)	
OTAHEITE	Malay apple (Pacific)	
OTOCONIA	concretions in mollusca	zo
OTOLITHS	tiny calcium crystals in (ear)	
OTORRHEA	discharge from ear	md
OTOSCOPE	ear examiner	md
OTOSCOPY	ear examination	md
OTTAVINO	It. small flute, piccolo	mu
OUISTITI	marmoset	zo
OUTBLUSH	outflush	
OUTBOARD	external, portable, boat motor	nt
OUTBOUND	outward bound	
OUTBRAVE	defy; dare; challenge	
OUTBREAK	fray; riot; broil; revolt	
OUTBURST	eruption; ebullition	
OUTCASTE	rejected; casteless Hindu	
OUTCLASS	excel; outvie; surpass	
OUTCROSS	(cross-breeding)	
OUTDARED	defied; flouted	
OUTDATED	outmoded; old-fashioned	
OUTDOING	surpassing; outstripping	
OUTDOORS	not at home; fresh airing	
OUTDWELL	outstay	
OUTFACED	braved	

OUTFIELD	(cricket); nearer to the boundaries	
OUTFLANK	overlap	
OUTFLASH	outshine	
OUTFLING	sharp retort	
OUTFLOWN	lost flying competition	
OUTFLUSH	sudden glow of heat	
OUTFROWN	win brow-creasing contest	
OUTGOING	expenditure; outlay	
OUT-GROUP	the excluded ones; pariahs	pc
OUTGROWN	become too constricting	
OUTGUARD	outpost	
OUTGUIDE	file marker for removed entries	
OUT-HEROD	be bigger stinker	
OUTHOUSE	shed; shack; shanty; barn	
OUTLAWED	beyond the pale	
OUTLAWRY	exile; banishment	
OUTLEAPT	jumped over	
OUTLEARN	excel in learning	
OUTLINED	delineated; sketched	
OUTLIVED	outlasted	
OUTLYING	far; remote; distant	
OUTMARCH	walk until drop	
OUTMODED	out of fashion	
OUTPACED	over-run; run faster	
OUT-PLANT	system with remote data terminals	cp
OUTPOINT	win (sport)	
OUTPOWER	overpower; vanquish	
OUTRAGED	insulted; maltreated	
OUTRANGE	extend further	
OUTRAZED	exterminated	
OUTREACH	exceed; surpass	
OUTREIGN	sit on throne longer	
OUTRIDER	mounted attendant	
OUTRIGHT	at once; utterly	
OUTRIVAL	excel; outvie; beat	
OUTROPER	kind of bailiff	lw
OUTSCOLD	upbraid excessively	
OUTSCORN	despise; disdain; contemn	
OUTSHINE	eclipse; overshadow	
OUTSHONE	outrivalled	
OUTSIDER	not a favourite; onlooker; as alien	
OUTSIDES	backs or three quarters (rugby football)	
OUTSIGHT	outlook	
OUTSKIRT	border	
OUTSLEEP	perchance to outdream	
OUTSLEPT	snored longer than	
OUTSLIDE	slide better than everyone else	
OUTSMART	diddle; outwit; overreach	
OUTSPEAK	speak boldly	
OUTSPENT	over tired	
OUTSPOKE	bad English	
OUTSPORT	outdo in sport	
OUTSTAND	resist; withstand	
OUTSTARE	look longer than	

OUTSTOOD	withstood	
OUTSTRIP	outrun; undress faster	
OUTSWEAR	collect cursing prize	
OUTSWELL	overflow	
OUT-TO-OUT	overall measurement	
OUTVALUE	appraise too highly	
OUTVENOM	opposite of invenom	
OUTVOICE	talk down	
OUTVOTED	won election	
OUTVOTER	imaginary elector	
OUTWARDS	externally	
OUTWATCH	peer superiorly	
OUTWEARY	bore stiff	
OUTWEIGH	} exceed in value;	
OUTWORTH	} offset; overbalance	
OUTWOUND	extricated	
OUTWREST	extort by violence	
OVARIOLE	egg-tube in insects	**zo**
OVARIOUS	consisting of eggs	**zo**
OVEN-BIRD	a tree-creeper	**zo**
OVER-AGED	time expired	
OVERALLS	garments	
OVERARCH	overhang	
OVERAWED	quelled; intimidated	
OVERBEAR	overwhelm; domineer	
OVERBLOW	cover with blossom; blow a	
	higher note, woodwind	**mu**
		bt
OVERBODY	embody excessively	
OVERBOIL	let kettle blow top	
OVERBOLD	impudent; presumptuous	
OVERBOWL	cricket	
OVERBRIM	overflow	
OVERBROW	project	
OVERBULK	loom large	
OVERBURN	burn with zeal	
OVERBUSY	officious	
OVERCAME	vanquished; subdued	
OVERCAST	lowering; cloudy	**mt**
OVERCLOY	to surfeit	
OVERCOAT	winter topcoat	
OVERCOLD	too cold	
OVERCOME	defeat	
OVERCROW	to insult; exult; brag	
OVERDATE	post-date	
OVERDONE	exaggerated	
OVERDOSE	too many pills	
OVERDRAW	take too much from bank	
OVERDREW	exaggerate in drawing	
OVER-FACE	requiring horse to jump	
	beyond its limits	
OVERFALL	tidal effect	
OVERFAST	insufficiently slow	
OVERFEED	glut; cloy; satiate	
OVERFILL	flood	
OVERFISH	cf. underdog	
OVERFLOW	overrun; inundate; swamp;	
	annex (space)	
OVERFLOW	reserve circuits; excess	
	(location); (audience)	**tc, cp**

OVERFOLD	inverted strata	**gl**
OVERFOND	doting	
OVERFULL	too full	
OVERGAZE	look over	
OVERGIVE	give lavishly	
OVERGROW	non-existent verb	
OVERHAIR	long outside hair	
OVERHAND	overarm	
OVERHANG	jut; impend	
OVERHAUL	repair; overtake; examine	
OVERHEAD	aloft	
OVERHEAR	eavesdrop	
OVERHEAT	scorch	
OVERJUMP	neglect; pass by	
OVERKILL	excess of casualties (nuclear	
	war)	
OVERKIND	indulgent	
OVERKING	control lesser kings	
OVERKNEE	(above the knee)	
OVERLADE	overburdened	
	smothered;	
OVERLAID	} with decorative layers,	
OVERLAIN	} (jewellery) (gems)	**mn,**
		gl, tx
OVERLAND	cross-country	
OVERLEAF	on the next page	
OVERLEAP	skip	
OVERLIVE	survive	
OVERLOAD	encumber	
OVERLOCK	lock up too much	
OVERLONG	too long	
OVERLOOK	to slight; connive; condone	
OVERLORD	feudal superior	
OVERMOST	highest; topmost	
OVERMUCH	in excess	
OVERNAME	nickname; recount	
OVERNEAT	finicky	
OVERNICE	fastidious	
OVERPAID	given excessive wages	
OVERPART	overtask	
OVERPASS	disregard	
OVERPAST	gone; spent	
OVERPEER	to look down on; overlook	
OVERPLAY	gambling	
OVERPLUS	remainder; surplus	
OVERRAKE	to sweep over like a wave	
OVERRATE	esteem too highly	
OVERREAD	peruse (Shak.)	
OVERRENT	exact too high a rent	
OVERRIDE	trample; quash; annul;	
	exhaust a horse	
OVERRIPE	passé; past the prime	
OVERRULE	prevail; repudiate; rescind	
OVERSEAM	a seam	
OVERSEAS	abroad	
OVERSEEN	observed; overlooked	
OVERSEER	superintendent; foreman	
OVERSELL	make excess profits	
OVERSEWN	sewn over the edge	

OVERSHOE	a galosh	
OVERSHOT	went too far	
OVERSIDE	overboard	
OVERSIZE	out-size	
OVERSKIP	leap-over; overtrip	
OVERSLIP	pass without notice	
OVERSMAN	overseer; umpire	
OVERSOLD	hyperpeddled	
OVERSOUL	divine principle	
OVERSPIN	cricket	
OVERSTAY	outstay	
OVERSTEP	exceed; transgress	
OVERSWAY	overrule	
OVERTAKE	pass	
OVERTASK	overtax; overtoil	
OVERTILE	imbrex; (It.); (Sp.)	**bd**
OVERTILT	upset	
OVERTIME	extra-pay and -play hours	
OVERTOIL	overexert	
OVERTONE	harmonic; partial tone, vibrating body	**mu**
OVERTRIP	to trip along	
OVERTURE	offer; proposal; prelude (opera)	**mu**
OVERTURN	upset; invert; perturb	
OVERVEIL	to cover	
OVERVIEW	an inspection	
OVERWASH	glacial formation	
OVERWEAR	outdoor clothing	
OVERWEEN	to be conceited	
OVERWIND	(springs)	
OVERWISE	too clever	
OVERWORK	overtask	
OVERWORN	threadbare	
OVERYEAR	last year's	
OVIPOSIT	to lay eggs	
OWL-GLASS	malicious character (Ger.)	
OWL-LIGHT	dusk	
OXIDABLE	oxidisable	
OXIDATOR	he who oxidates	**ch**
OXIDIZED	combined with oxygen	
OXIDIZER	oxidizing agent	
OX-PECKER	African bird	**zo**
OX-TONGUE	a plant	**bt**
OXYGONAL	having acute angles	
OXYMORON	bitter-sweet	
OXYTOCIC	causing muscle contraction	**zo**
OXYTOCIN	pituitary hormone strengthening uterus, mammary glands	**md**
OZOKERIT	waxen material	
OZONIZED	(ozone)	
OZONIZER	oxygen-to-ozone converter	**ch**

P

PABULARY	alimentary	
PABULOUS	nourishing	
PACHYOTE	thick-eared	

PACHYPOD	thick-footed	
PACIFIED	calmed; lulled; assuaged	
PACIFIER	tranquillizer; conciliator	
PACIFISM	appeasement	
PACIFIST	peace-maker	
PACKETED	made into a parcel	
PACK-LOAD	load for an animal	
PACK-MULE	beast of burden	**zo**
PAD-CLOTH	numnah	
PADDLING	propelling a boat	
PADELION	lady's mantle	**bt**
PADELOUP	inlaid leather book decoration	
PADISHAH	Turkish title; sultan; supreme ruler	
PADSTONE	kneeler; template	
PADUAKAN	coasting ketch (Celebes)	
PADUASOY	corded silk	**tx**
PAGANICA	feather filled leather ball	**ga**
PAGANISH	heathen	
PAGANISM	idolatry	
PAGANIST	paynim; infidel	
PAGANIZE	make give up true faith	
PAGINATE	to number the pages	
PAGODITE	pagoda-stone	**mn**
PAGURIAN	(hermit-crabs)	**zo**
PAHOEHOE	ropy or cordel lava (Hawaii)	**gl**
PAILLONS	spangles (Fr.)	
PAINLESS	pangless	
PAINTBOX	box of colours	
PAINTING	a picture; limning; coating; application of paints	**pt**
PAINTOUT	test of pigment	**pt**
PAIR-WISE	in pairs	
PAITRICK	a partridge (Sc.)	**zo**
PALAMATE	web-footed	**zo**
PALAMINO	beige-coloured horse (Sp.)	
PALATIAL	royal; magnificent; stately	
PALATINE	with royal privileges	
PALEBUCK	the oribi	**zo**
PALE-EYED	with bleached orbs	
PALE-FACE	a white man	
PALENESS	wanness	
PALESTRA	wrestling school	
PALIFORM	stake-shaped	**bt**
PALILOGY	repetition	
PALINODE	recantation	
PALISADE	a fortification; enclosure of paling; pales; (beyond the pale); obstacle for (horse-jumping)	
PALLIATE	extenuate; mitigate; gloss	
PALLIDLY	palely; wanly	
PALL-MALL	ancient croquet	**ga**
PALMETTE	palm-leaf decor	
PALMETTO	fan-palm; hat	**bt**
PALMIPED	web-footed	**zo**
PALMITIN	natural oil fat	
PALM-WINE	fermented palm juice	
PALOMINO	light-coloured horse (Sp.)	**zo**
PALPABLE	perceptible; evidently	

PALPABLY	obviously; tangibly	
PALPACLE	tentacle in siphonophora	zo
PALPATED	handled; felt	
PALPEBRA	eyelid	pl
PALPIFER	lobe of maxilla	zo
PALPLESS	absence of palpi	zo
PALPOCIL	sense hairlet in coelenterata	zo
PALSTAFF	} Celtic stone axe	
PALSTAVE		
PALSYING	paralyzing	
PALTERED	shuffled; quibbled	
PALTERER	dodger; prevaricator	
PALTRILY	equivocately	
PALUDINE	marshy	
PALUDISM	malaria	md
PALUDOSE	boggy	
PAMAQUIN	synthetic antimalarial drug	pm
PAMPERED	coddled; humoured	
PAMPERER	over-indulgent person	
PAMPHLET	a broadsheet; brochure	
PANAGHIA	bishop's pendant	rl
PANCAKED	landed flat	
PANCARTE	royal charter	
PANCHEON	earthenware pan	
PANCREAS	sweetbread	md
PANDANUS	(screw-pines)	bt
PANDEMIC	epidemic in an area	
PANDERED	procured; ministered	
PANDOWDY	apple-charlotte	
PANEGYRY	eulogy; encomium; adulation	
PANELESS	no glass	
PANELLED	(walls; a jury)	
PANEL-SAW	a cutting tool	to
PANGAMIC	of indiscriminate mating	zo
PANGOLIN	scaly ant-eater	zo
PANICKED	terrorized; affrighted	
PANICLED	in clusters	bt
PANIONIC	(Ionian people)	
PANMIXIA	cessation of natural selection	zo
PANNIKEL	brain-pan; skull	
PANNIKIN	small vessel	
PANOPTIC	all seeing	
PANORAMA	extensive view	
PANOTYPE	antique photograph	
PANPIPES	a scale of wood pipes	mu
PANSOPHY	all wisdom	
PANTHEON	complete mythology; burial place of monarchs	ar, rl
PANTONAL	synthesis of keys; atonal	mu
PANURGIC	skilled in all craft	
PAPABILE	suitable for papal/other office	
PAPAGAYO	northerly wind (Mexican plateau)	mt
PAPALISM	popery	l
PAPALIST	an R.C.	rl
PAPALIZE	proselytize (R.C.)	rl
PAPERBOY	newsagent's delivery boy	
PAPERING	decorating	

PAPILLAE	nipples	zo
PAPILLAR	warty	
PAPISHER	a papist	rl
PAPISTIC	popish	rl
PAPPADAM	} Indian bread wafer	ck
PAPPADUM		
PAPULOSE	pimply	
PAPYRINE	like paper	
PARABEMA	Byzantine sacristy	rl
PARABLED	used a parable	
PARABOLA	a conic section	
PARABOLE	similitude	
PARACHOR	molecular volume	
PARACONE	molar cusp in mammals	zo
PARADIGM	example; model; grammar pattern	
PARADING	displaying; flaunting	
PARADISE	Heaven; Eden; Elysium; oasis; open court; atrium	
PARAFFIN	an oil	mn
PARAFORM	fumigant; formaldehyde	ch
PARAGOGE	literal addition	
PARAGRAM	a pun	
PARAGULA	region of insect head	zo
PARAKEET	paroquet; small parrot	zo
PARAKITE	tailless kite	
PARALLAX	alternation; displacement	
PARALLEL	side by side	
PARALOGY	false reasoning	
PARALYZE	benumb; deaden; unnerve	
PARAMERE	an antimere	zo
PARAMOUR	a lover; mistress	
PARANEMA	paraphysis	bt
PARANGON	matchless jewel	
PARANOEA	} chronic monomania;	
PARANOIA	} hallucination	md
PARAPSID	reptile skull condition	zo
PARAPSIS	(thorax)	zo
PARAQUAT	weedkiller toxic to humans	ch
PARASANG	about 4 miles (Pers.)	me
PARASEVE	Jewish Saturday night	rl
PARASHOT	an anti-parachutist	
PARASITE	a sycophant; toady	zo
PARASTAT	gramophone record cleaner	ac
PARATYPE	not the type specimen	
PARAVAIL	inferior; cf. paramount	
PARAVANE	mine remover	nt
PARAXIAL	near to axis	pg
PARCENER	co-heir	lw
PARCHING	scorching; drying	
PARCLOSE	screen	rl
PARDONED	excused; absolved	
PARDONER	(papal indulgences)	rl
PARENTAL	affectionate; fatherly	
PARERGON	subsidiary work (Gr.)	mu
PARGETED	daubed; painted	
PARGETER	plasterer; artist-modeller on walls	
PARHELIA	mock suns	
PARIETAL	partitional	

PARIETES	organ/cavity walls	pl
PARISIAN	(Paris)	
PARISITE	a marble	mn
PARLANCE	mode of speech	
PARLANDO	articulation in singing	mu
PARLANTE	crisp (piano playing)	mu
PARLAYED	conferred; discussed	
PARMESAN	a cheese	
PARODIED	took off; burlesqued	
PARODIST	caricaturist	
PARONYME	similar sounding word	
PAROQUET	small parrot; parakeet	zo
PAROSMIA	smell sense abnormality	md
PAROUSIA	second Advent	rl
PAROXYSM	fit; convulsion	md
PARROTER	copyist	
PARROTRY	servile imitation	
PARRYING	warding; frustrating	
PARSONIC	like a parson	
PARTAKEN	consumed	
PARTAKER	sharer; partner	
PARTERRE	(flower beds, etc.) ground floor; stalls; auditorium	
PARTHIAN	(Parthia)	
PARTIBLE	divisible	
PARTIBUS	marginal note	lw
PARTICLE	an atom; scrap; fragment	
PARTISAN	votary; adherent; halberd	
PARTNERS	a framework	nt
PART-SONG	glee; for several parts	mu
PART-TIME	works for part of day only	
PARTYISM	party loyalty	
PASCUAGE	grazing	
PASCUOUS	growing in pastures	
PASHALIK	pasha's jurisdiction	
PASILALY	universal speech	
PASSABLE	tolerable, up to standard	
PASSABLY	acceptably; reasonably	
PASSAGER	free tripper (falconry)	zo
PASSBOOK	identity documents; pay, bankbook	
PASSCODE	secret entry requirement	
PASSER-BY	street pedestrian on his way	
PASSERES	perching birds (genus)	zo
PASSLESS	trackless; without pass, identity	
PASSOVER	Jewish festival	rl
PASSPORT	document of nationality, identity; visas	
PASSROLL	stroke in croquet	
PASSWORD	secret watchword for entry	
PASTICHE	comic imitation, entertainment	
PASTILLE	medicated lozenge	md
PASTORAL	rustic	
PASTORLY	pastorlike; priestly	
PASTRAMI	smoked/sun-dried seasoned meat	ck
PASTRIES	confectionery	
PASTURED	grazed	
PATAGIUM	wing membrane	zo

PATCH-BOX	collection of black spots	
PATCHERY	botchery	
PATCHING	repairing; cobbling	
PATELLAR	of the knee-cap	pl
PATENTED	protected by law	
PATENTEE	one to whom a patent	
PATENTER	is granted	
PATENTOR	issuer of a patent	
PATERERO	pederero; ancient gun	
PATERNAL	fatherly; parental	
PATHETIC	sad; grievous; emotional	
PATHLESS	no beaten track	
PATHOGEN	disease-causing parasite	zo
PATIENCE	cards; an opera	
PATOCOLE	forest-floor animal	ec
PATONCEE	heraldic cross	hd
PATOXENE	accidental forest-floor animal	ec
PATRONAL	condescending	
PATTAMAR	large 3-masted dhow (East India)	nt
PATTENED	wearing clogs	
PATTERED	(rain)	
PATTERER	cheap jack	
PATTY-PAN	baking dish	
PATULOUS	spreading	
PAULDRON	a shoulder plate	
PAUNCHED	obese	
PAVEMENT	footway; sidewalk	
PAVILION	large tent; canopy; sports house	
PAVILLON	grand opening of horns, bells (Fr.)	
PAVISADO	galley defence	
PAVONINE	like a peacock	
PAWNSHOP	usurer's	
PAYCLERK	employee charged with paying	
PAYPHONE	public coin callbox; telephone	
PAYSHEET	list of wages owed	
PEACEFUL	placid; serene; pacific	
PEACHERY	a hothouse	
PEACHICK	young peafowl	zo
PEACHING	divulging; informing	
PEAGREEN	a colour	
PEAK-LOAD	maximum activity	el
PEARL-ASH	potash	mn
PEARL-EYE	cataract	md
PEARLIES	coster's buttons	
PEARLING	diving for pearls	
PEARLITE	iron/steel microconstituent	ml
PEARLITE	granules of volcanic glass, insulation aggregate	mn, bd
PEARMAIN	an apple	bt
PEASECOD	pea-pod	bt
PEASTONE	limestone	mn
PEAT-MOOR	peat-bog	
PEAT-MOSS	sphagnum	bt
PEAT-REEK	peat smoke	
PECCABLE	weak; frail; erring	
PECCANCY	sinfulness; offence	

PECTINAL	like a comb	
PECTORAL	breast-plate	
PECULATE	embezzle; steal; purloin	
PECULIAR	odd; singular; unusual	
PECULIUM	prerogative; privilege	
PEDAGOGY	instruction	
PEDALFER	cyclist; iron-clay rich zonal soil	ag, gl
PEDALIAN	referring to feet	
PEDALIER	pedal keyboard	
PEDALITY	foot measurement	
PEDALLED	worked by foot	
PEDALLER	} cyclist	
PEDALFER		
PEDANTIC	finical; exact; precise	
PEDANTRY	priggishness; conceit	
PEDDLERY	hawking	
PEDDLING	retailing; trifling	
PEDERERO	paterero; swivel gun (Sp.)	
PEDESTAL	plinth; base	
PEDIATRY	childish diseases	md
PEDICURE	foot treatment	md
PEDIGREE	lineage; stock; genealogy	
PEDIMENT	portico decoration	
PEDIPALP	whip-scorpion	zo
PEDIREME	a crustacean	zo
PEDOLOGY	study of soil	
PEDUNCLE	stalk; nerve fibre stalks in brain	bt, pl
PEEK-A-BOO	punching cards with identity code	
PEEP-HOLE	a chink	
PEEP-O'-DAY	dawn	
PEEP-SHOW	galanty-show	
PEERLESS	unrivalled; matchless	
PEESWEEP	peewit	zo
PEETWEET	spotted sandpiper	zo
PEGAMOID	imitation leather	
PEGASEAN	(Pegasus)	
PEIGNOIR	loose wrapper	
PEINTURE	special consistent use of paints	
PEJORATE	deteriorate	
PEKINESE	small pug-nosed dog	zo
PELAGIAN	(deep sea)	
PELARGIC	stork-like	
PELASGIC	early Grecian	
PELERINE	a tippet or cape	
PELLAGRA	acute anaemia	md
PELLICLE	thin skin or crust	
PELL-MELL	} rapidly; confusedly;	
PELE-MELE	} in disorder	
PELLUCID	transparent; vitreous; clear	
PELORISM	abnormality	bt
PELTATED	shield-shaped	
PELT-WOOL	wool from a hide	
PEMMICAN	dried meat/berry food	ck
PENALIZE	handicap; punish	
PENCHANT	inclination; turn; bent	
PENCRAFT	penmanship	

PENDENCE	suspense	
PENDENCY	indecision	
PENDULUM	swinging weight	
PENELOPE	currasow-bird (S. Amer.)	zo
PENITENT	contrite; repentant	
PENJAJAP	square-lug trade vessel (Malaya)	nt
PENKNIFE	pocket-knife	
PENNORTH	a pennyworth	
PENNY-DOG	a kind of shark	zo
PENOLOGY	prison management	
PENSTOCK	duct to waterwheel	
PENTACLE	five-pointed star	
PENTAFID	cleft in five	
PENTAGON	five sided figure	
PENTELIC	(marble)	mn
PENTOSAN	polysaccharide	ch
PENT-ROOF	single sloped roof	
PENUMBRA	partial shadow; (partial solar eclipse)	as
PENWIPER	rag for pen user	
PENWOMAN	authoress	
PEOPLING	populating	
PEPERINO	granular tufa	mn
PEPPERED	hit with shot	
PEPTOGEN	} digestive principle,	
PEPTONIC	} digestive	
PEPYSIAN	(Samuel Pepys)	
PERACUTE	very sharp or violent	
PERCEIVE	apprehend; discern; descry	
PERCHING	roosting	
PERCLOSE	screen; railing	hd
PERDENDO	dying away	mu
PERDURED	endured; lasted	
PERFORCE	of necessity; forcibly	
PERFUMED	scented; odoriferous	
PERFUMER	perfume seller	
PERFUSED	sprinkled; bedewed	
PERIAGUA	} dugout canoe West	
PIROGUE	} Indies (Sp.)	nt
PERIANAL	region around anus	pl
PERIANTH	floral envelope	bt
PERIBLEM	portion of apical meristem	bt
PERICARP	seed-vessel	bt
PERICOPE	scriptural passage	rl
PERICYTE	small-blood-vessel cell	md
PERIDERM	outer bark	bt
PERIDIUM	outer wall of fungus fruitbody	bt
PERIGEAL	} (when moon's orbit is	
PERIGEAN	} nearest to the earth)	as
PERIGONE	perianth	bt
PERILLED	endangered; risked	
PERILOUS	hazardous; risky; parlous	
PERILUNE	point in lunar satellite orbit	as
PERIODIC	at stated intervals	
PERIOTIC	around inner ear	
PERIPETY	climax; solution	
PERIPLUS	circumnavigation	

PERISARC	chitinous layer in hydrozoa	**zo**
PERISCII	polar people	
PERISHED	decayed; died; expired	
PERISSAD	(odd atomic valency)	**ch**
PERITRON	special cathode-ray tube	**el**
PERJURED	perfidious; forsworn	
PERJURER	false witness	
PERKNITE	coarse-grained igneous rock	**gl**
PERLITIC	vitreous obsidian	**mn**
PERMEANT	highly mobile animal	**ec**
PERMEATE	penetrate; percolate; seep	
PERMUTED	exchanged; transmuted	
PERNANCY	rent in kind	**lw**
PERNETTI	kiln support	
PEROLENE	heat exchange organic fluid	**ch**
PERONATE	with thick-sheathed stipe	**bt**
PERONEAL	(fibula)	**md**
PERONEUS	fibula or leg muscle	**zo**
PERORATE	declaim; harangue	
PEROXIDE	a bleacher	**ch**
PERPENDS	face joints, corners (brick)	**bd**
PERRUQUE	peruke; a wig	
PERSICOT	peach cordial	
PERSIMON	date-plum	**bt**
PERSONAL	distinctive; individual	
PERSPIRE	sweat	
PERSUADE	induce; sway; entice	
PERTHITE	potassium/sodium-felspar intergrowth	
PERTNESS	sauciness; flippancy	
PERTUSED	punched	
PERUSING	reading; scrutinizing	
PERUVIAN	(Peru)	
PERUVINE	Peruvian balsam	**bt**
PERVADED	permeated; diffused	
PERVERSE	stubborn; vexatious	
PERVIOUS	porous; permeable	
PESSULUS	osseus trachea band in birds	**zo**
PESTERED	plagued; harassed; worried	
PESTERER	tormentor; teaser	
PESTLING	pounding; abrading	
PETALINE	(petal)	**bt**
PETALISM	banishment; ostracism	
PETALITE	silicate of alumina	**mn**
PETALODY	stamen-to-petal transformation	**bt**
PETALOID	petal-shaped	**bt**
PETALOUS	having petals	**bt**
PETANQUE	boule (Fr.)	
PETECHIA	tiny haemorrhage spot	**md**
PETERING	calling at cards	
PETERMAN	a fisherman	
PETIOLAR	having a leaf-stalk	**bt**
PETITION	supplication; ask; beseeching	
PETITION	(of Right)	
PETITORY	petitioning; craving	
PETRIFIC	turning to stone	
PETRONEL	horse pistol	
PETROSAL	otic-fusion bone	**zo**

PETTIFOG	quibble over details	
PETULANT	irritable; querulous; testy	
PETUNTSE	china clay	**mn**
PETWORTH	variety of marble	**mn**
PEWTERER	worker in pewter	
PEZIZOID	like cup-shape apothecium	**bt**
PHAKITIS	eye inflammation	**md**
PHALANGE	finger-bone	**pl**
PHANTASM	spectre; chimera	
PHANTASY	airy speculation; fancy	
PHARISEE	formalist	
PHARMACY	drug-store	
PHEASANT	a game bird	**zo**
PHELLOID	plant-surface cell crust	**bt**
PHENETIC	maximum observable similarity	
PHENGITE	species of mica	**mn**
PHENOLIC	plastic mould	
PHIALIDE	flask-shaped sterigma	**bt**
PHIALLED	bottled	
PHILABEG	} the kilt	
PHILIBEG		
PHILOMEL	the nightingale; unit of melody (Shak.)	**zo, mu**
PHLYCTEN	nodule on conjunctiva	**md**
PHOCENIC	(dolphins)	**zo**
PHONATED	gurgled	
PHONE-BOX	public telephone; call box	
PHONEMIC	phoneme minimal unit of speech in language	
PHONETIC	vocal	
PHORESIS	ion passage through membrane	**pl**
PHORMIUM	New Zealand flax	**bt**
PHOSGENE	poisonous gas	**ch**
PHOSPHAM	ammonia compound	
PHOSPHOR	morning star; Venus; fluorescent substance	**ch**
PHOTOGEN	phosphorescent organ	**zo**
PHOTOPIC	normal daylight vision	
PHOTOPSY	an eye trouble	**md**
PHRASING	expressing; uttering	
PHRYGANA	scattered thorn scrub (Greece)	**bt**
PHRYGIAN	a Montanist	
PHTHISIS	consumption	**md**
PHYLARCH	Greek tribal leader	
PHYLAXIS	body defence against infection protection	**md**
PHYLETIC	tribal	
PHYLITTE	clay slate	**mn**
PHYLLARY	bract outside capitulum	**bt**
PHYLLIUM	leaf insects	**zo**
PHYLLODE	a form of leaf	
PHYLLODY	} leaf-like structure	
PHYLLOID		**bt**
PHYLLOME	foliage	**bt**
PHYSALIA	Portuguese man-of-war	
PHYSALIS	Cape gooseberry	**bt**
PHYSETER	sperm whale	**zo**

PHYSICAL	material; corporeal; tangible	
PHYSIQUE	bodily structure	
PHYTOMER	phyton; plant unit	bt
PHYTOSIS	vegetable parasites	bt
PHYTOZOA	sea anemones, etc.	zo
PIACULAR	atrociously bad	
PIANETTE	small piano	mu
PIASSABA	} Brazilian palm; fibre used	
PIASSAVA	for ropes and brooms	bt
PIAZZIAN	like a piazza	
PIBLOKTO	culture syndrome (Eskimos)	
PICARIAN	(woodpeckers)	zo
PICAROON	small hooked pulling pole	fr
PICAROON	pirate; rogue	
PICCADIL	high collar	
PICIFORM	woodpecker type	zo
PICKEREL	pike; dunlin	zo
PICKETED	enclosed; guarded	
PICKLING	preserving	
PICKLOCK	skeleton key	
PICK-ME-UP	a cordial	
PICKWICK	a club	
PICOTITE	a spinel	mn
PICTURED	described; represented	
PIECENER	a piecer; joiner of threads	
PIECRUST	tart pastry	
PIEDMONT	zonal character at foot of mountain	gl
PIEDNESS	spotted diversity	
PIEDROIT	pier without cap or base	bd
PIERCING	keen; shrill; acute	
PIERHEAD	jetty	
PIERIDES	the nine Muses	
PIFFLING	trifling; peddling	
PIGEONED	fleeced; swindled	
PIGEONRY	pigeon loft	
PIG-FACED	swine-visaged	
PIGOTITE	aluminium compound	mn
PIGSTIES	pig-pens	
PIG'S-WASH	swill	
PIKEHEAD	head of a pike	
PILASTER	square column	ar
PILCHARD	sea-fish	zo
PILEATED	capped	
PILE-WORK	foundation of piles	
PILE-WORM	teredo; boring worm	zo
PILE-WORN	threadbare	
PILE-WORT	celandine	bt
PILFERED	filched; peculated	
PILFERER	purloiner; embezzler	
PILIDIUM	larval form of nemertea	zo
PILIFORM	slender as a hair	
PILING-UP	petrol deposition in manifold	au
PILLAGED	ransacked; looted	
PILLAGER	plunderer; rifler; robber	
PILLARED	columnar	
PILLCORN	oats	bt
PILLOWED	cushioned	

PILLWORT	a plant	bt
PILOSELY	hairily	
PILOSITY	hairiness	
PILOTAGE	pilot's fee	
PILOTING	directing; guiding; steering	
PIMELITE	aluminium silicate	mn
PIMPLING	fuel can surface swelling	nc
PINACOID	crystalline structure	
PINAFORE	apron; ship of line (Gilbert-rigged)	nt
PINASTER	the cluster-pine	bt
PINBOARD	bagatelle; plugboard (cordless)	cp
PINCE-NEZ	eye-glasses	
PINCHERS	pincers; pliers	
PINCHING	nipping; being frugal; sailing too close to the wind	nv
PINCH-OFF	breakdown point in field transmissions	el, ps
PINDAREE	mogul freebooter	
PINDARIC	in the style of Pindar	
PINE-CLAD	crowned with pines	
PINE-CONE	fir-cone	bt
PINE-WOOD	deal	
PINE-WOOL	fibrous substance	
PING-PONG	table tennis	
PINGPONG	twin tape multiple recording	cp
PININGLY	longingly; languishingly	
PINIONED	bound; shackled	
PINK-EYED	having small eyes	
PINK-ROOT	a vermifuge	bt
PINKSTER	Whitsuntide; a pink flower	
PINMAKER	who makes pins	rl
PIN-MONEY	an allowance	
PINNACLE	apex; acme; zenith; crown	
PINNATED	feathered	
PINNINGS	different coloured stones set in rubble wall	bd
PINNIPED	fin-footed; a seal	zo
PINOCHLE	card game (USA)	
PINOLEUM	wood and canvas sunblind	
PINPATCH	periwinkle	bt
PINPOINT	locate exactly	
PINTABLE	bagatelle gambling	
PIN-WHEEL	firework; clock part	hr
PINWHEEL	revolving coloured wheel on stick	
PIONNATE	fungal spore layer	bt
PIPE-CASE	pipe-holder	
PIPE-CLAY	a kaolin-like clay	mn
PIPE-FISH	sea-horse type	zo
PIPE-LINE	oil or water pipes	
PIPE-RACK	collection of pipes	
PIPERINE	extract of pepper	bt
PIPE-ROLL	Great Roll of Exchequer	
PIPE-TREE	the lilac	bt
PIPE-WINE	wine from the cask	
PIPE-WORK	a pipe-vein of ore	mn
PIPEWORT	pepperwort	bt

PIQUANCY	pungency; raciness	
PIRATING	infringing a copyright	
PIRIFORM	pearshaped	
PISCATOR	Izaak Walton; fisherman	
PISCINAL	(fishpond)	
PISIFORM	fishlike	**zo**
PISOLITE	coarse oolite	**mn**
PISTACIA	the pistachio-tree	**bt**
PISTOLET	small pistol	
PITCHING	flinging; casting; lurching	
PITCH-OUT	(baseball)	
PIT-FRAME	framework round mine	**mn**
PITHECUS	an ape	**zo**
PITHLESS	lacking energy; sapless	
PITIABLE	arousing pity or contempt	
PITIABLY	deplorably; movingly	
PITILESS	merciless; ruthless	
PITTACAL	a blue dye	
PITTANCE	dole; small allowance	
PITUITAL	(pituitary gland)	**pl**
PITYROID	branlike	
PIVOT-GUN	swivel-gun	
PIVOTING	moving around; hingeing	
PIVOT-MAN	key-man	
PIXY-RING	fairy-ring	
PLACABLE	relenting; forgiving	
PLACATED	pacified; appeased	
PLACEMAN	office-holder	
PLACENTA	the afterbirth	
PLACIDLY	serenely; tranquilly; calmly	
PLAGIARY	literary theft	
PLAGUILY	pestiferously	
PLAGUING	tormenting; pestering	
PLAINANT	plaintiff	**lw**
PLAITING	pleating; braiding	
PLANCHED	planked	
PLANCHET	disc; a blank	
PLANETIC	planetary; revolving	
PLANGENT	resounding; reverberating	
PLANKING	flooring; putting down	
PLANKTON	drifting organic life	**zo**
PLANLESS	unsystematic; aimless	
PLANNING	scheming; plotting; devising	
PLANTAIN	banana-like fruit; a weed	**bt**
PLANTING	inculcating; inserting	
PLANTLET	a small shrub	**bt**
PLANTULE	embryo of a plant	**bt**
PLANULAR	(embryo of hydrozoa)	**zo**
PLASHING	dabbling; splashing	
PLASHING	hurdle-making process	**bd**
PLASMOID	characteristic plasma section	**ps**
PLASTERY	plasterwork	**ar**
PLASTICS	industrial synthetic resins; organic polymer materials	**ch**
PLASTRON	breastplate (fencing)	
PLATBAND	impost; lintel; projecting; moulding	**bd**
PLATEFUL	a meal	

PLATELET	constituent of blood	**md**
PLATFORM	scheme of action	
PLATINIC	(platinum)	**ch**
PLATINUM	metallic element	**ch**
PLATONIC	philosophical	
PLATTING	plaiting; weaving	
PLATYPUS	duck bill	**zo**
PLATYSMA	dermal musculature	**zo**
PLAUSIVE	plausible	
PLAYABLE	dramatic	
PLAYBILL	programme	
PLAYBOOK	book of rules; log (Am. football); script	
PLAYBOOK	book of dramas	
PLAY-DEBT	gambling debt	
PLAYGOER	stage fan	
PLAY-MARE	hobby-horse	
PLAYMATE	sportive companion	
PLAYSOME	frolicsome; wanton	
PLAYTIME	recreation	
PLEACHED	interwoven; plaited; matted	
PLEADING	arguing; disputing	
PLEASANT	welcome; delectable	
PLEASING	grateful; charming	
PLEASURE	indulgence; gladness; joy	
PLEATING	folding	
PLEBEIAN	popular; vulgar; ignoble	
PLECTRUM	plucking quill for lute, lyre, mandolin, banjo	**mu**
PLEDGING	plighting; pawning	
PLEIADES	group of 7 stars	**as**
PLENARTY	(benefice)	**rl**
PLEONASM	verbosity	
PLEONAST	a sprouter; demagogue	
PLESSITE	entectic intergrowth in meteorites	
PLETHORA	super abundance; surfeit	
PLEURISY	lung inflammation	**md**
PLEXITIS	nerve plexus inflammation	**md**
PLIANTLY	easily bent; flexibly	
PLICATED	folded; involved; intricate	
PLIGHTED	betrothed	
PLIGHTER	one who pledges	
PLIMMING	becoming plump	
PLIMSOLL	rubber shoe; ship's load line	
PLIOCENE	a geological strata	**gl**
PLIOTRON	hot-cathode vacuum tube	**el**
PLODDING	slow but sure	
PLOPPING	dropping into water	
PLOTTING	contriving; planning	
PLOUGHED	furrowed; failed	
PLOUGHER	a husbandman	
PLUCKILY	courageously; valorously	
PLUCKING	glacial theft & misplacement of rocks; stripping; (examination); (strings)	**gl, mu**
PLUGGING	stopping; blocking; core; inserting a lead	**el**

PLUGMOLD	duct for laying cables; raceway (Amer.)	**el**	
PLUG-UGLY	thug; street ruffian; fister; slasher		
PLUGWIRE	two live sockets (also earth) circuits	**cp**	
PLUMBAGO	graphite; blue or violet flower	**mn, bt**	
PLUMB-BOB	test for vertical alignment	**pb**	
PLUMBEAN	leaden; dull; heavy		
PLUMBERY	lead work		
PLUMBING	sounding; piping for water, heating, sanitation	**bd**	
PLUMBISM	lead poisoning	**md**	
PLUMCAKE	fruit cake (Christmas) (wedding)	**ck**	
PLUMDUFF	suet and fruit pudding	**ck**	
PLUMELET	downy feather	**zo**	
PLUMIPED	feathered feet	**zo**	
PLUMMING	sinking a shaft		
PLUMPEST	fattest		
PLUMPING	going all out		
PLUNGEON	a sea-bird	**zo**	
PLUNGING	immersing; ducking		
PLURALLY	more than once		
PLUTONIC	infernal; dark; igneous		
PLUVIOUS	rainy; pluvial; humid		
PLYMETAL	metal-faced plywood	**bd**	
POACHING	stabbing; trespassing (It.)		
POCHETTE	(Fr.) (It.) pocket wallet,		
POCHETTO	book, violin, kit	**mu**	
POCKETED	filched; pouched		
POCKMARK	a scar	**md**	
POCKWOOD	a hard wood	**bt**	
PODAGRAL	gouty		
PODAGRIC		**md**	
PODALGIA	neuralgia in foot	**md**	
PODARGUS	genus of nocturnal birds	**zo**	
PODAUGER	grooved auger	**to**	
PODIATRY	chiropody; foot care		
PODISMUS	spasm of foot	**md**	
PODOCARP	stalk to a carpel	**bt**	
PODOMERE	limb segment in arthropoda	**zo**	
PODOSOMA	leg-bearing segments in acarina		
POEMATIC	poetical; lyric; metrical		
POETICAL	imaginative; rhyming		
POETIZED	versified		
POIGNANT	acutely painful; caustic		
POIGNARD	small dagger		
POINDING	distraining	**lw**	
POINTING	directing; aiming; indicating		
POINTING	exposed mortar treatment; allocation of syllables to notes	**bd, mu**	
POISONED	corrupted; envenomed		
POISONER	who gives poison		
POLARITY	united opposites		
POLARIZE	magnetize		

POLE-JUMP	high-flying sport		
POLEMAST	(without a topmast)	**nt**	
POLEMICS	controversies		
POLE-STAR	Polaris; a lode-star	**as, nv**	
POLICIES	lines of conduct; parks		
POLICING	maintaining order		
POLISHED	smooth; burnished		
POLISHER	shoe or furniture shiner		
POLITELY	courteously; urbanely		
POLITICO	opportunist politician		
POLITICS	art of government		
POLL-ADZE	blunt-headed adze	**to**	
POLL-BOOK	register of voters		
POLL-EVIL	bursa inflammation in horse	**vt**	
POLLICES	thumbs or great toes	**pl**	
POLLINAR	covered with pollen	**bt**	
POLLIWOG	tadpole; children's rag-doll		
POLLYWOG	(Moorish)	**zo**	
POLLSTER	opinion taker		
POLLUTED	contaminated; filth-laden		
POLLUTER	defiler; contaminator		
POLOCYTE	polar body	**zo**	
POLONIUM	radio-active element		
POLTROON	coward; dastard; craven		
POLYARCH	of many-stranded stele	**bt**	
POLYAXON	having many axes	**zo**	
POLYCARP	gonad form in urochorda; (philosophy)	**zo**	
POLYFOIL	circular ornamentation		
POLYGAMY	plurality of wives		
POLYGYNY			
POLYGLOT	in several languages		
POLYGRAM	many sided figure		
POLYMERS	organic, synthetic resins, rubbers		
POLYMERY			
POLYMERY	whorl of many members	**bt**	
POLYOPIA	multiple vision	**md**	
POLYPARY	hard covering of polyps		
POLYPIDE	compound polyzoan	**zo**	
POLYPODE	having many feet		
POLYPODY	a fern	**bt**	
POLYPOID	resembling polyps;		
POLYPOUS	octopus type	**zo**	
POLYPOSE	multi-pose portrait	**pg**	
POLYSEMY	multi meanings of word, root		
POLYSOME	cluster of ribosomes	**ch**	
POLYSOMY	multiple-chromosome state	**cy**	
POLYTENE	identical chromatids (genes)		
POLYTERM	unit concept heading		
POLYTYCH	many-leaved ancient book		
POLYTYPE	cast of an engraving		
POLYURIA	excessive urine secretion	**md**	
POLYZOAN	colony of polyzoa	**zo**	
POLYZOIC	zoolatrous; sporozoic	**zo**	
POLYZOON	barnacle type	**zo**	
POMANDER	perfumed ball		
POMIFORM	like an apple		
POMOLOGY	apple culture	**bt**	
POMPEIAN	(Pompeii)		

PONDERAL	ascertained by weight	
PONDERED	meditated; thought	
PONDERER	cogitator; ruminator	
POND-LILY	inhabitant of lily-pond	**bt**
POND-WEED	aquatic plant	**bt**
POND-WORT	water-soldier plant	**bt**
PONTIFEX	a Roman pontiff	
PONTIFIC	priestly; papal	**rl**
PONTINAL	bridging	
PONY-SKIN	soft hide	
PONY-TAIL	girl's hairstyle	
POOH-POOH	sneer at; deride	
POOL-ROOM	billiard-room	
POONSPAR	an Indian tree	**bt**
POOR-JOHN	salted hake	
POOR-LAWS	former legislation concerning paupers	**lw**
POORNESS	poverty; indigency	
POOR-RATE	a tax	
POPE-JOAN	a card game	
POPELING	a would-be pope	**rl**
POPE'S-EYE	fatty gland	**zo**
POPESHIP	popehood	**rl**
POPINJAY	parrot; coxcomb; fop	
POPISHLY	in popish style	**rl**
POPLITIC	(knee joint or ham)	**md**
POPODERM	dermal layer of hoof	**zo**
POPPLING	bubbling	
POPPY-OIL	slow-drying paint ingredient	
POPULACE	rabble; mob; masses	
POPULATE	propagate	
POPULINE	aspen bark extract	**bt**
POPULOUS	thronged; crowded; dense	
PORIFERA	the sponges	**zo**
PORIFORM	like a pore	
PORISTIC	porismatic; inferential	
PORK-CHOP	meat of pig	
PORKLING	young pig; piglet	**zo**
POROCYTE	tube-pierced cell in porifera	**zo**
POROGAMY	pollen-tube entry in micropyle	**bt**
POROROCA	tidal bore wave, Amazon	
POROSITY	porousness	
POROTYPE	a reproduction	
PORPHYRY	igneous rock	**mn**
PORPOISE	sea-hog	**zo**
PORRIDGE	Scotch oat dish; prison sentence (sl.)	
PORTABLE	easily carried	
PORTANDO }	carrying the voice;	
PORTAMENTO }	singing (lt.)	**mu**
PORTERLY	coarse; vulgar	
PORTESSE	a breviary	**rl**
PORTFIRE	an igniter	
PORTHOLE	gun-port; scuttle; ship's window	**nt**
PORTIERE	doorway curtain	
PORTLAND	(stone; cement)	**mn**
PORTLAST	gunwale	**nt**
PORTMOTE	court held in port	**lw**

PORTOISE	gunwale	**nt**
PORTOLAN	charts of bearing ports	**nv**
PORTRAIT	likeness; representation	
PORT-ROPE	rope for porthole lid	
PORTUARY	portable breviary	**rl**
POSEIDON	sea-god; Neptune	
POSHTEEN	sheepskin coat	
POSINGLY	so as to puzzle	
POSITING	postulating; affirming	
POSITION	spot; post; locality	
POSITIVE	actual; real; true; small organ	**mu**
POSITRON	radioisotope decay product	**nc**
POSOLOGY	science of quantity	**md**
POSSIBLE	feasible; likely	
POSSIBLY	practicably	
POSTABLE	mailable	
POSTBARK	mailboat	**nt**
POST-BILL	placard	
POST-CARD	card sent by post	
POST-DATE	cf. antedate	
POST-FACT	a later occurrence	
POST-FREE	postage paid	
POST-HORN	curled instrument	
POSTICHE	counterfeit; coil of false hair; wig	
POSTIQUE	added ornament	
POSTLUDE	conclusion	
POSTMARK	date stamp	
POST-NATI	born after a certain date	
POST-NOTE	promissory note	
POST-OBIT	payable after death	
POST-PAID	prepaid	
POSTPONE	defer; adjourn; shelve	
POST-TEST	final examination	
POST-TIME	hour of despatch	
POST-TOWN	district mail office	
POSTURAL	body position, reflexes, attitudes	
POSTURED	posed	
POSTURER	acrobat	
-POTAMOUS	living in streams	**cf, ec**
POTATION	drinking bout	
POTATOES	edible tubers	**bt**
POTATORY	draughty	
POT-BELLY	a paunch	
POTENTLY	forcibly; powerfully	
POTHERED	bothered; harassed	
POT-HOUSE	drinking booth	
POTLATCH	custom of giving presents (N. Amer. Indian)	
POT-METAL	lead and copper alloy	
POT-PLANT	(grown in a pot)	**bt**
POT-ROAST	braised meat	**ck**
POTSHARD }	broken piece of	
POTSHARE }	earthenware	
POTSHERD }		
POT-STICK	stirring stick	**ck**
POT-STILL	malt whiskey	
POTSTONE	soapstone	**mn**

POTTERED	dawdled	
POTTERER	desultory worker	
POTTOROO	rat kangaroo	**zo**
POTULENT	rather tipsy	
POUCHING	pocketing	
POUCHONG	black tea	**bt**
POULAINE	long pointed shoe	
POULTICE	a cataplasm	
POUNCING	sudden onset	
POUNDAGE	discount; taxation	
POUNDING	bruising; braying; hammering	
POWDERED	sprinkled	
POWERFUL	potent; puissant	
POWERGAS	coal-gas	
POYOK-OIL	W. African drying oil	**pt**
POZZOLAN	volcanic dust; hydraulic cement, fly-ash	**ce, mn**
PRACTICE	performance; wont	
PRACTICK	skilful; deceitful	
PRACTISE	to perpetrate; pursue	
PRACTIVE	adept; dexterous	
PRAECIPE	writ or instruction	**lw**
PRAEFECT	magistrate	**lw**
PRAISING	lauding; exalting; eulogizing	
PRANCING	bounding; capering	
PRANDIAL	concerning dinner	
PRANGING	crashing; bombing	
PRANKING	displaying; gambolling	
PRANKISH	freakish; impish	
PRASITES	type of wine	
PRATIQUE	clearance certificate	**nt**
PRATTLED	babbled; chattered	
PRATTLER	chatterbox	
PREACHED	proclaimed; exhorted	
PREACHER	pastor; divine; declarer	
PREAMBLE	an introduction; preface	
PREBOUND	(books) in a library binding	
PRECEDED	anticipated; headed; led	
PRECINCT	a close; enclosure	
PRECIOUS	dear; prized; treasured	
PRECLUDE	shut out; obviate; debar	
PRECURSE	a prognostication	
PREDABLE	raptorial; predacious	
PREDATED	antedated	
PREDATOR	carnivorous (preying) plunderer	
PREDELLA	altar decoration; stool	**rl**
PRE-ELECT	choose beforehand	
PREENING	tidying up; cleaning	
PRE-ENTRY	previous to joining	
PRE-EXIST	live before	
PREFACED	introduced by	
PREFACER	preface writer	
PREFINED	limited beforehand	
PREFIXED	anticipated; put before	
PREGNANT	prolific; fertile; fraught	
PREHNITE	silicate of alumina	**mn**
PREJUDGE	condemn unheard	
PRELUDED	prefaced; started	
PRELUDER	prelude player	
PREMIANT	incentive	

PREMIATE	to reward	
PREMIERE	first performance	
PREMISED	introduced	
PREMISES	a messuage	**lw**
PREMOLAR	bicuspid tooth	**md**
PREMORSE	ending abruptly	
PRENASAL	in front of your nose	
PRENATAL	before birth	
PRENOMEN	Christian name	
PRENTICE	apprentice	
PREORDER	arrange beforehand	
PREPARED	provided; planned; made	
PREPARER	arranger	
PREPENSE	premeditated	
PREPUBIC	prepubertal; preadolescence	
PRESAGED	foreboded; foretold	
PRESAGER	seer; soothsayer	
PRESBYTE	a far-sighted person	
PRESCIND	cut off; distract	
PRESENCE	mien; demeanour; company	
PRESERVE	conserve; defend; keep	
PRESIDED	controlled; officiated	
PRESS-BED	collapsible bed	
PRESS-BOX	reporter's box	
PRESSING	urgent; importunate; vital	
PRESSION	compression	
PRESSMAN	journalist	
PRESSURE	straits; urgency; stress; preparation for attack (fencing)	
PRESTIGE	reputation; fame; renown	
PREST-MAN	an enlisted man	
PRESTORE	deposit data temporarily	**cp**
PRE-STUDY	con; cogitate; ponder	
PRESUMED	surmised; thought	
PRESUMER	conjecturer	
PRETENCE	cloak; mask; guise	
PRETERIT	the past tense	
PRE-TRIAL	court case dry run	
PRETTIFY	beautify; adorn	
PRETTILY	neatly; daintily	
PREVIOUS	antecedent; prior; former	
PREVISED	foreseen	
PRIAPISM	chronically erect penis	**md**
PRICKING	inciting; spurring; needlepoint decoration; perforating	
PRICKLED	spiky	
PRIDEFUL	haughty; scornful	
PRIEDIEU	folding stool; praying desk	**rl**
PRIESTLY	sacerdotal	
PRIGGERY	super-respectability	
PRIGGING	larceny; pinching	
PRIGGISH	conceited; prim; affected	
PRIGGISM	coxcombry; pedantry	
PRIMATES	monkeys; archbishops	**zo**
PRIMEVAL	antediluvian; pristine	
PRIMMING	decking; pranking	
PRIMNESS	formality; demureness	
PRIMROSE	a badge	**bt**
PRINCELY	regal; stately; lavish	

523

PRINCEPS	the original	
PRINCESS	king's daughter	
PRINCOCK	a prig; coxcomb	
PRINKING	strutting; pranking	
PRINTIES	concave circles, ovals cut in glass	
PRINTING	typography	
PRINTOUT	reproduction of stored information	cp
PRIORATE	office of prior	rl
PRIORESS	lady prior	rl
PRIORITY	precedence	
PRISMOID	prismatic	
PRISONED	incarcerated; gaoled	
PRISONER	captive	
PRISTINE	original; ancient	
PRIZEMAN	a winner	
PROATLAS	bone between skull and vertebra	zo
PROBABLE	credible; likely	
PROBABLY	maybe; peradventure	
PROBATOR	examiner; approver	
PROCAINE	crystalline solid	pm
PROCEEDS	results; produce	
PROCHEIN	next; nearest	lw
PROCINCT	complete preparation	
PROCLAIM	bruit; trumpet; blazon	
PROCURED	got; obtained; acquired	
PROCURER	a pander	
PRODDING	goading	
PRODIGAL	wasteful; reckless; lavish	
PRODITOR	traitor	
PRODROME	preliminary treatise	
PRODUCED	created; caused; made	
PRODUCER	generator; manufacturer	
PROEMIAL	introductory	
PROFANED	violated; debased	
PROFANER	blasphemer; desecrater	
PROFILED	outlined; drawn; described in brief	
PROFITED	benefited; gained	
PROFITER	profiteer	
PRO-FORMA	advance checking for confirmation	
PROFOUND	deep; abysmal; occult	
PROGERIA	stunted; dwarfism; early senility	
PROGGING	begging food	
PROGONAL	of genital ridge portion	zo
PROGRESS	advancement; growth	
PROHIBIT	interdict; forbid; ban	
PROLAPSE	fall down	
PROLIFIC	productive; fertile; fecund	
PROLIXLY	at great length	
PROLOGUE	dramatic preface; poem	
PROLONGE	rope; rings and toggle	
PROMETAL	heat-resistant cast iron	ml
PROMISED	guaranteed; engaged	
PROMISEE	assured person	

PROMISER	} assuror; warranter;	
PROMISOR	} pledger; stipulator	
PROMOTED	elevated; preferred	
PROMOTEE	advanced person	
PROMOTER	active agent	
PROMPTED	suggested	
PROMPTER	encourager; (theatre)	
PROMPTLY	readily; quickly	
PROMULGE	announce; publish	
PRONATED	bent	
PRONATOR	an arm muscle	md
PRONG-HOE	a gardening tool	
PRONOTUM	prothorax notum in insects	zo
PRO-NYMPH	a stage of insect life	zo
PROOFING	testing; making waterproof	
PROPANOL	propyl alcohol	ch
PROPENOL	allyl alcohol	ch
PROPENSE	inclined; disposed	
PROPERLY	correctly; formally; exactly	
PROPERTY	quality; wealth; chattels	
PROPHAGE	inactive bacteriophage	bt
PROPHASE	mitosis/meiosis early stage	cy
PROPHECY	forecast; divination	
PROPHESY	to prognosticate; foretell	
PROPHYLL	bracteole	bt
PROPLASM	mould; matrix	
PROPOLIS	beeswax	
PROPOSAL	suggestion; tender	
PROPOSED	intended; meant; planned	
PROPOSER	mover; instigator	
PROPOUND	advocate; enunciate	
PROPPAGE	support	
PROPPING	shoring up	
PROPRIUM	self-hood; egotism	
PROPYLON	temple gateway	
PRORATED	assessed	
PROROGUE	adjourn; defer; postpone	
PROSAISM	prose writing	
PROSAIST	prosy person	
PROSEMAN	writer of prose	
PROSODUS	canal in porifera	zo
PROSPECT	aspect; outlook; survey	
PROSPORY	sporangia formation	bt
PROSTATE	male gland near bladder	pl
PROSTYLE	pillared portico	
PROTASIS	maxim; prologue	
PROTATIC	introductory	
PROTEASE	protein enzyme	ch
PROTEGEE	a ward	ch
PROTEIDS	} albuminoids	ch
PROTEINS	}	ch
PROTELES	the aard-wolf	zo
PROTENSE	extension (obs.)	
PROTEOSE	protein derivative	ch
PROTHECA	coral calyx rudiment	zo
PROTISTA	organisms	bt, zo
PROTOCOL	treaty; draft agreement	
PROTOCOL	etiquette, precedence; information flow	tc, tv

PROTOPOD	early abdominal phase in insects	
PROTOSET	mine rescue equipment	mn
PROTOZOA	early life forms	zo
PROTRACT	draw out; prolong; delay	
PROTRUDE	bulge; jut; project	
PROVABLE	demonstrable	
PROVABLY	verifiably	
PROVIANT	provender; fodder; provisions	
PROVIDED	if; supplied; yielded	
PROVIDER	furnisher; caterer	
PROVINCE	department; tract	
PROVINED	(vine culture)	
PROVISOR	purveyor; treasurer	
PROVOKED	exasperated; stung; vexed	
PROVOKER	inciter; annoyer; offender	
PROWLING	roving for prey; slinking	
PROXIMAL	adjoining; adjacent	
PRUDENCE	discretion; judiciousness	
PRUINOSE	} powdery; mealy	
PRUINOUS		
PRUNELLA	self-heal plant	bt
PRUNELLO	dried plum	bt
PRURIENT	interested in the obscene	
PRURITIS	persistent severe itching	md
PRYINGLY	inquisitively; curiously	
PSALMIST	inspired singer	rl
PSALMODY	psalms collectively	rl
PSALTERY	stringed instrument	mu
PSAMMITE	sandstone	mn
PSELLISM	stammering	md
PSITTACI	the parrot tribe	zo
PSYCHICS	mental phenomena	
PSYCHISM	spiritualism	
PSYCHIST	psychologist	
PTEROMYS	flying squirrel	zo
PTEROPOD	class of molluscs	zo
PTEROTIC	skull ear-wall bone	zo
PTERYLAE	clump of feathers	zo
PTILINUM	cephalic sac in dipters	zo
PTILOSIS	plumage	zo
PTOMAINE	organic poison	md
PTYALISM	salivation	md
PUBCRAWL	round of taverns	
PUBLICAN	collector of tribute	
PUBLICLY	open to all	
PUCELAGE	virginity	
PUCKBALL	puffball	bt
PUCKERED	wrinkled; crinkled	
PUDDLING	clay/iron refining process	mn
PUDICITY	modesty	
PUFF-BALL	lycoperdon	bt
PUFF-BIRD	S. American bird	zo
PUFF-PUFF	onomatopoeic locomotive	
PUG-FACED	monkey-faced	
PUGGAREE	scarf round helmet	
PUGILISM	the noble art	
PUGILIST	a pug; a boxer	
PUISSANT	powerful; forcible	

PULEGONE	terpene ketone in pennyroyal	ch
PULINGLY	fretfully; whiningly	
PULLBACK	a restraint	
PULL-LIFT	chain or rope-operator pulling device	to
PULLOVER	jersey; sweater	
PULMONIC	consumptive	md
PULPITER	preacher	
PULPITUM	stone screen in major church	
PULSATOR	vibrator	
PULSIFIC	throbbing	
PULVINAR	a cushion; brain fibres in visual sector	pl
PULVINUS	swollen leaf base	bt
PUMICATE	polish; make smooth	
PUMP-DALE	water trough	
PUMP-ROOM	mineral spring at spa	
PUMP-WELL	water pumped from well	
PUNCHEON	steel tool; large cask	
PUNCHING	perforating; striking	
PUNCTATE	pointed	
PUNCTUAL	punctilious; timely	
PUNCTURE	a hole; perforate; prick	
PUNGENCE	acridness	
PUNGENCY	keenness; acuteness	
PUNINESS	feebleness; frailty	
PUNISHED	chastised; penalized	
PUNISHER	disciplinarian	
PUNITIVE	punishing; penal	
PUNITORY	corrective	
PUNTILLA	lace-work	
PUNTSMAN	he who punts	
PUPARIAL	} a chrysalis; pupa	zo
PUPIFORM		
PUPARIUM		
PUPATION	incubation	zo
PUPILAGE	wardship; minority	
PUPILARY	in statu pupillari	
PUPILATE	having a central spot	
PUPIPARA	viviparous insects	zo
PUPPETRY	puppet-show; finery	
PUPPYISH	conceited	
PUPPYISM	affectation	
PURBLIND	dim-sighted	
PURCHASE	buy; procure; leverage	
PURENESS	purity; chastity	
PURFLING	embroidering	
PURIFIED	ceremonially cleansed	
PURIFIER	refiner	
PURIFORM	resembling pus	md
PURISTIC	scrupulously stylish	
PURPARTY	share of an estate	lw
PURPLING	dyeing with purple	
PURPLISH	somewhat purple	
PURPOSED	resolved; meant; intended	
PURPURIC	madder-purple	
PURSEFUL	enough to fill a purse	
PURSE-NET	purse with strings	
PURSLANE	salad herb	

PURSUANT	conformably	
PURSUING	prosecuting; chasing	
PURULENT	suppurating	md
PURVEYED	procured; retailed	
PURVEYOR	caterer	
PUSEYISM	tractarianism	rl
PUSEYITE	high church doctrinaire	rl
PUSHBALL	a great ball game	
PUSHBIKE	a cycle	
PUSHCART	barrow; handcart	
PUSHOVER	easy success; easily conned victim	
PUSHPULL	parallel amplifiers; two-way train	cp, ru
PUSS-MOTH	large hairy moth	zo
PUSS-TAIL	a bristle grass	bt
PUSSY-CAT	willow-catkin	bt, zo
PUSTULAR	pimpled	md
PUTATION	computation; sum	
PUTATIVE	reputed; alleged	
PUTCHOCK	root used for incense	bt
PUT-TO-BED	stopped press	pt
PUTTYING	fixing panes	
PUZZLING	bewildering; perplexing	
PYCNOSIS	staining-matter shrinkage	cy
PYELITIS	kidney pelvis inflammation	md
PYOGENIC	pus-producing; (inflammation)	md
PYRAMIDS	elevated medulla nerves (ear)	pl
PYRAMOID	of pyramid form	
PYRAZOLE	heterocyclic compound	ch
PYRENOID	refractive protein mass	bt
PYRENOUS	globular; nucleiform	bt
PYREXIAL	feverish	md
PYRIDINE	organic compound	ch
PYRIFORM	pear-shaped	
PYRITIZE	turn into pyrites	
PYRITOUS	like pyrites	mn
PYROGRAM	mechanical firework	
PYROLOGY	blowpipe analysis	
PYROSOMA	luminous animalculae	zo
PYROSTAT	a thermostat	
PYROTRON	thermonuclear device	nc
PYROXENE	augite	mn
PYROXYLE	gun-cotton	ch
PYRRHOUS	reddish	
PYTHONIC	oracular	
PYXIDATE	having a lid	bt
PYXIDIUM	lidlike capsule	bt

Q

QUACKERY	charlatanism; humbug	
QUACKING	boasting	
QUACKISH	somewhat bogus	
QUACKISM	medical pretence	
QUACKLED	almost choked	
QUADRANS	Roman farthing	nm

QUADRANT	quarter-circle	
QUADRATE	square; to agree	
QUADRIGA	four-horsed chariot	
QUADROON	(quarter negro blood)	
QUADRUNE	gritstone	mn
QUAESITA	to be decided on later	
QUAESTOR	treasurer	
QUAFFING	swallowing; imbibing	
QUAGMIRE	a bog; swamp	
QUAGMIRY	yielding; boggy	
QUAILING	flinching; blenching	
QUAINTER	odder; stranger	
QUAINTLY	whimsically; fancifully	
QUAKERLY	soberly	
QUALMISH	squeamish; queasy	
QUANDANG	Australian peach	bt
QUANDARY	dilemma; predicament	
QUANTIFY	determine quantity	
QUANTITY	measure; amount; bulk	
QUARRIED	hewn	
QUARRIER	quarryman	
QUARRIES	arrows; panes of glass	
QUARTERN	a gill; 4 lb (l.8 kg)	me
QUARTERS	living places	
QUARTILE	planetary aspect; point of quarter division	as
QUARTINE	a seed covering	bt
QUASHING	annulling; crushing	
QUASSINE	} extract of quassia;	
QUASSITE	} a febrifuge	md
QUATERON	a quadroon	
QUATORZE	a count in piquet	
QUATRAIN	four line stanza	
QUAVERED	quivered; shook; vibrated	
QUAVERER	a warbler	
QUAY-WALL	harbour-wall	
QUEASILY	squeamishly	
QUEBRADA	a ravine (Sp.)	
QUEEN-BEE	ruler of hive	zo
QUEENDOM	queenly state	
QUEENING	playing the queen	
QUEENLET	a petty queen	
QUEEREST	quaintest; oddest	
QUEERING	spoiling; disarranging	
QUEERISH	rather strange	
QUELLERZ	limonite	mn
QUELLING	crushing; subduing; curbing	
QUENCHED	extinguished; (fire); (appetite); (thirst)	
QUENCHER	a long drink; thirst or fire subduer	
QUENELLE	forcemeat	
QUERCITE	acorn extract	bt
QUERLING	twirling	
QUERYING	challenging; inquiring	
QUESTFUL	adventurous	
QUESTING	seeking; searching	
QUESTION	interrogation; catechize	
QUESTMAN	authorized inquirer	
QUEUEING	lining up	

QUIBBLED	evaded the question	
QUIBBLER	prevaricator	
QUICKEST	speediest; fastest	
QUICKIES	quickly done films, drinks, etc.	
QUICKSET	living plant	**bt**
QUIDDANY	a mess of quinces	
QUIDDING	food expulsion after chewing	**vt**
QUIDDITY	captious question; quibble	
QUIDDLED	wasted time; pottered	
QUIDDLER	a trifler	
QUIDNUNC	tattler; know-all	
QUIESCED	silenced; subsided	
QUIETAGE	tranquillity	
QUIETEST	calmest	
QUIETISE	pacify	
QUIETISM	placidness	
QUIETIST	a mystic	
QUIETIVE	sedative	
QUIETUDE	rest; repose	
QUILLING	crimping; goffering; decorating surface of glass with coloured glass ribbons (Amer.)	
QUILL-NIB	penpoint	
QUILTING	quilted work	
QUINABLE	interval of a fifth	**mu**
QUINCUNX	plantation of 5 trees	**fr**
QUINIEZA	pelota with bets	**ga**
QUINTAIN	balanced tilting beam	**ga**
QUINTILE	aspect of the planets	
QUINTOLE	five-stringed viol	**mu**
QUIPPING	taunting; jesting	
QUIPPISH	sarcastic	
QUIRINAL	Italian Court	
QUIRINUS	defied Romulus	
QUIRITES	Roman citizens	
QUIRKING	twisting	
QUIRKISH	evasive	
QUISLING	traitor; betrayer	
QUIT-RENT	rent in lieu of service	
QUITTING	deserting; ratting; hiatus; (golf)	
QUIXOTIC	} romantic and absurd	
QUIXOTRY	notions and actions	
QUIZZERY	ridicule	
QUIZZIFY	hoax; puzzle	
QUIZZING	bantering; chaffing	
QUOTABLE	citable	
QUOTIENT	how many times	
QUOTIETY	proportionate frequency	

R

RABATINE	turned-down collar	
RABBETED	grooved	
RABBINIC	Hebrew language, etc.	
RABBITER	rabbit catcher	
RABBITRY	enclosure for rabbits	

RABIDITY	raving madness; frenzy	
RABIETIC	maniacal; insane; demented	
RACE-CARD	record of runners	
RACEGOER	watcher of winners	
RACEMOSE	} in clusters	
RACEMOUS		**bt**
RACEMULE	small bunch	**bt**
RACHILLA	leaf-rib	**bt**
RACHITIC	rickety	**md**
RACHITIS	rickets	**md**
RACIALLY	pertaining to race (mixed)	
RACINAGE	acid technique for leather twig effects	
RACINESS	piquancy	
RACKETED	frolicked; clamoured	
RACKETER	a noisy person	
RACK-RAIL	toothed tail	
RACK-RENT	exorbitant rent	
RACK-TAIL	part of clock	
RACK-WORK	rack and pinion	
RACLETTE	cheese for melting; Swiss	**ck**
RACOVIAN	Polish Socinian	
RADARMAN	radar petty officer R.N.	
RADECHON	mesh-grid storage tube	**el**
RADIALLY	like spokes of a wheel	
RADIANCE	effulgence; lustre; energy in watts per steradian per m^2 directional intensity	**as, ps, el, me**
RADIANCY	brilliancy; glitter; sheen	
RADIATED	shone; sparkled	
RADIATOR	heating apparatus	
RADICANT	taking root	
RADICATE	to plant; emplant	
RADICOSE	having a large root	**bt**
RADICULE	a small root	**bt**
RADIOING	transmitting by wireless	
RADIOLUS	part of a feather	**zo**
RADULATE	(rasping tongue)	**zo**
RAFFLING	lottery for an article or articles	
RAFT-DUCK	black-headed duck	**zo**
RAFTERED	timbered	
RAFT-PORT	(timber loading)	**nt**
RAFT-ROPE	thickish piece of string	
RAFTSMAN	castaway	
RAGABASH	ragamuffin	
RAGGEDLY	in tatters	
RAGINGLY	furiously; rabidly	
RAGNAROK	twilight of the gods (Norse mythology)	
RAG-PAPER	high-quality paper	
RAGSTONE	impure limestone	**mn**
RAG-WHEEL	polishing wheel	
RAILHEAD	a terminus	**rw**
RAILLERY	banter; chaff; ridicule	
RAILROAD	railway; forceful insistence; overhead serve (tennis); (bowls)	**rw**
RAINBAND	band in solar spectrum	
RAINBIRD	Jamaican bird	**zo**

RAINCOAT	waterproof	
RAINDROP	single drop of rain	
RAINFALL	shower	
RAINLESS	state of drought	
RAINPOUR	downpour	
RAINTREE	S. American tree	**bt**
RAIN-WASH	gravity/rain soil creepage	**gl**
RAISINEE	a confection	
RAKEHELL	a rip; debauchée	
RAKISHLY	set at an angle	
RAKSHASA	Hindu ghoul	
RALLYING	reuniting; gathering; track & trek events; cycling; motor racing	
RAMAYANA	Indian epic poem	
RAMBLING	roaming; wandering	
RAMBOOZE	a cordial	
RAMBUTAN	Malayan fruit tree	**bt**
RAMENTUM	brown scale on ferns	**bt**
RAMICOLE	living on twigs	**bt**
RAMICORN	horny sheath	
RAMIFIED	diverse	
RAMIFORM	like a branch	
RAMPAGED	romped; rioted; gambolled	
RAMPANCY	excessive prevalence	
RAMPSMAN	highwayman	
RAMRODDY	stiff	
RAMSHORN	an ammonite	**mn**
RAMULOUS	ramulose; branching	
RANARIUM	frog aquarium	**zo**
RANCHERO	cow-puncher	
RANCHING	cattle-raising	
RANCHMAN	stockbreeder	
RANCIDLY	fustily; mustily; sourly	
RANDOMLY	at a venture; fortuitously	
RANGIFER	a reindeer	**zo**
RANIFORM	froglike	**zo**
RANKLING	festering; smouldering	
RANKNESS	overgrowth; exuberance	
RANSOMED	redeemed; released; purchased; (release money)	
RANSOMER	liberator; indemnifier	
RAPACITY	greed; avarice; voracity	
RAPE-CAKE	cattle fodder	
RAPE-SEED	(hence colza oil)	**bt**
RAPHANIA	ergotism; blight	
RAPHANUS	radish	**bt**
RAPHIDES	crystals in plants	
RAPIDITY	celerity; despatch; speed	
RAPPAREE	Irish robber; bandit	
RAPTORES	birds of prey	**zo**
RAPTURED	ravished; ecstatic	
RAQUETTE	(pelota); (rachet)	
RAREFIED	tenuous	
RARENESS	infrequency; scarceness	
RARERIPE	early ripe; untimely	
RASCALLY	knavish; roguish; dishonest	
RASHLING	reckless fellow	
RASHNESS	foolhardiness; unwariness	
RASORIAL	scratching	

RATAPLAN	beat of drum	
RATCHETY	jerky	
RATCHING	yarn-tightening process	**wv**
RATEABLE	assessable	
RATE-BOOK	book of valuations	
RAT-GOOSE	brent goose	**zo**
RATHRIPE	early ripe	
RATIFIED	confirmed; endorsed	
RATIFIER	approver; authorizer	
RATIONAL	reasonable; judicious; sane	
RATIONED	on an allowance	
RAT'S-BANE	rat poison	
RATSNAKE	rat-killing snake	**zo**
RAT'S-TAIL	tapering	
RATTINET	a woollen stuff	
RATTLING	quick; lively; clattering	
RAVAGING	despoiling; plundering	
RAVEHOOK	ripping iron	**to**
RAVELLED	entangled; untwisted	
RAVENING	plundering; devouring	
RAVENOUS	starving; voracious	
RAVINGLY	with fury; frantically	
RAVISHED	enchanted; charmed	
RAVISHER	abductor	
RAW-BONED	gaunt	
RAWLBOLT	} nail or screw	
RAWLPLUG	} wall fixing system	
REABSORB	soak up again	
REACCESS	fresh approach	
REACCUSE	indict again	
REACHING	extending; attaining; sailing, wind abeam	**nv**
REACTANT	substance involved in chem. reaction	**ch**
REACTION	counter-measure; recoil	
REACTIVE	capacity to react	
READABLE	well written; good style	
READABLY	clearly; legibly	
READ-HEAD	electro-magnetic	**cp**
READJUST	reset; modify	
READ-ONLY	on loan; unalterable	
READ-RATE	speed of reading	
READ-TIME	access to screen; delay	**cp**
REAFFIRM	swear on oath; state anew	
REAGENCY	reflex influence; reaction	**pc**
REALISED	felt; understood; comprehended	
REALLEGE	assert a 2nd time	
REALNESS	actuality; verity; fact	
REANOINT	relubricate	
REANSWER	reply again	
REAPPEAR	turn up again	
REAR-LINE	behind the army	
REARMING	re-equipping	
REARMOST	last; ultimate	
REAR-RANK	back line	
REARWARD	rearguard	
REASCEND	climb again	
REASCENT	a further climb	
REASONED	argued; disputed	

REASONER	debater	
REASSERT	re-affirm	
REASSESS	re-impose; revalue	
REASSIGN	give different job to	
REASSURE	console; comfort	
REATTACH	refix	
REATTAIN	get again	
REAVOWED	said so again	
REBATING	deducting from	
REBELLED	revolted; mutinied	
REBELLER	a rebel; insurgent	
REBELLOW	re-echo	
REBITING	re-engraving	
REBOILER	vessel at still bottom	ch
REBRACED	restrengthened	
REBUFFED	repulsed; snubbed	
REBUKING	chiding; carpeting	
REBURIED	re-interred	
REBUTTAL	refutation; retort	
REBUTTED	confuted; refuted	
REBUTTER	a legal reply	lw
RECALLED	revoked; annulled; denied	
RECANTED	retracted; abjured	
RECAPTOR	one who retakes	
RE-CASING	rebinding of book in original cover	
RECEDING	retreating; ebbing	
RECEIVED	got; allowed; welcomed	
RECEIVER	a recipient; receptionist; (bankruptcy); (telephone); (stolen goods)	lw
RECENTLY	lately	
RECEPTOR	sensory organ; nerve transmitter	
RECESSED	dimpled; secluded	
RECESSES	niches; vacations	
RECESSUS	a recess; a niche	
RECHAMPI	gold ornamentation on chair frames	
RECHARGE	attack anew; reload	
RECISION	cutting back; pruning	
RECITING	rehearsing; relating	
RECKLESS	heedless; rash; headstrong	
RECKLING	weakest in a litter	zo
RECKONED	considered; judged	
RECKONER	calculator; computer	
RECLINED	leant; lay; reposed	
RECLINER	a reclining dial	
RECLOSED	shut again	
RECLOTHE	provide new garments	
RECOALED	refilled the bunkers	
RECOILED	retreated; reacted	
RECOILER	flincher	
RECOINED	minted afresh	
RECOLLET	Franciscan monk	rl
RECOLOUR	repaint	
RECOMMIT	refer again; re-entrust	
RECONVEY	transfer back	
RECORDED	entered; minuted	lw
RECORDER	flageolet; judge	mu

RECOUPED	indemnified	
RECOURSE	reference; resort; refuge	
RECOVERY	convalescence; revival; body renewal; return (rowing)	
RECREANT	craven; apostate	
RECREATE	refresh; delight	
RECTIGON	thermionic gas diode	el
RECTORAL	rectorial	rl
RECUBANT	recumbent	
RECUMBED	reclined; reposed	
RECURRED	remembered; repeated	
RECURVED	bent back	
RECUSANT	Elizabethan R.C.	rl
REDACTOR	editor	
REDARGUE	to refute; disprove	
RED-BELLY	terrapin; char	zo
RED-CEDAR	pencil-wood	bt
RED-CHALK	reddle	mn
RED-CORAL	living coral	mn
RED-CROSS	humanitarian organization	
REDDENDA	rent clauses	lw
REDDENDO	(vassal's duties)	lw
REDDENED	blushed; flushed	
RED-EARTH	reddish loam	mn
REDEEMED	ransomed; freed; retrieved	
REDEEMER	liberator; saviour	
REDELESS	unwise; ill-advised	
REDEMAND	request again	
REDEMISE	reconveyance	lw
REDENTED	indented	
REDEPLOY	movement of army; industrial	
RED-FACED	florid; rubicund	
REDIGEST	reduce to form again	
REDIRECT	re-address	
REDITION	return	
REDIVIDE	re-allot	
RED-METAL	a copper alloy	
REDNOSED	nose red with cold	
REDOLENT	aromatic; fragrant	
REDOUBLE	a bridge call	
REDRIVEN	herded back again	
REDSHANK	red-legged sandpiper	zo
RED-SHIRT	follower of Garibaldi; athlete (USA)	
RED-SHORT	brittle	
RED-STAFF	millstone trimmer	
REDUBBER	old clothes merchant	
REDUCENT	reducing	
REDUCING	curtailing; abating	
REDUVIUS	predacious bug	zo
RE-DYEING	recolouring	
RE-ECHOED	reverberated; repeated	
REED-BAND	clarionets, etc.	mu
REED-BIRD	bobolink	zo
REEDLESS	no rush	
REEDLING	bearded titmouse	zo
REED-MACE	cat's tail	bt
REED-PIPE	an organ pipe	mu
REED-STOP	an organ stop	mu
REED-WREN	greater reedwarbler	zo

REEF-BAND	strip of canvas	**nt**
REEF-KNOT	secure flat knot	
REEF-LINE	a rope	**nt**
REELABLE	able to be wound	
REEL-LINE	fishing line	
REEL-RALL	topsy-turvy (Sc.)	
REEL-SEAT	reel housing on rod	
RE-EMBARK	get back in a boat	
RE-EMBODY	reform into a body	
RE-EMERGE	come out again	
RE-ENLIST	sign on again	
RE-EXPORT	ship out again	
REFASTEN	refix	
REFERRED	attributed; assigned	
REFERRER	enquirer	
REFIGURE	present anew	
REFILLED	replenished	
REFINERY	purification plant	
REFINING	purifying	
REFITTED	re-equipped	
REFLEXED	curved back	
REFLEXLY	reactively	
REFLOWED	ebbed	
REFLOWER	bloom again	
REFLUENT	flowing back	
REFOREST	plan anew	
REFORGED	kept signing false name	
REFORMED	remodelled; restored	
REFORMER	innovator	
REFRAMED	traduced all over again	
REFREEZE	make icebound again	
REFRINGE	infringe	
REFUGIUM	locality remaining unchanged despite climatic alteration	
REFUNDED	reimbursed; repaid	
REFUNDER	one who pays back again	
REFUSING	declining; repudiating	
REFUTING	gainsaying; rebutting	
REGAINED	retrieved; recaptured	
REGALIAN	regal; sovereign	
REGALING	faring sumptuously	
REGALISM	sovereignty	
REGALITY	royalty	
REGARDED	noticed; heeded; gazed	
REGARDER	observer; watcher	
REGATHER	recollect	
REGICIDE	killer of a king	
REGILDED	made golden once more	
REGIMENT	organize; a military unit	
REGIONAL	topographical	
REGIONIC	local	
REGISTER	record; chronicle; fit; list; filed data storage; range or compass of voice, instruments, organ stops	**cp, mu**
REGISTRY	labour agency	
REGLETTE	measuring tape scale	**sv**
REGNANCY	predominance; supremacy	
REGOLITH	mantle rock; topsoil	

REGORGED	vomited	
REGRATED	freshened; scraped	
REGRATER	huckster; regrator	
REGROUND	(razors); resharpened	
REGROWTH	new growth	
REGULATE	adjust; control; arrange	
REGULIZE	refine chemically	
REHANDLE	finger a 2nd time	
REHASHED	furnished up	
REHEARSE	recapitulate	
RE-HEATED	warmed up again; superheated	**ce**
REHEATER	part of steam or compressed air machines	**ce**
REHOUSED	given new homes	
REIGNING	prevailing; governing	
RE-IGNITE	rekindle	
REIMBODY	re-incorporate	
REIMPORT	bring back	
REIMPOSE	retax	
REINCITE	reanimate	
REINDEER	the caribou	**zo**
REINFECT	make sick again	
REINFORM	renotify	
REINFUND	pour in again	
REINFUSE	reanimate	
REIN-HOOK	bearing-rein hook	
REINLESS	unchecked	
REINSERT	put in again	
REINSMAN	accomplished driver	
REINSURE	make doubly certain	
REINVENT	create anew	
REINVEST	put money in again	
REINVITE	ask again	
REISSUED	put out again	
REJECTED	excluded; rebuffed	
REJECTOR	decliner; rejecter	
REJECTOR	impedance of circuit (due to overloading)	**el**
REJOICED	exulted; gloried; delighted	
REJOICER	reveller; merry-maker	
REJOINED	knit together; reunited	
REJUDGED	re-examined; reconsidered	
REKINDLE	arouse anew; relight	
RELANDED	came down twice	
RELAPSED	retrogressed	
RELAPSER	backslider	
RELATING	narrating; telling	
RELATION	connection; kinsman; (harmony)	
RELATIVE	comparative; kinsman; parallel common key-signature	**cp, mu**
RELATRIX	female informant	**lw**
RELAXANT	a loosener	
RELAXING	slackening; unbending	
RELAYING	transmit programmes	**ro**
RELEASED	emancipated; freed	
RELEASEE	discharged person	
RELEASER	releasor; liberator	

RELEGATE	consign; transfer		RENOUNCE	disclaim; forsake; abjure	
RELESSEE	releasee		RENOVATE	renew; repair; refresh	
RELESSOR	releaser	lw	RENOWNED	famous; eminent	
RELEVANT	applicable; apt; pertinent		RENOWNER	swaggerer; braggart	
RELIABLE	trustworthy; trusty; safe		RENTABLE	leasable	
RELIABLY	dependably		RENTERER	invisible mender	
RELIANCE	confidence; trust		RENT-FREE	living without paying rent	
RELICTED	left bare	lw	RENT-ROLL	list of tenants	
RELIEVED	palliated; soothed; eased		RENUMBER	put new numbers on	
RELIEVER	mitigator; assuager		RENVERSE	inverted; reverse	
RELIGION	faith		REOBTAIN	get again	
RELISHED	appreciated		REOCCUPY	move back in	
RELISTEN	hear once more		REOPENED	no longer shut	
RELIVING	experiencing again		REOPPOSE	not capitulate	
RELOADED	ready to fire again		REORDAIN	refrock the defrocked	
RELUCENT	transparent; shining		REORIENT	arising again	
RELUMINE	rekindle		REPACIFY	calm down again	
REMAINED	left over; stopped		REPAGULA	egg-protection bodies	zo
REMAKING	rebuilding		REPAIRED	redressed; went	
REMANENT	remaining		REPAIRER	restorer	
REMANNED	provided with a new crew		REPARTEE	witty retort; riposte	
REMARKED	said; declared; mentioned		REPASSED	went by twice	
REMARKER	commentator; observer		REPASTED	fed	
REMARQUE	marginal etching		REPAYING	refunding	
REMEDIAL	curative; healing		REPEALED	rescinded; annulled	
REMEDIED	repaired; rectified		REPEALER	abrogator; revoker	
REMEMBER	recall; recollect		REPEATED	iterated; echoed	
REMERCIE	to thank (obs.)		REPEATER	a watch; transmission channel	
REMIFORM	oar-shaped			amplifier	tc
REMINDED	brought to notice		REPELLED	repulsed; checked; rebuffed	
REMINDER	keepsake; souvenir		REPELLER	deterrer; rejecter	
REMISING	releasing	lw	REPENTED	truly contrite; rued	
REMISSLY	negligently; slackly		REPENTER	penitent person; (sect)	rl
REMITTAL	surrender; remittance		REPEOPLE	repopulate	
REMITTED	relaxed; forgave		REPERTOR	a finder	
REMITTEE	consignee		REPERUSE	read again	
REMITTER	pardoner; remittor		REPETEND	recurring decimal	
REMODIFY	remodel		REPINING	fretting; murmuring	
REMOLADE	salad dressing	ck	REPLACED	reinstated; restored	
REMOLTEN	remelted		REPLACER	a substitute	
REMOTELY	faintly		REPLEDGE	swear again	
REMOTION	remoteness (obs.)		REPLEVIN	a legal action	lw
REMOVING	dislodging; abstracting		REPLUNGE	dive again	
REMURMUR	complain again		REPLYING	answering	
RENAMING	rechristening		REPOLISH	shine up again	
RENDERED	translated; gave		REPONING	replacing	lw
RENDERER	supplier; assignor		REPORTED	communicated; related	
RENDIBLE	able to be torn; note not		REPORTER	announcer; journalist	
	renderable; degradable		REPOSING	reclining; resting	
RENDZINA	intrazonal dark soil on chalk		REPOSURE	repose; peace; tranquillity	
	(Poland)	gl	REPOTTED	(gardening)	
RENEGADE	⎫ quisling; apostate;		REPOUSSE	embossed	
RENEGADO	⎬ runagate; traitor;		REPRIEVE	respite; pardon; acquit	
RENEGATE	⎭ recreant; rebel		RE-PRIMER	recapping machine	
RENEGING	revoking at cards		REPRISAL	retaliation; revenge	
RENEWING	renovating; rejuvenating		REPROACH	reprimand; upbraid	
RENIDIFY	build a new nest		REPROVAL	admonition; censure	
RENIFORM	kidney-shaped		REPROVED	blamed; rebuked; chided	
RENIGATE	renegade		REPROVER	reprehender	
RENITENT	allergic; resistant		REPRUNED	lopped again	

531

REPTILIA	snakes and crocodiles, etc. **zo**	
REPUBLIC	democratic state	
REPUGNED	resisted; opposed	
REPUGNER	a rebel	
REPULPIT	restore a preacher	
REPULSED	checked; refused; rebuffed	
REPULSER	repeller	
REPURIFY	purify again	
REPUTING	esteeming	
REQUIRED	wanted; demanded; lacked	
REQUIRER	exactor; claimant	
REQUITAL	recompense; punishment	
REQUITED	reciprocated	
REQUITER	avenger	
RE-RAILED	got back on track	
REREFIEF	an under-fief (Sc.) **lw**	
REREWARD	rear-guard	
REROOFED	given new roof	
RESAILED	sailed again	
RESALUTE	put hand to head again	
RE-SCORED	rearranged **mu**	
RESCRIBE	rewrite	
RESCRIPT	edict; decree	
RESCUING	extricating; liberating	
RESEARCH	scientific enquiry	
RESEATED	given chair again	
RESEIZED	legal seizure of	
RESEIZER	disseized property **lw**	
RESEMBLE	liken; compare; collate	
RESENTED	strongly objected; resisted	
RESENTER	an injured party	
RESERVED	shy; distant; unsociable	
RESERVER	withholder	
RESETTER	receiver of stolen goods	
RESETTLE	repopulate	
RESHABAR	dry wind in Near East **mt**	
RESIANCE	residence	
RESIDENT	occupier; dweller; agent; routine **cp**	
RESIDUAL	left over; difference between observation and true value **ps**	
RESIDUUM	residue; surplus; excess	
RESIGNED	abdicated; relinquished	
RESIGNEE	he who gets resigned	
RESIGNER	renouncer; quitter	
RESILING	recoiling	
RESINATA	Grecian resinous white	
RESINATE	wine	
RESINIFY	to make resinous	
RESINISE		
RESINOUS	olfactory quality (pine, pitch)	
RESISTED	withstood; repelled; opposed	
RESISTER	opposer	
RESISTOR	non-conductor **el**	
RESMOOTH	smooth again	
RESOLDER	solder again	
RESOLUTE	steadfast; staunch	
RESOLVED	melted; determined	

RESOLVER	solver; mediator; catalyst; chord **mu**	
RESONANT	resounding; sonorous	
RESONATE	re-echo; vibrate	
RESORBED	absorbed	
RESORCIN	crystalline phenol **ch**	
RESORTED	betook; repaired; flew	
RESORTER	frequenter	
RESOURCE	expedient; means; natural wealth; ingenuity	
RESOWING	broadcasting again	
RESPECTS	compliments	
RESPERSE	disperse; sprinkle	
RESPIRED	inhaled	
RESPITED	postponed; reprieved	
RESPOKEN	repeated	
RESPONSE	answer; reply; rejoinder	
RESTATED	reaffirmed	
REST-CURE	convalescence	
RESTLESS	agitated; turbulent; uneasy	
RESTORED	returned; renewed; cured	
RESTORER	reviver; healer	
RESTRAIN	check; curb; suppress	
RESTRICT	limit; confine; hamper	
RESTRIKE	lay down work a second time	
RESTRING	tennis racket; violin	
RESULTED	caused; followed; ensued	
RESUMING	renewing; continuing	
RESUMMON	call again	
RESUPINE	lying on the back	
RESURVEY	review	
RETAILED	gossiped; peddled	
RETAILER	not a wholesale merchant	
RETAILLE	divided twice **hd**	
RETAINED	detained; kept; withheld	
RETAINER	henchman; lackey; servant	
RETAKING	recapturing	
RETARDED	slowed up; delayed	
RETARDER	hinderer; obstructionist; hardening reducing admixture	
RETENTOR	retaining muscle **md**	
RETEPORE	a coral **zo**	
RETICENT	taciturn; reserved; quiet	
RETICULE	lady's workbag; graticule; linked webs	
RETIERCE	heraldic arrangement **hd**	
RETIFERA	the true limpet **zo**	
RETIFORM	meshed; reticulated	
RETINENE	rhodopsin; pigment of retina (eye) **ch**	
RETINITE	obsidian; amber **mn**	
RETINOID	resin-like	
RETINULA	pigmented cells **zo**	
RETIRACY	retirement	
RETIRADE	a retrenchment	
RETIRING	shy; unobtrusive; diffident	
RETORTED	rejoined; replied **hd**	
RETORTER	responder	
RETOSSED	thrown back	

RETRACED	returned by same route	
RETRAXIT	loss of action	lw
RETRENCH	curtail; economize	
RETRIEVE	recover; regain; rescue	
RETROACT	oppose	
RETRORSE	bent back	
RETRUDED	thrust back	
RETRYING	attempting again	
RETUNDED	blunted	
RETURNED	rendered; reverted	
RETURNER	remitter; (reappeared)	
REUNITED	rejoined	
RE-UPTAKE	reabsorption of a substance	
REURGING	pressing on again	
REUSSITE	magnesium compound	mn
REVALUED	re-assessed	
REVAMPED	repatched	
REVANCHE	revenge (Fr.)	
REVEALED	disclosed; published	
REVEALER	betrayer; divulger	
REVEHENT	taking away	
REVEILLE	trumpet-call; dawn	
REVELLED	wantoned; feasted	
REVELLER	carouser	
REVENANT	returned from the dead; ghost	
REVENGED	requited; repaid	
REVENGER	vindicator	
REVEREND	respectful epithet	
REVERENT	submissive; humble	
REVERING	venerating; honouring	
REVERIST	a dreamer	
REVERSAL	complete change	
REVERSED	subverted; overthrew	
REVERSER	mortgager of land	lw
REVESTED	reappointed	
REVETTED	faced with masonry	
REVIEWAL	a critique	
REVIEWED	revised; edited; surveyed	
REVIEWER	an inspector; critic	
REVILING	aspersing; maligning	
REVISING	checking; amending	
REVISION	re-examination	
REVISORY	correctional	
REVIVIFY	reanimate; revive	
REVIVING	renewing; rousing	
REVOKING	repealing; quashing	
REVOLTED	felt disgust	
REVOLTED	rebelled	
REVOLTER	guerilla; partisan	
REVOLUTE	rolled back	
REVOLVED	rotated; wheeled; circled	
REVOLVER	a firearm	
REVULSOR	h. and c. apparatus	md
REWARDED	decorated; requited	
REWARDER	guerdon giver	
REWORDED	redrafted	
RHABDITE	rod-like structure	zo
RHABDOID	spindle-shaped body	zo
RHABDOME	lens supporter	md

RHAETIAN	(Rhaetia) Latin-Swiss linguistic area	
RHAGADES	fissures of the skin	md
RHAGODIA	grapelike genus	bt
RHAMNOSE	menthyl-pentose	ch
RHAPSODE	rhapsodist	
RHAPSODY	rambling composition	mu
RHEOBASE	minimal elect. response stimulus	
RHEOCORD	resistance wire	
RHEOLOGY	formation of matter	ps
RHEOSTAT	(variable resistance)	
RHEOTOME	a switch	
RHETORIC	florid oratory	
RHINIDAE	sharks	zo
RHINITIS	nasal inflammation	md
RHINODON	immense shark	zo
RHIZANTH	flowering root	bt
RHIZOGEN	parasite plant	bt
RHIZOMYS	genus of mole-rats	zo
RHIZOPOD	locomotive protozoa	zo
RHODANIC	roe-red colour	ch
RHODEINA	goldfish	zo
RHODEOSE	isomer of rhamnose	ch
RHODITES	genus of gall-flies	zo
RHOEADIC	(poppy extract)	ch
RHOMBOID	quadrilateral figure	
RHOMETER	molten-metal impurity measurer	ml
RHONCHAL	bronchial	md
RHONCHUS	a râle	md
RHOPALIC	a hexameter	
RHO-THETA	distance/bearing nav. system	nv
RHUBARBY	cathartic	bt, md
RHYOLITE	a quartz	mn
RHYTHMIC	harmonious; metric; lilting	
RHYTHMUS	rhythm; cadence; verse	
RIBALDRY	} irreverent jesting; obscenity	
RIBAUDRY		
RIBBONED	striped; streaked	
RIB-GRASS	ribwort	bt
RIB-NOSED	like a baboon	
RIBOSOME	nuclear source of protein synthesis	
RIB-ROAST	beat soundly	
RICE-BIRD	the bobolink	zo
RICEBOAT	backward-sailing river craft (Burma)	nt
RICE-DUST	rice-meal	
RICE-GLUE	a cement	
RICE-MEAL	oriental flour	
RICE-MILK	milk with rice	
RICERCAR(E)	} contrapuntal composition (research)	mu
RICERCATA		
RICE-SOUP	congee	
RICH-LEFT	richly endowed	
RICHNESS	wealth; opulence; affluence	
RICINIAE	mites; ticks, etc.	zo
RICINIUM	Roman mantle	

RICKETLY	shaky; weak; tottering	
RICK-RACK	openwork edging	
RICKSHAW	Indian or Chinese vehicle	
RICOCHET	rebound	
RICOLITE	ornamental stone	mn
RIDDANCE	deliverance; release	
RIDDLING	perforating; sieving	
RIDEABLE	broken in	
RIDICULE	deride; lampoon; mock	
RIFENESS	prevalence	
RIFFRAFF	sweepings; refuse; rabble	
RIFLEMAN	modern musketeer	
RIFLE-PIT	short trench	
RIGADOON	} lively English-French	
RIGAUDON	} dances	mu
RIGATION	irrigation	
RIGHTFUL	genuine; true; lawful	
RIGHTING	doing justice; rectifying	
RIGIDITY	stiffness; taughtness; contraction (muscle); social strictness	
RIGORISM	austerity	
RIGORIST	a martinet	
RIGOROUS	inflexible; severe; harsh	
RILL-MARK	corrugation	
RIMIFORM	having a rim	
RIMOSITY	roughness	
RIMULOSE	fissured	
RINABOUT	vagrant (Sc.)	
RIND-CALL	defect in timber; (callus)	
RING-BARK	make a circular cut	
RING-BILL	ring-necked duck	zo
RINGBOLT	embedded ring	
RINGBONE	exostosis on horse foot bones	vt
RINGBONE	callus on pastern	
RING-DIAL	portable sundial	
RING-DOVE	cushat; wood-pigeon	zo
RINGDOWN	operator-signalling method	tc
RING-GOAL	a ball game	
RINGLETY	with ringlets	
RING-LOCK	a puzzle lock	
RING-MAIL	chain armour	
RING-NECK	ring-plover	
RING-ROAD	by-pass	
RING-ROPE	a cable rope	nt
RING-SIDE	close to the scene	
RING-TAIL	hen-harrier	zo
RING-TIME	time for marriage	
RING-WALL	ring fence	
RINGWISE	experienced; of boxing	
RINGWOMB	incomplete cervix dilatation	vt
RING-WORK	mail construction	
RING-WORM	skin disease; fungoid	md
RIOMETER	ionosphere absorption measurer	ps
RIPARIAN	riparial; riverbanks	
RIPENESS	maturity; mellowness	
RIPPLING	flax cleaning	
RIPTOWEL	reaping gratuity	

RISE-BUSH	a faggot	
RISE-WOOD	hedge cuttings	
RISKIEST	most reckless	
RISORIAL	ludicrous	
RITENUTO	restrained, slower tempo	mu
RITUALLY	ceremoniously	
RIVALISE	compete	
RIVALITY	equality in rank	
RIVALLED	emulated; vied; matched	
RIVER-BED	a channel	
RIVER-GOD	tutelary deity	
RIVER-HOG	the capybara	zo
RIVERINE	riparian	
RIVER-MAN	river-liver	
RIVER-PIE	water-ousel	zo
RIVETING	clinching	
RIVULOSE	wavy; rivose	
RIXATION	brawl; quarrel	
RIZZERED	salted and sun-dried	
ROAD-BOOK	guide-book; route; list; itinerary	
ROADLESS	unwayed	
ROAD-POST	signpost	
ROADSIDE	footpath; wayside	
ROADSMAN	road repairer	
ROADSTER	coachdriver; cycle	
ROAD-WEED	plantago	bt
ROAD-WORK	highway repairs	
ROAN-TREE	rowan tree; mountain ash	
ROASTING	parching; bantering	
ROBURITE	an explosive	
ROBUSTLY	lustily; stoutly; sturdily	
ROCAILLE	scroll ornament	
ROCCELLA	dyers' lichen	bt
ROCK-ALUM	alum stone	mn
ROCKAWAY	American carriage	
ROCK-BIRD	a pigeon	zo
ROCK-CAKE	small, hard bun	
ROCK-CIST	a plant	bt
ROCK-COOK	rock-fish	zo
ROCK-CORK	asbestos	mn
ROCK-CRAB	stony crustacean	zo
ROCK-DOVE	pigeon nesting on rocks	
ROCKETED	shot away	
ROCKETER	a high flier	
ROCKETRY	science of rockets	
ROCK-FIRE	firework mixture	
ROCK-FISH	wrasse, bass, etc.	zo
ROCK-GOAT	ibex	zo
ROCK-HAWK	merlin	zo
ROCK-HEAD	bed-rock	mn
ROCK-HEWN	cut from rock	
ROCK-LARK	rock-pipit	zo
ROCKLESS	destoned; without rocks	
ROCK-LILY	(various types)	bt
ROCK-LING	cod; haddock	zo
ROCK-MOSS	lichen	bt
ROCK-ROSE	member of rock garden	bt
ROCK-RUBY	a garnet	mn
ROCK-SALT	native salt	mn

ROCK-SEAL	common seal	zo
ROCK-SOAP	a kind of bole	mn
ROCK-WOOD	ligniform asbestos	mn
ROCK-WORK	a rockery	
ROCK-WREN	stone-preferring bird	zo
RODENTIA	rats; mice; squirrels	zo
RODOMONT	vain boaster; braggart	
ROENTGEN	unit of radiation	me
ROE-STONE	oolite	mn
ROGAILLE	decorative work with rocks, shells	
ROGATION	litany; supplication	
ROGATORY	interrogatory	
ROISTING	blustering; bullying	
ROITELET	kinglet; gold-crest	zo
ROLLBACK	price legislation	
ROLL-CALL	a check of all present	
ROLY-POLY	suet and jam pudding	ck
ROMANCED	economized the truth	
ROMANCER	tall tale teller	
ROMANESE	Wallachian language	
ROMANIAN	} of Romania	
RUMANIAN		
ROMANISH	Catholic	rl
ROMANIST	R.C.	rl
ROMANIZE	Latinize; convert	rl
ROMANSCH	Swiss dialect	
ROMANTIC	quixotic; fanciful	
ROME-SCOT	Peter's pence	rl
ROMEWARD	verging on Romanism	
RONCADOR	Pacific fish	zo
RONDELET	form of poem	
RONDELLE	ladder rung	
ROOD-ARCH	(over rood-screen)	
ROOD-BEAM	beam supporting rood	
ROODEBOK	bush-buck	zo
ROOD-LOFT	gallery over screen	
ROOD-TREE	Holy-rood; the cross	
ROOFLESS	vulnerable to rain	
ROOF-RACK	automobile baggage holder	
ROOF-TREE	a beam	
ROOMSOME	spacious	
ROOSTING	perching; lodging	
ROOT-BEER	dandelion ale	
ROOT-CROP	(esculent roots)	
ROOT-FAST	firmly rooted	
ROOT-FORM	shape of a root	
ROOT-HAIR	delicate filament	bt
ROOT-KNOT	an abnormality	bt
ROOT-LEAF	a leaf that roots	bt
ROOTLESS	footloose	
ROPE-PUMP	(by an endless rope)	
ROPE-RIPE	fit to be hanged	
ROPE-WALK	shed for spinning ropes	
ROPE-YARN	manilla; hemp; sisal, etc.	
ROPINESS	stringiness	
ROQUETED	(croquet)	
RORIDULA	sundew plants	bt
RORULENT	dewy	
ROSARIAN	a rose fancier	
ROSARIUM	rose garden	
ROSASITE	copper/zinc carbonate	mn
ROSE-BUSH	source of roses	bt
ROSE-DROP	rose-flavoured orange	bt
ROSEFISH	redfish; Atlantic food fish	
ROSE-GALL	an excrescence	
ROSE-HUED	rosy	
ROSE-KNOT	a rosette	
ROSELITE	cobalt arseniate	mn
ROSEMARY	aromatic plant	bt
ROSE-PINK	sentimental	
ROSE-RASH	German measles	md
ROSE-ROOT	herbaceous plant	bt
ROSE-TREE	a standard rose	bt
ROSETTED	wearing a rosette (party colours)	
ROSEWOOD	Brazilian timber tree	bt
ROSE-WORM	a caterpillar	zo
ROSINESS	rubicundity	
ROSINING	impelling; hustling	
ROSIN-OIL	a lubricant	
ROSMARUS	walruses, etc.	zo
ROSOGLIO	red wine of Malta	
ROSTRATE	beaked	
ROSTROID	like a rostrum	
ROSULATE	having rosetted leaves	bt
ROSY-DROP	a grog blossom	
ROSY-WAVE	a moth	zo
ROTALIAN	} protozoan	zo
ROTALINE		
ROTALITE	fossil rotalian	
ROTARIAN	(Rotary Club)	
ROTATING	spinning; turning	
ROTATION	revolution; series	
ROTATIVE	in succession	
ROTATORY	circulatory	
ROT-GRASS	butterwort	
ROTIFERA	animalculae	zo
ROTIFORM	wheel-shaped	
ROT-STEEP	cotton purification	
ROTTENLY	putridly	
ROTTLERA	dye yielding plant	bt
ROTURIER	plebeian	
ROUGHAGE	litter	
ROUGH-DRY	not ironed	
ROUGH-HEW	back formation from rough-hewn	
ROUGHING	(ice-nails)	
ROUGHISH	rather boisterous	
ROULEAUX	bundles of fascines	
ROULETTE	a game of chance	
ROUND-ALL	acrobatic feat	
ROUND-ARM	(bowling)	
ROUNDERS	a game; 9 a-side forerunner of baseball (UK)	
ROUNDING	encircling	
ROUNDISH	not quite spherical	
ROUNDLET	a small circle	
ROUND-TOP	masthead platform	nt
ROUT-CAKE	cake for parties	

ROUTEING	selecting a route	
ROVINGLY	wanderingly	
ROWDY-DOW	hubbub; uproar	
ROWDYISH	riotous; noisy	
ROWDYISM	turbulence; brawling	
ROWELLED	spurred	
ROXBURGH	a book-binding	
ROYALISM	} king-supporter	
ROYALIST		
ROYALIZE	turn into a king	
RUBBISHY	trashy	
RUBECULA	robin redbreast	zo
RUBEDITY	ruddiness	
RUBELIAN	magnesia mica	mn
RUBEZAHL	mountain imp (Ger.)	
RUBIANIC	madder-coloured	
RUBICUND	ruddy; florid	
RUBIDIUM	metallic element	ch
RUBIFORM	like a ruby	
RUBRICAL	marked in red	
RUBSTONE	whetstone	
RUBY-TAIL	cuckoo-fly	zo
RUBY-WOOD	red sandalwood	bt
RUCERVUS	East Indian deer	zo
RUCKLING	crumpling; creasing	
RUCKSACK	knapsack	
RUDDLING	marking with ochre	
RUDENESS	unmannerliness	
RUDENTED	ornamented	
RUDIMENT	first principle; embryo	
RUEFULLY	sorrowfully; regretfully	
RUFFLING	disturbing; agitating	
RUFULOUS	somewhat rufous	
RUGBEIAN	(Rugby) (school)	
RUGGEDLY	jaggedly; unevenly	
RUGOSELY	wrinkly	
RUGOSITY	roughness	
RUGULOUS	creased; rumpled	
RUINABLE	of delicate virtue	
RUINATED	demolished	
RULE-CASE	a printing tray	
RULE-WORK	tabulation	
RULINGLY	dominantly	
RUMANIAN	} of Romania	
ROMANIAN		
RUM-BARGE	a warm drink	
RUMBLING	noise from stomach	
RUMINANT	chewing the cud	zo
RUMINATE	meditate; muse; ponder	
RUMMAGED	ransacked; rifled	
RUMMAGER	searcher	
RUMOROUS	vaguely heard	
RUMOURED	bruited; reported	
RUMOURER	a gossip; tattler	
RUMPLESS	having no tail	
RUMPLING	puckering; rimpling	
RUM-SHRUB	an odd decoction	
RUNABOUT	vagabond; convenient motorcar, motorboat	nt
RUNAGATE	renegade; vagabond	
RUNMAKER	cricket	
RUNNER-UP	second	
RUNOLOGY	rune-craft	
RUNRIDGE	open-field husbandry	
RUN-ROUND	railway shunting	
RUPICOLA	cocks of the rock	zo
RURALISM	country life	
RURALIST	country bumpkin	
RURALITY	ruralness	
RURALIZE	rusticate	
RUSH-HOUR	commuter-time	
RUSHLIKE	reedy; weak	
RUSH-LINE	football	
RUSH-TOAD	the natterjack	zo
RUSTICAL	rustic; sylvan	
RUSTLESS	stainless	
RUSTLING	cattle lifting	
RUST-MITE	gall-mite	zo
RUTABAGA	Swedish turnip; Swede	bt
RUTHLESS	pitiless; barbarous	
RUTILANT	shining	
RUTILATE	emit rays of light	
RYE-GRASS	fodder grass	bt
RYOT-WARI	} system of land	
RYOT-WARY	tenure of India	

S

SABAEISM	star worship	
SABBATIA	gentian	bt
SABBATIC	restful	
SABBATON	armoured boot	
SABELINE	sable type or skin	zo
SABINENE	terpene derivative	ch
SABLIERE	sand-pit	
SABOTAGE	wanton destruction	
SABOTEUR	a wrecker	
SABOTIER	a wearer of wooden shoes	
SABULOSE	growing in sandy places	bt
SABULOUS	sandy; gritty	
SACCATED	pouched	
SACCULAR	baggy; saclike; vesiculate	
SACCULUS	a small sac or cyst	zo
SACELLUM	makeshift altar	rl
SACKLESS	quiet; simple (Sc.)	
SACK-RACE	race run in sack	
SACREDLY	divinely; holily	
SACRISTY	the vestry	rl
SADDENED	mournful; downcast	
SADDLERY	horse furniture	
SADDLING	loading	
SADDUCEE	Jewish ritualist	rl
SADFACED	gloomy; depressed	
SAFENESS	security; trustiness	
SAFFRONY	saffron coloured	
SAFRANIN	saffron dye	ch
SAGACITY	wisdom; shrewdness	
SAGAMORE	American Indian chief	
SAGE-COCK	American grouse	zo

SAGENESS	sapience; sagacity; wisdom	
SAGENITE	crystals of rutile	mn
SAGE-ROSE	an evergreen	bt
SAGINATE	pamper; fatten	
SAGITTAL	like an arrow	
SAGO-PALM	food-giving tree	bt
SAGUINUS	marmoset	bt
SAHIB-LOG	Europeans	
SAIBLING	the char	zo
SAIKLESS	sackless	
SAILABLE	navigable	
SAIL-BOAT	yacht	nt
SAIL-FISH	basking shark	zo
SAIL-HOOP	mast-hoop	nt
SAILLESS	steam-driven	
SAIL-LOFT	(where sails are made)	
SAIL-PLAN	layout of sails	nt
SAIL-ROOM	storage place for sails	nt
SAIL-YARD	spar for sails	nt
SAINFOIN	a fodder-plant	bt
SAINTISH	rather saintlike	
SAINTISM	sanctimoniousness	
SALACITY	lustfulness	
SALADING	salad vegetables	bt
SALAD-OIL	vegetable oil for dressing	ck
SALARIED	receiving wages	
SALEABLE	marketable	
SALEABLY	vendibly	
SALE-ROOM	auction room	
SALESMAN	sometimes a drummer	
SALE-WORK	work carelessly done	
SALICINE	extract of willow bark	
SALIENCE	prominence	
SALIFIED	made into salt	
SALINITY	saltiness	
SALITRAL	saltpetre mine	
SALIVANT	⎫	
SALIVARY	⎬ referring to saliva	md
SALIVATE	⎪	
SALIVOUS	⎭	
SALLYING	dashing out	
SALMONET	young salmon	zo
SALOPIAN	from Shropshire	
SALPICON	Spanish savoury dish	ck
SALSILLA	edible tuber	bt
SALT-BUSH	Australian plant	bt
SALT-CAKE	sulphate of soda	mn
SALT-COTE	salt-pit	
SALT-FOOT	(below the salt)	
SALT-JUNK	salted beef	ck
SALTLESS	insipid; tasteless	
SALT-LICK	animals' rendezvous	
SALT-MINE	mine of rock salt	
SALTNESS	salinity	
SALT-WELL	salt spring	
SALT-WORK	salt factory	
SALT-WORT	(several species)	bt
SALUTARY	beneficial	
SALUTING	greeting; hailing	
SALVABLE	rescuable	

SALVAGED	saved	
SALVINIA	genus of ferns	bt
SAMARIUM	spectroscopic metal	ch
SAMAROID	(winged fruit)	bt
SAMAVEDA	Veda with chants	rl
SAMBUCUS	honeysuckle type	bt
SAMENESS	monotony; similarity	
SAMPHIRE	a herb	bt
SAMPLARY	an example (obs.)	
SAMPLING	matching selection of average; tasting; fixing value of a variable	cp
SANATION	a cure	
SANATIVE	healing	
SANATORY	curative; remedial	
SANATRON	valve circuit	el
SANCTIFY	make holy; hallow	rl
SANCTION	ratification; approve	
SANCTITY	holiness; godliness	
SANDARAC	realgar; resin	mn, bt
SANDARIC	N. Afr. resin for map varnishes	
SAND-BALL	pumice soap	
SAND-BAND	protecting band	
SAND-BANK	a shoal	go, nv
SAND-BATH	(used by chemists)	
SAND-BEAR	Indian badger	zo
SAND-BIRD	sandpiper	zo
SAND-COCK	redshank	zo
SAND-CRAB	the lady crab	zo
SAND-DART	a moth	zo
SAND-DUNE	a ridge of drifted sand	
SANDEVER	⎫ glass scum in state of	
SANDIVER	⎭ fusion	
SAND-FISH	dry land fish	zo
SAND-FLAG	a sandstone	mn
SAND-FLEA	chigoe or jigger	zo
SAND-HEAT	heat of sand-bath	ch
SAND-HILL	mound of sand	
SAND-IRON	a niblick	
SAND-LARK	a wading bird	zo
SAND-MOLE	S. African rodent	zo
SAND-PEEP	American stint	zo
SAND-PUMP	(rock drilling)	
SAND-REED	a shore grass	bt
SAND-REEL	a windlass	
SAND-ROLL	a casting	
SAND-SHOT	small shot	
SAND-STAR	starfish	zo
SAND-TRAP	sand eliminator	
SAND-WASP	the digger-wasp	zo
SAND-WELD	silica fusing	
SANDWICH	to interpose; intrude; snack between bread; bat with rubber layer (table tennis)	
SANDWICK	vertical sand drain construction	ce
SAND-WORM	lob-worm; lug-worm	zo
SAND-WORT	genus Arenia	bt
SANENESS	sanity; mental equilibrium	

SANGAREE	W. Indian drink	
SANGLANT	bleeding	
SANGLIER	wild boar	zo
SANGRAAL	holy grail	rl
SANGREAL	sangraal	
SANGUIFY	to make blood	
SANGUINE	optimistic; hopeful	
SANIDINE	potassium feldspar	mn
SANITARY	hygienic; healthful	
SANSERIF	serifless type face	pr
SANSKRIT	ancient Indian language	
SANTALIC	(sandal-wood)	bt
SANTALIN	red dye	
SANTALUM	sandal-wood genus	bt
SANTONIN	wormwood	ch
SAP-GREEN	yellow green	
SAPIDITY	tastiness	
SAPIENCE	wisdom; sagacity; intellect	
SAPINDUS	the soapberry	bt
SAPI-UTAN	wild ox (Celebes)	zo
SAPONIFY	convert into soap	
SAPONINE	soapwort extract	
SAPONITE	hydrous silicate of magnesium	mn
SAPOROUS	tasty; piquant (savour)	
SAPPHIRE	blue, green or red gem	mn
SAPPHISM	lesbianism; (Sappho)	
SAPREMIA	blood poisoning	md
SAPROPEL	stagnant water sediment	gl
SAPSTAIN	fungus-caused discoloration	fr
SAPUCAIA	Brazil nut-tree	bt
SARABAND	Spanish dance	
SARATOGA	American travelling trunk	
SARCELLE	a teal	zo
SARCENET	sarsenet; woven silk	tx
SARCINIC	fungoid	bt
SARCITIS	eye inflammation	md
SARCOCOL	gum Arabic	bt
SARCODIC	protoplasmic; resembling flesh	zo
SARCOSIS	a tumour	md
SARCOTIC	generating flesh	md
SARDELLE	herring-like fish	zo
SARDONIC	ironical; cynical	
SARDONYX	variety of onyx	mn
SARGASSO	sea of seaweed	
SARPLIER	packing cloth	
SARRASIN	a portcullis	
SARRIZIN	buckwheat	bt
SARSENET	sarcenet; woven silk	
SASH-DOOR	door having panes of glass	
SASSANID	a Persian ruler	
SASSOLIN	native boracic acid	mn
SASSOROL	rock-pigeon	zo
SASTRUGI	hard wind-ridges on winter snow surface (Russia)	go
SATANISM	devil worship	
SATANITY	devilry; diablery; (witchcraft)	
SATELESS	insatiable	
SATHANAS	Satan	
SATIABLE	appeasable	
SATIATED	glutted; gratified	
SATIRIST	lampoonist; ironic writer	
SATIRIZE	ridicule	
SATRAPAL	province of a satrap	
SATURANT	saturating	
SATURATE	soak; drench	
SATURDAY	Jewish sabbath	
SATURNIA	a moth genus	zo
SATURNIC	(lead poisoning)	
SATYRIUM	orchid genus	bt
SAUCEBOX	impudent fellow	
SAUCEPAN	cook-pot	
SAUCISSE	powder bag for use in mines	
SAUDADES	Port. 'remembrance of past' pieces	mu
SAURLESS	savourless; tasteless (Sc.)	
SAURODON	fossil fish	mn
SAURURUS	pepper plants	bt
SAUTERNE	white wine (Fr.)	
SAUTILLE	rebounding violin technique (Fr.)	mu
SAUTOIRE	heraldic ribbon	hd
SAVAGELY	barbarously; inhumanly	
SAVAGERY	ferocity; brutality	
SAVAGING	maltreating	
SAVANNAH	savanna; a treeless plain	
SAVEABLE	rescuable; salvable	
SAVINGLY	thriftily; frugally	
SAVOURED	tasted	
SAVOURLY	well seasoned	
SAVOYARD	Gilbert and Sullivan operas' enthusiast	
SAWBONES	a surgeon	md
SAW-FLIES	boring insects	zo
SAW-FRAME	blade holder	to
SAW-GRASS	a marsh grass	bt
SAW-HORSE	cradle for sawing logs	
SAW-TABLE	boring table	
SAW-WREST	a saw-set	
SAXATILE	rock-inhabiting	
SAXICAVA	mollusc genus	zo
SAXICOLA	the stone-chats	zo
SAXICOLE	growing on rocks	bt
SAXONDOM	Anglo-Saxon world	
SAXONISM	a Saxon idiom	
SAXONIST	Saxon scholar	
SAXONITE	coarse-grained igneous rock	gl
SCABBARD	sheath	
SCABBING	worn road surface; fretting; working non-strikers	ce
SCABBLED	rough hewn; scappled	
SCABIOSA	teasel plants	bt
SCABIOUS	scurfy; itchy	bt
SCAB-MITE	a parasite	zo
SCABROUS	rough; rugged	
SCAFFOLD	temporary structure for construction also ski-jumps	bd
SCALABLE	climbable; measurable	

SCALARIA	ladder-shells	zo
SCALAWAG	scallywag; scamp	
SCALDING	injuring with boiling water	
SCALDINO	Italian brazier	
SCALENUM	scalene triangle	
SCALENUS	a muscle	pl
SCALIOLA	imitation marble	
SCALLION	shallot; leek	bt
SCALLOPS	short withies (thatching willows)	bd
SCALPING	selling tickets at surcharge	
SCAMBLED	mauled; mangled	
SCAMBLER	gate-crasher	
SCAMMONY	convolvulus	bt
SCAMPING	shirking; skimping	
SCAMPISH	knavish; rascally	
SCANDENT	climbing	
SCANDIUM	a metal	ch
SCANNING	scrutinizing; viewing (tests)	md
SCANNING	action of a scanner	cp
SCANSION	rhythm	
SCANTIES	light attire	
SCANTILY	meagrely; sparingly	
SCANTING	stinting	
SCANTLED	in small pieces	
SCANTLET	a small pattern	
SCAPANUS	shrew-moles	zo
SCAPHISM	a Persian torture	
SCAPHITE	fossil ammonite	mn
SCAPHIUM	beetle genus	zo
SCAPHOID	boat-shaped	
SCAPPLED	rough hewn; scabbled	
SCAPULAR	(shoulder-blade); scarf	
SCARABEE	scarab; beetle	zo
SCARCELY	hardly; barely	
SCARCITY	dearth; rarity; lack	
SCARE-BUG	a bugbear	
SCARFING	uniting timber	
SCARF-PIN	male decoration	
SCARIDAE	parrot-fish	zo
SCARIOUS	dry; scaly	
SCARITID	(carabid beetles)	zo
SCARLESS	unwounded; scatheless	
SCARN-BEE	dung-beetle	zo
SCARPHED	(a timber joint)	bd
SCARRING	wounding; injuring	
SCATCHES	stilts	
SCATHING	bitterly severe; caustic	
SCATHOLD	open pasture ground	
SCATLAND	peat and pasture land	
SCATTERY	dispersed	
SCAVENGE	to collect refuse	
SCAWTITE	calcium silicate/carbonate	mn
SCELERAT	villain	
SCELIDES	the hind-legs	zo
SCENARIO	plan of a play	
SCENE-MAN	scene shifter	
SCENICAL	scenic; dramatic	
SCENT-BAG	animal's pouch	zo
SCENT-BOX	perfume pack	
SCENTFUL	highly odoriferous	
SCEPTRAL	regal	
SCEPTRED	kingly	
SCHEDULE	catalogue; inventory; list	
SCHELLUM	rascal; rogue	
SCHEMING	planning; intriguing	
SCHEMIST	projector; astrologer	
SCHEROMA	dryness of the eye	md
SCHIEDAM	schnapps; gin	
SCHILLER	bronze lustre	
SCHISTIC	laminated; slaty	mn
SCHIZOID	tendency to dementia	pc
SCHIZONT	trophozoite ready to reproduce	zo
SCHLAGER	duelling sword (Ger.)	
SCHMALTZ	grease (Ger.); sentimental	
SCHMELZE	enamel (Ger.)	
SCHNAPPS	akvavit; firewater	
SCHOENUS	a sedge genus	bt
SCHOKKER	fishing vessel, Holland	nt
SCHOLION	} marginal note in old classics	
SCHOLIUM		
SCHOOLED	disciplined; trained	
SCHOONER	large drinking glass	
SCHOONER	fore-and-aft rigged ship	nt
SCIAGRAM	X-ray picture	md
SCIATICA	neuralgia	md
SCIENTER	knowingly; deliberately	
SCIENTLY	fully aware	
SCILICET	to wit; namely	
SCIMITAR	curved sword	
SCINCOID	pertaining to the skink	zo
SCIOGRAM	radio photograph	
SCIOLISM	superficiality	
SCIOLIST	a know-all	
SCIOLOUS	shallow; skin-deep	
SCIOPTIC	(camera obscura)	
SCIRRHUS	cancerous tumour	md
SCISSILE	able to be cut	
SCISSION	division	
SCISSORS	acrobatic feat; forfex; cutters; secateurs; crossing	to, rw
SCISSURA	fissure; cleft	
SCISSURE	rupture division	
SCIURINE	} rodent mammals, squirrels, etc.	zo
SCIUROID		
SCLERITE	hardened tissue	md
SCLEROID	ossified	
SCLEROMA	sclerosis	md
SCLEROUS	bony	
SCOFFING	deriding; taunting; jeering	
SCOFF-LAW	contemptuous to law	
SCOLDING	nagging; chiding; rating	
SCOLEINA	earth-worms, etc.	zo
SCOLOPAX	woodcock genus	zo
SCOLYTUS	destructive beetle	zo
SCOMFISH	to nauseate (Sc.)	
SCONTION	inside quoin	bd
SCOONING	skimming	

SCOOPING	ladling	
SCOOP-NET	a hand-net	
SCOOTING	decamping	
SCOPARIA	sweet bromweed	**bt**
SCOPEFUL	with wide prospect	
SCOPIDAE	African wading birds	**zo**
SCOPIPED	having brushy feet	**zo**
SCORCHED	parched; charred	
SCORCHER	road-hog	
SCORDATO	out of tune	**mu**
SCORIOUS	ashy; clinkery	
SCORNFUL	mocking; insolent	
SCORNING	spurning; scouting	
SCORPION	stingtail	**zo**
SCOTCHED	wounded; blocked	
SCOT-FREE	untaxed	
SCOTOPIC	night vision	
SCOTSMAN	Scot	
SCOTTICE	in Scottish manner	
SCOTTIFY	Caledonianise	
SCOTTISH	Scots	
SCOURAGE	refuse water	
SCOURGED	chastised	
SCOURING	scurrying; scrubbing	
SCOUTHER	to scorn (Sc.)	
SCOUTING	rejecting; scorning	
SCOUT-LAW	Scout Code	
SCOWLING	glowering; frowning	
SCOWTHER	a brief shower (Sc.)	
SCRABBLE	scribble; scrawl	
SCRAGGED	strangled; throttled	
SCRAGGLY	rough-looking	
SCRAMBLE	hurry; strife; clamber; (eggs); (code); (jumble); (Amer. football)	**ck, mo**
SCRAMJET	spacecraft	**ae**
SCRAN-BAG	food sack	**nt**
SCRANNEL	squeaking; slender; meagre	
SCRAPING	abrading; rasping	
SCRAPPED	discarded; fought	
SCRAPPLE	to grub about; scrabble	
SCRATCHY	ragged; sketchy	
SCRATTLE	to scuttle	
SCRAWLED	scribbled	
SCRAWLER	slovenly writer	
SCREAMED	yelled; cried; squalled	
SCREAMER	tropical bird; monkey; human offspring	**zo**
SCREECHY	shrill and harsh	
SCREENED	veiled; hidden; sieved	
SCREEVER	begging-letter writer	
SCREWING	exacting; twisting; racking	
SCREW-KEY	a spanner	**to**
SCREW-POD	screw-bean	**bt**
SCRIBBET	painter's pencil	
SCRIBBLE	scrawl; write	
SCRIBING	recording	
SCRIBISM	Jewish literature	
SCRIGGLE	wriggle	
SCRIMPED	stinted	

SCRIMPLY	miserly	
SCRINIUM	scroll/relic container	
SCRIPTOR	ancient book-copier, handwriter	
SCRIVANO	Italian clerk	
SCRODDLE	to variegate	
SCROFULA	the king's evil	**md**
SCROGGIE	full of brushwood	
SCROLLED	convoluted	
SCROOPED	grated; cracked	
SCROUGED	squeezed	
SCROUGER	a whopper	
SCROUNGE	acquire by stealth; cadge	
SCRUBBED	scoured	
SCRUBBER	charlady; removal of gas impurities	**ch**
SCRUB-OAK	stunted oak	**bt**
SCRUPLED	hesitated; wavered	
SCRUPLER	demurrer; doubter	
SCRUTINY	close inquiry; search	
SCUDDICK	scuttock; a trifle; a shilling	
SCUDDING	speeding	
SCUDDING	pre-tanning hide treatment	**le**
SCUFFLED	tussled	
SCUFFLER	brawler	
SCULLERY	room for washing dishes	
SCULLING	rowing	
SCULLION	dish-washer	
SCULPSIT	he engraved it	
SCULPTOR	image maker	
SCUMBLED	painted over	
SCURRIED	scampered; hastened	
SCURRIES	pony races	
SCURRILE	scurrilous	
SCURVILY	basely; shabbily	
SCUTCHED	separated	
SCUTCHER	hedger	
SCUTELLA	sea-urchin genus	**zo**
SCUTIFER	shield-bearer	
SCUTIPED	having scaly shanks	**zo**
SCUTTLED	ran; bolted; scampered; sabotaged	
SCUTTLER	ship-sinker	
SCUTTOCK	see scuddick	
SCYELITE	coarse-grained igneous rock	**gl**
SCYTHIAN	(Scythia)	
SCYTODES	a genus of spiders	**zo**
SEA-ACORN	a barnacle	**zo**
SEA-ADDER	stickle-back	**zo**
SEA-APRON	a seaweed	**bt**
SEA-ARROW	flying squid	**zo**
SEA-BEACH	seashore	
SEA-BEAST	a sea monster	**zo**
SEA-BELLS	bindweed	**bt**
SEA-BOARD	the coast	**nv**
SEA-BORNE	shipped	**nt**
SEA-BRANT	brent goose	**zo**
SEA-BREAM	mackerel type	**zo**
SEA-CHART	marine map	**nv**
SEA-COAST	seashore	

SEA-CRAFT	seamanship	nt
SEA-DAISY	the lady's cushion	bt
SEA-DEVIL	ray; angel-fish	zo
SEA-DRAKE	sea-crow	zo
SEA-EAGLE	the osprey	zo
SEA-FARER	voyager; sailor	nt
SEA-FIGHT	marine engagement	nt
SEA-FRONT	shore promenade	
SEA-FROTH	foam	
SEA-GATES	(tidal basin)	nv
SEA-GAUGE	ship's draught	nt
SEA-GOING	deep water line ship	nt
SEA-GOOSE	a dolphin	zo
SEA-GRAPE	glasswort	bt
SEA-GRASS	the thrift	bt
SEA-GREEN	marine colour	
SEA-GROVE	under-water grove	bt
SEA-HEATH	beach plant	bt
SEA-HOLLY	the eryngo	bt
SEA-HORSE	the walrus	zo
SEA-HOUND	dog-fish	zo
SEA-JELLY	sea-blubber	zo
SEA-LEECH	an annelid	zo
SEA-LEMON	a doridoid mollusc	zo
SEA-LEVEL	mean tide level	
SEA-LOACH	a gadoid fish	zo
SEA-LOUSE	a parasite	zo
SEAL-PIPE	a dip pipe	
SEAL-RING	signet ring	
SEAL-SKIN	pelt; fur	
SEA-LUNGS	a comb-jelly	zo
SEAL-WORT	Solomon's seal	bt
SEAMANLY	seamanlike	
SEA-MARGE	seashore; tide-line	nv
SEA-MELON	sea-cucumber	zo
SEAMIEST	most sordid	
SEAMLESS	in one piece	
SEA-MOUSE	the dunlin; a worm	zo
SEAM-RENT	a tear at the seam	
SEAMSTER	one who sews	
SEA-NYMPH	an Oceanid	
SEA-ONION	a squill	bt
SEA-OTTER	marine otter	zo
SEA-OXEYE	seashore plant	bt
SEA-PEACH	sea-squirt	zo
SEA-PERCH	bass	zo
SEA-PIECE	seascape; poem; song; music	mu
SEA-PLANE	hydroplane; floatplane	
SEA-PLANT	a seaweed	bt
SEA-POWER	strategic	
SEA-PURSE	eggcase of skate	zo
SEA-QUAIL	the turnstone	zo
SEA-QUAKE	marine earthwake	
SEA-RAVEN	cormorant	zo
SEARCHED	quested; probed; sought	
SEARCHER	inquirer; examiner	
SEA-REEVE	customs officer	
SEARNESS	dryness, sereness	
SEA-ROBIN	gurnard fish	zo

SEA-ROVER	pirate; pirate ship	nt
SEARWOOD	dry wood	
SEASCAPE	marine view, painting	
SEA-SHARK	man-eater shark	zo
SEASHELL	marine shell	zo
SEASHORE	the beach	
SEA-SHRUB	a sea-fan	zo
SEA-SNAIL	the periwinkle	zo
SEA-SNAKE	sea-serpent	zo
SEA-SNIPE	sandpiper	zo
SEASONAL	not always available	
SEASONED	matured; inured	
SEASONER	a relish; strong flavouring	
SEA-SQUID	cuttlefish	zo
SEA-STICK	herring cured at sea	
SEA-SWINE	porpoise	zo
SEAT-BACK	loose cover	
SEA-TENCH	black sea-bream	zo
SEA-THONG	cord-like seaweed	bt
SEAT-LOCK	a catch	
SEAT-MILE	transport statistic	
SEAT-RAIL	a crosspiece	
SEA-TROUT	saltwater trout	zo
SEAT-WORM	pin-worm	zo
SEA-WATER	brine	
SEA-WOMAN	mermaid	
SEA-WRACK	coarse seaweed	
SEBESTAN	} a tree with plumlike fruit	
SEBESTEN	}	bt
SEBUNDEE	Indian militia-man	
SECAMONE	shrubby climber	bt
SECATEUR	pruning shears	to
SECEDING	withdrawing; retiring	
SECERNED	secreted	
SECESHER	a secessionist	
SECLUDED	aside; shut off	
SECODONT	with cutting teeth	zo
SECONDED	aided; transferred	
SECONDER	supporter; abettor	
SECRETED	cloaked; concealed	
SECRETIN	secretion-stimulating hormone	bc
SECRETLY	privily; covertly	
SECTATOR	an adherent	
SECTORAL	in a sector	
SECTROID	space between groins	bd
SECUNDUM	according to (Latin)	
SECURELY	fast; safely	
SECURING	acquiring; getting	
SECURITE	an explosive	
SECURITY	safety; surety; pledge; secrecy	
SECURITY	protection from risks of data losses	cp
SEDATELY	calmly; seriously; soberly	
SEDATIVE	tranquillizing; soothing	md
SEDERUNT	court session (Sc.)	lw
SEDGE-HEN	marsh-hen	zo
SEDILIUM	chancel seat	rl
SEDIMENT	lees; dregs; grounds	

SEDITION	treason; mutiny; rebellion	
SEDUCING	enticing; inveigling	
SEDUCTOR	tempter; corrupter	
SEDULITY	assiduity; diligence	
SEDULOUS	industrious; busy	
SEED-BIRD	water-wagtail	zo
SEED-CAKE	caraway cake	
SEED-COAT	husk	bt
SEED-CORN	corn for sowing	bt
SEED-DOWN	down on cotton, etc.	bt
SEED-FISH	spawn; roe	zo
SEED-FOWL	grain-fed bird	zo
SEED-GALL	plant disease	
SEED-LEAF	a cotyledon	bt
SEED-LEAP	seed-basket	
SEEDLESS	pipless	
SEEDLING	young plant	
SEED-LOBE	seed-leaf	bt
SEED-PLOT	a hot-bed	
SEEDSMAN	dealer; sower	
SEED-TICK	a parasite	zo
SEEDTIME	sowing season	
SEED-WOOL	cotton-wool and seeds	
SEEDY-TOE	a horse disease	vt
SEER-FISH	seir-fish	zo
SEERSHIP	(soothsaying)	
SEESAWED	oscillated	
SEETHING	boiling	
SEGREANT	rampant and salient	hd
SEIDLITZ	mineral water	mn
SEIGNEUR	lord of the manor	
SEIGNIOR	seigneur; feudal lord	
SEINE-NET	long shallow net	oc
SEIR-FISH	seer-fish	zo
SEIZABLE	apprehendable	
SEIZLING	the carp	zo
SEJUGOUS	(six pairs of leaflets)	bt
SEKITORI	sumo wrestler	
SELADANG	Malayan tapir; bison	zo
SELAMLIK	men's quarters (Turk.)	ar
SELANDER	post-Roman trireme, Mediterranean	nt
SELECTED	chosen; culled; preferred	
SELECTOR	picker and chooser; specified conditions finder	cp
SELECTOR	electromagnetic switching device	tc
SELENATE	a selenic salt	ch
SELENIDE	a compound	ch
SELENITE	gypsum	mn
SELENIUM	a chemical element	ch
SELF-BORN	self-begotten	
SELF-ENDS	endpaper leaves in books	
SELF-HEAL	burnet saxifrage	bt
SELF-HELP	unaided effort	
SELFHOOD	conscious personality	
SELFLESS	unselfish	
SELF-LIKE	indulgence	
SELF-LIKE	twin	
SELF-LOVE	self-seeking	

SELF-MADE	independent	
SELFMATE	hermaphrodite solves chess problem	
SELFNESS	egotism	
SELF-PITY	sorriness for self	
SELFSAME	identical; equivalent	
SELF-SOWN	plant from windblown seed	
SELF-WILL	obstinacy	
SELF-WISE	self-conceit	
SELLABLE	saleable; marketable	
SELVAGEE	untwisted rope	
SELVEDGE	woven border	
SEMANTIC	significant; expressive; symbol-meaning link	cp
SEMBLANT	resembling; like	
SEMESTER	period of six months	
SEMI-ACID	half-acid	
SEMI-ARID	between dessert & Savannah	go
SEMI-BULL	a papal bull	rl
SEMI-COPE	outer monastic garment	
SEMI-DOME	half-dome	
SEMI-FLEX	to half bend	
SEMI-MUTE	half deaf	
SEMINARY	academy; college; school	
SEMINATE	propagate; sow	
SEMINOLE	American Indian tribe	
SEMI-NUDE	barely clothed	
SEMI-OPAL	half-opal	mn
SEMI-OPEN	sport	
SEMIOTIC	sign language	
SEMI-OVAL	half-oval	
SEMI-PULP	ground-wood impurities in paper	
SEMI-RING	half-circle	
SEMITAUR	half-bull; half-man	
SEMITISM	Hebrew idiom	
SEMITIST	Hebrew scholar	
SEMITONE	musical interval	mu
SEMOLINA	granules of flour;	
SEMILINO	manna; grits	ck
SEMPLICE	simply	mu
SEMPSTER	seamstress	
SEMUNCIA	Roman coin	nm
SENARIUS	verse of six feet	
SEND-DOWN	expel; rusticate	
SENG-GUNG	Java badger	zo
SENGREEN	the houseleek	bt
SENILITY	dotage; old age	
SENNIGHT	a week	
SENONIAN	geological formation	gl
SENORITA	Spanish young lady	
SENSEFUL	judicious; rational	
SENSIBLE	intelligent; wise; discreet	
SENSIBLY	sagaciously; sanely	
SENSIFIC	exciting	
SENSUISM	sensuality	
SENSUIST	amorist; materialist	
SENSUOUS	aesthetic; voluptuous	
SENTENCE	doom; maxim; clause	

SENTIENT	perceptive; aware of; alert	
SENTINEL	sentry; watchman; warder	
SENTINEL	signal ending tape recording	
		cp
SENTRIES	watchers; guards	
SENTRY-GO	sentry duty	
SEPALINE	(leaf of calyx)	bt
SEPALODY	} reversion of petals to	
SEPALOID	} sepals	bt
SEPALOUS	sepaline	
SEPARATE	sort; divorce; sever	
SEPDUMAG	2-magnetic-sound-track film	cn
SEPDUOPT	2-optical-sound-track film	cn
SEPIACEA	cuttlefish	zo
SEPIIDAE	cephalopods	zo
SEPIMENT	hedge; boundary	
SEPTARIA	turtle-stones	mn
SEPTATED	divided into cells	bt
SEPTETTE	(seven performers)	mu
SEPTFOIL	the tormentil	bt
SEPTUARY	group of seven	
SEPTULUM	small cell	bt
SEPTUPLE	sevenfold	
SEQUENCE	continuity; series	
SEQUENZA	repetition in higher key; hymn for mass; solo pieces (It.)	
		mu
SERAFILE	serrefile	
SERAGLIO	Ottoman sultan's palace	
SERAPHIC	angelic; sublime	
SERAPHIM	celestial being	rl
SERAPIAS	genus of orchids	bt
SERENADE	} Nacht musik (Ger.); piece for woodwind	
SERENATA	} in several movements	mu
SERENELY	tranquilly; calmly; placidly	
SERENEST	calmest; most tranquil	
SERENISE	glorify	
SERENITY	peacefulness; quiet	
SERGEANT	serjeant	
SERGETTE	thin serge	
SERIALLY	consecutively	
SERIATIM	in regular order	
SERICATE	silky; downy	
SERICITE	potash mica	mn
SERIFORM	Chinese writing	
SERINGHI	Indian viol	mu
SERJEANT	sergeant	
SERMONER	preacher	rl
SERMONET	short address	
SERMONIC	admonitive	rl
SEROLOGY	study of blood, serum	md
SEROSITY	(exuding serum)	md
SEROTINE	species of bat	zo
SERPETTE	pruning knife (Fr.)	to
SERPLATH	80 stone (Sc.)	me
SERPOLET	wild thyme	bt
SERRANUS	perch; bass	zo

SERRATED	notched; like a saw	
SERRATUS	a thorax muscle	zo
SERRIPED	with serrated feet	zo
SERVIENT	subordinate; slavish; abject	
SERVIOUS	obsequious; sycophantic	
SERVITOR	waiter; henchman	
SESAMOID	(toe bones)	md
SESTERCE	Roman 2d. coin	nm
SESTETTE	sextet	mu
SESTOLET	sextuplet	mu
SET-ASIDE	reserve(d)	
SETIFORM	bristly	
SET-PIECE	stage scene	
SETTLING	colonizing; deciding; fixing	
SETULOSE	prickly; spinate; spicate	
SEVERELY	rigorously; strictly	
SEVERING	disrupting; sundering	
SEVERITY	harshness; austerity	
SEWELLEL	mountain beaver	zo
SEWERAGE	drainage	
SEWER-GAS	bad smell	
SEXAGENE	angle of 60 degrees	
SEXANGLE	a hexagon	
SEXOLOGY	study of sex and sexuality	
SEXTETTE	sextet	mu
SEXTOLET	sextuplet; group of 6 notes	
		mu
SEXTUPLE	sixfold	
SEXUALLY	in a sexual way	
SFORZATO	emphatically	mu
SGABELLO	stool or bench (It.)	
SHABBIER	more ragged	
SHABBILY	despicably; meanly	
SHABRACK	saddle-cloth	
SHACKING	tramping; hibernating	
SHACKLED	fettered; manacled	
SHAD-BIRD	American snipe	zo
SHAD-BUSH	the June-berry	bt
SHADDOCK	grapefruit	bt
SHADEFUL	umbrageous	
SHAD-FROG	jumping frog	zo
SHADIEST	most obscure	
SHADOWED	followed; obscured	
SHAFTING	(machinery)	
SHAGGING	shredding	
SHAGREEN	sharkskin & rayfish tea caddies; untanned leather (Persia)	
SHAKE-OUT	return to normal; economics	
SHALLOON	woollen fabric	tx
SHAMANIC	magical	
SHAMBLES	slaughter-house; ruin	
SHAMEFUL	humiliating; heinous; base	
SHAMMING	feigning; counterfeiting	
SHAMROCK	Irish emblem	bt
SHANGHAI	kidnap	
SHANKING	mishitting at golf	
SHANTIES	sea songs; huts	
SHANTUNG	coarse silk	tx
SHAPABLE	fashionable	

SHARKING	interception of ball (Australian football)	
SHARP-CUT	clearly defined	
SHARPING	tricking	
SHARP-SET	keen	
SHASHLIK	grilled lamb on skewer	ck
SHATRANJ	board game for two, like chess	
SHATTERY	brittle; rickety	
SHAW-FOWL	a wappenshaw fowl	zo
SHEADING	district, Isle of Man	
SHEALING	shepherd's hut (Sc.)	
SHEARHOG	shorn sheep	zo
SHEARING	clipping; shaving; fleecing	
SHEARMAN	cloth-cutter	
SHEATHED	encased; sheeted	
SHEA-TREE	butter tree	bt
SHEAVING	collecting; harvesting	
SHEDDING	discarding; diffusing	
SHEELING	shealing; shelter	
SHEEP-DIP	sheep's health bath	
SHEEPDOG	a chaperon	zo
SHEEPFLY	a parasite	zo
SHEEPISH	diffident; bashful	
SHEEP-PEN	an enclosure	
SHEEP-RUN	tract of pasture	
SHEERING	moving aside	
SHEER-LEG	a spar	
SHEETERS	steel poling boards for trenches	ce
SHEET-FED	separate-sheet printing	pr
SHEETING	cloth for sheets	
SHEETING	} vertical boards with	
SHEATHING	} struts for trenches	bd
SHEILING	shealing; hut	
SHEKINAH	Divine Aura	
SHELDUCK	female sheldrake	zo
SHELL-GUN	a cannon	
SHELL-ICE	(no water below it)	
SHELLING	bombarding; husking	
SHELL-OUT	spend cash; pay for (sl.)	
SHELTERY	affording shelter	
SHELVING	sloping; shelves	
SHEMITIC	Semitic; (Shem)	
SHEPHERD	a swain; shove, impede, shoulder (Australian football)	
SHERATON	furniture designer	
SHIELDED	sheltered; screened	
SHIELDER	protector	
SHIELING	Highland hut; sheiling	
SHIFTILY	deceitfully; evasively	
SHIFTING	moving; varying; changing	
SHILLALY	Irish blackthorn cudgel	
SHILLING	a bob	nm
SHIMMING	wedging	
SHIN-BONE	the tibia	md
SHINGLED	bobbed	
SHINGLES	herpes	md
SHINNING	climbing	
SHIPLESS	without boats	

SHIPLOAD	a full cargo	nt
SHIPMATE	fellow seaman	
SHIPMENT	embarkation	
SHIPPING	freighting; seaborne craft	nt
SHIP-TIRE	head-dress	
SHIP-WORM	the teredo	zo
SHIPYARD	building yard	nt
SHIREMAN	sheriff	
SHIRKING	evading; scamping	
SHIRTING	material for shirts	tx
SHIVAREE	mock serenade; charivari	
SHIVERED	shattered; quaked; trembled	
SHOALING	thronging	
SHOCK-DOG	a poodle	zo
SHOCKING	offensive; outrageous	
SHOEBILL	whale-headed heron	zo
SHOEHORN	footwear aid	
SHOELACE	a latchet	
SHOELESS	barefoot	
SHOGGING	shaking; jogging	
SHOGUNAL	(Japanese C. in C.)	
SHOOTING	a game-preserve; slaughter-sporter	
SHOOTOUT	police versus gangsters	
SHOP-BELL	bell at shop door	
SHOPGIRL	shop assistant	
SHOPLIFT	pilfer; rob a store	
SHOPPING	purchases	
SHOPWORN	faded	
SHORLING	newly shorn sheep	zo
SHORTAGE	deficiency; lack	
SHORT-AND	the ampersand; &	
SHORT-CUT	(tobacco); a quick way	
SHORT-LEG	(cricket)	
SHORT-RIB	a false rib	md
SHOT-BELT	bandolier	
SHOT-FREE	Scot free; untaxed	
SHOT-HOLE	hole for explosives	
SHOT-SILK	irridescent silk	
SHOTTING	loading with shot	
SHOULDER	carry; hump; a prominence	
SHOUTING	cheering; crying; calling	
SHOW-BILL	a showcard	
SHOW-CARD	card of patterns	
SHOW-CASE	display case	
SHOW-DOWN	cards on the table	
SHOWERED	bestowed liberally	
SHOW-ROOM	display salon	
SHOW-YARD	(horses and cattle)	
SHRAPNEL	a projectile	
SHREDDED	cut into strips	
SHREDDER	machine for shredding	
SHREWDLY	sagaciously; astutely	
SHREWISH	vixenish	
SHRIEKED	yelled; squealed; cried	
SHRIEKER	screamer	
SHRIEVAL	(sheriff)	
SHRILLED	squeaked; piped	
SHRIMPED	went fishing for shrimps	
SHRIMPER	boat or catcher	

SHRINING	enshrining	
SHRINKER	contractor	
SHRIVING	absolving; pardoning	
SHROUDED	veiled; hidden; screened	
SHROVING	Shrove-tide festivity	
SHRUGGED	uplifted	
SHUCKING	husking; stripping	
SHUFFLED	(cards); evaded	
SHUFFLER	palterer; quibbler	
SHUNNING	avoiding; evading	
SHUNPIKE	a byroad	
SHUNTING	switching railway cars	
SHUTDOWN	closure	
SHUTTING	fastening; barring	
SHWANPAN	Chinese abacus	
SIBERIAN	of Siberia	
SIBERITE	red tourmaline	**mn**
SIBILANT	hissing; buzzing	
SIBILATE	to hiss	
SIBILOUS	sibilant	
SIBYLLIC	oracular; prophetic	
SICANIAN	Sicilian	
SICELIOT	a Greek in Sicily	
SICILIAN	(Sicily)	
SICK-CALL	doctor's visit	
SICKENED	languished; ailed; wearied	
SICKENER	a cause of disgust	
SICK-FLAG	quarantine-flag	**nt**
SICKLIED	pallid; wan	
SICKLILY	languidly	
SICK-LIST	register of patients	
SICKNESS	malady; disease; illness	
SICK-ROOM	patients' room	**md**
SICULIAN	early Sicilian	
SIDE-ACHE	side stitch or pain	
SIDE-ARMS	sword or bayonet	
SIDEBAND	close frequencies	**ro**
SIDEBAND	signal for close transmission	**tc**
SIDE-BEAM	(above crank-shaft)	**au**
SIDE-COMB	ornamental comb	
SIDE-DISH	an entrée	
SIDE-DRUM	snare-drum; small drum	**mu**
SIDELINE	subsidiary activity	
SIDELING	sideways; sloping	
SIDE-LOCK	a curl	
SIDELONG	obliquely	
SIDE-NOTE	marginal note	
SIDEREAL	of interval between 2 transits	**as**
SIDERITE	ironstone	**mn**
SIDE-SEAT	seat not in front	
SIDE-SHOW	raree show at fair, circus, amusement park	
SIDE-SLIP	a skid; descending technique (skiing)	
SIDESMAN	deputy churchwarden	**rl**
SIDE-STEP	evade	
SIDE-SWAY	wind-caused side movement of frame	

SIDETONE	telephony	
SIDE-VIEW	profile	
SIDEWALK	pavement; footway	
SIDEWAYS	crabwise	
SIDE-WIND	undue influence	
SIDE-WIRE	wire staple stitching	**pr**
SIEGE-GUN	heavy gun	
SIFFLEUR	whistler	
SIFFLING	whistling	
SIGATOKA	fungal banana disease	**bt**
SIGHTERS	first six arrows on target (archery)	
SIGHTING	spotting; aiming; viewing	
SIGMATIC	(sigma)	
SIGNABLE	able to have a name written on	
SIGNALLY	eminently; notably	
SIGNIEUR	seignior; feudal lord	
SIGNLESS	making no sign	
SIGN-POST	modern milestone	
SIKYOTIC	plasma-fusing parasitic	**bt**
SILENCED	stilled; hushed	
SILENCER	(cars, guns, etc.)	
SILENTLY	mutely; dumbly; taciturnly	
SILICATE	silicon compound	**ch**
SILICIDE	silicon-content compound	**ch**
SILICIFY	make into silica	
SILICITE	labradorite	**mn**
SILICIUM	silicon	**ch**
SILICOLE	plant on silica-rich soil	**bt**
SILICONE	organo-silicon compound	**ch**
SILICULA	} seed vessel	**bt**
SILICULE		
SILKENED	made glossy	**tx**
SILK-MILL	cloth factory	
SILK-REEL	spool for silk	**zo**
SILKWORM	source of silk	**zo**
SILLABUB	syllabub; a drink; jelly sweetmeat	**ck**
SILLADAR	Indian cavalryman	
SILLY-HOW	a caul; foetal membrane	**pl**
SILPHIUM	rosin-weed	**bt**
SILURIAN	rock formation; geological era	**mn, gl**
SILURIST	a Silurian	
SILVANUS	a forest-god	
SILVERLY	like silver	
SIMARUBA	quassia; bitterwood	**bt**
SIMILIZE	compare; liken	
SIMMERED	boiled gently	
SIMONIAC	one guilty of simony	**rl**
SIMPERED	smiled fatuously	
SIMPERER	smirker	
SIMPLIFY	make plain and easy	
SIMPLING	gathering herbs	
SIMPLISM	affected simplicity	
SIMPLIST	herbalist	
SIMULANT	like unto	
SIMULATE	pretend; imitate; sham	
SINAITIC	(Mount Sinai)	**rl**

SINAPISM	mustard plaster	md
SINCIPUT	the skull	pl
SIN-EATER	(a Welsh custom)	
SINECURE	salary for no work	
SINEWING	strengthening	
SINEWOUS	strong; vigorous	
SINFONIA	a symphony	mu
SINFULLY	unrighteously; naughtily	
SINGABLE	vocable	
SINGEING	scorching; searing	
SINGERIE	monkeys represented as human	
SINGLING	selecting; picking	
SING-SONG	community singing	mu
SINGULAR	peculiar; unique; quaint	
SINICISM	a Chinese custom	
SINIGRIN	black-mustard-seed glucoside	ch
SINISTER	evil; unlucky; baneful	
SINK-HOLE	a vent; swallow hole, pot hole in depression	gl
SINN-FEIN	Irish home-ruler	
SINOLOGY	Chinese lore	
SINOPHIL	lover of China	
SINUATED	insinuated; wound	
SINUSOID	geometric curve	
SIPHONAL	working on the siphon principle	
SIPHONED	extracted to a lower level	
SIPHONET	aphid cornicle	
SIPHONIC	working on the siphon principle	
SIPYLITE	niobite of erbium	ch
SIRENIAN	mermaid-like sea mammal	zo
SIRENIZE	entice; allure	
SIRIASIS	sunstroke	md
SIRVENTE	troubadour's song	
SISCOWET	} a variety of trout from Lake Superior	
SISKIWET		
SISKOWET		zo
SISTERLY	affectionate; sororal	
SISYPHUS	stone-roller	
SITOLOGY	dietetics	md
SITTYBUS	papyrus-roll title label	
SITUATED	placed; located; sited	
SITZ-BATH	hip-bath	
SIXPENCE	a tanner	nm
SIXPENNY	worth sixpence	
SIXTIETH	ordinal number	
SIZEABLE	of some bulk	
SIZINESS	adhesiveness	
SIZING-UP	estimation; rapid evaluation	
SIZZLING	hissing; seething; frying	
SKEAN-DHU	Highland dirk	
SKELETAL	like a skeleton	
SKELETON	outline; nucleus; cadre	
SKELLOCK	squeal (Sc.)	
SKETCHED	drafted; depicted; drew	
SKETCHER	delineator	
SKEWBACK	an abutment	

SKEWBALD	piebald	
SKEWERED	impaled	
SKEWNESS	deviation of curve of frequency distribution	
SKIAGRAM	X-ray photograph	md
SKIATRON	type of cathode-ray tube	el
SKIDDING	side-slipping	
SKILLESS	maladroit; artless	
SKILLING	outhouse; bay of a barn	
SKIM-MILK	weightwatcher's drink	
SKIMMING	scan superficially	
SKIMMITY	a burlesque	
SKIMPING	scamping; stinting	
SKIN-DEEP	superficial	
SKINLESS	flayed	
SKINNING	flaying	
SKINTLED	of irregularly laid brickwork	bd
SKIN-WOOL	wool from dead sheep	
SKIPETAR	an Albanian	
SKIP-JACK	upstart; click-beetle	zo
SKIPJACK	sail cargo boat, Chesapeake, N. America	nt
SKIPPING	leaping; bounding; hopping	
SKIRLING	bagpipe music	mu
SKIRMISH	contest; brush; fray	
SKIRTING	bordering	
SKITTISH	mettlesome; fickle	
SKITTLES	ninepins	ga
SKUA-GULL	the great skua	zo
SKULKING	lurking; slinking	
SKULL-CAP	the sinciput	
SKUNKISH	like a skunk	zo
SKURFING	} skateboarding	
SKURFER		
SKYLIGHT	glazed hole in roof	
SKY-PILOT	aviator; padre	rl
SKYSCAPE	cloud painting	
SKY-SHADE	lens; hood	pg
SLABBING	cutting into slabs	
SLABLINE	a running rope	nt
SLACKING	relaxing; loosening	
SLAISTER	slovenly work (Sc.)	
SLAMMING	banging	
SLANGILY	colloquially	
SLANGING	vituperating	
SLANTING	sloping; tilting; oblique	
SLAP-BANG	violently	
SLAP-DASH	carelessly; rashly	
SLAPJACK	flapjack; pancake	ck
SLAPPING	large; strong; spanking	
SLASHING	showy; severe; gashing; swing of ice hockey stick	
SLATE-AXE	a seax	to
SLATTERN	slovenly person	
SLAVERED	dribbled	
SLAVERER	driveller; idiot	
SLAVONIC	(Czechs; Poles; etc.)	
SLEAVING	separating	
SLEDDING	sled-transport	
SLEDGING	sleighing	

SLEEKING	gliding; smoothing	
SLEEPFUL	somnolent	
SLEEPILY	drowsily	
SLEEPING	dormant; slumbering	
SLEETING	rain, snow and hail	**mt**
SLIDABLE	capable of sliding	
SLIGHTED	insulted; peeved	
SLIGHTLY	slenderly; faintly; scantily	
SLIGHTLY	superficial	
SLIME-PIT	pit of viscous mire	
SLIMMING	banting; reducing; dieting	
SLIMNESS	craftiness; artfulness	
SLINGING	throwing; flinging; tossing	
SLINKING	skulking; lurking; sneaking	
SLIP-DOCK	slipway	**nt**
SLIP-KNOT	sailor's device	**nt**
SLIPOVER	sleeveless sweater	
SLIPPERY	evasive; shifty; elusive	
SLIPPING	tripping; erring; sliding	
SLIP-RAIL	form of gate (Australian)	
SLIP-ROAD	minor by-pass; siding	**rw**
SLIPSHOD	down at heel	
SLIPSLOP	jejune; trash; slovenly	
SLIPWARE	lead glazed earthenware with relief slip pattern	
SLITHERY	slimy; deceitful	
SLITTING	splitting	
SLIVERED	cut into strips	
SLOBBERY	moist	
SLOGGING	smiting	
SLOP-BOWL	slop-basin	
SLOP-DASH	weak cold tea	
SLOP-PAIL	household bucket	
SLOPPING	spilling	
SLOPSHOP	(ready-made clothes) R.N.	
SLOPWORK	slovenly work	
SLOTBACK	(Am. football)	
SLOTHFUL	idle; dronish; dilatory	
SLOTTERY	squalid; dirty	
SLOTTING	grooving	
SLOUCHED	bent; depressed	
SLOUGHED	cast off	
SLOVENLY	negligently; unkempt	
SLOVENRY	slovenliness; disorder	
SLOWBACK	lazy lubber	
SLOW-DOWN	ca' canny; reduce capacity	
SLOWNESS	tardiness; sluggishness	
SLOW-WORM	limbless lizard	**zo**
SLUBBING	twisting	
SLUGFEST	high scoring (baseball)	
SLUGGARD	laggard; lounger; slacker	
SLUGGING	slogging	
SLUGGISH	slothful; inert	
SLUG-HORN	a trumpet	**mu**
SLUICING	flushing	
SLUMBERY	somnolent; soporous	
SLUMMING	visiting slums	
SLUMPING	falling heavily	
SLURGALL	knitted-fabric fault	**tx**
SLURRIED	smeared	

SLURRING	disparaging	
SLUTTERY	dirt and disorder	
SLUTTISH	slatternly	
SLY-BOOTS	a wag	
SLY-GOOSE	the sheld-duck	**zo**
SMACKING	tasting of; slapping	
SMALLAGE	wild celery	**bt**
SMALL-ALE	(no hops)	
SMALLEST	minutest; tiniest	
SMALLISH	on the small side	
SMALLPOX	variola	**md**
SMALTINE	} compound of cobalt and	
SMALTITE	} arsenic	**mn**
SMARTING	stinging; rankling	
SMASH-HIT	popular song; musical	
SMASHING	shattering (blow); excellent	
SMEARING	daubing; begriming	
SMECTITE	fuller's earth	**mn**
SMELLING	redolent; scenting	
SMELTERY	foundry	
SMELTING	producing metal	
SMIRCHED	soiled; clouded	
SMIRKING	simpering	
SMITCHEL	a particle	
SMITHERY	a smiddy; a smithy	
SMITHING	iron-working	
SMOCKING	pleating	
SMOKABLE	fumable	
SMOKE-BOX	(steam locomotive)	**rw**
SMOKE-DRY	cure; bloat	
SMOOTHED	palliated; levelled	
SMOOTHEN	to allay; mollify	
SMOOTHLY	suavely; blandly	
SMORBROD	open sandwich (Scand.)	
SMORZATO	diminuendo	**mu**
SMOTHERY	stifling; stuffy	
SMOULDER	hangfire	
SMOULDRY	slow burning	
SMUDGING	blotting	
SMUG-BOAT	smuggling boat	**nt**
SMUGGLED	brought in illegally	
SMUGGLER	an owler	
SMUGNESS	self-satisfaction	
SMUTBALL	a fungus	**bt**
SMUTCHED	blacken with soot	
SMYTERIE	many small people (Sc.)	
SNACK-BAR	buffet	
SNAFFLED	purloined; filched	
SNAGBOAT	(removing snags)	**nt**
SNAGGING	lopping trees	
SNAILERY	small farm	
SNAKE-EEL	sinuous fish	**zo**
SNAP-LINE	chalked-string design marker	**pt**
SNAPPING	biting; breaking; cracking	
SNAPPISH	short-tempered	
SNAPSHOT	amateur photograph; store data for correcting errors	**cp**
SNAP-VOTE	sudden vote	
SNAP-WEED	balsams, etc.	**bt**

SNARLING	entangling	
SNATCHED	plucked; clutched; wrested	
SNATCHER	grasper; grabber	
SNEAK-CUP	insidious scoundrel	
SNEAKING	telling; secret; slinking	
SNEERING	taunting; jeering; mocking	
SNEEZING	snuff	
SNICKING	cutting; nicking	
SNIFFING	indicating incredulity	
SNIGGLED	snared	
SNIPPETY	fragmentary	
SNIPPING	shearing; clipping	
SNIP-SNAP	smart sharp dialogue	
SNITCHER	handcuff; informer	
SNIVELLY	whining	
SNOBBERY	tuft-hunting	
SNOBBISH	feeling superior	
SNOBBISM	aping gentility	
SNOBLING	a little snob	
SNOOPING	furtive enquiry; prying	
SNOOZING	dozing; drowsing	
SNORTING	puffing	
SNOWBALL	guelder-rose	**bt**
SNOWBIRD	American finch	**zo**
SNOWBOOT	long boot; galosh	
SNOWCAPT	crowned with snow	
SNOWCOLD	cold as snow	
SNOWDROP	first sign of spring	**bt**
SNOW-EYES	snow goggles	
SNOWFALL	frozen precipitation	
SNOWLIKE	cold, white and soft	
SNOWLINE	line of perpetual snow	
SNOWSHED	railway protection	**rw**
SNOWSHOE	wide framed shoe for walking on snow	
SNOWSLIP	avalanche	
SNOWSUIT	winter garments	
SNUBBING	checking a rope	
SNUBBISH	petulant	
SNUB-NOSE	short nose	
SNUFFBOX	collector's item	
SNUFFERS	candle trimmers	
SNUFFLED	sniffed	
SNUFFLER	one who snuffles	
SNUFFLES	infantile breathing noise	**md**
SNUGGERY	cosy quarters	
SNUGGING	lying close	
SNUGGLED	cuddled	
SNUGNESS	warmth and comfort	
SOAKAWAY	dry well; rummel; pit	
SOAPSUDS	froth on soapy water	
SOAP-TEST	(for hardness of water)	
SOAP-TREE	a Chilean tree	**bt**
SOAPWORK	soap factory	
SOAPWORT	a genus of plants	**bt**
SOBERIZE	to calm down	
SOBRANJE	Bulgaria; Sobranye	
SOBRIETY	dispassion; temperance	
SOB-STORY	false, pathetic tale	
SOB-STUFF	synthetic emotion	

SO-CALLED	incorrectly known as	
SOCIABLE	companionable	
SOCIABLY	friendlily	
SOCIALLY	gregariously	
SOCIETAL	of society; social in nature	
SOCINIAN	a polemic theologian	
SOCKETED	shanked	
SOCMANRY	feudal tenure	**lw**
SOCRATIC	(Socrates)	
SODA-LIME	soda and quicklime	
SODALITE	a soda compound	**mn**
SODALITY	comradeship; association	
SODAMIDE	ammonia-sodium compound	**ch**
SODA-SALT	baking ingredient	**ch**
SODDENED	saturated; drenched	
SOFTBALL	rounders; derivative of baseball	
SOFTENED	molified; melted; assuaged	
SOFTENER	mitigator; mollifier	
SOFT-EYED	compassionate	
SOFTLING	weakling	
SOFTNESS	tenderness	
SOFT-SHOE	light tap-dancing	
SOFT-SOAP	flattery	
SOFTWARE	computer programs, subroutines	**cp**
SOFT-WOOD	sap-wood	**bt**
SOILLESS	untarnished	
SOIL-PIPE	drain-pipe	
SOLACING	consoling; comforting	
SOLANDER	case for prints	
SOLANINE	an alkaloid	**bt**
SOLANOID	potato-shaped	**md**
SOLARISM	solar myths	
SOLARIST	mythologist	
SOLARIUM	sun-dial; sun-parlour	
SOLARIZE	injure by sun's rays	
SOLASTER	starfish	**zo**
SOLATIUM	compensation	
SOLDANEL	blue moonwort	**bt**
SOLDERED	cemented	
SOLDERER	a joiner of metals	
SOLDIERY	the military	
SOLECISM	incongruity; impropriety	
SOLECIST	(breaches of manners or syntax)	
SOLECIZE		
SOLEMNLY	gravely; formally; staidly	
SOLENESS	singleness	
SOLENITE	fossil razor-shell	**mn**
SOLENOID	switch based on copper coil	**tc**
SOLFAISM	use of sol-fa for sight reading songs	**mu**
SOLFAIST		
SOLIDIFY	harden; congeal; petrify	
SOLIDISM	(medical theory of diseases)	**md**
SOLIDIST		
SOLIDITY	compactness	
SOLITARY	lonely; single; remote	
SOLITUDE	isolation; seclusion	

SOLLERET	foot armour	
SOLONIAN	(Solon, a lawgiver)	lw
SOLSTICE	an ecliptic point	
SOLUTION	release; elucidation	
SOLUTIVE	loosening	
SOLVABLE	explainable; resolvable	
SOLVENCY	all debts payable	
SOMACTID	bony fin rod in fish	zo
SOMATISM	a doctrine	
SOMATIST	materialist	
SOMATOME	homologous segment	
SOMBRELY	gloomily; darkly; gravely	
SOMBRERO	broad-brimmed hat (S. Amer.)	
SOMBROUS	gloomy; sombre; doleful	
SOMEBODY	more than a nobody	
SOMEDEAL	in some degree	
SOMEGATE	somewhere (Sc.)	
SOMERSET	sommersault	
SOMESUCH	similar	
SOMETIME	formerly; once	
SOMEWHAT	more or less	
SOMEWHEN	some time or other	
SOMNIFIC	inducing sleep; soporific	
SONATINA	short sonata	mu
SONG-BIRD	warbler	zo
SONG-BOOK	collection of songs	mu
SONGFORM	ternary; (3 sections)	mu
SONGLESS	not in good voice	mu
SONGSTER	vocalist	mu
SON-IN-LAW	daughter's husband	
SONOBUOY	underwater noise-fixing equipment	
SONORITY	resonance	mu
SONOROUS	melodious; audible	mu
SOOTHING	pleasing; calming; lulling	
SOOTHSAY	foretell; augur; predict	
SOPHERIM	Hebrew scribes	
SOPITION	lethargy	
SOPOROUS	drowsy; somnolent	
SORALIUM	group of soredia in lichen	bt
SORBITOL	hexahydric alcohol	ch
SORCERER	wizard; magician	
SORDIDLY	ignobly; basely; meanly	
SOREDIUM	a brood-bud	bt
SOREHEAD	disgruntled person	
SORENESS	regret; rancour	
SORICINE	(shrew-mice)	zo
SORORATE	marriage of widower to dead wife's sister	
SORORISE	be a sister to	
SORORITY	women's club (Amer. univ.)	
SORPTION	absorption, adsorption, etc.	ch
SORROWED	grieved; lamented; wept	
SORROWER	mourner; repiner	
SORTABLE	befitting; suitable	
SORTMENT	assortment; distribution	
SOTADEAN	satirical and malicious	
SOTERIAL	about salvation	
SOUCHONG	black China tea	
SOUGHING	moaning; sighing	

SOUL-BELL	passing-bell	rl
SOULLESS	dull; spiritless	
SOUL-SCOT	requiem fee	rl
SOUL-SHOT		
SOUL-SICK	morally diseased	
SOUND-BOW	part of a bell	
SOUNDING	swinging the lead; determination of sea depths and speed in knots of vessel	nt, me
SOUR-BALL	tart hard spherical sweet	
SOURDINE	a muffler; sordet	mu
SOUR-DOCK	sorrel	bt
SOUR-EYED	morose	
SOURNESS	tartness; asperity	
SOUR-PUSS	a kill-joy	
SOUTHERN	of the south	
SOUTHING	of star crossing meridian	as
SOUTHING	maintaining direction towards the south	
SOUTHPAW	boxer's stance in ring	
SOUVENIR	memento; relic; keepsake	
SOW-BREAD	a tuber	bt
SOW-DRUNK	beastly drunk	
SOYA-BEAN	protein/oil plant (Manchuria)	
SOZZLING	getting fuddled	bt
SPACE-AGE	era of astronautics	
SPACE-BAR	typewriter gadget	
SPACEMAN	astronaut	
SPACIOUS	vast; roomy; ample; wide	
SPADILLE	ace of spades in ombre & quadrille	
SPADILIO		
SPADROON	double-handed sword	
SPAGIRIC	chemical	
SPALLING	stonework fragmentation	
SPALPEEN	scamp; rascal (Ir.)	
SPANDREL	triangular space beside an arch	
SPANDRIL		
SPANEMIA	anaemia	md
SPANGLED	glittering	
SPANGLER	sparkler	
SPANIARD	an Iberian	
SPANKING	dashing; slapping	
SPANLESS	immeasurable	
SPAN-LONG	9 inches (22 cm)	me
SPANNING	bridging; extending	
SPAN-ROOF	roof with eaves	
SPARABLE	shoe nail	
SPAR-DECK	the upper deck	nt
SPARE RIB	a piece of pork	
SPARGING	sprinkling	
SPAR-HAWK	sparrow-hawk	zo
SPAR-HUNG	(with fluorspar)	
SPARKFUL	lively; gay	
SPARKING	playing the gallant	
SPARKISH	well-dressed; airy	
SPARKLER	a diamond	mn
SPARKLET	charge of gas	
SPARLING	a smelt	zo
SPARRING	boxing	

549

SPARSELY	thinly; meagrely	
SPARSILE	scanty; infrequent	
SPATHOSE	} foliated or lamular	**bt**
SPATHOUS		
SPATHURA	humming-birds	**zo**
SPAVINED	(leg swelling)	
SPAWLING	slobbering	
SPAWNING	putting forth eggs	
SPEAKING	hailing; addressing	
SPEARING	lancing	
SPEARMAN	he who spears	
SPECIFIC	distinctive; peculiar; particular; absolute address **cp**	
SPECIFIC	qualifier "per unit mass" for physical property	
SPECIMEN	sample; type; exemplar	
SPECIOUS	plausible; ostensible	
SPECKING	staining	
SPECKLED	variegated	
SPECTANT	expectant	
SPECTRAL	ghostly; spooky	
SPECTRAL	of spectrum or of monochromatic radiation; of separation of wavelengths	
SPECTRUM	(colour bands); of refracted light waves	
SPECULAR	reflective	
SPECULUM	a mirror	
SPEEDFUL	speedy; hasty; impetuous	
SPEEDIER	faster; quicker	
SPEEDILY	with rapidity	
SPEEDWAY	racing track; specially built light racing vehicles	
SPEKBOOM	S. African shrub	**bt**
SPELDING	} dried haddock; or fish	
SPELDRIN	split and dried in the	
SPELDRON	} sun	
SPELLING	charming	
SPEND-ALL	spendthrift	
SPENDING	exhausting; squandering	
SPERABLE	hopeful	
SPERGULA	spurry; sandweed	**bt**
SPERM-OIL	whale by-product	
SPHAGNUM	bog-moss	**bt**
SPHECIUS	digger-wasps	**zo**
SPHENOID	wedge-shaped	
SPHERICS	spherical geometry	
SPHEROID	almost a sphere	
SPHEROME	cell-inclusion causing oil globule	
SPHERULE	small globe	
SPHRAGID	ochreous clay	**mn**
SPHYGMIC	pulsative	**md**
SPIANATO	smoothed out evenness (It.)	**mu**
SPICATUM	herring-bone work	
SPICCATO	rapid detached notes (violin)	**mu**
SPICE-BOX	condiment-holder	
SPICEFUL	aromatic	

SPICKNEL	baldmoney plant	**bt**
SPICULAR	spiky; pointed	
SPICULUM	small spike	**bt**
SPIFFING	delightful	
SPIGELIA	worm-grass; pink-root	**bt**
SPIKELET	unit of grass inflorescence	**bt**
SPILIKIN	spillikin; splinter of wood	
SPILLING	upsetting; shedding	
SPILLWAY	overflow	
SPILOTES	a snake genus	**zo**
SPINDLED	tapering	
SPINETTO	It. spinet (harpsichord type) **mu**	
SPINIFEX	porcupine grass	**bt**
SPINITIS	spinal fever	**md**
SPINNERY	spinning mill	
SPINNING	whirling; twirling	
SPINSTER	unmarried woman	
SPINSTRY	spinning industry	
SPIRACLE	} breathing-hole; pore	
SPIRICLE		
SPIRALLY	whorled	
SPIRIFER	fossil brachiopod	**mn**
SPIRITED	sprightly; alert	
SPIRITUS	aspiration; breathing	
SPIRTING	spurting; sprinting	
SPITBALL	illegal pitch in baseball	
SPIT-CURL	soap-lock	
SPITEFUL	vindictive; malicious	
SPITFIRE	fighting aircraft; irascible	
SPITTING	piercing	
SPITTOON	a cuspidor; receptacle	
SPLASHED	spattered	
SPLASHER	a mud-guard; paddle wheel box, ditto steam loco's driving wheels; name plate	
SPLATTER	to splash	
SPLAYING	sloping	
SPLEENED	angered	
SPLENDID	lustrous; refulgent	
SPLENIAL	splint-like bone	**md**
SPLENIUM	posterior bend of commissure **zo**	
SPLENIUS	a neck muscle	**pl**
SPLICING	joining; binding	
SPLINTER	fragment, cleave	
SPLITTER	separator	
SPLOTCHY	unevenly daubed	
SPLUTTER	a bustle; a stir	
SPOFFISH	fussy; officious	
SPOILFUL	wasteful; rapacious	
SPOILING	marring; vitiating	
SPOLIARY	Roman mortuary	
SPOLIATE	plunder; pillage	
SPOLVERO	perforation cartoon technique	
SPONDIAC	(spondee)	
SPONDIAS	hog-plums, etc.	**bt**
SPONDYLE	a vertebra	**pl**
SPONGING	cadging; sorning	
SPONSION	sponsorship	

SPONTOON	kind of halberd	
SPOOFING	bluffing	
SPOOKISH	ghostly	
SPOOLING	winding on reels (cinema), (fishing), (recording) **cp**	
SPOONFUL	a bite	
SPOONILY	amorously	
SPOONING	courting	
SPORADIC	scattered; irregular	
SPOROSAC	a gonophore **zo**	
SPORTFUL	frolicsome; jocose	
SPORTING	generous	
SPORTING	romping; displaying	
SPORTIVE	wanton; hilarious	
SPOT-BALL	billiards	
SPOTLESS	pure; untainted	
SPOTTING	observing; raining; appearance of defect, disease; choosing correct moment to jump (parachuting) **pt**	
SPOUTING	orating; gushing	
SPRACHLE	} to clamber up with	
SPRACKLE	} difficulty	
SPRAGGED	scotched up	
SPRAINED	overstrained	
SPRAINTS	dung of an otter	
SPRAWLED	straggled; spread	
SPRAWLER	lounger	
SPRAYING	atomizing	
SPREADER	extender; distributor; disperser; trench strut **ag, ce, rw**	
SPRIGGED	adorned with sprigs	
SPRINGAL	catapult; youth	
SPRINGAR	Norw. folkdance	
SPRINGER	arch support; ornamental short note; spaniel dog **mu, zo**	
SPRINKLE	bedew; perfuse	
SPRINTED	speeded; spurted	
SPRINTER	racer	
SPROCKET	a cog; (film); (tape) **cp**	
SPRUCELY	neatly; tidily	
SPRUCIFY	to smarten	
SPRUCING	refurbishing	
SPRUNTED	sprang; sprouted	
SPUDDING	lifting potatoes; enlarging hole with piles **ce**	
SPUILZIE	to spoil (Sc.)	
SPUNYARN	loosely twisted rope	
SPUR-GALL	wound with a spur	
SPUR-GEAR	gear wheels	
SPURIOUS	bastard; faked	
SPURLESS	without incentive	
SPURLING	the smelt **zo**	
SPURNING	disdaining; scouting	
SPURRIER	spur-maker	
SPURRING	inciting	
SPURRITE	carbonate/silicate of calcium	
SPURTING	gushing	

SPURTLED	showered	
SPY-CRAFT	secret service	
SPY-GLASS	a telescope	
SPY-MONEY	pay to secret agent	
SQUABBED	stuffed; crashed	
SQUABBLE	wrangle; brawl; printing	
SQUAB-PIE	pigeon-pie	
SQUADDED	grouped	
SQUADRON	military grouping	
SQUALENE	symmetrical triterpine **ch**	
SQUALLED	yelled; cried	
SQUALLER	screamer; informer	
SQUALOID	like a shark **zo**	
SQUAMATA	reptile genus **zo**	
SQUAMATE	} scale-like	
SQUAMOID	}	
SQUAMOSE	} covered with scales;	
SQUAMOUS	} scaly **zo**	
SQUAMULA	} a small scale	
SQUAMULE	}	
SQUANDER	dissipate; lavish; fritter	
SQUARELY	evenly; quadilaterally	
SQUARING	adjusting; regulating; resetting; blade turning (rowing)	
SQUARISH	not quite square	
SQUARSON	squire-parson **rl**	
SQUASHED	compressed; squeezed	
SQUASHER	suppresser	
SQUATTED	covered; crouched; sat	
SQUATTER	settler without title	
SQUATTLE	to squat down (Sc.)	
SQUAWKED	squalled	
SQUAWMAN	N. American Indian	
SQUEAKED	shrilled	
SQUEAKER	informer	
SQUEALED	squalled	
SQUEEGEE	rubber mop	
SQUEEZED	crushed; constricted	
SQUEEZER	playing card	
SQUEGGER	self-quenching circuit	
SQUIBBED	wrangled	
SQUIGGLE	squirm; wriggle	
SQUILGEE	squeegee	
SQUINTED	peered with narrowed/crossed eyes	
SQUIREEN	a petty squire	
SQUIRELY	gallantly	
SQUIRING	escorting	
SQUIRMED	wriggled	
SQUIRREL	plume-tailed rodent **zo**	
SQUIRTED	ejected; gushed	
SQUIRTER	a syringe	
STABBING	piercing; thrusting	
STABLING	accommodation for horses	
STABLISH	establish	
STACCATO	abruptly **mu**	
STACKING	piling	
STADDLED	supported	
STAFFING	providing personnel	

551

STAFFMAN	surveyor's assistant	
STAG-EVIL	horse disease	vt
STAGGARD	4-year-old stag	zo
STAGGERS	giddiness	
STAGHORN	large fern	bt
STAGNANT	motionless; inert	
STAGNATE	become dull	
STAHLIAN	} medical theory	md
STAHLISM		
STAINING	sullying; discolouring	
STAIR-ROD	carpet retainer	
STAIRWAY	a staircase	
STAKE-NET	fishing net	
STALKING	approaching warily	
STALLAGE	stall rent	
STALL-FED	luxuriously nurtured	
STALLING	losing speed when flying; to remain motionless (basketball)	
STALLION	male horse	zo
STALLMAN	stall-holder	
STALWART	resolute; sturdy; valiant	
STAMENED	having stamens	bt
STAMINAL	constitutional; vigorous	
STAMPEDE	panic; rush; flight	
STAMPING	pounding; impressing	
STANCHED	staunched; stopped	
STANCHEL	next (Sc.)	
STANCHER	a tourniquet	
STANCHLY	steadily; staunchly	
STANDARD	banner; colours; size; quantity; U shaped metal casting	ce
STANDARD	normal; plant with treelike stem	
STANDING	rank; duration; status	
STAND-OFF	(Rugby football)	
STAND-PAT	decline to budge	
STANHOPE	dog-cart	
STANK-HEN	moorhen	zo
STANNANE	tin hydride	ch
STANNARY	tin mine	
STANNATE	a salt	ch
STANNINE	a tin alloy	
STANNITE	sulphostannate of copper/iron	
STANNOUS	containing tin	
STANZAIC	(stanzas)	
STAPELIA	milkweed plants	bt
STAPLING	sorting; binding	
STARCHED	formal; stiff	
STARCHER	stiffener	
STARCHLY	rigidly; punctiliously	
STAR-DUST	cosmic dust	
STARE-CAT	over-inquisitive neighbour	
STAR-FISH	an echinoderm	zo
STAR-FORT	angular redoubt	
STAR-GAZE	astronomise	
STARLESS	lacking stars	
STAR-LIKE	stellate	
STARLING	small heavenly body	as

STARLING	ring of piles; bird	zo
STAR-NOSE	N. American mole	zo
STAROSTA	Polish noble	
STAROSTY	life-estate	
STAR-REED	Peruvian plant	bt
STARRING	taking the lead	
STARTERS	introductory meal course	ck
STARTFUL	skittish; jumpy	
STARTING	beginning; (post); (price)	
STARTISH	nervous; fearful; scared	
STARTLED	affrighted; dumbfounded	
STARTLER	a shock; a rouser	
STAR-TURN	revue or circus act	
STARVING	famished; hungry	
STARWEED	star-shaped plant	bt
STARWORT	aster genus	bt
STASIMON	choral ode	rl, mu
STATABLE	declarable; affirmable	
STATEDLY	regularly	
STATICAL	in equilibrium; restful	
STATUARY	sculpture	
STATURED	full grown	
STAYBAND	mast hoop to take stay wires	nt
STAY-BOLT	a holdfast	
STAY-LACE	corset cord	
STAYSAIL	triangular upper mainsail (schooner)	nt
STEADIED	supported; upheld	
STEADILY	constantly; firmly	
STEADING	farm out-houses	
STEALING	filching; purloining	
STEALTHY	clandestine; furtive; sly	
STEAM-GUN	steam-propelled firearm	
STEAMING	evaporating; reeking	
STEAM-TUG	steam-driven boat	nt
STEANING	well-shaft lining	
STEAPSIN	fat-digesting enzyme	zo
STEARATE	a fatty acid	
STEARINE	tallow; suet; etc.	
STEATITE	soapstone	mn
STEATOMA	wen or tumour	md
STEELING	hardening; bracing; nerving	
STEEL-PEN	a nib	
STEENING	well-shaft lining	
STEEPING	soaking; macerating	
STEEPLED	having a sharp spire	
STEERAGE	third class at sea	nt
STEERING	directing; piloting; guiding	
STEEVELY	stiffly (Sc.)	
STEEVING	stowing	
STEINBOK	African antelope	zo
STEINGUT	lead glazed earthenware (Germ.)	
STEINING	process of well-lining	ce
STELLARY	starry	
STELLATE	radiated	
STELLION	a lizard	zo
STELLITE	zeolitic mineral	mn
STEM-HEAD	bow-post (forward end)	nt

STEM-LEAF	part of plant	**bt**
STEMLESS	no stalk	
STEMMING	techniques of stopping and turning (skiing)	
STENLOCH	overgrown coalfish	**zo**
STENOSED	contracted	
STENOSIS	constriction	
STEP-DAME	step-mother	
STEP-GIRL	doorstep cleaner	
STEPOVER	wrestling manoeuvre	
STEPPING	pacing; working; chorus dancing; (stones) (netball)	
STEPWISE	photocopying method	
STERCOME	faecal matter in sarcodina	**zo**
STEREOME	mechanical plant tissue	**bt**
STERIGMA	fungal-spore-bearing hypha	**bt**
STERLING	genuine; pure; sound	
STERNAGE	steerage	**nt**
STERNITE	part of an insect	**zo**
STERNWAY	backward movement	
STEROIDS	bile acids; vitamin D hormones; saturated hydrocarbons	**md**
STIBBLER	clerical locum tenens	**rl**
STIBNITE	antimony compound	
STICCADO	xylophone	**mu**
STICKBOY	oddjobs boy (ice hockey)	
STICKING	adhering; fixing; piercing	
STICKJAW	toffee	
STICKLED	interposed; obstructed	
STICKLER	purist over trifles	
STIFF-BIT	horse's bit	
STIFFISH	rather tight	
STIFLING	suffocating; muffling	
STIGMATA	sacred marks	**rl**
STILBENE	S-diphenylethylene	**ch**
STILBITE	zeolitic mineral	**mn**
STILBOID	having stalked spore-head	**bt**
STILETTO	small dagger; high heel	
STILLAGE	cask-storing platform	**br**
STILLING	calming; distilling; ceramics	
STILLION	stand for a cask	
STIMMUNG	tone; atmosphere, mood (Ger.)	
STIMULUS	spur; incitement; goad	
STINGILY	parsimoniously; miserly	
STINGING	pricking; wounding	
STING-RAY	a fish	**zo**
STINKARD	teledu; badger	**zo**
STINKPOT	a grenade; term of abuse	
STINTING	limiting; pinching	
STIPPLED	dotted	
STIPPLER	engraver	
STIPULAR	having pin-feathers; (leaf	
STIPULED	lobe)	**zo, bt**
STIRLESS	quiescent; still; dull	
STIRRING	rousing; exciting, lively	
STITCHED	united; sewn	
STITCHEL	a hairy wool	
STITCHER	seamstress	

STOCCADE	a thrust in fencing	
STOCCADO		
STOCKADE	palisaded defence	
STOCKIER	stouter built	
STOCKILY	thickset	
STOCKING	footwear; storing	
STOCKISH	stupid; blockish	
STOCKIST	a tradesman	
STOCKMAN	herdsman	
STOCKPOT	soup, stew of the day	**ck**
STOICISM	imperturbation	
STOLIDLY	impassively; obtusely	
STOLZITE	lead tungstate	**mn**
STOMATIC	mouth medicine	**md**
STOMIDIA	disc apertures in actinaria	**zo**
STONE-BOW	(for shooting stones)	
STONE-FLY	a lure for trout	**zo**
STONE-OIL	petroleum	**mn**
STONEPIT	quarry	
STOOGERY	clownish fraudulence	
STOOKING	corn gathering	
STOOLING	ramifying	
STOOMING	fermenting	
STOOPING	condescending; bending	
STOP-BATH	developing accessory	
STOP-BUTT	safety bank behind targets	
STOP-COCK	regulating valve; cystern system	**pb**
STOP-CODE	colours of traffic lights	
STOP-CODE	emergency stop signal	**cp**
STOP-OVER	intermediate landing	
STOPPAGE	a deduction of pay	
STOPPING	a filling; checking	
STOPPLED	corked	
STOP-SHOT	stroke in croquet	
STOP-TIME	deceleration time	**cp**
STORABLE	reservable	
STORMILY	angrily; tempestuously	
STORMING	assaulting; ranting	
STORYING	narrating	
STOVAINE	an anaesthetic	**md**
STOWAWAY	secret passenger	**nt**
STOWDOWN	arrange cargo	
STRADDLE	bracket; striddle	
STRAGGLE	stray; digress; wander	
STRAIGHT	direct; honest; upright	
STRAINED	stressed; exerted; taxed	
STRAINER	a filter; percolator	
STRAITEN	confine; perplex; constrict	
STRAITLY	narrowly; closely	
STRAMASH	a tumult (Sc.)	
STRAMMEL	straw	**bt**
STRANDED	driven ashore; aground	
STRANGER	odder; quainter; alien	
STRANGLE	choke; suppress; smother	
STRAP-OIL	a thrashing	
STRAPPED	secured; stropped	
STRAPPER	harness-maker	
STRATEGY	military art	
STRATIFY	laminate	

STRATOSE	of well-defined layers	**bt**
STRATULA	thin rock layer	
STRAVAIG	wander (Sc.)	
STRAW-HAT	Panama headgear	
STRAYING	roving; deviating; erring	
STREAKED	variegated; striped	
STREAKER	dare-naked runner	
STREAMED	flowed; poured; gushed	
STREAMER	a pennant; wind-drift indicator (parachuting)	
STREAMER	ecliptic corona; wet fly (angling)	
STRELITZ	Muscovite militia-man	
STRENGTH	power; vigour; might	
STREPENT	noisy; strident	
STREPERA	crow-shrikes	**zo**
STREPHON	love-sick swain	
STRESSED	emphasized; accented	
STRESSOR	factor of stress	
STRETCHY	elastic	
STREWING	scattering; broadcasting	
STRIATED	furrowed; streaked	
STRIATUM	brain ganglion	**md**
STRICKEN	afflicted; smitten; struck	
STRICKLE	a template	
STRICTLY	exactly; literally; severely	
STRIDDEN	strode	
STRIDDLE	straddle; bracket	
STRIDENT	harsh; grating; creaking	
STRIDING	bestriding; stalking	
STRIGATE	striped; variegated	
STRIGGED	with fruit stalks removed	
STRIGINE	owl-like	**zo**
STRIGOPS	owl-parrots	**zo**
STRIGOSE	bristly; setous; aciform;	
STRIGOUS	setiform	**bt**
STRIKING	impressive; forcible; breaking camp; removal of support structure	**bd**
STRINGED	(rackets; billiards)	**mu**
STRINGER	horizontal tie rod; binder; surfboard slat	
STRINKLE	sprinkle sparingly	
STRIPING	making stripes	
STRIP-OFF	dismantling; undressing	
STRIPPED	deprived; naked; fleeced	
STRIPPER	pillager; peeler; husker	
STROBILA	tape-worm	**zo**
STROBILE	hardened catkin	**bt**
STROKING	(rowing); caressing	
STROLLED	sauntered; wandered	
STROLLER	actor; vagrant	
STROMBUS	wing-shells, etc.	**zo**
STRONGLY	forcibly; mightily	
STRONTIA	strontium oxide	**ch**
STROPHIC	choral	
STROPPED	(razors)	
STROWGER	relay selectors in telephone exchanges	**tc**
STRUCKEN	struck	

STRUGGLE	wrestle; strive; contend	
STRUMMED	vamped	**mu**
STRUMOSE	with cushion-like swellings	**bt**
STRUMOUS	scrofulous	**md**
STRUMPET	trollop; fly-by-night	
STRUTHIO	ostrich genus	**zo**
STRUTTED	braced	
STRUTTER	proud walker	
STUBBING	uprooting	
STUBBLED	bristly	
STUBBORN	refractory; wilful; perverse	
STUB-IRON	(used for gun-barrels)	
STUB-NAIL	short thick nail (boots)	
STUCCOED	plastered	
STUDBOLT	headless bolt	
STUD-BOOK	pedigree book	
STUDDING	putting in studs	
STUD-FARM	(horse breeding)	
STUDIOUS	diligent; scholarly	
STUD-MARE	breeding mare	**zo**
STUDWORK	form of brickwork	
STUDYING	conning; learning	
STUFFING	cramming; taxidermy	
STULTIFY	deaden; dull the mind	
STUMBLED	tripped; lurched	
STUMBLER	blunderer	
STUMMING	fermenting	
STUMPING	(cricket); nonplussing	
STUNDISM	(Russian dissenters)	
STUNDIST		
STUNNING	dazing; marvellous	
STUNSAIL	studding-sail	**nt**
STUNTING	dwarfing; performimg	
STUPEOUS	with matted hair	**zo, bt**
STUPIDLY	doltishly; senselessly	
STUPRATE	to ravish	
STURDILY	stoutly; stalwartly	
STURGEON	caviare fish	**zo**
STURNOID	(starlings)	**zo**
SUASIBLE	persuasible	
SUBACRID	pungent	
SUBACUTE	slightly blunt; dull	
SUB-AGENT	an underling	
SUBAHDAR	Indian captain	
SUBCHORD	way-measuring chord length	**sv**
SUB-CLASS	subdivision	
SUBCOSTA	primary wing vein in insects	**zo**
SUBCRUST	layer between pavement and foundation	
SUBDUING	overpowering; mastering	
SUBDUPLE	ratio of one to two	
SUBDURAL	under dura mater	**zo**
SUB-ENTRY	subdivision	
SUB-EQUAL	nearly equal	
SUBERATE	compound derived from cork	
SUBERECT	half upright, half nodding	
SUBERINE	compound derived from cork	
SUBEROSE	somewhat gnawed	**bt**

SUBEROUS	corky	
SUB-FLOOR	basic underfloor; blind or rough floor	**bd**
SUB-FLORA	floral division	**bt**
SUBFRAME	fixing for cladding	**bd**
SUBGALEA	parastipes in insects	**zo**
SUB-GENUS	subdivision	
SUB-GIANT	bright star	**as**
SUB-GRADE	lower division; original natural road surface; strata	**ce**
SUB-GROUP	subsidiary part	
SUB-HUMAN	almost human	
SUBHYOID	under the tongue	**md**
SUB-IMAGO	a state of change	**zo**
SUBIMAGO	stage in mayfly life history	**zo**
SUB-INDEX	index within an index	
SUBITISE	not counting dots	**pr**
SUBLATED	taken away	
SUB-LEASE	an underlet	
SUBLIMED	exalted	
SUBLUNAR	under the moon	
SUBMERGE	plunge; drown; flood	
SUBMERSE	duck; douse; dive	
SUBNASAL	under your nose	
SUBNODAL	below a node	**bt**
SUBORDER	subdivision; sub-genus	
SUBORNED	bribed; lead astray	
SUBORNER	perjurer; false witness	
SUBOVATE	almost egg-shaped	
SUBPOENA	writ of attendance	**lw**
SUBPOLAR	adjacent to polar sea	
SUBPRESS	die set; punch & die unit	**eg**
SUBPRIOR	prior's deputy	
SUBRIGID	fairly stiff	
SUBSERVE	help forward; promote	
SUBSIDED	sank; abated; waned	
SUBSOLAR	under the sun	
SUBSONIC	slower than sound	
SUBSTAGE	microscopic device	
SUBSTYLE	line on sundial	
SUBSUMED	logically included	
SUBTENSE	chord of an arc	
SUBTEPID	lukewarm	
SUBTITLE	secondary title	
SUBTLETY	cunning; artfulness	
SUBTONIC	leading note of scale	**mu**
SUBTOPIA	suburban ideal	
SUBTRACT	withdraw; deduct; take	
SUBTRIBE	section of a tribe	
SUBTRIST	somewhat sad	
SUBTUTOR	under-master	
SUBULATE	awl-shaped	
SUBURBAN	subregional	
SUBURBIA	the suburbs	
SUBVENED	relieved; subsidized	
SUBZONAL	below the belt	
SUCCINCT	concise; compact; terse	
SUCCINIC	derived from amber	
SUCCUBUS	night demon; intercourse with the devil	**rl**

SUCHLIKE	in such manner; similar	
SUCHWISE	in like manner	
SUCKENER	a tenant (Sc.)	
SUCKERED	with suckers removed	
SUCKLING	unweaned child	
SUDAMINA	sweating fever	**md**
SUDANESE	(Sudan)	
SUDARIUM	sweat room of Roman bath	
SUDATION	perspiration	
SUDATORY	connected with sweating	
SUDDENLY	hastily; abruptly; quickly	
SUFFERED	underwent; allowed; bore	
SUFFERER	victim; martyr	
SUFFICED	satisfied; was adequate	
SUFFIONI	volcanic fumes	
SUFFIXED	added; subjoined; appended	
SUFFLATE	inflate; blow up	
SUFFRAGE	vote; prayers; intercession	
SUFFRAGO	hock joint	
SUFFUSED	permeated; overspread	
SUFISTIC	(Moslem pantheism)	**rl**
SUGARING	sweetening	
SUICIDAL	self-destructive	
SUILLINE	of the pig family	**zo**
SUITABLE	appropriate; convenient	
SUITABLY	fittingly; aptly	
SUITCASE	portable oblong bag	
SUKIYAKI	Jap. meat/vegetable dish	**ck**
SULCATED	grooved; furrowed	
SULCULUS	siphonoglyph of anthozoa	**zo**
SULLENLY	morosely; gloomily	
SULLYING	smirching	
SULPHATE	} sulphur compounds	**ch**
SULPHIDE		
SULPHITE		
SULPHONE	hexavalent sulphur compound	**ch**
SULPHURY	containing sulphur	
SULTANIC	despotic	
SULTANRY	Sultan's dominion	
SUM-CHECK	digit produced by summation check	**cp**
SUMERIAN	(Babylonian)	
SUMMERED	passed summer	
SUMMONED	bid; cited; arraigned	
SUMMONER	invoker; prosecutor	
SUMPITAN	Malay blow-pipe gun	
SUN-BLIND	window-shade	
SUNBURNT	tanned; bronzed	
SUNBURST	dazzling gleam	
SUNCRACK	a fissure	
SUNDERED	parted; severed; broken	
SUNDRIED	dehydrated	
SUNDRIES	miscellanea; odds and ends; extras on bill or in scores	
SUNLIGHT	illumination from Helios	
SUNNITES	orthodox Moslems	**rl**
SUNPRINT	photograph	
SUNPROOF	fadeless	
SUNSHADE	a parasol	

SUNSHINE	illumimation	
SUNSHINY	sunny	
SUNSPOTS	regions of cool gas as dark	
	patches	**as**
SUNSTONE	feldspar	**mn**
SUPERADD	increase the total	
SUPERBLY	magnificently; gorgeously	
SUPER-EGO	conscience	**pc**
SUPERHET	(wireless oscillations)	**ro**
SUPERIOR	senior by rank; (larger, finer	
	than); boss; head of a	
	monastery	**rl**
SUPERMAN	an admirable Crichton	
SUPERNAL	celestial; heavenly	
SUPERTAX	a gross imposition	
SUPINATE	bring palm upward	
SUPINELY	inertly; languidly	
SUPPLANT	displace by intrigue	
SUPPLIAL	provision; provenance	
SUPPLIED	bestowed; furnished; gave	
SUPPLIER	contributor; provider	
SUPPOSAL	supposition; conjecture	
SUPPOSED	assumed; opined; imagined	
SUPPOSER	surmiser; thinker; fancier	
SUPPRESS	quell; check; smother	
SURBASED	(pedestal moulding)	
SURCEASE	cessation	
SURCULUS	a botanical sucker	**bt**
SURENESS	certainty; infallibility	
SURETIES	sponsors	
SURFACED	smoothed	
SURF-BIRD	plover; sandpiper	**zo**
SURF-BOAT	shallow-draught boat	**nt**
SURF-DUCK	the scoter	**zo**
SURGENCY	hypothesised personality trait	
		pc
SURGICAL	chirurgical	**md**
SURICATE	the meercat	**zo**
SURMISAL	surmise; assumption	
SURMISED	took for granted	
SURMISER	conjecturer; supposer	
SURMOUNT	overcome; surpass; scale	
SURMULOT	brown rat	**zo**
SURNAMED	having as family name	
SURPLICE	linen vestment	**rl**
SURPRISE	shock; bewilder; astound	
SURREBUT	rebut a rebuttal	**lw**
SURRENAL	above the kidneys	**pl**
SURROUND	encircle; hem; beset; loop	
SURSOLID	fifth power	**ma**
SURVEYAL	review; scrutiny; prospect	
SURVEYED	scrutinized; scanned	
SURVEYOR	inspector; land measurer	
SURVIVAL	an outliving; relic	
SURVIVED	outlasted; endured; outlived	
SURVIVOR	who lives through	
SUSPENSE	uncertainty: indecision	
SUSPIRAL	breathing-hole	
SUSPIRED	sighed	

SUSURRUS	whispering; muttering;	
	rustling	
SUZERAIN	paramount ruler	
SWABBING	mopping	
SWADDLED	swathed; wrapped	
SWADDLER	a Methodist (nickname)	**rl**
SWADESHI	Indian boycott	
SWAGGING	sagging	
SWAGSHOP	where trash is sold	
SWAINING	lovemaking; courting	
SWAINISH	boorish; rustic	
SWAMPING	overwhelming; inundating	
SWAMP-OAK	semi-tropical tree	**bt**
SWAMP-ORE	bog-ore	**mn**
SWAN-HERD	tender of swans	
SWANKING	bragging	
SWAN-LIKE	as a swan	
SWAN-MARK	identification mark	
SWAN-NECK	curved; S-bend; handrail	**bd**
SWANNERY	nesting area, home for swan	
	colony	**zo**
SWANNING	moving around aimlessly	
SWAN-SHOT	buck-shot	
SWAN-SKIN	soft flannel	
SWAN-SONG	last act or appearance	
SWAPPING	bartering	
SWARDING	turfing	
SWARMING	thronging; crowding	
SWARTISH	tawny; swarthy	
SWASHING	splashing	
SWASHWAY	navigable channel	**nv**
SWASTIKA	Nazi emblem; triskele	
SWATHING	wrapping; binding	
SWATTING	killing flies	
SWEALING	melting; singeing	
SWEARING	profaneness; avowing	
SWEATILY	laboriously	
SWEATING	toiling; extorting; perspiration;	
	separation in paint; gloss	**pt**
SWEAT-OUT	plastic defect due to moisture	
SWEEPING	comprehensive; extensive	
SWEEP-NET	fishing gear	
SWEEP-SAW	curved-cut saw	**to**
SWEET-BAY	the tree laurel	**bt**
SWEET-GUM	a gum tree	**bt**
SWEETING	sweet apple	**bt**
SWEETISH	rather sweet	
SWEET-OIL	olive oil	
SWEET-PEA	an attractive flower	**bt**
SWEET-SOP	an evergreen shrub	**bt**
SWELLDOM	fashionable world	
SWELLING	bombastic; dilating	
SWELLISH	foppish	
SWELL-MOB	thieving gang	
SWERVING	deviating; diverging	
SWIFTEST	fastest; fleetest	
SWIFTLET	(bird's nest soup)	**zo**
SWIGGING	quaffing; drinking	
SWILLING	rinsing; toping	

SWIMMING	dizziness; waterborne mobility knack	
SWIMSUIT	bathing costume	
SWINDLED	defrauded; cheated	
SWINDLER	sharper; trickster	
SWINE-OAT	a coarse oat	bt
SWINE-POX	disease of pigs	vt
SWINE-STY	a pig-sty	
SWINGING	vibrating; dangling	
SWINGLED	flailed	
SWINGMAN	both guard and forward (baseball)	
SWINKING	drudging; moiling; toiling	
SWIRLING	twirling; gyrating; eddying	
SWISHING	birching	
SWITCHED	shunted; bypassed	
SWITCHEL	treacle beer	
SWOONING	a syncope	md
SWOOPING	descending; rushing	
SWOPPING	exchanging	
SWORD-ARM	right arm	
SWORD-CUT	a wound	
SWORD-LAW	violence	
SWOTTING	studying hard	
SYBARITE	a voluptuary	
SYBOTISM	pig culture	
SYCAMINE	mulberry tree	bt
SYCAMORE	species of maple	bt
SYCONIUM	figlike fruit	bt
SYENITIC	(syenite)	mn
SYLLABIC	in syllables	
SYLLABLE	to utter	
SYLLABUB	sillabub; a drink; jelly sweetmeat or glass to hold it	
SYLLABUS	an abstract; summary; programme of education	
SYLPHISH	} fairy like	
SYLPHINE		
SYMBATIC	of partly-like polymorphism types	
SYMBOLIC	emblematic; representative	
SYMMETRY	harmony; regularity	
SYMMORPH	similar notion	
SYMPATHY	fellow-feeling; affinity	
SYMPHILE	guest species among insects	
SYMPHONY	unison of sound	mu
SYMPHYLA	an insect genus	zo
SYMPLAST	multinucleate cell variety	cy
SYMPLOCE	rhetorical repetition	
SYNACRAL	(common vertex)	
SYNALGIA	sympathetic pain	md
SYNANCIA	fish genus	zo
SYNAPSID	reptile skull condition	zo
SYNAPTIC	of nerve-cell contact	zo
SYNAPTON	model imitating living matter	bl
SYNARCHY	joint rule	
SYNASTRY	stellar coincidence	
SYNCLINE	geological basin	

SYNCOPAL	} (alteration in rhythm)	mu
SYNCOPIC		
SYNDESIS	fusion of chromosomes	cy
SYNDETIC	linking together	
SYNDROME	concurrence	
SYNECHIA	an eye-disease	md
SYNEDRAL	(angularity)	
SYNERGIC	working together	zo
SYNGRAPH	signed deed	lw
SYNOCHAL	feverish	md
SYNODIST	(synod)	rl
SYNOMOSY	sworn brotherhood	
SYNONYME	} alternative word with	
SYNONOMY	} similar meaning	
SYNOPSIS	abstract; short outline	
SYNOPTIC	comprehensive	
SYNOVIAL	(synovia)	md
SYNTAXIS	syntax; grammar; mode of thinking, expression	
SYNTEXIS	emaciation	md
SYNTONIA	reactiveness to environment, surroundings	pc
SYNTONIC	intense sharp	mu
SYNTONIN	acid albumin	md
SYPHERED	flush jointed	
SYPHILIS	sex-transmitted venereal disease	md
SYRIARCH	a chief priest	rl
SYRIGMUS	noises in the ear	md
SYSTASIS	political union	
SYSTEMIC	pertaining to the system	md
SYSTOLIC	contractive	
SYZYGANT	(quadratic function)	

T

TABARDER	a herald	
TABASHIR	mostly silica	mn
TABBINET	damask-like fabric	tx
TABBY-CAT	a mouser	zo
TABBYING	watered fabric process	tx
TABITUDE	emaciation; atrophy	md
TABLEAUX	pictures (Fr.)	
TABLE-CUT	flat-faced	
TABLEDEX	co-ordinate book index for computers	
TABLEFUL	filling a table	
TABLEMAT	plate underlay	
TABLINUM	room by atrium (Roman)	ar
TABOOING	prohibiting; banning	
TABORINE	tambourine	mu
TABORING	drumming	mu
TABORITE	extreme Hussite	rl
TABOURET	embroidery frame; drum shaped stool	tx
TABULATE	enumerate; classify; list; group totals for items	cp
TACAHOUT	a leaf gall	bt
TAC-AU-TAC	(fencing)	

TACHISME	spilling, smearing painting technique	pt
TACITRON	type of thyratron	el
TACITURN	mute; reticent; silent	
TACKLING	harnessing; dealing with	
TACKMARK	dot(s) used in 'work & turn' system	pr
TACKSMAN	tenant (Sc.)	
TACTICAL	strategic	
TACTLESS	insensitive; indiscreet	
TAENIDIA	thickenings of eudotrachea	zo
TAENIOID	ribbonlike	
TAFFRAIL	tatereel; stern-rail	nt
TAGILITE	copper phosphate	ch
TAGMOSIS	grouping of somites	zo
TAIGLING	entangling	
TAILBACK	retreating (Am. football)	
TAILBAND	decorative back-cover band	pr
TAIL-BOOM	an aeroplane spar	
TAILCOAT	formal jacket	
TAIL-EDGE	lower edge	
TAILGATE	trombone technique	mu
TAILINGS	mining refuse	
TAILLESS	Manx; without end	
TAILORED	cut to figure	
TAILRACE	(mill stream)	
TAILROPE	guide-rope	
TAINTING	corrupting; sullying	
TAINTURE	taint; stain; blot	
TAKE-DOWN	dismantle prior to next job; hold after fall-back (wrestling)	cp
TAKE-OVER	acquire control	
TAKER-OFF	mimic; quantity surveyor	
TAKINGLY	captivatingly; winningly	
TALANDIC	of rhythrnic changes in cell	cy
TALAPOIN	Buddhist monk	rl
TALENTED	accomplished; gifted	
TALESMAN	a juror	
TALISMAN	charm; amulet	
TALKABLE	conversable	
TALK-DOWN	landing technique	ae, ro
TALLNESS	height; loftiness	
TALLOWED	fattened	
TALLOWER	tallow-chandler	
TALLYING	recording; agreeing	
TALLYMAN	pedlar	
TALMUDIC	(the Talmud)	rl
TAMANDUA TAMANOIR	} arboreal ant-eater	zo
TAMARACK	American larch	bt
TAMARIND	tropical tree	bt
TAMARISK	evergreen shrub	bt
TAMEABLE	submissive; docile	
TAMELESS	intractable; wild	
TAMENESS	dullness; monotony	
TAMPERED	interfered; machinated	
TAMPERER	meddler; schemer; plotter	
TANAISTE	deputy premier (Irish)	
TAN-BALLS	(refuse bark)	

TANGENCY TANGENCE	} a state of contact	
TANGIBLE	tactile; positive; corporeal	
TANGIBLY	palpably; obviously	
TANGLING	complicating; matting	
TAN-HOUSE	tan-bark store	
TANISTRY	Irish land tenure	lw
TANNABLE	able to be cured	le
TANNADAR	Indian policeman	
TAN-STOVE	used for tan-bark	
TANTALUM	metallic element	ch
TANTALUS	spirit-stand	
TANTICLE	stickleback	zo
TANTRISM	Indian doctrine	
TANTRIST	a devotee	
TANZIMAT	Turkish reform bill	
TAPADERA	leather stirrup guard	
TAP-DANCE	toe-tapping dance	
TAPE-LINE	tape measure	
TAPERING	slightly conical; pointed	
TAPESTRY	woven work	
TAPEWORM	a parasite	zo
TAPIROID	like the tapirs	zo
TARA-FERN	bracken (NZ)	bt
TAR-BLACK	coal-tar product for earthed posts	
TARBOOSH	a fez	
TARGETED	armed with a buckler	
TARGUMIC	(Bible in Aramaic)	rl
TARIFFED	dutiable; taxed	
TARLATAN	muslin; tarletan	tx
TAROGATO TARAGOT	} Hungarian clarinet	mu
TARPEIAN	(Roman rock)	
TARRAGON	savoury herb	bt
TARRYING	awaiting; loitering; halting	
TARSIPED	kangaroo-footed	zo
TARSIPES	small marsupial	zo
TARTARIC	(Tartar)	
TARTARIN	potash	ch
TARTARUM	tartar compound	
TARTARUS	sunless abyss	
TARTNESS	sharpness; piquancy	
TARTRATE	a tartar salt	ch
TARTUFFE	a hypocrite	
TARVIATE	of tar/stone surfacings	ce
TAR-WATER	an infusion	md
TASKWORK	piece-work	
TASTABLE	savoury; palatable	
TASTE-BUD	sensory bud on tongue	
TASTEFUL	discriminative; elegant	
TATTERED	in rags; rent	
TATTLERY	idle gossip	
TATTLING	chatting; prattling	
TATTOOER TATTOOED	} skin artist	
TAUNTING	deriding; flouting; reviling	
TAUROCOL	bull's glue	
TAUTENED	tightened; stretched	
TAUTNESS	strain; tenseness	

TAVERNER	inn-keeper; Boniface
TAWDRILY	gaudily; garishly; flashily
TAXATION	imposition; levy; toll
TAXIARCH	Greek commander
TAXIRANK	cab queue
TAXODIUM	swamp-cypress **bt**
TAXOLOGY	} classification
TAXONOMY	
TAXPAYER	one liable for taxation
TEA-BOARD	tea-tray
TEA-BREAK	refreshment pause (industrial)
TEA-CADDY	small tea box
TEA-CHEST	box of tea
TEACHING	instructing; enlightening; explaining
TEACHING	hardware for storage, display, response **cp**
TEA-FIGHT	a bun-worry
TEA-HOUSE	oriental pleasure dome
TEAMSTER	waggoner; drayman
TEAMWISE	harnessed together
TEAMWORK	cooperation
TEA-PARTY	(Boston 1773)
TEA-PLANT	source of tea
TEARDROP	a tear
TEAR-DUCT	lachrymal duct **md**
TEARLESS	unfeeling
TEA-SPOON	kitchen measurement
TEA-TABLE	where tea is served
TEATHING	fertilizing
TEA-TOWEL	towel for drying dishes
TECHNICS	doctrine of arts
TECTARIA	shellfish **zo**
TECTONIC	constructive
TECTONIC	of roofing, folds, faults **ar, gl**
TEENAGER	youngster
TEETHING	dentition
TEETOTAL	dry; total abstinence
TEETOTUM	small top
TEGUMENT	the skin **pl**
TEGUMERE	portion of tegumant in somite **zo**
TELALGIA	distant pain
TELAMONE	carved male figure as support
TELARIAN	web-spinner **zo**
TELEBLEM	membrane of hyphae in agarics **bt**
TELECAST	televised
TELECINE	TV cine film projector
TELEFILM	television film
TELEGONY	hereditary influence
TELEGRAM	a wire; cablegram message **tc**
TELEMARK	ski turn on slope; paddle stroke (canoe)
TELEOSIS	purposive development **bl**
TELESTIC	ending
TELETEXT	graphics, documents sent by television system **tv, tc**
TELETRON	TV cathode ray tube
TELETYPE	teleprint (Telex)

TELEVIEW	watch television programmes **tv**
TELEVISE	to broadcast **tv**
TELLTALE	revealer; indicator; earthquake indicator; glass in shifting wall; sneak; tin (squash rackets) **ar, bd**
TELLURAL	earthy
TELLURIC	(tellurium) **ch**
TELONISM	last letters of author's name; pseudonym
TELOOGOO	Dravidian dialect
TELOTYPE	printed telegram
TEMERITY	rashness; audacity
TEMEROUS	reckless; bold; foolhardy
TEMPERED	toughened; moderated
TEMPLATE	a pattern; a jig; similar pattern identifier **cp**
TEMPORAL	secular; transient; of cortex area of the temples; of the head; of time **pl, md**
TEMPTING	alluring; inveigling
TENACITY	adhesiveness; cohesion
TENAILLE	a rampart
TENANTED	occupied; dwelt
TENANTRY	the tenants
TENDANCE	attendance; care; attention
TENDENCY	bias; drift; inclination
TENDERED	offered; estimated
TENDERLY	leniently; gently; softly
TENEBRAE	R.C. service **rl**
TENEMENT	a flat or house-block
TENESMUS	ineffectual evacuation straining
TENONING	mortising
TENON-SAW	metal-backed saw **to**
TENORIST	a tenor **mu**
TENORITE	oxide of copper **mn**
TENOTOMY	tendon-cutting **md**
TENSIBLE	tensile; ductile
TENTACLE	a feeler **zo**
TENTERED	stretched
TENTILLA	branches of a tentacle **zo**
TENTWORK	embroidery
TENTWORT	a fern **bt**
TEOCALLI	Mexican temple
TEPEFIED	warmed up
TEPHRITE	andesite **mn**
TEPIDITY	lukewarmness
TERAPHIM	Hebrew idols
TERATISM	being a foetal monstrosity
TERATOMA	foetal tumour
TEREBENE	(turpentine) **ch**
TEREDINE	teredo, boring worm **zo**
TERGETIC	dorsal **zo**
TERMATIC	an artery
TERMINAL	binding screw; oil-; air-; end of line; (illness); growing point **bt, md, tel, cp**
TERMINAL	telephone, tele printer, (plug)

TERMINER	a determination	lw
TERMINUS	the end of a line	
TERMLESS	boundless	
TERRACED	having or being in terraces	
TERRAPIN	tortoise	zo
TERRAZZO	mosaic in cement; terrace	bd
TERRIBLE	formidable; dire; gruesome	
TERRIBLY	frightfully; awfully	
TERRIFIC	horrific; dreadful	
TERTIARY	third in order	
TERTIATE	triplicate	
TERYLENE	man-made cloth	
TERZETTO	a trio	mu
TESSELLA	} small tiles for paving	
TESSERAE		
TESSERAL	tesselated	
TESSULAR	like dice	
TESTABLE	can be proved; bequeathable	lw
TESTACEA	animals with shells	zo
TESTACEL	a little shell	zo
TESTAMUR	a certificate	lw
TESTATOR	will-maker; devisor ·	lw
TESTCASE	sample legal decision	lw
TESTICLE	male gonad	pl
TESTTUBE	laboratory vessel	ch
TESTWISE	by testing; test experience	
TETANISE	cause spasms (tetany)	md
TETANOID	convulsive	
TETCHILY	peevishly; testily	
TETHERED	restricted; tied; fastened	
TETRADIC	fourfold	ch
TETRAGON	quadrangle	
TETRALIN	organic solvent	ch
TETRAPLA	Bible in four versions	rl
TETRAPOD	four-footed	
TETRARCH	Roman governor	
TETRARCH	with 4 xylem strands	bt
TETRAXON	having 4 axes	zo
TETRONAL	hypnotic/sedative drug	pm
TEUTONIC	Germanic	
TEXT-BOOK	a manual	
TEXT-HAND	large script	
TEXTRINE	textile	tx, wv
TEXT-TYPE	type for bookprinting	pr
TEXTUARY	authoritative	
TEXTUIST	text reciter	rl
THALAMIA	layers of cells	bt
THALAMIC	of the brain	pl
THALAMUS	an inner room; brain	
THALLIUM	metallic element	ch
THANATOS	god of death (Gr.) (instinct)	rl
THANEDOM	thane's jurisdiction	
THANKFUL	grateful; beholden	
THANKING	acknowledging gratefully	
THATCHED	covered with straw	
THATCHER	straw-roof craftsman	
THEARCHY	theocracy	rl
THEBAINE	variety of morphine	pm
THEETSEE	black varnish	bt

THEIFORM	like tea	
THEMATIC	dissertative	
THEOCRAT	divine ruler	
THEODICY	a philosophy	
THEOGONY	(genesis of the gods)	
THEOLOGY	divinity	rl
THEORIES	speculations; hypothesis	
THEORIST	conjecturer	
THEORIZE	postulate	
THEOSOPH	inspired person	
THERBLIG	division of movement	
THEREFOR	for that purpose	
THEREMIN	electronic instrument	mu
THEREOUT	therefrom	
THERIACA	an opiate	md
THERMALS	reflected solar heat; ascending air currents (gliding)	
THERMION	ion from incandescent matter	ps
THERMITE	incendiary mixture	ch
THESPIAN	barnstormer; trouper	
THEURGIC	magical	
THEWLESS	weak; frail; feeble	
THIAMIDE	amide compound	ch
THIAMINE	vitamin B-1	
THIAZINE	heterocyclic compound	ch
THIAZOLE	pyridine-like liquid	ch
THICKEST	densest; closest	
THICKISH	rather thick	
THICKNEE	the stone curlew	zo
THICKSET	closely planted	
THIEVERY	larceny	
THIEVING	purloining; filching	
THIEVISH	sly; stealthy	
THIGGING	begging	
THIN FILM	glass plate memory storage	cp
THINGAMY	thingumabob; whatsitsname	
THINKING	ruminating; cogitating	
THINNESS	attenuation; emaciation	
THINNEST	lankiest; leanest	
THINNING	reducing; diminishing	
THINNISH	meagre; spare	
THIO-ACID	hydroxyl-replaced acid	ch
THIOCTIC	lipoic acid	
THIOPHEN	coal-tar constituent	ch
THIOPHIL	with affinity for sulphur	ch
THIOUREA	thiocarbamide; bismuth reagent ·	ch
THIRLAGE	milling rights	lw
THIRSTED	craved; yearned; longed	
THIRTEEN	the baker's dozen	
THISNESS	individuality	
THLIPSIS	compression	md
THOLE-PIN	rowlock	
THOMEANS	Malabar Christians	rl
THORACIC	(thorax)	
THORNBUT	turbot	zo
THORNSET	beset with thorns	bt

THOROUGH	complete; perfect	
THOUSAND	M; mille	
THRALDOM	slavery; bondage	
THRANITE	trireme rower	
THRAPPLE	windpipe; thropple	zo
THRASHED	drubbed	
THRASHER	fox-shark; thrush	zo
THRAWART	obstinate (Sc.)	
THREADED	strung	
THREADEN	made of thread	
THREADER	shuttle-worker	
THREAPED	contradicted (Sc.)	
THREATEN	menace; intimidate	
THREE-PLY	threefold; triple; treble; of wooden sheets	bd
THRENODY	} sad song	mu
THRENODE		
THRESHED	beat out grain; discussed	
THRESHEL	a flail	
THRESHER	mocking-bird	zo
THRESTLE	three-legged stool	
THRIDACE	lettuce juice	
THRILLED	agitated; stirred; excited	
THRILLER	a gripping story; curdler	
THRIVING	flourishing; prospering	
THROBBED	pulsated; beat; palpitated	
THROMBIN	blood clotting enzyme	md
THROMBUS	blood-clot	md
THRONGED	crowded; flocked	
THRONING	enthroning	
THROPPLE	windpipe; thrapple	zo
THROSTLE	missel thrush	zo
THROTTLE	garrotte; strangle; stifle	
THROWING	casting; hurling; slinging	
THROW-OUT	rejected product	
THRUMMED	strummed	
THRUMMER	vamper	mu
THRUSTED	intruded; drove; pushed	
THRUSTER	reckless rider	
THUDDING	reverberating	
THUGGERY	} brutality; violence; criminal assault	
THUGGISM		
THUMBING	fingering	
THUMB-NUT	screwed by hand	
THUMBPOT	small flower pot	
THUMPING	enormous	
THUNDERY	gloomy; frowning	
THURIBLE	incense censer	rl
THURIFER	incense bearer	rl
THURSDAY	one of the weekdays	
THUSWISE	like so	
THWACKED	thumped; belaboured	
THWARTED	frustrated; balked	
THWARTER	obstructionist	
THYROXIN	hormone; iodine containing amino acid	ch
THYRSOID	(Bacchus's ivied staff)	
TIBIALIS	tibial muscle	md
TICK-BEAN	horse bean	
TICKETED	labelled	

TICKLING	titillation	
TICKLISH	critical; risky	
TICK-SEED	coreopsis	bt
TICK-SHOP	(goods on credit)	
TICK-TACK	signalling system (racing)	
TICK-TICK	} watch or clock	
TICK-TOCK		
TIDEGATE	} dock	nt
TIDE-LOCK		
TIDELESS	not rising/falling	
TIDEMARK	low or high water border	
TIDEMILL	sea-operated mill	
TIDESMAN	customs officer	
TIDE-WAVE	tidal wave	
TIDINESS	neatness; trimness	
TIE-BREAK	extra play for winning points (tennis)	
TIED-DOWN	involved; restricted	
TIGELLUM	first bud on a stem	bt
TIGELLUS	an internode	bt
TIGER-CAT	margay; ocelot	zo
TIGERISH	ferocious	
TIGERISM	voracity	
TIGHT-WAD	a miser	
TILE-KILN	tile factory.	
TILLABLE	arable; cultivable	
TILLERED	produced offshoots	
TILT-BOAT	boat with roof; covered in excursion boat, Thames	nt
TILT-YARD	tilting yard	
TIMBERED	wooded	
TIME-BALL	time signal	
TIME-BILL	timetable	
TIME-BOMB	explodes by time-fuse	
TIME-BOOK	works record	
TIME-CARD	a register	
TIME-FUSE	time-fuze	
TIMELESS	untimely	
TIME-WORK	rate of pay	
TIMEWORN	decayed; weatherbeaten	
TIMIDITY	fearfuless; shyness	
TIMONEER	hehmsman	nt
TIMONIST	misanthrope	
TIMOROSO	hesitatingly; timidly	mu
TIMOROUS	fearful; pusillanimous	
TINCTURE	tinge; solution	md
TINE-TARE	the vetch	bt
TINEWALD	} Manx Parliament	
TYNEWALD		
TINGEING	colouring	
TINGLING	thrilling	
TINGLISH	sensation	
TING-TANG	two-note clock	hr
TINKERED	botched	
TINKERLY	clumsily	
TINKLING	clinking	
TINNITUS	ringing in the ears	md
TINPLATE	covered in tin	
TINSELLY	tawdry	
TINSMITH	tin worker	

TINSTONE	cassiterite	mn
TINSTUFF	tin ore	mn
TINTAMAR	confused noise	
TINTLESS	colourless	
TIPPED-IN	inserted by use of gum	pr
TIPPLING	toping; soaking steadily	
TIPSTAFF	court officer	lw
TIPULARY	(crane-flies)	zo
TIRELESS	inexhaustible	
TIRESOME	tedious; fretful	
TIRONIAN	(Roman shorthand)	
TIRRIVIE	tantrum (Sc.)	
TISSUING	interweaving	
TITANESS	giantess	
TITANIAN	(titanium)	ch
TITANITE	sphene	mn
TITHABLE	subject to tithes	rl
TITHONIC	actinic	
TITIVATE	tidy up	
TITLE-CUT	title-page woodcut decoration	pr
TITMOUSE	a small bird	zo
TITRATED	solution added from burette	ch
TIT-TAT-TO	a game; criss-cross	ga
TITTERED	giggled	
TITTEREL	whimbrel; curlew	zo
TITTERER	sniggerer	
TITTUPPY	frisky; lively	
TITUBANT	stumbling	
TITUBATE	stagger	
TITULARY	nominal; titular	
TIVERING	marking sheep	
TLACHTLI	Mexican court game like baseball	ga
TOAD-FISH	the sapo	zo
TOAD-FLAX	snapdragon	bt
TOAD-PIPE	a horsetail	bt
TOAD-SPIT	cuckoo-spit	
TOADYING	fawning	
TOADYISH	sycophantic	
TOADYISM	obsequiousness	
TOBOGGAN	(toboggin; taboggin) long light sled for snow transport	
TOCOLOGY	obstetrics	md
TODDLING	strolling aimlessly	
TOGETHER	in unison	
TOHU-BOHU	desolation; confusion; chaos; (Heb.)	
TOILETTE	ceremonial wear (Fr.)	
TOILLESS	workless	
TOILSOME	arduous; laborious	
TOILWORN	fatigued; tired; weary	
TOKOLOGY	tocology	md
TOKONOMA	flower alcove in a house (Jap.)	bt
TOLBOOTH	a toll-booth	
TOLERANT	forbearing; liberal	
TOLERATE	suffer; brook	
TOLEWARE	japanning on tinplate (Amer.)	

TOLL-DISH	(used in mills)	me
TOLLETAN	of Toledo	
TOLL-GATE	high road entry fees office	
TOLTECAN	early Mexican	
TOMAHAWK	war hatchet	
TOMALLEY	lobster-liver	zo
TOMATOES	love apples	bt
TOMBLESS	no tomb	
TOMENTUM	a downy covering	md
TOMMY-BAR	small lever	to
TOMMY-GUN	a handy weapon	
TOMMY-ROT	balderdash; nonsense	
TOM-NODDY	puffin; a dolt	zo
TOMOGRAM	X-Ray photograph	md
TOMORROW	the following day	
TOMUNDAR	Baluchi chief	
TONALITE	igneous rock	mn
TONALITY	pitch	mu
TONE-DEAF	unmusical	
TONELESS	unmusical	
TONGKANG	ketch; lighter; (Singapore)	nt
TONGUING	barking; licking	
TONICITY	healthiness; possessing tone	md
TONOTOPY	concerning pitch of a tone	mu
TONSILAR	(tonsils)	md
TONSURED	clerical; shaven	rl
TOONWOOD	Indian red wood	bt
TOOTHFUL	a short drink	
TOOTHING	decorative indenting of bricks	ar
TOOTH-KEY	forceps	md
TOOTLING	playing the flute	mu
TOPARCHY	small state control	
TOPAZINE	(topaz)	
TOP-BOOTS	longish boots	
TOP-DRESS	to manure	ag
TOP-HEAVY	tipsy; ill-proportioned	
TOP-LEVEL	} excellent	
TOPNOTCH		
TOP-LOFTY	bombastic	
TOPOLOGY	of distorted space; a child's outlook	ma, pc
TOPOLOGY	an aid to memory	
TOPONOMY	} topical terminology	
TOPONYMY		
TOPOTYPE	specimen from original locality	zo
TOPPLING	falling	
TOP-PROUD	very proud	
TOP-SHELL	a mollusc	zo
TOPSIDES	above waterline, upper works of ship	nt
TOP-STONE	a finial	
TORCHERE	ornamental lampstand	
TORCHING	night fishing	
TORCULAR	a tourniquet	md
TOREADOR	bullfighter	
TOREUTES	an artist in metal	
TOREUTIC	chased metal-work	

TORMINAL	colicky	**md**
TORNADIC	(tornadoes); very stormy	**mt**
TORNARIA	larval form of balanoglossida	
		zo
TOROIDAL	like an anchor-ring	
TOROSITY	muscularity	
TOR-OUZEL	the ring-ousel	**zo**
TORPIDLY	apathetically; dully	
TORQUATE	collared	
TORSHENT	youngest child (USA)	
TORTILLA	maize cake; omelette (Sp.)	**ck**
TORTIOUS	injurious	**lw**
TORTOISE	terrapin	**zo**
TORTUOSE	} twisted; winding;	
TORTUOUS	} wreathed; deceitful	
TORTURED	agonized; racked	
TORTURER	tommentor	
TORULOID	} somewhat cylindrical	
TORULOSE		
TOTALITY	full amount; sum	
TOTALIZE	to add up	
TOTEMISM	symbolism	
TOTITIVE	(no common factor)	
TOTTERED	reeled; staggered	
TOUCHILY	peevishly; petulantly	
TOUCHING	concerning; pathetic	
TOUCHPAN	priming pan	
TOUGHEST	most stubborn	
TOUGHISH	stiffish; leathery	
TOURELLE	slender tower	
TOURNURE	turn; contour; curver	
TOUSLING	ruffing; rumpling	
TOWARDLY	toward; docile; tractile	
TOWERING	soaring; mounting	
TOWN-HALL	council offices	
TOWNLAND	a township	
TOWNLESS	without a town	
TOWNSHIP	a municipality	
TOWNSMAN	urbanite	
TOWN-TALK	local gossip	
TOXAEMIA	blood-poisoning	**md**
TOXICANT	poisonous	
TOXICITY	poisonousness	
TOYISHLY	playfully	
TRACHEAL	} (windpipe)	**pl**
TRACHEAN		
TRACHOMA	eye disease	**md**
TRACHYTE	volcanic rock	**mn**
TRACKAGE	towing; traction	
TRACKING	spooring; trailing; liner of surface ways; horizontal progress during free fall (parachuting)	**ce**
TRACKMAN	(railroad track)	
TRACKWAY	path or open road	
TRACTATE	a treatise; a tract	
TRACTILE	ductile; tractable	
TRACTION	attraction; towage; hauling	
TRACTIVE	pulling	
TRACTORY	tractive	
TRACTRIX	geometrical curve	
TRADEFUL	commercial	
TRADITOR	traitor; quisling; renegade	
TRADUCED	defamed; slandered	
TRADUCER	calumniator; libeller	
TRAGICAL	calamitous; disastrous	
TRAGOPAN	Chinese pheasant	**zo**
TRAGSITZ	suspended alpine rescue stretcher (Ger.)	
TRAILING	hauling; dragging	
TRAIL-NET	a trawl	
TRAINING	drilling; schooling	
TRAIN-OIL	railway lubricant	
TRAIPSED	gadded about	
TRAKENER	cross country obstacle (steeple-chasing)	
TRAMPING	trudging; hiking	
TRAMPLED	trod under foot	
TRAMPLER	grape-treader	
TRAMROAD	tramway	
TRANCING	sleeping; dreaming	
TRANGRAM	a knick-knack	
TRANQUIL	placid; calm; serene	
TRANSACT	negotiate; conduct; enact	
TRANSECT	belt of vegetation for study	**bt**
TRANSEPT	cross-aisle; (church)	**ar, rl**
TRANSFER	make over; exchange; send; move across	
TRANSFER	convey; copy; control; data; peripheral	**cp**
TRANSFIX	penetrate; perforate; impale	
TRANSHIP	change conveyance	
TRANSIRE	customs pass	
TRANSMEW	transmute (obs.)	
TRANSMIT	despatch; forward; remit; broadcast	
TRANSMIT	send data, information to other location	**cp**
TRANSOME	} cross beam; fanlight	
TRANSOM		
TRANSUDE	to sweat	
TRANSVAR	power-transfer coupler	**tc**
TRAP-BALL	an old game	**ga**
TRAP-DOOR	door in the floor	
TRAPESED	traipsed; tramped	
TRAPEZIA	trapeziums	
TRAP-FALL	a trap	
TRAPPEAN	(traprock)	**mn**
TRAPPING	snaring	
TRAPPIST	Cistercian monk	**rl**
TRAPPOUS	like traprock	**mn**
TRAP-TUFA	} rock of volcanic	
TRAP-TUFF	} origin	**mn**
TRASHERY	rubbish; balderdash	
TRASHILY	in a rubbishy way	
TRASLING	freshwater perch	**zo**
TRAVERSA	} transverse flute (It.)	**mu**
TRAVESO		
TRAVERSE	crossing or lateral movement; grid survey	

TRAVERSE	sideways or diagonal climb (mountaineering)	
TRAVESTY	a burlesque; parody	
TRAWLING	fishing towing a submerged net	
TRAY-TRIP	a draughts game	ga
TREACLED	(moth catching)	
TREADING	trampling; pacing; stepping	
TREADLED	pedalled	
TREADLER	bicyclist	
TREASURE	preserve; hoard; garner	
TREASURY	money/gold office; repository	
TREATING	entertaining; dealing	
TREATISE	written discourse; essay	
TREBLING	doing 3-fold	
TRECENTO	14th Century Italian art	
TREE-CALF	leather binding	
TREE-CRAB	(lives on coconuts)	zo
TREE-DOVE	Indian pigeon	zo
TREE-FERN	tropical fern	bt
TREE-FROG	many species	zo
TREELESS	lacking forest cover	
TREE-NAIL	long wooden pin	
TREKKING	migrating; hiking	
TREMANDO	tremulously	mu
TREMATIC	of gill-clefts	zo
TREMBLED	quivered; shook; quaked	
TREMBLER	vibrator; oscillator	
TREMLELA	jelly-like fungi	bt
TRENCHED	encroached; furrowed	
TRENCHER	wooden platter	
TRENDING	inclining; tending	
TREPHINE	cutting tool	md
TREPHONE	cell-breakdown substance	bl
TREPTION	environment-change response	cy
TRESPASS	sin; intrude; transgress	
TRESPOLO	spindly 3 legged table (It.)	
TRESSURE	heraldic border	hd
TREVETTE	loop-pile wire knife	tx
TREWSMAN	(wearing trews)	
TRIADIST	composer of triads	
TRIALISM	(body, soul and spirit)	
TRIALITY	threeness	
TRIANGLE	flogging frame; 3-sided figure; metal percussion	mu
TRIAPSAL	having three apses	
TRIARCHY	rule of three	
TRIARIAN	of the third rank	
TRIASSIC	geological formation; era	gl, mn
TRIASTER	mitobic figure	cy
TRIAXIAL	having three axes	
TRIAZOLE	heterocyclic compound	ch
TRIBASIC	with 3 hydrogen atoms	ch
TRIBELET	a small tribe	
TRIBONYX	genus of water-hens	zo
TRIBRACH	three short syllables	
TRIBUNAL	court of justice	
TRIBUTED	contributed	

TRIBUTER	piece-work miner	
TRICHINA	parasitic worm	md
TRICHITE	hairlike fibre	mn
TRICHODA	hairy infusoria	zo
TRICHOID	hairlike	zo
TRICHOMA	hair disease	md
TRICHOME	hairy outgrowth	bt
TRICHORD	three-stringed lyre	mu
TRICKERY	chicanery; deception	
TRICKILY	artfully; cunningly	
TRICKING	duping; gulling	
TRICKLED	oozed; percolated	
TRICKLET	small rill	
TRICKSEY	wily; pretty	
TRICOLOR	flag of France	
TRICORNE	3-cornered hat	
TRICTRAC	variety of backgammon	ga
TRICYCLE	3-wheeled bicycle	
TRIDACNA	genus of molluscs	zo
TRIFLING	toying; trivial; paltry	
TRIGAMMA	wing-vein feature in lepidoptera	
TRIGENIC	controlled by 3 genes	gn
TRIGGING	stopping; skidding	
TRIGLOID	gurnard genus	zo
TRIGLYPH	Doric ornamentation	
TRIGNESS	trimness; neatness	
TRIGONAL }	triangular	
TRIGONIC }		
TRIGONON	a triangle	
TRIGRAPH	a triphthong	
TRILEMMA	(three alternatives)	
TRILLING	quavering; warbling	mu
TRILLION	million^3 (GB) million^2 (USA)	
TRILLIUM	a lily genus	bt
TRILOBED	trilobate	bt
TRIMARAN	racing yacht between two outriggers	nt
TRIMERIC	of 3 times molecular weight	ch
TRIMETER	(versification)	
TRIMMERS	rib holes for structure	ce
TRIMMING	decorating; adjusting; extra delicacies; (barber)	ck
TRIMNESS	neatness; tidiness	
TRIMURTI	Hindu Trinity	rl
TRINGINE }	genus of sandpipers	zo
TRINGOID }		
TRINODAL	treble-jointed	
TRINQUET	small covered court (pelota)	
TRIODION	Greek prayer-book	rl
TRIOLEIN	fatty oil	
TRIP-BOOK	(fishing records)	
TRIPEMAN	tripeseller	
TRIPHANE	spodumene	mn
TRIPLANE	an aeroplane	
TRIPLING	trebling	
TRIPLITE	a phosphate	mn
TRIPLOID	with triple chromosomes	cy
TRIPODAL	tripedal; three-footed	

TRIPPANT	heraldic trotting	hd
TRIPPING	lapsing; dancing; felling	
TRIP-SLIP	tram ticket (USA)	
TRIPTANE	trimethyl butane	
TRIPTOTE	having 3 cases only	
TRIPTYCH	painted screen	rl
TRIP-WIRE	obstacle; brake	nt
TRISEMIC	iambic	
TRISKELE	swastika	
TRISOMIC	of 3-chromosome type	cy
TRISTFUL	sorrowful; dejected; doleful	
TRITICAL	trite; common; hackneyed	
TRITICUM	wheat, etc.	
TRIUMVIR	one of three (Rome)	
TRIUNITY	trinity	
TRIVALVE	with three valves	
TROCHAIC	(verse)	
TROCHITE	sea-urchin's joint	zo
TROCHLEA	a cartilage	md
TROCHOID	cycloid	
TROILISM	sexhibitionism	pc
TROILITE	nonmagnetic iron sulphide	mn
TROLLING	singing; spinning; towing	
	metal bait (angling)	
TROLLOPY	slatternly	
TROMBLON	fire-arm support	
TROMBONE	a brass musical wind	
	instrument with slide valve	
		mu
TROOPIAL	American starling	zo
TROOPING	collecting; parading	
TROPHESY	indigestion	md
TROPHIES	emblems of victory	
TROPICAL	figurative; fervid	
TROT-COSY	head covering (Sc.)	
TROTTEUR	walking skirt, shoe	
TROTTING	walking quickly	
TROTTOIR	side-walk (Fr.)	
TROUBLED	incommoded; vexed	
TROUBLER	disturber; pest	
TROUNCED	thrashed; castigated	
TROUPIAL	American song-bird	zo
TROUSERS	} hose; legwear	
TROWSERS		
TROUTING	fishing for trout	
TROUTLET	small trout	zo
TROUVERE	French lyric poet	
TRUANTLY	lazily; evasively	
TRUCKAGE	cost of conveyance	
TRUCKING	bartering; hawking	
TRUCKLED	cringed; yielded; stooped	
TRUCKLER	servile agent	
TRUDGEON	a swimming stroke	
TRUDGING	foot-slogging	
TRUE-BLUE	faithful partisan	
TRUE-BORN	} not a mongrel	
TRUE-BRED		
TRUE-LOVE	sweetheart; a herb	bt
TRUENESS	honesty; accuracy; veracity	
TRUMPERY	rubbish; trash; trifling	

TRUMPING	ruffing	
TRUNCATE	lop; shorten; reduce; prune	
		bt
TRUNCATE	suppress insignificant digits	
		cp
TRUNDLED	rolled; bowled; revolved	
TRUNDLER	barrow-mover; slow bowler	
TRUNKFUL	enough to fill a trunk	
TRUNNION	gun support	
TRUSSING	binding; fastening	
TRUSTFUL	confiding; trusty	
TRUSTILY	faithfully; staunchly	
TRUSTING	relying on; believing	
TRYPTONE	pancreatic ferment	md
TRYSTING	rendezvousing; meeting	
TUBE-FORM	tubular	
TUBERCLE	tumour	md
TUBEROSE	Mexican lily	bt
TUBEROUS	knobbed	
TUBE-WELL	artesian well	
TUBICOLE	caddis-worm	zo
TUBIFORM	tubular	
TUBIPORE	a coral	zo
TUB-SIZED	dipped and strengthened	
	(handmade paper)	pp
TUBULATE	formed of tubes	
TUB-WHEEL	flat water-wheel	
TUCKAHOE	edible fungus	bt
TUCKSHOP	sweet-shop	
TUCOTUCO	small rodent	zo
TUG-OF-WAR	rope sport	
TUG-PLANE	gliders	ae
TUKUTUKU	tucotuco; rodent (SA)	zo
TULA-WORK	niello work	
TUMBLING	falling; tripping	
TUMEFIED	swollen; distended	
TUMIDITY	bombast; pomposity	
TUMOURED	distended; enlarged	
TUMP-LINE	carrying strap	
TUMULATE	make a barrow	
TUMULOSE	tumulous; many mounds	
TUN-BELLY	pot-belly	
TUNELESS	unharmonious; unmusical	
TUNGSTEN	same as wolfram	ch
TUNGSTIC	(tungsten)	ch
TUNICARY	ascidian; sea-squirt	zo
TUNICATE	coated; a mollusc	zo
TUNING-IN	adjusting to listen	ro
TUNISIAN	(Tunis)	
TURANIAN	family of languages	
TURANOSE	disaccharide	ch
TURBANED	wearing a turban	
TURBIDLY	disorderly; opaquely	
TURBINAL	scroll-like bone	md
TURBO-JET	gas engine	ae
TURCOMAN	} a Turk of central Asia	
TURKOMAN		
TURF-CLAD	grassy	
TURF-MOSS	boggy land	
TURGIDLY	pompously; grandiosely	

TURLOUGH	shallow pool (Irish)
TURMERIC	yellow dye; hot spice; ingredient of curry **bt, ck**
TURNAGRA	thrush (NZ) **zo**
TURNCOAT	renegade
TURNCOCK	water-man
TURNDOWN	fold down; reject
TURNMARK	logline mark **nt**
TURNOVER	a pasty; volume of sales; deliver; transfer **ck**
TURNOVER	(leaf); generation and loss of cells; running with ball (basket-ball) **pl**
TURNPIKE	toll-gate; a road
TURN-SICK	giddy
TURN-SKIN	a werewolf
TURNSOLE	sunflower **bt**
TURNSPIT	kitchen-boy
TURRETED	having little towers
TUSSOCKY	tufty
TUTELAGE	guardianship; charge; care
TUTELARY	protective
TUTORAGE	instruction
TUTORESS	governess
TUTORIAL	educational
TUTORING	teaching
TUTORISM	education; coaching
TWADDLED	gabbled
TWADDLER	tattler; chatter-box
TWANGING	making plucked-wire noise
TWANGLED	twanged
TWATTLED	prattled
TWATTLER	a gossip
TWEAKING	twisting
TWEEDLED	fiddled
TWEELING	twilling
TWEEZERS	forceps **to**
TWELVEMO	4 times folded for 12 leaves **pr**
TWENTYMO	paper folded into 20 leaves **pr**
TWIDDLED	twisted
TWIDDLER	thumb-twirler
TWIGGING	understanding
TWILIGHT	dusk
TWILLING	weaving
TWINBATH	2-solution processing method **pr**
TWIN-BORN	contemporaneous
TWINGING	twitching
TWINKLED	sparkled
TWINKLER	a star
TWINLING	twin lamb **zo**
TWINPLEX	radio-telegraph system **tc**
TWINWIRE	paper-holding system for offset **pr**
TWIRLING	revolving; whirling
TWISTING	writhing; contorting
TWITCHED	jerked; snatched
TWITCHER	angle trowel; involuntary jerker

TWITTING	upbraiding; taunting
TWO-EDGED	double-cutting
TWO-FACED	false; double-dealing
TWO-LAYER	twin-ply paper/board
TWOPENNY	cheap; worthless
TWO-PHASE	with 2 equal alternating voltages **el**
TWO-PIECE	costume; suit
TYCHONIC	astronomic; (Tycho Brahe)
TYMPANIC	like a drum; middle ear bone **pl**
TYMPANUM	eardrum **md**
TYNEWALD	Manx Parliament
TYPE-CAST	single-character actor
TYPE-HIGH	standard height
TYPHLOPS	earthworms, etc. **zo**
TYPHONIC	cyclonic **mt**
TYPIFIED	exemplified; symbolized
TYPIFIER	prototype
TYPOLITE	fossil footstep **mn**
TYPOLOGY	types and their classification
TYPORAMA	facsimile
TYRAMINE	amino-ethyl benzene **ch**
TYROCINY	pupilage
TYROLEAN	} (Tyrol)
TYROLESE	}
TYROLITE	Tyrol sandstone **mn**
TYRONISM	apprenticeship
TYROSINE	precursor of amino acid **ch**
TYRRANIC	despotic; autocratic
TYRTAEAN	(warlike verse)
TZAREVNA	} Empress of Russia;
TZARITSA	} Tsarina

U

UBIQUITY	omnipresence
UDOMETER	rain gauge
UGLIFIED	made hideous
UGLINESS	repulsiveness; unsightliness
UINTAITE	variety of natural asphalt **mn**
ULCERATE	cause or form an ulcer **md**
ULTERIOR	remote; hidden; indirect
ULTIMATA	plural of ultimatum
ULTIMATE	furthest; final; eventual
ULTIMITY	last consequence
ULTRAISM	extreme views
ULTRAIST	extremist
ULULATED	howled; yowled; lamented
UMBELLAR	form of inflorescence **bt**
UMBONATE	having a boss
UMBRATIC	shadowy; shady; obscure
UMBRELLA	a gamp; collapsable shade
UMBRETTE	African heron **zo**
UMBRIERE	vizor of helmet
UMPIRAGE	arbitration; adjudication
UMQUHILE	formerly (Sc.)
UNABASED	not degraded; unashamed
UNABATED	undiminished; persistent

UNACHING	free from pain
UNACTIVE	inactive; inert; torpid
UNADMIRE	view with tolerance
UNADORED	unloved; unvenerated
UNAFRAID	bold; valiant; undaunted
UNAIMING	purposeless; random
UNALLIED	alone; separate; isolated
UNAMAZED	composed; unruffled
UNAMUSED	not entertained; bored
UNANCHOR	let loose
UNANELED	unshriven; unanointed
UNARGUED	not disputed
UNARTFUL	simple; artless; naive
UNATONED	not expiated
UNATTIRE	disrobe; undress
UNAVOWED	unconfessed; secret
UNAWARES	suddenly; unexpectedly
UNBACKED	unaided; unassisted
UNBAGGED	trouserless; let loose
UNBANDED	disbanded; disembodied
UNBANNED	permitted; unrestricted
UNBARBED	unshaven; pointless
UNBARKED	stripped of bark
UNBARRED	unfastened; opened
UNBATHED	untubbed
UNBEATEN	untrodden; undefeated
UNBEDDED	uprooted
UNBEFOOL	undeceive
UNBEHELD	not visible
UNBELIEF	incredulity; scepticism
UNBENIGN	malignant; malevolent
UNBEREFT	not bereaved; unspoiled
UNBESEEM	to be unworthy
UNBIASED	impartial; unprejudiced
UNBIDDEN	spontaneous; unsolicited
UNBISHOP	deprive of a bishopric **rl**
UNBITTED	unbridled; uncurbed **nt**
UNBLAMED	uncensured; unrebuked
UNBLOODY	not cruel
UNBODIED	incorporeal
UNBODING	not expecting; unforeseeing
UNBOILED	raw
UNBOLTED	unfastened; unbarred
UNBONNET	remove the hat; uncap
UNBOOTED	stripped of boots
UNBOUGHT	not bribed; incorrupt
UNBOYISH	sedate; unchildish
UNBRACED	relaxed; unsupported
UNBREECH	debag
UNBREWED	pure; genuine
UNBRIBED	not corrupt
UNBRIDLE	free from restraint
UNBROKEN	inviolate; continuous
UNBUCKLE	unfasten; unclasp
UNBUDDED	not yet in bud
UNBUNDLE	unpack
UNBUOYED	notlifted **nt**
UNBURDEN	disclose; reveal
UNBURIED	uninterred
UNBURNED	uncharred

UNBURROW	to ferret out
UNBUSIED	idle; unemployed
UNBUTTON	unfasten
UNCAGING	releasing; liberating
UNCALLED	not awakened
UNCANDID	reserved; cautious
UNCAPPED	unbonneted
UNCARTED	unloaded
UNCASING	disengaging; unpacking
UNCAUGHT	still free
UNCAUSED	no reason for
UNCHANCE	misfortune
UNCHANCY	uncanny; dangerous
UNCHARGE	unload
UNCHASTE	impure; lewd
UNCHEERY	dull; gloomy
UNCHEWED	not masticated
UNCHIDED	unrebuked
UNCHURCH	excommunicate **rl**
UNCIATIM	ounce by ounce
UNCIFORM	hook-shaped
UNCINATA	marine worms **zo**
UNCINATE	hooked
UNCLENCH	} to open the hand
UNCLINCH	
UNCLEWED	unwound **nt**
UNCLOSED	open; ajar
UNCLOTHE	undress
UNCLOUDY	clear
UNCLUTCH	declutch
UNCOATED	dejacketed
UNCOIFED	headdressless; unkempt
UNCOILED	unwound
UNCOINED	not minted
UNCOMBED	unkempt
UNCOMELY	lacking grace
UNCOMMON	odd; rare; strange
UNCOOPED	set free
UNCORDED	unbound
UNCORKED	ready to pour
UNCOSTLY	inexpensive
UNCOUPLE	disconnect
UNCOWLED	unveiled
UNCREATE	kill
UNCTUOUS	greasy; oily; fulsome
UNCULLED	unpicked
UNCURBED	licentious; loose; unbridled; unchecked
UNCURLED	straightened
UNCURSED	not execrated
UNDAMPED	free to vibrate
UNDASHED	undaunted; undismayed
UNDECENT	indecent (obs.)
UNDECKED	not adorned **nt**
UNDEEDED	not noteworthy
UNDEFIED	unchallenged
UNDEFINE	make indefinite
UNDENTED	smooth
UNDERACT	perform inadequately
UNDER-AGE	immature

UNDERAID	help secretly	**UNFELLOW**	to dissociate
UNDERARM	(bowling); underside of arm	**UNFENCED**	not enclosed; open
UNDERBID	offer less	**UNFETTER**	unchain; unshackle
UNDERBUD	opposite of overbud	**UNFILIAL**	undutiful
UNDERBUY	cut the price	**UNFILLED**	empty
UNDERCUT	the tenderloin; hand-hold; (price); (tree) **mo**	**UNFILMED**	not photographed
		UNFIXING	detaching
UNDERDID	economized effort	**UNFLATED**	deflated
UNDERDOG	weaker contestant	**UNFLAWED**	flawless; faultless
UNDERFED	on short commons; starved	**UNFLESHY**	skinny; skeleton-like, thin
UNDERLAP	extend below	**UNFLOWER**	deflower (of virginity)
UNDERLAY	foundation	**UNFLUENT**	tongue-tied
UNDERLET	sublet	**UNFOILED**	not baffled
UNDERLIE	below the surface	**UNFOLDED**	deployed; disclosed; unwrapped
UNDER-LIP	to lip insufficiently		
UNDERMAN	(insufficient crew) **nt**	**UNFOOTED**	untrodden
UNDERPAY	remunerate inadequately	**UNFORCED**	easy; natural
UNDERPIN	support	**UNFORGED**	not yet made
UNDERRAN	opposite of overran	**UNFORMAL**	informal; unconventional
UNDERRUN	to run insufficiently	**UNFORMED**	shapeless; not yet composed
UNDERSAY	minimize	**UNFOUGHT**	uncontested
UNDERSET	a contrary current	**UNFOULED**	clean; unsullied
UNDERSKY	lower sky	**UNFRAMED**	frameless
UNDERTOW	tidal current; at beach level descending, after break of wave	**UNFRIEND**	an enemy
		UNFROZEN	uncongealed
		UNFRUGAL	prodigal; lavish; wasteful
UNDEVOUT	irreligious; unholy	**UNFUELED**	unfuelled
UNDIMMED	untarnished	**UNFUNDED**	floating; unmonied
UNDINISM	urophilia; erotic effect of urine **pc**	**UNFURLED**	displayed
		UNGAINLY	uncouth; clumsy
UNDINTED	undented	**UNGALLED**	unhurt
UNDIPPED	dry	**UNGEARED**	unharnessed; without gear system
UNDIVINE	secular		
UNDOCKED	(tails) **nt**	**UNGENIAL**	uncongenial; cold
UNDOCTOR	cf. undentist; unsurgeon	**UNGENTLE**	rude; rough
UNDOUBLE	unfold	**UNGENTLY**	harshly; unkindly
UNDRAPED	nude	**UNGIFTED**	without talent
UNDRIVEN	not propelled	**UNGILDED**	plain
UNDROSSY	free from impurity	**UNGILLED**	(free fish from net)
UNDULANT	wavy	**UNGIRDED**	beltless; unenclosed
UNDULATE	vibrate	**UNGIVING**	rigid
UNDULOUS	undulating	**UNGLAZED**	paneless; without window glass
UNEARNED	free; gain without work		
UNEASILY	restlessly	**UNGLOVED**	barehanded
UNEDIBLE	inedible	**UNGLUING**	ungumming
UNELATED	not puffed up	**UNGOADED**	not harassed; unurged
UNENDING	everlasting; ceaseless	**UNGORGED**	not sated
UNENVIED	viewed with complacency	**UNGOTTEN**	not gained
UNERRING	certain; sure; exact	**UNGOWNED**	unrobed
UNESPIED	not observed	**UNGRACED**	awkward
UNEVENLY	ruggedly; unequally	**UNGROUND**	not milled
UNEXEMPT	liable	**UNGUICAL**	(snail, claw, hoof) **zo**
UNEXPERT	unskilled	**UNGUIDED**	unregulated
UNFABLED	real; true	**UNGUILTY**	innocent; unproven **sc**
UNFADING	everlasting; constant	**UNGULATA**	hoofed mammals **zo**
UNFAIRLY	dishonestly; falsely	**UNGULATE**	having hoofs **zo**
UNFALLEN	still standing	**UNGUMMED**	unstuck; not sealed
UNFASTEN	open; let loose	**UNHACKED**	not notched
UNFAULTY	free from blemish	**UNHAIRED**	scalped
UNFEARED	not held in awe	**UNHALLOW**	profane

UNHANDED	let go; released
UNHANGED	not dependent; not executed
UNHARMED	scatheless; immune
UNHASPED	unlatched
UNHEADED	beheaded
UNHEATED	cold; without heating
UNHEDGED	hedgeless; without a border
UNHEEDED	disregarded
UNHEIRED	without an heir
UNHELMED	rudderless
UNHELMET	deprive of a helmet
UNHELPED	unassisted
UNHEPPEN	clumsy; maladroit
UNHEROIC	timid; shrinking
UNHINGED	unsettled
UNHIVING	unhousing
UNHONEST	dishonest (obs.)
UNHOODED	bareheaded
UNHOOKED	unfastened
UNHOOPED	hoopless
UNHORNED	uncuckolded
UNHORSED	dismounted
UNHOUSED	dislodged
UNHUNTED	unsought
UNHUSKED	still in shell
UNIAURAL	monaural; single ear
UNIAXIAL	having a single axis
UNIBASAL	having a single base **ch**
UNICYCLE	acrobat's cycle
UNIDEAED	thoughtless
UNIFYING	uniting; merging
UNILOBAR } having one lobe **bt**
UNILOBED
UNIMBUED	not saturated
UNIMODAL	only one mode; single 'peak' effect
UNINURED	not hardened
UNINVITE	cancel invitation
UNIONISM	combination; alliance
UNIONIST	confederate; conservative; (Ulster)
UNIONITE	lime silicate **mn**
UNIPOLAR	of one-process nerve cells **zo**
UNIQUELY	peculiarly; exceptionally
UNIQUITY	singularity
UNISONAL	harmonious
UNITEDLY	jointly; concertedly
UNITIZED	treated as a unit
UNIVALVE	a mollusc **zo**
UNIVERSE	the world
UNIVOCAL	unanimous
UNJOINED	uncoupled
UNJOYFUL	dull; mirthless; downcast
UNJOYOUS	gloomy; melancholy; glum
UNJUDGED	awaiting verdict
UNJUSTLY	prejudicially; unfairly
UNKENNED	unknown
UNKENNEL	release; of a dog
UNKINDLY	unfriendly; harshly
UNKINGED	deposed

UNKINGLY	non-regal
UNLACING	unloosing
UNLADING	unloading
UNLAPPED	unwrapped
UNLARDED	not intermixed
UNLASHED	unfastened
UNLAVISH	sparse; frugal
UNLAWFUL	illegal; illicit
UNLAYING	untwisting
UNLEARNT	forgotten
UNLICKED	ungainly; awkward
UNLIKELY	improbable; risky
UNLIMBER	get into action
UNLINEAL	not in succession
UNLINING	emptying
UNLINKED	disconnected
UNLIVELY	cheerless; listless
UNLOADED	discharged
UNLOCKED	open
UNLOOKED	unheeded
UNLOOSED	slackened
UNLOOSEN	set free
UNLORDED	not raised to peerage
UNLORDLY	undignified
UNLOVELY	unpleasing; hideous
UNLOVING	passionless
UNMAIMED	sound; whole
UNMAKING	destroying
UNMANNED	disheartened
UNMANTLE	unrobe
UNMAPPED	uncharted
UNMARKED	unobserved
UNMARRED	unsullied
UNMARTYR	debunk
UNMASKED	exposed; unveiled
UNMEDDLE	unmuddle
UNMEETLY	improperly
UNMELTED	undissolved
UNMILKED	fat-uddered
UNMILLED	unground
UNMINDED	forgotten
UNMINGLE	sort out
UNMISSED	good riddance
UNMOANED	not lamented
UNMODISH	out of fashion
UNMOORED	cast off
UN-MOSAIC	contrary to Mosaic law
UNMOVING	motionless; impassive
UNMUDDLE	coordinate
UNMUFFLE	(drums)
UNMUZZLE	take muzzle off of
UNNAPPED	smooth cloth **tx**
UNNATIVE	unnatural
UNNEEDED	superfluous
UNNERVED	frightened
UNNETTED	still flying/swimming around
UNNIMBED	without a nimbus
UNNOOKED	guileless; straightforward
UNNOTIFY	cancel
UNOPENED	closed

UNPACKED	taken out of wrappings	**UNRUFFLE**	render unflappable
UNPACKER	parcel-opener	**UNRUINED**	intact
UNPAINED	not hurting	**UNRUMPLE**	smooth
UNPAIRED	singly	**UNSADDLE**	remove saddle from
UNPANGED	without remorse	**UNSAFELY**	perilously
UNPARTED	together; unseparated	**UNSAFETY**	danger; hazard
UNPATHED	trackless	**UNSALTED**	fresh
UNPAWNED	not pledged	**UNSAPPED**	not undermined
UNPEELED	with skin intact	**UNSATING**	not filling
UNPEGGED	not stabilized	**UNSAYING**	recanting
UNPENNED	released	**UNSCARED**	not alarmed; unruffled
UNPEOPLE	depopulate	**UNSEALED**	still open
UNPICKED	not selected	**UNSEAMED**	ripped open
UNPINION	release from bondage	**UNSEARED**	uncharred
UNPINKED	not pierced	**UNSEASON**	mistime (obs.)
UNPINNED	loose	**UNSEATED**	unhorsed
UNPITIED	not felt sorry for	**UNSECRET**	not trusty
UNPLACED	not in the first three	**UNSECURE**	insecure
UNPLIANT	stubborn; stiff; rigid	**UNSEEDED**	not sown; unselected (tennis)
UNPLUMED	plucked	**UNSEEING**	blind
UNPOETIC	prosaic	**UNSEEMLY**	unbecoming
UNPOISED	out of balance	**UNSEIZED**	not grabbed
UNPOISON	detoxidify	**UNSERVED**	not waited on
UNPOLISH	make rough	**UNSETTLE**	unhinge; disturb
UNPOLITE	unmannerly; impolite	**UNSEXUAL**	not hot
UNPOLLED	not voted	**UNSHADED**	lit
UNPOSTED	not stuck up	**UNSHAKEN**	firm
UNPRAISE	crab; criticize	**UNSHAMED**	unabashed
UNPRAYED	impossible participle	**UNSHAPEN**	formless
UNPREACH	recant	**UNSHARED**	whole
UNPRETTY	plain	**UNSHAVED**	unbarbed
UNPRICED	priceless	**UNSHAVEN**	unshorn
UNPRIEST	unfrock	**UNSHELVE**	take away (from) shelves
UNPRINCE	cf. unqueen; unduke	**UNSHROUD**	unveil
UNPRISON	release	**UNSHRUNK**	full-size
UNPRIZED	not valued	**UNSIFTED**	not examined
UNPROPER	improper	**UNSINGED**	unseared
UNPROVED	untested	**UNSLAKED**	unquenched
UNPROVED	run wild	**UNSLUICE**	open a sluice
UNPUCKER	uncrease	**UNSMOKED**	fresh
UNPURGED	unpurified	**UNSMOOTH**	rough
UNRACKED	unharassed	**UNSOAPED**	unwashed
UNRAISED	low	**UNSOCIAL**	reserved
UNRANGED	in disorder	**UNSOCKET**	dislocate
UNREALLY	illusively	**UNSOILED**	clean
UNREAPED	not harvested	**UNSOLDER**	make unstuck
UNREASON	lack of sense	**UNSOLEMN**	merry; vivacious
UNREELED	unwound	**UNSOLVED**	enigmatic
UNREINED	unbridled	**UNSONCIE**	}
UNREPAID	not requited	**UNSONSIE**	} unlucky (Sc.)
UNREPAIR	in disrepair	**UNSORTED**	mixed
UNRIDDLE	solve; unravel; decipher	**UNSOUGHT**	not looked for
UNRIFLED	not ransacked	**UNSOULED**	spiritless
UNRIGGED	dismantled	**UNSOURED**	sweet
UNRIPPED	torn	**UNSPARED**	victimized
UNROBING	undressing	**UNSPEEDY**	deliberate
UNROLLED	spread out	**UNSPHERE**	remove spheres from
UNROOFED	topless	**UNSPIKED**	with barbs removed
UNROOTED	uprooted	**UNSPOILT**	natural
UNROUTED	still grouped	**UNSPOKEN**	untold

UNSPRUNG	ready-set trap	
UNSTABLE	inconsistent; irresolute	
UNSTARCH	destiffen	
UNSTATED	not mentioned	
UNSTAYED	unrestrained	
UNSTEADY	vacillating	
UNSTITCH	unsew	
UNSTORED	not warehoused	
UNSTRING	take strings off	
UNSTRUCK	not impressed	
UNSTRUNG	relaxed; loosed	
UNSUCKED	full, erect	
UNSUITED	unbecoming	
UNSUNNED	pale	
UNSURELY	unsafely	
UNSWATHE	unwrap	
UNSWAYED	unbiased	
UNTACKED	disjoined	
UNTACKLE	unhitch	
UNTALKED	unspoken	
UNTANGLE	unravel	
UNTANNED	pale	
UNTAPPED	unbroached	
UNTASKED	jobless	
UNTASTED	virginal	
UNTAUGHT	illiterate	
UNTENANT	evict	
UNTENDED	neglected	
UNTENDER	unsympathetic	
UNTENTED	uncared for (Sc.)	
UNTESTED	unproved	
UNTETHER	untie	
UNTHAWED	frozen	
UNTHORNY	smooth	
UNTHREAD	disentangle	
UNTHRIFT	a prodigal	
UNTHRONE	dethrone	
UNTHROWN	still in saddle	
UNTIDILY	disorderly	
UNTILING	unroofing	
UNTILLED	fallow	
UNTIMELY	premature	
UNTINGED	uncoloured; innocent	
UNTIRING	unwearied	
UNTITHED	10% not paid	rl
UNTITLED	common; no established right	
UNTOMBED	disenterred	
UNTONGUE	to silence	
UNTOWARD	perverse; froward	
UNTRACED	untracked	
UNTRADED	inexperienced; unexchanged	
UNTRUCED	without truce	
UNTRUISM	a fallacy	
UNTRUSTY	unfaithful	
UNTUCKED	unfolded	
UNTUFTED	tuftless	
UNTUNING	disordering	
UNTURFED	stripped of turf	
UNTURNED	straight	
UNTWINED	untwisted	
UNVAILED	untipped	
UNVALUED	not prized	
UNVARIED	monotonous	
UNVASSAL	free; emancipate	
UNVEILED	disclosed	
UNVEILER	revealer	
UNVENTED	unuttered; unreleased	
UNVERSED	unskilled	
UNVIRTUE	evil; sin; vice	
UNVIZARD	dehelmet	
UNVOICED	not spoken; mute	
UNWAITED	unattended	
UNWALLED	not enclosed	
UNWARILY	rash; reckless	
UNWARMED	unexcited	
UNWARNED	unadmonished	
UNWARPED	flat; original dry wood	nt
UNWASHED	dirty	
UNWASTED	made use of	
UNWEANED	unalienated	
UNWEDDED	unwed	
UNWEEDED	overgrown	
UNWIELDY	ponderous	
UNWILFUL	docile; pliant	
UNWILLED	involuntary	
UNWINDED	not blown	
UNWISDOM	folly; fatuity	
UNWISELY	irrationally	
UNWONTED	unusual	
UNWOODED	treeless	
UNWORDED	silent	
UNWORMED	with worms removed	
UNWORTHY	undeserving	
UNYOKING	relieving	
UPCAUGHT	caught up	
UPCOILED	coiled	
UPCOMING	impending; ascending	
UPCURLED	frizzed up	
UPHEAVAL	earthquake; extreme change	
UPHEAVED	lifted up; raised	
UPHOLDER	partisan	
UPLIFTED	exalted	
UPMAKING	filling pieces	nt
UPPERCUT	boxing blow	
UPPER-TEN	the aristocracy	
UP-PLOUGH	plough up	
UPRAISED	lifted	
UPRIDGED	in ridges	
UPRISING	insurrection	
UPROOTED	eradicated	
UPROUSED	awoken	
UPSNATCH	clutch	
UPSTAIRS	among the gentry	
UPSTAYED	upheld	
UPSTREAM	against the current	
UPSTROKE	alternates with downstroke	
UPTHRUST	upheaval	
UPTOSSED	upchucked	
UPTURNED	inverted	
UPWAFTED	borne aloft	

UPWARDLY	upwards	
URALITIC	(uralite)	mn
URBANISM	town planning	
URBANITY	suaveness; courteousness	
URBANIZE	derusticate	
URCEOLUS	floral envelope	bt
URETHANE	ethyl carbamate	ch
URGENTLY	momentously; pressingly	
UROBILIN	bile/urine pigment	
UROCHORD	(sea-squirt)	zo
UROCHROA	humming-birds	zo
UROCISSA	Asiatic magpie	zo
URODAEUM	urinary duct in cloaca	zo
UROESTON	a tail bone	zo
UROMERIC	(tail-piece)	zo
UROSCOPY	urine examination	md
UROSTEGE	a snake's scale	zo
UROSTYLE	lengthy tail	zo
URSIFORM	like a bear	zo
URSULINE	a nun, (St Ursula)	rl
URTICANT	irritating, stinging	zo
URTICATE	to sting; cause a rash	
USEFULLY	advantageously	
USHERDOM	schoolmastery	
USHERING	heralding; introducing	
USTILAGO	genus of fungi	bt
USTULATE	scorched	
USUFRUCT	temporary possession	lw
USURIOUS	at high interest	
USURPING	arrogating; assuming	
UTILIZED	employed; used	
UTOPIAST	(Utopia)	
UTRIFORM	bottle-shaped	
UTTEREST	furthest; remotest	
UTTERING	disclosing; issuing	
UXORIOUS	wife-loving	

V

VACATING	quitting; annulling	
VACATION	intermission; recess; holiday	
VACCINAL	pertaining to vaccine	md
VACCINIA	cow-pox	md
VAGABOND	vagrant; nomad; wanderer	
VAGANTES	itinerant clerics	rl
VAGARIES	whims; caprices; crotchets	
VAGILITY	power of movement	ec
VAGINANT	sheathing	bt, pl
VAGINATE		
VAGINULA	sheath of seta in bryophyta	bt
VAGOTOMY	division of vagus nerves	md
VAGRANCY	nomadism; itinerance	
VAINNESS	vanity; conceit; inanity	
VALENCED	decorated; draped	
VALENTIA	woven material	tx
VALERIAN	all-heal, medicinal plant	bt
VALETING	personal attendance	
VALHALLA	hall of heroes	
VALIANCE	bravery; intrepidity	

VALIANCY	courageousness; chivalry	
VALIDATE	confirm; legalize	
VALIDITY	soundness; justness; aptness within limits	
VALKYRIA	the Valkyries	
VALLANCY	large wig	
VALLATED	cup-shaped; circumvallated	
VALORIZE	make a currency reform	
VALOROUS	intrepid; bold; heroic	
VALUABLE	precious; costly; expensive	
VALUATOR	appraiser; assessor	
VALVELET	small valve	
VALVULAR	containing valves	
VAMBRACE	arm-armour	
VAMOOSED	decamped; skedaddled	
VAMPIRIC	extortionate	
VAMPLATE	hand-guard of lance	
VANADATE	vanadium salt	ch
VANADIUM	metallic element	ch
VANADOUS	of divalent vanadium	ch
VANDALIC	Hunnish; barbarous; savage	
VANDYKED	indented; notched	
VANGUARD	forefront; front line	
VANILLIC	flavoured with vanilla	
VANILLIN	compound from vanilla pods	ck
VANISHED	disappeared; dissolved	
VANISHER	absconder	
VANQUISH	overpower; rout; subdue	
VAPIDITY	insipidity	
VAPORIZE	turn into gas	
VAPOROSE	unsubstantial; gaseous	
VAPOROUS	unreal; steamy	
VAPOURED	evaporated; peevish	
VAPOURER	boaster; vaunter; braggart	
VAQUERIA	cattle ranch	
VARANOID	lizardlike	zo
VARDARAC	mistral wind (Macedonia)	mt
VARGUENO	writing table (Sp.)	
VARIABLE	mutable; fickle; mercurial; (field)	cp
VARIABLY	changeably; fitfully	
VARIANCE	discord; strife; dispute	
VARIANCE	average of deviation squares	
VARIANCE	discrepancy; deviant human behaviour	
VARIATED	altered; variegated	
VARIATIM	variations; in different ways	
VARICORN	a horned beetle	zo
VARICOSE	permanently dilated	md
VARICOUS		
VARIETAL	mutative; subgeneric	
VARIFORM	protean; diverse	
VARIOLAR	pox-marked	md
VARIORUM	commentated edition	
VARISTOR	2-electrode semi-conductor	el
VARLETRY	the rabble; the crowd	
VARTABED	Armenian priest	rl
VASALIUM	vascular tissue	md
VASCULAR	vessels; ducts, etc.	md

VASCULUM	specimen-box	bt
VASELINE	petroleum jelly	mn
VASIFORM	like a duct	md
VASSALED	enslaved	
VASSALRY	bondage; feudal system	
VASTNESS	immensity; spaciousness	
VATERITE	polymorph of calcium	
	carbonate	mn
VATICIDE	murder of a prophet	
VAT-SIZED	with sizing added to pulp	pp
VAULTAGE	arched work	ar, bd
VAULTING	leaping; bounding;	
	competition event (gymn.);	
	cross-arched ceiling	ar, bd
VAUNTERY	boastfulness; arrogance	
VAUNTFUL	ostentatious; swaggering	
VAUNTING	bragging; crowing	
VAUNTLAY	(hound movement)	
VAVASORY	(land tenure)	lw
VAVASOUR	feudal tenant	
VEALSKIN	a skin-disease	md
VEDANTIC	(Hindu philosophy)	rl
VEGETATE	to sprout; (secluded life)	
VEGETIVE	a vegetable (Shak.)	bt
VEHEMENT	impetuous; ardent	
VEILLESS	open to view; undisguised	
VEINLESS	lack of venation	bt
VELARIUM	awning; canopy	
VELATION	mystery; concealment	
VELATURA	picture glazing (It.)	
VELLEITY	volition; inclination	
VELLOPED	heraldic wattles	hd
VELOCERA	multi-rigged coaster (It.)	nt
VELOCITY	swiftness; rapidity; rate	
VELODYNE	tachogenerator	el
VELOGRID	a grid in a wireless valve	ro
VELVERET	ersatz velvet	
VELVETED	like velvet	
VENALITY	mercenariness; corruptness	
VENATION	veins as a whole	bt, zo
VENATION	hunting; pursuit of game	
VENDETTA	a blood feud; vengeance	
VENDEUSE	saleswoman, shop assistant	
	(Fr.)	
VENDIBLE	marketable; disposable	
VENDIBLY	saleably	
VENEERED	overlaid; disguised	
VENENATE	poisonous; poisoned; toxic	
VENERATE	esteem; respect; revere	
VENEREAL	venusian; sexual diseases	md
VENETIAN	(Venice)	
VENGEFUL	vindictive; retributive	
VENIABLE	pardonable	
VENIALLY	excusably; trivially	
VENOMING	poisoning (snake bite)	md
VENOMOUS	venemous; poisonous	
VENOSITY	full-bloodedness	
VENOUSLY	veined	
VENT-HOLE	air-hole	
VENTOUSE	vacuum-traction birth	md
VENT-PLUG	barrel-peg	
VENTURED	hazarded; dared	
VENTURER	speculator; adventurer	
VENUSIAN	pertaining to Venus, love	
	goddess	
VERACITY	truth; truthfulness	
VERANDAH	covered balcony	
VERATRIC	hellebore extract	ch
VERATRUM	hellebore, etc.	bt
VERBALLY	orally; by word of mouth	
VERBATIM	word for word	
VERBIAGE	verbosity; prolixity	
VERDANCY	greenness	
VERDERER	forest-keeper	
VERDITER	green pigment	
VERGENCE	turning the eye	
VERGENCY	border; verge	
VERGETTE	heraldic pallet	hd
VERIFIED	confirmed; authenticated	
VERIFIER	corroborator	
VERJUICE	sourjuice	
VERMINLY	verminously	
VERMOUTH	absinthe; wormwood	
VERNICLE	miraculous imprint	
VERONESE	(Verona)	
VERONICA	speedwell plants	bt
VERRUGAS	Peruvian skin disease	md
VERSABLE	reversible	
VERSELET	} brief ode	
VERSICLE		
VERTEBRA	segment of the spine	pl
VERTICAL	upright; erect; perpendicular	
VERTICES	summits; apices; zeniths	
VERTICIL	a whorl	bt
VESICANT	blistering	
VESICATE	to blister	
VESICULA	a pustule	md
VESPIARY	wasp's nest	
VESTIARY	a wardrobe	
VESTMENT	garment; robe; dress	rl
VESTUARY	vestiary	
VESTURAL	(robe; clothing)	
VESTURER	vestment keeper	rl
VESUVIAN	fusee; fuzee	
VEXATION	affliction; torment; worry	
VEXILLAR	feathery	zo
VEXILLUM	a banner; Roman standard	
VEXINGLY	provokingly; annoyingly	
VIAMETER	an odometer	me
VIATICUM	Eucharist	rl
VIBRATED	quivered; oscillated	
VIBRATOR	a trembler; buzzer	
VIBRATOR	device for producing A/C	el
VIBRISSA	whisker; bristle	
VIBROGEN	cellular tissue	bt
VIBRONIC	electronic vibrations	el
VIBURNUM	guelder-rose	bt
VICARAGE	vicar's house	rl
VICARIAL	substituted	
VICARIAN	deputy	

573

VICARIUS	a vicar	**rl**
VICE-DEAN	a canon	**rl**
VICE-KING	regent; viceroy	
VICENARY	based on twenty	
VICHYITE	(Vichy)	
VICINAGE	} neighbourhood;	
VICINITY	} proximity	
VICTORIA	a vehicle	
VICTRESS	woman conqueror; victrix	
VICTUALS	provisions; sustenance	
VIDENDUM	thing to be seen	
VIETMINH	people of Vietnam	
VIEWABLE	able to be seen	
VIEWLESS	vistaless	
VIEWSOME	panoramic	
VIGAROSO	forcibly	**mu**
VIGILANT	circumspect; alert; wakeful	
VIGNERON	wine-grower (Fr.)	
VIGNETTE	character sketch	
VIGOROUS	lusty; powerful; virile	
VIHYLITE	plastic glass	
VILENESS	baseness; depravity; vice	
VILIFIED	slandered; defamed; decried	
VILIFIER	traducer; maligner	
VILIPEND	disparage; calumniate	
VILLADOM	suburban villas	
VILLAGER	dweller in village	
VILLAINY	depravity; fraud; rascality	
VILLATIC	(village)	
VILLITIS	coronet inflammation in horse	**vt**
VINCIBLE	conquerable; surmountable	
VINCULUM	bond of union; link; chain	
VINE-CLAD	covered with vines	
VINE-GALL	vine disease	
VINE-GRUB	a parasite	**zo**
VINE-LAND	grape acreage	
VINEYARD	grape plantation	**bt**
VINOLOGY	art of wine making	
VINOSITY	wine flavour	
VINTAGER	grape gatherer	
VINTNERY	the wine trade	
VIOLABLE	transgressive	
VIOLATOR	ravisher; debaucher	
VIOLENCE	brute force	
VIPERINE	venomous	**zo**
VIPERISH	malignant	
VIPEROUS	treacherous	
VIREMENT	bookkeeping transfer	
VIRGINAL	early form of spinet	**mu**
VIRGINIA	tobacco; creeper	**bt**
VIRIDIAN	bluish-green colour	
VIRIDINE	green variety of andalusite	**mn**
VIRIDITY	verdure; greenness	
VIRILISM	male characteristics in woman	
VIRILITY	manhood; energy; manliness	
VIROLOGY	virus diseases	**md**
VIRTUOSE	expert in art	
VIRTUOSO	connoisseur; expert	
VIRTUOUS	upright; moral; chaste	

VIRULENT	bitter in enmity; toxic	
VISCACHA	pampas hare	**zo**
VISCERAL	abdominal	**md**
VISCOUNT	a title	
VISIGOTH	Spanish Goth	
VISIONAL	illusory; chimerical	
VISITANT	guest; frequenter	
VISITING	inspecting; haunting; calling	
VITALISM	} hypothetical vital principle	
VITALIST	}	
VITALITY	vigour; life; energy	
VITALIZE	animate; quicken	
VITELLIN	a protein in egg	
VITELLUS	the yolk of an egg	
VITIATED	impaired; spoilt; debased	
VITIATOR	a pervert	
VITICIDE	a vine pest	**zo**
VITILIGO	patchy skin depigmentation	**md**
VITREOUS	glassy	
VITULINE	(veal)	
VIVACITY	sprightliness; liveliness	
VIVARIUM	small zoo	**zo**
VIVA-VOCE	orally	
VIVIDITY	vividness; clarity; lucidity	
VIVIFIED	quickened; enlivened	
VIVIPARY	manner of bud/seed production	**bt**
VIVISECT	operate on the living	**md**
VIXENISH	quarrelsome; snappish	
VIZERATE	viziership	
VOCALISE	wordless composition (Fr.)	**mu**
VOCALIST	singer	**mu**
VOCALITY	utterableness	
VOCALIZE	voice; articulate	
VOCATION	profession; calling; pursuit	
VOCATIVE	(invocation); a case	
VOGESITE	hornblende-lamprophyre	**mn**
VOIDABLE	able to be annulled	
VOIDANCE	evasion; annulment	
VOIDNESS	nullity; emptiness	
VOIGTITE	form of mica	**mn**
VOLATILE	lively; fickle; changeable; unstable	
VOLATILE	memory lost; without power	**cp**
VOLCANIC	eruptive	
VOLITANT	able to fly	
VOLITION	freewill; choice; purpose	
VOLITIVE	wishful	
VOLLEYED	(tennis)	
VOLPLANE	glide	
VOLSUNGS	Norse legendary race	
VOLTAISM	galvanism	
VOLTZITE	zinc sulphide	**mn**
VOLULITE	petrified shell	**mn**
VOLUMIST	an author	
VOLUTION	convolution; spiral	
VOLVULUS	stoppage	**md**
VOMITING	ejecting	

574

VOMITION	sickness	md
VOMITIVE	vomitory	
VOMITORY	an emetic	md
VORACITY	rapacity; greed	
VORSPIEL	prelude; overture (Ger.)	mu
VORTEXES	whirlpools; vortices	
VORTICAL	turning	
VORTICES	eddies; maelstroms	go
VOTARESS	lady devotee	
VOTARIST	adherent; votary; zealot	
VOTIVELY	by way of vow	
VOUCHING	warranting; backing	
VOUSSOIR	arch stone	
VOWELISM	use of vowels	
VOWELIST	user of vowels	
VOWELLED	with vowels	
VRAICING	gathering seaweed (Ch. Is.)	
VULCANIC	volcanic	
VULGARLY	commonly; boorishly	
VULSELLA	forceps	md

W

WABBLING	wobbling	
WADDLING	walking like a duck	
WAESUCKS	alas (Sc.)	
WAFERING	sealing	
WAGE-FUND	(a theory)	
WAGELESS	unpaid	
WAGERING	betting; laying; staking	
WAGE-WORK	paid work	
WAGGLING	swaying	
WAGGONER	wagoner	
WAGGONET	wagonette	
WAGONAGE	cost of transport	
WAGONFUL	load	
WAGONING	carting	
WAGON-LIT	sleeping car (Fr.)	
WAHDEROO	langur monkey	zo
WAILMENT	lamentation	
WAINBOTE	timber for carts	
WAINROPE	cart-rope	
WAINSCOT	panelling	
WAIT-A-BIT	(various shrubs)	bt
WAITRESS	a female waiter	
WAKA-TAUA	Maori war canoe (New Zealand)	nt
WAKENING	rousing; stimulating	
WAKERIFE	wakeful (Sc.)	
WALDHORN	hunting horn (Ger.)	mu
WALHALLA	Valhalla	
WALKABLE	able to be walked	
WALK-MILL	fulling mill	
WALK-OVER	easy victory	
WALLAROO	large kangaroo	zo
WALLDPED	thrashed	
WALL-EYED	glaring; fierce	
WALL-GAME	Eton football	
WALL-KNOT	Turk's head	nt
WALL-MOSS	stonecrop	bt

WALL-NEWT	lizard; gecko	zo
WALLOPER	a slogger	
WALLOWED	floundered; weltered	
WALLOWER	groveller	
WALLSEND	house coal	mn
WALL-TREE	fruit tree	bt
WALL-WORT	dwarf-elder	bt
WALOGLAS	} green glass process	
WEALDGLASS	} (Ger.)	
WALTZING	dancing	
WAMBLING	rumbling	
WANDERED	strayed; roamed	
WANDERER	rambler; nomad	
WANGLING	winning by craft	
WANTLESS	fully satisfied; abundant	
WANTONED	frolicked	
WANTONLY	sportively; capriciously	
WAPPENED	tearful; beaten; wearied; done in	
WAPPERED	blinked	
WARBLING	quavering; trifling	
WAR-DANCE	tribal ceremony	
WARDCORN	castle guard	
WARDENRY	warden's district	
WARDMOTE	court of inquiry	
WARDROBE	clothes closet	
WARD-ROOM	mess-room	nt
WARDSHIP	guardianship	
WARE-ROOM	show-room	
WARFARER	combatant	
WAR-FIELD	battle-field	
WAR-HORSE	a charger	zo
WARINESS	alertness; craftiness	
WARM-DOWN	relaxing after exertion	
WARMNESS	warmth; ardour	
WARPAINT	battle make-up	
WAR-PLANE	fighting aircraft	
WAR-PLUME	plume de guerre	
WARPROOF	valorous	
WARRAGAL	the dingo	zo
WARRANTY	authority	
WARRENER	warren keeper	
WARRISON	healing (obs.)	
WARTLESS	unbumped	
WARTWEED	} spurge used for	
WARTWORT	} curing warts	bt
WAR-WEARY	tired of fighting	
WAR-WHOOP	a war-cry	
WASHABLE	non-shrink	
WASHAWAY	a breach	
WASHBALL	soap-ball	
WASHBOWL	washbasin	
WASH-COAT	pre-treatment primer	pt
WASH-DIRT	process	mn
WASHLAND	between river and flood	
WASH-ROOM	ablution room	
WASP-BITE	wasp-sting	
WASTEFUL	prodigal; improvident	
WASTEWAY	overflow weir; spillway	
WATCHBOX	sentry box	

575

WATCHDOG	a guardian	zo
WATCHFUL	vigilant; alert; wary	
WATCHING	wakefulness; vigil	
WATCH-KEY	antique implement	
WATCHMAN	a look-out; custodian	
WATER BAR	water or flood excluder	
WATERAGE	transport dues	
WATER-BED	bed filled with water	
WATERBUG	various types	zo
WATERCAN	yellow waterlily	bt
WATER-DOG	water spaniel	zo
WATERFLY	aquatic insect	zo
WATER-FOX	the carp	zo
WATER-GAS	illuminating gas	
WATER-GOD	Neptune	
WATER-HEN	moorhen	zo
WATER-ICE	a confection	
WATERING	diluting; irrigating	
WATERISH	insipid; moist; damp	
WATERLOG	saturate	
WATERMAN	ferryman; turncock	
WATER-POA	species of grass	bt
WATERPOT	watering can	
WATER-RAM	hydraulic ram	
WATER-RAT	water vole	zo
WATER-RUG	water spaniel	zo
WATER-TAP	spigot	
WATERWAY	a canal	
WATT-HOUR	measure of work	me
WATTLING	plaiting; hurdling	
WAVEBAND	group of wavelengths	
WAVEFORM	characteristic of radiowave	
WAVELESS	calm; undisturbed; serene	
WAVELIKE	undulating; rippling	
WAVE-LINE	stream-line	
WAVE-LOAF	a wave-offering	
WAVERING	tottering; vacillating	
WAVEROUS	fluctuating; unsteady	
WAVETAIL	fall in voltage of an unidirectional impulse	el
WAVE-TRAP	maritime hazard	
WAVETRAP	interference reducer for radios	el
WAVEWORN	of coastal rocks	
WAVINESS	unsteadiness	
WAVWISER	pedometer	
WAXCLOTH	oil-cloth	
WAXLIGHT	a taper	
WAX-PAPER	stencil paper	
WAX-PLANT	honeywort	bt
WAXWORKS	an exhibition	
WAY-BOARD	thin stratum	mn
WAYBREAD	common plaintain	bt
WAYFARER	traveller; pedestrian	
WAYGOING	departing	
WAYGOOSE	a printer's festivity	
WAYLAYER	interceptor; lurker	
WAYLEAVE	right of way	
WAYMAKER	a precursor	
WAY-SHAFT	an engine shaft	

WAYTHORN	buckthorn	bt
WAY-TRAIN	slow train	
WEAKENED	debilitated; enfeebled	
WEAKENER	enervator	
WEAK-EYED	needing glasses	
WEAKLING	delicate creature	
WEAKNESS	feebleness; frailty	
WEANLING	newly weaned	
WEAPONED	armed	
WEARABLE	fit to be worn	
WEARIFUL	wearisome; tedious	
WEARYING	tiring; fatiguing	
WEED-HOOK	garden tool	
WEEDLESS	well weeded	
WEEPHOLE	small drain hole for water	bd
WEEVILED	infested with weevils	zo
WEIGHAGE	a toll	
WEIGHING	balancing; pondering	
WEIGH-OUT	(horse racing)	
WEIGHTED	given due weight	
WEISSITE	iolite	mn
WELCOMED	greeted; hailed; saluted	
WELCOMER	polite host; receptionist	
WELDABLE	fusable	
WELD-IRON	wrought iron	
WELDMENT	welded assembly	eg
WELLADAY	alas; alackaday	
WELLAWAY	welladay	
WELL-BOAT	fishing boat	nt
WELL-BORN	of noble birth	
WELL-BRED	of good stock	
WELLCURB	ring of masonry	
WELLDECK	open-deck	nt
WELLDOER	a benefactor	
WELL-HEAD	source of a spring	
WELL-HOLE	(flight of stairs)	
WELL-KEPT	carefully tended	
WELL-KNIT	compact; sturdy	
WELLNIGH	nearly; almost	
WELL-READ	learned; scholarly	
WELL-SEEN	experienced; skilful	
WELLSIAN	(H. G.Wells)	
WELL-TO-DO	prosperous; affluent	
WELL-WORN	threadbare; shabby	
WELSHING	absconding	
WELSHMAN	a man of Wales	
WELTERED	wallowed; floundered	
WEREGILD	compensation for homicide	
WEREWOLF	a changeling	zo
WESLEYAN	(John Wesley)	rl
WESTERLY	in westward direction	
WESTWARD	toward the west	
WESTWORD	Wend of Carolingean, Romanesque church	ar, rl
WET-NURSE	breast-giver	
WET-ON-WET	short-interval spray-painting	
WHACKING	astounding; a beating	
WHALEMAN	Jonah	
WHALE-OIL	oil from blubber of whale	
WHANGHEE	bamboo cane	bt

WHANGING	whacking	
WHARFAGE	dock dues	
WHARFING	wharves	
WHATEVER	anything which	
WHEATEAR	fallowfinch	zo
WHEAT-EEL	a wheat disease	zo
WHEAT-FLY	a pest	zo
WHEEDLED	coaxed; cajoled; inveigled	
WHEEDLER	sycophant; fawner; toady	
WHEELAGE	a toll	
WHEELING	cycling; turning; twirling	
WHEELMAN	cyclist	
WHEEL-ORE	bournonite	mn
WHEEL-TAX	carriage tax	
WHEEZILY	asthmatically	
WHEEZING	breathing heavily	
WHELMING	overburdening; crushing	
WHELPING	littering	
WHENEVER	at any time that	
WHEREOUT	out of which	
WHEREVER	to whatever place	
WHETTING	sharpening	
WHEY-FACE	pale face	
WHIFFING	puffing	
WHIFFLER	prevaricator	
WHIGGERY	} Liberalism	
WHIGGISH		
WHIGGISM		
WHIMBREL	wimbrel; curlew	zo
WHIMSIES	notions; caprices; fancies	
WHIM-WHAM	a gadget	
WHINCHAT	singing bird	zo
WHINNIED	neighed	
WHINNOCK	a milk-pail	
WHINYARD	sword; dirk	
WHIPCORD	string; material	
WHIPHAND	advantage over; control	
WHIPLASH	crack of whip	
WHIPPING	lashing; castigating	
WHIPSTER	whippersnapper	
WHIPTAIL	slender tail	
WHIRLBAT	cestus	
WHIRLING	gyrating; rotating	
WHIRRING	spinning; twirling; turning	
WHISKERS	cats; minute single crystals	gl
WHISKERY	with whiskers, bristles	
WHISKING	brushing; seizing	
WHISTLED	piped	mu
WHISTLER	broken-winded horse	zo
WHITE-ANT	a termite	zo
WHITE-ARM	arme blanche	
WHITE-BOY	Irish white-shirt	
WHITE-HOT	hotter than red-hot	
WHITE-LIE	an evasion	
WHITE-MAN	a true and trusty man	
WHITENED	blanched	
WHITENER	bleacher	
WHITE-OUT	open space in display texts	
WHITE-OUT	polar blizzard when climber loses orientation of height, depth, etc.	mo

WHITEPOT	a confection	
WHITLING	sea trout; bull trout	zo
WHITSOUR	summer apple	bt
WHITSTER	a whitener	
WHITTLED	pared; cut; trimmed	
WHITTLER	reducer; trimmer (wood)	
WHITTRET	the weasel	zo
WHIZZING	speeding	
WHODUNIT	a crime novel	
WHOMEVER	whomsoever	
WHOOPING	yelling; hooting	
WHOPPING	beating; colossal	
WHURRING	pronounced word	
WICKEDLY	heinously; atrociously	
WICKERED	made of osiers	
WIDE-EYED	afraid; gullible	
WIDELINE	vertical mark in papermaking	pp
WIDENESS	breadth; width	
WIDENING	extending; broadening	
WIDOWING	bereaving	
WIELDING	brandishing; plying	
WIFEHOOD	wivehood	
WIFELESS	unmarried	
WIFELIKE	wifely	
WIG-BLOCK	wigmaker's block	
WIGGLING	wriggling	
WIGMAKER	perukist	
WILDBOAR	Richard III's badge; hog; swine	hd, zo
WILD-BORN	not born indoors	
WILD-DUCK	mallard and others	zo
WILDERED	bewildered (obs.)	
WILD-FIRE	sheet lightning	
WILD-FOWL	untamed birds	zo
WILD-LAND	uncultivated soil	
WILDNESS	savageness; recklessness	
WILD-WOOD	forest	
WILFULLY	obstately; deliberately	
WILINESS	craftiness; artfulness	
WILLIWAW	westerly blasting wind (Straits of Magellan)	mt
WILLOWED	full of willows	bt
WILLYARD	wilful; shy (Sc.)	
WIMBLING	boring	
WIMPLING	rippling	
WINCHMAN	windlass operator	
WIND BILL	guarantee	lw
WIND-BAND	instrumental ensemble	mu
WINDERED	} fanned, blown	
WINNOWED		
WINDFALL	fruit from trees; legacy	lw
WIND-GALL	puffy swelling	
WINDLASS	a winch; capstan	nl
WINDLESS	calm, still; winded (lungs)	
WINDMILL	wind-driven machine	
WINDOWED	fenestrated	
WINDPIPE	the access to lungs; trachea	

WIND-PUMP	small windmill	**nt**
WIND-RODE	anchored at sea, riding waves	**nt**
WIND-ROSE	a diagram of the compass	**nt**
WINDSAIL	ventilator; funnel	
WINDSCAB	snow surface crust; skiing	
WIND-SEED	carried by the wind	
WINDWARD	toward the wind, (course)	**nt**
WINE-CASK	barrel for wine	
WINELESS	undrunk; without wine	
WINE-RACK	wine bottle storage unit	
WINESKIN	bag for wine	
WINGBACK	half back (Amer. football)	
WING-CASE	horny cover of wing (beetles)	**zo**
WINGLESS	flightless bird; apterous	**zo**
WING-LOCK	wrestlers' hold	
WINGOVER	aerobatic, gliding manoeuvre	**ae**
WING-SHOT	threatening, flying shot	**nt**
WINNOWED	sifted	
WINNOWER	chaff remover	
WINTERED	hibernated	
WINTERLY	cheerless	
WIREDRAW	to make wire	
WIRE-HEEL	a foot disease	
WIRELESS	radio	
WIREMARK	horizontal mark in papermaking	**pp**
WIREROPE	tightrope; circus stay	
WIRESIDE	underside of paper	**pp**
WIRE-WORM	a centipede	**zo**
WIRE-WOVE	(glazed writing paper)	**pp**
WIRINESS	toughness	
WISEACRE	a simpleton	
WISELING	wiseacre	
WISERITE	manganese carbonate	**mn**
WISHBONE	merrythought; frame of racing cars; T formation (Amer. football)	
WISH-WASH	weak drink	
WISTARIA	a climbing plant	**bt**
WITCH-ELM	variety of elm tree	**bt**
WITCHERY	fascination; sorcery	
WITCHING	enchanting; charming	
WITHDRAW	retire; recall; retract	
WITHDREW	retreated; departed	
WITHERED	faded; shrunk; drooped	
WITHE-ROD	American shrub	**bt**
WITHHELD	kept back; detained	
WITHHOLD	restrain; reserve	
WITHWIND	bindweed	**bt**
WITTOLLY	complacently	
WIVEHOOD	wifehood	
WIVELESS	wifeless	
WIZARDLY	magically	
WIZARDRY	sorcery; necromancy	
WIZENING	withering	
WOAD-MILL	dye extracting mill	
WOBEGONE	woebegone; calamitous	

WOEFULLY	sorrowfully; tragically	
WOLF-FISH	catfish	**zo**
WOLF-SKIN	outer layer of wolf	
WOMANISH	effeminate	
WOMMERAH	stick for spear-throwing	
WONDERED	speculated; marvelled	
WONDERER	conjecturer; ponderer	
WONDROUS	marvellous; miraculous	
WONTLESS	unaccustomed; unused	
WOOD-ACID	acetic acid	**ch**
WOODBIND	} wild honeysuckle	**bt**
WOODBINE	}	
WOODBIRD	forest denizen	**zo**
WOODCHAT	shrike; woodpecker	**zo**
WOOD-COAL	charcoal; lignite	**mn**
WOODCOCK	bird allied to snipe	**zo**
WOOD-DOVE	stockdove	**zo**
WOOD-EVIL	cattle disease	**vt**
WOOD-HOLE	woodstore	
WOOD-IBIS	tantalus; stork	**zo**
WOOD-KERN	Irish outlaw	
WOODLAND	forest land	
WOODLARK	forest bird	**zo**
WOODLESS	treeless	
WOOD-LICE	wood-beetles	**zo**
WOOD-LILY	lily of the valley	**bt**
WOODLOCK	to stop	**nt**
WOOD-MITE	a beetle	**zo**
WOODMOTE	forest court	**lw**
WOODNOTE	bird call	
WOOD-OPAL	silicified wood	**mn**
WOOD-PULP	cellulose	
WOODROCK	asbestos	**mn**
WOODROOF	} a plant	**bt**
WOODRUFF	}	
WOOD-SEAR	} cuckoo-spit; an insect;	
WOOD-SEER	} a season	
WOOD-SERE	}	**zo**
WOOD-SHED	store for wood	
WOODSKIN	Guyana canoe	**nt**
WOODSMAN	a woodcutter	
WOOD-SOOT	charcoal soot	
WOOD-TICK	death-watch beetle	**zo**
WOOD-VINE	clematis	**bt**
WOODWALE	} golden oriole; green	
WOODWALL	} woodpecker	**zo**
WOODWARD	forest keeper	
WOODWIND	section of orchestra	**mu**
WOODWORK	carpentry	
WOOD-WORM	a grub	**zo**
WOOD-WREN	willow-warbler	**zo**
WOOINGLY	enticingly	
WOOLBALL	roll of yarn	
WOOLDING	binding	
WOOL-DYED	dyed in the wool	
WOOLFELL	skin with wool on it	
WOOL-MILL	cloth factory	
WOOLPACK	240 lb. of wool	
WOOLSACK	Lord Chancellor's seat	
WOOLWARD	wearing wool	

WOOLWORK	knitting, etc.
WORD-BOOK	a vocabulary
WORDLESS	silent; dumb; mute
WORD-PLAY	punning; repartee
WORKABLE	feasible
WORKADAY	prosaic; ordinary
WORKBOOK	duties of staff for the day
WORKCARD	report on work, defects, results
WORKFOLK	toilers
WORKGIRL	female employee
WORKMARK	title letter and catalogue number **pr**
WORKROOM	crafts workplace
WORKSHOP	tool workroom
WORM-BORE	damage by worms to books, furniture
WORMCAST	thrown by worms
WORMGEAR	gear wheels, etc.
WORM-HOLE	track of woodworm
WORMLIKE	vermicular **zo**
WORMSEED	santonica **bt**
WORMWOOD	absinthe; vermouth **bt**
WORRICOW	hobgoblin
WORRYING	harassing; fretting; chafing
WORSENED	deteriorated
WORSTING	besting; defeating
WORTHILY	deservedly; meritoriously
WORTHITE	silica compound **mn**
WOUNDILY	excessively; hurtful
WOUNDING	injuring
WRACKFUL	ruinous; destructive
WRACKING	gathering seaweed
WRANGLED	brawled; bickered
WRANGLER	disputant
WRANNOCK	the wren **zo**
WRAPPAGE	a wrapper
WRAPPING	enclosing; muffling
WRATHFUL	irate; incensed; wroth
WRATHILY	indignantly; furiously
WRAULING	caterwauling
WREAKFUL	revengeful; angry
WREAKING	inflicting; punishing
WREATHED	garlanded; festooned
WREATHEN	entwined
WRECKAGE	debris
WRECKFUL	causing ruin
WRECKING	sabotaging; destroying
WRENCHED	twisted; strained; wrung
WRESTING	extorting; forcing; usurped
WRESTLED	strove; grappled
WRESTLER	sturdy struggler
WRETCHED	miserable; paltry; sorry
WRICKING	spraining; straining
WRIGGLED	squirmed
WRIGGLER	shuffler
WRIGHTIA	tropical climber
WRINGING	twisting; squeezing
WRINKLED	furrowed; creased; rumpled
WRISTLET	wrist-band

WRIST-PIN	connecting pin of bracelet
WRITE-OFF	total loss
WRITHING	wriggling; squirming
WRITHLED	wrinkled
WRONGFUL	injurious; unjust; unfair
WRONGING	violating; maltreating
WRONGOUS	illegal (Sc.)
WURTZITE	sulphide of zinc **mn**

X

XANTHATE	a salt **ch**
XANTHEIN	yellow colour
XANTHENE	chemical dye
XANTHIAN	from Xanthus
XANTHINE	yellow dye
XANTHITE	yellow idocrase **mn**
XANTHIUM	a plant **bt**
XANTHOMA	skin disease **md**
XANTHOUS	yellowish
XANTHURA	American jay **zo**
XENOGAMY	cross-fertilization **bt**
XENOLITE	aluminium silicate **mn**
XENOPHYA	foreign particles **zo**
XENOTIME	yttrium phosphate **mn**
XENURINE	armadillo-like **zo**
XERANSIS	dryness **md**
XERANTIC	exsiccant **md**
XEROCOLE	animal living in dry place **ec**
XEROSERE	dry-land succession **bt**
XESTURGY	process of polishing
XILINOUS	of cotton
XIPHIOID	like a swordfish **zo**
XYLOCARP	hard woody fruit **bt**
XYLOIDIN	starch/nitric acid explosive
XYLONITE	form of celluloid
XYLOTYPE	wood engraving; print

Y

YACHTING	ice, ocean, or lake pastime
YAHOOING	howling and yelping
YAMMERED	lamented; whined
YANOLITE	axinite **mn**
YAPPEDGE	overlapping bookcover
YARDANGS	overhanging rock ridges (Central Asia) **gl**
YARDLAND	usually 30 acres (12 hectares) **mo**
YARDSMAN	scorer (Canadian football)
YARDWAND	yardstick **me**
YARWHELP	bar-tailed godwit **zo**
YATAGHAN	long Turkish dagger
YEANLING	eanling; a lamb **zo**
YEAR-BOOK	voluminous annual
YEARLING	one year old animal **zo**
YEARLONG	twelve months

YEARNFUL	mournful; distressing	
YEARNING	longing; craving; desirous	
YELDRING	} yowley; yorling;	
YELDROCK	} the yellow-bunting	**zo**
YELLOWED	dyed yellow	
YEOMANLY	sturdily; staunchly	
YEOMANRY	volunteer cavalry	
YESTREEN	last evening (Sc.)	
YIELDING	bearing; affording	
YODELLED	sang falsetto; (Swiss folkloric style)	
YOGEEISM	abstract meditation	
YOICKING	shouting encouragingly	
YOKELESS	unrestrained	
YOKEMATE	an associate; a partner	
YOKE-TOED	pair-toed	
YOKOHOMA	a breed of fowls	**zo**
YONDMOST	farthest; uttermost	
YOUNGEST	most youthful	
YOUNGISH	somewhat juvenile	
YOURSELF	reflexive pronoun	
YOUTHFUL	boyish; puerile; fresh	
YTTERBIA	oxide of ytterium	**ch**
YTTERITE	gadolinite	**mn**
YTTRIOUS	containing yttrium	**ch**
YUGOSLAV	Jugo-Slav	
YULETIDE	Christmas; Noel	**rl**

Z

ZALOPHUS	seal genus	**zo**
ZAMBOMBA	Spanish instrument	**mu**
ZAMINDAR	zemimdar; tax-collector	
ZAMPOGNO	Italian bagpipe	**mu**
ZANTIOTE	native of Zante	
ZARATITE	nickel compound	**mn**
ZARZUELA	Spanish operetta	**mu**
ZEALLESS	slack; apathetic	
ZEALOTRY	fanaticism; fervour; ardour	
ZECCHINO	sequin (Venice)	**nm**
ZEGIDINE	silver drinking cup (Hung.)	
ZELANIAN	(New Zealand)	
ZEMINDAR	Indian tax collector	
ZENITHAL	culminating; crowning	
ZEOLITIC	(felspar)	**mn**
ZEPPELIN	airship	
ZERUMBET	East Indian drug	**bt**
ZETICULA	a small room	
ZIBELINE	like a sable	**zo**
ZIGGURAT	Sumerian temple	

ZINCKIFY	cover with zinc	
ZINGIBER	ginger, etc.	**bt**
ZINNOBER	vermilion pigment	
ZIONWARD	heavenward	
ZIPHIOID	like a swordfish	**zo**
ZIRCONIA	zirconium oxide	**mn**
ZIZYPHUS	jujube tree	**bt**
ZOANTHUS	sea-anemone	**zo**
ZODIACAL	(zodiac)	**as**
ZOETROPE	early form of cinema	
ZOIATRIA	veterinary surgery	
ZOLOTNIK	Russian weight	**mo**
ZONATION	occurrence in bands	**bt**
ZONELESS	beltless	
ZOOBLAST	animal cell	**zo**
ZOOCHEMY	animal chemistry	**ch**
ZOOECIUM	wall/chamber of polyzoan individual	**zo**
ZOOGENIC	generative	
ZOOGLOEA	colony of bacteria	**md**
ZOOGRAFT	grafting tissue	**md**
ZOOLATER	animal worshipper	
ZOOLATRY	animal worship	
ZOOLITIC	(fossilized animals)	**mn**
ZOOMANCY	divination	**rl**
ZOOMETRY	animal mensuration	
ZOOMORPH	animal in decorative art	
ZOONITIC	articulated	**zo**
ZOONOMIA	animal physiology	
ZOOPHAGA	carnivorous animals	**zo**
ZOOPHILY	love of animals	
ZOOPHYTE	plantlike animal	**zo**
ZOOSCOPY	seeing snakes, etc.	**md**
ZOOSPERM	male seed-cell	**md**
ZOOSPORE	animated spore	**bt**
ZOOTOMIC	(vivisection)	**md**
ZOOT-SUIT	long coat and tight trousers	
ZOPFSTIL	pig-tail style (Ger.)	
ZOPILOTE	turkey-buzzard	**zo**
ZUCCHINI	green squash, marrow (It.)	**ck**
ZUGZWANG	compulsive move to disaster (chess)	
ZWIEBACK	biscuit rusk	**ck**
ZYGADITE	aluminium compound	**mn**
ZYGODONT	(molar teeth)	**md**
ZYGONEMA	zygotene phase of meiosis	**cy**
ZYGOTENE	2nd stage of meiotic prophase	**cy**
ZYMOLOGY	study of fermentation and enzymes	

GENERAL INFORMATION

A SWEEP AROUND THE WORLD IN MYTHOLOGY

Ass. Assyrian Fin. Finnish Jap. Japanese S. Am. South American Bab. Babylonian Ger. German
N.Am. North American Scan. Scandinavian C.Am. Central American Gr. Greek N.Z. New
Zealand Sem. Semitic Ch. Chinese Hung. Hungarian Pers. Persian Sum. Sumerian Eg. Egyptian
It. Italian Rom. Roman

2 Letters

AN ANU (Sum./Sem.) majestic supreme sky god & father of all the gods
AN (Brazil/Tupinamba Indian) the Soul
EA ENKI (Sem./Sum.) wise creator of mankind; see KINGU
EC (Siberia) Yemiseian high god who swallowed souls
EL (Sem.) the merciful, winged father of all the gods
FU HSING (Ch.) dispenser of happiness
GE GAEA/GAIA (Gr.) Mother Earth born of Chaos
HU (Ch.) deity of creative will; emperor/god of the North Sea
HU (Eg.) crew member, with SHIA, of the solar barque of RE
JE (Ch.) the Sun
LI (Ch.) the Earth
LU HSING (Ch.) dispenser of prosperity
MA Hittite/Hurrian HEBAT, goddess of war; (Rom. BELLONA)

NU NUN (Eg.) frog-headed male or female aquatic god, consort of NAUNET
NU & KUA (Ch.) incestuous couple whose relationship resulted in the human race
OT Mongolian Queen of fire
PO (Polynesia) the Void which gave birth to the world
RE RA/PHRA (Eg.) supreme celestial & solar god; creator; son of GEB (Earth) and NUT (Sky); see HAPI & MAAT
TU (Polynesia) chief warrior
UL (Oceania) lord of the moon and spirit of night
UO (C.Am.) trusted frog-mates of Mayan rain gods (CHACS)
VE (Norse) son of BOR & BESTLA; brother of ODIN; (Ger.) sacred places
YU (Ch.) horrible monster and great tamer of the flood

3 Letters

AIA (Sum.) see UTU
ANU (Sem.) see AN & ALALU & ANSHAR
ASK ASH/ASKR (Norse) forefather of man by his wife EMBLA; son of ODIN
AZI (Altaic) forest and mountain spirit
BAU GULA/NINKARRAK/NINURTA/NINGURSU (Sum.) gave the kiss of life to man; daughter of AN/ANU
BES BISU (Eg.) large-headed dwarf with bushy tail; god of recreation
BOR (Norse) father of ODIN by BESTLA
BEL (Sum.) see ENLIL
COU CUMHALL (Celtic) Gallic CAMULON, father of FINN
DIS Roman HADES, divinity of the Netherworld
DON DANU (Welsh/Irish) god of fertility & the forge; fiend of the Children of Darkness (LLYR); father of GWYDION
EOS (Gr.) the Dawn & mother of the winds ZEPHYRUS, NOTUS, BOREAS and HESPERUS (the evening star) & all stars, and PHAETHON by CEPHALUS; sister of HELIOS & SELENE; daughter of HYPERION & THEIA (Titans); (Rom. AURORA)

FAM (Africa/Bantu) an Adam, created by an invisible father; see NZAME
GEB KEB/SEB (Eg.) goose or male with head surmounted by a goose; earth god
HAP (Eg.) see HAPI
HEH NEHEH (Eg.) Infinity, Happiness & Long Life; husband of HEHET
HEL (Norse) Queen of Niflheim (nine worlds of Darkness); goddess of death and daughter of ODIN's rogue LOKI
HEP (Eg.) see HAPI
HOD (Norse) see HODER/HODUR
HSI (Ch.) human face with legs growing out of his head – no trunk or arms; son of LI (the Earth)
IAB (Samoyed) spirit of nature
IDA mountain on Crete & birthplace of ZEUS; Mt in Asia Minor near Troy; ancient Germanic temples
IFA (Nigeria/Yoruba) the Great Truth
ION (Gr.) forefather of the Ionian people; prince of Athens; son of CREUSA & APOLLO
ITI (Oceania) the Moon; see VATEA
KAL RUNDA/TUWATA Hittite hunting god
KEB (Eg.) see GEB

A SWEEP AROUND THE WORLD IN MYTHOLOGY

KEK (Eg.) deity of darkness married to KEKET

KUA see NU

KUL (Siberia/Ostyaks) genie that haunted big lakes & deep waters

KUN thousand li long whale monster transformed into yellow bear

KUU (Fin.) father of Kuutar; "moon" in Finnish

LER LIR Irish god of the sea; father of MANANNAN

LOA (Oceania/Marshall I.) creator of the world

LUA (Rom.) associated with Saturn, and plague & destruction

LUG LUGUS (Irish/Celtic) LAMFOTA, intellectual father of Ulster hero CU CHULAINN; as Welsh LLEU LLAW GYFFES, uncle of GWYDION and son of virgin ARANRHOD

MAH MAO (Pers.) moon god and assistant of VOHU MANAH

MEN Hittite/Hurrian mounted lunar god associated with ATTIS and Thracian SABAZIUS; (Pers. MAH/MAO)

MIN (Eg.) fertility & harvest god; patron of travellers; son of RE

MOT (Sem.) god of the Dead; son of EL; killed by BAAL (who was helped by his sister/wife ANATH/ANAT)

MUT (Eg.) sky goddess & wife of AMON-RE appearing as vulture, cow or lioness; adopted moon god KHONS

NIO (Jap.) Herculean spirits

NUM (Siberia) sky god, like TORUM and EC

NUT NUIT/NEUTH (Eg.) mother of OSIRIS, HORUS, SETH, NEPHTHYS, ISIS; goddess of the sky; (Gr. RHEA)

NYX (Gr.) see EREBUS

OPS Roman goddess of crops; wife of SATURN

ORO Tahitian deity who rules the Underworld

PAN (Gr.) musical herder; part man part goat; son of HERMES & PENELOPE

PAN (Africa) son of the Earth; god of the sky and cultivation

QAT (Siberia) spirits residing on high mountain tops

QAT (Australia/Melanesia) gave daylight & shaped trees, boulders, swine & humans

ROT Lappish deity of the Netherworld

SEB (Eg.) see GEB

SET (Eg.) see SETH

SHU (Eg.) god of light, air & supporter of the sky, unisexually created by RE; brother & husband of TEFNUT who bore him GEB and NUT

SHU (Ch.) god & emperor of the South Sea

SIA (Ass./Bab.) divinity of understanding & discernment

SIN NANNA (Bab./Sum.) moon god and Lord of the Second Cosmic Triad; see ISHTAR

SOL INDIGES, Rom. sun god (Gr. HELIOS)

TYR TIW (Norse) an AESIR and one-handed god whose other hand was severed by the hideous wolf FENRIR; (Rom. MARS); (Tuesday)

ULL (Norse) magician and patron of snowshoes

UNO (Hung.) female deer/heifer; ancestor of the Hungarians

UTU UTTU (Sum.) god of sun & justice with head of bison; son of NANNA/SIN & NINGAL; husband of SHENIRDA/AIA who produced SHAKAN, god of goats & wild steppe animals; see ISHTAR

YIN (Ch.) the Earth, moon being the essence of YIN

YUE (Ch.) the Moon and the lunar month

ZAM Persian earth spirit

4 Letters

ABUK (Africa) mother of AYWIL, founder of the Dinka religion

ACAT (C.Am.) god of life

ACIS (Gr.) see GALATEA

ADAD (Bab.) see HADAD

AGNI (India/Hindu) two-faced, many-tongued mouthpiece of the gods; god of fire & lightning; connected with RUDRA

AHTO AHTI (Fin.) chief water god

AJAX (Gr.) a) son of TELAMON & ruler of Salamis; b) son of OILEUS

AKKA (Fin.) see UKKO

AKNA (C.Am.) divinity of childbirth; wife of AKANCHOB

AMMA (Sudan) creator of the Earth; supreme god; father of the twins YURUGU and NONMO

AMON AMON-RE/AMEN/AMUN/AMANA/AMMON (Eg.) king of the gods and patron of the pharaohs; consort of MUT; father of adopted son KHONS; Ram

ANAT ANATH (Sem.) sister & wife of BAAL; see MOT

ANPU (Eg.) black jackal or male with jackal or dog's head; god of the Dead; son of RE (or OSIRIS)

ANUS Hittite king in Heaven who fought KUMARBIS

APEP (Eg.) see APEPI

APET (Eg.) see TAURT

APSU ABZU (Bab.) brought forth the gods; sweet water; consort of TIAMAT; see ANSHAR

ARES (Gr.) warrior god; see ENYO

ASIA (Africa) earth goddess; see also MAMALDI (Siberia); (Gr.) mother of ATLAS?

ATAR (Pers.) earth spirit

ATEA (Oceania/Marquesas I.) created Heaven & Earth; virile father and husband of ATANUA (Dawn)

ATEN ATON (Eg.) solar disc with rays ending in hands; an only god, associated with RE

ATUA (Polynesia) the gods

ATUM ATUM-RE/TEM/TUM (Eg.) male with head of mongoose (ichneumon); self-fertilizing creator god; the setting sun

AVIN (Oceania) see TORTALI

BAAL (Sem.) lord of the Earth & fertility god; won power as chief deity from YAMM; commissioned his divine craftsman KOTHAR to build superb palace for him; brother & husband of ANAT; see MOT

BAST SEKHMET (Eg.) cat or cat-headed woman; goddess of music & dance; wife of PTAH

BIAS (Gr.) brother of MELAMPUS, seer & descendant of AEOLUS (son of HELLEN)

BISU (Eg.) see BES

BOUS (Norse) son of ODIN & RINDA who killed the blind HODUR/HOD

BRAN (Celtic) see LLYR

BUNI (Siberia) chief of the Netherworld

BURI (Norse) grandfather of ODIN; see AUDUMLA

BUTO EDJO (Eg.) nurse of HORUS

CACA (Rom.) brother of CACUS

CAGN (Africa) omnipotent creator and chief Bushman deity whose abode is known only to antelopes; husband of COTI

CETO (Gr.) see PONTUS

CHAC (Yucatan/Maya) rain god; see UO

CHU-I (Ch.) patron of luck in examinations

CIMI (C.Am./Maya) Death

COTI (Africa) see CAGN

DANU Irish mother goddess; see DON

DENG (Africa) celestial creator & god of rain; ancestor of the Dinkas; son of AYWIL; see ABUK

DIVA DEVA/DEVONA (Celtic) divine Gallic rivers

DJOL (Samoyed) spirit of nature

DWYN DWYNWEN Welsh god of love; son of DAGDA

EDJO (Eg.) nurse of HORUS; see BUTO

ENKI EA (Sum./Sem.) divinity of liquid elements married to ARURU (NINTUE, NINMAKH); father of NINMA by ARURU and of UTTU (Spider) by his daughter NINDURRA; see ISHTAR & MARDUK

ENYO (Gr.) minor warrior associated with ARES

ERIS (Gr.) sister of ARES and daughter of Night; see LETHE

EROS (Gr.) god of love; son of Hermes & Aphrodite

ESUS (Celtic) last & least in Celtic triad

FINN (Celtic) see COU

FREA (Norse) see FRIGG

GAEA GAIA (Gr.) see GE and RHEA

GA-OH (N.Am./Iroquois) colossus ruling the winds

GARM GARMR (Norse) wolf destined to kill and be killed by TYR in Ragnarök; son of ODIN (or a giant)

GERD GERDR (Norse) daughter of the giant GYMIR; wife of FREYR; associated with the Netherworld

HAPI HAP/HEP (Eg.) bearded fertility god of the Nile; consort of NEKHBET (daughter of RE); as a bull, reincarnation of PTAH

HERA (Gr.) see ZEUS

HERO (Gr.) priestess of Aphrodite and beloved of LEANDER

HINA HINE (Polynesia) moon goddess and guardian of women; created by her husband TIKI; see TANE

HINO (N.Am./Iroquois) protector of the sky; thunder spirit

HIRO Tahitian chief of the Netherworld

IDUN (Norse) wife of divine poet BRAGI; keeper of apple trees for longevity; see AESIR

ILMA ILMARINEN (Fin.) weather god & creator of the Universe

INTI APU-PUNCHAU Inca sun god and ancestor of the Incas; brother & husband of moon MAMA-KILYA (-QUILLA)

INUA (Eskimo) master; SILAP INUA, master of the air

IRIS (Gr.) winged water-carrier for the gods; messenger & rainbow goddess

ISIS ASET/ESET (Eg.) Queen of the gods; wife of OSIRIS; mother of HORUS and great mother goddess

JORD FJORGYN (Norse) mother of THOR; beloved of ODIN; see AESIR

JUCK JUOK (Africa/Nile) supreme being; creator of all men on earth

JUNO (Rom.) deity of state & protectress of women (a female JUPITER)

KAPO (Hawaii) deity of fertility and abortion

A SWEEP AROUND THE WORLD IN MYTHOLOGY

LLEW (Irish/Celtic) see LUG/LUGUS

LLYR children of; father of MANAWYDAN (sea) (Irish LIR) (Irish MANANNAN) and BRAN (poetry) (Irish BENDIGEIDFRAN); his daughter BRANVEN badly treated by her husband MATLOLVCH, the sun god & king of Ireland; see DON

LOKI (Norse) bisexual tricky member of the AESIRs and son of the giant FARBAUTI; annoying and troublesome companion of ODIN & THOR; for causing the death of BALDR/BALDER he was bound to a rock; father of ANGRBODA (Anguish) and three evil offspring: HEL (Death), JORMUNGUND (evil serpent surrounding the world) & FENRIR (wolf); see HOENIR

LOTA (Tahiti) divine bird; (burbot fish)

LUNG (Ch.) dragon

MAAT MAYET (Eg.) patroness of law & order & counterweight on a divine scale to the hearts of the dead; daughter of RE; wife of THOTH

MAIA (Rom.) a female FAUNUS

MANA (Polynesia) all-penetrating dynamic force

MANU (India) ancestor of mankind; see SURYA

MARS MASPITER/MARSPITER/MAMAR/ MAVORS Rom. spirit of plants who grew to become god of war, subordinate only to JUPITER, receiving woodpeckers & wolves as sacrifice

MAUI (Polynesia) fished for the Earth and lifted up the Sky and made it his tutor; gave fire to mankind

MILK Altaic satans

MIRU (Polynesia) ruler of the Netherworld

MONT MENTU/MONTH-RE (Eg.) falcon (hawk) headed Theban war god of Upper Egypt; see BUKHE

NAGA Buddhist serpent deities

NIKE (Gr.) as ATHENA a portable, wingless owl, but as herself a winged goddess of victory & daughter of PALLAS (Giant) & STYX; (Rom. VICTORIA)

NINA fire god of the Incas

NUIT (Eg.) see NUT

ODIN WODAN/WODEN (Norse/Ger.) helped by his brothers VILI & VE he killed YMIR, first of all living beings & father of all giants; god of war living in Valhalla; made an Adam & Eve (ASKR & EMBLA) out of trees and lifted the earth from the sea; grandson of BURI & son of BOR by BESTLA; mistress GUNNIOD (like BESTLA a giant's daughter); see YMIR

OGMA OGMIOS (Irish/Celtic) close to Welsh GWYDION, son of DON (Sky)

OGUN (Africa/Nigeria) god of the Yoruba tribe

OPET (Eg.) see TAURT

PAHA (Fin.) bad spirit; "bad" in Finnish

PAPA (N.Z.) the Earth; see RINGI & VATEA

PTAH PHTHAH (Eg.) mummified maker of things, incl. the universe; god of fertility; patron of fine arts; husband of SEKHMET; father of NEFERTUM; see BAST & HAPI

PENG (Ch.) gigantic bird causing huge waves when rising from the sea

POIA (N.Am./Indian) son of young female SOATSAKI

P'O- (Ch.) Mrs Wind riding a tiger in the
P'O clouds; once male FENG PO

PURA (Oceania) originally sky god, later minor hero

QUAT (Polynesia) celestial deity

RAKI the Heaven in Polynesia and New Zealand

RAMA (India/Hindu) popular and a model of reason, with a devoted monkey HANUMAN; husband of SITA; half-brother of LAKSMANA and BHARATA (Bharata-varsha = India); as RAMACANDRA seventh incarnation of VISHNU

RHEA (Gr.) mother goddess (Phrygian CYBELE); daughter of URANUS & GAEA; sister and consort of CRONUS and mother of ZEUS; see NUT

RIGI (Polynesia) butterfly who separated the earth from the sea

RIGR (Norse) another name for HEIMDALL as father of three classes (bond-man, free citizen, royal) by three women

RITA (India) guardian of fire

ROHE (N.Z.) ruler of the middle world

RONA (N.Z./Maori) mother of TANE who ate the moon

SATI (India) wife of SIVA & daughter of DAKSA (Sage); places of pilgrimage sprung up where bits of her body, murdered by divine hands, fell; (Eg.) wife of KHNUM and sister of ANUKET

SETH SET/SETEKH/SETESH (Eg.) grey hound's body with long forked tail; rival of HORUS; brother or son of OSIRIS

SHEN (Ch.) gods

SHOU HSING (Ch.) patron of longevity

SIGI (Norse) formed the realm of Volsung; perhaps ODIN's son

SITA (India) see RAMA & HANUMAN

A SWEEP AROUND THE WORLD IN MYTHOLOGY

SIVA SHIVA (India) three-eyed ambiguous lord of Saiva sects; Vedic RUDRA (destruction), Agni (fire) & Prajapati (creator) absorbed by him; father of six-headed SKANDA & elephant-headed GANESA; bull NANDI was the mount for this half male, half female; husband of SATI; see BRAHMA

SOMA (India) earth & plant god; (Pers.) HAOMA

SPOR Slav deity guarding stables and fields

STYX (Gr.) hateful chthonian river & god; daughter of OCEANUS; mother of Victory, Force, Power & Rivalry; (Gulf of Corinth); see NIKE & TETHYS

T'AI-I (Ch.) took the place of SHANG TI as supreme god

TANE (Polynesia) coloured Heaven red and separated it from the Earth; mixed sand & clay to create HINA/HINE, an Eve, and then married her; creator of TIKI, messenger & guardian spirits; son of RONA

TARA (Himalayas/Mongolia) multi-eyed, multi-coloured Buddhist divinity dispensing relief from suffering and protecting travellers both on their earthly journeys and spiritual explorations

THAT (India/Hindu) the Absolute; Brahman

THOR THUNOR/DONAR (Norse/English/Ger.) red-bearded king of the gods travelling in a chariot drawn by goats; owner of magic hammer Mjöllnir; exterminator of giants; son of ODIN?; (Rom. JUPITER); see JORD

TIKI Polynesian protective spirits; see TANE & HINA

TILO (Mozambique) god of the sky, thunder & rain

TI-MU (Ch.) Earth Mother

T'U-TI (Ch.) gods of locality and an old couple

TYRO (Gr.) consort of CRETHEUS; mother of AESON; by POSEIDON mother of NELEUS & PELIAS (enemy of JASON); in love with ENIPEUS (river god); see JASON

UKKO (Fin.) sky god who supported the world and ruled the heavens; controlled rainfall & fertility; husband of AKKA/RAUNI

UMAI (Siberia/Orkhon) goddess of cradles and the hearth

UTTU (Sem.) see ENKI & UTU

VALI VELI/VILE (Norse) unkept son of ODIN waiting for his battle

VELA Lithuanian realm of the Dead

VELE Prussian aquatic and sylvan spirits

YAMA (India) red-eyed inventor of mortality astride a buffalo, with many-eyed dogs protecting his realm of the Dead; first of eight steps to full concentration, with him as judge; see SURYA

YAMM YAM (Sem.) hydra-like serpent ruler of the waters of the earth who was killed by BAAL

YANG (Ch.) Sky, and square (hence royal domain square); active masculine principles that permeate all being

YIMA (Pers.) son of the Sun; first man and father of the human race; accused by Zoroaster of causing the end of the golden age; replaced as first man by GAYOMART

YMIR AURGELMIR (Norse) first living being; father of all the giants, and dwarfs emanating from his corpse; great-grandfather of ODIN who killed him; see AUDUMLA

YOMI (Jap.) the Netherworld to which IZANAGI descended to look for his wife IZANAMI

ZEUS (Gr.) sky and weather god; "all things for all men"; avoided being swallowed by his father CRONUS; caught HERA disguised as a cuckoo

5 Letters

AEDON (Gr.) wife of ZETHUS (King of Thebes); daughter of Pandareos

AEGIR (Ger./Scan.) giant monster of the sea

AESIR (Norse) family of gods, enemies of the VANIR; together with BALDER, BRAZI/BRAGI, IDUN, JORD, HEIMDALL, LOKI, etc. the gods of battle ODIN, FRIGG, TYR, THOR inhabited ASGARD/VALHALLA, the top celestial abode

AESON (Gr.) son of TYRO and father of JASON; see ENIPEUS

AGAVE (Gr.) aunt of DIONYSUS; sister of SEMELE & mother of PENTHEUS

AHURA MAZDA/AURAMAZDA (Pers.) Zoroastrian creator of the universe and the twin spirits of evil and good fighting it out on Earth

ALALU Hurrian deity defeated by ANU (Sky) who descended to the Netherworld

AMANA (Eg.) see AMON

AMMON (Eg.) see AMON

A SWEEP AROUND THE WORLD IN MYTHOLOGY

ANATH ANAT (Sem.) sister & consort of BAAL whom she rescued from the Netherworld; goddess of war and patron of love who later merged with ASTARTE and was called Atargatis; see MOT

ANNWN (Celtic) the Netherworld; see PRYDERI

ANSUD (Sum.) NINURTA as a thunderbird

ARURU NINHURSAG/NINTUR etc. (Sum.) mother-goddess & deity of stony ground; wife of SHULPAE; mother of NINMU by ENKI and grandmother of NINDURRA

APEPI APEP/APOPHIS/REREK (Eg.) huge serpent; god of darkness & evil; enemy of RE

ARION (Gr.) swift horse, son of POSEIDON & DEMETER

ARTIO (Celtic/Helvetii) female bear

ASHUR ASSHUR (Ass.) Lord of the gods of Assyria and its capital Ashur; similar to ANSHAR (father of AN) or Sum. ENLIL

ASIAQ (Eskimo) protectress of the weather and the atmosphere

ATIRA (N.Am.) wife of TIRAWA

ATLAS (Gr.) a Titan condemned by ZEUS to support the pillars that separated Heaven & Earth; turned into a rocky mountain by PERSEUS; son of ISPETUS & nymph CLYMENE (or ASIA)

ATTIS ATTS (Gr.) Phrygian husband of CYBELE (Magna Mater) & son of NANA (river Sangarius) and twin-sexed AGDISTIS who killed him; solar divinity of the Roman Empire; see MEN & LYCUS

AYWIL (Africa) father of DENG

BALOR Irish divinity with an evil eye

BELUS (Gr.) king of Egypt; father of AEGYPTUS

BENNU (Eg.) heron-like sacred bird; soul of OSIRIS; (Gr. PHOENIX)

BINGO (Africa/Bantu) son of NZAME

BORVO BORMO/BORMANUS (Gallic) "boiling" god of thermal springs; wife DAMONA

BRAGI (Norse) like ODIN, a god of poetry; husband of IDUN

BRESS (Celtic) husband of BRIGIT/BRIDGET, pastoral poetic goddess

BUKHE (Eg.) bull sacred to MONT/MENTHU; (Gr. BUCHIS)

CACUS Roman cattle-thief and bandit who was killed by Hercules; son of fire god VULCAN and brother of CACA

CHONS (Eg.) see KHONS & MUT

CERES Roman goddess of crops associated with Gr. DEMETER

CH'UNG (Ch.) celestial administrator

CIAGA Nicaraguan water god, shared in creation

CREON (Gr.) father of Lycomedes; had many namesakes; sister of IOCASTE

CUNTI (India) mother of seven hundred thousand Buddhas

CUPID Roman arrow-shooting son of VENUS; roguish good spirit; (Gr. EROS)

DAGDA DAGDE/EOCHAID (Irish/Celtic) omnipotent father of OENGUS (Irish), DWYN (Welsh) and MORRIGAN, goddess of war; see DWYN & BRIGIT

DAITI (Pers.) river which flows from the centre of the world

DAKSA (India) see SATI

DATAN Polish divinity in charge of the welfare of fields

DEIVA Lithuanian werewolves

DELKA Lithuanian divine baby-minder

DIANA Roman huntress and helper of women; sister of APOLLO; (Gr. ARTEMIS)

DIEVS Baltic sky god

DIRCE (Gr.) wife of LYCUS; both were killed by ANTIOPE's twins (Amphion & Zethus) by ZEUS

DISIR (Ger.) female guardian spirits

DOMFE (Sudan) aquatic spirit

DONAR (Ger.) see THOR

DYAUS (India) Vedic father in the sky; (Gr. ZEUS/Rom. JUPITER)

DYLAN (Celtic) divinity of darkness and the sea; son of GWYDION and ARANRHOD

ECHUA (C.Am.) god of travellers

EGIME (Sum.) see NINMAKH

ELVES ALFAR (Ger./Scan.) water (wood & mountain) creatures

EMBLA (Norse) wife of ASK/ASH and thus mother of mankind

EMESU Hungarian queen

EMMA-O (Jap.) (Indian YAMA) King of Hell from which only the supplication of the living could release you; left the judgment of female souls to his sister

ENECH (Hung.) see HUNOR

ENLIL BEL (Sum.) god of sky & wind; second in the divine assembly of AN/ANU; husband of NINLIL, grain goddess; see ASHUR

A SWEEP AROUND THE WORLD IN MYTHOLOGY

EPONA AUGUSTA (Celtic/Rom.) mounted goddess connected with horses & donkeys; patroness of riders; see MACHA

ERLIK (Siberia/Altaic) father figure and an Adam; master of Death; sometimes in bird disguise

FAGUS Gallic divinity of the beech tree

FATUA (It.) see FAUNUS

FAUNA (It.) see FAUNUS

FAUNS (It.) see SATYRS

FLORA FERONIA Roman divinity of flowers

FREYR YNGRI (Norse/Swedish) a VANIR and son of NJORD and divine forefather of the Ynglingar kings of Sweden; bestower of fertility and guardian of crops; husband of GERD (daughter of giant GYMIR)

FRIGG FRIIA/FRIJA/FREA (Norse/Ger.) beloved wife of ODIN/WODAN; mother of BALDR/BALDER; (Friday)

FU-HSI (Ch.) deity with serpent's tail

GAMAB (Africa) vicious divinity

GANAS (India) attendants of SIVA; see GANESA

GARMR (Norse) see GARM

GAUNA (Africa/Bushmen) vicious divinity

GANGA GANGES (India) sacred river for the Hindus, 2506 km long; goddess

GYMIR (Norse) see GERD & FREYR

HADAD ADAD (Ass./Bab.) controlled rainfalls & tempest; withheld rains on orders of ENKI, causing famine

HADES PLUTO (Gr.) (TARTARUS) son of CRONUS & RHEA: King of the Netherworld with his queen Persephone; three-headed CERBERUS, guardian dog, stolen from him by HERCULES; allowed the Furies (Erinyes) to torment the wicked

HAKEA (Hawaii) chief of the Netherworld

HAOMA (Pers.) see SOMA

HALDI chief Urartian god depicted standing on a lion

HEBAT Hurrian Queen of gods and mother of SHARRUMA; stands on lion or lioness; see MA

HEHET (Eg.) see HEH

HEKET (Eg.) frog-headed goddess

HIISI (Fin.) vicious spirits

HODUR HODER/HOD (Norse) blind son of ODIN; see BOUS

HORON (Sem.) god of the Netherworld

HORUS HOR (Eg.) falcon-like sky god with solar & lunar vision; each Pharaoh a HORUS incarnate; brother (or nephew) of SETH/SET who murdered OSIRIS, his father; son of ISIS

HOU T'U (Ch.) supreme Earth

HSI-HO (Ch.) wife of TI CHUN/SHANG TI; gave birth to ten suns whom she polished by bathing them every morning

HUACA Incan mystic forces and guardian spirits

HUNOR ENECH (Hung.) horned forefather of the Hungarians

HYLAS (Gr.) a partner of HERACLES who was drowned by a naiad

INARI (Jap.) rice god

INDRA (India) storm, rain & sky god who gained mastery over the sun and killed the monsoon-preventing dragon VRTRA; chief thousand-eyed Vedic warlike god, rival of KRISHNA; husband of INDRANI; father of ARJUNA

INUAT (Eskimo) souls and spirits

IRENE EIRENE (Gr.) goddess of peace and one of the Horae (Seasons)

IXIOM (Gr) see CENTAURS

JANUS (Rom.) keeper of the universe and all beginnings who faced both the future and the past

JASON (Gr.) leader of the Argonauts in the quest for the Golden Fleece; see TYRO & ENIPEUS

JUMNA YAMUNA (India) river sacred to Hindus at its confluence with the Ganges

KALKI (India) giant with horse's head; AVATAR/VISHNU incarnation still to come

KALMA (Fin.) ruled over the graves with the spirits KALMANVAKI

KAMSA (India) see KRISHNA

KARMA (India) see SURYA

KAU-FU (Ch.) giant or composite animal; son of KUNG-KUNG (horned monster)

KEKET (Eg.) see KEK

KENOS (S.Am.) great forefather; an Adam

KHNUM KHNEMU (Eg.) elephantine lord of the cataracts and potter-god; shaped and gave life to his god models; husband of the sisters SATI (fertility) and ANUKET

KHONS (Eg.) moon god and adopted son of MUT and AMON-RE

KINGU (Sum.) husband of TIAMAT from whose blood ENKI/EA made Man; see MARDUK

KINTU (Mozambique) initially the only man on earth

KISIN (C.Am./Maya) helper of evil divinity USUKUN

KURKE Baltic divinity of the crops

A SWEEP AROUND THE WORLD IN MYTHOLOGY

KWOTH (Sudan) supreme god

LADON (Gr.) river god; father of the nymph who was the mother of EVANDER by HERMES

LAHAR (Sum.) god of cattle

LAHMU & LAHAMU (Sum.) divine couple who passed supreme power to MARDUK; see ANSHAR

LAIUS (Gr.) ruler of Thebes and father of OEDIPUS by IOCASTE/JOCASTA, sister of CREON

LARES (Rom.) household spirits; see PENATES

LAUME Baltic protective goddesses

LEMPO (Fin.) vicious spirit

LESKY Slav sylvan spirit and guardian of flocks & herds

LETHE (Gr.) river and spring of oblivion in the Netherworld; daughter of ERIS (Strife); sister MNEMONYME (Spring of Memory)

LIBER (It.) divinity of rural settlements, vines & fertility who, on his festival day LIBERARIA, presided over boys entering manhood

LINUS (Gr.) son of river god ISMENIUS; killed by HERACLES

LINUS (Gr.) son of APOLLO & Psamathe (daughter of ruler of Argos)

LODUR (Norse) fellow-traveller with ODIN, LOKI & HODUR on an unpopulated earth; gave warmth & colour of life to trees

LOTAN LEVIATHAN (Sem.) primeval serpent

LOUHI (Fin.) goddess in the land of the dead, MAAN-ALA (MANALA)

LUGUS LUG (Irish/Celtic) see ESUS & NUADU

LYCUS (Gr.) see DIRCE

MACHA MORRIGAN/BADB/NEMAIN (Celtic) three war goddesses: a) mother of twins and guardian of MACHA's fortress (Emain Macha/Ulster), b) wife of NEMHED, c) similar to Gallic EPONA (mare goddess)

MAIRA (Brazil) Indian paradise, a land with no evil

MAMAR (Rom.) see MARS

MAYET (Eg.) see MAAT & THOTH

MBOYA (Africa/Bantu) see NZAME

MEDEA (Gr.) murderous enchantress who helped JASON to overcome the obstacles to secure the Golden Fleece placed in their way by her father, king AEETES of Colchis; see AEGEUS

MIDAS (Gr.) gold-loving king of Phrygia to whom APOLLO gave ass's ears

MIMIR (Norse) giant wise water spirit of AESIR tribe; guardian of the fountain of knowledge (Mimisbrunnar); often consulted by ODIN whose eye lay in MIMIR's well; also a smith

MINOS (Gr.) lover of SCYLLA who drowned; enemy of the Athenians who killed his son Androgeus; son of ZEUS and EUROPA

MISCA Nicaraguan god of traders

MOGOR (Hung.) see HUNOR

MOIRA (Gr.) Fate that supersedes the gods

MOMUS (Gr.) symbol of guilt and son of Night

MONJU BOSATSU (Jap.) guide of all Buddhas; supreme wisdom

MUMMU (Sum.) male attendant of APSU

MUSUN (Samoyed) spirit of nature

NANDI (India) divine bull; mount of SIVA

NAKKI (Fin.) genie of the water

NANNA (Sum.) see SIN & ISHTAR

NEBTI (Eg.) vulture and cobra goddess

NEHEH see HEH

NEUTH see MUT

NIMMA (Sum.) see ENKI

NINMU (Sum.) see ARURU

NIOBE (Gr.) wife of AMPHION (Thebes) and sad mother of a dozen; see SIPYLON

NJORD (Norse) a VANIR and father of fertility deities FREYR & FREYJA

NUADU (Irish) came before LUG as King of the gods; fisherman

NUK-KUA (Ch.) deity with serpent's or dragon's tail (female)

NUSKU (Sum.) lunar god of fire & light who wards off the demons of night; shows himself when the Moon (SIN), his father, is new

NZAME (Africa/Bantu) invisible divinity who made FAM, an Adam; husband of MBOIA and father of BINGO

OMARA (Africa/Nile) descended from the sky and became the first man; grandfather of NYIKANG, ancestral god of the Shilluks tribe

OPHIS (Eg.) see OPHOIS

ORION (Gr.) son of POSEIDON by EURYALE, a Gorgon; given the power to walk on the sea by his father; mighty hunter who challenged ARTEMIS and was killed by her

PAIVA (Fin.) the sun and mother of Päivätär; "day" in Finnish

PALES (Rom.) rural festival spirits (Parilia)

PEMBA (Sudan) created all beasts & plants on earth and made the first woman; husband of MUSCO KORONI

A SWEEP AROUND THE WORLD IN MYTHOLOGY

PERUN PERKUNAS (Slav/Lithuanian) spirit of the sky governing lightning; Russian war god; see VARPULIS

PICUS (Rom.) woodpecker divinity of agriculture sacred to MARS; as myth. king, son of SATURN; father of FAUNUS and unwilling husband of sorceress CIRCE; grandfather of LATIMUS (king of the aborigines of Latium)

PINGA (Eskimo) protectress of game

PLUTO (Gr.) see HADES

PWYLL (Celtic) see PRYDERI

QUATO (C.Am./Aztec) has a remedy for headaches

RADHA (India) see KRISHNA

RAUNI (Fin.) see UKKO

RAVEN (N.Am./Indian) important hero associated with COYOTE & MINK

REMUS founder of Rome with his twin brother ROMULUS; later killed by him; adventurous sons of MARS and the vestal virgin RHEA SILVIA, daughter of the ruler NUMITOR whose brother AMULIUS wanted ROMULUS & REMUS drowned in the Tiber

REREX (Eg.) see APEPI

RERIR (Norse) seaside resident of NOATUN and husband of FREYJA; see VOLSUNG

RINDA RENDI (Norse) mother of BOUS who was raped by ODIN

RINGI (N.Z.) the Sky, in love with PAPA, the Earth

ROBUR Gallic divinity of the oak tree

RUDRA (India) destructive ancestor of SIVA, causing death & disease with his arrows; father of the storm gods MARUTS/RUDRAS

RUNDA (Hittite) see KAL

SAKTI (India) chief Hindu goddess and wife of SIVA

SEBEK SEBEQ/SEBEK-RE/SOBK-RE/SUCHOS (Eg.) crocodile or crocodile-headed man; protector of reptiles; son of NEITH/NEIT (goddess of war & the loom)

SEDMA (Eskimo) goddess of marine animals down below

SEKER SOKAR/SOKARIS (Eg.) hawk or hawk-headed mummy; god of Darkness and Decay

SHAIT (Eg.) goddess of destiny

SHEDU (Ass./Bab.) good demons

SHEOL Hebrew Hell

SHERI KHURRI, the bulls of the Hurrite storm-god TESHUP

SIBYL one of ten Roman female prophets

SILAP INUA (Eskimo) master of the air

SKADI (Norse) wife of NJORD after his defection to the AESIRS

SUANU (Africa) deity of sudden death

SURMA (Fin.) monster guarding the abode of KALMA; personification of Death

SURYA (India) important Hindu solar divinity and dissipator of Darkness who fathered the Aswin twins (heavenly horsemen), SURGIVA (ruler of monkeys), KARMA (fighter), YAMA (god of Death) and MANU (ancestor of mankind)

TAGES (Rom./Etruscan) self-appointed grandson of JUPITER who possessed magic and wisdom

TANIT (Sem.) see TIMMIT

TAURT APET/OPET/TAWERET/THOUERIS (Eg.) pregnant hippopotamus standing on his hind legs; deity of maternity & household

TELLA Hittite bull

TEPEU (C.Am./Maya) associated with powers of the sky

THEIA (Gr.) mother of SELENE

THOTH DJHOWTEY (Eg.) ibis-headed god of the moon & learning; created the languages and was the scribe of the gods; protector of ISIS; husband of MA'AT/MAYET; representative of RE on earth; (Gr. HERMES)

TORUM (Siberia) Ugrian sky god (like NUM & EC)

TUONI (Fin.) hellish river god and resident of TUONELA; husband of TUONETAR and father of LOVIATAR

TUPAN (S.Am.) spirit of lightning & thunder who rejects prayers

TYCHE (Gr.) winged goddess of chance & fortune; daughter of OCEANUS (or ZEUS) and TETHYS; (Rom. FORTUNA)

UMINA Ecuadoran divinity of medicine

VANIR (Norse) family of gods (NJORD, FREYR, FREIJA, etc.), enemies of the AESIR; associated with fertility & riches

VARUA (Polynesia) the spirits

VATEA (Oceania) perhaps father of PAPA; from his eyes emerged the Sun (TONGA) and the Moon (ITI)

VELNS Baltic/Teutonic devil

VENUS charming Roman goddess of gardens associated with Gr. APHRODITE; divine ancestor of the Roman Caesars through AENEAS (son of Aphrodite); beloved of ADONIS

A SWEEP AROUND THE WORLD IN MYTHOLOGY

VESTA Roman goddess of the hearth fire & patroness of bakers; her assistants, the six Vestal Virgins (priestesses)

VIDAR (Norse) son of ODIN who killed the monstrous wolf FENRIR

VOLKH VOLGA (Slav) werewolf; white bull with golden horns

VOLOS VYELYES (Slav) divinity of cattle

VRTRA (India) see INDRA

WEN-TI WEN CH'ANG (Ch.) god of literature

WODAN WODEN/WOTAN (Ger.) see ODIN; (Wednesday)

YAKSA (India) tree demon

YU-TZU (Ch.) rain maker with a magic sword

ZAMBA (Cameroon) god and creator, father of the Learned (N'KOKON), the Idiot (OTUKUT), the Gorilla (NGI) and the Chimpanzee (WO)

ZEMIS Haitian heroes and spirits

ZETES (Gr.) son of BOREAS, the North Wind

ZORYA (Slav) female triad of protectors of the whole universe

ZOSIM (Slav) patron of bee-keepers

6 Letters

ABNOBA Gallic goddess of hunting (Black Forest)

ADONIS (Gr.) beautiful lover of APHRODITE/VENUS (ATARGATIS/ASTARTE) and son of SMYRNA (MYRRHA) by her father THEIAS, ruler of Syria; claimed also by Persephone; originally associated with plant life and the Babylonian couple TAMMUZ & ISHTAR

AEGEUS (Gr.) King of Athens; like POSEIDON, claimant to fatherhood of THESEUS (Attic hero) by AETHRA from Argolis; husband of exorcist MEDEA of Colchis who tried to poison his son THESEUS

AEGINA (Gr.) see ASOPUS

AEOLUS (Gr.) wind god (Aeolian harp) who tried to help ODYSSEUS; eponymous ancestor of Aeolis; see BIAS, ALCYONE, MELAMPUS

AEROPE (Gr.) see ATREUS

AETHER (Gr.) see EREBUS

AETHRA (Gr.) suicidal mother of THESEUS and guardian & slave of HELEN; see AEGEUS

AGENOR (Gr.) see CADMUS & PERSES

AH-PUCH (C.Am./Maya) god of Death & the ninth hell; skeleton-like

ALALUS Hittite king in heaven

ALEYIN (Sem.) son of BAAL

ANANTA VASUKI (India) serpent; as "infinite" another name for VISHNU

ANSHAR (Bab.) supreme ruler of heaven above (an-), twin brother and husband of earth below (Ki-shar); both children of APSU (the waters around the earth) & TIAMAT (the sea) or their twins LAHMU & LAHAMI; each a parent of AN/ANU

ANUKET ANQET/ANQUET (Eg.) goddess of the Nile and the Cataracts; second wife of KHNUM; sister of SATI, his first wife

APOLLO (Gr. & Rom.) deity of light and later sun god; also associated with healing & prophecy & herds; see DIANA, ION, LINUS, MIDAS

ARAWAN (Gr.) see PRYDERI

ARJUNA (India) see INDRA

ASHMAN (Sum.) grain goddess

ASOPUS (Gr.) river god; husband of nymph MEROPE; father of AEGINA

ATABEI (Haiti) father of JOCA-HUVA, god in heaven

ATANUA (Oceania) see ATEA

ATHENA ATHENE (Gr.) unmarried & childless goddess of war; protectress of Athens and wise counsellor; see NIKE, CECROPS

ATREUS (Gr.) son of PELOPS of Mycenae & Hippodamia; father of Agamemnon & MENELAUS; his son Pleisthenes by AEROPE was killed by ATREUS' younger brother THYESTES, father of PELOPIA

ATUGAN Mongolian mother goddess

AUGEAS (Gr.) kept dirty stables; King of Elis

AURORA (Rom.) see EOS

AVATAR (India) bestial or human incarnation on earth of a god (VISHNU)

BACABS (Yucatan/Maya) four wind gods and brothers, placed by their supreme god at the four points of the compass to support the sky; patrons of bee-keepers

BAIAME DARAMULUN/NURUNDERA (E. Australia) father of all things and hero

BALDER (Norse) see BALDR

BANNIK (Slav) spirit of the baths

BENDIS (Gr.) divinity of the moon & war; Thracian associated with ARTEMIS

BESTLA (Norse) wife of BOR; see ODIN

BICUDO (Brazil/Indian) fish with beaklike jaw

BOREAS (Gr.) winged North Wind who kidnapped Oreithyia (daughter of the King of Athens) and had two sons by her, CALAIS & ZETES; see EOS

BRIGIT BRIGANTIA (Celtic) poetic goddess of arts & crafts (confused with DANU who had three namesakes, daughters of DAGDA; (Rom. MINERVA)

BRIXIA (Celtic) wife of LUXOVIUS

BRAHMA (India) Hindu four-faced creator god who emerged from a lotus of VISHNU's navel (or from a golden egg) to become part of the trinity after SIVA; identified with Vedic Prajapati (creator); married to SAVITRI and SARASVATI (or SATARUPA)

BROMIO (Gr.) DIONYSUS when roaring

CADMUS (Gr.) son of AGENOR (King of Tyre) who founded Thebes and married HARMONIA, and brought writing to Greece

CALAIS (Gr.) see BOREAS

CASIUS (Gr.) mountain abode of myth. Khazzi people; near Antioch/Antakya

CAUTES (Pers.) symbol of the rising sun; dawn

CH'ANG-O (Ch.) the Moon

CHASCA Inca male page to the Sun

CH'IH YU CHI-YOU (Ch.) monster with iron head

CHI-LIN (Ch.) friendly unicorn and, like the stork, herald of babies; patron of the saintly and wise

COCIJO (C.Am./Zapotec) rain god; (Maya CHAC)

CONSUS Italian deity of agriculture whose festival days spelt a holiday for horses & mules; colleague of OPS

COYOTE (N.Am.) greatest hero of N.Am. Indian tribes; clever trickster; see RAVEN

CREUSA (Gr.) see ION

CRONUS (Gr.) son of URANUS & GAIA and father of ZEUS; see RHEA & HADES

CURCHE (Baltic) see KURKE

CUYCHA Inca rainbow god

CYBELE CYBEBE Phrygian mother goddess; her husband ATTIS; later AGDISTIS, a monster

DAEMON DAIMON (Gr.) supernatural power

DAMONA (Gallic) wife of BORVO

DANAUS (Gr.) father of fifty murderous daughters & twin brother of AEGYPTUS; see AMYMONE

DAPHNE (Gr.) nymph of the mountain & beloved of Apollo; daughter of Thessalian river PENEUS

DEVANA a Czech DIANA

DOGODA (Slav) the West Wind

DUMUZI (Sum.) presided over fertility & regeneration in many forms; as Wild Bull, son of NINSUN; as shepherd, son of DUTTUR; as DUMUZI-ABZU, god of the marshland

EGERIA (Rom.) goddess of fountains & childbirth

EREBUS (Gr.) Darkness born of Chaos and incestuous brother of NYX (Night), fathering AETHER (Sky)

EUENUS (Gr.) river god; Idas of Messene challenged APOLLO for the hand of his daughter, MARPESSA

EUROPA (Gr.) beautiful daughter of PHOENIX or AGENOR (King of Phoenicia) mother of MINOS, SARPEDON and Rhadamanthus (Cyclades Islands); Cretan HELLOTIS

FAUNUS (It.) prophetic divinity of the countryside; father or husband of FAUNA/FATUA; (Gr. PAN); see MAIA, PICUS

FENG-PO (Ch.) releaser of winds from goatskin sack; transformed into female P'O-P'O

FENRIR (Norse) giant in disguise of wolf killed by VIDAR; see TYR

FREYJA (Norse) many-sided goddess with magic powers presiding over fertility, wealth, love & death; produced golden tears; wife of hammer-snatcher THRYM; daughter of NJORD

FYLGIA Germanic demonic creature (pl. FYLGJER)

GANESA (India) elephant-headed son of SIVA and PARVATI; ejects barriers

GARUDA (India) god and bird; mount of VISHNU

GAUNAB (Africa) Hottentot vicious demon

GEFION (Norse) fertility goddess & patroness of virgins whose sons were cloaked as oxen

GRAIAE (Gr.) the three grey sisters of the Gorgons with only one eye to share – taken from them by Perseus (DINO, ENYO, PEMPHREDO)

GRI-GRI (Sudan) clan spirit

GURUHI (Africa) vicious god able to poison humans

A SWEEP AROUND THE WORLD IN MYTHOLOGY

HAEMUS (Gr.) one of the mountain abodes (Thrace) of the hundred-headed monster TYPHON, son of TARTARUS & GAIA

HARITI KISHI-MOJIN (Jap.) Buddha changed her from child-eating monster to protectress of children; female counterpart of KAN-NON

HATHOR ATHYR (Eg.) mother goddess with cow's horns in attendance at the birth of a pharaoh; associated with festivity & love; daughter of NUT (Sky) and RE; linked with Aphrodite, ARTEMIS, DIANA, JUNO and Sem. ASTARTE

HECATE (Gr.) Carian divinity of fertility & witchcraft; daughter of PERSES (Titan) & ASTERIA (nymph); promoter of wealth & influential over heaven, earth and the sea; famous for her pillars (Hecataea) and protection of doorways & crossroads; see SCYLLA

HELIOS (Gr.) the Sun god who sailed to Rhodes in a crescent moon bowl where he mated with the nymph RHODAS and became the ancestor of the Rhodosians; see EOS

HELLEN (Gr.) ancestor of all the Greeks (named after his sons AEOLUS & DORUS, and grandsons ION & ACHAEUS); King of Phthia and grandson of PROMETHEUS

HEPATU Hittite Queen of gods standing on a panther; Hurrian HEBAT

HERMES (Gr.) bearded messenger and fertility god from Arcadia, linked with the Cabeiri and Roman MERCURY; see PAN & EROS

HOENIR (Norse) fellow-traveller with ODIN, LOKI and LODUR who gave a soul to the trees

HOLEYS (Africa) rulers of the soil

HUN-TUN (Ch.) Chaos, depicted as long-haired dog

ICARUS (Gr.) flew too high on homemade wings and drowned near Icaria island; son of DAEDALUS, sculptor and architect (Labyrinth/Crete)

IKTOMA (N.Am./Sioux) invisible being who formed the world

INANNA (Sum.) goddess of the Netherworld

INTOTA (N.Am.) Sun god

IOLAUS (Gr.) helped his labouring uncle HERACLES with the killing of the Hydra; son of IPHICLES (mortal half-brother of HERACLES)

ISHTAR (Ass./Bab.) (Sum. INANNA/Sem. ASTARTE) Queen of Heaven, daughter of the moon god SIN/NANNA and sister of the sun god SHAMASH/UTU (or daughter of ENKI by URUK/ERECH); see ADONIS

ITZANA (N.Am.) the Great God of the Lacandones Indians

IXCHEL (N.Am.) moon goddess and vicious woman

JUMALA (Fin.) ancestor of UKKO; "god" in Finnish

KAN-NON (Jap.) protective deity

KAUKIS Baltic dwarfs and guardians of homes

KEELUT (Eskimo) dog-like vicious earth demon

KHENSU (Eg.) see KHONS

KHEPAT Hurrian wife of TESHUP

KHEPER KHEPERA/KHEPRI (Eg.) sun-pushing scarab or man with a scarab on his head; the rising sun; RE

KHNEMU (Eg.) see KHNUM

KHONSU (Eg.) see KHONS

KHURRI (Hurrian) see SHERI

KOSHAR KOTHAR (Bab.) divinity of arts & crafts; palace-builder to BAAL

KRICCO (Slav) guardian of orchards

KRIMBA Bohemian house divinity

KUBABA Hittite CYBELE

KUPALA (Slav) associated with herbs & trees

KVASIR (Norse) divine sage murdered by midgets who made mead out of his blood

LAKSMI SRI (India) wife of VISHNU

LOTHIA (Fiji) ruler of the Netherworld

LYCAON (Gr.) Mountain and king of Arcadia whose family was turned into wolves by ZEUS

MANALA TUONELA/POHJOLA (Fin.) home of LOUHI, goddess of the dead – like TUONELA of TUONI; entered over bridge or by boat

MANNUS (Ger.) hermaphrodite Adam of three Germanic peoples; son of the giant TUISTO

MARAWA (Australia) strong, forceful spirit

MARDUK (Ass./Bab.) supreme creator god of Babylonia with many names; slayer of the sea monster TIAMAT and her husband KINGU; eldest son of EA/ENKI; married to ZARBANIT/ZARPANIT; see LAHMU

MARICI MARISHI-TEN Buddhist and Tibetan three-headed sunrise god

MARUTS RUDRAS (India) young storm gods of the clouds; rain-givers

MASAYA Nicaraguan lord of volcanoes

MAVORS (Rom.) see MARS

MEGARA (Gr.) wife of HERACLES

MEIDEN Baltic hare god

MENTHU (Eg.) see MONT & BUKHE

MERWER (Eg.) bull sacred to Ra-Atum; (Gr. MNEVIS)

METION (Gr.) see DAEDALUS

MEULER (Chile) god of waterspout (and whirlwinds & typhoons)

MINEPA (Mozambique) evil spirit

MITHRA (Pers.) Creator who killed the bull from whose blood life sprang; trusted helper of AHURA MAZDA; bestower of rain and patron god of the Roman army; sun god; see RASHNU

MITNAL (Yucatan) the Netherworld

MNEVIS (Eg.) see MERWER

MOKADI (Cameroon) a spirit

MOKOSH (Slav) divinity of domesticated animals

MOTRES MATRONAE (Gaul) Mother Goddess

MULUKU (Mozambique) the highest being

MYRRHA (Gr.) see ADONIS

NABAEO (Oceania) both good and bad demons

NAREAU (Oceania/Gilbert I.) maker of Heaven & Earth

NAUMET (Eg.) see NU

NANSHE (Ass./Bab.) goddess of springs & canals; daughter of ENKI/EA

NELEUS (Gr.) see TYRO

NEMAIN (Celtic) see MACHA

NEMHED (Celtic) see MACHA

NEREUS (Gr.) old Aegean sea god, son of PONTUS; father of the sea nymphs NEREIDS

NERGAL (Sum.) together with his consort ALLATUM he ruled the Kingdom of the Dead whom he could recall to life

NGAHUE (N.Z.) highest god

NIKKAL NINGAL (Sem./Sum.) moon goddess married to moon god YARIKH; see UTU

NINHAR NINGUBLA (Sum.) rain & weather god and roaring bull responsible for the greening of the desert; son of NANNA & NINGAL (or ENKI & NINHURSAG); husband of the dairy queen NINIGARA

NINIGI (Jap.) divine ancestor of the emperors of Japan whose grandmother was Amaterasu (sun goddess); her gifts, the jewel, mirror and sword, are Imperial emblems

NINLIL EGITUMMAL/SUD (Sum.) corn goddess and spouse of ENLIL; daughter of Haia (Stores) and Ninshebargunu (Barley)

NINMAR (Sum.) bird goddess and daughter of NANSHE; granddaughter of ENKI

NINSUN (Sum.) mother figure whose offspring was the wild bull DUMZI; wife of Lugalbanda; often appears as a cow

NINTUR (Sum.) see ARURU

NOATUN (Norse) see RERIR

NOMIOS (Gr.) APOLLO as lord of herdsmen

NYAMIA (Guinea) highest god; see KAK-GUIA

OENEUS (Gr.) King of Calydon; see ALTHAEA & DEIANIRA

OENGUS (Irish) son of DAGDA; an Irish EROS

OGMIOS (Celtic) see OGMA

OILEUS (Gr.) see AJAX

OLOFAD (Micronesia) went up to Heaven and divides his time between it and the Earth

ONATHA (N.Am.) deity of wheat and daughter of the Earth (Eithinoha)

OPHOIS OPHIS/UPUAUT (Eg.) wolf or jackal-headed warrior god associated with OSIRIS

ORENDA (N.Am./Iroquois) divine force and vigour in Nature

ORMAZD OHRMAZD (Pers.) omnipotent first man who sprang from ZURVAN

OSIRIS USIRE (Eg.) father of HORUS, supreme god and ruler of the Dead; son of NUT & GEB; see ISIS & BENNU

PADURI (Siberia/Altaic) lord of the reindeer

PALLAS (Gr.) four namesakes: a) son of EVANDER; b) a giant killed by ATHENE; c) a Titan; d) Attic idol, brother of AEGEUS; (Pallantids, his sons)

PANDIA (Gr.) see SELENE

PELEUS (Gr.) see ERIS

PELIAS (Gr.) see TYRO & ALCESTIS

PELOPS (Gr.) son of TANTALUS whom Poseidon befriended; uncle of Agamemnon

PERSES (Gr.) son of PERSEUS (King of Argos) & Andromeda; perhaps myth. founder of Persia

PHANES (Gr.) first divinity, born from an egg; married Night and begat Heaven & Earth

PHOEBE (Gr.) bright titaness & daughter of URANUS & GAIA; mother of LETO; associated with the moon

PILLAN (Chile/Araucanians) thunderbolt

A SWEEP AROUND THE WORLD IN MYTHOLOGY

PLUTUS (Gr.) wealthy son of DEMETER & the Titan IASION

POMONA Roman divinity of orchards

PONTUS (Gr.) most ancient divine embodiment of the sea (Black Sea) and waters; incestuous son of GAIA; father of NEREUS, EURYBIA, THAUMAS, PHORCYS and CETO

PURUSA (India) primal man from whose body the universe emerged

RAGANA Lithuanian werewolves

RASHNU (Pers.) one of a trio of judges (Mithra, Sraosha) deciding the fates of the souls of the deceased

RESHEF (Eg.) god of war with head of gazelle

RHODAS (Gr.) see HELIOS

RUDRAS (India) storm gods; see RUDRA & MARUTS

SABK-RE (Eg.) see SEBEK

SATURN SATURNUS Roman grain god and patron of sowing; colleague of OPS and CONSUS; (Gr. CRONUS); see LUA & PICUS

SATYRS (Gr.) creatures of the wild, part man, part goat; male counterparts of nymphs; (It. FAUNS)

SCYLLA (Gr.) six-headed sea monster with twelve legs, lived in a cave opposite Charybdis and snatched seamen like an octopus; daughter of HECATE; see MINOS

SEKHET SEKHMET/SAKHMIS (Eg.) lioness or woman with head of a lion; goddess of war; wife of PTAH, creator of the Universe

SEKUME (Africa) came second after FAM (the first man) and made his wife, MBONGWE, from a tree

SELENE (Gr.) moon goddess whom PAN lured into the forest with white fleece; wife of ZEUS; mother of PANDIA; daughter of HYPERION & THEIA (Titans); sister/daughter of HELIOS & EOS; (Rom. LUNA)

SEMELE (Gr.) see AGAVE

SETEKH SETESH (Eg.) see SETH

SHAKAN (Sum.) see UTU

SHE-CHI (Ch.) grain and oil deities

SILENIA (Gr.) like the SATYRS part man, part beast (horse) and associated with DIONYSUS

SIRENS (Gr.) birds with faces of beautiful women; spurned by the Argonauts; see ACHELOUS

SKANDA (India) see SIVA

SMYRNA (Gr.) see ADONIS; modern town of Izmir

SPHINX (Eg.) body of lion (or ram or goat), head of man; representation of royalty in Egypt

SRAOSH (Pers.) together with RASHNU & MITHRA a judge over the fates of the dead

SUCHOS (Eg.) see SEBEK

SVAROG (Slav) god of the sky; father of Svarogich, a fire god

TAATOA (Oceania/Society I.) made the earth and the sea

TAKARO (New Hebrides) he organized cosmos

TAMMUZ TAMMUZI (Sum.) forerunner of DUMUZI; pastoral grain god & shepherd with a large following; son of ENKI & DUTTUR; husband of INANNA/ISHTAR; see ADONIS

TARHUN TARHUND (Hittite) see TELEPINU & WURUSEMU

TAWALS Polish divinity in charge of the welfare of fields

TEFNUT TEFNET (Eg.) lioness or lion-headed woman with solar disc; deity of dew & moisture; sister and wife of SHU

TELLUS Roman earth divinity receiving pregnant cow as sacrifice

TENGRI (Siberia) both good and bad demons

TESHUB TESHUP Hittite weather god victorious over KUMARBI; see SHERI

TETHYS (Gr.) incestuous mother of the Oceanids & STYX; sister & wife of OCEANUS; daughter of URANUS & GAIA; see TYCHE

THEIAS (Gr.) see ADONIS

THEMIS (Gr.) consort of ZEUS; mother of the Seasons & the Fates; daughter of GAIA; prophetess

TIAMAT (Sum.) primeval salt water & sea who gave birth to the gods; wife and mother of KINGU (or APSU); killed by MARDUK

T'IEN-MU (Ch.) goddess of lightning with blazing mirrors

TINNIT TANIT/TINITH/TINT Carthagean chief goddess of fertility; consort of BAAL HAMMON; (Sem. ASTARTE)

TIRAWA (N.Am.) the Great Chief who at first lived in Heaven; husband of ATIRA

TITYUS (Gr.) son of GAIA by a giant; tried to assail LETO and was killed by her children APOLLO & ARTEMIS (or ZEUS); ended as a square meal of liver for vultures

TLALOC (C.Am./Aztec) god of rain, thunder & lightning

TODOTE Samoyed divinity of Death and illwill

A SWEEP AROUND THE WORLD IN MYTHOLOGY

TORANN (Irish) Thunder; (Gallo-Roman TORANIS/TARASUS)

TRITON (Gr.) half human, half fish merman; son of POSEIDON & Amphitrite

TUISTO (Ger.) giant father of MANNUS, the hermaphrodite first man

TUNGAT TUMRAT (Eskimo) spirits of locality

TUWATA (Hittite) see KAL

TYDEUS (Gr.) brain-eater & brother of Melanippus; father of DIOMEDES

TYPHON (Gr.) hundred-headed winged monster, half man, half serpent, with thunderous voice who threw ZEUS (later rescued by HERMES & PAN) into a cave in Cilicia; fled to Sicily and was crushed under Mt Etna by ZEUS; son of GAIA & TARTARUS; husband of ECHIDNA; see HAEMUS

URANUS (Gr.) god of an incestuous heaven; made his chaotic wife and mother GAIA fertile with rain; she gave birth to the Titans, Ceclopes and hundred-handed Hecatoncheires; attacked and overthrown by his son CRONUS; the giants and ash-tree nymphs arose from the blood of URANUS' testicles, and from the genital foam in the sea came Aphrodite, goddess of love; see RHEA & PHOEBE

USUKUN (C.Am./Maya) hater of humans & brother of HAPIKERN

VAHRAM (Pers.) bull, white horse, camel, ram, bird, wild goat; also youth and a warrior

VARUNA (India) Sky, one supreme being

VASUKI (India) see ANANTA

VISHNU (India) Hindu guardian of the world known through RAMA, KRISHNA and other incarnations (avatars); renewer of moral order; husband of LAKSMI/SRI and Bhumidevi; see ANANTA & GARUDA

VULCAN Roman god of fire and volcanic eruptions who liked fresh fish from Tiber; (Gr. HEPHAESTUS); see CACUS

VU-NUNA (Ugric/Votyak) water deity

VU-VOLO (Ugric/Votyak) water deity

XOLOTL (C.Am./Aztec) dog-headed god who created present mankind out of bloodied dried bones; twin of chief deity the Feathered Snake (Quetzalcoatl)

YANTHO (C.Am./Maya) brother of USUKUN & HAPIKERN

YARIKH (Sem.) see NIKKAL

YARILO (Slav) deity of love and happiness

YASODA (India) mother of KRISHNA by adoption

ZETHUS (Gr.) see AEDON & DIRCE

7 Letters

ABELLIO Gallic divinity of the apple tree

ACHERON (Gr.) river of Woe in HADES near Epirus

ADMETUS (Gr.) son of PHERES of Pherae and husband of ALCESTIS

AHRIMAN (Pers.) evil spirit; see GAYOMART

ALCYONE (Gr.) daughter of AEOLUS, god of the winds

ALLATUM (Sum.) see NERGAL

ALPHEUS (Gr.) river god and lover of nymph ARETHUSA

ALTHAEA (Gr.) mother of MELEAGER & wife of OENEUS, King of Calydon

AMPHION (Gr.) see DIRCE

AMYMONE (Gr.) fountain & spring; mother of NAUPLIUS by POSEIDON; one of fifty murderous daughters of DANAUS

ANDARTA ANDRASTA (Celtic) warrior goddess

ANULIUS (Gr.) see REMUS

APOPHIS APEPI/APEP/REREK (Eg.) reptile-like creature of Darkness and Evil, forever an enemy of RE

ARIADNE (Gr.) as thread-spinning spider led THESEUS out of the Labyrinth; daughter of King MINOS of Crete by PASIPHAE; wife of DIONYSUS on Naxos; see MINOTAUR

ASTARTE (Sem.) great goddess of fertility associated with ISHTAR/ATHTAR, ARTEMIS, DIANA, JUNO & Aphrodite, and also Hebrew ASHTORETH, and Atargatis; see ANATH and ADONIS

ASTERIA (Gr.) see HECATE

ATAKSAK (Eskimo) joyful spirit living in Heaven

ATHIRAT Semitic mother of the gods

AUDUMLA (Norse) cow and wet-nurse (made of molten hoar frost) of the giant AURGELMIR's (YMIR's) six-headed son; she formed BURI (grandfather of ODIN and his brothers who later killed Aurgelmir) by passing her tongue over stones; created the sky and the earth from his corpse

A SWEEP AROUND THE WORLD IN MYTHOLOGY

AUGUSTA (Celtic/Rom.) see EPONA

AUMANIL (Eskimo) land-based guide of whales

BACCHUS Roman wine god; (It. LIBER) (Gr. DIONYSUS)

BALANZA (Africa) lord of the trees

BANADED (Eg.) ram, incarnation of the soul of OSIRIS; (Gr. MENDES)

BELENUS (Celtic) connected with the sun & fire; widely revered pastoral god; (Gr. APOLLO)

BELLONA DUELLONA Roman goddess of war; perhaps sister or wife of MARS; see MA

BHARATA (India) see RAMA

BOCHICA (Colombia/Chibacha) creative divinity

BRANVEN (Welsh) see LLYR

BRIDGET (Celtic) see BRESS & BRIGIT

BUXENUS Gallic divinity of the box-tree

CABEIRI (Gr.) major divinities of Samothrace

CAMENAE (Rom.) goddess of sacred spring; power of prophecy

CAMILLA (Rom.) huntress taught by her father METABUS; warrior and friend of DIANA

CAMULON (Celtic) see COU

CECROPS (Gr.) cultured, dragon-like arbitrator between ATHENA & POSEIDON and first King of Attica

CHU-LUNG CHU-YING (Ch.) reptile with human face whose eyes when open brought daylight and, when shut, made night fall, and whose changing breath brought on the seasons

CLOELIA Roman virgin and hostage of Lars Porsena (Etruscan king)

COCYTUS (Gr.) tributary of ACHERON (NW Gr.) & one of the rivers of HADES

CORONIS (Gr.) mother of Asclepius (god of healing) who was shot by ARTEMIS

CUMHALL (Celtic) see COU

CURETES (Gr.) young protectors of the baby ZEUS

CYLLENE (Gr.) sacred mountain in Arcadia where HERMES was born in a cave to ZEUS & MAIA

DAPHNIS (Gr.) shepherd son of HERMES and a nymph from Sicily; in love with the nymph ECHENAIS

DAZBORG DAZHBOG Russian sun god

DEMETER (Gr.) great earth goddess of the Eleusinian Mysteries; mother of KORE/Persephone; see ARION & PLUTUS

DIIWICA Serbian DIANA

DOMOVOI (Slav) hairy spirit of the house in human shape, sometimes with horn & tail; silky fur even on palms of hands

DWYNWEN (Welsh) see DWYN

ECHIDNA (Gr.) half woman, half snake; wife of TYPHON; mother of CERBERUS, the Hydra, the CHIMAERA & the Nemean lion

EK-CHUAH (C.Am./Maya) divine patron of cacao growers & traders; also connected with war and death

EMAKONG (Australia) a traveller in the Netherworld of ophidian men who took back fire and the night

ENIPEUS (Gr.) river god of Elis; loved by TYRO; mother of AESON

ERIGONE (Gr.) suicidal daughter of the Athenian ICARIUS

EURYALE (Gr.) see ORION

EURYBIA (Gr.) see PONTUS

EVANDER (Gr.) son of HERMES and a daughter (nymph) of the river god LADON; associated with PAN; see PALLAS

FERONIA Roman/Etruscan divinity of springs and fertility

FJORGYN (Norse) see JORD

FORTUNA Roman TYCHE (Gr.)

FU-HSING (Ch.) see FU

FYLGJUR female Germanic protective spirit

GALATEA (Gr.) sea nymph who preferred ACIS (son of FAUNUS) to large one-eyed Polyphemus

GLAUCUS (Gr.) a) son of King MINOS by PASIPHAE & brother of ARIADNE; b) sea god, son of POSEIDON

GOIBNIU Irish smith; (Welsh GOFANNON)

GRANNUS (Celtic) associated with healing

GUMONGO (N.Am./Guacure Indians) rules the northern half of the sky

GUNNIOD (Norse) see ODIN

GWYDION (Welsh) cultured son of the sky god DON and brother & husband of ARANRHOD (Fertility); father of the twins DYLAN (Sea) and LLEU (Irish LUG) for whom he made a wife out of flowers

HANUMAN (India/Jap.) red-faced monkey in human shape, born of the wind and a nymph; adventurous – on solo flight to the Himalayas to collect healing herbs; giant jumper across to Ceylon, or clever spy to retrieve RAMA's wife SITA from the clutches of the demon RAVANA

A SWEEP AROUND THE WORLD IN MYTHOLOGY

HARPIES (Gr.) supernatural winged beings

HELICON (Gr.) highest mountain in Boeotia (Gulf of Corinth); favoured place of the Muses where PEGASUS gave them a fountain by stamping with his hoof

HIPPIOS (Gr.) POSEIDON when associated with horses

HUNAB-KU (C.Am./Maya) father of ITZAMNA

HURAKAN (C.Am./Maya) divinity of thunder and tornado

IACCHUS (Gr.) son of ZEUS & DEMETER (or DIONYSUS & KORE/Persephone) welcomed at the Eleusinian Mysteries

IAPETUS (Gr.) a Titan and son of URANUS & GAIA; father of ATLAS, Prometheus, Epimetheus and Menoetius

ICARIUS (Gr.) host to DIONYSUS, murdered by his friends; husband of PERIBOCA; father of ERIGONE

INDRANI (India) see INDRA

INTONAN (C.Am./Aztec) Earth goddess

IOCASTE JOCASTA (Gr.) see LAIUS, OEDIPUS

ISHARAS Hittite divinity of childbirth

ITZAMNA (C.Am./Maya) four-fold cultured lord of heaven who introduced writing and the calendar to mankind and patronized medicine; decided the points of the compass were Red in the East, White/North, Black/West and Yellow/South, and had a skilful female colleague in the moon goddess IXCHEL; married to Ix Chebel Yax (Weaving)

IZANAGI & IZANAMI (Jap.) eighth incestuous couple after the separation of Heaven & Earth who used a gem-studded spear to stir the primordial soup to create terra firma to stand on instead of their drifting bridge of heaven; on taking a bath, the sun (Amaterasu) sprang from IZANAGI's left eye, the moon from his right one and out of his nose came the storm god SUSANOVO; see YOMI

JOCASTA (Gr.) mother of OEDIPUS & wife of LAIUS; sister of CREON

JUPITER JOVIS Roman protector of the state & war god; chief of the triad with JUNO & MINERVA; also sky god (Gr. ZEUS) whose divine presence was welcomed at harvest & wine festivals; called FULGUR as master of the thunderbolt and LATIARIS when lording it over the Latin League; often busy with oaths & treaties; see TAGES

JUTURNA Roman goddess of springs and waters

KIVUTAR (Fin.) divinity of illness and pain

KHOVAKI SAVAKI (Siberia) creator and protective spirits of the shaman

KRISHNA (India) born of VASUDEVA & DEVAKI (sister of KAMSA, vicious king of MATHURA) but cared for by a cowherd (NANDA) and his wife YASODA; this eighth incarnation of VISHNU humiliated the storm god INDRA; in love with RADHA, but married RUKMINI

KUAN-YIN KUAN-SHIH-YIN (Ch.) female guardian of seamen and artisans

KUEI-HIU (Ch.) unfathomable crater into which all the waters of the world flow or emerge from

KUKUKAN (C.Am./Maya) feathered serpent divinity

KUMARBI Hurrian heir to ANU who was defeated by TESHUB; fathered monstrous stone ULLIKUMMI; depicted standing on the shoulders of UPELBURI (Atlas)

LAELAPS (Gr.) hound of CEPHALUS, given to him by his wife PROCRIS

LAMASSU (Ass./Bab.) protective spirit

LAPITHS (Gr.) see CENTAURS

LATIMUS (Rom.) see PICUS

LEANDER (Gr.) see HERO

LEI-KUNG (Ch.) lord of thunder and Taoist gruesome divinity who punishes men guilty of hidden crimes

LIBANZA god of Congo/Zaire

LOPEMAT Latvian protectress of cattle

LYNCEUS (Gr.) see AEGYPTUS

MAAN-ENO Estonian fertility deity and consort of UKKO

MAMALDI (Siberia/Amur) wife of KHADAU with whom, as the first human couple, she brought ASIA & SAKHALIN into existence before he killed her; shamans

MANITOU MANITOUS (N.Am./Algonquins) mystical & clever forces of nature

MARSABA (Oceania) divinity of the Netherworld and vile spirit

MARSYAS (Gr.) river god & satyr; defeated APOLLO in flute contest and was flayed alive by him; (tributary of the Meander river)

MELQART most important god of Tyre and chief of the Carthagean pantheon; (Rom HERCULES)

MERCURY Roman patron of traders; son of MAIA; (Gr. HERMES)

METABUS Roman; see CAMILLA

MEZAMAT Latvian protectress of wood

MICHABO (N.Am./Algonquin) the Great Hare spirit

MICTLAN (C.Am./Aztec) the Netherworld with nine rivers that the souls of the deceased must negotiate, and nine hells

MINERVA Roman divinity of the arts, war & victory; (Gr. ATHENA/NIKE)

MODEINA Polish god of the forest

MORRIGU (Celtic) see MORRIGAN

MULULIL (Sum.) see NINMAKH

MYCENAE (Gr.) see ATREUS

NAHUALS Mexican heroes and spirits

NEKHBET NEKHEBET (Eg.) vulture or vulture-headed goddess of childbirth; winged serpent protecting the pharaoh; daughter of RE; wife of HAPI; associated with MUT; counterpart of BUTCE/Lower Egypt

NEPTUNE (Rom.) god of water and the sea, perhaps of Etruscan origin

NEREIDS sea nymphs and daughters of NEREUS

NERTHUS Germanic peaceloving island-based mother goddess revered by several tribes, including invaders of England, the Angles

NGENDEI Polynesian high god

NINMAKH NINTUR/ARURU/NINHURSAG (Sum.) guardian of animal birth and bestower of desert wildlife; wife of SHULPAE and mother of MULULIL, EGIME and Ashshirgi

NINURTA NINGURSU/IMDUGUD/ANZU (Sum.) god of rain, floods & thunder; son of ENLIL & NINLIL and husband of BAU/NINNIBRU

NYIAMIA NYAMIA (Guinea) chief god

NYIKANG (Africa/Nile) his grandfather OMARA came from Heaven as the first man – or his ancestry traced to the first cow

OCEANUS (Gr.) the river surrounding the flat earth and forefather of the gods as son of URANUS & GAIA; husband of TETHYS (Titaness) & father of thousands of stream spirits & sea nymphs; see STYX

OEDIPUS (Gr.) incestuous son of LAIUS (King of Thebes) and JOCASTA who killed his father

OGYRVAN Arthurian giant; father of Guinevere

OHDOVAS (N.Am.) midgets below the earth who control poisonous monsters

OHRMAZD (Pers.) see ORMAZD

OLUKSAK (Eskimo) divinity of lakes

OLYMPUS (Gr.) site of the throne of ZEUS; abode of gods; highest mountain in Greece (2917 m/9370 ft); one of many namesakes in Greece & Asia Minor

ONUPHIS (Gr.) (EG AA NEFER) bull and soul incarnate of OSIRIS

ORPHEUS (Gr.) skilful musician and son of CALLIOPE (a Muse) and OEAGRUS, Thracian river god (or APOLLO); joined the Argonauts; killed by Thracian women; see EURYDICE

PARVATI (India) see GANESA

PEGASUS (Gr.) winged horse born of dying MEDUSA; see HELICON & SISYPHUS

PELOPIA (Gr.) wife of ATREUS

PENATES Roman spoilt protectors of the state and the penis & penetralia; household divinities like the LARES

PERSEUS (Gr.) son of DANAE who killed the Gorgon MEDUSA and with her head turned Polydeites of Seriphus and his followers to stone; made Mycenae his capital and became the forefather of the Perseids; see ATLAS

PHEBELE (Congo/Zaire) divine father who by MEBELI begat MAN, a son

PHORCYS (Gr.) see PONTUS

POLEVOI POLEVIK (Slav) grass-covered, black lord of the field

POUNTAN (Micronesia) ingenious divinity of cool, light winds

PRIAPUS (Gr.) unsightly product of DIONYSUS and Aphrodite (or a nymph) with huge phallus able to fertilize both animals and plants; garden gnome & guardian of seafarers

PROCRIS (Gr.) see CEPHALUS

PROTEUS	(Gr.) protector of sea creatures & assistant of POSEIDON; helped MENELAUS to reach Sparta
PRYDERI	(Celtic) son of RHIANNON and PWYLL, king of Dyfed (myth. land of abundance) who swopped home with his friend ARAWAN, the ruler of ANNWN (Netherworld)
PYRAMUS	& THISBE Babylonian couple who killed themselves under a mulberry tree
ROBIGUS	Roman divinity of corn rust and mildew
ROMULUS	twin brother of REMUS and co-founder of Rome
RUKMINI	(India) see KRISHNA
RUSALKA	(Slav) aquatic & sylvan divinity; drowned maiden
SAVITRI	(India) see BRAHMA
SEKHMET	SEKHET (Eg.) lioness or lion-headed goddess of war; wife of PTAH and mother of NEFERTUM, lotus deity; see BAST
SEMARGL	(Russia) wind god
SHAMASH	(Sem.) (Sum. UTU) a bestower of life and mounted sun god who belonged to the second cosmic triad together with his father SIN and sister & wife ISHTAR/AIA; sirened Justice & Right
SHANG-TI	TI CHUN (Ch.) husband of HSI-HO and father of ten suns
SHIKOME	(Jap.) demons
SHIVENI	Urartian sun god with winged solar disc
SHULPAE	(Sum.) see ARURU & NINMAKH
SIGMUND	(Ger./Scan.) son of VOLSUNG with magic weapon
SIPYLON	(Gr.) Lydian mountain on which NIOBE (daughter of TANTALUS) turned into rock after APOLLO & ARTEMIS had killed her children
SOKARIS	(Eg.) see SEKER
SRAOSHA	(Pers.) see RASHNU
STRIBOG	STRIBORG Russian wind god
SUGRIVA	(India) see SURYA
T'AISHAN	FUCHUN (Ch.) ruler of Mt T'ai where sacrificial ritual ceremonies and prayers for good crops were held; spiritual fountain of life
TARANIS	Welsh thunder & sky god; (Rom. JUPITER)
TARHUND	TARHUN (Hittite) see TELEPINU & WURUSEMU
TAUERET	APET/OPET (Eg.) divinity of childbirth
TAWERET	(Eg.) see TAURT
TELAMON	(Gr.) see AJAX
TELAVEL	Baltic heavenly smith who made the sun and the skies
T'EN-LUNG	(Ch.) heavenly dragon who may have produced the Universe and all life
TESHEBA	bull-mounted Urartian weather god
THAMMAS	(Gr.) see PONTUS
THAUNAS	(Gr.) see PONTUS
THEORIS	(Eg.) guardian of childbirth
THESEUS	(Gr.) Attic hero & son of AEGEUS, ruler of Athens, and AETHRA (or of POSEIDON & AETHRA); assailed the fire-breathing bull MARATHON & the Cretan MINOTAUR; fathered Hippolytus (partaker in the Argonautic expedition) by captured Amazon ANTIOPE
TOOTEGA	(Eskimo) little woman on island who can walk on water
TORTALI	(New Hebrides) ruler of the sun and mate of mortal AVIN
TUONELA	(Fin.) the Netherworld and home of TUONI & TUONETAR, his wife
TUPURAN	(N.Am.) killed by NIPARAYA; his disciples, absorbed with witchery & magic, were imprisoned in a subterranean cave
UYITZIN	(C.Am./Maya) friendly divinity
VEJAMAT	Latvian patroness of the wind
VELLAMO	(Fin.) wife of AHTO/AHTI
VIZ-ANYA	(Hung.) water mother
VIZETOT	Nicaraguan divinity of famine
VOLSUNG	(Ger./Scan.) fighter son of RERIR
VOSEGUS	protective divinity of the forest-covered Vosges
VU-KUTIS	(Ugric/Votyak) water divinity
WAKONDA	(N.Am./Sioux) great life force and father figure in the sky
XIBALBA	(C.Am./Quiche) the Netherworld
YEN-WANG	YEN-LO-WANG (Ch.) highest judge in hell; (Indian YAMA)
YU-HUANG	(Ch.) divine Jade Emperor
YUM-KAAX	(C.Am./Maya) god of the forests and maize
YUN T'UNG	(Ch.) a youth stirring up the clouds
ZIPACNA	(C.Am./Maya) twin brother of CAPAKRAN

A SWEEP AROUND THE WORLD IN MYTHOLOGY

8 Letters

ACHELOUS (Gr.) river god; father of the SIRENS (birds with faces of beautiful women)

ACHILLES (Gr.) warrior son of PELEUS, King of the Myrmidons, and THETIS, a sea nymph; murderer of MEMNON, King of Ethiopia, and the Amazon Penthesilea

AEGYPTUS (Gr.) twin brother of DANAUS whose daughters killed all their cousins except LYNCEUS; son of BELUS, ruler of Egypt

AETHLIUS (Gr.) ruler of Elis; see ENDYMION

AGDISTIS (Gr./Rom.) great mother goddess; see CYBELE

AGLOOLIK (Eskimo) lives under ice; good spirit of the seal cave

AITVARAI Baltic winged spirits

AKANCHOB (C.Am.) see AKNA

ALCESTIS (Gr.) wife of ADMETUS & daughter of PELIAS, king of Iolcus

AMAETHON (Welsh) god of agriculture and third son of DON

AMALTHEA AMALTHAEA (Gr.) she-goat (or nymph) and foster-mother of ZEUS whom she suckled in a cave on Crete

ANGRBODA (Norse) daughter of LOKI

ANTICLEA (Gr.) mother of ODYSSEUS

ANTIGONE (Gr.) daughter of JOCASTA by her son & husband OEDIPUS

ARDUINNA Gallic goddess of hunting; DIANA of the Ardennes

ARICONTE Brazilian divinity blamed for the deluge

ASTRAEUS (Gr.) see ZEPHYRUS

AULANERK (Eskimo) lives nude in the sea; cause for gladness

AWIKWAME North American Indian sacred mountain

BAGBARTU BAGMASHTU Urartian gods

BALARAMA (India) wine-loving, strong serpent-like (Sesa) incarnation of VISHNU; half-brother of KRISHNA

BHUSANDI (India) crow which flew into RAMA's mouth

CABAGUIL (C.Am.) associated with the core of the sky

CAPAKRAN (C.Am./Maya) divinity of earthquakes and mountains; twin brother of ZIPACNA

CATEQUIL Inca deity of thunder & lightning

CENTAURS (Gr.) part man, part horse anarchic mountain denizens and children of IXION, king of the LAPITHS; chariot-pullers for DIONYSUS; mounts for EROS

CENTEOTL (C.Am./Aztec) young maize gods

CEPHALUS (Gr.) beloved of EOS who made him kill his wife PROCRIS, who had given him a magic spear and the hound LAELAPS

CERBERUS (Gr.) hound of HADES; offspring of TYPHON and ECHIDNA

CERCOPES (Gr.) twin sons of OCEANUS & THEIA; thieves of Ephesus

CHIMAERA CHIMERA (Gr.) fire-breathing female monster (part lion, part goat, part dragon) of Caria & Lycia, killed by BELLEROPHON; see ECHIDNA

CIPACTLI (C.Am./Aztec) alligator-like divinity

CUKULLAN (Yucatan) bird and snake god

DAEDALUS (Gr.) father of ICARUS; son of METION & descendant of Hephaestus; sculptor, & architect of the Labyrinth in Crete

DARZAMAT Latvian protectress of the garden

DEIANIRA (Gr.) second wife of HERACLES who caused his death; sister of MELEAGER and daughter of OENEUS, ruler of Calydon

DIOMEDES (Gr.) Thracian king whose horses fed on human flesh; see TYDEUS

DIONYSUS (Gr.) wine god; see AGAVE & BACCHUS

DIVIRIKS Baltic rainbow deity

DZIEWONA Polish DIANA

ECALCHOT Nicaraguan wind god

ECHENAIS (Gr.) nymph; see DAPHNIS

ENDYMION (Gr.) shepherd son of ZEUS & nymph CALYCE (or of AETHLIUS, ruler of Elis) fathering fifty daughters in his sleep in a cave on Mt Latmus (Caria) with the moon goddess SELENE

ETEOCLES (Gr.) OEDIPUS' older son

EURYDICE (Gr.) wife of ORPHEUS killed by a snake bite

FARBAUTI (Norse) giant father of LOKI

GAHONGAS (N.Am./Iroquois) dwarfs who live

A SWEEP AROUND THE WORLD IN MYTHOLOGY

in water rocks

GAYOMART (Pers.) creative force dormant for three thousand years whose golden sperm became mankind after his losing battle with the evil spirit AHRIMAN; see YIMA

GLUS-KABE GLUS-KAP (N.Am./Algonquin/ Micmac) unselfish killer of a frog monster

GOFANNON Welsh smith; (Irish GOIBNIU)

GUCUMATZ (Guatemala) a plumose snake and maker of life who can take the form of different animals as he pleases

HAPIKERN (C.Am./Maya) fiend of the human race; brother of YANTHO & USUKUN

HARMONIA (Gr.) married CADMUS with all the gods in attendance; daughter of ARES and Aphrodite

HEIMDALL (Norse) divine, mead-drinking caretaker whose nine mothers were all sisters; see RIGR & AESIR

HELLOTIS (Gr.) see EUROPA

HERACLES (Gr.) strong son of ZEUS & ALCMENE (grandchild of PERSEUS) who had to labour for his half-brother Eurystheus; husband of MEGARA whom he killed together with their children

HERCULES Roman HERACLES; see ISMENIUS, CACUS & LINUS

HESPERUS (Gr.) see EOS

HUECUVUS (Chile) demon readily able to assume any other form

HYPERION (Gr.) see SELENE

IPHICLES (Gr.) father of IOLAUS and mortal half-brother of HERACLES

ISMENIUS (Gr.) river god; his son LINUS killed by HERCULES for trying to teach him how to play the lyre

JELPIN-JA (Ugric/Vogul) sacred rivers and lakes

JOCA-HUVA (Haiti) lord in heaven, son of ATABEI

JURASMAT Latvian mother of the sea

JUVENTAS Roman goddess of youth; (Gr. HEBE)

KAKA-GUIA (Guinea) bull-headed deliverer of the souls of the dead to the chief deity NYAMIA

K'RACOCHA Inca high god

KULLERVO (Fin.) shepherd and evil spirit

KUMARBIS Hurrite father of the gods; see KUMARBI & ANUS

KUNG-KUNG (Ch.) horned monster whose power-struggle with SHANG-TI put heaven askew; see KAN-FU

LAKSMAMA (India) see RAMA

LATIARIS (Rom.) see JUPITER

LAUKAMAT Latvian protectress of the field

LOMPSALO Lappish wizard

LOVIATAR (Fin.) black-faced creature with horrible skin, goddess of illness, who gave birth to nine monsters; see TUONI

LUKELONG (Oceania) female creator of heaven and earth

LUXOVIUS (Celtic) god of the baths and healing married to BRIXIA

MAMA-QORA Inca sea mother

MANANNAN MANAWYDAN (Celtic/Welsh) deity of the sea; see LLYR & LER

MARATHON (Gr.) fire-breathing bull assailed by THESEUS (son of AEGEUS)

MARPESSA (Gr.) see EUENUS

MARZANNA Polish patron of orchards

MASPITER (Rom.) see MARS

MELAMPUS (Gr.) seer who could understand the talk of animals; descendant of AEOLUS (son of HELLEN); see BIAS

MELEAGER (Gr.) descendant of AEOLUS who killed his uncles; see ALTHAEA

MENELAUS (Gr.) son of ATREUS & AEROPE; brother of AGAMEMNON; see PROTEUS

MERSEGER MERTSEGER (Eg.) human-headed snake goddess

MESHKENT (Eg.) divinity of childbirth

METSABOK (C.Am./Lacandones) divine master of rain and clouds

MEZAVIRS Latvian divinity of forest

MINOTAUR (Gr.) half human, half bull monster of Crete; offspring of PASIPHAE & POSEIDON's white bull; killed by THESEUS & ARIADNE

MORPHEUS (Gr.) patron of dreams about humans; see PHOBETOR

MORRIGAN MORRIGU (Celtic) war goddess & consort of Irish DAGDA; see MACHA

MYRTILUS (Gr.) charioteer of OENOMAUS (King of Pisa) killed by his son-in-law PELOPS and thrown into the Myrtoan sea by PELOPS

NAUPLIUS (Gr.) see AMYMONE

NEFERTUM NEFERTEM/NEFERTEMU (Eg.) lion-headed man; lotus god; son

NEKHEBET of PTAH & SEKHMET (or BAST) (Eg.) guardian of childbirth; (Gr. EILEITHYIA)

NGURVILU (S.Am.) god of water, rivers, lakes

NINDURRA (Sum.) see ENKI

NINGURSU NINURTA/IMDUGUD/ANZU (Sum.) as a rain cloud huge lion-headed bird with a thunderous roar; deity of tilling & ploughing

NINIGARA (Sum.) cream and butter goddess and spouse of NINHAR

NIPARAYA (Californian/Indian) god of heaven & earth; father of QUAAYAYP

NYALITCH NYALIC (Africa/Nile) chief god of the Dinka people

ODYSSEUS (Gr.) son of LAERTES & ANTICLEIA; King of Ithaca (or son of SISYPHUS and consort of CIRCE, CALYPSO etc.); brave and wise wanderer married to PENELOPE

OENONAUS (Gr.) see MYRTILUS

ORAMATUA Tahitian "forefathers"; spirits

PACA-MAMA Inca Earth Mother

PASIPHAE (Gr.) see ARIADNE, GLAUCUS, MINOTAUR

PELOPIDS (Gr.) see TANTALUS

PENELOPE (Gr.) mother of PAN; wife of ODYSSEUS or Telegonus, his son by the sorceress CIRCE; daughter of ICARIUS of Sparta and nymph PERIBOCA

PENTHEUS (Gr.) see AGAVE

PHAETHON (Gr.) killed by a thunderbolt (ZEUS) while searching for his father HELIOS; son of nymph CLEMENE; see EOS

PHILEMON & BAUCIS senior hospitable Phrygian couple who received ZEUS and HERMES

PHOBETOR (Gr.) provider of dreams about animals; see MORPHEUS

PORTUNUS Roman god of harbours (and city gates)

POSEIDON (Gr.) major sea god; brother of ZEUS; see TYRO

PSAMATHE (Gr.) see LINUS

QUAAYAYP (Californian/Indian) son of NIPARAYA, maker of Heaven & Earth

QUIATEOR Nicaraguan rain god

QUIRINUS Roman war and state god

RHIANNON (Welsh) Gallic mare goddess EPONA; Irish MACHA; wife of king PWYLL; mother of PRYDERI whom she killed

ROSMERTA (Celtic) goddess of abundance; (Rom. MERCURY)

SABAZIUS (Thrace) see MEN

SAKHALIN (Siberia) see MAMALDI

SATARUPA (India) see BRAHMA

SHARRUMA son of HEBAT, Hurrian Queen of gods

SHAUSHKA Hurrian lion-mounted winged god (Bab Ishtar)

SHENIRDA (Sum.) see UTU

SILVANUS Roman god of untilled earth associated with PAN

SISYPHUS (Gr.) trickster husband of MEROPE and son of AEOLUS; grandfather of Bellerophon, the hero who fought the CHIMAERA with PEGASUS

SLEIPNIR (Norse) magical, eight-legged horse of ODIN, born of trickster LOKI (as a mare) and swift & clever Svadilfari

SOATSAKI (N.Am.) handsome girl and mother of POIA

STRIBORG STRIBOG Russian wind god

SUCELLUS (Celtic) divinity with wooden hammer and husband of Nantosuelta

SUSANOWO (Jap.) nasal son of IZANAGI who was thrown out of Heaven for misbehaving — and got away with both the magic sword KUSANAGI, destined for emperors, and the girl he loved from the eight-headed dragon he killed; father of Okuninushi

TANGAROA (Polynesia, N.Z.) made the earth and lesser gods and mated with HINE, but sprouted mankind from himself

TANTALUS (Gr.) son of ZEUS (or TMOLUS of Lydia) and ruler of Sipylus in Lydia/Phrygia who abused his friendship with the gods and suffers never-ending hunger and thirst in HADES as a result; cursed ancestor of the PELOPIDS; father of PELOPS & NIOBE

TARTARUS (Gr.) see HAEMUS

TELEPINU TELIPINU son of the Hittite weather god TARHUN/TARHUND

TEUTATES TOUTATES (Celtic) god of the clan & messenger; (Rom. MARS,

MERCURY) (Gr. ARES, HERMES)

THOUERIS (Eg.) see TAURT

THUNNUPA (Chile/Aymara) bearded white puritan from the North who said No to polygamy and chica (popular drink)

THYESTES (Gr.) son of PELOPS of Pisa; brother of ALEATHOUS and ATREUS; killed their step-brother Chrysippus (of PELOPS by a nymph) and ATREUS and his son Pleisthenes; fathered AEGISTHUS by his own daughter PELOPIA

TONATIUH (C.Am./Aztec) sun god of the fifth age connected with the eagle

TPEREAKL (Micronesia) together with his wife LATMIKAIK, who emerged from a sea-lashed rock, they are the source of life and rule the world

T'SAI-SHEN (Ch.) divine lords of wealth

T'SAO-SHEN (Ch.) divine lords of the kitchen

UKEMOCHI (Jap.) food deity

UPELBURI (Hurrian) see KUMARBI

VAMMATAR (Fin.) deity of illness and pain

VARPULIS (Slav) wind god and follower of PERUN

VASUDEVA (India) father of KRISHNA

VODYANOI (Slav) huge fish and fearsome water deity covered with moss

WURUSEMU Hattic sun goddess (Hittite Arinnitti) and wife of TARHUN/ TARHUND, the weather god

YUNCEMIL (C.Am.) god of death

ZARBANIT (Sum.) see MARDUK

ZEPHYRUS (Gr.) the West Wind, suitor of Hyacinthus; son of EOS by ASTRAEUS

ZUTTIBUR (Slav) sylvan god

READ MORE IN PENGUIN

In every corner of the world, on every subject under the sun, Penguin represents quality and variety – the very best in publishing today.

For complete information about books available from Penguin – including Puffins, Penguin Classics and Arkana – and how to order them, write to us at the appropriate address below. Please note that for copyright reasons the selection of books varies from country to country.

In the United Kingdom: Please write to *Dept. JC, Penguin Books Ltd, FREEPOST, West Drayton, Middlesex UB7 0BR*

If you have any difficulty in obtaining a title, please send your order with the correct money, plus ten per cent for postage and packaging, to *PO Box No. 11, West Drayton, Middlesex UB7 0BR*

In the United States: Please write to *Penguin USA Inc., 375 Hudson Street, New York, NY 10014*

In Canada: Please write to *Penguin Books Canada Ltd, 10 Alcorn Avenue, Suite 300, Toronto, Ontario M4V 3B2*

In Australia: Please write to *Penguin Books Australia Ltd, 487 Maroondah Highway, Ringwood, Victoria 3134*

In New Zealand: Please write to *Penguin Books (NZ) Ltd, 182–190 Wairau Road, Private Bag, Takapuna, Auckland 9*

In India: Please write to *Penguin Books India Pvt Ltd, 706 Eros Apartments, 56 Nehru Place, New Delhi 110 019*

In the Netherlands: Please write to *Penguin Books Netherlands B.V., Keizersgracht 231 NL–1016 DV Amsterdam*

In Germany: Please write to *Penguin Books Deutschland GmbH, Friedrichstrasse 10–12, W–6000 Frankfurt/Main 1*

In Spain: Please write to *Penguin Books S. A., C. San Bernardo 117–6° E–28015 Madrid*

In Italy: Please write to *Penguin Italia s.r.l., Via Felice Casati 20, I–20124 Milano*

In France: Please write to *Penguin France S. A., 17 rue Lejeune, F–31000 Toulouse*

In Japan: Please write to *Penguin Books Japan, Ishikiribashi Building, 2–5–4, Suido, Tokyo 112*

In Greece: Please write to *Penguin Hellas Ltd, Dimocritou 3, GR–106 71 Athens*

In South Africa: Please write to *Longman Penguin Southern Africa (Pty) Ltd, Private Bag X08, Bertsham 2013*

FOR THE BEST IN PAPERBACKS, LOOK FOR THE 🐧

PENGUIN REFERENCE BOOKS

The New Penguin English Dictionary

Over 1,000 pages long and with over 68,000 definitions, this cheap, compact and totally up-to-date book is ideal for today's needs. It includes many technical and colloquial terms, guides to pronunciation and common abbreviations.

The Penguin Spelling Dictionary

What are the plurals of *octopus* and *rhinoceros*? What is the difference between *stationary* and *stationery*? And how about *annex* and *annexe*, *agape* and *Agape*? This comprehensive new book, the fullest spelling dictionary now available, provides the answers.

Roget's Thesaurus of English Words and Phrases   Betty Kirkpatrick (ed.)

This new edition of Roget's classic work, now brought up to date for the nineties, will increase anyone's command of the English language. Fully cross-referenced, it includes synonyms of every kind (formal or colloquial, idiomatic and figurative) for almost 900 headings. It is a must for writers and utterly fascinating for any English speaker.

The Penguin Dictionary of Quotations

A treasure-trove of over 12,000 new gems and old favourites, from Aesop and Matthew Arnold to Xenophon and Zola.

The Penguin Wordmaster Dictionary
Martin H. Manser and Nigel D. Turton

This dictionary puts the pleasure back into word-seeking. Every time you look at a page you get a bonus – a panel telling you everything about a particular word or expression. It is, therefore, a dictionary to be read as well as used for its concise and up-to-date definitions.